Look at that, you just opened this guide, and you've already found the best vacation ever. Get ready for awe-inclusive value, with world-class entertainment, gourmet food, top shelf liquor, and more fun stuff than you can shake a flip flop at. Like the FlowRider® Double Wave Simulator, and 27 holes of Jack Nicklaus Signature Golf. It's everything you need for the family vacation of a lifetime, a romantic escape, or a vacation completely unlike any other. So, who's with us?

PALACE
RESORTS®

MEXICO · JAMAICA

AWE-INCLUSIVE™

1.877.874.0579   PalaceResorts.com

# GRAND VELAS

### Riviera Nayarit

BEYOND ALL INCLUSIVE, BEYOND ALL COMPARE™

866 868 0992 | velasresorts.com

THE LEADING HOTELS
OF THE WORLD®

# Mexico

**Published by AAA Publishing**

1000 AAA Drive, Heathrow, FL 32746-5063
Copyright AAA 2015, All rights reserved

The publisher has made every effort to provide accurate,
up-to-date information but accepts no responsibility for loss or
injury sustained by any person using this book.

**Advertising Rate and Circulation Information: (407) 444-8280**

**Printed in the USA by Quad/Graphics**

*Photo Credit: (Cover & Title Page)*
*Mariachi Charro*
© *iStockphoto.com / JoseGirarte*

Printed on recyclable paper.
Please recycle whenever possible.

**This book is printed on paper certified by third-party standards
for sustainably-managed forestry and production.**

# Mexico

# Featured Information

## LET US STAY WITH YOU.®

*Let us show your kids how to help a turtle find its way to the sea.*

*Let us quench thirsty skin with the healing properties of a Mayan-inspired treatment.*

*Let us help you discover your inner chef at our mesmerizing seaside Culinary Center.*

*Let us make you fall in love with Cancun from sunrise to sunset.*

Nestled along the alluring Mayan coast is The Ritz-Carlton, Cancun. White sand beaches & charismatic Mexican hospitality combine to make this AAA 5-Diamond resort an exquisite location for your next vacation. For reservations, contact your travel professional, call The Ritz-Carlton at 800-241-3333 or visit ritzcarlton.com/cancun.

THE RITZ-CARLTON®
CANCUN

# Using Your Guide

## How the Guide is Organized

The guide is organized into three distinct sections.

The **Points of Interest** section helps you plan daily activities and sightseeing excursions and provides details about the city or attraction you are visiting.

The **Hotels & Restaurants** section helps you select AAA Approved accommodations and dining facilities meeting your specific needs and expectations.

The **Featured information** section provides indexes for locating information within this guide and items to aid the trip planning process.

## Locating the Attractions, Hotels & Restaurants

The guide is organized according to eight geographic travel regions. Attractions, hotels and restaurants are listed under the city in which they physically are located — or in some cases under the nearest recognized city. Most listings are alphabetically organized by region, then by city and establishment name.

A color is assigned to each region so you can match the color bars at the tops of pages to switch from the Points of Interest section to the corresponding Hotels & Restaurants section.

Spotting maps help you physically locate points of interest, hotels and restaurants in the major destinations.

The Comprehensive City Index located in the Featured information section contains an A-to-Z list of cities.

## Destination Cities and Destination Areas

Destination cities include metropolitan areas. Destination areas are regions with broad tourist appeal made up of several cities.

For cities that are within the Caribbean Coast Destination area, the city name will appear alphabetically within the Yucatán Peninsula region and a cross-reference will give you the exact page on which coverage of the city begins.

Orientation maps appear with each Destination city and Destination area and at the beginning of each of the eight geographic regions to familiarize you with what is covered.

## About Listed Establishments

AAA Approved hotels and restaurants are listed on the basis of merit alone after careful evaluation and approval by full-time, professionally trained AAA inspectors. An establishment's decision to advertise in the guide has no bearing on its evaluation or rating, nor does inclusion of advertising imply AAA/CAA endorsement of products and services.

Information in this guide was believed accurate at the time of publication. However, since changes inevitably occur between annual editions, please contact your AAA/CAA travel professional, visit AAA.com or download the AAA Mobile app to confirm prices and schedules.

## Location Abbreviations

Directions are from the center of town unless otherwise specified, using this highway abbreviation:

**Mex.**=Mexican highway

# Understanding the Diamond Ratings

Hotel and restaurant evaluations are unscheduled to ensure our professionally trained inspectors encounter the same experience members do.

- When an establishment is Diamond Rated, it means members can expect a good fit with their needs. The inspector assigns a rating that indicates the type of experience to expect.

- While establishments at high levels must offer increasingly complex personalized services, establishments at every level are subject to the same basic requirements for cleanliness, comfort and hospitality. Learn more at AAA.com/Diamonds.

## Hotels

◆

Budget-oriented, offering basic comfort and hospitality.

◆◆

Affordable, with modestly enhanced facilities, décor and amenities.

◆◆◆

Distinguished, multifaceted with enhanced physical attributes, amenities and guest comforts.

◆◆◆◆

Refined, stylish with upscale physical attributes, extensive amenities and high degree of hospitality, service and attention to detail.

◆◆◆◆◆

Ultimate luxury, sophistication and comfort with extraordinary physical attributes, meticulous personalized service, extensive amenities and impeccable standards of excellence.

## Restaurants

◆

Simple, economical food, often self-service, in a functional environment.

◆◆

Familiar food, often cooked to order, served in relaxed surroundings.

◆◆◆

Popular cuisine, skillfully prepared and served, with expanded beverage options, in enhanced setting.

◆◆◆◆

Imaginative, market-fresh food creatively prepared and skillfully served, often with wine steward, amid upscale ambience.

◆◆◆◆◆

Cutting-edge cuisine of the finest ingredients, uniquely prepared by an acclaimed chef, served by expert service staff led by maître d' in extraordinary surroundings.

## What's the difference?

◆ Red Diamonds mark establishments that participate in the AAA logo licensing program for increased visibility to members.

◆ Black Diamonds identify all other AAA Approved and Diamond Rated establishments.

## Attraction Listings

> **◆GEM ATTRACTION NAME,** (nombre de atracción) is at Manuel Doblado #1, about 2 blks. s.e. of Jardín Unión in an area of very limited street parking. Housing more than 700 pieces of art, this fascinating museum provides a look at the enduring literary character created by Spanish author Miguel de Cervantes as seen through the eyes of Pedro Coronel, Salvador Dalí, Pablo Picasso and other artists.
>
> The pieces are displayed in rooms surrounding a three-story courtyard. Quixote and trusty companion Sancho Panza are executed in a variety of media, including paintings, sculpture, stained-glass windows, clocks, painted eggs, woodcarvings and one large leaf, complete with veins, that shows Cervantes' hero in profile on horseback. There also are huge wall murals and quartz, bronze, silver and porcelain statuary. Exhibit information is in Spanish. Restrooms are provided. **Time:** Allow 1 hour minimum. **Hours:** Tues.-Sat. 9:30-6:45, Sun.-Mon. noon-6:45. Closed major holidays. Phone ahead to confirm schedule. **Cost:** 30 pesos (about $2.40 U.S.); free to all Tues. **Phone:** (473) 732-6721 or (473) 732-3376. ⃞

**◆GEM**

AAA travel experts may designate an attraction of exceptional interest and quality as a AAA GEM — *a Great Experience for Members®.*

Consult the online travel guides at AAA.com or visit AAA Mobile for additional things to do if you have time.

## Cost

Prices are quoted without sales tax in U.S. dollars or in Mexican pesos along with an approximate U.S. dollar equivalent. Some attractions and business establishments accept U.S. credit cards, but others may accept only local currency; in Mexico, it's always a good idea to have peso denominations on hand.

## Icons

GT Guided Tours available

🛆 Camping facilities

🍴 Food on premises

🏊 Recreational activities

🐾 Pets on leash allowed

🏕 Picnicking allowed

© Gennadiy Poznyakov / 123RF.com

## Information-Only Attraction Listings

Bulleted listings in the following category are listed for informational purposes as a service to members:

- **Wineries that offer tours and tastings**

# Multiply the Value

Upgrade to **Plus or Premier** for bigger benefits, and buy **Gift** and **Associate** memberships for friends and family.

AAA.com/CAA.ca • 800-Join-AAA

# Hotel and Restaurant Listings

**1** **Diamond Rating** – AAA Approved hotels and restaurants are assigned a rating of one to five Diamonds. Red Diamonds distinguish establishments that participate in the AAA/CAA logo licensing program. For details, see p. 8 or AAA.com/Diamonds.

[fyi] indicates hotels and restaurants that are not AAA/CAA Approved and/or Diamond Rated but are listed to provide additional choices for members:

- **Hotels** may be unrated if they are too new to rate, under construction, under major renovation or have not yet been evaluated; or if they do not meet all AAA requirements. Hotels that do not meet all AAA requirements may be included if they offer member value or are the only option; details are noted in the listing.
- **Restaurants** may be unrated if they have not yet been evaluated by AAA.

**2** **Classification or Cuisine Type** – Noted after the Diamond Rating.

- **Hotel Classifications** indicate the style of operation, overall concept and service level. Subclassifications may also be added. (See p. 12.)
- **Restaurant Cuisine Types** identify the food concept from more than 100 categories. If applicable, a classification may also be added. (See p. 13.)

**3** **Dollar Amounts** – Quoted without sales tax in U.S. dollars, rounded up to the nearest dollar. Most establishments accept credit cards, but a small number require cash, so please call ahead to verify.

- **Hotel Rates** indicate the publicly available two-person rate or rate range for a standard room, applicable all year.
- **Restaurant Prices** represent the minimum and maximum entrée cost per person. Exceptions may include one-of-a-kind or special market priced items.

**4** **Spotting Symbol** – Ovals containing numbers correspond with numbered location markings on hotel and restaurant spotting maps.

**5** **Parking** – Unless otherwise noted, parking is free, on-site self parking.

**6** **Hotel Value Nationwide** – Blue boxes highlight member benefits available at all AAA/CAA Approved locations across a hotel chain. (See p. 17 for details.)

**7** **Hotel Unit Limited Availability** – Unit types, amenities and room features preceded by "some" are available on a limited basis, potentially as few as one.

**8** **Hotel Terms** – Cancellation and minimum stay policies are listed. Unless otherwise noted, most properties offer a full deposit refund with cancellations received at least 48 hours before standard check-in. Properties that require advance payment may not refund the difference for early departures. "Resort fee" indicates a charge may apply above and beyond the quoted room rate.

**9** **Hotel Check-in/Check-out** – Unless otherwise noted, check-in is after 3 p.m. and check-out is before 10 a.m.

**10** **Restaurant Dress Code** – Unless otherwise noted, dress is casual or dressy casual.

**11** **Restaurant Menu** – Where indicated, menus may be viewed in a secure online environment at AAA.com or, if a mobile tag is provided, via the restaurant's website.

**12** **Hotel Icons** – May be preceded by CALL and/or SOME UNITS.

**Member Information**:

[SAVE] Member rates: discounted standard room rate or lowest public rate available at time of booking for dates of stay.

[ECO] Eco-certified by government or private organization.

[X] Smoke-free premises

**Services**:

[✈] Airport transportation

[🐕] Pets allowed (Call property for restrictions.)

[$🐕] Pets allowed (Call property for restrictions and fees.)

[🍽] Restaurant on premises

[🍽+] Restaurant off premises

[🛎] Room service for 2 or more meals

## HOTEL LISTINGS

**HOTEL NAME** (555)555-5555 **50**

▼▼▼▼▼
Hotel
$109-$199

**LOGO**

**AAA Benefit:** Members save a minimum 5% off the best available rate.

**Address:** 300 Main St 55555 **Location:** 1.6 mi w on Mex. 688 (Oak Rd). **Facility:** 149 units, some efficiencies. 3 stories, interior corridors. **Parking:** on-site (fee). **Terms:** check-in 4 pm, cancellation fee imposed, resort fee. **Amenities:** video games. **Pool(s):** heated outdoor. **Activities:** hot tub, exercise room. **Guest Services:** valet and coin laundry. **Featured Amenity:** continental breakfast.

SAVE ECO ⁜ CALL ⚷M BIZ sHS 🛜 ✕ 🎥
☕ / SOME UNITS 🛏 🧊 🍽

## RESTAURANT LISTINGS

**RESTAURANT NAME** 555/555-5555

▼▼▼▼▼
Continental
Fine Dining
$15-$35

**AAA Inspector Notes:** *Historic.* A romantic aura punctuates the modern and casual dining room, which is accented with floral arrangements and dramatic, freshly cut branches. The menu features seasonal ingredients. The pastry chef's decadent creations are popular. Semiformal attire. **Features:** full bar, patio dining, happy hour. **Address:** 26 N Main St 55555 **Location:** 2.7 mi s of jct Mex. 520. *Menu on AAA.com* SAVE ECO L D 🐾

---

🍸 Full bar

🏠 Child care

BIZ Business area

⚷M Accessible features (Call property for available services and amenities.)

**Activities**:

🎰 Full-service casino

🏊 Pool

🏋 Health club on premises

**In-Room Amenities**:

HS High-speed Internet service

sHS High-speed Internet service (Call property for fees.)

🛜 Wireless Internet service

📶 Wireless Internet service (Call property for fees.)

📡 No wireless Internet service

🎥 Pay movies

🧊 Refrigerator

🍽 Microwave

☕ Coffee maker

🅰 No air conditioning

📺 No TV

📞 No telephones

**Safety Features**:

S Sprinklers

SD Smoke Detectors

**13 Restaurant Icons**

SAVE AAA Discounts & Rewards® member discount

ECO Eco-certified by government or private organization.

🅰 No air conditioning

⚷M Accessible features (Call property for available services and amenities.)

◧ Designated smoking section

B Breakfast

L Lunch

D Dinner

24 Open 24 hours

LATE Open after 11 p.m.

🐾 Pet-friendly (Call property for restrictions.)

# Hotel Classifications

Quality and comfort are usually consistent across each Diamond Rating level, but décor, facilities and service levels vary by classification.

Berry Manor Inn, Rockland, ME / Courtesy of Berry Manor Inn

**Bed & Breakfast —** Typically owner-operated with a high degree of personal touches. Guests are encouraged to interact during evening and breakfast hours. A continental or full, hot breakfast is included in the room rate.

Killarney Lodge, Algonquin Provincial Park, ON / © Chris Dew / Killarney Lodge

**Cabin —** Often located in wooded, rural or waterfront locations. Freestanding units are typically rustic and of basic design. As a rule, essential cleaning supplies, kitchen utensils and complete bed and bath linens are supplied.

Divi Aruba Phoenix Beach Resort, Aruba / Courtesy of Divi Resorts

**Condominium —** Apartment-style accommodations of varying design or décor, units often contain one or more bedrooms, a living room, full kitchen and an eating area. As a rule, essential cleaning supplies, kitchen utensils and complete bed and bath linens are supplied.

Montpelier Plantation and Beach, St. Kitts and Nevis / Courtesy of Montpelier Plantation and Beach

**Cottage —** Often located in wooded, rural, or waterfront locations. Freestanding units are typically home-style in design and décor. As a rule, essential cleaning supplies, kitchen utensils and complete bed and bath linens are supplied.

Nottoway Plantation & Resort, White Castle, LA / © Elisa Rolle / Wikimedia Commons

**Country Inn —** Although similar in definition to a bed and breakfast, country inns are usually larger in scale with spacious public areas and offer a dining facility that serves breakfast and dinner.

The Westin Resort & Spa Los Cabos, Mexico / © Ken Bosma / Wikimedia Commons

**Hotel —** Typically a multistory property with interior room entrances and a variety of guest unit styles. The magnitude of the public areas is determined by the overall theme, location and service level, but may include a variety of facilities such as a restaurant, shops, a fitness center, a spa, a business center and meeting rooms.

Sheriva Luxury Villas & Suites Maundays Bay, Anguilla / Courtesy of Sheriva Luxury Villas & Suites

**House —** Freestanding units of varying home-style design. Typically larger scale, often containing two or more bedrooms, a living room, a full kitchen, a dining room and multiple bathrooms. As a rule, essential cleaning supplies, kitchen utensils and complete bed and bath linens are supplied.

Bryce View Lodge, Bryce Canyon City, UT / Courtesy of Bryce View Lodge

**Motel —** A one- or two-story roadside property with exterior room entrances and drive up parking. Public areas and facilities are often limited in size and/or availability.

Vista Verde Guest Ranch, Clark, CO / Courtesy of Vista Verde Guest Ranch

**Ranch —** Typically a working ranch featuring an obvious rustic, Western theme, equestrian-related activities and a variety of guest unit styles.

Courtesy of Divi Resorts

## Hotel Subclassifications

These additional descriptives may be added to the classification for more information:

- **Boutique** — Often thematic, typically informal yet highly personalized; may have a luxurious or quirky style that is fashionable or unique.
- **Casino** — Extensive gambling facilities are available, such as blackjack, craps, keno and slot machines.
- **Classic** — Renowned and landmark properties, older than 50 years, well known for their unique style and ambience.
- **Contemporary** — Overall theme reflects characteristics of present mainstream trends.
- **Extended Stay** — Offers a predominance of long-term accommodations with a designated full-service kitchen area within each unit.
- **Historic** — More than 75 years old with one of the following documented historical features: Maintains the integrity of the historical nature, listed on the National Register of Historic Places, designated a National Historic Landmark or located in a National Register Historic District.
- **Resort** — Extensive recreational facilities and programs may include golf, tennis, skiing, fishing, water sports, spa treatments or professionally guided activities.
- **Retro** — Overall theme reflects a contemporary design that reinterprets styles from a past era.

- **Vacation Rental** — Typically houses, condos, cottages or cabins; these properties are "home away from home" self-catering accommodations.
- **Vintage** — Overall theme reflects upon and maintains the authentic traits and experience of a past era.

## Restaurant Classifications

If applicable, in addition to the cuisine type noted under the Diamond Rating, restaurant listings may also include one or both classifications:

- **Classic** — Renowned and landmark operation in business for 25 plus years; unique style and ambience.
- **Historic** — Meets one of the following: Listed on National Register of Historic Places, designated a National Historic Landmark or located in a National Register Historic District.

## Mobile Tags

Scan QR codes throughout the guide to see online offers, menus, videos and more on your smartphone or tablet. If you need a QR scanner app, download one for free from your app store.

If you see a non-QR code in an ad, check the nearby text for details on which app you'll need to scan it.

# GET REAL
## REAL INSPECTORS, REAL RATINGS

**What makes Diamond Ratings more reliable than the rest?** Highly trained, professional inspectors who visit every AAA/CAA Approved property. We conduct on-site evaluations using extensive guidelines based on member priorities.

What matters to you matters to us. You're the reason AAA conducts inspections — to ensure the places you select provide the experiences you expect.

## Visit AAA.com/Diamonds

AAA Mobile App
CAA Mobile App

15

# Just For Members

## Member Discounts

Visit AAA.com/searchfordiscounts to find locations and member discounts available at your destination. Prior to travel, contact your local AAA/CAA office for reservations or other details regarding member discounts. Hard Rock Cafe savings may be used for up to six patrons. Other restrictions may apply. All offers subject to change. For complete restrictions, visit your local office or AAA.com/restrictions.

### DINING

**Hard Rock Cafe**
- Save 10% on food, nonalcoholic beverages and merchandise at all locations in the U.S. and Canada, plus select international locations. Visit AAA.com/HardRock for full listing.

### TRANSPORTATION

**Hertz**
- Save on daily, weekend, weekly and monthly rentals at AAA.com/Hertz or (800) 654-3080.

# Let the IDP Speak for You

## Traveling the world?

Before you go, purchase an International Driving Permit for a recognizable form of identification, even if you're not driving.

Translated into 10 languages, the IDP is valid in more than 150 countries — mandatory in some and highly recommended in others.

**U.S. residents apply at AAA offices. Canadian residents apply at CAA offices.**
**Or visit us online at: AAA.com/IDP or CAA.ca/travelling/idp**

## AAA Approved Hotels

For members, AAA Approved means quality assured.

- Only properties that meet basic requirements for cleanliness, comfort and hospitality pass inspection.
- Approved hotels receive a Diamond Rating that tells members the type of experience to expect.

### Guest Safety

Inspectors view a sampling of rooms during evaluations and, therefore, AAA cannot guarantee the presence of working locks and operational fire safety equipment in every guest unit.

If a hotel met AAA's security requirements at the time of inspection, the listing denotes "Meets AAA guest room security requirements" and includes icons for sprinklers and/or smoke detectors.

### Member Rates

AAA/CAA members can generally expect to pay no more than the maximum listed rate for a standard room. Member discounts apply to rates quoted within the rate range and are applicable at the time of booking. Listed rates are usually based on last standard room availability. Rates may fluctuate within the range and vary by season and room type. Obtain current AAA/CAA member rates and make reservations at AAA.com.

#### Exceptions

- Rates in this guide are not guaranteed and may fluctuate based on the currency exchange rate.
- Special advertised rates and short-term promotional rates below the rate range are not subject to additional member discounts.
- During special events, hotels may temporarily increase room rates, not recognize discounts or modify pricing policies. Special events may include holidays, holiday periods and festivals. Although some special events are listed in this guide and on AAA.com, it's always wise to check in advance with AAA/CAA travel professionals for specific dates.

**If you are charged more than the maximum listed rate**, question the additional charge. If an exception is not in effect and management refuses to adhere to the published rate, pay for the room and contact AAA/CAA. The amount paid above the stated maximum will be refunded if our investigation indicates an unjustified charge.

## Reservations and Cancellations

When making your reservation, identify yourself as a AAA/CAA member and request written confirmation of your room type, rate, dates of stay, and cancellation and refund policies. At registration, show your membership card.

To cancel, contact the hotel, your AAA/CAA club office or AAA.com, depending on how you booked your reservation. Request a cancellation number or proof of cancellation.

**If your room is not as specified and you have written confirmation of your reservation for a specific room type,** you should be given the option of choosing a different room or receiving a refund. If management refuses to issue a refund, contact AAA/CAA.

### Contacting AAA/CAA About Approved Properties

If your visit to a AAA/CAA Approved attraction, hotel or restaurant doesn't meet your expectations, please tell us about it — **during your visit or within 30 days**. Be sure to save your receipts and other documentation for reference.

Use the easy online form at AAA.com/TourBookComments to send us the details.

Alternatively, you can email your comments to: memberrelations@national.aaa.com or submit them via postal mail to: AAA Member Comments, 1000 AAA Dr., Box 61, Heathrow, FL 32746.

# AAA Preferred Hotels

All AAA/CAA Approved hotels are committed to providing quality, value and member service. In addition, those designated as AAA/CAA Preferred Hotels also offer these extra values at Approved locations nationwide. Valid AAA/CAA membership required.

- **Best AAA/CAA member rates for your dates of stay**.
- **Seasonal promotions and special member offers**. Visit AAA.com to view current offers.
- **Member benefit**. See the blue boxes in hotel listings for the chains shown in the right-hand column below to find values offered at AAA/CAA Approved locations nationwide, subject to availability. Details valid at the time of publication may change without notice.

- **Total satisfaction guarantee**. If you book your stay with AAA/CAA Travel and your stay fails to meet your expectations, you can apply for a full refund. Bring the complaint to the hotel's attention during the stay and request resolution; if the complaint is not resolved by the hotel, ask your AAA/CAA travel agent to request resolution through the AAA/CAA Assured Stay program.

DISCOUNTS ≫REWARDS
PREFERRED HOTELS

Rewards
PREFERRED HOTELS

ASSURED S T A Y
Total Satisfaction Guarantee

| | |
|---|---|
| **Best Western** | BEST WESTERN®, BEST WESTERN PLUS®, EXECUTIVE RESIDENCY, Vib, BEST WESTERN PREMIER® and BW Premier Collection^SM |
| **Hilton** | Hilton Hotels & Resorts, Waldorf Astoria™ Hotels & Resorts, Conrad® Hotels & Resorts, Canopy by Hilton, Curio - A Collection by Hilton™, DoubleTree by Hilton™, Embassy Suites Hotels™, Hilton Garden Inn™, Hampton Inn™, Homewood Suites by Hilton™, Home2 Suites by Hilton™ and Hilton Grand Vacations™ |
| **HYATT®** | Park Hyatt®, Andaz®, Grand Hyatt®, Hyatt Centric®, Hyatt®, Hyatt Regency®, Hyatt Place®, HYATT house®, Hyatt Zilara® and Hyatt Ziva® |
| **Marriott** | JW Marriott®, Autograph Collection® Hotels, Renaissance® Hotels, Marriott Hotels®, Delta Hotels and Resorts®, Gaylord Hotels®, AC Hotels by Marriott®, Courtyard®, Residence Inn®, SpringHill Suites®, Fairfield Inn & Suites® and TownePlace Suites® |
| **MGM RESORTS INTERNATIONAL®** | Bellagio®, ARIA®, Vdara®, MGM Grand®, The Signature at MGM Grand®, Mandalay Bay®, Delano™ Las Vegas, The Mirage®, Monte Carlo™, New York-New York®, Luxor®, Excalibur® and Circus Circus® Las Vegas |
| **starwood** Hotels and Resorts | St. Regis®, The Luxury Collection®, W®, Westin®, Le Méridien®, Sheraton®, Four Points® by Sheraton, Aloft®, element® and Tribute Portfolio™ |

# Take Your *Imagination* to New Destinations

**Use AAA Travel Guides online to explore the possibilities.**

> Tour popular places in the U.S., Canada, Mexico and the Caribbean from the comfort of your home.

> Read what AAA's professional inspectors say about area hotels, restaurants and attractions.

> Check out the best stuff to see and do, with itineraries to ensure you won't miss a thing.

 **Go to AAA.com/travelguide today to discover your next destination.**

---

**AAA Mobile App**
**CAA Mobile App**

# Mexico

## Popo's Splendor

Popocatépetl and its sister volcano Iztaccíhuatl are twin landmarks in this rugged nation

## Beaches Galore

Mexico's beaches range from Cancún's powdery sand and aquamarine water to the Pacific's rolling breakers

## Majestic Echoes of the Past

At Chichén Itzá, the remains of a great Mayan city wait to be explored

## Mountains & Sea

Puerto Vallarta blends old Mexico and modern amenities against a striking backdrop

## Head on Down to Cabo

Golf, great restaurants and luxurious accommodations, all set against a strikingly stark desert backdrop

© Vixit / Shutterstock.com

Mexico in the 21st century stands at a crossroads of sorts. Perhaps nowhere else on Earth is there such a difference between old and new, between the traditional past and the unpredictable future.

Timeless "Mexican" images still exist, of course. Donkeys amble down dusty paths, and ancient ruins stand silhouetted against the sky. But for every small village where a herd of goats comprises the local traffic, there is a vehicle-choked freeway. And for every local market displaying live chickens, hand-woven baskets and piles of dried chile peppers, there is a glitzy mall offering the latest in upscale merchandise.

The extremes of wealth and poverty here can be shocking. Half an hour away from Cancún's glittering resorts sit windowless, thatch-roofed huts with dirt floors. In bursting-at-the-seams Mexico City, high fashion and haute cuisine coexist with sprawling shantytowns lacking running water.

But while a Third World way of life is still unfortunately the norm for many Mexicans, visitors benefit from a strong and growing first world of hotels, restaurants and related amenities, as well as a cultural heritage richly expressed through fiestas and national celebrations. This makes Mexico a fascinating country that can be explored rather easily. What are you waiting for?

## Historical Overview

Historians don't know where Mexico's native peoples originally came from. But somewhere around 5000 B.C., in the valley of Tehuacán southeast of Mexico City, a straggling tribe of seed gatherers figured out how to domesticate maize, a grain plant, becoming corn farmers in the process and establishing permanent villages.

Eventually cities were built. At a time when much of Europe was decidedly primitive, civilizations in the New World were chalking up sophisticated architectural, scientific and artistic achievements. The ruins of pyramids, palaces and temples in central and southern Mexico left behind striking evidence of the Olmec, Maya, Toltec and Aztec cultures that flourished, in some instances, more than a thousand years before the arrival of Spain.

The Maya people were particularly accomplished; they developed the mathematical concept of zero and produced a calendar enabling their priests to predict eclipses and plot the movements of the solar system. But the Maya also participated enthusiastically in brutal games, human sacrifice and ritual bloodletting, which they believed helped them communicate with the gods. From about 200 B.C.

through the eighth century, the vast Mayan empire spread north from Guatemala to the Yucatán Peninsula.

In the early 1300s the fierce, nomadic Aztecs migrated from place to place in search of a prophetic vision foretold by the Toltec people: an eagle perched on a cactus pad, clutching a serpent in its beak. According to legend, that vision was seen on an island in the middle of Lake Texcoco, within the Valley of Mexico. The Aztecs settled at the site of present-day Mexico City, building a city that was well advanced by the beginning of the 16th century. Ironically, it was the Aztec thirst for ruthless dominance that led to their undoing at the hands of Spanish *conquistadores.*

The brutal conquest of the Aztecs gave Spain the infamous distinction of wiping out hundreds of years of Indian achievements in Mesoamerica. Spanish reign was insignificant politically but momentous socially. Mexico's colonial cities, its grand cathedrals and most of its historic buildings were constructed during 3 centuries of Spanish rule.

Spain justified its continued presence in Mexico on the basis of converting the natives—considered barbarians—to Christianity. The church thus played a singular role in the

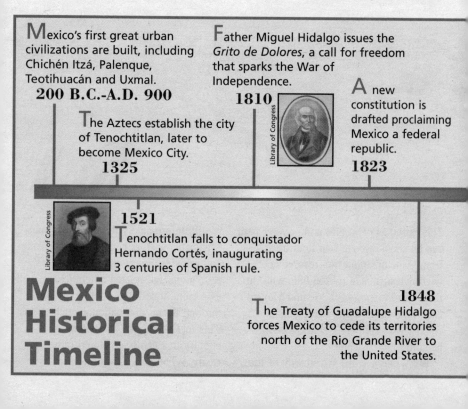

Mexico's first great urban civilizations are built, including Chichén Itzá, Palenque, Teotihuacán and Uxmal.
**200 B.C.-A.D. 900**

The Aztecs establish the city of Tenochtitlan, later to become Mexico City.
**1325**

Father Miguel Hidalgo issues the *Grito de Dolores*, a call for freedom that sparks the War of Independence.
**1810**

*Library of Congress*

A new constitution is drafted proclaiming Mexico a federal republic.
**1823**

*Library of Congress*

**1521**
Tenochtitlan falls to conquistador Hernando Cortés, inaugurating 3 centuries of Spanish rule.

# Mexico Historical Timeline

**1848**
The Treaty of Guadalupe Hidalgo forces Mexico to cede its territories north of the Rio Grande River to the United States.

colony of New Spain, which consisted of all Spanish possessions in North and Central America. Augustinian, Dominican and Franciscan friars (and later the Jesuits) all journeyed to New Spain to minister and teach, and missions were established in the depths of the wilderness.

Mexico's struggle for independence resulted from two things: the divisiveness bred by a rigid class system, and the continuing exploitation of a vast outpost off which only Spanish colonists profited. Freedom was finally achieved in 1821, but political turmoil was the rule rather than the exception throughout the remainder of the 19th century and into the 20th.

Rapid industrial growth and economic improvement came in the mid-20th century. The new Mexican prosperity was put on world view during the 1968 Summer Olympics, held in Mexico City. A guerrilla uprising, a political assassination and a devastating currency devaluation—all in 1994—threatened the country's leap from developing nation to world player, and in more recent years parts of the nation have been wracked by the violence of warring drug cartels.

## Natural Features

Mexico is a geographical transition point from the North American continent's topographic and climatic extremes to the more uniformly tropical features of Central America and the Caribbean basin. Its sun-scorched deserts and jagged mountain ranges are harsh, but they also have an austere beauty. In contrast are verdant valleys, cool highlands and mile after mile of sandy, palm-fringed beaches.

Roughly triangular in shape, Mexico narrows from 1,300 miles across its northern frontier to a mere 140 miles at the Isthmus of Tehuantepec. Two peninsulas—Baja (Lower) California and the Yucatán Peninsula—are appendages to the mainland. The terrain is mostly hills or mountain ranges broken by level plateaus, with the plateaus carved into many canyons and valleys.

The Sierra Madre comprises three great mountain ranges. The Sierra Madre Oriental and the Sierra Madre Occidental form the eastern and western boundaries of the central plateau region. The Sierra Madre del Sur frames the Pacific coast through the states of Guerrero and Oaxaca. The height of the mountains is accentuated by deep valleys and canyons, which can plunge more than 1,500

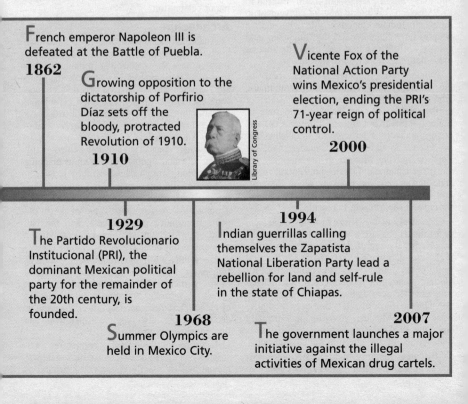

French emperor Napoleon III is defeated at the Battle of Puebla.
**1862**

Growing opposition to the dictatorship of Porfirio Díaz sets off the bloody, protracted Revolution of 1910.
**1910**

Library of Congress

Vicente Fox of the National Action Party wins Mexico's presidential election, ending the PRI's 71-year reign of political control.
**2000**

**1929**
The Partido Revolucionario Institucional (PRI), the dominant Mexican political party for the remainder of the 20th century, is founded.

**1994**
Indian guerrillas calling themselves the Zapatista National Liberation Party lead a rebellion for land and self-rule in the state of Chiapas.

**1968**
Summer Olympics are held in Mexico City.

**2007**
The government launches a major initiative against the illegal activities of Mexican drug cartels.

feet below the general level of the plateau. There are hundreds of volcanic peaks in Mexico; in the state of Michoacán alone there are more than 80.

The backbone of the Baja California Peninsula is formed by several westward-sloping mountain ranges. The Yucatán Peninsula, on the other hand, is primarily flat or rolling; its highest point is barely 1,000 feet above sea level. Much of the subsurface rock is limestone, and subterranean erosion creates many cenotes, sinkholes that fill with water and become natural swimming pools.

The Baja California and northwestern mainland coasts are marked by numerous bays and coves. Farther south, Pacific breakers crash against the feet of the Sierra Madre Occidental and the Sierra Madre del Sur. The Yucatán Peninsula's eastern coast boasts two outstanding natural features: powdery sand beaches and the clear, aquamarine waters of the Caribbean Sea.

## People

The Indians, or *indígenas,* living in Mexico today are direct descendants of the Aztec, Maya and other ancient civilizations. They speak a primary language other than Spanish, and many might express surprise if referred to as "Mexican." While it may be convenient to lump all Indians together, Mexico's native peoples are characterized by linguistic and cultural differences that can be as distinct as those defining Norwegians and Italians.

Ethnic groups populate different parts of the country. They include the Tarahumara, who dwell in the Copper Canyon region of northwest Mexico; the Yaqui, in the state of Sonora; the Huichol and the Tarasco, near and along the central Pacific coast; the Nahua and the Otomí, in the central plateau region; the Zapotec and the Mixtec, in the state of Oaxaca; the Chamula, Tzeltal and Tzotzil, in the state of Chiapas; the Huastec, along the eastern Gulf of Mexico coast; and the Maya, throughout the Yucatán Peninsula.

The status of *indígenas* in today's Mexico, unfortunately, is not a whole lot better than it was during the era of Spanish rule. Poverty is a chronic, debilitating fact of life for the majority of the country's Indian communities, including many in economically challenged southern Mexico. Indian rights—particularly the demand for self-rule—has been a thorny issue for the Mexican government, especially since the 1994 uprising in the state of Chiapas that was led by the guerrilla Zapatista group.

The great majority of Mexicans are *mestizos* of mixed European and Native American descent. They have perhaps the strongest sense of national identity, although occupying various levels of prosperity and social standing. The small percentage of citizens of purely European ancestry, sometimes referred to as the "Thousand Families," control much of the country's political power and economic wealth, just as the Spanish once did.

Many Mexicans have a strong streak of fatalism. Aztec ceremonies revolved around human sacrifice. The Spanish conquest wiped out entire cities. Post-independence Mexico endured war, revolution, assassinations and civil strife. The people have weathered hurricanes, erupting volcanoes and devastating earthquakes. Thus it's no surprise that death is both honored and mocked in such celebrations as the Day of the Dead, when decorated sugar skulls are sold, costumed children bear mock coffins in street parades and families pay tribute to deceased members in front of lavish home altars.

Priority is given to both family and holidays. On weekends city dwellers exit the concrete jungle en masse for beaches, parks and lakeside resorts. A minor saint's day is reason enough to hold a fiesta, and the birthday of a national hero or the date commemorating an important historical or religious event merits a major celebration.

## Architecture

Archeological sites—some little more than a few earthen mounds or a crumbling platform, others the spectacular remains of cities—offer intriguing clues as to how their creators lived. Mexico's first great architects were the Maya. They constructed ceremonial centers connected by straight, wide roadways of crushed limestone called *sacbe* (sack-BEH). These ancient roads were marvels of engineering, since the flat land denied builders an elevated vantage point while planning construction through dense, scrubby jungle.

Mayan buildings took three main forms: the pyramid, often with a temple capping the summit; the palace, consisting of a central court surrounded by chambers; and the ball court, a wide, flat area used for playing a mysterious but presumably sacred ball game.

Essentially a religious monument, pyramids frequently had steps built into the sides. Stone, particularly the porous, volcanic rock known as *tezontle,* was the building material of choice. Exterior carvings not only served as decoration but also depicted historical and mythological events.

Unfortunately, Spanish conquerors destroyed many Indian architectural achievements, and frequently chose razed ground as the spot to erect their own buildings. The Spanish conquest ushered in a 300-year period during which ecclesiastical architecture predominated, often imitating prevailing European trends.

Augustinian, Dominican, Franciscan and Jesuit friars built churches throughout Mexico as part of a large-scale attempt to convert the natives to Christianity. These structures, distinguished by thick walls and simple interiors with vaulted ceilings, were impressively fortified to serve as protection against Indian attack. A monastery built around an enclosed patio was usually connected to the church. Decoration also served an educational purpose, as frescoes and stone carvings vividly depicted the symbolic themes of the new religion.

Lavish ornamentation became the rule, and its ultimate expression was a Mexican development known as Churrigueresque. Named after Spanish artisan José de Churriguera, buildings in this style exploded with carved geometric forms, leafy vines, frolicking cherubs, scrolls and other imaginative accents. Churrigueresque interiors were a cornucopia of extravagant embellishment, often executed in gold; the overall intent was literally to knock one's eyes out.

During much of the 19th century Mexico was disrupted by war and political turbulence, and when relative prosperity returned under dictator Porfirio Díaz the new round of public buildings were mostly massive structures that again reflected what was happening in Europe. The Palace of Fine Arts (Palacio de Bellas Artes) in Mexico City was designed and executed by Italian architects following classic blueprints, while wealthy hemp exporters in Mérida gave their ornate mansions a refined Parisian influence.

The early 20th century found Mexican architects struggling for a style to call their own. Attempts at monumentality produced such misguided curiosities as the gigantic statue of José María Morelos, a hero of the Mexican War of Independence, built on an island in Lake Pátzcuaro.

In the last half of the century, however, innovative architecture resulted from the combination of old and new design elements in buildings like the National Museum of Anthropology in Mexico City and those on the campus of the National University of Mexico (UNAM) in the Mexico City suburb of San Angel. Large-scale resorts in Cancún, Los Cabos and Acapulco are striking examples of contemporary architecture, often incorporating ancient motifs in ultra-modern settings.

## Music and Dance

Mexico's musical traditions are exceedingly rich and abundantly varied. As with architecture and art, styles tend to originate elsewhere before being assimilated and frequently adapted to suit the national preferences: passion, romance and insistent rhythms. Popular folk and dance music in particular vividly evokes the country's sights, sounds and moods.

Indian musical expression is ceremonial in nature, often linked to religious rituals or village fiestas. But within the mixed *mestizo* population music has a genuinely mass appeal that is strengthened by a healthy recording industry, ceaseless radio play and impromptu performances that enliven the main plazas of practically every town in the country.

Little is known about what sort of sounds were created by pre-Hispanic civilizations. Music, singing and dancing did, however, play a large role in daily ceremonial life. The mesmerizing beat of the drum was foremost among ancient instruments. Drums were fashioned out of clay, wood, bones and turtle shells. Rattles complemented the beat, and simple reed or clay flutes added a melodic counterpoint. It might well have sounded similar to what is heard in some Indian villages today.

Spanish *conquistadores* and the missionaries who followed them imported European culture. Folk orchestras began to accommodate new instruments, chief among them various types of guitars. The *son* (also called *huapango*), a driving dance rhythm with plenty of instrumental flourishes, is the basic form of *mestizo* music. Regional styles have different names, but the guitar is usually the lead instrument, sometimes replaced by violin or harp.

Another traditional sound comes from the marimba, a percussion instrument similar to a xylophone. When struck with small rubber mallets, the marimba's hardwood bars produce clear, breezy-sounding tones. Marimba music is most commonly heard in southern Mexico and Guatemala, where town plazas resonate with its lively rhythms on fiesta days.

Popular Mexican songs have long evoked the trials and tribulations of daily life. The *corrido*, a folk narrative descended from Spanish balladry, emerged during the turbulent period of the 1910 Revolution and served as a news service of sorts in the days before radio. The *canción* is a slow, unabashedly sentimental ballad. No less dramatic are *rancheras,* nostalgic paeans to home and country originally sung by Mexican cattlemen.

But the music most associated with Mexico is the sound of the mariachis. The custom of hiring a group of professional musicians to play at weddings, birthdays and other special occasions began in the state of Jalisco. Mariachi bands deck themselves out in the costumes of the *charro,* or Mexican cowboy: tight-fitting pants, wide-brimmed sombreros and lots of silver spangles. They regale foreign tourists, play to homesick laborers in border towns and serenade the object of a young suitor's desire—all for a fee, of course.

Mariachi bands started out playing guitars, violins and harp, with the brassy sound of trumpets later replacing the harp. The style reached its peak in the 1950s, when Mexican matinee idols in Hollywood films sang love songs to the strains of mariachi music. A mariachi band worth its salt will be able to reel off a variety of songs from long-established classics to customer requests in styles from achingly sad to irresistibly upbeat—and all delivered with undeniable heart and soul.

*Cumbia,* a seductive, danceable import from the Caribbean, was the most popular music in Mexico in the 1980s; the songs are distinguished by flirtatious lyrics often spiced with double entendres. Equally danceable salsa is popular as well. And concerts given by brass bands fill parks and town halls throughout the country.

Native folk dances are one of Mexico's most enjoyable traditions for visitors. Although Spanish *conquistadores* initially tried to eradicate what they viewed as simply pagan rites, Franciscan and Dominican missionaries encouraged the continuation of Indian dances and wove these age-old rituals into their ongoing efforts to convert the natives to the Catholic church.

Like music, folk dances vary by region. Around Papantla in the state of Veracruz, Totonac Indians still perform the flying pole dance, originally a ceremony meant to appease the rain gods. In the states of Sonora and Chihuahua, Yaqui and Tarahumara Indians perform the deer dance, a ceremony once meant to impart good luck on the hunt. A dancer in this vivid re-enactment may even wear the stuffed head of a deer.

*Los Viejitos,* the "Dance of the Little Old Men," originated in the state of Michoacán. Danced by young boys wearing masks that resemble a much older visage, it begins with them moving slowly in a parody of old age, but by the end the pace enlivens considerably.

Popular traditional dances are based, not surprisingly, on Spanish steps. Everyone knows the *jarabe tapatío,* or Mexican hat

dance. The costumes for this passionate interlude are flamboyant: for men, the silver-embroidered shirt and trousers and wide-brimmed sombrero of the horseman *(charro);* for women, the national costume, a *china poblana* dress. It ends with the man's sombrero placed on the floor and the couple snappily parading around it.

## Food and Drink

Authentic Mexican dishes have many influences, among them Maya, Aztec, Spanish, French, Moorish and even Chinese. There is much more to the cuisine, however, than the commonly mistaken notion that it is always hot. Many items in use throughout the world originated in Mexico. Corn is the country's greatest contribution to global cookery, but the list also includes tomatoes, chocolate, avocados, squashes, beans, pumpkins, chiles and turkeys (the only bird bred in pre-Hispanic Mexico).

Corn, the centerpiece of the Indian diet, took on an almost magical significance in many cultures, being used in religious rituals and ceremonies. Called *teoxintle* until the Spaniards renamed it *maíz,* the different corn varieties enabled native cooks to put this versatile vegetable to assorted uses—grinding kernels to make tortillas, thickening soups, creating beverages.

A thin wrapper made from coarse cornmeal, the tortilla is universally known and appears in many guises. A tortilla wrapped around a filling is a taco, one of the earliest Mexican foods as well as the one most commonly embraced north of the border and around the world.

Flour tortillas are used for northern Mexican grilled meat tacos, replaced by smaller yellow or white corn tortillas in central and southern Mexico. These small, soft tortillas are often doubled to hold a filling and sold in orders of two or three. Tortillas also are rolled around fillings and then fried until the tortilla is crispy, a nod to the hard taco shells popular north of the border.

Chopped onion and cilantro are the classic toppings, augmented by salsas, chopped radishes and cucumbers, grilled green onions *(cebollitas)* and the juice of lime wedges *(limones).* Fresh chopped salsa with tomatoes, onions and cilantro is called *salsa casera.* Cooked red salsas utilize dried chiles, while *salsa verde,* made with tomatillos—the small, tart-tasting tomato native to Mexico—is green. Another garnish is guacamole, usually a thinner version than the chunky variety used as a dip.

There are numerous versions of the standard street taco, and different regional favorites throughout the country. Around dusk the storefront *taquerías* open, street vendor carts begin setting up and the air is filled with the tantalizing aroma of grilling meat. In the evening tacos can be the basis for a light supper (*cena*) and also are a preferred late-night snack.

*Tacos al pastor* and *tacos de carnitas* are twin favorites. A Mexican adaptation of Middle Eastern spit-grilled meat, *tacos al pastor* are made with marinated pork stacked on a vertical spit above a gas flame. As it roasts the meat is shaved off, heaped on a tortilla and topped with grilled onions, cilantro and often pieces of fresh pineapple. In Puebla a variation of *tacos al pastor* called *tacos arabes* is wrapped in a thicker tortilla similar to pita bread and served with a spicy, deep-red salsa flavored with *chipotle*, dried *jalapeño* chiles.

*Tacos dorados,* also called *taquitos* or *flautas,* are tortillas rolled around a filling, usually cooked chicken or beef, then fried and topped with shredded lettuce, cream (*crema*) and grated Mexican cheese. In Baja California and along the Pacific coast fish tacos are popular; batter-dipped, fried filets are wrapped in a tortilla along with shredded cabbage, guacamole, salsas and onions marinated in vinegar.

As long as you follow a couple of basic common-sense rules, indulging in street tacos—some of the tastiest food in Mexico—should not result in digestive problems. Trust the judgment of locals and look for a taco stand that has lots of customers, a sure sign the food is good. Pick one that specializes in a certain type of taco rather than offering a wide variety; fewer ingredients mean that they are likely to be fresher.

There are taco variations as well. When covered in tomato sauce and served with melted cheese, soft rolled tacos are called enchiladas. Crisp fried tortillas spread with minced chicken, meat or salad are *tostadas.* Tortilla dough turnovers filled with cheese are *quesadillas;* when filled with potato, pork sausage or refried beans and then fried in fat, they become *empanadas.*

Like tacos, *tamales* are made from a corn-based dough to which lard is added, creating a mealier texture. A *tamale* is filled with bits of chicken, pork or such sweets as chocolate, wrapped in corn husks or banana leaves and then steamed. *Sopes* are flat, thick disks of dough made from ground corn treated with lime juice (*masa*) that are baked on a griddle. Topped with various combinations of meat and vegetables and garnished with cheese, salsa and cilantro, *sopes* are best eaten right after they've been made.

*Tortas* are sandwiches prepared with a small loaf of bread called *telera* or *bolillo* and then filled with different meats, lettuce, onion, tomato, cheese and avocado. The *cemita,* which originated in the city of Puebla, is a sandwich on a soft, sesame-seed egg roll. The meat is usually pork or beef pounded thin and then deep-fried; fillings include onions, sliced avocado and mild white cheese.

Like the taco, two Mexican side dishes are known around the world. *Frijoles* (beans) are cooked in various ways and served either whole or mashed, or combined with rice, vegetables, chicken livers, plantains or eggs. Guacamole is usually seasoned with onions, hot peppers and chopped tomatoes.

Street food can be as simple as pieces of freshly peeled fruit sold in a plastic cup or threaded on a skewer. A popsicle vendor can be found on almost every city street corner. *Churros,* sold from carts, are ridged, tube-shaped pieces of fried dough that are dusted with sugar or filled with fruit or chocolate. Corn on the cob (*elote*) is roasted in the husk, then speared on a stick and spread with condiments like butter or sour cream and sprinkled with cheese or red chili powder. The kernels also are cut off the cob and served in a Styrofoam cup to which the condiments can be added.

### Festive and Regional Fare

A distinctly Mexican concoction is *chiles rellenos,* or stuffed chiles. A dark green chili pepper—not the sweet bell variety—is stuffed with cheese or ground meat, fried in a coating of egg batter and then simmered in tomato sauce. A variation of this dish is called *chile en nogada.* Instead of tomato sauce, the chili (stuffed with beef, pork and fruits) is covered with ground fresh walnuts and a pureed white cheese similar to cream cheese. When sprinkled with red pomegranate seeds and garnished with parsley, the dish represents the red, white and green colors of the Mexican flag. It is frequently served in conjunction with independence celebrations during the month of September.

At the time of the Spanish arrival, the staple diet of the Indians included such items as grasshoppers, ant eggs, rats, armadillos, monkeys, parrots and rattlesnakes. In Mexico City and Oaxaca you can sample crunchy fried grasshoppers (*chapulines*) dashed with chili powder and lime juice, ant eggs (*escamoles*) and worms (*gusanos de maguey*)—also crisply fried—that live on the maguey plant, from which tequila is made. *Huitlacoche* is a black, truffle-like fungus that grows on ears of corn; it is often served with crepes. In northern Mexico broiled goat *(cabrito)* is popular.

In and around Veracruz the specialty is *huachinango a la Veracruzana,* red snapper broiled in tomato sauce and served with onions, olives and capers. Acapulco and other seaside towns are known for their ceviche (say-VEE-cheh). Pieces of raw fish or shellfish are marinated in lime juice for at least eight hours, "cooking" the fish. Chopped tomatoes and onions, chiles and such herbs as cilantro are then added. It's served chilled, often as an appetizer.

In the Yucatán Peninsula the food has Cuban, Caribbean, European and Asian influences. The fiery habanero chile common in Yucatecan cookery grows nowhere else in Mexico. Achiote, the tiny red seed of the annatto tree, is the primary ingredient of a pungent paste with a distinctive orange-red color that seasons pork, chicken or fish cooked *pibil* style—a distant relative of American barbecue.

Yucatecan menus offer such authentic dishes as *cochinita pibil,* pork rubbed with achiote, wrapped in banana leaves and baked in an underground oven; *frijol con puerco,* a pork and black bean stew garnished with cilantro, radishes and onions and served with rice; and *huevos motuleños,* a filling breakfast dish featuring a tortilla covered with refried black beans, topped with a fried egg and smothered with tomato sauce or chile-spiked salsa, peas, diced ham and crumbled white cheese, usually served with slices of fried banana or plantain.

*Pozole,* a hearty soup native to the state of Jalisco but popular in many parts of Mexico, incorporates hominy and pork or chicken in a flavorful broth. Shredded lettuce, chopped onions, strips of fried tortilla and splashes of lime juice are frequently tossed in. This stew-like concoction also takes on red or green hues from the addition of ancho chiles or green tomatoes mixed with various greens, respectively. Most Mexican chiles are hot, and some are incendiary, so ask *"Es muy picante?"* ("Is it very hot?") if in doubt about their firepower.

## Beverages

*Cafe de olla* is flavored with cinnamon and sugar, although you'll have to ask for cream (which usually turns out to be evaporated milk). Espresso and cappuccino are widely available—and undistinguished instant is frequently served in restaurants—but Mexicans favor *cafe con leche,* a combination of strong black coffee and hot milk that is often poured into a tall glass. Another favorite is Mexican hot chocolate, which is not as sweet as the American version.

Freshly squeezed fruit juices are inexpensive and refreshing. Ask for a *licuado* (fruit shake) made with bananas or papayas. Also inexpensive are local soft drinks *(refrescos);* try Mexican coke, which is sweeter than Coca-Cola. They are not only safe to drink out of the can or bottle but one of the few luxuries that poorer citizens can afford. Tehuacán, in the state of Puebla, is famous for bottled mineral waters made with and without natural fruit flavors.

*Cerveza* (beer) is ubiquitous, and two Mexican varieties—Corona and Tecate—are sold everywhere; the latter is the country's No. 1 cheap alcoholic beverage. Dos Equis and Bohemia are two quality brews appreciated throughout the world.

Mexico's viticultural history was relatively late in developing. Although pre-Hispanic peoples enjoyed fermented beverages, those derived from the grape were not among them. Spanish colonists introduced the first vine cuttings, and Mexican wines soon began competing with those of the homeland. Today most of the domestic vintages are produced in the state of Baja California. Other major wine-producing areas are in the states of Aguascalientes, Querétaro and Zacatecas.

From the maguey (mah-GAY) plant come several highly intoxicating liquors. Tequila is the quintessential one, traditionally downed from a salt-rimmed glass and immediately followed by a bite into a lime wedge. Bottles of mezcal from the vicinity of Oaxaca sometimes include a worm that lives on the plant.

*Pulque,* manufactured in central Mexico from the maguey's unfermented juice, has less of a kick and is considered to have both nutritious and medicinal properties. *Colonche* is prepared in the states of Aguascalientes, Guanajuato, Jalisco and San Luis Potosí with fermented fruit from the prickly pear cactus. *Rompope* originated in the state of Puebla as a family beverage for festive occasions. Similar to eggnog, its ingredients include milk, egg yolks, sugar, vanilla, cinnamon and a dash of rum.

## Dining Tips

Local cuisine can be found in smaller restaurants called *cenadurías, taquerías* or *merenderos,* which cater more to Mexican customers than to foreign tourists. In such establishments diners can order *carne en su jugo* (meat in its juice), *tamales* and a great variety of *antojitos* (snacks). The sign "Antojitos Mexicanos" indicates that these and other specialties are on the menu.

For those accustomed to an early breakfast, restaurants are not particularly accommodating; many don't open until around 9 a.m. Markets, however, normally open early and are good places to pick up something for a morning meal. Another tip: Buy croissants or sweet rolls at a bakery the night before and have your own breakfast before starting the day.

If you follow the Mexican schedule for dining, you will have lunch no earlier than 2 p.m., cocktails at 7 p.m. and dinner at 9 or 10 p.m. *La comida* is the main meal of the day (*el almuerzo* also means lunch but tends to be a late morning snack eaten on the run). Many restaurants still offer a *comida corrida*, or lunch special, which usually includes soup, a main course, a dessert and coffee. For those on a budget, making this the big meal of the day is the most economical way to dine.

When you're ready for the check, say *"la cuenta, por favor"* ("the check, please"). Making scribbling motions on your hand to imply writing is commonly recognized international sign language. Regardless of the establishment, always ask about policies and double check the total amount of the bill. You might assume, for example, that there are free refills for coffee when in actuality you'll be charged for each cup you drink (a free second cup is more common at breakfast).

Some restaurants may compute the tab by adding up the number of glasses and plates on the table. The 15 percent IVA service tax (10 percent in the state of Quintana Roo and the Baja California Peninsula) may be added (sometimes the charge is 17 percent, which includes local tax); again, double check the individual amounts. This does not take the place of a tip, so leave what you think is appropriate, usually 10 to 20 percent of the bill.

## Celebrations

From the tiniest villages to the biggest cities, some sort of fiesta takes place practically every day of the year. And there's much to celebrate; in addition to observing national holidays and countrywide festivities like Carnaval and the Day of the Dead, every town salutes its patron saint's day.

Fiestas take on myriad forms, but almost every one includes a parade. The procession is usually in association with a revered religious image but also can be secular in nature, often capped off by fireworks. Music, dancing and an array of local edibles are essential elements. Costumed dancers may portray historical, mythological or imagined happenings to the accompaniment of indigenous instruments.

Regional and folkloric dances represent the area or state; mariachi or harp ensembles are the usual accompaniment. The Yucatán has its evocative *jaranas,* danced by couples in white costumes to the lilting sound of a band. Yucatecan fiestas, called *vaquerías,* are particularly joyous and colorful.

Mexico's best-known celebration, one in which both Indian and Catholic traditions blend into a unique expression of love for the deceased, is *Los Dias de Muertos,* or Days of the Dead, which are celebrated on Nov. 1 and 2. A straightforward approach to the uncomfortable subject of mortality, the holiday—celebrated in Mexico for centuries—mixes mourning with macabre humor and pagan rites with the Catholic observances of All Souls' and All Saints' days.

Families may honor departed loved ones by telling stories, eating candy skulls or even camping all night in the local cemetery while decorating gravesites, praying and sharing memories. The holiday is downplayed by some as superstitious ritual or quaint religious holdover, but that doesn't stop most of the country from celebrating each November with food, drink, flowers (specifically marigolds, the "flower of the dead") and skeleton figures known as *calaveras.*

The popular belief that the dead are permitted to visit their living kin provides the latter a chance to prepare culinary offerings, which usually include sweet loaves of *pan de muerto* (bread of the dead). A lavish home altar *(ofrenda)* could include candles, mementos, pictures of the departed, a bottle of favorite liquor, dancing skeletons, a portrait of the Virgin of Guadalupe and a display of marigolds. Everyone sings, dances and prays, simultaneously sending up and accepting the inevitability of death.

Some of Mexico's loveliest traditions center on Christmas, despite the American influence of Santa Claus and Christmas trees. Foremost are the *posadas,* which take place for 9 days beginning Dec. 16 and represent the search for an inn *(posada)* in preparation for the holy birth. Bearing candles and figures of Mary and Joseph, guests circle a house begging for a place to stay, but are refused until the Pilgrims are identified. After that the party begins, with hot punch, sweets and the breaking open of *piñatas*. More and more, gift giving is on Christmas Day, although in smaller towns presents are still exchanged on the traditional Twelfth Night, or Epiphany (Jan. 6).

Another Christmas season tradition is the presentation of *pastorelas* in public plazas, schools and theaters. Based on the events immediately before Jesus' birth, they often have a comic touch. Some *pastorelas* include in their cast of characters such historical figures as Aztec emperor Cuauhtémoc and revolutionary Emiliano Zapata, who take part as if they had lived during that first Nativity.

The Lenten season culminates in Holy Week *(Semana Santa)* from Palm Sunday to Easter Sunday, which is marked by solemn *pastorelas* or a re-enactment of the Passion from Judgment to Resurrection. The young man chosen to portray Jesus undergoes rigorous preparation for his role, which in some places includes being whipped and then tied to a cross. Again, the observance often ends with the burning of a papier-mâché figure, this time Judas. Holy Week celebrations also venerate the Virgin Mary, with processions bearing some form of her image.

Many Mexicans travel during Holy Week and the Christmas holidays, so make hotel reservations in advance if you'll be visiting during those times.

## Recreation

Mexico in the 21st century stands at a crossroads of sorts. Perhaps nowhere else on Earth is there such a difference between old and new, between the traditional past and the unpredictable future.

Timeless "Mexican" images still exist, of course. Donkeys amble down dusty paths, and ancient ruins stand silhouetted against the sky. But for every small village where a herd of goats comprises the local traffic, there is a vehicle-choked freeway. And for every local market displaying live chickens, hand-woven baskets and piles of dried chile peppers, there is a glitzy mall offering the latest in upscale merchandise.

The extremes of wealth and poverty here can be shocking. Half an hour away from Cancún's glittering resorts sit windowless, thatch-roofed huts with dirt floors. In bursting-at-the-seams Mexico City, high fashion and haute cuisine coexist with sprawling shantytowns lacking running water.

But while a Third World way of life is still unfortunately the norm for many Mexicans,

visitors benefit from a strong and growing first world of hotels, restaurants and related amenities, as well as a cultural heritage richly expressed through fiestas and national celebrations. This makes Mexico a fascinating country that can be explored rather easily. What are you waiting for?

### Outdoor Activities

In Mexico you can play **golf** at world-class courses, many of which are located at the beach resorts. Los Cabos is famed for its immaculately groomed and devilishly challenging courses designed by pros like Jack Nicklaus. Most of the better courses boast stunning backdrops, from Baja's stark desert landscapes to Cancún's gorgeous beaches to Puerto Vallarta's jungle and mountain backdrops.

The majority of golf courses in Mexico are private and can be played by visitors only if they are accompanied by a member. Hotel-owned courses give preference to guests, although the hotel might be able to arrange access to a nearby facility. Fees at the better courses are expensive and comparable to those in the United States. If you don't bring your own clubs, you'll find rental clubs available at virtually all major courses.

The horse was considered a strange, frightening beast to superstitious Aztecs who first laid eyes on the steeds brought over by Hernando Cortés. These fears were overcome, and many Mexicans are enthusiastic riders. **Horseback riding** is an invigorating way to explore the starkly scenic stretches of northern Mexico, and this part of the country has a number of stables and ranches that rent horses and arrange riding expeditions. You can go for a beachside horseback ride in Baja California and along the Caribbean coast in the Riviera Maya, and at resorts like Acapulco, Mazatlán and Puerto Vallarta.

### The Lure of the Water

There are beautiful beaches along the Pacific and Caribbean coasts. The major resorts all offer the usual water sports, from **water skiing** and **windsurfing** to **sailing** and **parasailing,** and any necessary equipment is easily rented. Pay close attention to local warnings regarding surf conditions; many Pacific beaches have dangerous undertows and strong currents.

**Snorkeling** is good around the islands of Cozumel and Isla Mujeres, where there are clear, shallow waters, brilliantly hued fish and intricate coral formations. The Baja California and Pacific coasts are more suitable for **scuba diving,** although Baja's Pacific waters are quite cold and the diving spots tend to be hard to reach. La Paz, in southern Baja on the Gulf of California, and Guaymas, on the northwestern mainland coast, have inviting waters, equipment rentals and resort facilities.

Other good bases for snorkeling and scuba explorations are Puerto Vallarta, situated amid the coves, rock formations and underwater ledges of the Bay of Banderas; Ixtapa/Zihuatanejo, where offshore rock formations create a variety of underwater sites; and Bahías de Huatulco, with nine lovely bays to explore.

**Note:** If you're taking scuba lessons or have a referral letter from your home training center, check to make sure that the instructor or dive center you choose in Mexico holds U.S.-recognized certification, such as NAUI, PADI, SSI or YMCA.

## Fishing

Mexico offers some of the best deep-sea **fishing** in the world, particularly around the southern tip of Baja California, in the Gulf of California, along the Pacific coast and off the eastern coast of the Yucatán Peninsula. Numerous tournaments are held each year. As part of a movement to protect the country's natural resources, a catch-and-release policy is advocated for sports anglers.

A Mexican fishing license is required to fish in Mexico (including the Mexican side of Falcon Lake). The license covers both freshwater and saltwater species and is valid anywhere in the country, including coastal waters. Licenses can be obtained by mail or in person through the National Aquaculture and Fishing Commission (CONAPESCA) office in San Diego. The address is 2550 Fifth Ave., Suite 15, San Diego, CA 92103; phone (619) 233-4324.

If you intend to fish in Baja California waters, contact the state tourism offices in Tijuana, Rosartio or Ensenada for fishing permit information. In Baja California Sur, contact the state's fishing permit office; phone (612) 123-3807. You also can obtain a Mexican fishing license at select fishing and tackle supply stores in San Diego.

License fees vary depending on boat size and time spent fishing (1 day to 1 year) and range from about $26 to $48 (U.S.). The cost is the same whether the angler is alone or part of a tour group. Everyone aboard private boats in Mexican waters must have a fishing license regardless of age and whether or not they are fishing. Licenses are not transferable. Skin divers and scuba divers who fish need a license as well. Boat operators normally provide licenses for people on chartered excursions, but double check before you go out on the boat. A license is not required when fishing from land.

The maximum catch per day varies by species. Generally authorized maximums are 10 fish caught per day, but not more than five of the same species. Catches of marlin, sailfish, swordfish and shark are limited to one per day per species; catches of tarpon, roosterfish, dorado and shad are limited to two per day per species. The limit on inland bodies of water is five fish per day, regardless of species.

Major hotels and independent companies at the resorts and in port cities can arrange fishing expeditions or provide boats and gear for hire. All nonresident private boats entering Mexican waters must obtain certification and a temporary boat permit from the Mexican Department of Fisheries in San Diego, a Mexican consulate office or a customs broker.

## Spas

For some, the focus of recreation is on relaxation and restoration rather than physical activity. Spa visitors can benefit from the same therapeutic resources used for centuries by indigenous peoples—Mexico's immense variety of native plants.

The country's botanical wonders are many. The nopal, a tropical prickly pear cactus, is a source of vitamin C and amino acids; helps the body pull fluids from tissues back into the bloodstream, thus diminishing cellulite and water retention; and is effective in regulating blood sugar for those who are diabetic. The so-called "magic bark" of the tepezcohuite tree, indigenous to the state of Chiapas, has skin-healing and regenerative properties used to treat sunburn, blisters and blemishes. Mineral-rich volcanic mud stimulates circulation and relieves muscular and arthritic pain.

Hot springs and mineral water bathing resorts still operate in Cuautla, Ixtapan de La Sal, Tepoztlán and other towns in central Mexico. Spa facilities at the beach resorts not only feature pre-Hispanic techniques like the *temazcal,* a type of sweat house that uses hot stones and herbs to purify the body, but also aromatic exfoliations, nontraditional plant medicine therapies and sacred healing rituals. And you can cleanse body and mind with the ocean or the mountains as a breathtaking natural backdrop.

# Fast Facts

**POPULATION:** 112,336,538 (2010 Mexican Census).

**AREA:** 1,972,554 sq km (761,603 sq. mi.).

**CAPITAL:** Mexico City, D.F.

**HIGHEST POINT:** Pico de Orizaba, Ver., 5,657 meters (18,555 feet).

**LOWEST POINT:** South of Mexicali, B.C., 13 meters (43 feet) below sea level.

**LANGUAGE:** Spanish; some 50 Indian languages and many more dialects are spoken outside of major cities and towns. English is widely spoken, particularly in larger cities and at resorts.

**CURRENCY:** The monetary unit is the peso. The exchange rate in May 2015 was about 13.5 pesos=$1 U.S., although small daily fluctuations in the rate are standard.

**BANK HOURS:** Most banks are open Mon.-Fri. 9-1:30; in some larger cities, they may reopen 4-6 and are open Sat. 10-1:30. Banks are closed on all national holidays, and also may close to celebrate local holidays.

**BUSINESS HOURS:** In most cities, businesses operate Mon.-Sat. 9-7; many are closed from 2-4 for the traditional long lunch break. In resort areas stores and shops are often open into the evening and on Sunday. Shop hours may not always correspond to what is advertised. Shopping malls are generally open daily; they are closed Jan. 1, Good Friday, May 1 (Labor Day) and Christmas.

**TAXES:** Mexico levies a 16 percent value-added (Impuesto de Valor Agregado, or IVA) tax on many goods and services, even telephone and Internet services (11 percent in the states of Baja California, Baja California Sur and Quintana Roo, and also along the northern border of Sonora). An additional tax on hotel and beverage services means that some items can carry a 17 percent IVA tax. The tax is supposed to be included in the posted price or rate but is not always itemized separately on your bill; inquire if you feel you are being doubly charged.

**HOLIDAYS:** New Year's Day; Constitution Day, Feb. 5; Birthday of Benito Juárez, Mar. 21; Holy Week (Semana Santa); Good Friday through Easter Sunday; Labor Day, May 1; Battle of Puebla (Cinco de Mayo), May 5; Independence Day, Sept. 16; Day of the Race (Columbus Day), Oct. 12; Christmas, Dec. 25. Banks, government offices and most stores are closed.

**MEDIA:** Mexico has no national English-language newspapers. USA Today is usually available in big cities or resorts. The Sanborn's chain, with outlets in the larger cities, carries English-language magazines. Hotels usually provide free magazines that list what is happening around town; most hotels also offer U.S. TV channels.

**ATTRACTION SCHEDULES:** Before setting out for a day of sightseeing, check with the front desk at your hotel regarding schedules for local museums, archeological sites or historic buildings. Many museums in Mexico are open 9-5 and are closed on Monday. Admission fees are inexpensive, usually less than $5 (U.S.). While free admission days or reduced fees for different age groups technically apply only to Mexican citizens, policies will vary depending on the attraction. The listings in this guide provide hours and admissions where known.

**PUBLIC RESTROOMS:** Take advantage of those in hotels, restaurants, airports or bus stations wherever possible, as public restrooms otherwise are difficult to find. Those in out-of-the-way places, particularly at gas stations, often have primitive plumbing and are definitely not up to the standards of public restrooms in the United States. Always carry a roll of toilet paper and a small bar of soap; both of these necessities can be in short supply away from your hotel.

**POLICE:** Few tourists ever run into trouble with the law, but you may need to ask police for directions or seek assistance for other reasons. While most officers are helpful, other encounters—mainly those involving alleged traffic violations—can be exasperating or intimidating if you don't speak fluent Spanish. Always cooperate if stopped, but try to resolve the situation right away.

**RESOURCES:** Bilingual telephone operators with the Mexico Ministry of Tourism (Secretaría de Turismo, or SECTUR) provide 24-hour information about tourist destinations and services. In Mexico City, phone (55) 5250-0123; elsewhere within Mexico, phone 01 (800) 903-9200 (toll-free long distance).

UNITED

STATES

Sonora

Baja
California

Rio

Rio

Chihuahua

Gran de

Bravo

del

Norte

Coahuila

Gulf

Baja

California

of

Sur

Sinaloa

Durango

California

Zacatecas

San

Pacific

Aguascalientes

Nayarit

Guana-
juato

Jalisco

Colima Michoacán

Guerrero

Ocean

## MEXICO TRAVEL REGIONS

Baja California

Northwestern Mexico

Northeastern Mexico

The Pacific Coast

Central Mexico

Mexico City & Vicinity

Southern Mexico

Yucatán Peninsula

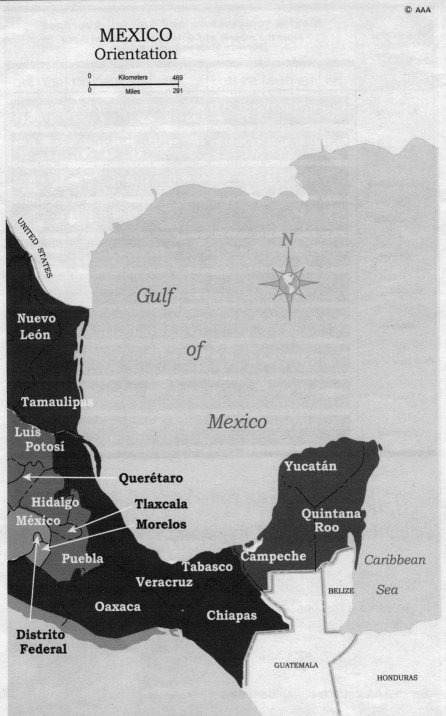

© AAA

MEXICO
Orientation

3022-16

## Mexico Temperature and Rainfall Averages
### From the records of Comisión Nacional del Agua
### (Servicio Meteorológico Nacional)

| | JAN | FEB | MAR | APR | MAY | JUNE | JULY | AUG | SEPT | OCT | NOV | DEC |
|---|---|---|---|---|---|---|---|---|---|---|---|---|
| **Acapulco** | 87/74 .5 | 87/74 .1 | 87/75 0 | 87/75 .2 | 89/77 .9 | 89/77 10.3 | 90/77 9.6 | 90/77 11.0 | 89/77 11.8 | 89/77 5.0 | 89/77 .7 | 88/75 .5 |
| **Cancún** | 82/69 5.4 | 84/69 1.8 | 86/71 2.1 | 89/74 1.5 | 91/76 3.5 | 91/77 5.4 | 92/77 2.2 | 93/77 4.3 | 91/77 8.8 | 88/75 8.7 | 85/73 5.2 | 83/70 3.8 |
| **Guadalajara** | 77/50 .8 | 80/52 .2 | 85/55 .2 | 88/59 .3 | 90/63 .7 | 87/64 7.3 | 81/62 10.8 | 81/62 8.6 | 81/62 6.5 | 81/60 .2 | 80/55 .6 | 77/52 .3 |
| **Mazatlán** | 75/60 .7 | 75/59 .2 | 76/60 .1 | 78/64 .1 | 82/69 0 | 86/76 1.2 | 88/77 7.4 | 88/77 7.6 | 88/77 8.9 | 87/75 3.2 | 82/68 .5 | 77/63 .7 |
| **Mérida** | 88/63 1.5 | 89/63 1.2 | 93/65 1.0 | 96/67 1.0 | 97/70 2.8 | 95/70 5.6 | 95/70 6.7 | 95/69 5.5 | 93/70 6.8 | 91/69 4.8 | 89/67 2.4 | 88/63 1.9 |
| **Mexico City** | 70/42 .4 | 73/45 .2 | 78/49 .4 | 80/51 1.0 | 80/53 2.2 | 76/54 5.3 | 73/53 6.9 | 74/53 6.7 | 72/53 5.7 | 72/50 2.6 | 71/46 .5 | 69/44 .2 |
| **Morelia** | 77/42 .6 | 80/43 .2 | 84/47 .4 | 87/51 .4 | 89/54 1.7 | 85/55 5.4 | 81/54 7.3 | 80/55 6.4 | 80/54 5.2 | 80/51 2.1 | 79/46 .4 | 78/43 .2 |
| **Puerto Vallarta** | 84/62 1.3 | 84/61 .2 | 85/62 .1 | 86/63 .1 | 88/68 .6 | 90/73 7.4 | 92/73 12.9 | 93/73 12.3 | 93/73 14.6 | 93/72 3.7 | 90/68 .8 | 86/64 .9 |
| **Tijuana** | 69/45 1.7 | 70/47 1.7 | 69/49 2.4 | 71/51 .8 | 75/56 .1 | 78/60 0 | 83/63 0 | 82/64 0 | 82/63 .2 | 78/56 .4 | 74/50 1.3 | 69/44 1.4 |
| **Veracruz** | 76/65 .9 | 77/66 .6 | 80/69 .6 | 84/73 .7 | 86/76 1.9 | 87/76 11.7 | 87/75 16.5 | 88/75 12.7 | 87/75 14.1 | 85/73 6.0 | 81/70 2.3 | 78/66 1.0 |

# Mexico State Chart

| State | Abbreviation | Area (sq. miles) | Population | Capital |
|---|---|---|---|---|
| AGUASCALIENTES | Ags. | 2,112 | 1,184,996 | Aguascalientes |
| BAJA CALIFORNIA | B.C. | 26,996 | 3,155,070 | Mexicali |
| BAJA CALIFORNIA SUR | B.C.S. | 28,369 | 637,026 | La Paz |
| CAMPECHE | Camp. | 19,619 | 822,441 | Campeche |
| CHIAPAS | Chis. | 28,653 | 4,796,580 | Tuxtla Gutiérrez |
| CHIHUAHUA | Chih. | 94,571 | 3,406,465 | Chihuahua |
| COAHUILA | Coah. | 57,908 | 2,748,391 | Saltillo |
| COLIMA | Col. | 2,004 | 650,555 | Colima |
| DISTRITO FEDERAL | D.F. | 571 | 8,851,080 | Mexico City |
| DURANGO | Dgo. | 47,560 | 1,632,934 | Durango |
| GUANAJUATO | Gto. | 11,946 | 5,486,372 | Guanajuato |
| GUERRERO | Gro. | 24,819 | 3,388,768 | Chilpancingo |
| HIDALGO | Hgo. | 8,038 | 2,665,018 | Pachuca |
| JALISCO | Jal. | 31,211 | 7,350,682 | Guadalajara |
| MEXICO | Mex. | 8,245 | 15,175,862 | Toluca |
| MICHOACAN | Mich. | 23,138 | 4,351,037 | Morelia |
| MORELOS | Mor. | 1,911 | 1,777,227 | Cuernavaca |
| NAYARIT | Nay. | 10,417 | 1,084,979 | Tepic |
| NUEVO LEON | N.L. | 25,067 | 4,653,458 | Monterrey |
| OAXACA | Oax. | 36,275 | 3,801,962 | Oaxaca |
| PUEBLA | Pue. | 13,090 | 5,779,829 | Puebla |
| QUERETARO | Qro. | 4,420 | 1,827,937 | Querétaro |
| QUINTANA ROO | Q.R. | 19,387 | 1,325,578 | Chetumal |
| SAN LUIS POTOSI | S.L.P. | 24,351 | 2,585,518 | San Luis Potosí |
| SINALOA | Sin. | 22,520 | 2,767,761 | Culiacán |
| SONORA | Son. | 70,290 | 2,662,480 | Hermosillo |
| TABASCO | Tab. | 9,756 | 2,238,603 | Villahermosa |
| TAMAULIPAS | Tamps. | 30,650 | 3,268,554 | Ciudad Victoria |
| TLAXCALA | Tlax. | 1,551 | 1,169,936 | Tlaxcala |
| VERACRUZ | Ver. | 27,683 | 7,643,194 | Jalapa |
| YUCATAN | Yuc. | 14,827 | 1,955,577 | Mérida |
| ZACATECAS | Zac. | 28,283 | 1,490,668 | Zacatecas |

Source: 2010 Mexican Census

# Planning Your Trip

Mexican travel planning depends on whether you'll be driving your own vehicle around the country, flying to one destination only, or flying to one destination and then driving a rental car to another. If you drive your own vehicle, specific regulations govern its temporary importation across the border. There's also your day-to-day, on-the-road itinerary to consider. Flying eliminates many of these additional details, particularly if a travel agency or tour operator is handling the logistics.

Expenses will be determined by your agenda. If you want frills or as many of the comforts of home as possible, travel exclusively by air or take a guided package tour, stay at internationally recognized hotels or all-inclusive resorts, and eat and shop at establishments that cater primarily to tourists. This ensures a hassle-free but likely very expensive vacation. But if you're willing to put up with the occasional lumpy bed or cold shower and don't mind giving up an orderly schedule, you'll reduce expenses and also experience Mexico on a much more intimate level.

While not essential, a knowledge of Spanish is helpful. English is spoken widely in large cities and at the major beach resorts. Hotel and restaurant staff and others in the tourism industry usually understand basic English. Small towns, Indian villages and rural areas in the Yucatán Peninsula and southern Mexico are another story, but if you know some words or phrases in the native tongue, Mexicans tend to overlook halting pronunciations and mixed tenses. The "Speaking of Spanish" section in this guide provides a handy list of common questions and needs.

## Mexico Travel Regions

There are eight geographic travel regions in this guide: Baja California, Northwestern Mexico, Northeastern Mexico, The Pacific Coast, Central Mexico, Mexico

© BlueOrange Studio / Shutterstock.com

# Practical Advice and Tips

City and Vicinity, Southern Mexico and the Yucatán Peninsula. Each of these regions is color-coded on the Mexico Orientation map. Mexico provides varying levels of visitor amenities and many different things to see and do, so a knowledge of what each region offers can aid in trip planning.

**Note:** The U.S. Department of State website provides information that might affect U.S. citizens traveling abroad; go to travel.state.gov and link to "International Travel." For updated information regarding Mexico travel and security issues

phone (888) 407-4747 (from the United States).

## Where To Go

Generally speaking, Mexico's priciest destinations are the big beach resorts like Cancún, Los Cabos, Puerto Vallarta, Acapulco and Ixtapa. For the first-time visitor, they offer the exotic lure of a foreign country without too much cultural displacement—you'll find American fast-food joints as well as thatch-roofed seafood shacks—and a greater percentage of locals who speak English. Also pricey is Mexico City, which is not a place for those seeking laid-back relaxation.

Much of Mexico away from the resorts and big cities provides a maximum of local flavor and a minimum of pampering. Getting close to nature at relatively remote and unspoiled areas is a trend that goes hand in hand with the understanding that preserving the environment also benefits tourism. Numerous tour companies offer specialized excursions based around biking, diving, hiking, kayaking and other outdoor activities; consult a travel agency for details.

Biosphere reserves like Sian Ka'an in the state of Quintana Roo protect a rich variety of indigenous flora and fauna. The El Rosario Monarch Butterfly Sanctuary, in the wooded mountains west of Mexico City, is a refuge for monarchs that annually migrate by the millions to the central Mexican highlands. Also protected are the California gray whales that migrate to Baja's Pacific coast each winter.

If you like or need a high level of comfort, an ecotour is not a wise choice. But for those who prefer unspoiled environments over five-diamond accommodations Mexico offers all kinds of options, from backpacking through the Baja desert to ziplining above the Yucatán jungle to mountain biking through the highlands of Oaxaca state.

Combine affordable and acceptable comfort with the pleasure of experiencing new cultural perspectives by visiting one of the colonial cities. Guanajuato, Querétaro, San Miguel de Allende, Taxco and Zacatecas, built by the Spanish, all have historical and architectural legacies. Oaxaca, San Cristóbal de Las Casas and Mérida are more off the beaten path, but each city is fascinating in its own right, and shoppers will find some of the best native handicrafts in Mexico. Guadalajara offers big-city amenities, authentically Mexican atmosphere and Western familiarity due to a large resident population of American retirees.

## When To Go

In most of Mexico the dry season—October through May—has the best weather. Rainfall patterns, however, vary greatly. In the highland region of central Mexico afternoon showers are likely at any time from June through September, but over a large portion of northern—and especially northwestern—Mexico, rain is infrequent throughout the year. In Chiapas and the normally wet coastal areas, heavy rains can wash out roads or cause mudslides.

Much of northwestern Mexico and Baja California is uncomfortably hot in the summer; in the coastal regions summer heat is exacerbated by high humidity. Conversely, fall and winter evenings in high-altitude locations can get quite nippy.

December through February or March is the high season at Mexico's beach resorts, and accommodation rates at tourist destinations like Cancún and Puerto Vallarta are at their peak. From April through November rates come down and crowds let up. Each resort has its own timetable; Cancún, for example, is crowded with U.S. spring breakers during March and April.

Easter week is perhaps the most popular time of the year for Mexican families to vacation. Many Mexicans also travel over the Christmas holiday period and during such major national celebrations as the Fiesta of the Virgin of Guadalupe on Dec. 12. For good weather, lower cost and crowd avoidance, a general rule of thumb is to go in the spring or fall.

It's a good idea to obtain advance confirmed reservations for accommodations at beach resorts and in most other Mexican cities during the peak travel seasons—roughly speaking, December through June at the resorts and June through August at the inland cities. Reservations are imperative for the week preceding and following Easter. All things considered, one of the nicest times to visit is in November; temperatures are moderate, summer rains have turned much of the normally brown landscape a lush green, and the busy holiday season is still a month away.

## Calling Mexico

To call Mexico from the United States and Canada, dial 011 (the international access code), then 52 (the country code), then the area code and local phone number. For credit card and operator-assisted calls, dial 0152, then the area code and local phone number. While major hotels in tourist areas normally have English-speaking staff, a basic knowledge of Spanish always comes in handy.

## What May Be Taken Into Mexico

If you're driving across the border your baggage will be examined at the Mexican customs checkpoint. Each vehicle must pass through an automated "traffic light" signal system. After submitting a customs declaration form or oral declarations, the driver presses a button that activates a randomly flashing signal. If the light flashes green there is no further action; if it flashes red your luggage will be inspected, regardless of previous declarations made to customs officials.

The best time to cross the border is early in the morning on weekdays. Weekends—and especially holiday weekends—are the worst time, and there may be a long wait depending on what time you arrive at the border. There's also the possibility of exasperating interactions with customs officials or time-consuming additional inspections at customs or immigration substations. But for the most part it's a streamlined process, especially if you're traveling light.

Airline passengers receive a customs declaration form (printed in English) on the flight listing all items that can be brought into Mexico duty-free and without prior authorization. The filled-out form is submitted to customs officials upon arrival at the entry point. At most airports (for example, Mexico City's), after retrieving your luggage you'll proceed to a similar automated mechanism and press a button that activates a randomly flashing signal. If the light flashes green simply hand in your declaration; if it flashes red your luggage will be inspected.

**Note:** Complaints regarding treatment by Mexican customs officials may be registered by contacting the Comptroller General's Office (SECODAM) in Mexico City; phone 01 (800) 001-4800 (toll-free long distance within Mexico), or (888) 594-3372 (from the United States).

**Money:** Up to $10,000 in U.S. currency and traveler's checks (or the equivalent in other currencies) may be taken into Mexico; any greater amount must be declared. U.S. traveler's checks, particularly those issued by the most recognized institutions, are normally easy to cash. It may be more difficult to cash Canadian currency and traveler's checks, so many Canadian travelers convert

# Weather Notes

Mexico encompasses some 760,000 square miles and varies in elevation from sea level to more than 18,000 feet above. This wide range of terrain guarantees a correspondingly wide range of climatic conditions. The weather can be oppressively steamy or refreshingly cool, extremely dry or persistently rainy. Because much of the country lies within the tropics, altitude rather than latitude tends to determine the temperature. Two characteristics more or less stand out: a large number of hours of annual sunshine, and distinct wet and dry seasons.

Many of Mexico's major inland cities, including Mexico City, Guadalajara, Puebla, Guanajuato, Morelia and Querétaro, are at altitudes that give them comfortable temperatures almost year-round. Northwestern cities such as Chihuahua and Hermosillo experience greater seasonal extremes; summers are sizzling, while temperatures during winter can drop below freezing and occasional light snow falls. Cancún, Acapulco, Puerto Vallarta and other coastal resorts, on the other hand, show little temperature variation from month to month. The nicest weather in these cities is from November through March, when humidity levels are fairly low and little rain falls.

Severe weather and natural disasters in Mexico are sporadic in nature. Localized heavy rains—particularly in low-lying, tropical coastal areas—can cause flooding, bridge washouts and mud or rock slides that adversely affect travel. Occasional hurricanes hit the eastern Yucatán Peninsula, the lower Gulf of Mexico coast, and the Pacific coast from the southern part of the normally arid Baja California Peninsula south to Acapulco. Earthquakes, however, cause the most catastrophic damage. While they are an ever-present possibility, the great majority of visitors will hopefully never experience one.

their money into U.S. currency beforehand.

When presented with sufficient identification, major credit cards are accepted provided that the credit card company normally operates in Mexico. Small-denomination traveler's checks and cash always come in handy, however.

You can make your dollars go further by exchanging them only as you need them. Exchange rates are posted at hotel front desks, currency exchange offices and banks. Banamex and Bancomer are two of the largest Mexican banks; most cities and towns have branches of one or the other.

If you transport or cause to be transported (including by mail or other means) more than $10,000 in currency or negotiable instruments such as traveler's checks into or out of the United States, you must file a copy of Customs Form 4790 with U.S. Customs and Border Protection, 1300 Pennsylvania Ave. N.W., Washington, D.C. 20229.

**Personal items:** You may take with you into Mexico duty free clothing, footwear and other personal items. The allowance includes jewelry, perfume, toiletries, books and magazines (in a quantity that does not indicate they are for commercial purposes), and medicines for personal consumption (accompanied by prescriptions as appropriate and in accordance with quantities prescribed).

Unless acceptable proof of prior ownership is presented upon return to the United States, duty may be required on personal articles that are foreign-made. This proof can be a bill of sale, insurance policy, jeweler's appraisal or original receipt of purchase. Items with serial numbers or other permanently affixed identification can be registered with the nearest Bureau of Customs and Border Protection office before departure. The certificate of registration will facilitate re-entry into the United States should any question of prior possession arise.

**Photographic equipment:** One camera, including the power source (for non-digital cameras, the allowance also includes up to 12 rolls of unused film). One video camera and 12 blank cassettes also are admissible. Foreign-made cameras can be registered at the point of departure to prove that they were not purchased in Mexico. Tripods and flash equipment require special permits for use at archeological sites, museums and monuments.

**Weapons:** The only way to legally import firearms and ammunition into Mexico is to secure a permit in advance. Tourists are not permitted to bring pistols, revolvers, automatic firearms or weapons of any type. Technically this includes all knives (pocket and Swiss Army knives, as well as switchblades and other knives that could be classified as weapons). Although tourists are not likely to be fined or incarcerated for bringing in knives for camping or personal use, you may want to purchase such a knife while in Mexico.

**Drugs:** Mexican law, to which tourists in Mexico are subject, deems that trafficking in and/or possession of illegal drugs is a federal offense. All such cases are prosecuted rigorously by the Mexican government regardless of the nature of the drug. During the extensive trial process, which can last more than a year, offenders are not eligible for bail; if found guilty, they are ineligible for parole.

If you require medicines containing habit-forming drugs or narcotics, take precautions to avoid any misunderstanding. Properly identify all drugs, carry only the necessary quantity and bring a prescription or written statement from a physician. These safeguards will also help to avoid potential customs problems upon return to the United States.

**Other duty-free items:** Also allowed are one tent and camping equipment, one surfboard, two tennis rackets, a pair of skis, one pair of binoculars, one new or used laptop or tablet computer, two cellphones, one portable digital audio player (such as an iPod), one CD player, one portable television set, one DVD player, up to 20 CDs or audiocassettes, up to five DVDs, a musical instrument that can normally be carried by one person, up to five used toys (if the tourist is a minor), and personal items that compensate for or aid individuals with a disability.

The duty-free limit for the above items is usually per person or per individual family member. Also admissible are gifts or items up to a total value of $300 (provided none are restricted) if arriving by air or sea, $50 if arriving by land. These duty-free limits apply per each crossing or arrival. There are no restrictions on the containers in which items are imported.

Each tourist, provided that he or she is not a minor, may bring in 3 liters of wine or another alcoholic beverage and two cartons of cigarettes, 25 cigars or 200 grams of loose tobacco. Recreational vehicle owners can bring in kitchen, dwelling and/or bedroom furniture or utensils, a videocassette player and a bicycle (with or without motor).

Tourists are *not* permitted to bring any type of live animal, fresh food products of animal or vegetable origin, or plants, flowers or fruits into Mexico. The following foodstuffs are allowed: dehydrated foods or canned fruit or vegetables, packaged roasted coffee, dried spices, dry herbal medicines, canned or bottled jellies or fruit preserves, canned or bottled nuts and sauces, and U.S.- or Canadian-processed cheeses.

## Packing Hints

Bring clothing items that are comfortable and easy to care for. In Mexico City and other high-altitude areas, a light coat is a good idea during the winter months, a sweater or jacket for other times. Sweaters also can ward off the chill of air conditioning, which can be icy in those establishments that have it. Lightweight summer clothing is all you'll need for the beach resorts. For dining in an upscale restaurant, casual evening clothes (a sports jacket for men, a dress or pantsuit for women) are appropriate. Bring an umbrella for the rainy-season months of June through September.

A pair of sturdy, comfortable walking shoes is essential for exploring ruins or even negotiating the frequently cobblestoned streets of cities and towns. A luggage cart is useful if traveling by bus—stations in smaller towns rarely have porters—and it can save money at airports. If you plan to be on the go much of the time, a shoulder bag may be more appropriate than a suitcase; make sure it fastens securely.

Take an extra pair of sunglasses, a hat and sunscreen, insect repellent (absolutely necessary in lowland and coastal areas and not always available in Mexico), a vacuum or plastic bottle for drinking water, and eyedrops to ease discomfort from wind or glare.

Bring your own prescription drugs. Toilet paper is often missing from restrooms in out-of-the-way locations; in such situations try to carry a roll with you. Purchase necessities like batteries before you leave, as they are usually more expensive in Mexico. Another useful item is a bathtub plug; in many hotel rooms they are missing or don't fit properly.

Electrical current in Mexico is 110-volt, 60-cycle AC—the same as in the United States and Canada—which permits the use of such small standard appliances as shavers, travel irons or hair curlers. In smaller towns, electricity may be weak or even unavailable, so bring a small flashlight and disposable razor.

## Crossing the Border

All U.S. and Canadian citizens entering Mexico by land must stop at the international border to show proof of citizenship and pay a fee to have their tourist permit validated. If you are planning on driving beyond the mainland border zone you also must

© Bruce Raynor / Shutterstock.com

provide the necessary forms for temporarily bringing a vehicle into the country, which necessitates a stop at a Mexican customs and immigration office. Hours of operation for these offices at major border crossing points are as follows:

### CALIFORNIA/MEXICO

Calexico/Mexicali—Daily 24 hours

San Diego/Tijuana—Daily 24 hours

### ARIZONA/MEXICO

Douglas/Agua Prieta—Daily 24 hours

Lukeville/Sonoyta—Daily 6 a.m.-midnight

Nogales/Nogales—Daily 24 hours

### TEXAS/MEXICO

Brownsville/Matamoros—Daily 24 hours

Del Rio/Ciudad Acuña—Daily 24 hours

Eagle Pass/Piedras Negras—Daily 24 hours

El Paso/Ciudad Juárez—Daily 24 hours

Laredo/Nuevo Laredo—Daily 24 hours

McAllen/Reynosa—Daily 24 hours

U.S. and Canadian citizens traveling to Mexico must carry proof of citizenship. A valid (unexpired) passport book is the most convenient, since it ensures problem-free re-entry into the United States, serves as a photo ID and facilitates many transactions, such as cashing traveler's checks.

You can request a passport application form by contacting the National Passport Information Center; phone (877) 487-2778, or TTY (888) 874-7793. The U.S. State Department website has comprehensive passport information and online application forms; link to "passports."

It's a good idea to keep a record of your passport number. Make two photocopies of your passport identification page and other personal documents before leaving home. Leave one set at home, and carry the other set with you in a separate place from your actual documents.

U.S. citizens who travel across the Mexican border regularly for business reasons can apply for a passport card, a wallet-sized document that will facilitate entry and expedite document processing at official land and sea points of entry. The passport card has the same validity period as the standard passport book: 10 years for adults, 5 years for children under 16. Passport cards cannot be used for air travel.

All U.S. and Canadian citizens traveling between the United States and Mexico by air, regardless of age, are required to show a valid passport. Acceptable forms of identification when entering Mexico by land or sea are a passport or passport card. When leaving Mexico and re-entering the United States by land or sea a passport or passport card, Enhanced Driver's License or Trusted Traveler program card is required. Children under 16 who are U.S. citizens can show the original or a copy of their birth certificate or other proof of citizenship, such as a naturalization certificate or citizenship card.

## Tourist Permits

A government-issued tourist permit, *Forma Migratoria para Turista*—commonly referred to as a tourist card, but actually a form—must be obtained in order to travel within Mexico. If you're entering Mexico by land, obtain your tourist permit prior to leaving the United States. Mexican consulates in the United States and Canada or immigration offices at official points of entry issue permits; proof of citizenship is required. An immigration office is identified as *Instituto Nacional de Migración/INM*.

When applying for a tourist permit, minors (under age 18) traveling without their parents—i.e., alone or with friends or relatives—must present proof of citizenship (a valid passport or birth certificate). Minors who are not Mexican citizens are not required to present any other documentation if traveling unaccompanied by one or both parents.

Canadian citizens, including parents, traveling abroad with a minor should be prepared to document their legal custody of that child. If a minor is traveling with a friend or relative, the individual with the minor must have a notarized letter of consent from both parents (including a telephone number) or a custody document. In all cases it is important for the minor to have a valid Canadian passport. Mexican citizens living in the United States must go to the Mexican consulate nearest their place of residence and sign the legal documents granting permission for their child to travel unaccompanied in Mexico.

When departing Mexico your tourist permit must be returned to Mexican immigration. All visitors departing through land points of entry should request that their passport be stamped with an "exit" designation. You can be fined by Mexican immigration officials on your next trip into the country via a land point of entry if your passport does not show the "exit" designation from a prior visit.

## Arriving by Air

There are international airports in all major Mexican cities and resort areas that receive regular flights from the United States and Canada, either directly or through Mexico City. Some airports receive charter flights as well. Unlike nonstop service, a direct flight stops at least once and may involve changing planes.

The following airlines provide service from selected cities in the United States and Canada to Mexican destinations:

**Aeroméxico,** (800) 237-6639 from the United States; aeromexico.com

**Alaska Airlines,** (800) 252-7522 from the United States; alaskaair.com

**American Airlines,** (800) 433-7300 from the United States; aa.com

**Delta Airlines,** (800) 241-4141 from the United States; delta.com

**Interjet,** (866) 285-9525 from the United States; interjet.com.mx

**JetBlue,** (800) 538-2583 from the United States; jetblue.com

**United,** (800) 864-8331 from the United States; united.com

**US Airways,** (800) 428-4322 from the United States; usairways.com

**Virgin America,** (877) 359-8474 from the United States; virginamerica.com

**Volaris,** (866) 988-3527 from the United States; volaris.com.mx

The major domestic airline is Aeroméxico, with flights linking the resorts and larger cities to Mexico City. The country's second largest domestic airline is Toluca-based, low-cost carrier Volaris, which flies to several mainland destinations, plus cities on the Baja peninsula. Low-cost, Mexico City-based carrier Interjet flies to some two dozen destinations throughout the country. Smaller regional airlines, such as Aeromar and Aeroméxico affiliate Aeroméxico Connect, operate in different parts of the country. Traveling between destinations within Mexico often involves changing planes in Mexico City;

schedules, fares and routes all are subject to change.

All arriving passengers must present valid proof of citizenship along with a filled-out tourist permit. Tourist permit and customs declaration forms are distributed on the flight (the tourist permit per individual, the customs declaration per individual or family). At the Immigration counter your tourist permit will be stamped with a "fee paid" designation before you proceed to the baggage claim area to retrieve your belongings.

The last stop is Mexican customs; make sure your declaration form is properly filled out. Mexico uses a random "Red Light-Green Light" system. If you are just bringing personal items and have nothing to declare, you will be asked or directed to push a button. If the light is green you may proceed without inspection. If the light flashes red your luggage will be routinely searched. If you do *not* declare items over and above the $300 allowance and pay all applicable duties and are caught by a red light, you will be fined.

Airports almost always offer fixed-rate transportation via bus, minivan or taxi to downtown or

hotel zone areas. Usually there is a booth at the airport where you can purchase a ticket or voucher. You also may have the option of riding in a private taxi (which costs more) or sharing the ride (and paying less). For safety reasons, never hail an unmarked cab outside the terminal.

There are frequent flights to Mexico from such "gateway" cities as Dallas/Fort Worth, Houston, Los Angeles and Miami. A bewildering array of fares, vacation packages and promotions also are available, and it often pays to search for a bargain. AAA/CAA members can obtain fare and schedule information and make reservations through AAA Travel Agencies. When making reservations, be sure you confirm all flights at least 72 hours prior to departure—particularly the return leg of a round trip.

Charter flights, while offering low fares, also are subject to the greatest number of restrictions. The charter operation can cancel a flight up to 10 days before it is scheduled to depart; if *you* cancel, you may not be able to recoup your money. When considering a charter flight, review the refund policy and contract stipulations carefully. Mexico also charges an airport tax on all departing flights; the nominal fee is normally included in the cost of your airline ticket.

## Car Rentals

U.S. rental cars generally cannot be driven across the border into Mexico. One exception is Hertz, which permits designated vehicles rented at airport facilities in San Diego, Tucson and Yuma to be taken across the border; special paperwork is required.

If you're flying into Mexico but plan on taking a side trip from your main destination, renting a car is an easy way to sidestep dealing with unfamiliar local transportation. AAA/CAA members can reserve a rental car through their local club; it is highly recommended that you make all necessary arrangements prior to your departure.

© Chepe Nicoli / Shutterstock.com

Major U.S. franchises are located in the larger cities. There are numerous Mexican companies as well, but although their rates may be less the vehicles also may be less reliable, and available insurance protection should be carefully reviewed. Overall, the cost of renting a car in Mexico is at least, if not more, expensive than in the United States.

U.S. car rental companies require a credit card. Few if any will accept a cash deposit, and if allowed it will be substantial. A U.S. or Canadian driver's license is acceptable. The usual minimum age limit is 25. With Hertz, renters ages 21-24 will incur an age differential charge, and certain restrictions may apply. Special restrictions also may be placed on drivers above a certain age. Extras such as air conditioning or automatic transmission may incur additional costs.

Also take your itinerary into account when deciding how long to rent. While most companies will allow you to rent in one location and drop off at another, the drop-off charge can be quite steep. Request that a copy of the reservation confirmation be mailed to you; this should reduce the chance of overcharging, since the rate will be printed on the confirmation slip.

Inspect the car carefully before you drive off the lot. Check the windshield for cracks; the windshield wipers; the body and fenders for dents, rust, etc.; the head and taillights; the tires for wear and pressure; and note any missing items, such as the gas cap or floor mats. Seat belts and a fire extinguisher are required by law. A thorough inspection is well worth the time, as you will be charged for anything that is perceived damaged or missing.

Mexican automobile insurance is required; it is provided by the rental company and is figured into the total cost of the contract. Standard contracts normally offer both liability coverage and collision coverage after payment of a deductible. Accepting an optional Collision Damage Waiver (CDW) will be an additional charge but

means that you won't have to pay the deductible (which can be as much as $5,000) in the event of an accident. Also, if you decline the CDW, some companies will apply an amount equal to 10 percent of the commercial value of the vehicle to your credit card.

It is strongly recommended that if renting a car you check with your personal automobile insurer to confirm that coverage is provided for a rental in Mexico; if not, definitely accept the Loss Damage Waiver option. Driving conditions in some areas of Mexico make it advisable to have the additional protection provided by the Loss Damage Waiver.

While the extras add up, they're worth it for peace of mind. In any event, the more coverage you have the better; speed bumps on many Mexican free roads, for example, can cause damage even if negotiated at slow speeds. Look into what your own automobile insurance covers—it might, for example, take care of damages to a rental car.

Keep the rental company's toll-free emergency number handy in case you run into trouble on the road. And when you return the vehicle, remember to fill the gas tank; the refueling charge will be much more expensive than any pump.

## Arriving By Personal Vehicle

If you're driving into Mexico, a little advance preparation can prevent crossing the border from becoming a lengthy process. Both a government-issued temporary vehicle importation permit and a promise to return vehicle form are required for travel beyond 20 to 30 kilometers (12 to 19 miles) of the mainland border (depending on the Mexican state).

The "Only Sonora" temporary vehicle permit program allows visitors to Sonora to drive within the state without obtaining the federal temporary vehicle importation permit. Sonora also has a designated "free zone" (west of Mex. 15 and north of Empalme) that includes the popular tourist

destinations of Puerto Peñasco (Rocky Point), San Carlos and Bahía Kino. A vehicle permit is not needed to drive to these destinations (although proof of citizenship, a tourist permit, a valid driver's license and proof of vehicle ownership are). For additional information about the "Only Sonora" program *see the Border Information section in the back of this guide.*

To be on the safe side, bring the original as well as two copies of your current vehicle license/registration receipt to present at the official point of entry (the immigration checkpoint as you leave the border zone), as Mexican officials may insist on seeing the original. Keep the original in a safe place while you are in Mexico and keep the copies with the temporary vehicle importation permit and the promise to return vehicle form.

For leased or company-owned vehicles, a notarized letter of authorization (printed on stationery showing the company's or leasing agency's letterhead) that permits the driver to take the vehicle out of the United States or Canada and into Mexico is required, and an employee ID card must be presented. If the vehicle is not fully paid for, a notarized letter from the lienholder authorizing use of the vehicle in Mexico for a specified period must be presented.

Rented vehicles require a rental agreement and a notarized affidavit from the rental company stating the company's permission to bring the car into Mexico. The same name must appear on the rental agreement and on the temporary vehicle importation permit.

If the owner does not have or does not wish to use a major credit card, a bond—based on the value of the vehicle—must be posted with a Mexican bonding firm (Afianzadora) at the point of entry. However, this is a costly procedure that involves much paperwork; fees range from $200-$400, depending on the vehicle's make and model year.

For the temporary importation of two vehicles at least two persons must travel as tourists, and separate permits must be obtained for each vehicle. For example, one individual will not be allowed with both a car and a motorcycle, even if he or she owns both vehicles. One of the vehicles must be registered to another qualified driver in the same party, or a second person can obtain a permit for the additional vehicle by presenting a notarized affidavit of permission from the owner.

It is not mandatory for a group of people arriving in Mexico in the same vehicle to leave in the same vehicle; however, the individual who obtained and filled out the temporary vehicle importation permit must leave the country in the same vehicle in which he or she arrived. The vehicle may be driven by the importer's spouse or adult children, as long as they have the same immigration status; other persons may drive the vehicle as long as the owner is in it. Drivers crossing and recrossing the border need not obtain a new temporary vehicle importation permit with each crossing, provided that the initial permit is still valid.

The temporary importation regulations for automobiles also apply to recreational vehicles.

Equipment and luggage should be packed to permit easy customs inspection. Vehicles exceeding 3.5 metric tons in weight require a special permit, as do buses. If in doubt as to how your vehicle will be classified, consult the nearest Mexican consulate office before starting your trip.

Trailers and motor homes can only stay in Mexico 6 months unless they are left in bond at an authorized trailer park. Such trailer parks have placed a bond with the nearest Mexican customs office, making them responsible for the storage of the recreational vehicle.

When you pay the administrative fee and enter Mexico with your own vehicle, a guarantee must be signed on your credit card, giving the Mexican government authority to track down the owner or driver if the vehicle is left behind. If a fine is incurred, it may be charged against the credit card. Should your vehicle become incapacitated, arrangements to leave without it can be made through the U.S. Embassy or one of its consulates, or through a Mexican customs (Aduana) office.

The Mexican government does not provide facilities for storing an automobile if you must suddenly leave the country due to emergency. It can, however, be left for up to 10 days after the temporary importation permit expiration date, provided that you apply for a *Retorno Seguro* permit at the nearest Mexican customs office.

Hacienda (the Mexican Treasury Department) has the authority to confiscate any vehicle that has been illegally imported into the country. Hacienda also has the authority to confiscate a vehicle whose owner (or driver) cannot produce the proper temporary vehicle importation documentation. It also is illegal for a foreigner to sell a motor vehicle in Mexico.

## Automobile Insurance

U.S. automobile insurance is *not* valid in Mexico. While some American companies may extend their coverage a certain number of miles from the border or number of days in Mexico, *only* a Mexico tourist automobile insurance policy is acceptable as evidence of financial responsibility if you have an accident in that country.

Arrange for a policy with full coverage issued through a reliable Mexican insurance company with complete adjusting facilities in cities throughout the country. AAA offices in border states, Nevada and Utah can provide Mexico automobile insurance to members.

To obtain Mexico insurance, you will need to provide the following: current vehicle title or registration, a valid U.S. or Canadian driver's license, and proof that you currently have U.S. or Canadian automobile insurance (the policy's declaration sheet lists all coverages). Call ahead to determine what additional specific information (vehicle identification number, included accessories, etc.) is needed so that the policy can be accurately written.

The Mexican government has no minimum requirement for insurance; the agent will help you

© James Mattil / Shutterstock.com

obtain the coverage best suiting your needs. If you obtain Mexico insurance through a AAA club office the policy will be written by the day, with a discount for more than 30 days' coverage, and will be issued immediately upon application. Towed vehicles *must* be identified in the policy; if not, the policy can be declared void.

Select Hertz locations in Southern California, Arizona, New Mexico and Texas allow customers to drive designated vehicles up to 250 miles south of the U.S./Mexico border. Members planning to drive a Hertz vehicle into Mexico must purchase a Mexico auto insurance policy directly from Hertz.

If the vehicle is leased or not owned by you, a notarized letter from the leasing company or the registered owner giving you permission to take the vehicle into Mexico must be provided, and must include the vehicle identification number and the dates of your entry into and departure from Mexico.

Unlike the prevailing tenet of U.S. and Canadian law, Mexican law is based on the Napoleonic Code, *which presumes guilt until innocence is proven*. As a result, *all* parties (operators of vehicles, but in some cases even passengers) involved in an accident in Mexico are detained for assessing responsibility. If the accident involves no personal injury, the drivers may be asked to go with the attending officer to the police station to complete the necessary accident report, and the vehicles will usually be impounded for investigation. Once blame is established, the negligent driver's vehicle will remain impounded until he or she pays the damages.

If the accident causes injury or death, the operators will be jailed until the authorities determine who was at fault. Then only the responsible driver will remain incarcerated until he or she guarantees restitution to the victims and payment of the fine imposed for causing the accident (under Mexican law an automobile accident is a criminal offense).

A Mexican insurance policy is recognized by the authorities as a guarantee of proper payment for damages according to the terms of the policy. When presented, it can significantly reduce red tape and help to bring about an early release. However, a Mexican insurance policy may not prevent a motorist from actually being detained *if* he or she is involved in an accident that results in injury or death.

If an accident in which a driver is at fault results in damage to government property, such as road signs, safety fences, light or telephone poles, toll stations, street pavement or sidewalks, he or she must pay for the repairs needed even if no other vehicle was involved or no injury or death occurred.

All accidents or claims *must* be reported before leaving Mexico. If you need assistance with a claim, you should obtain it *only* from an authorized agent or adjuster of the insurance company that issued the policy. Official release papers should be kept as evidence that the case is closed, especially if the car shows obvious damage from the accident.

Rates are based on the current value of the vehicle; towed vehicles are covered separately on the same policy as the towing vehicle. Policies are written in both English and Spanish. In the event of a disagreement, the Spanish text will prevail. Read your policy carefully before entering Mexico to discern what is and isn't covered. Some companies, for example, do not include lawyer's fees or bail to defend the policyholder against criminal charges, although adjusters in the larger cities may keep lawyers on a retainer who will act on behalf of the insured free of charge.

A separate policy may be required to pay for translating and notarizing a driver's license or other documents. A separate policy also may be required to cover personal accident insurance, baggage insurance and medical coverage.

## For Assistance

Ask at your hotel desk or consular office for the name and address of the nearest hospital and English-speaking doctor. Several Mexican and U.S. companies offer medical evacuation service by air; the U.S. Embassy in Mexico City provides a list of these firms. Tourist publications often print names and addresses of local hospitals. Most Mexican cities and towns also have a Red Cross (Cruz Roja) facility.

Assistance often is provided by Tourist Assistance (*Protección al Turista*). Offices are in Ensenada, Mexicali, Rosarito, San Felipe, Tecate and Tijuana on the Baja California Peninsula and in the capital of each state on the mainland, normally in the same building that houses the State Tourism Office. The U.S. Embassy and Mexican consulate offices in the United States and Canada can provide lists of attorneys who speak English. Federal Consumer Protection Agency (*Procuraduría Federal del Consumidor*) offices are in all state capitals and other major cities.

If detained or arrested, by international law you have the right to call a consular officer. The long distance access code for the United States and Canada from within Mexico is 95 (station to station). For Mexico from within the country the code is 91. To make a direct international call to the United States or Canada from within Mexico, dial 001 before the area code and phone number; to call long distance from one Mexican destination to another, dial 01 before the area code and phone number.

## State Department Services

The U.S. State Department's Office of Overseas Citizens Services office deals with such situations as notifying home if you are caught in a natural disaster or political disturbance, locating someone in the event of an emergency, delivering emergency messages, making emergency money transfers and providing emergency loans. The Office of Children's Issues handles international child abduction cases. To reach either office, phone (888) 407-4747 (from the United States) or (202) 501-4444 (within Mexico).

# Mexican Consulates in North America

## ARIZONA

**NOGALES**——Consul de Mexico, 135 W. Cardwell St., 85621; (520) 287-2521

**PHOENIX**——Consul General de Mexico, 320 E. McDowell Rd., 85004; (602) 242-7398

**TUCSON**——Consul de Mexico, 553 S. Stone Ave., 85701; (520) 882-5595

## CALIFORNIA

**LOS ANGELES**——Consul General de Mexico, 2401 W. Sixth St., 90057; (213) 351-6800

**SACRAMENTO**——Consul General de Mexico, 2093 Arena Blvd., 95834; (916) 329-3500

**SAN DIEGO**——Consul General de Mexico, 1549 India St., 92101; (619) 231-8414

**SAN FRANCISCO**——Consul General de Mexico, 532 Folsom St., 94105; (415) 354-1700

## COLORADO

**DENVER**——Consul de Mexico, 5350 Leetsdale Dr., Ste. 100, 80246; (303) 331-1110

## DISTRICT OF COLUMBIA

**WASHINGTON, D.C.**——Consul de Mexico, 2827 16th Street N.W., 20009-4260; (202) 736-1000

## FLORIDA

**MIAMI**——Consul General de Mexico, 1399 S.W. 1st Ave., 33130; (786) 268-4900

**ORLANDO**——Consul de Mexico, 2550 Technology Dr., 32804; (407) 422-0514

## GEORGIA

**ATLANTA**——Consul General de Mexico, 1700 Chantilly Dr. NE, 30324; (404) 266-2233

## ILLINOIS

**CHICAGO**——Consul General de Mexico, 204 S. Ashland Ave., 60607; (312) 738-2383

## MASSACHUSETTS

**BOSTON**——Consul de Mexico, 55 Franklin St., Suite 506, 02110; (617) 426-4181

## MICHIGAN

**DETROIT**——Consul de Mexico, 645 Griswold St., Ste. 830, 48226; (313) 964-4515

## MISSOURI

**KANSAS CITY**——Consul de Mexico, 1617 Baltimore Ave., 64108; (816) 556-0800

## NEBRASKA

**OMAHA**——Consul de Mexico, 7444 Farnam St., 68114; (402) 595-1841

## NEW MEXICO

**ALBUQUERQUE**——Consul de Mexico, 1610 4th St. N.W., 87102; (505) 247-4177

## NEW YORK

**NEW YORK**——Consul General de Mexico, 27 E. 39th St., 10016; (212) 217-6400

## NORTH CAROLINA

**RALEIGH**——Consul de Mexico, 336 E. Six Forks Rd, 27609; (919) 754-0046, ext. 222

## OREGON

**PORTLAND**——Consul de Mexico, 1305 S.W. 12th Ave, 97201; (503) 274-1442

## PENNSYLVANIA

**PHILADELPHIA**——Consul de Mexico, 111 S. Independence Mall East (in the Bourse Building), Suite 310, 19106; (215) 922-4262

## TEXAS

**AUSTIN**——Consul General de Mexico, 410 Baylor St., 78703; (512) 478-2866

**BROWNSVILLE**——Consul de Mexico, 301 Mexico Blvd. Ste. F-2, 78520; (956) 542-4431

**DALLAS**——Consul General de Mexico, 1210 River Bend Dr., 75247; (214) 932-8670

**EL PASO**——Consul General de Mexico, 910 E. San Antonio Ave., 79901; (915) 544-9299

**HOUSTON**——Consul General de Mexico, 4507 San Jacinto St., 77004; (713) 271-6800

**LAREDO**——Consul de Mexico, 1612 Farragut St., 78040; consul@srelaredo.org

**SAN ANTONIO**——Consul General de Mexico, 127 Navarro St., 78205; (210) 227-9145

## UTAH

**SALT LAKE CITY**——Consul de Mexico, 1380 S. Main St., 84115; (801) 521-8502

## WASHINGTON

**SEATTLE**——Consul de Mexico, 2132 Third Ave., 98121; (206) 448-3526

## CANADA

**MONTRÉAL**——Consul General de Mexico, 2055 Peel St., Suite 1000, Québec H3A 1V4; (514) 288-2502

**TORONTO**——Consul General de Mexico, 11 King St. W., Ste. 350, Ontario M5H 4C7; (416) 368-2875

**VANCOUVER**——Consul General de Mexico, 1177 W. Hastings St., British Columbia V6E 2K3; (604) 684-1859

Should you lose your money or other financial resources while in Mexico, the U.S. Embassy in Mexico City can help you contact your family, bank or employer to arrange for the transfer of funds. To transfer funds commercially to Mexico, contacts in the United States should go to the nearest Western Union office and have money sent to an "Elektra" store in Mexico. The funds should be sent in care of your name, either *Dinero en Minutos* (Money in Minutes) or *Va a Llamar* (Will Call). The embassy's website provides information (link to "Financial Assistance").

## Mexico's Highways

Roads in Mexico are generally not marked as clearly as those in the United States. Signs for turns and route directions sometimes consist of city or town names only. Route numbers are normally posted every 5 kilometers (3 miles) on small roadside markers, but these also can be few and far between.

Each Mexican state is responsible for the maintenance of its roads, and some are better kept than others. Weather conditions, especially heavy rains, as well as mud or rockslides keep some roadways in a constant state of disrepair. Lanes on nontoll roads tend to be narrow, and shoulders are either narrow or nonexistent.

Adventurous travelers who plan to drive little-used or unpaved roads should inquire locally about conditions before heading out. Even a good map may not be accurate regarding the condition of unpaved or ungraded routes; deep sand "roads" can stall even a four-wheel-drive vehicle, and seasonal downpours can render unpaved roads impassable. Put a protective covering over your luggage to keep out dust, and store camera equipment in plastic bags.

Do not expect most free roads in Mexico to compare to the interstate highway system in the United States. Following the dictates of mountainous terrain, these roadways are mostly rolling or winding, though there are

many straight and/or level stretches in northern Mexico and the Yucatán Peninsula. Some of them have a sandpaper texture that affords better traction on curves but is wearing on tires.

Try not to drive after dark if at all possible. Few roads aside from toll highways are equipped with street lights, and night visibility is poor. Vehicles are sometimes driven with no headlights, and potholes become invisible after dark. Bicyclists—on bikes without lights or reflectors—and pedestrians commonly use the roads at night. If you intend to cover a certain distance during any one day, get an early start and estimate your total driving time on the side of caution. *Never* pull off the road to sleep.

Livestock—mainly cattle, goats and donkeys—may unexpectedly appear on rural roadways at night and even during the day; slow down and give them a wide berth. Animals will be almost invisible on unlighted roads at night, and can cause tremendous damage to your vehicle if they are struck.

Drive defensively and always be alert to road conditions and other motorists. Bus, truck and other drivers who are familiar with local routes will drive faster and negotiate maneuvers more boldly than tourists on roads that are narrow, winding and weathered. **Note:** Using a cellphone while driving is a traffic violation in the state of Baja California.

Truckers in particular may drive aggressively or inconsiderately. If a truck begins to pass on a two-lane road, be prepared to pull off onto the gravel or graded dirt flanking the road surface if necessary to give the truck adequate room. Exercise caution; along the sides of roadways without shoulders there often is a full or partial covering of brush or undergrowth. Be particularly careful if you are attempting to pass a slow-moving truck—the driver isn't likely to pull over to give you more maneuvering room. Also be on the lookout for vehicles that are temporarily stopped in the roadway, particularly in rural areas.

At intersections with a left-turn lane there usually is a separate left-turn arrow; to turn left legally you must wait for the arrow. If making a left turn off a two-lane roadway where there is no separate left-turn lane, you are expected to pull over to the right as far as possible and wait for traffic to clear before making the turn. A right turn on red is generally not permitted unless there is a sign giving permission to do so; use your best judgment in situations when it is unclear whether you can legally turn right on red.

On two-lane roadways with paved shoulders, a solid white line runs along the right edge of each lane; this is an indication that drivers normally should not cross over to the right of this line onto the shoulder. In many instances, however, that solid line is now a dashed white line, which means that if you see a vehicle approaching you while passing a vehicle in the oncoming lane, you are required to move to the right of the dashed line onto the road shoulder while proceeding, giving the driver of the passing vehicle enough space to complete the maneuver. The driver of the vehicle being passed is supposed to move to his or her right as well. This essentially opens up the center of the roadway for safe passing maneuvers. This system works quite well once you realize why an approaching car appears to be heading straight at you.

Speed bumps *(topes)* and potholes *(baches)* constitute perhaps the greatest danger to motorists on Mexican highways. Speed bumps are at the entrance to almost every town, no matter how small, and also can be encountered within towns. Warning signs will say *Topes, Vibradores* or *Reductor de Velocidad* (speed reducer) and give the distance in meters. Instead of words, some signs show a picture symbol and the distance in meters. In small towns these signs can appear suddenly, and not just at the entrance to town. Some speed bumps may not be preceded by a warning sign, however.

# Embassies and Consulates

Note: If calling or faxing from outside Mexico, dial 01152 before the area code and phone number. The U.S. Embassy's fax number is (55) 5525-5040; the website address is www.usembassy-mexico.gov. Office hours vary but are indicated where known. Offices are closed on U.S. and Mexican holidays.

## U. S. EMBASSY:

Mexico City, Distrito Federal, Paseo de la Reforma #305, Colonia Cuauhtémoc, (55) 5080-2000; Mon.-Fri. 9-2 and 3-5

## CANADIAN EMBASSY:

Mexico City, Distrito Federal, Calle Schiller #529, Colonia Polanco, (55) 5724-7900; Mon.-Fri. 8:45-5:15

## U. S. CONSULATES:

Ciudad Juárez, Chihuahua, Paseo de la Victoria #3650, (656) 227-3000; Mon.-Fri. 8-4:45

Guadalajara, Jalisco, Progreso #175 at Avenida López Cotilla, (33) 3268-2100; Mon.-Fri. 8:30-noon and 2-3

Hermosillo, Sonora, Calle Monterrey #141 Poniente (between calles Rosales and Galeana), (662) 289-3500; Mon.-Fri. 8-4:30

Matamoros, Tamaulipas, Avenida Primera #2002 (at Calle Azaleas), (868) 812-4402; Mon.-Fri. 9-noon and 1:30-3:30

Mérida, Yucatán, Calle 60 #338 (near the Hyatt Regency Mérida), (999) 942-5700; Mon.-Fri. 7:30-4

Monterrey, Nuevo León, Avenida Constitución #411 Poniente, (81) 8047-3100; Mon.-Fri. 8-5

Nogales, Sonora, Calle San José, about 3 miles south of the border and a block west of Avenida Obregón, (631) 311-8150; Mon.-Fri. 8-5

Nuevo Laredo, Tamaulipas, Calle Allende #3330, Colonia Jardín, (867) 714-0512; Mon.-Fri. 8:30-11:30

Tijuana, Baja California, Paseo de las Culturas, Mesa de Otay, (664) 977-2000; Mon.-Fri. 8-4:45

## U. S. CONSULAR AGENCIES:

Acapulco, Guerrero, Costera Miguel Alemán #121 (in the Hotel Continental Emporio), (744) 481-0100; Mon.-Fri. 10-2

Los Cabos, Baja California Sur, Las Tiendas de Palmilla, Km marker 27.5 Carretera Transpeninsular, San José del Cabo, (624) 143-3566; Mon.-Fri. 9-2

Cancún, Quintana Roo, Boulevard Kukulcán, Km marker 13, Torre la Europea, (998) 883-0272; Mon.-Fri. 9-2

Mazatlán, Sinaloa, Avenida Playa Gaviotas #202, Golden Zone (in the Hotel Playa Mazatlán), (669) 916-5889; Mon.-Fri. 10-2

Oaxaca, Oaxaca, Calle M. Alcalá #407, Office 20, (951) 514-3054; Mon.-Fri. 10-3

Playa del Carmen, Quintana Roo, Calle 1 Sur (between Avenida 15 and Avenida 20), (984) 873-0303; Mon., Wed. and Fri. 10-1

Puerto Vallarta, Jalisco, Paseo de los Cocoteros #85 Sur in Paradise Plaza, Nuevo Vallarta, (322) 222-0069; Mon.-Fri. 8:30-12:30 (closed third Wed. of the month)

San Miguel de Allende, Guanajuato, Libramiento José Manuel Zavala #165, Plaza La Luciernaga, (415) 152-2357; Mon. Fri. 9-1

## CANADIAN CONSULATES:

Acapulco, Guerrero, Costera Miguel Alemán and Prolongación Farallón, Centro Comercial Marbella, (744) 484-1305; Mon.-Fri. 9-5

Cancún, Quintana Roo, Plaza Caracol II, 3rd floor (Boulevard Kukulcán, Km 8.5), (998) 883-3360; Mon.-Fri. 9-5

Guadalajara, Jalisco, Aurelio Aceves #225 on Minerva Circle (in the Hotel Fiesta Americana Guadalajara), (33) 3615-6215; Mon.-Fri. 8:30-2 and 3-5

Mazatlán, Sinaloa, Rodolfo Loaiza #202 (in the Hotel Playa Mazatlán), (669) 913-7320; Mon.-Fri. 9-1

Monterrey, Nuevo León, Constitución and Zaragoza #1300 Sur (Kalos Building), (81) 8344-2753; Mon.-Fri. 9-1:30 and 2:30-5:30

Oaxaca, Oaxaca, Pino Suárez #700, (951) 513-3777; Mon.-Fri. 11-2

Puerto Vallarta, Jalisco, Calle Zaragoza #160, (322) 222-5398; Mon.-Fri. 9-4

San José del Cabo, Baja California Sur, Boulevard Mijares at Plaza José Green, (624) 142-4333; Mon.-Fri. 9-1

Tijuana, Baja California, Avenida Germán Gedovius, Zona Río, (664) 684-0461; Mon.-Fri. 9-1

*Topes* are raised cobblestone bumps that can damage the underside of a vehicle unless negotiated at a very slow speed. *Vibradores* are corrugated, both lower and wider than *topes*. Speed bumps are prohibited on open sections of road and on toll roads, except at the entrance to toll stations.

Potholes are a particular problem along older free (nontoll) roadways and are exacerbated in areas that have a summer rainy season. Short-term maintenance may be nothing more than filling the pothole with sand or dirt, and some can be large enough to swallow a tire.

In the downtown sections of larger cities there are likely to be a number of one-way streets. Instead of signs, small arrows on the side of buildings or on lampposts often indicate traffic direction. Follow the flow; if in doubt as to whether you are driving in the right direction, note which way parked vehicles are facing.

## Toll Roads

Most newer highways in Mexico are toll roads (*autopistas*). Divided four-lane highways with road shoulders, they are comparable in quality to U.S. highways. These roads are safe and often scenic, and some are all but deserted because Mexican motorists can't afford to use them.

Toll roads are designated on signs by the word *cuota* (and also by the letter "D" following the route number), nontoll roads by *via libre* (free road). Toll routes usually have a free alternative route. *Libramiento* indicates a route that circumvents big city centers or bypasses smaller towns entirely. These bypasses, which sometimes are part of the toll route, can save time by avoiding congested areas.

Individual tollbooth (*plaza de cobro*) fees vary. Most booths near the U.S. border and in the vicinity of popular tourist resorts, such as Cancún and Cabo San Lucas, accept dollars in addition to pesos. However to be on the safe side, it is very wise to carry more than enough pesos to cover

all tolls regardless of your route. You will receive a receipt in return for payment, which also acts as an insurance certificate to avoid paying road repair charges if you are involved in an accident. Following are some major routes:

**Mex. 1-D** (Tijuana to Ensenada): Runs about 114 kilometers (71 miles) south from the U.S. border to Ensenada in the state of Baja California.

**Mex. 2-D** (Tijuana to Mexicali): Runs east-west along the U.S. border in the state of Baja California.

**Mex. 15-D** (Nogales to Mazatlán): Runs about 1,212 kilometers (727 miles) from the U.S. border south to Mazatlán through the states of Sonora and Sinaloa.

**Mex. 15-D** (Tepic to Guadalajara): Runs about 228 kilometers (137 miles) southeast through the states of Nayarit and Jalisco.

**Mex. 15-D** (Guadalajara to Mexico City): Runs about 668 kilometers (401 miles) southeast through the states of Jalisco, Michoacán and México.

**Mex. 40-D** (Durango to Mazatlán): Runs about 225 kilometers (140 miles) southwest through the states of Durango and Sinaloa.

**Mex. 57-D** (Mexico City to Querétaro): Runs about 210 kilometers (126 miles) northwest from Mexico City through the states of México and Querétaro.

**Mex. 85-D** (Nuevo Laredo to Monterrey): Runs about 235 kilometers (141 miles) south from the U.S. border through the state of Nuevo León.

**Mex. 55-D/95-D** (Mexico City to Acapulco): Runs about 415 kilometers (257 miles) south from Mexico City via Cuernavaca to Acapulco (states of Morelos and Guerrero).

**Mex. 180-D** (Mérida to Cancún): Runs about 242 kilometers (145 miles) from the junction with Mex. 180 east to the junction with Mex. 307 through the states of Yucatán and Quintana Roo.

**Arco Norte:** (Querétaro to Puebla): Runs about 223 kilometers (138 miles) from just outside Querétaro to just north of Cholula (near Puebla), bypassing the Mexico City metropolitan area to the east.

## Gasoline, Oil and Repairs

All gas stations in Mexico are concessions granted by the federally run oil company, Pemex. Fuel prices are fixed by the government. To avoid being overcharged by service station operators (a practice that targets foreign motorists in particular), you'll need to be vigilant. Make sure the pump has been turned back to zero before the attendant begins filling your tank, know exactly how many gallons/liters your tank holds and watch the station attendant closely up until the nozzle is pulled out and replaced on the pump. Also make certain you are being charged the correct amount.

keep smaller denominations of pesos in case attendants run out of change. Stations on major routes are spaced at adequate intervals, but it's a good idea to always keep your gas tank at least half full.

Most Pemex stations sell two grades of unleaded (*sin plomo*) gas. "Magna," dispensed from green pump handles, is the cheaper of the two; the "Premium" grade is dispensed from red pump handles. Pemex stations no longer offer Nova (leaded) gas, although diesel fuel is available.

Fuel quality is comparable to U.S. unleaded grades. In May 2015, a gallon of regular Magna was equivalent to about $3.40 (U.S.); a gallon of premium, about $3.60; a gallon of diesel, about $3.55. Gas prices in the northern border region tend to be a bit higher than in central and southern Mexico, but as is the case north of the border there are regional differences as well as frequent fluctuations in the price. Stations are full service; let the attendant fill the tank, but make sure he zeroes out the pump. Tipping is customary; a few pesos is fine.

Since unleaded pump nozzles in Mexico are sometimes larger than those in the United States, it's a good idea to keep a funnel in the car. Remember that pumps in Mexico register liters, not gallons; 10 liters is equal to about 2.5 gallons. For conversion information, see the metric equivalents chart in the back of this guide.

Stations with a "GasoPLUS" sign accept credit cards of the same name for gasoline purchases, but otherwise you'll have to pay cash, so keep peso amounts handy. Payments must be made in pesos, although some Pemex stations now accept credit cards. Along the border and in areas frequented by tourists (for example, in Cancún and Playa del Carmen) dollars also are accepted.

Service stations and private garages carry oils made in Mexico by foreign companies and by Pemex. Its brand, Brio, comes in several grades which are indicated by the color of the can; gold, black and blue are the best.

Propane gas is obtainable by vacationers traveling in recreational vehicles more than 50 kilometers (30 miles) south of the U.S. border. This policy ensures that tourists who use propane for their engines, stoves and heaters will have an adequate supply.

If your own vehicle or a rental car requires routine maintenance or major repairs while on the road, there are plenty of automotive repair shops (indicated by signs that say *taller mecánico*) in most parts of the country. Make sure you have a complete understanding about any work to be done as well as its cost. If a part must be ordered there could be additional expense and long delays, as permission from Mexican customs is needed to import parts.

A knowledge of Spanish is usually necessary when negotiating with car repair shops, and it could be difficult finding a mechanic familiar with the make and model of your vehicle. Also keep in mind that some businesses in Mexico still close from around 2-4 p.m. for *siesta*.

## The Green Angels

The idea of having a vehicle breakdown in Mexico can be unnerving, but motorists unfortunate enough to find themselves stranded do have a resource: the Green Angels. Since the early 1960s, these crews have patrolled roadways throughout the country. "Angeles Verdes" are identified by their green uniforms and green-and-white pickup trucks.

The Green Angels patrol a network of routes—both toll highways and nontoll roads—that collectively cover every Mexico state capital and all major tourist destinations. Most Green Angel patrols are linked to base stations in each of the 31 Mexican states plus the Federal District (Mexico City). Trucks are on the road daily 8-8, year-round.

Services offered include vehicle mechanical aid, towing, adjustment or changing of tires, road condition information, medical first aid and protection. Motorists pay for the cost of automobile parts, gasoline and oil, but service is rendered free of charge. A tip is customary, although not required. Although crew members are supposed to be bilingual, a knowledge of Spanish will still come in handy.

To enlist the assistance of a crew, pull completely off the highway and lift the hood of your vehicle. Contact the Mexico Ministry of Tourism (SECTUR) to obtain help or to have a crew dispatched; phone their national hotline, 01 (800) 903-9200 (toll-free long distance from within Mexico).

If you break down in a remote area and don't have a cellphone, it may be necessary to hail a passing motorist, or preferably a bus or truck driver, and ask that he or she stop at the nearest available location to place the call. You also may be able to use one of the emergency telephones found along most of the newer toll highways and also along some older roads. Since Green Angel crews constantly cover their assigned territory, chances are good that a patrol will soon locate you; repairs, unfortunately, are another matter.

## Road Signs

Road signs are a mix of international picture symbols and signs in Spanish. *Via Corta* indicates a short or alternate route. Right turns on red are prohibited unless a sign is marked *Continua*.

© Brandon Bourdages / Shutterstock

*Retorno* means a U-turn is permitted. Signs often posted just before entering small towns are *Poblado Proximo* (upcoming town), *Disminuya su Velocidad* (reduce your speed) or those that show the maximum speed limit allowed.

Common signs along highways include *Arbochate el Cinturon* (Buckle Your Seat Belt) and *No Deje Piedras Sobre el Pavimento* (Don't Leave Stones on the Pavement); the latter refers to the common practice of placing rocks in the road to denote a hazard or disabled vehicle. Some intersections without traffic signals have signs that say *Ceda el Paso a un Vehiculo* (Cede the Right of Way to One Vehicle); they are posted on each intersecting road and indicate that one vehicle at a time may proceed.

Bridges with signs marked *Un Solo Carril* or *Puente Angosto* are narrow, one-way bridges. When two cars approach such a bridge from opposite directions, the first driver to flick his or her headlights has the right-of-way. The other should pull to the side of the road, allowing the first driver to cross. Although not a regulation, it is a general practice.

Many traffic lights are positioned horizontally rather than vertically, and on some signals the green light flashes three times before the yellow light appears. Motorists stopped at red lights in cities will often be approached by people attempting to earn money by washing windshields. If you're not interested, mouth the words *"no tengo dinero"* or shake your head "no" and rub your thumb and index finger together—the international symbol for "I have no money."

## Parking

If possible, schedule daily activities so that your car does not have to remain unattended for any length of time. Heed "no parking" signs, which depict a red circle with a diagonal red line across a capital "E." Illegally parked cars will be towed, or their license plates will be removed. Recovering either item

can result in a nightmare of time, expense and frustration. If in doubt, park in a guarded lot rather than on the street. Never leave valuables in plain sight in a parked vehicle.

On a one-way street, make certain your vehicle is parked on the left side, not the right. Parking on the street also likely means being approached by a youngster who will offer to watch your vehicle while you're gone. This often is a good idea, since the couple of pesos you hand over are a small price to pay for peace of mind. If a group of boys appears on your return, however, pay only one.

## Law Enforcement

On main highways the speed limit is generally about 100 km/h (60 mph) or as posted. In many cities the limit is about 40 km/h (25 mph); in some small towns it may be as low as 30 km/h (18-20 mph). Always obey the speed limit; while local police are generally lenient toward tourists who commit minor traffic violations, they make an exception in the case of speeding.

In Mexico City and those parts of the state of Mexico falling within the greater metropolitan area (particularly north and east of the Federal District), motorists with foreign license plates may be stopped by police for alleged driving infractions. If you committed a violation and recognize it, accept the *boleta de infracción* (ticket) without arguing.

If you are stopped and did not do anything wrong, however, do not give in to a demand for graft. Write down the officer's identification number and ask to speak with his *jefe* (HEH-feh), or boss, or to be taken to the nearest *delegación de policía* (police station) to explain your situation. In Mexico City, the Secretaría de Turismo (the Ministry of Tourism, or SECTUR) may be able to provide assistance if you feel you have been unfairly accused of a traffic violation; phone (55) 5250-0123. From elsewhere within Mexico, phone 01 (800) 903-9200 (toll-free long distance), or contact the nearest State Tourism Office.

## Bus Service

Mexican bus lines offer frequent express service from U.S. border points to most cities, and also between major Mexican cities. Although service is less extensive in Baja California, buses travel practically everywhere. Among the major lines are Autobuses de Oriente (ADO), Enlaces Terrestres Nacionales (ETN), Transportes del Norte (TN) and Elite.

Most of these companies offer first-class service that is comparable in quality to first-class U.S. bus service. Referred to as *ejecutivo, lujo, primera plus,* "deluxe," "super first class" and similar terms, these buses often include such amenities and extras as air conditioning, reclining seats, footrests, restrooms, movies, free snacks and beverages, as well as controlled 95 km/h (60 mph) speed. First-class buses also make few—sometimes no—stops and carry fewer passengers.

Seats on first-class buses are usually reserved in advance. For long trips, bring your own food—in case you don't want to eat in the restaurant where the bus stops—drinking water and a roll of toilet paper. Even though first-class and luxury buses use toll highways and are thus less likely to encounter incidents of robbery or assault, travel only during the day and avoid overnight trips.

You can hail a second- or third-class bus just about anywhere simply by standing at the side of the road and waving, and they're certainly a great way to experience local life. However, these buses make interminable stops, the vehicles themselves are frequently antiquated and can be unpleasantly hot, and you may have to share your seat with a pig or chicken. Furthermore, they cost only slightly less than first-class or luxury buses, and without the convenience of making advance reservations.

Many Mexican cities have one central bus station (*Central Camionera* or *Central de Autobuses),* which may or may not be near the main plaza or center of town. The various bus lines have offices at the central station. In some cities several stations in different locations serve specific companies or destinations. If you're unsure where to go, ask for the *estación del autobús* and give your destination.

For trips between major cities, purchase a reserved-seat, round-trip ticket from the station in advance; this is imperative for long weekends and around school holidays, holiday seasons and important fiestas. You can search for available seats as well as reserve and pay for tickets on the major bus lines' websites.

Routes, fares and departure times are always subject to change, and the best way to obtain this information is directly from the station. A knowledge of basic Spanish is essential; it also helps to write down your destination and any other particulars and show the information to the ticketing agent to make certain you're getting on the right bus. Schedules usually indicate whether the bus is *local* or *de paso* (which means it is en route from another location). *Directo* or *expresso* indicate a nonstop route. *Salida* means departure; *llegada,* arrival.

Taxis, although more expensive, are a safer mode of in-town transportation than local buses. Exceptions are buses that travel specifically to tourist attractions; while these may be slow, they allow you to relax and enjoy the scenery.

Greyhound Lines Inc. can ticket passengers to most U.S. border cities; once across the border you need to make arrangements with a Mexican bus line. Often there are buses that shuttle between stations on both sides of the border. From Mexico City, bus trips to destinations throughout the country are easily arranged; the major bus lines operate out of four huge terminals located in the northern, southern, eastern and western sections of the city.

Another option to using buses as your main means of on-the-road transportation is to take a guided motor coach tour. Such U.S. companies as Gray Line Tours offer trans-border bus excursions that last from several hours to several days. Contact a travel agency for details.

Reservations can be made to various destinations in Mexico through Ticket Bus. For information phone (55) 5133-5133 or 01 (800) 009-9090 (toll-free long distance within Mexico); www.ticketbus.com.mx.

## Ferry Service

Passenger and vehicle ferry service is provided between the Mexican mainland and Baja California, connecting the ports of Santa Rosalía-Guaymas, La Paz-Topolobampo (Los Mochis) and La Paz-Mazatlán. Advance reservations are required and can be made by phone as well as in person at one of the ferry offices. As a knowledge of fluent Spanish is necessary, it's easier to make reservations through a local travel agency at the port of departure. The website www.bajaferries.com provides fare, schedule and contact information in English.

Fares are one way and per person, sharing the accommodation. *Salon* seats, the least expensive, are airplane-type seats. *Cabina,* cabin lodging with restroom facilities, also is available but is more expensive. Children ages 1-11 are charged half the adult fare. If you're prone to seasickness, bring the appropriate medications. Pregnant women are not allowed onboard. If transporting a vehicle, take everything you'll need out of it before the journey begins.

**Note:** If you plan on transporting a vehicle from Baja California to the Mexican mainland, it is necessary to obtain a temporary vehicle importation permit. To avoid frustration and disrupted travel plans, obtain the permit and have all related temporary vehicle importation documents

filled out at the border before entering Mexico. When applying for a vehicle permit, proof of citizenship, a copy of the current registration and a notarized letter of permission from the lienholder (if a vehicle is not fully paid for) all must be presented for each vehicle being transported (including motorcycles).

Your vehicle must be weighed before you purchase your ticket. Arrive at the ticket office as soon as possible (check in advance; opening times vary from location to location), and inquire where to park your vehicle for weighing (la balanza). Passenger and vehicle tickets are usually sold in separate lines. Also keep in mind that if you have entered Mexico via Baja California and then cross over to the mainland, you will have to go through customs before boarding the ferry and pay whatever duty fees are assessed.

## Health and Safety

Taking reasonable precautions should eliminate serious health risks for almost all foreign visitors. First and foremost: Don't eat anything that you haven't peeled yourself, or that cannot be cooked or boiled. This rule applies primarily to fruits, vegetables and seafood. Avoid unpasteurized dairy products as well. Unless you're used to it, it's best to avoid food sold by street vendors, but at restaurants in cities where tourism is big business, virtually anything on the menu can be enjoyed without fear.

Bottled water in liter or smaller sizes is sold throughout Mexico at gas station convenience stores, grocery stores and shops catering to tourists. Chemical disinfecting tablets also are available from pharmacies and supermarkets.

If the hotel has its own purification system, tap water can be used for brushing your teeth or rinsing contact lenses; ask to make sure, and also ask about the ice dispensed by ice machines. Most hotels routinely provide bottled water for drinking (some may charge for it when you check out). If in doubt about the water in smaller towns, ask for bottled water. Remember that this includes ice cubes. If you find yourself in an area where bottled water is not available, boil water vigorously for one full minute to kill disease-causing organisms.

These precautions should serve to ward off the most common visitor ailment, diarrhea (which Mexicans call turista). Bed rest and a liquid diet (unsweetened tea is best) will cure most cases. If these preventive measures fail, see a doctor. There are physicians, surgeons, specialists, good hospitals and Mexican Red Cross clinics in all the major cities and larger towns. In many villages, visitors can receive medical assistance from clinics or hospitals run by the Instituto Mexicano del Seguro Social (IMSS), the Instituto de Seguridad y Servicios Sociales de los Trabajadores del Estado (ISSSTE) or the Secretaría de Salud.

Most of the better hotels have house doctors; if not, your hotel manager or the local police will help you find medical assistance. It's not a good idea to buy over-the-counter antibiotics.

## Visiting High-Altitude Areas

If you live in or are used to a lower altitude, you may need a short adjustment period when visiting areas above 1,525 meters (5,000 feet). Don't push yourself too hard; a light diet and reduced intake of alcoholic beverages are recommended. Move about in a leisurely fashion for the first few days. If you're affected by the altitude (headache or nausea), rest quietly until you feel comfortable; it may take from 12 to 36 hours before you feel better. Another health consideration at high altitudes is overexposure to the sun; use a suntan lotion that has an effective sunscreen agent.

Persons with weak hearts or the elderly should consult their physician before undertaking prolonged visits to cities at high elevations. Travelers with specific health concerns should inquire about recommended immunizations or medications to carry with them.

Acute Mountain Sickness (AMS), which can strike at altitudes of 2,450 meters (8,000 feet) or more, is the body's way of coping with reduced oxygen and humidity. Also known as altitude sickness, its symptoms include headaches, double vision, shortness of breath, loss of appetite, insomnia and lethargy. Some people complain of temporary weight gain or swelling in the face, hands and feet. Even those used to high altitudes may feel the effects of AMS. If symptoms strike, stop ascending. A quick descent will alleviate the discomfort.

The negative reaction of your body to changes in altitude is lessened if you're in good physical shape and don't smoke. Ascend gradually, eat light but nutritious meals and drink plenty of bottled water. Alcohol consumption may aggravate AMS symptoms if they occur.

**Note:** The elevation for city and place descriptions in this guide is included if it is over 762 meters (2,500 feet).

## Diseases

The risk of contracting typhoid or cholera is minimal, despite sporadic cholera outbreaks. Vaccinations will offer protection in areas off the tourist itinerary, where running water and drainage systems frequently are inadequate, but vaccinations should not be considered a substitute for caution in selecting food and drink. In the case of cholera or other intestinal ailments, this means avoiding raw or undercooked seafood and cold seafood dishes.

The presence of mosquitoes that transmit malaria is dependent on such local conditions as weather, altitude, mosquito control efforts and the prevalence of disease. Mosquitoes also can spread dengue fever. In coastal areas, the risks of being bitten are greater. Use mosquito repellent if you plan on spending time outdoors. Brands containing DEET are the most effective; be sure to read and follow the directions and precautions on the label. Try to avoid being outside between dusk and dawn, when mosquitoes are most likely to bite.

Tourists arriving in Mexico from yellow fever-infected areas must have a yellow fever vaccination certificate; tourists arriving directly from the United States or Canada are not required to have the certificate.

The CDC operates a hotline with international health requirements and recommendations for foreign travelers. Topics include general vaccinations, food and water guidelines and current disease-outbreak reports. Phone (877) 394-8747, or (800) 232-4636 for the immunization hotline.

## Personal Safety

Crimes against tourists in Mexico are unlikely, but the possibility does exist. Cities that are centers of activity for Mexican drug cartels receive most of the negative publicity. And although not directed at tourists, the ongoing violence continues to grab news headlines and adversely affects the daily lives of many Mexicans.

The most hard-hit region is northern Mexico and the northern border cities. Foreign visitors are vulnerable in the Mexico City metropolitan area, where more than 20 million people are crammed together. Violence also

occurs regularly in the central and southern states of Guerrero, Veracruz and Michoacán—mostly in rural areas where vigilante groups combat the cartels, resulting in more violence and many innocent "collateral" victims. Tourist resorts like Acapulco and Mazatlán are affected as well.

Politically motivated violence, again not directed at foreigners, occurs from time to time, especially in southern Mexico. And tourist hot spots like Cancún and Los Cabos that are considered safe also are not immune from hotel room thefts, purse snatchings and pickpockets.

For visitors on vacation, good old common sense is the key to staying out of harm's way. In particular, it helps to look and act confident rather than bewildered when out in public. Don't flaunt expensive watches, jewelry or clothing; you're more likely to be targeted for robbery or assault if you appear well-off or wealthy.

Avoid putting your wallet in a back pocket or wearing a purse with a shoulder strap that can be grabbed by a passerby. Petty thieves and pickpockets often use a razor to slash pockets or bags, so keep your belongings close to you at all times. Put cameras in briefcases or bags with a chain-reinforced strap.

Always carry credit cards and cash on your person, never in a backpack, and hide money in different places; for example, in extra pockets sewn inside clothing. Keep photocopies of passports, credit cards and other documents in a separate place from the originals. Be very cautious around ATM machines. If possible, use one during the day inside a large commercial facility; avoid nighttime transactions at glass-enclosed street machines.

When planning a day of sightseeing, stay informed. Tense local political situations can sometimes result in rowdy demonstrations. Hotel staff, taxi drivers and tour guides are good sources of information in such instances and can offer practical advice should it be necessary to temporarily steer clear of certain parts of town for any reason.

If driving, never leave valuables in plain view in your car; stow possessions out of sight. Use parking lots or garages whenever possible. Legal parking is designated by a sign showing a red circle with a capital "E" inside; no-parking zones have signs with a diagonal red line through the "E."

Always lock your car, roll up the windows and park in a well-lighted area. Do not drive after dark. To avoid becoming a target

© David S April / Shutterstock.com

for robbery, stick to toll highways wherever possible, and never pull off the road to sleep. If traveling by bus, be especially careful at the station; don't leave your luggage unattended, and lock all items together with a chain or cable if possible.

On free roads you may be stopped at military checkpoints and approached by soldiers, police officers or other official-looking men in uniform who request identification and ask where you are going. This happens primarily if you're headed north toward the U.S. border. Most often these checkpoints are conducting random searches for firearms or drugs.

Be sure to slow down and stop if motioned to do so. Remain calm and polite, cooperate fully and speak as little Spanish as possible (or explain in English that you do not speak Spanish). If asked to hand over your wallet, provide *only* the proper identification; if necessary, remove all your money first. Get badge numbers and names, and report any irregularities to the U.S. Embassy in Mexico City, the nearest U.S. consular office in Mexico or to a Mexican consulate office upon your return home.

A potentially more dangerous situation involves criminal groups linked to drug cartels that control highways by setting up impromptu checkpoints. They may ask for papers or check trunks, illegally charge motorists to continue passing through their "territory" or, in worst-case scenarios, steal vehicles or abduct passengers. Cartel checkpoints operate along Mex. 2 in the state of Tamaulipas as well as in the states of Chihuahua, Coahuila, Durango, Sinaloa, Guerrero and Michoacán.

Poorly paid police may intimidate foreign motorists into paying "fines" for minor or alleged infractions. This is particularly true in and around Mexico City, where visitors with non-Mexican license plates may become victims of harassment. You could also be charged with an infraction that you are certain you did not commit.

Such an incident can be both frightening and infuriating, but if it happens, try to remain calm. Ask to be shown documentation of the rule you violated. Request to speak with someone of higher authority if necessary, and beware of "plainclothes policemen"; insist on seeing identification.

Very obviously writing down all the details of the incident—name, badge number, the nature of the alleged violation, the exact location where it occurred—may help defuse the situation. Avoid handing over an original driver's license, car rental contract, vehicle registration or any other document; always carry photocopies.

If resistance provokes further trouble, ask for the ticket, pay it at a bank and claim a receipt. To register a complaint, contact the Secretaría de Turismo (the Ministry of Tourism, or SECTUR). In Mexico City phone (55) 5250-0123; elsewhere in Mexico phone 01 (800) 903-9200 (toll-free long distance).

And while ethnic or sexual stereotyping is unfortunate, it can occur. Female travelers who look obviously foreign, or those with fair skin and hair, may attract unsolicited attention. If this happens, the best response is no response. In many *cantinas,* bars with a macho, often hard-drinking male clientele, female customers are unwelcome.

## Currency

The monetary unit is the peso (its symbol is the dollar sign, or $). One peso equals 100 centavos. There are 5-centavo, 10-centavo, 20-centavo and 50-centavo coins; peso coins are in denominations of $1, $2, $5, $10 and $100. Banknotes are in denominations of 20, 50, 100, 200, 500 and 1,000 pesos. All new banknotes issued by Banco de México are made of synthetic polymer, which gives the bills a longer life. The frequently used 20-peso and 50-peso notes have added safety features such as a transparent window.

The 5-, 10- and 20-centavo coins are not often used, but they come in handy as spare change to give to the needy, if you're so inclined. The 50-centavo coin can help facilitate small transactions like bus fares and souvenir purchases at markets. Hang on to smaller denomination banknotes

and coins as you accumulate them, or exchange a dollar amount that will yield smaller denominations.

Cash payments for amounts that include centavos are rounded off to the nearest 10 centavos. An item costing 11.52 pesos, therefore, would be rounded off to a cash payment of 11.50 pesos; an item costing 11.56 pesos would be rounded off to a cash payment of 11.60 pesos. Check and credit card payments will show the exact amount and must be paid in that amount. Credit card charges are converted into dollars by the bank issuing the card, usually at a favorable bank rate.

In border cities and some tourist resorts, prices in Mexican currency may carry the abbreviation "m.n." (moneda nacional); prices in American currency, "dlls." (dollars). As a general rule, Mexican establishments rendering services to tourists quote and charge in pesos. In many of Mexico's resort areas, though, U.S. dollars are as readily accepted as pesos—and taxi drivers will gladly take dollars almost anywhere in the country. Information sheets showing pictures of Mexican coins and bills are normally available at airports and border crossings, or appear in tourist publications.

**Note:** Attraction admissions in this guide are quoted in U.S. dollars or in pesos with a rounded-off dollar equivalent. In May 2015 the exchange rate was approximately 13.5 pesos to the dollar, although small daily fluctuations in the rate are standard. Attractions that do accept U.S. dollars may set their own exchange rate, often a straight 10 pesos-to-$1 conversion.

Credit cards should cover almost all hotel, restaurant and store charges, as well as airline tickets for flights within Mexico. Gasoline purchases normally cannot be charged unless you have a GasoPLUS credit card—issued only in Mexico—which can be used at Pemex gas stations. Some Pemex stations will accept U.S. credit cards, but have cash on hand just in case.

The best place to exchange dollars for pesos is at a reputable Mexican bank. It pays to find out if your bank has a "sister" bank in Mexico before leaving home (for example, Bank of America partners with Santander Bank in Mexico); you'll avoid service fees entirely or be charged a reduced fee per transaction. The Mexican banks Bancomer and HSBC require you to open an account before any business can be conducted, so inquire about this in advance. Mexican banks also require a copy of your personal identification; some may even ask you to provide the copy yourself.

Another option is to exchange money at home, just in case banks or casas de cambio (currency exchange houses) at airports are closed when you arrive. Wells Fargo Bank offers currency exchange at select branches for a fee.

Traveler's checks denominated in pesos can be purchased at banks and currency exchange offices in the United States and cashed at Mexican banks, hotels and currency exchanges. However, traveler's checks are quickly going the way of the dinosaur, and finding an establishment willing to cash them is becoming increasingly difficult.

Casas de cambio usually offer a better rate of exchange than banks. They often are located next to big hotels in cities, or in malls in resort areas. A driver's license is needed to cash U.S. traveler's checks. Some exchange houses may cash checks issued by all three major U.S. credit card companies (American Express, Mastercard and Visa), while others may not. Some also charge a commission on top of a service fee for transactions, so it's worth the time to find one that does not.

Some currency exchange houses also won't take bills that have marks or other blemishes on them. And there's always the chance that you will be ripped off, especially at airports. Always be very specific about telling the clerk (in Spanish if possible) exactly how many dollars you are exchanging for pesos. If you're traveling with someone, have your companion stand with you at the counter as a witness as you count out your money in front of the clerk.

Currency exchange used to be a standard service at hotel front

© Atomazul / Shutterstock.com

desks before a federal law went into effect prohibiting hotels from exchanging money. For most travelers finding the best rate boils down to a matter of convenience, since differences are normally minimal and the rate can fluctuate daily. If you're shopping around for the best rate or trying to save pennies a pocket calculator will come in handy.

Automated teller (cajero automático) machines are available in major cities and resort areas; most ATMs accept the widely honored Cirrus and PLUS cards. Expect peso denominations in return, and to be charged a hefty service fee by your bank for each transaction. If you don't want to carry around lots of cash, consider investing in a pre-paid Visa or Mastercard prior to your trip.

There is always the possibility that foreign travelers will be forced to withdraw money from an ATM. Make all transactions during daylight hours, preferably at machines inside commercial establishments.

The threat of purse or wallet snatching is ever present in crowded areas or a busy marketplace. Put money and important documents in separate places, and consider keeping extra currency and jewelry in your hotel room safe. When out in public, ignore remarks from strangers such as "What's that on your shoulder?" Or someone yelling "Thief!" in a crowded area—both may be set-ups used by pickpockets or scam artists to distract your attention or trick you into revealing where you carry your money.

## Tipping

The matter of whom, when and how much to tip varies depending on the situation. In Mexico waiters, maids, porters and other workers whose wages are low must rely to a great extent on tips for their living. Let your conscience be your guide, and don't hesitate to reward outstanding service or penalize poor service.

Percentages for hotel and restaurant staff are similar to those in the United States and Canada.

In restaurants, make sure that a service charge has not already been added onto the bill. Taxi drivers are not usually tipped unless they've performed some special service, such as waiting while a bit of shopping is done. Gas station attendants, however, expect a tip.

Sightseeing tour guides should be tipped. There also are individuals whom you would not normally tip at home but should in Mexico; for example, theater ushers, washroom attendants and parking attendants.

Economic reality makes it necessary for some people to resort to begging as a means of survival. Women or children will ask for coins on the street or outside the town cathedral. Another frequently employed location, particularly in larger cities, is a busy intersection. Here an entire family may gather—washing windshields or even putting on an impromptu performance in costume—in return for small change from motorists stopped at the red light. Whether to give under such circumstances is up to the individual, of course, but considering the very real poverty that is a daily fact of life, any gift will be much appreciated.

Street vendors can be ubiquitous, particularly in the main plazas of towns, at archeological sites and other places where tourists are likely to be, and at beaches where vending is not prohibited. If you do decide to purchase something from a roving vendor, be very discreet; otherwise you will be inundated by insistent hawkers pushing everything from fruit to straw baskets. If you don't intend to buy, firmly communicate your lack of interest.

Young children frequently will offer special services to visitors. Even if it is performed in an unsolicited manner—for example, cleaning your windshield while you're stopped at a red light—compensation is expected. Again, if you are not interested in what a child is offering, whether it be

carrying your bags at the airport or promising to guard your car while you shop or see the sights, be very firm about declining.

Youngsters also will charm coins or other gifts out of visitors, and it may be hard to resist these overtures. If you do succumb, hand something directly to a child. Children have been killed running across busy streets to pick up "gifts" tossed from car windows. Better yet, buy some pieces of fruit or other inexpensive foods at the local market. A few clothing items, pencils, pens or simple toys can be packed along with your own personal belongings if you enjoy contributing such gifts to the needy.

## Mail Service

All letter mail to Mexico travels by air. First class mail service from Mexico to other countries is by air; parcel post and second class mail is by land. If you want to send mail from Mexico, use post mail only in those cities with airline service. **Note:** Mail service is notoriously slow, and mail can take up to a month to reach destinations in the United States, even that marked "via air mail." Do not expect postcards, letters or packages to arrive back home before you do.

Postal codes in Mexican addresses should be placed before the name of the destination town or city, as in the following example: Hotel Imperial, Avenida Guadalupe #210, 45040 Guadalajara, Jal., Mexico.

## Addresses

If you've ever had difficulty hunting down an address in almost any large city in the United States, prepare for the same possibility in Mexico. Street names tend to change mysteriously on either side of a town's main square, or capriciously after traversing several blocks. Street signs may be outdated or even nonexistent. Addresses frequently do not include numbers. All of this can be frustrating if trying to locate an out-of-the-way shop or restaurant; however, there are some general guidelines that can be relied on to aid in the search.

Although used where known in this guide for purposes of clarification, designations such as *avenida* and *calle* usually are not posted, and streets are referred to by name only. That name may include a compass direction—*Nte.* or *Norte*, *Sur*, *Pte.* or *Poniente* and *Ote.* or *Oriente* for north, south, east and west, respectively.

When an address includes *s/n* it means there is no number. In numbered addresses, the number follows rather than precedes the name. Addresses on main routes outside of cities or towns will often be stated in terms of the number of kilometers from town; for example, *Km. 18 a Mérida.*

Sprawling urban areas (Guadalajara and Monterrey, for example) have their own inscrutable logic regarding street names and configurations, and trying to find something outside of well-known tourist areas can turn into an adventure. Mexico City in particular has a bewildering maze of thoroughfares, and existing streets are often renamed.

Streets in smaller cities are usually laid out in a simple grid pattern radiating from the central plaza. Specific locations within the core downtown area can thus be pinpointed relatively easily in terms of the number of blocks north, south, east or west of the plaza.

If you become lost in an unfamiliar city or town, asking a local taxi driver for directions or having him lead you where you want to go can save a lot of headaches. A knowledge of Spanish is helpful in these situations, and agree on a price first if he transports you anywhere.

If you need to ask directions from someone on the street, you may be steered off course; Mexicans tend to improvise rather than admit they don't know. But again, there are certain strategies that can increase your chances of success. Keep questions brief and to the point, and ask them with a smile; most people will be happy to try and help. Women who were brought up not to talk to strangers may ignore you, and don't bother asking a child, particularly if your Spanish is rusty. Maps are not likely to be understood; pointing is more direct. If you ask how long it will take to reach a specific destination, or what the exact distance is, the answer is likely to be subjective.

## Phone Service

If you need to make a phone call while you're in Mexico, keep three things in mind. First, they are frequently more expensive than back home. Second, do not expect that calls to attractions, tourist offices, etc. will always be answered; endless ringing or a repeated busy signal are two all-too-common occurrences. And third, if you do not speak fluent Spanish local calls to many businesses, police stations and public service agencies will quickly grind to a halt.

There are very few coin-operated public pay phones in Mexico, and they tend to be out of order. Most public phones are labeled Telmex, the name of the national telephone company, and are part of a system called Ladatel—literally, long distance (*lada*) telephone. Ladatel phones allow direct dialing without operator assistance and are less expensive than making phone calls from a hotel room. Local calls also can be made from Ladatel phones.

Most Ladatel pay phones have a slot in which to insert a disposable Ladatel phone card. Some have two slots—one for the Ladatel card and one for Mexican bank credit cards (Banamex, Bancomer or Carnet). They also may accept Mastercard or Visa, but not U.S. telephone calling cards. Ladatel phone cards can be purchased in various peso denominations (typically 30, 50 or 100 pesos) at most pharmacies and gas station mini-markets, as well as from machines at airports and bus stations.

To make a call with a Ladatel card, insert the card into the appropriate slot, with the computer chip facing up and toward the phone. Dial the access code (if necessary) plus the number you're trying to reach. The card is left in the slot while the call takes place. If the call does not go through, the card is returned. If the call is for less time than the value of the card, it

© Maciej Czekajewski / Shutterstock.com

is returned with a credit amount shown (the card does not expire). If the call is still in progress when the card's value has been used up, the phone will beep and another card must be inserted to continue the call. Some phones have a digital display window that monitors the cost of the call.

When calling long distance from one Mexican location to another, dial 01 (the access code), then the three-digit area code (two-digit area code in metropolitan Guadalajara, Mexico City and Monterrey), then the seven-digit local phone number (eight-digit local number in metropolitan Guadalajara, Mexico City and Monterrey). Mexican phone numbers shown in this guide include only the 10-digit format (area code plus the local number), not the access code that also must be dialed if making a long-distance call. Local calls in Mexico do not require dialing the access or area codes.

Free tourist publications often publish phone numbers for hotels, restaurants, attractions, travel agencies, airlines and so forth, as well as emergency and general information numbers.

All Mexican toll-free numbers have an 800 area code. You must first dial the 01 access code, then the 800 prefix and the seven-digit number. **Note:** Mexican phone numbers with an 800 prefix, such as SECTUR's national hotline number 01 (800) 903-9200, will work *only* if you are in Mexico; the call will not go through if dialed from outside the country.

If your cellphone is activated for international roaming and has worldwide capability it can be used in Mexico; otherwise you will need to have it programmed for a Mexican number. You also can rent one and prepay for the minute allotment you'll need. Calls to Mexican cell phone numbers—either locally or long distance within the country—must be prefaced by dialing 044, which replaces the access code 01. The 044 prefix does not need to be dialed if calling a Mexican cell phone number from outside the country, although you will still need to dial the international access number and the appropriate area code.

If you want to connect directly to an international destination without speaking to an operator, use your calling card and dial 01 (for AT&T) or 001 (for Verizon or Sprint) plus the 800 access number for your long-distance carrier. AT&T's USA DIRECT number is (800) 288-2872; Verizon, (800) 674-7000; and Sprint, (800) 877-8000. To avoid having expensive hotel surcharges tacked on to your bill, don't call from your room.

Some hotels may block one or more access code numbers if you try to call from the room; if that is the case, make the call from a public pay phone with a U.S. calling card. Some also add a charge for local calls made from the room in addition to the hefty surcharge placed on all international calls. Inquire when you check in whether local calls are extra. Avoid public phones claiming to offer low long-distance rates for calls to the United States and Canada; the cost per minute will be exorbitant.

If you have a problem trying to make a specific local or long-distance call, enlist the aid of an operator; there are few recordings advising callers of phone number or area code changes. To reach a long-distance operator within Mexico, dial 020; for directory assistance, dial 040; for emergency assistance, dial 060 or 066; for an international operator, dial 090. English will likely not be spoken.

To make an international call to the United States or Canada on a private phone line in Mexico, dial 001, then the area code and

phone number. If calling collect, dial 91, then the area code and phone number. If you call collect from your hotel room and the call is not accepted, however, you may still be charged.

## Time Zones

Most of Mexico's states are on Central Standard Time. Exceptions are the states of Chihuahua, Nayarit, Sonora, Sinaloa and Baja California Sur, which are on Mountain Standard Time; Baja California, which is on Pacific Standard Time; and Quintana Roo, which is on Eastern Standard Time. The country also observes daylight saving time (DST, referred to as *horario de verano,* or "summer time") from the first weekend in April through the last weekend in October. Ten northern border municipalities (including Ciudad Juárez, Mexicali, Nuevo Laredo, Reynosa and Tijuana) observe daylight saving time in accordance with the U.S., from the second Sunday in March through the first weekend in November. **Note:** The state of Sonora does not observe daylight saving time.

© Jose Ignacio Soto / Shutterstock.com

# Yucatán Peninsula

**M**exico's Yucatán (yoo-cah-TAHN) Peninsula is all about contradictions—it's a mix of old and new, natural and man-made, primitive and master-planned. Geographic, ethnographic and historical factors combine to separate the Yucatán from the rest of Mexico, and it's a feeling shared by many of the people who live here—many think of themselves as *yucatecos* first, Mexicans second.

Mayan civilization, which first evolved in central America and extreme southern Mexico, eventually migrated northward to the present-day states of Campeche and Yucatán. Between the 10th and 15th centuries the cities of Chichén Itzá, Cobá, Dzibilchaltún, Edzná, Ek Balam, Mayapán, Tulum and Uxmal were built. Over time the focus of Mayan life shifted from the observance of elaborate religious rituals toward commercial, governmental and militaristic concerns. But it all came crashing to the ground by the end of the 16th century, when Spanish conquest of the Yucatán was complete.

The Yucatecan people—direct descendants of the Maya—are one of Mexico's largest *indígena* groups. Short stature, dark-skinned complexions and sculpted cheekbones all bear witness to their

ancestors. Mayan dialects are as readily spoken as Spanish, although residents employed in the tourist industry usually speak English as well. Yucatecans are friendly; don't be afraid to ask for the time or for directions, but return the kindness with a smile and a thank-you.

Rising from the peninsula's flat scrubland are such archeological sites as Chichén Itzá, Ek Balam and Uxmal, where monumentally scaled buildings created without the basic assistance of the wheel or metal tools benefit from ongoing restoration. In contrast to the small rural villages dotting the Yucatán's rolling hills stands Mérida, one of the first cities to be built by the Spanish. Fine old buildings, ornate mansions and tropical vegetation give Mérida an exotic feel, and its lively

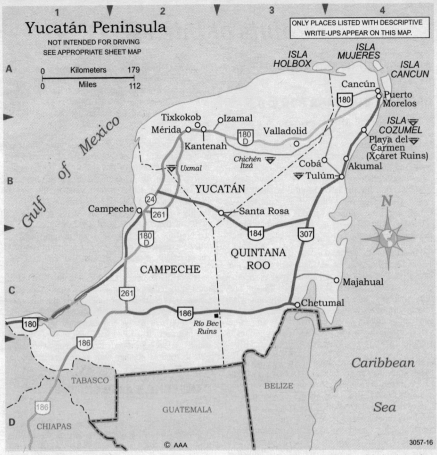

# Yucatán Peninsula

NOT INTENDED FOR DRIVING
SEE APPROPRIATE SHEET MAP

ONLY PLACES LISTED WITH DESCRIPTIVE
WRITE-UPS APPEAR ON THIS MAP.

Kilometers    0    179
Miles    0    112

© AAA

3057-16

plazas and numerous cultural offerings make the city a delightful place to explore.

But the Yucatán's vacation destination of choice is Cancún, which was just a small fishing village in the late 1960s. Since then it's become a major vacation destination for beach lovers, spring breakers and winter-weary gringos.

The stretch of Caribbean coast between Cancún and Tulum is a tourist magnet all its own, with lovely beaches and accommodations ranging from eco-friendly *casitas* to seriously upscale resorts. What to do? The Riviera Maya has family-friendly aquatic theme parks, cenotes in which you can swim and snorkel and an offshore barrier reef for divers, among other enticements.

In stark contrast to manufactured paradise is the very real wilderness of the Sian Ka'an Biosphere Reserve, designated a World Heritage Site in 1987 by the United Nations Educational, Scientific and Cultural Organization (UNESCO). Covering more than a million acres along the peninsula's eastern frontier, Sian Ka'an's tropical forests, lagoons and mangrove marshes are all protected from human encroachment and commercial development.

AAA recommends that travelers consult online U.S. State Department travel advisories when planning traveling abroad. Find this information at http://travel.state.gov/content/passports/english/alertswarnings/mexico-travel-warning.html.

# Points of Interest

## AKUMAL, QUINTANA ROO—

*See The Caribbean Coast p. 86.*

## BACALAR, QUINTANA ROO (C-3)

Bacalar (ba-cah-LAHR) barely registers a blip on the mass tourism radar, which means adventurous travelers who journey to this spot in southern Quintana Roo are rewarded with a gorgeous turquoise lagoon and an authentic town unspoiled by Cancún-like commercialism. Located on the lagoon's western shore, Bacalar has a handful of small hotels (some with lagoon views) that mainly cater to vacationing Mexican families, while a couple of rustic eco lodges with cabana-type accommodations appeal to international visitors.

Founded in 1528, Bacalar was the first Spanish colonial settlement in the region that became Quintana Roo. Although the colonists lived in relative peace for more than 100 years, Spanish-Mayan hostility simmered under the surface, exploding when four local farmers were savagely murdered. The Mayan community in Chetumal retaliated with equal savagery; the site was finally destroyed by pirates in 1652.

In 1726, Bacalar was resettled by Spanish expatriates from the Canary Islands. They built Fort San Felipe (Fuerte de San Felipe), a massive fortification completed in 1733 that was encircled by a most effective deterrent: a crocodile-filled moat. At the outbreak of the Castes War in 1848 the Maya, after brutal fighting, again reclaimed the settlement and the fort. Bacalar remained in Mayan hands until 1901, when the Mexican government reclaimed it peacefully.

Fort San Felipe, now surrounded by landscaped gardens rather than hungry reptiles, has a watchtower that overlooks the waters of Bacalar Lagoon. Inside is the small, interesting Pirate Museum (Museo de la Piratería), which focuses on the area's pirate past and contains displays of weapons and artifacts. Information is presented in Spanish and English. The museum is closed Monday.

Next to the fort is the main plaza. There's an ATM on the west side of the square. On the surrounding streets you may see a curious sight: horse-drawn buggies driven by Mennonites, a religious Christian group similar to the Amish. Seeking religious freedom, Mennonites began establishing communities in rural areas of northern Mexico, and also around Bacalar. Their small farming settlement is located west of Mex. 307.

Follow the signs from Mex. 307 to reach Bacalar Lagoon (Laguna de Bacalar). This 31-mile-long body of water is a spectacular natural wonder in the midst of the otherwise unremarkable jungle scrub of southern Quintana Roo. Salt and fresh water mix in the lagoon, accentuating beautiful hues from green to deep turquoise to almost black (thus the popular name "Lake of the Seven Colors"). The lagoon's clear water is ideal for swimming, boating, kayaking, snorkeling and scuba diving.

Along the western shore, a good swimming spot is the Balneario Magico beach club. Located a few minutes' drive north of the town plaza (take the waterfront road), the club has a simple restaurant, a pier and picnic tables with a view of the lagoon. Parking is about $1.50 (U.S.), and admission to the facility is about $1 per person. At the southern end of town, there's more good swimming in front of the bluff-top Hotel Laguna. Keep in mind that you will be expected to order something from the hotel's bar or restaurant to use the waterfront facilities.

About 5 kilometers (3 miles) south of town, almost at the edge of the lagoon, is Cenote Azul (Blue Cenote). This freshwater sinkhole is the largest in the Yucatán and reputedly the largest in the world. Some 600 feet across and estimated at more than 250 feet deep, it is filled with blue water that is unusually clear. Surrounded by green vegetation, Cenote Azul is popular with swimmers, snorkelers and divers. Camping facilities are available nearby.

## CAMPECHE, CAMPECHE (B-1)
**pop. 259,005**

Capital of the state of the same name, Campeche (kahm-PEH-cheh) is the largest city between Villahermosa and Mérida. Its waterfront, dotted by offshore oil rigs, is the base of Mexico's largest gulf coast shrimp fleet.

Hernández de Córdova and his *conquistadores* stopped in this area in 1517 to obtain fresh water. Founded in 1540 by Don Francisco de Montejo, the city flourished from the export of hardwoods and dyewoods to Europe. One of the foremost cities of New Spain in the mid-16th century, Campeche preserves buildings that date from this period in its old San Francisco section. One such structure was the house where Montejo planned his conquest of the Yucatán.

Campeche's most remarkable attraction is a massive 1.5-mile hexagonal wall with eight fortresses that was erected for protection against repeated sackings by European pirates in the 16th and 17th centuries. Begun in 1686, the fortification took 18 years to build. The historic fortified section of the city was designated a World Heritage Site by UNESCO in 1999.

Fort Soledad (Fuerte de la Soledad), 3 blocks north of the ancient Puerta del Mar entranceway, has been converted into a museum displaying Mayan artifacts, an arms collection and exhibits on colonial history. Fort San Carlos (Fuerte de San Carlos), a government-sponsored handicrafts market today, has intriguing secret underground passageways. Linked to many houses in the city, the tunnels provided a hiding place for women and children when pirate ships came to plunder. Most passageways are sealed off with bricks, but guides offer tours into the fort's basement for a small fee. The fort's roof, complete with ancient cannons, offers a spectacular view of the gulf.

Although the city is studded with ancient walls and fortresses, the Government Palace and the Legislative Palace are respectively referred to as "the jukebox" and "the flying saucer" for their modern architectural styles. Local markets sell such handicrafts as Panama hats and articles made of alligator skin. The regional cuisine features exotic dishes like shark stew.

Other points of interest include the 1540 Franciscan Cathedral, the oldest convent church in the Yucatán Peninsula; the 1546 Convent of San Francisco, the site of one of the first masses in Campeche; the Temple of San Francisquito, which now houses the Campeche Cultural Institute (Instituto Cultural Campechano); and the House of the King's Lieutenant (Casa del Teniente del Rey), which contains colonial furnishings. Alameda Park's Bridge of Dogs (El Puente de Los Perros), a colonial bridge guarded by carved stone dogs, honors the Dominican missionaries called the "Dogs of God" for their zealous hounding of converts.

Among the words coined in Campeche is *campechano,* used to describe a pleasant, easygoing person. Local tradition has it that the word "cocktail" originated here centuries ago because English pirates were served drinks adorned by palm fronds resembling cocks' tails. Happily, the root of Campeche's name, taken from the Mayan words *kim* and *pech,* meaning "serpent" and "tick," has no modern application.

**Campeche State Tourism Office:** downtown at Plaza Moch-Couoh, on Avenida Ruiz Cortines. **Phone:** (981) 127-3300.

**EDZNÁ RUINS** are about 61 km (39 mi.) s.e. of Campeche off Mex. 188; take Av. Central out of the city, following signs for the airport and then Edzná. This Mayan city was first inhabited about 400 B.C. and abandoned by the mid-15th century; as is true of other archeological sites in Mexico, the reasons for its decline remain a mystery.

The closest major ruins to Campeche may not be worth the trip if you've seen Chichén Itzá or Uxmal, but there is one standout building: the 98-foot-tall Temple of Five Stories (Templo de Cinco Cuerpos), a five-level structure with a central staircase and an impressive roof comb at the top. South of this temple is the Temple of Masks, with carvings of heads that have jaguar-like faces.

**Hours:** Daily 8-5. **Cost:** 52 pesos (about $3.85 U.S.). **Phone:** (981) 811-1000.

**FORT SAN MIGUEL** (El Fuerte de San Miguel) is off Av. Escénica, about 5 km (3 mi.) s. of downtown on the way to Lerma. This is one of the most impressive of the former Spanish fortifications that once guarded the city. Two ramps with steps lead up to the roof and a panoramic view of the city and the Bay of Campeche. Inside the fort is the Museum of Mayan Art, which displays priceless artifacts, including jade burial masks excavated from the Calakmul archeological site. **Time:** Allow 1 hour, 30 minutes minimum. **Hours:** Tues.-Sun. 8:30-5. **Cost:** 47 pesos (about $3.50 U.S.). **Phone:** (981) 816-9111 (INAH's Campeche office; only Spanish is spoken).

# Cancún

© javarman / Shutterstock.com

**City Population:** 661,176
**Elevation:** 7 meters (23 feet)

## Editor's Picks:

Does Cancún have more lives than the proverbial cat? Judging by how it has bounced back from the brink of meteorological disaster—twice—you might well think so. One of Mexico's most popular tourist destinations was ravaged by Hurricane Gilbert in 1988 and again by Hurricane Wilma in 2005. The aftermath of each storm plunged the city into near chaos—flooded hotel lobbies, palm trees tossed about like matchsticks, disrupted communications. And both times the city mopped up, remodeled, renovated and reopened for business with admirable resourcefulness. Apparently you just can't keep a good resort down.

History? At the beginning of the 1970s Cancún didn't show up on most maps. There were no throngs of vacationers. It was simply a coastal village with a handful of fishermen eking out a living along a stretch of gorgeous coast, once home to the Maya and later a refuge for pirates. The area appealed to committed beach bums, but a lack of all but the most basic amenities was an impediment to widespread leisure travel. Back then, those in search of inviting Mexican beaches that actually had hotels headed for Acapulco or Puerto Vallarta.

But a sandbar lying just offshore blessed with stunning natural attributes was paradise waiting to blossom. The Mexican government, in the midst of ambitious plans to maximize the country's tourism potential, determined that the location was a prime spot for a new resort and promptly handed over the little spit of land to eager developers.

Vacationers come to Cancún for several reasons: beaches of fine-grained sand and beautiful turquoise-hued water; accommodations from budget-priced to downright luxurious; high-energy nightlife; a dining scene encompassing both elegant hotel restaurants and local Yucatecan joints; shopping at bright, shiny malls; and sightseeing boat cruises and all sorts of water recreation. It's a spring break hot spot and a popular getaway for honeymooners.

Ciudad Cancún, or "El Centro," is on the mainland, a commercial and business center that is very much like any other Mexican town. Cancún Island (Isla Cancún), known as the Hotel Zone (Zona Hotelera), is where the major resorts are concentrated. An elbow-shaped sandbar nearly 15 miles long but just a quarter-mile wide, it is connected to the mainland by narrow causeways at either end.

In between are the calm waters of Nichupté Lagoon (Laguna Nichupté). The island's seaward side fronts Mujeres Bay from Ciudad Cancún east to Cancún Point (Punta Cancún). The point is the crook of the elbow; south of it the shoreline faces the open Caribbean.

The Hotel Zone is a mix of upscale luxury hotels and youth-oriented nightspots, trendy designer shopping and souvenir markets. There's buzzing energy as well as the relaxing sound of coconut palm fronds rustling in the breeze. Hotels—architecturally distinctive, lushly landscaped and opulently appointed—have the aquamarine Caribbean surf as a backdrop.

Although constant sea breezes temper the summer heat, humidity is high; the winter months are the most pleasant. The water is warm enough for swimming all year. Most visitors wear shorts and T-shirts; casual but stylish resort wear is appropriate at the

*Getting There* — starting on p. 67

*Getting Around* — starting on p. 70

*What To See* — starting on p. 72

*What To Do* — starting on p. 74

*Where To Stay* — starting on p. 376

*Where To Dine* — starting on p. 387

nicer restaurants or for an evening out. Bring your sunglasses and sunblock, and pack a sweater for the occasional cool, blustery winter day or icily air-conditioned summer interior. The greatest chance for a hurricane or tropical storm is from August through October.

This isn't colonial Mexico, steeped in time and tradition. From Subway to Starbucks, you'll see—at least in the Hotel Zone—fast food outlets and stateside franchises. For gringos there's also a comforting familiarity. English is commonplace, although Spanish might be spoken first. Dollars are routinely accepted. And you just can't beat that trio of sun, sea and sand.

© Pichugin Dmitry / Shutterstock.com

## Getting There

### By Air

Cancún International Airport (CUN) is on the mainland off Mex. 307, about 16 kilometers (10 miles) southwest of downtown Ciudad Cancún and about 10 kilometers (6 miles) from the southern end of Cancún Island. It receives regular flights from major cities in the United States and Mexico; many are daily.

Aeroméxico, 01 (800) 021-4000 (toll-free long distance within Mexico), offers nonstop flights from New York-JFK. Other airlines serving the airport include American, 01 (800) 904-6000 (toll-free long distance within Mexico); JetBlue, 01 (800) 861-3372 (toll-free long distance within Mexico); United, 01 (800) 900-5000 (toll-free long distance within Mexico); US Airways, 01 (800) 428-4322 (toll-free long distance within Mexico); and Virgin America, 001 (877) 359-8474 (from the United States).

Air Canada, 01 (800) 719-2827 (toll-free long distance within Mexico), flies nonstop from Calgary and Ottawa. A number of charter companies fly to Cancún as well.

To confirm schedules, contact the appropriate airline or a travel agency. *For additional information about airlines see Arriving by Air, page p. 42.*

Cancún's airport is modern and clearly marked with bilingual signs for arrivals, departures, gates, Immigration and restrooms. After arriving you must first proceed to Immigration and have your tourist permit validated before heading to the baggage claim area. The last stop is Mexican customs, where you will hand over your completed declaration form, put your luggage on a conveyor belt and push a button that activates the random green light/red light system; if the red light flashes your bags will be briefly searched.

Terminal 3 handles most, but not all, international arrivals/departures, while Terminal 2 handles most, but not all, domestic flights. Free shuttle service runs between the two terminals. Terminal 3 has

# The Informed Traveler

## WHOM TO CALL

**Police (emergency):** To contact the local police, dial 066 and ask to be connected to an English-speaking operator. American and Canadian tourists in Cancún also can call 911 in the event of an emergency.

**Consumer Protection Agency (Procuraduría Federal del Consumidor):** Av. Cobá #9 (2nd floor) in downtown Ciudad Cancún; phone (998) 884-2369. The office is open Mon.-Fri. 9-3.

**Immigration Office:** avenidas J.C. Nader and Uxmal in Ciudad Cancún; phone (998) 884-1404. The office is open Mon.-Fri. 9-2 and can provide assistance if you lose your tourist permit.

**Hospitals:** Most of the major hotels have their own in-house or on-call doctor. If in doubt, obtain a list of physicians from the U.S. Consular Agency, located at Plaza Caracol Two (third level, #320-323), Boulevard Kukulcán Km 8.5; phone (998) 883-0272. Local clinics do not accept U.S. health insurance, often charge fees well above U.S. rates and have been known to charge for services not rendered. In case of emergency, the Red Cross (Cruz Roja) is in Ciudad Cancún on Avenida Yaxchilán, between avenidas Xcaret and Labná. It is open 24 hours; phone (998) 884-1616.

## WHERE TO LOOK

### Newspapers

The *Miami Herald* and *USA Today* are available in the bigger hotels.

### Television

Most hotels have a cable TV system that offers the ABC, CBS, NBC and Fox networks via a U.S. affiliate, such staples as CNN and ESPN, and HBO or another movie channel, in addition to Spanish-language channels.

### Publications

*Cancún Tips* magazine has easy-to-read maps and information about restaurants, shopping, entertainment, sightseeing and local services. Pick up free tourist-oriented brochures at shopping centers and sidewalk booths. The open-air building on Boulevard Kukulcán just west of the Fiesta Americana Grand Coral Beach hotel has information about local attractions and guided tours down the coast.

## WHAT TO KNOW

### Currency Exchange

*Casas de cambio* (currency exchange houses) and banks are along Avenida Tulum in downtown Ciudad Cancún. Most banks are open Mon.-Fri. 9-5; currency exchange normally is confined to the morning hours. Currency exchange houses also are located in the Hotel Zone shopping areas around Cancún Point.

ATM withdrawals are in pesos, although some machines dispense dollars as well. Since the rates offered by exchange houses and banks usually differ only slightly and fluctuate daily, exchanging dollars boils down to a matter of convenience. You'll want to keep some peso coins and smaller denomination bills on hand, since not everything (bus and taxi fares and the ferry fare to Isla Mujeres, for example) can be paid for by credit card.

### Staying Safe

Crime directed at tourists is not prevalent, but do use common sense. Put jewelry and other valuables in the hotel safe, or don't bring them at all. Be on guard for potential pickpocket or purse-snatching incidents in crowded public places or when using public transportation. Car break-ins can occur in the Hotel Zone's shopping areas; don't invite one by leaving valuables in plain view. Always take a taxi after dark, whether in Ciudad Cancún or the Hotel Zone.

plenty of restaurants, gift shops and duty-free stores on the upper departure level. Rental car counters are in a consolidated location as you exit the baggage claim/customs area. Consider yourself lucky if you make it through Immigration without a wait; the lines are usually long.

**Note:** After a lengthy renovation, Terminal 1 recently reopened and primarily handles charter flights. Terminals 2 and 3 are in the midst of expansion projects. A new Terminal 4 is under construction and is scheduled to open sometime in 2017.

A noisy crowd of sign-bearing van drivers and shuttle bus operators congregate outside the airport. Shuttle service via passenger van (colectivo) is available to Ciudad Cancún and the Hotel Zone for a fixed rate of about $16 per person (U.S.). These vehicles usually take a maximum of 10 passengers. They are less costly than van pickup associated with your hotel or a private transfer, either of which will cost about $60-$65 (U.S.) to the Hotel Zone, plus tip.

You should arrange for a private transfer online or by phone prior to your trip. USA Transfers is a reputable outfit; phone (998) 914-0290. You can purchase a ticket for a colectivo or a chartered airport taxi at the taxi/transfers counter, located to your immediate left after exiting the airport doors. Colectivos do not provide service back to the airport, making a private transfer or hotel-associated fleet ride necessary upon departure. You can also take a regular city taxi back to the airport; the fare should be less than the trip from the airport. From the Hotel Zone, figure on $25 to $30 (U.S.).

Confirm your reservation and departure time with your airline at least 24 hours prior to departing Cancún. For international flights, plan on arriving at least 2 hours before your scheduled departure time. There are numerous snack carts, fast-food restaurants and places to pick up a sandwich and beverage. The airport also has a number of shops for last-minute souvenir purchases; prices are a bit steep, but U.S. dollars are accepted. Prices for duty-free merchandise—mostly liquor, cigars and perfume—may not be as much of a bargain as advertised, so shop carefully.

## By Car

Mexico's easternmost city is located at the Yucatán Peninsula's northeastern tip. From the west, the main route is Mex. 180 via Veracruz, Villahermosa, Campeche and Mérida; it ends at Punta Sam, north of Cancún. From Villahermosa, an alternate route is Mex. 186 east to Escárcega, Camp., and then north on Mex. 281 to Champotón. It carries heavy truck traffic and has very few gas stations or mechanical services. This route should only be driven during daylight hours.

Mex. 180 is two lanes between Mérida and the small town of Hoctún. Four-lane toll (cuota) highway Mex. 180-D begins about 60 kilometers (37 miles) east of Mérida and roughly parallels Mex. 180 for a distance of about 240 kilometers (144 miles). All of Mex. 180-D is in very good condition, lightly traveled and quicker than Mex. 180, which passes through small towns with lots of speed

bumps *(topes)*. It is, however, isolated if you happen to break down.

Kilometer markers are along the right side of the highway, and there are regular intervals, indicated by signs, to make a U-turn *(retorno)*. Signage is good (both speed limit and mileage signs and the international blue highway signs). Toll plazas are located at the Yucatán/Quintana Roo state line (Plaza de Cobro X-Can), which also is a customs checkpoint, and at the Chichén Itzá exit (Pisté). For automobiles, the toll charge is 262 pesos (about $19.40 U.S.) at the X-Can toll booth and 152 pesos (about $11.25 U.S.) at the Pisté toll booth. There are only a few gas stations along the length of the route, so make sure your tank is always at least half full.

Mex. 180-D ends about 16 kilometers (10 miles) west of the airport; follow the sign that says "Cancún/Puerto Juárez" to stay on the mainland, or the sign "Tulum/Aeropuerto" to get to the Hotel Zone.

An access route to Cancún from the south is Mex. 307, which begins about 19 kilometers (12 miles) west of Chetumal off Mex. 186 in southern Quintana Roo and proceeds north through Bacalar and Tulum. The section of Mex. 307 from Tulum north to Cancún offers easy access to attractions and beach resorts along the Riviera Maya coast.

A highway branching northwest at Tulum offers access to the Cobá archeological zone and joins Mex. 180 at the town of Xcan—a distance of about 85 kilometers (53 miles). It saves time and mileage if you want a more direct route from Tulum to Mérida.

## By Bus

The bus terminal is in downtown Ciudad Cancún at the intersection of avenidas Tulum and Uxmal, in front of the Plaza Caribe Hotel. The ADO line offers first-class service to and from various points on the Yucatán Peninsula, including Chetumal, Chichén Itzá, Mérida, Playa del Carmen, Tulum and Valladolid. Frequent first-class service is available from Mérida, with stops en route at Chichén Itzá and Valladolid. *For additional information about buses see Bus Service, page p. 52.*

## By Cruise Ship

Cancún has no docking facilities for cruise ships. If you're on a ship that docks at Cozumel and want to spend some time in Cancún, you can take a ferry from Cozumel to Playa del Carmen, about a 45-minute drive south of Cancún (or check with your ship's shore excursion desk to see if they offer a Cancún package). Depending on the length of shore leave, you could squeeze in a shopping trip or a visit to one of the beaches.

**Note:** If a shore excursion is arranged through the cruise line the ship will wait if you aren't back at the scheduled departure time. This is not the case, however, if you arrange the excursion yourself, so keep timing in mind.

## Getting Around

### City Layout

The main streets in downtown Ciudad Cancún, or "El Centro," are east-west Avenida López Portillo, the in-town section of Mex. 180, which extends from the western city limits northeast to Puerto Juárez and Punta Sam; and north-south Avenida Tulum, the in-town section of Mex. 307, which runs south toward the airport and on down the coast. Many souvenir shops and restaurants are along or near avenidas Tulum and Cobá; the latter street becomes Boulevard Kukulcán as it heads east and enters the Hotel Zone.

Ciudad Cancún is divided into districts called *super manzanas* (shortened to SM), each containing several blocks surrounding a central square or park. Driving can be daunting even if you know where you're going, however. There are numerous one-way streets and traffic circles *(glorietas)*, as well as crowds of pedestrians and unfamiliar traffic signals. For an excursion into El Centro for dinner or shopping, take a bus or taxi.

Parque las Palapas is centrally located a block west of Avenida Tulum, bordered by calles Tulipanes, Gladiolas, Margaritas and Alcatraces. This is a family-oriented park where craft sellers set up their wares and food vendors offer popcorn, fried bananas and *churros* (doughnut-like snacks). Casual restaurants line Calle Tulipanes, a pedestrian alleyway, and popular local eateries are within walking distance of the park.

Boulevard Kukulcán (also referred to as Paseo Kukulcán but usually just called "Kukulcán") is a four-lane divided thoroughfare running the length of narrow Cancún Island and is the Hotel Zone's only main traffic artery. It actually begins at the junction with Avenida Bonampak, on the eastern edge of Ciudad Cancún. Past Punta Nizuc (Nizuc Point), the island's southern tip, Kukulcán runs into southbound Mex. 307 at the overpass leading to the airport.

Kukulcán's four lanes divide briefly to encompass Cancún Point, the elbow of the island's "seven" configuration. Where U-turns are permitted, signs in the median say *retorno*. **Note:** The speed limit along most of Kukulcán is 40 km/h (25 mph); the limit increases to 60 km/h (37 mph) at the southern end of the island.

Lying between the Hotel Zone and the mainland is Nichupté Lagoon, a combination of fresh and salt water. Two smaller lagoons are connected to Nichupté by narrow waterways: Laguna Bojórquez, at the northeastern end, and Laguna Río Inglés, at the southwestern end. The lagoons form a habitat for many different bird species.

Numbered addresses are rarely given for places in the Hotel Zone. Kilometer markers installed in the median (from Km 1, just past the mainland, east and south to Km 25 beyond Nizuc Point) are used to designate locations. Directions also are given in reference to well-known landmarks or hotels. Because there is only one main road, it's almost impossible to get lost.

## Rental Cars

It's not really necessary to rent a car if you're limiting your vacation to Cancún and vicinity; bus and taxi service is frequent. But you'll need one if you plan a day or overnight trip down the coast toward Tulum or inland to the ruins of Chichén Itzá or Cobá and don't want to be part of an organized tour. The quality of most regional roads is good. Do not underestimate the amount of time it will take to arrive at your destination, however, and in general avoid driving after dark.

Rates are expensive if you rent on the spot; make reservations in advance through a U.S. 800 number to get the best deal. Arranging for pickup and dropoff at the airport will eliminate taxi fares. Make certain you fully understand the terms of any rental contract. If the car only has half a tank of gas when you pick it up, you can return it with half a tank; double check before you drive off.

Inspect the vehicle carefully inside and out for nicks and dents, and check for the required in-car fire extinguisher. Keep in mind that license plates on rental vehicles say *renta,* marking you as a visitor. It is becoming more common for major rental car agencies to provide (for an added charge) a driver; consider this option if you don't feel entirely comfortable driving in unfamiliar surroundings. In the event of damages caused by a hurricane, all insurance claims are void.

Hertz is one of several rental car agencies available, with offices at the airport, in downtown Ciudad Cancún and at three locations on Boulevard Kukulcán in the Hotel Zone. AAA/CAA members receive discounts through Hertz for vehicles booked in the United States or Canada; phone (800) 654-3080.

## Buses

*Ruta 1* and *Ruta 2* buses (marked R-1, *Hoteles* or *Zona Hotelera* on the windshield) run regularly from the mainland along Boulevard Kukulcán to the southern end of the Hotel Zone (around the Km 20 marker) and back daily 24 hours (buses are more frequent from 6 a.m.-10 p.m.). The fare is inexpensive—9.5 pesos (about 70c U.S.). The *Ruta 8* bus goes to Puerto Juárez and Punta Sam for the ferries to Isla Mujeres.

You'll need Mexican currency; drivers will return change up to a 20-peso bill. There are frequent designated stops along the length of Boulevard Kukulcán (or you can tell the driver where you want to get off), and buses can be flagged from hotel driveway entrances. Using the bus is much cheaper than taking a cab, especially if you're staying at the southern end of the Hotel Zone.

Buses are likely to be crowded mornings and evenings, when mainland locals use them to get to and from work. They jolt along and can stop suddenly,

so watch your footing. There also can be impromptu entertainment in the form of a guitar player who will board the bus, sing a song or two and then pass the hat for spare change.

## Taxis

Taxis within the Hotel Zone are very expensive, costing $7-$10 (U.S.) per ride, even if it's just from one hotel to the next. They also are not metered; fares are based on a zone system. Arranging for a cab directly at your hotel is convenient, but these cabs also tend to have the highest rates. Some hotels list fares to various destinations at the front entrance; if not, ask the doorman. Always confirm the rate with the driver before setting out. Better hotels will arrange "payouts," putting cab fares on the bill so they show up on your credit card receipt as a recorded expense.

Green city taxis can be hailed on the street in Ciudad Cancún. The driver should be able to provide a rate list if you ask, although it is likely to be in Spanish. If you're going from the Hotel Zone to Ciudad Cancún, Puerto Juárez or Punta Sam, take the Kukulcán bus to the mainland, then a taxi to your destination, since the city taxis have a cheaper rate structure (also based on a zone system) than the Hotel Zone taxis. A taxi also can be hired to Chichén Itzá or for a drive south along the Riviera Maya, although you'll pay a steep hourly rate for this convenience.

## Ferries

Enclosed, air-conditioned passenger ferries run between Puerto Juárez, about 3 kilometers (2 miles) north of Cancún via Avenida López Portillo (Mex. 180), and Isla Mujeres. The UltraMar ferry departs from the Gran Puerto dock on Avenida López Portillo every half-hour daily from 5 a.m. to 8:30 p.m., then hourly until 11:30 p.m. The final departure from Isla Mujeres back to Gran Puerto is at midnight. The trip takes about 15-20 minutes; one-way fare is 78 pesos (about $6.35 U.S.). Always double check the final departure time back to Cancún when you arrive. **Note:** The ride can be choppy even in good weather, so it's a good idea to take the proper precautions if you're prone to seasickness.

The dock at El Embarcadero, Km marker 4 on Boulevard Kukulcán, also is a departure point for UltraMar ferries, and it's a more convenient location if you're staying in the Hotel Zone. Ferries depart daily at 9:15, 11:45, 1, 2:15 and 4:30. The final departure from Isla Mujeres back to El Embarcadero is at 5:15 p.m. One-way fare is $14 (U.S.); round-trip fare is $19. For UltraMar ferry information phone (998) 881-5890.

UltraMar boats depart from the dock at Playa Tortugas, Km marker 7 on Boulevard Kukulcán. The ferry departs daily on the hour 9-5; it returns from Isla Mujeres approximately every 30 minutes 9:30-5:30. One-way fare is $14 (U.S.); round trip fare is $19.

## Parking

There are very few municipal parking lots in Ciudad Cancún or the Hotel Zone. Park on city streets at your own discretion. If you've rented a car or are driving your own vehicle, keep it in the hotel lot—most of them are guarded—and use buses or cabs for local excursions.

## Guides/Tours

The most popular day excursions from Cancún are to Xcaret, Xel-Ha and Tulum, all south along the Caribbean coast. Guided tours to Chichén Itzá and Isla Mujeres also are available. The Xcaret building next to the Fiesta Americana Grand Coral Beach Resort & Spa in the Hotel Zone is a convenient place to arrange a trip and purchase tickets. There also are numerous in-town tour operators, and many hotels have a travel agency on site or a concierge who can help with tour arrangements.

Gray Line Cancún, in downtown Cancún at Calle Robalo #30, offers motorcoach tours to various regional points of interest; including Chichén Itzá, Cozumel, the Riviera Maya, Xcaret and Xel-Ha, with pickup transportation available at most major Hotel Zone hotels. Phone (998) 887-2495 or (877) 240-5864 (from the United States).

The most popular day trip in the Mexican Caribbean is an organized bus excursion to Xcaret (see attraction listing under Playa del Carmen), which departs from a number of hotels in Cancún, Playa del Carmen and elsewhere along the Riviera Maya coast. This is the most convenient way to visit the park if you don't have a rental car.

Tour packages include round-trip transportation and park admission. Pickups in the Cancún Hotel Zone are daily between 7 and 9 a.m. Morning pickup times at Playa de Carmen and Riviera Maya hotels vary; check with your hotel regarding schedule. From Cancún, Playa del Carmen and Riviera Maya hotels the cost is around $140 (U.S.); around $70 (children 40 to 55 inches tall). For reservation information phone 01 (800) 212-9061 (toll-free long distance within Mexico). For additional information contact the Xcaret information center in Cancún, phone (998) 251-6560; in Playa del Carmen, phone (984) 147-6562. **Note:** Tour prices may vary depending on your booking method: online, phone or in-person.

Another tour that should be taken by anyone interested in Mexico's Mayan and Spanish colonial past is the Xichen Tour, which visits the Chichén Itzá archeological site and the town of Valladolid. It's an enriching and educational alternative to yet another day at the beach. The tour bus departs at 7 a.m. Mon.-Sat. from a lot just off Mex. 307 near the Cancún airport; round-trip transportation from your hotel and lunch at a restored mansion are included. The cost is $109 (U.S.); $54.50 (children 40 to 55 inches tall). For reservation information, phone (998) 251-6547 or 01 (800) 212-9061 (toll-free long distance within Mexico).

## What To See

**AQUA WORLD** is at Km 15.2 on the lagoon side of Blvd. Kukulcán. In addition to organizing deep-sea fishing trips and diving and snorkeling excursions, Aqua World rents equipment for windsurfing, jet skiing and wave running. The *Sub See Explorer* offers a snorkeler's-eye view of Caribbean coral reefs from the comfort of an air-conditioned, glass-bottomed boat. The sub departs from a floating platform, which is reached by taking a normal boat through Nichupté Lagoon and out to sea; a light lunch and beverages are included. The Skyrider offers both ocean and lagoon-side parasail "flights" high above Cancún Island.

Scuba diving instruction is available. Arrange cruise excursions or fishing trips in advance. Aqua World sales kiosks are located at most major hotels. **Hours:** Daily 7 a.m.-8 p.m. **Cost:** Fees for activities, cruises and equipment rentals vary. **Phone:** (998) 848-8326, or (844) 422-7235 (from the United States and Canada).

**Breathing Observation Bubble** (BOB) excursions depart from the Aqua World Marina. The tour begins with a ride aboard a motorboat through Nichupté Lagoon to Chitales, an offshore coral reef. At the reef site participants board the main BOB boat, where they receive instruction on how to operate the observation bubble, a submersible, scooter-like mini-submarine. The contraption is then lowered about 20 feet into the water for a 30-minute sightseeing session, with the plastic bubble around the rider's head supplying oxygen and a view of the reef's abundant marine life.

Beverages and a fresh fruit snack are provided after the session. A separate snorkeling trip is also part of the BOB package; equipment is provided. **Hours:** Departures daily at 9, 10:30, noon, 1:30 and 3. **Cost:** BOB session $68.10 (U.S.). Marine park/dockage fee $10. BOB participants must be between 12 and 60 years of age and at least 5 feet tall. Children under 5 are not permitted on the boat ride. **Phone:** (998) 848-8326, or (844) 422-7235 (from the United States and Canada).

**CANCÚN MAYA MUSEUM** (Museo Maya de Cancún) is on Blvd. Kukulcán at Km marker 16.5 in the Hotel Zone. This architecturally impressive museum, built over a 6-year period by Mexico's National Institute of Anthropology and History (INAH), was the largest INAH project undertaken since the construction of the Templo Mayor Museum in Mexico City in 1987. Around 350 archeological artifacts are displayed in three large exhibition halls; some were unearthed during recent excavations and others have never been exhibited before.

One of the highlights when visitors first enter is a collection of 14,000-year-old skeletal remains discovered in one of Tulum's underwater caves. Room 1 is dedicated to the Mayan civilization and contains items acquired over 30 years of archeological research, along with a historical timeline of human habitation on the Yucatán Peninsula.

Room 2 showcases the regions occupied by the Mayan people—southeastern Mexico, neighboring Belize and Guatemala, and parts of El Salvador and

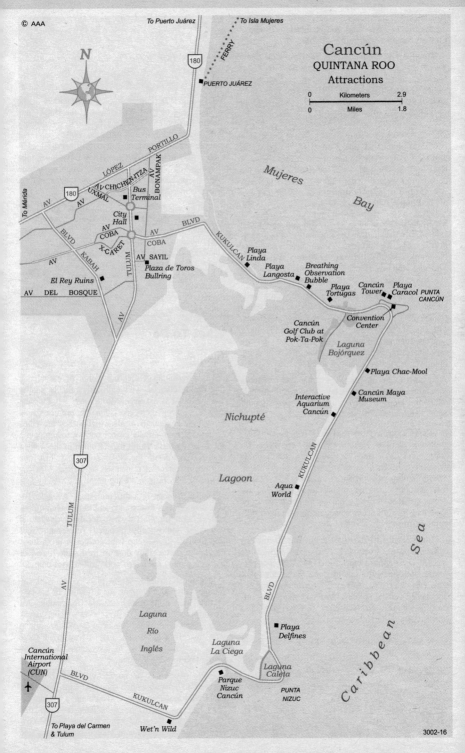

© AAA

N

To Puerto Juárez    To Isla Mujeres

# Cancún
## QUINTANA ROO
### Attractions

FERRY

PUERTO JUÁREZ

Kilometers 0 — 2.9
Miles 0 — 1.8

*Mujeres*

*Bay*

PORTILLO

LÓPEZ

AV CHICHEN-ITZA

AV BONAMPAK

AV UXMAL

Bus Terminal

To Mérida

AV

BLVD

AV

KABAH

AV COBA

X-CARET

City Hall

AV COBA

AV COBA

BLVD

KUKULCAN

*Playa Linda*

AV SAYIL

Plaza de Toros Bullring

AV

TULUM

El Rey Ruins

AV DEL BOSQUE

*Playa Langosta*

*Breathing Observation Bubble*

*Playa Tortugas*

Cancún Tower

*Playa Caracol*

PUNTA CANCÚN

Cancún Golf Club at Pok-Ta-Pok

Convention Center

*Laguna Bojórquez*

*Playa Chac-Mool*

Interactive Aquarium Cancún

Cancún Maya Museum

*Nichupté*

KUKULCAN

*Lagoon*

Aqua World

307

AV TULUM

BLVD

*Laguna Río Inglés*

*Laguna La Ciega*

*Playa Delfines*

Laguna Caleta

PUNTA NIZUC

Cancún International Airport (CUN)

BLVD

KUKULCAN

Parque Nizuc Cancún

*Caribbean*

*Sea*

307

To Playa del Carmen & Tulum

Wet'n Wild

3002-16

Honduras. Exhibits feature aspects of daily life and an overview of Maya art and architecture. Room 3 presents temporary changing exhibits.

**Time:** Allow 2 hours minimum. **Hours:** Museum Tues.-Sun. 9-5:30; ruins Tues.-Sun. 9-4:30. **Cost:** (includes admission to the adjacent San Miguelito ruins) 64 pesos (around \$4.75 U.S.); free (ages 0-12 and 61+). Cash only. **Phone:** (998) 885-3842 or (998) 885-3843. GT

**CANCUN TOWER** (Torre Escénica) is at the El Embarcadero municipal dock, on Blvd. Kukulcán at Km marker 4. From the top of this revolving tower there are panoramic views of the Hotel Zone and the aquamarine waters of the Caribbean. **Hours:** Daily 9-9. **Cost:** Single tower ride \$15 (U.S.); \$7.50 (ages 5-11). **Phone:** (998) 849-5582.

**EL REY RUINS** (Ruinas El Rey) are on the lagoon side of Blvd. Kukulcán at Km marker 17, a short distance past the Iberostar Cancún hotel (watch for the sign); take the stairway down to the entrance. The site, which is reached via a short trail, consists of a few temple platforms that once supported roofs.

El Rey is much smaller than the Yucatán's well-known archeological sites, and it's a nice, quiet change of pace from malls and rowdy nightspots. The chief attraction here is not ruins but the many iguanas sunning themselves on the rocks. Fed by park guards, they're used to people and will come running for bread, crackers or tortillas.

Restrooms are on site. Wear a hat and sunscreen and bring water. **Time:** Allow 1 hour, 30 minutes minimum. **Hours:** Daily 8-5. **Cost:** 47 pesos (about \$3.50 U.S.).

**INTERACTIVE AQUARIUM CANCÚN** is on the lagoon side of Blvd. Kukulcán at Km 12.5, in La Isla Shopping Village. Here you can swim with dolphins or observe sharks from a special underwater cage. Touch exhibits allow visitors to observe rays, starfish and other marine animals up close, and all guests can feed stingrays and young nurse sharks or have their picture taken with a macaw. Trained dolphins perform daily at 7 p.m.

**Hours:** Daily 10-7:30 (last admission 30 minutes before closing). **Cost:** 195 pesos (\$14 U.S.); free (ages 0-2). Dolphin swims \$85-\$135 (U.S.) per person (includes aquarium admission). Phone for shark tank encounter cost. Advance reservations are recommended for the dolphin swim and shark tank encounter. **Phone:** (998) 206-3311, or (888) 526-2330 (toll-free from the United States). ⊺↑

**SIAN KA'AN BIOSPHERE RESERVE**— *see Tulum p. 108.*

▼GEM **TULUM RUINS**— *see Tulum p. 107.*

▼GEM **XCARET**— *see Playa del Carmen p. 105.*

▼GEM **XEL-HA**— *see Tulum p. 109.*

▼GEM **XPLOR**— *see Playa del Carmen p. 105.*

**WET 'N WILD** (Parque Nizuc Waterpark) is at the southern end of Blvd. Kukulcán and the Hotel Zone at Km marker 25. Owned by Palace Resorts, it has thrill waterslides like Kamikaze, Twister and the Double Space Bowl, a lifeguard-supervised children's play area and the Lazy River for inner tube floating. You also can interact with dolphins and sea lions as part of a program run by the animal research center Atlantida.

Admission prices are all-inclusive; guests are given tickets redeemable for food and beverages in the park. **Hours:** Daily 10-5. Phone ahead to confirm schedule. **Cost:** \$49 (U.S.); \$43 (ages 3-11). One-hour dolphin swim \$95 (U.S.) per person (includes park admission); all-day dolphin swim \$209. Advance reservations are recommended for the dolphin swim. Lockers, towels and inner tubes can be rented. Prices may vary. **Phone:** (998) 881-3030. ⊺↑

# What To Do

## Dining

Hotel restaurants offer the gamut of casual and fine dining choices, with uniformly reliable quality and predictable expense. Most hotels go to great lengths to keep their guests on the premises, and some may charge for meals whether they are eaten or not. Dress is usually casual but not unkempt (no shorts or T-shirts). Don't expect much in the way of regional cookery in the Hotel Zone; U.S. fast-food and chain restaurant franchises, as well as Mexican chains like Sr. Frog's, are the norm.

Ciudad Cancún is a different story. Avenida Tulum is lined with restaurants, and most have outdoor tables. Look for places where locals congregate if you want authentically prepared Yucatecan dishes like *sopa de lima*—soup with a chicken broth base, vegetables and a tangy dose of fresh lime juice—or *poc-chuc,* spicy marinated pork grilled with onions.

One local favorite—and a place where you can sample home-style cooking for a fraction of the cost of the Hotel Zone restaurants—is Checándole, Av. Xpuhil #6 (SM 18). It serves tacos, steak *tampiqueña* and other Mexican standards, along with fresh fruit juices. The easiest way to get there from the Hotel Zone is to take a bus downtown, then a taxi to the restaurant.

For a reasonably priced Mexican-style breakfast try one of Cancún's coffee shops. At Vips, a popular chain with branches all over the country, you can order standards like *huevos motuleños*—two fried eggs, peas and diced ham atop a crispy tortilla covered in tomato sauce, with pureed black beans and slices of fried banana on the side. This, plus toast, orange juice and good *cafe americano,* will fill you up for about $10. The Hotel Zone Vips is next to the Cancún Center.

Restaurants in the large hotels use purified water for cooking and for washing produce; inquire about this health procedure specifically at places on the mainland. In general, avoid ice cubes in drinks unless you know purified water has been used. See the Lodgings & Restaurants section for AAA-RATED dining establishments.

## Shopping

Shopping in Cancún's Hotel Zone usually focuses on two things: pricey specialty items, or T-shirts and beach supplies. Window-shopping is a popular pastime, but don't expect a lot of bargains. For garden-variety souvenirs it pays to look around, as merchants compete vigorously for tourist dollars and prices can be on the steep side. Inspect carefully before buying; quality can vary greatly.

As a duty-free zone Cancún does offer potential bargains on international merchandise. High-quality tequila and cigars are two of the most popular purchases. Ultra Femme, downtown on Avenida Tulum, has good buys on cosmetics, jewelry and imported perfume; there also are branches in several of the Hotel Zone malls and at the airport.

In Ciudad Cancún, a variety of shops and open-air craft markets line Avenida Tulum. Ki-Huic, near the intersection with Avenida Cobá, is a flea market a block long with more than 100 vendors offering handicrafts, knickknacks, marble chess sets, men's *guayabera* shirts, *huipil* (ee-PEEL) dresses and Panama hats. Another downtown crafts market is Mercado Plaza, at the corner of avenidas Tulum and Uxmal. Bargaining is expected at the markets; never offer to pay the initial asking price.

If you feel the need to shop for basics, branches of three familiar stateside retailers also are in Ciudad Cancún: Costco, at the corner of avenidas Kabah and Yaxchilán; Sam's Club, at the corner of avenidas Xcaret and Yaxchilán; and Wal-Mart, at the corner of avenidas Kukulcán and Mayapán. Pick up convenience items at an Oxxo store (similar to 7-11); there are several branches in the Hotel Zone.

The Hotel Zone has both enclosed, air-conditioned malls and open-air complexes. Elegant Plaza Caracol is at Km 8.5 next to the Cancún Center. Cool marble walls and floors are the setting for shops and boutiques offering jewelry, designer clothing, resort wear, silver and decorative art. You'll also find pharmacies, art galleries, cafes and restaurants here.

Forum-by-the-Sea, Km 9.5 near the Cancún Center, is a three-level entertainment complex. There are specialty boutiques like Nike Store and Zingara Swimwear, but the emphasis is on restaurants, bars and nightspots, which include a branch of Carlos 'n

Charlie's. Flamingo Plaza, Km 11.5 on Kukulcán (lagoon side), is a smaller shopping center with several duty-free stores and boutiques, as well as a currency exchange office, an Internet cafe, an ATM and restaurants like Bubba Gump Shrimp Company.

Cancún's hottest mall is La Isla Shopping Village, Km 12.5 on Kukulcán (lagoon side). La Isla is as bright and shiny as anything you'll find in the states. The stores and shops are linked by crisscrossing bridges and walkways running over small canals. Johnny Rockets and Chili's are two of the several familiar stateside eateries here. There also is a movie multiplex, the Interactive Aquarium Cancún (see attraction listing) and other family-friendly features. It's upscale and expensive but a fun place to spend a few hours, especially on a rainy day.

At Km marker 13 is one of the largest malls, Kukulcán Plaza, which caters to tourists with stores and boutiques offering gifts, handicrafts, perfume, leather goods, jewelry and silver. It also contains a parking garage, bank, currency exchange offices, drugstores, a kiosk providing Internet access and a food court with a number of U.S. fast-food franchises. The mall's "Luxury Avenue" features such high-end retailers as Cartier, Fendi, Swarovski and Montblanc.

If you enjoy the bargaining experience, browse the many craft stalls at the Mercado de Artesanías Coral Negro (Flea Market), a peach-colored building just south of the Cancún Center (at the point where Blvd. Kukulcán splits). The selection of items is large, and it's open daily.

Most of the mall stores are open daily 10-8 or 10 p.m. Outside the Hotel Zone some stores observe the traditional siesta and close for a few hours in the afternoon. The sales tax is 10 percent, which may be waived at some shops if you pay in cash. Paying with cash instead of a credit card may also lower the price when bargaining with vendors. Almost all stores will accept U.S. dollars, and at some establishments prices are quoted in dollars rather than pesos.

## Beaches

Hurricane Wilma decimated Cancún's spectacular Caribbean beaches, which were literally replaced when sand dredged from the bottom 20 miles offshore was dumped on top of areas where the storm's fury had completely washed it away. That means they're artificial, which makes little difference to visitors. The white sand is soft and fine grained, and the water—warm enough for swimming all year—provides a gorgeous counterpoint, its ever-shifting hues ranging from opalescent green to vivid turquoise.

The beaches at the northern end of the Hotel Zone fronting Bahía Mujeres are narrow and have calm, shallow water. Those fronting the Caribbean are wider and more dramatic, with occasional crashing breakers and dangerous undertows.

The best beaches are in front of the big hotels. All beaches in Mexico, however, are federally owned and therefore public, even stretches that may seem like they are on hotel property. Keep in mind that you cannot use hotel facilities unless you are a guest, although changing areas and outdoor showers are available. Note the flags posted to indicate surf conditions. A green flag indicate safe conditions for swimming; yellow indicates caution; and red or black, dangerous conditions.

The "inner" coast of Cancún Island borders saltwater Nichupté Lagoon. Much of the lagoon is lined with stands of mangrove. Nichupté doesn't have the Caribbean's beauty, but the calm water is ideal for boating and water skiing, and the restaurants along the shore are popular places for sunset watching.

The following designated public beaches are described in the order they appear along Cancún Island, beginning at the top of the island's "seven" configuration after leaving the mainland. *See map page 73.*

**PLAYA LINDA** is just before the bridge over Canal Nichupté, at Km marker 4. Ferries to Isla Mujeres embark from the nearby El Embarcadero pier, and there are snack and dive equipment shops in the vicinity.

**PLAYA LANGOSTA** is next to the Casa Maya Hotel at Km marker 5. The beach is close to several yacht clubs, water sports facilities and restaurants. Tour boats leave from the dock here.

**PLAYA TORTUGAS** is off Blvd. Kukulcán at Km marker 6. Frequented by locals, the beach faces the calm waters of Mujeres Bay.

**PLAYA CARACOL** is close to the Fiesta Americana Grand Coral Beach. Farther east is Cancún Point, the crook of the Cancún elbow. The very tip of the point, behind the Hyatt Ziva Cancún resort, is where Mujeres Bay meets the open Caribbean. Isla Mujeres is visible in the distance. Waves crash against the rocks and send up plumes of spray on the Caribbean side, while just around the point the water is calm, shallow and translucent.

**PLAYA CHAC-MOOL** is at Km 9.5. This popular stretch is conveniently located and washed by the Caribbean surf, but also is subject to large waves and strong undertows.

**PLAYA DELFINES** is at Km marker 18 toward the southern end of the Hotel Zone. It offers some nice views, although swimming can be hazardous due to the rough surf conditions.

## Sightseeing

People come to Cancún not to sightsee but to sun, swim, eat, party and relax. One fun—and free—diversion is to go hotel hopping. The Hotel Zone is chock-full full of architecturally striking resorts, and even if you're staying at one it's worth checking out some of the others (consider it research for your next vacation). The public "Hoteles" buses that travel the length of Boulevard Kukulcán (see

*"Buses" under Getting Around*) are the best way to get from one property to another, as they stop frequently and will let you off right at the hotel entrance (keep in mind, however, that you must pay bus fare each time you reboard).

Cancún's resorts are state-of-the-art examples of imaginative design, with lavish public areas and swimming pool complexes looking out onto the Caribbean's aquamarine waters. It doesn't cost anything to tour a property, and you can take your pick of restaurants and lounges to indulge in a leisurely lunch or a relaxing pit stop. While you can enter most of the hotels if you're not a paying guest, many of the all-inclusive resorts, such as the Beach Palace and the Hotel RIU Cancún, do not allow non-guests to walk around their public areas.

Which ones should you see? The Fiesta Americana Grand Coral Beach Resort & Spa has a spacious, high-ceilinged lobby that radiates understated luxury—marble floors, giant flower arrangements and fine art displayed in recessed wall nooks, with cozy sitting areas scattered about. The ME by Meliá Cancún is hip and contemporary; its public areas have funky artwork, sleek furniture and fountains with sheets of water flowing over cool black marble slabs. The postmodern vibe extends to the pool complex, where there is an infinity pool—so named for the visual effect of water appearing to extend to the horizon and merge seamlessly with the sea.

The Paradisus Cancún Resort is one of the largest properties in the Hotel Zone, with the guest rooms housed in five soaring, pyramid-shaped buildings. The public areas here are towering and jungle-like, festooned with hanging plants, dripping with water and incorporating decorative elements—including oversized statues, frescos and calendars—that reflect Mayan motifs and culture. "Expansive" best describes the Iberostar Cancún, a dramatic pyramidal building with an enormous lobby and a series of interconnected pools that end up looking out on a spectacular stretch of beach.

Cancún is not a cruise ship stop, but that doesn't mean you can't take a cruise. Boats ply Nichupté Lagoon and the waters around Cancún Island, Cozumel and Isla Mujeres. Prices range from about $50-$70 (U.S.) per person, including beverages and entertainment. Boat operators and itineraries change, so check with your hotel or a local travel agency to see what's available.

Aqua World, at Km 15.2 on the lagoon side of Boulevard Kukulcán, offers an Isla Mujeres day trip that includes boat transportation to the island, a visit to a beach club and a buffet lunch; phone (998) 848-8327 for more information and to make reservations.

## Recreation

Water sports, not surprisingly, top Cancún's list of leisure activities. **Fishing** is excellent; the open Caribbean, Mujeres Bay, the channel between Cozumel and the mainland, and the waters of Nichupté Lagoon together are home to some 500 species, including all types of game fish. Bonito, dorado and sailfish run from March into July; bluefin tuna from April through June. Barracuda, grouper, mackerel and red snapper can be hooked all year.

Hotel Zone marinas offer a range of vessels and top-of-the-line equipment. Larger boats are 35-40 feet long; single-engine diesel boats average 26-28 feet. Four- and 8-hour charter excursions normally include a captain, first mate, gear, bait and soft drinks. Cost varies and the marinas compete for business, so it pays to shop around; ask at your hotel for recommendations.

**Scuba diving** and **snorkeling** are best at the southern end of Cancún Island around Nizuc Point, off Cozumel and Isla Mujeres, and in Nichupté Lagoon. Dive shops along Boulevard Kukulcán rent equipment, give lessons and schedule trips; some hotels also can arrange dive excursions. Check credentials, boats and equipment, and if possible get the inside scoop from a diver familiar with the area. Conditions are best from May or June through August.

Scuba Cancún, on the lagoon side of Kukulcán at Km marker 5 (across from Playa Langosta), offers daily two-tank dives that visit two local reefs. They also organize all-day snorkeling and cavern diving excursions (on Tuesday, Thursday and Saturday) to freshwater cenotes in the jungles just north of the Tulum ruins. Transportation, wet suits and gear are included; open water certification is required to participate in the cavern dive. Phone (998) 849-7508.

Other activities include **water skiing, windsurfing, parasailing, swimming** and **boating**. The best place for these activities is Nichupté Lagoon; ski clubs along Boulevard Kukulcán on the lagoon side rent boats and equipment. Windsurfing propels its participants across the water at exhilarating speeds, while the sailboard used by windsurfers is a masted

## DID YOU KNOW

The Mexican coastline is nearly four times longer than the combined coasts of California and Florida.

sail attached to a surfboard. Many Hotel Zone swimming pools have the added bonus of the Caribbean as a backdrop.

For landlubbers there's **golf** at the Cancún Golf Club at Pok-Ta-Pok, a championship 18-hole course designed by Robert Trent Jones Jr. Located on an island between Laguna de Bojórquez and Laguna Nichupté (access is off Kukulcán at Km 7.5), it offers fine views of both lagoons and the Caribbean. Shoes, carts and clubs are available for rent, and there is a pro shop. Reservations are advised; phone (998) 883-1230 or (998) 883-1277.

Another championship 18-hole course is at the Iberostar Cancún, off Kukulcán at Km 17; phone (998) 881-8000 for reservations information. Greens fees vary depending on the season and are less for hotel guests.

**Tennis** is offered at the big resort hotels; there are courts at the Crown Paradise Club Cancún, Fiesta Americana Condesa and the Fiesta Americana Grand Coral Beach, among others. A **jogging** and **bicycling** path—also used for roller blading—parallels the sidewalk along the northern (bay) side of Boulevard Kukulcán, extending as far as Cancún Point; a path also parallels the sidewalk along most of the southern half of the Hotel Zone.

If you just want to relax—and are willing to pay the price—the spa at the J.W. Marriott Cancún Resort & Spa, Km 14.5 on Kukulcán, offers hydrotherapy, massage and facial and body treatments, plus a state-of-the-art gym, an indoor pool, steam and sauna rooms and a natural juice bar. An appointment is required; for information phone (998) 848-9700.

## Nightlife

Cancún provides something for everyone after dark, from rowdy spring break hangouts to traditional Mexican and Caribbean-themed dinner shows. Hotels also get in the act with lobby bars, happy-hour specials and varied entertainment. Most clubs open around 10 or 10:30 p.m. and stay open until as late as 6 a.m. Cover charges begin at about $15 (U.S.), go up considerably with an open bar, and may be waived on certain nights in low season; at some places women are routinely admitted free of charge. Inquire about the dress code; some don't allow jeans or shorts.

Coco Bongo, at Km 9.5 on Kukulcán in the Forum-by-the-Sea shopping complex, draws young scenesters with a mix of recorded techno, hip-hop, house, salsa and '70s and '80s hits, as well as live bands. This cavernous space regularly packs in as many as 3,000 people. The cover charge (includes open bar) is about $70 to $80 (U.S.); women in short skirts or otherwise provocative attire can usually score discounts.

The City, also at Km 9.5 in front of Coco Bongo, attracts visiting international DJs who spin pulsating dance music accompanied by dizzying light shows. With nine bars and lounges and a beach club that has a wave pool, cabanas and food and drink service, this is a 24-hour hangout during spring break;

other times it opens around 10 p.m. and stays open until at least 4 a.m.

Dady'O, at Km 9.5 on Kukulcán (near the Cancún Center), is a granddaddy as far as longevity goes but is still very popular; like the other clubs it's loud and wild, and the sound and lighting are first-rate.

At La Isla Shopping Village, the La Madonna restaurant has a European-style ambiance and a well-stocked martini bar. If you prefer a quieter evening, most of the resort hotels have a nightclub or lobby bar with jazz or other live music; the lobby lounge at The Ritz-Carlton, Cancún is particularly elegant.

For those who love to party there are plenty of places that combine food, music and a frathouse sense of fun. Two Mexican chains—Carlos 'n Charlie's, at Km 8.5 in the Forum by the Sea mall, and Señor Frog's, at Km 9.5 on Kukulcán—are noisy and popular, with waiters who get as crazy as the patrons.

Cancún's spring break begins in mid-February and lasts for about 2 months. Excessive alcohol consumption associated with partying is common; the legal drinking age in Mexico is 18 but is not uniformly enforced. Much of the rowdy behavior takes place at nightspots that target a younger crowd.

For those who don't want to stand in line—or pay exorbitant cover charges three times over—the Party Hopper Tour does the work for you. It gets under way at 10 p.m. with bongo players, crazy waiters and free-flowing drinks at the XX Dos Equis Congo Bar (across Blvd. Kukulcán from the Coco Bongo club), then hits two other hotspots, usually Dady'O and Mandala night club. The cost is about $80 (U.S.) per person, which includes a reserved seating area at each club. Check with your hotel for details, or e-mail steve@cancuncare.com.

Romantics will enjoy a moonlit cruise. The Lobster Dinner Cruise sets sail for Nichupté Lagoon from the Aquatours Marina pier at Km 6.5 on Kukulcán (across from Playa Tortugas). A lobster or surf-and-turf dinner is served aboard the 60-foot galleon *Columbus,* along with dancing to live jazz music.

Departures are Mon.-Fri. and Sun. at 5 and 8 p.m. (also Sat. in spring high season). Arriving 30 minutes before scheduled departure is recommended. Reservations are required; under 14 are not permitted. Transportation to the pier is not included. You can book this excursion through a local tour company, many major hotels, or directly; phone 01 (800) 727-5391 (toll-free long distance within Mexico) or (866) 393-5158 (from the United States).

The Captain Hook Dinner Cruise departs from the Puerto Juárez Maritime Terminal, about 2 miles north of Ciudad Cancún via Avenida López Portillo. This terminal is about 100 yards north of the Gran Puerto dock, departure point for UltraMar ferries to Isla Mujeres. The 3.5-hour cruise includes dinner and drinks aboard twin galleons that are "attacked" by pirates. The boats light up after the sun sets, with live entertainment, music and dancing under the stars.

The cruise departs daily (except Jan. 1 and Christmas) at 7 p.m. and returns at 10:30; hotel pickup and drop-off is not included. The cost is $99 (U.S.) per person with a steak dinner; $114 with a steak and lobster dinner; $12 (ages 4-12) for the children's buffet. Adult dinner prices include an open bar. For reservations phone (998) 849-4451, or 01 (800) 010-4665 (toll-free long distance within Mexico).

## Special Events

The Day of the Kings (Feast of the Epiphany, or El Día de Los Reyes) on Jan. 6 is a day of gift-giving. Local restaurants serve a King's Cake (Rosca de Reyes) that contains a small plastic Jesus doll (El Niño) inside. The person receiving the piece with the doll acts as a host on Candlemas (La Candeleria), the season's final Christmas celebration held the first week in February, when a meal of *tamales* and hot chocolate is served in homes and restaurants.

Carnaval, a fiesta in the spirit of Mardi Gras, is held the week preceding Ash Wednesday. Residents dress up in elaborate costumes, floats parade down the streets of Ciudad Cancún, and there are street parties featuring dancing, fireworks and regional foods and beverages.

On Mar. 21 the Vernal Equinox (Inicio Primavera) is observed at Chichén Itzá. When the late afternoon sun shines on El Castillo, a shadow remarkably reminiscent of a slithering serpent appears on the side of the pyramid. Thousands of people attend this event.

As in all of Mexico, Independence Day (Patria de la Independencia) festivities take place Sept. 15-16 and include fireworks, a parade (on the 16th) and traditional food. Father Miguel Hidalgo's famous speech *Grito de Dolores* is re-enacted as people gather at midnight to shout out *"Viva México!"*

The Eve of All Souls' Day, Oct. 31, is observed throughout the Yucatán by adorning headstones with wreaths of marigolds and placing candles and offerings of food and tequila at gravesites. Day of the Dead graveside and church ceremonies take place amid a party-like atmosphere Nov. 1 and 2, with bakeries doing big business turning out various skull-shaped pastries.

Christmas celebrations begin 9 days prior to Dec. 25 and feature *posadas* (processions) of families and friends who take part in *pastorelas* (plays) portraying Jesus' birth, along with street fairs, *piñata* smashing and other festivities. One highlight of the season is the display of nativity scenes.

© BlueOrange Studio / Shutterstock.com

This ends listings for Cancún.
The following page resumes the alphabetical listings
of cities in Yucatán Peninsula.

# The Caribbean Coast

© BlueOrange Studio / Shutterstock.com

**Note:** Destinations in this region listed under their own names are Akumal, Cozumel, Isla Holbox, Isla Mujeres, Majahual, Playa del Carmen, Puerto Morelos and Tulum.

Cancún has one heck of a winning vacation formula. Begin with a string of glittering beachfront hotels where every amenity is provided. Add an assortment of restaurants offering a variety of cuisines, many with the added bonus of lovely water views. Stir in entertainment from sedate to slammin' and nightspots that extend the party into the wee hours. Provide numerous opportunities for shopping (humble souvenir stalls, ritzy malls and everything in between) and recreation (boating, fishing and snorkeling, to name just three). And it all takes place against a backdrop of sun, blue skies and turquoise water.

But Cancún isn't the only game in town; the stretch of Caribbean coast all the way south to the Belize border is speckled with beaches every bit as beautiful. A number of leisure activities lean toward the thrilling—anyone for zip lining above a jungle canopy or exploring the otherworldly depths of a freshwater sinkhole? And in an era where going green has become a burgeoning movement, protection of the natural environment is a key component of Mexican Caribbean tourism, along with the preservation and celebration of native Yucatecan culture.

## It's All in the Name

Two names define the Caribbean coast. The area known and promoted as the Riviera Maya covers the coastal strip from the town of Puerto Morelos south to the town of Tulum. The inland town of Felipe Carrillo Puerto, about 40 kilometers (25 miles) south of Tulum, also is considered part of the Riviera Maya. From a traveler's perspective, however, what constitutes the Riviera Maya is a somewhat fluid definition, as other points of interest—for example, the major archeological ruins at Cobá (*see separate listing under Yucatán Peninsula*)—are a fairly short distance from the coast and thus easily reached.

Between Tulum and the tiny lobster fishing village of Punta Allen is a 30-mile stretch of largely unspoiled coastline lying within the Si'an Kaan Biosphere Reserve, a protected area covering more than a million acres that is a haven for diverse plant and animal species. Long known to sport fishing enthusiasts, dedicated bird watchers and a few intrepid travelers, this stretch is known for small-scale, ecologically oriented tourism. It's the wilder side of the Caribbean coast—a swath of stunning empty beaches, mangrove forests and dense jungle scrub.

Farther south it gets wilder still. The length of coastline from Punta Herrero—another miniscule fishing village perched on a little sand spit at the head of Espíritu Santo Bay—south to the remote outpost of Xcalak, near the Mexico-Belize border, is referred to as the Costa Maya. The Costa Maya focuses on small-scale adventure tourism, but an international cruise ship pier at the small port of Majahual may bring bigger things to come.

Geographically speaking, this region embraces three islands as well: Cozumel, Isla Holbox and Isla Mujeres. All are less than 15 miles from the mainland, and the warm, clear Caribbean waters teem with myriad species of tropical and game fish.

Cancún itself isn't officially part of the Riviera Maya, but the great majority of Mexican Caribbean visitors arrive via Cancún International Airport. For many travelers it makes a convenient base from which to embark on day trips down the coast via such transportation options as rental cars and jeeps, public buses or private cabs. But Cancún shares a geographical proximity and the physical attributes that make it a kindred spirit of the Riviera Maya, the Costa Maya and the offshore islands.

## Thrill Seeking

Among this coastal region's most notable natural features are the sinkholes called cenotes (say-NO-tays). The underlying limestone's porous quality

leads to the formation of caverns and caves where fresh water collects. The water in cenotes is known for both its clarity and for colors ranging from deep blue to turquoise to emerald green. Furthermore, portions of limestone that weaken and collapse over time can form holes in a cavern ceiling, allowing shafts of light to penetrate otherwise dark surroundings and illuminate the numerous stalactite and stalagmite formations. These features lend a surreal aspect to the appearance of many underground cenotes.

Cenotes at land level, in contrast, look like any lake or pond. These sinkholes are often created when the ceiling of an underlying cave collapses. Specialized plants take root in the pile of rubble left behind by a collapse, their roots eventually splitting the rock to tap the cave water below. Then there are partially enclosed cenotes, which have some sections that are exposed to full sunlight and others where little natural light penetrates.

Land-level cenotes are common in the interior peninsula and function as swimming holes, while those along the coast frequently serve as entry points to extensive subterranean cave systems. Active underwater cave exploration along the Quintana Roo coast dates only to the early 1980s, but since then a number of cave systems have been discovered. While cave diving is a sport best left to experts, even landlubbers can enjoy snorkeling in the clear, cool waters of a cenote while exploring bizarrely beautiful rock formations. Cenote snorkeling and diving has quickly become one of this region's most popular recreational pursuits.

Zip-lining is popular as well. A steel cable mounted on an incline, a zipline propels users wearing a harness that is attached to a freely moving pulley; it provides a heart-thumping thrill of a ride as

© Dirima / Shutterstock.com

well as an elevated bird's-eye view of the scenery en route. Zipline outfitters along the Quintana Roo coast take advantage of scenic environments that range from jungle canopies to the open Caribbean.

Reputable operators provide all necessary safety equipment and offer a thorough demonstration, including zip-lining do's and don'ts, before anyone leaves the ground. You, on the other hand, should be in moderate to good physical condition, have some familiarity with adventure sport abilities and not be afraid of heights. Zipline excursions often include other activities like biking along unpaved jungle trails and swimming in a cenote. Selvática organizes various zipline tour packages; for details phone (998) 898-4312 or (866) 552-8825 (from the United States or Canada).

You can still do the tried-and-true tourist thing here—a sunset lagoon cruise, perhaps, or a snorkeling trip. But many tour companies along the Caribbean coast cater specifically to the active crowd. Playa del Carmen-based Alltournative specializes in vigorous outings like piloting a sea kayak to an offshore coral

# Destination Caribbean Coast

*C*aribbean Coast beaches are pretty close to paradise: sugar-white sand, intensely turquoise water and coconut palm fronds gently rustling in the breeze.

*T*he coast also has a rich historical backdrop. The ancient Maya built a city overlooking the sea, and today the cliff-top ruins of Tulum are a dramatic reminder of the past.

© BlueOrange Studio / Shutterstock.com

© mypokcik / Shutterstock.com

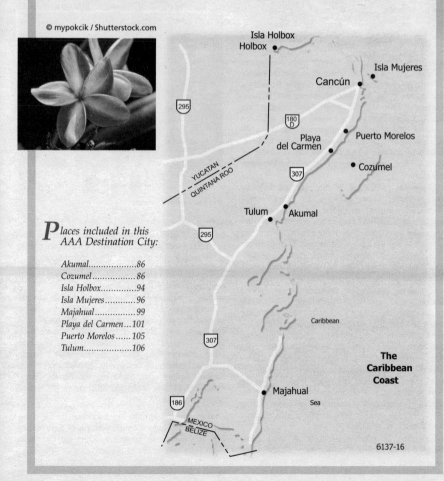

*P*laces included in this AAA Destination City:

The Caribbean Coast

6137-16

reef. Their guided day trips also involve the community, putting the focus not only on exciting fun but on education and giving back to local families. For more information phone (984) 803-9999 or (877) 437-4990 (from the United States).

## Touring the Riviera Maya

Organized bus tours departing from Cancún are plentiful, and this is certainly a convenient and hassle-free way to experience such established Caribbean coast tourist draws as Xcaret, Xel-Ha and the Tulum Ruins. But driving yourself offers greater flexibility and the opportunity to check out secluded spots the tour buses don't visit. Mex. 307, the main highway, hugs the coast from Cancún as far south as Tulum before turning inland and continuing all the way to the city of Chetumal, near the border with Belize.

All-inclusive beachfront resorts line the Riviera Maya. These accommodations add up to far more than simply a night's lodging—in addition to food and beverages, they offer everything from organized kid's activities to Spanish lessons to yoga classes on the beach. Ocean trampolines, catamaran excursions, theme parties under a starry night sky and just about any other diversion you can think of are part and parcel of the all-inclusive experience, making them very popular with families and groups.

If you've never driven Mex. 307, this four-lane divided highway is in good condition from Cancún south to Playa del Carmen. Speed bumps are present when approaching traffic lights at some intersections (road signs denote their presence). Speed limits vary from 70 kilometers per hour (about 45 mph) to 100 kilometers per hour (about 65 mph), but along most stretches the limit is 80 kilometers per hour (about 50 mph). It drops to 40 kilometers per hour (about 25 mph) when approaching Puerto Morelos, Playa del Carmen and Tulum.

International green road signs with picture symbols denote towns, points of interest, gas stations, resort hotels, etc. Practically every point of interest is a kilometer or two east or west of Mex. 307 via paved, dirt or rutted roads; they're designated by crude signs as well as prominent billboards. Mileage signs are posted in kilometers, and kilometer markers are installed along the right-hand side of the highway. Drive defensively—much of the route runs straight as a ruler, and many motorists tend to speed—and avoid driving after dark since lighting along most stretches is inadequate.

From Cancún it takes about 90 minutes (without stops) to reach the southern end of the Riviera Maya at Tulum. From Ciudad Cancún, take Avenida Tulum (which becomes Mex. 307) south. From the Hotel Zone, take Boulevard Kukulcán south toward the airport. After rounding Nizuc Point (Punta Nizuc), the southern tip of the island, Kukulcán curves west toward Mex. 307. Continue to the highway interchange and follow the signs for Playa del Carmen and Tulum.

The thick jungle that once blanketed this coastal region is largely gone; the flat terrain and scrub vegetation isn't unlike rural southern Florida in appearance. The highway offers no glimpses of the Caribbean; the

coastline is a mile or two to the east. Occasional road-side establishments along Mex. 307 offer hammocks, blankets and crafts for sale, and signs at turnoffs announce the latest upscale resort development that has either just opened or is under construction.

The main turn-off for Puerto Morelos (an intersection with a traffic signal) is about 36 kilometers (22 miles) south of Cancún's Hotel Zone. This laid-back village has a delightful setting—beaches backed by coconut palms, fishing boats, a municipal dock, and of course the turquoise hues of the Caribbean. The snorkeling and diving is excellent due to the coral reef that is less than 2,000 feet offshore. For a perfectly relaxed afternoon, stroll along the sandy beach in the center of town and then grab a bite to eat at one of the casual restaurants on the main square (zócalo).

The turn-off for Punta Beté, about 58 kilometers (36 miles) south of Cancún, is signed "Punta Beté/Xcalacoco." The bumpy dirt road leads to a rocky beach and inexpensive cabana-type lodgings.

## Playing in Playa

Either the first or second turn-offs (Avenida Constituyentes and Avenida Juárez, respectively) will take you to downtown Playa del Carmen, about 68 kilometers (42 miles) south of Cancún. Avenida Juárez goes straight to the main plaza. If you miss the inside left-turn lanes (easy to do) you can proceed south to the turnaround and then double back. An elevated overpass built directly over Mex. 307, some 6 kilometers (4 miles) in length, avoids the stoplights and traffic congestion on the older road and allows drivers en route to points south to bypass the city completely. There are entrance and exit ramps at key cross streets.

The Riviera Maya's largest city has a full quotient of glitzy resorts and a hopping nightlife. But in spite of Playa's rapid growth it remains a small town at heart. The pace along pedestrian-only 5th Avenue (Quinta Avenida), just a block off the beach, is leisurely. You can lunch alfresco, browse block after block of craft stalls or just relax on a bench at the palm-shaded plaza (zócalo), with its lovely view of the Caribbean.

South of Playa del Carmen Mex. 307 continues as a four-lane divided highway before eventually alternating between two- and three-lane stretches (with the middle lane used as a passing lane by both southbound and northbound vehicles). Be careful when passing, as drivers in the oncoming lane may cross over the center line unexpectedly. Also use caution when making left turns; turn lanes are marked by reflectors on the road.

The turn-off for Xcaret is about 72 kilometers (45 miles) south of Cancún. Once just a peaceful cove, Xcaret has grown over the years into a big aquatic theme park, albeit one that puts an emphasis on the preservation of Mayan heritage and the Yucatán Peninsula's natural resources. One of the highlights here is an underground river that flows through a series of caves to the beach; swimmers float along with the current.

Ten kilometers (6 miles) beyond Xcaret, just north of Puerto Aventuras, is the signed turn-off for Paamul (paul-MOOL), a sheltered cove with a rocky beach that is popular with RV owners. You can swim here when seas are calm, and the snorkeling is good due to the nearby presence of the offshore coral reef. The beach is sandier and less rocky at the south end.

The turn-off for Puerto Aventuras is about 85 kilometers (53 miles) south of Cancún. This planned resort community also is a sport fishing center and has the largest marina along the Riviera Maya coast. The marina is surrounded by shops and casual open-air restaurants. Much of the beachfront here is occupied by resort properties; the main beach area is along Fatima Bay between the Chac Hal condominium development and the Grand Peninsula residential complex.

A few kilometers south of Puerto Aventuras are several turn-offs for Xpu-Ha (take the one signed "La Playa" for public access to the beach). The Palace chain of all-inclusive resorts has properties here. The beach is lovely and clean (it's raked to remove seaweed). Like all beaches in Mexico it is open to the public, although beach chairs, palapas and other amenities are reserved for hotel guests.

South of Xpu-Ha and about 105 kilometers (65 miles) south of Cancún is the turn-off for Akumal. On the west side of the highway is the tiny pueblo (community) of Akumal, which consists of one main thoroughfare, a couple of small businesses and a few side streets; hotels and resort amenities are east of the highway.

**Note:** If you're heading southbound on Mex. 307, you'll need to continue a hundred yards or so beyond the Akumal turn-off to the signed turnaround (retorno), make a U-turn and head back north in order to turn right at the access road that leads to the beach.

A few kilometers south of Akumal is the signed turn-off for Xcacel, a lovely white-sand beach on a crescent-shaped bay with calm, clear water. The area is an important nesting site for Atlantic green and loggerhead turtles, both on the endangered species list, and ongoing efforts are made to ensure their preservation. At the south end of the beach is a path that leads through the jungle to a small cenote. The area is a nature preserve, and boating, sport fishing and overnight camping are prohibited.

About 122 kilometers (76 miles) south of Cancún is the well-marked turn-off to Xel-Ha, an ecologically oriented park centered around a large lagoon. Xel-Ha (shell-HAH) is a breeding ground for parrotfish and other tropical fish species. It's an ideal outing for kids and novice snorkelers. Tour buses regularly pack the parking lot, so try to get there early. On the west side of the highway and close to the park entrance is a group of restored Mayan ruins.

## An Outpost by the Sea

One look at the ruins of Tulum, about 131 kilometers (81 miles) south of Cancún (the turn-off to the ruins is prominently signed), and it's easy to see why the Maya chose this site: This is the only part of the low-lying Yucatán Peninsula where limestone deposits built up to form coastal cliffs. Tulum's most distinctive feature is its dramatic location over-looking the Caribbean. Explore the ruins, then hike to the beach below and enjoy a swim in the sea.

Many Tulum residents work at nearby resort properties. Mex. 307 is the town's main drag, lined with souvenir shops, open-air restaurants, fruit markets and local businesses (everything from muffler repair shops to Internet cafes). A gazebo stands in the middle of Tulum's small, palm-shaded plaza, just east of Mex. 307 behind the City Hall (Ayuntamiento) building/police headquarters. Kids play basketball during the day and families gather at the park in the cool of the evening, when vendors sell snacks from pushcarts.

Past the town of Tulum Mex. 307 angles southwest into the scrubby flatlands of interior Quintana Roo toward Felipe Carrillo Puerto. The wilderness along the coast south of Tulum is part of the 1.3 million-acre Sian Ka'an Biosphere Reserve. This vast tract of scrubland, honeycombed with cenotes, is a haven for wildlife that includes some endangered species.

If you want to explore Tulum's beaches and hotel zone (and you should, since it's a nice little drive), you can reach them via the paved road that intersects with Mex. 307 at the northern end of town. Take this road east (the sign at the intersection says "Playas/Punta Allen"). It passes through open scrubland for about 5 kilometers (3 miles) before reaching the Hotel Posada del Sol, where there also are several restaurants, a currency exchange house, a grocery store and a couple of mini-markets.

This is the beginning of the hotel zone, which extends south for several miles along a paved drive shaded by palms and other tropical vegetation; watch for occasional *topes* (speed bumps). Cabanas, thatched *palapa* huts, small hotels and other accommodations line the narrow road. Many advertise yoga and holistic massages, underscoring the relaxed, get-away-from-it-all feeling. The beachside properties are steps away from the surf, although you can't see the beach from the road. Several beachfront restaurants and a few nightspots also are mixed in.

After winding through the hotel zone the road continues south down the length of the Boca Paila Peninsula. This narrow isthmus of land constitutes Sian Ka'an's outer buffer zone, the only portion of this protected reserve that is open to visitors. Once past the hotel zone you must stop and pay the registration fee of around $4 (U.S.) per person at the reserve's official point of entry (marked by a guardhouse) if you intend to drive down to Punta Allen.

## The End of the Line

At the guardhouse, set your car's trip meter to zero. Ten kilometers (6.2 miles) down the road is a small visitor center with a handful of displays focusing on Sian Ka'an's flora, fauna and history. Information panels are in Spanish and English. A short trail leads inland to a wooden dock fronting an expansive lagoon. Here you can arrange kayak rentals (about $20 U.S. per hour) and 90-minute boat tours of the lagoon (about $40 U.S. per person). Reservations are not necessary.

Beyond the visitor center the setting is dense scrub jungle, with empty, palm-studded beaches and mangrove-lined estuaries along the Caribbean coast and a network of lagoons and waterways between the peninsula and the mainland. There are points where your peripheral vision will encompass sea, land and lagoon. Rustic eco lodges cater to dedicated birders (species common to this region include frigate birds, brown pelicans, woodpeckers, parrots and the Yucatán jay) and sportsmen who don't mind roughing it for the superb fishing.

Some 17 kilometers (10.6 miles) past the guardhouse there is easy beach access and good swimming at a gorgeous semi-sheltered cove. Park anywhere along the side of the road. Xamach Dos (24 kilometers south of the guardhouse) is a sleepy beachfront hotel with a few rental cabanas and a small *palapa* restaurant. There are picnic tables and beach chairs at the water's edge. If you've always fantasized about having a Caribbean beach all to yourself, continue toward Punta Allen and pull off at any of the small, unmarked turn-outs along the beach side of the road. Cancún this is not.

This truly off-the-beaten-path journey culminates at the hamlet of Punta Allen—a couple of restaurants, a handful of convenience stores and a few fishing and eco tour guide services—set smack dab in an idyllic setting of coconut palms, thatched *palapas* and stunning Caribbean views. The road comes to an end at a lighthouse with a *mirador* (viewing platform) that looks out over the vast saltwater flats of Ascension Bay (Bahía de la Ascensión). This is one of the best fly-fishing spots in the world for anglers seeking tarpon, bonefish and the elusive permit, a game fish with a deeply forked tail related to the pompano.

Trekkers take note: It is approximately 45 kilometers (28 miles) from the Sian Ka'an guardhouse to Punta Allen. Much of the route—which is gradually being paved and improved—is a narrow one-lane trail of packed dirt and sand over limestone. It winds through dense scrub jungle, passing deserted beaches, mangrove flats and even an occasional Mayan ruin. Iguanas scurry across the road. Ruts and potholes are more evident after crossing the Boca Paila bridge, about 24 kilometers (15 miles) south of the guardhouse.

You can make it in a car, but a jeep or four-wheel-drive vehicle is recommended. Be sure you have a full tank of gas and bring drinking water, food and insect repellent. Plan on at least 2 hours (not including stops) to reach Punta Allen from Tulum, although once you're familiar with the road it's safe to shave a good 20 minutes off your estimated return drive time. If you're not spending the night in Punta Allen allow enough time to get back to Mex. 307 before dusk.

Obviously this excursion isn't for the faint of heart, but that's the beauty of the Caribbean coast. You can hole up in sheltered luxury and pamper yourself, or leave your comfort zone behind for the shot of adrenaline that real adventure provides.

## AKUMAL, QUINTANA ROO (B-4)

A diving and snorkeling center, Akumal ("place of the turtles" in the Mayan language) is off Mex. 307 about 26 kilometers (16 miles) north of Tulum. Although centered around several resort complexes, you don't need to be a guest at any of them in order to enjoy the long, curving beaches or swim in the warm Caribbean surf. Akumal is laid-back and friendly, a great place to drop your anchor and get into the relaxed rhythms of the Riviera Maya coast.

If heading southbound on Mex. 307, drivers will encounter a concrete center median at the Akumal turn-off that prevents a left turn onto the access road. Continue a hundred yards or so beyond the turn-off to the signed turnaround (*retorno*); make a U-turn, head back north and turn right onto the access road.

Less than half a mile down the road you'll drive under a white arch. Stay to the left to get to the Akumal beach parking lot (there are spaces on either side of the road); an attendant will usually wave you in and collect a small parking fee. Past the parking lot, a dirt road continues on to Half Moon Bay. A short distance beyond Half Moon is Yal-ku Lagoon (*see attraction listing*).

The town of Akumal spreads out along the shore of exceptionally pretty Akumal Bay, the largest of three bodies of water comprising this stretch of coast. It has a beautiful white-sand beach and two full-service dive shops that provide scuba instruction as well as reef diving, sport fishing and snorkeling excursions. From shore it's an easy swim to Akumal's offshore reef, where the chances of spotting a sea turtle are high. As you snorkel, be mindful of boat traffic in the bay.

Grocery stores, restaurants, beach bars and other tourist amenities are plentiful in town. The beachfront bar at Restaurante Lol Ha is popular with Akumal regulars and has great views of Akumal Bay. To the north, Half Moon Bay is lined with a fine-sand beach backed by villas and condos. There's good snorkeling here as well. You can rent kayaks and other water sports equipment at both bays.

Akumal Dive Adventures, a PADI-certified dive center located on Half Moon Bay, offers a variety of scuba and snorkeling trips that emphasize a low-impact approach to the fragile offshore reef environment, as well as deep-sea fishing excursions for mahi mahi, marlin, sailfish and wahoo. Accompanied by a cave-certified instructor, divers can explore the wonderland of Dos Ojos (Two Eyes), a cenote (freshwater sinkhole) that leads to a vast subterranean cavern filled with intricate limestone formations in crystal-clear water. Phone (984) 875-9157, or (888) 425-8625 (from the United States).

**AKTUN CHEN** is about 4 km (2.5 mi.) s. of Akumal (watch for the signed turn-off on the right side of Mex. 307 going southbound), then another 4 km (2.5 mi.) down a narrow dirt road to the entrance. This nature park offers a guided half-mile walking tour through a dry cave festooned with stalactites, stalagmites and other natural limestone formations, all enhanced by indirect artificial lighting as well as natural light coming through openings in the cave ceiling.

The tour ends at a freshwater underground cenote with clear, green-hued water that reaches a depth of 36 feet; there is an extra fee to snorkel in the cenote. For daredevils, the park also offers a separate "Canopy" tour, which features 10 zip lines and two suspended bridges. The park's animal exhibits include deer, spider monkeys, toucans, parrots and snakes, and such local wildlife as wild turkeys and iguanas also can be seen.

Guided tours in English are available. A small restaurant is on the premises. On-site parking is available. Restrooms are provided. Insect repellent is recommended. **Time:** Allow 3 hours minimum. **Hours:** Mon.-Sat. 9-5 (last tour begins at 4), Sept.-May; 9-4 (last tour begins at 3), rest of year. **Cost:** Cave tour $33 (U.S.); $16.50 (ages 6-10). Cenote snorkeling $33. Canopy tour $44. Discounted combination tickets also are available. **Phone:** (984) 109-2061 or (984) 806-4962. ⑪

**YAL-KU LAGOON** is about 2 km (1 mi.) n. of town past Half-Moon Bay; take the marked Akumal exit off Mex. 307 and stay to the left past the center of town. The entrance to the lagoon is down a short, winding walking path. A brackish mix of fresh and salt water, Yal-ku offers the opportunity to snorkel in a sheltered environment (currents are stronger near the open sea). Sets of stairs lead down to a sandy bottom. Entry is easy and the water is calm, but due to poor water flow, clarity is on the murky side. You will, however, see rock formations and the usual small reef fish. It's a good choice for beginning snorkelers and families with kids. There also are sculptures and gardens on the grounds.

On-site parking is available. Restrooms are provided. Private cabanas are available for rent. No outside food or drink permitted, except for bottled water. **Time:** Allow 2 hours minimum. **Hours:** Daily 9-5. **Cost:** $14 (U.S.); $10 (ages 4-12). There are extra fees for snorkel equipment rental and life jackets. Cash only. **Phone:** (984) 875-9520. ⑪ ⊠ ⊞

## COZUMEL, QUINTANA ROO (B-4)
pop. 79,535

Cozumel (koh-soo-MEHL) is not only Mexico's largest inhabited island; many feel it's the country's most beautiful as well. Famed underwater explorer Jacques Cousteau would likely agree. His early 1960s documentary on Cozumel's spectacular coral reefs caught the attention of scuba fanatics, and today this tropical isle 12 miles off the Yucatán coast is one of the top diving destinations on the planet.

But if you step ashore at San Miguel de Cozumel, the island's only town, during the tourist high season (December through April), don't expect to see marine biologist types gearing up for a dive. Instead, you'll be surrounded by a human flood of cruise ship day-trippers shuffling past the wall-to-wall shops and restaurants lining the waterfront. And if this is all you see of Cozumel, you'll leave with the wrong impression.

Cozumel has two faces. There's San Miguel, and then there's the island's wild side, with its sugar-white beaches, ancient Mayan ruins and mind-blowing subaquatic scenery. For some, the highlight of an island visit is a drive (preferably in a jeep) along Cozumel's unspoiled windward coast. Dotted with rustic seafood restaurants and lashed by turquoise-blue breakers, the rugged eastern shore is worlds removed from tourist bustle.

Cozumel was an important Mayan ceremonial and trading center. The name is a derivation of the word Cuzamil, or "the island of swallows." In the 1500s Spanish explorers used the island as a base to launch attacks against mainland Indians. A port was established, but by the end of the 16th century European-introduced diseases had wiped out most of the local population. From the early 1600s through the mid-19th century, Cozumel was a favorite hide-out for fiendish pirates.

U.S. servicemen during World War II, and later Cousteau, spread the word about Cozumel's amazing reefs, and tourism took off. Hotel construction followed, but it is not on the massive scale found in Cancún. The island takes the daily arrival of massive cruise ships in stride, swaying to its own lazy tropical rhythm.

## Island Layout

Cozumel is located off the coast opposite Playa del Carmen; a 3,000-foot-deep channel separates it from the mainland. Mexico's largest populated island, it has a total area of 189 square miles (about one-sixth the size of Rhode Island), is approximately 29 miles long and averages 9 miles wide.

The interior is either patches of insect-ridden jungle or expanses of thorny, uninviting scrub. There are scattered Mayan ruins, none of them well preserved. This desolate landscape makes the beaches all the more inviting. Those on the island's western (leeward) side are protected from the open Caribbean; the water is calm and the shore sandy. The eastern (windward) coast is rockier and faces the open sea. Pounding surf and powerful undertows create dangerous swimming conditions, but these beaches also have a wild beauty.

San Miguel, Cozumel's only town, is a conglomeration of budget hotels, businesses, shops, restaurants and nightspots. Many of them line the main street, Avenida Rafael Melgar, which runs north-south along the waterfront. The *malecón,* a cement walkway, is between Melgar and the beach. Avenidas run north-south, calles east-west, forming an easy-to-negotiate grid pattern. (An exception is Avenida Benito Juárez, which begins at the passenger ferry pier and runs due east.)

Hotel zones with Cozumel's more exclusive accommodations are to the north and south of San Miguel. One paved road, the Carretera Transversal (the eastward extension of Avenida Benito Juárez), crosses the island west-east. At Cozumel's eastern (windward) shore, this paved road heads south along the coast, rounds the southern tip of the island and becomes the Carretera Costera Sur. Continuing north along the island's western (leeward) shore, the road offers access to Cozumel's best beaches before it becomes Avenida Rafael Melgar as it enters San Miguel. There are no paved roads in the northern half of Cozumel, and very little development.

## Practicalities

Cozumel International Airport is about 3 kilometers (2 miles) north of San Miguel via Boulevard Aeropuerto Internacional, which runs off Avenida Rafael Melgar. American Airlines offers direct flights from Dallas and Miami. Delta, United and US Airways offer nonstop service from Atlanta, Houston and Charlotte, respectively. Several charter airlines offer direct seasonal flights as well. Make airline and hotel reservations well in advance if you'll be visiting during the peak tourist season, mid-December through mid-April.

Ground transportation from the airport to your hotel is available via private taxi vans or shared passenger vans *(colectivos).* Fares for private van service are expensive and range from 150 pesos (about $12.20 U.S.) per person to downtown hotels to 475 pesos per person to the far southern hotel zone. Shared passenger vans wait until the vehicle is full; cost ranges from 60 pesos per person to downtown hotels to 141 pesos per person to the far southern hotel zone. Tickets can be purchased at the airport exit or from the drivers themselves. Take an inexpensive city taxi back to the airport upon departure.

Travel agencies, tour operators, hotels and airlines offer a variety of air/hotel package deals. *For additional information about airlines see Arriving by Air, page p. 42.*

Three ferry companies carry passengers between Cozumel and Playa del Carmen. The passenger ferry pier is off Avenida Rafael Melgar across from San Miguel's main plaza. A boat departs for Playa del Carmen every hour on the hour (and sometimes on the half-hour) beginning at 5:30 a.m.; the last scheduled departure is around 9 p.m. The last scheduled departure from Playa del Carmen back to Cozumel is around 10 p.m.

Tickets can be purchased from booths at the pier. Signs posted outside the ticket booths indicate each ferry's next departure time. If you're carrying luggage, you can check your suitcase with ferry baggage handlers free of charge. Double-check the schedule, and in particular confirm the time of the last departure from Playa if you're planning a day trip to the mainland.

All three companies—UltraMar, Mexico Waterjets and Barcos Caribe—operate modern, air-conditioned vessels. The trip takes about 35 to 45 minutes. UltraMar and Mexico Waterjets charge roughly the same one-way fare (including tax): 163 pesos (about $12 U.S.); 97 pesos (ages 6-11). Barcos Caribe fare is 135 pesos (about $10 U.S.); 70 pesos (children).

Buying a round-trip ticket is convenient, but the return ticket is nonrefundable and you'll be locked into a return departure time. If you're taking a day trip to Playa del Carmen, it's wise to leave your return time open in case you decide to stay longer or come back early. The boats accommodate plenty of passengers and very rarely sell out. Those prone to seasickness should take appropriate precautions on windy days.

A number of cruise lines, among them Carnival, Holland America, Norwegian, Princess and Royal Caribbean, dock at Cozumel and/or Playa del Carmen. AAA/CAA members receive exclusive savings on cruising vacations by booking through a AAA travel professional.

Mopeds, motorcycles and open-air jeeps are popular ways to get around the island, but streets crowded with people on bicycles, jaywalking pedestrians and the ubiquitous scooters can make them a risky means of transportation. Wearing a helmet is required. There are several moped rental establishments in San Miguel. The rate averages $25-$30 (U.S.) per day; insurance is not included.

If you're staying more than a day it might be worth your while to rent a car in town or at the airport, since the beaches and other points of interest are spread out. Hertz has a rental counter inside the airport.

Keep in mind that if stopped for a serious moving violation, your vehicle may be impounded and you'll be asked to accompany the police officer to the station to pay the fine. (Of course fines for minor infractions can often be paid on the spot, in cash; in Mexico a bribe is a common way of taking care of such situations.) Curbs painted yellow are for bicycle, motorcycle and moped parking only; curbs painted red are no parking zones. No parking signs feature a black capital "E" with a red line through it.

Taxis wait outside the major hotels, the passenger ferry pier and cruise ship piers, and can be hailed on the street in San Miguel. Taxi drivers are generally friendly and courteous, and fares are reasonable. Cabs are not metered; fares are per cab, not per person. Drivers do not carry a lot of change, so have smaller bills and coins available. Tips are expected and appreciated.

Fares within town average 40 pesos (about $3 U.S.). From downtown San Miguel to the airport the fare is about 90 pesos. To the San Gervasio ruins it is about 250 pesos. Fares to the north and south hotel zones range from about 50 to 80 pesos. To Chankanaab Lagoon Park, Playa Palancar, Playa San Francisco and other attractions at the southern end of the island, expect fares of about 150 pesos and up, depending on distance traveled.

If possible, share the cost with other passengers. You also can hire a taxi driver for a tour of the island; the standard fee begins at about $80 (U.S.) for a 3-hour tour. Most hotels will call a taxi for their guests. **Note:** Because Cozumel is a major cruise ship port, paying taxi fares in U.S. dollars often means a very unfavorable exchange rate of 10 pesos to the dollar.

Need to check e-mail or the weather? Most major hotels have a guest-use-only computer in the lobby. If you've brought along a laptop or tablet, several bars, restaurants and cafes (including Starbucks at the Punta Langosta Mall) offer free Wi-Fi.

The Red Cross (Cruz Roja) clinic is at Calle Rosada Salas and Avenida 20 Sur; phone (987) 872-1058. A 24-hour clinic and access to air ambulance service are available at the Cozumel Medical Center (Centro Médico de Cozumel), Calle 1 Sur #101; phone (987) 872-9400.

Since Cozumel is a major port of call for cruise ships, U.S. dollars are almost universally accepted. Even if you're staying for a week, there's really no need to exchange U.S. currency for pesos. Regardless of the small, daily official exchange rate fluctuations, the simple 10 pesos-to-$1 U.S. dollar exchange is common among many smaller businesses and taxi drivers, and you'll find some even make change with a mix of dollars and pesos. Canadian currency, however, will invariably draw blank stares.

There's an HSBC bank/ATM located at the southeast corner of the main plaza. There also is an ATM at the Bancomer bank, on the east side of the plaza behind the yellow clock tower; withdrawals at both are in pesos. Currency exchange houses (casas de cambio) are at the airport and at major hotels, but rates are often poor. Many tourist-oriented shops and restaurants accept credit cards.

Cozumel is balmy year-round. June through October, the rainy season, also is more humid. Afternoon showers during these months are generally brief and pose little interruption to leisure activities. Most of the year, however, is dry, warm and sunny, with an occasional cool evening December through February. The possibility of a hurricane or tropical storm is likeliest in September or October.

## Things to Do on the Island

When in Cozumel, dive. From the international cruise ship pier south to the island's southern tip are miles of offshore coral reefs that offer some of the most spectacular dive settings in the world. All of the reefs are part of a national marine park that includes the beaches and waters between Paradise Reef and Chiqueros Point. The entire area is governed by strict rules to ensure that the fragile environment remains protected at the same time it is enjoyed by visitors.

Cozumel has many rewarding dive sites that are classified primarily by skill level and the depth of the dive. The reefs are all off the western (leeward) coast. Paradise Reef, a series of three separate reefs lying about 200 yards offshore, is the only reef accessible from the beach. The marine life here is abundant, and the shallow depth (40 to 50 feet) is suitable for novice divers. Another good location for beginning divers is Yucab Reef, where the swift currents attract barracuda.

Tormentos Reef is suitable for intermediate divers. Colorful coral heads, valleys of sand and marine life that includes moray eels, angelfish, grouper and snapper can be found at depths of 50 to 70 feet. San Francisco Reef is the shallowest of Cozumel's wall dives—half a mile of reef broken into three sections that is teeming with sea life. The Santa Rosa Wall is a very popular deep dive; the wall begins at a depth of 50 feet and drops straight down, with sponge-covered coral overhangs and a myriad little caves and tunnels to explore.

Palancar Reef is one of the island's best known, and with good reason; the marine environment is full of caverns, tunnels and huge, tightly packed coral heads. Colombia Reef matches it in underwater grandeur; the towering pinnacles of coral are pocked with caverns and tunnels. Divers are joined by large turtles, rays and barracuda.

The peak diving season is June through August, when the Caribbean waters are calm and warm and hotel rates tend to be lower. A wetsuit top is recommended for winter diving, when water temperatures are slightly lower. Night dives, underwater photography or making a customized video are among the available options. A scale map of all of Cozumel's reefs, complete with water depths and other information, can be obtained from most of the local dive shops.

A variety of packaged excursions, which usually include airfare, accommodations and diving costs, can be booked in the United States. In addition, the island's dive outfits compete vigorously for both seasoned divers and beginners, offering equipment rentals, instruction, guides and organized expeditions that range from an afternoon to several days.

Many hotels organize their own dive trips as well, and their facilities, while likely to be more expensive, also are more convenient. If you're not on a packaged trip or making your own arrangements, take the time to investigate credentials, boats and equipment; if possible, get the inside scoop from a diver familiar with the area. It's customary to tip the dive crew, as they are responsible for your safety.

One in-town dive shop is Aqua Safari, in the Safari Inn at Av. Rafael Melgar #429 (at Avenida 5 Sur), phone (987) 869-0610. **Note:** Make certain the instructor you choose has PADI certification and is affiliated with the island's Buceo Médico Mexicano recompression chamber, located on Calle 5 Sur just off Avenida Rafael Melgar; phone (987) 872-1430 or (987) 872-2387.

Snorkeling is excellent in Chankanaab Bay, at Playa San Francisco and around the offshore reefs near Colombia Lagoon, at the island's southern tip. Morning feedings from the piers of the Presidente InterContinental and El Cid La Ceiba hotels attract schools of hungry fish, some of which are bold enough to break the surface of the water and take food from outstretched hands (but beware of sharp teeth). An upside-down plane, deliberately sunk for a movie production, sits on the sandy bottom a short distance from the La Ceiba pier. Those who want to view the colorful marine life but don't want to get wet can take a glass-bottom boat trip.

Snorkeling gear can be cheaply rented at Playa San Francisco, Chankanaab Lagoon Park (see attraction listing) or from the larger hotels. In addition, the dive shops and travel agencies provide organized snorkeling excursions to the various reefs. A representative agency is Turismo Aviomar, which has an office at Calle Felipe Angeles #1580, between Calle 5 Sur and Avenida Miguel Hidalgo (several blocks inland from the waterfront). For snorkel and dive trip information phone (987) 872-5445. The Fiesta Holidays agency has tour agents in a few of the major hotels; phone (987) 872-4311 for the main Cozumel office.

Sport fishing is superb, and Cozumel was an angler's paradise long before it gained renown as a dive destination. Catches differ according to the season. From April through June blue and white marlin, dorado, tuna and sailfish are hooked; fishing for amberjack, barracuda, bonito, mackerel, shark, snapper and wahoo can be done all year. Lagoon fishing yields bonefish, snook and tarpon.

Charters range from about $400 to $700 (U.S.) according to the length of the trip (half day or full day), size of the vessel, the number of people and the season. To get an idea of what's available and how much it costs, visit the Club Abrigo Náutico de Cozumel marina, north of downtown on Avenida Rafael Melgar (near the airport) in the late afternoon when the boats are returning and talk to a couple of the captains. Cozumel Charters departs from the marina and offers a range of guided sport-fishing trips; phone (987) 869-8560

Sightseeing excursions to Cancún, Playa del Carmen, Xel-Ha, Tulum and other nearby points of interest can be easily arranged; information is available at most hotels. Travel agencies also offer Cozumel tours that include such activities as sunbathing at the beach, snorkeling at Chankanaab Lagoon Park, a visit to the San Gervasio ruins or a day trip to the Xcaret ecological theme park on the mainland (see Playa del Carmen), which includes ferry transportation.

The Cozumel Country Club, on the north side of the island near the airport, has an 18-hole golf course, a pro shop, a driving range, and club and shoe rental. Carts are required. Guest privileges are available for those staying at the Playa Azul and Presidente InterContinental hotels. For greens fees (U.S. dollars are not accepted; payment is by credit card or cash in pesos only) and additional information phone (987) 872-9570.

Rancho Buenavista, on the island's east coast, offers a 4-hour guided horseback riding trek into the interior jungle scrub, with stops at several Mayan ruins. The tours include round-trip transportation from any of the cruise ship piers in San Miguel; phone (987) 872-1537.

Carnaval, the island's version of Mardi Gras, is held in February on the 3 days preceding Ash Wednesday. Colorful float parades along the *malecón*, masquerade balls, street dances and the "burning" of Juan Carnaval (a Carnaval king) take place during this exuberant fiesta. The Rodeo De Lanchas Mexicanas fishing tournament is held in mid-May. Cozumel also celebrates the patron saint of San Miguel with a fiesta on Sept. 29.

## Beaches and Ruins

All of Cozumel's beaches are public, even those that appear to be the property of hotels. North of San Miguel are several of the more luxurious accommodations and some condominium developments. Playa San Juan extends to Punta Norte, where the highway ends. This beach is good for swimming and water recreation. Beyond Punta Norte is miniscule Isla de la Pasión, in the middle of calm Abrigo Bay. Local boat owners can take you to this secluded spot, where there are deserted beaches and opportunities for fishing, but no facilities.

South of San Miguel, Avenida Rafael Melgar becomes the coastal highway (Costera Sur) and passes several beach and snorkeling spots. Heading south, the first beach club worth a stop is The Money Bar, next to the Fiesta Americana All Inclusive Hotel (watch for the signed hotel turn-off on the main road). This large *palapa* restaurant has beach chairs, umbrellas and a booth that rents snorkel equipment. The snorkeling is decent just offshore along the Dzul-Ha Reef.

The beach at Chankanaab Lagoon Park *(see attraction listing)* is studded with *palapas* that provide welcome shade, the sand is soft and powdery, and there are opportunities for snorkeling, diving and interactive dolphin swims. South of the park off the Costera Sur (coastal highway), beautiful Playa San Francisco is hugely popular with cruise ship passengers. Here you'll find public showers and changing rooms, as well as the Carlos 'n Charlies and Playa San Francisco beach clubs. Drinks, food, beach chairs, shade and snorkel gear can all be had for moderate prices.

For a mellower beach scene, continue south to the Playa Palancar beach club (watch for signs). You'll find the usual *palapa* seafood restaurant and beach chairs, minus the cruise ship crowds. For snorkelers, the main draw is an opportunity to see a relatively shallow section of the famous Palancar Reef. Boats leave from shore and charge about $40 (U.S.) per person for a guided 90-minute snorkel tour (usually not available on Sunday).

The eastern (windward) coast is far less developed and thus more dramatic. The beaches, interspersed among rocky coves, are frequently empty. The open Caribbean is intensely turquoise, but the surf and undertows are often strong; swim at your own risk.

Near the entrance to Punta Sur Park *(see attraction listing)*, hand-painted signs with images of Bob Marley direct day-trippers to Freedom in Paradise (also called "Rasta Bar"), Cozumel's very own mini Jamaica. The rustic two-story *palapa* restaurant has a relaxed tropical feel and sports the requisite red, green and yellow rasta colors, while the reggae icon's greatest hits seemingly play on a constant loop. The beach is gorgeous, but mostly rocky and not good for swimming.

From the southern end of the island at Punta Celarain, a paved road follows the coast north toward Punta Morena. Dotting the coastline are several beach clubs where you can grab a bite, sip a margarita, clock some serious hammock time and watch the surf roll in.

For sunbathing or a lazy beach stroll, try the long powder-white stretch of sand at the appropriately named Playa Bonita. For swimming, the calmest windward shore waters are usually found at Chen Río Beach, a protected cove farther up the road. There are *palapa* bars at both beaches, but there are better views and better food at Coconuts, a few minutes' drive north. Perched on a high bluff overlooking the Caribbean, Coconuts is a must for east shore first-timers. Ask for an outdoor table to fully absorb the unbeatable ocean panorama.

Located roughly halfway between Coconuts and the Carretera Transversal (cross-island road) turnoff, the Punta Morena beach club dishes up impressive lunches on a beachfront, white canvas-shaded patio. The fresh lobster tacos and chicken club sandwich are both delicious, and the new age background music encourages chilling out.

Near Punta Morena the road runs into the end of the east-west Carretera Transversal (cross-island road), about 15 kilometers (9 miles) from San Miguel. Playa Oriente, the rocky beach, is scenic but not safe for swimming. There also are two beach clubs here, and employees try hard to wave you in.

The San Gervasio Ruins *(see attraction listing)* are also north of and accessible from the cross-island road. At Km 17.5 on the Costera Sur, a turn-off leads about 3 kilometers (2 miles) east to the ruins of El Cedral. One small structure is all that remains at this site, believed to be the oldest on the island and the one first discovered by the Spanish. A tree grows from the roof, its roots snaking around the crumbled stones. Faint traces of paint and stucco are still visible. A small farming settlement named Cedral—the island's agricultural center—has grown up here, dominated by a rural church painted bright green.

## Dining

Cozumel's restaurant scene centers on San Miguel. Island eateries range from drop-in casual to suitable for a special occasion. There are a variety of cuisines (French, Italian, Japanese) in addition to Mexican, and also a number of local places dishing up terrific Yucatecan food that are off the beaten tourist path but definitely worth searching out.

Guido's, on the waterfront between calles 6 and 8 Norte, specializes in wood-fired pizzas but also offers fish and shellfish dishes. Another house specialty is *pan de ajo,* bread infused with olive oil, garlic and rosemary. The bougainvillea-draped outdoor dining area is a lovely spot for dinner. For a relaxing break from shopping, Pancho's Backyard, inside the Los Cinco Soles craft store, serves standard Mexican dishes in a courtyard garden setting complete with live marimba music—although you may have to share this place with the cruise ship crowd. Menu prices are listed in both dollars and pesos.

La Cocay ("the firefly"), Calle 8 Norte between avenidas 10 and 15 Norte, is a sophisticated spot where you can order a range of appetizers to nibble on, or entrees like sauteed sea scallops, lobster tail or a rib-eye steak.

Lobster aficionados will certainly want to try the Lobster House (La Cabaña del Pescador), in the hotel zone at the northern end of the island (on the east side of the road across from the Playa Azul Hotel). The atmosphere is romantic and candlelit, with starfish-studded fishing nets hanging from the ceiling (no air conditioning, though). The crustacean is the only thing on the menu—simply boiled and served with melted butter, steamed vegetables and bread. At market price, a jumbo lobster tail sure to satisfy two people will cost about $60 (U.S., cash only). After dinner, ask the waiter to take you for a walk through the gardens out front and shine a flashlight on the massive iguanas sleeping in the trees.

Casa Denis has traditional Yucatecan dishes like *cochinita pibil, poc chuc, sopa de lima* and phenomenal *papadzules* (warm tortillas stuffed with chopped hard-boiled egg and covered with a tasty pumpkin seed sauce). Family owned and operated, this longtime local favorite opened in 1945 and is on the pedestrian-only section of Calle 1 Sur, half a block east of the main plaza. Seating is available inside the historic *casa* or at the sidewalk tables out front. Service is fast and friendly.

Some of Cozumel's best eating is at the unassuming places that locals frequent. Taco lovers should seek out El Foco (The Light Bulb), on Avenida 5 Sur a few blocks south of the main plaza. Flour tortillas are filled with grilled meats, onions and peppers and topped with melted cheese. There are various combination plates, all for 80 pesos (about $6.50 U.S.).

For a morning pick-me-up, head to one of the island bakeries *(panaderías).* They offer fresh-baked French rolls *(bolillos),* sweet breakfast breads *(pan dulce)* and pastries; try *orejas,* crunchy morsels shaped like an ear and drenched with honey, or nut cookies topped with freshly grated coconut. Customers take a round metal tray and a pair of tongs, select the items they want from the bakery shelves and then take them to the counter to be bagged and paid for. Zermatt, at the corner of Calle 4 Norte and Avenida 5 Norte (a block east of the waterfront) has fresh bread, yummy desserts and pizza by the slice in the afternoon.

Ice cream parlors *(neverias)* serve ice cream *(helado)* made with milk or bottled water in flavors both standard (chocolate) and exotic (corn). A *paletería* is a shop that sells both ice cream and iced juice drinks *(agua frescas).* The *agua fresca de sandía*—watermelon juice mixed with sugar and water—tastes great on a hot day. Another refreshing treat is mango; when the fruit is in season (spring and summer), street vendors sell them on a stick, peeled and carved into different shapes.

Dress is casual at all island restaurants, and reservations are advised only at the most expensive places. Service is invariably relaxed and friendly. There's no need to worry about health concerns at restaurants that cater to tourists. At local joints, follow the standard rule—if it's cooked it should be safe to eat. English isn't spoken at the small family-run places, but it doesn't really matter; most have a wall menu, so just point to what you want to order and remember to add *"por favor."* Some restaurants close on Sunday. See the Lodgings & Restaurants section for AAA-RATED dining establishments.

## Shopping

Shops and boutiques lining Avenida Rafael Melgar offer duty-free imported goods, chic sportswear and high-quality folk art reproductions, as well as T-shirts and cheap souvenirs. The shops cluster around the main plaza and extend for about five blocks north and eight blocks south along the waterfront. Keep in mind, however, that prices will be more expensive here than in the shops on the side streets just a couple of blocks off Melgar. Also, prices at many shops magically drop on days when cruise ships are few and business is slow.

Five blocks north of the plaza is the Forum Shops, an air-conditioned, marble-floored mini mall on Avenida Rafael Melgar at Calle 8 Norte. Inside you'll find a Diamonds International outlet, plus shops selling quality beachwear, leather, silver, glass, tequila and cigars. Ride the escalator to the second floor for clean restrooms, a pharmacy, a restaurant/bar and a jewelry factory where you can peer through glass windows and watch jewelers at work.

Next door is Los Cinco Soles, a big, rambling store that sells a huge selection of crafts, art and clothing imported from all over Mexico. From furniture, ceramics, wood carvings and masks to textiles, hand-blown glass and obsidian figurines, prices on craft items are relatively reasonable. Clothing and jewelry prices, on the other hand, are high. For the budget-minded there's also an endless selection of affordable knickknacks.

Souvenir T-shirt shoppers flock to the Cozumel outpost of Florida's Ron Jon Surf Shop (at the corner of Avenida Rafael Melgar and Calle 4 Norte), where high-quality logo T-shirts, caps, souvenirs and beachwear fly off the shelves.

While doing the shopping shuffle along the waterfront, you'll notice there's no shortage of jewelry merchants in San Miguel. The salespeople posted in front of these stores can be annoyingly aggressive in their attempts to get you inside, often luring unsuspecting shoppers with promises of a "free gift." If your idea of a gift is a high-pressure sales pitch, by all means have at it. If not, it's best to ignore them and keep walking.

The plaza's northern side (the pedestrian-only section of Benito Juárez) is chock-a-block with souvenir shops and stalls, most selling identical merchandise (think blankets, sombreros, T-shirts and jewelry). While good quality is hard to come by, a little bargaining should yield low prices. There are gift shops and galleries in the white-trimmed, bright yellow Plaza del Sol building, on the east side of the plaza.

Galería Azul, on Avenida 15 Norte between calles 8 and 10 Norte (about 7 blocks northeast of the main plaza), is owned by Greg Dietrich, an exceptional Washington state artist who specializes in unique blown-glass pieces incorporating intricate undersea-themed designs. The gallery is open Mon.-Fri. 11-7, but he will gladly open the shop for you during non-business hours; phone (987) 869-0963.

Inspiración Galería de Arte, on Avenida 5 Sur near the corner of Calle 3 Sur (not far from the main plaza), deals in contemporary paintings and sculpture, plus Jicara gourd bowls. A few doors down, Puro Mar, at the corner of Avenida 5 Sur and Calle 3 Sur, sells top-quality swim trunks, bikinis, flip-flops, backpacks and other beach gear at tourist-inflated prices.

At the Punta Langosta Pier (Avenida Rafael Melgar, just south of Calle 7 Sur), cruise ship passengers disembark and walk directly into the Punta Langosta mall, a modern open-air building with shops, jewelry stores, clothing boutiques and eateries on two levels. Los Cinco Soles has a small satellite location here. Starbucks addicts can get their fix at the thatch-roofed franchise fronting the mall.

If you've docked at the southernmost cruise ship pier, Puerta Maya (about 5 miles south of San Miguel), you'll step ashore and find a modern, open-air mall with more than 50 shops, a convenience store and eateries, including a branch of downtown's ever-popular Pancho's Backyard.

The MEGA grocery store, on Avenida Rafael Melgar just south of downtown San Miguel, is a big, modern supermarket that stocks a variety of fresh produce, meats, seafood, cheeses and other staples. A little farther south is the smaller Chedraui grocery store; also in the shopping center is a movie theater that screens first-run Hollywood fare and Spanish language features.

El Mercado, at the corner of Avenida 25 Sur and Calle Rosado Salas, is the biggest of the traditional Mexican markets on the island. All kinds of fruits and vegetables are for sale here, along with cilantro, fresh and dried chiles, freshly squeezed fruit and carrot juices, honey and *jamaica* (dried hibiscus blossoms) sold by the kilo. When boiled in water and allowed to steep for at least several hours, strained into a pitcher along with sugar and lime juice and then served over ice, the blossoms make a refreshing tea. *Pescaderías* (fish markets) sell freshly caught fish like grouper (*mero*) and snapper (*huachinango*) as well as shrimp, octopus and conch.

## Nightlife

After a strenuous day of diving, swimming or exploring most visitors are content to turn in early. For after-dinner relaxation the outdoor cafes on the south side of the main plaza are pleasant places to enjoy the evening breeze. On Sunday evenings the plaza comes alive when families gather to hear Latin bands or be serenaded by mariachis. This is a good opportunity to dance and mingle with the locals, who take tourism in stride and are friendly toward visitors.

Fans of Polynesian-style tiki bars should drop by Tiki-Tok, a friendly second-floor *palapa* bar on Avenida Rafael Melgar between Calle 2 Sur and Calle 4 Sur. In addition to the usual lineup of tropical cocktails (mai tais, daiquiris and piña coladas), house specialties include original concoctions named after major Atlantic hurricanes (beware: Wilma packs a wallop). Tables along the front railing are situated in a sandbox and overlook the waterfront action below; there's live music on select nights.

Parrotheads belly up to the bar at Margaritaville (corner of Avenida Rafael Melgar and Calle 11 Sur), the Cozumel branch of Jimmy Buffett's wildly successful theme restaurant chain. This place draws big crowds during the day when cruise ships are in port. Revelers pack the outdoor waterfront terrace; DJs spin Buffett tunes and classic rock. A cheeseburger (in paradise?) and fries will set you back about $14 (U.S.).

**Tourist information office:** second floor of the Plaza del Sol building behind the main plaza, corner of Benito Juárez and Avenida 5 Norte. Open Mon.-Fri. 9-3. **Phone:** (987) 869-0211.

*ATLANTIS* SUBMARINE departs from the Atlantis office, Km marker 4 on Carretera Chankanaab (Chankanaab Highway), across the street from the Casa del Mar Hotel; passengers are taken from the pier to the submarine via a 12-minute ferry ride. The submarine accommodates 48 passengers for a 40-minute undersea tour of Chankanaab Reef at depths of up to 100 feet. Large portholes running the length of the sub offer views of coral formations and marine life in crystal-clear water.

**Note:** Entering involves climbing backwards down seven steep stairs (handrails are available). Children under age 4 or under 36 inches tall are not permitted, and the trip is not advised for those prone to claustrophobia or confined to a wheelchair. **Hours:** Sub departs daily on the hour 9-noon (weather permitting); also departs at 1 during busy spring break weeks. Phone ahead to confirm schedule. **Cost:** $105 U.S. (includes $2 entrance fee for visiting the reef area); $65 (ages 4-12). **Phone:** (987) 872-5671, or 01 (800) 715-0804 (toll-free long distance within Mexico) for reservation information.

◄▲▼ **CHANKANAAB LAGOON PARK** (Parque
GEM      Laguna de Chankanaab) is on the leeward
         side of the island, about 9 km (5.5 mi.) s.
of town off the Costera Sur (Coastal Highway), the southward extension of Avenida Rafael Melgar. The name, which means "small sea," refers to the natural saltwater lagoon inside the park.

Snorkeling is not permitted in the lagoon, nor is feeding the fish; observation areas are provided. Surrounding the lagoon is a shady botanical garden with tropical and subtropical plant species, many native to Cozumel; for a tip, local youths will give impromptu tours.

The beach fronting the bay is wide and pretty. In addition to swimming and snorkeling (submerged religious statues and encrusted anchors and cannons are popular dive sites), beach activities include snuba (a combination of snorkeling and scuba diving) and Seatrek, an underwater breathing helmet. A small museum has exhibits about local plant, animal and marine life. There also are hammocks for "frond snoozing" and a children's play area. Several dive shops on site, as well as restrooms, changing areas and showers.

**Time:** Allow 3 hours minimum. **Hours:** Mon.-Sat. 8-4. **Cost:** (includes access to the beach and use of park facilities) $21 (U.S.); $14 (ages 3-11). There are separate fees for snuba, Seatrek, a sea lion show and dolphin swim programs. Snorkel and scuba equipment can be rented; you also can bring your own. **Phone:** (987) 872-9760. 🍴 🏖

**DISCOVER MEXICO** is at Km marker 5.5 on the Carretera Costera Sur in the southern Hotel Zone. This private museum is best seen on a guided tour. After a video presentation in the museum's theater, visitors view displays of high-quality folk art from throughout Mexico. Replicas of pre-Hispanic archeological sites include Chichén Itzá, Cholula, Edzná, Palenque and Uxmal. Other exhibits feature architectural replicas from Cozumel, Guadalajara, Mexico City, Oaxaca and Taxco. The knowledgeable guides offer lots of historical background information. **Time:** Allow 1 hour, 30 minutes minimum. **Hours:** Mon.-Sat. 8-3. Phone ahead to confirm schedule. **Cost:** $26 (U.S.); $14 (ages 0-12). **Phone:** (987) 857-2820. 🍴

**MUSEUM OF THE ISLAND OF COZUMEL** (Museo de la Isla de Cozumel) is on Avenida Rafael Melgar just n. of the main ferry landing, between calles 4 and 6 Norte. The museum chronicles the island's history from its days as a revered Mayan religious destination to settlement by refugees from the 19th-century War of the Castes. An overview of natural history (with information in Spanish and English) focuses on endangered species and local plant and animal life.

A restaurant on the second floor has expansive waterfront views. There also is a bookstore and library with a few selections in English. Guided tours in English are available. Restrooms are provided. **Time:** Allow 2 hours minimum. **Hours:** Mon.-Sat. 9-4 (may vary seasonally). **Cost:** $4 (U.S.); free (ages 0-7). **Phone:** (987) 872-1434 or (987) 872-1475.

**PLAZA PRINCIPAL** is just inland from the malecón, bounded on the n. by Av. Benito Juárez and on the s. by Calle 1 Sur. A bright, mustard-yellow clock tower rises behind the plaza, a red tile-roofed gazebo sits at its center and a bust of lawyer and politician Benito Juárez, who was instrumental in resisting the French invasion of Mexico in 1862, is a tribute to one of the country's most beloved presidents. Tourists stroll the square while vendors hawk their wares in between relaxing and gossiping on wooden benches. **Hours:** Daily 24 hours. **Phone:** (987) 869-0211.

**PUNTA SUR PARK** (Parque Punta Sur) is at Km 28 at the southern end of the Costera Sur (coastal highway), about 28 km (17 mi.) s. of the main ferry landing; take the Punta Sur turn-off and proceed about 100 yards down a dirt road to the entrance ticket booth. This national ecological reserve focuses on the conservation of local wildlife, including crocodiles, iguanas, egrets and herons, and therefore has few tourist-oriented facilities.

The Celarain Lighthouse, built in 1934, stands guard at the island's southern point. The steep circular staircase can be climbed, and there are outstanding views from the top. Next to the lighthouse, the Navigation Museum has displays of ship models, nautical artifacts, maps and exhibits relating to lighthouse history.

Flatbed trucks with bench seating shuttle visitors to La Playa mas Hermosa ("The Most Beautiful Beach") for snorkeling. You can swim out to the reef from shore; two floating platforms anchored offshore provide a place to rest en route. Forty-minute pontoon boat rides explore the mangroves and bird life of Colombia Lagoon. **Note:** Cars are permitted only as far as the lighthouse parking lot.

A map of the park is handed out at the entrance booth. A snack bar at the snorkeling beach sells soda, cold beer and chips. Restrooms are on site. Snorkeling gear can be rented. **Time:** Allow 2 hours minimum. **Hours:** Park open Mon.-Sat. 9-4. Shuttle trucks run continuously between the lighthouse and the snorkeling beach, but there is no set schedule. **Cost:** $14 (U.S.); $8 (ages 3-11). Pontoon boat rides $5. Round-trip taxi service from San Miguel runs $60-$70. **Phone:** (987) 872-0914.

**SAN GERVASIO** is e. on the Carretera Transversal (Avenida Benito Juárez) to the well-marked San Gervasio turn-off, then n. 6.3 km (about 4 mi.) on a paved two-lane access road to the entrance gate. Not nearly as impressive architecturally as other archeological sites on the Yucatán Peninsula—Chichén Itzá this isn't—San Gervasio (san her-BAH-see-oh) was nevertheless inhabited for more than 1,000 years.

Bear left after walking through the site entrance and you'll come to Plaza Central. Nine spread-out structures sit low to the ground and are in various states of disrepair. From the back side of the plaza, take the well-marked, jungle-lined walking path that leads to Ka'Na Nah, a Post-Classic (1200-1650) temple reputedly built in dedication to the goddess Ixchel.

Another path leads east from Ka'Na Nah to Murcielagos, a building set deep in the jungle. Numerous iguanas sunning themselves on rocks offer good photo opportunities. A separate trail branching off to the left leads back to Plaza Central by way of Nohoch Nah.

This boxy temple, set atop a stepped pyramid-like platform, is classic Mayan architecture—with the out-of-character addition of a screen door that has been installed across the front entrance.

A thatch-roofed entrance pavilion has restrooms, vendor stalls and a snack bar that sells bottled water and sodas. Information plaques in Spanish and English provide historical background. The structures are roped off and cannot be climbed.

**Hours:** Daily 8-5. **Cost:** (paid at the entrance pavilion) 40 pesos (about $3 U.S.). A second fee of 52 pesos (about $3.85 U.S.) per person, charged by INAH (National Institute of Anthropology and History) must be paid at the official entrance to the ruins. Parking is free, but expect to give someone a few pesos to "watch your car" (standard procedure at attraction parking lots all over Mexico). San Miguel taxi drivers will take you to the site entrance and wait while you view the ruins; the fare is negotiable, but expect to pay about $60 U.S.

## ISLA HOLBOX, QUINTANA ROO (A-3)

The very definition of "laid back," Isla Holbox (hole-BOSH) lies in the Gulf of Mexico 7 miles off the northern tip of the Yucatán Peninsula, or about 40 miles northwest of Cancún as the crow flies. It was once visited by pirates who subsequently intermarried with Mayans living on the island, and descendants of the original families still live here. The first Europeans arrived in 1856 to harvest tropical hardwoods and founded a small village.

Although off the beaten path and not yet taken over by mass tourism, Holbox—some 7 miles long and about a mile wide—is growing, and not just in popularity: Land is being bought for multistory resort hotels, and efforts have begun to control both their construction and the island's ambience. For now, though, this is as good a spot as any to get away from it all.

And getting away from it all is the whole point. On Holbox the key word is relaxation. The exceptionally wide, sandy beaches are ideal for ambling. Shell collectors will delight in the variety of intact, unbroken seashells deposited on the beach by gulf currents. The water is warm, shallow, relatively clear and emerald green, without the dangerous undertows and large waves that can affect Quintana Roo's Caribbean coast beaches. The only thing the gulf lacks is the dazzling turquoise hues of the Caribbean.

Other pleasures are of the laid-back variety as well—paddle boating and kayaking, strolling around the village or just lazing the afternoon away in a hammock. A daily ritual is sunset watching from the beach or the main plaza in town, a view that takes in fishing boats silhouetted against the sky. A more adrenaline-fueled activity is the sport of kite surfing, which utilizes a surfboard with foot straps and a large kite that together propel a user both through the air and on the water.

Holbox Village has a prototypical tropical seaside look. The streets are sand; golf carts, bikes and walking are the preferred modes of transportation. Dogs nap in the shade. Dust devils swirl down the sandy streets. Local kids shoot hoops on the main plaza's basketball court. Tourists snooze on the beach. The wood and cinder block buildings are painted bright colors and roofed with either corrugated tin or traditional thatched *palapas*. Fancy? No—but a bit of paradise nevertheless.

## Practicalities

There's a reason that Isla Holbox is known for its tranquility—getting there involves a bit of effort. The island is about a 3-hour drive from Cancún via free Mex. 180 (not toll highway Mex. 180-D) west to the Nuevo X-Can exit (signed "Nuevo X-Can/ Kantunil"). The highway runs north to the land's end village of Chiquilá and south to the ruins of Cobá. Toward Chiquilá the road becomes very narrow, and sections of it are rough.

Vehicles can be left at a guarded parking lot in Chiquilá for a daily fee of about $6 (U.S.), cash only. Estacionamiento Cirilo has covered spaces and is located on the east (right) side of Avenida Delfines (Chiquilá's main drag) as you drive into the heart of town. The lot is next door to the Hotel La Puerta del Sol. If the lot is full, there are other lots along the waterfront, closer to the ferry pier. No matter where you park, do not leave valuables in your vehicle. There is also a twice-daily car ferry, but you won't need a car on the island.

Second-class buses travel to Chiquilá from the central bus station in downtown Ciudad Cancún (at the intersection of avenidas Tulum and Uxmal in front of the Plaza Caribe Hotel). There are normally three departures a day for Holbox; the earliest bus leaves around 7:30 a.m. A private taxi from downtown Cancún to Chiquilá costs about $85 (U.S.) one way; fare from the Cancún Hotel Zone is about $95. On the other hand, the fare for an airport-approved taxi departing from Cancún Airport is outrageous (several hundred dollars). It's best to arrange a private transfer prior to your trip; a few Holbox hotels offer this service.

From Chiquilá, a ferry service and water taxis take passengers on the 30-minute ride across Yalahau Lagoon to the island. The "9 Hermanos" ferry ticket booth is located on the pier; one-way fare is 100 pesos (about $8.15 U.S.). Departures are approximately every 2 hours; the last crossing departs at 9:30 p.m. It's also possible to hire a private water taxi; expect to pay $35 to $40 (U.S.) for a ride to the island. **Note:** Water taxis are not permitted on the lagoon after dusk. If you miss the last ferry the only lodging in Chiquilá is the Hotel La Puerta del Sol, where accommodations may not be up to AAA standards.

Golf cart taxi fares are inexpensive, and a ride from the ferry dock to your hotel (including properties outside of downtown) should cost no more than 35 pesos. While most everything of visitor interest on Holbox is within a 10- or 20-minute walk, renting a golf cart might be a good idea if the weather is too hot for foot travel or you're staying at a hotel on the beach east of town.

There are several rental agencies *(rentadoras)* that all charge basically the same rates. Turística Monkey's, on the west side of Calle Tiburon Ballena (just north of Aguilar), rents carts for 150 pesos (about $11 U.S.) per hour, 800 pesos for 8 hours and 1,000 pesos for 24 hours. Rentadora Moguel, across from the plaza at the corner of Calle Igualdad and Tiburon Ballena, also rents carts.

There are a handful of ATMs on Holbox (ask at your hotel for the locations), although it is wise to bring plenty of cash since ATMs in Mexico are notorious for being out of order. Most local businesses prefer cash (pesos or U.S. dollars), though a few establishments do accept credit cards. You can check your e-mail and the weather in air-conditioned comfort at Internet Cyber Shark, on Calle Igualdad just east of Avenida Carite.

Aerosaab, a regional airline, can arrange private flights from Cancún, Cozumel and Playa del Carmen to the small airstrip on Isla Holbox. The short flights (20 minutes to 1 hour) are aboard a four-seat Cessna aircraft. Aerosaab also offers all-day whale shark tours that depart from Cancún, Cozumel and Playa del Carmen.

During the whale shark off-season, consider the daylong tour that flies out of Playa del Carmen only and visits Bird Island, Yalahau spring and Holbox Village. For schedule, fare and reservations information phone (984) 873-0501.

## Recreation

Many of Holbox's approximately 1,500 permanent residents are fishermen. They set out each morning before sunrise, pulling in catches of grouper, barracuda, red snapper, yellowtail and shark. Most families on the island make their living from commercial fishing or diving for conch, lobster and octopus. Local skippers also serve as guides for sport-fishing excursions; the waters around Cape Catoche (Cabo Catoche), where the Gulf of Mexico and the Caribbean merge, are fertile fishing grounds. Boat trips for deep sea or fly fishing can be arranged at the main pier.

Yalahau is the name of the lagoon between Isla Holbox and the mainland as well as a natural spring-fed pond on the island that once was a source of drinking water for Mayan fishermen. According to folklore the pond was the private swimming pool of a Mayan king and later the refuge of a pirate, "Yellow Beard." Local legend also maintains that Yalahau is a fountain of youth. It can be reached by boat, and while swimmers may not feel any younger, the clear, cool water is decidedly refreshing on a hot day.

Isla Pájaros, or Bird Island, is a small islet only 200 feet wide that lies in a shallow portion of Yalahau Lagoon. This protected wildlife sanctuary is accessible only by boat. Covered by thick stands of mangrove, cacti and underbrush, it is a feeding and nesting haven for more than 150 different species. Flamingos visit from April to October; other frequently seen birds include frigates, white ibises, snowy egrets, spoonbills, pelicans and ducks. The island also is home to iguanas, horseshoe crabs and such plants as bromeliads and wild orchids.

Tours to Isla Pájaros depart from the main pier on Holbox Island. In order to protect the fragile ecosystem, visitors are not allowed to walk on the island; birds can be observed in their natural surroundings from elevated walkways and observation lookout points.

The most notable attraction Holbox offers is the opportunity to get up close and personal with whale sharks *(tiburon ballena* in Spanish). The world's largest living fish species, it attains a length of up to 45 feet. Also called domino shark for the distinctive pattern of pale yellow spots marking its body, the whale shark—unlike many of its more fearsome brethren—is harmless to humans. This shark is a filter feeder: It pumps sea water through five large pairs of gills that act as sieves, trapping plankton, algae, krill, small vertebrates and other food that are then swallowed.

The manta ray, another giant marine animal, is much less frequently spotted. A relative of the shark, it is the largest ray in the world—up to 25 feet wide when measured across the pectoral fins, and weighing more than 1.5 tons. The manta, unlike other species of ray, does not have a stinging spine. And like the whale shark, it too is a filter feeder, feasting on plankton, small fish and crustaceans that are swept into its wide mouth with the aid of two fleshy lobes that resemble horns (hence the nickname "devil ray"). These solitary creatures are harmless to swimmers and divers and thus a highly prized sighting.

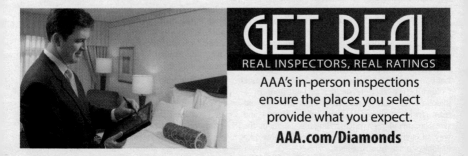

Whale sharks and manta rays visit the waters around Holbox from mid-June to early September. Boat trips to the whale shark feeding waters (about 1 hour away from the Holbox pier) allow visitors the opportunity to swim and snorkel alongside the surprisingly docile giants without touching them (scuba diving is not permitted). Only two snorkelers and a guide are allowed in the water at a time, and the first thing you'll notice is how fast these jumbo fish move. If you're not a strong swimmer, keeping up with them is out of the question. Regardless, simply being in the open water next to a whale shark is an incredible once-in-a-lifetime experience for most visitors.

**Note:** Although it is not guaranteed that you'll see a shark, the probability in the heart of the season (July and August) is high. If you're visiting at this time, make lodging and tour reservations far in advance.

There are about ten whale shark tour operators in town. Holbox regulars have their favorites, and two of them always rank at or near the top. Operadora Turística Monkey's (aka Monkey Tours) is the largest outfitter in town, and their red-and-white boats are manned by some of the best whale shark spotters on the island.

Excursions depart early in the morning and last 5 to 6 hours. Each boat takes a maximum of 10 people; snorkel equipment and lunch are included. Tours are not recommended for children under 8. Space is limited (especially in season), and advance reservations are necessary. No matter which tour operator you choose, expect to pay around $120 (U.S.) per person. For more information on Turística Monkeys and to make reservations, visit their office on the west side of Calle Tiburon Ballena, just north of Aguilar, or phone (984) 875-2442. Tours offered by Hotel Mawimbi also are well regarded; for information phone (984) 875-2003.

Holbox Tours & Travel on Calle Bravo offers all-inclusive trip packages that include ground transportation to and from Cancún International Airport and hotel accommodations in addition to a guided all-day whale shark excursion. Trips are offered June through August. For additional information or to book reservations phone (984) 168-4954 or (305) 396-6987 (from the United States).

## Shopping, Dining and Nightlife

On Calle Igualdad, east of the plaza, Artesanía Las Chicas specializes in handmade *henequen* clothing and also has a selection of purses, jewelry and incense. Artesanías Puesta del Sol sells beachwear, flip-flops, tote bags and jewelry, plus an array of good-quality Mexico keepsakes, including hand-painted margarita glasses.

West of the plaza, seashell collectors head for Lalo, on Avenida Canané just south of Avenida Coldwell. The shop is on the second floor of a thatch-roofed house. You can't miss the sign out front. Inside, polished seashells of all shapes and sizes command high prices. Bargains come in the way of souvenir knickknacks and cool items like handbags made from seashells.

Restaurants are simple and casual. Restaurante Zarabanda, a block south of the main plaza (look for the thatched roof and red-and-white trim) is a rustic, family-owned place that serves fresh seafood like grilled fish filets and conch or shrimp ceviche. You also can get breakfast here. Viva Zapata, just west of the main plaza, is a popular Mexican restaurant with sombrero-shaped lamps dangling over the tables and pictures of Pancho Villa covering the walls. Ask for a table on the breezy second-floor balcony and try the surf-and-turf platter for two. The food is very good, but service can be slow.

Always busy at dinner time, Restaurante y Pizzeria Edelyn bakes tasty thin crust pies in a log cabin-like building opposite the southeast corner of the plaza. While most first-timers order the house specialty, lobster pizza (covered with garlicky chunks of crustacean), don't overlook the linguine or the #10 pizza, loaded with the works. Seating is inside (hot in summer), on the front porch or at plastic tables set out in the street.

At funky La Isla del Colibre, opposite the southwest corner of the plaza, you can ponder the portraits of Frida Kahlo on the walls while you wait for your meal to arrive. Housed in a colorful clapboard building decorated with surrealist art, the restaurant specializes in seafood and also serves excellent breakfasts. This is a favorite haunt of street performers and musicians; bring change for *propinas* (tips).

In town, beachfront dining is limited to three restaurants: Cariocas (favored by locals), Buena Vista Grill (romantic but expensive) and the casual Villa Mar. Tables at the latter are shaded by mini *palapa* umbrellas and offer views of the beach and pier. Breakfasts are hearty, tasty and (late risers take note) served until 1 p.m. Mexican standards and drink specials draw a steady stream of tourists the rest of the day.

It won't take you long to figure out that there's no wacky Cancún-type nightlife on Holbox, but there *are* a handful of mellow bars on the west side of the plaza. On Saturday nights the plaza fills up with locals and tourists alike who come to watch live music and traditional Mayan dances performed under a white concrete bandshell. Think of it as the island's very own Hollywood Bowl.

# ISLA MUJERES, QUINTANA ROO (A-4)
pop. 16,203

Laid-back Mexican beach vacations don't get much better than Isla Mujeres (EES-lah moo-HEH-rehs). While single male travelers might be disappointed to find that the male-female ratio on the "Island of Women" is actually rather balanced, no one can deny Isla's considerable charms.

This little slip of an island in Mujeres Bay is within sight of Cancún's Hotel Zone, and getting there on a ferry boat is part of the fun. As soon as you leave the Cancún dock you're surrounded by intensely hued water that ranges from sea foam green to pastel aquamarine to deep, deep turquoise, the colors constantly shifting with the interplay of sun and clouds. The little boat bobs up and down on the waves, sending salt spray flying.

First appearing as an indistinct blur on the horizon, Isla Mujeres begins to take shape as the boat draws closer. Details emerge—palm trees, clapboard buildings, fishing boats. And before you know it you've reached another dock and disembark to a scene that is a bit different than the one you left.

Gold-seeking Spanish explorers led by Francisco Hernández de Córdoba accidentally discovered Isla Mujeres in 1517 after a storm blew their expedition off course. The origin of the name is based on two legends. One maintains that seafaring buccaneers used the island as a hideaway for stowing their female captives; slave trader Fermín Mundaca built a beautiful hacienda here in an effort to woo an island girl. But a more likely explanation is that it refers to the carved stone images of Ixchel, the Mayan goddess of love and fertility, discovered by the Spaniards.

After the era of pirates and smugglers passed, Isla Mujeres was quite content to be just another idyllic Caribbean island where people fished for a living. It was discovered again during the 1960s, this time by hippies and beach bums who dug the laid-back atmosphere. And since Cancún's ascendance to world-famous tourist destination Isla has gotten more and more spillover from its big, flashy mainland neighbor. But it's also a place where people live; while you're on vacation, for residents it's just another day. And the chance to be part of daily Mexican life—if only for a few hours—is what makes this island special.

You'll get into the spirit as soon as you start strolling along Avenida Rueda Medina, the *malecón*, which runs along the waterfront. The sidewalk is a jumble of sunburned gringos, locals and occasional dogs that might suddenly plop down under the shade of a coconut palm (the sound of palm fronds rustling in the ever-present breeze is a constant backdrop). Vendors sit next to their displays—bead necklaces, seashells, starfish, sandals, sombreros. The street is clogged with taxis, mopeds, golf carts and scooters, but no one is really in a hurry. Stop and breathe in the aroma of fresh fish grilling at a *loncheria* (casual open-air restaurant).

Then explore a few of the downtown side streets. Narrow Avenida Hidalgo, 2 blocks inland from the waterfront, is for pedestrians only, and thus invites browsers to linger at the many shops and vendor stalls. Turn a corner and you might see a group of school kids in immaculate uniforms skipping along the sidewalk. Many of the buildings have festive crayon colors—pink, peach, lime green, bright blue. Stop at a cafe for a cup of coffee or a freshly blended fruit smoothie. Above all, relax.

Many people spend their entire vacation on Isla Mujeres, since accommodations run the gamut from no-frills in-town motels to exclusive beachside retreats. But one of the island's calling cards is that it's just a half-hour boat ride away. You can leave Cancún in the morning, go shopping, have lunch and take an afternoon ferry back. You can leave around noon, go snorkeling or while away an afternoon sunning on the beach, and be back in time for dinner. Or you can leave in the late afternoon, enjoy dinner and a fun evening on Isla, and catch the last ferry back to the mainland. It's the perfect day trip.

## Practicalities

Located about 5 miles off the easternmost tip of the Yucatán Peninsula, Isla Mujeres is accessible by ferry from mainland Puerto Juárez; from the Cancún airport, a one-way taxi ride will run you about $60 (U.S.). There also are two Cancún Hotel Zone departure points for passenger ferries to the island: the El Embarcadero dock at Km marker 4 on Boulevard Kukulcán and the dock at Playa Tortugas, Km marker 7 on Boulevard Kukulcán.

UltraMar ferries depart from the Gran Puerto dock on Avenida López Portillo in Puerto Juárez every half-hour daily from 5 a.m. to 9:30 p.m., then depart hourly until 11:30 p.m. The final departure from Isla Mujeres back to Gran Puerto is at midnight. The trip takes about 15-20 minutes; one-way fare is 78 pesos (about $6.35 U.S.). Double-check the time of the final departure back to Cancún when you arrive.

UltraMar ferries depart from the El Embarcadero dock daily at 9:15, 11:45, 1, 2:15 and 4:30. The final departure from Isla Mujeres back to El Embarcadero is at 5:15 p.m. One-way fare is $14 (U.S.); round-trip fare $19. UltraMar boats also depart from the Playa Tortugas dock daily on the hour 9-5, returning from Isla Mujeres approximately every 30 minutes 9:30-5:30. One-way fare is $14 (U.S.); round-trip fare $19.

If you're basing a vacation in Isla Mujeres and have several pieces of luggage, taxis line up by the two town docks for the short ride to the hotels concentrated in town and scattered along the beaches. The fare shouldn't be more than a few dollars. Taxis also can be hired (at an hourly rate) for a tour of the island or to reach beaches at the southern end. A municipal bus travels from the Posada del Mar Hotel on Avenida Rueda Medina south to Playa Lancheros; the fare is inexpensive. Check with the tourist information office on Avenida Rueda Medina for bus schedules.

Renting a "moto," the local term for mopeds, or an electric golf cart is an easy way to get around, and there are several places in town that rent both (many of the hotels also rent golf carts). Keep in mind, however, that the rental fee does not include insurance. Some hotels also rent bicycles, which cost considerably less.

The "downtown" section of Isla Mujeres occupies the island's northern end. The main street, referred to locally as the *malecón*, is Avenida Rueda Medina, which runs the length of the island. The main streets are north-south avenidas Guerrero and Hidalgo, and east-west avenidas Madero and Morelos. These are all narrow, one-way, pedestrian-friendly streets where traffic (mostly taxis and mopeds) moves slowly. The ferry docks, in-town hotels, restaurants, shops, travel agencies, City Hall, the police station, the post office, a couple of *farmacias* (pharmacies), the island's one bank, *casas de cambio* (currency exchange offices) and several Internet cafes are all within a compact area of about four by six blocks.

*Islander,* a monthly magazine available at hotels, provides tourist information. A Red Cross (Cruz Roja) clinic is about 5 kilometers (3 miles) south of town, near Playa Lancheros; phone (998) 877-0280.

## Things to Do on the Island

The most popular beach is Playa Norte, located at the northern edge of town. It's a lovely white-sand beach sprinkled with coconut palms and thatch-roofed *palapas.* The water is clear, calm and shallow, perfect for swimming or wading. Umbrellas, chairs, jet-skis, three-wheeled water "trikes" and other equipment can be rented. You also may see discreet topless sunbathers at this beach.

Other options are Playa Lancheros and Playa Garrafón, both toward the opposite end of the island on the western (leeward) side. Playa Lancheros is the southernmost beach on the local bus route. The surf is rougher along Isla's eastern coastline, which faces the open Caribbean.

At the very southern tip of the island, on a bluff overlooking the sea, once stood the reconstructed remains of a Mayan temple believed to have been built in honor of the fertility goddess Ixchel. Archeologists believe that the Maya, en route to Cozumel on pilgrimages to worship Ixchel, stopped over at Isla Mujeres. In 1988 Hurricane Gilbert reduced it to a pile of stones, but there are fine views of the sea. A 30-foot-tall lighthouse nearby was left standing. A taxi ride from downtown costs about $10 (U.S.).

Branching east off Rueda Medina, a paved road follows the eastern edge of the island back toward town. If you've rented a golf cart, this is a nice route with plenty of pull-offs to take in views of the open sea.

Offshore coral reefs and the Cave of the Sleeping Sharks (Cueva de Los Tiburones Durmientes) attract scuba divers. The underwater cave, off the northern tip of Contoy Island National Park *(see attraction listing),* was discovered in the late 1960s. The reason for the sharks' seemingly narcotized state has been attributed to everything from varying salinity levels to lack of carbon dioxide in the underwater caverns to constant currents that supply the oxygen allowing the creatures to remain stationary. Whatever the cause, this is a challenging dive to depths of 150 feet or more, with no guarantee that the sharks will be around.

Another site for advanced divers is the Ultra-freeze (El Frio) wreck, a cargo ship that caught fire in 1979 and was towed to the open sea to be sunk. Many forms of marine life, including small and large fish, stingrays and turtles, can be seen.

Manchones Reef, just off the island's southern tip, is more than 2,500 feet long. Blue tangs, wrasses, parrot fish, angelfish and red snapper are among the tropical species that swarm over the reef, which exhibits a variety of coral formations. The water depth is 30 to 40 feet. Manchones also is the site of the underwater statue Cross of the Bay (Cruz de la Bahía).

The summer months of June, July and August, when the water is calm, are best for diving. Aqua Adventures Eco Divers, one block east of the Ultra-Mar ferry dock at the corner of Avenida Juárez and Avenida Morelos, offers certification classes. Their knowledgeable instructors can arrange trips to local dive sites, as well as snorkeling and whale shark excursions; phone (998) 236-4316. Carey Dive Center, Av. Matamoros #13-A at Avenida Rueda Medina (3 blocks north of the passenger ferry dock), also offers instruction and organizes snorkeling trips; phone (998) 877-0763.

The Boatmen's Cooperative (Cooperativa Isla Mujeres), on Avenida Rueda Medina at the foot of Avenida Madero (near the ferry dock), handles snorkeling and sport-fishing excursions as well as day trips to Isla Contoy. Some outings require a minimum number of passengers. Billfish (swordfish and marlin) are a good possibility in April and May; during the rest of the year catches include bonito, grouper and red snapper.

## Shopping, Dining and Nightlife

Although craft shop prices are lower than in Cancún, bargaining is still the best way to come out ahead. Wood carvings, ceramic and clay figurines, pottery, handmade clothing, T-shirts, and decorative objects made of sea and snail shells are among the possible purchases. Sidewalk vendors set up small displays along Avenida Rueda Medina in the vicinity of the passenger ferry dock, selling shells, jewelry, trinkets and souvenirs. The other side of the street is lined with gift shops.

Avenida Hidalgo, 2 blocks in from the waterfront, is a pedestrian-only thoroughfare with more shops and vendor stands, along with several restaurants that have outdoor tables. It's a pleasant little street to wander along. At Galería de Arte Mexico, Av. Guerrero #3, the handicrafts for sale include ceramics, silver jewelry, talavera tile and hand-painted Oaxacan rugs.

One of the nicest restaurants on the island is Zazil-Ha, in the Hotel Na Balam on Calle Zazil (at Playa Norte). The seafood dishes are well-prepared, and diners have a choice of eating indoors or in an open-air garden setting.

*Roticerias* are tiny joints that sell whole roasted chickens, which come with rice, beans, marinated onions and tortillas. It's a good takeout meal for a beach picnic. You'll find them along Avenida Hidalgo and at Plaza Isla Mujeres. The beachside restaurant at Playa Lancheros offers fresh ceviche and the Yucatecan style of fish preparation known as *tikin xic.* Look for the thatched *palapa* roof. If you want to sample local cookery, check out the food vendors at the Municipal Market (Mercado Municipal), on Avenida Guerrero next to the post office.

Isla Mujeres is not known for frenetic nightlife, which suits most visitors just fine. The *palapas* along

Playa Norte are a great place for sunset watching. Most of the restaurant bars have a late afternoon happy hour, and a few offer live music and dancing.

**Tourist information office:** Av. Rueda Medina #130, between Madero and Morelos (just north of the ferry dock). Open Mon.-Fri. 9-4. **Phone:** (998) 877-0307.

**CONTOY ISLAND NATIONAL PARK** (Parque Nacional Isla Contoy) is about 32 km (20 mi.) n. of Isla Mujeres. The uninhabited island is the site of a wildlife reserve and bird sanctuary. Four miles long and half a mile wide, Contoy has nature trails winding through tropical vegetation. Pelicans, egrets, cormorants and flamingos are among the species that nest here. In addition to park rangers, iguanas, turtles and hermit crabs live on the island, and marine life—which includes seasonal armies of migrating lobsters—is plentiful. There also is a fine outdoor nature museum.

Contoy is protected and can only be visited on a guided tour. Tours depart from Isla Mujeres, Cancún and Puerto Juárez. The Isla Mujeres tours are run by people familiar with the island and dedicated to preserving its natural environment, and the boats are smaller. But regardless of the operator, the itinerary is the same: snorkeling en route to the island, time to relax or explore, and a grilled fish lunch prepared Mayan style *(tikin-xic)*, plus an open bar. Activities include visiting an aviary, hiking along protected dunes, snorkeling or simply resting on the beach prior to the return voyage.

Life jackets and snorkeling gear are provided. Insect repellent is advised. The nature museum has restroom facilities. **Hours:** The boat trip is normally about 45 minutes one way but can take up to 2 hours if seas are rough. Kolumbus Tours offers an all-day trip that departs Tues., Thurs. and Sat. from the Marina Scuba Cancún dock, on Blvd. Kukulcán at Km marker 5 in the Hotel Zone. Daily departures (weather permitting) from Isla Mujeres are usually around 8 a.m. and can be arranged through Delfin Diving or Guadalupana Tours. **Cost:** Tours from Isla Mujeres average around $90 (U.S.) per person. The Kolumbus Tours excursion is $105; $60 (ages 6-12). Reservations are required for all tours. **Phone:** (998) 877-0374 for Delfin Diving, (998) 877-0229 for Guadalupana Tours, (998) 887-2127, or 01 (800) 715-3375 (toll-free long distance within Mexico) for Kolumbus Tours.

**DOLPHIN DISCOVERY** is at Villa Discovery on Discovery Island, reached via a bridge across Makax Lagoon. At this facility visitors can experience interactive encounters with dolphins. There are three different 1-hour programs that range from non-swimming sessions (includes touching the animals and watching them perform) to full-fledged water encounters. The program also features an educational video (watching it is required before you can enter the water). For trips from Cancún transportation is aboard the 110-foot cruiser *Discovery*.

Children must be accompanied by an adult. **Time:** Allow 2 hours minimum. **Hours:** Boat transportation

from Cancún departs daily at 9 and 11 a.m. from the Playa Tortugas dock, Km 6.5 on Boulevard Kukulcán; check-in at the Dolphin Discovery office is required 30 minutes prior to departure. Departures from Isla Mujeres back to Cancún are at 2:30 and 5:30 p.m. Dolphin programs take place daily beginning at 10:30, noon, 1:30 and 3:30. **Cost:** Basic dolphin encounter $117 (U.S.); $97 (ages 6-12); free (ages 1-5). Dolphin swim $147; $97 (ages 6-12). Children must be at least 48 inches tall and at least 6 years of age to participate in the dolphin swim. Round-trip boat fare and lunch is included in the admission price for dolphin program participants; $10 for nonparticipants. Reservations are required. **Phone:** (998) 193-3360, (866) 393-5158 (toll-free from the United States), or 01 (800) 727-5391 (toll-free long distance within Mexico). 🍴

**GARRAFÓN PARK** is at the southern end of the island off Carretera Garrafón, Km marker 6. This "natural park" is a haven for multicolored tropical fish that can be seen in calm, clear water with an average depth of 13 feet. Ziplines allow thrill seekers to skim above the island's coastal cliffs. Garrafón's swimming pool has a waterfall and a view of the Caribbean. Two ocean platforms anchored to a sandy bottom near the reef, one for sunbathers and one with a diving board, are connected by ropes that can be crossed "monkey" style, walking on one while hanging on to the other.

If all this sounds too strenuous, relax in the shady Garden of Hammocks and listen to the breeze rustling the palm fronds. In order to protect the environment, use of biodegradable sunscreen (available at the park's gift shops) is advised.

Locker rooms and showers are provided. **Time:** Allow 4 hours minimum. **Hours:** Park daily 10-5. **Cost:** Royal Garrafón package (includes use of beach, snorkeling area and equipment, pool, kayaks, hammocks and zip lines, plus continental breakfast, a buffet lunch and open bar) $97 (U.S.); $67 (ages 6-11). Other combination packages that include dolphin encounters are available. Round-trip transportation from Cancún's Playa Tortugas dock (every day except Sat., when no boats run) is included in all admission prices. There is a separate fee for guided snorkeling tours. **Phone:** (998) 193-3360, or (866) 393-5158 (toll-free from the United States). 🍴 🎟

# MAJAHUAL, QUINTANA ROO (C-4)

Majahual (mah-ha-WAL) sits at about the midpoint of an extensive, largely unspoiled stretch of shoreline lacking anything that remotely resembles an all-inclusive mega resort. Known as the Costa Maya, this coastal region encompasses Quintana Roo's southern Caribbean coast, from Punta Herrero (which is within the Sian Ka'an Biosphere Reserve) south to the village of Xcalak near the Mexico-Belize border.

The Costa Maya has a recurring motif of tangled mangroves, placid lagoons and swaying palms backing white-sand beaches. Just offshore, sea life thrives along one of the most pristine sections of the great

Mesoamerican barrier reef. Serene and sparsely developed, it's the 1970s version of the Riviera Maya coast.

The opening of the Puerto Costa Maya cruise ship pier in 2001 was the first major step in a tourism development plan cooked up by FONATUR, Mexico's tourism promoter. Six years later, category 5 Hurricane Dean roared ashore just north of Majahual, heavily damaging the pier and destroying most of the town's wooden buildings with sustained 170 mph winds and a massive storm surge. Rebuilding was swift, however, and cruise ships (including the Carnival and Disney lines) returned.

In an effort to make Majahual's sandy main street more tourist-friendly, FONATUR paved paradise and installed a concrete *malecón* (seaside promenade). Despite this concession to tourism, the Costa Maya as a whole retains a feeling of idyllic isolation and makes a nice change for cruise ship passengers weary of overcrowded Caribbean ports 'o call.

## Practicalities

Driving from the Cancún airport, it's a good 3.5-hour trip down Mex. 307 to the Majahual turn-off, on the east side of the road just beyond the tiny village of Limones. The paved, two-lane access road is not numbered, but is well signed. From the turn-off, the highway heads east toward the coast. It's about 57 kilometers (35 miles)—a 40-minute drive—to Majahual. There's a Pemex gas station on the south side of the Majahual road about 4 kilometers (2.5 miles) before you reach town.

If you're driving from the Riviera Maya south to Majahual, a Pemex station with restrooms is in the mainland town of Felipe Carrillo Puerto at the corner of Calle 70 (Mex. 307) and Calle 69. Next to the gas station is a bank with an ATM. From Felipe Carrillo the drive time to Majahual is about 1 hour and 30 minutes. When driving through rural areas in Mexico, always fill your tank whenever you have the chance.

From Bacalar, near Chetumal at the southern end of Quintana Roo, the distance to Majahual is about 137 kilometers (85 miles); drive time is about an hour and a half. There are Pemex stations on Mex. 307 in Bacalar; the station at the north end of town (on the east side of the highway) has a mini mart with an ATM.

There are a handful of ATMs in Majahual along the *malecón* as well as one at the Pemex gas station. ATMs in Mexico are often out of order, however, so don't come into town expecting to use them for convenient cash withdrawals.

Majahual (the official name, although the spelling shown on road signs and around town is "Mahahual") exhibits a dual personality. On cruise ship days, tourists shop and eat their way down the *malecón*, ATVs carrying sightseers buzz along the region's dirt roads, snorkeling boats bob near the reef and tour buses head inland to visit the Mayan ruins of Chacchobén *(see attraction listing)*. When there's no ship in port, Majahual becomes a ghost town.

Many restaurants and shops are closed and you'll probably be one of the few gringos on the beach.

Visitors arriving by cruise ship step ashore at the port facility, a modern complex with gift shops, restaurants, a Dolphin Discovery center and an ATM that can only be accessed by cruise ship passengers. But since Majahual is a cruise ship port of call, U.S. dollars are widely accepted. Some businesses may accept credit cards, but most don't. To be on the safe side, bring more cash than you think you'll need.

From the port it's a 5-minute taxi ride to Majahual (one-way fare about $5 U.S.), where a tall white lighthouse that miraculously survived Dean's fury marks the north end of town. From here the *malecón* winds its way south. Fringed with planted palms and offering views of the crystal clear Caribbean, the promenade is lined with *palapa* restaurants serving fresh seafood and a bevy of small shops hawking the usual beachwear, jewelry and trinkets. Pick up snacks, drinks and basic items at the Super Carolina convenience store (just south of Tequila Beach).

## Dining and Recreation

Restaurants are located on the inland side of the *malecón,* backed by a road that runs the length of town and continues south. If you want to sip a *cerveza* and wiggle your toes in the sand, most dining establishments also set up chairs, tables and umbrellas directly on the beach.

Near the lighthouse, the Tequila Beach Club occupies a huge, two-story *palapa* overlooking the *malecón* and a small wooden pier, a departure point for local snorkeling and sport-fishing trips. You can also rent Jet Skis. Many cruise ship passengers hang out here.

About halfway down the *malecón,* El Sabor de Mi Tierra sets up a half-dozen tables at the shoreline and operates out of a proper restaurant located a block behind the promenade. A fresh lobster tail swimming in a rich chipotle cream sauce costs about $30 (U.S.).

Farther south, La Posada de Los 40 Cañones is a hotel and restaurant that also operates the Pez Quadro Beach Club, which offers a few dozen umbrella-shaded lounge chairs. Mexican, Italian and seafood dishes dominate the menu; a lobster taco platter will set you back about $14 (U.S.). Top 40 and classic rock boom from the sound system.

If you're itching to snorkel the nearby reef and don't want to spend a half-hour swimming to it from shore, Dreamtime Diving offers 90-minute trips that usually visit two sites, where you'll see healthy coral and the usual posse of reef fish. Keep an eye peeled for rays. Dreamtime's boats are well maintained, guides are bilingual and most of the trip is spent in the water. Cost is $35 (U.S.) per person (tours require a four-person minimum); snorkel gear, bottled water and snacks are included. For more details phone (983) 124-0235 or (904) 730-4337 (from the United States).

The marquee attraction in these waters is Banco Chinchorro, the largest coral atoll in the Northern Hemisphere. Located some 31 kilometers (19 miles) from Majahual, Chinchorro's abundant marine life and eye-popping coral (including huge barrel sponges and compact car-sized brain coral) brings scuba divers and marine biologists from around the world. Chinchorro's distance from shore (between 1.5 and 2 hours) means the ocean must be calm for boats to go out, and because it's a protected federal marine reserve, dive operators need special permits.

Majahual-based Bucanero del Caribe offers an all-day, two-tank dive trip as well as a snorkeling trip to Chinchorro. Two-tank dive and snorkeling excursions in local offshore waters include a boat, equipment and a guide. The Bucanero del Caribe reservation booth is in front of the La Posada de Los 40 Cañones hotel.

The most highly regarded Chinchorro operator is XTC Dive Center, based in the tiny fishing village of Xcalak, about a 45-minute drive south of Majahual. XTC's all-day, two-tank Chinchorro excursions cost $239 per person. Snorkelers are welcome to ride along for $179. The fabled shipwrecks littering Chinchorro's shallow reefs are best explored sans oxygen tank. The summer months, when seas are at their calmest, is the best time of year to dive. The dive center has no phone; for information e-mail reserve@xtcdivecenter.com.

The small coastal town of Xcalak (shka-LAK) is about 55 kilometers (34 miles) south of Majahual and can be reached by two roads. The bumpy dirt-and-sand beach track that heads due south from Majahual will take you hours. Alternately, a narrow, two-lane paved road splits south off the access road to Majahual about 53 kilometers (33 miles) east of the Mex. 307 junction; taking this detour cuts the drive down to 45 minutes.

Xcalak was founded in 1900 as an outpost for the Mexican navy. Fishing and coconut plantations supported a healthy population until 1955, when Hurricane Janet wiped out this town at Quintana Roo's southernmost point, just a stone's throw from Belize. Xcalak has a ramshackle, end-of-the-road ambiance, with small hotels and bed-and-breakfast properties catering to adventurous travelers.

A laid-back vibe, excellent fishing and superb diving and snorkeling more than make up for beaches of hard-packed sand that lack picture-postcard beauty. Colorful clapboard homes and hurricane-proof cinder block houses line dirt roads. The restaurant at the Costa de Cocos Resort dishes up delicious seafood in a rustic setting.

North of Majahual, a paved inland road and a potholed beach road lead to the loose-knit coastal communities of Rio Indo, El Placer and El Uvero, the areas hardest hit by Hurricane Dean. Scores of beachfront homes, most built by expats, were completely leveled. While the vegetation will take years to fully recover, rebuilding commenced soon after the storm.

Farther north, within the Sian Ka'an Biosphere Reserve (see attraction listing under Tulum), you'll need a sturdy high-clearance vehicle to tackle the sandy road providing access to some of the most beautiful, unspoiled Caribbean beaches along the entire Yucatán Peninsula. If you make it to gorgeous Punta Herrero, a tiny fishing village at the mouth of Bahía del Espíritu Santo, congratulations are in order. You've reached the real Mexican Caribbean.

**CHACCHOBÉN RUINS** are about 73 km (45 mi.) w. of Majahual. The signed turn-off is on Mex. 307 just s. of the Mex. 307/Majahual access road junction; from this point, the site is 9 km (5.5 mi.) w. of the highway. Chacchobén is an old site, believed to have been settled around 200 B.C., although most of the nicely restored structures here date to around A.D. 200-700.

The most impressive pyramid (Templo 1) is in Group A, just beyond the Gran Plaza. The park-like setting, shaded by palms and banyan trees, is usually peaceful; however, the site does see large tour groups when cruise ships are in port at Majahual. If you're on a cruise ship that stops at Majahual, these are the Mayan ruins you'll most likely be visiting on a shore excursion.

**Hours:** Daily 8-5. **Cost:** 52 pesos (about $3.85 U.S.). Cash only.

# PLAYA DEL CARMEN, QUINTANA ROO (A-4)

Playa del Carmen once was the mainland departure point for Mayan pilgrims visiting the sanctuaries and temples on Cozumel. That connection is maintained today, but ferry boats have supplanted canoes and bear tourists, not worshippers. And "Playa," as it is usually referred to, has long surpassed its function as simply a ferry departure point. Growth in the last decade or so has been explosive, and while it might not rival Cancún in size or popularity, the town is very much a destination in its own right.

The mood here is relaxed and informal, the ambience decidedly international. Lots of Europeans visit Playa, and many hotels and restaurants have European owners. Environmentalism is actively promoted; visitors are encouraged to participate in activities like helping to preserve nesting sites of the threatened sea turtle population. Some accommodations promote a "back to nature" slant: at rustic, thatch-roofed seaside "eco-hotels," standard guest activities include yoga classes, meditation in a flotation tank or a full-body exfoliation treatment. If you want a crazy party scene, go to Cancún; Playa is primarily a beach hangout, but one with enough variety to satisfy all but the most jaded travelers.

## Practicalities

Most visitors fly into Cancún and then drive to Playa del Carmen, about 68 kilometers (42 miles) south via Mex. 307, the highway that connects the coastal communities. Several turn-offs run east into town. Avenida 34 accesses the northern end of Playa. Avenida Constituyentes and Avenida Juárez will take you downtown; Avenida Juárez goes straight to the main plaza and the ferry pier to Cozumel.

An elevated overpass built directly over Mex. 307, some 6 kilometers (4 miles) in length, avoids the stoplights and traffic congestion on the older road and allows drivers en route to points south to bypass the city completely. There are entrance and exit ramps at key cross streets.

Taxis from the Cancún airport are expensive, averaging about $75 (U.S.) one way. A far less expensive option is taking the bus. Autobuses Riviera provides frequent daily service between Cancún International Airport and Playa del Carmen. One-way fare is about $13 (U.S.). Bus tickets can be purchased at Terminals 2 or 3. Look for a bus ticket counter inside the terminal entrance doors, or purchase a ticket from the driver; the red buses, which have "Riviera" and "ADO" written on the side and the destination on the front, pick up passengers outside the terminals.

Playa has two bus stations. Buses from Cancún and other points north and from Tulum and other points south arrive at the Riviera bus station, at the corner of Avenida Juárez and 5th Avenue (Avenida 5), just up the street from the main plaza. Buses from Mérida and other interior points arrive at the newer ADO bus station, northwest of downtown on Avenida 20 between calles 12 and 14. *Colectivos* are an equally inexpensive alternative to the bus. These air-conditioned, government-regulated vans run the length of Mex. 307, providing transportation from Playa to various destinations between Cancún and Tulum.

Drivers on large yellow tricycles (*triciclos*), the Mexican version of a rickshaw, congregate in front of the downtown station; it's an inexpensive way to get to nearby hotels or take a spin around town. Playa is small enough, however, that practically everything of interest to casual visitors is within walking distance. There are several bike rental shops at the northern end of 5th Avenue, and bicycling is a pleasant way to get around.

Taxi fares within the downtown area shouldn't be more than 45 pesos (about $3.35 U.S.). From the Playacar resort area to downtown, fares average about 80 pesos. Make sure you confirm the rate with the driver before getting in the cab. Many drivers don't speak English, so it helps to have directions to your destination written down. You also can hire a taxi for the day, which is convenient if you don't have a rental car; the driver will take you to the places you want to visit and wait while you sightsee. Rates are negotiable, but expect to pay a minimum of about $75 (U.S.).

Three ferry companies carry passengers between Playa del Carmen and Cozumel. The centrally located ferry pier is off Avenida 5, a block south of the main plaza. Cars are not transported; there is a guarded parking lot across the street from the pier. Departures to Cozumel are approximately every hour (and sometimes on the half-hour) and begin around 6:30 a.m.; the last scheduled departure is at 11 p.m. The last scheduled departure from Cozumel

back to Playa del Carmen is at 10 p.m. Cold beverages can be purchased on board.

Tickets can be purchased at booths near the foot of the pier. If you're going on a day trip to Cozumel, simply arrive at the pier early and buy a ticket for the next available trip. Early morning rides may sell out due to workers commuting to the island, but in general seats are always available. Double-check the schedule at the pier, and in particular confirm the time of the last departure from Cozumel if you're planning a day trip to the island. On Cozumel tickets can be purchased at the dock where you board the ferry.

The trip takes about 45 minutes aboard modern, air-conditioned vessels. The one-way fare charged by UltraMar and Mexico WaterJets is 163 pesos (about $12 U.S.); 97 pesos (ages 4-11). Barcos Caribe has a fare of 135 pesos (about $10 U.S.); 70 pesos (children).

**Note:** Ferry schedules are subject to change due to weather conditions, as seas can sometimes be quite rough; make sure you carry appropriate medication if you're prone to seasickness.

Several banks are located on Avenida Juárez. Most have ATMs; withdrawals are in pesos. A Banamex bank branch with an ATM is at the corner of Avenida 10 and Calle 12. There also are several *casas de cambio* (currency exchange houses) in town. Many shops and restaurants accept U.S. and Canadian dollars.

## City Layout

Playa is somewhat of a hybrid—explosive growth has resulted in luxury resorts and a lively tourist scene, but it still has the workaday feel of a typical Mexican town. The small, compact downtown area bustles with traffic and pedestrians. Shoeshine men and vendors selling hot dogs and hamburgers from wheeled carts set up on the sidewalk. The nicest part of Playa is right along the beach; west of Avenida 10 (two blocks inland) the streets start to have a scruffier look.

Downtown is laid out in a simple grid pattern and is easy to negotiate. Avenidas run north-south, calles east-west. Traffic congestion is common, however, due partly to a number of newer unpaved, sandy streets and their water-filled potholes that require careful maneuvering. The busiest part of town is where Avenida Juárez ends at 5th Avenue (also called Avenida 5 or Quinta Avenida), in the vicinity of the Riviera bus station and the ferry pier to Cozumel. The public pay parking lot near the bus station, just north of Juárez and just west of 5th Avenue, is a convenient place to leave your car if you feel like getting out and exploring.

The tourist action centers on 5th Avenue, just inland from the beach. The 15-block stretch from Avenida Juárez north to Calle 26 has the greatest concentration of restaurants, hotels, shops and nightspots. Playa's small *zócalo* (main plaza), a block east of 5th Avenue and a block south of Avenida Juárez, is just off the beach. Shaded by coconut palms and a lush green canopy of almond trees, this little brick-paved plaza has benches, a gazebo with black wrought-iron trim and a view of the Caribbean; it's a lovely spot to relax. Next to the plaza vendors set up tables shaded by brightly colored umbrellas; in fact, almost everywhere you turn there are umbrella-shaded stands selling something.

The Playacar hotel zone is south of the ferry pier. Residential homes, condos, hotels and all-inclusive resorts are within this designated area; the cobblestoned main thoroughfare is called Paseo Xaman-Ha (sha-MAN hah). A genuine lodging bargain might be found here during the off-season (after Easter through November). Cruise ship passengers and day visitors from Cancún take advantage of Playacar Club de Golf, a public, 18-hole golf course designed by Robert Von Hagge that includes an outstanding clubhouse and pro shop. Greens fees drop significantly if you're a guest at a hotel affiliated with the club.

Playa's beaches have the powdery white sand and beautiful turquoise water characteristic of the entire Mexican Caribbean coast, and offshore reefs guarantee good snorkeling and diving. The main public beach, between the ferry pier and Calle 10, is the most crowded. It's wide and sandy near the pier, narrowing somewhat as it runs north past restaurants, beach bars, dive shops and varied water sports operators. If you prefer fewer crowds and more seclusion, keep walking north past the jetty at the Porto Real Hotel. The wide sand beach here is quieter as long as you avoid the activities around the Kool and Mamitas beach clubs. You can, however, rent an umbrella and a lounge chair from these places if you intend to stay the day; just get there early.

## Shopping and Nightlife

Avenida 5 is a pedestrian-only thoroughfare between calles 1 and 6. The numerous shops and souvenir stands here and on little side streets sell T-shirts, jewelry, knickknacks, handmade pottery, New Age paraphernalia and a wide variety of crafts from all over Mexico. While it's fun to browse the avenue checking out everything that's on display, some merchants can be quite persistent in their attempts to entice potential customers; be prepared to keep walking if you're not really interested in buying.

Strolling, shopping and the heat combine for a laid-back scene during the day. Avenida 5 really comes alive in the evening, when people flock to restaurants and congregate at sidewalk cafes. Reggae music fills the air, and a carnival-like atmosphere prevails. A number of dance clubs and beach bars offer a partying atmosphere and live music.

The Blue Parrot, on the beach between calles 10 and 14 (next to the Hotel Costa del Mar), is a popular bar that attracts a rowdy crowd. This longtime favorite has an outdoor beachside dance floor that throbs with techno music until the wee hours. For those over 30 it's a nice spot for lunch or a late afternoon drink on the beach. La Santanera, on Calle 12 between 5th and 10th avenues, has an open-air upper level where you can lounge on couches under

a *palapa* roof and a downstairs disco where DJs spin house and other dance music.

Like the original mega club in Cancún, the Playa del Carmen outpost of Coco Bongo, Av. 10 Norte #221 (at the corner of Calle 12 Norte), is a high-tech dance club with high-energy stage shows featuring Cirque du Soleil-style acrobats/dancers and pop icon impersonators. The steep cover charge includes an open bar; phone (984) 803-5939.

A popular daytime hangout is Mamita's Beach Club, on the beach at the end of Calle 28. It has a restaurant, bar, locker and shower facilities, a live DJ and canopied beds on the sand. In keeping with Playa's open-minded nature, topless sunbathing is permitted (although against the law in Mexico). Of course all the amenities aren't free; you'll pay rental fees for things like beach chairs, chaise lounges and shade-providing *palapas*.

## Dining

Playa has an impressive number of restaurants offering a smorgasbord of variety. Mexican, American, Italian, German, seafood, steak, pizza and taco vendors, ice cream and popsicle stands—it's all here. And the fine dining establishments in several of the big hotels along the coast north to Puerto Morelos rival the best that can be found in Cancún's Hotel Zone.

If you want something healthy to nibble on while walking around town, stop at a fruit stand. For about 10 pesos, women wearing traditional Mayan blouses (white with colorful embroidery) will give you a large cup filled with chunks of fresh pineapple, mango, coconut and watermelon.

*Churros,* sold from street carts, are sticks of dough pressed through a tube shaped like a star, then fried in oil and rolled in cinnamon sugar or filled with fruit jam or melted chocolate. Another tasty snack is *tacos al pastor,* shredded, marinated pork cooked on a rotisserie, heaped on a small corn tortilla and garnished with chopped onions, cilantro and a slice of pineapple.

There are restaurants up and down 5th Avenue. For dessert or a sweet break, walk up the avenue to 30th Street and Ah Cacao Chocolate Café. Pull up a chair at one of the little sidewalk tables, linger over an espresso, latte or iced coffee and sample one of the cafe's signature chocolate brownies.

And don't limit your restaurant sampling to 5th Avenue alone. Babe's Noodles and Bar, on Calle 10 between 5th and 10th avenues, is representative of Playa's international flavor. At this Swedish-owned restaurant—decorated with Barbie dolls and lava lamps—a Mexican server will bring you Thai-style noodles in green or coconut curry, or perhaps a shrimp salad with vegetables, rice noodles and a Vietnamese dressing. Eat in the Buddha Garden, an open-air terrace surrounded by tropical trees and hung with Asian lanterns.

More off the beaten path is La Pesca, on 30th Avenue between calles 14 and 16 (across from the Mega supermarket). Some locals say it serves the best seafood in town. Try the ceviche, octopus *(pulpo)* in a spicy sauce or *cazuela de camarones* (shrimp casserole).

Playa is very casual, and casual dress is appropriate even at the more expensive places. There's no need to watch what you order at restaurants targeting the tourist trade. Use your own judgment regarding local hangouts or street food, but as a general rule if it's cooked it should be safe to eat. See the Lodgings & Restaurants section for AAA-RATED dining establishments.

**Riviera Maya Tourism Board:** north of downtown in the Professional Building (Edificio Profesional), corner of Mex. 307 (Carretera Federal) and Calle #28. **Phone:** (984) 206-3150.

**ECOPARK KANTUN-CHI** is on the inland side of Mex. 307, 22 km (14 mi.) s. of Playa del Carmen, 2 km (1.2 mi.) s. of Puerto Aventuras and just n. of Xpu-Ha Beach. The park entrance road is prominently signed with a roadside billboard; a faux Mayan pyramid sits at the front entrance.

The 1-hour guided tour of Kantun-Chi's underground cavern system begins when you descend (via wooden ladder) a deep hole that resembles a well. Several pools feature ceilings dripping with stalactites and have cold water that is inhabited by tiny cave fish. The dry sections of the cavern are festooned with more stalactite and stalagmite formations illuminated by colored lights. You can swim and snorkel in the pools. In addition to the underground caverns, visitors can explore four above-ground cenotes—pools sheltered under limestone overhangs—that are linked by jungle-lined pathways.

Snorkel masks, life jackets and lockers are included. Waterproof sport sandals are highly recommended, but you can get by with flip-flops. Walking through the dry sections of the underground cavern involves negotiating some tight passageways and low overhangs. Restrooms are on site. Children under age 7 are not permitted on the cave tour.

**Hours:** Daily 9-5 (also 5-6 during the summer months). **Cost:** Guided cavern tour plus access to above-ground cenotes $71 (U.S.); $36 (ages 5-11). Access to cenotes only $44; $22 (ages 0-12). Admission packages that include round-trip transportation from Riviera Maya hotels also are available. **Phone:** (984) 873-0021.

**PUERTO AVENTURAS** is 20 km (12 mi.) s. of Playa del Carmen off Mex. 307. This planned resort community of hotels, condominiums and residential areas has its own golf course, marina, dive centers, shops and restaurants. The landscaped grounds are adorned with imported palms and orchids. Tennis, swimming, scuba diving, deep-sea fishing and swimming with dolphins are among the recreational activities offered.

**CEDAM Museum** is 2 blks. s. of the Omni Puerto Aventuras Resort. Known locally as the Shipwreck Museum, this small space exhibits artifacts and wreckage obtained from shipwrecks that have occurred off the Quintana Roo coast. Cannons, dinnerware, gold coins and an elephant tusk are some of the objects on display from wrecks that include the *Matanceros* (which means "the killers"), a Spanish merchant ship that ran into the coral reefs just offshore in 1741. **Time:** Allow 1 hour minimum. **Hours:** Mon.-Sat. 10-1 and 2:30-5:30, although hours may vary. **Cost:** Donations. 🎟

**RANCHO PUNTA VENADO** is at Mex. 307 Km marker 286 (on the e. side of the highway), about a 10-minute drive s. of Playa del Carmen. This large, rustic working ranch is also a tourist-oriented eco-park that encompasses more than 2 miles of uninterrupted coastline. The main activity is a guided horseback riding excursion through tropical scrub jungle and along a stretch of unspoiled beach. If you have riding experience be sure to mention it; you'll go with a different guide on a spirited horse and have more of an adventure.

Other activities include Waverunner tours, ATV rides through a jungle habitat, and snorkeling and kayaking at a nearby protected reef. And if you just feel like kicking back on a chaise lounge in the shade under a comfy *palapa,* there's a secluded beach club on the premises.

**Time:** Allow 4 hours minimum. **Hours:** Daily 9-4. **Cost:** (includes snacks at the beach club) Horseback riding trips $96 (U.S.) per person (includes snacks at the beach club). Fees for other activities vary. If you're not participating in a tour, there is a cover charge for beach club use, and you'll be expected to order food and/or drinks. There are small fees for locker and towel rentals. Advance reservations are required for all trips. Cash only. **Phone:** (984) 879-3998, or 01 (800) 841-5797 (toll-free long distance within Mexico). 🎟

**RIO SECRETO** is about 5 km (3 mi.) s. of Playa del Carmen and just s. of Xcaret, at Mex. 307 Km marker 282 (watch for the Rio Secreto sign). At this nature preserve an underground river flows through a cavern that is millions of years old but was only recently discovered by a local rancher. This eerily silent environment is highlighted by otherworldly stalactite and stalagmite formations. Guided excursions led by a knowledgeable, bilingual guide explore the 2,000-foot-long route, allowing visitors to float in a small pool, experience pitch blackness for a moment and observe shrimp, bats and other creatures that have adapted to the cavern's very specialized conditions.

**Note:** There is a long, bumpy, 30-minute ride in a 10-passenger van from the reception area to the cavern entrance. After showering and changing into a wet suit, life vest, waterproof shoes and a light-equipped helmet, guests are escorted down a jungle trail that leads to the cavern opening. The trek through the cavern proceeds in single file, with each person holding on to the wet suit strap of the person in front. Some climbing up and down narrow, rocky trails is required. Guests must be able to walk without assistance, weigh less than 250 pounds and be free of physical limitations. Under 4 are not permitted.

**Time:** Allow 4 hours minimum. **Hours:** Excursions depart daily at 9, 10, noon, 1 and 2. Excursions from

Cancún depart Mon.-Fri. at 9, with hotel pickup times starting at 7 a.m. Excursions from Riviera Maya locations depart daily at 9 and 1, with hotel pickup times starting at 7:20 a.m. **Cost:** $79 U.S. (includes entry to the preserve, trip-related equipment, towel, showers, lockers and a light buffet lunch); $39.50 (ages 4-11). Admission plus transportation from Cancún locations $129; $64.50 (ages 4-11). Admission plus transportation from Riviera Maya locations $109; $54.50 (ages 4-11). Advance reservations are required. **Phone:** (984) 877-2377, or (888) 844-5010 (from the United States and Canada). 🍴 ⊠

**XCARET** is about 6 km (4 mi.) s. of Playa del Carmen at Mex. 307 Km marker 282 (follow the marked turn-off). At Xcaret (ISH-kah-ret), preserving the natural environment is as important as showcasing it, and equally important is this water park's dedication to educating visitors regarding Mayan history, culture and traditions.

One of the most popular activities for swimmers, snorkelers and divers is paddling through interconnected cenotes (freshwater sinkholes) and two natural underground rivers. There also are beaches and inlets for swimming and snorkeling, along with educational programs that include interaction and swimming with dolphins.

In addition to water-based recreation, Xcaret offers a living coral reef aquarium; jaguar, deer and monkey island habitats; an aviary; a bee farm; regional wildlife exhibits, including tapirs, flamingos, manatees and sea turtles; a nature trail through tropical jungle; a bromeliad and orchid greenhouse; a Butterfly Pavilion; and several small archeological sites on the grounds.

A replica of a Mayan village (Pueblo Maya) depicts how life is still lived in many rural Yucatán towns. The re-created village cemetery, with colorful grave displays and catacombs running underneath, has a hilltop setting. Entertainment features performances of the ceremonial flying pole dance by the Papantla Flyers and the rousing evening show "Xcaret Mexico Espectacular," with traditional music and dance performances and an overview of Mexican history as seen through the eyes of a young girl.

**Note:** Using suntan lotion is not permitted in the lagoons and other waterways because of its effect on the marine habitat. Visitors are not permitted to bring food, beverages, audio devices or sunblock lotions into the park. Allow a full day.

**Hours:** Daily 8:30 a.m.-9 p.m. Phone ahead to confirm schedule. **Cost:** $99 (U.S.); $49.50 (ages 5-11). The basic admission includes use of showers, changing rooms, beach chairs and hammocks, as well as all water, wildlife and botanical areas, the Butterfly Pavilion, archeological sites and entertainment. There are separate rental fees for snorkeling equipment, lockers, towels, wheelchairs and baby strollers. Depending upon crowds, however, the park may run out of supplies; bring your own towels and snorkeling gear if possible. There also are separate fees for scuba diving instruction, guided diving and snorkeling excursions and the dolphin swim programs (which should be reserved in

advance). **Phone:** (998) 883-3143 in Cancún, (984) 206-0038 in Playa del Carmen, (888) 922-7381 (toll-free from the United States and Canada), or 01 (800) 292-2738 (toll-free long distance within Mexico). 🍴

 **XPLOR** is 7 km (4 mi.) s. on Mex. 307 to Km marker 282; take the exit signed "Xplor/Xcaret" and follow signs. This eco-adventure park caters to families with a variety of safe, well-organized outdoor activities. Two zip line circuits have towers of varying heights up to 147 feet and include water features and a waterslide plunge. A 6.2-mile-long ATV trail runs through the jungle as well as a couple of underground tunnels.

Visitors can maneuver a hand paddle raft along an underground river and cave system and through a grotto with clear, cool water and amazing rock formations. A mini zip line features a hammock chair instead of a harness and ends up with a cooling dunk in the water. And you can chill out with a brief siesta in a hammock before starting all over again.

The all-inclusive experience includes a buffet lunch, and there are smoothie and snack stations located throughout the park. Safety helmets and lockers are provided. Bring towels, an extra pair of shorts, appropriate footwear and a waterproof camera.

**Note:** Arrive early, as lines at the entrance can be long and slow, and put the zip lines first on your agenda, since they're the most popular activity and lines can again be long. Some zip line towers require quite a bit of climbing. The ATV trails are dusty during the dry season (roughly November through May). Some activities are not recommended for children under 8. Ages 0-4 not permitted. Those with certain health conditions should heed posted warnings.

**Time:** Allow 5 hours minimum. **Hours:** Mon.-Sat. 9-5. **Cost:** Full-day, all-inclusive general admission $139 (U.S.); $69.50 (ages 5-11 and under 55 inches tall). Other packages include transportation to the park (hotel pickup and drop-off from Cancún); prices vary. **Phone:** (984) 147-6560, (888) 922-7381 (toll-free from the United States), or 01 (800) 212-8951 (toll-free long distance within Mexico). 🍴 ⊠

## PUERTO MORELOS, QUINTANA ROO (A-4)

About halfway between Cancún and Playa del Carmen, Puerto Morelos (PWEHR-toh moh-REH-los) is a peaceful, unhurried fishing village with palm-shaded beaches and restaurants serving fresh seafood. It's the perfect place to while away a lazy afternoon in the shade of a thatched *palapa* on a white-sand beach while gazing at the beauty of aquamarine water.

Puerto Morelos is also the serene eye in the midst of a storm of tourism development. Flashy resorts and boutique hotels dot the Caribbean coast north toward Cancún, their manicured grounds occupying prime beachfront locations. These upscale properties are a world away from the humble *posadas* and economical motels in town.

An offshore reef, part of the Great Mesoamerican Reef system that runs along Mexico's Caribbean coast, is a protected national marine park. In addition to creating excellent snorkeling and diving opportunities, the reef acts to break up waves before they reach the shoreline, which makes Puerto Morelos beaches safe for wading and swimming.

Frequent first-class bus service is available from Puerto Morelos to both Cancún and Playa del Carmen. Two stations, one for northbound buses and one for southbound buses, are on Mex. 307. The fare to either city is around 50 pesos (about $3.70 U.S.). *Colectivos* (white minivans) also provide transportation both in town and between towns; the in-town fare is an inexpensive 10 pesos. Taxi rates are set, not metered; agree on a price before you get in the cab.

The main square is the local hangout. Alma Libre Books has a large selection of used paperbacks and other titles in English. It's open daily 10-6 during the high tourist season. Also on the square is the Casa Martín grocery market.

Dive shops in town provide guided deep-sea fishing trips on local *pangas* or a larger vessel with a cabin; catches include barracuda, billfish and grouper. They also offer scuba and snorkeling excursions to the reef, which teems with brilliantly colored tropical fish, all sorts of crustaceans, rays, eels, nurse sharks and sea turtles, plus a wrecked military vessel that divers can explore.

Dive In Puerto Morelos, Av. Rojo Gómez #14 (several doors north of the town square), has knowledgeable, PADI-certified guides. A reef snorkeling trip (plus a 20-peso park fee) costs $30 (U.S.); an open water one-tank dive is $70; a half-day excursion to dive at a local cenote (two tanks, plus lunch) is $160. For information and reservations phone (998) 206-9084 (cellular number), or (801) 738-0169 (from the United States).

**CROCO CUN** is just n. of the Puerto Morelos turn-off on Mex. 307, at Km marker 31. This small zoo, which also functions as a crocodile-raising farm, emphasizes environmental education. On display are crocodile specimens of all ages and sizes, along with rattlesnakes, boa constrictors, iguanas, macaws, tapirs, spider monkeys, tarantulas and other regional species. Visitors can hold young crocodiles and feed baby deer. Guided tours in English are available. Insect repellent is strongly advised. **Hours:** Daily 9-5. **Cost:** $30 (U.S.); $20 (ages 6-12). **Phone:** (998) 850-3719. ⓣ

**DR. ALFREDO BARRERA BOTANICAL GARDEN** (Jardín Botánico Dr. Alfredo Barrera) is just s. of the Puerto Morelos turn-off; the entrance is right off Mex. 307. This protected area features a nature trail that winds through a variety of native and regional plants, including a grove of sapodilla trees (from which the sticky substance used to make chewing gum is extracted), a mangrove swamp, an orchid garden, a section where epiphytes (air plants) grow and an area containing a reproduction of a Mayan dwelling. It will be of most interest to visitors familiar with the flora, although bird-watching is rewarding and there are occasional monkey sightings.

Signs give plant names in Spanish and English. Wear plenty of insect repellent. **Hours:** Mon.-Sat. 8-4. **Cost:** 150 pesos (about $11 U.S.); 100 pesos (ages 2-7). **Phone:** (998) 206-9233.

## TULUM, QUINTANA ROO (B-3)
### pop. 28,263

Bustling Tulum (too-LOOM) anchors the south end of the Riviera Maya. The town benefits not only from the robust tourism industry along the Mexican Caribbean coast but from its proximity to the Tulum Ruins and several other nearby attractions.

Tulum is small enough that it's easy to walk around and soak up the local atmosphere. Mex. 307 is the main thoroughfare, and for about a mile it is lined with restaurants, souvenir shops and small businesses. Internet cafes sit next to laundromats, *loncherías* (open-air lunch counters), tortilla stands, ice cream parlors, *zapaterías* (shoe stores) and auto repair shops. Produce markets are filled with clusters of bananas on stalks, green coconuts, tropical fruits and sacks of beans. Craft shops offer the usual array of hammocks, textiles, rugs, jewelry, masks and ceramics, while other stores sell housewares and everyday items.

Explore the side streets, which extend a couple of blocks on both sides of the highway. Tulum's town plaza is just east of Mex. 307 behind the Ayuntamiento (City Hall) building. Shaded by coconut palms, it has a gazebo and is a community gathering place where kids play basketball and vendors set up shop on the sidewalk. Many locals work in nearby resorts or in construction. The local neighborhoods are a mix of cement block houses, traditional Mayan huts and dwellings with thatched roofs and walls made of sticks. **Note:** Lateral streets with diagonal parking spaces run along either side of Mex. 307; use caution when entering the highway from one of these streets.

Evening is a pleasant time to stroll around town. The restaurants along Mex. 307 are casual, and several of them have open-air seating in a garden setting. Some feature live music and dancing on certain nights. Sidewalk taco vendors fill the air with the tantalizing aroma of grilling chicken and pork, and reggae music wafts out of doorways and courtyards. Tulum is a bit of an international melting pot; you'll see American tourists, young European backpackers and elderly local matriarchs wearing a *huipil*, the embroidered white cotton blouse that is standard garb for Yucatecan women.

To reach the beaches, take the Cobá/Boca Paila road east (the intersection with a traffic signal at the northern end of town; make a left turn if traveling southbound or a right turn if traveling northbound). The paved road has no highway number; the sign at the intersection says "Playas/Punta Allen." It runs through open scrub for about 3 kilometers (2 miles) before forking north (toward the Tulum Ruins, with access to beaches along the way) and south to the hotel zone.

Take the right fork (south), a narrow, winding paved road that follows the coast. Campgrounds, cabanas and small spa hotels line this lovely drive, bordered by lush growths of palms and other tropical vegetation. Some properties are nothing more than a grouping of *palapa* huts just steps away from the beach. Several of these laid-back accommodations have signs designating them as "eco chic" resorts—which means that they might rely on a generator for electricity and dispense with such amenities as TVs and phones.

Even if you're not staying in the Tulum hotel zone, it's well worth stopping at one of the casual hotel restaurants for lunch and picture-postcard Caribbean views. Head south along the coast road to Zamas; it draws a loyal following to a breezy dining deck overlooking an unspoiled stretch of beach. Farther down the road, Ana y José Beach Club serves great seafood and cocktails. You can eat inside the big *palapa* restaurant, or if you prefer, in a king-size beach bed. Bring lots of cash. Near the southern end of the hotel zone, rustic-chic La Zebra attracts vacationing hipsters, but the excellent food and drink will satisfy anyone. And La Zebra's beach is gorgeous.

Some of the beaches along this stretch of coast, in addition to boasting powdery white sand and luminous turquoise water, are all but deserted. South of the entrance to the buffer zone of the Sian Ka'an Biosphere Reserve *(see attraction listing)*, miles of uninhabited beaches edge the Boca Paila Peninsula.

**Note:** These are natural beaches, unlike the "groomed" stretches that front resort hotels; foot protection is recommended since the bottom can be rocky. Swim or snorkel only when seas are calm, beware of strong currents and stay close to shore; there are no lifeguards. Do not park along the coast road, and do not leave valuables in your car. There are no facilities at these beaches; bring your own water and food.

Numerous cenotes dot the jungles outside Tulum. Technically a cenote (pronounced say-NOH-tay) is a sinkhole that forms when the ceiling of an underlying cave collapses. The Yucatán Peninsula, honeycombed with an underground network of porous limestone rock, also has many cavern systems through which subterranean rivers often flow. The pile of rubble left by a collapsed cave ceiling typically contains very few nutrients, so trees and plants that do manage to sprout send their roots through the rocks to tap the water below; this is why you'll often see tree roots descending into an underground cave from above.

From above ground many cenotes look just like normal ponds, and locals use them as swimming holes. Small tropical fish—such species as tetras and mollies that are commonly seen in home aquariums—live in these freshwater sinkholes, making them great places to snorkel. Most also have remarkably clear water, although the tannin from fallen dead leaves can stain the water in some cenotes, giving it the appearance of freshly brewed tea, and in the heat of summer warm water temperatures promote algae bloom that can turn it a cloudy green.

Cenote Cristal and Cenote Escondido are about 4 kilometers (2.5 miles) south of Tulum on opposite sides of Mex. 307 and can be reached via short gravel walking paths. These are typical cenotes of the "pond" variety, and the cool, clear water is good for a refreshing dip. Snorkelers will see turtles and small tropical fish. Watch for the parking area on the right side of the highway, where you pay the 120-peso entrance fee; lock your car and do not leave valuables inside. Cenote Cristal has a sloping path to the water's edge; at Cenote Escondido a ladder descends from a stone platform to the water. There are no facilities, so bring your own drinking water and snacks. Both are open daily 9-5.

**GRAN CENOTE** is about 3.6 km (2.1 mi.) w. of Tulum via the road to the Cobá ruins (the jct. with Mex. 307 is at the n. end of town); watch for the signed turn-off on the right side of the road. This freshwater limestone sinkhole—shaped like a half moon—leads to a huge underground cave system. It offers good swimming and snorkeling in cool, clear blue water. Beneath the surface are caverns and passageways, limestone stalactites and stalagmites, and schools of tropical fish. From the entrance/parking area, access to the cenote is down a short path. Divers suit up on the wooden decks overlooking the cenote, and ladder steps lead down to the water. Wear nonslip shoes while swimming or snorkeling.

About 3 kilometers (2 miles) farther down the road (watch for the turn-off on the left) is Car Wash Cenote, so named because locals once washed their vehicles here and you can drive right up to the water's edge. A diving platform has been installed for swimmers. This freshwater pond is home to lots of small tropical fish. Algae growth is heavy in the summer; the water is clearer during the winter months.

Snorkel gear and life jackets can be rented, or bring your own mask and gear. Parking, a snack bar and very basic restrooms are on site. **Time:** Allow 2 hours minimum. **Hours:** Gran Cenote open daily 8-5; Car Wash Cenote open daily 9-5. **Cost:** Gran Cenote 150 pesos (about $11 U.S.). Car Wash Cenote 50 pesos (about $4.05 U.S.). Prices may vary. Cash only. **Phone:** (984) 146-2323 (cellular number). 🗙 🛱

**TULUM RUINS** are about 60 km (37 mi.) s. of Playa del Carmen and about a mile n. of the town of Tulum. The well-marked turn-off is on the e. side of Mex. 307; a large parking lot is less than 100 yds. e. of the highway. While not nearly as impressive or varied architecturally as Chichén Itzá or Uxmal, Tulum is notable for its dramatic setting overlooking the turquoise Caribbean.

One of the later Mayan outposts, this small but powerful city-state rose to prominence sometime during the 12th century. It was fortified on three sides by a wall—rather uncommon among Mayan cities—due to the coastal location, which was both strategic and vulnerable. A center for maritime commerce, Tulum was never conquered by the Spaniards, although it was abandoned some 75 years after the Spanish conquest of Mexico in 1521.

Some 60 structures are spread over a level, grassy area. The most imposing is The Castle (El Castillo), a pyramidal structure capped by a small temple that stands at the edge of a cliff above the sea. Also worth seeing is the Temple of the Frescoes (Templo de los Frescos) near the site entrance. It features interior murals that display typical Mayan motifs and exterior statues bearing still-discernible traces of paint. Just north of El Castillo is the Temple of the Descending God; the winged stucco figure over the doorway suggests a plummeting diver.

**Note:** The structures cannot be climbed, and most have roped-off areas that visitors must stand behind, obscuring the view of some interior details. Wear non-slip walking shoes; the sandy, rocky terrain can be unexpectedly slippery. You'll also be on your feet, as there aren't really any places to sit. The porous limestone has created a few blowholes through which geysers of sea water can unexpectedly erupt and drench bystanders. Weather permitting, bring a swimsuit—the lovely beach below can be reached by walking down a long staircase. Licensed, English-speaking guides are available, although the information you receive may or may not be historically accurate. The ruins are a popular day trip from Cancún and can be crowded depending on the time of year.

There are restrooms, a bookstore, a restaurant and a few souvenir stands in the visitor center at the far end of the parking lot; the entrance to the site is about a 10-minute walk from the parking lot. **Time:** Allow 2 hours minimum. **Hours:** Daily 8-5. **Cost:** 64 pesos (about $4.75 U.S.). Shuttle ride from the visitor center to the site about $2.25 (U.S.). Guided tour fee about $30 (U.S.); the fee for using a video camera is about $4. Cash only. **Parking:** 40 pesos. 🍴

## Nearby Destinations

**MUYIL** is about 22 km (13 mi.) s. of Tulum on the east side of Mex. 307. This archeological site—also known as Chunyaxché (choon-yahsh-CHEH)—is on the banks of Muyil Lagoon (there also is a pueblo called Muyil on the west side of Mex. 307). The main structure is the Castle (El Castillo), a well-restored pyramid about 70 feet tall. Lesser structures in varying degrees of repair surround it. From the site a path leads to the lagoon (technically a bay since it opens to the sea).

**Note:** This is a tropical scrub jungle environment, and visitors may encounter large horseflies or the occasional poisonous snake. About 300 feet south on Mex. 307 is a turn-off; head left (east) on this narrow road to a large two-story building on the waterfront constructed entirely from bamboo sticks. Locals gather here on weekends and holidays and will take visitors on a bay cruise.

Parking and restrooms are on site. There are no other facilities; bring your own water and food. **Time:** Allow 1 hour minimum. **Hours:** Daily 8-5. **Cost:** 39 pesos (about $2.90 U.S.); free (ages 0-11). There is an additional 40-peso fee to access the walkway down to the lagoon. The fee for a 1-hour boat cruise is negotiable and runs about $25 (U.S.). Cash only.

**SIAN KA'AN BIOSPHERE RESERVE** (Reserva de la Biosfera Sian Ka'an) encompasses the Boca Paila Peninsula and mainland Quintana Roo s. of Tulum

and e. of Mex. 307. Designated as a protected area by the Mexican government in 1986, Sian Ka'an (the name means "place where the sky is born") includes a variety of habitats: tropical jungle, drier areas of tree-speckled savanna, coastal mangrove flats and some 70 miles of offshore coral reefs.

Most of the reserve is off limits to tourists, but the beaches and jungles on the Boca Paila Peninsula can be explored by visitors. Take the Boca Paila/Punta Allen road off Mex. 307 (turn left if traveling southbound, right if traveling northbound; the intersection has a traffic signal and is signed "Playas/Punta Allen"). The road runs east for a few miles and then continues south through Tulum's hotel zone. About 15 kilometers (9 miles) from the Mex. 307 junction is the entrance to the reserve, marked by a guardhouse building (Caseta de Control). Day visitors must register at the guardhouse; from this point there is access to secluded beaches, and kayaks and bikes can be rented.

Sian Ka'an Community Tours offers guided excursions that include lagoon kayaking around mangrove islands, an all-day canal boat trip through mangrove swamps and savanna grasslands to palm-lined beaches, and a bird-watching excursion. **Hours:** Guided tours are offered on a seasonal basis. **Cost:** Day visitors must register at the guardhouse and pay a registration fee of about $4 (U.S.). **Phone:** (984) 871-2202 for tour information and reservations.

**XCACEL** (ISH-ca-sell) is about a quarter mile e. of Mex. 307 between Playa Chemuyil and Xel-Ha, about 19 km (12 mi.) n. of the town of Tulum; watch for the signed turn-off if approaching from the south. Access to the beach is via a short access road to a gate with a welcome sign in Spanish; a security guard is usually on duty. The long stretch of beach is beautiful and rarely crowded. There is good snorkeling at the north end, but be mindful of the currents and stay close to shore.

Toward the south end of the beach is a path into the jungle; a 5-minute walk leads to a cenote (freshwater sinkhole) where you can swim and snorkel. The small fish living in the sinkhole will nibble your toes.

Xcacel has long been a protected refuge and nesting site for endangered loggerhead and green turtles. From May through October, female turtles laboriously leave the sea at night to build nests on the beach and lay their eggs in the sand, but many turtle nesting sites are being destroyed by the tourism-related development.

**Note:** Park within sight of the security guard shack, do not leave valuables in your car and avoid disturbing the raised mounds of sand that indicate turtle nesting areas. There are restrooms at the entrance. Bring your own food, water and snorkel gear. **Hours:** Daily 6 a.m.-10 p.m., Nov.-Apr.; 9-6, rest of year (during turtle nesting season). **Cost:** Suggested day use fee donation about 20 pesos ($1.50 U.S.).

**XEL-HA** is about 16 km (10 mi.) n. of the town of Tulum via a well-marked turn-off on the e. side of Mex. 307 (Km marker 240). The centerpiece of this water park (pronounced shell-HAH) is a beautiful lagoon surrounded by jungle. A natural aquarium with a mix of salt and fresh water, it allows visitors to observe schools of brightly colored tropical fish that gather around the underwater rock formations. Snorkeling can be enjoyed without the undertows or strong currents that can make the beaches dangerous, and the clarity of the water is excellent. Snuba gear enables snorkelers to stay under water longer by breathing air through tubes that run to air tanks floating on the surface. Platforms built over the lagoon offer easy underwater viewing for landlubbers.

Another favorite activity at Xel-Ha is river floating. Visitors are taken to a drop-off point by a shuttle train and then float slowly along with the current toward the sea. Mo's Flight, a rope swing, and the Cliff of Courage both offer an exhilarating plunge into the lagoon waters. Xel-Ha also has an interactive dolphin swim program. Other activities include visiting a nursery/apiary where honey is harvested from stingless bees, hiking the Path of Conscience bordering the lagoon and

relaxing in the shade on appropriately named Hammock Island.

Xel-ha is a popular day trip from Cancún and is often combined with a stop at the Tulum ruins; contact a local travel agency for information. Dress casually and bring comfortable shoes. Life jackets are provided, and there is a first-aid station on site. An ATM accepts international credit cards.

To fully enjoy Xel-ha get there early; when the tour buses arrive it can become very crowded. All food services close at 5 p.m. **Hours:** Daily 9-6. **Cost:** (includes entry fee, use of showers, changing rooms and hammocks, life jacket, river float, river shuttle and a bag for transporting personal belongings, plus food and beverages) 1,175 pesos (about $89 U.S.); 587 pesos or about $44.50 U.S. (ages 5-11). Package tours from Cancún and Playa del Carmen can be arranged that include admission and round-trip transportation. Snorkeling gear and locker rentals are available; photo identification and a $25 (U.S.) deposit are required (refundable on return of gear). There are separate fees for Snuba snorkeling, the dolphin swim and other underwater activities. Make reservations in advance for the dolphin swim. **Phone:** (998) 884-7165, or (888) 922-7381 (toll-free from the United States). ⑪

© Helen Filatova / Shutterstock.com

This ends listings for The Caribbean Coast.
The following page resumes the alphabetical listings
of cities in Yucatán Peninsula.

## CHETUMAL, QUINTANA ROO (C-3)
pop. 134,412

One of the oldest cities on the Yucatán Peninsula, Chetumal (cheh-too-MAHL) was a former Mayan stronghold. Three centuries of back-and-forth battles—some viciously barbaric—were waged as the Spanish attempted to wrest control of the region from the Maya. The city was renamed Payo Obispo in 1898 and recast as a border town dealing in jungle hardwoods, arms and smuggled goods. These checkered but profitable dealings came to an abrupt end in 1955, when a hurricane all but flattened the city.

The capital of Quintana Roo is at once a thriving port and a steamy backwater. Rickety clapboard buildings huddle under tropical trees ablaze with blooms in the older part of town. Belize, with which Chetumal shares tourist and commercial traffic, is just across the river. Waterfront Boulevard Bahía is bordered by small plazas. The large, modern bus terminal is north of downtown near the intersection of avenidas Héroes and Insurgentes; first-class bus service to Cancún and Mérida is offered by ADO.

**Quintana Roo State Tourism Office (Secretaría de Turismo):** Av. del Centenario #622. **Phone:** (983) 835-0860, ext. 1809 or 1810.

**Shopping:** Stores line Avenida Héroes, which begins at the bay and runs west through the market area. An incongruous touch in this downtown shopping district are the numerous shops selling Dutch cheeses, Japanese stereo equipment, French perfume and other international products, all at duty-free prices. The chance to purchase such items draws crowds of Mexican and Belizean tourists. While it is possible to find good buys on Yucatecan hammocks, U.S. and Canadian visitors should save their pesos and purchase Mexican crafts elsewhere. Like most Mexican markets, Chetumal's enormous and lively central market, across the street from the Museum of Mayan Culture, is fun to wander through.

**MUSEUM OF MAYAN CULTURE** (Museo de la Cultura Maya) is downtown on Av. de los Héroes between calles Colón and Gandhi, 5 blks. e. of Av. Alvaro Obregón (across from the Holiday Inn). Occupying an entire city block, it presents an excellent historical account of all things Mayan from around 1,000 B.C. to the conquest of the Yucatán in 1590. Touch screens, interactive exhibits and displays of paintings, sculpture and stela provide a detailed understanding of Mayan astronomy, architecture, mathematics, art, music, politics and religion. The central courtyard features a re-creation of a typical Mayan village complete with thatch-roofed huts, mini altars and work areas.

Most (not all) of the stela and artifacts are reproductions. There is a small museum bookstore near the ticket window that has books about the Maya in English. Exhibit information is in English and Spanish. The museum also is air conditioned, a rarity in this Third World border city. **Time:** Allow 2 hours minimum. **Hours:** Tues.-Sun. 9-7. Phone ahead to confirm schedule. **Cost:** 66.50 pesos (about $4.90 U.S.). **Phone:** (983) 832-6838.

## ▼GEM CHICHEN ITZA, YUCATÁN (B-3)

The pyramids, temples and shrines at Chichén Itzá (chee-CHEHN eet-SAH)—the magnificent remains of a once-great Mayan city—were designated a World Heritage Site by UNESCO in 1988. It is believed that Chichén Itzá was founded sometime around A.D. 435; the first large-scale excavations of the site began around the turn of the 20th century. Of the several hundred buildings believed to have once stood, only about 30 are fully restored. A few more remain as they were found, and the rest are hidden under rough, underbrush-covered mounds in the thick jungle scrub of the north-central Yucatán Peninsula.

### Northern Zone

Chichén Itzá is remarkable for both monumental scope and architectural variety. The ruins consist of two complexes connected by a dirt path. Generally speaking, the older southern section contains mostly Mayan ruins and the structures in the northern section combine Mayan and Toltec influences, although the blending of pre-Hispanic cultures is apparent throughout. The militaristic Toltec influence is evident in the images—jaguars, sharp-taloned eagles, phalanxes of marching warriors, feathered serpents—employed to decorate the exteriors of pyramids and temples.

El Castillo dominates the other Northern Zone ruins sprinkled over a level, grassy area. That this pyramid's builders were mathematically precise in their construction is borne out by a natural phenomenon that occurs at the spring and fall equinoxes (on or around Mar. 21 and Sept. 21). As the sun begins its descent, the shadows cast by the terraces on the north staircase form the body of a serpent, whose actual sculpted head rests at the base of the stairs. In the spring, the serpent appears to be slithering down the stairs; in the fall, the illusion is reversed. **Note:** Visitors from around the world attend this semiannual event, and although it is well worth seeing, expect large and boisterous crowds.

El Castillo also is deceptively steep; the large stone steps ascend to the top at a 45-degree angle. Visitors have traditionally been able to climb the 100-foot-tall pyramid using the staircases on three of its sides, with most people climbing the steps on the western side (the side you see as you first enter the site). But because of erosion to the steps and a fatality that occurred in 2006, the base is roped off and climbing is not permitted on the pyramid or any other structure at the site.

Temples are at both ends of the ball court near El Castillo. The temple at the northern end has a short stairway ascending to two columns supporting a roof. It retains only a few remnants of its former murals and sculptures. The Temple of the Jaguars, at the southeastern corner of the ball court, has columns carved in the shape of serpents and panels depicting jaguars and Mayan warriors.

Just east of the ball court is the Temple of the Skulls (Tzompantli), decorated in macabre fashion

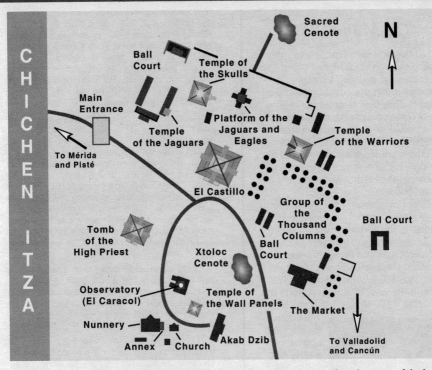

with rows of human skulls. This artistic rendering reflects the gruesome act of human sacrifice that was integral to Mayan religious rites, as the heads of victims were often stuck on the ends of poles. The adjacent Platform of the Eagles and Jaguars has carvings showing these creatures grasping human hearts. A short distance east of this structure and north of El Castillo is the Platform of Venus, which has depictions of a feathered serpent (a reference to the god Quetzalcóatl) holding a human head in its mouth. Serpent carvings ascend the stairways.

Just south of the Temple of the Warriors are the partially restored remains of what archeologists believe were steam baths and a market complex. Further to the southeast are unrestored mounds of rubble beneath the trees.

## Central Zone

The southern complex of ruins (often mistakenly referred to as Old Chichén), accessible from the northern complex via a short dirt pathway, consists of mostly Mayan ruins. The first structure you come to is the Ossuary (High Priest's Grave), thought to be a burial ground. This partially reconstructed pyramid is topped with the remains of a temple and has distinctive serpent head carvings at the base. Its interior (not open to the public) leads to an underground cave in which human skeletons and offerings have been found.

Across the path and south of this pyramid is El Caracol, an astronomical observatory dating from the 10th century that may have been one of the last Mayan buildings erected at this site.

East of El Caracol a winding path leads north through dense underbrush to the Cenote Xtoloc. Unlike the Sacred Cenote, this well was not used for human sacrifice; it provided Chichén with its drinking water. South of El Caracol is the Nunnery (Casa de Las Monjas), so named by the Spaniards because it reminded them of a European convent. This large complex has exquisitely carved facades of animals, flowers and designs that are reminiscent of latticework. Next to the Nunnery is The Church (La Iglesia), also named by the Spanish. While it in no way resembles a church, this small building is lavishly decorated, primarily with beak-nosed carvings of Chac.

The exterior carvings on the Temple of the Carved Panels (Templo de Los Tableros Esculpidos), east of the Nunnery, are more difficult to discern, but may refer to Toltec warrior symbology. A rough path, also beginning east of the Nunnery, runs through the scrub for several hundred feet to the Akab-Dzib, a classically designed Mayan temple believed to be one of Chichén Itzá's oldest structures. Traces of red handprints are faintly visible in some of the interior rooms, and above one doorway are carved Mayan hieroglyphics that have yet to be deciphered.

## General Information and Activities

Arrangements to join a group tour aboard a first-class bus can be made in Mérida, about 120 kilometers (75 miles) west, and Cancún, about 200 kilometers (125 miles) east. A group tour eliminates the

# The Maya World

At the same time Europe was stumbling through the Dark Ages, the Maya people were enjoying a creative flowering without precedent in the known world. They built temples and ceremonial centers that evoke wonder to this day; developed an astronomical calendar and predicted both solar and lunar eclipses; produced a highly refined hieroglyphic writing system; and were accomplished artists, historians and road builders.

Maya civilization spread as far south as northern Central America and as far north as the northern Yucatán Peninsula. Its history can be divided into Preclassic, Classic and Postclassic eras. The earliest Maya settlements date from around 1800 B.C.; one important Preclassic site was Dzibilchaltún, north of Mérida.

© Jo Ann Snover / Shutterstock.com

The Classic period, from approximately A.D. 300 to 900, represented the peak of independent Maya city-states. For unknown reasons—theories range from peasant revolt against the elite to crop failure caused by climate change to an epidemic of disease—major ceremonial centers such as Palenque in the state of Chiapas and Tikal in Guatemala declined by the early 10th century, as Mayan civilization shifted northward to the Yucatán Peninsula and such cities as Chichén Itzá and Uxmal.

hassle of driving but can make for a long, hectic day and requires sticking to a rigid schedule. Gray Line Cancún Tours offers a day trip package that includes round-trip transportation from Cancún or Mérida, guide service, park admission, a buffet lunch and a swim at a local cenote—a nice refresher after touring the hot, humid site. For reservations information phone (998) 887-2495 (in Mexico) or (800) 719-5465 (toll-free from the United States).

The ruins are a few miles south of the Chichén Itzá exit off Mex. 180-D; Yuc. 79 is the local road. One of the highway's two toll plazas is at this exit; from Cancún the tolls total 326 pesos (about $24 U.S.). You'll first pass through the small town of Pisté, on Mex. 180 about 2 kilometers (1.2 miles) west of the Chichén Itzá entrance. Here there are budget accommodations, restaurants and basic travel services for those who prefer to stay overnight. Taxi service also is available from Pisté to the site entrance. Several more upscale hotels are located east (and within walking distance) of the southern complex of ruins.

Chichén Itzá can be explored on your own or as part of a group led by a staff guide. A guide isn't necessary to appreciate the grandeur of the major landmarks, however, and information plaques in Spanish and English give a general architectural and historical background.

If you're visiting on your own, begin early in the morning if possible, before it gets too hot and the tour buses begin arriving. Wear a hat or other headgear and sturdy walking shoes. Bring bottled water and/or snacks as well as insect repellent for any extended walking excursions. Two to three hours is enough to see everything, although archeology buffs could easily spend the entire day.

A sound-and-light show is presented nightly. The ruins are bathed in colored lights, and Spanish narration recounts the history of and legends associated with the site. Headsets in several languages can be rented. Confirm the start time at the visitor center ticket window. There are occasional performances by big-name international musical stars as well.

The visitor center at the main entrance has an information desk (where admission tickets are purchased); a small museum; an air-conditioned auditorium, Chilam Balam, where an audiovisual presentation is shown; and a bookstore, restaurant and restrooms. There also are restrooms off the path between the northern and central zone complexes.

Food is available. Site open daily 8-5 (last admission at 4:30). Sound-and-light show begins at 7 or 8 p.m. (depending on season) and lasts about 45 minutes. Admission (includes museum) 216 pesos (about $16 U.S.). Sound-and-light show 193 pesos. Parking fee 30 pesos. Video camera fee 45 pesos. Phone (985) 851-0137.

**THE CASTLE** (El Castillo) is a short walk from the visitor center at the main entrance. Also called Kukulcán, the Mayan name for the Toltec king Quetzalcóatl, this 100-foot-tall pyramid has a perfectly symmetrical design. Each of the four sides is scaled by 91 steps; the total of 364 steps plus the top platform equaled the number of days in the Mayan year. El Castillo also is deceptively steep; the large stone steps ascend to the top at a 45-degree angle. Due to safety concerns, climbing El Castillo is not permitted.

An additional step underneath the pyramid, the 365th, signified a trip to the underworld. Each side also has 18 terraced sections—nine on either side of a central staircase, equaling the 18 months of the Mayan year—and 52 panels, corresponding to the number of years in the Mayan calendrical cycle.

Inside El Castillo is an older temple (not open to visitors) with a very narrow set of steps ascending to two claustrophobic inner chambers; one contains a reclining Chac Mool figure, the other a reddish throne in the shape of a jaguar with green jade eyes.

**GREAT BALL COURT** (Gran Juego de Pelota) is a short distance from the visitor center. Two walls run parallel to the playing field. The object of this ancient game was for two teams of players to maneuver a heavy rubber ball—without using their hands—through one of two stone rings placed high on each wall. Some participants (opinion is divided on whether they were winners or losers) apparently suffered death by decapitation. Stone carvings depict this act as well as players sporting protective padding and feathered headdresses. The acoustics are startling: Two people standing on opposite sides of the field and speaking in normal voices can easily hear each other.

**OLD CHICHÉN** (Chichén Viejo) is about a 15-minute walk down a dirt path that begins southwest of the Nunnery. A sincere interest in archeology and a local guide are both recommended for a trek to this area of little-restored buildings, which is mosquito-infested (wear plenty of insect repellent) and overgrown with jungle scrub. Avoid exploring during the June-through-September rainy season, when the narrow pathways can become difficult to navigate.

The barely uncovered buildings feature masks of Chac and gargoyle-like creatures carved along cornices. The Date Group of ruins includes the House of the Phalli, so named for some well-endowed sculptures carved into the walls of one room. The earliest date discovered in Chichén Itzá—the equivalent of A.D. 879—is carved into a lintel supported by columns; the rest of what was once a pyramid no longer remains.

**SACRED CENOTE** is about a 5-minute walk due n. of the Platform of Venus along a dirt path. This path was once a Mayan *sacbe*, or paved causeway. Two cenotes, or limestone sinkholes, served Chichén Itzá. The Sacred Cenote is a 190-foot-wide pit that was used for human sacrifice to appease the rain god Chac. The skeletons of men, women and children have been excavated, which suggests that in addition to young maidens—the preferred sacrificial victim—the diseased and mentally ill also may have been drowned in the well.

## The Maya World (continued)

The Postclassic period from the 10th to early 16th centuries saw the rise of such sites as Cobá, Edzná, Mayapán and Tulum. After being conquered by Spanish *conquistadores* in the 16th century the surviving Maya peoples retreated to the jungles of Quintana Roo, where fierce revolts continued until Mexico finally won its freedom in 1821. The fighting continued, however, and the Yucatán twice declared its own independence in the 19th century.

The buildings the Maya left behind are all the more notable when one considers they were constructed without benefit of draft animals, wheeled conveyances, metal tools or pulleys. The El Castillo pyramid at Chichén Itzá was designated one of the "new seven wonders of the world" in 2007. The buildings at Uxmal have an intricately detailed beauty. And while the ruins of Tulum pale in comparison architecturally, the location—on top of a cliff overlooking the turquoise waters of the Caribbean—is breathtaking.

Excavations of the cenote have unearthed bones, idols, jewelry, jade objects and other artifacts from different parts of Mexico, leading archeologists to believe that pilgrimages to Chichén Itzá continued long after its abandonment.

**THE SNAIL** (El Caracol) is in the southern group of ruins. Also called "The Winding Stair," its name is a reference to the interior winding staircase (not open to the public) that leads to the dome. This ruin's round construction is quite possibly unique in Mayan architecture. Stones could be removed from slits within the dome—nine in all—enabling Mayan astronomers to study different parts of the heavens. Some interesting carvings decorate the dome's exterior.

**TEMPLE OF THE WARRIORS** (Templo de los Guerreros) is a short distance e. of El Castillo. This Toltec-influenced temple has impressive rows of carved warriors and a roof boasting fine sculptural details of the rain god Chac, feathered serpents and mythical animals; it is guarded by a reclining Chac Mool figure. Next to the temple is the Group of the Thousand Columns, thought to have housed the residences of Chichén's ruling elite. The rows of Toltec-style pillars (in actuality, far fewer than 1,000) are covered with bas-relief. Climbing is not permitted.

## Nearby Destinations

**BALANCANCHÉ CAVES** (Grutas de Balancanché) are about 6 km (4 mi.) e. of the Chichén Itzá ruins via Mex. 180 (the free road to Valladolid), then down a very short gravel road to the entrance; follow signs. In 1959 a Chichén Itzá tour guide was exploring a network of caverns and discovered a secret passageway that led to a huge floor-to-ceiling stalagmite surrounded by Mayan ceremonial objects, offerings to the rain god Tlaloc. The artifacts are exhibited in the same locations in which they were found. There also is a small museum and a botanical garden at the site.

**Note:** The cave is hot and humid, with a dimly lit but well-maintained trail that includes many steep stairways; wear sturdy shoes. The tour is not recommended for those who are claustrophobic.

**Time:** Allow 1 hour minimum. **Hours:** Guided tours in English are offered daily at 11, 1 and 3 for groups of between six and 30 persons (make sure to double-check these tour times at the Chichén Itzá visitor center). Self-guiding tours are not permitted. **Cost:** 150 pesos (about $11 U.S.). Cash only. **Phone:** (999) 930-3760 (Merida Secretary of Tourism office; only Spanish is spoken).

## COBÁ, QUINTANA ROO (B-3)

Cobá (coh-BAH) translates roughly as "waters stirred by wind." This small village is about 66 kilometers (40 miles) northwest of Mex. 307; the Tulum/Cobá road branches off Mex. 307 just north of the town of Tulum. From Cancún, take Mex. 180 west to Xcan, then the paved road south about 43 kilometers (26 miles). The village is about a mile west of the road via a turn-off.

**COBÁ RUINS** are 43 km (27 mi.) n.w. of Tulum via the paved, well-marked road that branches off Mex. 307 just n. of Tulum and runs n. to Mex. 180 (near Valladolid); follow signs to the ruins entrance. Spreading east from the shore of a lagoon just outside the small town of the same name, this city/ceremonial center dates from between A.D. 600 to 900—older than both Chichén Itzá and the Tulum ruins—and at its height may have supported as many as 50,000 inhabitants.

Excavations began in earnest in the early 1970s. It is believed that as many as 6,500 structures exist. Temples, pyramids and elaborately carved stela (vertical stone tablets) are surrounded by palm tree thickets, tropical hardwoods and roping vines. Cobá has a much more primeval feel than other Yucatan ruins, increasing its sense of mystery.

Nohoch Mul ("large hill"), a 138-foot-high pyramid towering above the flat landscape (about a half-hour walk from the site entrance), is the tallest structure of its kind in the northern Yucatán—rising even higher than the Pyramid of the Magician at Uxmal. It can be climbed; hold onto the rope that runs up one side. The Cobá Group, a cluster of ruins on the right after you enter the site, contains another massive pyramid, the Temple of the Churches (Templo de las Iglesias). Climbing is permitted on the lower levels of many structures, but some sections are blocked off; heed the signs that prohibit climbing.

Bicycle taxi guides can be hired at the entrance, and bikes are available for rent. A bike is the best way to see these ruins; get here early enough and you'll practically have the place to yourself.

**Note:** If you're not part of an organized tour group, arrive as early as possible to avoid the hordes of tour buses that start showing up between 10 and 11 a.m. The heat, humidity and mosquitoes can be formidable; wear sturdy walking shoes and bring insect repellent and drinking water. **Time:** Allow 2 hours minimum. **Hours:** Daily 8-5. **Cost:** 64 pesos (about $4.75 U.S.). Guided tour fee 400 pesos (about $30 U.S.). Cash only. **Parking:** 40 pesos. GT ⑪

## COZUMEL, QUINTANA ROO—
*See The Caribbean Coast p. 86.*

## ISLA HOLBOX, QUINTANA ROO—
*See The Caribbean Coast p. 94.*

## ISLA MUJERES, QUINTANA ROO—
*See The Caribbean Coast p. 96.*

## IZAMAL, YUCATÁN (B-3) pop. 25,980

A significant pre-Columbian political and religious center, Izamal (ee-sah-MAHL) developed around a Franciscan monastery. Diego de Landa, the Spanish bishop responsible for the annihilation of most of the Mayan civilization's *codices* (picture books) and documents, deliberately chose Izamal as the seat of his diocese because it was a religious center of the Maya-speaking tribe known as the Itzae.

Izamal was a center of commerce and trade during the Spanish colonial period. But when Mérida took over as the Yucatán's chief city it slipped into obscurity. One recent momentous event in this slow-paced town was a 1993 visit by Pope John Paul II. The mustard-colored government buildings surrounding the central plaza give it the nickname "Ciudad Amarilla" (Yellow City). A relaxing way to view the colonial-era architecture is by horse-drawn carriage; rides can be arranged at the plaza, where the guides congregate.

Dilapidated houses and commercial buildings attest to the poverty that most Yucatecans endure. Downtown clusters around the small central plaza, shaded by trees and furnished with wrought-iron benches.

Izamal is about 74 kilometers (46 miles) east of Mérida via two-lane Mex. 180. From Mérida, watch for the signed turn-off that says "Yuc. 53"; if approaching from Cancún, the signed turn-off from toll highway Mex. 180-D says "Izamal" and also merges into Yuc. 53. The narrow, two-lane road, which has no shoulders and occasional potholes, passes through thick green scrubland interspersed with fields of spiky, blue-green agave plants.

Between the 180-D turn-off and Izamal—a distance of about 18 kilometers (11 miles)—are three small villages: Xanaba, Sudzal and Cuauhtémoc. Cobbled *topes* (speed bumps) force vehicles to slow to a crawl when entering each one, as do the wandering dogs, chickens, turkeys and children. Xanaba has a large yellow church with white trim opposite its small central plaza. In Sudzal and Cuauhtémoc you'll see typical Mayan houses—thatch-roofed huts with open doorways, dirt floors and walls constructed of upright wooden stakes—surrounded by banana trees and other tropical vegetation. This is rural life at its most basic, a world away from Cancún's glitter and Mérida's big-city bustle.

From Izamal, there are two ways to return to Mex. 180: Backtrack on Yuc. 53, or take another local road to the small town of Hoctún (which is on Mex. 180). The latter route passes through Citilcum and Kimbila en route; all three villages are representative of the rural Yucatán countryside. Make certain you're back on Mex. 180 before dark.

Because of the slow-paced driving conditions and the fact that it's easy to lose your orientation in Izamal—small as it is—this trip is most conveniently taken with a hired taxi driver or guide from Mérida. Check with one of the city's tour operators or arrange for a driver through your hotel.

**FRANCISCAN MONASTERY** dominates the main plaza. It was originally dedicated to St. Anthony of Padua and was later known as the Church of Our Lady of Izamal. It was completed in 1561 atop a Mayan pyramid. In 1618, monks added the monastery and an arcade. The atrium of this enormous church is reputed to be second in size to that of St. Peter's Basilica in Rome. The church's simple, mustard-colored exterior contrasts with the rough-hewn, fortress-like monastery compound; the original access ramps and stairways built by the Maya remain.

**KINICH KAKMO PYRAMID** (Pirámide Kinich Kakmo) is about 4 blocks n. of the plaza. In the Mayan language, its name means "Solar-Faced Macaw of Fire." Kinich Kakmo is one of Mexico's largest pyramids—some 115 feet high and almost 660 feet wide. It sits in the middle of town; there are houses just across the street. One of the four sides remains unexcavated and is covered with a thick green matting of tangled underbrush. **Hours:** Daily 8-5. **Cost:** Free.

## MAJAHUAL, QUINTANA ROO—
*See The Caribbean Coast p. 99.*

## MÉRIDA, YUCATÁN (B-2) pop. 830,732

Capital of the state of Yucatán and metropolis of the Yucatán Peninsula, Mérida (MEH-ree-dah) is an intriguing mix of modern and timeless, presenting visitors with sights that are both comfortingly familiar and exotically foreign.

Founded in 1542 by Francisco de Montejo at the site of T'ho, an ancient Mayan city, Mérida became the commercial, governmental and religious center of the Yucatán. The city became wealthy in the last half of the 19th century thanks to henequén, a tough, thorny member of the agave family. The fibrous leaves of this plant, which thrives in the rocky soil and seasonally dry conditions prevalent in the northern Yucatán, were made into twine, burlap sacks, furniture stuffing, hammocks and other products. In the late 19th-century heyday of the large haciendas (plantations), field workers manipulated this intractable plant by hand.

Plantation barons were an island unto themselves, since the Yucatán Peninsula still lacked road and rail access and remained isolated from the rest of Mexico. Privileged Meridanos looked to Europe as their model for cultural sophistication, building imposing, Moorish- and rococo-style mansions with arched doorways and marbled tile interiors. These buildings still line Paseo Montejo, Mérida's wide showcase boulevard, and give the city its air of graceful elegance.

Mérida's tropical ambience and variety of cultural offerings make it an appealing destination for travelers. The city also is a convenient base from which to explore nearby, notable Mayan ruins.

### Planning Your Stay

There are plenty of things to do here, like visiting the museums and public buildings that cluster around the main square, Plaza de la Independencia (also called Plaza Grande), wandering through the bustling market district, taking a horse-drawn carriage ride down Paseo Montejo and sampling authentic Yucatecan cuisine at local restaurants.

For *Mérida en Domingo* (Mérida on Sunday), the streets surrounding the plaza are closed to traffic. Mexican families dressed in their Sunday best make for a great people-watching promenade as they stroll among the pushcart vendors selling *tortas* (sandwiches), fruit drinks, corn on the cob, fried cornmeal balls and little cups of sliced mango dusted with chile powder.

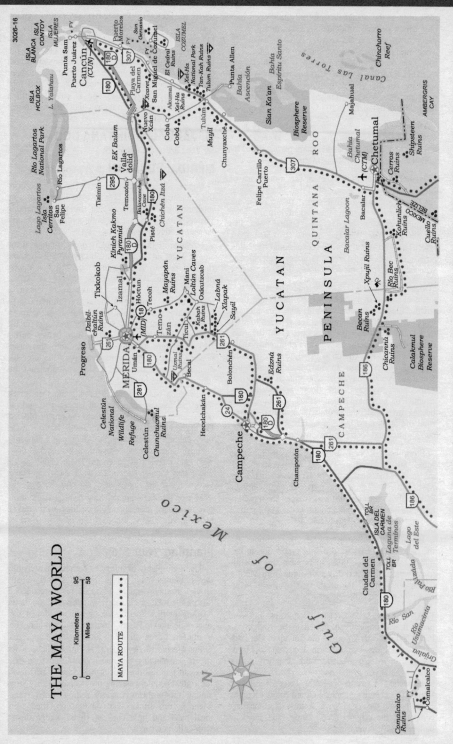

THE MAYA WORLD

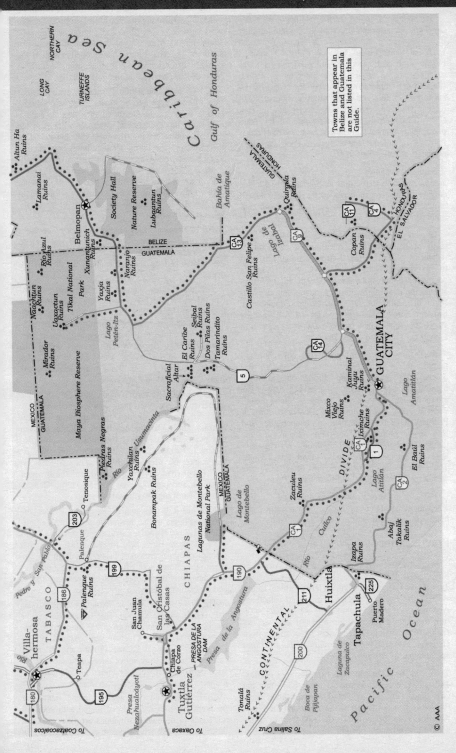

Towns that appear in Belize and Guatemala are not listed in this Guide.

Sunday also is one of the high points of Mérida's excellent public events program. In the late morning the city police orchestra performs typical Yucatecan music in Santa Lucía Park, on Calle 60 about 3 blocks north of Plaza de la Independencia. Groups of musicians in front of the Government Palace (Palacio del Gobierno) play everything from classical to jazz. A folkloric ballet interpretation of a Yucatecan wedding celebration is enacted at City Hall (Palacio Municipal), on the west side of the main plaza, while marimba music can be heard at Hidalgo Park (also called Cepeda Peraza Park), a block northeast at calles 59 and 60.

Saturday evenings also are active; the downtown area is closed to traffic, and restaurants move tables outside so diners can listen to the bands scattered around the plazas. The music starts at 8:30 and continues until around 2 a.m.

Guided tour operators abound in Mérida, and many of them offer the same itineraries with differing forms of transportation (from economical buses to luxurious private vehicles). City tours last a couple of hours and take in the public buildings around the main plaza, Paseo Montejo, and the Museum of Anthropology and History. Popular day trips travel to Chichén Itzá or Uxmal, with admission to the ruins, lunch, a guide and often a swim at a hotel pool included in the price.

April through September can get quite hot and humid, and in May temperatures soar toward 100 degrees. If you're visiting during one of these months, sightsee in the morning, take it easy in the afternoon and venture out again in the evening, when it cools down somewhat. December through February have the most pleasant temperatures and also lower humidity. The rainy season is June through September, but precipitation isn't usually heavy or persistent enough to affect travel plans. The greatest chance for hurricanes or other stormy weather is in September and October.

The city is very crowded in July and August, when many Mexican families go on vacation; make hotel reservations in advance for these months.

## Practicalities

Manuel Crecencio Rejon International Airport is off Avenida Benito Juárez, also called Avenida Itzaes (Mex. 180), about 7 kilometers (4 miles) southwest of the city center. The Aeroméxico subsidiary Aeroméxico Connect, phone 01 (800) 021-4000 (toll-free long distance within Mexico), offers direct flights from Miami. United offers direct flights from Houston. *For additional information about airlines see Arriving by Air, page p. 42.*

By car, the main approach from the east is Mex. 180, which becomes east-west Calle 65 within the city limits. To get to the downtown hotel zone (where such major hotels as the Hyatt and the Fiesta Americana are located), take Calle 65 west to north-south Calle 60 and turn right.

Mex. 180 also approaches Mérida from the southwest via Campeche. Mex. 261 approaches from the south, joining Mex. 180 at the town of Umán, just south of the city limits. North of downtown, the northern extension of Calle 60 continues north as Mex. 261 to Progreso on the gulf coast.

A loop road, the Anillo Periférico, encircles Mérida, offering access to regional destinations without having to negotiate the downtown area. It can be confusing, however, unless you're familiar with the exits. If you're driving, the most direct way out of the city from the Paseo Montejo/hotel zone area is to take east-west Avenida Colón west to Avenida Itzaes, a major north-south thoroughfare on the west side of town. Turn left (south); you'll pass Centenario Park and the turn-off to the airport before reaching the Anillo Periférico—a distance of about 12 kilometers (7 miles).

**Note:** Avenida Itzaes changes names twice without warning—to Avenida Internacional and then to Avenida Benito Juárez—as it proceeds south. Don't get sidetracked by the name changes; stay on the avenue.

At the periférico junction there are signs for Cancún (Mex. 180 east), Progreso (Mex. 261 north) and Campeche (Mex. 180 southwest). To head south toward Uxmal and nearby archeological sites, continue south a mile or two on Avenida Itzaes/Internacional/Juárez to Umán. Watch for signs saying "To Campeche via Uxmal on Mex. 261," "Zona Arqueologica Uxmal" and "Ruta Puuc." Follow these signs to access Mex. 261 south.

To head east toward Cancún, turn left onto the periférico at the sign that says "Cancún/Motul." Take this four-lane divided highway about 15 kilometers (9 miles) to the Mex. 180/Cancún exit. From this point, two-lane Mex. 180 runs about 48 kilometers (30 miles) east to the town of Hoctún. At Km marker 66, Mex. 180 divides. The two-lane "libre" (free) road continues east toward the town of Kantunil, and the four-lane divided Mérida-Cancún "cuota" (toll) highway begins.

City bus #79 (designated "Aviación") takes airport passengers to the downtown area but is unreliable and slow; if you're carrying any amount of luggage it's more convenient to take a taxi. *Colectivo* (group) minivans transport passengers from the airport to downtown hotels for about $8 (U.S.) per person; taxi fare runs about $18 between the airport and downtown hotels.

The first-class bus station, Terminal CAME (CAHme), is on Calle 70 between calles 69 and 71, about 7 blocks southwest of the main plaza. Buses travel frequently to and from Chichén Itzá, Uxmal, Cancún, Campeche, Playa del Carmen, Tulum and Palenque. "Deluxe" service to many of these destinations is offered by ADO's GL and UNO lines. *For additional information about buses see Bus Service, page p. 52.*

*Sitios* (taxi stands) are located in the vicinity of the main plaza, or use a cab affiliated with your hotel. Rates to in-town destinations are fixed and can be expensive; ask what the fare is before getting in the cab. *Colectivo* taxis (usually white Volkswagen minivans) also take passengers to various city destinations on a first-come, first-serve basis; look for these around the main plaza.

Mérida has a tourist police force that patrols on foot and motorcycle in the downtown core and also in the hotel zone, the area along Avenida Colón between Paseo Montejo and Calle 60. Officers wear white-and-brown or blue uniforms and a sleeve patch that says "Policia Turística." To contact police in case of an emergency, phone (999) 925-2034.

To register a complaint with the Consumer Protection Agency (Procuraduría del Consumidor), phone (999) 923-2323. If you lose your tourist permit, contact the Mexican Immigration Office; phone (999) 928-5823. In case of medical emergency, contact the Red Cross (Cruz Roja); phone (999) 924-9813.

The rates offered at the airport and by banks and *casas de cambio* (currency exchange houses) do not differ greatly, so exchanging dollars for pesos comes down to a matter of convenience. There are several *casas de cambio* in the vicinity of the big downtown hotels.

The Mérida English Library, Calle 53 #524 (between calles 66 and 68), functions as a meeting place for the English-speaking community throughout the city. The library offers English-language books and Internet access as well as community information, and also sponsors guided house and garden tours on Tuesdays from November through April; tour fee is 200 pesos (about $14.80 U.S.) per person. It is open Mon.-Fri. 9-1 (also Mon. 6:30-9 p.m. and Thurs. 4-7), Sat. 10-1; phone (999) 924-8401.

## City Layout

El Centro, Mérida's downtown core, is compact and dense. A standard grid pattern of streets radiates out from the central plaza and are numbered rather than named. Even-numbered streets (calles) run north-south, odd-numbered streets run east-west. All are lined with many beautiful old buildings, and many more shabby ones. Most of these streets also are narrow and one way. Vespa motor scooters and beat-up bikes abound, and traffic is heavy and slow. Elsewhere in the city thoroughfares are not well signed and change names without warning. They also can twist and turn confusingly, so know where you're going.

Where buildings stand close together and sidewalks are very narrow, exhaust spewed by green city buses is a near-constant irritant. This area is roughly bounded by Calle 49 on the north, Calle 67 on the south, Calle 52 on the east and Calle 66 on the west.

Fortunately Mérida also is a city of tree-filled plazas that are oases of relative tranquility amid the street noise and traffic jams. Plaza de la Independencia is bounded east and west by calles 60 and 62 and north and south by calles 61 and 63. Here and at other city plazas you'll see *confidenciales*, S-shaped white stone benches that allow two people to face each other while

talking. The cathedral and the aristocratic facades of government buildings border the plaza.

A good way to experience the local atmosphere is to stroll up and down Calle 60, a busy street filled with restaurants, handicraft shops selling clothing, jewelry and trinkets, and several fine examples of colonial architecture. From the northeast corner of Plaza de la Independencia, walk north. In the next block is cozy little Hidalgo Park, where there are several outdoor restaurants. At the corner of calles 60 and 57 is the imposing, Italianate Peón Contreras Theater (Teatro Peón Contreras); climb the marble steps and wander around inside.

Mérida's "show street" is four-lane Paseo Montejo, which begins at Calle 47, about 7 blocks northeast of the main plaza. Broad and tree-lined, it also has much wider sidewalks than you'll encounter in other parts of the city, a relief from the cramped spaces of the *centro*. Montejo runs north for 10 blocks past hotels, shops, sidewalk cafés and several large, ornate 19th-century mansions. It culminates at the Monument to Patriotism (Monumento a la Patria), a grouping of sculptures within a traffic circle that depict various stages of Mexican history.

Along Paseo Montejo is the Mérida Sculpture Walk, a collection of changing outdoor art. It begins with the large sculpture in the traffic circle at Montejo and Calle 47; from there walk south along Montejo to the corner of Avenida Colón, near the U.S. Embassy. The final sculpture is the beautifully carved trunk of a tree that was killed by Hurricane Isidore in 2002.

For a peek inside one of the street's impressive residences, take a guided tour of Quinta Montes Molina, Paseo de Montejo #469 (at Calle 56). Still owned by the same family, the mansion now functions as a location for wedding receptions and "sweet 16" parties. The lavish rooms are filled with European furniture, alabaster and porcelain sculptures, sumptuous crystal chandeliers and Art Deco

## DID YOU KNOW

Mexico is divided into 31 states. The largest, Chihuahua, is slightly smaller than Oregon; the smallest, Tlaxcala, is slightly larger than Rhode Island.

decorative accents. One-hour tours in English are given Mon.-Fri. at 9, 11 and 3, Sat. at 9 and 11; the fee is 50 pesos (about $3.70 U.S.). Other times are available by appointment; phone (999) 925-5999.

Sunday is the best day to take a ride on a *calesa* (horse-drawn carriage). Most of them can be found in the vicinity of Plaza de la Independencia or along Calle 60, and they have designated routes. A 45-minute ride should cost about $20 (U.S.); determine the fare before you set out.

## Shopping

Mérida is particularly known for hammocks *(hamacas)*, clothing (especially the men's shirt called a *guayabera),* Panama hats *(jipis)* and henequén handicrafts. The market district extends roughly from calles 63 to 69 north-south and from calles 54 to 62 east-west (the area just southeast of Plaza de la Independencia) and encompasses hundreds of shops and open-air stalls.

The Municipal Market (Mercado Municipal), centered at calles 65 and 56, is a hodgepodge of fruit, vegetables, live chickens, tortilla stands, spices and candy, all presided over by *huipil*-clad *señoras* who bring their wares from the small Mayan villages around Mérida. Here you'll find baskets, pottery, gold earrings, gold and silver filigree jewelry, and pieces of amber-colored incense.

Native handicrafts from all over Mexico, but particularly the Yucatán region, are in a separate building at calles 56 and 67. Look for table mats, purses, leather goods, hammocks, piñatas, clothing, ceramics and *huaraches* (sandals with leather straps and soles made from old tires).

Fixed prices prevail at many shops, but you can bargain at some of the market stalls and with street vendors. Haggling in this crowded, noisy atmosphere is not for everyone. Although many vendors speak English, a knowledge of Spanish would be very handy for asking specific questions about merchandise. If you're uncomfortable around high-pressure sales tactics, stick to the fixed-price shops.

Hammocks—often used in the rural Yucatán in place of beds—are fashioned from various materials and come in several sizes. To judge the proper size, hold one end of the hammock even with the top of your head. Let the other end drop—if it reaches the floor and then some, it's probably big enough. Those made from cotton tend to be the most durable.

Street vendors will harangue prospective hammock purchasers, but their low prices may also indicate low quality. Shops specializing in hammocks offer a greater selection. Wherever you buy a hammock, check the workmanship carefully, since a poorly made or loosely woven one will wear out quickly.

The *guayabera,* a loose, lightweight cotton shirt, is about as formal as men's clothing gets in sweltering Mérida. Upper-class Yucatecans in the late 19th century bought them during trips to Cuba. The garment is worn by businessmen and local politicians instead of a shirt and tie. Traditionally it is white, with a bit of colored embroidery around the front buttons, and has four pockets—two at the chest and two at the waist. Guayaberas Jack, on Calle 59, is one of the few city factories that still produces custom-made shirts.

Just as traditional as the *guayabera* is the *huipil,* a white cotton dress with a squared neck that often is edged with embroidered flowers. A similar but longer and more elaborate garment is the *terno.* Many women who live in rural areas still wear these garments. Handmade dresses have largely been supplanted by machine-made ones, although the latter are usually of good quality.

A jauntily positioned *jipi* (HEE-pee) provides an effective screen against the hot Yucatán sun. The hats are made in several small towns in neighboring Campeche; residents store palm fronds in damp basements until they become soft and pliable, then weave them. Panama hats cost anywhere from about $6 to more than $60 (U.S.); the price is determined by the closeness of the weave and the quality of the fibers (coarse to fine). A good-quality, closely woven hat should bounce back into shape even after being folded into a suitcase or rolled up and stuck in a pocket.

Mexican markets are known for their exotica, and Mérida is no exception; here you can buy live "jeweled" beetle pins called *maquech* (ma-KETCH). The insects are displayed in glass bowls along with a few pieces of wood (their food). Bits of multicolored glass are glued to their backs, and the beetle is attached to a gold chain which hooks to a safety pin. If you purchase a live lapel ornament, find another buyer before you leave the country; U.S. Customs and Border Protection officials won't allow it across the border.

## Dining and Nightlife

This is a great place to sample some of the Yucatán's culinary specialties. *Papadzules* are tortillas stuffed with chopped hard-boiled eggs and topped with pumpkinseed or tomato sauce. *Poc-chuc* is slices of pork marinated in sour orange juice and served with pickled onions; *pollo pibil* is herb-infused chicken wrapped in banana leaves and baked.

*Sopa de lima* is a soup containing shredded chicken and strips of fried tortilla and flavored with lime juice. *Salbutes* are puffy fried tortillas topped with shredded turkey, lettuce and pickled onions. The incendiary habanero chile is provided on the side rather than in the dish at most establishments (ask to make doubly sure).

Beverages are intriguing as well. While *licuados*—liquified fruit drinks—are sold in many parts of Mexico, they are especially refreshing in Mérida, where the vendors can draw from a variety of melons, pineapple and other tropical flavors. *Licuado* stands are marked by rows of colorful fruit. Another common beverage is *horchata,* a blend of ground rice and almonds, water and ice, sweetened with raw sugar, cinnamon, vanilla or honey. See the

Lodgings & Restaurants section for AAA-RATED dining establishments.

Mérida is a fairly safe city to walk around in after dark. At dusk, Plaza de la Independencia and adjoining Hidalgo Park are alive with families watching street performers, listening to musicians, grabbing a bite to eat or just relaxing on benches. Sidewalk vendors set up along nearby streets, selling everything from *tortas* to heavy metal CDs.

There is free evening entertainment at downtown parks and plazas several nights a week. On Monday beginning at 9 p.m. a folkloric dance troupe performs *vaquerías* (traditional Yucatecan dances) in front of City Hall (Palacio Municipal), on Calle 62 across from Plaza de la Independencia. For event schedule information, check at the Peón Contreras Theater or one of the city tourist offices.

**Yucatán State Tourism Office:** in the Peón Contreras Theater, on Calle 60 between calles 57 and 59. The office is open daily 8 a.m.-9 p.m. **Phone:** (999) 924-9290 (English spoken).

The publication *Yucatán Today*, available at the airport and most hotels, has detailed information about city and state attractions and includes maps.

## Downtown

**CATHEDRAL** (Catedral) is on the e. side of Plaza de la Independencia, opposite the Government Palace. Much of the stone used in its construction came from the ruined buildings of T'hó, the ancient Mayan city upon which Mérida was built. The interior is stark, in marked contrast to the lavish decoration of other Mexican colonial churches. One painting, hanging over a side door to the right of the main altar, depicts a meeting between the Spanish and the Xiu Indians.

To the left is a chapel containing a replica of the Christ of the Blisters (Cristo de las Ampollas), an image of Christ carved from a tree that was said to be struck by lightning but did not burn; it survived a fire in another church and was brought to the cathedral in 1645. **Hours:** Daily 6 a.m.-noon and 4-7. **Cost:** Free.

**CITY HALL** (Palacio Municipal) is on Calle 62 on the w. side of Plaza de la Independencia. More commonly known as the Ayuntamiento, it was built atop a Mayan pyramid. The exterior, yellow with white trim, shows a Moorish influence, and the clock tower is typical of Mexican government buildings. Adjoining it is the Olimpo, a cultural center with space for concerts and art exhibitions; schedules for upcoming performances are posted on the bulletin board in the pretty courtyard.

**CITY MUSEUM** (Museo de la Ciudad) is at calles 61 and 58 across the street from Plaza de la Independencia. It has paintings, photographs and drawings illustrating Mérida's history, with exhibit information in English. **Hours:** Tues.-Fri. 9-6, Sat.-Sun. 9-2. **Cost:** Free. **Phone:** (999) 923-6869.

**GOVERNMENT PALACE** (Palacio de Gobierno) is on the n. side of Plaza de la Independencia. It dates from 1892. Take the wide stairway to the second floor, where the walls of one room are adorned with murals by Meridano artist Fernando Castro Pacheco depicting traditional Mayan symbols as well as the violent appropriation of their culture by the Spanish. A hall of history, also on the second floor, chronicles the destruction by Spanish bishop Diego de Landa of the Mayan *codices*, pictorial history books. **Hours:** Daily 8 a.m.-9 p.m. **Cost:** Free.

**MACAY MUSEUM** (Museo de Arte Contemporáneo Ateneo de Yucatán) is on Calle 60 next to the cathedral. It exhibits the work of Yucatecan artists in two floors of rooms built around an interior patio. There are paintings by Fernando Castro Pacheco, who created the murals in the Government Palace. The museum also presents temporary exhibits of art from other parts of Mexico. The Revolution Passage (Pasaje de la Revolución), a pedestrian walkway connecting the museum and the cathedral, is an outdoor exhibit space for various sculptures.

**Hours:** Wed.-Mon. 10-6. **Cost:** Free. **Phone:** (999) 928-3258.

**MONTEJO HOUSE** (Casa de Montejo) is on Calle 63 (s. side of Plaza de la Independencia). It was built in 1549 by the son of Francisco de Montejo, the Yucatán conqueror. Montejo the Younger employed Indian labor to create the richly ornamented facade and doors, fine examples of Plateresque decoration. A reminder of Spanish cruelty are the carvings of *conquistadores* with feet firmly planted on top of wailing Mayan heads. This restored family home now houses a Banamex Bank branch with a huge, lushly landscaped patio. There's also a small museum. **Hours:** Bank business hours Mon.-Fri. 9-4, Sat. 9-2. Museum Tues.-Sat. 10-7, Sun. 10-2. **Cost:** Free.

**NATIONAL MUSEUM OF POPULAR ART** (Museo Nacional de Arte Popular) is 5 blks. e. of the main plaza at Calle 50-A #487 (across from Parque de la Mejorada). It is housed in the handsomely restored Casa Molina, a mansion built in 1900 for Carmela Molina as a wedding gift from her father, a wealthy sisal tycoon and local politician. The collection of Yucatecan and Mexican handicrafts includes ceramics, textiles and wood and stone carvings. A highlight is El Cuarto de Nacimientos, a room devoted to beautifully detailed Nativity scenes.

**Time:** Allow 1 hour minimum. **Hours:** Tues.-Sat. 10-5, Sun. 10-3. Closed major holidays. **Cost:** Free. **Phone:** (999) 928-5263.

**PEÓN CONTRERAS THEATER** (Teatro Peón Contreras) is on Calle 60 between calles 57 and 59, just n. of Cepeda Peraza Park (Hidalgo Park). It was built in the early 20th century in the grand Italianate style of European opera houses. The main entrance features a staircase of Carrara marble, and the interior is typically and richly ornate. Changing exhibitions feature the work of contemporary painters, sculptors and photographers from all over Mexico. This venue for the performing arts also houses a tourist information center that is a good place to find out what's going on around town.

## In and Around the City

**ANTHROPOLOGY MUSEUM** (Museo Regional de Antropología) is on Paseo Montejo at Calle 43. It is housed in the Palacio Cantón, the former home of Mérida's prominent Cantón family. The museum has an extensive collection of stone carvings, figurines and relics, including jade and gold objects retrieved from the Sacred Cenote at Chichén Itzá. Particularly interesting are the sections devoted to daily Mayan life, showing how babies' heads were elongated and how teeth were filed to achieve their rather bizarre standards of beauty.

Exhibit information is mostly in Spanish. **Hours:** Tues.-Sun. 8-5. **Cost:** 52 pesos (about $3.85 U.S.); free (ages 0-12). **Phone:** (999) 923-0557.

**CENTENARIO PARK AND ZOO** is about 12 blks. w. of Plaza de la Independencia, running along Av. Itzaes between calles 59 and 65. Handsome, colonial-style yellow stone archways flank the park entrance. It is large, shady and particularly fun for children. The zoo displays a variety of animals and birds, from peacocks and flamingos to alligators, lions and jaguars, as well as species native to the Yucatán Peninsula. A miniature train offers rides through the park. **Hours:** Park open Tues.-Sun. 6-6, zoo Tues.-Sun. 8-5. **Cost:** Free. A small fee is charged for the train ride. **Phone:** (999) 928-5815.

**DZIBILCHALTÚN RUINS** (zeeb-eel-chal-TOON) are about 15 km (9 mi.) n. of Mérida; take Calle 60 n. out of the city, following signs for Progreso and Mex. 261. The paved turn-off is marked by a sign that says "Dzibilchaltún/Universidad del Mayab." The site entrance is another 5 km (3 mi.) e. Although this is one of Mexico's largest archeological discoveries, not much remains of its former glory. More than 8,000 ruins, mostly mounds of rubble or the remains of low platforms, have been uncovered so far. The cluster of excavated altars and other structures are aligned along a walkway.

The reconstructed House of the Seven Dolls (Templo de las Siete Muñecas), a raised temple, was named for the seven primitive figures discovered buried under the structure's floor. Exhibiting such deformities as a hunchback and a swollen belly, they may have served as spiritual "messengers" during ceremonies to cure illness. There is a good site museum that exhibits carved stone tablets and stela, panels and finely detailed limestone carvings (including a life-size gorilla carrying a human); paintings and Yucatán artifacts from the Spanish colonial period; weapons associated with the 19th-century War of the Castes; and machines used to harvest henequén.

Public transportation to the site is readily available via taxi or shuttle van; *colectivo* vans departing from San Juan Park in downtown Mérida (Calle 69 between calles 62 and 64) go directly to the ruins. **Time:** Allow 2 hours minimum. **Hours:** Site daily 8-5. Museum daily 9-4. **Cost:** 172 pesos (about $12.75 U.S.). **Parking:** 10 pesos. **Phone:** (999) 922-0193. GT ⑪

**HERMITAGE OF SANTA ISABEL** (La Hermita de Santa Isabel) is s. of Plaza de la Independencia at calles 66 and 77. It was built in 1748. In colonial days it became known as the Convent of Safe Travel, since travelers on their way to the busy port of Campeche would stop to pray for a safe journey. The restored hermitage is surrounded by a serene, pretty garden accented with Mayan and Toltec statues and a waterfall.

**MAYAPÁN RUINS** are about 64 km (40 mi.) s.e. of Mérida. To get there from downtown, take Calle 59 e. to the Anillo Periférico (the loop road around the city). Take the Anillo Periférico s. to the exit for Mex. 18. Continue s. on Mex. 18, a two-lane blacktop, past the villages of Kanasin, Acanceh, Tecoh and Telchaquillo; a short distance past Telchaquillo watch for the prominent sign (on the right) directing you to the ruins entrance. From Cancún or Chichén Itzá, take Mex. 180-D w. to the Ticopo exit and follow signs to Mex. 18; continue s. on Mex. 18 past Acanceh, Tecoh and Telchaquillo.

This walled city flourished after the heyday of Chichén Itzá and Uxmal; it was reduced to rubble in the 16th century by Spanish conqueror Francisco de Montejo's forces. The site is impressively large, with eight buildings more than 30 feet tall and another two dozen smaller ruins and platforms. The structural similarities with Chichén Itzá are evident: high, sloping walls with steep steps built into the sides.

Most of the pyramidal structures can be climbed, although the very narrow steps make it difficult to do so. The remote location and slow pace of ongoing restoration work means there are few visitors, and those fascinated by ruins will have these crumbling temple platforms and weathered sculptures basically to themselves.

**Time:** Allow 2 hours minimum. **Hours:** Daily 8-5. **Cost:** 39 pesos (about $2.90 U.S.). The fee to use a video camera is about $5 (U.S.). **Parking:** 10 pesos. **Phone:** (999) 942-1900.

**MUSEUM OF THE MAYAN WORLD** (Gran Museo del Mundo Maya) is about 12 km (7 mi.) n. of downtown at Calle 60 #299, at the e. end of the Siglo XXI Convention Center. Four permanent exhibition halls in this daringly contemporary museum showcase a collection of more than 500 Mayan artifacts, from textiles and religious relics to ancient stone sculptures and sumptuous gold and jade objects. Each hall focuses on a different theme: The Mayans, Nature and Culture; Mayans of Today; Yesterday's Mayans; and Ancient Mayans.

One of the galleries features rotating exhibits. A highlight is the spectacular, five-act sound-and-light show shown in the MAYAMAX Theater, which depicts the creation of the Mayan world. On Tuesdays, when the museum is closed, the show is projected on the outside wall at 9 p.m.

**Note:** The museum is north of downtown; if you don't have a car, the easiest way to get there is by bus. Yellow "Mini 2000" buses travel up and down Calle 60; look for one with the destinations Xcumpich, Tapetes or Komchen on the windshield, and make sure you tell the driver to announce the museum stop. **Hours:** Wed.-Mon. 8-5. **Cost:** (includes MAYAMAX Theater show) 150 pesos (about $11 U.S.); 50 pesos (ages 0-11). Tues. evening show free. Cash only. **Phone:** (999) 341-0435. ⑪

## Nearby Destinations

Mérida makes a good base for day trip excursions to the small towns and villages in the state of Yucatán. Most of them have interesting churches and bustling markets, and it's a nice opportunity to get out of the city, see the countryside and mingle with the locals.

If you want to visit a typical Yucatecan *pueblo* located just outside the Mérida city limits, take Avenida Itzaes (Mex. 180) southbound past the airport to the Anillo Periférico loop road, then follow the directional signs for Umán. In the vicinity of the town's main plaza, which is dominated by a large church, are small shops and sidewalk vendors selling food and trinkets. *Triciclo* drivers line up waiting to transport locals. A *triciclo* is the reverse of a tricycle—two wheels in front supporting a cargo/carrier area, and one in the back below the driver's seat. People, live chickens and crates of produce are all transported by means of this cheap transportation.

Hacienda Yaxcopoil is about 32 kilometers (20 miles) south of Mérida. From downtown take Avenida Itzaes southbound to the Anillo Periférico. Access Mex. 180 (the road is signed "Libramiento Umán" but bypasses the town of Umán), continue south and exit at Mex. 261. Stay on Mex. 261, following the signs for Uxmal. The small village of Yaxcopoil (yawsh-koe-poe-EEL) is about 11 kilometers (7 miles) south of the exit; watch for the marked turn-off to the hacienda ("Antigua Hacienda y Museo Yaxcopoil"), distinguished by a Moorish double arch, on the right at Km marker 186.

# The Art of the Retablo

Churches and cathedrals in Mexico are renowned for their beauty both inside and out. Many of them positively brim with stone carvings, statues and extravagant ornamentation. And a particularly lovely feature in some churches is the display of *retablos,* or devotional paintings. Combining centuries-old Catholic iconography, traditional religious beliefs and indigenous artistry, the *retablo* is a distinctly Mexican example of popular folk art.

Vibrantly colorful and rife with symbolic overtones, these small oil paintings of Catholic saints were created on zinc, wood, copper and tin. *Retablos* were employed by Spanish priests as part of an effort to convert the Indians to Christianity after Spain's conquest of Mexico in the early 16th century. Tall,

 multi-paneled structures displaying an array of saints and other religious figures were typically erected behind a church's main altar; the word *retablo* means "behind the altar."

Small factories sprang up to mass produce *retablos* (also called *laminas* in Mexico). *Retableros,* artists who were both skilled and unskilled, made their living reproducing the images of many different saints, from venerated individuals like St. Francis of Assisi, founder of the Franciscan order, and biblical translator St. Jerome (San Jerónimo) to San Ysidro Labrador, the patron saint of farmers. Over a lifetime a *retablero* might end up creating the same image literally thousands of times. At the height of their popularity in the late 19th century *retablos*—in addition to being placed in churches and at shrines—were sold to devout believers who graced home altars with the likeness of their patron saint.

Operating first as a cattle ranch and later as a henequén plantation, this was once one of the most important haciendas in the Yucatán. Although now showing great age and some ruin, the Moorish-style architecture of Casa Principal, the main building, and its drawing rooms, high-ceilinged corridors and lush garden areas hint at the gracious lifestyle enjoyed by wealthy late 19th-century plantation owners.

The Maya Room in the main building has displays of pottery and artifacts excavated from nearby Mayan ruins. The property is safe to visit and interesting to explore. Hacienda tours are given Mon.-Sat. 8-6, Sun. 9-6. Admission 75 pesos (about $5.55 U.S.). Phone (999) 900-1193 (cellular number).

## The Convent Route

The Convent Route (Ruta de Los Conventos) south from Mérida via Mex. 18 passes through a string of rural towns and villages. From the downtown historic center, take Calle 59 east to the Anillo Periférico loop road, then take the Anillo Periférico south to the exit for Mex. 18 (signed "Kanasin"). Two-lane Mex. 18 heads south, passing through small Yucatecan communities distinguished by their impressively large churches.

About 22 kilometers (14 miles) south of Kanasin is the town of Acanceh (ah-con-KAY). A Mayan pyramid, a colonial-era church and a present-day church all stand on the town plaza. About 8 kilometers (5 miles) beyond Acanceh is Tecoh (tay-KO), where the town market is dwarfed by a large church and convent dedicated to the Virgin of the Assumption. The church is built atop the raised platform that was once the foundation for a Mayan pyramid and is reached by a broad stone stairway.

This 16th-century building has a rough stone exterior capped by twin towers similar in appearance to the cathedral in Mérida. Inside is a soaring, beautifully ornamented *retablo* that was restored in the late 1990s. It features four large paintings that are the work of Mexico's famed baroque artist Miguel Cabrera. In addition to the main altarpiece, the church also is graced with two smaller *retablos* dedicated to the Virgin Mary, both resplendent with gold decoration in the extravagant Mexican Churrigueresque style.

Several miles south of Tecoh is the small village of Telchaquillo (tel-chah-KEY-yoh). On the plaza stands a small, plain-looking chapel, and nearby is a cenote (limestone sinkhole) with stone stairs leading down into the water. A short distance south of Telchaquillo is the turn-off (on the right) for the Mayapán Ruins.

About 18 kilometers (11 miles) south of Telchaquillo is a larger village, Tekit (teh-KIT). Tekit's parish church of San Antonio de Padua has a simple altar and elaborately decorated statues of saints. About 7 kilometers (4 miles) south of Tekit is Mamá, another small village dominated by a large church and convent built in the 17th century. The exterior is crowned by lovely decorative stonework; inside are wall frescoes, baroque *retablos,* recessed wall niches holding statues of saints and a spectacularly ornate altar.

About 13 kilometers (8 miles) south of Mamá is Teabo (tay-AH-bow), which like other towns in this region is known for the manufacture of the *huipil* dress, the traditional white cotton shift with colorful embroidery around the neckline worn by Yucatecan women. Teabo's 17th-century Temple of St. Peter the Apostle is part of a complex of colonial buildings. There are beautiful frescoes in the sacristy.

From Teabo, it's another several miles to Maní. It was here in 1562 that Diego de Landa, a Spanish bishop, ordered the destruction by fire of the Mayan *codices,* or hieroglyphic picture books, believing them profane. The historical loss resulting from this act was incalculable, leaving Landa's own treatise on Mayan history, *"Relación de las Cosas de Yucatán"* ("Yucatán Before and After the Conquest"), the only known account.

Maní is a quiet, peaceful town that sees little tourist traffic. Visit the town church, which has artwork displaying both Mayan and Spanish influences. The carefully preserved *retablos,* each replete with red and gold ornamentation, are noteworthy. Be sure to look up at the vaulted ceiling above the gilded gold *retablo* behind the altar; it is covered with exquisite frescoes. The church's adjacent open-air Indian chapel dates from the late 16th century. The park on the main plaza, complete with the bust of an unidentified Mexican statesman atop a green stone pedestal, is a shady spot to relax.

From Maní continue south to Oxkutzcab (osh-koots-KAHB), located in a fertile farming region that produces sugar cane, tobacco, corn, bananas and citrus fruits. It's a bustling place, with fleets of foot-pedaled *triciclos* and motorized three-wheeled taxis waiting to pick up passengers.

Oxkutzcab's market, near the main plaza, has stacks of plump green watermelons, wooden crates filled with fruits and vegetables, and vendor stalls in an open-air building with a long, colorful mural extending across the front. Go in the morning, before it gets too hot or crowded, for a Yucatecan breakfast of *salbutes*—handmade corn tortillas fried and topped with lettuce, chopped tomatoes and shredded chicken. Also on the plaza is the Church and Convent of San Francisco de Asis, which has a tan exterior. Inside this meticulously renovated church are several beautiful *retablos,* the statues of saints surrounded by gold-leaf ornamentation.

From Oxkutzcab, take the Mérida-Chetumal Highway (Mex. 184) north about 19 kilometers (12 miles) to Ticul. This busy regional center specializes in the manufacture of pottery and women's shoes. It's also larger than most of the other towns; the streets are filled with *triciclos* (and dogs).

A domed 18th-century church stands next to Ticul's central plaza. An interesting exterior decoration is the facial features—two half-moon eyes and a nose—carved below the roof. Many of the shops lining the downtown streets sell nothing but shoes. Craft shops offer ceramic bowls, and street vendors

## The Art of the Retablo (continued)

A similar expression of devotion is the *ex-voto,* a painting on canvas or a sheet of tin that was accompanied by a written testimonial. The assistance of a particular saint might be requested to help cure a health problem, or an expression of thanks was offered in return for a perceived benevolent act or answered prayer. In addition to featuring the saint's image, an *ex-voto* also told a story through pictures, depicting such scenes as a person rising miraculously from a sickbed or a farmer praying for rain for his crops.

Churches with fascinating collections of *retablos* include the Basilica of Our Lady of Guadalupe in Mexico City; the Parish of the Immaculate Conception in Real de Catorce, a former mining town in the state of San Luis Potosí; and the Temple and Ex-Convent of Santo Domingo in San Cristóbal de Las Casas. The Church of La Valenciana, just outside of Guanajuato, features three soaring *retablos*—one behind the main altar and two in the transepts to either side—adorned with life-size statues of saints and biblical figures and a profusion of ornate gold-leaf decoration.

And in Tecoh (tay-KO), a little Yucatán village southeast of Mérida, stands a huge fortress-church and convent that was built in the 17th century atop a Mayan pyramid. Inside the imposing structure stands a tall, four-tiered *retablo* highlighted by four large paintings depicting St. John the Baptist and three archangels. Painstakingly restored, this visual feast of elaborate red-and-gold ornamentation is a stunning reminder of Mexico's rich legacy of colonial art.

hawk embroidered *huipiles* and Panama hats made from woven palm fronds.

From Ticul continue north on Mex. 184 to Muna, then take Mex. 261 from Muna north to Mérida. From Ticul you also can get to the ruins at Uxmal *(see separate listing within this region)*.

## Celestún

A day trip also is possible to the fishing village of Celestún, on the western Yucatán coast. To get there, take Mex. 281 (Calle 59A within the city) about 97 kilometers (60 miles) west. En route are the towns of Hunucma and Kinchil, as well as fields of hene-quén and old haciendas that drove this once-thriving industry.

The village sits at the tip of a strip of land sepa-rating the Celestún Estuary (*ría* in Spanish) from the Gulf of Mexico. The atmosphere is decidedly laid-back; there are no resort amenities here. A stretch of white-sand swimming beach is at the north edge of town, although constant winds make the water choppy and silt-laden. The harbor is picturesque in a scruffy sort of way, filled with small boats and fish-ing nets drying in the sun.

The main reason to visit Celestún is the surround-ing wildlife refuge, home to a large colony of fla-mingos. While these spindly-legged, coral-plumaged birds are the area's most spectacular residents, nu-merous species of waterfowl also live here. In addi-tion, Celestún is on the flyway of many species mi-grating from northern climates to South America.

Tours of the estuary can be arranged just past the bridge leading into town, where there is a parking lot, ticket window, restrooms and a snack bar. The fare for a 75-minute tour is about $45 (U.S.) per boat (cash only), in canopied boats that accommodate up to six passengers. Bring sunscreen and water. The tour in-cludes bird-watching (in addition to flamingos, you're likely to see pelicans, herons, egrets, spoonbills and ducks) as well as an excursion through dense man-groves to a freshwater spring welling up within the saltwater estuary. The number of flamingos seen de-pends on the season, tide and time of day. Refrain from encouraging your boat captain to get too close, which causes the birds undue stress.

## PLAYA DEL CARMEN, QUINTANA ROO— *See The Caribbean Coast p. 101.*

## PUERTO MORELOS, QUINTANA ROO— *See The Caribbean Coast p. 105.*

## RÍO BEC, CAMPECHE (C-2)

Discovered at the turn of the 20th century, Río Bec (REE-oh bek) is the collective designation for an archeological zone comprising several Mayan sites. All but two are in the state of Campeche. They generally flourished between about A.D. 400 and 1000 and are believed to have served as trade routes between Mayan outposts established along the Ca-ribbean and Gulf of Mexico coasts. The most inter-esting of these—Kohunlich, Dzibanché, Xpujil, Be-can, Chicanná and Calakmul—are all accessible from east-west Mex. 186.

Architecturally the sites exhibit what is referred to as the "Río Bec" style. Features include tower-like structures more visually pleasing than functional and temple entrances carved to look like the open jaws of a snake, dragon or other monstrous creature. These ruins are largely unexplored and little visited, although more and more restoration efforts are being made. What remains intact is the mystery and sense of wonder surrounding these ancient cities.

One or more of the Río Bec sites can easily be vis-ited in the course of a day. As far as staying overnight (highly recommended if you plan on visiting the far-flung Calakmul ruins), there are tourist-class accom-modations and a restaurant at the Chicanná Ecovillage Resort, located across the highway from the Chicanná ruins *(see attraction listing)*. The rooms lack air condi-tioning, but the resort is surprisingly luxurious consid-ering its remote location. Non-guests are welcome to eat at the restaurant; simply tell the guard at the front gate that's what you want to do.

Each archeological site has a parking/entry area and restrooms. Water and food are not available; bring your own. Insect repellent and sturdy shoes are essen-tial for those who plan to do any amount of walking or ruin climbing, which is allowed at all the sites.

**Note:** Mex. 186 is a long, hot route with few ser-vices of any kind. ADO operates first-class bus ser-vice from Chetumal west to Escárcega and Villaher-mosa; while the buses may stop at ruins along the way, it is much more convenient to drive your own vehicle. Make sure the car is in good condition and the tank is full (there is a gas station shortly before reaching Xpujil, near the Quintana Roo-Campeche state line). It is strongly recommended that Mex. 186 only be traveled during daylight hours. The sites below are listed based on their distance from Chetumal. One-way drive time (with no stops) from Chetumal to Xpujil is about 90 minutes.

**DZIBANCHÉ** ruins are about 64 km (40 mi.) w. of Chetumal on Mex. 186 to the well-signed turn-off, then about 19 km (12 mi.) n. of the highway via a paved road. Only open to the public since the mid-1990s, Dzibanché dates to between A.D. 300 and 1200. It receives few visitors despite containing a small but impressive collection of structures. Temples 1 and 6 soar above the wooded site (the ceiba trees that grow here were sacred to the ancient Maya). Just beyond Dzibanché is the smaller Kinichná archeolog-ical zone.

**Hours:** Daily 8-5. **Cost:** (good for both sites) 52 pesos (about $3.85 U.S.). Cash only.

**KOHUNLICH** ruins are about 66 km (41 mi.) w. of Chetumal to the signed turn-off (just before the village of Francisco Villa), then about 8 km (5 mi.) s. of the highway via a paved road. Park-like and shady, Kohunlich (koh-hoon-LEECH) may once have been an oasis. The most notable structure among the rubble-strewn mounds is the pyramid-like Temple of the Masks (Templo de Los Mascarones), which has a central stairway flanked with carved faces, strongly Olmec-influenced, that resemble masks. Hints of red are still visible on these figures, which are protected by thatched coverings. **Hours:** Daily 8-5. **Cost:** 62 pesos (about $4.60 U.S.). Cash only.

**XPUJIL** ruins are about 72 km (45 mi.) w. of Kohunlich, on the n. side of the highway just past the village of Xpujil. Xpujil (sh-pooh-HEEL), which means "place of the cattails" in the Mayan language, flourished between A.D. 400 and 900. The largest building at the site consists of three towers that once had steep ornamental stairways extravagantly decorated with jaguar masks; traces of its former grandeur remain. **Hours:** Daily 8-5. **Cost:** 47 pesos (about $3.50 U.S.). Cash only.

**BECÁN** ruins are about 7 km (4 mi.) w. of Xpujil on the n. side of the highway and can be reached via a short road (watch for the turn-off sign). Surrounded by a dry moat that probably was used as a fortification (the name means "ravine formed by water"), the site once was accessed by seven causeway bridges. This is the most developed of the Río Bec sites and has some of the largest structures, including a twin-towered temple (Structure IX), plazas surrounded by low-rise buildings and a ball court. There also is a nicely preserved stucco mask on display (behind glass) at Structure X.

**Hours:** Daily 8-5. **Cost:** 52 pesos (about $3.85 U.S.). Cash only.

**CHICANNÁ** ruins are about 2 km (1.2 mi.) w. of Becán on the s. side of the highway; a short road leads to the site. They stand within an enticing grove of tropical trees and other vegetation. The buildings are a mix of Río Bec and Chenes architectural styles. Most notable is Structure II, which stands in the main plaza. It features elaborate carvings and a huge doorway fashioned after the jaws of a monster's open mouth, complete with stone teeth. Other buildings include a twin-towered temple and Structure XX, which also has a monster mouth doorway. **Hours:** Daily 8-5. **Cost:** 47 pesos (about $3.50 U.S.). Cash only.

**CALAKMUL** ruins are a good 2-hour drive w. of Chicanná; from the Mex. 186 turn-off (watch for signs), a winding road heads s. about 60 km (37 mi.) into the Calakmul Biosphere Reserve. This huge archeological zone—a UNESCO World Heritage Site—sits in the state of Campeche near the Guatemala border. A Classic-era superpower that often battled nearby Tikal, Calakmul is one of the largest Mayan cities ever discovered and boasts the tallest Mayan pyramid (180 feet) in Mexico. Allow a full day to explore the ruins. **Hours:** Daily 8-5. **Cost:** 52 pesos (about $3.85 U.S.). The toll charge for the biosphere reserve road is about 30 pesos per person.

## TULUM, QUINTANA ROO—

*See The Caribbean Coast p. 106.*

## ◆GEM UXMAL, YUCATÁN (B-2)

If Chichén Itzá is considered the Yucatán Peninsula's most impressive archeological site, Uxmal (oosh-MAHL) is the most beautiful. Unlike the structures at Chichén Itzá, with their Toltec-influenced images of violent conquest, Uxmal's architecture is more purely Mayan, with richly ornamented stone facades and a majestic pyramid. The ruins were designated a World Heritage Site by UNESCO in 1996; don't miss them.

Uxmal rose to prominence concurrently with the great civilizations at Palenque (in the state of Chiapas) and Tikal (in Guatemala), flourishing between A.D. 600 and 1000. Little is known about its history. The name means "thrice built" in Maya, although it was actually reconstructed five times, suggesting that drought forced abandonment followed by resettlement. The subsequent importance of Chichén Itzá and the increased intermingling of Mayan cultures with those from the central Mexican highlands were likely contributors to the city's decline, which appeared to be complete by the 14th century.

The first excavations were begun in 1929 by Danish archeologist and explorer Frans Blom, who also conducted research at other Mayan archeological sites. The Mexican government has since worked with a number of archeologists to reconstruct the site, and the main buildings have all been restored.

Uxmal is the defining example of the Puuc architectural style (the name refers to the region's hilly terrain), which emphasized elegant, horizontal proportions and intricately detailed building exteriors of cut stones assembled in geometric patterns. Cornices and entryways often feature beak-nosed representations of the rain god Chac. The detail of the stonework is even more amazing when one considers that the Maya created their buildings without benefit of metal tools.

This part of the peninsula has a hot climate with seasonal precipitation and is subject to prolonged dry spells. Unlike other Mayan cities, Uxmal did not have ready availability to a source of water. Instead, they depended upon the *chultun* (a man-made cistern) to collect precious rain.

Visitors enter the site via a short path that begins at the visitor center. The first building is immediately evident: The Pyramid of the Magician (*see attraction listing*). This structure probably functioned as a ceremonial building where Uxmal's rulers were crowned.

The Nunnery (*see attraction listing*), named by the Spaniards, was probably used by Uxmal's elite ruling class. Just south of the Nunnery is a ball court, smaller and simpler than the one at Chichén Itzá. South of the ball court is the small, classically designed House of the Turtles (Casa de las Tortugas), named for the border of turtles carved along its upper molding. Stand on the south side of this temple and look through the central doorway (of three) for a nicely framed view of the Nunnery.

The Governor's Palace *(see attraction listing)* was most likely Uxmal's administrative center and may also have served an astrological purpose; it faces east while the other buildings face west, perhaps to better sight the planet Venus, which the Maya associated with war. From this elevated vantage point there is an expansive view of the Nunnery and the Pyramid of the Magician.

The Great Pyramid, partially restored, is just southwest of the Governor's Palace. Originally terraced with nine levels, it is topped by a palace decorated with Chac masks and bird carvings that probably represent parrots. The climb to the palace level is steep but doable (be particularly careful descending if you're prone to vertigo), with sweeping views of the surrounding jungle scrub.

Just west of the Great Pyramid are the remains of a building called the Dovecote because its lattice design somewhat resembles a bird nesting house. The view of this ruin is particularly fine from the summit of the Great Pyramid.

Other buildings at the site are only partially reconstructed, or unexcavated mounds hidden in the brush. The House of the Old Woman (Casa de la Vieja), an old, ruined pyramidal structure southeast

of the Great Pyramid, is reached by an overgrown path. Further southeast is the Temple of the Phalli, another ruined structure with phallic-shaped sculptures along the cornices, presumably to divert and collect rainwater from the roof.

## General Information and Activities

Mérida is the most convenient base from which to explore the Puuc region. Gray Line tours offers two packages: a day tour of Uxmal and the nearby Kabah archeological site that departs at 9 a.m., and a two-day tour of Uxmal that departs at 9 a.m. and includes the evening sound-and-light show and an overnight hotel stay. Both tours include round-trip transportation, guide service and meals. For reservation information phone (998) 887-9162 (in Mexico) or (800) 472-9546 (from the United States). Tour groups usually have access to a swimming pool; bring a suit and towel, as they aren't provided.

Uxmal is about 80 kilometers (50 miles) south of Mérida via Mex. 261. If driving, take Avenida Itzaes (Mex. 180) south from downtown Mérida past the airport to the Anillo Periférico (loop road) and the junction with Mex. 261.

Newer highway construction gives motorists the option of bypassing Umán, Yaxcopoil, Muna and other villages en route to Uxmal. This cuts some time off the trip, which takes about an hour from Mérida. If you want to experience rural Yucatán take

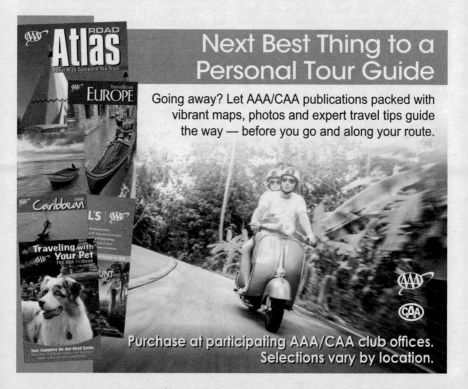

old Mex. 261, which runs through largely undeveloped scrub country. Muna is a typical Yucatecan small town that has thatch-roofed stone dwellings and a large Franciscan church.

For those who want to spend the night near the ruins, there are AAA Approved lodgings along Mex. 261 near the site entrance. For budget-minded travelers the nearby town of Ticul, about a 15-minute drive from Uxmal, offers very basic motels.

Guide fees are posted on a board next to the ticket window. Although you don't need a guide to appreciate the architecture, and the information may be embellished with fanciful details, a guide's general knowledge will be helpful to those unfamiliar with Mayan history. The main buildings have informational plaques in English, Spanish and Maya. Plan on spending half a day at the ruins if not part of an organized tour group, or devote a full day to see Uxmal and the other sites along the "Puuc Trail."

A 45-minute sound-and-light show is presented nightly from a vantage point overlooking the Nunnery quadrangle. Colored lights, recorded symphonic music under the stars and melodramatic narration provide an appropriate backdrop for Mayan legends. Although the "history" can be taken with a grain of salt, the artificial lighting illuminates architectural details that are missed under sharp sunlight. The narration is in Spanish, but headsets offering the show in several languages (including English) can be rented.

Most of the site is unshaded; bring a hat or other headgear for protection from the strong sun. An early start will allow you to beat not only the heat but the tour bus crowds that begin arriving before noon. Comfortable, nonslip walking shoes are a must if you plan to do any climbing. It's also a good idea to bring bottled water and insect repellent (particularly if you're attending the sound-and-light show).

The visitor center at the entrance has very clean restrooms, a bookstore, first-aid station, gift shop, coffee shop, casual restaurant and convenience store. A few souvenir and T-shirt stands set up next to the visitor center parking lot. Uxmal is open daily 8-5. The sound-and-light show begins at 7 or 8 p.m., depending on the season. Site admission 188 pesos (about $14 U.S.). Sound-and-light show 78 pesos (about $5.75 U.S.). Parking fee 20 pesos. Video camera fee 50 pesos (about $3.70 U.S.).

**GOVERNOR'S PALACE** is s. of the Nunnery and just s.e. of the House of the Turtles. This building is widely considered to be among the finest Mayan architectural achievements. The low, narrow structure, more than 300 feet long, is built on three levels. Its upper facade is covered with intricately carved stone figures and geometric designs. Serpents, masks and mosaic patterns all blend into a beautifully harmonious whole. Stand back from the palace's eastern side to discern the 103 stone carvings of Chac that together form the image of an undulating serpent (dramatically illuminated during the sound-and-light show).

**NUNNERY** (Casa de las Monjas) faces the western stairway of the Pyramid of the Magician. Get thee to these long, low buildings that surround a large quadrangle and stand in the center of the courtyard to appreciate the overall harmony that prevails, even though the structure is terraced and on different levels. The exteriors of each wing have beautiful decorative details, including stone masks of Chac (recognized by their elongated noses), entwined serpents, mosaic patterns and latticework designs. The southern wing has an arched entryway, once the complex's main entrance.

**PYRAMID OF THE MAGICIAN** is near the site entrance. Also called The Sorcerer (Templo El Adivino), this impressive structure is both taller (some 125 feet) and steeper than El Castillo, the pyramid at Chichén Itzá. It actually contains five superimposed layers that correspond to Uxmal's five separate periods of construction. The walls are rounded rather than sharply angular, an unusual feature. Stairways ascend the eastern and western sides. The western stairway is very steep (a 60-degree angle); the eastern stairway is not quite as steep. Climbing the pyramid is not permitted.

**CHOCOLATE MUSEUM** (Choco-Story México) is just off Mex. 261, across the road from the Uxmal Ruins. This open-air museum, on the grounds of a cacao plantation, showcases the history of cacao production in the Yucatán region. After passing through the neo-colonial entrance building, visitors walk along a trail where thatched *palapas* contain exhibits about cacao's sacred link to the Mayan people and a more general overview of chocolate production. Background information is in both Spanish and English.

Along with demonstrations of how the dried and fermented fatty seed of the cacao tree—one of the fundamental building blocks in the creation of chocolate—is processed, visitors can sample a traditional Mayan drink made from organic cocoa and spices that is not the sweet beverage one might expect. A re-enactment of a traditional Mayan ceremony is also presented. The lovely grounds feature a variety of orchids and labeled plants as well as habitats for spider monkeys and jaguars rescued from the wild.

Bus transportation via ADO (the Puuc Route bus) departs Fri.-Sun. at 8 a.m. from the Union Terminal in downtown Mérida, at Calle 69 #554 (between calles 68 and 70). **Time:** Allow 1 hour, 30 minutes minimum. **Hours:** Daily 9-6. Closed Jan. 1, Christmas Eve, Christmas and Dec. 31. **Cost:** 120 pesos (about $8.90 U.S.); 90 pesos (ages 6-12 and 65+). Tours led by a guide are available for an additional fee. **Phone:** (999) 192-5385 (cellular number; in Mexico dial 045 before the number). 🍴

## Nearby Puuc Ruins

For true aficionados of Mayan history and culture, a full day can be spent exploring the ruins along the Puuc Route south and east of Uxmal, all within easy driving distance. Bus service visits these small archeological sites, but driving allows you to see them at your own pace. Roadside services are minimal, so make sure your gas tank is full and bring food, water, insect repellent and comfortable, nonslip walking shoes. The following sites are listed in order of location from Uxmal.

**KABAH** is about 19 km (12 mi.) s. on Mex. 261; park in the small dirt lot on the e. (left) side of the road. Although small—there are only two main buildings—it is well worth visiting to see the lavishly decorated Palace of the Masks, or Codz-Pop (in Maya, "rolled mat"). Its entire west exterior is emblazoned with elaborately carved stone masks of the rain god Chac. The busy architectural style reflects the ornate Chenes influence, which is not often seen in this region.

As amazing as the front is, make sure you walk around to the back (east) side. There are no Chac masks here, but jutting off the upper facade are the sculptures of two warriors who seem to be guarding the palace. Below them on one of the side panels (at ground level) are bas-reliefs depicting one warrior subjugating another in classic Mayan fashion.

The other major building on this side of the road is the well-restored Palace (El Palacio), built on two levels, which features a Puuc-style colonnaded facade. Across Mex. 261 is the Great Temple, a large conical mound rising above the thick scrub. It is only partially restored. Beyond the Great Temple is a freestanding arch marking the spot where a Mayan *sacbe* (limestone causeway) road once entered Kabah from Uxmal; compare it to the one at Labná.

**Hours:** Daily 8-5. **Cost:** 47 pesos (about $3.50 U.S.). The fee to use a video camera is 50 pesos.

**SAYIL** is about 5 km (3 mi.) from Kabah; take Mex. 261 to the junction with Mex. 184 (the road to Oxkutzcab), then e. about 4 km (2.5 mi.) to the ruins. The aptly named site, which means "place of ants," contains several hundred known structures, almost all on the south side of the road. There is one standout: the Palace (El Palacio), a grand three-level building more than 200 feet long. The second level features rows of Grecian-style columns as well as a profusion of stone carvings. Most are of the rain god Chac, but there are additional depictions of an upside-down "diving god."

Most of the other buildings are in ruins or obscured by jungle. South of the Palace is El Mirador, a small temple, and beyond it a primitive stele (carved stone). Also at this site are a number of man-made cisterns that were built to catch seasonal rainfall. **Hours:** Daily 8-5. **Cost:** 47 pesos (about $3.50 U.S.). The fee to use a video camera is 50 pesos.

**XLAPAK** is about 6 km (3.5 mi.) e. of Sayil. Xlapak (shla-PAHK) means "old walls" in Maya. The notable structure at this small site on the south side of the road is the partially restored Palace of Xlapak, which is decorated with Chac masks, some flaunting curled noses. The restored portions are lighter in tone than the weathered, unrestored sections. **Hours:**

Daily 8-5. **Cost:** Free. The fee to use a video camera is 50 pesos.

**LABNÁ** is about 3 km (2 mi.) e. of Xlapak. Here the best-known ruin is a restored, freestanding stone arch larger than the one at Kabah. It displays ornate decoration on the west side and a more geometric pattern on the east side. Pass through the arch to El Mirador, a pyramidal structure resting on a pile of rubble. Labná, like Sayil, contains the remains of many *chultunes* (cisterns) that collected rainwater.

Labná's impressive Palace building is similar to the one at Sayil, although not in as good condition. See it for the ornamentation, which is—as on so many Mayan buildings—bizarrely imaginative. **Hours:** Daily 8-5. **Cost:** 47 pesos (about $3.50 U.S.). The fee to use a video camera is 50 pesos.

**LOLTÚN CAVES** (Grutas de Loltún) are about 6 km (10 mi.) s.w. of Oxkutzcab via the Sayil-Labná road. The entrance to the caves is reached from a gravel path that branches off the n. side of the road; the turnoff is not signed. Hieroglyphic inscriptions and carvings of flowers on the cave walls are estimated to be some 1,000 years old; the name, loosely translated, means "one flower in the stone." Throughout the caves are *chultunes* (cisterns), stone troughs which were placed to collect water dripping from the roof. Natural formations include giant stalactites and stalagmites that emit an echoing hum when struck.

The caverns can be seen by guided tour only. Tours are given daily at 9:30, 12:30 and 3:30; double-check this schedule at the Uxmal visitor center. Some passages are dark and the paths may be slippery or steep; wear comfortable, nonslip walking shoes. Most tours are given in Spanish; ask at the front ticket office regarding the availability of an English-speaking guide. **Hours:** Daily 8-5. **Cost:** 115 pesos (about $8.50 U.S.).

## VALLADOLID, YUCATÁN (B-3)
### pop. 74,217

Valladolid (vah-yah-doh-LEED) was founded in 1543 by Francisco de Montejo, who established Spanish rule over much of the Yucatán Peninsula. The Spaniards constructed their churches over the site of a former Mayan town, Zací. Many revolts occurred in this region during the mid-19th-century War of the Castes, when rebellious and oppressed descendants of the Maya clashed with privileged landowners. Here too was one of the first uprisings against dictator Porfirio Díaz, which foreshadowed the Mexican Revolution of 1910.

The commercial center for an agricultural district, Valladolid is on Mex. 180; there is also an exit off toll highway Mex. 180-D. A colonial atmosphere, somewhat gone to seed, pervades this unpretentious market town. Old buildings still bear weathered Spanish coats of arms above their doorways. The main plaza is bounded by calles 39, 40, 41 and 42;

here visitors can browse among shops selling leather goods or sit on one of the curved stone benches and observe the local scene.

Several kilometers north of Valladolid on Mex. 295, on the way to the Ek Balam ruins *(see attraction listing)* is the little village of Temozón. It's worth stopping here for a look at the beautifully weathered church that dates from the early 18th century. The small plaza in front makes a good photo opportunity.

The ruins themselves are the most noteworthy attraction in the Valladolid vicinity. Ongoing restoration work at this archeological site deep in the jungle began in 1997. Still primitive, Ek Balam receives relatively few visitors and thus retains more of a sense of mystery than other Yucatán ruins.

**CENOTE DZITNUP** is about 4 km (2.5 mi.) s.w. of town on free Mex. 180, then about a km s. on an unnamed road (follow the signs). This is a better alternative than Cenote Zací if you want to try swimming. The natural pool of clear, blue water is inside a cavern where artificial lighting illuminates the stalactites hanging from the roof. The short flight of stone steps leading down into the cavern can be slippery. There are modern facilities, including restrooms, on site. **Hours:** Daily 7-6, during the summer months; 8-5 rest of year. **Cost:** 59 pesos (about $4.35 U.S.). Cash only.

**CENOTE ZACÍ** is downtown between calles 34 and 36 and calles 37 and 39 (Mex. 180), about 3 blks. e. of the main plaza. This huge underground sinkhole is reached by worn stone stairs that descend to a dark, spookily atmospheric cavern, with upper walls populated by bats. The somewhat murky water is suitable for swimming but is flecked with green scum that the locals call "lake lettuce." It is located in a park that has a restaurant as well as examples of traditional thatch-roofed Mayan houses. **Hours:** Daily 8-5. **Cost:** 25 pesos (about $1.85 U.S.). Admission is free to restaurant patrons. Cash only.

**CHURCH AND CONVENT OF SAN BERNARDINO DE SIENA** is about 1 km (.6 mi.) s.w. of the main plaza via Mex. 180 to Calle 41A. The fortifications of this massive complex, built between 1552 and 1560 by the Franciscan Order, were meant to ward off the warring Mayas, who sacked it repeatedly. It was constructed next to a large cenote, with a paddle wheel over the opening providing fresh water.

A recent underwater excavation revealed weapons and munitions discarded during the War of the Castes in the mid-19th century; a large exhibit of these items along with photos of the excavation can be seen in the onsite museum. The church and chapels contain a number of religious artifacts.

**Time:** Allow 1 hour minimum. **Hours:** Daily 9-5. **Cost:** 30 pesos (about $2.20 U.S.).

**EK BALAM** is about 15 km (9 mi.) n. of the Mex. 180-D Valladolid exit via Mex. 295, following signs. To get there from Valladolid, take Calle 40 out of town to Mex. 295 and proceed n. about 18 km (11 mi.) to the Ek Balam turn-off (watch for the sign marking the turn-off). Archeologists believe the site achieved its greatest prominence sometime between A.D. 400 and 900; the name Ek Balam means "black jaguar."

Stony, muddy walkways connect ruins unusual in the fact that the buildings have round corners where there are normally sharp right angles. Structure 1 (known as the Acropolis) dominates the main plaza. About 100 feet tall, this enormous pyramid has steep stairs that can be climbed for fantastic views of the surrounding area. Thatched roofs protect statues and carvings on the different levels.

About two-thirds of the way up is the recently uncovered tomb of Ukit Kan Lek Tok, one of Ek Balam's rulers. The opening, designed to look like a stylized jaguar head, is flanked by stucco sculptures of winged warriors intriguingly reminiscent of angels. Decorative features include skulls, a doorway lined with "teeth" and a wall covered with intricate carvings.

Smaller edifices surround the base of the main pyramid. Large thatched roofs protecting new excavation sites provide welcome shade. At the entrance is a restored Puuc-style gateway arch that once was connected to an ancient road, or *sacbe* (sock bay); the Maya built these slightly raised roads of limestone gravel to connect their cities.

There are restrooms in the ticket building. Wear comfortable walking shoes and bring drinking water. The small village of Ek Balam, just before the entrance to the ruins, is a good place to stop for cold refreshments. **Time:** Allow 2 hours minimum. **Hours:** Daily 8-4:30. **Cost:** 152 pesos (about $11.25 U.S.); free (ages 0-12). The fee to use a video camera is 35 pesos.

**RÍO LAGARTOS NATIONAL PARK** is about 100 km (62 mi.) almost due n. of Valladolid at the end of Mex. 295. **Note:** The *topes* (speed bumps) along Mex. 295 can significantly damage the underside of a vehicle if negotiated at too fast a speed. Mexico's largest flamingo sanctuary comprises some 120,000 acres of protected mangrove swamps, sand dunes, mud flats and shallow estuaries along the Yucatán Peninsula's northern coast. In addition to flamingos, the park is home to herons, egrets, cormorants, ducks, pelicans and many other bird species.

Boat tours can be arranged with local guides at the dock area in the fishing village of Río Lagartos. Bring a hat or other protection from the sun, your own water and a snack. The winter months are a better—and cooler—time to observe young flamingos and other bird species. Don't allow the boatman to scare flamingos into flight for a photo opportunity, as this will eventually drive them from their habitat. **Cost:** Park entrance fee about $2.50 (U.S.). Tour rates vary according to boat, destination and tour size, but an excursion for five people should be about $90 (U.S.).

© Sorin Colac / Shutterstock.com

# Baja California

I n 1535 a shipwreck survivor regaled Hernando Cortés with reports of an island populated by Amazonian women and brimming with gold and pearls. The *conquistador,* believing it to be the fabled land of California, set sail for the elongated peninsula known as Baja (Lower) California with three galleons and 600 prospective settlers.

Cortés landed near the present site of La Paz, toward the peninsula's southern end. Finding neither pearls, gold nor Amazons—but encountering impoverished land and fierce Indians—Cortés abandoned the area. And the Spanish, busy plundering other parts of Mexico, all but forgot Baja. It was not until 1697 that a permanent settlement was established, a Jesuit mission and presidio at Loreto.

Except for border town Tijuana and seaside Ensenada, Baja for the most part remained a lonely outpost for hardy fishermen through the first half of the 20th century. But in 1974 Mex. 1, the Transpeninsular Highway, opened the more far-flung parts of the peninsula to visitors.

Nearly 800 miles in length and varying from about 30 to 110 miles in width, the Baja Peninsula extends south from the U.S. border like a

giant appendage paralleling the northwestern Mexican mainland. It broke off millions of years ago, in the process creating the Gulf of California (also known as the Sea of Cortez). The gulf and Pacific coastlines are indented by an endless string of bays and coves, with many islands scattered offshore. Both bodies of water are home to an amazing variety of fish, making the peninsula a sport-fishing paradise.

The state of Baja California, comprising all territory north of the 28th parallel, consists mostly of rugged mountains or harsh desert, although irrigation of the hot, arid valleys around the border city of Mexicali has turned them into a productive agricultural region. Day trippers, the partying college crowd and souvenir hunters trek across the border to Tijuana. The port of

Ensenada is a cruise ship stop and weekend destination. Between the two is casual hangout Rosarito Beach.

The state of Baja California Sur, occupying the southern portion of the peninsula, is even more barren. Occasional oases such as the village of San Ignacio, a mirage of date palms and pastel-colored buildings, pop up in the middle of the desert. Toward the peninsula's end is La Paz, the capital and a traditionally Mexican city.

At Baja's dramatically beautiful southern tip is its most popular vacation spot, and one of Mexico's most popular destinations. Los Cabos (the Capes) refers to the twin resort towns of Cabo San Lucas and San José del Cabo, full of championship golf courses and pricey all-inclusive resorts.

Vagabundos Del Mar RV, Boat and Travel provides assistance to RV travelers in Baja. Services include roadside aid, RV park information, insurance needs, and medical air services and evacuation. For information phone (800) 474-2252 (from the United States).

AAA recommends that travelers consult online U.S. State Department travel advisories when planning traveling abroad. Find this information at http://travel.state.gov/content/passports/english/alertswarnings/mexico-travel-warning.html.

3050-16

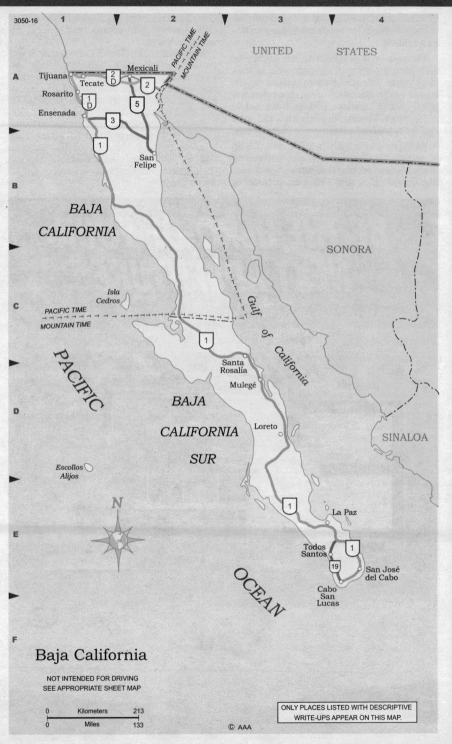

UNITED        STATES

Tijuana
Tecate        Mexicali
Rosarito
Ensenada

San
Felipe

*BAJA*

*CALIFORNIA*

SONORA

PACIFIC TIME
MOUNTAIN TIME

Isla
Cedros

*PACIFIC*

Gulf

of

California

Santa
Rosalía
Mulegé

*BAJA*

*CALIFORNIA*

Loreto

*SUR*

SINALOA

Escollos
Alijos

N

La Paz

Todos
Santos
19              San José
del Cabo
*OCEAN*
Cabo
San
Lucas

Baja California

NOT INTENDED FOR DRIVING
SEE APPROPRIATE SHEET MAP

Kilometers    213
0
Miles         133

© AAA

ONLY PLACES LISTED WITH DESCRIPTIVE
WRITE-UPS APPEAR ON THIS MAP.

# Points of Interest

## CABO SAN LUCAS, BAJA CALIFORNIA SUR (E-3)

*See map page 136.*

Cabo San Lucas (KAH-boh sahn LOO-kahs) perches at the southern tip of Baja California, where the waters of the Gulf of California (Sea of Cortez) and the Pacific Ocean converge. Although offering some of Mexico's nicest luxury resorts and a full slate of outdoor-oriented recreational activities, it is still very much a laid-back place where local fishermen go about their daily business. The stark, stunning scenery—rocks, water and big blue sky—is, of course, the stuff of tourist brochure dreams. And Cabo has a well-deserved reputation for attracting those who like to party, if only for a getaway weekend.

Cabo San Lucas and neighboring San José del Cabo *(see separate listing within this region)*—plus the 20-mile stretch of highway between them—are collectively known as Los Cabos. This is one of Mexico's leading resort areas, rivaling such hotspots as Cancún and Puerto Vallarta, and its popularity shows no sign of slowing down.

Each Cabo has a distinctly different personality. Cabo San Lucas draws golfers and sport-fishing fans as well as Generations X and Y, who come for the surfing, beaches and rowdy nightlife. San José del Cabo is a much more traditional Mexican small town, complete with a central plaza and cathedral. It's quieter and more family-oriented than Cabo San Lucas, but also offers a growing number of sophisticated shops, galleries and restaurants.

Between the two Cabos runs divided four-lane Mex. 1. "The Corridor" has developed into its own destination. The wild, rocky landscapes along the highway once hid only secluded fishing lodges and a few hotels. Now the views of rugged cliffs and the glimpses of steely blue gulf water and white-sand beaches are punctuated by a string of lushly groomed and lavishly appointed resorts. The Corridor also is where you'll find Cabo's championship golf courses. The resort communities of Cabo Real and Cabo del Sol are centers of tourist-oriented development.

Due to geographic isolation from the Mexican mainland and a tourism infrastructure with close ties to California and other Western states, there is a more pronounced "north of the border" sensibility here than at other Mexican resorts. American cars, products and dollars are all highly visible. But Los Cabos also has a by-the-seaside feel that is distinctly Mexican, aided immeasurably by the unspoiled grandeur of its desert setting.

It's a setting that comes at a price, however. If you're in search of a bargain Mexican vacation, you won't find it in Los Cabos. Hotels, restaurants, taxis, shops and tour operators charge some of the steepest prices in Mexico; locals jokingly refer to Cabo San Lucas as "*Caro* San Lucas" (*caro* means expensive). That said, prices for goods and services do drop the farther you stray from the main tourist areas.

In September 2014 Hurricane Odile made landfall near Cabo San Lucas as a Category 3 storm with maximum sustained winds of 125 mph. Damage to hotels, buildings and beaches was widespread, especially along "The Corridor" (Mex. 1 between Cabo San Lucas and San José). Recovery was swift, however, and by early 2015 most tourism-related services (including the airport) were back to normal. A few heavily damaged resorts along The Corridor were not expected to reopen until fall 2015.

## Practicalities

San José del Cabo International Airport is about 13 kilometers (8 miles) north of San José del Cabo and 48 kilometers (30 miles) northeast of Cabo San Lucas. Alaska, American and United airlines offer nonstop flights from Los Angeles. Alaska Airlines flies direct from San Diego, San Francisco and Seattle. US Airways handles flights from Phoenix. American and Delta offer service from U.S. East Coast cities, with most connecting flights via Atlanta, Dallas or Houston. *For additional information about airlines see Arriving by Air, page p. 42.*

**Note:** Avoid the time share sellers who bombard arriving visitors, unless you're really interested in spending 4 hours enduring an aggressive sales pitch for a new condominium development. The lure of free lunches and drinks or so-called discounted activities is definitely not worth it.

Private taxis from the airport to your hotel are very expensive; a ride to San José del Cabo can cost up to $60 (U.S.), while fares to Cabo San Lucas reach into the $90 stratosphere and beyond. Returning to the airport via private taxi is slightly cheaper. Rates from San José are in the $30 to $35 (U.S.) range; from Cabo San Lucas prepare to shell out $50 to $60.

Los Cabos Express provides bus and private shuttle van transportation from the airport to hotels based on a zone system. Shuttle vans can only be booked for round-trip service, and rates range from $90-$170 (five-person maximum) depending on the destination; for information phone (624) 163-7200. If you arrive at the airport without a reservation, look for the green-and-white Los Cabos Express bus, which is usually parked outside the terminal; buy your ticket from the driver. One-way rates average $16-$18. Another less expensive option than a cab is an airport transfer, which some hotels offer for a fee; inquire about this service when you make your reservations.

Because the Los Cabos area is spread out and expensive taxi fares will quickly add up, renting a car

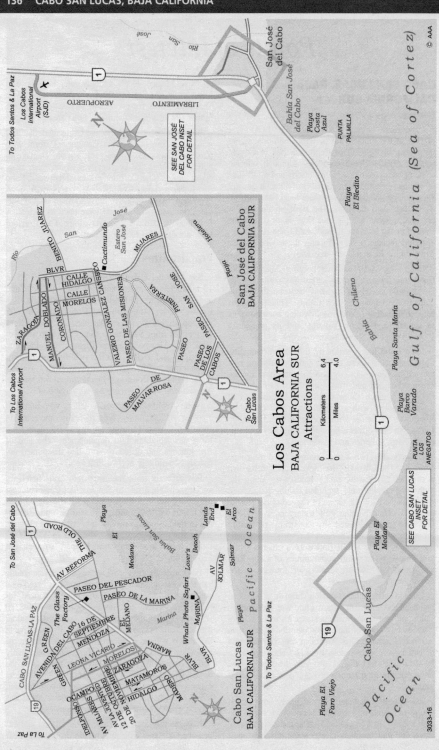

© AAA

San José del Cabo

To Todos Santos & La Paz
Los Cabos International Airport (SJD)

AEROPUERTO

LIBRAMIENTO

SEE SAN JOSÉ DEL CABO INSET FOR DETAIL

Bahía San José del Cabo

Playa Costa Azul

PUNTA PALMILLA

Playa El Bledito

Gulf of California (Sea of Cortez)

**San José del Cabo**
**BAJA CALIFORNIA SUR**

Río San José

BENITO JUAREZ

BLVR
CALLE HIDALGO
CALLE MORELOS

Cactimundo

Estero San José

MIJARES

VALERIO GONZALEZ CANSECO

PASEO DE LAS MISIONES

FINISTERRA

SAN JOSÉ

Hidalgo

Playa

ZARAGOZA

MANUEL DOBLADO

CORONADO

To Los Cabos International Airport

PASEO

PASEO DE LOS CABOS

PASEO DE MALVARROSA

To Cabo San Lucas

Playa Santa Maria

Playa Chileno

Bahia

**Los Cabos Area**
**BAJA CALIFORNIA SUR**
**Attractions**

Kilometers
6.4
4.0
Miles
0
0

Playa Barco Varado

PUNTA LOS ANEGATOS

SEE CABO SAN LUCAS INSET FOR DETAIL

To San José del Cabo

THE OLD ROAD

AV REFORMA

Playa El Medano

El Medano

Bahía San Lucas

Lover's Beach

Lands End

El Arco

pacific Ocean

Playa

The Glass Factory
PASEO DEL PESCADOR
PASEO DE LA MARINA

Whale Photo Safari

MARINA

AV SOLMAR

Solmar

Marina

CABO SAN LUCAS-LA PAZ

GREEN
GREEN
AVENIDA DEL CABO
16 DE SEPTIEMBRE
MENDOZA
LEONA VICARIO
MORELOS
ZARAGOZA
MATAMOROS
HIDALGO

EL MEDANO

BLVR MARINA

MARINA BLVR

IDELFONSO
AV MIJARES
AV JUVENTUD
12 DE NOVIEMBRE
20 DE NOVIEMBRE

OCAMPO

MADERO

Playa El Medano

**Cabo San Lucas**
**BAJA CALIFORNIA SUR**

Playa

pacific Ocean

To Todos Santos & La Paz

19

Cabo San Lucas

Playa El Faro Viejo

Pacific Ocean

To La Paz

19

3033-16

is a viable option if you're staying more than a few days or want to explore the surrounding area. If you only want a car for a day or two, consider renting one in town at the end of your trip and dropping it at the airport on your departure day. The car rental company's one-way drop-off fee will usually be cheaper than a taxi ride back to the airport.

If you've rented a car at the airport and want to by-pass the stoplights and frequently heavy traffic on Mex. 1, take the Los Cabos Airport-San José del Cabo toll road. This modern, four-lane highway departs the airport (watch for signs) and travels about 20 kilometers (12 miles) to San José, where it terminates at Mex. 1, just west of the waterfront hotel zone. The toll booth is at the southern end of the road; the toll is around 30 pesos ($2.20 U.S.). To reach Cabo San Lucas, just continue southwest on Mex. 1. There are no gas stations along the toll road.

**Note:** AAA/CAA members enjoy discounts through Hertz for vehicles booked in the United States. Consult your local AAA/CAA club or phone Hertz, (800) 654-3080. *For additional information about renting a car see Car Rentals, page p. 43.*

It's a long drive to Los Cabos from the border at Tijuana—some 1,050 miles via Mex. 1 (also called the Carretera Transpeninsular). From La Paz, the quicker and less winding route to Cabo San Lucas is Mex. 1 south to the junction with Mex. 19, then Mex. 19 south through Todos Santos to Cabo San Lucas.

Except for the four-lane Corridor and four-lane Mex. 1-D from Tijuana to Ensenada, Mex. 1 is a two-lane road that runs through frequent desolate stretches. Gas stations and traveler facilities can be few and far between. A temporary vehicle importation permit is not required anywhere on the peninsula, unless the vehicle is put on a ferry bound for the mainland.

Mex. 1 is narrow compared to highways in the United States and Canada, and road shoulders are nonexistent along many stretches. The quality of the road is generally good, but there are potholes in the vicinity of Cataviña in the state of Baja California. Avoid driving at an excessive speed (above 50 mph), and do not drive after dark. This and other roads are not lit at night, and cows standing on the road surface pose an ever-present danger.

While it seldom rains much of the year in southern Baja, streams (called *arroyos*) are subject to flash floods during infrequent storms. Flooding, although rare, can make vehicle travel impossible when it occurs. Elevated bridges have solved this problem along the Corridor (the stretch of Mex. 1 between San José del Cabo and Cabo San Lucas).

Baja's main overland bus line, Autotransportes de Baja California (ABC), travels from Tijuana to La Paz twice a day; the trip (including stops en route) takes about 24 hours. From La Paz, the Aguila bus line provides frequent service to both San José del Cabo and Cabo San Lucas for about $20 (U.S.); this trip takes another 2 to 3 hours. A valid tourist permit is required. Greyhound buses take passengers from the Greyhound terminal at 120 W. Broadway in downtown San Diego to Tijuana's Central Bus Terminal (Centro de Autobuses) in La Mesa; for fare and schedule information phone (800) 231-2222 (from the United States). *For additional information about buses see Bus Service, page p. 52.*

Taxis from Cabo San Lucas to San José del Cabo or the Corridor hotels are convenient but expensive, averaging $25-$30 or more depending on destination. The local Suburcabos buses are a much cheaper alternative, running regularly between the two Cabos; the fare for the 45-minute trip is 33 pesos (about $2.85 U.S.). The Aguila bus line provides service from Cabo San Lucas to San José del Cabo and also to Todos Santos. The central bus station is at the junction of Mex. 19 and Mex. 1.

Currency can be exchanged at banks during their normal Mon.-Fri. business hours, but make sure this service is offered before getting in line. *Casas de cambio* (currency exchange houses) are another option; their exchange rates may not be as favorable, but they're more convenient. ATMs are plentiful, and some dispense dollars in addition to pesos. Avoid using an ATM after dark.

As in other parts of Mexico, making phone calls from your hotel room, calling collect or using a credit card can all end up being prohibitively expensive. Instead, buy a prepaid Ladatel/Telmex calling card, available in various denominations at mini markets, pharmacies and other local businesses. The cards offer relatively low per-minute rates and can be used at any public phone marked "Telmex" or "Ladatel." Avoid phones on which the message "To call long distance to the USA and Canada, simply dial 0" is inscribed; the charge will be exorbitant.

The English-language *Gringo Gazette* is published every other week. There are two separate editions covering southern and northern Baja. The newspaper is a good source for local tourist-related news, plus restaurant and entertainment listings. The website visitloscabos.travel/ also has travel information about the Los Cabos area. If you need to use the Internet stop by the Cabo Coffee Co., at the corner of Avenida Madero and Calle Hidalgo (across the street from the main square), which also serves java made from organically grown Mexican coffee.

In case of emergency dial 066 to reach local police, the fire department or the Red Cross. The AmeriMed Cabo San Lucas Hospital, on Avenida Lázaro Cárdenas near the Bancomer bank branch and a McDonald's outlet, offers a wide range of routine and emergency services and has a 24-hour pharmacy. Insurance is required for medical emergencies; phone (624) 105-8550.

To contact the municipal police, phone (624) 143-3977. The Red Cross (Cruz Roja) is at Mex. 19 Km marker 221 (on the way to Todos Santos); phone (624) 143-3300. As is the case with most local offices in Mexico, the ability to speak fluent Spanish will come in handy.

Cabo San Lucas is warm all year. Daytime highs are around 80 degrees in winter but can soar to over

100 during the summer months; bring plenty of sunscreen. The Gulf of California waters warm well into the 80s in summer and are close to 80 degrees the rest of the year, making conditions for diving and snorkeling ideal. The Pacific is about 10 degrees cooler. The high tourist season is primarily November through April; bring a sweater for occasional cool evenings if visiting in January or February. September and October are the rainiest months, but in general the climate is arid.

## City Layout

Despite its popularity as an exclusive resort area, Cabo San Lucas is still a small town at heart. It spreads north and west from Cabo San Lucas Bay (Bahía de Cabo San Lucas). The main street is Avenida Lázaro Cárdenas, the westward extension of Mex. 1. Boulevard Marina branches off it, curves around the harbor and leads to a few beachfront hotels located beyond downtown. Almost everything of visitor interest clusters around the harbor; the streets in the vicinity of Plaza Amelia Wilkes, the central square; and along the Mex. 1 Corridor.

Downtown Cabo lends itself to strolling. The shopping centers, restaurants and nightspots along Boulevard Marina and on the surrounding streets can all be easily reached on foot. In addition, a pedestrian walkway (malecón) wraps around the large Cabo San Lucas Marina, a modern harbor packed with everything from humble pangas to huge luxury yachts. The harbor malecón can be traversed in about an hour and the people-watching is always interesting.

Stop by the sport-fishing docks at the harbor's southern end in late afternoon, when local boats return from a day's fishing, for a firsthand look at the many game varieties found in the surrounding waters. If you're driving in from one of the Corridor hotels, there is a large free parking lot off Boulevard Marina, next to the Plaza Nautica shopping center.

## Beaches

The beaches of southern Baja are renowned for their beauty as well as their tranquility. The scenery is magnificent: intensely blue water, a backdrop of mountains and rugged cliffs, stands of huge cacti. It's still not all that difficult for solitude seekers to find a secluded beach and spend the day picnicking, surfing or snorkeling sans crowds.

You will, however, need a car for beach exploring. With the exception of Medano Beach, private taxi rides to and from the Corridor beaches are expensive. Public bus transportation is an option and drivers will generally let you disembark at beach turn-offs. However, walking from the highway to the beaches themselves often involves a long trek without any shade (i.e., miserably hot).

Cabo's most popular sunbathing spot is Medano Beach (Playa El Medano), which curves gracefully along the shore of Cabo San Lucas Bay just north of town and encompasses the beachfront hotel zone. The water here is usually safe for swimming, the sand is soft, and people-watching from the outdoor bars and restaurants lining the beach is always entertaining.

Cruise ships anchor just off shore. Parasailers soar overhead. Beach vendors trudge through the sand. Catamarans, sea kayaks and pangas ply the bay. Rowdy co-eds rent wave runners and other water toys. To reach the beach from Avenida Lázaro Cárdenas, head south on Paseo de Pescador. During college spring break weeks Medano's raucous beachfront bars are party central.

Land's End (see attraction listing), or "Finisterra," is literally that—the tip of the Baja California Peninsula. Both the approach to Cabo San Lucas via Mex. 1 and elevated spots in town offer panoramic views of Baja's final frontier. Some of the beaches in this area, however, are accessible only by boat.

Located just west of Land's End, Lover's Beach (Playa del Amor) may well be the most idyllic, although it's almost always crowded unless you arrive early in the day. A water taxi can be hired either at Medano Beach or the Cabo San Lucas marina to take you to the beach, drop you off and then return at a predetermined time; bring along drinking water and a lunch. Swimming and snorkeling are usually safe along the cove that faces the Gulf of California side, although the water can occasionally get a bit rough.

At Lover's Beach it's also possible to walk coast to coast—literally and in a matter of minutes. From the gulf shore, the sand extends across the cape to another beach facing the Pacific Ocean. Known as Divorce Beach, this stretch's white sand is great for strolling or beachcombing, but crashing waves and strong rip currents make swimming dangerous.

Solmar Beach (Playa Solmar) is a wide stretch of sand running west from the rocks at Land's End. Several large hotels, including the Gran Solmar resort, the Hotel Finisterra, the Terra Sol Beach Resort and the Playa Grande Resort, front this beach. The powerful Pacific undertow and currents make swimming here dangerous as well, but the views are spectacular.

Land's End is noted for two dramatic rock formations sculpted by the elements. El Arco, Cabo's signature landmark, is the famous natural rock arch featured on everything from tourist brochures to souvenir shot glasses. The other photogenic formations here are the pinnacles of The Friars (Los Frailes)—chiseled granite formations shaped like hooded monks. Deep blue water surrounds them at Land's End, a point where the Gulf of California mingles with the mighty Pacific.

For close-up views of El Arco you'll need to hit the water. Everything from water taxis and kayak tours to booze cruises and glass-bottom boats make the short trip from either Medano Beach or the Cabo San Lucas marina. Glass-bottom boat tours last an hour, cost about $15 (U.S.) per person and depart from the docks at the far southern end of the marina. You'll find ticket booths along the malecón.

If you have a car, the Gulf of California coast between Cabo San Lucas and San José del Cabo is sprinkled with surfing areas, hidden beaches and secluded little coves that can be explored. Turn-offs branching off the Corridor (Mex. 1), some no more than dirt paths, lead to these spots. Generally these beaches are not considered safe for swimming (there are no lifeguards, for one thing), but they offer excellent snorkeling and diving opportunities. Heading northeast on Mex. 1 from Cabo San Lucas toward San José del Cabo, here are a few worth visiting.

**Note:** The Cabo Corridor beaches took an especially heavy beating from Hurricane Odile; in March 2015 Chileno Bay was crawling with bulldozers in an effort to rehabilitate the beach. Double check conditions at these beaches before planning an excursion.

Shipwreck Beach (Playa Barco Varado) is at Km 11, about 7 miles north of downtown Cabo. It's a long drive from the highway to the entrance of the Cabo del Sol resort development; access to the beach is via the southwest side of the Sheraton Hacienda del Mar Golf & Spa Resort (follow the signs). The beach is named for a Japanese tuna boat that ran aground in the 1960s; until recently the rusted hulk still remained on the rocks, providing golfers at Cabo del Sol's Ocean Course with a spectacular backdrop on the last few holes. There are tide pools to explore and swimming in the surf is possible, although not recommended for young children due to waves and occasional rough conditions.

Widow's Beach (Playa las Viudas) also is known as Twin Dolphin Beach because of its location near the now-demolished Hotel Twin Dolphin. Swimming is usually good at this series of scalloped, coarse sand beaches separated by rocky outcroppings. When the surf's up, however, the pounding shore break will surely finish you off. But the wild beauty of Viudas make it a worthwhile stop at any time, regardless of ocean conditions. The turn-off for the unpaved beach access road (signed "Acceso a la Playa") is just past the Km 12 marker.

Snorkelers are drawn to Playa Santa Maria, a picturesque horseshoe-shaped bay endowed with colorful underwater scenery. Around mid-day tour boats arrive at the cove, blasting high-decibel party music and dispensing pods of snorkelers. In other words, it's best to visit in the morning or late afternoon. There are no snack bars, so pack a cooler. Shade is nonexistent, but roving umbrella rental boys will set you up for a few pesos. The signed beach turn-off is on Mex. 1 just past Playa la Viudas. Parking is available in a "guarded" lot near the highway, or farther down the dirt road at the beach itself.

Chileno Bay, about 14 kilometers (9 miles) northeast, is one of the most beautiful areas along the Los Cabos coast, and a prime swimming, snorkeling and scuba destination. A gorgeous bay backed by rocky bluffs and a shady palm grove, Playa Chileno caters to civilized beachgoers with bathrooms, showers and a booth renting snorkel equipment. The Mex. 1 Chileno turn-off is clearly signed "Chileno Bay Playa Público"; a paved road leads down to a free parking lot.

Playa Palmilla, about 27 kilometers (17 miles) northeast, is near the luxurious, long-established One&Only Palmilla resort hotel. A long crescent of sand, Palmilla's dependably calm surf makes it one of the best swimming beaches along the Corridor. If you've brought your mask and fins, there's decent snorkeling along the rocks toward the point. Thatched *palapa* umbrellas provide welcome shade, and if you're in the mood to fish, the Fisherman's Cooperative in the beach parking lot will gladly arrange a trip. The well-signed turn-off (look for the Palmilla resort signs) is near the Km 27 marker. The paved access road winds through Palmilla's golf course before reaching the beach.

Most of the beaches facing the Gulf of California are safe for swimming; those facing the open Pacific should be appreciated only for the view. Pay attention to any warning signs: Some beaches are prone to riptides and dangerous breakers, or have deep drop-offs close to shore. All beaches in Mexico are the property of the government and consequently are accessible to the public. Parking at or camping on deserted beaches is perfectly legal; it is not legal, however, to leave behind garbage of any kind. Driving on beaches in Mexico also is illegal.

## Outdoor Recreation

Two pursuits define the outdoor life at Los Cabos: sport fishing and golf. The waters of the Gulf of California and the Pacific Ocean are home to some 850 species of fish. The gulf in particular has a rich and varied marine population, including whale sharks, manta rays, schooling hammerhead sharks, stingrays, moray eels and sea turtles.

Of the two dozen or so game species widely caught in Baja waters, striped marlin run year-round. The season for the majestic blue marlin is June through mid-November. Others commonly hooked include amberjack, black marlin, bonito, black sea bass, corbina, dorado (mahi mahi), roosterfish, sailfish, snapper, wahoo, yellowfin tuna and yellowtail.

During the season it is advisable to book fishing trips well in advance; some participants reserve boats as much as a year in advance for the Bisbee's Black and Blue Marlin Jackpot Tournament and the Los Cabos Offshore Tournament, both held the second half of October. These are among the world's richest marlin fishing tournaments, with base entry fees of several thousand dollars.

A catch-and-release policy is strongly emphasized; anglers experience the thrill of battle, but after their catch is reeled in it is tagged and set free, helping to preserve billfish species and ensure the continuation of the sport.

Most of the larger resort hotels have their own sport-fishing fleets, making it easy to plan an excursion if you're a guest. The Fiesta Americana Grand Los Cabos, the Solmar resort properties and the One&Only Palmilla have fleets with boats anchored at the Cabo San Lucas marina.

If you prefer to make your own arrangements, several fleet operators operate from the marina's docks on the south side of the harbor. *Pangas* (small, outboard motor-powered skiffs) holding two or three people can be rented by the hour, including equipment and a fishing license (required). ABY Charters is at the marina's main dock, next to the Flea Market (Mercado de Artesanías); phone (624) 143-0831 or (866) 751-3505 (from the United States).

More expensive sport-fishing cruisers normally rent for parties of four to six people so expenses can be shared; the cost usually includes tackle, bait, licenses, lunch and a captain and mate, but not taxes or tips. Rates range from $700 to more than $1,000 per day, depending on the size of the boat. Trips depart around 7 a.m. and return by 2 or 3 in the afternoon. Most boats either head east to the fertile fishing grounds of the Gordo Banks or around Los Arcos toward the open Pacific.

Several water sports centers provide a full range of rental equipment as well as organized snorkeling and scuba trips. Manta SCUBA Diving specializes in scuba and snorkeling excursions to Chileno Bay. They also conduct two-tank boat dives with an English-speaking guide to nearby sites, twice daily. Bringing your own dive gear is recommended, although rental equipment is available. The dive shop is located near the south end of the marina at Plaza Gali #37; phone (624) 144-3871 or (877) 287-1120 (toll-free from the United States).

Amigos del Mar, on Boulevard Marina across from the sport-fishing docks, offers guided natural history, scuba and snorkeling tours. These excursions venture to such prime spots as the Socorro Islands, about 200 miles southwest of Cabo San Lucas, inhabited by 400-pound tuna and exotic species of reef fish; Land's End, home to octopus, tropicals and sea lions; and Cabo Pulmo National Marine Park, site of a living coral reef that offers experienced divers some of the clearest water and richest marine life in the world.

Most trips are aboard a 25-foot canopied skiff that accommodates four people, or a newer 30-foot boat that can carry up to ten divers. For additional information and reservations phone (624) 355-3975, or (513) 898-0547 (from the United States).

Gray whales complete their long-distance migration from the Bering Sea to the warm Pacific waters of the mid- and lower Baja coastline each year from January through March. They can sometimes be spotted from the beaches and rocky overlooks along the Mex. 1 Corridor and the rocks around Land's End.

As popular as sport fishing—if not more so—is golf. A few decades ago the nine-hole Mayan Palace Golf Course in San José del Cabo was it. Now world-class courses are scattered along the Corridor between the two Cabos. Some—like the new Tiger Woods-designed El Cardonal course in the Diamante condo community—are open to members only.

Golfing in Los Cabos also is a very expensive pastime; greens fees for 18 holes average more than $225 (somewhat less in the low season), cart and bottled water included.

The signature hole at the Nicklaus-designed Palmilla Golf Club, at the One&Only Palmilla resort, is the par-4 fifth. The tee shot must carry over a cactus-filled canyon, which also wraps around in front of the green. The desert vegetation, Gulf of California vistas and view from the mountaintop clubhouse are all breathtaking, and the play is a strategic challenge. For information phone the resort at (624) 144-5250.

The Golden Bear also designed the highly regarded Ocean Course at the Cabo del Sol resort development. The final three holes offer dramatic waterfront scenery as well as an assortment of hazards in the form of cactus, rock cliffs and treacherous bunkers. Instead of negotiating long fairways, players tee off over deep ravines to landing pads and then chip to the green. Even the short par 3 holes are formidable.

The Tom Weiskopf-designed Desert Course features an inland layout that nevertheless provides a view of the gulf from every hole. For information about either course phone the resort at (624) 145-8200, or (877) 703-4394 (toll-free from the United States).

The Cabo Real Golf Course, at Corridor Km marker 19.5, was designed by Robert Trent Jones. It winds its way among beautiful homes and the exclusive Las Ventanas al Paraiso resort. Average players can handle the layout, which doesn't mean play is easy. The palm-flanked 14th-hole fairway sweeps down to the beach, while the 15th tee, right at the surf, offers the most spectacular view of the course. Reservations can be made by phoning 01 (800) 543-2044 (toll-free long distance within Mexico) or (877) 795-8727 (toll-free from the United States).

The Nicklaus-designed course at the members-only Eldorado Golf Club, next to the Westin Resort & Spa at the northeast end of the Cabo Real development, has six holes right along the beach. The layout winds from seaside to rocky canyons and back, with the green at the par-3 16th hole framed by the gulf's cobalt-blue waters. For reservations, phone (624) 144-5464 or (866) 513-4434 (from the United States).

The Cabo San Lucas Country Club is just a short distance east of Cabo San Lucas. This is the only course in Los Cabos with a view of the Land's End rocks, which look particularly impressive from the 18th hole. The gently sloping fairways look out on a desert landscape that features giant cardon cacti. The seventh hole, a par 5 double dogleg that wraps around a lake, is a whopping 620 yards. Greens fees range from $95 to $166 (U.S.), a tad lower than at the other championship courses. For information phone (624) 143-4653 or (888) 239-7951 (from the United States). **Note:** The course does not accept U.S. dollars; payment is by credit card or pesos only.

## Dining

Hotel restaurants in Los Cabos are expensive and, on the whole, predictably good. For more local fare, hit the streets. Cabo is famed for fish tacos, but you'll also find shrimp, pork, chicken and beef varieties. For the most part, the food at the bars and restaurants lining Medano Beach and the marina *malecón* is very good, but also overpriced. For better *comida* at more digestible prices, try the open-air restaurants in the downtown area, many run by families. These are good places for late night tacos or a hearty morning meal of *huevos rancheros,* eggs and black beans drenched in tomato salsa, sprinkled with cheese and served with tortillas.

El Pollo de Oro ("The Golden Chicken"), at the corner of Morelos and 20 de Noviembre, specializes in juicy, fall-off-the-bone Sinaloa-style barbecued chicken. Seating is in a large patio courtyard perpetually packed with locals and a sprinkling of tourists. In addition to the must-order *pollo*, the menu is loaded with tempting Mexican dishes—all authentic and affordable.

*Torta* (sandwich) stands also pop up on downtown street corners after dark. Ham and cheese is a common and tasty variety. Many stands grill hot dogs and whip up tacos as well. Use the same common sense at these places that applies whenever sampling street food in Mexico—if there's a crowd hovering around a cart and the food looks hot and fresh, it should be fine. Squeezing lots of lime juice over the meat helps kill any lingering bacteria. See the Lodgings & Restaurants section for AAA-RATED dining establishments.

## Shopping

A one-stop destination for shopping and entertainment in downtown Cabo is the Puerto Paraiso mall, off Avenida Lázaro Cárdenas between Plaza Bonita Mall and the Marina Fiesta resort. On a par with American malls, Paraiso is a modern, three-level collection of clothing chains (Kenneth Cole, Nautica, Tommy Bahama), boutique-type shops, gift stores, high-end jewelry merchants and restaurants. The center is designed for open-air strolling along attractively landscaped terraces, as well as window shopping in air-conditioned comfort.

On the lower level, American restaurant chains like Johnny Rockets, Harley-Davidson Restaurant & Bar and Ruth's Chris Steakhouse front the marina. There's also an outpost of San José del Cabo's Baja Brewing Co. here. For kids there is a bowling alley and video arcade, a 10-screen movie theater complex and a fast-food court. Puerto Paraiso is open daily 9-9, with extended hours at major restaurants.

Plaza Bonita, an open-air shopping center next door to Puerto Paraiso, has a few interesting shops, including the Sergio Bustamante Gallery. The famed Guadalajaran artist is known for his whimsical ceramic, wood, bronze and papier-mâché sculptures, which elicit opinions as wildly mixed as his art.

Check out the two-level gallery and decide for yourself.

The Souvenir Outlet, across the street from Puerto Paraiso at the corner of Avenida Lázaro Cárdenas and Vicario, occupies a faux lighthouse packed with all manner of souvenir cheese. We're talking fridge magnets, twisted Corona beer bottles, El Arco paperweights, snow globes and other assorted dust collectors. If this is what you're after, the prices here are noticeably lower than at other gift shops around town. There's also a well-stocked pharmacy (*farmacia*) inside.

No shopping tour of Cabo is complete without wandering the streets in the vicinity of Plaza Amelia Wilkes, a traditional Mexican square with a gazebo at its center. Magic of the Moon, in the vicinity of the plaza on Madero (between Guerrero and Marina Boulevard) sells designer women's fashions—casual, colorful outfits with tropical motifs that fit right in at a beachside resort. The vivacious owner, Pepita, will gladly show you around.

Zen Mar, near the corner of Avenida Lázaro Cárdenas and Calle Matamoros, is a combination art gallery and museum with an outstanding variety of ethnic masks from all over Mexico, including Day of the Dead designs. *Ex-votos* have facial writings describing why the mask was made for a particular religious ceremony; *retablos* (small devotional paintings) depict emotions without the use of words. Most of the works are for sale.

## Nightlife

Bars and rock 'n' roll—that pretty much sums it up. The Cabo Wabo Cantina, on Calle Vicente Guerrero just south of Avenida Lázaro Cárdenas, is owned by rocker Sammy Hagar. Young crowds pack the place for regular live shows by a rock cover band and occasional visits from big-name acts, including Hagar himself; hard rock and dance pop blasts from the sound system on other nights. It's open daily until 2 a.m.

The Giggling Marlin, on Boulevard Marina at Calle Matamoros, blasts classic rock and dance hits, has frequent live music and puts on a saucy audience-participation show. The attraction here is a pulley device that dangles patrons upside down—rather like a captured fish—to the great amusement of the masses. There's also a restaurant on the premises that serves good Mexican and seafood dishes. To find it, look for the beer bottle-toting marlin atop the entrance.

Also high on the see-and-be-seen circuit is El Squid Roe, on Avenida Lázaro Cárdenas at Boulevard Marina (across from Plaza Bonita Mall). This three-level nightclub is loud, raucous and invariably packed. Be forewarned: It's the kind of place where waiters brandishing spray tanks of tequila move through crowds of people dancing on top of tables. An open-air dance floor is on the main level.

Another dance club on the Cabo party scene is Pink Kitty, on Boulevard Marina across from Burger King. The atmosphere is decidedly upscale—Italian blown-glass chandeliers, plush leather seating, an all-female staff and VIP service. The roster of visiting international DJs changes weekly, drawing a young, dressed-to-impress crowd that parties until dawn.

For a decidedly mellower evening, the Don Diego Terrace restaurant's bar in the Sandos Finisterra hotel, off Boulevard Marina heading out toward Land's End, is an ideal place to watch the sun slowly drop into the Pacific. Wager on game outcomes at the Caliente Sports Book in the Puerto Paraiso mall. Clean, well-lit, air conditioned and loaded with TVs, Caliente also offers off-track betting in case you've got a hot tip on a horse. There's a full bar.

**THE GLASS FACTORY** is on Av. Gen. Juan Alvarez (behind the hospital), a short distance w. of Av. Lázaro Cárdenas (Mex. 1). Multiple teams of glass blowers work in shifts to produce hundreds of pieces of glassware and decorative items every day. Visitors can watch as these artisans melt down recycled bottles, blend the molten liquid with colored chips and blow it into various shapes, and then temper the pieces in glass-fired kilns for 24 hours. This is a popular stop for both locals and tourists to stock up on glassware and accessories. The workers gladly accept tips and in return will answer questions and let you try your hand at glass blowing.

**Time:** Allow 30 minutes minimum. **Hours:** Glass-blowing demonstrations given Mon.-Fri. 7-3:30, Sat. 7-1. Closed holidays. **Cost:** Free. **Phone:** (624) 143-0255.

**LAND'S END** (Finisterra) is at the confluence of the Pacific Ocean and the Gulf of California (Sea of Cortez). This southernmost tip of the Baja California peninsula generally refers not just to one specific outcropping, but rather the slender chain of rocks protruding from the waters south of Cabo San Lucas. The most well-known of this group is El Arco (The Arch).

Although visible from shore, the best way to see the eroded formations that constitute Land's End is from the water. Fleets of water taxis (many of the "glass-bottom" variety) line up at the marina to take passengers on a roughly 45-minute trip for up-close looks at these unusual rocky outcroppings. Among the formations along the way are Pelican City, a group of rocks where members of that large-billed species congregate; another clump of rocks where a colony of seals likes to hang out; a cave said to have been a favorite of pirates; Lover's and Divorce beaches; and, of course, El Arco.

Since these water taxi excursions are extremely popular, in order to provide good views the guide may have to maneuver his craft past numerous other water taxis; boats carrying snorkelers and scuba divers to nearby offshore locations; fishing boats; and other watercraft towing parasailers. Before returning to shore, the boat swings by a small rock jutting up from the water, the actual "land's end."

El Arco (The Arch) is part of the Land's End formation stretching offshore near the point where the Gulf of California and the Pacific Ocean meet. The iconic image of Cabo San Lucas, El Arco is a natural granite arch that has been carved by wind and water.

While the arch is readily visible from shore, its size and beauty are best appreciated close up. Water taxis, available at the marina, take passengers past the arch and will drop guests off on request at nearby Lover's Beach (Playa del Amor), which faces the swimmable Gulf of California. The opposite side of the beach fronting the rough waters of the Pacific is not safe for swimming. **Note:** If you opt to linger at Lover's Beach, remember to set a time for the water taxi to pick you up for the trip back to Cabo San Lucas.

**WHALE PHOTO SAFARI** departs from the Cabo Dolphins building at the marina on Paseo de la Marina (the *malecón*). This fun adventure takes you off the southern tip of the Baja Peninsula to view gray and northern humpback whales; both species migrate to the warm waters of the Sea of Cortez to breed and to nurse their young. An inflatable all-weather speed boat moves quickly and easily among the gentle giants; the most frequent whale sightings are in January and February.

Other marine animals you'll likely encounter are wild dolphins (they seem to love small boats), sea turtles and manta rays that fling themselves out of the water for an occasional somersault. Experienced guides provide background information about the whales, their habits and their habitat.

Bring a camera, hat, sweater or light jacket, sunscreen and a towel. Snacks and bottled water are provided. **Time:** Allow 3 hours minimum. **Hours:** Trips depart Mon.-Fri. at 9, noon and 3, Dec. 15-Mar. 31. **Cost:** Fare $89 (U.S.); $69 (ages 5-11). Ages 0-4 are not permitted. Reservations are recommended. **Phone:** (624) 173-9500, or (888) 526-2238 (from the United States and Canada).

**WILD CANYON ADVENTURES** is located in El Tule Canyon, an ecological preserve about a 20-minute drive from Los Cabos. Fans of extreme sports will get the most out of this adventure park, where the main draw is eight lengthy zip lines. The final line, called Big Ocho, is more than half a mile long, and riders can reach speeds of up to 50 miles per hour while zipping along suspended from twin cables high above stark desert scenery.

Equally adrenaline inducing is Bungee Bombers; thrill seekers jump from a glass-floored gondola for that free-falling sensation. Camel Quest and Camel Encounter feature camel rides through the oasis at the canyon bottom as well as interactive encounters with these desert beasts. The young camels are trained to be ridden by kids, making this a good activity for families.

The 1,082-foot-long Los Cabos Canyon Bridge is a wooden suspension bridge that accommodates both pedestrians and ATVs. Just under 7 feet wide, it stands 164 feet above the canyon floor at its lowest point. An animal sanctuary is home to rescued parrots, macaws, prairie dogs and iguanas.

**Note:** Bilingual guides are present for all organized activities. Trails between the zip line landing and launching platforms are steep and involve uphill hiking, which can be strenuous in the summer heat; wear comfortable, lightweight clothing. Taking photographs with a personal camera or smartphone is not permitted.

**Hours:** Daily 9-6. Tour times for zip lines and other scheduled activities are at 9, noon and 3 (weather permitting). **Cost:** Tortugas zip line and Bungee Bombers $100 (U.S.) per person. Camel Quest $100 per person; $75 (children). Camel Encounter $75 per person; $55 (children). Fees for other activities vary. Day pass (includes three main activities at scheduled times as well as use of other park facilities) $235 per person. A $10 (U.S.) park entrance fee (includes access to the animal sanctuary and Los Cabos Canyon Bridge) must be paid at check-in. Round-trip transportation from hotels in Cabo San Lucas, San José del Cabo and The Corridor is included, along with bottled water and zip line equipment. **Phone:** (624) 144-4433, (866) 230-5253 (from the United States and Canada), or 01 (800) 838-4645 (toll-free long distance within Mexico). 🍴 ✉

## ENSENADA, BAJA CALIFORNIA (A-1)
**pop. 466,814**

Ensenada (ehn-seh-NAH-dah) spreads over scrub-covered hills that slope down to the shores of Bahía de Todos Santos (Todos Santos Bay). The city (its name, not surprisingly, means "bay") boasts a scenic setting, pleasant weather, duty-free shopping, fine sport fishing and close proximity to the United States; Ensenada is the farthest many weekend visitors ever get into Mexico.

The first real roots were put down by ranchers, who began settling the area in the early 19th century. Ensenada temporarily boomed in 1870 with the discovery of gold at nearby Real del Castillo. The town became a supply depot for miners and was designated the capital of the Baja California Territory in 1882. By the early 20th century, however, the mines had given out, the capital was relocated to Mexicali and Ensenada lapsed back into obscurity.

After U.S. Prohibition went into effect in the late 1920s, Ensenada—along with Tijuana—became a favored drinking and gambling destination for Hollywood stars and other well-heeled types. Real revitalization came with agricultural reform and development in the Mexicali Valley. A nearby port was needed to handle the export of farm produce to the United States and mainland Mexico, and Ensenada's harbor facilities made it an obvious choice for development.

The completion of paved highway Mex. 1 from Tijuana opened the city up to American vacationers and sport-fishing enthusiasts. Ensenada is a little far for a day trip; a weekend getaway allows you to dine, stroll, shop, do some fishing, visit a winery or attend one of the city's many annual events.

## Practicalities

Ensenada is about 109 kilometers (68 miles) south of Tijuana. The city's small airport, south of town off Mex. 1, accommodates only private planes. A tourist permit is not required for stays of less than 72 hours or if you do not travel any farther south than the town of Maneadero, south of Ensenada. *For additional information about border crossing regulations see the Border Information section in the back of this guide.*

Four-lane toll highway Mex. 1-D is a quick, convenient route south from Tijuana. From the border, follow the prominent "Ensenada Toll Road" (*Ensenada Cuota*) signs along westbound Calle Internacional, which parallels the border fence to the junction with Mex. 1-D. Make sure you choose the proper exit lane, or you could be routed back to downtown Tijuana. The first of three toll plazas between the two cities is at Playas de Tijuana. The second is on the southern edge of Rosarito Beach; the third is at the village of San Miguel, about 13 kilometers (8 miles) north of Ensenada. The toll at each plaza is 31 pesos (about $2.30 U.S.). The final stretch from San Miguel to Ensenada is via four-lane, non-toll Mex. 1.

Alternative free Mex. 1 (look for signs that say *Libre*) parallels Mex. 1-D most of the way, although it turns inland south of the village of La Misión, about 44 kilometers (27 miles) north of Ensenada. The driving time is longer, and the road has some rough spots. Avoid night driving along this and other two-lane secondary roads in northern Baja, as both cattle and pedestrians frequently cross them.

The main bus station is in the northern part of town on Avenida Riveroll, between calles 10 and 11. Bus service is inexpensive; local routes are designated by street name, usually painted on the windshield. The Autotransportes de Baja California bus line provides regular service to cities up and down the peninsula. *For additional information about buses see Bus Service, page p. 52.*

Taxis, many of them minivans, congregate near the hotels along Avenida López Mateos. Although their ubiquitous solicitations can be annoying, drivers are normally courteous and knowledgeable. Make sure, however, that the fare is decided before you set off. Taxis can be hired for trips to such outlying destinations as La Bufadora (*see attraction listing*) and the Guadalupe Valley wineries. Round-trip rates run $40-$50 (U.S.), depending on the number of passengers.

In the event of emergency, dial 066 (English may not be spoken). For tourist assistance that isn't of an emergency nature or help with legal problems, dial 078; you should then be connected to the nearest State Tourism Office during normal office hours. A calling card is not needed to dial either of these three-digit numbers from a public phone. For medical emergencies, Clinica Hospital Cardiomed is located downtown at Av. Obregón #1018. Phone (646) 178-0351 (English spoken).

The English-language *Gringo Gazette* publishes two editions, one for northern and one for southern Baja, containing travel-related information and lots of local advertising. *Casas de cambio* (currency exchange houses) offer the best rates. ATM machines dispense pesos and also may charge a withdrawal fee.

One of Ensenada's best features is its mild climate, similar to coastal Southern California and with fewer extremes of heat than almost any other Baja city. Winter evenings can be chilly, but the temperature seldom drops below 40 F. Summers are warm and dry, with occasional hot spells caused by Santa Ana winds blowing in from the desert. Almost all of the annual precipitation falls between December and March. Fierce Pacific storms sometimes bring torrential winter rains, and early summer can be quite foggy.

Personal safety is a matter of common sense. Tourists are invariably welcomed, as their dollars sustain many local businesses. If traveling by car, the best advice is to drive safely and defensively; traffic accidents are one of the biggest sources of vacation headaches in Mexico. One way to minimize risk is to stop at every intersection, even those that don't have stop signs.

## City Layout

The preferred route into downtown Ensenada (signed "Centro") branches off Mex. 1 about 2.5 miles north of the city and follows the coastline. It becomes Boulevard Lázaro Cárdenas (more commonly known as Boulevard Costero), one of two main thoroughfares traversing the waterfront tourist zone. Boulevard Costero runs along the harbor; Avenida López Mateos is a block inland. These two streets are lined with hotels, restaurants, bars, shops, nightspots and other businesses catering to visitors.

Heading south, Boulevard Costero ends at Calle Agustín Sangines (also called Calle Delante), which proceeds east to Mex. 1. Mex. 1, the Transpeninsular Highway, then continues south to Maneadero and on down the peninsula.

The *malecón,* a bayside walkway running for half a mile between Boulevard Azueta and Avenida Castillo, has been widened and refurbished. Here are the sport-fishing piers, a towering flagpole and huge Mexican flag, Plaza Cívica *(see attraction listing)* and the cruise ship terminal. It's the best place in town for a breezy stroll, and there are benches for relaxing.

Away from the waterfront, Ensenada is easy to negotiate. The terrain is flat, and the layout is a basic grid. Avenues (avenidas) are named and run north-south; streets (calles) are numbered and run east-west. Streets and avenues are often unmarked, however. To orient yourself, count off city blocks inland from

Avenida López Mateos, which is also known as Calle 1; successive streets are Calle 2, Calle 3, etc. The commercial business district centers around avenidas Ruíz and Juárez (the in-town extensions of Mex. 1) at the western end of downtown.

Driving tips to keep in mind: As in other Baja cities, traffic lights are small and often hard to spot from a distance. Stop *(alto)* signs placed at intersections can be obscure, so always proceed slowly and with caution. Some downtown streets are one way. The pay lot at the Plaza Marina shopping center, on Boulevard Costero just north of the sport-fishing piers, is convenient for nearby waterfront wandering.

The city's low skyline is distinguished by the twin spires of Our Lady of Guadalupe (Nuestra Señora de Guadalupe), at the corner of Calle 6 and Avenida Floresta. The cathedral, built in typical Spanish colonial style, is one of Ensenada's most prominent structures and can be used as a downtown orientation landmark. Named for the Virgin of Guadalupe, Mexico's patron saint, it is the focus for celebrations on Dec. 12 *(see Special Events).*

## Shopping

The main tourist shopping area is along Avenida López Mateos. Gift shops lining the blocks between avenidas Castillo and Ruíz feature such imported items as silver and gold jewelry, onyx chess sets, leather boots and fine liquor. Some of the shops have fixed prices; English is usually spoken and credit cards are welcomed. Los Castillo, Avenida López Mateos #815, carries Taxco silver jewelry guaranteed to be at least 92.5 percent pure (designated by the numerals ".925").

This upscale merchandise is augmented by curio shops that stock traditional Mexican craft and clothing items like baskets, ceramics, guitars, jewelry, wrought-iron furniture and leather jackets, purses and sandals. On Boulevard Costero at Avenida Castillo is the Handicrafts Center (Centro Artesanía), a cluster of craft stalls. In particular, take time to wander through Galería de Pérez Meillon, which sells Nuevo Casas Grandes pottery, Kumeyaay baskets and other handmade items fashioned by northern Mexican artisans using age-old techniques.

Ensenada's outdoor flea markets offer a chance to find the odd treasure amid piles of utilitarian wares. Los Globos, bordered by Calle 9, Calle Coral, Avenida Morelos and Avenida Juárez (3 blocks east of Avenida Reforma and about a mile from the waterfront), is especially busy on weekends. In one area there are foodstuffs—fruit, vegetables, nuts, grains, freshly made tacos and *churros,* a sweet tube-shaped fritter similar to a doughnut. Although you won't find many souvenirs, this full-blown Mexican marketplace is a change of pace from the tourist district.

## Outdoor Recreation

Todos Santos Bay and the Pacific yield such cool-water species as albacore, barracuda, bonito, rockfish and yellowtail. Summer is the best time for sport fishing, although such bottom dwellers as sea bass, ling cod, rock cod, halibut and whitefish can be caught all year.

Charter arrangements can be made at the piers off the *malecón*. Rates for private groups range from about $200 (U.S.) to upward of $550 per day, depending on the size of the craft (an outboard-powered *panga* or a larger cruiser) and the number of passengers. Party boats for bigger groups cost about $50 per person for an 8-hour day of fishing, plus an extra $10 or so for a required Mexican fishing license. Bait and tackle are usually included, as is pick-up and drop-off from your hotel.

In addition to fishing trips, Gordo's Sport Fishing Fleet offers privately chartered sightseeing boat tours of the bay; phone (646) 178-3515, or (949) 678-1187 from the United States. Sergio's Sportfishing runs daily trips all year to Punta Banda, San Miguel Reef and the Todos Santos Islands, plus longer trips to the Outer Banks (about 35 miles offshore), usually from late May through September; phone (646) 178-2185, or (619) 399-7224 (from the United States).

Northern Baja diving conditions are similar to those off the coast of Southern California. Within easy reach of Ensenada are thick kelp forests sheltering a wide range of marine life. The tip of the Punta Banda Peninsula is a favored dive site; underwater mountains (sea mounts) are blanketed with colonies of anemones and sponges, and a variety of fish swim through growths of brilliant blue algae. Water temperatures are bracing—around 55 to 64 degrees F. The La Bufadora Dive shop, near the end of the road to La Bufadora *(see attraction listing)*, offers half-day diving and fishing trips. Equipment, wet suit and kayak rentals also are available; phone (646) 154-2092, or (619) 730-2903 (from the United States).

Punta Banda also has an abundance of hot springs; at spots along the beaches here, it is possible to dig into the sand and create your own hole from which soothing hot waters bubble. There are a couple of RV parks and camping areas along BC 23, the paved road that traverses the peninsula. Several unmarked hiking trails also lead off this road.

Ensenada is on the last leg of a gray whale migration journey that begins in the Bering Sea and ends at coastal bays and lagoons along the southern half of the Baja Peninsula. From late December through March the whales pass between the shoreline and the Todos Santos Islands, a little more than a mile offshore. Some of them come close enough to scratch their backs along the bay floor, removing barnacles and parasites. The rugged coastline north and south of town, and especially the end of the Punta Banda Peninsula, provides some excellent lookout points. Gordo's Sport Fishing Fleet, Sergio's Sportfishing and La Bufadora Dive all offer whale-watching trips in tour boats during the peak viewing months.

There are no beaches within the city proper. Most visitors head for Estero Beach, about 12 kilometers (7 miles) south of downtown Ensenada via Mex. 1; the turn-off, about 7.5 kilometers (4.5 miles) south, is well marked. Along the shore of Estero Inlet there are gentle waves and a long stretch of sand.

Southern California surfers gravitate to several spots in the vicinity of Ensenada, including Punta San Miguel, a point next to the village of the same name; Punta Salsipuedes, north of Punta San Miguel; and Estero Beach. But the ultimate surf location in northern Baja is off the Todos Santos Islands (Islas Todos Santos), located at the mouth of Todos Santos Bay. These twin islands catch the full brunt of winter swells from the north Pacific, and waves can reach 30 feet. The San Miguel Surf Shop, on Avenida López Mateos between avenidas Miramar and Gastélum, is the local surfer hangout.

## Dining and Nightlife

Ensenada's traditional open-air Seafood Market, at the north end of Boulevard Costero at Avenida Miramar, is just north of the sport-fishing piers. Known to locals as the Mercado de Mariscos, the covered sheds displaying freshly caught fish and shellfish have a suitably salty ambience. Handcart vendors hawk fresh clams, oysters shucked on the spot and seafood cocktails.

Fish tacos are an Ensenada staple. Stands opposite the Seafood Market offer strips of savory fried fish wrapped in a folded tortilla along with sour cream, guacamole, salsa (both *verde* and *roja*, green and red), cabbage, onions and cilantro. Avoid the mayonnaise that is left out on the tables, though. You also can get fish tacos, soups *(caldos)* and other reasonably priced seafood at the nearby outdoor food court Plaza del Marisco.

Stumbling into a small, out-of-the-way seafood restaurant hidden on a side street is one of the joys of exploring the city. Check the customers; if a place is full of locals, it's likely to be good. Mariscos Bahía Ensenada, at the corner of avenidas López Mateos and Riveroll, is a downtown fixture with an extensive menu and a lively atmosphere complete with roving string trios. See the Lodgings & Restaurants section for AAA-RATED dining establishments.

Bars and clubs catering to tourists are downtown in the vicinity of Avenida López Mateos and Boulevard Costero. Hussong's Cantina, on Avenida Ruíz just east of Mateos, treats the designated driver in a group to free soft drinks while his or her companions indulge in margaritas and *cerveza*. Sawdust covers the hardwood floor and mariachi bands provide the music at a watering hole that has atmosphere to spare. Across from Hussong's is Papas & Beer, three floors of fun with free-flowing margaritas, blasting rock and high energy dance music, occasional live bands and numerous theme events.

An alternative to all this raucousness can be found at Bar Andaluz, in the Riviera del Pacífico *(see attraction listing).* This low-key lounge is a relaxed place to have an early evening drink. It's open noon-8 Sun.-Thurs., noon-9 Fri.-Sat.

Mexican dance, ballet and theatrical productions take place at the City Theater (Teatro de la Ciudad), on Calle Diamante between avenidas Pedro Loyola and Reforma. For event information phone (646) 177-0392.

## Special Events

Carnaval (Mardi Gras) is usually celebrated in mid-February on the 6 days prior to Ash Wednesday. A downtown street fair takes place each night, with midway rides, live entertainment, food vendors, parades of flower-covered floats and other merriment. The festivities climax with a masquerade ball; prizes are awarded for the best costume.

The Newport to Ensenada Race from Newport Beach, Calif., to Ensenada is held the last weekend in April. Hundreds of yachts depart from Newport Beach at noon, ending up in Ensenada about 11 hours later. Most remain in the city for a day or two, and a huge party with food, music and dancing follows. For information contact the Newport Ocean Sailing Association; phone (949) 644-1023 (from the United States).

Thousands of cyclists make the 50-mile trek from Rosarito to Ensenada along Mex. 1 (the free road) during the Rosarito-Ensenada Bike Ride, which is held twice a year, in May and late September. Following the event, participants and supporters party at the Finish Line Fiesta, held at the Corona Hotel near the cruise ship terminal.

Franciscan and Dominican missionaries first introduced wine culture to Baja California in the 16th century as a way to celebrate holy Mass, and today a thriving wine industry is centered in the Guadalupe Valley. With an ideal climate for grape production and rich volcanic soil, vineyards in northeastern Baja California state produce some 90 percent of Mexican wines.

For 2 weeks in the first half of August the Grape Harvest Festival (Fiesta de la Vendimia) celebrates this bounty. Area wineries, many with vineyards in the nearby Guadalupe and El Escondido valleys, also offer tours *(see Wineries).* For more information contact the Association of Wine Growers of Baja California (Asociación de Viticultores), downtown at Av. de la Marina #10, third floor; phone (646) 178-3038. Restaurants from all over Mexico enter dishes for judging at the Baja Seafood Expo, which normally takes place in late September.

The deceased are honored during Day of the Dead celebrations Nov. 1-2. Beginning in mid-November is the SCORE Baja 1000 (commonly known as the Baja Mil), one of the world's most prestigious off-road races. There are separate categories for cars, trucks, motorcycles and ATVs. The course alternates between an 800-mile loop beginning and ending in Ensenada and a longer run from Ensenada to La Paz that takes place every third year. For information contact SCORE International in the United States; phone (775) 852-8907.

Another major festival is the Feast Day of Our Lady of Guadalupe (Día de Nuestra Señora de Guadalupe), celebrated Dec. 12. It honors the nation's patron saint, the Guadalupe Virgin. All manner of amusement rides are set up in front of Our Lady of Guadalupe Church, and another attraction is the array of culinary specialties from all over Mexico.

**Baja California State Tourism Office:** at Boulevard Lázaro Cárdenas (Boulevard Costero) #609, this office also can provide legal assistance to tourists. Open daily 8-8. **Phone:** (646) 178-8578.

The Tourism and Convention Bureau (Comité de Turismo y Convenciónes) operates a booth on Boulevard Lázaro Cárdenas near the western entrance to the city. Open Mon.-Fri. 9-7, Sat. 10-4, Sun. 10-3 (but may vary by season); phone (646) 178-2411 (English spoken).

**CIVIC PLAZA** (Plaza Cívica) is off Blvd. Lázaro Cárdenas (Costero) at the foot of Av. Riveroll. Also known as Three Heads Park, it has a small landscaped court with 12-foot-high bronze busts of Mexican freedom fighter Father Miguel Hidalgo and former presidents Benito Juárez and Venustiano Carranza. Horse-drawn sightseeing carriages, or *calandrias,* depart from the plaza. There also are public restrooms.

**LA BUFADORA** (The Buffalo Snort) is about 32 km (20 mi.) s.w. of downtown Ensenada. Take Mex. 1 s. to the jct. with BC 23, which branches w. just n. of Maneadero. The two-lane road, offering spectacular views of Bahía Todos Santos and the Pacific, winds past olive orchards, cultivated fields, trailer parks and the private Baja Beach and Tennis Club before ending at a paved parking lot near the western tip of the Punta Banda Peninsula.

From the parking lot it's a short walk to a viewing area where you can observe a hollow rock formation that acts as a natural sea spout. During incoming tides, water rushes into an underground cavern, sending spray shooting into the air like a geyser. Snack vendors congregate along the path to the blowhole, and there are curio shops where you can browse for souvenirs, but the main attraction is the dramatic mountain scenery en route. Public restrooms are on site. **Cost:** A small parking fee is charged.

**REGIONAL HISTORICAL MUSEUM** (Museo Histórico Regional) is on Calle Gastélum, a blk. s. of Calle Ambar and 2 blks. w. of Av. Riveroll. The oldest public building in the state of Baja California, it was built in 1886 and served as an army barracks during its early years. It also was a prison, and the cellblocks and guard towers remain. Exhibits focus on city history. **Hours:** Tues.-Sun. 9-5. **Cost:** Free. **Phone:** (646) 178-8294.

**RIVIERA DEL PACÍFICO** is in the center of town at Blvd. Lázaro Cárdenas (Costero) and Av. Riviera.

Also called the Civic, Social and Cultural Center (Centro Cívico, Social y Cultural), this elegant Moorish-style mansion was formerly a gambling casino and hotel as well as a favored gathering place for wealthy Americans and Mexicans during the Prohibition era. Visitors can admire the painted, beamed ceilings and tile mosaics, view historic photos and murals that line the walls, wander through the beautifully landscaped gardens and have a drink at the Andaluz bar.

The building also houses the Museum of History (Museo de Historia), which has artifacts and dioramas recalling Baja's early days. **Time:** Allow 1 hour minimum. **Hours:** Grounds and building daily 8:30-8. Museum Tues.-Sat. 10-5, Sun. noon-5. **Cost:** Grounds and building free. Museum 20 pesos (about $1.60 U.S.); 10 pesos (children). Cash only. **Phone:** (646) 176-4310 (mansion), or (646) 177-0594 (museum).

## WINERIES

- **Bodegas de Santa Tomás** is downtown on Av. Miramar #666 (at Calle 7). Baja's oldest and largest winery began selling wine by the barrel in 1888, and today the firm's huge Ensenada aging and storage facility produces a variety of wines and liquors. **Hours:** One-hour guided tours in English are given on the hour Mon.-Sat. 11-4. **Cost:** Tour free. Tasting fee $10-$20 (U.S.). **Phone:** (646) 174-0836, ext. 22. GT

- **Casa Pedro Domecq** is on Mex. 3 (Carretera Tecate-El Sauzal), Km marker 73, a few miles n. of the town of Guadalupe; from Ensenada, take Mex. 1-D n. about 10 km (6 mi.) to the junction with Mex. 3 , then proceed n.e. toward Tecate. **Hours:** Tours and tastings Mon.-Fri. 10-4, Sat. 10-1:30. **Phone:** (646) 155-2249. GT

- **Château Camou** is off Mex. 3 in the Guadalupe Valley. The deluxe tour (reservations required) includes lunch. **Hours:** Tours and tastings Mon.-Sat. 9-4:30, Sun. noon-3. **Cost:** Tastings $5 (U.S.). Tour fees $10-$40. **Phone:** (646) 177-3303 or (646) 177-2221. GT

- **L. A. Cetto Winery** is on Mex. 3 at Km 73.5. **Hours:** Tastings and tours of the facility daily 10-5. **Phone:** (646) 155-2179. GT

- **Monte Xanic Winery** is off Mex. 3 near the village of Francisco Zarco. **Hours:** Tours (reservations required) and tastings Mon.-Fri. 9:30-4. **Phone:** (646) 155-2080. GT

## GUERRERO NEGRO, BAJA CALIFORNIA SUR (C-2)

Guerrero Negro (geh-REH-roh NEH-groh) is located within the barren Vizcaíno Desert (Desierto Vizcaíno), just south of the Baja California Sur state border. The name, which means "black warrior" in Spanish, was the moniker of an American whaling ship wrecked at the entrance to nearby Scammon's

Lagoon (Laguna Ojo de Liebre). Summer temperatures here are much cooler than in the interior of the peninsula due to the cold California Current, which extends north off the Pacific coast.

The area around Guerrero Negro is part of the El Vizcaíno Biosphere Reserve, designated a World Heritage Site by UNESCO in 1993. Encompassing bays, lagoons, vast expanses of the Sonoran Desert and the rugged Sierra mountains, El Vizcaíno is an important breeding and wintering site for the California gray whale and also is home to four species of endangered sea turtle.

The easiest way to experience the whales up close is to take part in an organized trip from Guerrero Negro. Malarrimo Eco-Tours offers 4-hour excursions with English-speaking guides aboard a 23-foot outboard boat with a maximum of 10 passengers. In addition to the whales, marine birds, sea lions and dolphins can be seen. Van transportation to and from Scammon's Lagoon is included.

Warm clothing, a waterproof jacket or windbreaker, sunblock and rubber-soled shoes are recommended. Trips depart daily Dec. 15-Apr. 15 from the Malarrimo Restaurant and campground complex on Boulevard Zapata. Tour prices and reservations should be made several months in advance; phone (615) 157-0100.

An all-inclusive package excursion under the guidance of an experienced naturalist is significantly more expensive, but worth it if you want convenience and a complete experience. Most of these trips depart from San Diego and include transportation and accommodations. A representative package tour company is the environmentally oriented, San Diego-based Baja Expeditions, Inc.; phone (800) 843-6967 (from the United States).

## LA PAZ, BAJA CALIFORNIA SUR (E-3)
pop. 251,871

La Paz (lah PAHS) is the commercial and governmental capital of the state of Baja California Sur. Its name means "peace," and the Dove of Peace Monument, a large contemporary sculpture of a dove in flight just off Mex. 1 at the northern entrance to town, serves as a gateway to the city. A plaque greets visitors with the following inscription: "And if you want peace, I offer it to you in the sunny peace of my bay."

Rich oyster beds below the surface of the Gulf of California attracted a handful of fortune seekers throughout the 17th century. The Jesuits founded a mission at La Paz in 1720 and kept it going despite a series of Indian uprisings. It was abandoned nearly 30 years later after disease had virtually wiped out the area's indigenous population; the city's cathedral stands on the site today.

Southern Baja's remoteness hindered any large-scale development. But as was the case with Ensenada and Cabo San Lucas, sportsmen and tourists slowly discovered the area's balmy winter climate and fine fishing. After years of existence as a neglected territory, the state of Baja California Sur experienced economic and population growth in the last half of the 20th century, and La Paz evolved from a sleepy port into a modern state capital.

Despite its commercial bustle, this is a laid-back city. Shady plazas and the palm-fringed *malecón*, the waterfront promenade along the bay, still retain some of the colonial grace of old. The old-fashioned charm is most evident on Sunday evenings, when couples and families go for a stroll against the backdrop of an often-spectacular sunset.

## Practicalities

Marquéz de León International Airport is about 13 kilometers (8 miles) southwest of downtown off Mex. 1 (north toward the town of Ciudad Constitución). Aeroméxico flies direct from Los Angeles twice a week (Thursdays and Sundays). Aeroméxico Connect and Volaris offer service from Mexican cities, including Guadalajara, Mexico City and Tijuana. *For additional information about airlines see Arriving by Air, page p. 42.*

*Colectivos* (shared shuttle vans) transport passengers from the airport into the city for about $12 (U.S.), but not the other way around; you'll need to take a taxi when departing. Taxi rides to the airport average $20-$25.

The central bus station (Central Camionera) is southwest of downtown at Calle Jalisco and Héroes de la Independencia. Another station is on Paseo Alvaro Obregón, just south of Avenida 5 de Mayo. Autotransportes de Baja California buses provide regular service between La Paz and Tijuana-a 22-hour trip that includes stops at towns along the route. *Aguila* buses travel to San José del Cabo and Cabo San Lucas, about 209 kilometers (130 miles) to the south. In-town fares are inexpensive, but a knowledge of both Spanish and the city's layout is helpful.

Taxis are plentiful, especially along Paseo Alvaro Obregón. Rides within the downtown area average less than $5 (U.S.), to the port of Pichilingue about $15. A car will come in handy for exploring outlying beaches, but keep in mind that rental cars tend to be more expensive in Mexico than in the United States. Major car rental agencies have offices on Paseo Alvaro Obregón.

Ferry service links La Paz with the mainland ports of Mazatlán and Topolobampo, near Los Mochis. Reservations to Mazatlán and Topolobampo can be made in person at the Baja Ferries ticket office, which is downtown at Allende #1025 (corner of Allende and Rubio). The office is open Mon.-Fri. 8-5, Sat. 8:30-3; phone (612) 123-6600 or 01 (800) 337-7437 (toll-free long distance within Mexico). Reservations and tickets also are available at the Baja Ferries Pichilingue Terminal office. The office is open daily 8-4; phone (612) 125-6324.

The ferry terminals are in Pichilingue, about 16 kilometers (10 miles) north of La Paz via Mex. 11, and are located on opposite sides of the harbor. A knowledge of Spanish is essential when making reservations, which should be booked at least a couple of days in advance. The easiest way to buy ferry tickets is online at bajaferries.com. *For additional information, see Ferry Service, page p. 53.*

The southern Baja edition of the English-language *Gringo Gazette* has tourist-related articles and advertisements pertaining to La Paz and other cities in the state of Baja California Sur. Allende Books, on Avenida Independencia 2 blocks northeast of Plaza Constitución, stocks English-language books. The shop also carries a nice selection of travel guides, area maps and gift items. The satellite dishes at the large hotels bring in TV stations from Mexico City as well as the United States.

Banks with ATM machines are concentrated a block or two inland from Paseo Alvaro Obregón. Most major hotels offer free Wi-Fi to guests. You'll also find a handful of Internet cafes along the *malecón*. For medical emergencies, the Hospital Especialidades Médicas is in the Fidepaz Building at the north end of town, on Mex. 1 at Km marker 5.5; phone (612) 124-0400.

November through April or May is the best time to visit La Paz, when days are warm and nights can be comparatively cool. Summer's sticky heat and humidity is uncomfortable, to say the least, despite afternoon breezes coming off the bay. Rainfall in this desert region is scant and varies from year to year, although violent tropical storms called *chubascos* bring occasional downpours in late summer or fall.

## City Layout

La Paz appears as somewhat of a mirage in the midst of the barren, cactus-covered foothills of southern Baja. The city spreads out from the curving shoreline of beautiful Bahía de la Paz, the largest bay along the Baja Peninsula's eastern coast. Situated at the bay's southern end, La Paz faces northwest rather than east. While this location is ideal for viewing the frequently impressive sunsets, it can be somewhat confusing when it comes to getting your bearings.

Fortunately, city streets are laid out in a simple grid pattern, oriented northwest-southeast and southwest-northeast. Hotels and tourist-oriented facilities are concentrated along Paseo Alvaro Obregón and the bayside *malecón* promenade, roughly between northwest-southeast avenidas Sinaloa and Colegio Militar. Adjoining the bayfront is downtown, a congested maze of streets that is more easily navigated on foot than by car.

The *malecón*, a traditional feature of every Mexican port town, is the city's gathering place. The boardwalk runs parallel to Paseo Alvaro Obregón in the heart of the tourist and shopping district. A pair of wharves serve tour boats and commercial vessels. Benches and statuary along the length of the *malecón* make it the most scenic spot in La Paz, just the place for an early morning or evening walk.

Many streets are one way, although clearly marked. Besides Paseo Alvaro Obregón, the major thoroughfares are Avenida 5 de Mayo, Avenida 16 de Septiembre and Avenida Bravo. Most visitor points of interest are a few blocks inland from the waterfront, but you'll need a car for trips to the outlying beaches and the port of Pichilingue.

## Recreation and Beaches

La Paz, like Los Cabos and Ensenada, is famed for its sport fishing. Blue marlin weighing up to 1,000 pounds are found in offshore waters from mid-March through October; sailfish can be hooked from the end of May through October. Bonito, roosterfish and yellowtail are available all year. Other fish anglers may encounter include black marlin, cabrilla, dorado, grouper, red snapper, wahoo and yellowtail. Although the northern end of the bay still offers good fishing, the open gulf is where the real action is, especially in the waters off Isla Cerralvo southeast of the city.

Boats for a day of deep-sea fishing—either an outboard motor-powered *panga* or a more expensive cruiser for four or more people—usually include tackle, bait and a fishing license, but double check when you make arrangements. A *panga* for two or three anglers averages about $250 (U.S.) for a day; a 30-foot cruiser accommodating four will cost about $450-$550. Many boats depart from beaches north and southeast of the city.

Baja Diving & Service, which operates from the Club Cantamar Resort & Sports Center, offers a variety of sport-fishing excursions. Their downtown office is at Paseo Alvaro Obregón #1665-2 at Plaza Cerralvo; phone (612) 122-1826. Fishermen's Fleet operates out of the Hotel La Perla on Paseo Alvaro Obregón. Their guided charters to Isla Cerralvo, Muertos Bay and Bahía de la Paz aboard a 22-foot *panga* include bait, tackle, breakfast and lunch; phone (612) 122-1313, or (408) 884-3932 (from the United States).

Diving is rewarding in the La Paz area, which has perhaps a dozen spots where coral reefs and sunken shipwrecks can be explored and sea lions, sharks and numerous tropical fish can be viewed. Among the most popular locations are Isla Espíritu Santo north of the Pichilingue Peninsula; Los Islotes, a group of islets off that island's north coast; El Bajo, a grouping of underwater rock pinnacles east of Isla Espíritu Santo; and around the northern and southern tips of Isla Cerralvo.

Scuba gear can be rented from a handful of area outfitters, and basic instruction courses are available. The Cortez Club, Carretera Pichilingue Km. 5 next to the La Concha Beach Resort, offers two-tank dives for $140 (U.S.). If you'd rather snorkel alongside whale sharks (in season) or sea lions, half-day excursions are available; phone (612) 121-6120, or (877) 408-6769 (from the United States).

Sea kayaking is another popular activity. Due to its scenic qualities, numerous sheltered coves, prime diving conditions and easy shore access, Isla Espíritu Santo is one of the best kayaking destinations in Baja California. Isla la Partida, a smaller island just north, is home to a large colony of friendly sea lions. El Mogote, a spit of sand across the bay from

downtown La Paz, and Playa Balandra, a few miles north of La Paz, are good nearby destinations. Both single-seat and tandem models can be rented. The outfitters referenced above also organize kayak trips. A few hotels offer kayaks to their guests for local use; check when you make reservations.

Although gray, sperm, humpback and enormous blue whales are sometimes spotted off local waters, La Paz is not considered a primary whale-watching destination. Bahía Magdalena, a shallow, protected bay on the Pacific coast about 160 miles north, offers a much better opportunity for whale observation. Here gray whales mate and give birth from January through March. Baja Diving & Service offers full-day trips including transportation, meals and viewing time aboard a local licensed *panga*.

San Diego-based Baja Expeditions offers a number of different excursions with a focus on environment, education and adventure. Most trips include accommodations, equipment, meals and a knowledgeable trip leader. Operations are based in La Paz; many trip organizers live in the city and are well acquainted with the area. For additional information, e-mail travel@bajaex.com, or phone (800) 843-6967 (toll-free from the United States and Canada).

The nicest beaches are north of the city via Mex. 11 (known locally as the Pichilingue Highway) as it heads to the northern end of the Pichilingue Peninsula. The highway is not marked, although signs indicate that you are heading in the direction of Pichilingue, the city's deep-water port, and the ferry docks. Mex. 11 continues north all the way to Playa Tecolote.

A short distance north of the tourist wharf in town is the sandy stretch of Playa El Coromuel. Parque Acuático El Coromuel has water slides, a restaurant and plenty of gringo-friendly facilities. About 13 kilometers (8 miles) north of town via Mex. 11 is Playa El Tesoro, a crescent-shaped beach with some *palapas* for shade.

About 5 kilometers (3 miles) north of Pichilingue is Playa Pichilingue. Stop here for a dip in the clear blue water followed by a cold beer and some freshly grilled fish at one of the beachside *palapa* eateries. Next is Playa Balandra, which fronts a narrow inlet. In addition to a small coral reef that is one of the few good spots for snorkeling close to La Paz, this beach is known for a distinctive mushroom-shaped rock formation that balances on an almost absurdly tiny base.

At the peninsula's northern tip is Playa El Tecolote, where conditions for swimming and diving are just about ideal. The gently sloping beach is equipped with *palapas*, there are casual open-air restaurants, and the water is beautifully blue and crystal clear. The water sports center here rents ski boats, kayaks and other craft and also can arrange trips to Isla Espíritu Santo.

## Shopping, Dining and Nightlife

La Paz offers the savvy shopper good buys on such handicrafts as coral jewelry, seashell knickknacks, leather goods and woven baskets. Tourist-oriented shops cluster along the stretch of Paseo Alvaro Obregón between avenidas Bravo and 5 de

Mayo. Antigua California, Paseo Alvaro Obregón #220 (at Avenida Arreola), carries a good selection of folk art from different parts of the country.

Ibarra's Pottery, about 6 blocks inland from the waterfront at Calle Guillermo Prieto #625, is a workshop where the Ibarra family fires pottery the old-fashioned way. Artisans carefully hand-paint exquisite floral designs on plates, mugs, tiles and vases. At Artesanía Cuauhtémoc (The Weaver), southwest of downtown on Avenida Abasolo (Mex. 1) between calles Jalisco and Nayarit, Fortunato Silva creates and sells handwoven cotton and woolen articles—rugs, tablecloths, placemats, blankets, *sarapes* and the like.

Local restaurants are big on steak, seafood and traditional Mexican favorites. You'll find Burger King and other fast-food franchises as well. The open-air restaurants at the beaches have a decidedly casual ambience and are good places to go for fresh grilled fish and other simply prepared seafood. See the Lodgings & Restaurants section for AAA-RATED dining establishments.

Nightlife here doesn't compare to Cabo San Lucas, but there are still options. Local and visiting performing arts groups take the stage at the 1,500-seat City Theater (Teatro de la Ciudad), at Miguel Legaspy and Héroes de la Independencia.

Las Varitas, on Avenida Independencia at Belisario Domínguez, is a dance club that plays everything from salsa to Mexican rock. There is a cover charge to get in. The nightclub La Cabaña, which also has a cover charge, is on the lobby floor of the Hotel Perla, on Paseo Alvaro Obregón between Avenida Arreola and Callejón La Paz. The music is a mix of salsa, disco and oldies.

The most enjoyable activity might just be taking a seat at an outdoor café along the *malecón* at sunset and watch the bay turn to spectacular hues of red and gold. La Terraza, at the Hotel Perla, is a good spot.

**Baja California Sur State Tourism Office (Coordinadora de Promoción al Turismo):** on Mex. 1 at Km marker 5.5, at the north end of town in the Fidepaz Building (near the marina); staff are helpful and bilingual. Open Mon.-Fri. 8-8. **Phone:** (612) 124-0100.

Another office is on Paseo Alvaro Obregón at Calle Nicolas Bravo. It has information about various city tour packages and is open Mon.-Fri. 8 a.m.-10 p.m., Sat.-Sun. noon-10; phone (612) 122-5939.

**OUR LADY OF LA PAZ** (Nuestra Señora de la Paz) is on the s.e. side of Plaza Constitución. The church, originally a Jesuit mission, has lovely stained glass. The present building dates from 1861; a second tower was added in the early 20th century. Large bilingual plaques relate the church's history as well as La Paz's beginnings.

Plaza Constitución is a traditional main square, with tiled, tree-shaded paths and a gazebo. It's a peaceful spot to relax while city life goes by, or to gather with the locals and listen to a band concert. On the plaza's northwest side is the old state capitol

building, which houses the Historical Library of the Californias (Biblioteca de Historia de las Californias). In addition to historical documents, the library has some striking paintings depicting Baja California Sur's early days.

**REGIONAL MUSEUM OF BAJA CALIFORNIA SUR** (Museo de Antropología y Historia de Baja California Sur) is at Ignacio Altamirano and Av. 5 de Mayo. It features exhibits on the geology, geography, flora and fauna of the state. Evocative murals and dioramas depict the region's Indian cultures and La Paz's early days. Spanish mission settlement, Mexican ranch life and three major conflicts—the War of Independence, the Mexican-American War and the Mexican Revolution—are among the historical subjects covered. Most exhibit information is in Spanish.

**Hours:** Daily 8-6. **Cost:** Free. **Phone:** (612) 125-6424.

**SEA & ADVENTURES, INC.** (Mar Y Aventuras) excursions depart from the Posada Luna Sol Hotel near the Marina de La Paz, half a blk. w. of jct. Blvd. 5 de Febrero and Calle Abasolo. The opportunity to interact with whale sharks at close range is well worth taking this guided trip into La Paz Bay. Small *lanchas* holding up to 10 passengers patrol the water searching for these gentle giants, offering the opportunity to observe them at close range as they float in shallow, crystal-clear water while peacefully feasting on plankton.

Although shark sightings are not guaranteed, they are likely during the winter season, when whale sharks visit the waters off the Baja peninsula as part of their annual migration cycle. The boat also cruises past an offshore rock where you can jump in the water and snorkel with sea lions. In addition to the whale shark trip, the company organizes kayaking trips and an all-day snorkeling tour to Espiritu Santo Island.

**Note:** If you don't speak fluent Spanish, be sure to request an English-speaking guide; you'll get more out of the experience. The trip can also be arranged through some hotels in San José del Cabo and Cabo San Lucas; ground transportation to La Paz is provided. **Hours:** Three-hour whale shark trip departs daily (weather permitting), Oct.-Feb. **Cost:** $55 (U.S.) per person (includes snorkel gear). Wet suit rental (recommended during the winter months) $15 (U.S.). Advance reservations are required; trips cannot be booked more than 7 days in advance. **Phone:** (612) 122-7039, (406) 522-7596 (from the United States), or (800) 355-7140 (from the United States).

# LORETO, BAJA CALIFORNIA SUR
(D-3) pop. 16,738

Loreto (loh-REH-toh) dates from 1697, when a mission was founded by Jesuit padre Juan Maria Salvatierra. It became the first capital of both Alta (the present state of California) and Baja California. Loreto also was the departure point from which

Junípero Serra launched his northward quest in 1769 to establish a chain of missions in Alta California. Today its impressive natural attributes and outstanding fishing attract U.S. sportsmen.

Loreto is easily reached from points north via the transpeninsular highway (Mex. 1). The airport is about 7 kilometers (4 miles) southwest of town. Nonstop flights from Los Angeles are offered by Alaska Airlines on select days of the week. Regional airline Aéreo Calafia flies from La Paz and Tijuana on small prop planes; phone (624) 143-4302, or 01 (800) 560-3949 (toll-free long distance within Mexico).

The *malecón* (boardwalk) has benches for taking in the view, but beach lovers should skip the rocky public stretches in town and head for the indented shores of Bahía Concepción, about an hour's drive north up the Gulf of California coast toward Mulegé.

At Nopolo Bay, about 8 kilometers (5 miles) south of Loreto, there is a championship 18-hole golf course at the Loreto Bay Golf Resort & Spa. The challenging course features numerous sand traps and is laid out along the Gulf of California coastline, blending into the surrounding desert and the Sierra de la Giganta mountains. For information on tee times and facilities, phone (613) 133-0016.

The Baja Big Fish Company, on the *malecón* 3 blocks south of the marina, has several boats and knowledgeable guides; phone (613) 135-1603. Arturo's Sport Fishing, on Calle Hidalgo between the main plaza and the marina, is a family-owned business that offers snorkeling, kayaking and whale-watching excursions in addition to fishing trips; phone (613) 135-0766.

A boat excursion can be taken to Coronado Island, about a mile and a half offshore, part of Bay of Loreto National Marine Park. The clear, tranquil water harbors a great variety of tropical fish. The best months for snorkeling and scuba diving are June through October, when the water is warmest. Whale sightings are possible in winter. Trip arrangements can be made through local hotels or Arturo's Sport Fishing.

Few merchants in town take credit cards for payment, although both pesos and U.S. dollars are readily accepted. The Bancomer bank, on the main plaza, has an ATM; currency can be exchanged Mon.-Fri. during the morning.

Adventurous travelers can make the trip to the San Javier Mission (Misión San Javier), which is west of town; from a signed junction about 2 kilometers (1.1 miles) south of the Loreto turn-off on Mex. 1, a rough access road (recommended only for high-clearance vehicles) proceeds southwest through stunning canyon and mountain scenery for about 37 kilometers (23 miles). The beautifully restored structure of dark volcanic rock in the *mudéjar* (Moorish) style sits at the bottom of a deep valley.

The second oldest of the Jesuit missions established on the peninsula, it was founded in 1699 but not completed until 1758. The towering walls feature exemplary stonework, and the gilded altar was brought from Mexico City. It's possible to climb the winding stairs to the roof and bell tower, which offers a panoramic view of the valley below. A guided tour can be arranged through Loreto hotels or Desert and Sea Expeditions; phone (613) 135-1979.

**Tourist information office:** in the Palacio de Gobierno building across from the main plaza. Hours vary. **Phone:** (613) 135-0411.

**MISSION MUSEUM** (Museo de Las Misiones) is next to the Mission of Our Lady of Loreto. Artifacts and manuscripts on display relate to Baja California's historic missions. Other exhibits include religious art and saddles used in colonial times. **Hours:** Tues.-Sun. 9-1 and 2-6. **Cost:** 47 pesos (about $3.50 U.S.).

**MISSION OF OUR LADY OF LORETO** (Misión de Nuestra Señora de Loreto) is a block w. of the main plaza. Severely damaged by earthquakes, the 1752 mission—including the tower with its modern clock—has been almost completely rebuilt and still functions as an active church. It features baroque stone ornamentation, a bell tower and a collection of gilded altar paintings.

# MEXICALI, BAJA CALIFORNIA (A-2)
pop. 936,826

A remote and blazingly hot desert seems an unlikely location for a big city, but Baja California's second largest city has grown up in just such an environment. Mexicali (meh-hee-CAH-lih) is an unlikely metropolis developed as a market center for surrounding farms in the early 20th century. Visitors from across the border were attracted by legalized alcohol and gambling as well as by land speculation, and *maquiladoras,* foreign-owned businesses established in Mexican border areas because of low production costs, further bolstered the economy.

Capital of the state of Baja California, Mexicali is opposite Calexico, Calif. Mexican and U.S. Customs

## DID YOU KNOW

One-fifth of Mexico's total population lives in or around Mexico City.

and Border Protection offices are open 24 hours daily.

Shops and restaurants are near the international border in an irregular rectangle bounded by avenidas Cristóbal Colón and Alvaro Obregón, the Río Nuevo and Calle C. Mexico's largest Chinatown (La Chinesca) also is near the border, concentrated south of Calzada López Mateos around avenidas Juárez and Altamirano.

**Secture (Secretaría de Turismo del Estado):** calzadas Montejano and Benito Juárez in the Hotel Zone (Zona Hotelera), south of Plaza Azteca. Open Mon.-Fri. 8-6, Sat. 9-1. **Phone:** (686) 566-1116.

**REGIONAL MUSEUM, UNIVERSITY OF BAJA CALIFORNIA** is at Av. Reforma and Calle L. It has exhibits focusing on paleontology, archeology, ethnography, landscape photography and the missions of Baja California. **Hours:** Tues.-Fri. 9-6, Sat.-Sun. 10-4. **Cost:** 15 pesos (about $1.10 U.S.). **Phone:** (686) 552-5715.

## MULEGÉ, BAJA CALIFORNIA SUR
(D-3) pop. 59,114

Mulegé (moo-leh-HEH) is an old, traditional Mexican town and an oasis in the middle of the inhospitable Baja California desert. Perched on a terrace above the Río Mulegé—one of the peninsula's few rivers—it has dirt streets and a laid-back air. Mulegé also offers easy accessibility to the stunning beaches and tucked-away coves of Bahía Concepción, which begins 19 kilometers (12 miles) south of town.

About 3 kilometers (2 miles) northeast of town is the public beach, at the end of a dirt road where the Río Mulegé empties into the Sea of Cortez. The beach has dark sand, a few waves and, in summer, jellyfish. Nearby El Sombrerito, at the mouth of the river, is a hat-shaped monolith with stone steps leading to a lighthouse at the summit.

Mulegé offers outstanding fishing and boating opportunities. Fishing arrangements can be made through most hotels or at one of the many RV parks along the river south of town. The area also attracts scuba divers and snorkelers; the underwater life in Bahía Concepción includes impressively large sea turtles.

The shell-studded beaches of coarse white sand south off Mex. 1 along the shores of the bay are known for warm, clear and gloriously blue water. For a backdrop, there are mountains tinted shades of rose by the sun. All are accessible from Mex. 1, with signs posted at each turn-off; however, the access roads are likely to be sandy, rutted or both. If you wish to hike from the highway (wear sturdy shoes), bus drivers will make drop-offs at the access roads; double-check the time the last northbound bus heads back to town. Expect to share these beaches with an army of RVers and campers.

The first beach south of Mulegé is Playa Punta Arena, about 16 kilometers (9 miles) south. Palm-thatched *palapas* line the sand, and hillside caves

south of the beach are littered with shells discarded by ancient inhabitants. Playa Santispac, crowded with campers, is the most active; craft from sailboats to yachts cruise on the bay.

Playa El Coyote fronts a cove and has several trees, rare on Baja's desert beaches. Playa El Requesón, a narrow point of land connected to an offshore island that can be reached by vehicle at low tide, is a prime windsurfing location. Don't expect much in the way of tourist facilities at any of these beaches, aside from some *palapa* shelters and a few toilets.

**MISSION OF SANTA ROSALÍA MULEGÉ** (Misión Santa Rosalía de Mulegé) is just upstream from the Mex. 1 Bridge over the Mulegé River. It can be reached by a pathway shaded by broad-leafed banana plants. Sunday services are still held in the solid stone structure, which was abandoned as a mission in 1828. The hilltop view takes in date palm groves spreading toward the mountains.

## ROSARITO, BAJA CALIFORNIA (A-1)
pop. 90,668

Once a Prohibition-era hideaway for Hollywood's Golden Age elite and now home to a large community of American expatriates, the beach resort of Rosarito (roh-sah-REE-toh) has traditionally been an easy sell for local tourism boosters. Only a 29-kilometer (18-mile) drive south of the U.S./Mexico border? Check. Tasty waves and warm, sunny Southern California-type weather? Check. Fantastic fish tacos and cheap *cerveza*? Si, señor. It's *not* Tijuana? Perfect.

Up until 2008, weekends and spring break months saw bumper-to-bumper traffic on Boulevard Juárez (Rosarito's main drag) as sun and fun seekers from San Diego and L.A. flocked here for tequila shooters at the massive Papas & Beer beach club, or perhaps a romantic horseback ride along the shore. While you can still do both, negative news headlines generated by Mexico's warring drug cartels have kept Americans away in recent years, and local merchants welcome visitors to what they jokingly call *"un pueblo fantasma"* (a ghost town).

Rosarito (the town is also called Rosarito Beach and Playas de Rosarito) is located at the junction of Mex. 1 (free) and Mex. 1-D (toll), both four lanes from Tijuana. Approaching from the north on the toll road, the outstanding Pacific views are periodically obstructed by high-rise condo and hotel complexes. Some are open for business. An equal number are half-completed construction projects, abandoned due to lack of funding. Faded real estate "For Sale" banners flap in the breeze outside the gated beachfront communities favored by American expats. The toll charge is 31 pesos (about $2.30 U.S.); the free road is not recommended due to often-heavy local traffic.

The picture brightens once you hit town. Waves tumble ashore. Local fishermen cast off from the pier. In the distant ocean haze are the jagged silhouettes of the Coronado Islands. A few gringos buzz down the beach on rented ATVs. Beach bar hucksters reel in afternoon imbibers with 2-for-1 drink specials. The scene is *tranquilo* (calm), quite the opposite of the drug war mayhem depicted in the international media.

The *municipo* of Rosarito stretches more than 25 miles south to the village of La Misión, but the main tourist strip is little more than a mile long and manageable on foot. Walking the downtown area and beach is generally safe during the day. Rosarito's mayor claims to have cleaned up the city's notoriously corrupt police department. While most locals remain skeptical, there's no denying that the special Tourist Police force (Policía Turística) maintains a highly visible presence.

Regardless, a late night stroll around downtown Rosarito is not advised. The dramatic downturn in tourism has forced many restaurants and nightlife spots out of business. The streets can be dark and eerily deserted, particularly on weeknights.

Driving here from the U.S. can be a hassle. Enhanced security measures at the San Ysidro/Tijuana border crossing have resulted in long waits in both directions. Visitors who cross on foot can easily hire a taxi from Tijuana to Rosarito for about $35 (U.S.) one way. In general, it's safest to use one of the yellow-and-white tourist taxis; there's a cab stand just beyond the final gates into Mexico. Taxis are not metered; always settle on a fare before you get in.

In Rosarito taxis are easily flagged down along Boulevard Juárez. The main cab stand is across the street from the Rosarito Beach Hotel.

If you're hunting for tacky souvenirs, there's no shortage of curio shops lining the west side of Juárez. Most shops don't take plastic, but the U.S. dollar is universally accepted. Although not obvious from the street, the Handicrafts Market (Mercado de Artesanías), on the west side of Juárez between calles Acacias and Roble, is home to a maze-like shopping arcade with more than 100 vendor stalls. Merchandise ranges from cheap "Made in China" gifts to surprisingly exquisite handcrafted items.

Plaza de los Artístas, on Juarez next to the security gate for the Rosarito Beach Hotel, houses a few art galleries and a small wine tasting shop. The tiny La Quinta Luz gallery sells fine Day of the Dead-inspired art. Also inside the building you'll find quality jewelry, handmade furniture and a shop packed to the rafters with crafts from the state of Michoacán. If you're running low on cash, there are banks with secure, glass booth-enclosed ATMs along the east side of Boulevard Juárez; withdrawals are in pesos.

The historic Rosarito Beach Hotel, opened in 1925, is well worth a look even if you don't spend the night. The ornate lobby is vintage Baja California, replete with arched entryways, lovely tile work, beautiful hand-painted ceilings and wall murals depicting everything from Spanish missions to mythic Zapotec gods of death.

Out the hotel's back exit is the Rosarito Beach Hotel Pier, a 500-yard-long wooden pier supported by towering metal pylons. At pier's end, local fishermen haul up their catch. Pelicans dive-bomb for lunch around the offshore rocks. A lone surfer tucks into a nice hollow wave. Pier access is free to hotel guests; non-guests are charged 12 pesos, about a dollar. Just south of the pier you'll find salesmen offering guided horseback rides along the beach ($15 U.S. per half hour) and ATV rentals ($20 per half hour).

North of the pier, Rosarito's three main beach bar clubs wage a daily, high-decibel audio war. While one club attempts to lure party people with ear-splitting Jay-Z beats, the bar next door has Michael Jackson's "Thriller" cranked way past 10.

Papas & Beer, an offshoot of the Ensenada original, is on the beach where Calle Nogal meets the sand. This 47,000-square foot mega club claims to be the biggest bar in Baja. On weekdays the place is lucky to see 47 customers all day. However, plenty of locals and some dedicated Southern Californians still come on weekends to boogie in the faux tropical setting. The other beach party spots are Club Corona and Iggy's; the latter sometimes has live music.

*Carne asada* hounds should sniff out Tacos El Yaqui, a simple stand one block east of Juárez at the corner of Calle de la Palma and Avenida Mar del Norte. Two fresh flour tortillas loaded with melt-in-your-mouth-meat, beans, guacamole, onion, cilantro and (if you dare) grilled jalapeños will set you back $6 (U.S.).

In May, the Rosarito Art Fest features more than 100 arts and crafts booths, plus food stands and live music. Traditional Mexican eats, along with carnival rides and music concerts, add up to a month of fun during the Rosarito City Fair in July.

**Rosarito Tourist Office:** downtown on Mex. 1 (Boulevard Juárez) at Oceana Plaza #29. The office is open Mon.-Fri. 8-6, Sat.-Sun. 9-1. Brochures, maps and tourist information also are available in the lobby of the Rosarito Beach Hotel. **Phone:** (661) 612-0200 for the tourist office.

**PUERTO NUEVO** is about 18 km (11 mi.) south of Rosarito via free Mex. 1. This tiny, unremarkable fishing village is known for one thing: some 30 restaurants specializing in Pacific lobster (*langosta*). Some have an ocean view and a touch of elegance; others are down-home places operated by local families. The menu at each is similar—a clawless lobster (ordered by size) sliced lengthwise and pan fried in lard, along with rice, refried beans and flour tortillas, plus melted butter and chile sauce on the side. Beverages are equally standardized, running to soft drinks, wine or beer.

Hucksters shout the merits of their particular establishment to potential customers, but the final decision boils down to ambience—or a line indicating popularity. Expect to pay about $20 to $25 (U.S.) per person for dinner. Dollars are accepted, but few restaurants take credit cards. Summer weekends are the peak dining time.

## SAN FELIPE, BAJA CALIFORNIA (B-2)

Although nomadic fishermen first gravitated to the area around San Felipe (sahn feh-LEE-peh) in the mid-19th century, the town was not permanently settled until the 1920s. The completion of Mex. 5 from Mexicali in 1951 brought a steady stream of American sportsmen who have helped transform San Felipe into a major winter vacation destination. Rapid expansion that began in the 1980s has produced a slew of waterfront trailer parks, condominiums and hotels. Even so, do not expect a luxury-style resort: San Felipe's style is distinctly no-frills.

About 193 kilometers (120 miles) south of Mexicali, the town's location combines the inviting—the Gulf of California's shimmering blue waters—with the forbidding—an extremely arid desert environment. Mex. 5 south from Mexicali is in excellent condition, including an initial stretch of four-lane divided highway. **Note:** There aren't any gas stations between the village of La Puerta and San Felipe, a distance of some 100 miles; make sure your tank is full before starting out.

After traversing open desert, an archway heralds the arrival into town. The steep eastern flank of the Sierra San Pedro Mártir range—which includes Baja California's tallest mountain, Picacho del Diablo—is clearly visible to the west. The town spreads out under 940-foot-tall Punta San Felipe, a promontory that forms the northern end of Bahía San Felipe. Yellow-sand beaches line the coast southeastward from the crescent-shaped bayfront to Punta Estrella, about 19 kilometers (12 miles) distant. A splendid view of the town and coastline is available from the Virgin of Guadalupe Shrine, atop a hill just north of San Felipe.

The bay, along with the entire northern Gulf of California, has an extreme tidal range that often reaches more than 20 feet, requiring an experienced boater to successfully navigate the waters. At high tide waves break against the shore; at low tide it is possible to wade far out over sand and mud flats.

South of town, a paved but rough road passes the airport and continues 85 kilometers (53 miles) to Puertecitos. Along the way are turn-offs leading to vacation home communities and trailer camps, but very few motorist facilities.

About 21 kilometers (13 miles) south of San Felipe via the Gulf of California coast road is the Valley of the Giants (El Valle de Los Gigantes). Watch for the sign for Colonia Gutierrez Polanco, then take the sandy road going in the opposite direction—southwest—about 5 kilometers (3 miles). The cluster of very large, very old cardón cactuses and other desert vegetation makes for an intriguing sight. It is

recommended that this excursion be made only in a sturdy, high-clearance vehicle.

San Felipe attracts campers, anglers, road racers and beachcombers. Dwellings are modest, vegetation scarce, and litter sometimes an eyesore. The town attracts a rowdy crowd of motorcyclists and dune buggy fanciers on holiday weekends like Presidents Day and Thanksgiving and also during the 2 weeks around Easter; at these times San Felipe is noisy and congested. Also avoid the blistering summer months, when temperatures can soar to 120 degrees under cloudless skies. The weather November through April is much more pleasant.

At this major fishing center shrimp are caught commercially, and surf fishing and package or chartered fishing trips are available. Cabrilla, white sea bass, yellowtail, dorado and other game species are found in the gulf waters. Boat rentals range from oar-propelled *pangas* to large craft that can accommodate a party for several days. Local boating outfits are concentrated along Mar de Cortés, as are San Felipe's restaurants, bars and nightspots.

**Tourist information office:** downtown at Calzada Chetumal #101, at the corner of Avenida Mar de Cortés, the waterfront *malecón*. **Phone:** (686) 577-1155.

## SAN JOSÉ DEL CABO, BAJA CALIFORNIA SUR (E-4)

Fronting the steely blue Gulf of California at the eastern end of the Los Cabos resort area, sedate San José del Cabo (sahn hoh-SEH dehl KAH-boh) is the anti-Cabo San Lucas *(see separate listing within this region)*. While young couples and rowdy college kids dance and drink themselves into a Mexi-coma near Land's End, San José attracts a slightly older tourist crowd that bypasses hyper-Americanized Cabo in favor of a more relaxed resort. That's not to say that San José is a sleepy Baja backwater: It's plenty modernized, but the town's colonial roots and pockets of late 19th-century architecture remind visitors they are indeed vacationing in Mexico.

In contrast to its party animal sibling, the "other" Cabo manages to retain some small-town charm, even if its sleepy days are pretty much a thing of the past. While San José has certainly benefited from the tourist surge in recent decades, and residents take pride in preserving its small-town character—evident in the vicinity of Plaza Mijares, the large main square—growth *does* bring change.

And change is exemplified by Puerto Los Cabos, which extends along 3 miles of beachfront just east of town. This 2,000-acre, master-planned resort community is anchored by a 535-slip marina sandwiched between the untamed San José Estuary (Estero San José) and the small fishing village of Pueblo La Playa. A breakwater built at the mouth of the marina has created dependably calm surf at adjacent La Playita *(see Beaches and Recreation)*.

As for Pueblo La Playa, local residents banned together and rejected lucrative offers to sell their land. The pueblo is surrounded by homes and condos stretching back into the hills and spreading eastward along the coast.

For the serene flip side to progress, head to Cabo Pulmo National Marine Park *(see Beaches and Recreation)*, a colorful coral realm teeming with sea life that lies beneath the Sea of Cortez. Driving to Cabo Pulmo from San José entails a long, bumpy journey along the unpaved East Cape Road, but it's doable in one very full day. Those who make the trip will be rewarded with some of the finest diving and snorkeling in Baja—in an unspoiled environment blissfully free of T-shirt shops, raucous watering holes and gaggles of sunburned, camera-toting tourists.

## Practicalities

San José del Cabo International Airport is about 13 kilometers (8 miles) north of San José del Cabo and 48 kilometers (30 miles) northeast of Cabo San Lucas. Aeroméxico, Alaska Airlines, American, Delta and United all offer either direct or connecting flights from various U.S. cities. *For additional information about the airport see the Cabo San Lucas listing; for additional information about airlines see Arriving by Air, page p. 42.*

Because the Los Cabos area is spread out and expensive taxi fares will quickly add up, renting a car is a viable option if you're staying more than a few days or want to explore the surrounding area. **Note:** AAA/CAA members enjoy discounts through Hertz for vehicles booked in the United States. Consult your local AAA/CAA club or phone Hertz, (800) 654-3080. *For additional information about renting a car see Car Rentals, page p. 43.*

Taxis from San José del Cabo to Cabo San Lucas or the Corridor hotels are convenient but expensive, averaging $25-$30 depending on destination. The local Suburcabos buses are a much cheaper alternative, running regularly between the two Cabos; the fare for the 45-minute trip is 33 pesos (about $2.70 U.S.). The Aguila bus line also provides service between the two towns.

Walking from the far eastern end of the beachfront hotel zone to downtown San José will take about 20 minutes. If you're staying at a hotel located west of town, you'll save time, energy and a $6 (U.S.) taxi fare by taking the bus. San José employs a fleet of converted yellow school buses, which you'll see running during daylight hours along Paseo San José, the wide boulevard behind the hotel zone. Flag down any eastbound bus and simply tell the driver, *"La Plaza, por favor."* The fare is 10 pesos per person. **Note:** Unless you're familiar with the city, taking the bus beyond Plaza Mijares is not recommended.

Currency can be exchanged at banks during their normal Mon.-Fri. business hours, but make sure this service is offered before getting in line. Banks also may be open Saturday morning. You'll find branches of Mexican banks (with attached ATMs) all over downtown and along Mex. 1 west of town. If you're staying in the beachfront hotel zone, head for the modern, two-level Mega Comercial shopping center at the junction of Mex. 1 and Paseo de Los Cabos. There's an ATM inside the Mega grocery store, plus two banks/ATMs in a strip mall next door. Some ATMs dispense dollars in addition to pesos, but beware of stiff transaction fees.

In case of emergency dial 066 to reach local police, the fire department or the Green Angels. There is a 24-hour medical clinic and pharmacy (Médica Los Cabos) on Calle Zaragoza near the corner of Avenida I. Green, about 3 blocks west of the main plaza. English is spoken; phone (624) 142-2770. The Red Cross (Cruz Roja) is on Boulevard Mijares next to the post office; phone (624) 142-0316. To contact the local police at City Hall, phone (624) 142-0361.

## City Layout

A more quiet alternative to the fiesta-like atmosphere of Cabo San Lucas 20 miles down the road, downtown San José is about a mile from the Gulf of California (Sea of Cortez), separated from the beachfront hotel zone by a series of low hills and the condos and private homes surrounding the Mayan Palace Golf Course. Some of downtown's narrow streets are lined with historic Spanish-colonial style buildings that have been converted into stylish shops and restaurants. Flowering trees, including the purple-blossomed jacaranda, arch overhead. The orderly grid of streets is small and compact, and conducive to walking.

Mex. 1 runs along the western edge of town before turning west toward Cabo San Lucas to form the Corridor. Another main thoroughfare is north-south Boulevard Mijares. It begins at Avenida Zaragoza and heads south to Paseo San José, which follows the waterfront. San José's hotel zone is along this wide boulevard.

Avenida Zaragoza borders the south side of Plaza Mijares. The name commemorates Mexican naval officer José Antonio Mijares, who prevailed in a bloody skirmish against U.S. forces deployed from the frigate *Portsmouth* during the Mexican-American War. Tourists tote shopping bags through the cobbled square, pausing to snap pictures or rest on the wrought-iron park benches.

On the south side of the plaza a yellow clock tower rises above the traditional Palacio Municipal (City Hall), built in 1927. Inside, city offices surround a shady courtyard where you'll find an ATM and racks full of tourist brochures. The east side of the square is graced with a large fountain backed by the Jardín del Los Cabaños, a half-dozen bronze busts of historical big shots. A giant Mexican flag waves overhead. There is a small but ornate wrought-iron bandstand near the plaza's east side.

Across Avenida Miguel Hidalgo from the plaza stands the twin-steepled San José Church; it was rebuilt in 1940 on the spot where the town's original mission stood. Above the entrance is a tiled mural depicting the unwelcome fate of San José mission founder Nicolás Tamaral—being dragged to his death toward fire by Indians. The church is usually open if you want to peek inside.

The Arroyo San José, more a stream than a river, flows along the eastern side of town and empties into San José Inlet (Estero San José). The estuary, east of the Presidente InterContinental Los Cabos Resort, was long ago a pirate hideout and more recently a waterfowl sanctuary. The Puerto Los Cabos Marina has displaced some of the wetlands on the estuary's eastern side, but the grassy marshes near town remain unspoiled.

## Beaches and Recreation

The stretch of beach along the San José del Cabo waterfront is impressive to look at, but pounding shore breakers make it generally unsafe for swimming. Guided horseback rides along the shoreline are popular and can be booked on the beach or through your hotel.

La Playita is a calm, pretty curve of sand at Pueblo la Playa, a small fishing village about 4 kilometers (2.5 miles) east of San José and adjacent to the Puerto Los Cabos Marina. A cobbled walkway runs behind the beach, and there's an oceanfront playground for kids right on the sand. *Palapa*-shaded picnic tables, showers and restrooms are set back near the marina.

To reach La Playita, take Avenida Juárez heading east out of town, which almost immediately becomes a modern, elevated access road. On the other side of this bridge, continue following Juárez through several *glorietas* (traffic roundabouts) for about 2.4 kilometers (1.5 miles) to the beach turnoff (signed "La Playa"), then take the paved beach access road about a mile.

The most popular surfing beach is Playa Costa Azul, a short distance south of San José at Mex. 1 Km marker 29. The Costa Azul Surf Shop at Km marker 28 rents boards by the day, and also offers lessons. Since surfing is a tricky art, most visitors will be content to watch the experts take on the waves from a lookout point at the top of a hill just south of the beach.

The diving and snorkeling are superb at Cabo Pulmo National Marine Park, which protects the only coral reef in the Sea of Cortez. There are several reef fingers in Pulmo Bay (Bahía Pulmo), most of which are best left to divers. However, the inner reef can be easily accessed by snorkelers. A handful of dive shops offer tours that depart from the tiny town of Cabo Pulmo itself. Boats stop for exceptional snorkeling off rocky Mermaid Beach (Playa La Sirenita) and then visit a sea lion colony where you'll actually swim alongside the barking beasts. The Cabo Pulmo Dive Center is a long-established local dive shop; phone (624) 141-0726, or (562) 366-0722 (from the United States).

It's also possible to reach beautiful Mermaid Beach by car and a short hike. Just five minutes south of Cabo Pulmo village, look for the well-signed turn-off to Playa Arbolitos. A short dirt road leads to the beach, where *palapa* umbrellas and good snorkeling await. To

find Mermaid Beach, face the ocean and look to your right. There's a narrow unmarked trail that climbs a hill and heads south along the bluffs. The hike takes about 15 minutes **Note:** Sections of the trail are narrow, with steep drop-offs; use caution. This trail is only recommended for people in fairly good physical condition.

To reach Cabo Pulmo by car, you can take one of two routes. The paved option involves driving north out of San José on Mex. 1 toward La Paz. At the town of Las Cuevas, head east toward the coast on a paved road that eventually veers south and approaches Cabo Pulmo from the north. Only the last 10.5 kilometers (6.5 mi.) are unpaved, but can still be negotiated by a regular passenger car.

The scenic route follows the unpaved East Cape Road (usually passable in a regular car), which heads east out of San José (follow Avenida Juárez out of town), veers north, skirts the coast and affords gorgeous views of stark, cactus-studded desert hills tumbling into the deep blue Sea of Cortez. One-way drive time is between 2.5 and 3 hours. You'll see an ever-growing number of luxury beachfront homes along the coastal road, but visitor services and gas stations are nonexistent.

Baja Wild offers full-day Cabo Pulmo kayak and snorkel trips that depart from the San José area and include round-trip, air-conditioned van transportation to the marine park. The company also organizes ATV, jeep and whale-watching tours. Phone (624) 172-6300 for tour fees and additional information.

**Note:** All beaches in Mexico are the property of the government and consequently are accessible to the public. Driving on beaches in Mexico is illegal. *For information about other beaches in Los Cabos, see the Cabo San Lucas listing.*

Due to a combination of game fish migration patterns, bait supply, water temperature and ocean currents, the Gordo Banks, about 10 miles east of San José del Cabo, are considered to be among the richest fishing grounds in the Gulf of California. Gordo Banks Pangas, headquartered in the village of Pueblo la Playa, offers chartered 6-hour sportfishing trips in outboard motor-powered *pangas* that are launched from the Puerto Los Cabos marina.

Rates for a standard 22-foot *panga* holding up to three passengers begin at about $210 (U.S.). Tackle and equipment are included; lunch, live bait and transportation to and from the launch area are not. Reservations should be made several months in advance for the October-November peak season; phone (624) 142-1147 or (619) 488-1859 (from the United States).

The nine-hole Mayan Palace Golf Course is the granddaddy of Los Cabos links. Although not the caliber of the world-class courses down the road, this public course suits duffers as well as intermediate golfers—and it's much cheaper to play. Tee times are on a first-come, first-served basis; phone (624) 142-0905.

The Puerto Los Cabos Golf Club has a Jack Nicklaus signature layout, plus a second course designed by

Greg Norman. Nine holes of each course are complete and can be played together for a combined 18 holes. Both courses are currently open to the public, but the Norman course will eventually be restricted to members and residents. For rates and reservations, phone (624) 105-6440, 01 (800) 543-2044 (toll-free long distance within Mexico), or (877) 495-8727 (toll-free from the United States). *For information about other courses see the Cabo San Lucas listing.*

## Shopping

Shops of varying quality can be found along Calle Zaragoza near Plaza Mijares, and also up and down Boulevard Mijares. Necri Fine Mexican Handicrafts, Av. Obregón #17 (between Morelos and Hidalgo), specializes in hand-painted Talavera tile, Majolica ceramics, dinnerware sets and pewter creations—all made in Mexico. Prices are a bit steep, but the craftsmanship is superior.

If you want a good deal rather than pricey quality try Curios Carmela, at the corner of Boulevard Mijares and Coronado. It's a huge store packed to the rafters with ceramic plates, glassware, blankets, toys, clothing, decorative items and cheap Mexico mementos.

More than a dozen art galleries dot Avenida Obregón and the narrow streets behind the San José Church. Easily explored on foot, the area is known as the San José del Cabo Art District, and behind its pastel storefronts you'll find some of the most interesting shopping in all of Los Cabos. A free guide map is available at the galleries.

At the corner of Avenida Obregón and Morelos, a colorful mural featuring Frida Kahlo serves as a backdrop for the gourmet coffee patio at El Armario, the self-proclaimed "cutest shop in town." Housed in an old gas station building, the gallery sells handmade folk art, unusual gift items and jewelry, plus eye-pleasing abstract paintings by up-and-coming local artists.

Old Town Gallery, Avenida Obregón #1505, features paintings by local artists and a nice selection of original crystal sculptures. The Arenas Mata Ortiz Art Gallery sells much sought-after Mata Ortiz pottery, as well as paintings and exquisite jewelry.

Corsica Galería de Arte deals in contemporary works by internationally known Mexican artists like Leonardo Nierman and Manuel Felguerez. Unless you've got a few thousand extra U.S. dollars burning a hole in your pocket, you'll have to be content with simply admiring Corsica's museum-quality paintings, large-scale sculptures and various *objets d'art*.

Art Walk, which takes place Thursday evenings from 5-9 during the high tourist season (November through June), is a good time to check out the district. The galleries stay open late, and many provide cocktails or wine to sip as you stroll. Several also offer artist-in-residence demonstrations, and all will happily wrap purchases for shipping or carrying home.

For a more down-to-earth shopping experience, walk through the Municipal Market (Mercado Municipal), off Calle Manuel Doblado. Locals gather here to buy fish, produce and flowers. Next door, a large yellow building houses a half-dozen *loncherìa* stands where you can get a fairly inexpensive lunch. Lonchería Ely dishes up outstanding *pozole* (hominy stew), while Lonchería Sonia makes a mean fish taco. Seating is at communal tables, packed with locals at lunchtime.

## Dining and Nightlife

Many downtown restaurants are either on or a block or so away from Plaza Mijares. Open-air courtyards, garden patios, sidewalk tables and distant Gulf of California views all make dining out a delightfully relaxed affair. See the Lodgings & Restaurants section for AAA-RATED dining establishments.

Even more casual is Zippers, just south of town on the road to Cabo San Lucas (Mex. 1 Km marker 28.5). This surfer and gringo hangout at Playa Costa Azul serves up burgers, fries, ribs, steaks, seafood and Mexican standards, usually with a helping of TV sports events, and you can chow down in your bathing suit if you wish.

Compared to Cabo San Lucas, nightlife in San José is downright sedate. The TVs at Shooters Sports Bar, at the corner of Boulevard Mijares and Doblado, are tuned to NFL, NHL, NBA and MLB action. The Tropicana Bar & Grill at the Tropicana Inn, Blvd. Mijares #30, is a longtime local gathering place that sometimes has live music.

Baja Brewing Co., on Morelos just north of Avenida Obregón (in the Art District), is owned by a couple of beer aficionados from Colorado. The on-site brewery produces impressive ales and lagers, and the kitchen (open late) turns out tasty pub grub and thin-crust pizzas. There's sports on TV as well as live salsa and reggae music on most nights.

Live bands also occasionally play beachside at Zippers. For most visitors, however, a stroll around Plaza Mijares caps off a pleasant evening—it's safe, the trees are wrapped in twinkling lights, and the square is filled with vendors and families.

## SANTA ROSALÍA, BAJA CALIFORNIA SUR (C-3)

A mining town that has been designated a national historic monument, Santa Rosalía (SAHN-tah roh-sah-LEE-ah) was established by the French-owned El Boleo Copper Co. during the 1880s. Prosperity reigned until the mines gave out in 1953. Mining operations were later reactivated with the discovery of new copper and manganese deposits, but these too failed. Commercial fishing and boat building contribute to today's economy.

The French left their mark on Santa Rosalía's narrow, bustling streets. Instead of Mexican-style stucco walls and tiled roofs, many houses are built of wood painted in pastel shades, and gardens are enclosed by picket fences. One of these residential neighborhoods sits on a plateau north of town and offers a panoramic view of the old copper smelter. Another European touch shows up on some of downtown's 19th-century buildings, which are topped with square clock towers.

Santa Rosalía also is known—somewhat incongruously—for bread. The El Boleo Bakery (Panadería El Boleo), Avenida Obregón and Calle 4, has earned a regional reputation for its fresh-baked specialties, particularly baguettes (arrive early if you want to stock up; they tend to sell out quickly).

The small harbor serves as the terminal for ferry service to Guaymas *(see separate listing under Northwestern Mexico)* on the Mexican mainland. Reservations are recommended; double-check rates and schedules prior to departure. The ferry office is in the terminal building just south of town on Mex. 1; phone (615) 152-1246. For reservations information phone 01 (800) 505-5018 (toll-free long distance within Mexico). *For additional information see Ferry Service, page p. 53.*

A pleasant side trip is the farming community of San José de Magdalena, reached via a well-marked turn-off that branches west off Mex. 1, about 27 kilometers (17 miles) south of Santa Rosalía. The road is graded dirt and can be negotiated by a high-clearance vehicle, but it becomes rough past the village. An oasis sheltered by palm groves, the village dates from Baja California's Spanish colonial period, when it served as a visiting station of the Mission Santa Rosalía Mulegé *(see Mulegé listing)*. In the vicinity are the ruins of a chapel built by the Dominicans in 1774.

**SANTA BARBARA CHURCH** (Iglesia Santa Barbara) is in the center of town at Av. Obregón and Calle 1. Santa Rosalía's most interesting architectural feature is this prefabricated, galvanized-iron church designed by Gustave Eiffel for the 1898 Paris World's Fair. It was shipped in pieces from France and reassembled here. Note the stained-glass windows.

# TECATE, BAJA CALIFORNIA (A-1)
pop. 101,079

In downtown Tecate (teh-KAH-teh)—sitting on a shady restaurant patio at the edge of Hidalgo Park, the main plaza, chomping tortilla chips, sipping a Tecate beer and overhearing conversations in Spanish—it's easy to forget California is just a few blocks to the north. The only reminder of los Estados Unidos' close proximity is the bright yellow Subway sandwich franchise next door.

For some people zebra-striped burros, drunken sailors on shore leave and seedy adult establishments typically spring to mind when picturing a Mexican border town. Not so in this relaxed community 30 miles east of Tijuana and only a 75-minute drive from the steel-and-glass skyscrapers of downtown San Diego. With its traditional colonial-style plaza and laid-back vibe, Tecate has the feel of any random small town you'd encounter in mainland Mexico.

Set in a valley surrounded by rolling chaparral and boulder-covered hills, the downtown district is packed with restaurants, clothing shops, cheap electronics stores, pharmacies and mini-marts. While this sounds a lot like Tijuana, low-key gringos who prefer to travel under the radar (or as incognito as Nike shoes and a Nikon camera allow) will be pleased to find that Tecate lacks the in-your-face street vendors and pushy cantina hucksters of its infamous neighbor.

Judging by the long line at lunchtime, Tecate's most popular *taquería* is Taquería Los Amigos, a block south of Hidalgo Park at the northeast corner of Calle Rubio (Mex. 3) and Avenida Hidalgo. Here you order at a counter where the food prep and cooking is done before your eyes in assembly-line fashion. The *carne asada,* chicken and *al pastor* are all outstanding.

The El Mejor Pan de Tecate bakery is on Avenida Juárez between calles Rodriguez and Portes Gil (about 2 blocks east of Hidalgo Park). It sells fresh-baked cakes, donuts, *bolillos* (rolls), *pan dulce* (lightly sweetened breakfast breads) and other treats in traditional serve-yourself style.

**Note:** Tecate is a small, relatively safe town that does not attract a lot of visitors. However, if being the only tourist on the street makes you uneasy, you will likely feel uncomfortable in Tecate.

## Practicalities

Tecate is accessible from the Otay Mesa border crossing into Tijuana *(see "Border Tips" under Tijuana).* From the border, proceed south about a mile on Boulevard de los Aztecas to Boulevard Industrial and turn left (east). Toll Mex. 2-D begins after about 2 miles. The toll for cars and light trucks is 80 pesos (about $6.10 U.S.), but this is a faster, non-congested alternative to free Mex. 2. Once you leave the industrial zone behind the route enters open countryside, first tracing a narrow canyon (watch for falling rocks along the roadside) and then continuing past rolling hills dotted with farms and ranches. The total distance is about 34 kilometers (21 miles).

It is also possible to drive from San Diego to the Tecate border crossing, park your vehicle in a pay lot and walk into Mexico (recommended for day trips). From downtown San Diego take SR 94 east. The freeway ends in San Diego's eastern suburbs and SR 94 becomes Campo Road, a major four-lane street. At Jamacha Junction, Campo Road veers south (watch for the SR 94 sign and turn right) and becomes a rural two-lane road that traverses rolling hills. At the SR 94/SR 188 junction, turn right (south) on SR 188 and follow it about 2 miles to the border crossing. The total distance from downtown San Diego is about 40 miles.

On the U.S. side of the border (also called Tecate) you'll find currency exchange houses,

Mexico automobile insurance agents and a couple of parking lots that charge about $5-$7 (U.S.) per day. The crossing for both vehicles and pedestrians is at the junction of Calle Cárdenas and SR 188 in California. From the border, Calle Cárdenas runs south 4 blocks before ending at the junction with Mex. 2. A block east is the northern terminus of Mex. 3, which runs southwest through the Guadalupe Valley and connects with Mex. 1 just north of Ensenada.

The northbound border crossing for vehicles returning to the United States is at the northern terminus of Calle Rubio, located a block east of the southbound crossing; there can be a long wait to cross the border back into the U.S. on busy weekends. The border crossing is open daily 5 a.m.-11 p.m. Mexican customs offices are open daily 8-4; U.S. Customs and Border Protection offices are open daily 5 a.m.-11 p.m.

**CUAUHTÉMOC BREWERY** (Cervecería Cuauhtémoc) is 6 blks. s. of the border at Dr. Arturo Guerra and Calle Carranza. This is where the famed Tecate beer is brewed. The Tecate logo—a red and gold symbol with a stylized eagle—is a familiar sight throughout Baja. Guided tours begin with an orientation film and then visit various aspects of the brewing process, including stainless steel boiling vats, towering fermentation tanks and a huge room where cans and bottles fly by at light speed.

Visitors wear safety glasses and headphones, and the tour guides provide entertaining narration not only about beer production but about Tecate history. At the end of the tour each person receives a ticket for one free beer in the beer garden.

Tours are offered in both Spanish and English; specify your preference when setting up an appointment. Cameras, cell phones and other personal items are not permitted inside the production facility. Closed-toe shoes must be worn. **Hours:** Beer garden open daily 10-3:30. Free 1-hour tours are given Mon.-Fri. at noon and 3, Sat.-Sun. at 11 and noon. All tours are by appointment only and require a minimum of five people. **Phone:** (665) 654-9478.

## TIJUANA, BAJA CALIFORNIA (A-1)
pop. 1,559,683

**Note:** For current information about safety/security issues in Tijuana, refer to the U.S. State Department website (travel.state.gov).

The First World meets the Third World in Tijuana (tee-HWAH-nah), arguably the most notorious international border city on the planet. The name alone conjures a blizzard of images, from white-knuckle taxi rides and burros painted to look like zebras to super-sized sombreros and throngs of American teenagers tanked on tequila shooters.

Downtown Tijuana is crass, bawdy, cheap, touristy and then some—which of course is all part of the fun. Tijuana's illicit reputation has been luring Californians south of the border since the 1890s, and generations of them have the wild stories and barroom brawl scars to prove it.

"TJ" (as the city is often called) is about 18 miles south of downtown San Diego. From the pedestrian bridge spanning U.S. I-5 and the border crossing, the view to *el norte* is the orderly San Diego Trolley plaza and a tidy freeway. The view to the south is ramshackle sprawl behind an imposing metal border fence. Your first instinct may be to turn and run, and you can't be blamed if you do. But for adventurous travelers an interesting city awaits exploration, one that isn't as squalid and simple as it first appears.

Most day-trippers stick close to the border or head directly to Avenida Revolución, downtown's main drag. For decades boisterous cantinas, sleazy strip joints and the dirt-cheapest of souvenirs ruled on "La Revo." And while you can still knock back one too many margaritas at a loud nightspot or score a $5 Che Guevara poncho, these days the avenue is somewhat more sedate, with wide, well-maintained sidewalks dotted with trees and wrought-iron park benches.

**Note:** Drug cartel-related violence peaked in Tijuana in the late 2000s and ebbed dramatically thereafter, but as far as many Americans are concerned the massive PR damage has been permanent. The only gringos hitting La Revo and the Zona Río these days are San Diego college kids, Americans seeking inexpensive south-of-the-border medical and dental procedures, and a handful of adventurous foodies in search of eateries featured on Anthony Bourdain's Travel Channel show "No Reservations."

Although Tijuana remains on the U.S. State Department's travel warning list, in 2015 the Avenida Revolución tourist zone doesn't feel any more dangerous than the downtown area of a major U.S. city. Travelers have varying comfort levels, however, and if the mere thought of visiting Tijuana makes you nervous, you'll probably want to stay away.

If you *do* choose to cross the border, be aware that as one of the few tourists walking La Revo, you'll be constantly approached by nightclub barkers and souvenir vendors. They're harmless, but the aggressive solicitations can be annoying in the extreme.

## Practicalities

Tijuana International Airport is on the eastern edge of the city near the Otay Mesa border crossing. Aeroméxico and Volaris are among the airlines serving the airport, flying to cities on the Baja Peninsula and mainland Mexico. *Colectivos* (shared shuttle vans) and taxis provide transportation to downtown hotels. *Colectivo* fares are about $5 (U.S.). Taxis are more expensive; fares are posted at the counters where you purchase tickets. *For additional information about airlines see Arriving by Air, page p. 42.*

**Note:** In 2014 construction began on a cross-border airport terminal, the Cross Border Xpress, that will link Otay Mesa in the U.S. with Tijuana International. Tentatively scheduled to open in late 2015, the facility will only be accessible to ticketed airline passengers. Check the airport website for updates.

Greyhound buses travel frequently between Tijuana and San Diego; for fare and schedule information phone (800) 231-2222 (from the United States). Tijuana's Central Bus Terminal (Centro de Autobuses) is on Calzada Lázaro Cárdenas at Río Alamar in La Mesa, en route from downtown to the airport. Regular passenger service is offered to the nearby cities of Ensenada, Mexicali and Tecate. The Autotransportes de Baja California line (ABC) offers first-class service; phone (800) 025-0222 (toll-free long distance within Mexico). *For additional information about buses see Bus Service, page p. 52.*

Five Star Tours provides charter shuttle service and bus tours from San Diego to locations in northern Baja. Bus tours depart from San Diego's Amtrak depot, Broadway at Kettner Boulevard, or complimentary transportation from San Diego area hotels is available. Tour destinations include Avenida Revolución in downtown Tijuana, Rosarito, Ensenada and the Puerto Nuevo lobster village. For schedule and fare information phone (619) 232-5040 or (877) 704-0514 (in the United States).

For day visitors who want to avoid traffic congestion and the hassle of finding a parking space, it's much more convenient to park on the U.S. side and enter the city on foot. After exiting the border crossing's pedestrian walkway, you'll first cross to the west side of the northbound vehicle lanes via a footbridge. At the bottom of the bridge ramp is a tourist taxi stand.

**Note:** A new pedestrian walkway that will adjoin the west side of I-5 is under construction and is tentatively scheduled to open in early 2016. When using that border crossing, the tourist taxi stand will be dead ahead after visitors exit the new Mexico Customs facility.

Yellow tourist taxis are not metered. Always ask how much the fare is (*"Cuanto?"*) and state your destination before getting in, as drivers may try to get more money out of tourists or take you somewhere other than where you want to go.

Fares from the border to Avenida Revolución and the Zona Río run about $6 to $7 (U.S.). Within the downtown area fares are $4 to $5; from downtown to the racetrack about $10; and to the airport or Bullring-by-the-Sea about $15.

If you're crossing the border in your vehicle, most shopping centers have free parking lots, and there are pay lots along Avenida Revolución downtown; either option is preferable to parking on the street.

In addition to the yellow tourist taxis, there are red and white *taxis libres,* which are metered. You won't find these taxis at the border crossing cab stand, but they travel all over town and the metered fare is often a little cheaper than the set rates charged by the tourist taxis. "Route taxis" are solid-colored (red, brown, etc.) *colectivo* cabs that follow set routes and are mainly used by locals.

The weather in Tijuana is similar to that in southern California—mild, overcast and rather wet in winter, warm and dry in summer. Daily maximums are usually in the 60s during the winter months, rising to the low 80s in summer. While there are occasional hot spells, the moderating influence of the Pacific Ocean largely spares the city from the blazing temperatures common in many other parts of Baja. Precipitation averages only about 10 inches a year, with almost all of it occurring during the winter; from May through September practically no rain falls.

## Border Tips

There are two border crossings—at Tijuana-San Ysidro and at Otay Mesa, just east of Tijuana International Airport and south of SR 117 (Otay Mesa Road). U.S. Customs and Border Protection offices are open 24 hours daily. Mexican customs offices are open Mon.-Fri. 8 a.m.-9 p.m., Sat. 8-5. Both crossings are open to travelers daily 24 hours. *For additional information see the Border Information section in the back of this guide.*

**Note:** The entire Tijuana-San Ysidro border crossing complex is in the midst of a major renovation scheduled to be completed at some point in 2016. The change that most affects day visitors crossing the border on foot is the closure of the old southbound pedestrian walkway on the west side of I-5. This walkway has been moved to the east side of I-5, next to the U.S. Customs building. The southbound pedestrian walkway adjoining the west side of I-5, scheduled to open by early 2016, will funnel visitors through a new Mexico Customs facility.

Also on the near horizon is a planned third pedestrian walkway that will adjoin the rerouted southbound vehicle lanes, which are now located just west of the old lanes. The new vehicle crossing is called Puerto Mexico El Chaparral.

Keep in mind that crossing the border by car south into Tijuana or north back to the United States can involve significant delays (as long as several hours) at both crossings. Enhanced security measures are in effect in an effort to curb the flow of illegal firearms and huge amounts of drug cartel cash. Mexican customs officials may conduct thorough vehicle searches, including X-rays.

Travelers also are likely to encounter routine backups in the morning and late afternoon on weekdays, as thousands of commuters travel between their Tijuana homes and jobs on the U.S. side of the border. Friday afternoon backups are especially common. The best times to cross the border north into the United States are in the very early morning and after 8 p.m.

Crossing on or around major holidays—Memorial Day, July 4, Labor Day, Thanksgiving and Christmas—also can entail long waits. The 2-week college spring break and the first 2 weeks of December, when citizens of both countries are traveling back and forth doing their Christmas shopping, are other times when significant delays can be expected, as are Mexican holidays.

For day visitors walking across, a safe place to leave your vehicle is Border Station Parking, next to the San Diego Factory Outlet Center at the San Ysidro crossing. Open and attended 24 hours daily, it's fenced, lighted and equipped with surveillance equipment. Both short- and long-term pay parking is available; day parking Mon.-Fri. is $7, Sat.-Sun. $10.

Closer to the border is a fenced parking lot next to a large duty-free store; day parking is $8. Both the duty-free store and Border Station lots are on the west side of I-5, on the opposite side of the freeway from where the southbound pedestrian border crossing is located. To reach the crossing, use the footbridge spanning I-5; if you park in the Border Station lot, pedicab rides are available for a few bucks. Phone (619) 428-9477.

More convenient are the fenced parking lots on the east side of I-5 (all-day fees range from $8 to $10 on weekdays, and up to $20 on busy weekends). If you park in one of these lots, you'll simply walk toward the San Diego Trolley station and U.S. Customs building to the southbound pedestrian crossing.

Pedestrians returning from Mexico will exit the U.S. Customs building on the east side of I-5. If you parked in the Border Station or duty-free store lots on the west side of I-5, use the footbridge to cross back over the freeway and return to your vehicle.

San Diego Trolley's blue line provides transportation to the San Ysidro station (East Beyer Boulevard and East San Ysidro Boulevard) from various downtown San Diego stations, including the Santa Fe Depot, America Plaza (West C Street and Kettner Boulevard), Civic Center (C Street and 3rd Avenue) and 5th Avenue (5th Avenue and C Street at the north end of the Gaslamp Quarter).

There are public parking lots at each station; daily rates range from $7 to $10. One-way fare from downtown San Diego is $2.50; over 59, $1.25. Day passes good for unlimited trolley rides are $5. Trolley tickets are available from self-serve kiosks at each stop. For information and schedules phone (619) 595-4949 or (619) 685-4900 (recorded information), or TTY (619) 234-5005. Closed Thanksgiving and Christmas.

## City Layout

El Centro, the old downtown part of the city, is less than a mile from the San Ysidro border crossing. Roving bands of kids selling chicle (gum) approach you every few minutes. Vendors call out, offering a great deal on that San Diego Chargers blanket big enough to cover your front lawn.

The Monument Arch (Arco Monumental, also called Reloj Monumental) marks the north end of Avenida Revolución. Stretching for some 10 blocks south, "La Revo" is packed with bars, restaurants, discount pharmacies and—of course—shops and vendors selling everything from stuffed Tweety birds to Bob Marley paintings on black velvet.

In the decades before cartel violence scared off most Americans, TJ's famed "zonkeys" (burros painted with black and white zebra stripes) were a common sight on every other Avenida Revolución corner, their handlers urging gringos to don a giant sombrero and pose for a souvenir photo on the poor burro's back. These days, however, the zonkey is an endangered species; only a couple of the spray-painted beasts remain employed.

The vanishing zonkeys are part of a wider trend. In an ironic twist of fate, the downturn in tourism has encouraged Tijuana residents to take back the heart of their own city. The nightlife scenes along La Revo and adjacent Calle 6 (La Sexta) are seeing a renaissance—young Mexican artists and musicians conversing at a coffeehouse rather than drunk gringos trading punches outside the strip clubs of yore.

About a mile to the southeast is the Zona Río. Along the main thoroughfare, Paseo de los Héroes, four massive monuments (think Aztec emperors and Mexican generals) punctuate the major traffic circles. The most unexpected monument is a towering statue of Abraham Lincoln, a gift from U.S. president Jimmy Carter. Most tourists never visit the Zona Río, which is a shame. With its upscale restaurants, contemporary shopping mall and impressive cultural center, it's the sophisticated flip side of brash Avenida Revolución.

If you're driving, you'll enter Mexico at the Puerto Mexico El Chaparral vehicle crossing. To reach Avenida Revolución and the Zona Río, move to the far left-hand lanes and follow the "Zona Centro" signs. If you're heading toward Playas de Tijuana and/or Rosarito/Ensenada, immediately move to the far right-hand lanes and follow the signs for Mex 1-D. If you're headed for the airport, stick to the middle lanes.

Streets in the immediate border vicinity, plus north-south Revolución and Avenida Constitución, are all very congested, and traffic signals are not always readily visible. The traffic circles, or glorietas, along northwest-southeast Paseo de los Héroes and Paseo de Tijuana also can be confusing; always bear right when entering a traffic circle, following the flow of traffic counterclockwise. There are many one-way street signs as well, so make sure you have a good downtown street map.

Mex 1-D, a divided, fully access-controlled toll highway, provides a quick and safe route to Ensenada and points south and is preferable to the older, free Mex. 1 roadway. From the international border, it proceeds west, paralleling the border fence and bypassing much of Tijuana's congestion (follow the "Ensenada Cuota" signs along Calle Internacional).

Mex. 1-D continues west to Playas de Tijuana, then turns south, with the ocean in view along most of the scenic route. There are three toll plazas between the two cities; the total charge is 93 pesos (about $6.90 U.S.). Toll highway Mex. 2-D runs parallel to the border from Tijuana east to Mexicali; expect to pay 190 pesos (about $14 U.S.) in tolls between the two cities.

## Shopping

Avenida Revolución is lined with souvenir stalls and maze-like arcades filled with curio shops. Many have closed because of the drop in tourism, but there are still enough shopkeepers left to keep browsers busy, calling out from doorways or pacing the sidewalk pleading with you to stop and look. And no matter what the item, they always have "the best price, amigo."

Keep expectations in mind; if you're looking for authentic silver jewelry instead of a simple trinket, avoid the street vendors whose arms are garlanded with necklaces. Leather boots, shoes, sandals, luggage, purses, wallets, briefcases, belts and jackets can all be bargained for—but again, check for quality before committing your dollars.

A standout shop with fixed prices is Casa del Angel, Av. Revolución #1026 (near Calle 4), where you'll find a nice selection of decorative masks, Oaxacan wood carvings and Day of the Dead-related items. This isn't museum-level workmanship, but prices are fair and the quality is of a higher pedigree than most of the stuff the street vendors peddle.

Across the street, Emporium carries fine silver jewelry and some nice stained-glass pieces, and the owner speaks English. Phone (664) 685-1324. Hand Art, a block north on Avenida Revolución between calles 3 and 4, specializes in traditional, hand-embroidered men's and women's clothing, along with lovely handmade tablecloths.

If you'd rather browse in a more concentrated area and avoid the irritating street vendors, outdoor Plaza Río Tijuana, along Paseo de los Héroes next to the Tijuana Cultural Center, has shops, restaurants, several department stores and a movie theater multiplex. Baseball fans from north of the border will find a San Diego Padres team store selling discounted logo gear.

A block southwest of the cultural center on Avenida Independencia is the Hidalgo Market (Mercado M. Hidalgo). This lively public market is filled with bins of fresh produce, heaps of fresh and dried chiles, a mind-boggling array of spices and candy, and craft stalls that feature, among many other things, a great selection of piñatas.

Pueblo Amigo, a 5-minute walk from the border, has shops, restaurants, nightspots and a Caliente Sportsbook betting facility. At Plaza Viva Tijuana, which you'll walk through on the way from the border to Avenida Revolución, there are craft stalls, curio shops, liquor stores and a few casual bars.

The Mexican peso and the American dollar are practically interchangeable in Tijuana, and visitors rarely have to worry about currency exchange. Haggling is expected if you're buying from street vendors or open-air stalls; in more established shops, ask if bargaining is accepted. The only ground rule is to maintain a serious yet light-hearted approach, for a merchant's initial offering price will usually be about twice what the item is worth. Some stores accept U.S. credit cards.

## Sports and Recreation

Occasional bullfights take place at Bullring-by-the-Sea (Plaza de Toros Monumental) on selected Sunday afternoons; July and August are the likeliest months. The bullring is 10 kilometers (6 miles) west of downtown via Mex. 1-D. Reserved and general admission seating is available. Ticket prices range from $15-$60 (U.S.); seats on the shady side of the arena are more expensive. Tickets can be purchased at the bullring or by phone: (664) 633-4000 (no English spoken).

Matches are a thing of the distant past at the Jai Alai Palace (Frontón Palacio), at the corner of Calle 7 and Avenida Revolución, but the building itself remains a Tijuana landmark, a Moorish-inspired structure with tile mosaics adorning its front. Now it's a venue for concerts, boxing and *lucha libre* (wrestling) matches. Next to the building is a Caliente Sportsbook betting facility. Wagers can be placed for most major U.S. and Latin American sporting events; multiple giant-screen TVs broadcast the action. Other locations are scattered throughout the city, including three within walking distance of the border.

The Caliente Racetrack (Hipódromo de Caliente), about 5 kilometers (3 miles) east of downtown off Boulevard Agua Caliente, presents greyhound racing. First post time at matinee races is 1:30 p.m.; evening races begin at 7:45. General admission is free. Race days vary by season; check race forms or the Caliente website for additional information, or phone (664) 633-7300.

## Dining and Nightlife

A Tijuana time warp not to be missed, Caesar's Restaurante Bar, on Avenida Revolución between calles 4 and 5, is a good choice for a relaxed drink and bite in a classy atmosphere that feels more like Old Hollywood than tawdry TJ. Originally opened in 1927, its claim to fame is inventing the Caesar salad, which is prepared at your table. Locally brewed Caesar's Cervezas (try the dark *morena*) are best enjoyed at the polished wood bar, backed by antique espresso machines.

Restaurante Chiki Jai, Av. Revolución #1388 (across Calle 7 from the old Jai Alai Palace) has been a La Revo fixture since 1947. Behind the classic blue-and-white tiled facade, excellent Spanish dishes are served in a cozy dining room. Try the seafood *paella* or a freshly grilled fish filet. If it's a nice day, sit at one of the half-dozen sidewalk tables for two.

For those in search of quick, inexpensive street food, there are taco stands along the pedestrian walkway from the border to Avenida Revolución, as well as on La Revo itself. Street tacos are cheap, filling and often better than what you'll find in restaurants; look for food that is hot and freshly prepared.

Want to feast on what many consider TJ's best street tacos? Head for Las Ahumaderas, a string of six connected taco stands near the Zona Río on Avenida

Prieto (about a block south of Boulevard Agua Caliente). This spot can be tricky to find on your own, so definitely take a taxi; every cabbie knows the place. One-way fare from La Revo should run about $5 to $6 (a buck or two more from the border).

Since 1960, Las Ahumaderas (Spanish for "the smokehouses") have cooked taco and *torta* meats on simple wood-burning grills that give everything—from carne asada to chorizo—a fantastic mesquite flavor. There are also exotic fillings like *cabeza* (cow head meat) and *lengua* (beef tongue), plus tender *al pastor* (pork) cooked on a proper rotisserie spit—difficult to find in the states. Grab a counter stool at one of these inexpensive, open-air taquerias (the "El Paisa" and "Las 3 Salsas" stands are best) and ascend to taco heaven. All are cash only.

If you're leery of street food, stateside franchises like TGI Friday's, Burger King, McDonalds and Starbucks can be found in Tijuana.

When deciding what to tip in restaurants, do not include the 11 percent IVA tax that is automatically added to the check. A 20 percent tip is not expected in Mexico; 10 percent is acceptable, unless you feel the service has been truly outstanding. See the Lodgings & Restaurants section for AAA-RATED dining establishments.

Loud music—both recorded and live—booms from a handful of clubs on Avenida Revolución Thursday through Saturday nights. Shills stationed at every door lure potential customers with free drink cards and frequent shouts of "$1 beers!" Traditionally high cover charges have also dropped in recent years.

If thumping dance beats aren't your thing, party bars are a good alternative. Local institution Tia Juana Tilly's, next to the Jai Alai Palace on Avenida Revolución at Calle 7, attracts an all-ages crowd with standard Mexican dishes, strong margaritas and fun waiters. During the day and early evening, sports fans gather at the sleek El Copeo bar (Av. Revolución #1240, near the corner of Calle 6), which is loaded with HDTVs.

Feeling lucky? Casino Caliente, Avenida Revolución between calles 3 and 4, has rows of video slot machines to reward or rob you of a few pesos. **Note**: To enter the casino you'll need to pass through a security metal detector. Also, smoking is not permitted.

The nightlife scene along Calle 6 (aka "La Sexta") stretches for a few blocks both east and west of Avenida Revolución. The epicenter of TJ's bar and nightclub rebirth is a hangout for the city's young artists, musicians and DJs. La Mezcalera (Calle 6 #8267) is a trendy, colorful spot to chill with friends over mezcal cocktails.

If you crave the classic Tijuana dive bar experience, make your drinking destination El Dandy Del Sur (Calle 6 #8274, just east of La Revo). Although the exterior looks sketchy, once inside you'll knock back cheap drinks alongside a friendly mix of Mexican hipsters, local *borrachos* (drunks) and a few

tourists. If dance clubs are your thing, walk the street and take your pick.

**Note:** While Tijuana promotes fun, remember that you are in a foreign country where a different set of rules and laws are in effect. The police invariably arrest those who are inebriated and causing a disturbance in public, and nothing will ruin a vacation like a night in a Mexican jail and the ensuing bureaucratic hassle to get out.

**Tijuana Convention & Visitors Bureau:** Paseo de los Héroes #9365-201. **Phone:** (664) 684-0537.

The bureau operates a small visitor center with English-speaking staff where you can pick up brochures and maps, and obtain information about local attractions and tours. The kiosk is on Avenida Revolución (between Calles 3 and 4) and is open daily 9-6; phone (664) 685-3117.

There also is a tourist information booth at the Border Station Parking facility just north of the San Ysidro border crossing, though it is not always staffed; phone (619) 428-6200.

**TIJUANA CULTURAL CENTER** (Centro Cultural Tijuana, or CECUT) is on Paseo de los Héroes between calles Javier Mina and Centenario, just n. of the Plaza Río shopping center in the Zona Río section of downtown. This modern, clean, well-signed cultural/museum complex is a refreshing contrast to Tijuana's raucous bars and myriad souvenir stands. It includes a history museum, an aquarium, the giant, orb-shaped Cine IMAX theater (with daily showings in English), a 1,000-seat performing arts theater (Sala de Espectáculos), a photography gallery, the El Cubo temporary exhibit gallery, a bookstore and an outdoor sculpture garden (Jardín Caracol).

The Museum of the Californias (Museo de las Californias) has varied exhibits on the Baja peninsula's natural history, the Spanish conquest of Mexico (including a large-scale replica of a 16th-century sailing ship), scale models of Baja missions and historical artifacts from bowls, baskets and battle armor to flags, antique mining tools, period weaponry and hand-drawn maps.

An exhibit about the history of Tijuana features a panoramic rendering of downtown TJ circa 1924, vintage postcards and restaurant menus, bullfight posters and other memorabilia. Exhibit information is given in both Spanish and English. A children's interactive play area has a Spanish galleon that kids can climb inside and a playroom with tables for coloring and other activities.

At the rear of the complex is a dark, cave-like aquarium displaying more than 500 aquatic species, including many native to Baja California waters. A few dozen tanks hold everything from eels and seahorses to small sharks and rays; information is given in both Spanish and English.

Sunday jazz, pop and rock concerts take place on the paved concourse in front of the main entrance, which also is the setting for art and craft fairs and other events. "Baja P" buses drop passengers off here from the border. Yellow tourist taxi fare from the border is about $6 (U.S.).

**Hours:** Complex daily 10-7; hours for specific facilities vary. Museum of the Californias Tues.-Sun. 10-6:15. Outdoor sculpture garden daily 10-7. Aquarium Tues.-Fri. 3-7, Sat.-Sun. 10-7. IMAX film showings Mon.-Fri. on the hour 4-9, Sat.-Sun. on the hour 11-9. Phone ahead to confirm schedule. **Cost:** Complex and sculpture garden free. Museum admission 27 pesos (about $2 U.S.), 17 pesos (children). IMAX films 52 pesos (about $3.85 U.S.); 33 pesos (ages 3-11). Aquarium admission 42 pesos (about $3.10 U.S.); 26 pesos (ages 3-11). Temporary exhibits in the El Cubo gallery 48 pesos (about $3.55 U.S.); 27 pesos (ages 3-11). Parking 20 pesos for 3 hours. **Phone:** (664) 687-9650. 🍽 🚻 San Ysidro, 22

**TIJUANA WAX MUSEUM** is downtown at the corner of Calle 1 and Av. Madero, along the pedestrian walkway connecting the international border crossing with Av. Revolución. Figures depict both the famous and infamous from Mexico, the United States and around the world. The first room, filled with figures from early Mexican history, features ancient ruler Moctezuma II in a giant headdress as well as a convincingly gory diorama depicting Aztec sacrifice, right down to the unlucky victim with a ripped-open chest.

The galleries featuring Hollywood stars and musical legends are where you'll have the most fun deciding who is acceptably—or unacceptably—lifelike. Eddie Murphy and Whoopi Goldberg come off fairly well, but Sylvester Stallone, Harrison Ford, Julia Roberts and Madonna look downright frightening, and Michael Jackson resembles a clone of sister La Toya rather than the pop superstar of the "Thriller" era. This is an enjoyable way to spend an hour in Tijuana.

**Hours:** Mon.-Fri. 10-6, Sat.-Sun. 10-7, in summer; Mon.-Fri. 10-5, Sat.-Sun. 10-6, rest of year. Phone ahead to confirm schedule. **Cost:** 20 pesos (around $1.50 U.S.); free (ages 0-5). **Phone:** (664) 688-2478.

## WINERIES

- **L. A. Cetto Winery** is downtown at Av. Cañon Johnson #2108, about 2 blks. s.w. of Av. Revolución. This large, modern building is the aging facility for the L.A. Cetto Vineyards in northern Baja's Guadalupe Valley. **Note:** Although the building is located only a few blocks from the southern end of Avenida Revolución, you'll briefly walk through a ramshackle business district that may make some people feel uncomfortable. If you're the nervous type, definitely take a taxi; winery staff will be happy to call a cab for you. **Hours:** Mon.-Sat. 10-5. Guided tours are available by request. **Cost:** Tastings $2-$5 (U.S.). Tour free. **Phone:** (664) 638-5848. GT

## TODOS SANTOS, BAJA CALIFORNIA SUR (E-3)

An old farming and fishing community about 80 kilometers (50 miles) north of Cabo San Lucas, Todos Santos (TOH-dos SAHN-tos) was long isolated from visitors. That changed in 1986 with the completion of Mex. 19 from La Paz south to Cabo San Lucas. Even though large-scale resort development has begun to take shape south of town, Todos Santos ("All Saints") retains a relaxed air and the charms of a traditional Mexican town.

Located just south of the Tropic of Cancer, Todos Santos is tropical but not quite as torrid as the towns lying next to the warm Gulf of California waters. Underground water from the Sierra de la Laguna range, which rises to the east, provides irrigation for groves of mangoes, papayas and avocados. The town's 19th-century status as a sugar cane producer is evidenced by the ruins of a few sugar mills.

The peak tourist season is from October through February; many businesses are closed or open irregular hours from July through September, when the weather is hotter and more humid and the beaches are plagued by mosquitos. Occurring over the second weekend of October, the 4-day Fiesta Todos Santos celebrates the town's 1723 founding with live music, dancing and sports competitions.

A persistent urban legend claims that the Hotel California, on Calle Juárez, is the lodging with "plenty of room" referred to in the Eagles song and shown on the cover of the band's same-named 1976 album. The Hotel California opened in 1950, closed in the late 1990s for an extensive renovation and reopened in 2004. Standing under the arches is a popular photo op. The La Coronela Restaurant has live music on Saturday evenings.

Café Todos Santos, on Calle Centenario at Calle Topete (across from the Todos Santos Inn), is where many visitors head for breakfast. The cafe latte comes in a cup the size of a bowl; pair it with a cinnamon bun, sit in the charming garden and while away the morning.

Local galleries include Galería de Todos Santos, on Juárez next to the Centro Cultural (Cultural Center) between calles Obregón and Topete, where works by Mexican and American artists are on display. Galería Santa Fe, Centenario #4 next to Café Santa Fe, has a delightful collection of Mexican folk art.

About 3 kilometers (2 miles) west of town on a dirt road is Playa Punta Lobos. Here local fishermen embark in their *pangas* for the day's catch; visitors can enjoy the dramatic Pacific surf. South of town via Mex. 19, dirt-road turn-offs offer access to unspoiled, unpopulated beaches—good for surfing— along the rocky coastline. Just 23 kilometers (14 miles) east the Sierra de la Laguna Mountains rise to 6,000 feet; pack trips to explore the area can be arranged in town.

© Bruce Raynor / Shutterstock.com

# Northwestern Mexico

Northwestern Mexico encompasses three of the country's four largest states—Chihuahua, Durango and Sonora—and vast expanses of insurmountable territory. Desolate plateaus stretch for miles, and the sun sets over panoramic mountain and desert vistas. This part of Mexico also is economically rich; irrigated river valleys produce flourishing crops of cotton, peanuts, sugar cane, tobacco, fruits and vegetables, and extensive ranchlands in Sonora yield what is considered to be the country's best beef cattle.

One way to view the rugged scenery is from the window of a passenger train traversing the Copper Canyon region, a complex of interconnected canyons almost four times larger and some 280 feet deeper than the Grand Canyon. Copper Canyon travel packages feature coach tours, and some also include guided hiking or horseback riding expeditions.

Durango's historic center is filled with carefully preserved 17th- and 18th-century buildings. San Carlos is a laid-back beach resort, while Puerto Peñasco—better known as Rocky Point—is especially popular with nearby California and Arizona residents due to its easy accessibility.

For a taste of authentic Mexico head to Alamos, in the foothills of the Sierra Madre Occidental. About 52 kilometers (32 miles) east of Navojoa via Mex. 10, it's a 5-hour drive from the U.S. border at Nogales. Cottonwood trees and restored colonial-era mansions make this expat community an oasis in the otherwise barren landscape of coastal Sonora.

AAA recommends that travelers consult online U.S. State Department travel advisories when planning traveling abroad. Find this information at http://travel.state.gov/content/passports/english/alertswarnings/mexico-travel-warning.html.

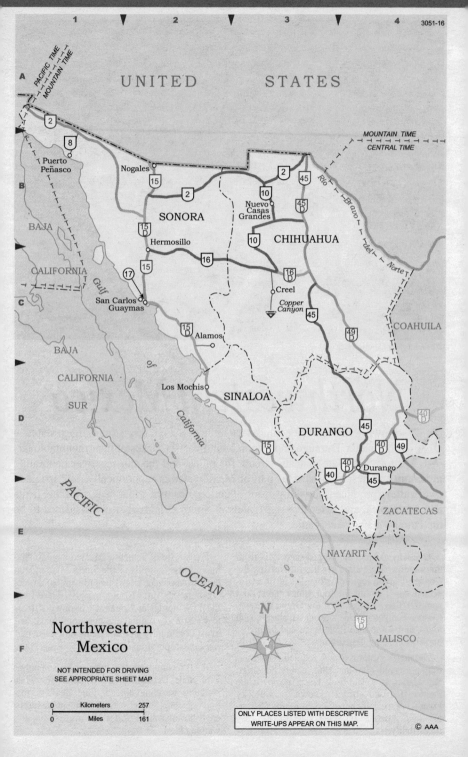

3051-16

UNITED STATES

PACIFIC TIME
MOUNTAIN TIME

MOUNTAIN TIME
CENTRAL TIME

Puerto
Peñasco

Nogales

SONORA

Hermosillo

San Carlos
Guaymas

Nuevo
Casas
Grandes

CHIHUAHUA

Creel

Copper
Canyon

Alamos

Los Mochis

SINALOA

DURANGO

Durango

COAHUILA

ZACATECAS

NAYARIT

PACIFIC

OCEAN

JALISCO

BAJA
CALIFORNIA

BAJA
CALIFORNIA
SUR

Gulf of California

Rio Bravo del Norte

N

Northwestern
Mexico

NOT INTENDED FOR DRIVING
SEE APPROPRIATE SHEET MAP

| Kilometers | |
|---|---|
| 0 | 257 |

| Miles | |
|---|---|
| 0 | 161 |

ONLY PLACES LISTED WITH DESCRIPTIVE
WRITE-UPS APPEAR ON THIS MAP.

© AAA

# Points of Interest

## ALAMOS, SONORA (C-2) pop. 25,848

Alamos (AH-lah-mohs), an early Spanish stronghold in the vastness of northwestern Mexico, was once a remote settlement that supplied services for regional silver-mining operations. The mines were all but depleted by the turn of the 20th century; the town's wealthier citizens pulled up stakes, leaving their colonial-style mansions to deteriorate. A turnaround took place following World War II, when U.S. artists and expats began restoring the old homes to their former glory.

On arcaded Plaza de Armas, the main square, stand the Church of the Immaculate Conception (Iglesia de la Inmaculada Concepción) and City Hall (Palacio Municipal). Mocuzari Dam (Presa Mocuzari), accessed by a gravel road branching north off Mex. 10, offers fishing and outdoor recreation activities.

**Tourist information office:** Calle Guadalupe Victoria #5. Open daily 9-7 (reduced hours in summer). **Phone:** (647) 428-1371.

**HOME AND GARDEN TOUR** departs from Plaza de Armas. Community residents open their restored Spanish colonial homes and gardens to the public; volunteer guides lead the tours. The nonprofit organization Los Amigos de Educación uses the proceeds to provide scholarships to local students. For additional information contact the Alamos tourist information office. **Hours:** Tours depart Sat. at 10 a.m., mid-Oct. to May 1. **Cost:** Tour fee $10 (U.S.).

**MUSEUM OF SOCIAL CUSTOMS OF SONORA** (Museo Costumbrista de Sonora) is at Guadalupe Victoria #1 on Plaza de Armas. It occupies a 19th-century colonial house with three patios. The state's past is preserved through displays of furniture, photographs, machinery and work tools, clothing, documents and ethnographic displays. There is also a reproduction of a typical 19th-century Mexican kitchen and a collection of coins from the former mints in Alamos and Hermosillo. Exhibit information is in Spanish. **Hours:** Wed.-Sun. 9-6. **Cost:** 10 pesos (about 75c U.S.); 5 pesos (children). **Phone:** (647) 428-0053.

## CHIHUAHUA, CHIHUAHUA (C-3)
pop. 819,543

**Note:** For current information about safety/security issues in Chihuahua, refer to the U.S. State Department website (travel.state.gov).

Chihuahua has figured prominently in Mexico's history despite its geographical isolation. Miguel Hidalgo y Costilla, champion of Mexican independence, was executed here in 1811. It served as headquarters for Benito Juárez when French troops invaded Mexico between 1862 and 1867. Outlaw Pancho Villa frequented the surrounding countryside in the early 20th century and once captured the city by disguising his men as peasants going to market.

Industrial plants clog Chihuahua's outskirts, but like many Mexican cities it has a well-preserved historic center that manages to evoke a bit of 19th-century atmosphere. Downtown is divided by northwest/southeast Avenida Independencia; Plaza de Armas, the main square, is a block below this street. Take a taxi to reach such outlying points of interest as the Museum of the Revolution (*see attraction listing*).

Rising from the plaza is a 115-foot-tall marble column topped by the bronze Angel of Freedom. The statue stands on a slowly revolving base; at night a laser beam shoots out from the angel's sword. About 3 blocks northwest of Plaza de Armas at Av. Juárez #321 is the Juárez House (Casa de Juárez), also known as the Museum of the Republican Loyalty. Between October 1864 and December 1866 president Benito Juárez took refuge in this house while in exile during the brief reign of Archduke Maximilian. It exhibits historic objects, documents signed by Juárez and a replica of the carriage he rode in during a trip through the state. The museum is open Tues.-Sun. 9-6; phone (614) 410-4258.

The small Temple of Santa Rita, Calle 10 de Mayo #1601-A, Colonia Santa Rita, is very significant for Chihuahuans, who consider St. Rita the city's patron saint. The site was originally occupied by a hacienda and a smelting plant. The daughter of a general who acquired the property had a chapel built in honor of Santa Rita. In 1837 it became a hospice for the poor, initiating the popular devotion for Santa Rita. The chapel was restored in 1949 and retains its original beams. The family-oriented, 2-week Santa Rita Fair, which takes place in mid-May, offers rides, arts and crafts, traditional food and cultural events.

The city's ancient aqueduct was begun in 1706; prior to its construction canoes carried water from the Chuvíscar River to a smelting hacienda. The ditches dug for the canoes provided the foundation for a stone aqueduct completed in 1854; some of the semicircular arches can still be seen.

Lerdo Park, on Paseo Bolívar southeast of Plaza de Armas, is the scene of Sunday concerts. Seasonal Sunday afternoon bullfights take place at the 7,500-seat Plaza La Esperanza. For a good selection of Tarahumara and other regional crafts, visit the House of Crafts of the State of Chihuahua (Casa de las Artesanías del Estado de Chihuahua), at Av. Niños Heroes #1101 (near the Federal Palace). The shop is closed Sunday; phone (614) 437-1292.

The El Tarahumara Trolley is a convenient way to see the sights. Service begins in front of the city's cathedral, facing the main plaza; the 19-passenger trolley completes the tour loop in 1 hour and runs Tues.-Sat. 10-6, Sun. 10-3. One ticket allows passengers to get on and off at different stops up to four times in the same day; the fare is 100 pesos (about $8 U.S.) per person.

Day trips can be made to Aquiles Serdán (also known as Santa Eulalia), east of the city via Mex. 45, and to Aldama, north via Mex. 16. Reputedly the oldest mining town in northern Mexico, Santa Eulalia has been restored and has a cathedral, the Templo de Santa Eulalia de Mérida, that contains impressive religious artwork. Near Aldama are the ruins of the Santa Ana de Chinarras Mission, founded by Jesuits in 1717. These highways run through desert areas with very few facilities; driving at night is not recommended.

**Chihuahua State Tourism Office (Información Turística del Estado):** On the ground floor of the Government Palace building, located on the n. side of Plaza Hidalgo at Calle Aldama and Calle Venustiano Carranza. **Phone:** (614) 429-3596, or 01 (800) 508-0111 (toll-free long distance within Mexico).

**CASA REDONDA MUSEUM** (Museo Casa Redonda) is n.w. of Plaza de Armas via Av. Independencia to Av. Escudero; the museum is at Av. Escudero and Av. Tecnológico/Colón. The name (Round House) is a reference to the building's circular shape and original purpose: It was once a maintenance and repair shop for steam locomotives. In addition to a permanent exhibit documenting the history of railroads in the region, there are rotating displays of contemporary art.

**Time:** Allow 1 hour minimum. **Hours:** Tues.-Sun. 10-7. **Cost:** 15 pesos (about $1.10 U.S.). **Phone:** (614) 414-9061.

**CATHEDRAL** faces Plaza de Armas. This ornate, twin-towered church of pink-hued stone is perhaps northern Mexico's finest example of baroque architecture. Although it was begun in 1725, Indian wars delayed completion until 1826. To the left of the main entrance is the beautiful Christ of Mapimí Chapel, where a cross-shaped niche holds a venerated image of Christ. **Hours:** Daily 7 a.m.-8 p.m. **Cost:** Free. **Phone:** (614) 410-3877 (no English spoken).

**CHIHUAHUA HOUSE MUSEUM** (Museo Casa Chihuahua) is several blks. n.e. of Plaza de Armas via pedestrian-only Calle Libertad, at Av. Juárez and Vicente Guerrero. This neoclassic building dates from 1910 and served as the Palacio Federal, a federal building housing Chihuahua's main post office, until 2004. It was subsequently renovated and reopened in 2006 as a cultural center and museum presenting primarily traveling exhibits.

In the basement is Hidalgo's Dungeon, which preserves the cell in which Father Miguel Hidalgo was held prisoner by the Spanish while awaiting execution. The freedom fighter's crucifix, pistol and other personal belongings are displayed, along with a plaque inscribed with a message Hidalgo dedicated to his captors for their humane treatment.

**Hours:** Wed.-Mon. 10-6. **Cost:** 40 pesos (about $3 U.S.); free to all Sun. **Phone:** (614) 429-3300.

**CHURCH OF SAN FRANCISCO** (Iglesia de San Francisco) is n.e. of Plaza de Armas on Calle Libertad (at Calle 15). Begun by Franciscan missionaries and dedicated to St. Joseph, it was consecrated in 1721. Architecturally similar to Franciscan missions in northern Mexico, the church's exterior is relatively plain. The interior has a roomy cross-shaped nave, beamed roofing, 18th-century altarpieces and a majestic cupola. Bricklayer Nicolás Muñoz built the bell tower in 1740. **Hours:** Open daily. **Cost:** Free.

**GOVERNMENT PALACE** (Palacio de Gobierno) is a block s. of the Chihuahua House Museum, on the n. side of Plaza Hidalgo at Calle Aldama and Calle Venustiano Carranza. The Chihuahua state capitol was built 1881-92; a third floor was added during reconstruction after a 1941 fire destroyed a large part of the building. Inside are enormous archways, a large central patio and first-floor walls covered with noteworthy murals depicting the state's history. A beautiful stained-glass window above the main staircase illustrates themes of law and justice.

It was here that Father Miguel Hidalgo was executed by firing squad in 1811 during the War of Independence. The Nation's Altar (Altar de la Patria) on the ground floor marks the exact spot where he died. The Hidalgo Museum has a re-creation of the church facade in Dolores Hidalgo from which the priest turned freedom fighter issued his call for independence, while the Gallery of Arms displays an impressive array of weapons. Both museums incorporate state-of-the-art interactive media displays.

**Time:** Allow 1 hour minimum. **Hours:** Daily 8-8. **Cost:** Free.

**HISTORICAL MUSEUM OF THE REVOLUTION** (Museo Histórico de la Revolución) is about 1 km (.6 mi.) s. of the historic city center at Calle 10a #3010, 2 blks. n. of Av. Ocampo and 2 blks. e. of Av. 20 de Noviembre. The mansion was the home of Pancho Villa, a revolutionary leader who sympathized with the hardships endured by the Mexican peasant majority. It also is referred to as Quinta Luz in honor of Villa's wife Dona Luz, who lived here until her death in the early 1980s.

The mansion's front portion is arranged around an open courtyard in which stands the bullet-riddled Dodge Villa was riding in when he was ambushed and killed. Two floors of exhibit rooms are dedicated to the Mexican Revolution of 1910 and include displays of military uniforms, period firearms (revolvers and some machine guns), and a collection of photographs of Villa and his cohorts.

Exhibit information is in Spanish and English. **Time:** Allow 1 hour minimum. **Hours:** Tues.-Sat. 9-1 and 3-7, Sun. 10-4. Closed May 1 and Christmas. **Cost:** 10 pesos (about 75c U.S.). **Phone:** (614) 416-2958.

**NOMBRE DE DIOS CAVERNS** (Grutas de Nombre de Dios) are in the northeastern part of the city, about a 20-minute drive from downtown Chihuahua via Calzada H. Colegio Militar, then along dirt roads following the blue-and-white signs. Stalactite and stalagmite formations in these small caves are said to resemble Don Quixote, a dinosaur head and the Leaning Tower of Pisa, among other things. Tours with English-speaking guides are available.

The path through the caverns is fairly dark and has some tight passages and a couple of steep inclines; the tour is not recommended for those prone to claustrophobia. **Time:** Allow 1 hour, 30 minutes minimum. **Hours:** Tues.-Fri. 9-3, Sat.-Sun. and Mexican holidays 10-4. **Cost:** 50 pesos (about $3.70 U.S.); 25 pesos (ages 5-10). **Phone:** (614) 432-0518.

**QUINTA GAMEROS** is at Paseo Simon Bolívar #401, about 8 blks. n.w. of the main plaza. The cultural center for the University of Chihuahua occupies a restored turn-of-the-20th-century mansion—named for Manuel Gameros, the wealthy mining engineer who commissioned its construction—furnished in Art Nouveau style. The main reason to visit is not the university's collection of art on the second floor but the building's stained-glass windows, intricately carved wooden staircases and lavish interior decoration and furniture.

**Hours:** Tues.-Sun. 11-2 and 4-7. **Cost:** 26 pesos (about $1.90 U.S.); 10 pesos (children). **Phone:** (614) 416-6684.

## CIUDAD JUÁREZ, CHIHUAHUA (B-3)
pop. 1,332,131

**Note:** For current information about safety/security issues in Ciudad Juárez, refer to the U.S. State Department website (travel.state.gov).

In 1581 Juan de Oñate crossed the Rio Grande in the vicinity of present-day Juárez (HWAH-res), the first Spanish explorer to do so. It wasn't until 1668, however, that Franciscan friar Father Garcia de San Francisco founded the Mission of Our Lady of Guadalupe (Misión de Nuestra Señora de Guadalupe), which still stands on the west side of Plaza de Armas in downtown Juárez. This sprawling border city is on the Rio Grande opposite El Paso, Tex.

## Border Tips

There are several border crossings between El Paso and downtown Juárez, including the Ysleta-Zaragoza Bridge, the Bridge of the Americas, the Stanton Street Bridge and the Santa Fe Street Bridge (also called the Paseo del Norte Bridge).

The port of entry at Santa Teresa in nearby New Mexico is on the western edge of the El Paso/Juárez metropolitan area; take exit 8 (Artcraft Road) off I-10 and proceed west about 13 miles. Since it bypasses the city, this is the recommended crossing point for tourists and other travelers who are driving to Chihuahua and beyond or otherwise headed for interior Mexico. Banjercito offices at this border crossing and at the 30-kilometer (19-mile) mark on Mex. 45 (the Juárez-Chihuahua Highway) can process the paperwork necessary for vehicle travel into the interior.

Dollars or pesos are accepted when entering or departing Mexico or the United States. Baggage may be inspected at the customs offices. Both Mexican and U.S. Customs and Border Protection offices are open daily 24 hours at Ciudad Juárez. U.S. Customs and Border Protection offices at Santa Teresa are open daily 6 a.m.-midnight. AAA/CAA members can obtain Mexican automobile insurance at AAA Texas offices.

**Destination El Paso:** 400 W. San Antonio Ave., El Paso, TX 79901. **Phone:** (915) 534-0600, or (800) 351-6024 outside of Texas.

## COPPER CANYON, CHIHUAHUA (C-3)

The Copper Canyon (Barranca del Cobre) area of northwestern Mexico was created by more than 60 million years of geological upheaval. Over time the ash deposited by volcanic eruptions built up to form massive plateaus; further volcanic activity created gaping cracks that were subsequently eroded by rain and subterranean water to carve twisting canyons. Within this extensive canyon system are rivers that are rendered all but unnavigable due to boulder fields and lofty waterfalls.

The name "Copper Canyon" is something of a misnomer; although one canyon along a section of the Urique River is named Barranca del Cobre, the Copper Canyon as a whole actually comprises more than 20 canyons covering some 25,000 square miles. There are six main canyon systems: the Urique, Copper, Cusarare and Tararecua canyons; Batopilas Canyon; Candamena Canyon; Huapoca Canyon; the Oteros, Chínipas and Septentrion canyons; and Sinforosa Canyon. Mountain elevations within the entire region range from 7,500 to 9,500 feet, with a few peaks reaching 12,000 feet.

This rugged and forbidding region has long been inhabited by the Rarámuri Indians. Also known as the Tarahumara, these mountain dwellers have managed to preserve their ancient way of life more successfully than other Native American groups. Although sharing a common ancestry with the warrior-like Aztecs, the peaceful Tarahumara could not have been more different. Settling the plains of central Chihuahua, they grew corn, beans and squash, constructing irrigation canals to make the arid land productive. The Tarahumara took advantage of more than 250 varieties of edible and medicinal plants, and also were renowned for their stamina, chasing down game through sheer dogged determination until the animals collapsed from exhaustion.

During the 17th century Spanish settlers enslaved many Tarahumara, forcing them to toil in mines and carry goods across terrain that was too rough for even horses to negotiate. To escape servitude many

COPPER CANYON
AREA ▽
Attractions

0    Kilometers    73
0    Miles    45

Cumbres de
Majalca
Nat'l Park

To Ciudad Juárez

To Delicias

Chihuahua
Airport
(CUU)

16

45

★ CHIHUAHUA

16

16
D

Cuauhtémoc

N

CONTINENTAL

HIGHEST POINT OF
RR ROUTE

Basaseachic
Falls
National Park

Creel    San Ignacio Arareco

Cusárare
Basihuare

DIVIDE

Posada
Barranca

360°
Loop

8671 FT

El Divisadero

23

Copper Canyon Railroad

Barranca del Cobre
National Park

Urique

Bahuichivo    Cerocahui    Batopilas

Témoris

Chínipas

CHIHUAHUA
SONORA

Rio Urique

CHIHUAHUA
SINALOA

LONGEST BRIDGE
1,650 FT

LONGEST
TUNNEL
5,986 FT

23

SONORA
SINALOA

Fuerte

El Fuerte

23

To Guamúchil

15
D

Rio    Fuerte

15    Guasave

To Navojoa

PUNTA
AHOME

Los
Mochis    ✈ Federal del Valle
del Fuerte
Int'l Airport
(LMM)

Topolobampo

PUNTA
SAN IGNACIO

Gulf

of

California

FERRY
(TOLL)

© AAA    • To La Paz    3019-16

of them retreated deep into the remote Copper Canyon sierra country. Their descendants continue to live here today, working small ranches or farms and living in simple huts. Some of the more reclusive Tarahumara still dwell in remote mountain caves in the summer, migrating to the warmer *barrancas* (canyon bottoms) in winter.

It was not until the beginning of the 20th century that this vast and inhospitable region was penetrated by a railroad. Construction of the Chihuahua-Pacific Railway (Chihuahua al Pacífico) began in 1898 but was not completed until 1961. A noteworthy engineering feat, the 941-kilometer (588-mile) rail line begins at Ojinaga, just across the border from Presidio, Tex., and ends at the Pacific coast port of Topolobampo. It boasts 99 tunnels and 39 bridges. Within a distance of less than 125 miles, numerous switchbacks drop from an elevation of more than 7,000 feet in the mountains to near sea level on the coastal plain.

One of the railway's most dramatic stretches is the approach to the station at Témoris, where three different levels of track hug one mountainside. Another breathtaking view unfolds at the small mountain village of Divisadero, at an elevation of about 7,400 feet. Here the Urique, Copper and Tararecua canyons are all visible, a vast overlapping series of rust-colored walls and pine-clad ridges.

In 2010 a Swiss-built aerial tram opened at Divisadero. The tram's 60-passenger gondolas travel between the village and a tram station located in the canyon some 1,150 feet below. The ride takes about 20 minutes, with a stop at the midway point for picture taking. The tram departs daily 9-4:30. The cost is 250 pesos (about $18.50 U.S.); 125 pesos (ages 0-10). At the lower tram station is Barrancas del Cobre Adventure Park *(see attraction listing under Creel)*.

One fascinating aspect of the Copper Canyon is the dramatic difference between environments. On canyon rims and atop high plateaus—where the altitude exceeds 8,000 feet—winters are cold and summers mild, with abundant rain. Fragrant forests of pine and Douglas fir cloak these highlands, the mesa tops are bright with wildflowers from the end of September into October, and alders and poplars add fall foliage color.

In contrast, canyon bottoms, often a mile below the rim, are subtropical. Palms and towering fig and ceiba trees—the ceiba is known for its buttressed roots and huge, spreading canopy of leaves—grow where water is available. Wildlife ranges from badgers, otters, skunks and the seldom-seen ocelot to such endangered bird species as the military macaw and the thick-billed parrot.

The town of Creel is a major stop on the rail line and functions as a base for excursions to other towns and villages. Hotels in Creel can arrange guided day or overnight trips to towns on the canyon floor. Lodgings can lack electricity and telephones; the key word is rustic.

The mode of transportation is often a school bus, and the ride can be dusty and bone-jarring. Sturdy walking shoes are absolutely essential for exploring; even guided hikes may involve anything from fording a brook to clambering over fallen logs. If you hire a guide make certain that he is familiar with your destination; much of this region remains authentic wilderness.

From the train station at Bahuichivo, a trip can be arranged to the mountain village of Cerocahui, where a Jesuit mission was established in the late 17th century. Local hotels can arrange round-trip excursions from Bahuichivo to the canyon-bottom village of Urique. Cusárare, about 19 kilometers (12 miles) from Creel, also has a Jesuit mission that was built in order to minister to the Tarahumara. Lake Arareco (see Creel) is located in an area of volcanic rock formations that resemble mushrooms.

A trip to the town of Batopilas, about 129 kilometers (80 miles) southwest of Creel, is an 8-hour adventure if taken by local bus. The narrow, dusty dirt road to the canyon bottom passes Cerro El Pastel (Cake Mountain), named for its alternating layers of pink and white volcanic rock. The Urique and Basíhuare rivers trace tight, meandering paths before their headwaters lose themselves in unnamed chasms. As the route descends temperatures rise, and forest of pine are replaced by stands of cactus.

Batopilas itself is a former silver-mining town. It began to boom in the 1740s, although mining operations had been in existence for more than 100 years before that. According to local legend, the town's cobblestone streets were once paved with silver. Distinctly different from the canyon-top villages, Batopilas has whitewashed houses, palm trees and gardens of subtropical flowers—temperatures here are some 30 degrees warmer than at the top of the canyon. Local ranchers ride into town on horseback, and an occasional goat or pig wanders the streets. Accommodations for overnight stays are modest.

## Practicalities

Allow plenty of time to take this rail journey. First-class trains depart from both Chihuahua and Los Mochis in the early morning (around 6 a.m.) and take anywhere from 14 to 17 hours (depending on whether there are weather-related delays) to cover the 654-kilometer (406-mile) distance between the two cities. Because of the length of the journey it's necessary to spend at least one night en route to better experience what the region has to offer. Creel has the most lodging options, but hotels in the vicinity of the train stations also can be quite expensive. More rustic cabin accommodations are a short taxi ride from the stations, but amenities are likely to be quite basic.

During the winter months, leaving from Los Mochis or El Fuerte guarantees seeing the most spectacular scenery in full daylight; coming from Chihuahua, towering canyon walls can block the last rays of the sun and magnify the gathering gloom of evening. Summer's extended daylight hours, however, make this decision less crucial. Also keep in mind that you will not really experience the true magnificence of the Copper Canyon from either a train car or a station platform; take a bus or horseback tour to one of the various canyon rim viewing points in order to fully appreciate the views.

Temperatures can be quite cold December through February at the higher elevations, and the canyon bottoms are uncomfortably hot in May and June. The best times of the year to take this trip are March and April or late September through October, when both the sierra wildflowers and fall foliage are at their colorful peak. There may be fewer travelers from August into September, and the landscape will be green from summer rains. Avoid May and June, the driest time of the year; browned-out vegetation and hazy skies are not the best showcase for the Copper Canyon's natural beauty.

The easiest way to arrange a tour of the Copper Canyon is through a travel agency or rail tour company that offers an all-inclusive trip package. These packages normally include applicable ground transportation (but not airfare to and from the point of departure), lodgings, meals and sightseeing excursions. Mexico-based Camp David provides organized train tours on the Chihuahua-Pacific rail line that depart from Los Mochis and also feature sightseeing in Cerocahui, Creel and at the Gulf of California coast; phone (866) 247-3464 (from the United States or Canada).

Fully escorted, all-inclusive tours also are offered by Los Angeles-based California Native International Adventures. Their standard Copper Canyon itinerary departs from Los Mochis and includes stays at Divisadero and Creel plus sightseeing trips to a Tarahumara cave dwelling and the village of Cusárare. Tours wrap in Chihuahua. For further information phone (310) 642-1140 or (800) 926-1140 (from the United States).

**Note:** Tour companies outside of Mexico do not sell individual train tickets, only tickets that are part of a tour package that includes lodgings and transportation. They cannot provide information regarding point-to-point travel along the Chihuahua-Pacific Railway route.

**PIEDRAS VALLEY TOUR** (Valle de Piedras) departs from Best Western The Lodge at Creel, Calle López Mateos #61. This is one of several Copper Canyon guided tours offered by the hotel. You'll get an up-close look at the striking volcanic rock formations that comprise the Valle de Hongos (Mushroom Valley), the Valle de Ranas (Valley of Frogs) and the Valle de Monjes (Valley of the Monks). Other stops include the San Ignacio Mission (Misión de San Ignacio), built by the Jesuits in 1746, and a cave dwelling that is home to Tarahumara Indians.

**Time:** Allow 2 hours minimum. **Hours:** Tour departs daily at 9. **Cost:** Tour fee 165 pesos (about $12.20 U.S.) per person; tours require a four-person minimum. **Phone:** (635) 456-0071 (English not likely to be spoken).

**URIQUE CANYON LOOKOUT TOUR** departs from the Hotel Misión in the village of Cerocahui, which is accessible only by train. If you've just seen the Copper Canyon from a train window, this guided bus tour—offered to hotel guests only—is well worth it for breathtaking views of the region's deepest canyon from the Urique Canyon Lookout. The tour includes a visit to a cave home and shop where you can visit with local Tarahumara basket weavers. The journey by bus from the hotel to the lookout point—along a narrow, rutted dirt road that winds through pine forests—takes about 2 hours each way and is not for the faint-hearted, as there are numerous steep drop-offs.

**Hours:** Tour departs daily at 8 a.m. **Cost:** 345 pesos (about $25.50 U.S.) per person. **Phone:** (635) 456-5294, or (800) 896-8196 from the United States for Balderrama Hotels & Tours (English not likely to be spoken).

## CREEL, CHIHUAHUA (C-3)

**Note:** For current information about safety/security issues in Creel, refer to the U.S. State Department website (travel.state.gov).

The logging village of Creel (creh-EHL) was once the western terminus of the Chihuahua al Pacífico Railway; it is now the approximate midway point. Although the quantity of pine shipped from the vicinity has diminished over the decades, active lumber camps still operate. The concrete statue of Christ gazing down from the cliffs north of town bears testimony to the Jesuit priests who first came to this area in the early 17th century.

Creel retains a raw charm; men ride down López Mateos, the main street, on horseback, and Tarahumara women in native dress sell pottery and baskets from the curbside. Shops also sell Tarahumara arts and crafts like rugs, wood carvings, necklaces, dolls and violins. Indians benefit from all sales at the Tarahumara Mission Store.

Creel functions as a base for trips to other parts of the region; dirt-gravel roads lead to Tarahumara

---

## DID YOU KNOW

There are four mountain peaks within Mexico greater than 15,000 feet in elevation. The tallest, the 18,850-foot extinct volcano Citlaltépetl, is the third-highest point in North America.

---

villages at the edges of scenic canyons. **Note:** If you plan to drive to this area in your own vehicle, fill the gas tank in Chihuahua or the town of La Junta, on Mex. 16. Drive time from Chihuahua to Creel is about 3.5 hours; a sturdy vehicle is recommended.

Basaseáchic Falls National Park is about 5 hours away via a paved road running from Creel north to the Mex. 16 junction, then west on Mex. 16 to the park. The falls plunge some 800 feet into an open cylinder formed by huge rock columns. The spray nourishes pine trees growing at the base of the falls, and a marked footpath allows hikers access to the bottom of the canyon. At the top there are basic camping facilities.

**BARRANCAS DEL COBRE ADVENTURE PARK** (Parque de Aventuras Barrancas del Cobre) is in Divisadero, 2 km (1.2 mi.) s. of the Barrancas train station. A Swiss-built aerial tram (teleférico) in Divisadero consists of 60-passenger gondolas that travel between the village and the canyon some 1,150 feet below. The tram trip takes about 20 minutes. The park is at the lower tram station. For thrill seekers and adventure junkies the unquestionable highlight is the seven zip lines (tirolesas), one of them almost a mile in length. It's an amazing way to see the Copper Canyon by literally flying through it.

There are many other activities available, including rock climbing, rappelling, mini-golf, bungee jumping for kids and an events amphitheater. The fact that the park is built on the edge of the canyon means that all of these activities also come with incredible views. **Time:** Allow 2 hours minimum. **Hours:** Trams depart daily 9-4:30. Zip lines operate daily 9-1. **Cost:** Park entrance fee 20 pesos (about $1.50 U.S.); free (ages 0-10). Tram ride 250 pesos (about $18.50 U.S.); 125 pesos (ages 0-10). There are separate fees for the zip lines and for other activities. **Phone:** (635) 589-6805. 🍴 ✂

**LAKE ARARECO** is 7 km (4 mi.) s. on a paved road. This horseshoe-shaped, man-made lake is surrounded by diversified forest and oddly-shaped rock formations. Lodging, horseback riding, boat rental and food service facilities are available. Fishing and camping are permitted.

## DURANGO, DURANGO (D-3) pop. 582,267

**Note:** For current information about safety/security issues in Durango, refer to the U.S. State Department website (travel.state.gov).

Not many travelers make it to Durango (doo-RAHN-goh), situated in the high desert country of north-central Mexico. Comparative isolation is one of the main reasons: Mazatlán, the nearest city of any size, is nearly 200 miles away, and the Sierra Madre Occidental mountains form an inhospitable barrier to the west. So despite being an important commercial crossroads due to the fact that it sits at the junction of two major highways (Mex. 40 and Mex. 45), Durango's location makes it a bit of a diamond in the rough for visitors.

Local legend maintains that it was in a cave in one of the buttes punctuating the countryside north of Durango that revolutionary Pancho Villa traded his soul to the Devil in return for mastery over other men. Villa was born Doroteo Arango in 1877 on a hacienda near the village of San Juan del Río, 110 kilometers (68 miles) north of Durango on Mex. 45. He grew up an uneducated peasant, working as a sharecropper. After killing a man who had seduced and then abandoned his younger sister, Villa began a life on the run from the law.

After becoming involved in the fight to overthrow the iron rule of dictator Porfirio Díaz Villa went on to become one of the Mexican Revolution's foremost figures, envisioning himself as a Mexican Robin Hood who took from the rich hacienda owners and gave back to poor farmers and sharecroppers. Commanding a fiercely loyal band of supporters collectively known as the Division of the North (División del Norte), Villa was an able military leader as well as a flamboyant personality who today is one of Mexico's most admired folk heroes.

## City Layout

Durango—officially Victoria de Durango—sits in a valley strewn with craggy buttes that have an unusual orange color. It's a beautiful natural setting that initially seems compromised by modern industry; like other Mexican cities founded during the colonial era, the outskirts of town look grimy and industrial. To experience the best of what the city has to offer head straight for the historic downtown core, where the 17th- and 18th-century colonial architecture has for the most part been handsomely preserved.

Plaza de Armas, the main plaza, is between avenidas 20 de Noviembre and 5 de Febrero and calles Constitución and Juárez. It has pretty gardens and a circular bandstand, and is the scene of Sunday band concerts. The major visitor points of interest are all within several blocks of the plaza, making Durango easy to explore on foot.

A block southwest of Plaza de Armas, facing the north side of Plaza Centenario, is the Government Palace (Palacio de Gobierno), an 18th-century baroque building distinguished by its arcades. Inside are murals illustrating Durango state history.

A block north of the Government Palace on Avenida 20 de Noviembre, between calles Zaragoza and Bruno Martinez, is the Ricardo Castro Theater (Teatro Ricardo Castro), originally called the Teatro Principal but renamed for a Durangueño pianist and composer when it was renovated in 1990. Used for performances by visiting music, theater and dance troupes, it has beautiful marble and tile flooring.

Shoppers can browse through the Municipal Market (Mercado Gómez Palacio), 3 blocks east of Plaza de Armas (entrances on Calle Pasteur and Calle Patoni). In addition to the standard displays of produce and foodstuffs the market has stalls selling *charro* (Mexican-style rodeo) clothing, leather goods, wool *sarapes*, locally made handicrafts and souvenirs with scorpion motifs; the stinging arachnids are a common sight in this desert country.

The surrounding countryside has long been used by filmmakers for location shooting, particularly Hollywood westerns *(see Movie Sets attraction listing)*. Golden age icons Lillian Gish, John Wayne and Clark Gable as well as more recent stars like Jack Nicholson, John Belushi and John Travolta have all starred in movies filmed on location.

A downtown restaurant popular with Durangueños is Los Farolitos, on Calle Bruno Martinez near the intersection with Avenida 20 de Noviembre. Huge, freshly made flour tortillas are wrapped around a variety of tasty fillings, from *carne asada* (grilled steak) to cheese spiked with bits of green chiles *(queso con rajas)*. A branch of the Mexican chain Sanborn's on Avenida 20 de Noviembre offers a reliably standard menu and good coffee.

The central bus station is east of downtown near the junction of avenidas Felipe Pescador and Colegio Militar (Mex. 40). Transportes del Norte offers first-class bus service from Chihuahua, Mazatlán, Mexico City, Zacatecas and other Mexican cities. The *Ruta 2* line runs west from the station along Avenida 20 de Noviembre (downtown's main east-west thoroughfare) to Plaza de Armas. It makes stops within easy walking distance of downtown points of interest. The fare is inexpensive (about 50c U.S.).

**Durango State Tourism Office (Dirección General de Turismo y Cinematografía):** downtown at Calle Florida #1106, on the second floor of the Barrio del Calvario. Open Mon.-Fri. 9-8, Sat.-Sun. 10-6. **Phone:** (618) 811-1107.

**CATHEDRAL** (Catedral Basílica Menor) is on Av. 20 de Noviembre facing the n. side of Plaza de Armas. Construction was begun in 1695 and completed in 1750. The massive structure is surmounted by two square towers. The exterior is a mixture of styles, with baroque predominating. The entrance is richly decorated. Inside are choir stalls adorned with finely carved wooden figures of saints and apostles. Bell ringers in the towers are visible from the plaza.

The ghost of an 18th-century nun *(monja)* is said to inhabit the church. According to local legend she fell in love with a French soldier who had deserted the Napoleonic army. He was killed by his countrymen before returning to France and seeking a pardon for deserting; unaware of his fate, the nun climbed one of the cathedral's towers each night to await his return, finally dying of a broken heart. Her silhouette is supposedly visible on nights when there is a full moon. **Hours:** Open daily. **Cost:** Free.

**GANOT-PESCHARD MUSEUM OF ARCHEOLOGY** (Museo de Arqueología Ganot-Peschard) is 2 blks. w. of Plaza de Armas at Calle Zaragoza #315 Sur, between avs. 20 de Noviembre and 5 de Febrero. It chronicles the indigenous cultures of this part of Mexico from prehistoric times through the Spanish conquest. Highlights are an underground recreation of tombs and their contents and an exhibit detailing the methodology of archeological research. Background information is in Spanish. **Time:** Allow 1 hour minimum. **Hours:** Tues.-Fri. 10-6, Sat.-Sun. 11-6. **Cost:** 10 pesos (about 75c U.S.). **Phone:** (618) 813-1047.

**HOUSE OF THE COUNT OF SUCHIL** (Casa del Conde del Valle de Súchil) is 2 blks. e. of Plaza de Armas at Av. 5 de Febrero and Calle Francisco I. Madero. This is a fine example of mid-18th-century Spanish colonial architecture. Built for a wealthy landowner, the restored mansion's former grandeur is evident in such exterior features as the roof-line sculptures and elaborate molding around the main doorway. The building houses a Banamex bank branch, but visitors are welcome to wander around the interior courtyard. **Hours:** Mon.-Fri. 9-3.

**MERCADO HILL** (El Cerro de Mercado) is just n. of the city. A mound of high-content iron ore said to be one of the largest single iron deposits in existence, it rises some 700 feet above the surrounding plain and is still producing. The hill was named for the man who discovered it in 1552, Ginés Vázquez del Mercado.

**MOVIE SETS** (Escenarios) in the city vicinity are permanent fixtures. Durango's heyday as a movie-making center began in the 1950s and continued through the '70s, as actors like John Wayne, Burt Lancaster and Robert Ryan came here to film Hollywood westerns. Among the classics shot in the vicinity were Raoul Walsh's "The Tall Men" and Sam Peckinpah's "The Wild Bunch" and "Pat Garrett and Billy the Kid." For information contact the Durango State Tourism Office.

**Note:** These locations are remote and difficult to reach via dirt roads; they should only be visited on a guided excursion arranged through the Durango State Tourism Office. **Phone:** (618) 811-1107.

**Chupaderos** is about 14 km (9 mi.) n. of Durango off Mex. 45. An actual Mexican village, it has been used for filming more than any other area location. The town's original structures have been augmented over the years by Old West-style buildings fabricated for the movies, which ironically are occupied by local families. Among the Westerns filmed here was the 1970 oater "Chisum," starring John Wayne.

A few kilometers to the south on Mex. 45 is Villa del Oeste, a village that first came into being as a constructed "Western" town. It's now a tourist attraction offering shops, restaurants and re-enactments of Old West-style shootouts and barroom brawls on weekends.

## Nearby Destinations

Opened in the 1940s, the 312-kilometer (195-mile) journey from Durango west to Mazatlán via two-lane Mex. 40 passes through some of Mexico's most spectacular scenery, courtesy of the Sierra Madre Occidental mountain range. Locals—quite appropriately—call it the Road of 3,000 Curves (Camino de Tres Mil Curvas).

From Durango, the road ascends through stands of pine to the logging town of El Salto, about 100 kilometers (62 miles) west. The surrounding region is noted for waterfalls, thick forests and interesting geological formations at elevations of up to 8,500 feet. Continuing west, La Ciudad is another mountain town with a couple of bare-bones diners (comedores) with wood-burning stoves and cement floors.

The most unnerving part of the route begins a short distance west of La Ciudad. The Devil's Backbone (El Espinazo del Diablo) is a narrow mountain ridge with precipitous drop-offs falling away from both sides of the road. The Pacific Ocean, more than 90 kilometers (55 miles) to the southwest, can be seen on clear days from this height.

Countless switchbacks, twisting hairpin turns and little to no shoulders—not to mention numerous encounters with trucks, buses, burros, cows and bicycles—made driving the Devil's Backbone an extreme adventure. Sections were frequently closed due to accidents or mudslides, and thick clouds can reduce visibility to near zero.

A triumph of man's ingenuity over a challenging environment, it was a spectacular trek for motorists with nerves of steel and plenty of experience negotiating mountain roads. It was also not without danger, as drug cartels have firm control in this remote region, setting up their own roadblocks and engaging in highway robbery while many locals eke out a living cultivating marijuana and opium.

Fortunately, the road trip between the two cities became safer—and somewhat easier—in late 2013, when Mex. 40-D, the Durango-Mazatlán toll road, finally opened to motorists. The new toll sections branch off of and intersect with portions of the free road; they are clearly marked, much less serpentine and are equipped with ample shoulders. The route includes an astounding number of bridges, eight of them with a clearance of over 900 feet, and 63 tunnels that total nearly 11 miles; the longest is the 1.7-mile Sinaloense Tunnel.

The spectacular highlight of this massive engineering project is the four-lane Baluarte Bridge (Puente Baluarte). Straddling the Durango/Sinaloa state border, it is the world's second-tallest highway bridge, spanning the Baluarte River at a dizzying height of 1,322 feet. When crossing this bridge, keep in mind that there is no separate viewing area (and the views are jaw-dropping). As a result some motorists will stop in the right lane to get out and take photographs.

There are four toll plazas, and the total fee from Mazatlán to Durango is 506 pesos (about $37.50 U.S.). But while toll charges are hefty, the drive time is also reduced considerably, from almost 8 hours on the old road exclusively to approximately 3 hours taking advantage of the new highway sections. For the time being gas stations and other road services are few and far between, so make sure your tank is full before setting out on this journey from either Durango or Mazatlán.

## GUAYMAS, SONORA (C-1) pop. 149,299

Guaymas (GWAY-mahs) is one of Mexico's principal seaports. The old city sits along the shore of a fine natural harbor crowded with freighters, tankers and shrimp boats. A mountainous peninsula divides this part of Guaymas from the newer resort area, which spreads out to the northwest along Bacochibampo and San Carlos bays. The mountain backdrop, brilliant blue sky and equally blue gulf waters are best appreciated on a stroll along the waterfront section of Avenida Aquiles Serdán, the main east-west thoroughfare.

Two blocks north of Serdán, on the east side of Plaza de Armas (between calles 24 and 25) stands the 19th-century Church of San Fernando (Iglesia de San Fernando). In front of the church is Plaza de Armas 13 de Julio (the date refers to a battle fought against the French in 1854). This small park has a white wrought-iron bandstand and benches beneath trees that provide welcome shade.

Nearby, at Avenida Serdán and Calle 23, is the Plaza of the Three Presidents (Plaza de Los Tres Presidentes). In front of City Hall (Palacio Municipal), on the plaza's west side, are statues honoring Plutarco Elías Calles, Adolfo de la Huerta and Abelardo Rodríguez, all former Mexican presidents born in Sonora.

Native heritage is evident in the celebrations and ritual dances of the Yaqui Indians, who still inhabit the villages in the Yaqui River valley southeast of Guaymas. One of Mexico's most fiercely independent ethnic peoples, the Yaqui staged frequent rebellions against ruling governments during the 18th and 19th centuries.

Yaqui culture is on display during the Deer Dance (*Danza del Venado*), performed both locally and at folkloric festivals throughout the country. The featured participant wears a deer's head to enact the dance's symbolic representation of the battle between good and evil.

The offshore waters are well known to deep-sea fishing enthusiasts for prized catches like marlin, sailfish, yellowtail, corbina, sea bass and red snapper. The local shrimp are celebrated for both their

size and flavor. Fishing excursions and sunset cruises can be arranged in nearby San Carlos (see separate listing within this region).

## Practicalities

Regional carrier Aéreo Calafia offers flights from Mexican cities, including La Paz. For additional information about airlines see Arriving by Air, page p. 42. Taxis provide service to and from the airport, which is located west of town. First-class bus service to border cities and other Mexican destinations is provided by several bus companies, including Elite, TAP, Transportes del Pacífico and Tufesa. Schedule and fare information can be obtained at one of the city's three downtown bus stations, all located in the vicinity of Calle 14 and Avenida 12. In addition, local buses to Playa Miramar and San Carlos make stops at various points along Avenida Serdán.

The Santa Rosalía ferry provides automobile-passenger service linking Guaymas and Santa Rosalía (see separate listing under Baja California) on the Baja California Peninsula. The ferry terminal is just east of downtown on Avenida Serdán. There are normally three departures a week; sailing time is 8 hours. Schedules and rates are subject to change and should be double-checked in advance. Phone (622) 222-0204, or 01 (800) 505-5018 (toll-free long distance within Mexico) for reservations information. For additional information about ferries see Ferry Service, page p. 53.

**Tourist information office:** downtown at Av. Aquiles Serdán #349. For information about the San Carlos area, contact the Sonora State Tourism branch office in San Carlos, located at Hacienda Plaza #264 Int. 6, Sector Crestón. **Phone:** (622) 226-0202.

## HERMOSILLO, SONORA (B-2)
pop. 784,342

Capital of the state of Sonora, Hermosillo (ehr-moh-SEE-yo) rises abruptly from the sparsely settled terrain of northwestern Mexico. Big and spread out, the city is not conducive to sightseeing but is a convenient stop for motorists on the way south to Mazatlán and other Pacific coast resorts. Aeroméxico flies non-stop from Los Angeles. US Airways offers non-stop service from Phoenix. Aeroméxico Connect, Aéreo Calafia and Volaris fly from several Mexican cities, including Cancún and Mazatlán. First-class bus service from Nogales is provided by the Elite, Norte de Sonora, TAP and Tufesa lines.

Aside from the colonial-era architecture of the 18th-century Cathedral of the Assumption (Catedral de la Asunción), the Government Palace (Palacio Gobierno) and the pink-hued City Hall (Palacio Municipal), most of Hermosillo looks blandly modern. Plaza Zaragoza, the central plaza, provides welcome shade trees and an oasis from the crowded and frequently dusty downtown streets. Also check out the colorful murals depicting Sonoran history in the Government Palace courtyard.

Mex. 15/15-D, also called the Pacific Coast Highway, extends from the U.S. border at Nogales south

and then east to Mexico City. It is mostly a divided four-lane highway except when passing through some small towns and villages. Watch for occasional potholes and rocks, especially in the vicinity of hills or low mountains. Highway repair work is frequent, and traffic may be diverted to the two-lane stretch that is open.

It costs 761 pesos (about $56 U.S.) in tolls to drive an automobile on Mex. 15-D from Nogales south to Mazatlán. Dollars are usually accepted at toll booths near the U.S. border, but it's best to have pesos on hand for the entire route. **Note:** Toll charges can go up without warning, and rates for different types of vehicles aren't always posted. Avoid the toll road SIN-1 (Sinaloa Express Highway 1) between Guamúchil and Culiacán, which is targeted by robbers.

Saltwater fishing is the main attraction at the Gulf of California resort town of Kino Bay (Bahía Kino), some 105 kilometers (65 miles) southwest of Hermosillo via Mex. 16. Named for Jesuit missionary Francisco Eusebio Kino, this was long a hideaway known only to a few intrepid RV owners. There are condominiums and secluded vacation homes here, although the mountain-backed beaches of tan-colored sand are mostly undeveloped.

Tourist facilities are concentrated in Kino Nuevo (New Kino), separated by some 4 kilometers (2.5 miles) of open beach from Kino Viejo, the Mexican village. The beaches are practically deserted during the summer months, but they also are uncomfortably hot.

**Sonora State Tourism Office (Subsecretaría de Fomento al Turismo):** on the third floor of the State Government Building, North Wing, located on Calle Comonfort between Blvd. Francisco Serna and Paseo Río Sonora Norte (about 7 blocks south of Plaza Zaragoza and 3 blocks west of Mex. 15). **Phone:** (662) 289-5800.

To receive visitor information from the Sonora Department of Tourism, phone (800) 476-6672 (from the United States) or 01 (800) 716-2555 (toll-free long distance within Mexico).

**REGIONAL MUSEUM OF THE UNIVERSITY OF SONORA** (Museo Regional de la Universidad de Sonora) is on the University of Sonora campus off Blvd. Luis Encinas Johnson. It has exhibits relating to the Yaqui, Mayo, Pima, Pápago and Seri Indian groups. Also on view are photographs of Mexican Revolution activities in Sonora, exhibits pertaining to the local history of the area and the university, and numismatic collections. **Hours:** Mon.-Sat. 9-2. **Cost:** Free. **Phone:** (662) 212-0609.

**SONORA ECOLOGICAL CENTER** (Centro Ecológico de Sonora) is about 3 km (2 mi.) s. of downtown off Mex. 15. This zoological park exhibits flora and fauna native to northwestern Mexico's varied ecosystems, from arid desert to the rich marine environment of the Gulf of California. Snakes, tortoises, sea lions and the Mexican gray wolf can all be seen. Notable are the more than 300 species of cacti, many of them labeled. The zoo covers a large area and thus is more pleasant to walk during the cooler winter months. Bottled water is available. **Hours:** Daily 8-5. **Cost:** 50 pesos (about $3.70 U.S.); 35 pesos (ages 4-12 with U.S. or Mexican school ID). **Phone:** (662) 250-1225. GT

## LOS MOCHIS, SINALOA (D-2)

Los Mochis (los MO-chees) was founded in 1893 by Benjamin Johnston, who arrived from Pennsylvania to grow sugar cane. Johnston also founded the Ingenio Azucarero, an enormous sugar refinery around which the city developed. Los Mochis is the major coastal terminus of the Chihuahua al Pacífico Railway, which travels across the rugged Sierra Madre Occidental to Chihuahua via the Barranca del Cobre (Copper Canyon) region.

Technically the end of the rail line is 24 kilometers (15 miles) south at Topolobampo. This deep sea port, known for its shrimp and fishing fleets, is connected by ferry to La Paz, B.C.S. Los Mochis is an agricultural boomtown and the export center of the state of Sinaloa. A dam on the Río Fuerte, part of a tri-river federal irrigation program in northern Sinaloa and southern Sonora, has increased the productivity of this semiarid region.

Aeroméxico flies to Los Mochis (via Mexico City) from the United States. Baja Ferries service links Topolobampo with La Paz; the trip takes about 6 hours. Schedules and rates are subject to change and should be double-checked in advance with the Topolobampo ferry office; phone (668) 862-1003 or 01 (800) 337-7437 (toll-free long distance within Mexico).

**Tourist information office:** in the back of the State Government (Gobierno del Estado) building on Calle Allende. **Phone:** (668) 815-6507.

## NOGALES, SONORA (B-2) pop. 220,292

**Note:** For current information about safety/security issues in Nogales, refer to the U.S. State Department website (travel.state.gov).

The border city of Nogales (noh-GAH-lehs) is sometimes referred to as Ambos Nogales ("both Nogales") in recognition of the sister city of Nogales, Ariz. on the other side of the international boundary fence. Established in 1882, the city is not only significantly larger than its U.S. counterpart but also retains a strong sense of Mexican identity.

The gateway into northwestern mainland Mexico and points south is primarily a day visit for tourists. A tourist permit is not needed for in-town stays of less than 72 hours, but proof of citizenship is required.

Mexican and U.S. Customs and Border Protection offices are open 24 hours daily. For southbound motorists, the official immigration checkpoint is 21 kilometers (13 miles) south of Nogales on Mex. 15.

You can obtain a tourist permit here if you don't already have one, and must present a federal temporary vehicle importation permit or an "Only Sonora" temporary vehicle importation permit (if you intend to stay within the state of Sonora) and accompanying windshield sticker.

A vehicle permit is not required for travel to the following destinations in the state of Sonora: Rocky Point (Puerto Peñasco), Guaymas, San Carlos, Bahía Kino and other locations west of Mex. 15, as well as cities along Mex. 15 (Magdalena, Santa Ana, Hermosillo). An "Only Sonora" permit is required if driving within Sonora east of Mex. 15 as well as south of Empalme (about 350 miles south of the U.S. border). The permit can be obtained at Banjercito offices in Agua Prieta (opposite Douglas, Ariz.), Cananea (southwest of Agua Prieta on Mex. 2) and Empalme (on Mex. 15 at Km marker 98, just south of the Guaymas bypass).

From Tucson, I-19 south ends at Nogales, Ariz.; signs point the way to the border crossing. Mex. 15 begins at the border, but the downtown Nogales crossing passes through the most congested part of the city. Motorists intending to bypass Nogales for points south can save time by using the international truck crossing, known as the Mariposa crossing; take exit 4 off I-19, then proceed west on SR 189 (Mariposa Road), following signs that say "Border Truck Route" and "International Border." This route reconnects with Mex. 15 south of Nogales at the 21-kilometer (13-mile) immigration checkpoint. The charge at the toll booth approximately 6 miles south of the border is about $2 (U.S.).

If you're driving through downtown Nogales back to the United States, watch for the sign that says "Linea International"; follow the directions for the road that leads to the border crossing.

Since almost all of the tourist-oriented shopping is within easy walking distance of the border, it is recommended that day visitors park on the Arizona side and head into Mexico on foot. From the Nogales-Santa Cruz County Chamber of Commerce and Visitor Center, 123 W. Kino Park Way (just off the intersection of Grand Avenue and US 82) in Nogales, Ariz., it's about a 1.5-mile drive south to a series of guarded lots; all-day parking fees average about $8, and cash is expected. The turnstiles to Mexico are at the foot of the Port of Entry.

Shops and vendor stalls catering to tourists are concentrated along north-south Avenida Obregón. They sell pottery, baskets, fabrics, ceramics, leather goods, glassware, carved pine furniture, rugs, jewelry and more. Most business is conducted in English, bargaining is acceptable and even expected, and American currency is preferred. More exclusive establishments have fixed prices and carry crafts and gift items from all over Mexico. When buying at stalls or from street vendors, always check for quality.

Along with shopping, Nogales offers such standard tourist experiences as having your picture taken astride a donkey and listening to mariachi bands.

And like other Mexican border cities, it's a place to get prescriptions filled at a cost that is often far less than stateside.

La Roca Restaurant is just across the border on a side street off Avenida Ruiz Cortines (look for the large magnolia trees in front of the restaurant). Built into the base of a cliff, it has an elegant atmosphere, expert service by white-jacketed waiters and a menu emphasizing Sonoran specialties.

## NUEVO CASAS GRANDES, CHIHUAHUA (B-3) pop. 59,337

**Note:** For current information about safety/security issues in Nuevo Casas Grandes, refer to the U.S. State Department website (travel.state.gov).

A harsh climate, an equally harsh landscape and a remote setting long impeded large-scale settlement of northern Mexico, and this vast region has few ancient ruins or cultural reminders of past greatness. One notable exception is the Paquimé Archeological Site near Nuevo Casas Grandes (see attraction listing). Designated a World Heritage Site by UNESCO in 1999, this former city was once an important trade and cultural link between the Pueblo culture of the southwestern United States and the more advanced civilizations of Mesoamerica. Paquimé was mysteriously abandoned about a century before the arrival of the Spanish, and excavation and reconstruction of the extensive ruins left behind is ongoing.

The most convenient way to get to Paquimé from the United States is to use the Columbus, New Mexico/Palomas, Chihuahua border crossing. The paperwork to obtain tourist and temporary vehicle importation permits can be processed at the Mexico port of entry, which is open daily 8 a.m.-midnight (the U.S. border station is open daily 24 hours).

Palomas, which means "city of the doves," is a typically dusty Mexican border town with one paved street (the main drag) and a rustic plaza where vendors sell cold drinks, cactus candy and cheap sunglasses. A must stop is The Pink Store (La Tienda Rosa); you can't miss the bubblegum-colored exterior. The restaurant here has quite a reputation for authentic and tasty regional cuisine (the cheese comes from a nearby Mennonite community). And in addition to souvenirs like sombreros and paper flowers, the store itself carries an outstanding selection of folk art, jewelry, clothing, furniture, leather goods and handicrafts handpicked by the owners from all over Mexico.

Across the street from The Pink Store is a bronze statue of Doroteo Arango Arámbula, better known as Francisco "Pancho" Villa. As commander of the División del Norte (Division of the North) during the Mexican Revolution, Villa led an attack on neighboring Columbus, New Mexico, in 1916, seizing horses and mules and burning part of the town. The revolutionary is depicted on horseback at full gallop. It's said that the statue faces east because

Americans objected to it facing north and Mexicans did not want it facing south.

From Palomas, proceed south about 32 kilometers (20 miles) to the junction with Mex. 2, then take Mex. 2 west about 90 kilometers (56 miles) to the town of Janos. At Janos, follow Mex. 10 south about 61 kilometers (38 miles) to Nuevo Casas Grandes. Driving at night on these paved but narrow two-lane roads is not recommended.

From El Paso, use the Santa Teresa, New Mexico border crossing, about 13 miles west of I-10 exit 8 (Artcraft Road). Crossing here allows you to bypass Ciudad Juárez and avoid having to navigate that city. At Santa Teresa (where you also can complete the necessary paperwork for tourist and temporary vehicle importation permits) you can either take Mex. 2 west toward Nuevo Casas Grandes, or stay in New Mexico and take SR 9, which parallels the border, west about 60 miles to Columbus/Palomas.

Combine an exploration of the Paquimé ruins with a visit to Mata Ortiz, about 20 kilometers (12 miles) southwest of Nuevo Casas Grandes and 17 kilometers (11 miles) southwest of the much smaller town of Casas Grandes, locally called el pueblo viejo ("the old village") or just el pueblo. More than 400 potters of various ages live in Mata Ortiz, and they all create the distinctive style of pottery that is known by the same name.

The pottery-making tradition here is young—going back only to the 1970s, when a local man, Juan Quezada, began to re-create the pottery-making techniques once practiced by the people of Paquimé after he found some ancient pots near his village. In the process Quezada became a self-taught potter and artist, passing on what he learned to family members and other families throughout the village.

Many of these artisans fashion their beautifully designed creations using age-old methods. Pots are shaped without the use of a wheel; intricate designs are painted by hand with brushes made of human or horse hair; firing is done on the ground utilizing cow manure. Native clay and the minerals used in making paints come from the surrounding mountains.

A couple of galleries in town sell the work of village artists, and if you're a first-time visitor this is the easiest way to discover the world of Mata Ortiz pottery. Besides pottery, the Jorge Quintana Gallery sells woven goods from Oaxaca and Mexican crafts. Juan and Mauro Quezada maintain galleries out of their respective homes. All three galleries are just off the main street that runs through town; inquire locally and someone can point you in the right direction.

Dollars are readily accepted (travelers checks are not), but most potters have no means of shipping purchases to the United States. The Jorge Quintana Gallery will pack and ship purchases for their customers. If you're transporting your treasures across the border, keep in mind limits and exceptions for bringing back duty-free articles. Pottery is duty-free but must be declared; keep receipts for any large purchases.

If you just want to visit Mata Ortiz for the experience, don't intend to buy pottery and don't want to drive, a taxi can take you to the village and the driver will wait while you walk around and explore. The cost can be negotiated with the driver, but expect to pay around 650 pesos (about $48 U.S.) for the round-trip fare, plus another 150 or so pesos per hour for him to wait. In Nuevo Casas Grandes there are taxi stands (sitios) in the vicinity of the main plaza and train station.

**PAQUIME ARCHEOLOGICAL SITE** (Zona Arqueología Paquimé) is about 8 km (5 mi.) w. of Nuevo Casas Grandes on Mex. 37, then about half a mile s.w. of the main square in the old village of Casas Grandes, following signs. Relatively little is known about these shadowy ruins, which make them all the more fascinating.

Paquime emerged early in the 13th century, becoming the largest and most advanced settlement in what is now northern Mexico. These ruins bear the influence of both the Puebloan culture of the American Southwest and the Mesoamerican civilizations of southern Mexico and Central America. Paquimé collapsed sometime during the mid-15th century, about a century before the arrival of the Spanish; drought, warfare that ruined commerce and sacking by a nomadic tribe are all possible causes for its downfall.

Mazelike adobe walls are one of the site's most defining features. Their rounded contours were achieved by laboriously applying the building material a handful at a time. Also distinctive are the T-shaped doorways dotting the terraced building compounds, each of which surrounded a central plaza. Stone aqueducts and reservoirs supplied water for drinking and irrigation, and stone pits were used for roasting agave leaves, a desert plant used to produce the alcoholic drink mescal. Some of the large stone structures had an astrological function.

The site museum (Museo de las Culturas del Norte) has detailed exhibits chronicling Paquimé's connection to both Puebloan and Mesoamerican cultures, with background information in both Spanish and English. The site retains a great air of mystery, inviting speculation as to what life might have been like in its heyday.

Snacks are available at the museum. **Time:** Allow 2 hours minimum. **Hours:** Tues.-Sun. 10-5. **Cost:** 62 pesos (about $4.60 U.S.); free to all Sun. **Phone:** (636) 692-8003.

# PUERTO PEÑASCO, SONORA (B-1)
pop. 57,342

Puerto Peñasco (PWEHR-toh peh-NYAHS-coh) is situated in the midst of some of Mexico's most inhospitable territory: blazingly hot, extremely arid and impressively desolate. But because of close proximity to the U.S. border—about a 4-hour drive from Tucson and 4 to 5 hours from Phoenix—it attracts campers and RVers.

The beaches in this area are generally wide and flat, with both sandy and rocky areas. While the coarse, tan-colored grains are no match for the powdery sand at some of Mexico's other beach resorts, the blue-green water is calm and shallow, waves are gentle and there are no riptides—ideal conditions for wading and swimming. Beachcombers take note: The northern Gulf of California coast experiences an extreme tidal range of more than 20 feet, which exposes a treasure trove of shells and marine life at low tide.

Playa Hermosa, just west of Puerto Peñasco, is the locals' beach and the one closest to town. It has restrooms, showers and snack stands. To the east at Playa Las Conchas are tide pools teeming with crabs, mussels, sponges and other creatures. Farther east, the Morua Estuary (Estero Morua) and the La Pinta Estuary (Estero La Pinta) provide habitats for shore and wading birds, fish and invertebrates. In between the two estuaries are three beaches—Playa Encanto, Playa Dorada and Playa Miramar—lined with condos, resort complexes and rental homes. Keep in mind that all beaches in Mexico are public, even stretches that may seem like they are on hotel property.

The Intercultural Center for the Study of Oceans and Deserts (CEDO) is on the eastern edge of town at Playa Las Conchas; from Boulevard Benito Juárez take Boulevard Fremont and then an access road east, following signs. This biological field station is devoted to researching and conserving the surrounding marine and desert environments. Free public tours of the facility are offered Tuesdays and Saturdays. The center also organizes occasional tide pool explorations, bird-watching excursions, coastal desert walks and other guided activities. Reservations are required; for information phone (638) 382-0113 or (520) 320-5473 (from the United States).

Other things to do in Puerto Peñasco include shore fishing, chartered sport-fishing excursions, sailing, snorkeling, scuba diving, kayaking and, during the winter months, whale watching. Or you could just kick back and enjoy the sunset.

The Old Port section of town, perched at the tip of a rocky cape overlooking the gulf, is the site of the original fishing settlement. Browse the craft shops along waterfront Malecón Kino, where vendors sell—in addition to the ubiquitous T-shirts, ceramics and seashell necklaces—carvings fashioned from ironwood, a desert tree known for its extremely hard and dense wood. Another interesting place to wander through is the open-air seafood market and its displays of freshly caught fish.

Taquerias set up along the malecón and around the harbor area. These stands dish up handmade corn tortillas filled with strips of meat or fish cooked on a charcoal griddle and garnished with such toppings as grilled onions and peppers, beans, chopped cabbage, radishes, cilantro and salsa. The tacos are an inexpensive and tasty on-the-spot snack. They also should be safe to eat as long as you avoid adding the lettuce, tomatoes or carrots that are often provided (and may not be rinsed with purified water). Another good rule of thumb is to patronize a stand that is popular with Rocoportenses (locals).

## Practicalities

Easy access is perhaps Puerto Peñasco's biggest lure. Sonoyta, the small town just across the border from Lukeville, Ariz., has the usual assortment of tourist-oriented shops but lacks the excitement of bigger and more bustling border cities like Nogales, Mexicali and Tijuana. Unless you're intent on scoring a souvenir, stay on Boulevard de las Américas, following the signs for Puerto Peñasco.

A temporary vehicle importation permit is not needed if traveling to Puerto Peñasco from the United States. Motorists must, however, carry Mexican automobile insurance. If you plan on bringing a boat, ATV or other type of recreational vehicle, take along a copy of the ownership documents.

Mex. 8, the direct route to the Gulf of California, is a two-lane road that has a couple of sharp turns. The approximately 105-kilometer (65-mile) drive through open range country takes over an hour; note the lower speed limit of 65-75 kilometers per hour (about 45 mph). Because of the lack of roadside facilities, the trip from the border should be made only during the daytime.

Mar de Cortés International Airport (Sea of Cortez Airport) is a small airport catering to light aircraft. The facility is equipped to accommodate regularly scheduled air service by major carriers, but with the dramatic downturn in tourism to Mexico's border region, major airlines are reluctant.

The summer heat in Puerto Peñasco can be extreme; the best time to visit is from November through May, when the weather is cooler. The months with the most visitors are March and April.

The Santander Bank at Boulevard Benito Juárez and Calle 13 has an ATM machine; withdrawals are in pesos. Many local businesses, however, accept or even prefer U.S. dollars. In case of medical emergency, contact the Red Cross (Cruz Roja); phone (638) 383-2266. To reach the local police department, phone (638) 383-2626.

**Rocky Point Convention & Visitors Bureau:** Boulevard Freemont #4, in Plaza Freemont. **Phone:** (638) 388-0444, or (602) 539-0027 (from the United States).

**PINACATE BIOSPHERE RESERVE** is part of northwestern Mexico's Gran Desierto; the information center is about 52 km (32 mi.) s. of Lukeville, Ariz., just off Mex. 8 at Km marker 52. This trackless, otherworldly region was created over time by subterranean pools of molten rock that exploded up through the desert floor and then cooled, leaving behind a wasteland of towering sand dunes, lava tubes, cinder cones and dormant volcanic craters.

The area was designated as a biosphere reserve in 1993 to preserve both its volcanic rock formations and such endemic species as the desert octopus (which lives in the Sonoyta River), the flat-tail chameleon and the Gila monster. From the top of El Pinacate, a hill about 3,960 feet above sea level, there are panoramic views of the Baja California Peninsula.

**Note:** Day visitors must pay admission at the visitor center before hiking or driving into the reserve. A high-clearance vehicle is recommended. There are no facilities; bring plenty of water, a hat and sun protection and wear comfortable hiking shoes. Camping is permitted at two designated locations (a permit is required). The best time to visit is January through April. **Hours:** Reserve and visitor center daily 9-5. **Cost:** Reserve access 56 pesos (about $4.15 U.S.) per person. **Phone:** (638) 108-0011.

## SAN CARLOS, SONORA (C-1)

San Carlos, "just over the mountain" from the port city of Guaymas, is actually about 8 kilometers (5 miles) north via Mex. 15, then 24 kilometers (15 miles) west on four-lane Mex. 124. Guaymenas Indians occupied this area for a few thousand years before the Spanish arrival in the mid-16th century; Jesuit priests built a mission in 1710. San Carlos flourished as a major supply center during the Mexican-American and U.S. Civil wars, but following the Mexican Revolution of 1910 sport fishing took precedence over port activities.

Quiet San Carlos "went Hollywood" in the late 1960s when the movie "Catch 22" was filmed at nearby Playa Algodones. A Club Med followed, and today's resort was born. Natural beauty remains in the form of tranquil white-sand beaches and the clear, blue-green waters of the Sea of Cortez, inhabited by more than 650 species of game fish. You'll find upscale condos and Sonora's most luxurious accommodations in San Carlos, but there also are inexpensive motels and RV parks that cater to budget travelers.

Marina San Carlos, one of Mexico's largest yacht marinas, has extensive docking facilities as well as moorings on outer San Carlos Bay. The San Carlos Country Club, Avenida Cristobal #1390, has an 18-hole golf course; most hotels in the area can arrange a temporary membership. Gary's Dive Shop, on Boulevard Fabio Beltrones (at Km marker 10), offers a variety of fishing and scuba excursions; phone (622) 226-0049.

**Sonora State Tourism Office:** A branch office is located on Blvd. Fabio Beltrones (Mex. 124). **Phone:** (622) 226-0202.

# Northeastern Mexico

Northeastern Mexico is not the Mexican vacation paradise touted in glossy travel brochures. Whereas resorts like Cancún and Cabo San Lucas lure vacationers from all over the world, the beaches along the low-lying, marshy Gulf of Mexico coastline in the state of Tamaulipas are muddy and mosquito-ridden. Sprawling Coahuila is arid and sparsely populated, with tourist facilities few and far between.

Saltillo, in a broad valley surrounded by the imposing peaks of the Sierra Madre Oriental, was founded as a Spanish outpost in 1577. By the early 17th century the settlement was a strategic center for Spanish expeditions embarking on explorations to the north, and from 1835 to 1847 Saltillo was capital of a territory that included Texas and extended as far northward as present-day Colorado.

Capital of the state of Nuevo León, industrial Monterrey is Mexico's third largest city. Sheer size makes it a daunting choice for the casual tourist. But the plazas and narrow thoroughfares of Monterrey's old center retain some of the flavor of Spanish colonial days, and a handful of pedestrian-only streets provide relief from big-city congestion.

AAA recommends that travelers consult online U.S. State Department travel advisories when planning traveling abroad. Find this information at http://travel.state.gov/content/passports/english/alertswarnings/mexico-travel-warning.html.

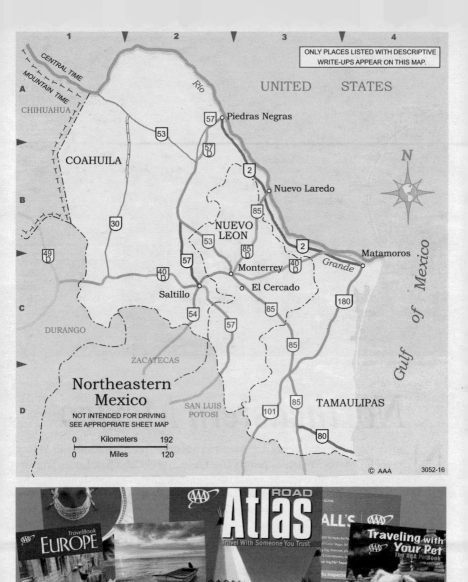

ONLY PLACES LISTED WITH DESCRIPTIVE
WRITE-UPS APPEAR ON THIS MAP.

UNITED STATES

CENTRAL TIME
MOUNTAIN TIME

CHIHUAHUA

Rio

A

COAHUILA

53

57 Piedras Negras

57

2

Nuevo Laredo

N

B

30

NUEVO LEON

85

53

85

2

Matamoros

49

57

85

40

Monterrey

40

Grande

Gulf of Mexico

Saltillo

El Cercado

180

C

54

85

57

85

DURANGO

ZACATECAS

**Northeastern Mexico**

NOT INTENDED FOR DRIVING
SEE APPROPRIATE SHEET MAP

SAN LUIS
POTOSI

101

85

TAMAULIPAS

D

80

| 0 | Kilometers | 192 |
| 0 | Miles | 120 |

© AAA          3052-16

# Points of Interest

## MATAMOROS, TAMAULIPAS (C-4)
pop. 489,193

**Note:** For current information about safety/security issues in Matamoros, refer to the U.S. State Department website (travel.state.gov).

Main port of entry to Mexico from the lower Rio Grande Valley, Matamoros (mah-tah-MOH-rohs) is connected with Brownsville, Tex. The B & M Bridge enters Matamoros via Mexico Street in Brownsville; the Gateway Bridge, also called the International Bridge, enters via International Boulevard. Toll fees on the B & M Bridge are $2.25 (U.S.) for automobiles and pickups and 50c for pedestrians; the Gateway Bridge fees are $3 (U.S.) for automobiles and pickups and 75c for pedestrians.

U.S. Customs and Border Protection offices as well as Mexican customs and immigration offices at both bridges are open daily 24 hours. Baggage must be inspected if you plan to travel into the interior.

The Casamata Museum, about 6 blocks east of Plaza Hidalgo (the main plaza) at avenidas Guatemala and Santos Degollado, is housed in the remains of a fort dating from 1845; never completed, it was supposed to help defend the city from U.S. attack. Exhibits include weapons, early city photographs and memorabilia associated with the 1910 Mexican Revolution. The museum is open Tues.-Fri. 9-5, Sat.-Sun. 9-2, and admission is free; phone (868) 816-2071.

The Reforma Theater (Teatro Reforma) is a block north of Plaza Hidalgo at Calle 6 and Avenida Abasolo. It was built in 1861, demolished in 1956 and replaced with a movie theater, and then restored to its original architectural style in the early 1990s. It now serves as the venue for events associated with the International Autumn Festival in October.

## MONTERREY, NUEVO LEÓN (C-2)
pop. 1,135,550

*See map page 184.*

Founded in 1596 by Don Diego de Montemayor, Monterrey (mohn-teh-REY) was named for the Viceroy of New Spain, Don Gaspar de Zúñiga y Acevedo, Count of Monterrey. Real development began in the 18th century, when El Obispado, or the Bishop's Palace *(see attraction listing)*—initially built as a place of retirement for Catholic bishops—became the seat of the religious diocese.

The city lies in a valley ringed with craggy mountains, including 5,700-foot Hill of the Saddle (Cerro de la Silla) and 7,800-foot Hill of the Miter (Cerro de la Mitra). The former is saddle-shaped; the latter resembles a bishop's headdress. The mountains trap smog created by the dense concentration of industry, creating a significant pollution problem, and with an estimated metropolitan area population of nearly 3.5 million, there is formidable congestion. Contrasting with these urban pains are a couple of impressive natural attractions outside the city.

## Practicalities

Monterrey's Mariano Escobedo International Airport is about 6 kilometers (4 miles) northeast of the downtown area. Taxis shuttle passengers between the airport and the central city. Aeroméxico, phone 01 (800) 021-4010 (toll-free long distance within Mexico), American, Delta and United airlines offer direct or connecting flights from U.S. cities. The Aeroméxico subsidiary Aeroméxico Connect flies nonstop from Houston, New York/JFK and Las Vegas; reservations can be made through Aeroméxico. *For additional information about airlines see Arriving by Air, page p. 42.*

Motorists can access the city via two major toll highways—Mex. 85-D from Laredo/Nuevo Laredo or Mex. 40-D from McAllen/Reynosa. These highways more or less parallel free Mex. 85 (the Pan-American Highway) and Mex. 40. Although the less scenic of the two, Mex. 40-D is convenient to downtown Monterrey.

Metro, the city's subway system (also referred to as Metrorrey), consists of two lines. Elevated Line 1 runs east-west along Avenida Colón, north of the downtown core, and then toward the northwestern suburbs. Underground Line 2 originates at Gran Plaza (the Zaragoza station) and runs west to Avenida Cuauhtémoc, then north-south to the vicinity of the Cuauhtémoc Brewery (the General Anaya station).

Metro is used primarily by office workers and is not particularly helpful for the visitor interested in sightseeing, although Line 2 does provide access to the Zona Rosa, downtown's upscale shopping/dining area. Magnetic one-way ticket cards can be purchased from vending machines at the entrance stations for 4.5 pesos; multiple-trip cards also are available. Trains run daily from 5 a.m.-midnight. Check with the State Tourism Office for further information.

The downtown streets, wedged within a ring of expressways, tend to be narrow, one way and congested. Street parking in this area is difficult, and overnight parking is prohibited. The best way to see the sights is by taxi or bus tour. Taxis are plentiful and can be hailed on the street; always determine the fare in advance. First-class bus service to Monterrey from Dallas, Houston and San Antonio is offered by Transportes del Norte. Greyhound Bus Lines in Laredo, Tex., can provide information about bus lines serving northeastern Mexico; phone (956) 723-4324.

## City Layout

At first glance Monterrey is all factories, grimy housing projects and noisy traffic congestion. The city

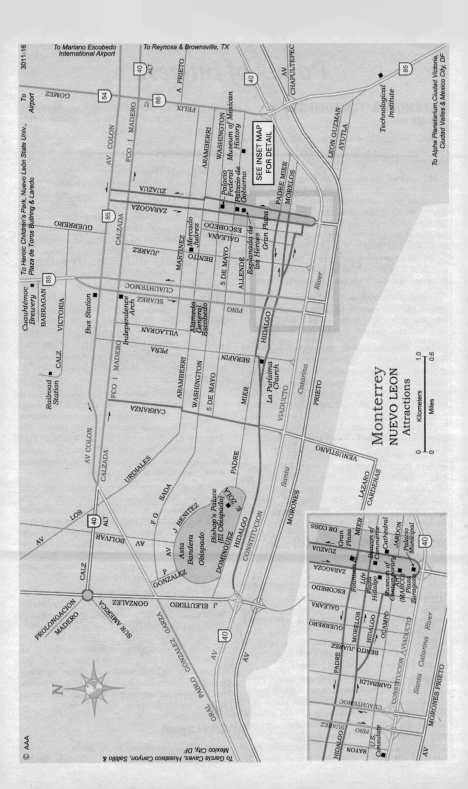

# Monterrey
## NUEVO LEON
### Attractions

© AAA

3011-16

Kilometers  0   0.6   1.0
Miles

To Mariano Escobedo International Airport

To Reynosa & Brownsville, TX

To Alpha Planetarium, Ciudad Victoria, Ciudad Valles & Mexico City, DF

To Airport

To Heroic Children's Park, Nuevo León State Univ., Plaza de Toros Bullfighting & Laredo

To García Caves, Huasteco Canyon, Saltillo & Mexico City, DF

**SEE INSET MAP FOR DETAIL**

GOMEZ
GUERRERO
BARRAGAN
VICTORIA
CALZ
Railroad Station
FCO I MADERO
CALZADA
AV COLON
LOS
CALZADA
CALZ
PROLONGACION MADERO
SUR AMERICA
GRAL PABLO GONZALEZ GARZA
J ELEUTERIO
GONZALEZ
P GONZALEZ
AV BOLIVAR
F G SADA
J BENITEZ
DOMINGUEZ [El Obispado]
HIDALGO
CONSTITUCION
PADRE
MORONES
Santa Catarina
VENUSTIANO
LAZARO CARDENAS
PRIETO
VIADUCTO
La Purísima Church
SERAFIN
MIER
5 DE MAYO
WASHINGTON
ARAMBERRI
PEÑA
CARRANZA
FCO I MADERO
URDIALES
Cuauhtémoc Brewery
Bus Station
Independence Arch
SUAREZ
VILLAGRAN
Alameda General Escobedo
PINO
CUAUHTEMOC
MARTINEZ
JUAREZ
BENITO
5 DE MAYO
ALLENDE
GALEANA
ESCOBEDO
ZARAGOZA
Mercado Juárez
Esplanada de los Héroes
Gran Plaza
HIDALGO
River
ZUAZUA
AV COLON
FCO I MADERO
CALZADA
A PRIETO
FELIX
WASHINGTON
Museum of Mexican History
Palacio Federal
Palacio de Gobierno
PADRE MIER
MORELOS
CHAPULTEPEC
LEON GUZMAN
AYUTLA
Technological Institute
AV
54
85
40 ALT
85
40
40
85
40 ALT
85
85
40

Asta Bandera

Bishop's Palace (El Obispado)

N

**Inset map:**

DR COSS
MIER
Gran Plaza
Beacon of Commerce
ZUAZUA
Plaza Commonfort
Plaza Hidalgo
Museum of Contemporary Art (MARCO)
Palacio Municipal
Plaza Zaragoza
Cathedral
JARDIN
ZARAGOZA
ESCOBEDO
GALEANA
GUERRERO
MORELOS
HIDALGO
BENITO JUAREZ
OCAMPO
PADRE
GARIBALDI
CUAUHTEMOC
SUAREZ
PINO
HIDALGO
RAYON
U.S. Consulate
CONSTITUCION
VIADUCTO
Santa Catarina River
MORONES PRIETO
AV
40

center, where hotels and office buildings stand next to old flat-roofed houses, is a haven of sorts from this industrial sprawl. One landmark symbolizes Mexico's break from Spain—the figure of "Patria" (Fatherland) holding a broken chain, which sits atop the Independence Arch (Arco de la Independencia) at Avenida Pino Suárez and Calzada Francisco Madero.

La Purísima Church, at Calle Serafín Peña and Avenida Hidalgo (west of Gran Plaza on the way to the Bishop's Palace), is considered an outstanding example of modern ecclesiastical architecture. Pastora Park (Parque la Pastora), east of downtown off Avenida Chapultepec, is a naturally landscaped recreation area featuring a lake and a zoo.

## Shopping

Folk arts and handicrafts such as leather articles, blown glass and pottery are available at two downtown markets. Mercado Juárez is off Avenida Benito Juárez between avenidas Martinez and Aramberri; the more tourist-oriented Mercado Colón is on Avenida Constitución west of Gran Plaza. Other craft shops can be found around Plaza Hidalgo near the big downtown hotels; Carapan, Av. Hidalgo #305 Oriente, offers a variety of high-quality merchandise. The House of Crafts (Casa de las Artesanías) is just east of Gran Plaza at avenidas Dr. Coss and Allende.

The Zona Rosa runs along Calle Morelos in the vicinity of Gran Plaza. Craft shops, fashionable boutiques, restaurants and nightclubs line an open mall several blocks long and 2 blocks wide, reserved for pedestrians only.

## Special Events

Starting on Palm Sunday, the 2-week Spring Fair (Feria de Primavera) festivities offer parades, art expositions, auto races and other sports events. The Festival of the Virgin of Guadalupe take place during the first half of December.

Bullfights are held periodically between May and December at the Plaza de Toros bullring, located south of Niños Heroes Park at avenidas Ruíz Cortines and Alfonso Reyes; phone (81) 8374-0505 for schedule information, or visit ticketmaster.com.mx. Feats of horsemanship characterize *charreadas,* or Mexican-style rodeos, held Sunday mornings at ranches in the eastern suburb of Villa de Guadalupe. To reach them, follow the signs reading "Lienzo Charro" posted along free Mex. 40 in the direction of Reynosa. For more information, including dates and times, contact Monterrey Infotur.

**Monterrey Infotur:** Av. 5 de Mayo #525 Oriente (West) between avs. Mariano Escobedo and Ignacio Zaragoza, on the third floor of the Elizondo Páez building. The office is open Mon.-Fri. 9-6:30. **Phone:** (81) 8345-0870, or 01 (800) 832-2200 (toll-free long distance within Mexico).

**ALFA PLANETARIUM** (Planetario Alfa) is s.w. of downtown via Av. Manuel Gómez Morín to Av. Roberto Sada #1000. Housed in a building that looks like a leaning cylinder, this large walled complex contains, in addition to one of Mexico's better planetariums, a museum with an excellent collection of pre-Hispanic art, a large aquarium, a domed IMAX theater and multiple hands-on, interactive displays demonstrating lightning, optics and mechanical sciences. On the grounds is an outdoor aviary and plenty of tree-shaded green areas.

Free bus service to the complex departs from Alameda Park, just west of Avenida Pino Suárez between avenidas Aramberri and Washington, Tues.-Fri. at 2:30, 3:30 and 4:30, Sat.-Sun. on the half-hour from 10:30 to 5:30. **Note:** The weather in Monterrey can be extremely hot from May until September; plan accordingly. **Time:** Allow 2 hours minimum. **Hours:** Tues.-Fri. 2:30-7, Sat.-Sun. 10:30-7. Phone ahead to confirm schedule. **Cost:** Museum admission 70 pesos (about $5.20 U.S.); free (ages 0-3). Museum plus IMAX film 100 pesos (about $7.40 U.S.); free (ages 0-3). **Phone:** (81) 8303-0001. 🍴

**BISHOP'S PALACE** (El Obispado) is in the western part of the city at the w. end of Av. Padre Mier. It was built by Fray José Rafael Verger in 1787, a year of famine, to employ Indian victims of a severe drought. During the Mexican-American War, it resisted an onslaught by the invading U.S. Army for 2 days after the city had fallen. The building also served as a stronghold against the French in 1864, as a hospital during a 1903 yellow fever epidemic, and as temporary quarters for Pancho Villa during the 1910 Revolution. On smog-free days it offers a wonderful view of the city.

**Regional Museum of Nuevo León** (Museo Regional de Nuevo León) is inside the palace. It has displays tracing the industrial, cultural and artistic development of the Monterrey area. Of note are the guns that were used to execute self-proclaimed Emperor Archduke Maximilian. **Hours:** Tues.-Sun. 9-6. **Cost:** 52 pesos (about $3.85 U.S.); free (ages 0-12). **Phone:** (81) 8346-0404.

**CUAUHTÉMOC BREWERY** (Cervecería Cuauhtémoc) is n. of downtown at Av. Universidad #2002 Norte, following signs; there is no street parking, but limited free parking is available within the entrance gate. Bohemia, Tecate and Carta Blanca beers are produced at the rate of more than a million bottles a day; free samples are served in the large beer garden.

Visitors taking the brewery tour must wear an orange vest and safety goggles and be able to climb steep, narrow metal stairs. **Time:** Allow 2 hours minimum. **Hours:** Guided brewery tours are available Mon.-Fri. by reservation only; phone to arrange a tour time. Beer garden open daily 10-4. **Cost:** Tour and beer garden free. **Phone:** (81) 8328-5355. 🍴

**GRAN PLAZA** is bounded by Av. 5 de Mayo on the north and Av. Constitución on the south. Monterrey's immense central plaza is one of the world's largest city squares. Also known as the Macro Plaza, its construction during the 1980s helped revitalize the downtown area. Graced by fountains, statuary, gardens and boldly modern buildings, the 100-acre expanse stretches from City Hall (Palacio Municipal) north to the Government Palace (Palacio de Gobierno). Several streets pass beneath the raised plaza, helping to alleviate traffic congestion.

**Beacon of Commerce** (Faro del Comercio) stands in the center of Plaza Zaragoza. This 230-foot-tall, bright-orange laser beam tower dominates the plaza and bathes it with green light in the evenings.

**Cathedral** is on Calle Zuazua at the southern end of Gran Plaza. Built over a period of more than 2 centuries, it exhibits different architectural styles; the pale yellow facade is baroque, while Plateresque decoration adorns the entrance door.

**Esplanade of the Heroes** (Explanada de Los Héroes) is just s. of the Government Palace. This is the most formal looking part of Gran Plaza in terms of its resemblance to a traditional Mexican plaza. It contains monuments to Mexican historical figures Father Miguel Hidalgo, Benito Juárez and José María Morelos. Just south is the Hidden Garden (Bosque Hundido), a relaxing green space with trees, burbling fountains and sculptures.

**Fountain of Life** (Fuente de la Vida) is in the center of Gran Plaza between avenidas Matamoros and Padre Mier. This impressive fountain boasts a bronze statue of Neptune surrounded by cavorting steeds and nymphs.

**Government Palace** (Palacio Gobierno) anchors the n. end of Gran Plaza, just south of Av. 5 de Mayo. The Nuevo León state capitol, this Spanish colonial-style building was built in 1908 of pink stone quarried from around San Luis Potosí; it has a typically Spanish patio.

**Plaza Hidalgo** is across Gran Plaza from the cathedral. Another traditional Mexican square, Hidalgo is framed with colonial-style buildings and dotted with shops and little outdoor cafes.

**HEROIC CHILDREN'S PARK** (Parque Niños Héroes) is on Av. Alfonso Reyes, about 4 km (2.5 mi.) n. of downtown and just s. of Nuevo León State University. It was named in honor of the young cadets

who defended Mexico City's Chapultepec Castle from U.S. forces during the Mexican-American War; they committed suicide by leaping from the castle battlements rather than surrendering.

This large, fenced-in recreational complex is family oriented and one of the best places in the city to go for outdoor activities. There are playgrounds, plenty of picnic areas, several adjoining man-made ponds stocked for fishing and an athletic area for jogging and track events.

Also within the park are botanical gardens; an aviary; a baseball stadium; a museum of automobiles; the Museum of Fauna and Natural Sciences (Museo de la Fauna y Ciencias Naturales), with numerous animal displays; and the Nuevo León Art Gallery (Pinacoteca de Nuevo León), which surveys the state's artistic heritage. The facilities are scattered throughout the extensive park grounds, connected by tree-shaded paths.

**Hours:** Tues.-Sun. 9-6. **Cost:** Park entrance fee about 50c (U.S.); free (ages 0-12). Small additional fees are charged at the museums. 🍴

**MUSEUM OF CONTEMPORARY ART** (Museo de Arte Contemporaneo) is at calles Zuazua and Ocampo at the southern end of Gran Plaza, next to the cathedral. MARCO, as this museum is popularly known, is a spacious, ultramodern building designed by noted Mexican architect Ricardo Legorreta. Exhibits in the 14 galleries emphasize Mexican and Latin American artists, including works by 20th-century masters Diego Rivera and David Alfaro Siqueiros. Cutting-edge artist Juan Soriano created the gigantic bronze sculpture of a dove, "La Paloma," that stands at the front entrance.

**Time:** Allow 2 hours minimum. **Hours:** Tues.-Sun. 10-6 (also Wed. 6-8 p.m.). Last admission 45 minutes before closing. **Cost:** 80 pesos (about $5.90 U.S.); 55 pesos (ages 6-15). Free to all Wed. **Phone:** (81) 8262-4500. 🍴

**MUSEUM OF MEXICAN HISTORY** (Museo de Historia Mexicana) is in the center of the downtown historic area at Calle Dr. Coss #445. The top floor of this large, two-story building across from the main plaza is devoted to the history of Mexico from prehistoric times to the present. Exhibits organized by century feature ancient clay artifacts, tools and foods; the evolution of Mexican textiles; transportation, religion and politics; and such cultural mainstays as music and TV shows.

Underground burial vaults and grain storage are depicted through the use of a Plexiglas floor. The downstairs section has rotating exhibits and the Hall of Ivories (Sala de Marfiles), displaying silver crowns and other decorative objects. Next door is the Museum of the Northeast (Museo de Noreste), with exhibits focusing on northern Mexican history and the region's cultural ties to Texas. Across the street is the Palace Museum (Museo del Palacio). **Hours:** Tues.-Sun. 10-6 (also Tues. and Sun. 6-8 p.m.). **Cost:** (includes Museo de Noreste) 40 pesos (about $3 U.S.); free (ages 1-11).

Free to all Tues. and Sun. Palace Museum free. Cash only. **Phone:** (81) 2033-9898.

## Nearby Destinations

GARCÍA CAVES (Grutas de García) are n.w. of downtown Monterrey via Mex. 40. A paved road runs to the caves, which are about 8 km (5 mi.) east of the village of Villa de García. Discovered about 1843 by parish priest Juan Antonio Sobrevilla, these caves are among the largest and most beautiful in Mexico. Their estimated age is 50 to 60 million years; it is presumed the caves were once submerged due to the shellfish fossils scattered over the walls and ceilings. Ten "rooms" contain stalagmite and stalactite formations.

A swimming pool, restaurants, and picnic and recreational areas cluster at the foot of the mountain where the caves are located. From the parking area, a cable car transports visitors past rugged scenery to the cavern entrance, tucked high on the side of a cliff. The cement passageways connecting the caves are well lighted. **Hours:** Daily 9-5 (last cable car departs at 4). **Cost:** Guided tour fee (includes cable car ride) 80 pesos (about $5.90 U.S.); 60 pesos (ages 4-10).

HUASTECA CANYON is about 32 km (20 mi.) w. of Monterrey on Mex. 40 to the village of Santa Catarina, then 3 km (2 mi.) s. The magnificent rock gorge of Huasteca (wahs-TEH-kah) is located in Monterrey Heights National Park (Parque Nacional Cumbres de Monterrey). The sheer walls reach heights of 750 to 1,000 feet. In places the softer rock has been eroded into curious formations. Restrooms, a snack bar and picnic areas are on site.

## NUEVO LAREDO, TAMAULIPAS (B-3)
pop. 384,033

**Note:** For current information about safety/security issues in Nuevo Laredo, refer to the U.S. State Department website (travel.state.gov).

Nuevo Laredo (noo-EH-voh lah-REH-doh) is a major point of entry to the Mexican mainland from the United States. It is connected to Laredo, Tex., by four international toll bridges across the Río Grande. International Bridge 1 (Gateway to the Americas) is open to vehicular and pedestrian traffic; International Bridge 2 (Juárez Lincoln) is open to vehicular traffic only. Either one can be used if you plan on driving beyond the border zone.

International Bridge 3 (Columbia Solidarity) primarily serves commercial vehicles, and International Bridge 4 (World Trade Bridge) is reserved for commercial vehicles only. Tolls for International Bridge 1 and 2 are $3 (U.S.) southbound, $2.25 northbound. The toll for pedestrians using International Bridge 1 is 75c southbound, 30c northbound.

For shopping day trips, it is recommended that you leave your car in Laredo and walk across the border, which eliminates the time-consuming wait to return to the United States. The Mexican customs and immigration office at Bridge 1 is open 24 hours

daily. U.S. Customs and Border Protection offices at Bridge 1 and Bridge 2 are open 24 hours daily.

## PIEDRAS NEGRAS, COAHUILA (A-2)
pop. 152,806

**Note:** For current information about safety/security issues in Piedras Negras, refer to the U.S. State Department website (travel.state.gov).

Piedras Negras (pee-EH-drahs NEH-grahs) faces Eagle Pass, Tex., across the Rio Grande. Two bridges extend across the border. International Bridge One is a two-lane bridge with pedestrian walkways that connects the towns' shopping areas; it is open daily 7 a.m.-11 p.m. International Bridge Two (Camino Real International Bridge) carries vehicle traffic into Mexico; it is open daily 24 hours. Tolls are $2.50 (U.S.) for automobiles and pickups, 50 cents for pedestrians. If you're traveling into the interior the Mexican customs office is open Mon.-Fri. 8-8, Sat. 10-2. For those returning from Mexico the U.S. Customs and Border Protection office is open 24 hours daily.

This typical border city is notable chiefly as the setting for Laura Esquivel's novel "Like Water for Chocolate," which also was made into a popular film. Kike's Tacos, downtown on Calle Bravo, has a devoted local following. The small taco shells, filled with ground meat, lettuce, onions, tomatoes and an authentically fiery salsa, are usually ordered by the dozen or half dozen.

## REYNOSA, TAMAULIPAS (B-3)
pop. 608,891

**Note:** For current information about safety/security issues in Reynosa, refer to the U.S. State Department website (travel.state.gov).

On the Rio Grande just south of McAllen, Tex., Reynosa (reh-NOH-sah) is reached via the McAllen International Toll Bridge. The toll for automobiles and pickups is $3 (U.S.), pedestrians $1. Both Mexican and U.S. Customs and Border Protection and immigration offices are open 24 hours daily. About 81 kilometers (50 miles) west of the city via Mex. 2 is El Azucar (Sugar) Dam, where anglers seek bass and other freshwater game species.

## SALTILLO, COAHUILA (C-2) pop. 725,123

**Note:** For current information about safety/security issues in Saltillo, refer to the U.S. State Department website (travel.state.gov).

About 85 kilometers (53 miles) southwest of Monterrey on Mex. 40, Saltillo (sahl-TEE-yoh) is the capital of and leading industrial city in the state of Coahuila. Because of altitude and the resulting dry, mild climate, golf, tennis, polo and swimming are popular summer recreational pursuits. The city's annual *feria* (fair) takes place the first half of August.

There are two downtown plazas. Dignified monuments and well-preserved colonial buildings line the streets around Plaza de Armas. The feeling of formality is reinforced by its paved surface, a central fountain overlooked by four female statues, and the lack of trees and benches. The plaza is flanked by the city's grand 18th-century cathedral and the Government Palace (Palacio de Gobierno), which contains murals illustrating regional history.

Much livelier is Plaza Acuña, 2 blocks northwest. Here there are an abundance of shops, and the square is ringed with little cafes and bars. Occupying one corner is Mercado Juárez, which is a good place to browse for handicrafts, *sarapes* (woolen blankets), rugs, pottery, silverwork and bizarre-looking tin masks. Wandering musicians entertain families and visitors soaking up the local atmosphere.

A monument to Emilio Carranza, who made the first nonstop flight from Mexico City to New York, stands along Calle Victoria. The street begins at the Alameda, a shady park just west of Plaza de Armas that is frequented by students and joggers. Here stands an equestrian statue of General Ignacio Zaragoza, hero of the 1862 Battle of Puebla. Zaragoza was born in 1829 in Bahía del Espíritu Santo, near what is now Goliad, Tex. The central bus station is southwest of downtown on Boulevard Luis Echeverría.

**Coahuila State Tourism Office (Instituto Estatal de Turismo):** Blvd. Venustiano Carranza #3206 in the Latinoamericana district of the city. **Phone:** (844) 439-2745, or 01 (800) 718-4220 (toll-free long distance within Mexico).

**FUENTE ATHENEUM** (Fuente Ateneo) is on Boulevard Venustiano Carranza on the University of Coahuila campus. This Art Deco-style building contains an art gallery with works by well-known European and Mexican painters. **Hours:** Mon.-Fri. 10-4, Sat. 10-1. **Cost:** Free. **Phone:** (844) 415-7631.

**HERRERA MUSEUM** is at General Victoriano Cepeda #105. It showcases paintings by early 20th-century Mexican artist Rubén Herrera, primarily Italian landscapes and pastoral scenes representing Herrera's apprenticeship in Rome. **Hours:** Tues.-Sun. 10-7. **Cost:** Free.

**LA ANGOSTURA BATTLEGROUND** is about a half-hour drive south of the city off Mex. 54. A monument on the east side of Mex. 54 marks the site of a bloody Mexican-American War battle on Feb. 22-23, 1847.

**SANTIAGO CATHEDRAL** is at calles Hidalgo and Juárez facing Plaza de Armas. Built 1746-1801, it exhibits a mix of architectural styles, most notably the Mexican Churrigueresque. Decorative baroque carvings representing plants and shells adorn its facade and doors. The interior features a gilded altarpiece and a pulpit covered in gold leaf. The 1762 chapel contains a Spanish image of Christ associated with numerous legends. A 200-foot tower dominates the church and offers a panoramic view of the city.

© photomatz / Shutterstock.com

# The Pacific Coast

A lso known as the Mexican Riviera, Mexico's Pacific Coast boasts hundreds of miles of surf-pounded shoreline and a string of destinations stretching from Mazatlán south to Bahías de Huatulco. They range from funky beach communities—traditional getaways for the budget conscious and Mexican families of modest means—to luxurious oceanfront retreats catering to the well-heeled international set.

The Mexican Riviera unofficially begins at Mazatlán, "the Pearl of the Pacific." The name is derived from the Náhuatl Indian word *mazatl,* meaning "place of deer"—a reference to former inhabitants, as these fleet creatures are nowhere to be seen in the midst of today's oceanfront bustle. Strung along miles of scenic Pacific shoreline, the city is northwestern Mexico's major beach destination.

In Manzanillo sun, sea and sand mix with the matter-of-fact grime of a real working city. Sport fishing is one of the big draws. The place all but shuts down on Sunday, when practically everyone heads to the beach.

Puerto Vallarta was a tiny fishing village blessed with a stunning natural backdrop when director John Huston filmed "The Night of the Iguana" on location in 1963. The torrid romance between star Richard Burton and tagalong Elizabeth Taylor—both of whom were married to others—titillated millions and generated an avalanche of publicity. Visitors came pouring in, hoping to glimpse a movie star, and an international destination was born. PV combines an idyllic locale with a full spectrum of resort amenities.

Ixtapa and Zihuatanejo are twin resorts, only 4 miles apart but decidedly different in atmosphere. Ixtapa, created in the early 1970s, has an upscale but planned look; Zihuatanejo, founded by Spanish *conquistadores* in the early 16th century, is much more down-home.

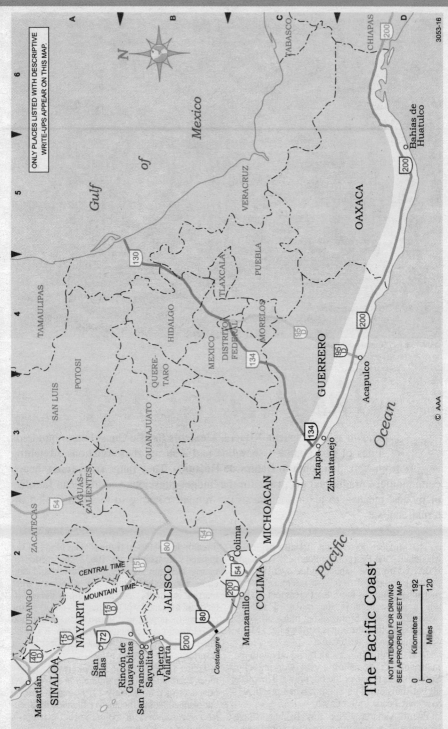

The Pacific Coast

NOT INTENDED FOR DRIVING
SEE APPROPRIATE SHEET MAP

0    Kilometers    192

0    Miles    120

ONLY PLACES LISTED WITH DESCRIPTIVE
WRITE-UPS APPEAR ON THIS MAP.

3053-16

© AAA

Certainly Acapulco fulfills the scenic requirements for a tropical resort. Lofty mountains and green foothills extend to the sparkling blue of bay and ocean waters. Tall palm trees stand silhouetted against picturesque sunsets. And the view of Acapulco Bay at night, set off by thousands of city lights, is breathtaking.

Rounding out the Riviera is Bahías de Huatulco, built along a series of bays that scallop the Pacific coast like a necklace of aquamarine jewels. Located on the Pacific Coast in Oaxaca, one of Mexico's poorest states, Huatulco is visited mostly by Mexican families, European tourists, diving enthusiasts and backpackers.

AAA recommends that travelers consult online U.S. State Department travel advisories when planning traveling abroad. Find this information at http://travel.state.gov/content/passports/english/alertswarnings/mexico-travel-warning.html.

# Acapulco

**City Population:** 789,971
**Elevation:** 13 meters (43 feet)

## Editor's Picks:

Acapulco Historical Museum........*(see p. 198)*
La Quebrada .........................*(see p. 198)*
Pie de la Cuesta ....................*(see p. 199)*

© Rafal Kubiak / Shutterstock.com

**Note:** For current information about safety/security issues in Acapulco, refer to the U.S. State Department website (travel.state.gov).

Acapulco has been around since the turn of the 16th century, when it was established as an authorized trading port between the Americas and Asia and galleons laden with exotic goods began sailing back and forth across the Pacific. But it wasn't until 1927 that a road was cut through the rugged Sierra Madre Mountains, connecting Mexico City to this unremarkable fishing village located on a sheltered bay. And when international air service was established in 1964, Acapulco was catapulted head-first into the resort age.

In the 1960s and '70s this was Mexico's most notorious party spot, the darling of the international and Hollywood jet sets. Movie stars like John Wayne, Johnny Weissmuller, Elizabeth Taylor and Rita Hayworth lounged at luxurious hotels. Elvis Presley and Ursula Andress had "Fun in Acapulco," a 1963 movie starring the King as a lifeguard and hotel singer who serenaded audiences with the ditty "Bossa Nova Baby." The shore along Acapulco Bay was transformed into a 9-mile swath of glitter and indulgence patronized by *la gente bonita* (the beautiful people).

Take a random poll today and you'll likely find that Cancún is Mexico's beach of choice for many tourists. But the city retains its popularity, especially among Mexicans. The weather is always balmy, and the water is warm enough for swimming year-round. November is one of the nicest months to visit, as high-season prices haven't yet kicked in. Formality can be left at home with your coat; standard attire consists of shorts, T-shirts and the occasional scandalous bathing suit.

Acapulco doesn't have dignified historical monuments. It's a big city and an important commercial center, but the economy depends most heavily on the tourist trade. In addition to letting life's cares melt away at the beach, water recreation and watching the *clavadistas* (cliff divers) hurl themselves from the top of La Quebrada are some of the city's favorite diversions.

As is the case at some of Mexico's other resort destinations, there are two Acapulcos. The flashy, pretty Acapulco along the immediate bayfront caters to tourists, while the Acapulco that spreads over the hills above the beaches—poverty ridden, with dusty, potholed streets and little police protection—is where many of the taxi drivers, chambermaids, waiters and other workers who depend on the tourist industry live. It also is where almost all of the city's highly publicized incidents of drug-related violence have taken place.

But it's a heady place if you have money to burn. Big resort hotels shepherd guests to private villas bedecked with fresh flowers and offer some of Mexico's most impressive swimming pool complexes. And alfresco tables at intimate little restaurants like Su Casa—tucked away on a mountainside with a swooning view of Acapulco Bay—turn dining out into a romantic special event.

## Getting There

### By Air

Acapulco International Airport is about 23 kilometers (14 miles) southeast of the city and the hotel

Getting There — *starting on this page*

Getting Around — *starting on p. 195*

What To See — *starting on p. 196*

What To Do — *starting on p. 198*

Where To Stay — *starting on p. 448*

Where To Dine — *starting on p. 449*

© prochasson frederic / Shutterstock.com

zone, near Puerto Marqués. Major carriers frequently fly into Mexico City, where connections can be made to Acapulco.

United offers seasonal nonstop flights from Houston. Providing service from Mexico City are Aeroméxico, phone 01 (800) 021-4000 (toll-free long distance within Mexico), and Interjet, phone 01 (800) 011-2345 (toll-free long distance within Mexico). Charter flights from Canada are available seasonally. *For additional information about airlines see Arriving by Air, page p. 42.*

Best Day is an airport shuttle/taxi service that transports visitors from the airport to the city's hotel zone along Costera Miguel Alemán. The 30-minute ride in a shared minivan *(colectivo)* costs about $18-$22 (U.S.) per person; a non-shared cab starts at about $60, depending on the destination. Phone 01 (800) 237-8329 (toll-free long distance within Mexico) or (800) 593-6259 (from the United States).

## By Car

From Mexico City, toll highway Mex. 95-D, the Autopista del Sol (Sun Highway), is by far the quickest and best option. Between Mexico City and Cuernavaca the funnel highway is toll Mex. 55-D. Mex. 95-D splits off from old Mex. 95 near Puente de Ixtla, proceeds south to Chilpancingo and Tierra Colorada, and then on to the international airport. Total driving time is a little over 4 hours.

The four-lane, largely traffic-free highway twists and turns through beautiful valleys and around mountainous curves. Signs denote scenic stops. About halfway to Acapulco a suspension bridge 600 feet above a river affords a spectacular view; acrophobes will probably want to keep their eyes shut.

The one drawback to traveling this well-maintained, 415-kilometer (257-mile) route is the cost. There are six toll plazas with a total charge of about 450 pesos (about $33 U.S.). Tolls must be paid for and gas must be purchased in pesos. The highway is economically out of the question for the average Mexican driver; most of the traffic is luxury buses, long-distance trucks and tourists willing to pay for convenience.

Mex. 95, an older, free highway, begins at Mexico City and proceeds south through Cuernavaca, Taxco, Iguala and Chilpancingo to Acapulco, roughly paralleling toll Mex. 95-D. It's scenic, but also very winding.

Acapulco is a long way from the United States; from McAllen, Tex., one of the closest U.S. border points, the distance is nearly 900 miles.

## By Bus

First-class *(ejecutivo)* buses operated by Tres Estrellas de Oro make daily runs on the Autopista del Sol between Mexico City's southern bus terminal and Acapulco; the trip takes 5 to 6 hours and costs about $30 (U.S.) one way. This bus line also has service to

# The Informed Traveler

## WHOM TO CALL

**Police (emergency):** Dial 060 and ask to be connected to an English-speaking operator.

**Police Assistance:** (744) 485-0650. English-speaking tourist police on the streets wear white uniforms and safari hats and are very helpful to tourists.

**Highway Patrol (Policía Federal de Caminos):** (744) 486-0647 or (744) 485-0439

**LOCATEL:** (provides assistance in locating vehicles or missing persons, or to those in need of public services): (744) 481-1111

**Hospitals:** Hospital Privado Magallanes, Calle Wilfrido Massieu #2, (744) 485-6544; IMSS (Mexican Social Security Hospital), downtown at Av. Cuauhtémoc #95, (744) 483-5550; Red Cross (Cruz Roja), Av. Ruíz Cortines #126, (744) 485-4100. Most hotels have an in-house doctor or a doctor on 24-hour call.

**Local Phone Calls:** Many public phones take Ladatel/Telmex credit cards only. They can be purchased in stores and other locations that display the Ladatel logo.

## WHERE TO LOOK

### Newspapers

The bigger hotels offer *USA Today*, the *New York Times* and the *Los Angeles Times*.

### Publications

Sanborn's, a Mexican restaurant chain, has English-language books and periodicals. There are branches on Boulevard Miguel Alemán near Playa Condesa and in the old downtown area.

### Visitor Information

**Guerrero State Tourism Office (Secretaría de Fomento Turístico):** Boulevard Miguel Alemán #4455, in the Acapulco International Center (Centro Internacional de Acapulco). **Phone:** (744) 484-2423 (English may not be spoken).

**State Attorney General's Tourist Office (Procuraduría del Turista):** Boulevard Miguel Alemán #4455 (in the Acapulco International Center). The office provides maps as well as tourist assistance daily 8 a.m.-11 p.m. **Phone:** (744) 484-4416.

## WHAT TO KNOW

### Currency Exchange

Most banks along the Costera, both in the downtown area and the hotel zone, are open Mon.-Fri. 9-5 (some also Sat. 10-2). *Casas de cambio* (currency exchange houses) line the Costera in the vicinity of the big hotels; these are open daily and often until 8 p.m. ATM machines are plentiful and accept international credit cards; withdrawals are in pesos.

### Staying Safe

If you leave your hotel, stick to areas frequented by visitors; in Acapulco this means the beaches and tourist-oriented businesses along Costera Miguel Alemán. The old downtown area is also safe during daylight hours. Tourists often are targeted for petty theft; stay alert if you happen to be in a crowded public place, like a market. Never carry large sums of money or personal valuables and always keep your hotel room key with you, preferably in a hidden pocket or other safe place.

Taxco, Ixtapa and Zihuatanejo. Buses coming from Mexico City on Friday and departing Acapulco on Monday are often very crowded. **Note:** This highway is very steep and winding in places. *For additional information about buses see Bus Service, page p. 52.*

## By Cruise Ship

Due to ongoing Mexican drug cartel violence and wary American tourists, many major cruise lines have omitted Acapulco from their Pacific Mexico itineraries. At press time (May 2015), Oceania Cruises and the Norwegian Cruise Line still occasionally visit the city, docking at Puerto Acapulco near the old downtown area. Your ship's excursion manager can book you on a tour of the city; onshore visits typically include Fort San Diego (across the street from where the cruise ships are moored); La Quebrada, where the cliff divers perform; the city market; and the Mercado de Artesanías (flea market).

## Getting Around

### City Layout

Acapulco is divided into three main sections. The oldest part, appropriately referred to as Old Acapulco (or "Tradicional") fills a peninsula that forms the western side of the bay. This is where locals as well as U.S. and Canadian retirees attend to their daily business. It's compact, bustling and has a very Mexican feel, a striking cultural contrast to the more tourist-oriented parts of the city.

The downtown waterfront contains the docks and fishermen's wharves, reminders of Acapulco's continuing importance as a commercial port. This is where both cruise ships and smaller fishing boats dock. Historic Fort San Diego is in this area. Old Acapulco also includes Caletilla and the other city beaches as far east as the first hotel high-rise.

Boulevard Miguel Alemán runs through the Dorado (or Golden Zone) section of the city. This wide boulevard following the northern shore of Acapulco Bay is also called the Costera and was named for the former Mexican president who was responsible for initiating much of the city's resort development. Luxury hotels, restaurants, shops, family-oriented attractions and beaches like Playa Hornos and Playa la Condesa are located in the Golden Zone, which continues as far as the Las Brisas hotel, east of the junction with Mex. 95 (the highway to Taxco and Mexico City).

Beyond this point is the newest section, Punta Diamante (the Diamond Zone). Here the coastal drive is called the Carretera Escénica and continues along Acapulco Bay toward Puerto Marqués and the airport. Another group of luxury hotels, like the Acapulco Princess and the Fairmont Pierre Marqués, are clustered in the Punta Diamante area.

As in many other parts of Mexico, streets change names frequently and street signs are difficult to locate. Orient yourself by using the Costera as a reference point—the great majority of Acapulco's accommodations, restaurants and nightspots are on or a short distance off it.

© Humberto Ortega / Shutterstock.com

## Rental Cars

Hertz is one of several rental car agencies with offices in Acapulco. Be sure you fully understand the terms of any rental contract. Some luxury hotels provide jeeps for their guests.

**Note:** AAA/CAA members enjoy discounts through Hertz for vehicles booked in the United States. Consult your local AAA/CAA club or phone Hertz, (800) 654-3080.

## Buses

Local buses connect the city with the beaches and various points of interest; fares are inexpensive (7 pesos), and the newer tourist buses are air-conditioned. If you are taking a bus to one of the outlying areas, such as Pie de la Cuesta or Puerto Marqués, find out when and where to board the last bus going back into town. Buses run regularly all along the Costera, and maps at covered bus stops illustrate routes to major hotels and tourist attractions. Stay alert while on the bus and beware of pickpockets, who sometimes target foreign tourists.

## Taxis

Taking a *sitio* taxi associated with your hotel is more expensive but also much safer, especially after dark. VW taxis as well as the yellow-and-white cabs that cruise the streets picking up passengers for a negotiated rate are not recommended, as robberies can occur. A list showing the rates for *sitio* taxis is usually posted in the hotel lobby.

## Parking

Old Acapulco has narrow streets and is better suited to walking than driving. It is illegal to park anywhere along Miguel Costera Alemán. An easier alternative is to use city buses or take a taxi where you want to go.

## Guides/Tours

With the focus on sunning, shopping and eating out, a guide is not really necessary in Acapulco. If you do hire one, make certain he or she is a reputable, bonded guide licensed by the State Department of Tourism. Guides can usually be found in the lobbies or at the entrances of the more expensive hotels.

Better yet, take an organized excursion. A standard city tour, a day trip to Taxco or an evening tour of the city's nightclubs are all easily arranged. Local tour operators often have desks at the large hotels. Acuario Tours is a representative company. Their office is at Costera Miguel Alemán #186-3; phone (744) 469-6100.

## What To See

**CATHEDRAL OF OUR LADY OF SOLITUDE** (Catedral Nuestra Señora de la Soledad) stands at the n. end of Plaza Juan Alvarez, the Zócalo. The cathedral's appearance—complete with an onion-shaped blue dome and Byzantine towers—is a bit misleading; it was constructed in 1930 from parts of an uncompleted movie theater. The simple interior features a yellow-tiled floor, blue and white walls, religious statues and an image of the Virgin of Solitude, patron saint of Acapulco. This is a fully functioning church, and visitors should be respectful of worshippers.

Palm trees tower above the plaza, a local meeting place where vendors peddle their wares and people stop and socialize or read the newspaper over a cup of coffee. Band concerts take place on Sundays. This is the oldest part of the city (appropriately referred to as Old Acapulco, or "Tradicional"). The neighborhoods in the vicinity of the plaza are lined with vintage, architecturally interesting houses, making the streets conducive to a pleasant early evening stroll. **Hours:** Cathedral open daily; mass times vary. **Cost:** Free.

**CHAPEL OF PEACE** (La Capilla de la Paz) is off Costera Miguel Alemán in the exclusive Las Brisas residential neighborhood. Standing high on a hilltop, this modern, non-denominational open-air chapel is distinguished by a white cross standing 130 feet tall, a landmark that can be seen from almost anywhere in the city. Overlooking the southern end of Acapulco Bay at an elevation of 1,200 feet above sea level—the city's highest point—the chapel grounds offer spectacular views and the best photo ops in town. Cascading water and well-kept gardens add to the beauty of this peaceful spot.

The best way to visit the chapel is to hire a driver/guide for the steep drive to the mountaintop, complete with glimpses of beautiful homes precariously perched on hillsides. The best time to go is in the evening in order to witness the sun setting over the bay. For a truly stunning photo, stake out a spot near The Hands of Brotherhood (Las Manos de la Hermandad) sculpture; the clasped hands provide a perfect framing feature. **Hours:** Chapel open daily 10-1 and 4-6. Grounds open daily dawn-dusk. **Cost:** Free.

**EL ROLLO ACAPULCO** is on Costera Miguel Alemán at Calle Cristóbal Colón. This water park contains a wave pool, waterslides, swimming pools with water pistols and boats, and a small aquarium. There also are shows featuring performing dolphins and seals. The most popular activity is swimming with dolphins, which includes a half-hour orientation and another half hour of swimming time. **Hours:** Daily 10-6. **Cost:** (includes inner tube for water slides) 200 pesos (about $14.80 U.S.). Admission packages including food and drink also are available. One-hour dolphin swim 1,600 pesos (about $120 U.S.); reservations are required. **Phone:** (744) 484-1970. [T]

**FORT SAN DIEGO** (El Fuerte de San Diego) stands on a hill e. of the main square in Old Acapulco, overlooking the harbor and the oldest section of the city's port. Originally built in 1616 as a series of ramparts to ward off Sir Francis Drake and other marauding pirates, the fort was extensively damaged by an earthquake and rebuilt in 1776 as a stout, star-shaped fortress. In 1813, during the War of Independence, Gen. José María Morelos attacked the fort; after a 4-month

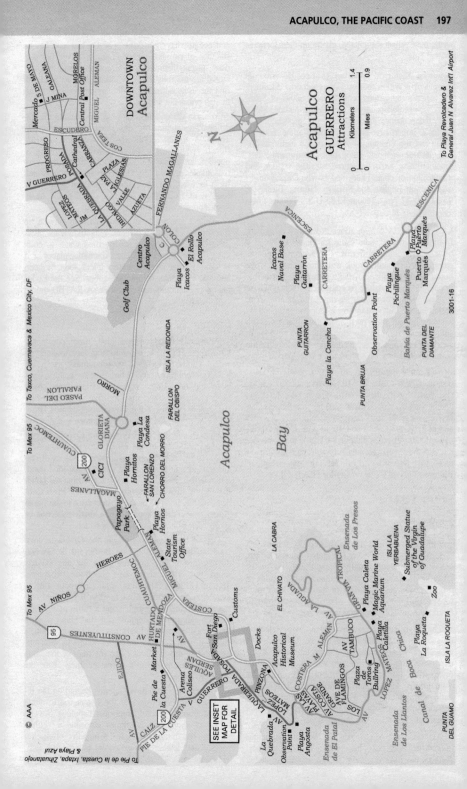

DOWNTOWN ACAPULCO

Mercado 5 DE MAYO
MORELOS
GALEANA
J MINA
Central Post Office
MIGUEL ALEMAN
ESCUDERO
CARRANZA
Cathedral
COS TERA
PROGRESO
INSURG
PLAZA
IGLESIAS
HIDALGO
VALLE
PAZ
AZUETA
V GUERRERO
LA QUEBRADA
LOPEZ
J M MATOS

Acapulco GUERRERO Attractions

FERNANDO MAGALLANES

Kilometers
Miles
0          0.9          1.4

To Playa Revolcadero &
General Juan N Alvarez Int'l Airport

ESCENICA

Centro
Acapulco
COLON
C COLON

El Rollo
Acapulco
Playa
Icacos

Icacos
Naval Base
Playa
Guitarrón

ESCENICA
CARRETERA
CARRETERA

Puerto O Playa
Marqués  Puerto
Marqués

Playa
Pichilingue

Observation Point

PUNTA
GUITARRÓN

Bahía de Puerto Marqués

PUNTA DEL
DIAMANTE

Golf Club

ISLA LA REDONDA

FARALLON
DEL OBISPO

Playa la Concha

PUNTA BRUJA

3001-16

To Taxco, Cuernavaca & Mexico City, DF

PASEO DEL FARALLON

MORRO

GLORIETA DIANA

Playa La
Condesa

FARALLON
DEL MORRO

To Mex 95

CUAUHTEMOC

200

CICI

Playa
Hornitos

FARALLON
SAN LORENZO
CHORRO DEL MORRO

Acapulco Bay

MAGALLANES

AV

Papagayo
Park

Playa
Hornos

State
Tourism
Office

HEROES

To Mex 95

AV NIÑOS

95

AV CONSTITUYENTES

MIGUEL ALEMAN

COSTERA

Customs

Ensenada
de Los Presos

LA CABRA

ISLA LA
YERBABUENA

Submerged Statue
of the Virgin
of Guadalupe

Magic Marine World

Playa Caleta

Aquarium

Zoo

EL CHIVATO

LA LAGUNA

VIA TROPICAL

GRANDE

AV M ALEMAN

AV TAMBUCO

Playa
Caletilla

Playa
La Roqueta

Playa
La Roqueta

ISLA LA ROQUETA

HURTADO
DE MENDOZA

CUAUHTEMOC

AV

Pie de la Cuesta
Market

Arena
Coliseo

AGUILAS
ROSADA

GUERRERO

PINZONA

LA QUEBRADA
PIE DE LA CUESTA

200

CALZ

AV

EJIDO

© AAA

To Pie de la Cuesta, Ixtapa, Zihuatanejo
& Playa Azul

Fort
San Diego

Docks

Acapulco
Historical
Museum

PINZONA

COSTERA M ALEMAN

AVE DE
FLAMINGOS

AVE GRANDE

AV COSTA

PALLAS

LOS

Plaza
Toros
Bullring

LOPEZ MATEOS

Boca
Chica

Canal de

Ensenada
de Los Llantos

PUNTA
DEL GUAMO

La
Quebrada

Observation
Point

Playa
Angosta

Ensenada
de El Patal

SEE INSET
MAP FOR
DETAIL

V GUERRERO

LOPEZ MATEOS

AV

siege, the Spanish capitulated, giving up their lucrative trading base.

**Acapulco Historical Museum** (Museo Histórico de Acapulco) is within the fort. Various rooms document the region's indigenous peoples, the exploits of Spanish *conquistadores* and swashbuckling pirates, Mexico's independence from Spain, and especially Acapulco's importance along the trade route between Spain and the Philippines. Artifacts and items on display include cannons, navigational instruments, religious artifacts, Asian-influenced Mexican textiles, and a collection of china plates and bowls. Display information is in English and Spanish. **Hours:** Tues.-Sun. 9-6. **Cost:** 52 pesos (about $3.85 U.S.). **Phone:** (744) 482-3828.

**LA QUEBRADA** is high above downtown Acapulco; from the cathedral, take Calle La Quebrada about 4 blks. w. Watching cliff divers *(clavadistas)* plunge from atop this natural rock wall into a narrow cove bordered by treacherous rocks some 135 feet below is perhaps the signature Acapulco experience. These fearless young men (after saying a prayer at a small shrine on the cliffs) stand on a ledge illuminated by a spotlight and then perform a dive that relies on split-second timing; the tide fills the cove with swirling surf and then recedes quickly, leaving the water level as low as 12 feet for a brief period.

You can watch the divers from a public observation deck next to the El Mirador Acapulco hotel; arrive early for the best views. The hotel's La Perla restaurant also offers meal seatings for the evening performances. **Hours:** Divers perform daily at 12:45 and at 7:30, 8:30, 9:30 and 10:30 p.m. **Cost:** Observation deck 40 pesos (about $3 U.S.); many people also tip the divers, as they rely solely on tips in return for providing death-defying entertainment. **Phone:** (744) 483-1260 (Mirador Hotel). 🍴

## What To Do

### Dining

Although Acapulco has its share of local hangouts dishing up tacos and other regional Mexican fare, it's worth getting casually dressed up (no tie or jacket, but no shorts or jeans either) and splurging at a hotel restaurant. The view of the bay from a rooftop establishment at dusk, when city lights start to twinkle, is reliably breathtaking.

The bigger hotel restaurants offer a wide selection of standard international and trendy fusion cuisine as well as local specialties. Prices tend toward the expensive side (dinner for two without drinks, wine or tip will be upwards of $60), but food quality and a luxurious setting help compensate. Atmosphere and entertainment vary with the establishment. Dinner rarely begins before 9 p.m., although some hotel restaurants begin serving around 6 or 7.

Along Costera Miguel Alemán there are numerous *palapa* (thatch-roofed) places with a seafood menu and a funky air. Look for those where people are eating

and not just having a drink. The Costera also has no shortage of rib and hamburger joints, where big portions, potent libations, wild decorations and a wilder crowd are the rule. Those homesick for fast food will find the usual American outlets lining the Costera, although prices are not cheap.

You can get an authentic Mexican meal at the traditional restaurants around Plaza Alvarez in Old Town Acapulco. Typically the *comida corrida* (lunch special) is a bargain, with soup, rice or noodles, an entree and dessert or coffee for a very reasonable price. Neighborhood street stands sell fresh seafood, but use caution when purchasing any food item from street vendors—if it's *not* fresh, your stomach could regret it.

In most restaurants it is customary to leave a tip *(propina)* of 10 to 15 percent. Establishments catering to tourists normally use purified water to cook vegetables and wash produce. At smaller places or if in doubt, order bottled water, juice, soda or beer, and ask for drinks without ice cubes. See the Lodgings & Restaurants section for AAA-RATED dining establishments.

### Shopping

Artesanías Finas de Acapulco, more commonly known as AFA-ACA, is a one-stop department store where you'll find carved wooden masks, folk art, jewelry, furniture, onyx chessboards, pottery, luggage and other items. Quality varies, from cheap mass-produced souvenirs to fine craftsmanship. AFA-ACA is just off the Costera on Avenida Horatio Nelson, near the downtown Sanborn's.

Plaza Bahía, on the bay side of Costera Miguel Alemán just west of the Hotel Crowne Plaza Acapulco, is an enclosed mall with stores and small restaurants on four levels. There's also a fast-food court, a movie theater and a bowling alley; within the bowling alley is a bar and a sports book facility. Plaza Condesa, on the bay side of the Costera next to the Fiesta Americana Villas Acapulco, has a small collection of sportswear, swimwear and fashion outlets.

One of the nicest malls is in the Diamante area. La Isla Shopping Village on Boulevard de las Naciones (just a few minutes from the airport) has more than 150 shops and boutiques (Lacoste, Tommy Hilfiger, Quiksilver), plus Liverpool, a high-end Mexican department store. You'll also find restaurants, a cinema multiplex and a turtle pool. For a fee you can go for a gondola ride that glides along a man-made waterway. Everything is laid out along a canal in a landscaped setting of fountains and outdoor cafes, and if it looks like the mall of the same name in Cancún, there's a reason: they share the same developer.

Another snazzy mall is Galerías Diana, on the inland side of the Costera at the Diana traffic circle (across from the Hotel Emporio Acapulco). Several levels of shops and boutiques surround a vaulted atrium. The movie multiplex Cinépolis offers bar service and leather lounge chairs outside the individual theaters. There's also a video arcade for kids, slot machines and a sports book for grown-ups and a Starbucks outlet (on the main floor of the atrium) for homesick coffee aficionados.

La Gran Plaza, on the inland side of the Costera facing Playa Icacos (near the El Rollo Acapulco water park), has six different "plazas" spread out on two levels. Retailers range from fashion boutiques and jewelry stores to craft shops run by Huichol Indians, and there also are drugstores, currency exchange offices, travel agencies and other businesses. The mall has plenty of ATMs as well. There's a nice food court and a game-oriented playground for kids.

Most hotels have their own specialty shops; the plush shopping arcade at the Fairmont Acapulco Princess is worth stopping by just to ogle the merchandise. Some establishments may shut down in the early afternoon for the traditional long lunch break from about 2-4 p.m.

## Beaches

Acapulco Bay is anchored by a commercial port at one end and a naval base at the other. Still, there is plenty of room in between for a swath of sand that is broken only by a few rock outcroppings, and more secluded beaches stretch northwest of the bay along the Pacific coastline. Keep in mind that all beaches in Mexico are federally owned property and therefore public, even stretches that may seem private because they are in front of one of the big hotels.

Chairs, umbrellas, showers, hammocks and refreshments are available at most locations; avoid isolated beaches. Due to unpredictable or rough surf conditions, the beaches facing the open Pacific—northwest of more protected Acapulco Bay—are better suited for watching the sky turn a pretty pink at sunset or taking a romantic stroll along the shore than for swimming. The following beaches are listed alphabetically.

**PIE DE LA CUESTA** is about 16 km (10 mi.) n.w. of Acapulco off Mex. 200. This village (its name means "foot of the hill") is an easy day trip by car or taxi. The open beach stretches for about 6 miles; on the opposite side of the coastal road is the large expanse of Coyuca Lagoon, its shoreline edged with palms and mangroves. It's a nice place to chill out in a hammock, although crashing breakers and treacherous currents make swimming or body surfing very risky, and there are no lifeguards.

Much safer—and a popular daily ritual—is watching the sun set. Families line up rows of chairs, and vendors mill around selling snacks and trinkets. If there are clouds, the patterns of color are often magnificent; if the sky is clear the Pacific turns to pale gold as the sun drops below the horizon.

**PLAYA CALETA** is along the peninsula in Old Acapulco. Caleta Beach and its twin, Playa Caletilla, were the jet setter beaches of choice in the 1960s, but today they cater more to families. The ocean water is very calm here, since the island of La Roqueta deflects the brunt of Pacific currents. Inner tubes and other water sports equipment can be rented.

La Roqueta can be reached by a 15-minute trip aboard a motorboat or glass-bottom boat. It's a peaceful place to sunbathe, snorkel, windsurf or just take a walk to the lighthouse. Beach chairs, inner tubes and canoes can be rented on the island.

Standing submerged in the harbor near La Roqueta is a bronze statue of the Virgin of Guadalupe. The shrine is best seen on a glass-bottom boat ride, as it is not easily visible from the surface. Round-trip boat tickets can be purchased at Caleta Beach; the boat stops for a look at the statue en route to the island. **Hours:** Boats to La Roqueta stop running around 5 p.m.

**PLAYA HORNOS** is just off Costera Miguel Alemán near Papagayo Park. Twin beaches Hornos and Hornitos are packed with tourists and families. Here the bay is calm, palm trees shade the sand and numerous casual, thatched-roof restaurants line the beach.

**PLAYA LA CONDESA** is in the center of the Golden Zone. Popular La Condesa Beach is crowded with attractive young singles flaunting daring swimwear—although you could say this about most Acapulco beaches—and is a place to watch parasailers do their adrenaline-fueled thing. The waves can get fairly big, which makes boogie boarding popular. Vendors hawking trinkets also roam this beach. There are numerous restaurants and bars along nearby Costera Miguel Alemán.

**PLAYA PUERTO MARQUÉS** stretches along a narrow neck of little Puerto Marqués Bay e. of Acapulco. The beach has a backdrop of mountains, the waves are gentle and suitable for swimming, water skiing and sailing, and seafood restaurants are literally at the water's edge. Another attraction is the drive along the Carretera Escénica (Scenic Highway), the eastward extension of Costera Miguel Alemán that winds past Icacos Naval Base; it offers magnificent views looking back toward the city and Acapulco Bay.

**PLAYA REVOLCADERO** is just beyond Playa Puerto Marqués. On the ocean side of the airport highway, Revolcadero Beach is popular for swimming and surfing, although the waves can be rough and there is a powerful undertow; stay close to shore. The long, wide strip of sand is ideal for a beachside horseback ride.

## Sightseeing

Acapulco's sights are scenic, not historic. Brightly decorated *calandrias* (horse-drawn carriages) regularly parade along Costera Miguel Alemán, and this is a leisurely way to tour the wide bayfront boulevard lined with beaches, hotels and restaurants.

The Historic Naval Museum of Acapulco has exhibits about Acapulco's role as a principal port of commerce on the Pacific coast. Displays include ancient and modern ship models and old drawings of the port. It's located near the intersection of Av. Costera Miguel Alemán and Calle Mateo F. Maury, a short distance south of the El Rollo Acapulco water park and across the Costera from the Real de

Cascadas Hotel; phone (744) 484-0356. **Note:** The museum is currently closed for renovations and a re-opening date has not been set.

Mexican muralist Diego Rivera asked art patron Dolores Olmedo, a longtime friend, to marry him after the death of his wife, painter Frida Kahlo. The Casa de Los Vientos (House of Winds) is surrounded by a wall covered with seashell murals that Rivera created while living here the last 2 years of his life. This small art museum and cultural center is occasionally open to the public for exhibitions, but the exterior murals can be viewed any time. The house is on Calle Inalámbrica in the La Pinzona neighborhood, in the old downtown area of Acapulco (a short cab ride from the central plaza).

Freshwater Coyuca Lagoon, near Pie de la Cuesta, is one of the most scenic spots in Acapulco, threaded with jungle-lined canals choked with masses of floating water hyacinths. Within the lagoon is Isla de los Pajaros, a bird sanctuary home to black and white herons, pelicans and marabou storks. Lagoon sightseeing cruises include lunch at a beachfront restaurant and time to walk along the beach or just laze in a hammock. Local travel agencies book tours, or check to see if your hotel offers an excursion.

Yachts that depart daily from the *malecón* offer morning, afternoon and moonlight cruises around Acapulco Bay. Tickets can be purchased at the boat or from any hotel travel agent. Lunch or dinner, music and dancing are frequently part of the package. The water also is a prime vantage point from which to view Acapulco's sunsets or the La Quebrada cliff divers. Glass-bottom boat tours of the bay are available at Caleta Beach and several other waterfront locations.

## Outdoor Recreation

Big-game **fishing** for marlin, sailfish, dolphin, barracuda, yellowtail, shark, red snapper and pompano is excellent all year. An international sailfish tournament takes place in October. Besides deep-sea fishing, there's freshwater fishing in Tres Palos Lagoon and Coyuca Lagoon. Small boats can be rented, with catfish the frequent catch. Favored spots for inland river fishing are along the Río Papagayo, east of Acapulco just beyond Tres Palos Lagoon, and the Río Coyuca, just beyond Coyuca Lagoon and west of Pie de la Cuesta.

Guides are available for hire, and fishing trips also can be arranged through your hotel or the Pesca Deportiva, near the dock across from the main square. Rates at the dock are negotiable; select a reliable outfit whose equipment is in good, safe condition. Deep-sea boats with experienced crews can be rented by the day; these excursions usually leave in the early morning and return in the early afternoon. Make arrangements ahead of time. A fishing license is required, but local companies frequently will take care of this for you.

Almost every type of **boating** can be enjoyed. Sailboats, speedboats, catamarans and other pleasure craft prevail on the bay. Yachts and deep-sea fishing vessels are available as well; some host sunset and moonlight cruises complete with champagne. Arrange boat rentals through hotels or travel agents. For larger vessels with fully-equipped crews, make reservations in advance. An information booth at Caletilla Beach rents canoes, paddleboats and other small craft and can arrange water skiing and scuba diving excursions.

**Swimming** in Acapulco Bay is popular due to the enticing hue of its waters. The rougher surf at Playa Revolcadero is favored by surfers. Pay particular heed to any warning flags posted, which can refer to hazardous water conditions or the occasional shark sighting. As an alternative, almost every hotel has a pool, if not several. Some of them are huge, set against a backdrop of rustling palms and tropical plantings, and have swim-up bars for the truly indolent. Luxury hotels feature private or semiprivate pools.

All of the major hotels offer **scuba diving** lessons and equipment. The waters off Roqueta Island are especially suited to diving. Acapulco Scuba Center provides dive packages with English-speaking instructors; phone (744) 482-9474. Boats for **water skiing** can be booked at hotels as well. The gentler waters at Puerto Marqués and Caleta Beach are good for beginners. Exhibitions of barefoot skiing can be viewed at Coyuca Lagoon. **Surfing** is not permitted in Acapulco Bay; the best place to surf is Revolcadero Beach, near Puerto Marqués.

Another popular sport is **parasailing,** although it is not without risks. From a standing position, a speedboat hauls a "sailor" to an altitude of more than 325 feet. This thrill can be had at almost any beach, although many parachute operators set up at La Condesa. **Windsurfing** is good at Puerto Marqués and also can be arranged at Caleta Beach. **Horseback riding** is best at Playa Revolcadero and Pie de la Cuesta.

## Nightlife

Acapulco's glitzy dance clubs feature elaborate light shows, mirrored walls, fireworks and dance beats pounding from state-of-the-art sound systems. The music ranges from techno to house to hip-hop to Top 40. They start hopping after 10:30 p.m. and stay open until the wee hours. A dress code is standard (jeans and T-shirts are usually frowned on). Cover charges are steep ($30 or more during the winter high season, less at other times), although they are sometimes waived to draw customers. Women normally pay a reduced charge. Bar drinks, of course, are extra.

One of the hottest hot spots is the Palladium, on Carretera Escénica (the Costera) at Las Brisas. High on a hillside, it has glass windows 160 feet wide that look out over Acapulco Bay, giving dancers the feeling of being suspended in mid-air. Lighting and sound are top of the line, and as a result there's always a line to get in. Baby'O, Costera Miguel Alemán #22, is a mainstay that has been around since the disco days of the '70s and is still going strong. The atmosphere here is akin to a very high-class cave pierced by laser lights, rumbling to the throb of techno, hip-hop and dance music.

The city's most celebrated nighttime attraction is the diving from La Quebrada cliff (*see attraction listing*). Professionally trained young men perform these spectacular dives, which date back to 1934, when La Quebrada first became a popular spot for local divers to display their talent.

A successful dive depends as much on timing as on skill, since a diver enters a channel less than 25 feet wide and must wait for an opportunity when the water is deep enough to permit a safe entry at a speed of about 55 miles an hour. Getting to the top of the cliff is risky as well—barefoot divers scale the steep, vertical cliffside by grasping at rocky outcrops that occasionally snap off. Evening dives feature blazing torches that enhance the theatrical effect.

The traditional place to view the cliff divers is from the bar or terraces of the La Perla restaurant at the El Mirador Acapulco hotel, but you'll be required to pay a cover charge (which includes two drinks) or have dinner. Reservations are advised during the winter high season; phone (744) 483-1260.

The major hotels frequently offer nightly entertainment, such as Mexican-style fiestas or theme parties. Live music accompanies the happy hour at these establishments, which also have the usual poolside cocktail bars and evening floor shows.

## Special Events

The year's greatest influx of visitors is during Holy Week and the week after, marked by several religious observances. Many local businesses close, and the city becomes so crowded that some people sleep on the beach. Those wishing to visit during this time should make reservations far in advance.

For music lovers the Festival Acapulco (Acafest), which takes place in May, draws participants from many countries. The offerings encompass everything from top-of-the-charts pop to traditional boleros, and are performed by orchestras, bands, trios and individual artists. Concerts are given at the Acapulco International Center, the Plaza de Toros bullring and at beaches, hotels and other open-air spots around the city.

The Virgin of Guadalupe is the focus of a nationwide pilgrimage on Dec. 12 to the Basilica of Our Lady of Guadalupe in Mexico City. The event, celebrated with dancing and other forms of merriment, is observed with special exuberance in Acapulco. Acapulco closes out the year with a huge party on New Year's Eve.

© dubassy / Shutterstock.com

This ends listings for Acapulco.
The following page resumes the alphabetical listings
of cities in The Pacific Coast.

## BAHÍAS DE HUATULCO, OAXACA
(D-5)

FONATUR, Mexico's government-funded tourist development agency, officially inaugurated Bahías de Huatulco (wah-TOOL-co) in 1988, selecting a 22-mile stretch of bays, coves and inlets as the site for a master-planned vacation getaway. But while its resort aspects are a recent development, the settlement of Huatulco has been around for quite awhile.

Zapotec, Mixtec and Aztec merchants established a trade route through this region during pre-Hispanic times, and the coastal settlement of Santa Cruz Huatulco became a thriving port and shipyard. By the late 16th century, however, Acapulco had absorbed the galleon trade, and pirate attacks brought about a further decline. Until recently, Huatulco and other small villages along this stretch of coast remained forgotten outposts.

Jagged boulders and small islands characterize this section of Mexico's Pacific coastline, much of which is backed by dense tropical forest. The resort area comprises nine bays in all. Thanks to their natural layout, large-scale development will be broken into a series of resort areas targeting budget, mid-range and upper-end travelers. Ecotourism is promoted heavily, and there are increasing opportunities for jungle hikes, river rafting, rappelling and other vigorous activities.

## Practicalities

Huatulco International Airport is off Mex. 200, about 19 kilometers (12 miles) northwest of the Tangolunda resort area. United flies nonstop from Houston. From Mexico City, both Aeromexico Connect, phone 01 (800) 021-4000 (toll-free long distance within Mexico), and Interjet, phone 01 (800) 011-2345 (toll-free long distance within Mexico) offer nonstop service. To those travelers arriving by air, Huatulco from above resembles more than anything a vast green carpet of jungle descending from the foothills of the Sierra Madre del Sur to the ocean shore.

The tropical feeling is reinforced by the airport's appearance. The two terminals—one for international flights, one for domestic flights—are large, *palapa*-style hardwood structures with high ceilings and thatched roofs. Unfortunately, arriving visitors may encounter roaming time share representatives; avoid their high-pressure sales tactics. *For additional information about airlines see Arriving by Air, page p. 42.*

Transportes Terrestres, phone (958) 581-9014, operates shared minivan *(colectivo)* service that shuttles passengers from the airport to the resort hotels; expect to pay about $12 (U.S.) per person. A private taxi (often a Chevrolet Suburban) is much more expensive—about $40 and up, depending on the amount of luggage you have—and drivers can be aggressive about soliciting fares.

Taxi service also links the three separate areas of Tangolunda, Santa Cruz and La Crucecita. Cabs wait in front of the big hotels and also congregate around the plazas in Santa Cruz and La Crucecita. Fares average about $5 (U.S.) from La Crucecita to Tangolunda and $3 from Santa Cruz to Tangolunda or Santa Cruz to La Crucecita. Rates are posted at the travel booth on the main plaza in La Crucecita.

Since Huatulco is spread out and also has a good road network, a rental car can come in handy for exploring as well as for trips to nearby destinations. AAA/CAA members can reserve a rental car through their local club; it is recommended that you make all necessary arrangements prior to your departure. It also helps to know the peso equivalent of the dollar rate you are charged, since the charge in Mexico will be in pesos.

The climate is tropical, with an average annual temperature of 82 degrees. Temperatures in May, the hottest month, can reach 100. January through May is practically rainless; heavy rains fall July through September. As in Mexico's other Pacific coast resorts, the "winter" months, December through March, are the sunniest, driest and least oppressive. Mosquitoes can be fierce all along the coast. Pack an effective insect repellent or pick up Autan Classic, a widely available Mexican brand.

## Beaches and Recreation

From east to west, the nine bays of Huatulco are Conejos, Tangolunda, Chahué, Santa Cruz, El Organo, El Maguey, Cacaluta, Chachacual and San Agustín. Conejos, Tangolunda, Chahue, Santa Cruz, El Maguey and El Organo are accessible by car; others can be reached only by boat. Bahía Conejos has minimal tourist facilities but offers excellent snorkeling, diving and fishing at its four beaches.

Luxury hotel development in Huatulco is focused along Bahía Tangolunda, which means "place where the gods live" in the Zapotec dialect. High-rise buildings are absent—no structure here is more than six stories tall. As a result, the Mediterranean-, Moorish- and Mexican-style resorts that hug the bay offer unobstructed views from many different vantage points. Careful attention has been given to paving and landscaping, with sculptured rocks separating the roads running to and from the resort properties.

Several beaches line this bay, including Playa La Hierbabuena, Playa del Amor (Love Beach), Punta Paraiso and Playa La Entrega, where a coral reef lies just a few feet offshore. Most of the resorts are all-inclusive, with shuttle service to the beach and such diversions as themed evening shows and Mexican Fiesta nights.

Bahía Chahué (Chah-WAY) is the largest of the nine, with three separate stretches of sandy beach and a marina catering to private yachts. Many hotel employees live in La Crucecita, a planned town and residential area a mile or so inland off Mex. 200. Its main square, while not particularly authentic, is attractive, graced with a central bandstand, brick walkways, green lawns, shade trees and white stone benches.

Surrounding this plaza are modest hotels, restaurants and shops specializing in Oaxacan handicrafts.

The area is lively in the evening, when locals and tourists mingle at the restaurants and in the square.

Bahía Santa Cruz is the site of the original fishing settlement of Huatulco. Day cruises to the other eight bays depart from the marina here; arrangements can be made at your hotel or through local travel agents.

The village of Santa Cruz has a shady main square surrounded by shops, restaurants, bars and a few Mexican-style, middle-class hotels. Playa Santa Cruz, the main beach, is a short distance from the marina. It has clear, calm water and refreshment facilities, making it a pleasant spot to snorkel or simply lay around after lunch. Nearby Playa Yerbabuena and Playa La Entrega are accessible by boat, either an outboard motor-propelled *panga* (skiff) or a deluxe cruise vessel.

Bahía El Organo has gentle surf, nearby parking facilities and a few open-air *palapa* restaurants. The four westernmost bays—El Maguey, Cacaluta, Chachacual and San Agustín—were designated a national park in 1998, protecting them from commercial development, although they can still be visited. Cacaluta and Chachacual have long, deserted stretches of beach; San Agustín is excellent for diving. All of the beaches boast lovely golden sand and pristine water, the result of a sewage system that permits nothing to be dumped into the ocean.

In the mountains above Huatulco are coffee plantations begun by German immigrants. The tropical highlands in the vicinity offer ideal conditions for growing coffee, an evergreen shrub native to East Africa.

The best way to enjoy the cove-pocked coastline is to take a cruise. Boat tours visit El Maguey and Chachacual bays, with time for swimming or snorkeling and lunch on the beach. Guided kayaking trips explore the Copalita River, which winds into the nearby mountains.

Isla La Blanquita, off Bahía Santa Cruz, looks white from a distance, crowded as it is with seagulls, ducks, pelicans and albatrosses. Bahía El Organo's U-shaped Playa Violín has very fine sand and gentle waves not unlike a natural swimming pool. El Bufadero, a blowhole in a shoreline cliff, occasionally spouts jets of water; the aptly named Stone Face is a rock formation just above the water.

Surf conditions can fluctuate greatly at Tangolunda Bay; heed the colored flags posted along the beach that advertise swimming conditions. Tangolunda and Santa Cruz bays have the most extensive equipment rental facilities. Among the prettiest beaches are Bahía Chahué's Playa Esperanza and Playa Tejón, and Bahía Chachacual's Playa la India. Swimming is best at Conejos, Tangolunda, Santa Cruz, El Organo and El Maguey bays.

The easiest way to arrange most activities is through a travel agency. Bahías Plus has offices in the major hotels and offers various tours, including snorkeling, diving and sport-fishing trips, sunset cruises, bird-watching excursions, ATV jungle adventures, wildlife observation eco-tours, and day trips to Puerto Angel and Zipolite Beach. The all-purpose "Huatulco Discovery" sightseeing tour includes a swim at El Maguey Bay, a stop in downtown La Crucecita and time out for shopping.

If necessary, bring comfortable shoes, sunblock, insect repellent and/or a bathing suit or change of clothes. Expect to get dusty riding in an ATV. Some excursions are advised only for those in good physical condition. Bahía Plus agency's main office is at Av. Carrizal #704 in La Crucecita; phone (958) 587-0216.

## Dining and Nightlife

Dining choices in Huatulco are not necessarily limited to the expensive hotel restaurants. Restaurant Ve El Mar, on the water's edge at Playa Santa Cruz, is a casual, friendly place serving lobster, ceviche, shrimp and other seafood dishes.

Airy, colorfully decorated El Sabor de Oaxaca, Avenida Guamúchil #206 in La Crucecita (just east of the plaza, in the Hotel Las Palmas), features such regional fare as chicken in *mole* sauce, *tlayudas* (big corn tortillas with cheese and other toppings), *chiles rellenos* (stuffed chiles) and tamales. Café Huatulco is on the plaza in Santa Cruz (near the marina). It serves a variety of caffeinated concoctions utilizing good locally grown coffee, and also sells whole beans.

As far as nightlife goes, most of the hotels have their own bars, and the bigger ones stage Mexican Fiesta nights. **Note:** Finding a cab late at night can be difficult. Make any necessary arrangements for transportation back to your hotel before stepping out for the evening.

One local hangout that has been around awhile is the La Crema Bar, Calle Gardenia #311 (on the main plaza in La Crucecita, across from the Hotel La Flamboyant). You can't miss the guitar-playing dude hanging from the outside of the building. The inside is colorful and kitschy, with a bar serving everything from *cervezas* to tequila shots. Loud rock and occasional live bands draw a young crowd, but the festive atmosphere is fun for all ages, and the bar is a good place to mingle with locals.

**Huatulco Hotel and Motel Association:** office (Asociación de Hoteles y Moteles de Huatulco) is at Blvd. Benito Juárez #8 (in the Crown Pacific Huatulco hotel). The staff can provide information about a variety of local excursions, including day trips to Puerto Escondido and Puerto Angel. The office is open Mon.-Fri. 9-6, Sat. 9-1; phone (958) 581-0486, or (866) 416-0555 (from the United States). **Phone:** (958) 581-0176.

**NATIONAL MEXICAN TURTLE CENTER** (Centro Mexicano de la Tortuga) is about 12 km (7 mi.) west of Puerto Angel on the Puerto Angel-San Antonio highway, in the small seaside village of Mazunte. It is dedicated to the ongoing preservation of endangered sea turtle species inhabiting Mexican coastal waters. Prior to 1990, when the government imposed a ban on turtle hunting, the local economy depended upon the slaughter of turtles for their meat and leathery hides; the center's opening refocused efforts toward conservation. Sea turtles are on view in large tanks.

Guided tours in English are available. **Hours:** Wed.-Sat. 10-4:30, Sun. 10-2:30. **Cost:** about 35 pesos ($2.60 U.S.). **Phone:** (958) 584-3376.

## Nearby Destinations

Northwest of the airport off Mex. 200, sitting at the foot of the jungle-carpeted Sierra Madre del Sur, is Santa María Huatulco, which functioned as a trade center for the coastal region during pre-Hispanic times. Today the town serves as the governmental center for the different districts that make up Huatulco. It is about 10 kilometers (6 miles) from the airport and west of the developed bays; watch for the marked turn-off on Mex. 200.

Unlike the resort area, Santa María Huatulco has the look of a typical Mexican small town. Activity centers on the main square, where there is a museum housing an interesting collection of masks. Also on the square is the 18th-century, red-and-white cathedral; inside is a fragment of wood that is said to be part of Jesus' cross.

A day trip can be made to the coastal town of Puerto Angel, about 49 kilometers (30 miles) west of Huatulco via Mex. 200 to the town of Pochutla, then about 12 kilometers (7 miles) south on the Puerto Angel-San Antonio highway. Buses travel from Huatulco to Pochutla, from which a taxi can be taken to Puerto Angel. This small fishing village was rebuilt after being severely damaged by Hurricane Pauline in 1997. The beaches are rocky but pretty, and the bay is dotted with *pangas*—small, motor-propelled skiffs.

Morning activity centers around Playa Principal and the town pier, where fishing boats arrive with the day's catch. The most popular in-town swimming and sunning beach is Playa Panteón, where there are sandy-floored *palapa* eateries and an oceanfront graveyard filled with colorful tombstones.

Playa Zipolite, about 5 kilometers (3 miles) west of Puerto Angel toward Mazunte, is one of the few beaches in Mexico where nudity is tolerated. In addition to *au naturel* sunbathers (who congregate at one end of the beach), Zipolite attracts a young crowd of surfers and backpackers. Strung along the sand are huts where one can eat, drink or just lounge in a hammock. Camping is permitted at the beach's trailer park. If you do venture here, don't bring anything valuable, as petty theft is common, and avoid walking on the beach after dark. The undertow is treacherous, so swimming is not advised.

## COLIMA, COLIMA (C-2) pop. 146,904

Although the city of Colima (koh-LEE-mah) is little visited, it makes a very pleasant day trip from Manzanillo and a nice break from the beach. The 70-minute drive—via the Manzanillo-Colima toll highway to the town of Tecomán, then north on

Mex. 110—passes beautiful tropical and mountain scenery. If you don't have a car, trips to Colima can be arranged through travel agencies at Manzanillo resorts *(see What To Do under the Manzanillo listing)*. The toll fee is about $6.75 (U.S.); have pesos on hand to pay the charge.

Colima itself lies in a fertile valley. Although tropical in appearance, it is cooler than the lowlands along the coast. The Río Colima divides the city in two, running through tropical fruit orchards and clusters of coconut palms (the region is an important producer of coconuts, bananas and lemons). Entering the city via Mex. 110 from Manzanillo, the first landmark visitors see is the King Colima Monument, a sculpture erected in 1955.

What makes Colima especially enticing—besides the notable cleanliness of its streets and parks—is the carefully preserved colonial atmosphere of the town center. Many of the downtown buildings were constructed in the neoclassic style during the later years of dictator Porfirio Díaz's regime. Earthquakes in 1932 and 1944 leveled some of the structures, which were later rebuilt.

Jardín Libertad, the main plaza, is located between avenidas Francisco I. Madero, Miguel Hidalgo, Santos Degollado and Reforma. The plaza, landscaped with palm trees and tropical shrubs, has walkways lined with white wrought-iron benches and fountains shooting streams of water. A domed gazebo stands at its center. Beneath arcades on the north and south sides of the plaza are shops and commercial businesses.

The Government Palace *(see attraction listing)* is on the plaza's east side. Bordering the west side is the cathedral (Catedral Basilica Menor de Colima), built by the Spanish in 1527 and subsequently rebuilt several times. The Hidalgo Theater (Teatro Hidalgo), a block southwest of Plaza Principal at the corner of Degollado and Independencia, was completed in 1883 and reconstructed after earthquakes in 1932 and again in 1941. The opulent interior has a 19th-century elegance. For theater schedule and ticket information phone (312) 312-1231.

Four blocks east of the main plaza between avenidas Benito Juárez and Revolución is Jardín Nuñez, a park with lush greenery that makes it a good spot for relaxing. For lunch try Samadhi, about 2 blocks north of Jardín Nuñez on Avenida Filomena Medina (where it branches off Avenida Juárez). This vegetarian restaurant has a shady courtyard and serves a tasty, inexpensive *comida corrida*. Have a *licuado* (fruit shake) or juice rather than taking a chance on the water.

Just south of the House of Culture complex *(see attraction listing)*, on the east side of Calzada Pedro Galván, is Piedra Lisa Park (Parque La Piedra Lisa). The name means "sliding stone," and those who do slide on the namesake rock will supposedly return to Colima one day.

The Main Bus Terminal (Central Camionera Foránea), also called Terminal Nuevo, is a little over a mile east of the city center via Avenida Guerrero to Avenida Niños Heroes.

About 7 kilometers (4 miles) north of Colima (via Avenida Herrera out of town) is the village of Comala ("the place of the griddles"). It's a quick trip by car or bus; "suburban" buses leave from the Central Camionera Suburbana station at Plaza Colimán, on the western outskirts of town via Carretera a Coquimatlán.

Comala was once known as El Pueblo Blanco ("The White Town") for its white buildings (although with red-tiled roofs). Passing time in the central plaza, with its benches and shade trees, makes for a pleasant afternoon outing. A group of small restaurants on the plaza's south side serve a variety of *botanas,* or appetizers, for the price of potent Mexican libations. As the afternoon lingers on, the square fills with the sound of music as mariachi bands try to outdo each other for customers' business.

The Sociedad Artesanías Cooperativa Pueblo Blanco, a short walk south from the Comala town center, is a factory and crafts school. Local artisans create colonial-style wood furniture and ironwork using traditional methods, and good buys are possible.

Twin volcanoes just 3 miles apart are the focus of Volcán Nevado de Colima National Park, about 40 kilometers (25 miles) north of the city via Highway 16 (the road to the villages of Comala, Suchitlán and San Francisco). Dormant Volcán Nevado de Colima, 14,365 feet tall, has flanks cloaked with forests of conifers.

Neighboring Volcán de Fuego, on the other hand, has acted up numerous times since a disastrous eruption in 1941. The most recent major outburst occurred in June 2005, spewing rocks and lava, necessitating the evacuation of nearby villages and creating spectacular night scenes for intrepid photographers. In early 2015, this 12,989-foot-tall volcano erupted three times, covering towns as far as 15 miles away in ash.

From May through July orchids line the paved, winding road to the tiny village of San Antonio, just outside the national park. The clear, dry winter months, when the volcanoes are snowcapped, is the best time for viewing them. Experienced mountaineers often hike or climb to the summit of Nevado de Colima.

**Colima State Tourism Office (Secretaría de Turismo):** is inside the Government Palace building on the west side of the main plaza. Open Mon.-Fri. 8:30-8, Sat. 10-2. **Phone:** (312) 312-4360 (English spoken).

**COLIMA REGIONAL HISTORY MUSEUM** (Museo Regional de Historia de Colima) is on Calle 16 de Septiembre at Av. Reforma, on the s. side of Jardín Libertad, the main plaza. It exhibits archeological and craft displays and a group of pre-Hispanic ceramics (primarily dogs and human figures), smaller than the collection at the Museum of the Western Cultures but just as fascinating. **Hours:** Tues.-Sat.

9-6. **Cost:** 51 pesos (about $3.80 U.S.). **Phone:** (312) 312-9228.

**GOVERNMENT PALACE** (Palacio de Gobierno) is on the w. side of the main plaza. Built between 1884 and 1904, it has a cool inner courtyard. Covering four walls around an interior staircase is a mural by Jorge Chavez Carrillo illustrating scenes from Mexican history, beginning with the Spanish conquest and ending with the 1910 Revolution.

**HOUSE OF CULTURE** (Casa de la Cultura) is at Calzada Pedro Galván and Av. Ejército Nacional, about half a mile e. of the main plaza; it is most easily reached by bus. This is the University of Colima's arts center. The modern buildings of this extensive complex include a theater and an art gallery displaying a permanent collection of paintings by Colima artist Alfonso Michel, all set among landscaped grounds. Temporary art exhibits and traditional music and dance performances are regularly scheduled; contact the State Tourism Office for information.

**Museum of the Western Cultures** (Museo de las Culturas de Occidente) is part of the Casa de la Cultura complex. It has a superb collection of pre-Columbian pottery and artifacts. Male and female statues depict many aspects of daily life in pre-Hispanic western Mexico. Noteworthy are the Izcuintli, or "Colima dog" figurines, playful representations of dancing canines. Deposited in the tombs of the departed, they were said to guide the dead in the journey toward *tlalocan* (paradise). Exhibit information is in Spanish.

The museum's cafe has a smoky ambience accentuated by Salvador Dalí posters hanging on the walls. **Hours:** Tues.-Fri. 10-1:30 and 4-6, Sat.-Sun. 2-8. Phone ahead to confirm schedule. **Cost:** 15 pesos (about $1.10 U.S.). **Phone:** (312) 314-1533.

**LA CAMPANA RUINS** are on the city's n.w. edge in the village of Villa de Alvarez, next to the Technological Center on Av. Tecnológico, following signs. The earliest remains of this important pre-Hispanic settlement are believed to date from around 1500 B.C. Seven pyramid-like buildings and a tomb have been excavated; structures No. 5 and 6 are the largest, and Structure No. 7 has a tunnel tomb beneath it. Buses run from downtown Colima to the site.

Background information is presented in Spanish and English. **Time:** Allow 30 minutes minimum. **Hours:** Tues.-Sun. 9-6. **Cost:** 47 pesos (about $3.50 U.S.). **Phone:** (312) 313-4945.

**UNIVERSITY MUSEUM OF POPULAR ARTS** (Museo Universitario de Artes Populares) is about 8 blks. n. of Plaza Principal at calles 27 de Septiembre and Manuel Gallardo. Here the emphasis is on traditional masks; there also are displays of musical instruments, textiles and furniture. Exhibit information is in Spanish. **Hours:** Tues.-Sat. 10-2 and 5-8, Sun. 10-1. **Cost:** 20 pesos (about $1.50 U.S.). **Phone:** (312) 316-1000.

## COSTALEGRE, JALISCO (B-1)

The Costalegre (Happy Coast)—also known as the Costa Careyes, or Turtle Coast—extends from Chamela south to Barra de Navidad. A few expensive, exclusive, secluded resorts catering to the wealthy are tucked among a string of modest beach towns that are popular weekend getaways for residents of Guadalajara.

By car, take Mex. 200 south from Puerto Vallarta. (Buses traveling between Puerto Vallarta and Manzanillo also make stops along the coast.) At Boca de Tomatlán, south of Puerto Vallarta, the road swings inland, bypassing Cabo Corrientes (the southern tip of Banderas Bay) before nearing the Pacific again in the vicinity of Chamela. Although not strictly a coastal route, the highway does offer occasional views of the ocean.

The scenery is varied—hills spiked with cactus give way to palm groves as the route winds south, and views shift from craggy mountains to waterfowl-filled lagoons. Many of the villages, beaches and private resorts along the Costa Alegre are accessed from dirt roads branching off Mex. 200.

The village of Chamela sits on bluffs overlooking Bahía Chamela. First settled in 1525, it served as a fortified anchoring ground for Spanish galleons returning from the Orient. Sea turtles and good-sized oysters inhabit the local beaches. During February and March, huge flocks of migrating sea birds settle on the small islands in the bay. A few rustic bungalows, restaurants and campsites accommodate travelers.

The next major development is Costa Careyes, where an all-inclusive resort development and luxury villas are situated along a series of rocky, jungle-edged coves protected from the open ocean. Further south is the tranquil, mile-long beach at Tenacatita, which is reached by a 8-kilometer (5-mile) dirt road turn-off. There are a number of restaurants at the western end of the beach.

The most popular stretch of the Costalegre is anchored by the towns of Barra de Navidad and San Patricio Melaque (meh-LAH-keh), just north of the Colima state border. They lie about 2 miles apart along the shore of crescent-shaped Bahía de Navidad, which is edged by a long, curving beach. Small, inexpensive hotels and thatch-roofed restaurants line the beach, known for its blazing sunsets. This area is much less crowded during the week than it is on weekends (and particularly during the Easter and Christmas holidays).

Barra de Navidad, on a sandbar lying between the bay and a lagoon, is the more picturesque of the two towns and the one most dependent on tourism. While not luxurious, it has more upscale accommodations than San Patricio Melaque. Hotels line Avenida Lopez de Legazpi, the beachfront street (although it is actually a short walk to the beach from most of them).

The redbrick-tiled Zócalo, on Calle Jalisco, is part of a pedestrian mall closed to traffic. This plaza is the place to relax, browse the many small shops (tiendas), have a cup of coffee or a cold cerveza, or perhaps have your hair braided by one of the local women. A street market sets up along Calle Guanajuato between avenidas Veracruz and Tampico on Thursdays.

There are views of the bay and beaches along the length of the malecón (sea wall), where pangas (small open-air ferries) and yachts can be seen entering and leaving the harbor. On the ocean side of the malecón stands "Triton & Nereida." The sculpture commemorates the 400th anniversary of the discovery of the Philippine islands by a Spanish expedition that departed from this area in 1554.

The panga docks are at the south end of Avenida Veracruz, on the lagoon side of the sandbar. The local cooperativa—an association of individual boat operators—is further up the street. They can arrange fishing excursions, a tour of the lagoon or a quick trip across it to one of the half-dozen seafood restaurants in the little village of Colimilla. Lagoon tours are about 220 pesos (about $16.30 U.S.).

Local buses connect Barra de Navidad with San Patricio Melaque, toward the northern end of Bahía de Navidad. Melaque, with its main plaza, church, municipal market and bus station, is more like a typical Mexican town, and has a greater number of hotels in the budget range.

## IXTAPA/ZIHUATANEJO, GUERRERO (C-3)

Ixtapa (eeks-TAH-pa) and Zihuatanejo (see-wah-tah-NEH-ho) are geographically close resorts on Guerrero's Pacific coast, but they are altogether different in character. Ixtapa materialized in the 1970s, largely through the efforts of FONATUR, the Mexican government's tourism development agency. Zihuatanejo, in contrast, was a quaint little fishing town long before its northern neighbor's first lofty hotel rose from the sand. While Ixtapa indulges visitors with luxurious amenities at world-class hotels, Zihuatanejo beguiles them with centuries-old traditions and—despite its own increased growth—a relaxed village feel.

Like Cancún, Ixtapa appeals to the traveler who craves a getaway from daily concerns. Beauty and pampering come with a price, of course, but for those willing to pay it, the big-league resort trappings definitely satisfy. With Ixtapa's air-conditioned luxury and Zihuatanejo's down-to-earth informality, vacationers have the best of both worlds.

## Practicalities

Ixtapa-Zihuatanejo International Airport is off Mex. 200 (referred to as the Carretera Costera, or Coastal Highway), about 10 kilometers (6 miles) east of Zihuatanejo and 17 kilometers (10.5 miles) southeast of Ixtapa. United, phone 01 (800) 900-5000 (toll-free long distance within Mexico), flies direct from Houston, with connecting flights linking other U.S. cities.

Alaska Airlines, phone 01 (800) 252-7522 (toll-free long distance within Mexico), and Delta, phone 01 (800) 266-0046 (toll-free long distance within Mexico) offer seasonal nonstop service from Los Angeles. In addition, a handful of U.S.-based carriers offer seasonal service from Dallas, Phoenix and Denver. Aeroméxico, phone 01 (800) 021-4000 (toll-free long distance within Mexico), offers flights to Mexico City, where connections can be made to Zihuatanejo on AeroméxicoConnect. *For additional information about airlines see Arriving by Air, page p. 42.*

Fixed-price *colectivos* (minivans) shuttle groups of passengers from the airport to hotels in either Ixtapa or Zihuatanejo. Tickets are purchased at the transportation desk in the arrival area. It will cost slightly more for a ride to Ixtapa. Private taxis from the airport are more than twice as expensive. Arrange transportation back to the airport through your hotel.

Taxis are a convenient way to shuttle between Zihuatanejo and Ixtapa's Hotel Zone (about a 10-minute ride), but they're expensive. It costs at least $7 (U.S.) to travel between the two, and fares average about $4 within each town. Rates go up after midnight. Current rates are posted in hotel lobbies. Fortunately, both the Hotel Zone and downtown Zihuatanejo are easily negotiated on foot. Regardless of where you're going, agree to a fare before getting in the cab.

City buses run frequently between Ixtapa and Zihuatanejo. The fare is inexpensive, about 90c (U.S.) one way. Buses make numerous stops along Boulevard Ixtapa; in Zihuatanejo, they stop near the intersection of avenidas Morelos and Benito Juárez, some 3 blocks north of the city market.

Currency can be exchanged at banks and *casas de cambio* (exchange houses). Banks usually have the best rates and are open Mon.-Fri. 9-1. A Banamex branch is at the corner of Ejido and Vicente Guerrero in downtown Zihuatanejo. In Ixtapa, there are 24-hour Banamex automatic teller *(cajero automático)* machines on Boulevard Ixtapa next to the Hotel Fontan and at other locations. In Zihuatanejo, there are ATMs at Ejido and Vicente Guerrero and on Benito Juárez in the Comercial Mexicana, as well as several other locations. The machines accept Mastercard or Visa and dispense pesos.

For assistance or in case of an emergency, contact the Ixtapa tourist police; phone (755) 554-5360. The Red Cross (Cruz Roja), in Zihuatanejo, provides 24-hour ambulance service; phone (755) 554-2009. Major hotels should be able to provide the names and phone numbers of English-speaking doctors.

The average annual temperature at this tropical location is a balmy 79 degrees. Summers are hot, with temperatures ranging from the upper 70s to the low 90s. The winter months—high tourist season—are slightly cooler, with lows in the low 70s, highs in the upper 80s. The rainy season, from June through October, turns the normally brown countryside a brilliant green. The rain frequently falls at night, guaranteeing sunny days almost all year. Pacific hurricanes occasionally strike this section of the coast.

## Layout

An impressive string of high-rise hotels, surrounded by clusters of palms, make up Ixtapa's Hotel Zone, which fronts broad Palmar Bay. Boulevard Ixtapa is the main street and runs behind the hotels. On the other side of this thoroughfare are a number of small shopping malls. At the Hotel Zone's eastern end is the Ixtapa Golf Club. Almost anything of interest to visitors will be on either side of Boulevard Ixtapa.

About a mile before the end of the Hotel Zone (if you're heading north), a road branching to the right off Boulevard Ixtapa leads to Mex. 200, and also is the way to get to Playa Quieta, Playa Linda and other beaches north of Ixtapa proper (watch for signs indicating the destination). Boulevard Ixtapa itself ends in a traffic circle at the 450-acre Marina Ixtapa complex, where luxury villas and condominiums share space with a 622-slip yacht marina, the Marina Golf Course and a dockside promenade lined with restaurants. Overlooking the marina is El Faro, an 85-foot-tall tower that offers a 360-degree view of the surrounding area.

Ixtapa is connected with Zihuatanejo, about 7 kilometers (4 miles) to the southeast, by Mex. 200, which is referred to as the *carretera*. Zihuatanejo, or "Zihua," spreads along the shores of oyster-shaped Bahía de Zihuatanejo, a naturally protected harbor. Less than 2 miles wide, this is one of the more picturesque bays along Mexico's Pacific coast.

Zihuatanejo's small downtown lies north of the bay; to the east are unobstructed beaches and the foothills of the Sierra Madre del Sur. Locals and tourists alike congregate along the *malecón* (waterfront promenade), officially called Paseo del Pescador. In Zihuatanejo, the basketball court fronting the

---

## DID YOU KNOW

Mexico is a young nation, gaining independence from Spain 45 years after the United States broke free of England.

beach right in the center of town takes the place of the traditional Mexican main square.

East-west Avenida Juan Alvarez, a block north of and paralleling the *malecón*, is one of the main traffic arteries; it takes traffic out of the commercial area while Avenida Ejido, a block farther inland, takes traffic in. The main north-south thoroughfares are 5 de Mayo, Cuauhtémoc (which is pedestrian-only for a couple of blocks), Vicente Guerrero and Benito Juárez.

Hotels perch atop the cliffs surrounding the bay. A clifftop *mirador* (lookout point) along Camino a Playa la Ropa, the road that connects Zihuatanejo and La Ropa Beach, offers a spectacular view of the town and the bay. A bronze plaque (in Spanish) commemorates the first commercial maritime expedition that departed from the port, bound for the Philippines.

## The Beaches

The coastline between Ixtapa/Zihuatanejo and Acapulco is known as "La Costa Grande" because of its broad, open beaches. The swath fronting the Ixtapa Hotel Zone is called Playa el Palmar. The dramatic arc of white sand forms a wide curve, with clusters of rock formations rising from the offshore waters. This beach faces the ocean, and the surf is rough at times. At the eastern end of the Hotel Zone, near the Ixtapa Golf Club, is Playa Vista Hermosa. Between Ixtapa and Zihuatanejo is secluded Playa Majahua.

Outboard motor-powered skiffs *(pangas)* depart from the small jetty at Playa Linda, several miles up the coast, for the 10-minute boat ride to Isla Ixtapa, a short distance offshore. This is a pleasant place to spend a day sunning, snorkeling or diving; basic snorkeling gear is available for rent. Playa Cuachalalate, the main beach, is lined with *palapa* restaurants.

Round-trip tickets for the boat ride to Isla Ixtapa can be purchased at the Playa Linda pier landing for around 40 pesos (about $3.20 U.S.). The last boats depart back to the mainland around 5 p.m.; keep your ticket stub for the return trip. It's recommended to take a boat displaying the local *Cooperativa* emblem.

Zihuatanejo's main beach is Playa Principal, a sandy stretch in front of the *malecón* (Paseo del Pescador). At the *malecón's* western end is the town pier *(muelle)*. Local fishermen store their boats and gear on the sand after returning with the morning's catch. At the western end of the *malecón*, a concrete bridge crosses a narrow canal; to the south is the Puerto Mío resort and marina.

Just east of Playa Principal and the main part of town is Playa la Madera (Wood Beach). The name is a reference to the time when wood cut from mountain forests was shipped back to Spain. Small hotels, private bungalows and restaurants crowd Cerro la Madera (Madera Hill), which rises behind the narrow beach. A bayside footpath (known as "Continuación del Paseo del Pescador") cuts

through the rocks and is a pleasant walk if not attempted at high tide, when you're bound to get wet. Also avoid the footpath after dark.

Particularly pretty is Playa la Ropa (Clothes Beach), on the protected eastern side of the bay and a 5-minute taxi ride from downtown Zihuatanejo. The name refers to the cargo of silks that were strewn all over the beach when a Spanish galleon shipwrecked here. Palm trees fringe the mile of soft white sand, and several sand-floored, thatch-roofed eateries offer both seafood and Mexican cooking. Playa la Ropa is good for swimming, water skiing, jet skiing, parasailing and windsurfing. A steep rock bluff separates this beach from Playa la Madera.

Divers and snorkelers head for the crystalline waters of Playa las Gatas, which is reached by boat. Harmless nurse sharks once populated the shallow, rocky bay bottom, hence the name. There are a number of open-air restaurants here. Small, canopied *pangas* depart from Zihuatanejo's town pier for the scenic 10-minute ride across the bay to the small dock at Las Gatas. Round-trip tickets cost around 40 pesos and can be purchased at the *Cooperativa* office at the head of the pier. These "water taxis" run frequently; keep your ticket stub for the return trip.

## Outdoor Recreation

Sailfish is the pre-eminent big-game catch in these offshore waters, along with blue and black marlin, dorado (mahi-mahi) and yellowfin tuna; smaller species like barracuda, grouper, roosterfish, Spanish mackerel and wahoo also put up a spirited fight. An environmentally friendly tag-and-release policy is promoted.

The Boat Cooperative (Cooperativa de Lanchas de Recreo) at the Zihuatanejo town pier can arrange an excursion. Prices vary based on the size of the boat and the number of people and can be negotiated with the boat owners. Most of the boats depart the bay by 7 a.m. and return around 3. Your hotel may be able to arrange a fishing trip, although it will cost more.

Ixtapa Aqua Paradise arranges local scuba trips. Visibility is best from May through December, although diving is possible year-round. Scuba sites range from shallow reefs to submerged shipwrecks to canyons 100 feet below the surface. Night dives and certification courses also are available. The dive center is located in the Hotel Barceló Ixtapa Beach at the south end of the hotel zone. For information and reservations phone (755) 555-2078.

Yates del Sol's trimaran *Picante* departs from Zihuatanejo Bay for a 4.5-hour sailing and snorkeling cruise to Playa Manzanillo, accessible only by boat. The trip includes lunch; snorkeling gear is available for rent. A 2.5-hour "magical sunset" cruise sails from the bay into the open Pacific for sunset watching, a view of Ixtapa's Hotel Zone and onboard hors d'oeuvres. Both cruises include an open bar and transportation from Ixtapa hotels. Reservations are required. Cruises can be arranged through a local travel agency, or phone Yates del Sol at (755) 554-2694 or (755) 554-8270.

Water and jet skiing, windsurfing and parasailing can be enjoyed at both Ixtapa and Zihuatanejo. Facilities and equipment rentals are usually available at Playa del Palmar, Playa la Ropa and Playa las Gatas. Surfers favor Playa Troncones, which faces the open ocean northwest of Ixtapa. **Note:** Make certain that parasailing is arranged only through a reputable outfit. Not all boat operators have the required level of experience, and accidents have occurred.

The Ixtapa Golf Club (Campo de Golf Ixtapa), at the eastern end of the Hotel Zone, extends to the ocean's edge. The grounds, lush with tropical vegetation, are considered a wildlife preserve and are home to numerous exotic birds. Crocodiles inhabit some of the water hazards, discouraging any attempts to search for balls lost in the drink; zoologists from Mexico City visit once a year and retrieve the largest specimens for relocation to Mexican zoos. Clubhouse facilities include a pro shop, restaurant and pool with a lounge deck. For reservations information phone (755) 553-1062.

Tennis courts are located at the Ixtapa Golf Club, the clubhouse at Marina Ixtapa, at the major Ixtapa hotels, and at the Viceroy Zihuatanejo hotel at Playa la Ropa in Zihuatanejo. Most courts are illuminated for night play; nonguests can usually play at the hotel courts for a fee.

At Playa Linda and Playa Larga, both northwest of Ixtapa's Hotel Zone, horses can be rented by the hour for rides along the beach or through one of the nearby coconut plantations. Sunset rides are especially nice (wear insect repellent). Local travel agencies can arrange a trip, or make reservations through Rancho Playa Linda; phone (755) 554-3085 (only Spanish is spoken).

A crocodile farm (*cocodrilario*) at Playa Linda provides the opportunity to observe these armor-plated reptiles in a jungle estuary habitat from the safety of an elevated boardwalk. A bike is the best way to explore Aztlán Ecological Park, near the Marina Ixtapa complex, a wildlife sanctuary inhabited by iguanas, turtles and various bird species.

## Shopping

There are no malls in the traditionally sprawling sense in either Ixtapa or Zihuatanejo. Instead, small complexes with (usually) air-conditioned shops line Boulevard Ixtapa, across the street from the big hotels. Fashionable resort wear, sportswear, jewelry, art and handicrafts fill the boutiques at Ixpamar, La Puerta, Las Fuentes and Los Patios, among other shopping plazas.

La Fuente, in the Los Patios shopping center, has a fine selection of talavera pottery, hand-blown glass, ceramics and papier-mâché figures. Mic Mac, in the La Puerta center, offers native handicrafts, embroidered clothing and wall hangings. All of the shopping centers contain restaurants and snack shops for those in need of refueling. Most of the stores are open daily; many of them close from 2-4.

Downtown Zihuatanejo has its share of souvenir stands and T-shirt emporiums, but it's also a good place to search out Mexican crafts. Shops and stalls line Paseo del Pescador and the adjacent streets. Mario's Leather Shop, Calle Vicente Guerrero #12, features custom-made saddles, hats, vests, purses and belts. Galería Maya, Av. Nicolas Bravo #31, and Arte Mexicano Nopal, just inland from the waterfront at Av. Cinco de Mayo #56, display such items as pewter frames, straw baskets, wooden sculptures and handmade leather bags.

Casa Marina, Paseo del Pescador #9 (near the main plaza), consists of five family-owned folk art and handicraft shops under one roof. There are displays of pottery, rugs, pillows, regional costumes, silver jewelry, hammocks, hand-painted lacquer boxes and masks created by Guerrero artisans. Visitors can observe weaving demonstrations at La Zapoteca, one of the stores. Within the complex is Café la Marina, where you can have a pizza and a beer and then browse through the large collection of used books for sale and trade.

Vendors hawk their wares at specially designated handicrafts markets. At the Mercado de Artesanía Turístico, on Boulevard Ixtapa across from the Bay View Grand condo development, there are numerous souvenir and handicraft stands. In Zihuatanejo, a similar tourist-oriented market is located along Calle 5 de Mayo across from the church. Families operate many of the stalls at these markets, producing hand-painted ceramics, seashell knickknacks and embroidered goods.

## Dining and Nightlife

For an expensive but reliably good dining experience, the Ixtapa Hotel Zone is an obvious choice. Zihuatanejo has a lower price range and a greater variety of eateries; imported fast-food chains are conspicuously absent. Fresh seafood—lobster, clams, squid, *huachinango* (red snapper) and a local specialty, *camarones al ajo* (garlic shrimp)—are on many Zihuatanejo menus.

La Sirena Gorda (The Fat Mermaid), on the *malecón* next to the town pier, is known for its fresh seafood tacos—fish, shrimp, octopus and conch—and also is a pleasant spot for breakfast. Nueva Zelanda, Calle Cuauhtémoc #23 (at Avenida Ejido), is casual and family-oriented, specializing in *tortas* (sandwiches), enchiladas and *licuados* (fruit shakes). There is a branch in Ixtapa as well (in the Los Patios shopping center).

*Pozole* is a hearty, hominy-thickened soup with a chicken or pork stock base. Toppings include avocado slices, chopped onion, white cheese, lettuce and cabbage; herbs and spices vary depending on who is making the *pozole*. Less adventurous diners will appreciate the fact that pickled pig knuckles are normally served on the side. The addition of chile peppers gives *pozole* three different colors—red, green or white. Thursday is the traditional day to eat this thoroughly Mexican dish, and most lunch spots in Zihuatanejo include it on their Thursday *comida corrida* menu.

Mexican "Fiesta Nights" are popular evening entertainment in Ixtapa during peak tourist season (December to March). They start around 7 p.m. with a lavish buffet spread, after which live music and folkloric dance performances are presented. The cost, about $35-$45 (U.S.) per person, normally includes dinner, drinks and the show. The Las Brisas Ixtapa and the Krystal hotel in Ixtapa both offer occasional fiestas in high season. Ixtapa's Sunscape Dorado Pacifico resort hosts a fiesta once a week in high season. The Barcelo Ixtapa Beach hotel presents entertainment year-round. Reservations or advance tickets are necessary; call the hotel or make arrangements through a local travel agency.

Casual is the standard attire in both Ixtapa and Zihuatanejo, although you'll want to dress up a little for an evening out at an expensive restaurant or fashionable nightspot. Most restaurants use purified water to make the ice in drinks (check to see if the cubes have holes). If in doubt, order bottled mineral water (the brands Agua de Taxco or Tehuacán are good), beer or a soft drink; the *limón* flavor of Yoli, a soft-drink brand sold only in the state of Guerrero, is similar to 7-Up. See the Lodgings & Restaurants section for AAA-RATED dining establishments.

Nightlife is concentrated in Ixtapa. Christine, in the Krystal hotel, has a laser light show set to music beginning at midnight; after that dancing takes over. Tiers of tables overlook the dance floor. The club is open only during the tourist high-season (spring) on Fridays and Saturdays. The doors open around 10:30 p.m.; there is a cover charge of about 300 pesos (about $22 U.S.). Shorts, jeans and tennis shoes are not allowed.

## Special Events

In February, the Zihuatanejo Sailfest features boat races and the requisite hoopla. The International Sailfish Tournament draws hardcore sports fishermen in May. Other sporting events include a national triathlon in Ixtapa in late May. Check with the convention and visitors bureau for specific dates, which tend to be erratic.

Cultural Sunday takes place every Sunday at the basketball court in downtown Zihuatanejo. Young children are in the spotlight at this delightful event, performing regional dances from all over Mexico in full, colorful costume. The festivities begin around 6 p.m.

**Convention & Visitors Bureau:** in Ixtapa in the Plaza Zócalo building, behind the Plaza La Puerta shopping center on Boulevard Ixtapa. Open Mon.-Fri. 9-2 and 4-7. Avoid booths with "Tourist Information" signs (found mostly at the airport), which are essentially pushing time-shared properties. **Phone:** (755) 553-1270.

**ARCHEOLOGICAL MUSEUM OF THE COSTA GRANDE** (Museo Arqueológico de la Costa Grande) is on the Zihuatanejo waterfront just off Av. Juan Alvarez (near Calle Vicente Guerrero). This small but nicely organized museum contains artifacts, pottery and paintings relating to the Costa Grande, the section of coastline between Zihuatanejo and Acapulco. Exhibit information is in Spanish.

**Time:** Allow 30 minutes minimum. **Hours:** Tues.-Sun. 10-6. Closed Christmas. **Cost:** 10 pesos (about 75c U.S.); free (ages 0-12). **Phone:** (755) 554-7552.

**DELFINITI IXTAPA** is at the n. end of the Hotel Zone, adjacent to the Posada Real Ixtapa hotel; from Blvd. Ixtapa, follow the driveway to the hotel and Dolphinarium. Three different encounters are offered. Visitors can stand on a submerged platform for an underwater observation, pet dolphins as they swim in front of you, or swim with them by holding onto their fins. There also is a dolphin encounter for children.

Before the dolphin encounter begins you can have your picture taken with colorful parrots. Guests are accompanied to an area with lockers and seating, and a brief instructional program about dolphin interaction is given. Photos are taken throughout the program and are available for purchase.

Dolphin encounters can be reserved by phone or booked through your hotel; a major credit card is required to hold a reservation. Programs are offered in English and Spanish. **Time:** Allow 1 hour minimum. **Hours:** Programs are given daily at 10, noon and 4. **Cost:** Dolphin encounter for kids ages 3-7 $62 (U.S.); underwater observation and petting encounters $82; 45-minute dolphin swim $124. Reservations are required. **Phone:** (755) 553-2736.

## MANZANILLO, COLIMA (C-1) pop. 161,420

Manzanillo (mahn-sah-NEE-yoh) began attracting foreign visitors in the 1970s, thanks to such natural attributes as twin bays, golden-sand beaches and a lush backdrop of tropical jungle. What really put this commercial port on the tourist map was the 1974 opening of Las Hadas, a luxurious vacation hideaway conceived by Bolivian tin magnate Antenor Patiño. Manzanillo gained further exposure when the hotel was chosen as the setting for the 1979 film "10," although for many the movie's most striking image was Bo Derek, her hair braided in corn rows, jogging down the beach.

## Practicalities

Playa de Oro International Airport is about 47 kilometers (29 miles) northwest of Manzanillo, on the way to Barra de Navidad. Inside the small terminal building are rental car counters, several shops and a restaurant. Alaska Airlines, United and US Airways fly nonstop from Los Angeles, Houston and Phoenix, respectively. All other major airlines servicing Manzanillo arrive via Mexico City.

The domestic commuter airline Aeromar, phone 01 (800) 237-6627 (toll-free long distance within Mexico), offers regular flights to Manzanillo from Mexico City. Charter packages to Manzanillo from various Canadian cities are available during the winter months; consult a travel agency for details. *For additional information about airlines see Arriving by Air, page p. 42.*

Transportes Turísticos Benito Juárez provides shuttle service from the airport. The fare averages about $20-$25 (U.S.) per passenger; phone (314) 333-1999. Make advance arrangements for a ride back to the airport upon your departure; a taxi ride between the airport and most hotels averages about $25 (U.S.).

First-class bus service from Manzanillo to Puerto Vallarta and Guadalajara is provided by ETN. The bus station is in the Santiago area, on Mex. 200 at Km marker 13.5. *For additional information about buses see Bus Service, page p. 52.*

From Guadalajara, Manzanillo can be reached by car via two-lane Mex. 80, which runs into coastal Mex. 200 at Barra de Navidad, or by toll highway Mex. 54-D, which passes through Colima. Driving on coastal road Mex. 200 from Puerto Vallarta is recommended only for the adventurous—particularly during the July-through-September rainy season, when downpours can create hazardous potholes and unexpected detours.

## City Layout

Downtown Manzanillo occupies a narrow isthmus at the southern end of Manzanillo Bay. It's a noisy, bustling jumble of shipyard activity and railroad tracks. There are few tourist amenities to be found here, although an ongoing port beautification project—undertaken to help establish the city as a port of call for cruise ships—has resulted in a landscaped promenade.

Jardín de Obregón, the main plaza, is at the north end of downtown overlooking the harbor, which is studded with Mexican military vessels. This small square has an elaborate bandstand and a gazebo. Near the plaza are courts where pickup basketball and *fútbol* games attract lively crowds of spectators. Avenida México, the city's main commercial thoroughfare, runs south from the plaza.

The resort area spreads out north and then west of town along the shores of twin bays, Bahía de Manzanillo and Bahía de Santiago. Manzanillo Bay encompasses the harbor and is where the reasonably priced hotels are located. Santiago Peninsula separates the bays. This tourist-oriented area has restaurants and shopping centers. The more luxurious homes, condos and resort properties are in the vicinity of Santiago Bay.

**Note:** Mex. 200 is referred to as the Santiago-Manzanillo Highway or the Costera Highway; the official name is Boulevard Miguel de la Madrid. There are three major crossroads along this highway: with the road to the Santiago Peninsula and Las Hadas resort; with the road to the Las Brisas Peninsula, the resort area closest to town (known as the *crucero*); and heading into downtown Manzanillo. Mex. 200 then continues southeast along the coast toward Colima.

Roads, many of them dirt, branch off Mex. 200, leading to resort and condominium developments. City buses (the newer ones are blue and white) make a circuit from downtown north along Mex. 200 and the shores of the two bays. Destinations are marked on the left side of the windshield; for example, "Centro" (downtown), "Las Brisas," "Las Hadas" or "Santiago." The fare is inexpensive—less than $1 (U.S.) from the main resort areas to downtown—and it's a convenient way to get a look at the coastline without driving.

## The Beaches

There are several beaches to choose from along the wide curve of Manzanillo's two bays. Playa las Brisas is the closest to town, although to reach it by road requires detouring around Laguna de San Pedrito to the narrow strip of land fronting Manzanillo Bay. Older hotels and restaurants line both sides of the bayfront drive, a popular destination for weekenders from Guadalajara.

Beyond Playa las Brisas is the long curve of golden-brown sand called Playa Azul. The water gets rougher heading north toward the Santiago Peninsula, and the bottom drops off sharply along much of this stretch, making it problematic for wading or swimming.

The water in Santiago Bay, which is not used for shipping, tends to be cleaner than at the beaches fronting Manzanillo Bay closer to town. One of the area's best swimming beaches is Playa la Audiencia, which occupies a pretty, sheltered cove below jungle-covered hills on the north side of the Santiago Peninsula. The rocky outcroppings here are one of Manzanillo's few good snorkeling spots.

Farther around Santiago Bay is Playa Miramar, popular with windsurfers and boogie boarders. Beyond Playa Miramar, the shoreline curves to form the Juluapan Peninsula. Here the water becomes tranquil and the beach is dotted with thatch-roofed souvenir shops. Locals crowd this area on Sundays.

Swimmers should exercise care due to occasional rough surf, and flags are posted at most beaches to indicate conditions. A red flag means potentially hazardous conditions; a white flag means safe conditions.

About 49 kilometers (30 miles) southeast of Manzanillo and accessible by bus is Playa Cuyutlán, a beach known for the *Ola Verde*, or "Green Wave." This mountainous wave—with crests that are said to reach 30 feet or more from March through May—seems to be more talked about than actually seen. The greenish hue is due to the glow of phosphorescent marine organisms.

Despite their color, the waves pounding this beach are impressive at any time. The black sand is the result of crushed volcanic rock. The long, open beach, backed by coconut palms, is all but deserted during the summer; lifeguards are normally present during the high season (December to May). Swimmers should heed the rough seas and strong undertows.

The village of Cuyutlán, which consists of a few budget hotels and a handful of seafood shacks, drowses away most days, although *Semana Santa* (Holy Week) brings an influx of Mexican families. Facilities are very basic, but it's an appealing day trip for those seeking solitude. To get there, take a local bus to the town of Armería, south of Manzanillo on Mex. 200; buses leave frequently from Armería for Cuyutlán. There is a signed turn-off for Cuyutlán on Mex. 200, about 5 kilometers (3 miles) north of Armería; it can also be reached via the Manzanillo-Colima toll highway (Mex. 200-D) that parallels the railroad line.

## Recreation

In Manzanillo it's easier to arrange activities like tennis, horseback riding, scuba and fishing trips, sunset cruises and golf outings if you're staying at an all-inclusive hotel that provides them. If not, try one of the local travel agencies, which have offices along Boulevard Miguel de la Madrid. They can arrange tours of the city and trips to such nearby destinations as Colima, the state capital, and Barra de Navidad.

The peak season for sport fishing in the self-proclaimed "sailfish capital of the world" is November through March. Marlin, dorado, tuna and wahoo can also be hooked. There are two annual fishing tournaments, one in November and one in January. Reservations for fishing excursions can be arranged through any of the resorts; booking as part of a group will lower costs.

Ocean Pacific Adventures offers deep-sea fishing excursions departing from the La Perlita dock in downtown Manzanillo; phone (314) 335-0605. They'll also cook your catch for free at the Colima Bay Café. Again, going with a group will be less expensive. Cheaper still are the *pangas* (outboard motor-powered launches) operated by individual owners; determined haggling can lower the fee.

Honeycombed with lagoons, the coastal region offers good bird-watching. Laguna de Cuyutlán, just south of Manzanillo, attracts different species depending on the season. Herons, pelicans and flamingos can be seen at Laguna de las Garzas (Lagoon of the Herons), the waterway separating the Las Brisas Peninsula from the mainland. The views here are especially nice at sunset.

The 18-hole La Mantarraya golf course, at the Las Hadas resort, offers plenty of water hazards, notably the water-encircled tee-off at the finishing hole. The course is open to the public, although hotel guests receive preferred tee times. To make reservations phone (314) 331-0101.

The 27-hole course at the Grand Isla Navidad Resort, about 30 kilometers (19 miles) north of the airport and a 45-minute trip from Manzanillo, was designed by Robert von Hagge. Laid out along the ocean, with breathtaking views at the 13th and 14th holes, the course is lushly landscaped and immaculately maintained; phone (314) 331-0500.

Tennis courts, all lighted for night play, are located at the following resorts: Gran Festivall, on Boulevard Miguel de la Madrid at Playa Miramar; Las Hadas Resort, on the Santiago Peninsula off Boulevard Miguel de la Madrid; and the Tesoro Manzanillo, on the Santiago Peninsula at Av. de la Audiencia #1.

Although Manzanillo is geared more toward relaxing at the beach than to sightseeing, its premier resort, Las Hadas, is an attraction in itself. Standing on the eastern side of the Santiago Peninsula, it resembles a Moorish village bristling with minarets, cupolas and turrets. If you're not a guest you can still stroll the luxuriously landscaped grounds, although restaurant reservations are needed to enter the property through the guarded gate. The marina here accommodates vessels for a fee, and adjacent to the marina is a calm bay where boats can be moored without a fee.

The University Museum of Archeology is on Avenida Niños Héroes a few minutes north of the downtown area, on the San Pedrito campus of the University of Colima. Displays include numerous metal and shell artifacts from western Mexico as well as fabrics, looms and fabric-making implements. Hours vary, so call ahead to make sure the museum is open; phone (314) 332-2256.

## Shopping, Dining and Nightlife

Clothing and gift boutiques pop up here and there along Boulevard Miguel de la Madrid, and there is a shopping arcade at the Las Hadas resort.

Vendors at the beaches peddle everything from jewelry to shell ornaments. Playa Audiencia has a group of vendor stalls, including one where you can have a weave of Bo Derek-style cornrow braids *(trensitas)* added to your natural tresses. More vendor stalls at Playa Miramar sell jewelry, beachwear and Mexican handicrafts.

The resort hotels all have reliably good (and reliably pricey) restaurants, but for fresh seafood in a casual atmosphere try Bigotes 1, Boulevard Miguel de la Madrid # 3157 (Mex. 200) at Playa Las Brisas. One of the house specialties is shrimp breaded with shredded coconut and then fried. American-owned Juanito's, on Boulevard Miguel de la Madrid at Km 14, Playa Olas Altas, is a relaxed hangout popular for breakfast as well as burgers, fries, crispy chicken tacos, ribs, milkshakes and fresh fruit smoothies. You also can check your e-mail and access the Internet here.

Casual dress is standard at Manzanillo restaurants (resort wear at the more expensive places). Keep in mind that a service charge may automatically be added to the bill (in addition to the 16 percent IVA tax). While purified water is used at the well-known restaurants, you might want to steer clear of the *enramadas* (beach shack restaurants) and outdoor taco stands unless you have a cast-iron stomach. See the Lodgings & Restaurants section for AAA-RATED dining establishments.

Nightlife centers around the resorts. A Mexican "Fiesta Night" is offered at the Gran Festivall All Inclusive Resort during the high tourist season. Clubs include TEQUE, also at Gran Festivall, and Disco Vog, in the vicinity of Playa Azul (open Friday and Saturday nights only). There is a cover charge at both, and shorts and sandals are not permitted (this dress code is more likely to apply to men than to women). Hours may vary even during the high season.

**Colima State Tourism Office:** Blvd. Miguel de la Madrid #1033, in the vicinity of Playa Azul. Open Mon.-Fri. 9-3 and 5-7, Sat. 10-2. **Phone:** (314) 333-2277 (English spoken).

## MAZATLÁN, SINALOA (A-1) pop. 438,434

Mazatlán (mah-saht-LAHN) is the Mexican beach resort that typifies the good old days, when all you needed was a clean hotel room, reliable sunshine and cheap tacos. Unlike Cancún and Los Cabos, gringo-friendly destinations that have gone increasingly upscale with a glut of all-inclusive luxury resorts and over-the-top nightlife, this Pacific port's pleasures are more subdued. It also has something those other two lack: a historic downtown core that's well worth your precious time.

German immigrants had helped transform Mazatlán into an international shipping port in the late 19th century, and today the German influence is still evident in Old Mazatlán. The European architecture and wrought-iron balconies also have a French Quarter feel. The refurbishment of the once-crumbling Angela Peralta Theater *(see attraction listing)* and ongoing restoration efforts have sparked a blossoming cultural scene. Art galleries and specialty shops ensure that you'll bring home something more unique than a Pacífico beer T-shirt, while beautiful Plazuela Machado, ringed with breezy sidewalk cafes, is the Mexico you won't find in Cancún.

## Practicalities

Besides affordability, one of Mazatlán's attractions is its relative proximity to the U.S. border. As a result, a greater percentage of the city's tourist traffic arrives by motor vehicle, at least when compared to beach resorts farther south and the colonial cities of the southern interior. Mazatlán is about 750 miles from the border at Nogales via Mex. 15/15-D. Toll fees along the entire stretch total 752 pesos (about $56 U.S.). Although dollars are usually accepted at toll booths near the U.S. border, it's best to have pesos on hand for the entire route.

**Note:** Toll charges can go up without warning, and fees for different types of vehicles aren't always posted. As in the rest of Mexico, night driving is not recommended. Plan on a 2-day journey from the United States.

Rafael Buelna International Airport is about 40 kilometers (25 miles) south of downtown via Mex. 15 and is a good 30- to 40-minute drive to the major resort areas. Alaska Airlines, American Eagle, Delta and US Airways offer nonstop flights from some U.S. cities. Aeroméxico and Volaris fly from U.S. cities via Mexico City. WestJet and Sunwing Airlines offer seasonal nonstop service from select Canadian cities. *For additional information about airlines see Arriving by Air, page p. 42.*

*Colectivo* shuttle van service to downtown Mazatlán or the hotel zones costs about $12 (U.S.) per person. Private taxis hired in front of the airport cost about $30-$40, which can be cut by sharing the ride; the driver usually will carry up to four people. A taxi is the only way to get back to the airport, and will cost $25-$30.

Elite provides first-class bus service to many inland Mexican cities, including several daily departures for Mexico City and Guadalajara. Elite also offers service north to the border at Nogales, Ariz. The main bus terminal (Central de Autobuses) is just off Carretera Internacional (Mex. 15, also called Avenida Ejército Méxicano) and just south of Avenida de Los Deportes, 3 blocks inland from the *malecón* (Avenida del Mar) at Playa Norte. *For additional information about buses see Bus Service, page p. 52.*

Baja Ferries provides automobile-passenger service linking Mazatlán with La Paz *(see separate listing under Baja California)* on the Baja California Peninsula. The ferry departs 3 days a week from the Playa Sur terminal, at the southern end of town near the sport-fishing docks; sailing time is about 15-18 hours. Schedules and rates are subject to change. Double-check both prior to departure and purchase tickets in advance; for details phone (669) 985-0470 (English may not be spoken). *For additional information see Ferry Service, page p. 53.*

The city is a port of call for cruise ships, including Carnival, Holland America and Norwegian. To find out which ships will be calling on Mazatlán in 2016 and beyond, check with the cruise lines or your travel agent.

Banks are generally open Mon.-Fri. 9-6 and set aside morning hours—normally 8:30 to 11:30 a.m.—to exchange foreign currency. Almost all banks have ATM machines that accept most bank cards; withdrawals are in pesos. Some machines also dispense U.S. dollars, which are widely accepted in Mazatlán. *Casas de cambio* (currency exchange houses) stay open longer than banks, although their rates are usually not as good; you pay for the convenience.

The post office is downtown on Avenida Benito Juárez, in front of the cathedral and across the street from the main plaza.

Mazatlán's weather can be characterized as tropical, although not as hot as points farther down the coast. From November through May, daytime temperatures are in the 70s, nighttime temperatures in the 60s. It's hotter and more humid during the summer months, but afternoon highs are usually in the 80s rather than the sultry 90s. The ocean water is warmest in late summer and fall. Leave your heavy coat at home; the temperature at this seaside location has never dropped below 50 F.

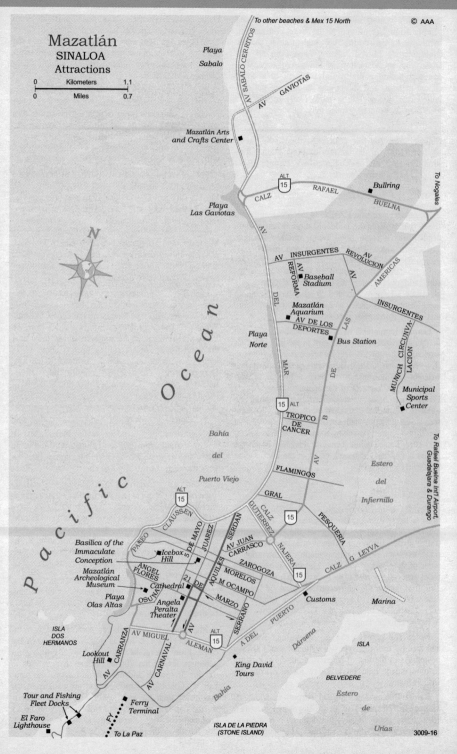

Mazatlán
SINALOA
Attractions

© AAA

To other beaches & Mex 15 North

Playa
Sabalo

AV SABALO CERRITOS

AV GAVIOTAS

Mazatlán Arts
and Crafts Center

ALT
15

CALZ

RAFAEL

BUELNA

Bullring

To Nogales

Playa
Las Gaviotas

AV

DEL

AV INSURGENTES

AV
REFORMA

AV
REVOLUCION

Baseball
Stadium

AV

AMERICAS

INSURGENTES

Mazatlán
Aquarium

AV DE LOS
DEPORTES

LAS

Playa
Norte

MAR

DE

Bus Station

MUNICH

CIRCUNVA-
LACION

Municipal
Sports
Center

Bahía

del

15 ALT

TROPICO
DE
CANCER

B

To Rafael Buelna Int'l Airport,
Guadalajara & Durango

Pacific Ocean

Puerto Viejo

FLAMINGOS

AV

Estero

del

Infiernillo

ALT
15

GRAL

PESQUERIA

CLAUSSEN

PASEO

DE MAYO

JUAREZ

AV SERDAN

CALZ
GUTIERREZ

15

NAJERA

15

Basilica of the
Immaculate
Conception

Icebox
Hill

AV JUAN
CARRASCO

ZAROGOZA

CALZ G. LEYVA

Mazatlán
Archeological
Museum

ANGEL
FLORES

21 DE

AQUILES

MORELOS

M OCAMPO

15

Cathedral

DE

Customs

Marina

Playa
Olas Altas

OSUNA

Angela
Peralta
Theater

MARZO

SERRANO

A DEL

PUERTO

Dársena

ISLA

ISLA
DOS
HERMANOS

AV MIGUEL

AV

ALT
15

BELVEDERE

Lookout
Hill

AV CARRANZA

AV CARNAVAL

ALEMAN

King David
Tours

Estero

de

Tour and Fishing
Fleet Docks

FY.

Ferry
Terminal

El Faro
Lighthouse

To La Paz

ISLA DE LA PIEDRA
(STONE ISLAND)

Bahía

Urías

3009-16

Kilometers    1.1
Miles         0.7
0
0

N

July, August and September are the rainiest months; the rest of the year rain is infrequent and seldom a threat to vacation plans. Clothing is decidedly informal—bathing suits, shorts, jeans and T-shirts—unless you wish to "dress up" in casual resort wear for an evening out to dinner or a club.

**Note:** Due to Mexico's ongoing drug war there is a police and military presence in Mazatlán, and visitors may see armed officers both on foot and in trucks, even in the city's tourist zones.

## City Layout

Mazatlán occupies a peninsula that juts into the Pacific Ocean, forming Bahía del Puerto Viejo, a natural bay and protected harbor. The main approach into the city is via Mex. 15, which becomes the International Highway (Carretera Internacional).

Mex. 15 essentially loops around the city, changing names in the process. As Avenida Rafael Buelna, it veers west off Carretera Internacional, passing the bullring and ending at the Sábalo traffic circle at the waterfront. It then proceeds south as Avenida del Mar and Paseo Claussen. It skirts the southern edge of downtown as Avenida Miguel Alemán, running east to Port Avenue (Avenida del Puerto). At the customs office it becomes Avenida Gabriel Leyva and continues east toward the airport. Once out of town, Mex. 15 heads south to Tepic and Guadalajara.

The *malecón,* or waterfront boulevard, runs along the coast for some 17 kilometers (11 miles). In Mazatlán this thoroughfare also changes names— four times. At the southern end of the city (the old downtown area), it is called Paseo Claussen. North of downtown it becomes Avenida del Mar. At Punta Camarón (Shrimp Point), the name changes to Avenida Camarón Sábalo. At this point it runs inland and is paralleled by Avenida Playa las Gaviotas (formerly called Rodolfo Loaiza), along which several of the city's luxury hotels sit. After a mile or so the two streets rejoin. Farther north the name changes again to Avenida Sábalo Cerritos as the street runs north to the marinas.

Stroll the *malecón* for a look at some seafront sculptures. While this is not the avant-garde statuary you'll see farther south in Puerto Vallarta, these creations make for an interesting walk. Along Playa Olas Altas, sculptures depict a deer, mermaids and "La Mujer Mazatleca," a woman dramatically embracing the heavens. "La Continuidad de la Vida" (The Continuity of Life) features a nude man and woman perched atop a huge seashell, the man gesturing to a pod of leaping dolphins.

The Fisherman's Monument (Monumento al Pescador), on Avenida del Mar north of Playa Olas Altas, is a local landmark. This sculpture of a woman and a fisherman dragging his net—both of them again sans clothing—is a curious sight. Farther north, along Avenida del Mar across from Avenida Lola Beltran, suds lovers will find a tribute to Mazatlán's very own Pacífico Brewery in the form of a huge copper beer vat.

The section of town north of the *malecón* along Avenida Camarón Sábalo is known as the Golden Zone (Zona Dorada). Welcome to *turista* central. Here, a chain of high-rise hotels and mega resorts front some of Mazatlán's finest beaches. Running behind the hotels is a garish commercial drag jam-packed with fast food joints, bars, restaurants, mini markets, souvenir shops, car rental offices and banks. While the comforts of home are certainly convenient, the area isn't exactly picture postcard material.

Near the Golden Zone's southern end, where Avenida Playa las Gaviotas splits off from the main thoroughfare and runs behind the hotels fronting Playa Gaviotas, are more restaurants and several nice shops. But no matter where you go in the Golden Zone, be aware that you're also in the "Time Share Zone"—and the sharks here are particularly aggressive. If you're not interested in a "free tour" (read: time share presentation), it's advisable to give them the cold shoulder.

Icebox Hill (Cerro de la Nevería), in the Olas Altas area, is residential. A gradually ascending road reaches its summit, from which are views of a great part of the city, the immense blue bay and awe-inspiring sunsets that tint the sea and clouds a brilliant orange-red. Nearby El Mirador, off Paseo Claussen, is where daring locals plunge from a platform 45 feet above turbulent water surrounded by dangerous rocks. The feat requires expert timing; without the cushioning effect of a wave, a diver meets just 6 feet of water. In the evening these young daredevils carry flaming torches for a theatrical effect. Tips are expected.

Old Mazatlán, just inland from Playa Olas Altas, is the oldest part of the city. Blocks of buildings and private residences—including rows of town houses with wrought-iron and stone trim—line the narrow streets, especially along avenidas Heriberto Frias, Venus and Niños Héroes.

Plaza Principal, the main plaza (also called Plaza Revolución), is in the heart of the historic center across the street from Mazatlán's 19th-century cathedral, the Basilica of the Immaculate Conception. With its wrought-iron benches, shoeshine stands and vendor carts shaded by bushy trees and palms, the plaza is the city's communal hub.

If you're trying to find the "other plaza," Plazuela Machado, walk to the south end of Plaza Principal (away from the cathedral) and head west 2 blocks on Calle Angel Flores. Make a left on Avenida Carnaval and follow it for 2 blocks to this beautiful little plaza, a shady oasis surrounded by colorful colonial buildings housing cafes and restaurants. Teenagers smooch on the wooden benches, and in the late afternoon local expatriates walk their dogs. Outdoor art shows are held regularly, and occasional music concerts take place under the green wrought-iron gazebo. After dark the atmosphere *es muy romántico.*

The Mazatlán Art Museum (Museo de Arte de Mazatlán), Calle Sixto Osuna and Avenida Venustiano

Carranza, displays works by Mazateco artists as well as such nationally known figures as José Luis Cuevas. Film screenings, concerts and other cultural events also take place; phone (669) 985-3502.

At the southern end of town are the ferry terminal, tour boat operators, sport-fishing fleets and commercial port activities. Standing guard over the harbor's entrance is El Faro, said to be the tallest lighthouse in the Western Hemisphere and second only to Gibraltar in the world, with a range of some 35 nautical miles. Those undertaking the strenuous half-hour hike up the rocky pinnacle will be rewarded with an expansive view of the harbor and ocean.

Another vista of the city and its watery surroundings—particularly lovely in the evening—can be seen from the top of Lookout Hill (Cerro de Vigía), a short distance north of El Faro. This climb, also steep, is better made via taxi.

There are more great city views at the historic Hotel Posada Freeman, now part of the Best Western chain. An elevator whisks you to the 12th-floor "Sky Room," a casual bar with big picture windows offering panoramas of city and sea. The rooftop has a swimming pool and lounge chairs; the latter are available to non-hotel guests who order drinks. Nicknamed "Mazatlán's Skyscraper," the Freeman welcomed its first guests in 1944.

Waterfront sprawl makes walking an ill-advised means of exploration. Fortunately, there are several public transportation options. *Pulmonías*, the city's signature taxis, are essentially souped-up golf carts powered by Volkswagen Bug engines. They make the Zona Dorada circuit, travel up and down the *malecón* and seat three passengers comfortably (four is a squeeze).

The vehicles were nicknamed *pulmonía* by rival cabbies, who told potential fares that riding in a chilly open-air car would result in the flu (it apparently didn't, judging from their ubiquity, and the name stuck). Always negotiate the fare in advance, as *pulmonías* tend to be more expensive than a taxi. A word of caution: *Pulmonías* do not have seat belts and they emit strong exhaust fumes; if either is a concern, opt for a regular taxi instead.

For 10 pesos one can get to just about any place in the city via local bus lines. The "Sábalo-Centro" route is the most useful for tourists. These buses run along the waterfront between the Zona Dorada hotels and downtown. Buses marked "Sábalo-Cocos-Centro" or simply "Centro" also travel between the two areas, but unless you're interested in a lengthy detour through the city's working class neighborhoods, avoid them.

"Cerritos Juárez" buses follow a route from Mazatlán's coffee factory to the Zona Dorada and then north to the marinas, ending at Playa Los Cerritos. The fare for the comfier, air-conditioned green buses, which are only available on the "Sábalo-Centro" and "Sábalo-Cocos-Centro" routes, is 10.5 pesos. A knowledge of Spanish is helpful if you intend to get around by bus. During rush hour, about 5

to 7 p.m., buses that are full may pass waiting passengers. During off hours it's often possible to hail a bus as you would a taxi.

## Beaches

Mazatlán's beaches offer something for everyone and accordingly attract different groups of sun seekers. Some are visited mainly by Mazatlecos; others draw tourists. The following beaches are described as they are located from south to north along the coast.

Stone Island (Isla de la Piedra), at the southern end of the city, is actually a peninsula offering miles of mostly undeveloped oceanside beaches that can be explored on horseback. Small motorboats carry passengers to and from the island (about a 5-minute ride), departing from a launch along the harbor channel north of the ferry terminal. On weekends— and particularly Sunday—entire families spread out along the sand or under the coconut palm groves. Open-air restaurants offer smoked fish, shrimp and beer along with music and dancing.

Playa Olas Altas was the city's first tourist beach and is where the *malecón* begins. The name means "high waves," and surfers congregate here during the summer. This is not the best beach for swimming; instead, enjoy the tremendous views of the surf from one of the many outdoor cafes that line the seaside walkway.

Playa Los Piños, located between the Marine House and the Fisherman's Monument, is where local fishermen sell their catch. If you're interested in purchasing fresh fish without angling for it, arrive early; the catch disappears quickly. Just north of Playa Los Piños is Playa Norte, which stretches between the Fisherman's Monument and Punta Camarón. This beach is popular with locals who play impromptu baseball and soccer games in the sand or take to the water on a three-wheeled floating trike.

Playa Martín fronts the seaside promenade along Avenida del Mar. A tunnel connects the beach with the Hotel Hacienda Mazatlán. Big Pacific rollers crash against the rocks at Punta Camarón. On the north side of this outcrop jutting into the water is Playa las Gaviotas, popular with tourists who want to soak up some sun or play a game of beach volleyball.

Farther up is Playa Sábalo, where the wide, white sand beach attracts droves of tourists and what seems like an equal number of Mexican vendors. Parasailers and windsurfers utilize this stretch fronting the Golden Zone. It is protected from the open surf by Bird, Deer and Goat islands, which rise out of the water a short distance offshore.

Beyond Playa Sábalo, at the north end of Mazatlán, are Playa Brujas (Witches' Beach) and Playa Los Cerritos, which stretch north to Cerritos Point (Punta Cerritos). To reach these beaches, either hire a taxi (about $8-$10 U.S. one way from the Golden Zone) or hop on the "Cerritos-Juárez" bus heading north. The line ends near Playa Los Cerritos. To get to the shore, walk straight ahead past a long, squat building packed with souvenir stalls. Rustic *palapa* restaurants sit on a low bluff overlooking the beach, which is crowded with

Mexican families on weekends. During the week, swimming is good at this mostly unspoiled stretch of sand protected by rocky outcroppings.

Playa Brujas also is within walking distance of the bus stop. Head west up the only narrow paved road in sight and follow it to Restaurant Playa Bruja, a nice *palapa* bar overlooking the sand. Playa Brujas was once an isolated surfing outpost, but condo and hotel development continues to creep ever closer.

## Sports and Recreation

Fishing in Mazatlán ranks among the best anywhere. Striped marlin are hooked between November and April; sailfish and black marlin are caught between May and October. Other game species taken from the Pacific waters include blue marlin, bonito, dolphin and yellowfin tuna. Well-equipped fleets are headquartered at the docks at the southern end of town, where the ferry and charter tour boats are moored, and at Marina El Cid in the Golden Zone.

Charter fishing boat rates start at about $300 (U.S.) a day for a small boat (up to four people) and include bait and tackle, but not fishing licenses or refreshments. Tipping the captain and first mate is customary, particularly if the day's catch has been bountiful. A catch-and-release policy is emphasized. Make fishing arrangements in advance of your arrival with either the fleet itself or through your hotel. Hotels will usually try to arrange group excursions, thereby sharing the cost of boats.

The El Cid Resort offers a variety of fishing packages utilizing its own Aries fleet of boats. For information and reservations phone (669) 916-3468, or contact a travel agency. Local charter companies include Star Fleet, phone (669) 982-2665, and Flota Bibi Fleet, phone (669) 148-2055. Sport-fishing guides depart from Marina Mazatlán in the Golden Zone; for marina information phone (669) 916-7799.

Baseball in Mazatlán is considered something of a tradition. Loyal fans fervently support the local Pacific League team, the Mazatlán Venados, which has produced players who have gone on to the American majors. Games are played at Teodoro Mariscal Stadium, off Avenida del Mar and convenient to the tourist zone. For game schedules, ask at your hotel or check the team's website; the season runs October through January.

A popular activity is parasailing, which provides 15 minutes of sheer thrills for those not prone to vertigo. Arrangements can be made in front of the Playa Mazatlán and Las Flores hotels in the Golden Zone.

The Aqua Sports Center at the El Cid Resort rents a variety of water sports equipment, from jet skis and Hobie Cats to kayaks and snorkeling gear. The resort also has a challenging 27-hole golf course—18 holes designed by Robert Trent Jones Jr. and nine by Lee Trevino. It is open to the public on a limited basis, although preferred tee times are given to hotel guests. Phone (669) 989-6969, extension 3261, for equipment rental or golf reservation information.

Another Jones-designed championship course is at the Estrella del Mar resort community on Isla de la Piedra, just south of Old Mazatlán. Six of the 18 holes border the ocean, offering spectacular views. Amenities include a pro shop and clubhouse. For information, phone 01 (800) 727-4653 (toll-free long distance within Mexico) or (888) 587-0609 (from the United States).

Good for a casual round is the nine-hole course at the Mazatlán Country Club (Club Campestre Mazatlán), and the 290-peso (about $21.50 U.S.) greens fee is significantly less expensive; the course can be played twice (a combined 18 holes) for 390 pesos; a motorized cart costs extra. The club is on Mex. 15 at the south end of town but is hard to find; take a taxi. Walk-ons are typically not a problem, but if you'd like to schedule a tee time, phone (669) 980-1570 (no English spoken).

## Shopping

Shopping in Mazatlán is centered primarily along avenidas Playa las Gaviotas and Camarón Sábalo in the Golden Zone. The shops and galleries here feature the usual assortment of T-shirts, sportswear, resort wear, jewelry, handicrafts and leather goods. Most are open Monday through Saturday; some do not accept credit cards.

Be sure to stop by Sea Shell City, a combination museum and shop on Av. Playa las Gaviotas #407. A kaleidoscopic variety of shells from around the world are on display, and there are many shell craft items as well as Mexican handicrafts for sale. Upstairs is an amazing fountain covered in shells that holds colorful koi.

Across the street, the open-air Las Cabañas Shopping Center is a narrow corridor lined with small gift shops, some of them interesting, others stocked with the usual trinkets. At the far end of this mini shopping arcade you'll find Pancho's Restaurant and steps leading down to Playa las Gaviotas, where roving beach vendors are waiting to pounce.

The nearby Mazatlán Arts and Crafts Center, on Avenida Playa las Gaviotas, stocks everything from tablecloths and rugs to pottery, *guayabera* shirts, embroidered dresses and footwear. Artisans can sometimes be seen creating both artwork and jewelry designs. Purchases here are cash only.

If you're looking for jewelry of a better pedigree than what the beach vendors are peddling, Cielito Lindo, Av. Playa las Gaviotas #311, has a huge selection at surprisingly reasonable prices.

For a more authentic Mexican shopping experience, head downtown. In the Central Market (*mercado*), at avenidas Ocampo and Juárez in Old Mazatlán, you'll find aisle after aisle crammed with vendor stalls selling everything from fresh meat, seafood and produce to *piñatas,* shoes and Che Guevara T-shirts. More stalls line the outside walls of the market building. As far as non-food items go, good quality can be hard to find, but for dedicated bargain hunters the opportunity to haggle with local merchants is the real fun.

Art galleries are located on the streets west of Plazuela Machado; pick up a free map published by Art Walk Mazatlán, available many of the galleries. Nidart (Nido de Artesanos) occupies a bright purple and red-trimmed building next to the Angela Peralta Theater in Old Mazatlán. This gallery and studio complex (the name means "nest of artisans") features leather masks, sculptures, burlap dolls, decorated coconut shells, jewelry, clay figurines and other crafts expertly fashioned by local artisans. It's open Mon.-Sat. 10-3 during the high tourist season.

Casa Etnika, Calle Sixto Osuna #50, is a contemporary Mexican art gallery that occupies a large 19th-century house. The ground-floor rooms are filled with fine furniture, sculpture, paintings, wildlife photography prints, baskets, jewelry and more. You'll also find gifts for children (Mazatlán coloring books) and high-quality T-shirts (a rarity in Mexico). There's a small gourmet coffee bar next to the gallery entrance.

South of Avenida Rafael Buelna on Avenida de los Deportes, about 3 blocks inland from the *malecón* (Avenida del Mar), is La Gran Plaza, a mall offering American-style shopping. The supermarket and department stores make this a convenient place to stock up on basics. It is easily reached by taxi or the Sábalo Cocos bus.

## Dining and Nightlife

Mazatlán calls itself the "shrimp capital of Mexico." In addition to the big hotel restaurants and fine dining spots, there are numerous establishments along the *malecón* serving fish filets, various shrimp concoctions or such Pacific coast specialties as *pescado zarandeado*, filleted and grilled snapper coated with a chile/achiote marinade.

In and around Old Mazatlán's Central Market, food stands sell tasty tacos, *tortas* and the like. Better yet, head a few blocks southwest to Plazuela Machado and dine alfresco at one of the sidewalk cafes.

The Hotel Playa Mazatlán, on Avenida Playa las Gaviotas in the Golden Zone, presents "Fiesta Mexicana" three times a week beginning at 7 p.m. from November through May (less frequently the rest of the year). An all-you-can-eat buffet is followed by folkloric dance and music performances from various regions of Mexico. The entertainment includes an amazing display of rope twirling by a *charro*, or Mexican cowboy, and a flamboyantly costumed troupe who re-enact a bit of Carnaval.

Admittance to the shows is first-come-first served. Dress is casual, but shorts are not permitted. For information and tickets phone (669) 989-0555, or stop by the tour desk inside the hotel lobby.

Most of the restaurants and hotels in Mazatlán offer purified water and ice. There should be no cause for concern about drinking the water in these establishments, but double check if in doubt. Purified water can be bought in any of the mini markets around town. See the Lodgings & Restaurants section for AAA-RATED dining establishments.

**Note:** Some restaurants add a standard 10 to 15 percent gratuity to the bill. Be sure to differentiate between this charge and the 16 percent IVA tax that is added to every check, and tip accordingly.

Many of the big hotels in the Golden Zone have bars or lounges with happy hours featuring two-for-one drink prices. For a more rocking good time head to Joe's Oyster Bar. There's a well-signed entrance on Avenida Playa las Gaviotas, or you can enter this thatch-roofed *cantina* from the Golden Zone beachfront. The music is mostly hip-hop, with a few Latin jams mixed in for the local clientele. Late afternoon happy hour sees college kids dancing on tables, older tourists eating jumbo oysters and two-man volleyball teams engaged in heated matches on the sand volleyball court. The scene gets much wilder after the sun sets.

Gus y Gus, in the Golden Zone at Av. Camarón Sábalo #1730 (across the street from the Costa de Oro Hotel), is a casual bar and grill with a fun atmosphere and a menu of well-done Mexican staples. Classic rock cover bands provide the music.

## Events

The year's biggest party is the pre-Lenten Carnaval, or Mardi Gras, held in late February or early March. All Mazatlán—not to mention revelers from around the world—gathers for 5 days and nights of fireworks, parades with elaborate floats, the coronation of a festival queen (*La Reina de Carnaval*) and of course, plenty of music and dancing. If you'll be visiting around this time, make hotel reservations several months in advance and inquire regarding exactly when Carnaval begins. Expect prices to climb as well.

Historical records of the event date to 1827, when military men demanding salaries staged a protest by masquerading. Over the years the tradition grew, with mask wearing becoming part of the festivities at both public assemblies and private parties. By the end of the 19th century, French, German and Italian immigrants were adding facets of their own culture to Carnaval, and today the city claims that its celebration is the world's third largest after those in Rio de Janeiro and New Orleans. The revelry culminates on Shrove Tuesday, when the *malecón* is packed with merrymakers.

Mazatlán recognizes Day of the Dead celebrations Nov. 1 and 2 with a combination of feasting and somber remembrances. Several sport-fishing tournaments also occur in November.

## Nearby Destinations

A guided tour is a good way to see both the city and towns in the surrounding area. Information about tours of Mazatlán and vicinity can be obtained at the major hotels or any local travel agency. **Note:** Beware the numerous sidewalk entrepreneurs who offer free tours; their real goal is to pitch the sale of time share units.

Day excursions also can be arranged to the islands off the Golden Zone section of the coast: Goat

Island (Isla de Chivas), Bird Island (Isla de Pájaros) and Deer Island (Isla de Venados), a nature preserve where seashell collectors can search along the shore and snorkelers will find decent submarine scenery when waters are calm.

The El Cid Resort offers a trip to Deer Island aboard an amphibious vehicle for 150 pesos (about $11 U.S.) per person; snorkeling gear is available for rent. Daily departures are at 10, noon and 2. There are no services or restaurants on the island, so pack a cooler with drinks and snacks. If you forget, the men who rent out beach umbrellas also sell beer and soda on the sly. For information contact the resort's Aqua Sports Center; phone (669) 913-0451.

Perhaps the most popular guided day trip from Mazatlán takes in the former mining outposts of Concordia and Copala, both on Mex. 40 as it heads east toward Durango (see place listing under Northwestern Mexico). These two colonial-era towns offer a charming, laid-back contrast to Mazatlán's seaside partying atmosphere.

Concordia, in the foothills of the Sierra Madre Occidental, is surrounded by mango and banana plantations. Founded in 1565 by Spanish conquistador Francisco de Ibarra, it is still a furniture, brick and pottery making center; roadside stands sell furniture, pottery and fresh mangos. The main plaza contains a gazebo and an enormous wooden chair that provides an amusing photo opportunity. Across from the plaza is the baroque Church of St. Sebastian, a lovely old building that has an ornate stone facade.

Copala, about 24 kilometers (15 miles) east of Concordia, is smaller and not as bustling but just as picturesque. A walk down this village's cobblestoned main street past red tile-roofed, whitewashed buildings is like a journey back in time. Little has changed in the town's more than 400 years of existence. Cars are few and far between. Dogs, chickens, pigs and donkeys wander the streets, and dawn is greeted by the sound of crowing roosters. Adding to the scene is the brilliantly colored bougainvillea that spills over roofs and cascades down walls.

Up until the late 19th century Copala was a center for silver mining operations in the surrounding mountains, and old homes still cling precariously to the hillsides. The tree-shaded town plaza has wrought-iron lampposts and an ornate bandstand and is bordered by small gift shops selling silver jewelry and regional handicrafts. At one end of the plaza stands the baroque Church of San José, which was completed in 1775; it has a vaulted interior with gold leaf decoration and colorful polychrome statues of saints.

South of Mazatlán via Mex. 15 is Rosario, another old mining community. At the end of the 18th century it had a population of 7,000 and was one of the richest towns in northwest Mexico. Mining activities ceased in the 1940s. Of particular interest is Our Lady of the Rosary, the town's beautiful colonial church, with a marvelous altarpiece completely covered with intricate gold-leaf designs. Some 70 kilometers (43 miles) of underground tunnels, dug over a 300-year period to aid in extracting gold and

silver, remain behind; locals attest that they outnumber the surface streets.

Mex. 40-D, the toll road from Mazatlán to Durango, is an exhilarating road trip for drivers who have experience with challenging mountain roads (see description under the Durango place listing). The clearly signed toll sections branch off portions of old, free Mex. 40, allowing motorists to avoid the more treacherous switchbacks and hairpin curves that make a journey along the aptly named "Devil's Backbone" such a gut-clenching experience.

The arguable highlight of this spectacular journey across the Sierra Madre Mountains is the Baluarte Bridge (Puente Baluarte). A suspension marvel, it straddles the Sinaloa/Durango state border at a dizzying 1,322 feet above the Baluarte River. All told, an amazing number of bridges and tunnels were required to negotiate these impressively rugged mountains.

The drive time to Durango is approximately 3 hours (versus the 6-8 hours it formerly took to negotiate the serpentine length of old Mex. 40). There are four toll plazas between the two cities; fees total 506 pesos (about $37.50 U.S.).

**Sinaloa State Tourism Office (Coordinación General de Turismo de Sinaloa):** at Av. del Mar #882 (between downtown and the Golden Zone). The staff speaks English. Open Mon.-Fri. 9-5. **Phone:** (669) 981-8883.

**ANGELA PERALTA THEATER** (Teatro Angela Peralta) is 3 blks. s. of Plaza Machado at Av. Carnaval #47 (at Calle Libertad). It opened in 1874 as the Teatro Rubio. Renowned opera singer Angela Peralta, dubbed "the Mexican Nightingale," arrived for an engagement in 1883 but contracted cholera and tragically died (along with most of her company) before uttering a single note.

After stints as a Mardi Gras ballroom, movie palace, boxing arena and parking garage, the theater was

abandoned and in ruins before being restored and re-opening in 1992. The performance schedule includes ballet, folkloric dance, concerts, operas and plays. Rehearsal schedule permitting, the opulent interior can be viewed; photo displays on the second-floor mezzanine chronicle the theater's history and restoration.

**Time:** Allow 30 minutes minimum. **Hours:** Daily 9-6. **Cost:** Free; ticket prices for performances vary. **Phone:** (669) 982-4446.

**BASILICA OF THE IMMACULATE CONCEPTION** (Basilica de la Inmaculada Concepción) is downtown on the n. side of Plaza República, at Calle Benito Juárez and Av. 21 de Marzo. It is easily recognized by its gold-colored twin spires. The late 19th-century exterior is rather plain, but the beautifully preserved interior is very ornate, with numerous gold accents. **Hours:** Open daily. **Cost:** Free.

**KING DAVID TOURS,** Av. Camarón Sábalo #333, offers various sightseeing tours that include pickup and drop-off at your hotel or (in the case of cruise passengers) the cruise ship terminal. The guides are knowledgeable and speak English.

A 3-hour City Tour aboard an air-conditioned bus visits such landmarks as the Old Mazatlán historic center, Plazuela Machado, the cathedral and several sites along the *malecón*. The 5-hour Jungle Tour is not really a jungle excursion but a waterfront sightseeing trip. The tour boat passes shrimp fleets and the navy base, and also cruises through inlets and waterways lined with mangroves. A mesquite-grilled fish lunch is included, along with time for beachcombing and wading.

Another boat tour visits Stone Island (Isla de la Piedra), where visitors are transported to the island's beach. Guests have the option of choosing two activities from a list of options like beachside horseback riding, snorkeling, boogie boarding, a banana boat ride or a ride through the island's village via horse-drawn carriage; lunch at the Molokay Restaurant also is included. The Tequila Tour visits a tequila factory where the finished product can be sampled, then stops at the picturesque country town of El Quelite for lunch and time to stroll around the cobblestoned main square.

**Note:** The City Tour requires a five-person minimum; the Tequila Tour requires a four-person minimum. **Hours:** Tours depart around 9 a.m. (hotel or cruise ship terminal pickup at 8:45), with city tours returning around noon and boat tours around 2:30. Schedule varies according to season but city and Stone Island tours are normally offered daily; the Jungle Tour is available Tues., Thurs. and Sat. **Cost:** City Tour $25 (U.S.); $15 (ages 6-12). Jungle Tour $45; $30 (ages 6-12). Stone Island Tour $35; $25 (ages 6-12). Tequila Tour $50; $40 (ages 6-12). Round-trip transportation is included. Reservations are required. **Phone:** (669) 914-1444, or (866) 438-7097 (from the United States).

**MAZATLÁN AQUARIUM** (Acuario Mazatlán) is half a blk. e. of Av. del Mar at Av. de los Deportes #111. It displays 250 species of fresh and saltwater marine life,

from colorful reef fish to moray eels to sea turtles, in some 50 tanks. A sea lion show is presented several times daily in an open-air amphitheater. There also is an exotic bird show utilizing birds confiscated from vendors who captured them illegally. **Hours:** Daily 9:30-5. **Cost:** 100 pesos (about $7.40 U.S.); 70 pesos (ages 2-11). **Phone:** (669) 981-7815.

**MAZATLÁN ARCHEOLOGICAL MUSEUM** (Museo Arqueológico de Mazatlán) is at Calle Sixto Osuna #76, just e. of Paseo Olas Altas. The small collection focuses on paintings, clay figurines and regional artifacts. There also is an exhibit that covers the Mexican Revolution and Mazatlán's early history. Most background information is in Spanish. **Hours:** Tues.-Fri. 9-6, Sat.-Sun. 10-2. Phone ahead to confirm schedule. **Cost:** 39 pesos (about $2.90 U.S.). **Phone:** (669) 981-1455. GT

## PUERTO ESCONDIDO, OAXACA (D-5)

Puerto Escondido (PWEHR-to ehs-cohn-DEE-doh) means "hidden port," and until fairly recently the translation was quite appropriate. The town was named for Punta Escondida, the rocky outcrop that protects a half-moon bay. A port was established here in 1928 as a shipping point for coffee grown on the forested seaward slopes of the Sierra Madre del Sur. Coastal Mex. 200 came through in the 1960s, opening up the area to tourism.

Among the first visitors were surfers, who were drawn by the big waves and dirt-cheap lodgings. Today they're still here, but Puerto Escondido is no longer a hideaway and not quite as cheap. Instead, it's an established destination, frequented by an international group of travelers preferring a more laid-back alternative to the shiny expense of Bahías de Huatulco and other carefully planned seaside resorts.

## Practicalities

The international airport is about 3 kilometers (2 miles) west of town off Mex. 200, near the newer hotel and resort development around Playa Bacocho. It receives flights from Mexico City via Aeromar (usually on twin-turboprop airliners), VivaAerobus and Interjet. Taxis and less expensive *colectivos* (minibuses) operated by Transportes Terrestres shuttle airport passengers to and from hotels. *For additional information about airlines see Arriving by Air, page p. 42.*

Puerto Escondido is about 113 kilometers (70 miles) west of Huatulco via Mex. 200, often referred to as the Carretera Costera (Coastal Highway). Driving from Acapulco or Huatulco is not recommended for safety reasons; the winding road is also potholed, particularly during the July-through-September rainy season. If you do drive, avoid doing so after dark.

Mex. 200 divides the town roughly in half. The older, upper section, above the highway, is where most residents live and conduct their daily business. Below the highway is the newer, tourist-geared waterfront. Hotels, restaurants and shops spread for about a mile along the main thoroughfare, Avenida Perez Gasga. At noon each day, chains are raised at the eastern and western ends of the beachfront strip, closing the street to vehicular traffic. At the western end of this pedestrian zone, Gasga begins winding uphill and crosses Mex. 200, where its name changes to Avenida Oaxaca (Mex. 131). The junction, marked by a traffic signal, is known as El Crucero.

The local bus stations are all within a block or so of the El Crucero intersection. Estrella Blanca provides first-class service along Mex. 200 between Acapulco and Bahías de Huatulco (be sure to specify the La Crucecita terminal as your destination if you're taking a bus to Huatulco from Puerto Escondido). The station is on Avenida Oaxaca, just north of the El Crucero junction.

*Casa de cambio* (currency exchange) houses are on each side of Peréz Gasga near the Rincón Pacífico Hotel.

## The Beaches

A lighthouse atop Punta Escondida at the western end of the bayfront affords a panoramic view of town. Running east from the rocky cove beneath the lighthouse is Playa Principal, the in-town beach. Here the stretch of sand is narrow, the water calm and the beach backed by rustling palms. It can be crowded: Mexican families flock here on Sundays and holidays to wade and paddle in the shallows, and local fishermen cast their nets at the sheltered west side of the bay or launch small, colorfully painted boats. Do not walk along the beaches at night because of the possibility of robberies or muggings.

To the east of Playa Principal is Playa Marineros, which begins at the jutting rocks below the Hotel Santa Fe. Here the shoreline begins curving toward the south and increasingly faces the open ocean. The surf gets rougher, and swimmers should exercise caution.

Farther to the southeast is Playa Zicatela, considered to be one of the world's best surfing beaches. The wide expanse of golden-colored sand stretches for miles, and the thundering Pacific breakers crashing onto it are impressive indeed. The biggest waves occur between August and November. Spectators line the beach to watch daredevil surfers finesse the "pipeline," a long tubular swell of water. Needless to say, swim here at your own risk.

West of town are the coves of Puerto Angelito and Carrizalillo. These sheltered spots are ideal for snorkeling and scuba diving; bring your own gear, as facilities are limited at best. They can be reached either by taxi, a boat launched from Playa Principal or a circuitous concrete footpath (wear a hat and bring water if you decide to walk). Farther west is Playa Bacocho, another open strip of sand; the waves and undertow make it better for sunning and hiking than swimming. Most of the more expensive hotels cluster around this beach.

## What To Do

The main reason to visit Puerto Escondido is to relax at the beach; shopping and entertainment are not high on the list of diversions. The local *mercado* (municipal market) is in the upper section of town on Avenida 10 Norte, several blocks west of Avenida Oaxaca. It sells mostly produce, but one group of stalls offers a selection of regional handicrafts. Along the tourist strip, there are a few clothing shops and the usual hodgepodge of T-shirts, postcards and souvenirs.

Several restaurants line beachside Avenida Peréz Gasga, with fish and seafood—from sushi to octopus—the main menu items. Most places provide a view of the beach and the activity along it. The restaurant in the Hotel Santa Fe, on Avenida del Morro at the eastern end of the bay (about half a mile southeast of the town center), has good food and a breezy atmosphere, with tables overlooking the Playa Zicatela surf.

The best places to watch the sun sink into the Pacific are along Playa Zicatela, where there is an unobscured view of the western horizon. The cliff-top lawn on the grounds of the Posada Real Hotel, west of town overlooking Playa Bacocho, is an ideal perch for sunset watching. A taxi can get you there. There are a couple of noisy bars and dance clubs in the tourist zone along Avenida Peréz Gasga and in the hotels around Playa Bacocho.

The surrounding coastal region is a natural paradise, and because most locations are inaccessible except by boat, eco-tourism is actively promoted. Hidden Voyages Ecotours offers seasonal (mid-Dec. through March) guided bird-watching and nature trips to some of the lagoons that indent the Oaxacan coast. Early morning motorboat trips visit Manialtepec Lagoon, about 15 kilometers (9 miles) west of Puerto Escondido, which is encircled by mangroves and home to a rich variety of wetland bird species and tropical vegetation. The company also offers kayak tours of the lagoon.

Round-trip transportation is provided from Puerto Escondido hotels. Food is not included; the restaurant at the departure dock sells beverages to go. Bring a hat and sunblock. Binoculars are provided. The motorboat tour fee is 650 pesos (or $50 U.S.) per person; kayak tour fee 800 pesos (about $65 U.S.) per person.

Reservations are required. From mid-December through March phone (954) 582-2962 in Puerto Escondido (English is spoken). The rest of the year phone (519) 326-5193 in Canada (English is spoken). Reservations can also be made through the Dimar Travel Agency, Av. Peréz Gasga #905 on the beachfront. Office hours vary; phone (954) 582-2305. This agency also can arrange three- or four-person fishing trips to the waters off Puerto Escondido for mackerel, sea bass, snook or tuna. Boats depart from Playa Principal.

**Tourist information office:** near the airport, at the intersection of Mex. 200 (Carretera Costera) and Avenida del Pacífico. Open Mon.-Fri. 9-2 and 5-8, Sat. 9-1. **Phone:** (954) 582-0175.

# Puerto Vallarta

**City Population:** 255,681
**Elevation:** 6 meters (20 feet)

## Editor's Picks:

© Eugene Kalenkovich / Shutterstock.com

On the shores of sparkling blue Bahía de Banderas (Bay of Flags), jungle-cloaked mountains plunge into the Pacific. Here lies the treasure at the foot of the Sierra Madre: Puerto Vallarta. Luxury resorts fronted by warm water and golden-sand beaches are the main draw for visitors content to simply unwind, soak up the sun and watch waves wash ashore—and we can't say we blame them. But dig a little deeper and it won't take long for the city's alluring combination of modern sophistication and vintage character to get under your skin.

Adventurous travelers began trickling here during the 1940s and '50s, but it took a Hollywood director and a scandalous romance to put Vallarta on the mass tourism radar. Long before TMZ photogs chased celebutants and washed-up pop stars around the globe, the paparazzi pursued real movie stars. Elizabeth Taylor came to Puerto Vallarta in 1963 to be near Richard Burton, who was on location filming John Huston's "The Night of the Iguana," as the two were having a highly publicized extramarital affair. Photographers followed their every move, and Vallarta instantly became world famous.

Along cobbled streets you'll find the usual line-up of gringo-friendly businesses, from casual Mexican restaurants and hip clothing boutiques to American chain stores and party-til-dawn nightclubs. But Vallarta (as the locals call it) also has an artistic bent. Surrealistic sculptures dot the bustling beachfront *malecón* (boardwalk), a prime location for sunset strolls.

One-of-a-kind art galleries and shops pepper the compact downtown area. Souvenir stalls line shady Isla Río Cuale, a long, slender islet in the middle of the Río Cuale, the river that bisects the downtown area on its journey from mountains to sea.

The Marina Vallarta complex sits just north of the Hotel Zone. Here, discount chains like Costco and WalMart serve an ever-growing population of Mexican transplants and expatriates from *el norte*. Yet somehow such name-brand consumerism doesn't overshadow Vallarta's prevailing Old Mexico charm.

The weather is balmy year-round, but it's nicest from mid-December through mid-April. This is also the time preferred by migrating humpback whales that swim down from the frigid Arctic to the warm Pacific waters. Book your reservations several months in advance if you intend to visit during the winter high tourist season.

Vallarta is very casual; most visitors wear shorts and T-shirts. Slacks or nice jeans for men and summer-type dresses for women are appropriate for more upscale restaurants and some nightclubs. A sweater comes in handy for winter evenings; an effective sunblock is a must all year.

Pack a hat and bring along an effective insect repellent, as mosquitoes can be a nuisance at any time of year. A formula containing at least 40 percent DEET will usually do the trick. If you arrive without bug dope, Autan Classic is a widely available Mexican brand.

© Chris Howey / Shutterstock.com

## Getting There

### By Air

Gustavo Díaz Ordaz International Airport is on the main highway about 7 kilometers (4 miles) north of downtown. Aeroméxico, Alaska Airlines, American, Delta, Frontier and United all provide service to Puerto Vallarta from U.S. cities. Connections for flights from the United States are normally via Mexico City. Regular flights from Canada are available via WestJet; several Canadian charter airlines offer nonstop flights (seasonal) as well. Aeroméxico provides service from several cities within Mexico, including Guadalajara, Mexico City and Monterrey.

For flight information contact the individual airline; phone 01 (800) 021-4000 (toll-free long distance within Mexico) for Aeroméxico, 01 (800) 904-6000 (toll-free long distance within Mexico) for American, 01 (800) 266-0046 (toll-free long distance within Mexico) for Delta, 01 (800) 432-1359 (toll-free long distance within Mexico) for Frontier, 01 (800) 900-5000 (toll-free long distance within Mexico) for United and 01 (800) 514-7288 (toll-free long distance within Mexico) for WestJet. *For additional information about airlines see Arriving by Air, page p. 42.*

The ticketing and arrival area is on the main level; customs is located in the baggage claim area. Beyond customs is the main lobby, where you'll be approached by overly friendly men offering to arrange discounted ("almost free") ground transportation. These are time share salesmen. Unless you're willing to endure a high-pressure time share sales pitch, ignore them. Just beyond the hustler gauntlet you can pick up tourist brochures, make arrangements for no-strings-attached ground transportation and exchange currency. The upper level is the departure area, which requires a boarding pass to enter. Phone (322) 221-1537 for airport information.

*Colectivos* (minivans) operated by Transportes Terrestres provide shared transportation for a per-person fare from the airport to area hotels. Tickets can be purchased at booths just outside the terminal. Specially licensed airport taxis also take passengers to hotels. In both cases, fares are based on a zone system. Zones are posted at the minivan and taxi ticket booths; ask if you don't know the zone in which your hotel is located.

Airport taxis are notoriously expensive; don't be surprised to fork over as much as $20 (U.S.) for a ride to the main Hotel Zone north of town, and about $26 to either the downtown Romantic Zone or the Nuevo Vallarta area. For budget-friendly taxi transportation to your hotel, exit the far end of the airport lobby and walk over the pedestrian bridge to the other side of the main highway. Here you can hire a regular city taxi for about $12 to $15 (U.S.) depending on your destination.

# The Informed Traveler

## WHOM TO CALL

**Police (emergency):** Dial 060 and ask to be connected to an English-speaking operator. For non-emergencies, phone (322) 290-0507.

**Consumer Protection Agency (PROFECO):** Calle Morelos #883; phone (322) 225-0000 (English may not be spoken fluently). The office is open Mon.-Fri. 9-3 and can assist with time share, taxi, store and other consumer-related issues.

**Hospitals:** Ameri-Med Hospital, in Plaza Neptuno at the entrance to Marina Vallarta (Boulevard Francisco Medina), (322) 226-2080; CMQ Hospital, Basilio Badillo #365 at Insurgentes, (322) 223-1919 or (322) 222-3572; Red Cross (Cruz Roja), (322) 222-1533. All of these facilities are open 24 hours.

**Local phone calls:** Use public Telmex phones marked "Ladatel" rather than calling from your hotel room, which almost always incurs a hefty charge (as much as $7 U.S. per minute). These phones require a Ladatel phone card, available in various denominations from most local stores. Avoid phones showing pictures of credit cards or plastered-on decals saying "3 minutos gratis" that advertise long distance calling to the United States and Canada. You'll pay dearly for the convenience.

## WHERE TO LOOK

### Newspapers

*Vallarta Today* is an English-language daily newspaper geared toward tourists; it has information on everything from restaurants to currency exchange rates. The English-language *Vallarta Tribune* is a free weekly containing local news as well as restaurant and entertainment listings.

### Visitor Information

**Municipal Tourist Office:** in the City Hall (Presidencia Municipal) building at avenidas Juárez and Independencia. The office is open daily 8 a.m.-9 p.m. **Phone:** (322) 223-2500.

The Web site www.virtualvallarta.com provides local news and comprehensive information about everything from airlines to restaurants to city services. There also are Internet cafes where you can check e-mail and surf online for about $4 (U.S.) per hour. Aquarius Internet, Av. Juárez #523 (on the west side of the street between avenidas Corona and Galeana) is open daily; phone (322) 223-5700.

Banderas Bay American Legion Post 14 meets on the third Tuesday of the month at noon at Steve's Sports Bar, Basilio Badillo #286 (across from Memo's Pancake House).

**Riviera Nayarit Convention & Visitors Bureau:** Av. Cocoteros #85 Sur (in Paradise Plaza), Nuevo Vallarta, Nayarit. The office is open Mon.-Fri. 9-6, Sat. 9-2. **Phone:** (322) 297-2516.

## WHAT TO KNOW

### Currency Exchange

Banks and currency exchange houses (*casas de cambio*) are located throughout the city and at the airport. Banks are usually open Mon.-Fri. 9-5, although hours for exchanging foreign currency may be restricted. Currency exchange houses are open longer hours. Stores, restaurants, taxi drivers and even street vendors will often take U.S. dollars, and credit cards are widely accepted. ATMs are plentiful; withdrawals are in pesos. Some machines dispense U.S. dollars as well, but this option usually requires a Mexican bank-issued ATM/credit card.

### Staying Safe

Tourist crime is uncommon, and it's safe to walk the downtown streets. However, visitors would do well not to carry large amounts of cash in public. Avoid walking back streets after dark. If your hotel provides safety deposit boxes, they are a good place to keep money, passports, airline tickets, tourist permits and so forth. Bilingual "tourist police" wearing white safari outfits and baseball caps patrol the downtown area and are generally friendly and helpful.

## By Car

Reaching Puerto Vallarta by car involves a lengthy journey; the city lies some 1,200 miles south of the border at Nogales, Ariz., via Mex. 15/15-D and Mex. 200. Traffic on the Mex. 15 free road (*libre* in Spanish) slows considerably in the city of Mazatlán and beyond. Alternately, the Mex. 15-D toll road (*cuota*) is usually wide open. Tolls are hefty, however; the fees from Nogales to Mazatlán alone total 752 pesos (about $56 U.S.). While dollars are usually accepted at toll booths near the U.S. border, it's best to have pesos on hand for the entire route.

State and federal police conduct frequent inspections, particularly at state lines. Trucks can slow traffic down around Tepic, the Nayarit state capital. From Tepic, Mex. 200 proceeds south to Puerto Vallarta.

Mex. 161 connects San Blas, on the Nayarit coast, with Puerto Vallarta, bypassing Mex. 15's uphill slog through Tepic. While it's not any faster than 15, the Mex. 161 route is incredibly scenic. The generally well-maintained two-lane road snakes through jungle-cloaked hills, then skirts the coast while passing through arid farmland. If heading south from San Blas (which is accessible from Mex. 15 via Mex. 54), take the marked Puerto Vallarta turn-off just before the entrance to town and head south. Mex. 161 connects with Mex. 200 at the town of Las Varas; from there, proceed south. Plan on a 3-hour drive from San Blas to Puerto Vallarta.

To reach Puerto Vallarta from Guadalajara, take toll highway Mex. 15-D west toward Tepic. At Chapalilla, take the Mex. 200-D turn-off (toward Compostela); at Compostela, proceed south on Mex. 200 for about 130 kilometers (80 miles) to Puerto Vallarta.

**Note:** Mex. 200 is a precipitously winding two-lane road that passes through mountainous terrain. In addition to numerous twists and turns, road shoulders are narrow and have steep drop-offs. Only experienced motorists familiar with mountain driving should attempt to navigate this route, and never drive it at night. Plan on a 6-hour drive to get to Puerto Vallarta from Guadalajara.

## By Bus

Puerto Vallarta's modern central bus station, Central Camionera de Puerto Vallarta, is located just off the Tepic Highway about a kilometer north of the airport. It has a ticket office, baggage storage, restaurants, long distance phone and fax services and guarded overnight parking. The major first-class lines operate out of this station.

Vallarta Plus is a popular line offering daily first-class bus service to and from Guadalajara (about 5 hours). Elite travels the route as well, and also offers service north to Tepic, Mazatlán, Mexicali and Tijuana and south to Manzanillo, Zihuatanejo, Acapulco and Puerto Escondido. Some buses require transfers or stop along the way, while others do not; the ticketing agent will be able to clarify routes and answer questions.

ETN (Enlaces Terrestres Nacionales) specializes in "executive-class" service to Mexico City, Guadalajara and Manzanillo. Travel agencies around

© karamysh / Shutterstock.com

town can sometimes provide bus routes and schedules. *For additional information about buses see Bus Service, page p. 52.*

## By Cruise Ship

Puerto Vallarta is a port of call for cruise ships, most arriving from Los Angeles during the peak tourist season. Cruise lines dock at the Terminal Marítima (Maritime Terminal), north of downtown at the Marina Vallarta complex, and include Carnival, Celebrity, Holland-America, Norwegian and Princess. From the dock, a road lined with gift shops and guided tour kiosks leads to the main highway. Taxis congregate around the terminal area; a ride downtown will cost about $8 (U.S.).

## Getting Around

### City Layout

North of the Río Cuale, different sections of the city are connected by one primary thoroughfare. Officially called Avenida Francisco Medina Ascencio, it changes names several times. The stretch of busy four-lane highway heading south from the airport and running behind the beachfront Hotel zone is also known as the Carretera Aeropuerto (Airport Highway). South of the Hotel Zone, the road narrows and becomes Avenida México and then Paseo Díaz Ordáz as it runs along the waterfront.

El Centro *(see attraction listing),* the central downtown area, is small and compact, hemmed in as it is between the mountains and the bay. The Río Cuale divides it into two sections. The *malecón* (oceanfront boardwalk) runs along Paseo Díaz Ordáz from north of the river south to the Romantic Zone. Widened and landscaped a couple of years ago, it creates a pedestrian-only esplanade along this stretch of Ordáz. Drivers heading through downtown should use either Calle Morelos (one-way southbound) or Avenida Juárez (one-way northbound) as alternate routes.

Vacationers and locals alike come to enjoy the sea breeze, people watch and ponder the beautiful—and often bizarre—collection of bronze sculptures. Master sand castle artists create additional eye candy on the narrow shore below the seawall. Across the street you can browse boutiques and souvenir shops, scout the nightclubs or sip a margarita on one of several restaurant balconies and watch the sun set over the bay.

The heart of Vallarta, tree-shaded Plaza de Armas (also called Plaza Principal), sits just off the *malecón* between avenidas Morelos and Juárez. A central gazebo and a statue of Don Ignacio L. Vallarta, for whom the city was named, adorn this traditional town square where schoolchildren chase pigeons and overheated street vendors nap on wrought-iron benches. Tourists stroll by on their way to the Church of Our Lady of Guadalupe *(see attraction listing),* its crown-topped spire soaring over the city.

On Avenida Juárez, facing the north side of the plaza, is City Hall (Presidencia Municipal). The mural of Puerto Vallarta hanging above the stairwell was painted by local artist Manuel Lepe. On the west side of the plaza between Avenida Morelos and the southern end of the *malecón* is an outdoor amphitheater, the site of evening concerts. The white arches (Los Arcos) backing the amphitheater were rebuilt after being destroyed by Hurricane Kenna in 2002.

The area known as Gringo Gulch was named for the intellectual and artsy Americans who settled in Puerto Vallarta during the 1950s and '60s. This steep ravine overlooking the Río Cuale is lined with red tile-roofed, colonial-style villas, many of them tucked away off cobbled alleyways festooned with blooming bougainvillea.

To reach the gulch, walk up Calle Zaragoza toward the hillside above town. The street appears to dead-end, but look closely and you'll see a steep stone staircase. Climb it to continue on Zaragoza.

Río Cuale Island (Isla Río Cuale), a long, narrow island-oasis in the middle of the Río Cuale, can be accessed from the northern and southern sections of El Centro by two road bridges, a pair of wood-plank suspension foot bridges and a concrete pedestrian bridge that spans the mouth of the river. The island's main attraction is its meandering fig and rubber tree-shaded walkway, lined with colorful souvenir stalls and a handful of riverside eateries.

Just east of the Avenida Insurgentes road bridge, a shady plaza is home to a statue of Hollywood legend John Huston, who directed "The Night of the Iguana." At the island's western end, where the river meets the sea, local kids play and swim in water that appears less than pristine.

The area south of the Río Cuale, the Zona Romantica, is one of Vallarta's oldest neighborhoods. Although the whitewashed building facades don't look radically different from what you see north of the river, the narrow cobbled streets exude more of a ragged "Old Vallarta" feel. An eclectic mix of shops, restaurants and bars can be found along east-west Basilio Badillo, 5 blocks south of the river.

The Zona Romantica's main beach is Playa los Muertos, a popular stretch of sand lined with casual *palapa* (thatched-roof) restaurants and mid-range hotels. North of El Centro, luxury properties fronting pretty Playa de Oro (Golden Beach) form the upscale Hotel Zone. High-rise resort towers boast sweeping views of palm-fringed Banderas Bay.

Running behind the Hotel Zone is busy, four-lane Avenida Francisco Medina Ascencio. While it's not exactly ideal for a romantic stroll, the boulevard does offer a convenient assemblage of shopping centers packed with a predictable lineup of mini-markets, banks, gift shops, restaurants and American fast-food joints. Plaza Caracol, near the Fiesta Americana Hotel, is anchored by a Gigante supermarket.

Feeling more like a yachtsman's enclave in the United States rather than part of Mexico, Marina Vallarta aims to be a resort destination unto itself and wholly succeeds. This modern development near the airport encompasses major chain hotels, upscale condos, an enormous marina and yacht club and the 18-hole Marina Vallarta Club de Golf.

Deluxe mega-resorts occupy beachfront estate, while the pleasant marina boardwalk is lined with tourist-geared shops, galleries, cafes and restaurants. Hotel shuttles, city buses and taxis provide service to downtown. The marina is a good choice if you're a first-timer or part of a package tour, although it lacks the charm of Puerto Vallarta proper.

Nuevo Vallarta, about 19 kilometers (12 miles) north of the airport, is just over the Nayarit state line at the mouth of the Río Ameca. This planned resort area is a mix of condominiums, time share units, private bayfront homes and fancy all-inclusive accommodations.

A bit farther north is the village of Bucerías ("place of the divers"), an enclave of cobblestone streets, walled villas and tidy little hotels. Some travelers prefer this lower-cost alternative to Puerto Vallarta for its many shops, town square market and casual open-air restaurants. The 5-mile stretch of white sand is the longest along the Banderas Bay coastline. The shallow shoreline is perfect for wading, body surfing and shell collecting, and the beach draws throngs of local families on Sundays. Bucerías is most easily reached by bus; minivans also shuttle passengers from the airport to the village and back.

## Rental Cars

If you've driven your own vehicle or rented one for exploring areas to the north or south, avoid driving after dark; cows wandering onto the roadway can be a very real hazard. Keep in mind that rental cars are expensive, and downtown parking is difficult. For sightseeing in and around the city, take advantage of the green-and-white or blue-and-white city buses that cover the area from Marina Vallarta south to Mismaloya Beach.

**Note:** AAA/CAA members enjoy discounts through Hertz for vehicles booked in the United States. Consult your local AAA/CAA club or phone Hertz, (800) 654-3080.

## Buses

City buses are inexpensive and take passengers to almost all points along Banderas Bay, from the airport south through the Hotel Zone, into downtown via the Ignacio Vallarta Bridge, and to points as far south as Mismaloya Beach. The fixed fare is 7.5 pesos. The exact amount is appreciated, but drivers will make change for a $20 peso note. Change for a $50 peso bill comes with a heavy sigh and a side of grumbling. In addition to the newer minibuses (*combis* or *colectivos*) that are equipped with emission controls, there are still old public buses on the streets spewing clouds of exhaust.

Stops are designated by a white bus outlined on a dark blue sign. If traffic is light, it's often possible to flag down a bus anywhere along the street. Destinations and routes (for example, *"Olas Altas," "Ixtapa," "Zona Hoteles"* or *"Aeropuerto"*) are posted on the front of the bus or painted on the windshield. As you climb aboard and pay your fare, tell the driver where you want to be let off. Most drivers don't speak English but they do understand, for example, "El Sheraton Hotel, por favor." Local routes are normally covered from 6 a.m. to 11 p.m.

The local bus station is on Avenida Olas Altas at Plaza Lázaro Cárdenas, south of the Río Cuale and just inland from the beach. City buses also depart from Plaza de Armas, the main square.

## Taxis

Taxis are plentiful and cover the same routes as buses, but are more expensive. Fares are based on set rates and defined zones. The average fare within town is about $5 to $6 (U.S.); trips from downtown north to the Hotel Zone or Marina Vallarta will run up to about $8, depending on the destination. A ride across town from Marina Vallarta south to Playa los Muertos is about $12 to $14.

Fares *should* be posted in each taxi and are printed in the *Vallarta Today* newspaper. Many hotels post a list of rates to specific destinations, which can come in handy if you're unfamiliar with the city. Taxis also can be hired by the hour or by the day for out-of-town trips.

Always ask how much the fare is (*"Cuanto?"*) and come to a decision before you get in the cab, which might save a few pesos. Resist efforts by any driver to steer you to a particular restaurant; some restaurateurs pay commissions to drivers for bringing them customers. It also is customary not to tip drivers.

## Parking

Parking in the compact downtown area is scarce, and driving around the city in general presents a

## DID YOU KNOW

With a population of more than 112,000,000, Mexico is the most populous Spanish-speaking country in the world.

challenge. During the winter tourist season from December through April the narrow streets are jammed; from July through October heavy rains can make them flooded and muddy. Many roads leading in to Puerto Vallarta are just two lanes and descend from the mountains; drive with caution.

## Guides/Tours

The standard city tour provides an all-purpose Puerto Vallarta orientation. A short version of the tour covers the local sights by air-conditioned minibus, including the main plaza, cathedral and the exclusive neighborhoods of Conchas Chinas and Gringo Gulch. A shopping trip is usually made to either Isla Río Cuale or the Municipal Market.

The jungle tour is a longer version that throws in trips to a tequila tasting room and Mismaloya Beach, plus lunch in a tropical setting at Chico's Paradise. Hotel pickup and drop-off is included in the fee; lunch is not. Several companies offer daily city and jungle tours lasting 4 and 6 hours, respectively. Make arrangements through your hotel or at one of the guided tour reservation booths you'll see all over town.

Canopy Tours de los Veranos offers daily 4-hour excursions to their zipline course near Mismaloya Beach. Transportation from the tour office on Mex. 200 (just south of downtown) is included. Reservations are required; phone (322) 223-0504 or (619) 955-6993 (from the United States).

## What To See

**CHURCH OF OUR LADY OF GUADALUPE** (La Iglesia de Nuestra Señora de Guadalupe) is on Calle Hidalgo, a block e. of Plaza Principal. It took 33 years to build. The church is noted for the large crown atop the steeple, modeled after one worn by Carlota, wife of Archduke Maximilian, Mexico's ruler for 3 years in the 1860s. Made of fiberglass, it replaced the original crown, which collapsed during an earthquake in 1995. Angels clasping hands decorate the exterior. Do not wear shorts or T-shirts if you wish to enter the church. **Hours:** Open daily. **Cost:** Free.

**CUALE MUSEUM** (Museo del Cuale) is on Isla Río Cuale at the island's far western end, near Oscar's restaurant. Focusing on the indigenous peoples of western Mexico, this tiny archeology museum displays ancient pottery, figurines, jewelry and other objects. Information panels are in Spanish and English. **Hours:** Tues.-Sat. 9-6. **Cost:** 39 pesos (about $2.90 U.S.). **Phone:** (322) 135-0762 (cellular number).

**EL CENTRO** encompasses the area inland from the *malecón* and n. of the Río Cuale. Puerto Vallarta's old downtown core is a delightful contrast to the newer resort development that has spread both north and south along the beaches. An irregular grid of narrow streets, lined with whitewashed stucco buildings with red-tiled roofs, extends some 6 blocks up into the hills above the bay. The cobblestone streets, full of little shops and offering vistas of lush green hills tumbling down to the bay, are a pleasure to stroll (wear comfortable shoes). Street names are denoted on Mexican tiles on the sides of buildings.

El Centro exudes charm despite sputtering taxicabs, aggressive bus drivers and occasional construction; such sights as the odd donkey clopping along the cobblestones are a flashback to a more prosaic Mexico.

*MALECÓN* **SCULPTURES** dot the boardwalk along Paseo Díaz Ordáz. Walking from south to north, you'll see a beautiful collection of bronze public sculptures that includes the "Fountain of Friendship" (Fuente de la Amistad), a dome-shaped fountain crowned with three leaping dolphins. The romantic "Triton & Nereida" depicts the son of Neptune reaching for his mermaid lover, perched atop a curling wave just beyond his grasp.

A Vallarta icon, "El Caballito del Mar" is the famous statue of a young boy riding a seahorse. Farther along the sculptures take a surrealistic turn. "In Search of Reason," by Guadalajara artist Sergio Bustamente, features a ladder to nowhere being climbed by two pillow-headed children. Perhaps the *malecón's* strangest installation is Alejandro Colunga's "Rotunda of the Sea" (La Rotunda del Mar); ringed by alien creatures with twisted shapes that form high-backed chairs, this is by far Vallarta's most bizarre photo-op. Nearby is an 8-foot-high, Dali-esque statue of a man filling his black obsidian pot belly with rocks; Jonás Gutierrez's 2006 installation is called "Eating Stones" (Come Piedras).

At the northern end is Mathis Lidice's "Millennium"; a wave twists and arcs toward the sky, topped by a female figure releasing a dove to the heavens. The sculpture represents "the feminine energy that will lead us into a new age."

**NAVAL HISTORY MUSEUM** is in the center of town (Colonia Centro) at Calle Zaragoza #4. This small but well-maintained museum has three rooms with exhibits about Acapulco pirates, the history and development of Mexican navigation and the role the Mexican Navy has played in the country's naval battles. Exhibit information is in Spanish, but a book with the information in English is available. **Time:** Allow 30 minutes minimum. **Hours:** Tues.-Sun. 9-8. Phone ahead to confirm schedule. **Cost:** Free. **Phone:** (322) 223-5357. 🏛

**OCEAN FRIENDLY TOURS** depart from Los Peines pier, about a 10-minute taxi ride from the downtown waterfront. This company's guided whale-watch excursion is one of the best in Vallarta. Led by a professional researcher who has an infectious passion for these gentle giants, the trip begins with information about the whales' migration, mating and birthing activities, with emphasis on conservation and species protection. A hydrophone and speaker system on board allows passengers to listen to underwater humpback vocalizations.

In addition to humpback whales, dolphins, sea turtles, manta rays and varied bird species are likely

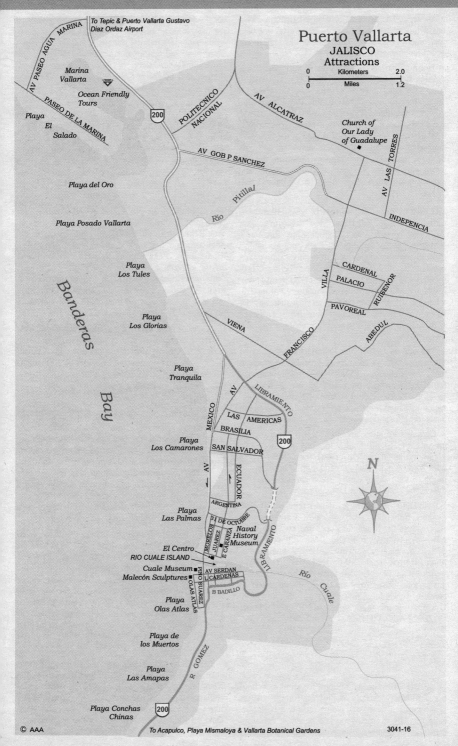

Puerto Vallarta
JALISCO
Attractions

Kilometers 0 2.0
Miles 0 1.2

To Tepic & Puerto Vallarta Gustavo Diaz Ordaz Airport

AV PASEO AGUA MARINA

Marina Vallarta

Ocean Friendly Tours

PASEO DE LA MARINA

Playa El Salado

200

POLITECNICO NACIONAL

AV ALCATRAZ

Church of Our Lady of Guadalupe

AV LAS TORRES

AV GOB P SANCHEZ

Playa del Oro

Río Pitillal

INDEPENCIA

Playa Posado Vallarta

CARDENAL
VILLA
PALACIO
RUISEÑOR
PAVOREAL
ABEDUL

Playa Los Tules

Playa Los Glorias

VIENA

FRANCISCO

Banderas Bay

Playa Tranquila

AV LIBRAMIENTO
MEXICO
LAS AMERICAS
BRASILIA
SAN SALVADOR
200

Playa Los Camarones

AV

ECUADOR

ARGENTINA

Playa Las Palmas

BI DE OCTUBRE
MORELOS
JUAREZ
CARANZA
Naval History Museum

El Centro
RIO CUALE ISLAND
Cuale Museum
Malecón Sculptures
PINO SUAREZ
OLAS ALTAS
AV SERDAN
L CARDENAS
B BADILLO
LIBRAMIENTO

Río Cuale

Playa Olas Atlas

Playa de los Muertos

R GOMEZ

N

Playa Las Amapas

Playa Conchas Chinas

200

© AAA

To Acapulco, Playa Mismaloya & Vallarta Botanical Gardens

3041-16

to be seen. The 30-foot, customized fiberglass boat has a tiny restroom on board. Life vests, dry bags for camera protection, water, soft drinks and an onboard lunch are provided.

**Hours:** Trips depart daily at 9 a.m., early Dec. through late Mar., and last 4 to 5 hours. Arrive at least 15 minutes prior to departure and allow at least 30 minutes for transportation time to the pier from downtown Vallarta. **Cost:** $129; $115 (ages 2-13). Ages 0-1 are not permitted on the tour. There also is a 10-peso fee per person that is paid at the pier. Prepaid advance reservations are required and can only be made online via the company's website using a credit card. Phone for tour space availability and general information (English spoken). **Phone:** (322) 225-3774.

**VALLARTA BOTANICAL GARDENS** is 19 km (12 mi.) s. of Puerto Vallarta at Mex. 200 Km marker 24, following signs. Set in a tropical dry forest ecosystem 1,300 feet up in the Sierra Madre mountains, this 20-acre botanical garden features native and non-native collections of orchids, palms, ferns, bromeliads and succulents. The Tree Fern Grotto is representative of a tropical mountain environment, while the Blue Agave Hills is an area that was deforested for cattle grazing before being replanted with agaves, mountain pines, and tababuia and mahogany trees.

The newest facility, the Vallarta Conservatory of Mexican Orchids, provides a greenhouse environment for numerous varieties of orchids that are found nowhere else on Earth; Mexico is home to more than 1,200 orchid species. Promoting conservation of native flora, this professional operation appeals to both serious gardeners and nature lovers.

Getting here is an adventure, via a winding road up into the Sierra Madre foothills past a jungle gorge and an impressive granite formation covered with wild orchids, plumeria and vanilla bean. In addition to touring the gardens, you can take a dip in the crystal-clear Río Los Horcones.

"El Tuito" tourist buses depart regularly for the gardens from the corner of calles Carranzas and Aguacate in the Romantic Zone; one-way fare is 20 pesos. A taxi ride from Old Town will cost about $25 (U.S.) each way. **Time:** Allow 2 hours minimum. **Hours:** Daily 10-6, Dec.-Mar.; Tues.-Sun. 10-6, rest of year. Guided tours are offered once a day; phone ahead for tour times. Phone ahead to confirm schedule. **Cost:** 80 pesos (about $5.90 U.S.); 20 pesos (ages 4-12). Cash only. **Phone:** (322) 223-6182. 🍽 ✉

## What To Do

### Dining

Vallarta offers many options for dining well, if not particularly cheaply. A plus for foreign visitors is the purified water—including ice—that is universally used by licensed food and beverage establishments. (If in doubt, ask for bottled water, juice, beer or a soft drink.) While food quality is dependable, it is the striking ocean views that distinguish many restaurants. Most hotel establishments offer a standard steak and seafood menu. Seafood, Mexican and Argentinian are some of the choices at eateries along the 3 blocks of Calle Basilio Badillo between Pino Suárez and Insurgentes.

If you want to sample authentic Mexican cooking and rub elbows with locals, try Cenaduria Doña Raquel, at Leona Vicario #131 (half a block east of the *malecón*). Along the back wall of a small, simple dining room, Mexican women whip up delicious *flautas*, enchiladas and *tostadas* in an open kitchen. The *pozole* (pork, cabbage and hominy stew) is excellent—and for the adventurous eater, also available with a "triple portion of head meat."

For some of the city's tastiest and cheapest cuisine, grab a quick lunch at a sidewalk taco stand. You'll find them all over town, with an especially high concentration on the streets south of the Río Cuale in the Zona Romantica. At the southern end of the *malecón* a congregation of food vendor carts sells everything from fish on a stick to fresh-cut fruit. As is the usual case with street food and hygiene, use your best judgment. Does the operation look clean? Is it busy? If so, it's usually fine.

A casual dress code is the rule, although wearing shorts to dinner may be frowned on at some of the nicer places. Some restaurants shut down for a month during the summer. See the Lodgings & Restaurants section for AAA-RATED dining establishments.

### Shopping

Shoppers can browse for jewelry, especially silver; clothing ranging from the ubiquitous beach T-shirts to designer fashions; colonial-style furniture; pottery and ceramics; hand-tooled leather goods, including *huaraches* (sandals); shoes (keep in mind that sizes are measured in centimeters); and sombreros and other hats. Fine handicrafts include beaded tapestries from Nayarit, lacquered boxes and ceremonial masks from Michoacán, and handwoven baskets, rugs and shawls from Central America.

For a typical Mexican shopping experience, head to the open-air Municipal Market (Mercado Municipal), which spreads out under the trees below the steps leading down from the northern end of the Avenida Insurgentes Bridge. Clothes, crafts, leather goods, silver jewelry and trinkets fill the two-level maze of stalls—everything from piñatas to whips. Experienced hagglers may be able to persuade vendors to lower their prices *un poquito* (just a little bit). If that doesn't work, simply walk away and prices magically drop.

A similar but more atmospheric shopping experience lies just across the river on Isla Río Cuale. The island's shady *paseo* is chock-a-block with vendor stalls hawking all those must-have Mexico souvenirs like Corona beer wall clocks, *lucha libre* masks and Oakland Raiders ponchos. Some vendors offer quality items, but you'll have to seek them out.

Interested in more than a souvenir? You could spend an entire day visiting Puerto Vallarta's wide assortment of fine art galleries and distinctive shops and still not even scratch the surface. As home to one of the largest resident communities of painters, sculptors and craftspeople in all of Mexico, art is *big* here.

Galleries are spread throughout the entire downtown area; a handy "Old Town Art Walk" map is available at many galleries and also is printed in the *Vallarta Tribune* newspaper. However, with fine art pieces come eye-popping price tags and the challenge of getting your new treasures home safely. Most (if not all) gallery owners accept credit cards and can arrange shipping. Don't bother trying to haggle over price, as it's usually fixed and you will surely offend the proprietor—not to mention embarrass yourself.

North of the Río Cuale, standouts include Galería Vallarta, at Guerrero #110. Located near the main plaza, this casual gallery carries traditional and contemporary paintings, plus fine art prints and beautiful handmade jewelry; phone (322) 222-5125. Galería Uno, Calle Morelos #561 (at Calle Zaragoza),

occupies a huge space exhibiting a range of Mexican contemporary art, including paintings, graphics and sculptures. It is open Mon.-Sat. 9-8; phone (322) 222-0908.

Galería Pacífico, Aldama #174, specializes in contemporary works by Mexican and Latin American artists; phone (322) 222-1982. Galería de Ollas, Corona #176, carries the exquisite work of potters from the village of Mata Ortiz; phone (322) 223-1045.

A cluster of galleries near the corner of Leona Vicario and Guadalupe Sánchez includes Corsica Galería de Arte, at Guadalupe Sánchez #735. Favored by serious collectors, it specializes in museum-quality work by big-league Mexican artists. Unless you flew to PV on a private jet, sky-high prices will relegate you to browsing only. Phone (322) 222-9620.

South of the Río Cuale, Galería Dante, Basilio Badillo #269, should be on every gallery hound's short list. Vallarta's largest (and many claim its best) gallery, Dante features a sculpture garden filled with contemporary pieces by international artists, plus high-quality re-creations of classical statues. The

painters represented are primarily Mexican; phone (322) 222-2477. From here, more galleries, boutiques and jewelry shops line Basilio Badillo all the way down to the beach.

Downtown shops carry an excellent selection of home decor. Prices tend to be high, but so does quality. The warehouse-like Mundo de Cristal, south of the river at Insurgentes #333 (at the corner of Basilio Badillo) is the place to go for all things glass—from plates, stemware and vases to art glass hand-blown on site.

Mundo de Azulejos (World of Tiles), Venustiano Carranza #374 (also south of the river), has a huge selection of hand-painted Talavera tiles, as well as plates and murals. On display at Alfarería Tlaquepaque, Av. México #1100 (just off the *malecón*), are baskets, woodcarvings, glassware and ceramics from various Mexican states.

Huichol (pronounced we-CHOL) bead and yarn art is hand-crafted by Huichol Indians, who live in the Sierra Madre Mountains not far from Puerto Vallarta. Shamanistic traditions and peyote-fueled visions inspire the Huichol to create colorful yarn "paintings." Threads of yarn are pressed into a wax-coated wood tablet to create mythological imagery. The same general process is employed when using tiny, colored beads to decorate wooden animal figures with psychedelic patterns.

A good place to learn more about the animistic Huichol and the symbolism reflected in their art is the Folklore Bazaar, Paseo Díaz Ordaz #732 (on the *malecón*). Deer, snake, wolf, jaguar and iguana figures fill the shelves. Larger items can cost hundreds of dollars, but smaller pieces can be had for about $20 (U.S.). Huichol artisans demonstrate their craft at a worktable in the center of the gallery.

Puerto Vallarta's shopping centers feature boutiques offering sportswear and casual yet fashionable evening wear. They are located primarily along the *malecón* and north into the Hotel Zone. Most stores are open until at least 8 p.m., and some may close from 2-4 for *siesta*. Many stores are closed on Sunday.

Among the arcades with browsing potential are Plaza Malecón, on the oceanfront at Paseo Díaz Ordaz and Calle Allende; Plaza Marina, within the Marina Vallarta complex; and Villa Vallarta, on Avenida Francisco Medina Ascencio in the Hotel Zone. Just north of the cruise ship terminal and WalMart, the sleek Galerías Vallarta mall is anchored by Mexican department store Liverpool (think Nordstrom).

Worlds removed from the hustle and bustle of downtown, the relaxed Marina Vallarta boardwalk caters to tourists staying in the Marina Vallarta resort area. Yachts glisten in the sun, couples stroll hand in hand along the water's edge and families dine alfresco at gringo-friendly eateries. Roving souvenir vendors are nonexistent.

Finding the boardwalk can be tricky, as it's hidden behind a string of condominium developments. From the marina's main thoroughfare, Paseo de la Marina, access is via calles Timón, Ancla or Vera. Restaurants outnumber retail establishments, but there are a handful of shops, clothing boutiques and galleries worth investigating. Galería EM deals in gorgeous high-end art glass; prepare to dole out serious *dinero* for one of their elaborate stained-glass windows, fused-glass creations or eye-catching "floating crystal" sculptures.

A small flea market offering the usual T-shirts and souvenirs sets up at the Maritime Terminal docks where the cruise ships anchor. And finally, swarms of vendors peddle their wares at all Vallarta beaches, but they're practically a plague at Playa de los Muertos, and their persistence can be annoying. If you're not interested in purchasing anything, shake your head "no," say "*Gracias, no*" or ignore them completely.

Also be aware that if you eat at one of the *palapa* restaurants fronting the beach boardwalk, vendors will approach you constantly. If this bothers you ask for a table located well inside, away from the front row action.

## Beaches

Beaches are divided into three zones: north of town, in town and south of town. In summer there are efforts at all of the beaches to protect the eggs of endangered sea turtles, evidence of an increased ecological awareness throughout the country. Puerto Vallarta's sea turtle release programs involve regular patrols of turtle nesting grounds. Eggs are taken to protected nurseries, and hatchlings are released in the open water.

**PLAYA DE ORO** is n. of downtown, backed by the Hotel Zone. Although it may seem like the stretches of sand in front of the big hotels are private, they are not; all beaches in Mexico are federal property and thus open to the public. The wide, flat beach is divided into sections by rocky jetties and faces the open bay; waves can be surprisingly rough.

**PLAYA DE LOS MUERTOS** (Beach of the Dead) is s. of the Río Cuale and can be accessed from Calle Olas Altas. City officials have long tried to rename this popular beach Playa del Sol. Better for sunning than for swimming (the water is somewhat polluted), Playa de los Muertos attracts locals, European tourists and budget travelers. Sunbathers crowd the sand (particularly on Sundays and holidays), parasailers soar above it and roaming vendors hawk barbecued fish on a stick—the PV equivalent of a Coney Island hot dog. At the southern end of the beach is El Púlpito, a rock formation shaped like a pulpit.

**PLAYA MISMALOYA** (Mismaloya Beach) is about 10 km (6 mi.) s. of town off Mex. 200 (the southward extension of Av. Insurgentes). "The Night of the Iguana" was filmed here. A walking path along the southern end of a pretty cove leads to the ruins of the movie set, most of it surrounded by chain-link fencing hung with signs warning visitors to stay out.

Although the spot's tranquil beauty has been compromised by hillside home development and the sprawling La Jolla de Mismaloya hotel complex, the water is clear, the sand white and the beach backed by jungle-cloaked hills. A string of shoreline *palapa* restaurants sell beer and seafood, and also rent out tables and beach chairs. At the far southern end of the beach, Teos Restaurant & Bar serves delicious jumbo shrimp wrapped in greasy bacon and drizzled with pineapple juice. In the rugged country above Mismaloya another movie was made—Arnold Schwarzenegger's 1987 action opus "Predator."

## Sightseeing

Terra Noble is an arts center and spa situated on a high plateau at the north end of town, surrounded by mountains and jungle. Visitors can attend hands-on clay or painting workshops utilizing pre-Hispanic techniques, or relax with a massage and an invigorating sea salt exfoliation. Reservations can be made through local travel agencies, or phone (322) 223-0308.

Nearby beaches and islands make easy day trip destinations from Puerto Vallarta. More and more eco-tourism activities allow participants to explore or learn about the local environment without disturbing it. Vallarta Adventures organizes a variety of sightseeing and eco tours; phone (322) 226-8143, or (888) 526-2238 (from the United States).

About 16 kilometers (10 miles) south of the city, just before Mex. 200 veers inland, is the village of Boca de Tomatlán, at the mouth of the Río Tomatlán. It is easily reached by taxi or bus (buses post their destination in the window or above the windshield). Lush hillsides, freshwater pools and water burbling past huge rocks all evoke a relaxed tropical atmosphere.

The small but enticing beach at Boca de Tomatlán is sheltered by a narrow cove. Here you can hire a *panga* (skiff) for trips to the remote beaches of Playa de las Animas, Playa Quimixto (key-MISH-toh) and Playa Yelapa, all located southwest of town and only accessible by boat. Prices range from about $10 to $20 (U.S.).

All three beaches also can be reached by slightly larger and more expensive water taxis that depart from the pier at Playa de los Muertos. Tour booths at the foot of the pier can offer more details; look for booths advertising "Tour information only. No time share." Separate catamaran and boat cruises set sail daily for the coastal villages of Animas, Quimixto and Yelapa from both Playa de los Muertos and Marina Vallarta's Maritime Terminal. Cruises typically depart between 9 and 10:30 a.m. and return around 4 or 5; they usually include lunch and use of snorkeling equipment.

The coastline here is a series of small coves set against a jungle backdrop. Cruceros Princesa, phone (322) 224-4777, offers a daily yacht cruise that visits Animas and Quimixto beaches. You'll also drop anchor for a half hour of snorkeling at Los Arcos, an underwater eco-preserve surrounding the huge offshore rocks that lie just north of Mismaloya Cove.

Playa de las Animas is a striking stretch of sand backed by a string of *palapa* restaurants and a small

fishing village. Water activities abound; swimming, jet skiing (rentals are available) and snorkeling are popular. Quimixto's main draw, besides the beach, is a pretty waterfall reached by an easy half-hour hike or horseback ride (about an extra $25 U.S. per person).

Yelapa, the farthest afield of the three main beaches, sees the fewest day trippers. That doesn't mean you'll have the beach to yourself; not by a long shot. But its distance from Vallarta means that all-day Yelapa cruises typically *only* visit Yelapa, and those that do number far fewer than the Animas/Quimixto/Los Arcos boats—something to consider if you desire fewer crowds.

Vallarta Adventures offers a day-long catamaran tour that departs Puerto Vallarta's Maritime Terminal, cruises the coast, stops for snorkeling off Playa Majahuitas and spends between 2 and 3 hours (although often longer) at Yelapa. Jungle-cloaked hills surround the small bay, and a half-dozen *palapa* restaurants line the coarse-sand beach. Chico's Restaurant accepts credit cards (there are no ATMs here). Rogelio's serves fresh ceviche and fish tacos. For dessert, Yelapa's roaming "pie ladies" sell slices from lemon meringue and pecan pies that they balance on their heads.

Yelapa itself is reached by a short water taxi ride from the main beach. The steep, sandy streets of the tiny pueblo are blissfully free of cars. A 10-minute walk along the Yelapa River leads to a 150-foot-high waterfall. Tempted to stay the night? There are rustic accommodations, and you can catch a water taxi back to Vallarta in the morning. Reservations for the Vallarta Adventures catamaran can be made at most of the tour booths around town, or by calling (322) 226-8143.

## Recreation

Water sports are a given in an environment where there is access to modern marine facilities within a protected bay. The Bay of Banderas extends north to Punta de Mita (Mita Point) and south to Cabo Corrientes (Corrientes Cape), where the foothills of the Sierra de Cuale range begin. Water depths of up to 1,500 feet give the bay characteristics normally associated with oceans, but it also is protected due to its shape and the surrounding geography. The result

is generally calm water and clear visibility, which makes it ideal for **boating.**

For snorkelers, the bay teems with tropical fish. Dolphins, sea turtles, giant manta rays and migrating humpback whales also can be seen. A favorite **snorkeling** destination is the underwater park at Los Arcos (also called Las Peñas), a short distance offshore from Mismaloya Beach. The oddly eroded formations jutting out of the bay served as an early landmark for ships. Colorful marine life is particularly evident around these rocks.

A favored destination for kayakers and experienced divers is the Marietas Islands (Islas Marietas), off Punta de Mita at the bay's northern end. Comprising the tips of an undersea mountain range, these islets were once used as a hiding place by pirates who plundered galleons loaded with silver from Sierra Madre mines. Tropical fish thrive here, dolphins are frequently sighted, and the islands also are a protected bird sanctuary. Chico's Dive Shop, Paseo Díaz Ordaz #772 at the northern end of the *malecón*, rents equipment and organizes dive trips to the Marietas; phone (322) 222-1895.

Boats for **sport fishing** can be hired through the Fishing Cooperative (Cooperativo de Pescadores), at the northern end of the *malecón*. There are reservation booths out front; phone (322) 222-1202. Fishing charters can also be booked through your hotel or travel agent. Rates for fishing vessels depend on the size of the boat, where you fish, and whether bait and tackle are supplied. Bring your own refreshments, since most trips don't include them.

Sailfish and blue marlin are hooked November through February; smaller game species such as dorado, roosterfish and tuna can be caught seasonally most of the year. A catch-and-release policy is stressed if the fish is not going to be eaten.

Marina Vallarta has more than 500 slips and offers boaters fresh water, as well as cable TV and telephone hookups. Hardware and boating supply outlets are located along the boardwalk of this sprawling complex, which also has an 18-hole golf course, luxury hotels and condominiums. Tour boats and fishing excursions depart from the marina's Maritime Terminal. Boaters can explore a variety of tiny coves and hidden beaches along the shore of Banderas Bay, or drop anchor for awhile at Bahía de Banderas in Nuevo Vallarta.

**Swimming, water skiing, parasailing** and other watery pursuits can be enjoyed at many spots along the bay. Surfers head for the open waters and bigger waves around Punta de Mita. For those who would rather view the bay than venture into it, saddle horses for shoreline rides can be rented through a travel agency or the beachfront hotels.

Rancho El Charro and Rancho Ojo de Agua organize guided 2- to 3-hour **horseback riding** excursions into the foothills of the Sierra Madre, past jungle plantations and rural villages. Transportation is included and reservations are necessary; phone (322) 224-0114 for Rancho El Charro, (322) 224-0607 for Rancho Ojo de Agua.

There are several 18-hole **golf** courses in the area. Water comes into play on 11 holes at the Marina Vallarta Club de Golf course. Member privileges are extended to guests staying at certain hotels. Greens fees range from $72-$135 (U.S.) and include a shared cart. Golfers wishing to play outside peak tourist season should check with the club; phone (322) 221-0073.

The Flamingos Golf Club is about 13 kilometers (8 miles) north of the airport off Mex. 200, in the state of Nayarit. Greens fees (motorized cart included) at this older, par-72 course range from $65-$150 (U.S.); caddies are available. (**Note:** Nayarit observes Mountain Standard Time, which is an hour earlier than Puerto Vallarta and the rest of Jalisco.) Reservations and transportation can be arranged through your hotel, or phone (329) 296-5006.

The Vista Vallarta Club de Golf, 653 Circuito Universidad, Colonia San Nicolas, is about 3 miles inland from Marina Vallarta. There are two courses, one designed by Jack Nicklaus and one by Tom Weiskopf. Greens fees (motorized cart included) range from $110-$205 (U.S.). For tee times and hotel package information phone (322) 290-0030.

Most of the resorts provide clay **tennis** courts for their guests. PV also has two tennis centers: the Canto del Sol Tennis Club, at the Canto del Sol Plaza Vallarta resort in the Hotel Zone; and the Los Tules Tennis Center, near the Fiesta Americana Hotel.

## Nightlife

The cheapest after-dark option is strolling along the *malecón* (Paseo Díaz Ordaz). Sunday evenings in particular bring out local families, mariachi bands, street performers and the ubiquitous vendors.

The loud, flashy nightclubs along the *malecón* tend to attract younger crowds. Hip-hop booms at Mandala, a sleek, partially open-air dance club where flat-screen TVs play the latest rap videos and a giant Medusa statue towers over the bar. Next door, techno pulses in the cave-like Zoo, a safari-themed club complete with a bouncer in a gorilla suit and an elevated "dance cage."

These and other clubs usually stay open into the wee hours, and often until dawn during spring break weeks. Dress codes aren't strict, but don't show up in your soggy swim trunks and flip-flops. There's usually no cover charge; however, drink prices are steep.

Vallarta's party bars cater to a diverse demographic—from frat boys to boomers in tacky Hawaiian shirts—with rock, reggae and pop hits. Gringo-friendly grub, drinking contests, conga lines and over-the-top party boy waiters are all part of the fun. Señor Frog's is at Galeana #518, across the street from the seahorse statue.

Puerto Vallarta also has American-style sports bars where you can grab a bite to eat, play a board game, watch sports on TV or just sit and chat. El Torito, on Ignacio L. Vallarta (#290), features satellite broadcasts of sports events and a casual menu with the likes of nachos, ribs and beer-battered shrimp. Steve's Sports Bar, at Basilio Badillo #286 across the street from Memo's Pancake House, is a casual sports pub frequented by local expats and NASCAR, NHL and NFL enthusiasts.

For a more romantic evening, catch a live jazz combo at Le Bistro, a stylish supper club at the eastern end of Isla Río Cuale. Mexican-style fiestas with dinner buffets, folk dancing and live music take place at big hotels like the Krystal Vallarta and the Sheraton Buganvilias. For schedule and reservation information, check with the hotels or a local travel agency.

Pirates of the Bay sets sail nightly on a 4-hour dinner cruise and pirate show. Passage on the replica pirate ship includes live entertainment, a buffet meal, open bar, dancing and a fireworks display launched from the boat. Cruises depart the Maritime Terminal at 7 p.m. Monday through Saturday (reduced schedule in low season); a more family-friendly version of the cruise is available Monday through Saturday mornings at 9 a.m. Make reservations through your hotel, or phone (322) 223-0309 or (866) 915-0361 (toll-free from the United States).

## Special Events

Luckily for visitors, Puerto Vallarta's biggest events occur during the peak tourist season. The Festival of the Sea (Fiesta del Mar) is celebrated during November. Golf tournaments, art exhibits, an international boat show and a gourmet dining festival all take place, as well as the International Sailfish & Marlin Tournament, which attracts anglers from all over Mexico and the United States. For dates and details on specific events, contact the Puerto Vallarta Tourist Office.

The patron saint of mariachis is honored Nov. 23 during the Festival of Santa Cecilia, when a lineup of mariachi bands plays at the cathedral. In February, the San Diego to Puerto Vallarta Annual Regatta heralds the arrival of some impressive craft.

Perhaps the year's biggest celebration is the Fiesta de Guadalupe, honoring the Virgin of Guadalupe, Mexico's patron saint. Daily evening processions, called *peregrinaciones,* make their way to the Church of Our Lady of Guadalupe from various *colonias* (neighborhoods) and local businesses the week prior to Dec. 12. Young and old alike participate in the celebration, many carrying candles or offerings of food and flowers to be exchanged for a blessing by the priest. Mass is held in front of the cathedral, accompanied by dancing and singing. The festivities culminate on Dec. 12 with a grand fireworks display.

© Six Drive / Shutterstock.com

This ends listings for Puerto Vallarta.
The following page resumes the alphabetical listings
of cities in The Pacific Coast.

## RINCON DE GUAYABITOS, NAYARIT (B-1)

While the "Riviera Nayarit" towns of Sayulita and San Francisco court tourists with gringo-friendly amenities (read: cute shops), Guayabitos sits on pretty Jaltemba Bay and mainly draws vacationing Mexican families in search of budget beachfront accommodations and mild surf. Guayabitos is also popular with Canadian snowbirds, who are attracted by the town's affordability.

Guayabitos is about 61 kilometers (39 miles) north of the Puerto Vallarta airport via Mex. 200—just over an hour's drive. You'll find the usual *palapa* bars serving seafood and cold *cerveza*, although not on the wide, flat beach itself; local law doesn't allow alcohol sales on the sand. Instead, vendor carts hawking fish-on-a-stick, fresh fruit and inflatable beach toys are the norm.

There's decent snorkeling around Isla Islote, which is a few kilometers offshore and accessible by *pangas* that depart from Guayabitos beach. You should be able to hire a boat for about $30 (U.S.) round-trip. Los Ayala, about 2 kilometers south of Guayabitos, is an attractive curve of sand lined with thatch-roofed restaurants serving fresh seafood at non-inflated prices. Local kids play beach soccer. Fishermen repair their nets. On weekdays, you'll likely be the only *gabachos* there.

For those who really want to get away from it all, gorgeous Playa Chacala is the stuff of Mexico coffee table books. Tall palms sway behind a golden crescent of sand. The deep blue Pacific is framed by jungle-covered points at both ends of a picturesque bay. Children play in the shore breakers. Pelicans dive for lunch. A smattering of tourists and RVers sip *cervezas* at a string of rustic *palapa* restaurants. And there isn't a time share hustler in sight.

Playa Chacala is slightly less than a 2-hour drive north of Puerto Vallarta. From the airport, take Mex. 200 about 103 kilometers (64 miles) to the Chacala turn-off. The turn-off sign is badly faded; when you reach a large collection of roadside produce markets, watch for a paved road heading west. A 9-kilometer (5.5 mile) stretch of blacktop leads to the little town of Chacala; the main thoroughfare is a dirt loop road running behind the beach. Rough, cobbled side streets lead up into the residential areas.

Among the *palapa* bars, Las Brisas caters to gringos with comfy lounge chairs, good seafood and clean bathrooms. But don't overlook the excellent grilled lobster at Chico's. On the beach, you can rent kayaks or arrange snorkeling excursions with local fishermen. Shopping is limited to a few stalls selling the usual souvenir T-shirts and trinkets. Lodging options range from a beachfront campground to a pair of "eco-resorts" in the hills just south of town.

There are no ATMs in Chacala. The nearest machines are in the town of Las Varas, on Mex. 200 about 5 minutes north of the Chacala turn-off.

## SAN BLAS, NAYARIT (A-1) pop. 43,120

San Blas (sahn BLAHS) was an important 18th-century port, and galleons from the Philippines once made regular stops. The town was also a garrison for the Spanish navy, which fended off attacks from French, Dutch and British pirates. The ruins of a Spanish fort stand on a hillside overlooking the harbor.

Surfers and hippies have trekked to this sleepy fishing village since the 1960s. It's also an ecotourism destination; the surrounding mangrove swamps, lagoons, estuaries and jungles provide habitats for about 300 species of birds.

Adventurous travelers wishing to avoid the hubbub of Mazatlán to the north or Puerto Vallarta to the south will find peace and quiet at San Blas, which is accessible via Mex. 15-D to the Mex. 11 turnoff. **Note:** This road is isolated and jungle-lined; make sure the gas tank is full and your vehicle is in tip-top shape.

Tan-colored beaches encircle nearby Matanchen Bay. Playa Borrego is the most convenient to town. This typical Mexican beach has few amenities but plenty of open-air shacks serving cold beer and whole smoked fish. Playa Los Cocos, reachable by taxi, has a backdrop of palm trees. The rainy summer season is plagued by mosquitoes; *jejenes* (hey-HAY-nays), or "no-see-ums," are bothersome biting gnats that materialize at dawn and dusk year-round. As a result, insect repellent is a necessity.

U.S. and Canadian expats appreciate the laid-back pace and the fact that you can walk just about everywhere in town. The main plaza is a pleasant place to hang out and observe daily life. Stalls sell handicrafts, hammocks, jewelry, ceramic plates and woodcarvings, and on Saturday nights the plaza is lively with music and food vendors.

**LA TOVARA BOAT TRIP** excursions depart from the boat launch at the bridge leading into town. This jungle trip along the La Tovara River in a motorized boat (panga) is a favorite of bird-watchers, nature photographers and fans of adventure tourism. The small boats (usually holding six passengers) pass through swampy lagoons, dense mangrove forests inhabited by herons, ducks, turtles, iguanas, crocodiles, fish and a great variety of birds. The itinerary often includes a stop at a small crocodile reserve where injured crocs are rehabilitated and babies are raised until they are old enough to be released back into the wild.

Excursions can be arranged directly with local boat owners/guides. The best wildlife viewing is on a trip that departs early in the morning.

**Hours:** Round trips from the San Blas dock take between 2 and 3 hours, including the short stop at the crocodile reserve. **Cost:** The fee is negotiable and starts at about $8 (U.S.) per person.

## SAN FRANCISCO, NAYARIT (B-1)

Christened the "Riviera Nayarit" by Mexico's tourism developer, FONATUR, the string of beach villages along the southern coast of Nayarit state have largely escaped the condo construction evident at places like Punta Mita and Sayulita. Low-key Playa San Francisco (nicknamed "San Pancho") isn't quite what Puerto Vallarta was like before the big tourist invasion, but it comes close.

From the signed turn-off on Mex. 200, 38 kilometers (23 miles) north of the Puerto Vallarta airport (about a 45-minute drive), the town's cobbled main street leads to a wave-pounded, deep sand beach beloved by surfers. Book-ended by jungly headlands, the long, palm-backed strand is refreshingly crowd free. A pair of *palapa* restaurants provide fine spots for sunset watching.

You'll find more dining along the drowsy main drag, curiously named Avenida Tercer Mundo (translation: Third World Avenue). Expatriates get their American-style breakfast fix at Maria's, a homey diner that whips up outstanding chorizo-and-potato omelets and pours an eye-opening Bloody Mary (closed Wednesday).

There's a sprinkling of small shops and galleries. And if you're inclined to spend a night or two, a couple of hotels and bed & breakfasts are just north and south of town. The Costa Azul Adventure Resort and Bungalows Lydia are solid choices.

**Note:** San Francisco has two ATMs. One is located inside the Mini-Super Mary convenience store on the main street. The other machine is at the Costa Azul resort, just north of town. If the ATMs are out of service (common in Mexico), the nearest machine is at the Pemex gas station about 11 kilometers (7 miles) north of town on Mex. 200.

### SAYULITA, NAYARIT (B-1)

Sayulita was a little-known fishing village until surfers "discovered" its extra-long waves in the early 1970s. Good paved roads connect the town to Puerto Vallarta, 33 kilometers (20 miles) northwest of the airport via Mex. 200 (about a 40-minute drive) and to the nearby Four Seasons Punta Mita resort, a favorite of celebrities hiding from paparazzi.

Back in the '70s, surf pilgrims made do with a case of beer and a beach tent, grooving on the beautiful views of Banderas Bay and the rich tropical forest environment that characterizes the base of the coastal Sierra Madre mountains. Nowadays, Sayulita's scruffy beach town charm attracts hippie dropouts, families, bohemian hipsters and rich retirees from los Estados Unidos who demand certain creature comforts.

You'll also find upscale bed and breakfasts, cafes and boutiques (think deep tissue massages, chai lattes and designer handbags). But it's Sayulita's bay that remains the star attraction. A string of *palapa* restaurants and a handful of surf schools line the gray-sand shoreline. When waves are small, boogie boarders and beginning surfers head for the water en masse.

Painted in red, green and yellow pastels, Plaza Pública is in the center of town. After services at the church front door, local families head to the plaza's palm-shaded benches. Huichol Indian artisans on cell phones hurry past, carting their wares to the small vendor market at the plaza's northeast corner. The narrow streets leading down to the beach are peppered with real estate offices, clothing boutiques and shops.

The funky Gypsy Galería (Calle Marlin #10) is packed with hand-painted plates, masks, tiles and figurines from all over Mexico, plus Guatemalan handbags, Chiapan shawls and a slew of Dia de Los Muertos (Day of the Dead) crafts from Michoacán. Overlooking the beach, two-story Don Pedro's Restaurant & Bar (Calle Marlin #2) dishes up Mexican and seafood classics; there's live salsa music on Monday nights.

### ZIHUATANEJO, GUERRERO—

*See Ixtapa/Zihuatanejo, Guerrero p. 206.*

© Barna Tanko / Shutterstock.com

# Mexico City and Vicinity

Floating on a lake bed a mile and a half high, Mexico City is, in a word, unique. This ancient land of the Aztecs is a thoroughly modern world capital, yet a city with roots deeply entrenched in its indigenous and colonial Spanish cultures. It is the oldest (more than 675 years) and second highest (7,350 feet) capital in North America, and one of the most populous cities in the world.

Distinguished colonial buildings fill Mexico City's historic center. More than 2,000 years of history unfurl at the city's wealth of museums and their collections of priceless artifacts. The world-famous Ballet Folklórico celebrates the history of Mexican folk music and dance. If you are a gourmand on a culinary quest, the capital offers memorable gastronomic experiences. And ardent shoppers will find a treasure trove of brightly colored bargains.

Mexico City's neighborhoods are as varied as the city itself. Polanco is a small residential area filled with art galleries, hotels, restaurants and foreign embassies. The shopping malls and exclusive international boutiques along Presidente Masaryk, the main street, are Mexico City at its most chic. Condesa is a middle-class neighborhood filled with parks and lovely turn-of-the-20th-century homes. San Angel and Coyoacán, two distinctive neighborhoods in the southern part of the city, reflect the Spanish colonial era in the form of venerable plazas, colorful markets and a vibrant sense of artistic expression. This is "old Mexico" at its most beguiling.

Sunday is the best time to visit Coyoacán, when it is the site of a lively street bazaar. City residents converge at Plaza Hidalgo against a heady backdrop of sights, colors and aromas. Vendors display their wares—clothing, jewelry, balloons, trinkets, plants, paintings, puppies, paper flowers, incense, carved figurines, housewares and myriad other items—in stalls or spread on the ground on blankets.

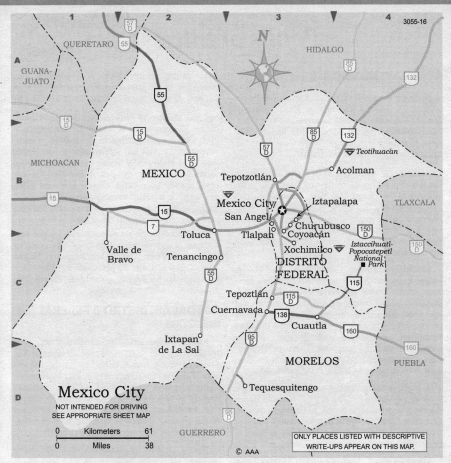

3055-16

Mexico City

NOT INTENDED FOR DRIVING
SEE APPROPRIATE SHEET MAP

| 0 | Kilometers | 61 |
| 0 | Miles | 38 |

© AAA

ONLY PLACES LISTED WITH DESCRIPTIVE
WRITE-UPS APPEAR ON THIS MAP.

Side trips are a relatively short hop away. Perhaps the most impressive is Teotihuacán, easily reached from Mexico City. While it lacks the lush jungle backdrop of Palenque, in southern Mexico, Teotihuacán is the most monumentally scaled of all the country's archeological zones. The temple remains and two majestic pyramids rise from a flat, open plain, with little surrounding vegetation to obscure the view. The wide open spaces and awe-inspiring ruins are the perfect antidote to the city's sometimes claustrophobic congestion.

AAA recommends that travelers consult online U.S. State Department travel advisories when planning traveling abroad. Find this information at http://travel.state.gov/content/passports/english/alertswarnings/mexico-travel-warning.html.

# Points of Interest

## ACOLMAN, MÉXICO (B-4) pop. 136,558

Acolman is a small village off Mex. 132-D on the way to the ruins of Teotihuacán. From downtown Mexico City, take Avenida Insurgentes Norte (Mex. 85-D) northeast to the Mex. 132-D turn-off. The route is pleasantly scenic, although slow going because of heavy bus and truck traffic.

**CONVENT OF SAN AGUSTÍN ACOLMAN** is on Calzada de Los Agustinos, just off Mex. 132 at the entrance to the village. This large, fortresslike structure displays Mexico's first plateresque ecclesiastic facade. It was completed in 1560 and deteriorated over time before being restored. Two sets of columns, with the statue of a saint between each, flank the elaborate entrance.

Several of the inner courtyards are planted with orange trees, which perfume the air with their blossoms during winter and early spring. Small, stark dormitory rooms containing one bed, one chair and one small table show the frugal lifestyle lived by convent residents. Dozens of labyrinthine corridors throughout the convent lead to large assembly rooms and immense granaries. There are fine examples of Renaissance art, including somber frescoes in black and gray inks.

A small museum displays paintings and artifacts. Standing next to the building is a tall, beautiful church that dates from the same period. At Christmas the convent chapel provides the setting for nativity plays, or *pastorelas*. This is a delightful stop either en route to or returning from the pyramids at Teotihuacán.

**Time:** Allow 1 hour minimum. **Hours:** Daily 9-5:30. **Cost:** 47 pesos (about $3.50 U.S.); free (ages 0-12).

## CHURUBUSCO, DISTRITO FEDERAL (B-3)

After having fought valiantly on the side of Gen. Antonio López de Santa Anna in several battles of the U.S.-Mexican War, members of St. Patrick's Battalion—a group of Mexican sympathizers—met disaster in Churubusco (choo-roo-BOOS-coh) in 1847. American forces captured and hanged most of the battalion of 260 Irish immigrants who had deserted the U.S. Army to fight for Mexico. Churubusco is much more tranquil today; major Mexican film studios are located in this suburb just east of Coyoacán.

**EX-CONVENT OF CHURUBUSCO** is on Calle 20 de Agosto (M: General Anaya, line 2), about a 5-minute walk from the Metro station. It was built in 1678 over the ruins of an ancient Aztec temple. This former Franciscan convent, which includes the Church of St. Matthew, served as a fortress against invading U.S. forces in August 1847. There are

lovely gardens on the grounds of the restored structure. Some of the convent rooms have been left intact and show the frugal lifestyle the friars followed.

**National Museum of Interventions** (Museo Nacional de las Intervenciones) is within the convent complex. Ornate rooms chronicle the exploits of those adventurers, pirates and foreign armies—the United States and France chief among them—who have invaded Mexico over the past 4 centuries. Display cases contain large battle swords, guns and rifles, and there are mounted bayonets, cannons, horse carriages, military uniforms from various eras and photos of war heroes. Exhibit information is in Spanish.

**Note:** Photographs are permitted, but visitors may not take photos of themselves or of others next to the displays. **Time:** Allow 1 hour minimum. **Hours:** Tues.-Sun. 9-6. **Cost:** 52 pesos (about $3.85 U.S.); free (ages 0-13). Free to all on Sun. **Phone:** (55) 5604-0699.

## COYOACÁN, DISTRITO FEDERAL (B-3) pop. 620,416

About 10 kilometers (6 miles) south of downtown Mexico City and west of Avenida Insurgentes Sur, Coyoacán (coh-yoh-ah-KAHN) lies on the northern edge of the Pedregal. Established in 1521 by Hernando Cortés, Coyoacán was the third seat of Spanish government in New Spain. The name is loosely derived from the Náhuatl Indian term *coyohuacan*, or "place of the coyotes." Francisco Sosa, the main thoroughfare, connects it with neighboring San Angel.

This is an artsy neighborhood where the stucco buildings are painted bright purple, blue and yellow. Tall trees line the narrow streets. Bookstores, sweet shops, restaurants and sidewalk cafes all compete for the stroller's attention. The area is very congested; the easiest way to explore it is to hire a taxi driver who will drive you there, wait while you have a look around and then take you back to your hotel.

On Plaza Hidalgo stands the Palace of Cortés, now the Town Hall (Delegación de Coyoacán). The Spaniards allegedly tortured Aztec emperor Cuauhtémoc at the palace in an effort to obtain treasure.

Also of interest are the 1583 Church of San Juan Bautista, the 1530 Dominican Monastery and the Alvarado House, now a private home. The Alvarado House belonged to Pedro de Alvarado, Cortés' right-hand man in his conquest of Mexico and later governor of Guatemala.

Two blocks east of Plaza Hidalgo on Calle Higuera is the Malinche House (Casa de la Malinche), the former home of Cortés' Indian mistress, interpreter and chief aide on his march through Mexico. Malinche, a major and much-maligned figure in Mexican legend, was supposedly condemned to 300 years of martyrdom for her act of betrayal. The solemn-looking dwelling sits across from Plaza de la Conchita, a peaceful little park.

**DIEGO RIVERA MUSEUM** (Museo Anahuacalli) is on the s. side of the city, off Av. División del Norte at Calle del Museo #150 (access is via Calle Arbol de Fuego). Designed by Rivera and constructed from dark volcanic stone, this imposing three-story structure with narrow walkways was built to house the artist's 39,000-piece collection of pre-Hispanic art.

Although you won't see any Rivera works, the building itself is an art form, replete with mosaic floors and ceilings depicting images of snakes and frogs (a Rivera trademark given that the artist's birthplace was Guanajuato, which means "place of frogs"). The art collection is remarkable. The objects on display include urns and decanters; stone, clay and marble pieces; smiling *xoloitzcuintle* dogs (a mid-size breed dating from pre-Hispanic times); and warriors and ceremonial ballplayers in full regalia.

Rivera also set up a studio on the upper floor of the building; mementos and works in progress now occupy

the restored space. On clear days there are spectacular views from the building's hilltop location, particularly of twin volcanoes Popocatépetl and Iztaccíhuatl.

**Note:** The museum can be seen only on a docent-led guided tour Wednesday through Friday; all tours are given in Spanish. Weekend visits are self-guiding. Photography without flash is permitted. **Hours:** Wed.-Sun. 11-4:30. Guided tours depart Wed.-Fri. at 11, noon, 1, 2, 3, 4 and 4:30 (no 4:30 tour on Fri.). Closed Mexican holidays. Phone ahead to confirm schedule. **Cost:** 60 pesos (about $4.45 U.S.); free (ages 0-5). **Phone:** (55) 5617-4310.

**FRIDA KAHLO MUSEUM** (Museo Frida Kahlo) is at Calle Londres #247 (at the corner of Allende), 5 blks. n. of Plaza Hidalgo (M: Coyoacán, line 3). This adobe house was the celebrated Latin American painter's life-long residence; from 1929 until her death in 1954 she shared it with her husband Diego Rivera, Mexico's equally celebrated muralist. Through their tempestuous relationship Rivera and Kahlo forged the nucleus of contemporary Mexican art.

"Casa Azul" is an explosion of color, not the least of which is the cobalt-blue, red-trimmed exterior. Personal possessions include the four-poster bed in which Kahlo was born and died. *Calaveras* (papier-mâché skeletons) and carved death masks are reminders of the physical suffering that plagued Kahlo's everyday life and provided the fuel for her creativity. Works on display by this self-taught artist include some surrealistic self-portraits.

A spacious studio contains the artist's wheelchair, paintbrushes and an easel on which rests an unfinished portrait of Joseph Stalin. Wooden spoons and ceramic jugs and bowls fill the kitchen. Be sure to stroll through the garden, full of luxuriant vegetation, sculptures, pre-Hispanic pottery and descendants of Kahlo's beloved cats. There is a cafe on the museum's first floor. The surrounding neighborhood, with its bookstores and coffee shops, has a bohemian air well suited to this iconoclastic figure. **Hours:** Tues.-Sun. 10-5:45. Closed Jan. 1, Christmas Eve and Christmas. **Cost:** 80 pesos (about $5.90 U.S.); free (ages 0-5). **Phone:** (55) 5554-5999.

**LEON TROTSKY MUSEUM** (Museo Casa de Leon Trotsky) is about 8 blks. n. of Plaza Hidalgo at Av. Río Churubusco #410, between avs. Gómez Farías and Morelos (M: Coyoacán, line 3). The Russian revolutionary took up residence here after being exiled from the Soviet Union in 1929. He was murdered at home on Aug. 20, 1940. An ice pick-wielding assassin (a Spanish communist) accomplished the deed, which had been attempted months earlier when Stalinist sympathizers showered the house with a hail of bullets.

The fortresslike dwelling is capped with turrets once occupied by armed guards. Inside are Trotsky's kitchen, bedroom and study, with modest belongings preserved largely as he left them; newspaper clippings recount the event. You'll also see the bullet holes resulting from the first attempt on his life. A garden courtyard contains Trotsky's tomb. **Hours:** Tues.-Sun. 10-5. **Cost:** 40 pesos (about $2.95 U.S.). The fee to use a camera (still or video) is 15 pesos. **Phone:** (55) 5554-0687 or (55) 5658-8732.

## CUAUTLA, MORELOS (C-3) pop. 175,207

**Note:** For current information about safety/security issues in Cuautla, go to the U.S. State Department website (travel.state.gov).

Cuautla (coo-WOW-tlah), popular with the Aztecs for its mineral springs, became a fashionable Spanish spa early in the 17th century. The city witnessed one of the most dramatic battles of Mexico's War of Independence when patriot José María Morelos and 3,000 rebels managed to withstand a 58-day siege by Royalist troops.

Some 31 kilometers (19 miles) south of Cuautla is Chinameca, the hacienda where Emiliano Zapata was assassinated; the site has been designated a national historic monument. Another historical site is Ayala, about 6 kilometers (4 miles) south of Cuautla. In 1910, Zapata issued a declaration of land reform here; later

the townsite was a battlefield during the Revolution of 1910.

**AGUA HEDIONDAS** are about 3 km (1.9 mi.) e. of town. The "stinking waters" are a series of connected thermal pools. Aztec emperor Moctezuma is said to have spent time improving his health in the spa's sulfurous waters. Facilities include swimming pools, bathhouses, dressing rooms, a pavilion and gardens. **Hours:** Open daily 6:30-5:30. **Cost:** 75 pesos (about $5.55 U.S.); 40 pesos (children). **Phone:** (735) 352-0044.

## CUERNAVACA, MORELOS (C-2)
### pop. 365,168

The list of those who have owned summer homes in Mexico includes presidents, Aztec emperors, Hernando Cortés, Archduke Maximilian and his wife Carlota, Taxco "silver king" José de la Borda and any number of affluent Mexico City residents. And these homes all have one location in common: Cuernavaca (kwehr-nah-VAH-cah). The capital of Morelos is a city of mountain views, pastel-colored buildings with red-tiled roofs and gardens lush with tropical vegetation (although many are hidden behind high walls). Benevolent weather not only nourishes the greenery but provides Cuernavaca with the nickname "city of eternal spring."

At Mex. 95 and Avenida Fundadores a grand equestrian statue pays tribute to Emiliano Zapata, the leader of the Revolution of 1910. Zapata's battle cry of "Land and liberty, and death to the haciendados" struck at hacienda owners throughout the country. His Plan de Ayala, aimed at agrarian reform, was signed near Cuautla on Nov. 28, 1911. In 1914 Zapata briefly joined Pancho Villa in occupying Mexico City before returning to Cuernavaca to prevent its seizure by federal troops.

Plaza de Armas, the main square, is shaded by flowering trees and dotted with park benches. Both the plaza and adjoining Juárez Garden (Jardín Juárez) are pleasant spots to relax over coffee or enjoy a Sunday band concert. The plaza teems with vendors, especially on weekends when stalls set up selling handicrafts, jewelry, balloons and every conceivable kind of trinket.

The Flower Fair (Feria de la Flor), held the first week in April, is a colorful and aromatic event that features garden-themed exhibits and competitions as well as a sound-and-light show staged at the main plaza. This also is a good time to visit the Borda Gardens, which has special horticultural displays in honor of the fair.

On the outskirts of town in the suburb of Acapantzingo is the Olvido House, Maximilian and Carlota's summer home. The restored structure is now the Museum of Traditional and Herbal Medicine (Museo de Medicina Tradicional y Herbolaria). There's a botanical garden on the grounds as well. The museum is open Monday through Friday, and admission is free; phone (777) 312-3108 for more information.

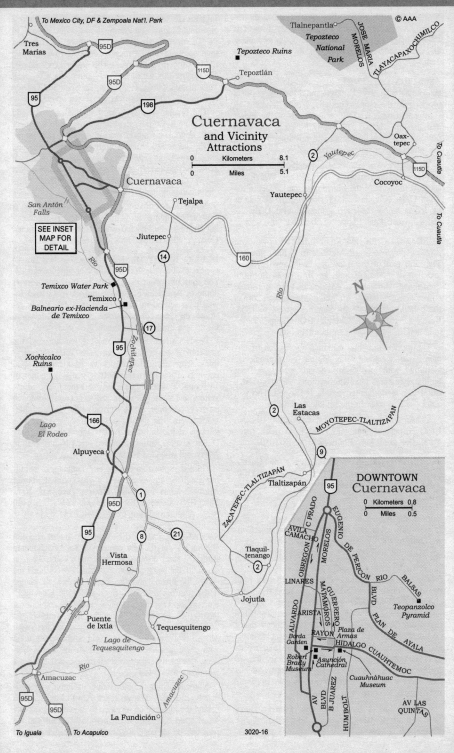

© AAA

To Mexico City, DF & Zempoala Nat'l. Park

Tres Marías

95D

95D

95

198

Tlalnepantla

Tepozteco Ruins

115D

Tepoztlán

Tepozteco National Park

JOSE MARIA MORELOS

TLAYACAPAXOCHIMILCO

## Cuernavaca
### and Vicinity
### Attractions

| 0 | Kilometers | 8.1 |
| 0 | Miles | 5.1 |

Cuernavaca

Yautepec

Oax-tepec

2

115D

To Cuautla

Cocoyoc

To Cuautla

Tejalpa

Yautepec

San Antón Falls

SEE INSET MAP FOR DETAIL

Jiutepec

14

160

Rio

Rio

95D

Temixco Water Park

Temixco

Balneario ex-Hacienda de Temixco

17

N

Xochicalco Ruins

95

Zochitepec

Lago El Rodeo

166

Alpuyeca

Las Estacas

2

MOYOTEPEC-TLALTIZAPAN

9

1

ZACATEPEC-TLALTIZAPÁN

Tlaltizapán

95D

8

21

Vista Hermosa

Tlaquil-tenango

2

Jojutla

95

DOWNTOWN Cuernavaca

| 0 | Kilometers | 0.8 |
| 0 | Miles | 0.5 |

95

EUGENIO DE PERCON

C PRADO

OBREGON

AVILA CAMACHO

MORELOS

RIO

BLVD PLAN DE AYALA

BALSAS

Teopanzolco Pyramid

LINARES

ALVARDO

MAYAMOROS

GUERRERO

ARISTA

RAYON

Plaza de Armas

Borda Garden

HIDALGO

CUAUHTEMOC

Puente de Ixtla

Lago de Tequesquitengo

Tequesquitengo

Robert Brady Museum

Asunción Cathedral

Cuauhnáhuac Museum

AV BLVD

B JUAREZ

HUMBOLT

AV LAS QUINTAS

Rio

Amacuzac

Amacuzac

95D

95D

La Fundición

**Morelos State Tourism Office (Subsecretaría de Turismo):** Av. Morelos Sur #187 (Mex. 95) in the Las Palmas neighborhood, south of the downtown plaza and the cathedral. Open Mon.-Fri. 8-7. **Phone:** (777) 314-3872 (English spoken).

**ASUNCIÓN CATHEDRAL** (Catedral de la Asunción de María) is at avs. Hidalgo and Morelos, about a block from the Borda Gardens. It was founded by Hernando Cortés in 1529 and is one of the oldest churches in Mexico. The cathedral was the focal point of activities by Franciscan missionaries in Far Eastern countries during the colonial era.

The interior was renovated in the 1960s in a spare, modern style, but remains of early frescoes can still be seen. At the back of the cathedral is the Chapel of the Third Order (Capilla de la Tercer Orden). Sculptures by Indian artists flank the atrium. **Hours:** Daily 8-2 and 4-7. **Cost:** Free. **Phone:** (777) 318-4590.

**BORDA GARDEN** (Jardín Borda) is downtown, across Calle José María Morelos from the cathedral. They are part of the mansion, landscaped grounds and botanical gardens built by José de la Borda, a Frenchman who came to Mexico in 1716 and made a fortune in mining. Archduke Maximilian turned the palatial estate into his summer retreat in 1864. Borda is buried in the Church of Guadalupe (Parroquía de Guadalupe) next to the main house.

The gardens are laid out in a succession of terraces; maintenance is limited, but most plants are identified with labels. An art gallery in the front buildings features changing exhibits. Rowboats at a small man-made lake are available for rent. This is a quiet place to relax in the middle of the city.

Snacks are available. **Hours:** Tues.-Sun. 10-5:30. **Cost:** 30 pesos (about $2.20 U.S.); 15 pesos (ages 4-12); free to all Sun. **Phone:** (777) 318-1050.

**CUAUHNÁHUAC MUSEUM** (Museo de Cuauhnáhuac) is downtown at Av. Francisco Leyva #100; it flanks the e. side of the main plaza. This museum with the tongue-twisting name (pronounced kwown-NAH-wak) is housed in the Cortés Palace (Palacio Cortés), the former home of the Spanish conqueror. It was built over the remains of a pyramid. Construction of the medieval-style stone fortress began in 1530, but its appearance has been considerably altered since then.

The museum's 26 rooms chronicle everything from the age of dinosaurs to Mexico's contemporary Indian cultures. There are pre-Hispanic and religious artifacts; an exhibit about sugar plantations; 18th-century paintings from New Spain; traditional 19th-century dance costumes; pottery dating from the ninth century; a hat and gun that belonged to Emiliano Zapata; and objects associated with Cortés. Diego Rivera murals donated by former U.S. Ambassador Dwight Morrow depict the conquest of Mexico, the War of Independence and the Mexican Revolution of 1910.

**Time:** Allow 1 hour minimum. **Hours:** Tues.-Sun. 9-5:30. **Cost:** 48 pesos (about $3.55 U.S.). **Phone:** (777) 312-8171. GT

**LAKES OF ZEMPOALA NATIONAL PARK** (Parque Nacional Lagunas de Zempoala) is about 22 km (14 mi.) n. on old Mex. 95 to the town of Huitzilac, then some 15 km (9 mi.) w. on a narrow, winding road to the park entrance. The seven lakes *(lagos)* comprising this national park—Zempoala, Compela, Tonatihagua, Quila, Hueyapan, La Seca and Ocoyotongo—lie about 9,500 feet above sea level.

The bracing scenery—lofty mountain peaks and thick stands of tall green pine trees—looks more like Oregon or Canada than it does Mexico. Some of the lakes are stocked with bass and trout, and simple roadside restaurants hawk the latter (known as *trucha*) grilled, fried and smoked. The park offers plenty of opportunities for boating, hiking, bicycling, camping and jet-skiing.

**Note:** Do not drive after dark, as the access road is extremely winding and is in an area that is experiencing ongoing drug-related crime and high insecurity. **Cost:** A toll is charged at a forest ranger station.

**ROBERT BRADY MUSEUM** (Museo Robert Brady) is next to the cathedral at Calle Netzahualcóyotl #4. The museum occupies Casa de la Torre, the former home of American artist Robert Brady, a native Iowan who settled in Cuernavaca in 1960. Brady restored the 16th-century stone and adobe mansion, formerly a Franciscan convent.

Brady collected as well as created art, and the museum displays more than 1,300 pieces—everything from Balinese masks to Mexican colonial carvings. They adorn the shelves, walls and tables of 14 rooms, essentially as Brady left them. The bright yellow and deep red walls and exuberantly colorful artwork combine for a surreal effect. Also noteworthy are the hand-painted tiles covering the kitchen and bathrooms. Artists represented include Diego Rivera, Rufino Tamayo, Frida Kahlo, Milton Avery and Marsden Hartley.

Guided group tours in several languages, including English, are available by appointment. **Time:** Allow 2 hours minimum. **Hours:** Tues.-Sat. 10-6, Sun. 10-5. **Cost:** 40 pesos (about $2.95 U.S.); 20 pesos (children). **Phone:** (777) 318-8554. T

**SAN ANTÓN FALLS** (Salto de San Antón) is 3 km (1.8 mi.) w. of the city center via the Ayuntamiento Bridge, a short distance n., then just s.w. on Avenida del Salto; the entrance is near Plazoleta del Salto at the end of the street. The falls, about 120 feet tall, plunge down a *barranca* (narrow river gorge) against a backdrop of lush vegetation, tropical butterflies and unusual basalt rock formations. Near the falls, just off the walkway, are a couple of tables and altars to the Virgin Mary. Locally made pottery is sold on the street, along with plants and coconut juice. From the Borda Gardens, this pretty retreat is a 10-minute taxi ride or a 30-minute walk away.

**Note:** Reaching the falls requires climbing approximately 10 flights of steep stairs. A walkway that runs behind the falls can be accessed by descending another set of steep staircases. There are no handrails and the path can be slippery. Restrooms are located near the

entrance. **Time:** Allow 45 minutes minimum. **Hours:** Daily during daylight hours. **Cost:** Free. 🅰

**TEMIXCO WATER PARK** (Ex-Hacienda de Temixco Parque Acuatico) is in the town of Temixco, about 11 km (7 mi.) s. of Cuernavaca. From downtown Mexico City, take the Autopista del Sol highway (Mex. 95-D) s. to the Las Brisas exit (Brisas/Temixco-Utez), then follow signs for Temixco Centro; the entrance is on Av. Temixco.

This water park has the usual assortment of slides, game and wave pools, a lazy river and children's play areas, plus miniature golf, sports courts, and picnic and barbecue areas. The grounds are attractive and nicely maintained. It can get very crowded on weekends and holidays, when Mexico City families pay a visit.

**Time:** Allow 2 hours minimum. **Hours:** Daily 9-6. **Cost:** 195 pesos (about $14.45 U.S.); 145 pesos (children under 37 inches tall). Admission to all on Mon. 100 pesos (about $7.40 U.S.). **Parking:** 30 pesos (about $2.45 U.S.). **Phone:** (777) 325-0355. 🅸🅸

**TEOPANZOLCO PYRAMID** (Pirámide de Teopanzolco) is e. of downtown just off Calle Río Balsas, at the jct. with Calle Ixcateopan; from Mexico City, take Av. Tlalpan s., then the Mex 95-D toll highway to Cuernavaca. Presumably built by the Aztecs, it was never completed. The remains were discovered in 1910 during the Mexican Revolution, when a large hill on the outskirts of Cuernavaca was used as a platform for attacks on the city. Tremors resulting from gunfire shook away some of the earth and revealed the ruins underneath.

The pyramidal base upon which twin temples once rested was constructed in the same style as other pyramids in central Mexico, such as the Great Temple (Templo Mayor) in Mexico City. The north

temple was dedicated to the rain god Tlaloc, and the one on the south side to the war god Huitzilopochtli. A couple of signs in English provide a brief historical explanation. Because of its proximity to the city, this is a convenient archeological site to visit. **Hours:** Daily 9-5:30. **Cost:** 47 pesos (about $3.50 U.S.). **Phone:** (777) 314-1284.

**XOCHICALCO RUINS** are about 37 km (23 mi.) s.w. of Cuernavaca and can be reached from downtown Mexico City via two different routes. Take Av. Tlalpan s. to toll highway Mex. 95D and continue s. to the town of Xochitepec, following signs to Mex. highway 166 (Xochitepec exit); from that point, follow signs to Xochicalco. There is a 16-peso toll at the Xochitepec exit. The alternate route is to take Mex. 95D to the exit for the town of Alpuyeca (toll 52 pesos), then follow the paved road that winds n. about 8 km (5 mi.) to the ruins site, which sits atop a mountain.

In terms of sheer grandeur, Xochicalco (so-chee-KAHL-coh, which means "place of flowers" in the Náhuatl Indian language) rivals the more famous archeological zone of Teotihuacán. After Teotihuacán's fall Xochicalco became one of the leading urban centers of the central high plains. These white-stone ruins epitomize the Classic Period in Mesoamerican history, which lasted from about the second through the eighth centuries and produced Mexico's first noteworthy urban civilizations. Xochicalco was designated a World Heritage Site by UNESCO in 1999.

Upon entering, buy your ticket to the ruins at the site museum (Museo de Xochicalco). The well-labeled (in Spanish) exhibits feature pottery, carvings and artifacts that have been excavated, and there is also a diorama of the entire site. There are excellent views of the ruins from the museum grounds.

The Pyramid of the Plumed Serpent (Pirámide de Quetzalcóatl) is the dominant structure, with well-preserved bas-reliefs and traces of hieroglyphs representing dates and eclipse signs. Close by is the entrance to a mazelike tunnel ending at a stone-hewn, stepped chamber with a "telescope" orifice; the astrologer-priests of Xochicalco made corrections to their calendar by examining the heavens through this aperture. From Xochicalco's fortresslike location the sweeping vistas of the Valley of Cuernavaca are spectacular.

**Time:** Allow 2 hours minimum. **Hours:** Site daily 9-5:30. Museum daily 9-5. Phone ahead to confirm schedule. **Cost:** 64 pesos (about $4.75 U.S.); free (ages 0-12). Free to all Sun. **Phone:** (737) 374-3090. 🅸🅸

## IXTAPAN DE LA SAL, MÉXICO (C-2)
pop. 33,541

Ixtapán de La Sal (ees-tah-PAHN deh lah SAHL) is a *balneario* (spa) town known for its warm mineral waters; bathing in them is certainly soothing, and reputed to aid arthritis and rheumatism as well.

---

**DID YOU KNOW**

Hurricane Wilma, which hit Cancún, Cozumel, Isla Mujeres and the Quintana Roo coast in October 2005, caused nearly $3 billion in damage.

Public pools, flowing fountains, flowers and lush landscaping lend a cool, refreshing appearance to this popular resort. Golf, tennis, horseback riding and a variety of spa facilities are available at the Ixtapan Spa Hotel & Golf Resort, which has been in business for more than 60 years.

The Ixtapan Parque Acuatico, off Mex. 55 (Boulevard Arturo San Román) next to the Ixtapan resort property, is a public spa along the lines of a Turkish bath. In addition to thermal pools of varying temperature and such traditional spa treatments as massages and facials, it offers waterslides, a lazy river for inner tubing and other water park features.

Although Ixtapán de La Sal makes a nice day trip from either Taxco or Cuernavaca, weekends and holidays can be quite crowded. Tonatico, a town about 5 kilometers (3 miles) south via Mex. 55, also has swimming facilities.

**STAR GROTTOES** (Grutas de la Estrella) are s. of town via Mex. 55 (Carretera Taxco-Ixtapan de la Sal); about 12 km (7 mi.) s. of Tonatico, watch for the signed turnoff at Km marker 14.5. They are most dramatic during the July-September rainy season, when waterfalls cascade among such spectacular rock formations as "The Holy Family" and "The Human Ear." Ancient Matlaltzinca Indians may have conducted religious ceremonies in the grottoes. Guided walking tours in Spanish proceed along a lighted, protected footpath. **Note:** Accessing the caves requires climbing a number of steps. **Hours:** Tues.-Sun. 10-4. **Cost:** 20 pesos (about $1.60 U.S.). **Phone:** (721) 141-8018.

## IZTACCÍHUATL-POPOCATÉPETL NATIONAL PARK, MÉXICO (C-4)

Embracing the pass between Mexico's two most famous volcanoes, Iztaccíhuatl-Popocatépetl (shortened locally to Izta-Popo) National Park is about 83 kilometers (52 miles) east of Mexico City. Popocatépetl (po-po-kah-TEH-pet-el) and Iztaccíhuatl (iss-tah-SEE-hwat-el) together form the Valley of Mexico's eastern rim. The volcanoes are Mexico's second and third highest mountains, and although located in a tropical latitude, both are high enough to be perpetually snowcapped.

Iztaccíhuatl (The White Lady), which rises 17,343 feet, is dormant. The mountain got its name from the legend of Popo, a warrior, and Izta, an Aztec princess, who fell in love and were turned into mountains by the gods, so the story goes, after Popo was betrayed by one of his enemies. Supporting the tale is the shape of Iztaccíhuatl, which bears a superficial resemblance to a reclining female form.

Immense quantities of sulfur have been taken from the crater of 17,887-foot Popocatépetl (The Smoking Mountain); Hernando Cortés' soldiers used it to make gunpowder. Aztec runners made daily trips up the mountain to fetch ice for Emperor Moctezuma's drinks and to preserve fish. The last significant eruption occurred in 1802, but sporadic spewings of smoke, ash and glowing red rocks that resumed in the 1990s—and more recently in mid-2013—have resulted in evacuations.

The town of Amecameca, about 60 kilometers (37 miles) east of Mexico City via Mex. 190 and Mex. 115, lies at the foot of the national park at an elevation of about 7,500 feet. Although it doesn't offer much to do, there are views of Izta and Popo from the main plaza.

The Sanctuary of El Sacromonte (Santuario del Sacromonte) stands on a hill above Amecameca. From the arch on the southwest side of the plaza, walk about 2 blocks to the steps that ascend the hill to the sanctuary; the inspiring vistas en route are worth the effort.

To get to the park from downtown Amecameca, take Mex. 115 south to the Pemex gas station at the city's southern edge, then take the paved road east toward Tlamacas (watch for the highway sign). The narrow, two-lane blacktop passes through the town of San Pedro Nexapa; watch for the highway signs that say "Ruta de Acesso" (route access). The road ascends to the town of Paso de Cortés, where the main park office is located; this is where visitors check in. The office has wall-mounted maps of the park.

Dirt and cobblestone hiking and bicycling trails branch out into various sections of the park, offering beautiful views of rugged mountains and thick pine forests. Interestingly, the terrace farms and fruit orchards in this region are more reminiscent of Europe than Mexico. Burnt-out land and lava flows are evidence of Popo's recent activity, and the mountain remains off limits to the public.

**Note:** Military checkpoints may be encountered. Watch for electric cattle fences that are scattered throughout the park. Picnicking is permitted. Allow 2 hours minimum. Izta-Popo National Park is open daily 7 a.m.-8:30 p.m. Admission is 30 pesos (about $2.20 U.S.). For information phone (597) 978-3829 (Spanish only spoken).

## IZTAPALAPA, DISTRITO FEDERAL (B-3) pop. 1,815,786

Long before it became absorbed by the sprawl of greater Mexico City, Iztapalapa (ees-tah-pah-LAH-pah) was a flourishing Aztec town. Atop nearby Star Hill (Cerro de la Estrella), the Aztecs lighted fires to mark the beginning of their 52-year cycle. During the New Fire Ceremony, priests would ignite kindling on the chest of the unfortunate sacrificial victim. If the flame continued to burn, the continued existence of the world was assured. Flames would then be carried by runners to other temples. Instead of human sacrifices, the hill today is the scene of a Passion Play performed on Good Friday.

The views of volcanoes Popocatépetl and Iztaccíhuatl are exceptional from the hilltop; a road leads to the summit. Many visitors ascend the hill by foot, as there are caves and small ruins that can be explored along the way.

# Mexico City

**City Population:** 8,851,080
**Elevation:** 2,240 meters (7,347 feet)

## Editor's Picks:

Metropolitan Cathedral.............*(see p. 261)*
National Museum of
   Anthropology......................*(see p. 271)*
Palace of Fine Arts...................*(see p. 268)*

© Noradoa / Shutterstock.com

Mexico City lies in the Valley of Mexico, or Anáhuac, a great basin about 60 miles long and 30 miles wide, hemmed in by mountains on all sides except the north. From the air, the vastness of the city's sprawl is startling—a solid sea of buildings stretching across the valley floor to the distant horizon. The most conspicuous landmarks, however, are natural: the snowcapped peaks of Popocatépetl and Iztaccíhuatl to the southeast. At elevations ranging from about 7,200 to 8,000 feet, this is one of the world's loftiest major cities.

Although most Mexican cities and towns have a central plaza that may be locally referred to as the *zócalo,* it is only Mexico City's that receives the official designation. This is the world's second largest public gathering place after Moscow's Red Square. Once a verdant green common strolled by privileged aristocrats, the *Zócalo* is a vast expanse of concrete (the plaza was paved over during the Revolution of 1910) that is best known as a very public stage for political rallies.

The metropolis is defined by its contrasts. It's both a world business center with a distinctly international air and a place where millions suffer rampant poverty. Expensively dressed socialites have lunch in fancy restaurants; ragged children and the destitute elderly beg for a few coins at street corners. The green expanses of Chapultepec Park and the serene charm of colonial plazas are counterbalanced by ceaseless traffic congestion and some of the worst gridlock you'll see anywhere.

Much of the valley is an old lake bed with no underlying bedrock. The combination of unstable subsoil and the region's volcanic nature makes sinking and earthquakes the two greatest threats to the city's buildings. Mexico City is literally settling under its own weight even as it continues to rise story upon steel, glass and stone story—although the ground yields about an inch each year. Despite the preponderance of concrete it's surprisingly green, at least

when it rains. Tamarind, cypress and rubber trees lines the streets. Date palms adorn parks; sculpted shrubs border sidewalks.

One of the newer additions to an increasingly impressive downtown skyline is the Pillar of Light (locals call it the Estela de Luz). Located on Paseo de la Reforma at Calle Lieja, near the entrance to Chapultepec Park, it commemorates Mexico's bicentennial, although the monument wasn't officially unveiled until more than a year after the Sept. 16, 2010, anniversary. This soaring metal structure, approximately 430 feet tall, is covered with translucent quartz panels that are back-lit at night, giving off an eerie glow. The panels also create a waffled appearance amusingly reminiscent of *Suavicremas,* a cream-filled cookie with a rectangular, wafer-like appearance.

Mexico City's sheer size can be overwhelming to the first-time visitor, but there are pleasant retreats amid the hubbub. One such area is Condesa, a *colonia* (neighborhood) centered along Avenida Michoacán off Calzada J. Vasconcelos, southeast of Chapultepec Park's eastern end. This part of the city was the early 20th-century home of well-to-do residents who later abandoned the area, leaving behind dilapidated mansions.

As recently as the 1980s Condesa (which means countess) was largely run-down. Since revitalized by

*Getting There* — *starting on p. 254*

*Getting Around* — *starting on p. 256*

*What To See* — *starting on p. 260*

*What To Do* — *starting on p. 274*

*Where To Stay* — *starting on p. 505*

*Where To Dine* — *starting on p. 509*

an influx of young, hip artists and expatriates, it has tree-lined boulevards, plenty of sidewalk bistros, a hopping gallery scene and the Federal District's largest concentration of Art Deco buildings.

Condesa is one of the best places for tourists to mingle with Mexico City's middle class. Leafy Parque México, on Avenida Michoacán near Avenida Insurgentes Sur, is delightfully well-kept and has plenty of benches. Families gather at the park on Sundays, when there are all sorts of arts and crafts activities for kids. But Condesa also is a magnet for sleek, well-dressed 20-somethings who congregate for a night out at one of the fashionable *cantinas* and bars, many of which are open until the wee hours.

The high altitude results in year-round mild weather, with a very occasional heat wave in May or early June. The arrival of spring somewhat diminishes the severe smog and pollution problem, which peaks from mid-November through January and is exacerbated by the tremendous amount of automobile traffic. Afternoon showers are most likely from June through September.

Earthquakes—the result of unfortunate geography—are in the back of every resident's mind. Mexico City's greatest natural catastrophe in modern times was the massive earthquake and aftershocks that occurred on Sept. 19 and 20, 1985. Some 10,000 people died, and scores of buildings were destroyed or later razed.

Despite the unavoidable big-city headaches, it is the obvious draws of history, culture and world-class museums that make Mexico City such a fascinating experience overall. Pride-filled residents like to say *"Como México no hay dos,"* or "There is no place like Mexico."

© Transcendental Media / Shutterstock.com

## Historical Overview

The Aztec people, like the Toltecs before them, migrated south over centuries. A band of Aztecs eventually ended up in the Valley of Mexico in 1168 to fulfill a priestly prophecy: They were destined to settle where an eagle, carrying a serpent in its beak, was perched on a cactus (an image that appears on the Mexican flag). According to legend that spot was on an island in the middle of Lake Texcoco. It was there that the Aztec capital of Tenochtitlan was founded.

The Aztecs soon controlled the riches of the Valley of Mexico, an important trade center, and by the end of the 15th century Tenochtitlan was a beautiful city of fountains, gardens and canals occupying the small islands that dotted the lake. Eventual land reclamation resulted in the creation of one large island, connected to the mainland by causeways. Tenochtitlan's population was about 300,000—possibly the world's largest city at its time. Then the Spanish arrived.

On Nov. 8, 1519, explorer Hernando Cortés became the first white man to enter Tenochtitlan's ceremonial center, today's *Zócalo*. Moctezuma II, the Aztec emperor,

# The Informed Traveler

## WHOM TO CALL

**Tourist Protection (Protección Legal al Turista):** Secretaría de Turismo (SECTUR) headquarters, Presidente Masaryk #172; phone (55) 3002-6300 (English spoken). Persons needing legal assistance should contact this department at the Ministry of Tourism. SECTUR's 24-hour hotline also can help tourists in difficulty or coordinate aid in an emergency; phone (55) 5250-0123 or (55) 5250-0151.

**Police (emergency):** Dial 060 and ask to be connected to an English-speaking operator if you need immediate assistance.

**Police (non-emergency):** In general, the police in Mexico City should be contacted only as a last resort. If your car is stolen, however, you must report it to the police, as you will be liable for any subsequent crimes committed in or with the vehicle. To reach the highway police phone (55) 5684-2142; to report a robbery, assault or mugging, phone (55) 5625-8008 or (55) 5625-8646.

**U.S. Embassy:** Paseo de la Reforma #305 (M: Sevilla or Insurgentes, line 1); phone (55) 5080-2000. The embassy is open for general business Mon.-Fri. 8:30-4:30; closed U.S. and Mexican holidays. There is a protection officer on 24-hour duty to advise you in the event of robbery, assault, major loss, accident, illness or death; Mexican law takes precedence in such instances. Information regarding attorneys and translators also can be obtained.

**Canadian Embassy:** Calle Schiller #529, just north of the National Museum of Anthropology (M: Auditorio, line 7); phone (55) 5724-7900. The office is open Mon.-Fri. 8:45-5:15; closed Canadian and Mexican holidays.

**LOCATEL:** Phone (55) 5484-0400. This government-operated agency can help coordinate a search for missing persons or lost, stolen or towed vehicles and is available 24 hours.

**Consumer Protection Office (Procuraduría del Consumidor):** Phone (55) 5625-6700 if you feel that you've been cheated or ripped off regarding a service or purchase.

**Hospitals:** American British Cowdray (ABC) Hospital, in the southern part of the city at Calle Sur #136 and Avenida Observatorio (M: Observatorio, line 1, west bus terminal); phone (55) 5230-8000. All major credit cards are accepted. The Mexican Red Cross (Cruz Roja), Ejército Nacional #1032 in the Polanco neighborhood, is open 24 hours; phone (55) 5395-1111.

A list of doctors and hospitals in Mexico City is available from the U.S. Embassy, phone (55) 5080-2000, ext. 4780 (during working hours) and the Canadian Embassy (see phone number above). The British Embassy is at Rio Lerma #71 (2 blocks north of Paseo de la Reforma near the Sheraton María Isabel Hotel); phone (55) 1670-3200 Mon.-Thurs. 8-4:30, Fri. 8-2. Hotel front desks should be able to provide information as well.

**Local Phone Calls:** Card-operated Ladatel phones have replaced most coin-operated phones. Ladatel phone cards in 20-, 50- and 100- peso denominations can be purchased at pharmacies or newsstands. To reach information, dial 040.

## WHERE TO LOOK

### Newspapers

*The News* is an English-language newspaper published Monday through Friday in Mexico City. Major U.S. newspapers are available at many newsstands the day after they are printed. The Spanish-language weekly *Tiempo Libre* has information about restaurants, museums, galleries and cultural events.

# The Informed Traveler

## Publications

The American Bookstore, Av. Bolívar #23 near Avenida Francisco Madero (M: Allende, line 2), has U.S. newspapers and magazines, books and a selection of travel guides. The Sanborn's chain of restaurants also carries newspapers, magazines and books. Mexico City has numerous branches; one is in the House of Tiles, Av. Madero #4 (M: Bellas Artes, lines 2 and 8). Gandhi Bookstore, Av. Juárez #4 at Avenida Lázaro Cárdenas (across from the Palace of Fine Arts), has books about Mexico as well as an international selection of CDs and DVDs.

## Visitor Information

**Mexico Ministry of Tourism (Secretaría de Turismo, or SECTUR):** Av. Presidente Masaryk #172 (ground floor), near the northeastern edge of Chapultepec Park in the Chapultepec Morales neighborhood (M: Polanco, line 7). Printed information can be obtained during office hours (Mon.-Fri. 8-6, Sat. 10-3). **Phone:** (55) 3002-6300, ext. 1133.

Contact SECTUR 24 hours a day for answers in English to questions about tourist attractions, destinations and services. In Mexico City, phone (55) 5250-0123; elsewhere within Mexico, phone (800) 006-8839 (toll-free long distance).

Most of the big hotels offer Internet access in their business centers. Java Chat, an Internet cafe at Calle Génova #44 in the Zona Rosa (near Calle Hamburgo), is open daily until 11 p.m.; an hour of surfing costs about $3 (U.S.).

## WHAT TO KNOW

## Currency Exchange

The rates charged by banks and *casas de cambio* (currency exchange houses) don't differ that much, so currency exchange is a matter of convenience. Most banks exchange currency Mon.-Fri. 9-noon, but you may have to wait in line; exchange houses often are open weekdays until 5 and may be open Saturdays as well. Exchange houses and ATMs are concentrated along Paseo de Reforma, in downtown's Historic Center and in the Zona Rosa. The Sanborn's chain also provide ATMs.

Almost all ATMs take Visa and Mastercard; withdrawals are in pesos. Only use ATMs inside commercial establishments and be alert for suspicious behavior around the machine—criminals may target tourists withdrawing cash. Above all, do not make street transactions at night. Also be careful when leaving banks or exchange houses, which can be targeted by petty thieves.

## Staying Safe

Street crime—from relatively benign offenses like pickpocketing and purse snatching to dangerous armed robbery—is an ever-present risk. No part of the city is immune, even the upscale Polanco neighborhood and other areas frequented by tourists. If going out for the evening, arrange designated hotel taxi transportation to and from your destination, particularly if you're unfamiliar with your surroundings. One way to avoid being mugged or robbed is not to wear expensive jewelry or watches.

Taxi robberies are among the most frequently reported crimes. The Zona Rosa and the area behind the U.S. Embassy are particularly vulnerable to street crime against foreigners; also avoid taxis parked in front of the Palace of Fine Arts. For safety's sake, it is advisable to arrange any excursion—even if only several blocks away—with a driver affiliated with your hotel.

Avoid participating in any demonstrations, strikes or other disputes that might be deemed political by Mexican authorities. Avoid the *Zócalo* and surrounding streets if protest activity is taking place. The Mexican Constitution prohibits foreigners from engaging in political activities; those who do may be detained and/or deported.

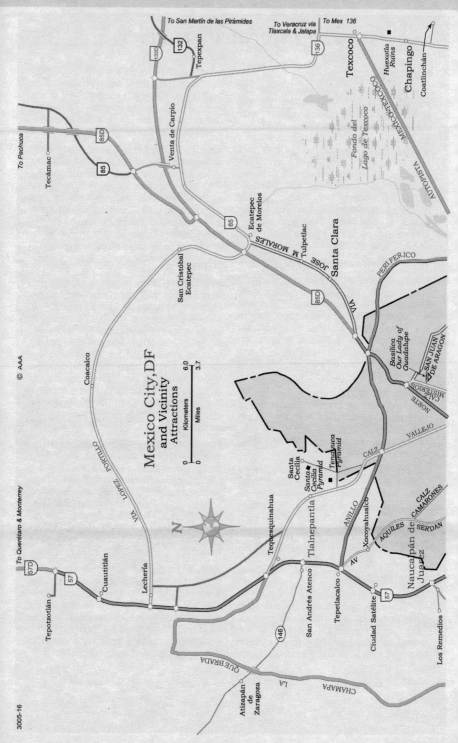

Mexico City, DF
and Vicinity
Attractions

Kilometers  6.0
Miles       3.7

© AAA

3005-16

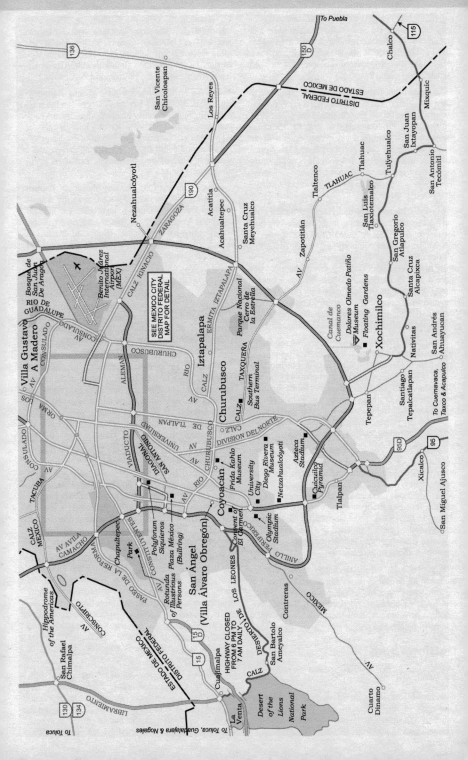

To Puebla

115

136

150 D

San Vicente Chicoloapan

Los Reyes

DISTRITO FEDERAL

ESTADO DE MEXICO

Chalco

Mixquic

190

ZARAGOZA

Nezahualcóyotl

Acatitla

Acahualtepec

Santa Cruz Meyehualco

San Juan Ixtayopan

San Antonio Tecomitl

Tlaltenco

TLAHUAC

Tlahuac

Tulyehualco

San Luis Tlaxialtemalco

Benito Juárez International Airport (MEX)

CALZ IGNACIO

CONSULADO

Bosque de San Juan De Aragón

RIO DE GUADALUPE

AV. CONSULADO

SEE MEXICO CITY DISTRITO FEDERAL MAP FOR DETAIL

ERMITA IZTAPALAPA

Parque Nacional Cerro de la Estrella

AV. Zapotitlán

San Gregorio Atlapulco

Santa Cruz Alcapixca

Dolores Olmedo Patiño Museum

Floating Gardens

**Xochimilco**

Canal de Cuemanco

Nativitas

San Andrés Ahuayucan

Villa Gustavo A Madero

AV CONSULADO

Iztapalapa

RIO CHURUBUSCO

ALEMAN

AV

CALZ

Churubusco

TAXQUEÑA

Southern Bus Terminal

CALZ

DIVISION DEL NORTE

Tepepan

Santiago Tepalcatlapan

To Cuernavaca, Taxco & Acapulco

95 D

95

Xicalco

San Miguel Ajusco

AV TLALPAN

UNIVERSIDAD

SAN ANTONIO

DIAGONAL

VIADUCTO

Frida Kahlo Museum

University City

Diego Rivera Museum

Netzahualcóyotl

Azteca Stadium

Cuicuilco Pyramid

Tlalpan

CONSULADO

TACUBA

AV

DE LOS

REFORMA

CALZ MEXICO

AV AVILA CAMACHO

Chapultepec Park

Polyforum Siqueiros

Plaza México (Bullring)

CONSTITUYENTES

PASEO DE LA REFORMA

Rotunda of Illustrious Persons

**Coyoacán**

Convent of El Carmen

Olympic Stadium

ANILLO PERIFERICO

MEXICO

AV

Hippodrome of the Americas

AV CONSCRIPTO

San Rafael Chimalpa

130

134

ESTADO DE MEXICO

DISTRITO FEDERAL

LIBRAMIENTO

Cuajimalpa

15 D

15

**San Ángel (Villa Álvaro Obregón)**

LOS LEONES

DESIERTO

HIGHWAY CLOSED FROM 6 PM TO 7 AM DAILY

La Venta

San Bartolo Ameyalco

CALZ

Contreras

Desert of the Lions National Park

Cuarto Dinamo

To Toluca

To Toluca, Guadalajara & Nogales

met Cortés with rich gifts and offered no resistance to his entry into the city. He believed the Spaniard to be a divine envoy of Quetzalcóatl, the fair-skinned, golden-haired god of civilization who according to legend was to return in the year of One Reed (Ce Acatl). On the Aztec calendar, 1519 was that year.

This case of mistaken identity brought about Moctezuma's downfall. Taking the ruler captive, Cortés and his troops remained in Tenochtitlan. After a long siege, a once-mighty city collapsed on Aug. 13, 1521. The Spaniards built their own city atop the ruins of the capital, leaving the outer periphery to the vanquished. Aztecs gradually intermingled with the Spanish, resulting in *mestizos,* persons of mixed Spanish and Indian blood who comprise the great majority of Mexico's present-day population.

Mexico City remained under Spanish rule for exactly 3 centuries, culminating in the decade-long fight for independence that followed *Grito de Dolores,* Father Miguel Hidalgo's impassioned speech advocating Mexican freedom, in 1810. It was finally taken by an army of patriots under Gen. Agustín de Iturbide, who entered the city on Sept. 27, 1821. Iturbide appointed himself emperor of the new nation in 1822 and was crowned in Mexico City as Agustín I, but his power was short lived; in December 1822 the republic was proclaimed and Iturbide was forced to abdicate.

During the 1860s the first *colonias,* or residential districts, began to appear. Modernization began on a large scale under the reign of dictator Porfirio Díaz from 1876 to 1910. Mexico City benefited from the establishment of such amenities as electric lighting, streetcars and a drainage system. The Palace of Fine Arts (Palacio de Bellas Artes) and other monumental public buildings were constructed, their design modeled after prevailing European neoclassic styles.

Modernization continued after adoption of the Constitution of 1917, bringing a steady stream of impoverished *mestizos* and Indians from the countryside. They crowded into working-class *colonias,* while luxurious residential districts housed the wealthy few. Skyscrapers began to define the city's skyline in the 1930s. The first sections of a modern subway system were completed in 1971; today Metro's nine lines provide inexpensive public transportation to millions of people daily.

In the last half of the 20th century Mexico city exploded in all directions, absorbing separate towns like Churubusco, Coyoacán, Iztapalapa, San Angel, Tlalpan, Villa de Guadalupe and Xochimilco. Today's metropolitan area encompasses hundreds of individual residential neighborhoods.

## Getting There

### By Air

Benito Juárez International Airport is about 13 kilometers (8 miles) east of the *Zócalo.* Some 30 airlines, both international and domestic, maintain regular flights to and from Benito Juárez.

Aeroméxico, (55) 5133-4000 or 01 (800) 021-4000 (toll-free long distance within Mexico) and low-cost Mexican carriers Interjet and Volaris offer service from multiple U.S. cities. Major U.S. carriers offering nonstop flights include Alaska Airlines, American, Delta, United and US Airways.

The T2 terminal handles all outbound Aeroméxico flights. Numerous facilities cater to foreign travelers, including Banamex and Bancomer bank branches, cellular phone rental, Internet access, ATMs and *casas de cambio* (currency exchange offices), a food court, short-term parking garage, and a variety of gift and duty-free shops. Rental car agencies include Hertz.

Representatives of the Mexican Ministry of Tourism (SECTUR) and the Hotel Association in the arrivals area can assist in booking a room according to location and price specifications. Authorized baggage handlers are identified by the "Union" ID placard attached to their hand carts. Phone (55) 2482-2400 for recorded airport information in English.

Contact the airline directly when making reservations for flights to other cities within Mexico, or if you need price or schedule information. This can be frustrating if you reach someone who doesn't speak good English; airline numbers also change frequently. If possible, make all flight arrangements prior to your departure; then the only reason you may need to call is to confirm times.

Allow for sufficient travel time to the airport—a minimum of 45 minutes if you're based in the downtown area. Arrive at least an hour before departure for domestic flights, 90 minutes before departure for international flights. If you have an early morning flight, staying at the Camino Real Aeropuerto hotel is convenient; an elevated skywalk connects the hotel and Terminal B. *For additional information about airlines see Arriving by Air, page p. 42.*

Authorized airport taxis are the safest way to reach the downtown area. The yellow-and-white vehicles, sedans or minivans, have a black aircraft symbol on the door and are labeled *"Transportación Terrestre"* (Ground Transportation). Taxis require prepayment at the official airport taxi counter; look for the *Taxi Autorizada* booth in the baggage claim area.

Rates are based on a zone system and vary according to distance; consult the map at the taxi counter to verify your destination. The fare to downtown Mexico City is about $20 (U.S.). Yellow-outfitted escorts show you to an available taxi; vouchers are given to the driver. Do not negotiate with anyone who approaches you with the offer of a ride into town. The ride to the city center takes 25 minutes to an hour, depending on the time of day. Tipping is customary if the driver helps with your luggage.

Metrobús buses run between the airport and downtown. Color-coded orange buses (Line 4) depart from both terminals approximately every 20 minutes daily, 4:30 a.m.-midnight. The ride takes about 30 minutes and the fare is 30 pesos (about $2.20 U.S.). Bus drivers only accept Metrobús boarding cards as payment; the cards can be purchased in both terminals from vending machines that only accept Mexican pesos.

If you're traveling light you might consider using Metro, Mexico City's rapid transit system. Large pieces of luggage aren't allowed on board, however, and riding a crowded subway car weighed down with anything more than an overnight bag is not only cumbersome but unsafe. The airport station is Terminal Aérea (Air Terminal Building, line 5) on Boulevard Puerto Aéreo. The main terminal is within walking distance; follow the signs. To reach the downtown area from the airport, take the subway to the Pantitlán station and switch to line 1.

## By Car

Mex. 15-D, 57/57-D and 85-D are the major highways approaching Mexico City from the west and north. From the south and east come Mex. 95-D and Mex. 150-D. Other routes are likely to be slow, winding or of substandard quality, and one—Mex. 134, which travels northeast to Mexico City from Mex. 200 along the Pacific Coast—should be avoided entirely.

Leaving the city, the main thoroughfares are Avenida Insurgentes Sur, which becomes Mex. 95-D as it heads south to Cuernavaca, Taxco and Acapulco; running north, Avenida Insurgentes Norte becomes Mex. 85-D/85 heading toward Pachuca. The Periférico loops around the city's western and southern sides. It is called Avenida Avila Camacho within

the city and becomes Mex. 57-D heading northwest toward Querétaro. Avenida Constituyentes runs west past Chapultepec Park and becomes Mex. 15 as it heads toward Toluca; Calzada Ignacio Zaragoza leads east out of the city, becoming Mex. 190-D as it heads toward Puebla.

Try to time both arrival and departure times into and out of Mexico City as early in the morning as possible to avoid the near-constant traffic.

**Note:** Seat belt use by the driver and all passengers is required within the Federal District.

## By Bus

With interconnections between Mexican and U.S. bus lines, it is possible to travel economically by bus from several U.S. border cities to Mexico City. Transportes del Norte, Tres Estrellas de Oro, Transportes Chihuahuenses and Omnibus de México are linked with Greyhound Lines Inc. From Tijuana it takes about 40 hours to reach Mexico City; from Ciudad Juárez, across the border from El Paso, Tex., about 24 hours; from Matamoros, across the border from Brownsville, Tex., about 14 hours.

Bus travel is available from Mexico City to nearly every town in the republic, but reservations must be made. Most major Mexican lines offer first-class (lujo) bus service; these companies include Autobuses Cristóbal Colón, Autobuses del Oriente (ADO), ETN, Omnibus de México, Primera Plus and Tres Estrellas de Oro. Arrivals and departures at bus stations in Mexico are usually announced in

© Frontpage / Shutterstock.com

Spanish only. *For additional information about buses see Bus Service, page p. 52.*

Mexico City has four main bus terminals that correspond to the four compass points. Each terminal has luggage storage facilities, a post office, ATMs, a cafeteria and long-distance (Ladatel) telephones.

By far the largest of the four is the Terminal Central de Autobuses del Norte, Av. Cien Metros #4907 (M: Autobuses del Norte, line 5). Most of the buses traveling from the northern border arrive at this terminal, also known as "Terminal Norte" or "Camiones Norte." From here, buses travel to almost every destination north of the capital, including the Pacific Coast resorts from Manzanillo northward; inland cities such as Aguascalientes, Guadalajara, Guanajuato, Monterrey, Morelia, Querétaro and San Miguel de Allende; and the nearby archeological sites of Teotihuacán and Tula.

The terminal offers currency exchange services (during normal banking hours) and has a hotel reservations booth. Taxis charge standard fares based on a zone system; tickets are purchased at booths inside the station. Count your change carefully, as overcharging is common.

Terminal de Autobuses de Pasajeros de Oriente (TAPO) is at Calzada Ignacio Zaragoza #200, near the airport (M: San Lázaro, line 1). The most modern of the four stations, it handles buses to and from such eastern destinations as Jalapa, Puebla, Veracruz, Villahermosa and cities on the Yucatán Peninsula, as well as Oaxaca, San Cristóbal de Las Casas, Tuxtla Gutiérrez, Guatemala and other places to the south. Taxi ticket booths and currency exchange services are available.

Terminal Central de Autobuses del Sur is at Av. Taxqueña #1320 (M: Taxqueña, line 2). At the end of Metro's line 2, this also is a major terminus for local city buses from downtown and other points north. From here buses arrive and depart for Acapulco, Cuernavaca, Ixtapa/Zihuatanejo, Taxco and other points south of Mexico City. For day trips to the tourist destinations of Cuernavaca and nearby Cuautla and Tepoztlán, take one of the Pullman de Morelos buses, which depart frequently for Cuernavaca. Estrella de Oro has first-class service to Acapulco and Zihuatanejo. The terminal also has a travel agency.

The smallest of the four is the western station, Terminal de Autobuses del Poniente, Av. Sur #122 at Tacubaya (M: Observatorio, line 1). This is the easiest way to take a day trip to Toluca by bus. Service also is available to Morelia and Guadalajara; the going is slow but the scenery is pleasant.

## Getting Around

### City Layout

Mexico City's *colonias,* or neighborhoods, are threaded by a maze of *calles, avenidas* and *calzadas.* Some narrow alleyways, or *callejones,* are cobblestoned relics from earlier days. Major thoroughfares, on the other hand, can have eight lanes.

Most of the signs tend to be more confusing than enlightening. There is no real logic to the city's streets, which are named after rivers, mountains, foreign cities and countries, musicians, writers, doctors, composers, the states of Mexico and just about everything else. They also change names frequently.

Connected highways form the Circuito Interior, which roughly encircles the central city. Beginning at the airport, on the east side of town, Avenida Río Consulado runs north and then west, becoming Calzada Melchor Ocampo. Ocampo swings south, passing east of Chapultepec Park and intersecting Paseo de la Reforma, at which point it continues as Calzada Vasconcelos. Angling off Vasconcelos is Avenida de la Revolución, which runs south to Avenida Río Churubusco. Churubusco then proceeds east before turning north to connect with Río Consulado, southwest of the airport, and completing the circuit.

Theoretically, this loop provides a less congested alternative to the jam-packed streets within it. However, these roads themselves are usually crowded, particularly during the morning and evening rush hours.

Also within the Circuito Interior are axis roads *(ejes),* a series of numbered boulevards running one way only, with special lanes reserved for trolleys and buses circulating in the opposite direction. East-west Eje 1 Norte and Eje 2 Norte are north of the *Zócalo,* Eje 2 Sur through Eje 8 Sur run progressively south of the *Zócalo.* North-south Eje 1 through 3 Oriente are east of Eje Central Lázaro Cárdenas, which divides the central city in half; Eje 1 through 3 Poniente are to the west.

Paseo de la Reforma intersects the central city. A legacy of French emperor Maximilian, this broad artery runs southwest to northeast for more than 7 miles. From the eastern end of Chapultepec Park to past Alameda Park, Reforma is exceptionally wide and is punctuated by several *glorietas* (traffic circles).

One good point of reference is the Independence Monument at the intersection of Reforma, Florencia and Tiber. The 150-foot-tall spire, topped by a gold angel, is easy to spot. Another is the major intersection at Paseo de la Reforma and Avenida Insurgentes, marked by the Cuauhtémoc Monument.

Insurgentes, the capital's longest thoroughfare, runs north/south, bisecting western and eastern sections of the city. East-west Viaducto Miguel Alemán runs south of downtown, connecting Calzada Ignacio Zaragoza at the eastern end of the city with the Anillo Periférico at the western end. The Periférico (Mex. 57) traverses the city's western and southern sections.

Driving just about anywhere within Mexico City is a daunting prospect and not recommended. The sheer number of vehicles makes for an extremely slow pace. Add to that aggressive tactics (the locals often disregard traffic signals), frequent construction, detours and a plethora of one-way streets, and visitors are far better off relying on taxi transportation provided by their hotel. Above all, never drive alone after dark due to the risk of car hijacking, robbery or assault.

If you must drive, carry a good city map and always park the vehicle in a guarded lot. Street parking is not only rare but chancy, as vandalism often occurs. Any vehicle parked illegally is likely to have its license plate removed by police; expect to pay a fee to get it back. Never leave valuables in your car, even if hidden.

At many downtown intersections, motorists stopped at a red light will be besieged by everyone from beggars to performing children (whose parents are often sitting on a nearby corner) to vendors selling newspapers, flowers, candy and trinkets. The best defense if you're part of this captive audience is to keep your door locked, your window rolled up and look straight ahead, avoiding eye contact.

Speed limits are shown in kilometers. If a road, avenue or street is unmarked, follow these general guidelines: school zones, 20 km/h (10-12 mph); residential streets, 30 km/h (20 mph); main streets, 50 km/h (30 mph); avenues, bypasses, loop roads and overpasses within the city, 60 km/h (35 mph); main roads, 100 km/h (60 mph); selected main roads and toll roads, 110-120 km/h (65-75 mph).

## Taxis

The most important safety advice for visitors is to never hail a cab on the street. Avoid the constantly cruising green and white Volkswagen Beetle taxis (often referred to as *ecologicos* or *magna sins*), or cabs with license plates containing the letter "L" (*libre* cabs). While residents must use them to get around an overcrowded city, drivers often are involved in robberies against passengers. The drivers themselves also are frequent victims of assault, making this a dangerous profession.

Major hotels maintain fleets of *turismo* taxis associated specifically with the hotel. These can be used for short hops to a nearby restaurant and back, or for longer excursions to shop or sightsee. For an hourly rate (and normally a 2-hour time minimum), you can arrange to have the driver wait at a specific location in addition to providing transportation. Rates for individual trips are negotiated with the driver; establish the fee for any excursion in advance. Although *turismo* taxis are expensive (a ride just a few blocks in length can cost several dollars), the peace of mind is well worth the cost.

J.R. Taxi is a reliable service; the owner/driver speaks English, is familiar with all of the city's major tourist attractions, and can pick up passengers at the airport or at designated bus stations. Favorable rates are offered to AAA members, and American Express, Mastercard and Visa are accepted. Phone (044) 55-5100-7542 (cellular number) in Mexico City, (044) 5100-7542 elsewhere within Mexico, or (155) 5100-7542 outside of Mexico.

If your hotel doesn't provide transportation or you otherwise need a cab, the U.S. Embassy strongly urges that you ride only in a taxi summoned by phone from a designated *sitio* (SEE-tee-oh) stand. They are considered safer than taxis that circulate because the driver can be easily traced back to the stand. Many of the stands list telephone numbers where the taxi can be called. Arrangements also can be made to have these cabs pick you up at a predetermined time and place.

Ask for the license plate number and the cab driver's name, and only use cabs with plates beginning with the letter "S," which are assigned to a particular site—such as a hotel—and registered. The number on the license plate should match the number painted on the side of the cab. It's much easier to negotiate for a *sitio* taxi if you speak fluent Spanish.

Authorized taxis at the airport and at bus stations charge fees based on a zone system; tickets to pay the fee are purchased at booths inside the terminal.

## Rental Cars

There are many car rental agencies in Mexico City. The larger companies also have branches in major cities where you can leave your car at trip's end. Be sure you fully understand the terms of any rental contract, especially in regard to insurance coverage. It's much less expensive to reserve before you leave home; make reservations at least 1 week in advance. AAA/CAA members enjoy discounts through Hertz for vehicles booked in the United States. Consult your local AAA/CAA club or phone Hertz, (800) 654-3080.

**Note:** Although having a vehicle at your disposal can be convenient for sightseeing trips outside the metropolitan area, keep in mind that a rental car driven by a foreigner may unfortunately become a target for police who will try to extract a bribe.

Vehicles in the Mexico City metropolitan area, including the Distrito Federal (Federal District) and parts of the state of Mexico, may *not* be driven on certain days based on the last digit of the license plate. Make certain your rental car can be driven when you wish to use it; a rental agency may inadvertently provide a vehicle with a license plate that has a last digit corresponding to the day on which it cannot be driven.

## Buses

City buses go just about everywhere and are inexpensive, but the system is not user-friendly for visitors. Routes and bus numbers change frequently, and route maps are practically nonexistent. Some signs at the downtown bus stops bear route descriptions. Buses run daily 5 a.m.-midnight, but show up much less frequently after 10 p.m.

Two major bus routes put visitors within walking distance of many of the city's attractions. The east-west route links the *Zócalo* with the National Auditorium in Chapultepec Park and continues to the Observatorio Metro station (line 1), traveling along avenidas Francisco I. Madero and Juárez and Paseo de la Reforma. These buses are usually marked "*Zócalo.*"

Buses running north-south along Avenida Insurgentes connect the huge Terminal Norte station with the southern suburbs of San Angel and University City via the Zona Rosa. These buses are usually marked *"Indios Verdes-Tlalpan."* Routes are marked on the windshield.

Never carry valuables onto a city bus, and know exactly where you're going before you board. But unless you simply want to have the experience, it's safer and much more convenient to use a taxi associated with your hotel for getting around.

## Peseros

These vehicles resemble a minibus or van. *Peseros,* also called *colectivos, combis* or *rutas,* travel along established routes and charged flat rates (according to distance) that are a bit more than the bus but less than taxi fares. Route destinations (often a Metro station) are marked on the windshield or shown on a sign. Flag down a *pesero* as you would a bus, and tell the driver your destination when you board.

Major routes include the principal east-west and north-south tourist corridors (the *Zócalo* to Chapultepec Park and Avenida Insurgentes Sur, respectively). This is an alternative to the crowded and often chaotic city buses, although using a designated taxi is still the safest way to travel. Try to have the exact change in pesos, and never pull out a wallet, which will attract the attention of pickpockets.

## Metro

Metro—one of the world's busiest subway systems—is faced with the formidable task of moving millions of riders daily over both surface and subterranean track. Metro lines cover most of the city. In addition, a *tren ligero* (light rail) line provides service to the popular tourist attraction of Xochimilco. The two lines visitors will find most convenient are Lines 1 and 2, as they cover major sightseeing points of interest.

Line 1 runs roughly west-east from the Observatory, near Chapultepec Park, to Pantitlán in the eastern suburbs, passing south of the Zona Rosa and the *Zócalo*. Subway riders bound for the airport switch to line 5 at the Pantitlán station. Line 2 begins in the northwest part of the city at the Cuatro Caminos station, proceeds east, burrows under the *Zócalo* and then runs above ground due south to the Taxqueña station.

Line 3 runs from the Indios Verdes station, north of the Basílica of Guadalupe, south past Alameda Park to University City (National University of Mexico campus). Line 4 runs north-south east of downtown, from the Martín Carrera to the Santa Anita stations. Line 5 runs from the Politécnico station south to the La Raza station, then east and south to Pantitlán, with a stop (Terminal Aérea) at the airport. **Note:** To switch from line 3 to line 5—or vice versa—at the La Raza station requires a 10- to 15-minute walk through a long tunnel.

Line 6 runs north of downtown, proceeding east from the El Rosario station to the Martín Carrera station via the Instituto del Petróleo and Deportivo 18 de Marzo stations. Line 7 runs north-south along the city's western edge from the El Rosario station to the Barranca del Muerto station. Line 8 runs from

the Garibaldi station (one stop north of the Bellas Artes station on line 2) south and east to the Constitución de 1917 station, in the southeast section of the city. Line 9 parallels line 1 and runs south of it, from the Tacubaya station in the west to the Pantitlán station in the east.

Two additional lines provide light rail service. Line A runs from the Pantitlán station (the eastern terminus of lines 1, 5 and 9) south to the La Paz station; Line B serves the Buenavista Railroad Station and runs east to the Garibaldi station (the northern terminus of line 8), then north to the Ciudad Azteca station. The *tren ligero* line runs south from the Taxqueña station south to Xochimilco.

The flat fare, which includes transfers, is 5 pesos (about 40 cents U.S.). Ticket vending machines dispense prepaid electronic cards in various denominations. The cards are swiped at long rows of turnstiles for access to the boarding ramps. If you plan on using the system, purchase several tickets at one time to avoid spending time standing in lines. You also can purchase an *abono* ticket, which allows use of the entire system for a multiple-day period. (With this type of ticket, enter Metro stations only through the blue turnstiles; otherwise the ticket will be taken and not returned.)

Metro is handicap accessible and people over 65 ride free by going through the turnstiles with police officers. Present a legal ID and an officer will swipe the machine for you. Once inside the turnstile, riders can access any of the system's lines.

At the stations, on signs and in guidebooks and brochures, Metro lines are designated by the following colors: lines 1 and A, bright pink; line 2, blue; line 3, olive green; line 4, light blue; line 5, yellow; line 6, red; line 7, orange; line 8, dark green; and line 9, brown. You can consult a color-coded subway guide at Metro information booths, or try obtaining a map of the system from the ticket booths at the larger stations.

The most striking aspect is the sea of people. There are restrictions on carrying personal items like luggage and backpacks, but they aren't enforced; many people tote large bundles and plastic bags filled with goods. The modern rail cars show some wear and tear as well as graffiti, but the ride is smooth and quiet. Keep in mind, however, that Metro is used daily by millions for commuter travel, so sardine-can conditions usually prevail. During weekday rush hours (both morning and evening) the trains are crammed and guards are employed to control the crowds; avoid using the system during these times and also after dark.

There are plenty of restrooms and the ubiquitous stands selling food and snacks. Most areas are well illuminated and ventilated. Cellphones generally do not work underground. Taking photographs is not permitted.

Pairs of police officers are at station entrances, and there are more police at turnstiles and patrolling the ramps, but they do not in general ride on the rail cars. Single women, unfortunately, may have to fend

# METRO LINES

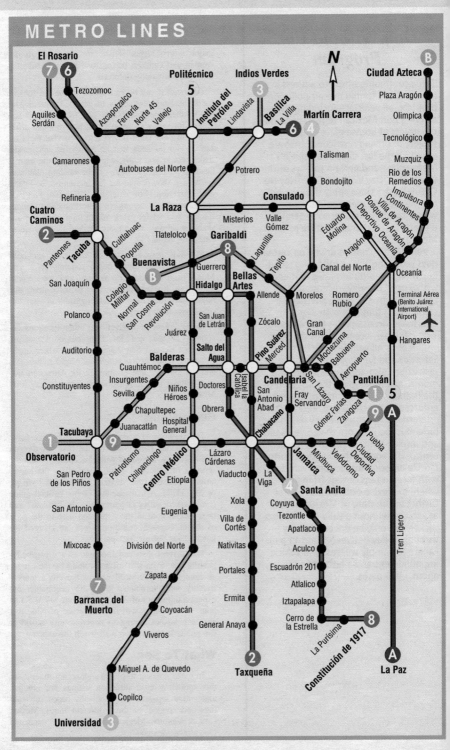

# "Day Without Car" Program

In a continuing effort to address Mexico City's formidable air pollution problem, all vehicles—including those carrying non-Mexican registration and regardless of license plate origin—are subject to driving restrictions that are based on the last digit of a vehicle's license plate and pertain to days of the week. The "Day Without Car" (Hoy No Circula) restrictions apply throughout the Mexico City metropolitan area, which includes the Distrito Federal (Federal District) and the state of México.

Vehicles may not be driven on certain days according to the following schedule: Monday—license plates that end with 5 or 6; Tuesday—license plates that end with 7 or 8; Wednesday—license plates that end with 3 or 4; Thursday—license plates that end with 1 or 2; Friday—license plates that end with 9 or 0. All vehicles may be driven Saturday and Sunday; however, the restrictions also apply one Saturday a month, again based on the last digit of the license plate. Restrictions are not enforced between 10 p.m. and 5 a.m.

In order to be driven every day, a vehicle must be no more than 5 years old and display a sticker issued by a *Verificentro*, the agency that conducts automobile emission inspections. Vehicles with foreign tags or tags from anywhere in Mexico outside the Federal District or the state of México, as well as vehicles without a valid *Verificentro* sticker, can only be driven Monday through Friday between 5 and 11 a.m. Failure to comply will result in vehicle impoundment and a hefty fine of about 1,000 pesos.

off unwelcome advances or inappropriate male conduct. Foreign visitors are prime targets for pickpockets and purse snatchers, especially at stations near major tourist sights. There are separate cars for women and children during rush hours, but regulations are not strictly enforced.

Although it can be convenient to use the subway for sightseeing, especially to get to Xochimilco or the southern neighborhoods of Coyoacán and San Angel, for safety's sake it's best to hire a taxi affiliated with your hotel if you intend to visit these areas. If you do need to take Metro for any reason, make certain you know which direction the train is heading. Check the signs on the loading platforms *(andenes);* they denote the last station on the line in each direction. For example, *Dirección Pantitlán* and *Dirección Observatorio* indicate the last stations for line 1. Transfer gates, where more than one line shares a subway station, are marked *Correspondencia;* exits, *Salida.*

Metro is least crowded on weekends and holidays. In general trains begin running at 5 a.m. Mon.-Fri., 6 a.m. Sat., 7 a.m. Sun., and operate until 12:30 a.m. It's best not to carry personal items that hinder movement, and remain cognizant of your surroundings at all times.

**Note:** Points of interest and other locations described in the text for Churubusco, Coyoacán, Mexico City and San Angel include, where applicable, the name of the individual Metro station (M) and the subway line (1 through 9). Attraction listings without this designation are located away from Metro routes.

## Guides/Tours

The services of a good guide can be expensive but invaluable, particularly for the first few days in this huge city. If you go with this option, obtain the services of a bonded guide licensed by the Secretaría de Turismo (the Mexican Ministry of Tourism, or SECTUR). Ask to see his or her official guide card marked with "Departamento de Turismo" and take special note of the expiration date to the right of the photograph. Additional fees are charged for guided trips outside Mexico City.

Taxi drivers also can function as a driver/bodyguard/guide, even if it means waiting by the car for an hour while you stroll one of the city's tourist-friendly neighborhoods. Rates are negotiable, but expect a minimum of 230 pesos (about $17 U.S.) an hour. Most visitors will find the peace of mind that comes from not having to negotiate city traffic or use public transportation well worth the expense.

## What To See

To make it easier to plan a sightseeing itinerary in this sprawling city, attraction listings are grouped under nine separate, geographically based subheadings and spotted on three different maps: Mexico City & Vicinity, Mexico City Distrito Federal and Downtown Mexico City.

## Around the Zócalo

**GRAN HOTEL CIUDAD DE MEXICO** is just w. of the *Zócalo* at Av. 16 de Septiembre #82 (M: Zócalo, line 2); the parking entrance is located between avenidas 5 de Febrero and Palma. Renovations have ensured that this five-story building—a grand example of turn-of-the-20th-century architecture in the Chicago style—retains much of its original splendor. Take a peek inside the spacious atrium lobby; it boasts a spectacular Tiffany stained-glass ceiling and gilded, open-cage elevators. The rooftop terrace restaurant overlooking the *Zócalo* is a great choice for lunch with a view. **Cost:** Parking is available for an hourly fee. **Phone:** (55) 1083-7700.

**GREAT TEMPLE** (Templo Mayor) encompasses a city block just n. of the *Zócalo;* the site entrance is on Av. Seminario (M: Zócalo, line 2). The only available parking is a commercial underground garage near the Palace of Fine Arts. The Great Temple, or Teocalli, of the Aztecs was a monumental pyramid that served as a religious, political and sacrificial center. The ruins, located in the heart of today's metropolis, are striking evidence of a separate civilization that flourished hundreds of years earlier.

Demolished and buried by the conquering Spaniards, the structure—originally thought to be beneath the nearby Metropolitan Cathedral—was rediscovered in 1978 by a subway construction worker. The excavated ruins reveal successive layers of older temples, each built atop the other, and include other structures as well as a stone replica of a *tzompantli,* or wall of skulls. Plaques in Spanish explain the origin of the different temples. English audio guides are available. **Note:** Visitors must proceed through the complex in one direction and are not permitted to turn around and go back once inside the site.

**Time:** Allow 1 hour, 30 minutes minimum. **Hours:** Site open Tues.-Sun. 9-5. **Cost:** (includes site and Great Temple Museum) 64 pesos (about $4.75 U.S.); free (ages 0-12). The fee to use a video camera is 45 pesos (about $3.35 U.S.). **Phone:** (55) 5542-0606.

**Great Temple Museum** (Museo Templo Mayor) is at avs. Guatemala and Seminario within the site. The museum provides a valuable historical perspective, especially for those unfamiliar with Aztec lore. On display are more than 7,000 items recovered from the site and locations as far away as the present-day states of Veracruz and Guerrero. There are eight exhibit rooms (*salas*) on three levels, organized around a central open space dominated by the original discovery, the enormous stone depicting a beheaded and limbless Coyolxauhqui.

Among the more impressive artifacts are life-size, terra-cotta eagle warrior statues and stone masks that were offered as tributes by subjugated tribes. **Hours:** Open same hours as the site.

**METROPOLITAN CATHEDRAL** (Catedral Metropolitana) is on the n. side of the *Zócalo* (M: Zócalo, line 2). This enormous church seems even bigger rising up from the vast

## "Day Without Car" Program (continued)

The regulation applies to both permanent and temporary plates. There is no specific provision regarding plates with letters only. If you plan to rent a car and drive anywhere in the greater Mexico City metropolitan area, contact the rental car agency in advance and make certain the vehicle can be driven when you wish to use it.

Physically disabled drivers are not exempted from the regulation. Whether you're driving your own vehicle or a rental, keep in mind that police officers within the greater metropolitan area often stop drivers with foreign plates for alleged violations of driving restrictions in an attempt to extract a bribe in the form of a "fine."

When pollution is extremely heavy (particularly during the winter months), emergency driving restrictions may be mandated. "Double Day Without Car"

© Africa Studio / Shutterstock.com

(Doble Hoy No Circula) means that driving is prohibited a second day during the week, based on whether the last digit of the license plate is odd (1, 3, 5, 7 or 9) or even (2, 4, 6, 8 or 0). Before any such decision is made, announcements are broadcast on radio and TV specifying the contingency days added to the normal restriction, and those vehicles affected.

expanse of the *Zócalo*. A church built in 1525 was demolished in 1573 to make way for the present structure, which was not completed until some 215 years later. The exterior is a mingling of architectural styles, from baroque ornamentation to a neo-classic clock tower.

Along the interior side aisles are five naves and 14 chapels (two additional chapels on the cathedral's east and west sides are not open to the public), each dedicated to a saint and variously adorned with statuary, ornate altars, paintings, gilded surfaces, priceless tapestries and representations of Christ, including a black Christ figure. The Chapel of the Kings, at the end of the nave behind the main altar, is graced by gilded wood carvings and an extravagantly Churrigueresque altarpiece. **Note:** Visitors to the cathedral (or any church in Mexico) should respect those who are there to worship.

All manner of crystals, herbs, gemstones and religious paraphernalia are sold in front of the cathedral. On the west side more vendors set up shop, selling everything from crafts to Mexican jumping beans, and laborers sit on the curb next to small signs advertising their trade.

A sound-and-light presentation, "Voices of the Cathedral," features choral music and actors in period costume. Check local newspapers for schedule information, or phone Ticketmaster, (55) 5325-9000. **Hours:** Daily 8-8. **Cost:** Free. **Phone:** (55) 5510-0440.

**Sacristy** (El Sagrario) adjoins the cathedral. This church, built in the mid-18th century to house vestments and sacred relics, has an elaborate baroque facade. Both the Sacristy and the cathedral were damaged in the 1985 earthquake, and each has also tilted over decades as the buildings ever so slowly sink into the underlying lake bed, requiring repair work to mitigate the .effects of uneven settling. **Hours:** Daily 8-8. **Cost:** Free.

**MUNICIPAL PALACE** (Palacio del Ayuntamiento) faces the *Zócalo's* s. side (M: Zócalo, line 2). It serves as City Hall. The original building at the square's southwest corner dates from 1724. On the front arcade are coat-of-arms mosaics depicting Mexican cities, states and regions, including Coyoacán, site of the first city hall in the Valley of Mexico; the 1168 founding of Aztec capital Tenochtitlan; and the Villa Rica de la Vera Cruz, said to be the first city hall in the continental Americas.

In order to see the Hall of Rulers (Salón Virreyes) and the Legislative Assembly Hall (Sala de Cabildos) visitors must present identification and sign in at the visitor desk on the first floor. The exhibit halls are located on the second floor. The Hall of Rulers is a collection of paintings—including one of Hernando Cortés—displayed in two rooms. Adjacent to these rooms is the room where the Mexican legislative assembly met until 1928; it contains original furniture. Spanish-only guided tours are available. **Time:** Allow 30 minutes minimum. **Hours:** Tues.-Sun. 10-5. Closed major holidays. **Cost:** Free.

**NATIONAL MUSEUM OF CULTURES** (Museo Nacional de Las Culturas) is at Calle Moneda #13, near the cathedral and just e. of the *Zócalo* (M: Zócalo, line 2). The museum displays permanent and rotating exhibits offering an overview of the world's cultures. Three floors of exhibit halls are grouped around a lovely central patio; the Pacific Cultures Hall is particularly noteworthy. All displays are professionally mounted and well illuminated. A striking Rufino Tamayo mural in the lobby depicts the 1910 Revolution. Exhibit information is in Spanish only. **Time:** Allow 2 hours minimum. **Hours:** Tues.-Sun. 10-5. Closed major national holidays. **Cost:** Free. **Phone:** (55) 5542-0422.

**NATIONAL PALACE** (Palacio Nacional) is along Av. Pino Suárez, facing the e. side of the *Zócalo* (M: Zócalo, line 2). It has housed the offices of government officials since 1821. It took Diego Rivera some 25 years to execute the sweeping, lavishly detailed historical murals decorating the upper level of the central courtyard and the walls of the main staircase, which depict everything from romantically idealized views of Aztec life before the arrival of Hernando Cortés to the bloody 1910 Revolution.

Hanging over the central doorway is the Independence Bell, tolled by Father Miguel Hidalgo in 1810 to proclaim Mexican independence from Spain; on Sept. 15 Mexico's president rings the bell in an annual ceremonial re-enactment of Hidalgo's plea for freedom.

There also are two museums inside the palace. The Benito Juárez Museum consists of several large rooms displaying furnishings, manuscripts, artwork and other artifacts associated with the former Mexican president; the Parliamentary Museum has elegant fabric-covered walls, gold chandeliers, flags and the formal "well" used for parliamentary sessions. At the palace's far end is a lovely, relaxing garden with benches and stone fountains.

**Note:** A photo ID is required to enter the building. Public restrooms are available. **Time:** Allow 1 hour, 30 minutes minimum. **Hours:** Daily 9-5; museums Tues.-Sun. 9-5. **Cost:** Free.

**ZÓCALO** is bounded by avs. Corregidora, Seminario (Pino Suárez), Madero and Monte de Piedad (M: Zócalo, line 2). The *Zócalo* (SOH-cah-loh), officially Plaza de la Constitución, is a vast, open expanse of concrete covering nearly 10 acres; only Moscow's Red Square is larger. Emperor Moctezuma's palace and the Templo Mayor stood on the site when the Spanish made their way into the city of Tenochtitlan and proceeded to tear it to the ground.

The *Zócalo* (the word means "base of a pedestal") follows the Spanish blueprint for colonial settlements staked out in the Americas: a central plaza surrounded by a cathedral and government buildings. A Mexican flag stands in the center of the square; residents come here to participate in *manifestaciones*—street marches and demonstrations—as well as to just hang out.

Commemorative events, like the 200-year anniversary of Mexico's declaration of independence from Spain celebrated in 2010, are held regularly. A flag-lowering ceremony performed daily at 6 p.m. is filled with flourishes of pomp. Hundreds of thousands assemble for Sept. 15 and 16 Independence Day celebrations. This massive plaza also is regularly filled with the sound of music; former Beatle Paul McCartney and tween idol Justin Bieber are among the superstars who have put on shows here before tens of thousands of fans.

For a bird's-eye perspective, head to the seventh-floor dining terrace at the Majestic Hotel (Avenida Madero on the west side of the square). You'll enjoy a panoramic view away from the swarms of people that fill the Zócalo for major events.

**Note:** This is a very crowded, congested part of the city. Do not even attempt to negotiate the traffic or find a place to park on your own. If you want to walk around and explore for an hour or so, hire a licensed guide, a private driver or a hotel taxi to drop you off, wait and then take you back to where you're staying. Avoid the Zócalo and surrounding streets after dark.

## Within the Historic Center

**BANAMEX PALACE OF CULTURE** (Palacio de Cultura Banamex) is w. of the Zócalo at Av. Madero #17 near Av. Bolívar (M: Bellas Artes, lines 2 and 8). Commissioned by the Count of San Mateo de Valparaíso as a dowry for his daughter, the Iturbide Palace is a fine example of the 18th-century baroque architectural style. It became a hotel in 1850, was purchased by the National Bank of Mexico (Banco de Mexico) in 1966 and today houses a bank-underwritten museum promoting all types of Mexican culture. Exhibits are on two floors surrounding a colonnaded courtyard.

The longer-term exhibits on the second floor include framed art, sculpture, photographs, audiovisual presentations and interactive displays. The main floor features rotating exhibits often focusing on traditional popular art.

Guided tours in Spanish are given daily at noon, 2 and 4. Guided tours in English are available by advance reservation; phone a few days prior to visiting the museum. Children are not permitted on guided tours. **Hours:** Daily 10-7. **Cost:** Free. **Phone:** (55) 1226-0091.

**CHURCH AND HOSPITAL OF JESUS THE NAZARENE** (Iglesia y Hospital de Jesús Nazareno) is 3 blks. s. of the Zócalo on Avenida República del Salvador; the entrance is at Salvador and Calles Mesones (M: Pino Suárez, lines 1 and 2). The first hospital in Mexico is said to stand on the site where Hernando Cortés and Aztec emperor Moctezuma had their first meeting in 1519; a large stone tablet on Pino Suárez next to the church commemorates the occasion. The chapel has an entrance on Salvador at Pino Suárez; inside are Cortés' remains. A plaque marking the tomb of the conquistador can be seen on the left wall of the main altar.

The dramatic José Clemente Orozco mural "Apocalypse" covers the ceiling and upper walls of the church's choir mezzanine. **Time:** Allow 30 minutes minimum. **Hours:** Mon.-Sat. 7 a.m.-8 p.m., Sun. 7-1 and 5-8. Rectory open Tues.-Fri. 11-noon and 1:15-2. **Cost:** Free.

**EX-CONVENT AND TEMPLE OF REGINA COELI** (Ex-Convento y Templo de Regina Coeli) is about 5 blks. s.w. of the Zócalo at calles Regina and Bolívar (M: Isabel la Católica, line 1); street parking is very limited. Construction began in 1655, although it was not consecrated until 1731. Once the Convent of the Nuns of the Conception in Mexico, it received its present name in 1756.

The sumptuous Medina-Picasso Chapel, built in 1733, encompasses an entire block and is considered a masterpiece of Churrigueresque architecture. It contains three altarpieces with works by Villalpando Rodríguez Juárez and other 18th-century painters. A striking niche in the main altar is adorned with tortoiseshell and mother-of-pearl. **Time:** Allow 30 minutes minimum. **Hours:** Daily 8-1 and 4-8. **Cost:** Donations.

**JOSÉ LUIS CUEVAS MUSEUM** (Museo José Luis Cuevas) is at Calle Academia #13, 2 blks. e. of the Zócalo. The former Convent of Santa Inés was completed in 1612. The richly carved doors on the corner of Called Moneda depict the saint's life and death and portraits of the convent's founders. Cuevas, a highly regarded contemporary artist, created the monumental sculpture "The Giantess" that stands in the center of the courtyard. About a third of the museum's approximately 3,000 works are by Cuevas. **Hours:** Tues.-Sun. 10-5:30. **Cost:** 20 pesos (about $1.50 U.S.). **Phone:** (55) 5522-0156.

**MINISTRY OF PUBLIC EDUCATION** (Secretaria de Educación Pública) is n. of the Great Temple at República de Argentina #28 (M: Zócalo, line 2). The walls of this building were perhaps Diego Rivera's greatest canvas; almost every space on the three floors is covered with murals symbolizing Mexican life, history and culture.

The first floor contains images of daily rural life, depictions of industry and the celebration of such truly Mexican festivities as the Day of the Dead. Notably missing from these scenes is Rivera's customary political satire; instead, he emphasized national pride. Panels on the second and third floors focus on Mexican workers, the nation's heroic leaders, the 1910 Revolution and such familiar Rivera targets as capitalist greed.

**Note:** Due to security concerns, visitation is by appointment only and a photo ID is required. Phone ahead or appear in person at the front security desk to arrange your visit. This is not a guided tour; once visitors have gone through the appointment formality they are permitted to view the murals. **Hours:** Building open Mon.-Fri. 10-5. **Cost:** Free. **Phone:** (55) 3601-1000 (only Spanish is spoken).

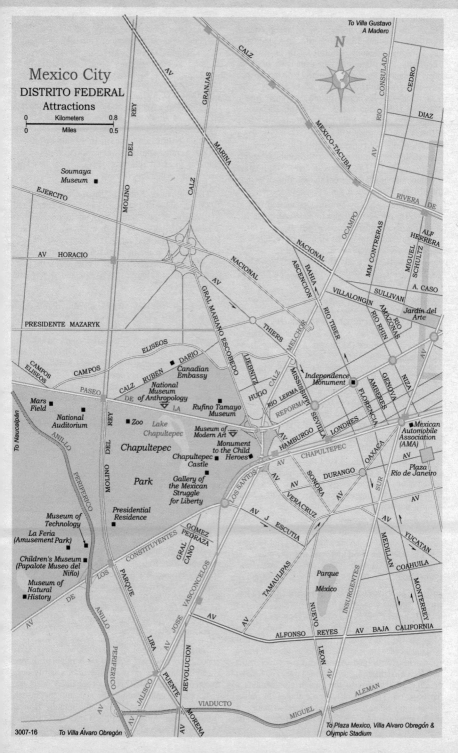

# Mexico City
## DISTRITO FEDERAL
### Attractions

Kilometers
0          0.8
Miles
0          0.5

N

To Villa Gustavo
A Madero

CALZ

AV

GRANJAS

CALZ MARINA

RIO CONSULADO

CEDRO

DIAZ

MEXICO-TACUBA

AV

RIVERA DE

OCAMPO

MM CONTRERAS

ALF HERRERA

MIGUEL SCHULTZ

A. CASO

Soumaya
Museum

EJERCITO

MOLINO DEL REY

CALZ

NACIONAL

AV NACIONAL

BAHIA

ASCENCION

VILLALONGIN

SULLIVAN

Jardín del
Arte

AV HORACIO

AV GRAL MARIANO ESCOBEDO

THIERS

MELCHOR

RIO TIBER

RIO AMAZONAS

RIO RHIN

PRESIDENTE MAZARYK

ELISEOS

DARIO

LIBERTZ

CALZ

MISSISSIPPI

GENOVA

NIZA

AV

CAMPOS ELISEOS

CAMPOS

PASEO

CALZ RUBEN

Canadian
Embassy

National
Museum
of Anthropology

HUGO

RIO LERMA

REFORMA

FLORENCIA

AMBERES

Independence
Monument

DE LA

Rufino Tamayo
Museum

SEVILLA

LONDRES

Mexican
Automobile
Association
(AMA)

Mars
Field

National
Auditorium

Zoo

Lake
Chapultepec

Museum of
Modern Art

HAMBURGO

AV CHAPULTEPEC

OAXACA

Chapultepec
Park

MOLINO DEL REY

ANILLO

To Naucalpán

PERIFERICO

Monument
to the Child
Heroes

Chapultepec
Castle

Gallery of
the Mexican
Struggle
for Liberty

LOS SANTOS

AV

SONORA

VERACRUZ

DURANGO

SUR

AV

AV

Plaza
Río de Janeiro

Museum of
Technology

Presidential
Residence

GOMEZ PEDRAZA

GRAL CANO

AV J ESCUTIA

MEDELLIN

YUCATAN

COAHUILA

La Feria
(Amusement Park)

Children's Museum
(Papalote Museo del
Niño)

Museum of
Natural
History

CONSTITUYENTES

JOSE VASCONCELOS

LOS

PARQUE

DE

TAMAULIPAS

Parque
México

NUEVO LEON

INSURGENTES

MONTERREY

AV

AV

ANILLO

PERIFERICO

LIRA

PUENTE

JALISCO

REVOLUCION

MORENA

VIADUCTO

ALFONSO REYES

AV BAJA CALIFORNIA

MIGUEL

ALEMAN

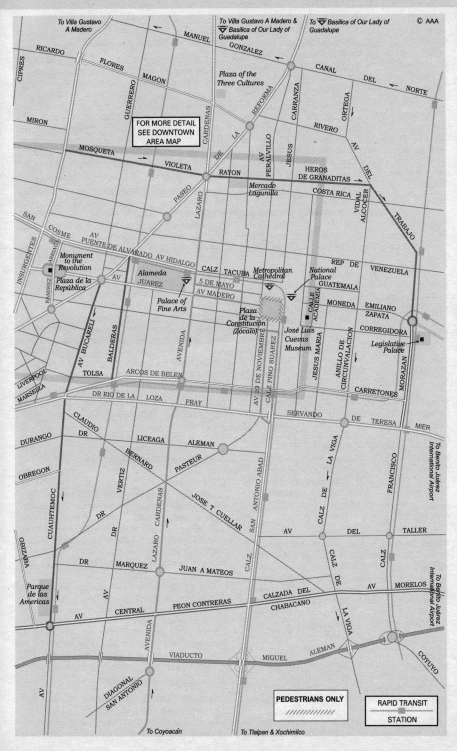

© AAA

**MUSEUM OF MEXICO CITY** (Museo de la Ciudad de México) is 3 blks. s. of the *Zócalo* at Pino Suárez #30, near República del Salvador (M: Pino Suárez, line 2). The building housing this museum was originally given by Hernán Cortés to a member of his crew; in the late 19th century it was converted into a two-story palace with stone archways and several interior courtyard gardens.

The vast collection surveys the history, culture and people of both the ancient and modern city. Large exhibits that can be observed from overhead catwalks depict daily life in the early 1500s in the Aztec city of Tenochtitlan, where canoes were the primary means of conveyance for people and goods. Displays show how neighborhoods that exist today, like Tacuba and Coyoacán, looked back then.

Other exhibits feature 19th-century carriages and traditional costumes. Artwork on view includes Aztec sculptures, feather-adorned pieces, gold bracelets, murals and paintings by Frida Kahlo and Diego Rivera.

A permanent display features black-and-white images of gridlocked cars, turbulent political scenes, earthquake damage and a sea of humanity in the *Zócalo,* all dramatically evoking the day-to-day challenges of living in this enormous metropolis. Temporary rotating exhibits are presented regularly. **Time:** Allow 2 hours minimum. **Hours:** Tues.-Sun. 10-5:30. **Cost:** 26 pesos (about $1.90 U.S.); free (ages 0-2). Free to all Wed. **Phone:** (55) 5542-0487.

**OLD COLLEGE OF SAN ILDEFONSO** (Antiguo Colegio de San Ildefonso) is just n. of the Great Temple (Templo Mayor) and 2 blks. n. and just e. of the *Zócalo* at Avenida Justo Sierra #16, between avenidas República de Argentina and del Carmen (M: Zócalo, line 2). This outstanding colonial edifice was built in 1749 as the Jesuit School of San Ildefonso. Converted to a museum, the renovated structure has three floors exhibiting colonial works of art, paintings by Fernando Leal and traveling exhibitions.

José Clemente Orozco murals depicting post-Revolutionary Mexico surround the main patio. The Patio of the Undergraduates (Patio de Los Pasantes), with just three corridors, has a small courtyard featuring Orozco and Diego Rivera murals painted in the 1920s. Guided tours in Spanish are available. **Time:** Allow 2 hours minimum. **Hours:** Tues.-Sun. 10-5:30 (also Tues. 5:30-7:30). Closed major Mexican holidays. **Cost:** 45 pesos (about $3.35 U.S.); free (ages 0-12). Free to all Tues. **Phone:** (55) 5702-6378.

**SANTO DOMINGO CHURCH** (Iglesia de Santo Domingo) is on República de Brasil (M: Allende, line 2), facing the n. side of Santo Domingo Plaza. The original church, destroyed by a flood, was the first founded in Mexico by the Dominicans. The present building, dating from 1736, has a beautiful baroque exterior highlighted by ornately carved Corinthian columns. Inside is a chapel containing *milagros,* offerings given by the devout in thanks for a miraculous cure from infirmity or disease.

**SANTO DOMINGO PLAZA** is 3 blks. n.w. of the *Zócalo,* bounded by República de Venezuela, República de Peru, República de Chile and República de Brasil (M: Zócalo, line 2). It is one of the best preserved colonial squares in the city. Dating from about 1550, the plaza is surrounded by charming old buildings. It also is the home of *los evangelistas.* These professional typists, writers and editors ply their trades from under arcades on the west side of the plaza, a service begun by public scribes in the 1850s for citizens unable to write.

**Museum of Mexican Medicine** (Museo de Medicina Mexicana) is at the opposite end of the plaza at República de Brasil and República de Venezuela. Formerly a college of medicine, it has rooms dedicated to medical equipment—some of it archaic—and a re-creation of an old pharmacy. Other displays include an old dentist's office with antique chair, laboratory set-ups, amputation and ophthalmological tools, early needles and a 19th-century respirator with a turn wheel.

Some of the exhibits, such as skulls showing the results of brain surgery, mannequins afflicted with various skin diseases and one detailing aborted fetuses at different stages, are quite graphic. **Time:** Allow 1 hour minimum. **Hours:** Daily 9-6. **Cost:** Free. A small fee is charged for special exhibitions. **Phone:** (55) 5623-3123.

**SUPREME COURT OF JUSTICE** (Suprema Corte de Justicia) is just s. of the National Palace at Pino Suárez and Corregidora. Built between 1935 and 1941 at the site of ancient Plaza del Volador, this building has a sober exterior, but the interior features an interesting set of staircases leading to the Hall of Lost Steps (Salón de los Pasos Perdidos), which contains two José Clemente Orozco murals depicting workers' rights, nationalism and concepts of justice.

Calle Corregidora runs between the court building and the National Palace. Prior to the Spanish conquest a canal traversed this area, part of a system that connected Tenochtitlan to other Aztec centers around Lake Texcoco. Today evidence of the ancient waterway can still be seen, although Corregidora is now a pedestrian-only thoroughfare filled with vendor stalls.

Free self-guiding audio tour devices are available in English, Spanish and French; after passing through courthouse security, request one at the front information desk. **Hours:** Mon.-Thurs. 9-5, Fri. 9-4. A photo ID is required to enter the court building; foreigners must present a valid passport issued by their respective country. **Cost:** Free. **Phone:** (55) 4113-1100, Ext. 5811.

## Alameda Park and Vicinity

**ALAMEDA PARK** is just w. of the Palace of Fine Arts between avs. Juárez and Hidalgo. Two Metro stations are close by: Hidalgo (lines 2 and 3) is at the intersection of Hidalgo and Paseo de la Reforma, a block off the park's northwest corner; Bellas Artes (lines 2 and 8) is at the park's northeast corner. A green retreat in the middle of Mexico City's concrete jungle, this rectangular, centrally located green space—formerly an Aztec market—is surrounded by museums, theaters, hotels and restaurants.

The park is large, clean and well maintained, landscaped with poplar, ash and willow trees. There are benches, fountains, 19th-century French sculptures and a Moorish kiosk. Weekends bring the best people watching; food and drink stands set up and myriad vendors peddle their wares to the assembled crowd of families, couples and roving packs of teenagers. Public restrooms are available, and there are plenty of police (who patrol on horseback on weekends). **Hours:** Daily 24 hours.

**Juárez Monument** (Hemiciclo de Juárez) faces Av. Juárez along the park's southern boundary. "Hemiciclo" refers to the monument's semicircular design. It honors the man who was president of Mexico from 1858 to 1872; his marble statue sits on a pedestal surrounded by columns. Benito Juárez's Mar. 21 birthday is celebrated at the park.

**CHURCH OF THE CONVENT OF CORPUS CHRISTI** is at Av. Juárez #44, opposite the s. side of Alameda Park (M: Bellas Artes, lines 2 and 8). Part of the first convent to accept noble indigenous women and the daughters of Indian chieftains, this sober baroque building was later a training college for teachers and until 1985 housed the National Museum of Popular Art and Industries. The central portal has arched doors flanked by pilasters supporting a cornice and a small pediment.

**DIEGO RIVERA MURAL MUSEUM** (Museo Mural Diego Rivera) is at calles Balderas and Colón, just w. of Alameda Park (M: Hidalgo, lines 2 and 3). It was built specifically to house the epic mural "Dream of a Sunday Afternoon in the Alameda Central," which had originally been painted on a wall of the Hotel del Prado across the street. Although the hotel was torn down following damage caused by the 1985 earthquake, the mural weathered the disaster and was carefully moved to this museum. The central figures—among a gallery of Mexican historical characters—enjoying a Sunday promenade in the park are the artist (portrayed as a child); his wife, fellow painter Frida Kahlo; and Catrina, a clothed skeleton (*calavera*) representing the works of satirist José Guadalupe Posada.

Publications and lithographs on the walls provide information about the historical characters depicted in the mural. The second floor has information about Rivera's life and work and also is used for temporary art exhibits. **Time:** Allow 30 minutes minimum. **Hours:** Tues.-Sun. 10-6. Closed major Mexican holidays. **Cost:** 19 pesos (about $1.40 U.S.); free to all Sun. **Phone:** (55) 5512-0754. GT

**FRANZ MAYER MUSEUM** (Museo Franz Mayer) is at Av. Hidalgo #45 (Plaza de la Santa Veracruz), opposite the n. side of Alameda Park (M: Bellas Artes, lines 2 and 8). A former convent dating from the second half of the 16th century, it was a hospital for much of its existence until closing in 1966; in 1989 it was restored to house an enormous and valuable collection of viceregal, European and Asiatic paintings and sculptures.

Among the objects on view are ceramics, silver, textiles, maps and navigation instruments. The museum also presents temporary exhibits. **Hours:** Tues.-Sun. 10-5. **Cost:** 45 pesos (about $3.35 U.S.); free (ages 0-11, ages 60+ and to all Tues.). **Phone:** (55) 5518-2266. ⁇

**HOUSE OF TILES** (Casa de Los Azulejos) is at Av. Francisco I. Madero #4, about 2 blks. e. of Alameda Park (M: Bellas Artes, lines 2 and 8). This is one of the city's finest colonial mansions. It was built in 1596 to be the residence of the Counts of Orizaba. The entire exterior is covered with decorative blue and white tiles from Puebla; the bronze balustrade was brought from China.

The flagship of the Sanborn's restaurant chain has occupied the building since 1919. Stop in for a look at the main dining room, which has carved stone columns, large frescoes, an elaborate staircase and a bar/lounge on the second level. **Hours:** Restaurant open daily 7 a.m.-1 a.m. **Cost:** Free. **Phone:** (55) 5512-1331. ⁇

**LATIN-AMERICAN TOWER** (Torre Latino) is at avs. Madero and Lázaro Cárdenas (M: Bellas Artes, lines 2 and 8); entrances are on both streets. At 545 feet, this slender, 44-story glass skyscraper was once the city's tallest. The tower rests on floating piers sunk deep into the underlying clay; as the city's first building to have an adequate foundation, it has survived every earth tremor that has occurred since its 1956 construction. An elevator takes visitors to the 37th floor, where there is a cafe; a small museum is on the 38th floor.

The open-air observation deck on the 44th floor offers magnificent views of the city and the surrounding mountains on rare smog-free days; the 42nd and 43rd floors are enclosed for rainy day viewing. **Time:** Allow 1 hour minimum. **Hours:** Daily 9 a.m.-10 p.m. Phone ahead to confirm schedule. **Cost:** Observation deck admission 80 pesos (about $5.90 U.S.); 60 pesos (children and senior citizens). Tickets can be purchased at a booth near the elevators. **Phone:** (55) 5518-7423.

**MAIN POST OFFICE** (Correo Mayor) is on the corner of Calle Tacuba and Av. Eje Central Lázaro Cárdenas across from the Palace of Fine Arts (M: Bellas Artes, lines 2 and 8). Designed by Italian architect Adam Boari—who also was responsible for the Palace of Fine Arts—and in operation as a post office since 1907, the building incorporates Gothic, Moorish, Renaissance, Spanish and Venetian elements and has an exterior of yellow-rose quarry stone from the state of Hidalgo. Most of the interior ironwork, banisters and furnishings were imported.

On the second floor, the Philatelic Museum (Museo Filatélico) displays stamp collections and antique Mexican postal equipment, including enormous stamp machines that dispensed 1-centavo stamps. The post office is the point of reference for the city's street numbering system. **Hours:** Philatelic Museum open Tue.-Fri. 10-6, Sat.-Sun. 10-4. **Cost:** Free. **Phone:** (55) 5512-0091.

**Mexico City Naval Museum,** on the fourth floor of the Main Post Office, has a number of exhibits that chronicle the country's naval history. Among the many replicas is a scale layout of the first naval battle in the New World. Displays of model ships, weapons, uniforms and other artifacts tell the story of significant Mexican naval conflicts, including the French invasion in 1862 and the U.S. occupation of Veracruz in 1914. **Hours:** Tues.-Fri. 10-5, Sat.-Sun. 10-2. **Cost:** Free. **Phone:** (55) 5512-8178.

**NATIONAL ART MUSEUM** (Museo Nacional de Arte) is at Calzada Tacuba #8, directly e. of the Palace of Fine Arts (M: Bellas Artes, lines 2 and 8). This outstanding museum, formerly the Palace of Communications and Public Works, has 33 exhibit halls displaying national art treasures. The halls are large and uncluttered, focusing on just one or two magnificent pieces per wall. Works include paintings, sculptures, pre-Columbian figures, metal work and even ornately framed video screens that flicker with constantly changing images. This museum is fun and surprising; one of the exhibits is a video of an apartment building showing residents beginning and ending their day.

Also noteworthy are the rooms devoted to 17th-century painters Juan Correa and Cristóbal de Villalpando, both of whom were inspired by the sensual style of Peter Paul Reubens, and 20th-century artist María Asúnsolo. Two elegant curved staircases at the back of the museum lead to the upper levels; at the bottom are two lions supporting a buttress with five lamps. The underside of one stairwell is decorated with the painting "Peace Defeating War." **Time:** Allow 2 hours minimum. **Hours:** Tues.-Sun. 10-5:30. **Cost:** 42 pesos (about $3.10 U.S.); free (ages 0-12); free to all Sun. **Phone:** (55) 5130-3400.

**El Caballito** stands in the center of the square fronting the museum. "The Little Horse" is the work of Manuel Tolsá. The 30-ton sculpture, showing King Charles IV of Spain astride his horse, is considered one of the world's finest equestrian statues. It was cast in 1803 from a single piece of bronze. **Cost:** Free.

**NATIONAL MUSEUM OF ENGRAVING** (Museo Nacional de la Estampa) is at Hidalgo #39 across from Alameda Park (M: Bellas Artes, lines 2 and 8). Housed in a handsomely restored 16th-century building, it focuses on lithographs, sketches and engravings utilizing silk screen, rubber, wood and metal for multiple transfers. The second floor has permanent exhibits, including posters and the pointed political cartoons and cavorting skeleton figures of 19th-century Mexican artist José Guadalupe Posada. Temporary exhibits are on the first floor.

**Hours:** Tues.-Sun. 10-5:45. **Cost:** 13 pesos (about $1 U.S.); free (ages 0-12). **Phone:** (55) 8647-5220.

**PALACE OF FINE ARTS** (Palacio de Bellas Artes) is on Calle Lopez Peralta at the e. end of Alameda Park (M: Bellas Artes, lines 2 and 8). It was begun in 1904 by Italian architect Adamo Boari, interrupted by the Revolution of 1910 and finally dedicated in 1934, a legacy of Porfirio Díaz's economically progressive but politically oppressive regime. Because of enormous weight and a swampy subsoil, the building has settled considerably since its construction.

The decorative sculptures on the facade are the building's highlight. They include garlands, flowers, masks and a sculptural group called "Harmony." A sculpture of Pegasus stands in the outdoor esplanade. Inside the look is pure 1930s Art Deco, augmented by second- and third-floor murals by Diego Rivera, José Clemente Orozco and David Alfaro Siqueiros. Note in particular "Man in Control of His Universe," Rivera's caustic rendering of capitalism, originally commissioned for New York City's Rockefeller Center in 1933.

The city's premier cultural center is the home of the National Opera Company, the National Ballet of Mexico, the National Dance Company and the National Symphony Orchestra. The building also houses the National Museum of Architecture, which contains models, sketches, photographs and draft plans. Temporary exhibitions of art, sculpture and photography are regularly mounted.

**Hours:** Tue.-Sun. 10-5. **Cost:** Museum 25 pesos (about $1.85 U.S.). Admission to view the murals 45 pesos (about $3.35 U.S.). Museum and murals free to all Sun.

**Ballet Folklórico de México** is presented in the Palace of Fine Arts theater. This theatrically colorful spectacle showcases many forms of Mexican folk music and dance. The theater is famed for its 22-ton crystal curtain; actually a double-walled steel curtain, the side facing the audience was crafted from 1 million pieces of opalescent glass that resemble a large window and depict snowcapped peaks Popocatépetl and Iztaccíhuatl. The half-hour curtain show is given only before the Sunday morning performance. *Also see Concerts, p. 278.*

**Hours:** Performances are usually given Sun. at 9:30 and 8:30 p.m., Wed. at 8:30 p.m. The ballet is occasionally moved to another venue, usually the National Auditorium or the Museum of Anthropology; performance times may vary. **Cost:** Tickets 360-700 pesos (about $27-$52 U.S.). **Phone:** (55) 5325-9000 for Ticketmaster.

**SAN FERNANDO CHURCH AND CEMETERY** is n.w. of Alameda Park at Vicente Guerrero #39 (M: Hidalgo, lines 2 and 3). At one end of the plaza is the church, a former monastery built in the mid-18th century. The Churrigueresque facade survived the monastery's dismantlement after the monks were expelled in 1860. The adjacent cemetery holds the remains of several prominent Mexican families; the last person buried here was former president Benito Juárez. **Hours:** Daily 8-3. **Cost:** Free.

**SAN FRANCISCO CHURCH** is on Av. Madero, 2 blks. e. of Alameda Park and almost directly across from Sanborn's (M: Bellas Artes, lines 2 and 8). Begun in 1524 with money granted by Hernando Cortés, it was long the center of Catholicism in America and headquarters of the Franciscan Order. The original complex, fragments of which are still visible, also comprised a monastery and training school for Franciscan missionaries. The present church dates from the 18th century and has an elaborately Churrigueresque facade.

## Chapultepec Park and Vicinity

**CHAPULTEPEC CASTLE** (Castillo de Chapultepec) is within Chapultepec Park (M: Chapultepec, line 1). It stands atop a 200-foot-high hill overlooking the central part of the city; the stony outcrop was once used by Aztec emperors as a summer retreat. Construction of the castle began in 1783. Completed in 1840, it was fortified and became a military college. When it was attacked and taken in 1847 by U.S. forces during the Mexican-American War, the castle was defended solely by its young cadets. After passing through a succession of leaders it was finally bequeathed to the nation in 1939 by President Lázaro Cárdenas.

The climb to the castle along a paved walkway winding up Chapultepec Hill is fairly steep and takes about 20 minutes. En route there are frequent views of the downtown skyline. For a small fee, visitors can ride a tourist train that is boarded inside the park entrance and transports passengers up the hill.

**Caracol Museum/Gallery of History** (Museo de Caracol/Galería de Historia) is within Chapultepec Park, about halfway up the hill to Chapultepec Castle. The name "caracol" refers to the building's spiral shape, which resembles a snail's shell.

Twelve descending *salas* (exhibit halls) offer detailed, colorful dioramas that depict memorable past events in Mexican history, including Father Miguel Hidalgo's military campaign to secure independence from Spain, the Mexican-American War, French intervention in the 1860s and the Mexican Revolution of 1910. The chamber of red *tezontle* (volcanic) stone at the end of this walk through the past is covered with an impressive dome and is dominated by three objects: the national flag, a carved-stone eagle and a facsimile of the 1917 Constitution. Explanations are in Spanish.

**Time:** Allow 1 hour minimum. **Hours:** Tues.-Sun. 9-4:15. **Cost:** 52 pesos (about $3.85 U.S.); free (ages 60+ and 0-13). The fee to use a video camera is 45 pesos. **Phone:** (55) 4040-5241.

**National Museum of History** (Museo Nacional de Historia) is the first building before Chapultepec Castle and adjacent to it; there is no sign. A guided tour proceeds through 12 *salas* (exhibit halls) tracing Mexican history from the Spanish conquest to the Revolution of 1910 and the adoption of the 1917 constitution. Weapons, paintings, clothing, furniture and maps are displayed. The *Salón de Virreyes* contains portraits of historical figures and rulers from Hernando Cortés to 20th-century Mexican presidents, while the *Salón de Malaquitas* has doors and other objects fashioned out of malachite.

Murals depict important events in the nation's history, and there also is a striking mural painting of Mexican artists such as Jorge Gonzalez Camarena and José Clemente Orozco. Exhibit information is in Spanish. Visitors will find self-employed, English-speaking tour guides for hire near the museum's front doors; expect to pay about $30 U.S. per hour.

Flash photography is not permitted. **Time:** Allow 2 hours minimum. **Hours:** Tues.-Sun. 9-5. **Cost:** 64 pesos (about $4.75 U.S.); free (ages 0-13 and 60+). **Phone:** (55) 5061-9200.

**CHAPULTEPEC PARK** (Bosque de Chapultepec) sprawls on either side of Paseo de la Reforma beginning about 4 blks. w. of the Zona Rosa (M: Chapultepec, line 1; Auditorio and Constituyentes, line 7). It is the oldest natural park in North America and one of the largest and most varied in the world. After the establishment of Tenochtitlán, Aztec emperors used Chapultepec Hill, within today's park, for summer relaxation.

Despite the wear and tear it's fascinating to stroll along the cobbled walkways, as much for the people-watching as anything else. You won't see many foreign tourists here; the park is very much a gathering place for city residents. Sunday is the best day to visit, as families converge to enjoy their day off at this enormous green space.

Chapultepec is divided into three sections. Some of the city's most notable museums are grouped in the oldest (eastern) section ("1a Sección"), including the National Museum of Anthropology, the Museum of Modern Art and the National Museum of History in Chapultepec Castle. The section of the park west of Calzada Molino del Rey ("2a Sección") is newer and contains many of the kid-oriented attractions. The Pines (Los Piños), the Mexican president's residence, is just east of Molino del Rey; it is not open to the public.

If you plan to spend most of the day and would rather not sample the offerings of food vendors, bring a lunch. **Hours:** Eastern section open daily 5-5; some attractions are closed Mon. **Cost:** Free. Separate admissions charged for attractions.

**Chapultepec Park Zoo** (Parque Zoológico de Chapultepec) is in the eastern section, s. of Paseo de la Reforma off Calzada Chivatito (near the National Museum of Anthropology). It displays giant pandas—this is one of the few zoos to have successfully bred them in captivity—a white tiger and other animals in natural habitats. There's also an aviary, a venomous snake exhibit and a miniature train ride. **Hours:** Tues.-Sun. 9-4:30. Closed Jan. 1 and Christmas. **Cost:** Free. **Phone:** (55) 5553-6263. 🍴

**Children's Museum** (Papalote Museo del Niño) is at Av. Constituyentes #268 in the park's second (western) section (near the Anillo Periférico). Themed areas explore the human body, science, computers and artistic expression, among other subjects. Kids will love the contraption that makes giant soap bubbles. In addition to the many interactive, hands-on activities, the museum also has an IMAX theater and hosts special exhibitions.

**Hours:** Mon.-Fri. 9-6 (also Thurs. 6-11 p.m.), Sat.-Sun. 10-7. Hours may vary, especially during school holiday weeks. Phone ahead to confirm schedule. **Cost:** 129 pesos (about $9.55 U.S.); free (ages 0-2). Separate admission for IMAX movies. **Phone:** (55) 5237-1773. 🍴

**Don Quixote Fountain** (Fuente de Don Quijote) stands in Quixote Square, just off Gran Avenida, w. of Lake Chapultepec and s. of the Botanic Garden. The fountain is within a pavilion designed in the shape of a simple cube. A mural by Diego Rivera covering its bottom depicts the evolution of life by water. The hydraulic works in the vicinity receive water from the Río Lerma. Also on the square is a metallic structure housing two small sculptures of Quixote and sidekick Sancho Panza in the midst of an argument.

**La Feria** is in the park's second (western) section off the Circuito Bosque de Chapultepec, w. of the Anillo Periférico. This amusement park is dominated by a pair of huge roller coasters, the wooden Russian Mountain (Montaña Rusa) and the steel, triple-loop Infinitum. There are numerous other rides, as well as a haunted house. **Hours:** Generally open Tues.-Sun. 10-8, although hours vary by season; extended hours during Mexican school holidays. Phone ahead to confirm schedule. **Cost:** (includes access to all park rides) 200 pesos (about $14.80 U.S.). Ninety- and 150-peso tickets offer access to fewer rides, with separate fees (15 to 30 pesos each) for roller coasters and other premium rides. **Phone:** (55) 5230-2121. 🍴

**Lake House** (Case del Lago) is in the heart of the park's old section, on the western shore of Lake Chapultepec (Lago de Chapultepec). It functions as a cultural center and as a setting for public events. Rowboats can be rented. A short distance west of the lake is the park's Botanical Garden (Jardín Botánico).

**Monument to the Child Heroes** (Monumento de Los Niños Héroes) is near the park's main entrance. The group of columns memorializes six cadets who were among those defending Chapultepec Castle, then a military college, against American troops at the height of the Mexican-American War in 1847. They reputedly leaped to their deaths wrapped in the Mexican flag rather than be captured.

**Museum of Natural History** (Museo de Historia Natural) is in the park's second (western) section off the Circuito Bosque de Chapultepec. It consists of 10 interconnecting domes that house nature dioramas and biological, geological and astronomical exhibits. The museum's insect collection is a highlight. **Hours:** Tues.-Sun. 10-5. **Cost:** 23 pesos (about $1.70 U.S.); free to all Sun. **Phone:** (55) 5515-2222.

**Museum of Technology** (Museo Tecnológico) is in the park's second (western) section off the Circuito Bosque de Chapultepec, s. of the amusement park. Housed in a pyramidal structure, the museum has a planetarium and exhibits on aviation, energy, science and industry. The grounds feature installations of railroad cars and other industrial equipment. **Hours:** Daily 9-4:15. **Cost:** Free. **Phone:** (55) 5516-0964.

**Rotunda of Illustrious Persons** (Rotonda de las Personas Ilustres) is in the western section of the park at avs. Constituyentes and Civil Dolores (M: Constituyentes, line 7). Dolores Cemetery (Panteón Civil de Dolores), Mexico's national cemetery, is where many of the country's military leaders, political figures and important citizens have been laid to rest. The markers are arranged in circular fashion around an eternal flame. Artists Diego Rivera, David Alfaro Siqueiros and José Clemente Orozco are just a few of the notables interred. A map is available at the entrance building. **Hours:** Daily 6-6. **Cost:** Free.

**Tlaloc Fountain** (Fuente de Tlaloc) is in Section II of Chapultepec Park, next to the Carcamo municipal water pump station. Created in the early 1950s by Diego Rivera, this large and intricate mosaic of Tlaloc, the Aztec rain god, had long been abandoned but is now being restored along with the concave fountain that contains it as well as the surrounding park area.

Measuring approximately 100 by 100 feet, the likeness of Tlaloc is a relief, situated about 3 feet above ground level in a position that indicates running or perhaps dancing. Behind the artwork is a domed pump house (Carcamo de Dolores) that once housed a large water tank. Inside the pump house, wall-mounted organ pipes softly echo natural sounds derived from the movement of water, and posters depict Rivera's intent to merge practical functionality with cultural expression via a single work of art.

**Hours:** Pump house open Tues.-Sun. 9-5. **Cost:** Fountain free. Pump house 45 pesos (about $3.60 U.S.). Cash only.

**INDEPENDENCE MONUMENT** (Monumento a la Independencia) is in the circle at Paseo de la Reforma and Tiber (M: Insurgentes, line 1). A 150-foot-high column dating between 1901 and 1910, it is topped by a winged statue of Victory. The central figure at the base is Father Miguel Hidalgo; he is flanked by other leaders in the war for independence, including José María Morelos and Nicolás Bravo. The female statues represent Law, Justice, War and Peace.

This is one of several commanding landmarks that stand in the middle of *glorietas* (traffic circles) at principal intersections along Reforma; locals and visitors alike use them as geographical reference points.

**MUSEUM OF MODERN ART** (Museo de Arte Moderno) occupies a circular building on the s. side of Paseo de la Reforma (at Calle Gandhi), near the entrance to Chapultepec Park (M: Chapultepec, line 1). It celebrates the diversity of 20th-century Mexican modern art and also presents temporary exhibitions by important international artists.

The permanent collection is housed in Xavier Villaurrutia and Carlos Pellicer halls. Among its many highlights are works by Mexico's three leading muralists—Diego Rivera, David Alfaro Siqueiros and José Clemente Orozco. Paintings by another major Mexican modern artist, Rufino Tamayo, include "The Sleeping Musicians" and "The Man Radiant in Happiness." This museum also contains Frida Kahlo's "The Two Fridas," one of the surrealist's most striking works.

José Guadalupe Posada, José Luis Cuevas and Juan Soriano are other well-known artists represented, along with contemporary figures like Oliverio Hinojosa and Irma Palacios. There is a sculpture garden surrounding the museum. Exhibit information is in Spanish. **Hours:** Tues.-Sun. 10-5:15; closed major holidays. **Cost:** 28 pesos (about $2.05 U.S.); free to all Sun. **Phone:** (55) 8647-5530.

**NATIONAL MUSEUM OF ANTHROPOLOGY** (Museo Nacional de Antropología) is in Chapultepec Park off Calz. Mahatma Gandhi, facing the n. side of Paseo de la Reforma (M: Chapultepec, line 1 or Auditorio, line 7). A must-see stop for any Mexico City visitor, this is one of the world's finest museums.

The halls (*salas*) devoted to Mexico's early civilizations exhibit every conceivable type of artifact, including temple reconstructions, stone carvings, sculptures, ceramics, antique furniture, jewelry, masks, decorative objects, and arts and crafts. Dramatic lighting accentuates the remarkable artistry of the larger sculptures. Upstairs exhibit areas focus on the country's Indian cultures, showcasing musical instruments, traditional costumes and giant papier-mâché dolls.

Guided tour tickets can be purchased in the main entrance hall, which also has a bookstore selling English-language museum guides and an orientation theater where a 20-minute orientation film is shown. Most exhibit labeling is in Spanish; newer exhibits also include an English translation. The museum is very crowded on Sundays, when admission is free to Mexican nationals.

English language audio guides are available. Wheelchairs are available. Flash photography and tripods not permitted. **Time:** Allow 3 hours minimum. **Hours:** Tues.-Sun. 9-6:45. **Cost:** 64 pesos (about $4.75 U.S.); free (ages 0-12 and 60+). Guided tour fee 75 pesos (about $5.55 U.S.). Audio tour fee 75 pesos. The fee to use a personal video camera is 60 pesos. **Parking:** 16 pesos per hour. **Phone:** (55) 5553-6381, or (55) 5553-6386 for guided tour information. [GT]

**Aztec Hall** (Sala Mexica), on the ground floor, has as its focal point the 24-ton Aztec calendar stone, the Stone of the Sun (Piedra del Sol), with the face of the sun god carved in its center. The vivid statue of the goddess Coatlicue is rendered beheaded and wearing a skirt of snakes, and a scale model of the center of pre-Hispanic Tenochtitlan includes hundreds of detailed miniatures and an accompanying mural depicting the lake that once covered the area.

**Maya Hall** (Sala Maya), on the ground floor, spotlights a culture that was arguably the most advanced in all Mesoamerica. While the artifacts displayed here may not equal the grandeur of their lavishly decorated temples—the singular Mayan architectural achievement—they affirm the beauty of Mayan art. Many of the ceramic figurines, pieces of jewelry and death masks were retrieved from burial sites.

**Teotihuacán Hall** (Sala Teotihuacána), on the ground floor, is devoted to the first of Mexico's great pre-Hispanic cities. Here visitors can see a reproduction of the site's Temple of Quetzalcóatl, a huge statue of Chalchiuhtlicue, the Teotihuacán goddess of the "running waters," and displays from Cholula (*see separate listing under Central Mexico*).

**RUFINO TAMAYO MUSEUM** (Museo Rufino Tamayo) is in Chapultepec Park, on the n. side of Paseo de la Reforma and west of Calzada Gandhi (M: Chapultepec, line 1). It displays the personal modern art collection of the Oaxacan painter and muralist, who died in 1991. Although Tamayo's work was initially criticized for its lack of political content, his reputation as a key figure of 20th-century Mexican art has grown over the years. In addition to Tamayo's own paintings, the large, well-lit halls display works by Pablo Picasso, René Magritte, Max Ernst, Mark Rothko and Joan Miró, as well as changing exhibitions devoted to international artists.

The museum also has rooms where you can watch videos about the art on display and a cyber lounge with interactive monitors and headsets.

**Time:** Allow 2 hours minimum. **Hours:** Tues.-Sun. 10-6. **Cost:** 21 pesos (about $1.55 U.S.). **Phone:** (55) 5286-6519.

## North of Downtown

**BASILICA OF OUR LADY OF GUADALUPE** (Basilica de Nuestra Señora de Guadalupe) is at Plaza de las Américas #1, about 10 km (6 mi.) n. of the Historic Center (M: La Villa-Basilica, line 6). The site is located on a rocky hill (Cerro del Tepeyac) in the neighborhood (*colonia*) of Villa de Guadalupe. From the La Villa-Basilica Metro station, walk n. 2 blks. to the plaza. If you're unfamiliar with the city, take a taxi. The basilica, one of Roman Catholicism's holiest shrines, honors the Guadalupe Virgin, Mexico's patron saint.

Mexican Catholics believe that at this site in December 1531 the Virgin appeared to Juan Diego, a peasant Indian, and asked him that a church be built. After hearing this story, the local bishop requested

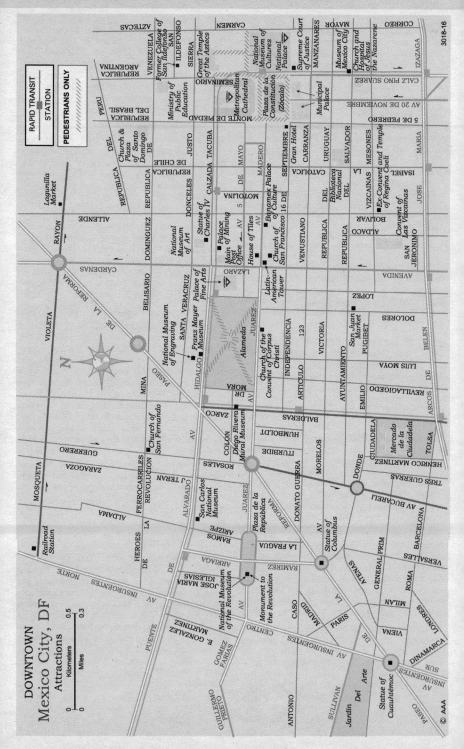

# DOWNTOWN
# Mexico City, DF
## Attractions

RAPID TRANSIT

STATION

PEDESTRIANS ONLY

proof. Diego returned on Dec. 12, his cape filled with roses that the Virgin had directed him to pick (a rather miraculous occurrence itself, considering the time of year). When the cape was opened, the roses had disappeared and a vivid image of the dark-skinned Virgin appeared on the folds of cloth.

A plaza with a visitor information center and a museum anchors the sprawling complex. A large underground parking lot is filled with a bazaar-like assemblage of religious-themed shops and street vendors selling handicrafts. Visitors enter the plaza through steel gates manned by armed guards. At the far end of the plaza is the ornate Old Basilica (Basilica Antigua), built about 1709 to house the sacred image.

Near the main entrance soars the New Basilica (Basilica Nueva), which can accommodate more than 10,000 people. Daringly modern in contrast, it was built in 1976. The cloth, in a gold frame and protected by bulletproof glass, hangs above the main altar; visitors pass beneath it via two moving walkways going in opposite directions. To the rear of the Old Basilica is a museum that displays religious artworks, including a collection of *retablos* (small devotional paintings). Other churches within the complex are the Church of the Indians (Parroquía de Indios) and the Chapel of the Well (El Pocito).

**Time:** Allow 1 hour minimum. **Hours:** Churches daily 6 a.m.-8 p.m., museum Tues.-Sun. 10-5:30. **Cost:** Churches free, museum admission 5 pesos (about 40c U.S.).

**CONVENT OF SAN AGUSTÍN ACOLMAN—** *see Acolman listing p. 240.*

**PLAZA OF THE THREE CULTURES** (Plaza de Las Tres Culturas) is 3 blks. n. of Paseo de la Reforma on Av. Lázaro Cárdenas, at the intersection with Ricardo Flores Magón (M: Tlatelolco, line 3); a taxi will take you to the entrance. The name comes from three vastly different influences—pre-Hispanic Aztec, colonial Spanish and contemporary Mexican—that have left their individual imprints on this plaza.

The ceremonial and trading center of Tlatelolco (tlah-tay-LOHL-koh) considerably predated the Aztec capital of Tenochtitlan. Even after it was absorbed by the Aztec city in 1473, Tlatelolco continued to function as an important market. It was from Tlatelolco that the Aztecs made their final stand against Spanish forces on Aug. 13, 1521.

Nearly 450 years later, the plaza was the scene of another massacre. On the eve of the 1968 Summer Olympic Games—with Mexico City in the world spotlight—a massive student protest over prevailing economic and social policies turned deadly when government troops were ordered to open fire.

The site ruins can be seen from raised walkways and give an indication of its former size. The Church of Santiago Tlatelolco, dating from 1609, has a restored interior that contains several frescoes and a strikingly simple stone altar. Next to the church are the remains of a monastery and former college where Franciscan friars taught the sons of Aztec nobility. The modern high-rise at one time

housed the Secretariat of Foreign Relations. **Time:** Allow 2 hours minimum. **Hours:** Daily 8-6. **Cost:** Free. **Phone:** (55) 5583-0295.

**SOUMAYA MUSEUM** (Museo Soumaya) is at Blvd. Miguel de Cervantes #303, in Plaza Carso. Named in honor of his late wife, the Soumaya Museum showcases the eclectic art collection of businessman Carlos Slim, allegedly the world's richest man. The dramatic, free-form aluminum exterior is seven stories tall and resembles a Rodin sculpture. Inside, various exhibit halls display an enormous collection of life-size sculptures, precious metals and framed art from across history and around the world.

Cultural displays feature valuable ceramics and crafts as well as utilitarian objects and implements. Most of the exhibits are very well illuminated and displayed on low stands for 360-degree viewing. Some sections are devoted to specific artists and artistic movements, such as Rodin and the Dutch Masters, while others focus on temporary exhibits. The blocks surrounding the museum, once economically depressed, now boast gleaming high-rise office buildings and apartments, with Plaza Carso (named after Slim's holding company) as the centerpiece.

The museum is located in the northern part of the city, away from the downtown core; it's best to arrange taxi transportation from your hotel. **Time:** Allow 3 hours minimum. **Hours:** Daily 10:30-6:30. **Cost:** Free. **Phone:** (55) 5616-3731, or (55) 5616-3731, ext. 308 or 309, for guided tour reservations. GT ⛔

**TEOTIHUACÁN—** *see Teotihuacán listing p. 282.*

## West of Downtown

**REVOLUTION MONUMENT** (Monumento a la Revolución) stands in the Plaza de la República, n. of Paseo de la Reforma and w. of the Alameda (M: Revolución, line 2). Topped by an imposing copper dome that surmounts four arches, it rises 250 feet. Buried under the four columns are four former presidents—Venustiano Carranza, Plutarco Calles, Lázaro Cárdenas and Francisco I. Madero—as well as revolutionary Pancho Villa. Porfirio Díaz, the dictator deposed by the Revolution of 1910, intended the building to house the government's legislative offices, but the uprising halted construction; it was dedicated as a monument in the 1930s.

**National Museum of the Revolution** (Museo Nacional de la Revolución) is inside the lower part of the monument. It houses a collection of weapons, along with paintings and sculptures depicting the revolution's leading figures. **Hours:** Tues.-Sun. 9-5. **Cost:** 26 pesos (about $1.90 U.S.). **Phone:** (55) 5566-1902.

**SAN CARLOS NATIONAL MUSEUM** (Museo Nacional de San Carlos) is about 3 blks. n. of Plaza de la República at Puente de Alvarado #50 (M: Revolución, line 2). It houses an impressive collection of paintings by European artists spanning the 15th through the 19th centuries, including works by Francisco José de Goya, Tintoretto, Titian, Anthony Van Dyck, Rembrandt and Peter Paul Rubens.

The lovely neoclassic building was the private home of such notable Mexican military figures as Gen. Agustín de Iturbide and Gen. Antonio López de Santa Anna. A small public park off Puente de Alvarado faces the rear facade. **Hours:** Tues.-Sun. 10-6. **Cost:** 35 pesos (about $2.60 U.S.); free (ages 0-13). Free to all Sun. The fee to use a personal video camera is 30 pesos. **Phone:** (55) 5566-8522.

**STATUE OF COLUMBUS** stands within the *glorieta* (traffic circle) on Paseo de la Reforma at Av. Morelos (M: Revolución, line 2). The work of Charles Cordier, it depicts the explorer (Cristóbal Colón in Spanish) and is one of several statues commissioned by Porfirio Díaz to grace major intersections along this stretch of the city's widest boulevard.

**STATUE OF CUAUHTÉMOC** (Monumento a Cuauhtémoc) is on Paseo de la Reforma at Av. Insurgentes (M: Insurgentes, line 1). Cuauhtémoc, the last Aztec emperor, was tortured by Hernando Cortés in an unsuccessful attempt to force him to reveal the hiding place of the vast treasure of Moctezuma. The statue, created by Miguel Moreña, shows the proud ruler garbed in a plumed robe and standing imperiously with his spear, surrounded by warriors. Pedestal engravings depict Cuauhtémoc's torture and the burning of his feet. The circle at Insurgentes and Reforma is a major crossroads for city traffic.

## South of Downtown

**POLYFORUM SIQUEIROS** is at Av. Insurgentes Sur #701 (at the corner of Av. Filadelfia), on the grounds of the World Trade Center Mexico building complex. Housed in a twelve-sided, polyhedron-shaped exposition hall for the arts, it is the work of and a monument to muralist David Alfaro Siqueiros (1896-1974). The vivid Siqueiros murals covering the building's exterior walls make for a good photo opportunity. Inside on the upper level a revolving floor permits an unimpeded view of the artist's 26,150-square-foot ceiling mural "March of Humanity." A sound-and-light show is projected on the mural Saturdays and Sundays at noon and 2 p.m.

**Note:** The building is in the southern part of the city, a considerable distance away from the main tourist areas in the vicinity of Chapultepec Park; if you're a Siqueiros fan and want to see the art, take a taxi associated with your hotel and have the driver wait while you view the mural. **Hours:** Daily 10-6. The museum closes occasionally for special events; phone ahead to confirm schedule. **Cost:** 15 pesos (about $1.10 U.S.); sound-and-light show admission 30 pesos. **Phone:** (55) 5536-4520.

## The Southern Suburbs

Churubusco, Coyoacán, Iztapalapa, San Angel, Tlalpan and Xochimilco, all within the Mexico City limits, were once individual *pueblos* (towns) that for the most part have maintained their own identities despite now being part of the Federal District, the 571-square-mile seat of national government.

North-south Avenida Insurgentes Sur is a direct line to the tourist hotspots of San Angel and Coyoacán. Restaurants, museums and weekend arts and crafts shopping make them a popular destination for visitors. Take a taxi; for an hourly fee you can hire a driver who will not only navigate the urban sprawl but wait while you shop or sightsee. For more information about these destinations, see their individual listings.

# What To Do

## Dining

The most buzzed-about restaurants in this sprawling city—elegant or otherwise—specialize in authentic Mexican cookery. This is not the cheese-slathered, chile-spiked food that many people think of as generically "Mexican," nor is it necessarily the regional specialties that have ended up on menus across the country as well as north of the border.

For one thing, ingredients are often exotic, like *nopales,* fleshy pads of cactus, or *cajeta,* a sweet caramel flavoring made from goat's milk. Menu items can be unusual, too: squash flowers, *chapulines* (grasshoppers), *gusanos de maguey* (worms) fried and served with guacamole. And street food comes in every imaginable form, including some choices that will challenge the most adventurous palate (tacos featuring organ meats like eyeballs or pig snouts).

Of course diners still crave classic fare, and El Bajío is one of the best places in the capital to sample the glories of traditional Mexican cooking, whether it's plantain turnovers stuffed with earthy black beans, *gorditas* (thick, fat little corn tortillas) filled with white cheese or a jet-black, chocolate-infused mole sauce ladled over chicken enchiladas. And dessert is not something to be turned away—*capirotada* is a scrumptious concoction of fried bread drizzled with honey, studded with peanuts and plump raisins and layered with cheese. This popular chain has several locations.

If you're looking for a traditional fine-dining experience—with prices to match—the dependable choices are in the big, expensive hotels along Paseo de la Reforma or in the Polanco neighborhood north of Chapultepec Park. At such establishments reservations are advised, and a jacket and tie are usually required for men.

The Mexican chains Vips and Sanborn's have locations throughout the city and are good for a casual meal. Another casual alternative is the taco stands found on almost every street corner. *Tacos al pastor,* shreds of roast pork, grilled onions and cilantro heaped on a small tortilla, cost around 10 pesos apiece and are a popular late-night snack.

The El Globo bakery chain, with locations throughout the Federal District, offers good-quality breads and pastries at low prices. For the homesick, there are plenty of American fast-food outlets, including Burger King, McDonald's, Pizza Hut and Subway.

Reservations are needed for the trendy and popular spots in downtown's Polanco, Zona Rosa, Condesa and Roma neighborhoods. Another cluster of good restaurants and cozy sidewalk cafes are in the southern suburbs of San Angel and Coyoacán. Casual, family-style places are the rule in the vicinity of the *Zócalo.* Many restaurants close on Sunday.

Approach cocktails and liquors with caution if you are unaccustomed to the altitude. Also be aware that imported wines and spirits are heavily taxed; Mexican beers and wines are much less expensive. Although the better restaurants customarily use purified water, avoid green salads, unpeeled raw vegetables and unpeeled fruit if you have a sensitive stomach. To be completely safe order drinks without ice cubes, or drink bottled water.

Restaurants often cater to the local custom of eating the main meal of the day in the early afternoon, then a lighter supper around 9 p.m. or later. Most begin to serve breakfast around 7:30 a.m., *comida* (lunch) about 1 p.m. and dinner after 7:30 p.m. From 2 to 4, restaurants can be crowded with a lingering lunch crowd; if you eat dinner before 9, on the other hand, you might have the place to yourself.

Don't expect every server to have a fluent command of English. A knowledge of basic Spanish or a handy phrase book not only helps in communication but also in deciphering menus. See the Lodgings & Restaurants section for AAA-RATED dining establishments.

## Shopping

Shops and boutiques abound in the Zona Rosa, off Paseo de la Reforma and encompassing calles Amberes, Génova, Hamburgo, Niza and Londres (M: Sevilla or Insurgentes, line 1). Outdoor cafes provide a relaxing break. A more exclusive shopping area is the Polanco neighborhood (M: Polanco, line 7). Armani, Cartier, Perry Ellis, Hermes and other chic fashion boutiques line a section of Avenida Presidente Masaryk that is Mexico City's version of L.A.'s Rodeo Drive.

Condesa (M: Juanacatlan, line 1), which spreads east from the eastern end of Chapultepec Park, is another neighborhood that is both pedestrian and shopper friendly. The trendiest shops are concentrated near the intersection of avenidas Michoacán and Atlixco and along Avenida Tamaulipas. Avenida Michoacán also has retail outlets selling clothes, CDs and other merchandise.

Downtown, hundreds of shops and vendor stalls line avenidas Juárez and Francisco I. Madero in the vicinity of the *Zócalo.* From the *Zócalo* west to Avenida Lázaro Cárdenas, every other side street is closed to traffic and paved with brick tiles. The

government-run FONART stores offer a variety of arts and crafts—rugs, glassware, folk art, pottery—from all parts of the country at reasonable prices. A centrally located outlet, also known as Exposición Nacional de Arte Popular, is at Av. Juárez #89, just west of Alameda Park (M: Hidalgo, line 2); phone (55) 5521-0171.

The major department stores are Liverpool and Palacio de Hierro; each has several branches. The Mexican restaurant chain Sanborn's has numerous locations throughout Mexico City, including the original outpost in the House of Tiles *(see attraction listing)* and several along Paseo de la Reforma and in the Zona Rosa. Almost all branches have an attached store that is a convenient place to pick up toiletries and English-language publications, as well as quality craft items and ceramics. Many also have a pharmacy and an ATM.

One of the largest suburban shopping malls is Centro Santa Fe, in the western part of the city. Although inconvenient for tourists because there is no Metro station nearby, it does have nearly 300 stores, as well as movie theaters, restaurants and play areas for kids. To get there, take the Anillo Periférico expressway (Avenida Avila Camacho) south to the exit marked *Centro Santa Fe*. Another big, pricey mall is Perisur, located on the southern outskirts close to where the Periférico expressway crosses Avenida Insurgentes Sur (just south of the National University of Mexico).

Practice the time-honored art of bargaining at the San Juan Market (Mercado de Curiosidades San Juan). The main section is in a modern three-story building at Ayuntamiento and Dolores, 4 blocks south of Alameda Park (M: Salto del Agua, line 1). It offers an assortment of baskets, leather goods, jewelry, linens, shawls and other wares, and is open Mon.-Sat. 9-7, Sun. 9-4.

The city's biggest food market is La Merced, several blocks east of the *Zócalo* along Circunvalación (M: Merced, line 1). The huge buildings are crammed with a multitude of vendors selling produce, housewares and other everyday items. The selection of fruits, vegetables and spices in particular is staggering. While you're not likely to find many souvenirs, the sheer scope of the commerce makes it a fascinating place to wander through.

The Mercado Insurgentes, also called the Mercado Zona Rosa, fills an entire block along Calle Londres between Florencia and Amberes in the Zona Rosa (M: Insurgentes, line 1). A typical neighborhood crafts market, it has a maze of stalls selling everything from baskets to ponchos. Bargaining is expected, and good buys are possible. It's open Mon.-Sat. 9:30-7:30, Sun. 10-4.

The Lagunilla Market is east of the intersection of Lázaro Cárdenas and Paseo de la Reforma, between República de Chile and Calle Allende (M: Allende, line 2). A triple-roofed building of enormous proportions, Lagunilla is especially busy on Sunday, when vendors from all over the city set up tables or booths to sell used clothing, silver of varying quality

and other goods. Antiques, coins, blankets and rare books are good buys here. Watch out for pickpockets. Within walking distance, north of Paseo de la Reforma, is the Plaza of the Three Cultures *(see attraction listing)*.

Silver fanciers should head for Tane, in the Hotel Presidente InterContinental at #218 Campo Elíseos (in the Polanco district) and several other locations. Jewelry, candelabras and museum-quality reproductions are all expensive but exquisitely crafted. Also in the hotel you'll find a gallery selling the striking work of contemporary Mexican artist and sculptor Sergio Bustamante.

Handcrafted items from all over the country are sold at the Mercado de la Ciudadela, about 6 blocks southwest of Alameda Park on Plaza de la Ciudadela at Avenida Balderas (M: Balderas, line 1). Covered booths display everything from leather moccasins to custom guitars. Some of the coolest items at La Ciudadela are the colorful, hand-carved wooden masks. Expect to bargain here.

Scores of Mexican artists exhibit and sell paintings and sculpture in the city's many art galleries. Of special interest is the Saturday Bazaar (Bazar Sábado), at Plaza San Jacinto #11 (M: Miguel A. de Quevedo, line 3) in San Angel. Set up in a beautifully renovated 18th-century mansion—but usually spilling out of it as well—the bazaar is held only on Saturdays from 10-7.

The emphasis here is on art and features works by a tightly knit group of contemporary artisans, some of them U.S. expats. Paintings, sculpture, ceramics, textiles, garments, rugs and high-quality jewelry are sold; prices are high, but so is quality. Search out the *animalitos*, bizarrely carved and painted wooden creatures for which Oaxaca is famous, and "Tree of Life" candelabras exploding with flowers, animals and other figures.

Gilded statues of the Virgin Mary, Our Lady of Guadalupe and other Mexican patron saints are exquisite examples of handiwork and command high prices. More affordable merchandise—and a greater chance to bargain—can be found outside the bazaar, where merchants offer wooden toys, decorative gourds and beaded bracelets. Local artists exhibit their work, and the lively scene frequently includes dancers and other entertainment.

## Sightseeing

Mexico City's enormous size makes it difficult to plan a sightseeing itinerary. Although many museums and other points of interest are concentrated in certain areas—the Historic Center, Chapultepec Park, the southern suburbs of San Angel and Coyoacán—getting to them can take time and effort.

The best day to sightsee is Sunday, when many attractions are free. Another good reason to plan your sightseeing for Sunday is that the traffic lanes of Paseo de la Reforma, the city's famed boulevard, are closed to motor vehicles for 6 hours (from 8 a.m. to 2 p.m.). The pedestrian-only stretch extends from Chapultepec Park to the Zócalo, a distance of about 3 miles.

You'll see every type of non-motorized wheeled conveyance imaginable. Vendors sell "jicamasicles"; the native Mexican vine's edible, tuberous root is cut into thick slices that are squirted with fresh lime juice and sprinkled with cayenne pepper for a snack that is simultaneously cool, spicy and refreshing. Numerous kiosks provide free bike rentals (with your driver's license left as a deposit). This is the ideal way to view the boulevard's gleaming skyscrapers and historic monuments without the distraction of ceaseless traffic congestion and honking horns.

If the prospect of hitting the streets on your own still seems too stressful, consider taking a guided tour. Check with the staff at your hotel; the hotel may either have its own travel agency or be able to recommend a reliable one. An alternative is to visit one of the city's tourist information modules (Módulo de Información y Orientación Turística) operated by the Tourism Secretariat of Mexico City. A number of these modules are located in the Historic Center, in the vicinity of Alameda and Chapultepec parks, in the Pink Zone (Zona Rosa) and along Paseo de Reforma.

Guided tours of the Historic Center (via Tren Turístico) and Coyoacán (via Paseo por Coyoacán) depart daily aboard trolley buses built to resemble the trams that crisscrossed Mexico City streets in the early 20th century. The narrated tours are in Spanish; the fare is 140 pesos (about $11 U.S.). For schedules and other information, check at any tourist information module.

Turibuses travel a route that takes in the Historic Center, Paseo de la Reforma, Chapultepec Park and the Condesa and Roma neighborhoods—an area filled with museums, monuments, art galleries, parks and restaurants. Each red, double-decker Turibus can hold up to 70 passengers, and the tour includes a simultaneous translation in several languages. One ticket allows you to use the service all day, disembarking and reboarding at 26 stops.

Buses run daily 9-9 and pass each stop approximately every half hour. Tickets Mon.-Fri. cost 140 pesos (about $11.25 U.S.); ages 4-12, 70 pesos. Tickets Sat.-Sun. cost 165 pesos (about $13.30 U.S.); ages 4-12, 85 pesos. Two-day tickets also are available. For more information check with your hotel or at a tourist information module.

Another easy way to see the sights is to have your hotel arrange for a private car and a guide, either by the hour or by the day. Although you'll pay for the convenience, this option allows greater flexibility and more personal service. The larger hotels should be able to arrange such an excursion; check with the concierge. Guests at the Four Seasons Hotel, for example, can take advantage of guided weekend cultural tours.

## Sports and Recreation

In addition to the major sports mentioned below, Mexico City offers basketball games, boxing and wrestling matches and a growing collegiate schedule of American-style football. Refer to the sports pages of the newspapers for current activities and schedules; your hotel can help you get tickets.

The best **bullfighting** in the republic can be found at Plaza México (M: San Antonio, line 7). Accommodating about 50,000 spectators—one of the world's largest bullrings—it is located on Calle Augusto Rodín a few blocks west of Avenida Insurgentes, about 6 kilometers (4 miles) south of the traffic circle at Paseo de la Reforma (the Cuauhtémoc Monument).

The season for top matadors runs from early November through March. During other months novice bullfighters *(novilleros)* take the ring. Bullfights start promptly at 4:30 p.m. on Sunday; buses marked "Plaza México" travel along Insurgentes Sur throughout the afternoon. Plan on arriving early to get a good seat, and hang on to your ticket stub so you can reclaim your seat if you need to leave it.

To avoid long lines at the bullring's ticket windows *(taquillas),* buy tickets in advance through ticketmaster.com.mx, or book a tour that includes a bullfight through your hotel or a travel agency. Ticket prices range from about $8 to $60 (U.S.); they vary according to proximity to the ring and the side on which you sit. Sun *(sol)* is cheap, shade *(sombra)* is expensive. Seats in the sun tend to attract the more unruly fans. **Note:** The bull is traditionally killed during these performances; plan not to attend if you find the spectacle's inherent cruelty upsetting.

**Soccer** *(fútbol)* is played almost every weekend by the big leagues at Azteca Stadium, in the southern part of the city on Calzada de Tlalpan, north of the Periférico Sur. Shuttles are available from the Taxqueña Metro station (line 2). There are winter (August to December) and summer (January to May) seasons. The city's most popular team, América—nicknamed Las Aguilas (the Eagles)—draws huge crowds, especially when they play arch-rival Guadalajara in a match called El Clásico.

The university-sponsored Pumas play soccer at Olympic Stadium (Estadio Olímpica) on the National University of Mexico campus. Reconstructed and enlarged for the 1968 Summer Olympics, it can accommodate some 72,500 people. The oval design somewhat resembles the crater of a volcano. A Diego Rivera mosaic of colored rocks, illustrating human endeavor in sports, covers the stadium's sloping walls. Tickets for all games are normally available right up to game time and range from about $10 to $20 (U.S.).

Professional **baseball** is popular in Mexico City, where teams in the Mexican League play from the beginning of April through mid-September. Games are announced in Spanish, but little is lost in the translation as the rules are the same. Some key terms: *el lanzador* is the pitcher, *la entrada* is the inning, *pegar* means hit, *un sencillo* is a single.

Many games are played at the Parque Foro Sol, a very modern facility on Avenida Río Churubusco in front of the Sports Palace. It is home field for the Diablos Rojos; the season is from March through August. General admission seats are inexpensive, less than $5 (U.S.). Tickets can be purchased through Ticketmaster; phone (55) 5325-9000.

**Horse races** are held at the lovely Hippodrome of the Americas (Hipódromo de las Américas). The track is in the northwestern part of the city between avenidas del Conscripto and Industria Militar, west of the Anillo Periférico. Buses and *peseros* (minivans) marked "Hipódromo" travel west along Paseo de la Reforma to the track. Races are held Friday through Sunday throughout the year beginning at 3 p.m.; first post times may vary.

General section admission is 20 pesos; box seats are more expensive. Tickets are available through Ticketmaster. There are fast-food outlets, the fashionable restaurant La Terraza and a sports book facility on the premises. For further information phone (55) 5201-7800.

**Tennis** and **golf** clubs are typically semi-private. If your heart's set on playing tennis, it's best to stay at a hotel that offers courts. The Bella Vista Golf Club, northwest of the city off Mex. 57-D (the Querétaro Highway), has an 18-hole course. For rates and to make a reservation for a tee time, phone (55) 5366-8050.

## Nightlife

More often than not, nightlife in Mexico City means nightclubs—both independent establishments and the lobby bars in the big hotels. Nightclub tours are an easy way to visit some of the city's hot spots, since transportation and reservations are arranged for you. These tours usually last several hours and include dinner at a nice restaurant and perhaps a floor show or a stop at the city's famed Plaza Garibaldi. For more information check with your hotel desk or a travel agency.

Clubs usually don't kick into high gear until around midnight. Many nightspots are closed on Sunday. The weekly publication *Tiempo Libre* (Free Time), available at newsstands, provides entertainment, performing arts and event listings in Spanish.

**Note:** Always be careful when venturing out after dark anywhere in Mexico City, even in tourist-frequented areas like the Zona Rosa and Polanco.

Metro is not recommended as a way of getting around at night, and never hail a taxi on the street. The safest way to travel is to make drop-off and pickup arrangements with your hotel taxi service. Thieves also frequent the popular nightlife districts, so carry a minimum of cash and guard your personal belongings carefully.

Hotel lobby bars offer an elegant atmosphere, a sophisticated clientele and music for dancing. Good bets include the bars in the Presidente InterContinental Mexico City, Campos Elíseos #218, Colonia Polanco; the Camino Real Mexico, Mariano Escobedo #700 (near the main entrance to Chapultepec Park); the Sheraton María Isabel Hotel and Towers, Paseo de la Reforma #325 (opposite the Independence Monument); and the Galería Plaza, Hamburgo #195 in the Zona Rosa.

Avoid *cantinas,* small, dimly lit places that tend to be filled with hard-drinking patrons. An exception is the La Opera Bar, Av. 5 de Mayo #10 at Filomeno Mata, 3 blocks east of Alameda Park (M: Bellas Artes, lines 2 and 8). By day this is a crowded lunch spot, with jacketed waiters and formal service. In the evening dinner is served, but the gilded ceiling, mirrored walls, dark paneled booths and clubby feel also make La Opera an intimate place for an early evening cocktail. Your waiter is likely to show you the bullet hole Pancho Villa supposedly fired into the ceiling.

El Hijo del Cuervo, Jardín Centenario #17 in Coyoacán, is frequented by hip students and a mix of locals and foreigners. The music is hip as well; there is a cover charge for occasional live shows. Bar Jorongo, in the Sheraton María Isabel Hotel and Towers at Paseo de la Reforma #325, is a popular nightspot where well-known mariachi trios play in upscale surroundings. There is a cover charge. The rooftop bar at the Hotel Majestic, Av. Francisco I. Madero #73 (M: Zócalo, line 2), often has live entertainment in a setting overlooking the Zócalo.

For those seeking an indubitably Mexican nightlife experience, Plaza Garibaldi offers it. Bounded by calles República de Peru and República de Honduras, about 5 blocks north of the Palace of Fine Arts (M: Garibaldi, line 8), this square is ruled by the city's mariachi bands, who serenade paying customers every night of the week. The typical outfit includes violin, trumpet, guitar and a heart-tugging vocalist, and the songs almost always address the travails of love (usually at the hands of an unfaithful woman—a nod to Mexican *machismo*).

Decked out in tight, silver-spangled costumes and wide-brimmed sombreros, the musicians unabashedly solicit business from the throngs of people crowding the plaza (about $5 U.S. for a song). Sunday night is the best time to hear music in the square itself. Mariachis also perform in the surrounding *cantinas* and clubs, which stay open into the wee hours. El Tenampa nightclub, across Calle Amargura from the plaza, puts on first-rate mariachi shows. At other establishments you can sit and listen to the mariachis while nibbling *botanas* (snacks).

**Note:** Plaza Garibaldi is at its most exuberant late at night and is a traditional last stop for an evening on the town, but the surrounding neighborhood has long been a sketchy one, filled with cheap hotels and gaudy burlesque theaters. In recent years an overhaul spruced up both the plaza and the surrounding blocks. Even so, guard closely against pickpockets, and arrange for round-trip taxi transportation with your hotel. Some places will try to gouge money from tourists by raising quoted prices for food and/or drinks, so stick to the larger, well-known establishments.

## Concerts

Your hotel or a travel agency may be able to obtain tickets for popular performances, such as those by the Ballet Folklórico de México, which should be obtained in advance. Tickets for many events also can be purchased through Ticketmaster. Phone (55) 5325-9000; ticketmaster.com.mx. There is a Ticketmaster outlet in the National Auditorium, Paseo de la Reforma #50 in Chapultepec Park (M: Auditorio, line 7).

The Palace of Fine Arts (M: Bellas Artes, lines 2 and 8) is the home of the National Symphony Orchestra. The National Opera Company also stages productions here, usually January through March and August through October. The Mexico City Philharmonic Orchestra (Filarmonica de la Ciudad de México) gives concerts at Silvestre Revueltas Hall (Sala Silvestre Revueltas). It is located at Anillo Periférico Sur #5141, just east of Avenida Insurgentes at the southern end of the city (near San Angel).

International symphony, ballet and opera companies also perform at the National Auditorium. Tickets can be purchased at the auditorium box office Mon.-Sat. 10-7, Sun. 11-6; for information phone (55) 5280-9250.

The acclaimed National University Symphony mounts its concert program at Justo Sierra Auditorium (M: Universidad, line 3, south terminal), on the National University of Mexico campus. The hall is famed for its acoustics. Nezahualcoyotl Hall regularly presents performing artists and groups, including the University of Mexico Philharmonic Orchestra. It is located within the University Cultural Center, which is off Avenida Insurgentes south of the main campus buildings.

Music alfresco is particularly popular and can be heard on the street or at parks throughout the capital. Better yet, many of these performances—which range from mariachi music to heavy metal—are free. Sunday concerts often take place in Alameda Park, usually around noon, and near the Lake House (Casa del Lago) in Chapultepec Park.

The central plazas in the southern suburbs of Coyoacán and San Angel often are the scene of weekend musical offerings. International pop, rock and hip-hop acts take the stage at the National Auditorium; at the Sports Palace (Palacio de Los Deportes), Avenida Río Churubusco and Calle Añil; and at Parque Foro Sol stadium, in front of the Sports Palace.

The state-of-the-art Mexico City Arena, Avenida de las Granjas #800 (northwest of downtown in the Azcapotzalco neighborhood) is a 22,000-seat indoor arena hosting major pop and rock concert tours, ice skating shows, circuses, and occasional boxing matches and NBA exhibition games. For a full lineup of events, check the arena's page on ticketmaster.com.mx.

The Ballet Folklórico de México (see Palace of Fine Arts attraction listing) is one of the city's standout offerings. Although tickets are sold in advance at the Palace of Fine Arts box office (on the ground floor at the main entrance), they may be difficult to obtain unless you purchase them at least a day ahead or book a tour that includes the ballet. **Note:** The troupe occasionally moves to the National Auditorium or the National Museum of Anthropology to accommodate visiting performing arts groups. Contact Ticketmaster for specific schedule information.

## Theater and Cinema

Theaters are not centralized in an entertainment district but are located throughout the city. Plays are almost always presented in Spanish, but other theaters present shows in a cabaret or variety format that can be enjoyed by non-Spanish speakers.

The Insurgentes Theater (Teatro de Los Insurgentes), Av. Insurgentes Sur #1587, presents plays and musicals in a building that boasts a striking Diego Rivera mosaic on its facade. The Blanquita Theater (Teatro Blanquita), 4 blocks north of the Latin-American Tower on Avenida Lázaro Cárdenas (M: Bellas Artes, lines 2 and 8), offers variety shows performed by Mexico's top singers, dancers, comedians and magicians.

Other theaters include the Hidalgo, Av. Hidalgo #23 (M: Hidalgo, line 2); and the Virginia Fábregas Theater, Calle Velasquez de León #29, a few blocks from the Zona Rosa (M: Allende, line 2).

American and foreign films are shown in their original language with Spanish subtitles, though some children's movies are dubbed in Spanish; ask when you buy your tickets. Hollywood blockbusters and first-run films open in Mexico soon after they do in the United States, and admission is inexpensive (about $6 U.S.). The Spanish-language Tiempo Libre magazine, available at newsstands, has entertainment listings.

Cineteca Nacional, Av. México-Coyoacán #389, the southern extension of Avenida Cuauhtémoc (M: Coyoacán, line 3), is a multiplex with a wide range of movie choices and offers half-price admission on Wednesday; phone (55) 5688-3212. Closer to the city center is Cinépolis Diana, Paseo de la Reforma #423, Colonia Cuauhtémoc; phone (55) 2122-6060. Cinemex Casa de Arte, Av. Anatole France #120 at Avenida Presidente Masaryk in the Polanco neighborhood, is a complex of four theaters that show both Hollywood blockbusters and art house films from around the world; for recorded movie schedule information phone (55) 5257-6969.

## Special Events

Flower-garlanded cows, beribboned dogs and cats and irreverent roosters are paraded on Jan. 17 for the Feast of San Antonio Abad, or the "blessing of the animals." This whimsical ceremony takes place at the Metropolitan Cathedral on the Zócalo. Holy Week *(Semana Santa)* celebrations take place in mid-April.

On May 1, Labor Day *(Día del Trabajo)*, the president reviews a huge parade of workers from the central balcony of the National Palace. For the Feast of Corpus Christi, families dress children in native costumes or their Sunday best and gather at the Metropolitan Cathedral for a priest's blessing. The date is variable, occurring between late May and mid-June.

The fall of Tenochtitlan to Hernando Cortés and his followers is commemorated on Cuauhtémoc Day, Aug. 21, with wreath-laying ceremonies at the Plaza of the Three Cultures and the Cuauhtémoc Statue at the intersection of Paseo de la Reforma and Avenida Insurgentes.

Father Miguel Hidalgo's *"El Grito de Dolores,"* the rallying cry of Mexican independence, is repeated by the president of Mexico and echoed by hundreds of thousands on the evening of Sept. 15 in Plaza Constitución (the *Zócalo*). One of the year's biggest events, it is nationally televised. A morning military parade on Independence Day, Sept. 16, proceeds from the *Zócalo* to the Independence Monument, past buildings draped with streamers in the national colors of red, green and white.

Columbus Day *(Día de la Raza)* on Oct. 12 commemorates Christopher Columbus' discovery of the Americas. Families build altars in their homes and decorate the graves of loved ones with extravagant flower garlands to celebrate the Day of the Dead Nov. 1. Revolution Day, Nov. 20, features a spirited parade down avenidas Madero, Juárez and Reforma in commemoration of the start of the Revolution of 1910.

The venerated Virgin of Guadalupe, patron saint of the country, is the focal point of a nationwide celebration of dancing, fireworks and religious processions on Dec. 12, the Feast Day of the Virgin of Guadalupe. Devout believers from throughout the country and abroad make the journey to the Basilica of Guadalupe, in the northern suburb of Villa de Guadalupe. Mexico City is decorated in high style for Christmas and the 9 days leading up to it, during which there are traditional re-enactments of the Holy Family's search for an inn *(posada)*.

© Noradoa / Shutterstock.com

This ends listings for Mexico City.
The following page resumes the alphabetical listings
of cities in Mexico City and Vicinity.

## SAN ANGEL, DISTRITO FEDERAL (B-3)

San Angel (sahn AHN-hehl) was once a small town far removed from colonial Mexico City. Like other southern suburbs, however, it has been overtaken by the capital's inexorable growth. Even so, a leisurely stroll past San Angel's elegant colonial mansions and bougainvillea-draped walls is a trip back through history and a welcome respite from downtown Mexico City's noise and congestion.

In the beautifully leafy Bombilla Park (Parque de la Bombilla), at the junction of avenidas La Paz and Insurgentes Sur, stands a granite monument honoring Gen. Alvaro Obregón. Obregón helped draft the Constitution of 1917 and was the first president of post-revolutionary Mexico. He was assassinated in San Angel by a religious fanatic in 1928.

A few blocks southwest of the park off Avenida La Paz is Plaza San Jacinto, a pleasant square bordered by cobblestone streets, tucked-away restaurants and outdoor cafes. A plaque in the square honors members of St. Patrick's Battalion, a group of Irish immigrants who deserted the U.S. Army and sided with Mexico during the Mexican-American War. Today the plaza is known for its Saturday Bazaar, or Bazar del Sábado (described under the Mexico City Shopping section).

**CARRILLO GIL ART MUSEUM** (Museo de Arte Carrillo Gil) is about 3 blks. n. of Plaza San Jacinto at Av. Revolución #1608 (Metro: Miguel A. de Quevedo, line 3). It displays the collection amassed by Dr. Carrillo Gil, focusing on paintings and graphics by noted 20th-century Mexican artists but including European works as well. José Clemente Orozco, Diego Rivera, David Alfaro Siqueiros and Pablo Picasso are among those represented. **Hours:** Tues.-Sun. 10-6. **Cost:** 21 pesos (about $1.55 U.S.); free to all Sun. **Phone:** (55) 5550-6260.

**CASA DEL RISCO** is at Plaza San Jacinto #15 (Metro: Miguel A. de Quevedo, line 3). The building contains an extensive library and one of Mexico City's finest collections of European paintings from the 14th through the 17th centuries. Don't miss the colorful, wildly abstract fountain in the patio that appears to be made primarily of broken crockery. **Hours:** Tues.-Sun. 10-5. **Cost:** Free. **Phone:** (55) 5616-2711.

**DIEGO RIVERA STUDIO MUSEUM** (Museo Casa Estudio Diego Rivera) is on Calle Diego Rivera, across the street from the San Angel Inn (Metro: Miguel A. de Quevedo, line 3). Designed by architect Juan O'Gorman in 1931, it was Rivera's last home, where he died in 1957. Surrounded by different kinds of cacti, it has interior and exterior staircases leading up to the artist's large studio, which contrasts sharply with the small bedrooms. A roof bridge links the house to one occupied by fellow artist and partner Frida Kahlo. Temporary exhibitions are mounted.

**Hours:** Tues.-Sun. 10-6. **Cost:** 14 pesos (about $1.05 U.S.); free to all Sun. Camera fee 30 pesos. **Phone:** (55) 5550-1518.

**EL CARMEN MUSEUM** (Museo del Carmen) is just s. of Av. La Paz at Av. Revolución #4 and Monasterio (Metro: Miguel A. de Quevedo, line 3). It occupies a former Carmelite convent dating from 1615. The building is distinguished by carved doors, baroque altarpieces, a fine collection of religious paintings and three domes, each tiled in a different color. The cloister's garden has a tropical look, unusual for Mexico City. **Hours:** Tues.-Sun. 10-5. **Cost:** 52 pesos (about $3.85 U.S.); free (ages 0-12 and 65+). Free to all Sun. **Phone:** (55) 5616-7477.

**NATIONAL UNIVERSITY OF MEXICO** (Universidad Nacional Autonoma de México, or UNAM) spreads out s. of Av. Universidad and e. of Av. Insurgentes Sur (M: Copilco or Universidad, line 3). Covering some 800 acres, the complex is commonly referred to as University City (Ciudad Universitaria).

The chief attractions for visitors are the mosaic murals decorating the exterior of the main campus buildings, most of which are concentrated just east of Insurgentes Sur. One of the most visually arresting is the Main Library (Biblioteca). This rectangular tower is covered with stone mosaic work, augmented in places by colored tiles.

Near the library is the Administration Building (Rectoría), dominated by a huge David Alfaro Siqueiros mural that incorporates pieces of colored glass. A mosaic that includes a three-headed mask symbolizing Indian, Spanish and *mestizo*—the three peoples of Mexico—adorns one wall of the School of Medicine.

The easiest way to get to the university is to take a taxi or line 3 of the Metro, getting off at one of the last two stops. City buses marked "Ciudad Universitaria" travel regularly down Avenida Insurgentes Sur and stop in front of the main complex of buildings. Weekends, when students are noticeably absent, are the best time to view the buildings.

## TENANCINGO, MÉXICO (C-2) pop. 90,946

Tenancingo (teh-nahn-SEEN-goh)—its name an Indian term meaning "place of little walls"—was founded in 1425. Overlooking the town from atop a hill is a large Christ statue; this vantage point provides a sweeping view. Wood furniture, *rebozos* (shawl-like woven garments) and fruit liqueurs are among the many items for sale at the town's huge open-air Sunday market.

**MALINALCO** is about 25 km (16 mi.) e. of Tenancingo via a graded road to the village of Malinalco, then approximately 2 km (1.2 mi.) w. on a good dirt road. Buses from Toluca travel to Malinalco. Partially restored, the site is hewn into a cliffside.

The Temple of the Eagles and Jaguars, one of the world's few archeological remains carved from solid stone, has a reconstructed thatch and wood roof entrance, in front of which sits a headless stone figure. The doorway resembles an open-mouthed serpent. A beautifully carved wooden drum retrieved from the

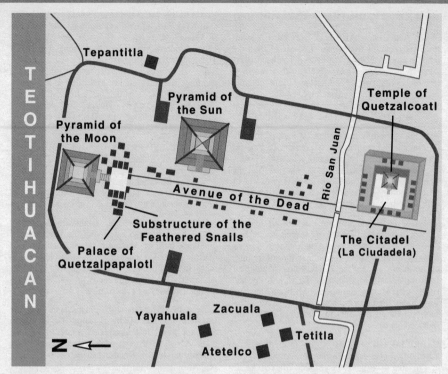

Temple of the Sun (Building IV) resides in the Museum of Anthropology at the Mexiquense Cultural Center in Toluca *(see attraction listing under Toluca).*

The staircase that leads to the site is carved into the mountainside. It's an arduous climb of more than 400 steps that takes 30 minutes, but the view of the surrounding valley is magnificent. **Hours:** Tues.-Sun. 10-5. **Cost:** 52 pesos (about $3.85 U.S.).

**SANTO DESIERTO DEL CARMEN MONASTERY NATIONAL PARK** is about 12 km (7 mi.) southeast of Tenancingo on a graded road, a short distance from Malinalco. The park's main feature is a late 18th-century Carmelite monastery that stands in a lovely wooded setting.

## ◆GEM TEOTIHUACÁN, MÉXICO
(B-4) pop. 53,010

San Juan Teotihuacán (teh-oh-tee-wah-KAHN) is one of the most widely known and easily accessible of Mexico's major archeological zones. Very little is known about this religious center, the people who built it, or even what the city was originally called. It was designated a World Heritage Site by UNESCO in 1987.

Teotihuacán is thought to have been founded as early as 700 B.C., although it was not until around 100 B.C. that construction of its two great pyramids began. Archeologists estimate that at its height around A.D. 500, up to 200,000 people lived there, making it bigger than Rome at the time and one of the largest cities in the world. The city was burned and abandoned for unknown reasons around A.D. 750; it is believed the decline was gradual and perhaps facilitated by overpopulation and a resulting depletion of natural resources.

The area was later inhabited by the Toltecs; by the time the Aztecs discovered the site, it was in such an advanced state of ruin that they named it Teotihuacán, which means "place of the gods," or more broadly, "where men become gods." The gray stone structures seen today are to a large degree reconstructed, and the barren landscape barely hints at what the city must have looked like during its heyday some 1,500 years ago.

## Exploring the Site

Teotihuacán was once paved with volcanic stone and mica slabs, and buildings were plastered with lime and mortar and then decorated with bas-relief sculptures and murals, often painted red; traces of the color are still discernible. The typical structural arrangement was often a courtyard surrounded by several levels of temples and rooms.

The ruins are aligned along a north-south axis traversed by the Avenue of the Dead (Avenida de Los Muertos). The name was given by the Aztecs, who believed that the low structures lining both sides of the avenue were burial sites. All similar in size and style, they accentuate the grandness of the pyramids. Touches of paint can still be detected on some of the building fragments. This wide thoroughfare (paved for today's visitors) is more than a mile long; it seems even longer when you're trekking from one building to another.

The Pyramid of the Sun, on the east side of the Avenue of the Dead, dominates the ruins and is the oldest of Teotihuacán's structures. It is the world's third-largest pyramid; only those at Cholula and Cheops, Egypt, are bigger. The structure rises in five sloping levels to a height of more than 250 feet; each side of its base measures about 735 feet.

Built of adobe brick faced with volcanic stone, the pyramid is visible for some distance from the highway approaching the site. When first discovered it was a gigantic mound covered with vegetation, but even the subsequent reconstruction fails to detract from the achievement of those who originally built this enormous monument without benefit of the wheel or metal tools.

A stairway on the west flank begins at the pyramid's base and leads to the summit, where a temple probably once stood. The 248 steps make for an arduous climb, but the five levels each provide a chance to stop, take a breather and take in the view. In clear weather, the panorama from the top is simply breathtaking. Because of the gentle slope, descending is significantly easier than clambering down the steeper sides of some of Mexico's other pyramids. If you still feel vulnerable, hold onto the link chain that runs the length of the stairway.

The Plaza of the Moon is surrounded by staired platforms and has a square altar in the middle. The Pyramid of the Moon, at the north end of the Avenue of the Dead, is 140 feet high; stairs scale its south face. It appears as tall as the Pyramid of the Sun because it was built on higher ground. The pyramid is connected to a temple with sloping walls. The climb to the summit of this pyramid is shorter (although no less taxing). It's worth the effort, though, for the panoramic vista of the Avenue of the Dead. **Note:** The apex is rocky and uneven; watch your footing.

At the southwest corner of the Plaza of the Moon is the restored Palace of Quetzalpapalotl, Teotihuacán's most elaborate building. Presumed to have been the home of a prominent citizen or supreme priest, it has some well-preserved murals. In the inner courtyard are pillars decorated with bas-reliefs depicting the *quetzal-papalotl,* a feathered butterfly, and various symbols related to water.

Beneath this palace is the Palace of the Jaguars, so called because of the jaguar images in the rooms ringing the courtyard, and the Substructure of the Feathered Snails, part of a beautifully decorated temple beneath the Quetzalpapalotl Palace that features carvings of large snails garlanded with feathers.

In 1998 excavations uncovered a tomb and offerings inside the Pyramid of the Moon that archeologists hope will provide additional clues to help solve the riddle of the site's origination. Objects at what

has initially been described as a burial site—most likely someone of high social standing—include obsidian and jade sculptures and skeleton fragments.

At the southern end of the zone is The Citadel (La Ciudadela). Teotihuacán was ruled from this vast sunken square, which encompassed nearly 17 acres and was surrounded by a low wall. The inner esplanade once held thousands of standing people.

Within the courtyard are several temples; the most elaborate is the restored Temple of Quetzalcóatl (the Feathered Serpent). The god Quetzalcóatl was worshipped by the Mayan, Toltec and Aztec civilizations, although it is unknown whether the inhabitants of Teotihuacán paid tribute to the same being. Carved stone slabs face part of the structure; writhing serpents, their heads sticking out from ruffles of feathers, adorn some of the walls.

Other structures are located off the Avenue of the Dead. Tepantitla, east of the Pyramid of the Moon, may have been the residence of a high priest. Several walls have traces of paintings showing Tláloc, the rain god, amid swimming male figures and water imagery.

Tetitla, west of the loop road that surrounds the archeological zone, has a labyrinthine maze of rooms with patchy murals depicting jaguars, snakes, quetzals and aquatic life. Also west of the loop road is Atetelco, another large-sized group of structures with murals that portray priests. Nearby are Zacuala and Yayahuala, fortresslike one-story structures with many rooms, halls and passageways.

The museum (Museo Teotihuacán) near the Pyramid of the Sun has archeological, historical and diagrammatic exhibits, some of them interactive, that pertain to the peoples who once inhabited the area. Scale models of the zone (which you walk above and view through a glass floor) will help orient the first-time visitor.

## General Information and Activities

The archeological site is about 49 kilometers (30 miles) northeast of downtown Mexico City. Buses for Teotihuacán depart regularly from the Terminal Central de Autobuses del Norte in Mexico City, on Avenida de los 100 Metros; Metro has a subway station at the terminal (Autobuses del Norte, line 5). The trip takes about an hour. Ascertain from the bus driver when the last bus returns to Mexico City and where it picks up passengers. Numerous Mexico City travel agencies offer Teotihuacán sightseeing tours.

To get there by car, take Avenida Insurgentes Norte/Mex. 85-D out of the city and get off at the exit for Mex. 132-D. From the toll plaza, the site entrance is about 22 kilometers (14 miles) east (about a 30-minute drive); signs along the way are marked "Pirámides."

Wear sturdy, nonslip walking shoes if you plan to climb the pyramids, because the rocks can be slippery. On warm, sunny days wear lightweight clothing, sunscreen and a hat. During the summer months

(June through September) afternoon showers are frequent. Fall and winter days can be cloudy, chilly and breezy. The altitude is more than 7,000 feet, so walk and climb at a relaxed pace.

**Note:** Numerous souvenir vendors roam the site, and you will be approached on many occasions to purchase items ranging from jewelry to carved figurines to lace shawls. The vendors are persistent but usually not aggressive. If you have no intention of buying anything, keep walking; a negative shake of the head and a polite *"gracias"* will convey a "thanks, but no thanks" response. If you stop, chances are you'll never get away. But if you want to buy something, by all means bargain; a vendor will initially offer three to four times what he or she is willing to settle for.

Avoid going on weekends, which can be very crowded. Try to visit during the week and early in the day before the tour buses begin arriving.

Snacks are available at the entrance and there are a few restaurants just outside the site, but most hotels will pack a box lunch to take along on a bus tour. Bring bottled water, particularly if it's a hot day. There are very basic restrooms at the entrance. The site and museum are open daily 8-5. Admission (includes museum) 64 pesos (about $4.75 U.S.). There is an additional fee of 45 pesos for the use of a video camera. Parking fee 45 pesos. Phone (594) 956-0276.

## TEPOTZOTLÁN, MÉXICO (B-2)
pop. 88,559

Tepotzotlán (teh-poht-soh-TLAHN), about 35 kilometers (22 miles) north of Mexico City, is an easy day trip destination from the capital. From the downtown area, take Avenida Avila Camacho (Mex. 57-D) northwest out of the city and watch for the Tepotzotlán turn-off; the center of town is about a mile west. Buses depart regularly for Tepotzotlán from the Cuatro Caminos Metro station (the western terminus of line 2); ask for the bus going to Tepotzotlán. To return, take a bus going to the Cuatro Caminos station.

This is the perfect antidote for visitors tired of Mexico City's grinding congestion and noise: clear air, wonderful mountain views and a laid-back atmosphere. After visiting the Church of San Francisco Xavier, have a relaxed lunch at one of the eateries surrounding the downtown plaza.

**CHURCH OF SAN FRANCISCO XAVIER** is between avs. Benito Juárez and Insurgentes, facing the main plaza. It was founded by the Jesuits in the late 16th century, serving as a seminary for the religious training of the children of Otomí Indians. The richly detailed stone carvings of angels and saints on the building's facade—a masterful example of Mexican baroque architecture—reflect the Jesuit order's wealth and influence.

A tree-lined atrium leads to the Aljibes Cloister (Claustro de Los Aljibes), which contains paintings by Miguel Cabrera. The interior is filled with gold gilt, carvings of cherubs and saints, and five extravagant altarpieces. A highlight is the Camarín de la Virgen, or altar room, behind the Chapel of the Virgin of Loreto (Capilla de la Virgen de Loreto). This small, octagonal-shaped chamber is a jewel box of intricate interior design.

Outside the Orange Cloister (Claustro de Los Naranjos), planted with orange trees, are carefully tended gardens. **Hours:** Church and National Museum of the Viceroyalty open Tues.-Sun. 9:15-5:45. **Cost:** Museum 62 pesos (about $4.60 U.S.); free (ages 0-13 and 60+). The fee to use a video camera is 35 pesos (about $2.85 U.S.). **Phone:** (55) 5876-2770 (museum).

**National Museum of the Viceroyalty** (Museo Nacional del Virreinato) is adjacent to the church, within the restored monastery. It houses 3 centuries' worth of colonial and religious art. Rare 16th-century vestments and altar hangings, gold and repoussé silver monstrances from the 17th century and a painting of the Virgin attributed to Bartolomé Esteban Murillo are among its many treasures.

*Pastorelas,* traditional re-enactments of Christ's birth, are performed during the Christmas season. Travel agencies in Mexico City can arrange for reservations, which should be booked well in advance. **Cost:** Admission is charged for the *pastorela* performances.

## TEPOZTLÁN, MORELOS (C-3) pop. 41,629

Tepoztlán (teh-pos-LAHN), a name that means "place of copper," is secluded on the lush green slopes of the Sierra del Ajusco mountains and sheltered by the Sierra de Tepoztlán. The latter's scarred cliffs make up Tepozteco National Park, which surrounds the village of Tlalnepantla, northeast of Tepoztlán. This sequestered location was perfect for Emiliano Zapata, regarded locally as a folk hero, who made the village his revolutionary stronghold in 1910.

Despite proximity to urban Cuernavaca and Mexico City, some traditional customs of Tepoztlán's pre-Hispanic predecessors hang on. This is, after all, the reputed birthplace of the Aztec god Quetzalcóatl *(see sidebar p. 336).* Older residents still speak Náhuatl, the ancient Aztec tongue, and mingle Christian and pagan religious practices.

Religious celebrations, in fact, are a way of life here, observed through somber processions to the town cathedral as well as raucous fiestas punctuated by the music of brass bands and the explosive sound of bottle rockets. During Mardi Gras, held on the 5 days preceding Ash Wednesday, people perform Aztec dances and dress as Spanish *conquistadores.* On Sept. 8 a celebration honors both the Nativity of the Virgin and the god Tepoztécatl, the town's patron saint, a Mexican version of Bacchus credited with the creation of pulque, a fermented alcoholic drink extracted from the maguey plant.

The panoramic setting—a lush green valley hemmed in by volcanic peaks—lures artists and other creative types, along with devotees of meditation and yoga and followers of New Age philosophies. The altitude and mild year-round weather nurture both tropical and temperate vegetation; everywhere there are exuberant growths of palms, bananas, orchids and bougainvillea, as well as pine and cedar trees and rose bushes. The sandstone cliffs visible from just about any location in town emerge sharply from early morning fog and cast a mellow glow at sunset.

Tepoztlán also is well known for various health treatments, particularly its Aztec sweat lodges, or *temazcales*. These small, round stone structures, which resemble igloos, are scattered around town. An hour's immersion in sauna-like heat includes short breaks when participants rub fresh aloe, eucalyptus and rosemary leaves on their skin. *Temazcal* aficionados swear by this cleansing ritual.

The Saturday and Sunday market, which sets up in and around the main square, is one of the best in the region. It overflows with locally made clothing and handicrafts—pottery, hand-carved wood figures, woolen sweaters, carvings etched on tree bark, incense, '60s-style hippie jewelry—as well as mounds of produce and an amazing variety of food stands. Natural healers and shamans (Tepoztlán and the surrounding towns have a reputation for their *brujos*, or witches) also congregate at the market, selling herbs and potions. It can get very crowded, as many Mexico City families head here on weekends.

The mystical vibe even extends to ice cream. Tepoznieves, on Avenida 5 de Mayo near the main square, offers myriad flavors of ice cream and sorbet, including such unusual choices as tequila and chili. Many are made from exotic native fruits like the green, grapefruit-sized guanabana. No artificial colorings or preservatives are used, lending the different varieties a rainbow of pale, pastel hues. Ice cream made here is packed in freezers and shipped to Tepoznieves outlets all over Mexico. It's worth dropping in just to see this ice cream parlor's wildly colorful tables and counters, tile floors and yellow walls covered with fanciful artwork.

## Practicalities

Tepoztlán is about 80 kilometers (50 miles) south of downtown Mexico City via toll highway Mex. 95-D to the exit for Mex. 115-D. The turn-off to Tepoztlán is clearly marked. First-class Pullman de Morelos buses depart daily for Cuernavaca/Tepoztlán from Mexico City's Taxqueña bus station, in the southern part of the city; the fare to Tepoztlán is 84 pesos (about $6.20 U.S.). Buses to Cuernavaca also leave from Mexico City's airport. For Pullman de Morelos information and reservations, phone (55) 5549-3505 or 01 (800) 624-0360 (toll-free long distance within Mexico). Bus reservations also can be made through Ticket Bus; phone (55) 5133-5133 or 01 (800) 009-9090 (toll-free long distance within Mexico).

From Cuernavaca, taxi fare for the 40-minute drive to Tepoztlán averages $12-$15 U.S. (including the toll). The Tepoztlán bus terminal is on Avenida Tepozteco near the entrance into town; a free shuttle runs regularly from the terminal to the main plaza daily until 5 p.m.

**EX-CONVENT OF TEPOZTLÁN** (Museo de la Natividad) is just e. of the main plaza, off Av. Revolución 1910 next to the church. Built by Dominican friars, it was completed in 1588. Some walls of this massive structure are more than 6 feet thick. It has a crumbling beauty—much of the plaster has peeled away over time—and walls covered with beautiful murals. Upstairs is the small Historical Museum of Tepoztlán, with five rooms of interesting exhibits that depict the region's religious, ethnological and natural history. Information is in Spanish.

The church adjoining the monastery has twin spires, a barrel-vaulted interior and a walled atrium filled with aromatic eucalyptus trees. Religious paintings done by local artists also are on display. The mural at the entry gate is a portrait of the convent's history created entirely from dried beans, corn kernels and other grains. **Hours:** Complex open Tues.-Sun. 10-6. Closed Jan. 1 and Dec. 31. **Cost:** Free. **Phone:** (739) 395-0255.

**TEPOZTECO PYRAMID** (Pirámide de Tepozteco) stands at the top of a hill n. of town; the walking trail begins at the n. end of Av. 5 de Mayo/Del Tepozteco. Built around 1200 by the Tlahuica Indians, it honored the god Tepoztécatl.

The pyramid is about a 1.3-mile hike from the parking lot. Approximately 35 feet tall, it rises from a stone platform and can be climbed (the 13 steps are very tall). At the top are the remains of a two-room temple, still showing evidence of carved door jambs and pedestals. Your reward for all of this exertion is the view of the valley below, which is simply magnificent. Peanuts are for sale to feed the coatimundis *(tejones);* these long-snouted, tree-dwelling relatives of the raccoon, native to Mexico and Central America, beg for food from visitors.

**Note:** The walking trail is very steep and very rocky the entire way; wear sturdy shoes and bring a large bottle of water. The trek takes a little over an hour and is recommended only for people who are in reasonable physical shape. The trail ends at a steep staircase that leads up to the pyramid. But trees provide shade along the way and the countryside is beautiful, so plan on several stops to both conserve energy and admire the views.

**Hours:** Daily 9-5:30. **Cost:** 47 pesos (about $3.50 U.S.), paid when you reach the top. **Phone:** (777) 312-3108.

## TEQUESQUITENGO, MORELOS (D-3)

South of Cuernavaca lies the resort area of Tequesquitengo (teh-kehs-kee-TEHN-goh), on Lake Tequesquitengo. The village was moved to its present location in 1820 when rising lake waters forced the abandonment of an earlier site. Between 1957 and 1958 the lake rose nearly 13 feet, inundating lakeside homes and the first floor of a hotel. To restore the water level, a 1.7-mile tunnel was bored through a nearby mountain rim.

The lake, about 3,000 feet above sea level, has calm, spring-fed waters ideal for water skiing; it is the site of championship exhibitions. Swimming, boating and fishing also are possible.

## TLALPAN, DISTRITO FEDERAL (B-3)
pop. 650,567

Tlalpan (TLAHL-pan), south of University City, can be reached by bus from the Taxqueña Metro station (line 2). The name means "place of solid ground"; in this area south of the Valley of Mexico, regional civilizations flourished as early as 1200 B.C. The Olympic Village (Villa Olímpica), built to

house athletes during the 1968 summer games, is now a residential area.

Near Plaza de la Constitución, Tlalpan's main square, is the 1532 church of San Agustín de las Cuevas, which contains paintings by Miguel Cabrera. To the southwest is the extinct 13,097-foot Volcán Ajusco. Buses that leave from Azteca Stadium on Calzada de Tlalpan travel to the volcano, which offers excellent views of the surrounding area if the weather is clear.

**CUICUILCO PYRAMID** is near the intersection of Av. Insurgentes Sur (Mex. 85) and the Anillo Periférico, close to Olympic Village. The city of Cuicuilco was a major urban center, believed to have developed as early as 700 B.C. It eventually had a population estimated to be 20,000, but was abandoned around the end of the fourth century after several eruptions by the volcano Xitle.

Today the site consists of a round platform, discovered in the early 1920s, and a ramp that once led to an altar at the temple's summit. The original structure was some 370 feet in diameter and 59 feet high; it was enlarged several times over the centuries. A small museum at the site has geologic exhibits and displays objects found during the excavations. **Hours:** Daily 9-5. **Cost:** Free. **Phone:** (55) 5606-9758.

**SIX FLAGS MEXICO** is off Paseo del Pedregal (the Picacho-Ajusco Highway), adjacent to Pedregal Park. It consists of five villages—Mexican, French, Polynesian, Swiss and Cowboy—plus two theme areas, Hollywood and Bugs Bunny's Circus. In addition to roller coasters and various thrill rides, attractions include bumper cars, go-karts, laser tag, a Ferris Wheel, a dolphin show and live entertainment. **Hours:** Opens daily at 10 a.m.; closing times vary. Closed on some Mondays and Tuesdays. **Cost:** 499 pesos (about $37 U.S.); children under 47 inches tall 369 pesos (about $27.50). **Phone:** (55) 5339-3600.

## TOLUCA, MÉXICO (B-2) pop. 819,561

Capital of the state of México, Toluca (toh-LOO-cah)—about 65 kilometers (40 miles) west of Mexico City—is a commercial center in the middle of the flat Toluca Valley. One of the highest Mexican cities in elevation, it thus enjoys cool weather despite the tropical latitude. Although it is heavily industrial, low buildings characterize Toluca's skyline, and there are many little plazas and manicured parks.

Toluca was an Indian settlement as early as 1200; the name is derived from the Náhuatl Indian expression *tollocan,* or "those who bow their heads." Spaniards under Hernando Cortés began settling the region in the early 16th century after the conqueror was granted 22 towns in central and southern Mexico by King Carlos V.

Plaza of the Martyrs (Plaza de Los Mártires), the main plaza, is between avenidas Sebastian Lerdo de Tejada and de la Independencia. It was named for a group of revolutionaries who were executed in 1811 for their part in Mexico's struggle to win freedom from Spain, an uprising started by Father Miguel Hidalgo. On the plaza's south side is the cathedral, where traditional dances are presented on various Mexican holidays. Check with the State Tourism Office for more information about these colorful spectacles.

The Museum of Fine Arts (Museo de Bellas Artes) is on Avenida Santos Degollado a block north of the plaza. The collection of paintings and sculptures spans the 16th through the 19th centuries. Phone (722) 215-5329.

A block or so south of the plaza along Avenida Miguel Hidalgo is Los Portales, a pedestrian-only walkway fronting an arcade of shops and restaurants protected by arches and buzzing with sidewalk vendors. It's an interesting place to stroll. Here rows of candy stands offer Toluca's local fruit confections, and liquor stores sell an orange-flavored liqueur called *moscos*.

From Mexico City, the easiest way to reach Toluca by car is to take toll highway Mex. 15-D. This direct route takes about an hour, and the toll fee for automobiles is 72 pesos (about $5.35 U.S.). Buses to Toluca depart regularly from Mexico City's Terminal de Autobuses del Poniente, the western bus terminal; to get there, take Metro to the Observatorio station (at the western end of Line 1). Buses marked "Toluca—Directo" make the trip in the least amount of time.

Nevado de Toluca Park is about 25 kilometers (16 miles) southwest of Toluca on Mex. 134 to the junction with Mex. 10, then south on Mex. 10 about 8 kilometers (5 miles) to the park entrance. The 15,032-foot-tall, extinct volcano for which the park is named is Mexico's fourth highest mountain peak.

Nevado de Toluca was designated a national park in 1936 but lost this status in 2014 due to a combination of deforestation, chemical contamination and mining and farming activities that have decimated large areas. But there are still alpine meadows and forests of pine and fir, and with care and a good guide it's possible to drive to the top of the mountain on a rough, unsurfaced road and then hike down into the crater.

Mexico City-based outfitter Ecotura offers full-day Nevado de Toluca tours that include transportation from your hotel, lunch and a visit to the crater. Participants must be in good physical shape. The tour is offered once per month; phone (55) 5555-9382 (English may not be spoken) to confirm the schedule and make the required reservations. The cost is $245 (U.S.) per person.

Several towns and villages east and south of the city offer a firsthand look at the way Mexico's rural population has engaged in manufacturing and marketing since pre-Hispanic days. Visiting these places during the morning is a good way to acquire locally made items at the various *tianguis* (open-air markets), even without benefit of bargaining expertise. East of Toluca on Mex. 15 to the paved turn-off for the village of San Pedro Cholula, then south, is appropriately named Tianguistenco. The Tuesday market fills roughly half the streets in town with baskets, *sarapes* and other crafts from throughout the Toluca Valley.

**México State Tourism Office (Secretaría de Turismo del Estado de México):** Calle Primero de Mayo #731 at the corner of Calle Robert Bosch, second floor, Industrial Zone. **Phone:** (722) 275-8108 or (722) 275-8109.

**BOTANIC GARDEN** (Cosmovitral Jardín Botánico) is just e. Plaza de los Mártires at calles Lerdo de Tejada, Degollado and Ignacio Rayón. Hundreds of plant species native to Mexico are exhibited within the walls of this Art Nouveau-style building. Most impressive, however, are the magnificent stained-glass panels, which replaced the original windows. They were designed and built in 1980 by local artist Leopoldo Flores, who utilized some 45 tons of glass, 65 tons of metal and 25 tons of lead in their creation. **Hours:** Daily 10-6. **Cost:** 10 pesos (about 75c U.S.); 5 pesos (ages 0-11). **Phone:** (722) 214-6785.

**CALIXTLAHUACA ARCHEOLOGICAL ZONE** is 8 km (5 mi.) n. on Mex. 55 to the site turn-off, then about 3 km (2 mi.) w. The site is located on a hilltop above the village of the same name. Not much is known about its origins, although it was taken over by the Aztecs around 1476. Several buildings have been uncovered: the conical Temple of Quetzalcóatl-Ehecatl; the Pyramid of Tláloc; and the Altar of Skulls (Tzompantli), which was probably used for human sacrifice. Buses make frequent trips from Toluca to Calixtlahuaca; there is a short uphill walk to get to the site entrance. **Hours:** Tues.-Sun. 10-5. **Cost:** 47 pesos (about $3.50 U.S.).

**CASA DE ARTESANÍAS** is at Paseo Tollocan Oriente #700, at the corner of Calle Urawa. This government-run crafts store offers contemporary crafts produced in the state of México, including textiles, carved wood figures, ceramics and blown glass. It also is possible to watch the artisans as they work. The store is staffed with multilingual personnel. **Hours:** Mon.-Sat. 10:30-7, Sun. 10:30-3.

**FELIPE SANTIAGO GUTIÉRREZ MUSEUM** is downtown at Calle Nicolas Bravo #303, at the corner of Av. Lerdo de Tejada. It features works by the 19th-century portrait painter who taught figure drawing to José María Velasco. Gutiérrez was one of the first Mexican artists who rendered his subjects' Indian lineage, making no attempt to give them European features. **Hours:** Tues.-Sat. 10-6, Sun. 10-3. **Cost:** 10 pesos (about 75c U.S.); free to all Wed. and Sun. **Phone:** (722) 213-2647. GT

**JOSÉ MARIA VELASCO MUSEUM** is at Av. Lerdo de Tejada #400, adjoining the Felipe S. Gutiérrez Museum. It exhibits paintings and sculptures by one of Mexico's most influential 19th-century painters. One of Velasco's more notable works, "Vista desde Molino del Rey," was donated to the museum by former president Ernesto Zedillo. One room contains a re-creation of the artist's workshop. **Hours:** Tues.-Sat. 10-5:45, Sun. 10-3. **Cost:** 10 pesos (about 75c U.S.); free to all Wed. and Sun. **Phone:** (722) 213-2814. **GT**

**METEPEC** is about 8 km (5 mi.) s.e. of Toluca via Mex. 55. It is best known for the Trees of Life *(Arboles de la Vida)* meticulously created by local artisans. Against a backdrop of clay trunks and branches, these delightful trees depict stories populated by a diverse cast of religious and secular characters and inanimate objects. Many families in town are engaged in the craft.

Buses depart frequently for Metepec from Toluca's central bus station. The town is an easy day trip from Mexico City as well. By car, leave the capital via Paseo de la Reforma or Avenida Constituyentes, picking up either toll Mex. 15-D or free Mex. 15 west toward Toluca. Take the Mex. 15-D exit for Taxco/Ixtapan de La Sal and follow signs for Metepec. Pottery shops line the main street; ask for directions to the artisans' workshops *(alfarerías)*, where bargaining for purchases is expected. **Note:** Many are closed from 2-4 for afternoon *siesta*.

**MUSEUM OF WATERCOLOR** (Museo de la Acuarela) is at Melchor Ocampo #105. It occupies one of Toluca's oldest buildings, a two-story house with a central courtyard. It is known as "El Gallito," a reference to the brand of thread that was once distributed from the building. The permanent collection of 176 paintings is displayed in six halls, each named after a popular artist from the state of México. **Hours:** Tues.-Sat. 10-5:45, Sun. 10-2:45. **Cost:** 10 pesos (about 75c U.S.); 5 pesos (children). Free to all Sun. **Phone:** (722) 214-7304. **GT**

**STATE OF MÉXICO CULTURAL CENTER** (Centro Cultural Mexiquense) is off the Paseo Tollocan loop road; from its s.w. section (between the monument to Christopher Columbus, at the junction with Mex. 134, and the University of the State of México), follow the signs about 1.6 km (1 mi.) s.w. to the cultural center. This large, spread-out complex comprises a mix of architectural styles from colonial to contemporary.

The center can be reached from downtown Toluca via bus or taxi. Guide service in English is available. **Hours:** Museums open Tues.-Sat. 10-5:45, Sun. 10-2:45. **Cost:** (good for all three museums) 10 pesos (about 75c U.S.); free to all Wed. **Phone:** (722) 274-1277.

**Museum of Anthropology** (Museo de Antropología), within the State of México Cultural Center, exhibits artifacts from the state's archeological zones, including Malinalco and Calixtlahuaca. It was designed by Pedro Ramírez Vasquez, the architect who supervised construction of Mexico City's National Museum of Anthropology.

**Museum of Modern Art** (Museo de Arte Moderno), within the State of México Cultural Center, has works by Mexican muralists José Clemente Orozco, Diego Rivera and David Alfaro Siqueiros, among others.

**Museum of Popular Arts** (Museo de Artes Popular), within the State of México Cultural Center, is housed in a hacienda dating from the 17th century. Colorful murals decorate its walls, and a variety of regional handicrafts are on display. A huge "tree of life" sits in the front hall. The museum's exhibits of saddles, clothing and other items used by *charros* (cowboys) are considered among the best of their type in the country.

**TEOTENANGO ARCHEOLOGICAL ZONE** is about 25 km (16 mi.) s.e. of Toluca via Mex. 55, the highway to Ixtapan de La Sal, following signs to just n. of the village of Tenango. One of the few archeological zones in Mexico not owned and managed by INAH, the National Institute of Anthropology and History, Teotenango was excavated and developed in 1975. This walled, hilltop site is spread across a flat bluff and comprises the largest group of pyramids in central Mexico after those at Teotihuacán. Multiple low-rise pyramids cover several acres and have a backdrop of snowcapped mountains.

A museum at the site entrance has professionally mounted displays of artifacts found at the site. Clean, orderly and very well maintained, these ruins make an excellent day trip from Mexico City. Bus transportation also is available from Toluca.

**Note:** A long and steep cobblestone path leads from the parking area up to the pyramids; wear comfortable walking shoes. At an altitude of about 7,000 feet, the 15-minute hike will be arduous for those not in reasonably good shape. **Time:** Allow 2 hours minimum. **Hours:** Tues.-Sun. 10-6. **Cost:** (site and museum) 10 pesos (about 75c U.S.). **Parking:** Free. **Phone:** (722) 274-1262.

**ZACANGO ZOO** (Zoológico de Zacango) is about 7 km (4 mi.) s.e. of Toluca via Mex. 55 to the Metepec exit, then approximately 6 km (3.5 mi.) w. on Carretera Metepec to Km marker 7, following signs. The zoo displays more than 200 species of animals on the grounds of the former Hacienda de Zacango, home of the Order of Franciscan Priests in the 16th century. There ae six different zones: an African compound with free-roaming animals; a walk-through aviary; habitats for carnivorous animals, herbivores and primates; and a reptile exhibit. **Hours:** Daily 10-4. **Cost:** 42 pesos (about $3.10 U.S.); 27 pesos (ages 4-11). **Phone:** (722) 298-0631. **fi**

## VALLE DE BRAVO, MÉXICO (C-1)

pop. 61,599

Situated on a forested mountain slope about 140 kilometers (87 miles) west of Mexico City, Valle de Bravo (VAH-yeh deh BRAH-voh) overlooks large, man-made Lake Avándaro, part of a vast hydroelectric project serving the Valley of Mexico. The town is a popular weekend resort for well-to-do residents of Mexico City and Toluca.

Hang gliding, hiking, horseback riding, kayaking mountain biking, sailing and windsurfing are among the recreational activities available. Nearby Aván-daro Hotel Golf & Spa Resort has an 18-hole golf course. Valle de Bravo also hosts an international hang-gliding competition. Due to the elevation, the region is blessed with some of Mexico's nicest weather—mild, dry and sunny.

Buildings with whitewashed stucco walls and red-tiled roofs give the town an attractive colonial look. Further color is supplied by masses of bougainvillea cascading over walls and terraces. In the vicinity of Plaza Independencia, the main square, are boutiques, restaurants, a two-story artisans' market and a bookstore.

## XOCHIMILCO, DISTRITO FEDERAL
(C-3) pop. 415,007

Xochimilco (soh-chee-MEEL-coh) is about 24 kilometers (15 miles) southeast of downtown Mexico City, within the Federal District but outside the city limits. Designated a World Heritage Site by UNESCO in 1987, the "place where the flowers grow" was once a Chichimec Indian stronghold.

The best way to reach Xochimilco is to take Mexico City's Metro (line 2) to the Taxqueña station, then board a light rail train *(tren ligero)* and get off at the Xochimilco stop. *Peseros* (minibuses) also make the trip from the Taxqueña Metro station to Xochimilco, as do buses that travel down Avenida Insurgentes Sur and Calzada de Tlalpan to the Anillo Periférico.

By car, Xochimilco can be reached via the Periférico, exiting at Jardines del Sur. The tourist-oriented "floating gardens" area is busiest on Sunday, when Mexican families take their traditional day off. It's much less crowded in the middle of the week.

Xochimilco is threaded by numerous waterways, the last remains of a once-extensive lake. *Chinampas,* rafts woven from twigs, were covered with earth and planted with flowers or vegetables. The rafts often carried a small hut and were propelled about the lake with oars. The roots of willows planted around the perimeter of some rafts gradually attached to the lake bottom, and the so-called "floating gardens" became islands threaded by canals.

For a real taste of Mexican merrymaking visit on Sunday, when Xochimilco is thronged by families and a free-wheeling carnival atmosphere prevails. Signs marked "Embarcadero" point the way to the boat launches. The rental rate is per boat rather than per person, so it's cheaper—and more fun—to join a group.

Restaurants and souvenir stands line the canals. Everywhere there are hawkers, ashore and afloat in canoes, peddling tacos, beer, drinks, trinkets, balloons, flowers and fruit. Music is an integral part of the fun, and some boats are occupied by mariachi bands or guitar trios, in full costume and of varying degrees of polish, who paddle up to prospective customers and serenade them for a fee.

The government sets authorized rates for the boats, called *trajineras.* If an operator tries to charge more, complain to the police, who usually patrol the principal pier. If a police officer is not available, you must resort to bargaining, at which the boat operators are uncannily skillful; many have learned some English for just this purpose. Be sure to agree on the price and the length of the ride before embarking. Most rides will cost around 350 pesos (about $26 U.S.) per hour.

North of the town center is a more recently developed area of canals and *chinampas* where produce is raised, most of it bound for Mexico City markets. Boats can be hired to cruise these canals as well, although the area is kept separate from the tourist-targeted floating gardens. Picnicking is permitted along the banks of a man-made lake, where there also is a visitor center.

Although the floating gardens are the reason most people come here, Xochimilco has other attractions. Facing the main square is the early 16th-century Franciscan Convent and Church of San Bernardino, one of the first in New Spain. Stone carvings of angels and flowers adorn the church's exterior. Inside are several chapels and a main altar resplendent with gold gilt, sculptures and paintings. Also in the central part of town are garden centers and the market, liveliest on Saturdays when Indians come from miles around to sell their wares.

**DOLORES OLMEDO PATIÑO MUSEUM** is at Av. México #5843; take Metro line 2 to the Taxqueña station, then the *tren ligero* (light rail) to the La Noria station. The museum is several blocks from the light rail station. Since street parking is limited, it's easier to hire a hotel taxi driver for the trip. Philanthropist, art collector and benefactor of Diego Rivera, Olmedo bequeathed her hacienda, La Noria, and her outstanding art collection to the Mexican people upon Rivera's death in 1957.

Featured are Rivera paintings, drawings and engravings; paintings by Frida Kahlo (including some of her best-known works); watercolors and engravings by Russian artist Angelina Beloff; sculptures; and Mexican folk and religious art. The lovely grounds of this immense complex are alone worth a visit, with their lush gardens, orange and fig trees, Aztec and Mayan artifacts, wandering peacocks and a friendly pack of *xoloitzcuintle,* a rare, mid-size hairless dog with black skin dating from pre-Hispanic times. Children's programs, concerts and other special events take place Sat.-Sun.

Guided tours are available in Spanish only. Restrooms are provided. **Time:** Allow 2 hours minimum. **Hours:** Tues.-Sun. 10-6. **Cost:** 75 pesos (about $5.55 U.S.). **Phone:** (55) 5555-0891.

© Noradoa / Shutterstock.com

# Central Mexico

The "heartland of Mexico" has more reminders of Spain's legacy than any other part of the country. It is in this region that Spanish explorers capitalized upon abundant mineral resources, particularly silver, and built Mexico's first colonial cities. Many of Mexico's grand cathedrals and historic buildings date from some 300 years of Spanish rule.

The push for independence began with secret meetings in Morelia, Querétaro and San Miguel de Allende, where revolutionaries plotted Spain's downfall to coincide with the rising of Nueva España ("New Spain"), an independent nation. It was in the town of Dolores Hidalgo that Father Miguel Hidalgo first declared Mexico's freedom from Spain in his 1810 proclamation *Grito de Dolores.*

The Treaty of Guadalupe Hidalgo was signed in the city of Querétaro in 1848. It ended the Mexican War and forced Mexico to give up its territory north of the Rio Grande to the United States. In May 1862, invading French forces under emperor Napoleon III were soundly defeated at Puebla, a triumphant event celebrated in today's *Cinco de Mayo* festivities both north and south of the border.

The colonial cities of Guanajuato, Morelia, Puebla, Querétaro, San Miguel de Allende and Zacatecas feature well-preserved historic centers, pretty plazas, and beautiful cathedrals and churches. Puebla is known for buildings covered with Talavera tiles arranged in geometric patterns, a Spanish import. Guadalajara is the home of the *jarabe,* or Mexican hat dance, mariachi music and the flashy horsemanship of the *charreada* (Mexican rodeo).

AAA recommends that travelers consult online U.S. State Department travel advisories when planning traveling abroad. Find this information at http://travel.state.gov/content/passports/english/alertswarnings/mexico-travel-warning.html.

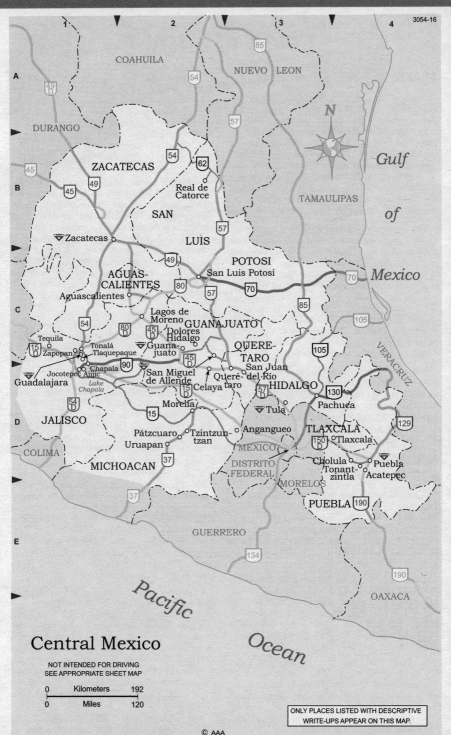

3054-16

# Central Mexico

NOT INTENDED FOR DRIVING
SEE APPROPRIATE SHEET MAP

| 0 | Kilometers | 192 |
|---|---|---|
| 0 | Miles | 120 |

ONLY PLACES LISTED WITH DESCRIPTIVE
WRITE-UPS APPEAR ON THIS MAP.

© AAA

# Points of Interest

## ACATEPEC, PUEBLA (D-4)

The small villages of San Francisco Acatepec (ah-kah-teh-PEHK) and Tonantzintla *(see separate listing within this region)* are just off Mex. 190 a few miles south of Cholula. Both are distinguished by baroque churches that are magnificent examples of Indian craftsmanship—local artisans employing pre-Hispanic imagery to depict Christian beliefs—and are well worth seeing for their visual splendor. The two towns are only about a mile apart, and both churches can be visited by taking a local bus or taxi from either Cholula or Puebla.

The beautifully preserved and refurbished Church of San Francisco Acatepec, in the center of this little town, dates from the 18th century and is considered one of the most ornate in the Americas. The facade is an extravagantly colorful feast of blue, yellow and orange ceramic tiles arranged in intricate geometric patterns, reminiscent of Puebla's trademark talavera tile building exteriors. The interior is more restrained but still lovely, with paneled doors, wall paintings and folk art decoration. Both this church and the one in Tonantzintla strongly reflect the culture of the Indians who labored to build them.

Bus tours to the churches depart from Cholula's main plaza Tuesday through Sunday approximately every 45 minutes beginning at 10. Bus tour tickets cost 110 pesos (about $8.15 U.S.). The church is open daily 10-1 and 3-5; admission is free. To confirm the bus tour schedule and cost, phone (222) 273-8300 (English not spoken).

## AGUASCALIENTES, AGUASCALIENTES (C-1) pop. 797,010

Aguascalientes (ah-guahs-ka-lee-EHN-tehs) was founded in 1575 as a way station for Spaniards traveling the "Silver Route" between Zacatecas and Mexico City. This manufacturing center still has impressive reminders of its colonial past; many are in the vicinity of Plaza de la Patria, the main plaza, which is best explored on foot.

The Government Palace (Palacio de Gobierno), on the plaza's south side, is built of red sandstone; it features hand-carved pillars and a fine interior patio. A highlight is the mural by Chilean painter Oswaldo Barra, which depicts all manner of mercantile scenes as well as miners grimly ascending from underground. The building is open Mon.-Sat. 9-4; closed holidays.

Next door is City Hall (Palacio Municipal), which has an attractive fountain inside the entrance. The baroque Cathedral, on the plaza's west side, is the oldest church in Aguascalientes and contains noteworthy religious paintings. The plaza itself, with another fountain and a park-like setting furnished with benches, is a pleasant spot to relax.

The House of Culture (Casa de la Cultura), 2 blocks west of the plaza on Calle V. Carranza, is housed in an old colonial convent and is worth a stop for the beauty of the building, which has courtyards festooned with vividly colored bougainvillea. The Church of San Antonio, about 6 blocks northeast of the plaza, has a cupola adorned with stained-glass windows.

The annual San Marcos Fair (Feria de San Marcos), honoring the city's patron saint, has been held since 1604. Mexico's oldest and largest state fair takes place from mid-April to early May at the Expo Plaza, southwest of Plaza de la Patria near the bullring. The celebrations include fireworks, live music concerts, amusement rides, craft exhibits, agricultural and industrial expositions, cultural events (including an international film festival), the crowning of a festival queen and a huge parade on Apr. 25, the saint's day. Bullfights and cockfights generate a great deal of wagering. If you're planning to visit during this time make reservations for accommodations well in advance.

### Practicalities

Jesús Terán International Airport is about 34 kilometers (21 miles) south of the city via Mex. 45 (the Aguascalientes-León Highway). Aeroméxico Connect, 01 (800) 021-4000 (toll-free long distance within Mexico) flies nonstop from Mexico City. American Eagle, 01 (800) 904-6000 (toll-free long distance within Mexico), and Volaris, 01 (800) 122-8000 (toll-free long distance within Mexico), offer nonstop service from Dallas and Los Angeles, respectively *(see Arriving by Air, page p. 42)*. One-way taxi fare between the airport and downtown will cost about $17 (U.S.).

It's easy to get lost in and around Aguascalientes if you're depending on highway signs and especially if you're a first-time visitor; obtain specific directions before attempting to negotiate the city on your own. Roadways within the state are narrow, with little or no shoulders and much truck traffic, but are well maintained. Toll highway Mex. 45-D links Aguascalientes with Lagos de Moreno to the southeast.

### Day Trips

Ojocaliente Sports Center (Centro Deportivo Ojocaliente) is about a kilometer east of downtown on Mex. 70. This spa has thermal pools, steam baths, saunas and tennis courts. Plaza Vestir, about 10 kilometers (6 miles) south on Mex. 45, is a collection of shops selling locally made clothing, embroidered items and shoes. A city bus or taxi will take you to the center. Peñuelas Hacienda is a breeding ranch said to produce some of Mexico's most spirited bulls; make arrangements to visit beforehand, either through your hotel or the State Tourism Office.

In the nearby town of Pabellón de Hidalgo, 33 kilometers (20 miles) north of Aguascalientes on Mex. 45, then 5 kilometers (3 miles) west, is the Hacienda San Blas de Pabellón, which houses the Museum of the Insurgency. Here, after losing two important battles against the Spanish in 1811, insurgent leader Father Miguel Hidalgo y Costilla was relieved of his command and replaced by Ignacio Allende. The hacienda produces woolen goods on hand-powered looms.

Asientos, easily reached by bus, is about 45 kilometers (28 miles) northeast. A colonial atmosphere prevails in this mining town, and you can view 16th- and 17th-century paintings on display in the local churches. Encarnación de Díaz, about 42 kilometers (26 miles) south on Mex. 45, has old baroque churches and a central plaza with topiary trees sculpted into various shapes, including Christopher Columbus' ships the *Niña*, the *Pinta* and the *Santa María*.

**Aguascalientes City Tourism Office:** In the Government Palace building (Palacio de Gobierno), within the historic city center on the south side of Plaza de la Patria. Open Tues.-Sun. 9-8. **Phone:** (449) 915-9504.

**CITY MUSEUM** (Museo de Aguascalientes) is about 6 blks. n.e. of Plaza de la Patria at Calle Zaragoza #505, opposite the Church of San Antonio. It exhibits 20th-century art, including a collection of paintings by Saturnino Herrán, who was born in the city. His work depicts the common people with uncommon sensitivity and fostered a sense of nationalist pride. **Hours:** Tues.-Sun. 11-6. **Cost:** 10 pesos (about 75c U.S.); free to all Sun. **Phone:** (449) 915-9043.

**JOSÉ GUADALUPE POSADA MUSEUM** is about 6 blks. s. of Plaza de la Patria on Plaza Encino, next to Encino Church (Templo del Encino). It houses a fascinating collection of works by Posada, a 19th-century Mexican engraver and cartoonist who was another native son. He was best known for his *calaveras*, skeletal-like figures that satirized events leading up to the Mexican Revolution of 1910. These humorous political scenarios influenced public opinion in their day. **Hours:** Tues.-Sun. 11-6. **Cost:** 10 pesos (about 75c U.S.); free to all Wed. **Phone:** (449) 915-4556.

## AJIJIC, JALISCO (D-1)

Ajijic (ah-hee-HEEK) is about 8 kilometers (5 miles) west of Chapala on the northern shore of Lake Chapala. This artists' and writers' colony, one of several resort/retirement communities along the lake, is populated by many former U.S. residents.

Along Calle Morelos between the main square and the waterfront are shops and boutiques selling everything from local handicrafts to designer fashions. Easily reached from Guadalajara, Ajijic has a picturesque waterfront area and cobblestone streets and is a pleasant destination for shopping, strolling and perhaps lunch. The town's Fiesta of St. Andrew, held in late November, is celebrated with parades, dancing and fireworks.

## ANGANGUEO, MICHOACÁN (D-3)

**Note:** For current information about safety/security issues in and around Angangueo (including the El Rosario Monarch Butterfly Sanctuary) as well as the state of Michoacán, refer to the U.S. State Department website (travel.state.gov).

Angangueo (ahn-gahn-GEH-oh), which sits in a canyon carved by the Río Puerco, was a pueblo inhabited by Tarascan Indians long before the arrival of the Spanish. The name means "mouth of the cave." Towering above are the 10,000-foot peaks of Cerro de Guadalupe, El Campanario and Cerro de la Gotera.

Angangueo's heyday was in the early 20th century, when it was a mining center. Today this hamlet, dominated by two imposing Catholic churches facing each other across the main plaza, survives as a tourist departure point for trips to the surrounding monarch butterfly sanctuaries, most of them in the state of Michoacán.

Every winter the generation of monarchs that have spent the spring and summer in Canada and the United States east of the Rockies arrive in this mountainous, forested region of Mexico as part of their remarkable migratory life cycle. Scientists do not know for sure what inner navigational system guides the insects into making this 2,500-mile journey, although one possible explanation is that more than half of North America's species of milkweed—the caterpillars' food source—are native to Mexico, indicating that the urge to migrate is passed along genetically.

After reaching their wintering grounds the monarchs hibernate, forming enormous colonies that completely cloak the tall pines and firs. In a semi-dormant state they burn almost no energy, but begin to grow more active as the weather warms, preparing for the northward migration in the spring. Several generations hatch along the way, thus continuing the monarch's life cycle for another year.

The monarch has a remarkable ability to survive decimating losses; in the winter of 2002, heavy rainstorms and freezing winter weather killed millions

and millions of butterflies. However, both scientists and environmentalists worry that herbicide use in the United States and Canada, which kills milkweed plants, as well as illegal Mexican logging operations that destroy the butterflies' sanctuaries will have a devastating long-term effect on their numbers.

**EL ROSARIO MONARCH BUTTERFLY SANCTUARY** (Santuario de Las Mariposas Monarca, El Rosario), accessible from Angangueo, is located near the tiny village of El Rosario. The easiest way to visit this ecological preserve is to book a guided bus or van tour from Mexico City or Morelia; arrangements can be made through travel agencies in those cities. Alternatively, tour guides can be hired in Angangueo, and the Hotel Albergue Don Bruno, in the center of town at Calle Morelos #92, has basic rooms for an overnight stay. From Angangueo the slow, steep route to the sanctuary by truck or four-wheel-drive vehicle takes about an hour.

On cold, cloudy days the butterflies cling to tree branches; when the sun is out they're more active. The best chance of seeing impressive swarms of monarchs is February into early March. Wear sturdy, comfortable walking shoes and dress appropriately for the weather. On weekends the refuge is often crowded with visiting Mexico City residents; plan a trip during the week if possible.

**Note:** Check the U.S. State Department website for current travel advisories or warnings before planning any trip to this region. **Hours:** Daily 9-6, late Nov.-Mar. **Cost:** 45 pesos (about $3.35 U.S.); 35 pesos (children and senior citizens). **Phone:** (715) 156-0026 (for Hotel Albergue Don Bruno reservations).

## CHAPALA, JALISCO (D-1) pop. 48,839

Chapala (chah-PAH-lah) is one of three resort communities (along iwth Ajijic and Jocotepec) on the northern shore of Lake Chapala. During the early 20th century it was the summer residence of dictator Porfirio Díaz. At that time the town attracted a rich international clientele who spent weekends at lavish estates, enjoying the area's tranquil beauty and delightfully spring-like weather, a bit cooler in summer and warmer in winter than Guadalajara.

Chapala has an established resident population of American and Canadian retirees. Commercial activity is centered along Avenida Madero, which leads to the lake and town pier. The street is lined with shops and small cafes. Near the pier is the main square, a pleasant spot to relax; band serenades are held here on Sunday evenings. Along the lakeshore is Cristiania Park, where vendors gather on the weekend.

The lake itself, some 53 miles long and 18 miles wide, is the largest natural lake in Mexico, surrounded by forested mountains. Mezcala Island can be reached by boat from the Chapala pier. The ruins of a fort and bastion here date from the Mexican War of Independence, when rebels successfully defended the island against the Spanish army and navy

from 1812-16. Hunger and sickness finally forced these 1,500 courageous souls to surrender, but their valor prompted the Spaniards to present them with an honor guard and a military pardon.

## CHOLULA, PUEBLA (D-3)

The Cholula (choh-LOO-lah) of today is practically a suburb of ever-expanding Puebla, but at the time of its destruction in 1519 by Hernando Cortés it was a religious city built on the foundations of a ceremonial center that had flowered by the second century A.D. At its peak Cholula was inhabited by 100,000 Cholultecs—a mixture of Olmec, Toltec, Aztec, Mixtec and Mazatec Indians.

When Cortés arrived in Cholula en route to Tenochtitlan, the Aztecs mistook the conqueror for the god Quetzalcóatl, which their mythology described as being fair skinned and with light hair. Consequently, the 100,000 inhabitants showed deference to Cortés and his band of 500 men. The conqueror promptly shattered this illusion by having his second in command, Pedro de Alvarado, carry out the slaughter of 6,000 Indians and the destruction of their temples and shrines.

Following custom, the Spanish conquerors erected a church atop the rubble of each temple they razed. An example sits atop Tepanapa Pyramid, one of the New World's largest structures. Burrowing into the earth near the base of this brush-covered hill, archeologists discovered that the Cholultecs, in fact, appeared to be better builders than the Aztecs who last occupied the city.

**CHOLULA ARCHEOLOGICAL ZONE** is in the center of town off Calzada San Andres Cholula to Av. 14 Poniente, near the main square. It is completely dominated by the Great Pyramid of Tepanapa (officially, the tongue-twisting Tlachihualtepetl), a massive structure that has a base length of about 1,315 feet—each side is some 500 feet longer than the Pyramid of the Sun at Teotihuacán. This is one of the three largest pyramids in the world by total volume.

Looking more like a wide hill than a traditional pyramidal structure, it was built around 100 B.C. By the time Hernando Cortés arrived in Cholula in 1519, temples built by the Toltecs and later the Aztecs surrounded the Great Pyramid, and it escaped the destructive wrath the Spanish conqueror unleashed on the buildings around it.

Hike up the stone trail to the top and the Santuario de Nuestra Señora de los Remedios (Sanctuary of Our Lady of Remedies), which crowns the hill 217 feet above ground level. This lovely parish church, built in the late 16th century, has twin domes adorned with mosaic tiles and a breathtaking interior replete with gold-leaf ornamentation. The view of the city and surrounding countryside from the pyramid's summit is well worth the climb.

Archeological excavations undertaken in the 1930s to study the pyramid created some 5 miles of zigzagging subterranean passageways that reveal various stages of construction over centuries. The passageways open to visitors feature models of the pyramid built into the walls. You'll also catch glimpses of narrow stairways and ancient chambers.

The site museum, near the entrance, has a cutaway view of the pyramid showing its different levels and displays pre-Hispanic artifacts, knives and arrowheads. Vendors set up booths under the trees behind the pyramid, selling handicrafts and homemade sweets, and a team of *voladores* ("flying men") regularly performs the dramatic and dangerous flying pole dance for tourists. Freelance tour guides, who congregate at the entrance, will identify various structures and point out decorative highlights.

**Time:** Allow 1 hour, 30 minutes minimum. **Hours:** Daily 9-5:30. **Cost:** 52 pesos (about $3.85 U.S.); free (ages 0-12). Negotiable guided tour fees begin at 250 pesos (about $18.50 U.S.). Cash only. **Phone:** (222) 247-9081. GT

**ROYAL CHAPEL** (Capilla Real) faces the main square. The chapel is within the walls of the Church of San Gabriel. Originally built for defensive as well as religious purposes, it contains seven naves and has 49 domes.

## DOLORES HIDALGO, GUANAJUATO
(C-2) pop. 148,173

Known in Mexico as Cuna de la Independencia Nacional (The Cradle of National Independence)

and designated a national historic monument, Dolores Hidalgo (doh-LOH-rehs ee-DAHL-goh) lies in the valley of the Río Laja. Just before midnight on Sept. 15, 1810, Father Miguel Hidalgo y Costilla called together his parishioners by ringing the village church bell. He then gave the venerated *Grito de Dolores,* a speech announcing Mexican independence that ignited the 11-year war to achieve it.

A statue of Hidalgo stands in Plaza Principal, the main plaza, where various vendors ply their wares among comfortable old benches and square-trimmed trees. The former homes of other Mexican heroes are here as well; guides are available for town tours.

The annual Independence Day celebrations held Sept. 15-16 re-create Father Hidalgo's historic rallying cry, and the president of Mexico often officiates.

**HIDALGO HOUSE MUSEUM** (Museo Casa de Hidalgo) is a block s. of the main plaza at Calle Morelos #1 (at Calle Hidalgo). Miguel Hidalgo lived here when he was the town's parish priest. It contains many items relating to the life of the patriot, including paintings, portraits, books, period furniture and a room filled with wreaths and other memorials. **Hours:** Tues.-Sat. 9-5:45, Sun. 9-4:45. **Cost:** 39 pesos (about $2.90 U.S.). **Phone:** (418) 182-0171.

# Guadalajara

**City Population:** 1,495,189
**Elevation:** 1,552 meters (5,091 feet)

## Editor's Picks:

Cabañas Cultural Institute .......... *(see p. 301)*
Degollado Theater .................... *(see p. 301)*
Plaza Tapatía ......................... *(see p. 305)*

Guadalajara's (gwah-dah-lah-HAH-rah) history dates to 1530, just 38 years after Christopher Columbus first reached North America and 9 years after the conquest of Mexico by Hernando Cortés. Another Spanish explorer, Nuño de Guzmán, founded the settlement that today is Mexico's second largest city.

Guzmán was a cruel conqueror; he and his soldiers slaughtered entire Indian communities in the course of exploring the lands west and north of Mexico City. The settlement was relocated several times in the aftermath of Indian attacks and finally ended up in the Valley of Atemajac in 1542. The move was a wise choice, as the valley offered room for unimpeded expansion.

Spanish expeditions left from Guadalajara to gain control of such far-flung lands as the Philippine and Molucca Islands and the island of Guam, and to establish missions in northern Mexico and present-day California. Wealth from the region's farms and silver mines was channeled into the construction of lavish churches, mansions and monuments.

In the late 1850s and early 1860s the city withstood army attacks led alternately by Archduke Maximilian and Benito Juárez; the latter made the city the capital of his reform government for a few months during his forced exile from Mexico City. Today it's a sprawling metropolis, surrounded by high plains noted for horse, cattle and grain ranches.

Guadalajara, a mile above sea level, enjoys abundant sunshine most of the year. High temperatures are normally in the 70s and 80s; uncomfortably humid days are rare. In April and May, the warmest months, it can creep into the low 90s, but always cools off in the evening. The rainy season is June through September. Air pollution is a problem, although not as severe as in Mexico City. A sweater or light jacket will come in handy on chilly nights.

Guadalajara even has its own word: *tapatío*. Reputedly derived from *tlapatiotl*, a term used to denote cacao or other small objects frequently used as

© Noradoa / Shutterstock.com

units of exchange in Indian marketplaces, it now refers to any person, thing or quality that is indisputably Guadalajaran, like the *jarabe*, or Mexican hat dance, and mariachi music.

## Getting There

### By Air

Miguel Hidalgo International Airport is about 17 kilometers (11 miles) southeast of the city off Mex. 23. Aeroméxico, Alaska Airlines, Delta, United, US Airways and Volaris offer direct flights from U.S. cities. International connections are usually via Mexico City. Numerous half-hour flights connect Guadalajara with Puerto Vallarta. Always check with a travel agency or the airline prior to booking a flight, as routes and direct-flight availability differ depending on the time of year. *For additional information about airlines see Arriving by Air, page p. 42.*

Airport Transportation (Autotransportaciónes Aeropuerto) offers shared-ride shuttle van service to and from any place in the metropolitan area. Tickets are sold at a booth outside the terminal exit; fares are based on a zone system and average about $15 per person (U.S.). For details phone (33) 3812-4278. Taxis also take passengers to and from the airport; the fare to the downtown area is about $30 (U.S.).

Getting There — *starting on this page*

Getting Around — *starting on p. 299*

What To See — *starting on p. 300*

What To Do — *starting on p. 305*

Where To Stay — *starting on p. 523*

Where To Dine — *starting on p. 526*

## By Car

Guadalajara's location between the Pacific coast and central Mexico makes it an ideal base from which to explore Jalisco and the surrounding states of Nayarit, Zacatecas, Aguascalientes, Guanajuato, Michoacán and Colima. Mex. 15/15-D is the major highway from the northwest; Mex. 54 from the north and northeast. Mex. 80 proceeds southwest to coastal Mex. 200, which heads south to Manzanillo or north to Puerto Vallarta. With the exception of Mex. 15-D, all of the above routes are old (free) highways.

The Guadalajara-Manzanillo toll highway, Mex. 54-D, begins at El Cuarenta, on Mex. 15 south of the city. Although the distance to Colima is not much shorter than that traveled on free Mex. 54, the toll road avoids the latter's narrow, winding stretches.

Toll highway Mex. 15-D provides a direct link between Guadalajara and Mexico City. It takes between 5 and 6 hours to drive the 540-kilometer (335-mile) route. Toll charges total approximately 941 pesos (about $70 U.S.).

South of and roughly parallel to Mex. 15-D is old Mex. 15, a winding road that hugs the southern shore of Lake Chapala and passes through the cities of Morelia, Zitácuaro and Toluca on its way to Mexico City—a scenic but much more time-consuming alternative. The road is in poor condition in places, and driving the stretch from Morelia to Mexico City is not recommended because of safety and security concerns.

## By Bus

The big, modern New Bus Station (Nueva Central Camionera) is about 10 kilometers (6 miles) southeast of downtown outside the suburb of Tlaquepaque (on

© Elena Elisseeva / Shutterstock.com

the way to Tonalá). Bus lines service practically every destination in the country; several of the bigger companies are connected with Greyhound Lines Inc. Cross-country buses make frequent trips between Guadalajara and border points. First-class travel compares favorably with major U.S. lines; these buses are the standard size but carry fewer passengers.

Seven terminal buildings (*módulos*) in the U-shaped station accommodate different bus companies; some have a presence at several terminals, so you need to find the terminal associated with your specific destination. Amenities include shuttle bus service, luggage storage (*guarda equipaje*), restaurants, restrooms, Ladatel long-distance phones and tourist and hotel information (although the booths are not always staffed). City buses and *colectivos* designated "Centro" or "Central" travel between the bus station and downtown. You also can take a taxi from this station to the downtown area. Taxi tickets are sold inside each terminal building; fares are based on a zone system.

For shorter bus trips to Tequila, the Lake Chapala suburban communities or other towns within a 60-mile

# *The Informed Traveler*

## WHOM TO CALL

**Police (emergency):** Dial 060, 066 or 080 (emergency services) and ask to be connected to an English-speaking operator if you need immediate assistance.

**Police (non-emergency):** (33) 3668-0800.

**Hospitals:** Hospital México-Americano, Calle Colomos #2110, (33) 3641-3141, and the Red Cross (Cruz Roja), (33) 3345-7777 or 065 (ambulance assistance), both provide 24-hour emergency service. Major hotels and the U.S. Consulate should have information regarding doctors who are on 24-hour call.

## WHERE TO LOOK

### Newspapers

English-language newspapers, including the weekly *Guadalajara Reporter*, are available at newsstands and the Hotel Fenix, downtown at avenidas Corona and López Cotilla. The monthly *Lake Chapala Review* has information about the communities around Lake Chapala.

### Publications

Sandi Bookstore, Av. Tepeyac #718 in the Chapalita neighborhood west of downtown, has English-language newspapers and books. The Sanborn's restaurant chain has several area locations and also offers books, newspapers and magazines in English; the downtown branch is at avenidas Juárez and 16 de Septiembre, a block south of Plaza de Armas.

### Visitor Information

**Jalisco State Tourism Office (Secretaría de Turismo):** Calle de Morelos #102 on Plaza Tapatía (near the Degollado Theater). **Phone:** (33) 3668-1600, or 01 (800) 363-2200 (toll-free long distance within Mexico).

A tourist information booth is inside the southern doorway of the Government Palace (Palacio de Gobierno), facing Plaza de Armas; it is open Mon.-Fri. 9-3 and 6-8 p.m., Sat. 9-1.

**U.S. Consulate:** Calle Progreso #175 at Avenida López Cotilla. **Phone:** (33) 3268-2100.

## WHAT TO KNOW

### Currency Exchange

A number of *casas de cambio* (currency exchange houses) are located downtown along Avenida López Cotilla between calles Corona and Degollado, about 3 blocks south of the cathedral. Most of them post their rates, and they normally don't have the lines that banks often have. Dollars and traveler's checks can be exchanged at branches of Banamex banks Mon.-Sat. 9-1. A Banamex branch is at Calle Corona and Avenida Juárez. ATMs are the quickest and most convenient way to get cash; withdrawals are in pesos.

### Staying Safe

The rules in Guadalajara are the same as those in any big city. At night, avoid urban neighborhoods that are away from the downtown core or other tourist areas; dark side streets in particular can be dangerous. If going out for the evening or taking a side trip during the day, it's a good idea to hire a taxi driver affiliated with your hotel. Keep an eye on personal items at all times, especially in the crowded shopping districts, and avoid wearing jewelry or carrying large sums of money. Women are not welcome in *cantina* bars and other bastions of heavy drinking and *machismo* attitudes.

radius of the city, use the Old Bus Station (Antigua Central Camionera), located off Avenida Dr. R. Michel at calles Los Angeles and 28 de Enero (in the city center and just northeast of Parque Agua Azul). Also shaped like a U, it consists of two wings (*salas*) and has luggage storage, restrooms and food stands. There are taxi stands on either side of the terminal. Inexpensive shuttle service is provided to the New Bus Station.

Route, schedule and fare information can be obtained at two offices located on Calzada de la Independencia where it runs beneath Plaza Tapatía. Hours are daily 9-2 and 4-7. *For additional information about buses see Bus Service, page p. 52.*

## Getting Around

### City Layout

The city is divided into four sectors; street names change when a new sector is entered. The major north-south routes are Calzada Independencia/Calzada Gobernador Curiel, which divides Guadalajara into east and west sectors; Avenida Alcalde/Avenida 16 de Septiembre, which passes through the Historic Center (Centro Histórico); Avenida Federalismo/Avenida Colón, which runs a few blocks west of Alcalde; and Avenida López Mateos, the main thoroughfare passing through a concentration of malls, upscale shops and restaurants west of downtown.

The major east-west routes are Avenida Circunvalación, which runs north of downtown; Avenida Avila Camacho, which provides access to the northwestern suburb of Zapopan; Avenida Independencia/Avenida Industria (not to be confused with Calzada Independencia), which runs through the historic center a block north of the cathedral; Avenida Vallarta/Avenida Juárez/Avenida Javier Mina, which also runs through the historic center and divides the city into north and south sectors; and Avenida Guadalupe/Avenida Niños Héroes/Calzada González Gallo, which links points of interest in the southern part of the city.

The carefully preserved downtown historic district is the chief tourist attraction. Forming a shape somewhat like a giant cross are four plazas, each offering a distinct personality: Plaza Tapatía, Plaza de la Liberación, Plaza de Armas and Plaza Guadalajara. They all surround the cathedral, the heart of the old city. Here, amid narrow cobblestone lanes and weathered two- and three-story buildings, street vendors and shoeshine boys are an integral part of the urban landscape.

Plaza Tapatía is conveniently located close to museums, monuments and grand examples of colonial architecture. It features tree-shaded parks, stone walkways and burbling fountains as well as numerous restaurants. On Sundays, dressed-up families stroll up and down Plaza de la Liberación, just east of the cathedral at Tapatia's western end. A narrow waterway runs along this plaza, which is bordered on both sides by shops and more restaurants. A statue of Father Miguel Hidalgo shows the priest holding a broken chain, a symbol of his call to end slavery in Mexico.

Plaza de Armas, a block south of the cathedral, is the city's traditional main square, bordered on the east side by the Government Palace. Plaza Guadalajara (just west of the cathedral) was formerly called Plaza de los Laureles for the Indian laurel trees that shade it. The church on the plaza's north side, built in the mid-20th century, is one of the newer buildings in the historic center.

West and south of the historic center the boulevards are wider and the buildings taller. Along north-south Avenida Chapultepec between Avenida Niños Héroes and Avenida México—about 20 blocks west of the cathedral—are office buildings interspersed with stores and restaurants. Farther west, along Avenida López Mateos between Avenida Vallarta and Avenida Mariano Otero, are major hotels, nightlife venues and the big Plaza del Sol mall.

Two thoroughfares loop around Guadalajara. The inner Avenida de la Patria travels around the western half of the city between Avenida de las Américas and Avenida López Mateos. The outer Anillo Periférico encircles the entire metropolitan area; navigating this two-lane route can be slow going, however, due to potholes and heavy truck traffic. *Glorietas* (traffic circles) mark busy city intersections.

**Note:** Due to air pollution levels, all vehicles with Jalisco license plates must pass a tune-up test. Vehicles with out-of-state plates, however, are exempted.

## Rental Cars

Hertz is one of many rental car agencies with offices at the airport and downtown. Be sure you fully understand the terms of any rental contract, especially with regard to insurance coverage. It's significantly less expensive to reserve before you leave home; make reservations at least 1 week in advance.

**Note:** AAA/CAA members enjoy discounts through Hertz for vehicles booked in the United States. Consult your local AAA/CAA club or phone Hertz, (800) 654-3080.

## Buses

Buses are the most economical means of local transportation, and they cover every part of town. City buses run daily every 5 to 10 minutes from 6 a.m.-11 p.m. School bus-style vehicles have the cheapest fares (about 50c U.S.), but also are quite likely to be very crowded.

*Tur* buses (operated by Linea Turquesa), turquoise in color and with the letters "TUR" designated on the side, cost more (about 90c U.S.) but are air conditioned, do not carry standing passengers and travel to such outlying tourist destinations as Tlaquepaque, Tonalá and Zapopan. *Par Vial* buses travel a central east-west route along avenidas Independencia/Hidalgo as far west as Minerva Circle (at Avenida López Mateos); from there, they double back along Avenida Vallarta/Juárez, a few blocks south.

Privately operated *colectivos* (minivans) cost about the same as city buses; some have their destination marked on the windshield, although routes and pick-up points change frequently.

## Taxis

Compared to the bus, a taxi ride in Guadalajara is expensive. Even short 10-minute rides are likely to cost at least $8 (U.S.). Rates go up at night. All cabs are equipped with a meter, but drivers can be reluctant to use them, quoting a flat fee instead; make certain you agree on a destination and a fare with the driver before entering the cab. Check at your hotel's front desk for current fares; bellboys can often assist those who don't speak Spanish.

Most cabs are found at or called from a cab stand (*sitio*). *Sitios* are located near all the major hotels and attractions. The safest option is to stick with cab drivers who are affiliated with your hotel.

## Parking

On-street parking in the city center is scarce. Public parking garages generally charge a fixed rate per hour; few are insured for customers. Parking lots charge less than garages. An underground lot is below Plaza de la Liberación, just east of the cathedral. Always avoid areas marked "No E," "Estacionamiento Prohibido" (No parking) or "Exclusivo" (Reserved). License plates are removed from illegally parked vehicles, and a fine must be paid to retrieve them.

## Public Transportation

Guadalajara's *tren ligero* (light rail) rapid-transit system has two lines. Line 1 runs north-south along Avenida Federalismo-Colón for a distance of about 10 miles, between the northern and southern stretches of the Periférico. More helpful to visitors is Line 2, which runs east-west along avenidas Vallarta/Juárez and Javier Mina (the street name changes at Calzada Independencia). Trains run about every 15 minutes or so daily 6 a.m.-11 p.m. The fare is 7 pesos (50c U.S.); 1-peso coins are needed to purchase tickets. Stops are marked by a "T" symbol.

## Guides/Tours

Tour guides with name tags who congregate at the airport and bus terminal are likely to be agents on commission with hotels. The major hotels usually have a list of licensed bilingual guides. Bus tours of the downtown area as well as nearby Tlaquepaque and Zapopan are offered by Tapatío Tours. The company's red double-decker buses depart from Plaza Tapatía; phone (33) 3613-0887 for schedule and fare information. For visitors without a car, this is an easy way to experience the city.

Rides in horse-drawn *calandrias* (carriages) can be taken throughout the central downtown area for about $20 (U.S.) for up to four people and are a relaxing way to see the sights. Excursions depart from the Regional Museum of Guadalajara, Liberty Market and San Francisco Park. Few drivers speak English, so you may want to familiarize yourself with the layout of the city before embarking.

## What To See

**AGUA AZUL PARK** (Parque Agua Azul) is at the southern end of downtown, adjacent to the intersection of calzadas Independencia Sur and González

Gallo. This is the oldest of the city's parks. Trees, flowers, fountains and a man-made lake make it a popular spot for city residents and a pleasant place to while away an afternoon. On the grounds are an orchid house, an aviary and an outdoor amphitheater where band concerts take place. On the other side of Calzada González Gallo is Plaza Juárez, which has a monument encircled by the flags of other Latin American countries. **Hours:** Daily 10-5:30. **Cost:** 7 pesos (about 50c U.S.); free (ages 0-11). **Phone:** (33) 3619-0328.

**Jalisco House of Handicrafts** (Casa de las Artesanías de Jalisco) is at the northern end of the park, with a separate entrance on Calzada González Gallo. This state-run store sells fixed-price regional handicrafts, including leather saddles, furniture, blown glass, ceramics, pottery, textiles, tinwork and woodcarvings. **Hours:** Mon.-Sat. 9-4, Sun. 9-3. **Phone:** (33) 3030-9090.

**ARCHEOLOGICAL MUSEUM OF WESTERN MEXICO** (Museo de Arqueología del Occidente de Mexico) is at Av. 16 de Septiembre #889, just n. of Plaza Juárez and across from Agua Azul Park. It exhibits a small but select group of figurines, pottery and other artifacts from sites in Colima, Jalisco and Nayarit. **Hours:** Tues.-Sat. 10-6, Sun. 11-4. Phone ahead to confirm schedule. **Cost:** 20 pesos (about $1.50 U.S.); free (ages 0-11). **Phone:** (33) 3619-7043.

**CABAÑAS CULTURAL INSTITUTE** (Instituto Cultural Cabañas) is at the e. end of Plaza Tapatía at Cabañas #8; take a taxi, as this is a congested area. It was built in the early 19th century and financed by Bishop Juan Cruz Ruíz de Cabañas. Originally offering shelter for crippled, destitute and orphaned men, women and children, Hospicio Cabañas provided education and medical care for children through the 1970s before being renovated for use as a cultural center.

This architecturally fascinating complex encompasses 23 patios linked by pink-tiled corridors. It is the showplace for some of José Clemente Orozco's most powerful murals, particularly *"El Hombre de Fuego"* ("Man of Fire"), which graces the lofty ceiling. The art is memorable, although it depicts scenes of horrific violence from Mexico's history.

In addition to contemporary art and changing exhibitions, the institute has a movie theater, performing arts theater and an outdoor patio where ballet, music and dance performances take place. **Hours:** Tues.-Sun. 10-6. **Cost:** 70 pesos (about $5.20 U.S.); free to all Tues. **Phone:** (33) 3668-1647.

**CATHEDRAL** faces Av. Alcalde. Begun in 1561, it was consecrated in 1618. Its twin 200-foot towers were erected in 1848 after an earthquake destroyed the original, much shorter structures. Emblazoned with yellow and blue tiles, they are a city landmark. Inside are three cavernous naves and 11 elegantly appointed altars, a gift from King Ferdinand VII of Spain. A lovely sculpture, "Our Lady of the Roses," was given to the city by the 16th-century Spanish

king Carlos V. The priceless painting "The Assumption of the Virgin" in the sacristy is thought to be by Bartolomé Murillo. **Hours:** Open daily. **Cost:** Free.

**CHURCH OF OUR LADY OF ARANZAZU** (Iglesia de Nuestra Señora de Aranzazu) is at avs. 16 de Septiembre and Prisciiano Sánchez, bordering the s. side of San Francisco Park (Parque San Francisco). It has a plain exterior, but inside is an extravagantly ornate *retablo* (altarpiece) that is a dazzling example of Spanish baroque design; its niches contain lifesize statues of the saints. Also impressive are the colorful walls and ceilings.

Next to this church stands the less-ornate San Francisco Church (Iglesia de San Francisco). San Francisco Park is a starting point for horse-drawn carriage rides.

**CITY MUSEUM** (Museo de la Ciudad) is w. of the historic center at Av. Independencia #684 (at Av. Mariano Bárcena) in an area with street parking only. It opened in 1992 to commemorate Guadalajara's 450th anniversary. The old stone convent housing the museum is a fine example of late 17th-century colonial architecture. *Salas* (halls) on two floors display photographs and other exhibits that present a chronological timeline of the city's history and development.

Background information is in Spanish. **Time:** Allow 30 minutes minimum. **Hours:** Tues.-Sat. 10-5:30, Sun. 10-2:30. Closed major holidays. **Cost:** 20 pesos (about $1.50 U.S.); free (ages 0-11). **Phone:** (33) 3658-2531.

**JOSÉ CLEMENTE OROZCO MUSEUM** (Casa Museo José Clemente Orozco) is at Av. Aurelio Aceves #27, just e. of Minerva Circle off Av. Vallarta. This is the former workshop and residence of José Clemente Orozco, Jalisco's leading muralist (1883-1949). Distinguished by a three-story window, it displays photographs, tools, clothing and his personal easel. The wall facing the window is covered by a huge mural entitled *"Alegoría del Vino"* ("Wine Allegory"). Also on display are documents, handwritten letters, posters, diplomas and other tributes to the artist.

**Note:** The museum was expected to reopen in late summer 2015 following a closure for renovation work. Phone ahead to confirm reopening schedule. **Hours:** Tues.-Sat. 10-4. **Cost:** Free. **Phone:** (33) 3616-8329.

**DEGOLLADO THEATER** (Teatro Degollado) is on Calle Belén between Calle Morelos and Av. Hidalgo, just e. of the cathedral. This impressive neoclassic structure, completed in 1866, has been compared to Milan's La Scala Opera House, although it has the grimy look of stone buildings exposed to decades of vehicle exhaust. The relief above the columned entrance depicts Apollo and the Nine Muses. The plaque on the outside back wall commemorates Guadalajara's 1542 founding ceremony.

Inside are opulent red and gold balconies and a dome with murals painted by Gerardo Suárez that depict Dante's "Divine Comedy." The remodeled

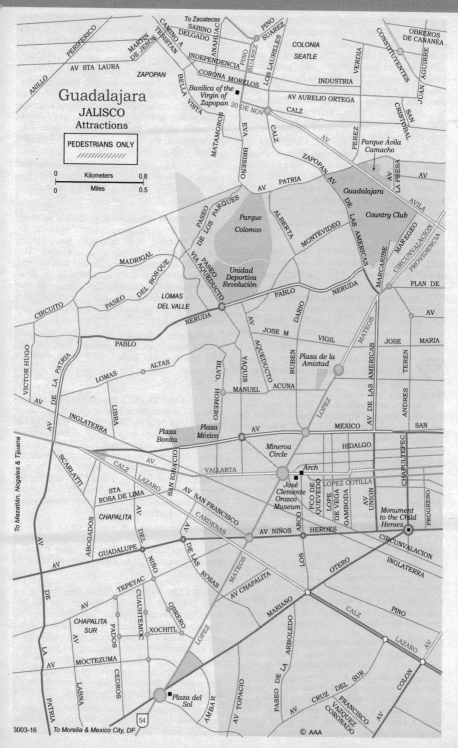

# Guadalajara
## JALISCO
### Attractions

PEDESTRIANS ONLY

| Kilometers | | |
|---|---|---|
| 0 | | 0.8 |
| 0 | Miles | 0.5 |

To Zacatecas

Basilica of the Virgin of Zapopan

Parque Ávila Camacho

Parque Colomos

Guadalajara Country Club

Unidad Deportiva Revolución

LOMAS DEL VALLE

Plaza de la Amistad

Plaza México

Plaza Bonita

Minerva Circle

Arch

José Clemente Orozco Museum

Monument to the Child Heroes

To Mazatlán, Nogales & Tijuana

Plaza del Sol

54

To Morelia & Mexico City, DF

3003-16

© AAA

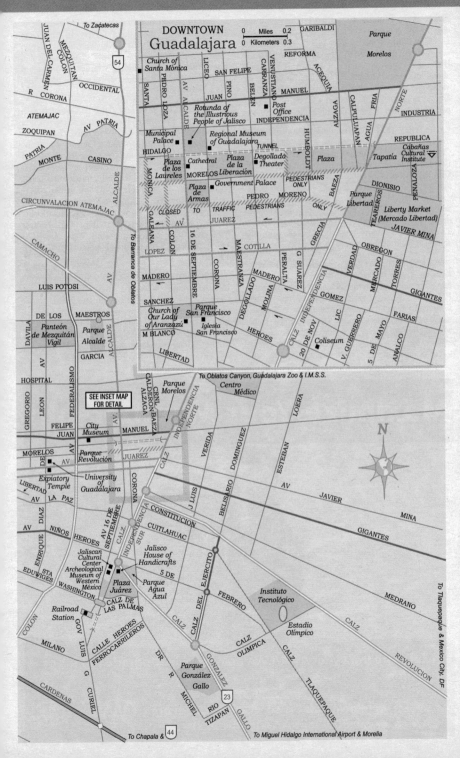

theater is the home of the Jalisco Philharmonic Orchestra and presents concerts, live theater performances and film festivals year-round. Performances are given by the University of Guadalajara Folkloric Ballet usually every Sunday at 10 a.m. If you can't attend an event, the theater's interior can usually be viewed (rehearsal schedule permitting) daily from around noon to 2 p.m. **Phone:** (33) 3614-4773 for performance and ticket information.

**EXPIATORY TEMPLE** (Templo Expiatorio) is w. of the historic center, bounded by Av. López Cotilla, Calle Madero, Av. Enrique Díaz de León and Av. Escorza. This massive structure covers a city block. One balcony of the Gothic-style church, built at the turn of the 20th century, features mechanical representations of the 12 Apostles who make an appearance, accompanied by a carillon playing classical music, three times daily (9 a.m., noon and 6 p.m.). The clockwork figures can be viewed from the square in front of the church.

**GOVERNMENT PALACE** (Palacio de Gobierno) faces the e. side of Plaza de Armas. This Spanish baroque building dates from 1643 and was completed in 1774. Note the stone gargoyles, used to divert water from the roof, and the pillared front entrance. An enormous mural by José Clemente Orozco depicts Father Miguel Hidalgo, bearing a flaming torch, symbolically leading Mexico's struggle against such 20th-century forces of oppression as communism and fascism.

Two important historical events took place here: Hidalgo's decree abolishing slavery in 1810 and Guillermo Prieto's plea saving president Benito Juárez from assassination in 1858. The cannon and armor carved on the building's facade are a symbol of colonial authority. **Hours:** Tues.-Sat. 10-6, Sun. 10-3. **Cost:** Free.

**GUADALAJARA ZOO** (Zoológico de Guadalajara) is about 6 km (4 mi.) n. of Plaza Tapatía at the junction of Calzada Independencia Norte and Paseo del Zoológico. Overlooking Huentitan Canyon, it contains a variety of large mammals, reptiles, monkeys and birds, including brightly colored toucans and macaws. A train and well-marked footpaths traverse the major viewing areas. There also is a children's petting zoo.

Next to the zoo is a planetarium and the Selva Mágica amusement park, which has a pool with performing dolphins. Parking is provided. **Hours:** Wed.-Sun. 10-6; daily during Holy Week. **Cost:** 70 pesos (about $5.20 U.S.); 42 pesos (ages 3-11). **Phone:** (33) 3674-4488.

**JALISCAN CULTURAL CENTER** (Casa de la Cultura Jalisciense) is at avs. 16 de Septiembre and Constituyentes, near Agua Azul Park. This state-supported center houses a movie theater, two art exhibition halls, artists' studios and the offices of various culture-oriented organizations. The Guadalajara Public Library also is in this building. **Hours:** Art exhibition halls Mon.-Fri. 10-6. **Cost:** Free.

**OBLATOS CANYON** (Barranca de Oblatos) is 10 km (6 mi.) n.e. of downtown Guadalajara via Calzada Independencia Norte, near the Guadalajara Zoo. This 2,000-foot-deep gorge was cut by the Santiago and Verde rivers. Thermal rivulets plunge down the red walls (except during the dry season). The greater the depth, the more tropical the climate: Papayas, oranges, guavas, bananas, mangoes and other fruits grown at the canyon bottom are marketed in Guadalajara.

A cable car leaves the rim in the morning to take workers to the power plant on the canyon floor. The best views are from the Parque Huentitán el Alto Mirador lookout area at the top of the gorge.

**PLAZA TAPATÍA** extends along Av. Miguel Hidalgo. A 7-block-long pedestrian walkway connects the Degollado Theater at the west end to the Cabañas Cultural Institute at the east end. The walkway enables visitors to see several of Guadalajara's downtown attractions without having to cross major streets. Underground parking lots also are along the route.

Plaza Tapatía is a prime spot for strolling and people watching. Vendors sell everything from candy to canaries. The festive atmosphere unfolds against a backdrop of flower beds, statues, fountains and reflecting pools, and there are myriad storefronts in which to browse or window shop.

*Escritorios* set up shop in the arcade close to the State Tourism Office. For centuries these typists, writers and editors have helped illiterate people fill out documents or write messages and correspondence, particularly love letters.

**REGIONAL MUSEUM OF GUADALAJARA** (Museo Regional de Guadalajara) is at Av. Liceo #60, a block north of the Government Palace. Housed in a former theological seminary dating from around 1700, it has been a museum since 1918. Exhibits focus on the history of Jalisco and western Mexico, and include pre-Hispanic artifacts, ethnological displays and a 1,715-pound meteorite discovered in the state of Zacatecas in 1792.

A collection of Spanish and Mexican art on the second floor features paintings from the school of Bartolomé Murillo. **Hours:** Tues.-Sat. 9-5:30, Sun. 9-4:30. **Cost:** 52 pesos (about $3.85 U.S.).

**ROTUNDA OF THE ILLUSTRIOUS PEOPLE OF JALISCO** (Rotonda de Los Jaliscienses Ilustres) is on the n. side of the cathedral in a park bounded by Calle Hidalgo and avs. Alcalde, Independencia/Industria and Liceo. The mausoleum is where six of Jalisco's foremost native sons—representing artistic, philanthropic and musical fields as well as the military—are buried. Surrounding the circular grouping of stone columns are sculptures of the men, along with other Jaliscan notables. The original name was the Rotunda of Illustrious Men; it was changed in 2000 when teacher Irene Obledo Garcia became the first woman honored.

**SANTA MONICA CHURCH** (Iglesia de Santa Monica) is at calles Santa Mónica and Reforma, about 4 blks. n.w. of the cathedral. It dates from around 1720. The baroque facade features some exquisite stone carvings; the interior is elaborately decorated as well.

**UNIVERSITY OF GUADALAJARA** is on Av. Juárez at Av. Enrique Díaz de León, behind the Expiatory Temple and 4 blks. w. of Revolución Park. The main building, French Renaissance in style, contains an Orozco mural. On the north side of Avenida Vallarta is the university tower, where cultural events are held regularly.

**University of Guadalajara Museum of Arts** (Museo de las Artes de la Universidad de Guadalajara) is opposite the main building. It occupies a beautiful early 20th-century edifice that was once a primary school. The permanent collection consists primarily of contemporary Jaliscan and Mexican artists; traveling exhibitions are mounted regularly. Also on display are early Orozco murals. **Hours:** Tues.-Fri. 10-6, Sat.-Sun. 10-4. **Cost:** Free. **Phone:** (33) 3134-1664.

## What To Do

### Dining

Guadalajaran restaurants specialize in hearty *tapatío* fare. Specialties include grilled steaks; *carne asada a la tampiqueña,* broiled or roasted meat served with bacon and beans; *pozole,* a thick, hominy-based soup with hunks of *carnitas* (pork), tomatoes, cilantro and frequently chickpeas; and *birria* (stewed goat or pork in a spicy tomato broth).

*Restaurantes campestres* are country-style establishments that serve steaks and side dishes like beans, quesadillas and tortillas. The food is accompanied by mariachi music and entertainment—sometimes in the form of a *charreada,* or rodeo, giving willing customers the opportunity to go *mano a mano* with a young bull. *Restaurantes campestres* are located within the city and also along main highways outside the urban area.

There is also an astounding variety of street food. Inexpensive *taquerías* operate up and down the length of Plaza Tapatía; the freshly made corn tortillas are wrapped around a variety of meat or vegetable fillings. The Mercado Libertad *(see Shopping)* has a myriad tiny stands offering full-course *comida corrida* meals, tamales, enchiladas, quesadillas and other treats. You can also find cheese, fruit and pastries. Cleanliness levels vary, however, and anyone planning to nibble their way from stall to stall should keep in mind the possibility of bacterial contamination, especially if the food has been sitting for a long time.

Except at first-class hotels and restaurants where purified water is customarily used, be careful of drinking water; this includes the ice cubes in drinks. Avoid unpeeled raw vegetables and fruit as well as untreated milk and dairy products. See the Lodgings & Restaurants section for AAA-RATED dining establishments.

### Shopping

Fashionable shops and boutiques line Avenida Chapultepec between avenidas México and Niños

Héroes in Guadalajara's Zona Rosa (Pink Zone). This upper-class area west of the historic center is frequented by tourists.

Malls dot the metropolitan landscape as well. La Gran Plaza is a sleek three-story collection of stores and a movie theater multiplex on Avenida Vallarta near the Camino Real Hotel. The largest is Plaza del Sol, at avenidas López Mateos Sur and Mariano Otero southwest of downtown. Restaurants and outdoor garden areas offer a break from shopping. City buses designated "Plaza del Sol" travel to the mall from Calzada Independencia in the vicinity of the Liberty Market.

Guadalajara also has an amazing number of shoe stores. Calle Esteban Alatorre, northeast of the historic center, is known locally as "shoe street." Galería del Calzado, at the corner of avenidas México and Yaquis (on the west side of town near Plaza México), is a shoe shopping center covering a square block.

El Baratillo, Guadalajara's Sunday morning flea market, offers shopping that is more for fun than for serious purchasing, unless you're an expert haggler. It stretches for blocks along Avenida Javier Mina in an area east of the Liberty Market; take a local bus along Avenida Gigantes, 2 blocks south of the market, to get there. Just about everything is here, much of it used.

**LIBERTY MARKET** (Mercado Libertad) is just e. of Calzada Independencia, between Avenida Javier Mina and Calle Dionisio Rodriguez (on the s. side of Plaza Tapatía; an elevated pedestrian walkway provides access from the plaza to the market). Locals call it Mercado San Juan de Dios, the name of the neighborhood and a nearby church (Templo San Juan de Dios), and also the Mercado Taiwan because of the abundance of cheap imported electronic gadgets for sale.

This huge, three-level building stands on the site occupied for centuries by Guadalajara's traditional *tianguis* (open-air markets). It is one of the largest enclosed markets in Latin America and attracts tourists from around the world. And it's no wonder, because everything under the sun is sold here: clothing (embroidered, traditional, utilitarian and otherwise), blankets, housewares, handicrafts, ceramics, silver, hardware, leather goods, shoes, office supplies, flowers, musical instruments, trinkets.

The number of stalls—more than 2,600—is staggering. Food stalls are on the first floor, food vendors on the second. Produce sellers display an encyclopedic array of fruits and vegetables, from familiar dried beans, yams and spices to exotica like the chewy *zapote* fruit from the sapodilla tree. Those with weak stomachs will want to avoid the section where butchers display every animal body part imaginable and the aroma of delicacies like tripe stew is quite strong.

Look for candy vendors selling sugar skulls and other traditional Mexican sweets. There's also an amazing variety of prepared food, from tacos and other *antojitos* (snacks) to delicately carved mango slices to sandwich stands where *tortas* are assembled on large, fresh rolls.

**Note:** There are restrooms in the market, but you'll need to pay an attendant to enter, and pay another small fee to use toilet paper or soap. **Hours:** Daily 6 a.m.-8 p.m. **Cost:** Free.

## Sightseeing

Guadalajara is a convenient base for day excursions to the Lake Chapala communities of Ajijic, Jocotepec and Chapala; to the suburban handicraft centers of Tlaquepaque and Tonalá; to the town of Tequila, known for the production of one of Mexico's more potent brews; and to the suburb of Zapopan, home of the revered Virgin of Zapopan. Casual clothes are suitable for just about any sightseeing excursion in the Guadalajara area, but shorts are frowned upon in churches.

## Sports and Recreation

**Bullfighting** fans head for the 25,000-seat Plaza de Toros Nuevo Progreso, northeast of downtown on Avenida Pirineos between Calzada Independencia Norte and Avenida Fidel Velasqués (across from Jalisco Stadium). From October through March, bullfights *(corridas)* take place most Sunday afternoons starting at 5. Tickets are sold at the bullring, or in advance through Ticketmaster; phone (33) 3818-3800. Spectators can opt for seats in the sun *(sol)* or shade *(sombra);* those in the shade are more expensive. Ask at your hotel about dates and ticket prices.

Although similar to the Western rodeos of the United States, the *charreada* is unmistakably Mexican. When Spanish explorers and conquerors reintroduced the horse (which had roamed the North American plains some 45,000,000 years earlier), only noblemen were permitted to ride. By the 19th century, the development of large *haciendas* (estates) for agricultural purposes made horses an everyday necessity, and the *charro* (male rider) evolved from the requirements of raising livestock in open country.

*Charros* were resourceful, self-reliant men, familiar with the land and able to live off it. *Charro* contingents fought in the war to achieve Mexican independence, and *charreadas,* where native horseback riders gathered to show off their skills, became part of Mexican culture. The National Association of Charros (Asociación Nacional de Charros) was founded in Mexico City 1921, and in Guadalajara these events are still very popular.

Both *charro* and *escaramuza* (female) riders are expert at fancy horsemanship and roping. The focus is on style and finesse rather than competition, although some of the sidesaddle riding feats performed are of the daredevil variety. One of the chief pleasures of a *charreada* is viewing the elegantly ceremonial costumes on display (on both horses and riders). Men are decked out in white pleated shirts, black pants encrusted with silver buttons and a sombrero embroidered with gold or silver thread. Women wear lacy petticoats and brightly colored skirts decorated with lace and ribbons, and wear their hair braided and beribboned.

The arena Lienzo Charros de Jalisco, Av. Dr. R. Michel #577 (near Agua Azul Park), presents a *charreada* most Sundays at noon with different events as well as mariachi music. Admission begins at about $3 (U.S.); phone (33) 3619-0315.

**Soccer** (*fútbol*) is the most popular spectator sport. Professional team Club Deportivo Guadalajara (nicknamed "Chivas") plays home matches at 49,000-seat Omnilife Stadium. Somewhat resembling a volcano in shape, it has an exterior largely covered by grass. The stadium is on Guadalajara's west side, just off the *periférico* ring road (Avenida Periférico Poniente Manuel Gomez Morin) via Avenida Circuito JVC. For schedule and ticket information, visit the stadium's website or phone (33) 3777-5700.

Guadalajara's year-round mild, sunny weather is ideal for **golf**. Some private courses allow visitors to play for a greens fee and proof of membership in a U.S. club; others are closed to nonmembers on weekends and holidays. Admittance to the immaculately maintained, 18-hole course at the Guadalajara Country Club is through a member, although the better hotels may be able to get their guests in. The country club is off Avenida Avila Camacho, about 8 kilometers (5 miles) northwest of the downtown historic center.

The Atlas Country Club (18 holes) is southeast of the city, on Mex. 23 just south of Tlaquepaque (on the way to Lake Chapala); phone (33) 3689-2620. The Santa Anita Golf Club is on Mex. 15, about 7 kilometers (4 miles) south of the Periférico loop road; phone (33) 3686-0321. Colomos Park (Parque Colomos), south of Avenida Patria and west of the country club in the city's western sector, has a track and tree-lined paths for **jogging.**

## Nightlife

Inquire at the front desk or ask a bellboy what's happening in town during your stay. Bars and clubs tend to be concentrated in two places: in the historic downtown center, and along Avenida Vallarta in the vicinity of Minerva Circle, an area of hotels and shopping west of downtown. La Maestranza, Calle Maestranza #179 at the corner of Avenida Madero (3 blocks south of the Government Palace), is a classic *cantina* that also is filled with bullfighting memorabilia.

The lobby bar in the Fiesta Americana Hotel, Av. Aurelio Aceves #225 on Minerva Circle, is a classy club/lounge with live music. Cantina María Bonita in the Camino Real Hotel, Avenida Vallarta #5005, has a romantic atmosphere and occasionally music for dancing. Maxim Cabaret, downtown at Calle Maestranza #35 (near Plaza de la Liberación and next door to the Hotel Frances), has live music and a dance floor. Piano music provides the backdrop at the intimate lobby bar in the Hotel Frances.

Several theaters show foreign and repertory films, including the Cine Cinematógrafo, Av. Vallarta #1102 (2 blocks west of the University of Guadalajara Museum of Arts), and Cine-Teatro Cabañas, in the Cabañas Cultural Institute at the eastern end of Plaza Tapatía. Malls such as Plaza del Sol have multiplexes showing the latest American releases.

Soak up the local ambience at Plaza de los Mariachis, on Calzada Independencia Sur between avenidas Javier Mina and Alvaro Obregón (on the south side of the Mercado Libertad). This pretty plaza is staked out by the roving bands of musicians. For a fee (usually about $5 U.S.) they will perform with guitar, violin, trumpet and an enthusiasm second to none. It costs nothing to listen to these serenades from another table, but if you're the one requesting a song, negotiate the price first.

Sidewalk cafés clustered around the plaza are pleasant places to relax during the day, but it's advisable not to linger in this area after dark. Use the pedestrian overpass from the market to avoid the heavy traffic congestion. Pickpockets frequent the plaza, so keep an eye on your valuables.

On Thursday and Sunday evenings the Jalisco State Band gives free performances at Plaza de Armas, across from the Government Palace. The music starts at 6:30 p.m., but if you want a seat at one of the benches arrive at least half an hour early.

## Theater and Concerts

Probably the grandest spectacle in town is the presentation of the University of Guadalajara's Ballet Folklórico in the Degollado Theater. Regional dances are complemented by *estudiantinas* or *rondallas* string ensembles, the Mexican counterpart of American high school marching bands or drum-and-bugle corps. Performances take place Sunday mornings at 10 a.m. in July and August; phone the box office at (33) 3614-4773 for more information.

The Jalisco Philharmonic Orchestra (Orquesta Filarmónica de Jalisco) performs on Sundays at 12:30 p.m. (and seasonally at other times) at the Degollado Theater. National and international artists appear at the theater as well. The Cabañas Cultural Institute presents various theater, dance and musical performances throughout the year. Chamber music recitals take place in the institute's Tolsá Chapel. The English-language *Guadalajara Reporter* publishes schedules of current events.

For something a little out of the ordinary, take in a performance at the Experimental Theater of Jalisco (Teatro Experimental de Jalisco), on Calzada Independencia Sur next to the entrance to Agua Azul Park. The University of Guadalajara's theater company is headquartered here. Performances are in Spanish; phone (33) 3619-1176.

## Special Events

Guadalajara's biggest annual event is the October Fair, or Fiestas de Octubre. This month-long artistic and cultural festival offers concerts, ballet, opera, theater, movies, folk art expositions and live music. Events take place at various locations, many in the vicinity of Plaza Tapatía, where outdoor stages and pavilions sprout. Hotel and ticket reservations are highly advised for the entire month of October and should be made in advance.

Major celebrations include Independence Day in mid-September and the return of the Virgin of Zapopan to the Basilica of Zapopan on Oct. 12 *(see Zapopan)*. Cultural events take place the last 2 weeks of February before the beginning of Lent.

Other festivities with a special *tapatío* flavor are the Day of the Three Wise Men on Jan. 6; the Tlaquepaque Ceramics Fair, in mid-June; the Day of St. James the Apostle in Tonalá on July 25, which features a mock battle between Indians and Spaniards; and Day of the Dead celebrations Nov. 1-2. Most of these are characterized by *tianguis* (open-air markets), *charreadas* (rodeos), fireworks, dancing, mariachi bands and tempting spreads of regional food.

The Christmas holidays in Guadalajara are celebrated with *pastorelas,* folk representations of the birth of Christ, and *posadas,* re-enactments of Mary and Joseph's search for an inn. The city's museums often participate, offering traditional dance programs and providing special refreshments. Families also get together to take part in candlelight processions to each other's homes, and nativity scenes are set up in churches and plazas. If you'll be visiting during December, check with your hotel, the Jalisco State Tourism Office or the bulletin boards at museums for further information.

© stacyarturogi / Shutterstock.com

This ends listings for Guadalajara.
The following page resumes the alphabetical listings
of cities in Central Mexico.

# GUANAJUATO, GUANAJUATO (C-2)
pop. 171,709

Guanajuato (gwah-nah-HWAH-toh), capital of the same-named state, is one of Mexico's most beautifully preserved colonial cities, with leafy plazas and flowerpot-bedecked alleyways that exude charm. In an age of global information sharing and pop culture predominance, it is a city that has remained thoroughly Mexican in character.

Founded by the Spanish in 1548, Guanajuato (the name means "place of frogs") enjoyed early prosperity thanks to the rich deposits of silver that were extracted from surrounding mines. The establishment of a university by the Jesuits in 1732 ensured its reputation as an intellectual center and seat of learning.

Ironically, the city that became wealthy under Spanish rule also played an integral role in the struggle for Mexican freedom. In 1810, Guanajuato was invaded by a motley army of peasant farmers, miners and other disenfranchised citizens under the leadership of Father Miguel Hidalgo de Costilla. The town was sacked, and many Spanish Royalists—mining barons and the landowning elite—were massacred. But the revolutionaries didn't remain in control for long; the following year Hidalgo and three of his leaders were executed and their heads were hung from hooks protruding from the four corners of the town granary, where they remained impaled until Mexico finally won its independence in 1821.

Guanajuato is built on the slopes of a narrow, rugged canyon. Houses hug the canyon's different levels, with the foundation of one house sitting at the rooftop level of the one below. Gas stations and other concessions to contemporary life are restricted to the suburbs and outlying areas, allowing the downtown core to maintain a Spanish-influenced architectural integrity, and the twisting streets are a delight to explore.

## Practicalities

The nearest airport is Del Bajío International Airport (also known as Guanajuato/León International), about 30 kilometers (18 miles) from downtown. American, Delta and United offer nonstop service from select U.S. cities. Aeroméxico and low-cost carrier Volaris offer flights from Mexico City and Tijuana, respectively. The taxi ride to Guanajuato takes about 30 minutes and the fare is around 400 pesos (about $30 U.S.). *For additional information about airlines see Arriving by Air, page p. 42.*

Central Camionera, the main bus station, is about 6 kilometers (3.5 miles) southwest of downtown. First-class bus service is offered by ETN and Omnibus de México. There is frequent service between Mexico City's Terminal del Norte (North Bus Terminal) and Guanajuato. The Flecha Amarilla line has service from Guanajuato to San Miguel de Allende several times daily. *For additional information about buses see Bus Service, page p. 52.*

© AAA

Avenida Subterránea Miguel Hidalgo is for inbound traffic only with street level exits just beyond the Hidalgo Market, at Plazuela de los Ángeles, at Jardín Unión and terminus at Plaza de Allende. It is 3 km. long.

**Guanajuato**
GUANAJUATO
Attractions

| Kilometers | |
|---|---|
| 0 | 0.3 |
| Miles | |
| 0 | 0.2 |

3017-16

Local buses navigate several routes. One runs from downtown east along Mex. 110, passing several hotels along the way, and heads in the direction of the La Valenciana Church, the La Valenciana Mine and the town of Dolores Hidalgo. Buses designated "Presa-Estación" basically travel from one end of town to the other; they use the subterranean avenue if going toward the La Olla Reservoir and above-ground streets if going toward the train station. Another line takes tourists to the popular Mummy Museum. All schedules are subject to frequent change; the State Tourism Office can provide helpful bus information.

The city's high altitude guarantees mild weather year-round. Daytime highs are usually in the low or mid 70s except in April and May, when they climb into the low 80s. Nighttime lows are usually in the 40s and 50s, although winter nights can be chillier. Showers or thunderstorms occur from June through September, but the weather is usually dry and sunny. Bring a couple of sweaters and a jacket or light coat if you're visiting in the fall or winter. Comfortable walking shoes are a must, not only for the cobblestoned street surfaces but for climbing the numerous hills.

Guanajuato has a large student population and an active social and cultural life. The city is small, and most establishments are casual and friendly. Tourist crime occurs infrequently, and personal safety is essentially a matter of taking the usual common sense precautions.

## City Layout

Attempting to negotiate Guanajuato's narrow, congested and utterly illogical streets by car is a classic exercise in frustration. Furthermore, there are practically no local car rentals available. Most maps, including those available from the State Tourism Office, fail to show the winding, often unmarked streets in perspective. If you're staying at a hotel outside of the city, use local transportation for forays into and around downtown. Taxi stands (sitios) are located around Plaza de la Paz and the Jardín Unión, and taxis also can be hailed on the street. Always establish the fare before setting out.

Unlike many Mexican cities, where the streets are laid out in an orderly grid pattern radiating from a central plaza, downtown Guanajuato's twisting thoroughfares simply follow the dictates of the terrain. The two main streets, Avenida Juárez and Calle Pocitos, run one way roughly east to west. Juárez is closed to vehicular traffic east of the basilica, and past Jardín Unión its name changes to Avenida Sopeña. Pocitos runs north of Juárez and changes names from Lascuraín de Retana to Pocitos to 28 de Septiembre as it travels from east to west.

Traffic going west to east uses Avenida Subterránea Miguel Hidalgo, an antiquated tunnel which in the mid-1960s was transformed into a vehicular route for inbound traffic. It follows the original course of the Río Guanajuato under the city—roughly parallel with Avenida Juárez/Sopeña—for about 1.5 miles. Mexican engineers rerouted the river following a flood in 1905.

Street-level exits are just beyond the Hidalgo Market, at Plazuela de los Angeles, at Jardín Unión and at the subway terminus at Plaza Allende.

A confusing network of subsidiary tunnels attempts to alleviate the heavy traffic; the city's layout was never intended to accommodate automobiles. Even horse-drawn carriages cannot fully negotiate the steep streets. It's much easier for visitors to explore on foot. Another option is to take a guided tour. Transportes Turísticos de Guanajuato offers excursions in and around the city aboard a streetcar called "El Quijote." The office is underneath the Basilica of Our Lady of Guanajuato (Basílica Nuestra Señora de Guanajuato) on Plaza de la Paz; phone (473) 732-2134.

The best starting point for the Panoramic Highway (Carretera Panoramica), the scenic loop road that travels around Guanajuato's periphery, is from Mex. 110 just south of the Real de Minas Hotel (north of downtown). This route offers easy access to such attractions as the El Pípila Statue, Acacia Park, La Olla Dam, the Mummy Museum at the city cemetery (El Panteón) and the Church of La Valenciana.

Grupo Turístico Minero offers guided, 4-hour van tours of the city that include a visit to such attractions as the La Valenciana Mine, the Mummy Museum and the Statue of El Pípila. Tours depart daily; the fee is 280 pesos (about $20.70 U.S.) per person. Advance reservations are required; phone (473) 734-1669.

Discovered in 1760, La Valenciana Mine at one point was said to produce more than a fifth of the world's silver. The outer walls were peaked to symbolize the crown of Spain. It was reactivated in the late 1960s after decades of lying in ruin, and still brings up silver, lead and nickel. The mine shaft is exceptionally wide and more than 1,500 feet deep; visitors can look down it but are not permitted to descend.

## Events

Guanajuato's biggest cultural event is the annual Cervantino International Arts Festival (Festival Internacional Cervantino). University of Guanajuato students first began presenting entremeses— skits—of Spanish author Miguel de Cervantes' work in the early 1950s at the Plaza de San Roque.

For 2 to 3 weeks in October (sometime extending into early November), Mexican as well as international actors, dance companies and symphony orchestras perform at plazas and in theaters across the city. Theater performances are reserved, paying events, but the open-air performances in the plazas are often free. The farcical entremeses, presented mostly in pantomime, are easily grasped even if you don't understand Spanish. Ballet, films and classical, jazz and rock concerts round out the offerings.

The festival draws huge crowds and the narrow streets can become extremely congested, something to keep in mind if you're staying in the city. Reservations need to be made months in advance for the top events; if Guanajuato hotels are full, an alternative is to stay in San Miguel de Allende. For additional information contact Festival Cervantino, Plaza

San Francisquito #1, Colonia Pastita, 36090 Guanajuato, Gto.; phone (473) 731-1221. Tickets can be ordered through Ticketmaster in Mexico City; phone (55) 5325-9000.

Day of the Dead, or Día de Los Muertos, is celebrated Nov. 1 and 2. *Posadas*, re-enactments of Mary and Joseph's search for an inn, take place during the Christmas season. The arrival of the Virgin of Guanajuato is commemorated in late May and again on Aug. 9. These festivals usually include fireworks, regional dance groups and sometimes a parade.

## Shopping

The Hidalgo Market (Mercado Hidalgo), on Avenida Juárez west of the city center, occupies a building that resembles, with its glass windows and elaborate iron grillwork, a Victorian train station. There are two levels, with a peripheral walkway above roamed by souvenir vendors and containing shops selling crafts, clothing and sombreros.

The produce, meat and sweet stands are where local families do their grocery shopping. Little eateries offer quick bites of typical Mexican fare. Everything from fruit to honey-laced candy is sold along row after row of these tidy stalls. Outside, flower vendors set up on the sidewalks. The market is open daily.

Bargainers may want to focus their skills on pottery purchases. Numerous types are sold, including the highly glazed, pale green and blue ceramic designs known as majolica or Talavera. Ceramic mugs and other items fashioned by Gorky González, a local artisan renowned for his Talavera-influenced work, are available at lower prices here than at his studio, which is located on Calle Pastita near Embajadoras Park (Parque de las Embajadoras).

## Touring Guanajuato's Parks and Plazas

Jardín Unión, in the center of town, is the city's lively focal point. This elegant park has old-fashioned lampposts, tiled, tree-shaded walkways, outdoor cafes and a band shell that is the scene of frequent musical performances. Most of Guanajuato's downtown attractions are within easy walking distance. It's just off Avenida Juárez/Sopeña, and can be used as a point of orientation while exploring the downtown area.

Facing one side of this triangle-shaped plaza are the opulent Teatro Juárez and the Church of San Diego. Commissioned by Franciscan missionaries, the church was almost destroyed by floodwaters and rebuilt in the late 18th century. The doorway is a good example of the flamboyant Churrigueresque architectural style. Just off Jardín Unión is Plazuela del Baratillo, a peaceful spot for relaxing in the *sol* (sun) or *sombra* (shade) to the sounds of a gurgling fountain, a gift to the city from Emperor Maximilian.

West of Jardín Unión is Plaza de la Paz, anchored by the Basilica of Our Lady of Guanajuato, or Parish Church (La Parroquia). Adjacent to the plaza is the University of Guanajuato. Opulent private residences dating from the 18th and 19th centuries are a reminder of the days when silver poured out of the region's mines.

Continue down Avenida Juárez to Plazuela de Los Angeles, where the walls of the shops and houses are painted in bright colors. Close by is the Alley of the Kiss (Callejón del Beso), an intimate passageway narrow enough to permit a smooch from balconies on either side of the street; according to local legend, two lovers who were kept apart did just that.

Near Jardín de la Reforma, a shady park along Avenida Juárez a block or so from the Hidalgo Market, is Plaza de San Roque, a small square that is the site of many of the *entremeses* presented by university students as part of the Cervantes festival in October.

Equally engaging are the *callejoneadas* (kah-yeh-hoh-neh-AH-dahs), or serenades, that take place at Guanajuato's plazas or in the city streets on various weekend evenings. During these frolics, strolling student ensembles called *estudiantinas* dress in medieval costumes and sing songs with guitar and mandolin accompaniment. The public is welcome to join in the merriment.

The reservoir impounded by La Olla Dam (Presa de la Olla), built in the mid-18th century, provides Guanajuato's supply of drinking water as well as a recreational setting favored by local weekenders. This residential area at the east end of town can be reached via Paseo de la Presa or by taking a city bus designated "Presa."

Antillón Park is just below the dam. Flower gardens and a large statue of Father Miguel Hidalgo distinguish Acacia Park; picnicking is permitted, and rowboats can be rented for paddling around on the man-made lake.

**Guanajuato State Tourism Office (Coordinadora Estatal de Turismo):** Plaza de la Paz #14, across from the Basilica of Our Lady of Guanajuato. Open Mon.-Fri. 9-7:30, Sat. 10-5, Sun. 10-2. **Phone:** (473) 732-1982.

**BASILICA OF OUR LADY OF GUANAJUATO** (Basilica Nuestra Señora de Guanajuato) is on Plaza de la Paz. Construction of the church began in 1671 and was completed 25 years later, financed by the region's wealthy miners. The baroque-style exterior features an impressive dome and is a beautiful yellow-orange in color. The celebrated image of the Virgin of Guanajuato, brought from Granada, Spain, in 1557, was a gift from King Philip II. Mounted on a pedestal of solid silver, the jewel-bedecked wooden statue is said to date from the seventh century and is considered to be the oldest piece of Christian art in Mexico. The interior also contains magnificent chandeliers, ornamental frescoes and Miguel Cabrera paintings.

Late afternoon is a good time to visit; after viewing the interior, take a stroll around the plaza, where vendors sell grilled corn on the cob, fresh mango slices, souvenirs and handicrafts. **Hours:** Open daily. **Cost:** Free.

**CHURCH OF LA COMPAÑIA** (Iglesia de la Compañia) is at Calle Pocitos and Navarro near the University of Guanajuato. It was built by the Jesuits 1747-65 and then abandoned when the order was expelled from New Spain. Restored in the 19th century, the church has a lovely, typically ornate Churrigueresque exterior of rose-colored stone, intricately carved wooden doors and a large dome. The interior contains paintings by 18th-century artist Miguel Cabrera.

**CHURCH OF LA VALENCIANA** (Iglesia de la Valenciana) is about 4 km (2.5 mi.) n.w. of downtown on Mex. 110, toward Dolores Hidalgo; some parking is available along the road by the church. The Church of San Cayetano (Iglesia de San Cayetano) is commonly referred to as La Valenciana. It dates from 1788 and was constructed by the Don Antonio de Obregón Alconcer family, wealthy owners of the La Valenciana Mine.

The pink-stone facade, with its profusion of delicate carvings, is a fine example of the florid Churrigueresque architectural style. But it is the interior that is truly breathtaking, adorned with a soaring gilt and gold-leaf, ornately carved *retablo* (wall behind the main altar), which includes many life-size statues of saints and biblical figures. Two additional *retablos*, each as tall and as magnificent as the central decoration, grace the transepts on either side. Three huge oil paintings by Luis Monray Pinto depicting biblical stories hang along the side walls of the narthex.

On Dec. 8 a fiesta honors The Immaculate Conception (La Purísima). Buses designated "Valenciana" run from downtown Guanajuato to the church, which has provided services since its inception in the late 18th century. **Time:** Allow 30 minutes minimum. **Hours:** Mass daily at 10 a.m.; church open daily 7-7. **Cost:** Free.

**CUBILETE MOUNTAIN** (Cerro del Cubilete) is about 16 km (10 mi.) w. of Guanajuato off Mex. 110, on the way to Silao. It is said to be the geographical center of Mexico and draws many pilgrims. A gravel road climbs to the 9,440-foot summit, which is surmounted by a 65-foot-tall bronze statue of Christ the King (Cristo Rey). From here are superb views of the Bajío region, a fertile green plain dotted with lakes and isolated mountain peaks. City buses travel to the summit; the trip takes about 90 minutes.

**DIEGO RIVERA MUSEUM** (Museo Casa Diego Rivera) is at Calle Pocitos #47, 3 blks. n. of the Guanajuato State Museum; street parking is very limited. The city's most celebrated native son and one of Mexico's most esteemed muralists lived here the first 9 years of his life. The first floor of the home has been restored and is furnished with turn-of-the-20th-century antiques. The second and third floors contain more than 90 paintings, sketches and watercolors that trace the development of his style, influenced by both 20th-century Cubism and ancient Mayan techniques.

Political beliefs strongly informed Rivera's work, as evidenced by a sketch for the 1933 mural commissioned by Rockefeller Center in New York City that was destroyed because it included a portrait of Vladimir Lenin. Exhibit information is in Spanish. Restrooms are provided. **Time:** Allow 1 hour minimum. **Hours:** Tues.-Sat. 10-6:30, Sun. 10-2:30. **Cost:** 20 pesos (about $1.50 U.S.). **Phone:** (473) 732-1197.

**DON QUIXOTE ICONOGRAPHIC MUSEUM** (Museo Iconográfico del Quijote) is at Manuel Doblado #1, about 2 blks. s.e. of Jardín Unión in an area of very limited street parking. Housing more than 700 pieces of art, this fascinating museum provides a look at the enduring literary character created by Spanish author Miguel de Cervantes as seen through the eyes of Pedro Coronel, Salvador Dalí, Pablo Picasso and other artists.

The pieces are displayed in rooms surrounding a three-story courtyard. Quixote and trusty companion Sancho Panza are executed in a variety of media, including paintings, sculpture, stained-glass windows, clocks, painted eggs, woodcarvings and one large leaf, complete with veins, that shows Cervantes' hero in profile on horseback. There also are huge wall murals and quartz, bronze, silver and porcelain statuary. Exhibit information is in Spanish. Restrooms are provided. **Time:** Allow 1 hour minimum. **Hours:** Tues.-Sat. 9:30-6:45, Sun. noon-6:45. Closed major holidays. Phone ahead to confirm schedule. **Cost:** 30 pesos (about $2.20 U.S.); free to all Tues. **Phone:** (473) 732-6721 or (473) 732-3376.

**GOVERNMENT PALACE** (Palacio de Gobierno) is on Paseo de la Presa near the La Olla Dam. It stands on the site of the old house of the Marqués of San Clemente. The original building was destroyed by a flood; the present structure was completed in 1903. It evokes a European elegance, enhanced by the use of Guanajuato green sandstone.

**GUANAJUATO CITY MUSEUM** (Museo del Pueblo de Guanajuato) is at Calle Pocitos #7 near the University of Guanajuato. Housed in a 17th-century mansion, this art museum is the former home of Mexican muralist José Chávez Morado. Three floors of exhibits include Morado's personal collection of colonial-era religious paintings, dramatic Morado murals, works by contemporary Mexican artists, and collections of miniatures and folk art. **Hours:** Tues.-Sat. 10-6:30, Sun. 10-2:30. **Cost:** 20 pesos (about $1.50 U.S.). **Phone:** (473) 732-2990.

**HOTEL POSADA SANTA FE** is at Plaza Principal #12 at Jardín Unión. The hotel houses a collection of paintings by Don Manuel Leal, a Guanajuato native who dramatically documented his perceptions of the city's history. The paintings hang in the hotel's lavishly appointed, colonial-style public areas. **Phone:** (473) 732-0084.

**JUÁREZ THEATER** (Teatro Juárez) faces Jardín Unión; street parking in the vicinity is very limited. Very European in appearance, it is a deliciously opulent reminder of Guanajuato's late 19th-century prosperity. The exterior is impressive, with tall columns, ascending steps, branching lampposts, bronze lions and statues of the Greek muses at the roof line.

Inside there are four levels of seating, private boxes and a smoking room with circular velvet settees, heavy drapes and a marble floor. The Moorish-style ornamentation includes dazzlingly intricate red-and-gold patterns on the walls and ceiling. It's a suitably grand setting for performances associated with October's Cervantino International Arts Festival.

Call for festival performance schedule. **Hours:** The interior can be viewed Tues.-Sun. 9-1:45 and 5-7:45, rehearsal and performance schedules permitting. **Cost:** 35 pesos (about $2.60 U.S.). **Phone:** (473) 732-0183.

**MARFIL** is about 3 km (2 mi.) s.w. of Guanajuato off Mex. 110; the old road to Marfil (Camino Antiguo a Marfil) winds into a valley. At the height of this former mining town's prosperity in the late 19th century, numerous silver mines operated and luxurious mansions lined the streets. Marfil was devastated in 1905 when La Olla Dam burst, killing many of the residents. In recent years Marfil has experienced a rebirth, with ongoing renovations sprucing up some of the long-neglected haciendas of the mine owners.

**Ex-Hacienda of San Gabriel de Barrera** (Museo Ex-Hacienda San Gabriel de Barrera) is at Camino Antiguo a Marfil Km marker 2.5, opposite the Hotel Misión Guanajuato. This former hacienda, which contains paintings and elegant Victorian-era furniture as well as a small chapel with an ornately carved *retablo* (decorative wall) behind the altar, offers a peek at the lifestyle enjoyed by privileged late 19th- and early 20th-century Mexicans. The gardens are a delight—more than a dozen, all beautifully maintained, whimsically named and distinctive with regard to plants and statuary.

**Time:** Allow 1 hour minimum. **Hours:** Daily 9-6. **Cost:** 30 pesos (about $2.20 U.S.). The fee to use a camera is 21 pesos, a video camera 26 pesos. **Phone:** (473) 732-0619. 🍴

**MUMMY MUSEUM** (Museo de Las Momias) is w. of downtown on Calzada del Panteón, next to the city cemetery (El Panteón). This is the city's ghastliest attraction. Dryness, minerals and natural salts in the soil all helped preserve some 120 corpses, which escaped decomposition to a remarkable degree.

The mummies—men, women and children, some still with shoes and hair—are displayed behind glass with various frozen expressions, giving visitors the morbid thrill of viewing them face to face. This museum is not recommended for the squeamish or the claustrophobic (it's small and often crowded). City buses and taxis that can be boarded or hailed along Avenida Juárez will stop within walking distance of the museum. **Hours:** Daily 9-6 (also Fri.-Sun. 6-6:30 p.m.). **Cost:** 56 pesos (about $4.15 U.S.); 37 pesos (ages 6-12). The fee to use a still camera (no flash) is 21 pesos. **Parking:** 7 pesos per hour. **Phone:** (473) 732-0639.

**STATE HISTORICAL MUSEUM** (Alhóndiga de Granaditas) is at Mendizábal and 28 de Septiembre (Calle Pocitos), n.w. of the city center; street parking in the immediate area is very limited. This massive 1809 structure was originally a seed and grain warehouse.

Among the varied exhibits are Indian weavings, saddles, leather clothing, hats, tools, pottery, *Carnaval* masks and a full-sized kitchen with period displays of pots and foods. Upstairs are historical exhibits and a number of pre-Columbian stone artifacts. Murals by José Chávez Morado depicting revolutionary themes embellish the Alhóndiga's stairwells. Bronze busts of War of Independence heroes Hidalgo, Jiménez, Aldama and Allende preside in a hall illuminated by an eternal flame.

Permanent and temporary exhibitions feature the work of Mexican and international artists, and a fine exhibit depicts Guanajuato's historical, social and mining importance through photographs and various artifacts. Exhibit information is in Spanish. Restrooms are provided. **Time:** Allow 1 hour minimum. **Hours:** Tues.-Sat. 10-5:30, Sun. 10-2:30. Closed major holidays. **Cost:** 57 pesos (about $4.20 U.S.). **Phone:** (473) 732-1180.

**STATUE OF EL PÍPILA** (Estatua de El Pípila) overlooks Guanajuato from a steep hill to the e. of the Jardín Unión. It immortalizes Juan José Martínez, a miner who set fire to the front door of the Alhóndiga de Granaditas, the massive granary where Spanish Royalists took refuge in 1810 during an attack on the city by Mexican revolutionaries. The dramatic, 30-foot-high figure, bearing a torch, keeps watch over the city below. This vantage point affords an outstanding view of Guanajuato's architectural landmarks.

Buses designated "Pípila" take visitors to the monument; parking for other vehicles is free. El Pípila also is accessible by a steep climb on foot (wear sturdy walking shoes). To get there, take Calle Sopeña east to Callejón del Calvario and watch for the sign that says "Al Pípila." An incline railway (funicular) takes passengers up the hill to a terminal just below the monument. **Hours:** Funicular runs Mon.-Fri. 8 a.m.-10 p.m., Sat. 9 a.m.-10 p.m., Sun. 10-9. **Cost:** Monument free; funicular 18 pesos (about $1.35 U.S.) one way, 36 pesos round trip.

**UNIVERSITY OF GUANAJUATO** is on Calle Pocitos/Lascurain de Retana. The school has been in almost continuous operation since it was opened by Jesuits in 1732 at the request of Spain's King Philip V. It became a state university in 1945. Ten years later a modern new addition with interconnecting patios and open-air hallways was built, complete with Moorish-style facade. The city's cultural arts showcase, it offers theater, symphonies and student performances of Cervantes' *entremeses* (short comic presentations).

## JOCOTEPEC, JALISCO (D-1) pop. 42,164

Founded in 1528, Jocotepec (hoh-koh-teh-PEHK) sits at the western end of Lake Chapala. This popular retreat is known for hand-woven items, which are still produced on old-fashioned looms. Local artisans turn out bedspreads, table coverings, wall hangings and *sarapes*. There are several small shops along Calle Hidalgo, and it's possible to watch the weavers at work.

## LAGOS DE MORENO, JALISCO (C-2)
pop. 153,817

An attractive city in the Jaliscan highlands, Lagos de Moreno (LAH-gos day moh-REH-noh) is located at the intersection of two major highways, Mex. 45 and Mex. 80. Designated a national historic monument, it has a downtown riverside park, colonial mansions and tiny plazas that pop up in unexpected places.

Montecristo's House, downtown at Calle Hidalgo #494, has beautiful exterior stonework; this former government building houses an antique shop. On the main plaza stands a massive baroque-style church, and surrounding it are handsome colonial mansions. About 10 blocks north of the plaza is the Templo del Calvario. Although the monastery, which overlooks the city from a steep hillside perch, is not open to visitors, those who make the long, somewhat arduous climb up the hill will be rewarded with beautiful views, especially around sunset.

## MORELIA, MICHOACÁN (D-2)
pop. 729,279

**Note:** For current information about safety/security issues in Morelia and the state of Michoacán, refer to the U.S. State Department website (travel.state.gov).

Capital of the state of Michoacán, Morelia (Moh-REH-lee-ah) was founded in 1541. It was first known as Valladolid, after the Spanish birthplace of New Spain's first viceroy, Antonio de Mendoza. The name was changed in 1828 to honor native son José María Morelos, who became a general for and hero of the Mexican War of Independence.

Local building ordinances require that all new construction in the historic downtown area conform to the prevailing, richly decorated Spanish colonial architectural style. The Church and College of las Rosas (Templo y Colegio de las Rosas), established in the late 16th century as a Dominican convent, is home to the oldest school for liturgical music in the Western Hemisphere. This impressive building is on Avenida Santiago Tapia, 2 blocks north of Plaza de Armas, the main plaza. Visitors are welcome to attend rehearsals of Morelia's famed Boys' Choir, which has given performances in Rome and at Carnegie Hall.

An aqueduct (El Acueducto) dating from 1789 was once the primary means of bringing water to the city. It extends for more than a mile and is made up of 253 arches—the tallest 25 feet in height—that are illuminated at night. Some of the arches line two sides of Parque Villalongín and shelter small shops and private homes.

Extending east from this small park is Calzada Fray Antonio de San Miguel, a tree-shaded, three-block-long pedestrian street lined on both sides with stone benches. It runs to the Guadalupe Sanctuary (Santuario de Guadalupe) on Calzada Ventura Puente. This typically lavish baroque church was built in the early 18th century, although the highly ornate interior dates from the early 20th century.

The Michoacán State Museum (Museo del Estado) is half a block west of Plaza de Armas at Av. Guillermo Prieto #176. It has some nice examples of pre-Columbian pottery, as well as a collection of clothing and household items and a few paintings of local 18th- and 19th-century notables. The building housing the museum was once the residence of self-designated Mexican emperor Agustín Iturbide. Phone (443) 313-0629.

Folkloric dance performances and music recitals take place regularly; check with the State Tourism Office for schedule information. Band concerts enliven Plaza de Armas on Sundays. The Morelia Fair (Feria de Morelia), held in mid-May, is an old-fashioned state fair showcasing livestock and produce displays; it also features regional dance performances and a celebration of the city's founding in 1541. Musicians perform at various locations during the International Music Festival (Festival Internacional de Música) in late July and early August.

## Practicalities

Aeroméxico Connect offers daily flights between Mexico City and Morelia's Francisco Mújica Airport, about 30 kilometers (19 miles) north of the city. United flies nonstop from Houston. Volaris offers nonstop flights from Chicago and Los Angeles. Schedules change frequently, and flight times should be confirmed in advance. Airport taxi services charge about $25 (U.S.) between the airport and the city center.

First-class bus service is offered by ETN between Morelia and Mexico City's Terminal de Autobuses del Poniente (Western Terminal), as well as to Guadalajara and Guanajuato. The central bus station is near the intersection of avenidas Eduardo Ruíz and Gomez Farias, a couple of blocks northwest of the main plaza; a newer bus station is on Periférico República, across from the football stadium on the northwestern city outskirts.

Buses, taxicabs and *combis* (usually white VW vans) all provide public transportation. Buses can be helpful for getting to and from Cuauhtémoc Woods Park and the Aqueduct via Avenida Madero, but they move slowly along the crowded streets during rush hours. *Combi* vehicles have different-colored stripes depending on their destination. Taxis are not metered. The average in-town fare is normally about $3-$5 (U.S.); agree on the amount before getting in the cab.

## City Layout

Large, tree-lined Plaza de Armas is bounded on the north by Avenida Francisco I. Madero and on the south by Calle Allende. It also is known as the Plaza of the Martyrs (Plaza de los Mártires) in honor of the rebel priests who were executed during Mexico's War of Independence. The square is surrounded by colonial-era buildings, and this part of the city is pedestrian-friendly (although congested with vehicles

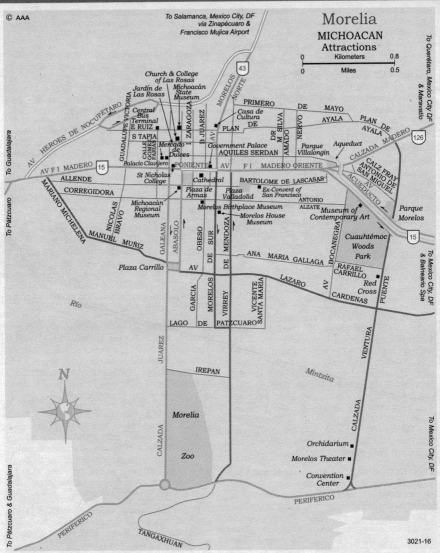

Morelia
MICHOACAN
Attractions

and vendors). Almost all of Morelia's visitor attractions are within walking distance of the plaza.

Downtown street names change north and south of Avenida Madero (Mex. 15), which is the principal east-west artery. Two blocks west of Plaza de Armas, Avenida López Rayón becomes Gómez Farias north of Avenida Madero. A block west of the plaza, Calzada Galeana becomes Nigromante north of Madero. Avenida Abasolo, which runs along the west side of Plaza de Armas, becomes Guillermo Prieto north of Madero; a block east of Plaza de Armas, Avenida García Obeso becomes Juárez north of Madero.

East-west thoroughfares change name at the cathedral. West of the cathedral Avenida Madero is Poniente (Pte.); to the east it is Oriente (Ote.). Calle Allende, which runs along the south side of Plaza de Armas, becomes Valladolid once east of the cathedral.

**Michoacán State Tourism Office (Secretaría de Turismo):** adjoining Clavijero Palace, downtown at Calle Nigromante #79. In addition to maps and visitor information, the office can provide details about free guided walking tours of the city center. Open Mon.-Fri. 9-8, Sat.-Sun. 9-4. **Phone:** 01 (800) 450-2300 (toll-free long distance within Mexico).

**BALNEARIO SPA** (Balneario Cointzio) is about 9 km (6 mi.) w. of Morelia on Mex. 15 to the junction with Avenida Cointzio, then about 6 km (4 mi.) s. The spa, at the base of a cliff where mineral waters of 100 F (37 C) emerge, includes two swimming pools, a wading pool, bathhouse, refreshment facilities and bungalows. **Hours:** Daily 8-6. **Cost:** (pool and bathhouse access) 50 pesos (about $3.70 U.S.); 30 pesos (children). Private bungalow rentals cost extra. **Phone:** (443) 320-0623.

**CATHEDRAL** is on the e. side of Plaza de Armas, facing Av. Madero. One of Mexico's most beautiful churches, it took more than a century (1640-1744) to build. Exterior highlights are the rose-colored stone facade, two elaborately decorated towers, and a colonial fence and gates.

Inside are religious relics and paintings as well as a magnificent three-story organ with 4,600 pipes, reputed to be one of the largest in the world. The cathedral is the site of the International Organ Festival, held annually in early May. A music program and fireworks display takes place every Saturday evening.

**Time:** Allow 1 hour minimum. **Hours:** Daily 6 a.m.-9 p.m. **Cost:** Free; donations are accepted. GT

**CLAVIJERO PALACE** (Palacio Clavijero), downtown at Calle Nigromante #79, is a former Jesuit college. The main patio features lofty colonnades and beautiful pink stonework. Cultural events take place in the large open-air gallery.

Under the arcade on the western side of the complex is the Candy Market (Mercado de Dulces). Candy-making traditions begun by European nuns are still carried out at this shrine to Mexican confections. Worth trying are the many flavors of *ate*, a pasty concoction made with fresh fruit to which sugar and water are added. Perhaps the biggest holiday for sweets shops is the *Day of the Dead* Nov. 1-2, when they turn out an array of sugar skulls, skeletons and other ghostly creations. **Hours:** Clavijero Palace open Tues.-Sun. 10-6. Closed Christmas and Dec. 31. Candy Market open daily 9 a.m.-10 p.m. **Cost:** Free. **Phone:** (443) 312-0412.

**CONVENTION CENTER** (Centro de Convenciones) is s.e. of downtown, at the intersection of Calzada Ventura Puente and the Periférico (loop road) that encircles the city. This complex of buildings is situated in a reasonably well-groomed park. Convention meetings and cultural events take place at the Morelos Theater (Teatro Jose María Morelos). The Orchid House (Orquidario) is a greenhouse containing more than 3,000 varieties that bloom at various times. The Planetarium (Planetario de Morelia) presents IMAX movies and star shows on a domed screen.

**Hours:** Orchid greenhouse open Mon.-Fri. 9-6, Sat.-Sun. 3-6; phone for planetarium show schedule. **Cost:** Greenhouse admission 10 pesos (about 75c U.S.). Planetarium show and IMAX movie prices vary. **Phone:** (443) 314-6150 for general Convention Center information, or (443) 314-2465 for the planetarium.

**CUAUHTÉMOC WOODS PARK** (Bosque Cuauhtémoc) is about 12 blks. e. of Plaza de Armas, just s. of Av. Acueducto (Mex. 15). This is the city's largest green space and a popular Sunday picnic spot.

On the park's northeast side, in the small Plaza Morelos, is a statue of the patriot on horseback. **Hours:** Daily during daylight hours. **Cost:** Free.

**Museum of Contemporary Art** (Museo de Arte Contemporaneo) is on the park's northern border at Av. Acueducto #18. Housed in an early 19th-century mansion, it exhibits works by both local and international artists. **Hours:** Mon.-Fri. 10-8, Sat.-Sun. 10-6. **Cost:** Free. **Phone:** (443) 312-5404.

**EX-CONVENT OF SAN FRANCISCO** (Ex-Convento de San Francisco) is on Calle Bartolomé de las Casas at Plaza Valladolid, 2 blks. e. of the cathedral. It dates from 1531. The founding of Morelia took place in the square in front of the church. Closely set columns give its interior courtyard a medieval look, unlike the open archways that characterize others in the city.

**House of Crafts** (Casa de las Artesanías) is in the church cloister. This combination museum and workshop displays lacquerware, woodcarvings, pottery, copper items, ceramics and other crafts from throughout the state. Artisans also can be observed at work. The quality of the handicrafts is excellent, and prices are accordingly high. **Hours:** Mon.-Sat. 8-4 and 5-8, Sun. 9-3:30. **Phone:** (443) 312-2486.

**GOVERNMENT PALACE** (Palacio de Gobierno) faces the cathedral across Av. Acueducto (Mex. 15). This baroque building, a former seminary, serves as the state capitol and is the colonial prototype for all new city edifices. Murals painted by Alfredo Zalce, Morelia's famed artist, depict scenes from Mexico's often violent history. **Hours:** Mon.-Fri. 8-5.

**HOUSE OF CULTURE** (Casa de Cultura) is 4 blks. n. of Plaza de Armas on Av. Morelos Norte. This peach-colored, architecturally striking building was salvaged from the ruins of a 350-year-old Carmelite monastery. The central courtyard serves as an open-air theater for drama, dance and music groups, and also provides studio space for artists. Ask about the free monthly brochure that lists upcoming city events.

Within the complex is the Museum of Masks, which displays a collection of ceremonial masks from around the country. **Hours:** Mon.-Fri. 10-3 and 4-8, Sat.-Sun. 10-6. **Cost:** Free. **Phone:** (443) 313-2141.

**MICHOACÁN REGIONAL MUSEUM** (Museo Regional Michoacano) is at Calle Allende #305, just s. of Plaza de Armas. A palace dating from the 18th century, it contains an art gallery, archeological and natural history exhibits, displays of colonial-era furniture and weaponry, and other historical items. Note the stairway mural by Alfredo Zalce depicting figures who have made a positive contribution to Mexico's national identity, as well as those who have not.

**Hours:** Tues.-Sun. 9-4:30. **Cost:** 47 pesos (about $3.50 U.S.). **Phone:** (443) 312-0407.

**MORELIA ZOO** (Zoológico de Morelia) is about 3 km (1.9 mi.) s. of the city center via Av. Juárez to Av. Camelinas. A variety of animal and bird species are displayed on the landscaped grounds. The zoo also has an aquarium, a small lake (rowboats are available for rent), a children's playground and the Casita Ecológica (Ecological House), where exhibits relate to the conservation of natural resources.

**Time:** Allow 2 hours minimum. **Hours:** Daily 10-5 (last admission one hour before closing). **Cost:** 22 pesos (about $1.65 U.S.); 12 pesos (ages 2-9). The aquarium, Ecological House and train and sightseeing shuttle transportation each have a small additional fee. **Phone:** (443) 299-3616. ⓘ 🏧

**MORELOS BIRTHPLACE MUSEUM** (Museo Casa Natal de Morelos) is at Corregidora #113 at García Obeso, a block south of Plaza de Armas. The Mexican revolutionary was born here in 1765. The house, erected more than a century earlier, is a national monument and contains a public library. An eternal flame burns in a courtyard garden behind the building. Eight rooms are devoted to Morelos memorabilia, portraits and documents. **Hours:** Mon.-Fri. 9-7:30, Sat.-Sun. 10-6:30. **Cost:** Free. **Phone:** (443) 312-2793.

**MORELOS HOUSE MUSEUM** (Museo Casa de Morelos) is 3 blks. s.e. of Plaza de Armas at Av. Morelos Sur and Calle Aldama. An example of Spanish colonial architecture, this was José María Morelos' residence beginning in 1801. His descendants lived in the house until 1910, when it was converted into a museum. Inside are personal belongings, manuscripts and exhibits relating to the War of Independence. All exhibits include background information in English.

**Hours:** Tues.-Sun. 9-4:45. Closed Christmas. **Cost:** 39 pesos (about $2.90 U.S.); free (ages 0-12 and 60+). Free to all Sun. **Phone:** (443) 313-2651.

**ST. NICHOLAS COLLEGE** (Colegio de San Nicolas) is at the corner of Calle Nigromante and Av. Madero Poniente, a block n.w. of Plaza de Armas. This is the oldest Mexican university still in operation, and was the second educational institution to be established in the Americas. Among its distinguished alumni were War of Independence leaders José María Morelos and Father Miguel Hidalgo. Interesting frescoes decorate the inner walls of the main building's colonial patio. **Hours:** Open Mon.-Fri. **Cost:** Free.

## Nearby Destinations

About 32 kilometers (20 miles) north of Morelia on Mex. 43 is an unusual 19th-century causeway across Lake Cuitzeo. The town of Cuitzeo, on the lake's north shore, contains one of the region's two 17th-century Augustinian monasteries; the other is in the city of Yuríria, north of Cuitzeo and a short distance east off Mex. 43.

Two national parks with scenic views are east of Morelia on Mex. 15. José María Morelos National Park (Parque Nacional Insurgente José María Morelos) is about 26 kilometers (16 miles) east of the city. Cerro de Garnica National Park (Parque Nacional Cerro de Garnica), which has two *miradores* (observation points) overlooking the rugged Mil

Cumbres (Thousand Peaks) landscape, is another 24 kilometers (15 miles) farther east. From here, Mex. 15 continues winding through steep mountains and dense forests to the town of Ciudad Hidalgo.

## PACHUCA, HIDALGO (D-3) pop. 267,862

Capital of the state of Hidalgo, Pachuca (pah-CHOO-kah) is the center of a rich mining district that once produced much of the world's silver. It is believed that silver was mined before the arrival of the Spanish, who founded the city in 1534, and the surrounding hills are honeycombed with tunnels and heaped with slag piles. Although operations declined markedly by the mid-20th century, mining's influence remains in everything from museums to such historic buildings as the Cajas Reales, where miners once deposited one-fifth of their finds in the form of taxes to the Spanish crown.

The narrow, winding streets of the city center are lined with well-preserved buildings dating to the colonial era; some of the most impressive are along Calle Hidalgo in the vicinity of Plaza de la Constitución, the main plaza. Standing in the middle of the plaza is a local landmark, the Reloj Monumental (Monumental Clock). It was dedicated in 1910 to commemorate the centennial of Mexico's independence. The neoclassic-style tower, approximately 125 feet tall, was built from white cantera stone (a type of volcanic rock) and features four sculpted female figures.

City government offices are housed in the Casa Colorada (Red Houses) complex, built toward the end of the 18th century by the Count of Regla, who made his fortune from Pachuca's silver mines. The name refers to the building facades, which have a reddish color.

Also of interest is the 1596 Church and Ex-Monastery of San Francisco, begun in 1596 and completed around 1660. The Spanish baroque-style stone exterior is impressive, but the interior is breathtaking, the white walls decorated with a profusion of gold-leaf ornamentation. Much of the adjoining monastery now houses Fototeca, Mexico's national photography archive. The Casasola Archives (Archivo Casasola) contains an extensive collection of photographs chronicling Mexican history from the late 19th to early 20th centuries; the Mexican Revolution of 1910-20 is particularly well documented.

## Nearby Destinations

Northwest of Pachuca via Mex. 85 is the town of Actópan (ahk-TOH-pahn). The name means "in thick and fertile soil," appropriate considering the surrounding agricultural region. It was founded July 8, 1546, 10 years after Augustinian friars had first journeyed to the area to Christianize the indigenous people. The Toltecs, meanwhile, had arrived even earlier—perhaps as far back as the seventh century.

In the nearby mountains are rock formations known locally as "The Friars," or Los Frailes. According to legend, these rocks were formed when God, angry with two friars who fell in love with a beautiful woman, turned all three people into stone.

Actópan's St. Nicholas Church and Monastery (Templo y Convento de San Nicolas), built in 1546, is distinguished by massive yet harmonious proportions. Impressive features include the patio, Renaissance-style doorway, frescoes and Gothic cloisters.

The 125-foot-tall bell tower, between the church entrance and the door to the monastery, resembles a giant vertical prism and suggests a Moorish influence. In the chapel ruins outside the church, parts of a mural fresco painted on the walls and ceiling can still be seen. Painted to impress newly converted Indians, it depicts the various punishments their souls would receive in hell if they were not good Christians.

Farther west on Mex. 85, between Actópan and Ixmiquilpan, is El Mezquital, an Otomí Indian region known for its embroidered clothing. Ixmiquilpan (ees-mee-KEEL-pahn) was once the Otomí capital. The town's Church and Monastery of St. Michael the Archangel is a huge, medieval-style fortress/complex and former monastery dating from 1550 and founded by the Order of St. Augustine. Inside the main church are Indian frescoes depicting imaginary beasts and warriors engaged in classic combat. The Church of El Carmen, graced by gilded altars, also is noteworthy.

Monday is market day in Ixmiquilpan; beautifully worked bags, mother-of-pearl-encrusted miniatures, guitars, wine bottle racks and Otomí belts are all for sale. Maguey is an important local crop. From this versatile plant paper, vinegar, molasses, medicines, rope and thread all are made. More potent derivatives include such alcoholic drinks as aguamiel, pulque and mezcal.

About 11 kilometers (7 miles) northeast of Pachuca via Mex. 105 is Mineral Real del Monte, an old mining town with narrow, extremely steep cobblestone streets and aged buildings reminiscent of a Cornish village. Most of the houses were built more than 200 years ago, after the Count of Regla abandoned area mining operations and an English firm took over. Mex. 105 continues on to the picturesque town of Omitlán.

About 3 kilometers (1.9 miles) past Omitlán a road branches eastward off Mex. 105 to Huasca, another village, and the nearby 18th-century smelting haciendas of Santa María Regla and San Miguel Regla. The two complexes are now historical lodgings, with rooms, restaurants and other facilities occupying many of the original buildings.

From Mineral Real del Monte a paved road travels northwest to another old mining town, Mineral El Chico. En route is El Chico National Park, an area of enormous rock formations and cool pine woods.

**Tourism Office (Secretaría de Turismo y Cultura del Estado de Hidalgo):** Blvd. Everardo Márquez #202. Open Mon.-Fri. 8:30-4:30. **Phone:** (771) 717-6400 (toll-free long distance within Mexico).

# PÁTZCUARO, MICHOACÁN (D-2)
pop. 87,794

**Note:** For current information about safety/security issues in Pátzcuaro and the state of Michoacán, refer to the U.S. State Department website (travel.state.gov).

Pátzcuaro (PAHTZ-kwah-roh), built on the hills sloping back from Lake Pátzcuaro, has red and cream-colored churches, mansions and other buildings erected during 3 centuries of Spanish rule. It also boasts one of Mexico's loveliest colonial plazas: Plaza Vasco de Quiroga, named for the first Spanish bishop of Michoacán, who introduced Christianity and various craft industries to the region's Tarascan Indians. A statue of "Tata Vasco" gazes down from a stone fountain in the center of the plaza.

A block north of Plaza Vasco de Quiroga is Plaza Gertrudis Bocanegra, named in honor of a woman who was executed by firing squad in 1818 for staunchly supporting the War of Independence. This is the commercial center of town; the market on the plaza's west side bustles with food, clothing and craft stalls.

Many of the colorful native dances performed throughout Mexico originated in this area. One of the most widely known is "Los Viejitos" (the little old men), a witty commentary on the manners and foibles of age.

First-class bus service is provided by the Herradura de Plata line between Mexico City's Terminal de Autobuses del Poniente (Western Terminal) and Pátzcuaro's Central Bus Station (Central Camionera), on the southwest outskirts on Avenida Circunvalación, a loop road encircling town.

**Michoacán State Tourism Office:** A branch office (Delegación Regional de Turismo) is at Calle Buena Vista #7, on the northwest side of Plaza de la Basilica (a block northeast of Plaza Vasco de Quiroga), near the parish church. Open Mon.-Fri. 10-3 and 4-7, Sat.-Sun. 10-2. **Phone:** (434) 342-1214 (English may not be spoken).

**BASILICA** (Parroquía de María Inmaculada de la Salud) stands on a hill a block n.e. of Plaza Vasco de Quiroga. The church dates from 1554. A likeness of the venerated Virgin of Health, positioned on the main altar, is made from a paste of crushed cornstalks mixed with a substance extracted from orchids. On Dec. 8 a fiesta honors the Virgin.

Every morning local women set up shop on the plaza adjacent to the church selling *corundas*. These triangular-shaped *tamales* are made of cornmeal dough, filled with meat or beans, then wrapped in cornhusks and steamed; they are frequently served with thick cream. An accompanying beverage might be *atole*, which is made from ground cornmeal or rice, served warm and often flavored with vanilla.

**HOUSE OF THE ELEVEN COURTYARDS** (Casa de Los Once Patios) is about a block s.e. of Plaza Vasco de Quiroga on Calle Madrigal de las Altas

Torres. Once a Dominican convent, it now houses the studios and galleries of painters and artisans, whom visitors can watch at work. The building also contains small shops (artesanías) selling regional handicrafts. **Hours:** Most shops open daily 10-7.

**JANITZIO ISLAND** (Isla Janitzio) is in the middle of Lake Pátzcuaro. The town of the same name is built in terraced fashion. Day of the Dead ceremonies held Nov. 1-2 include an all-night candlelight vigil in the village cemetery. The island is accessible by launch and is crowded with day visitors on weekends and holidays.

**Statue of José María Morelos** is on Janitzio Island. It has been called "quite an accomplishment in ugliness." The priest turned freedom fighter's raised arm tops the 130-foot-tall figure. A spiral staircase leads to the top; a balcony offering a panoramic view of the lake is in the cuff of his sleeve. The climb is arduous, and along the way the stairway walls are adorned with deteriorating murals depicting the man's life. **Hours:** Daily during daylight hours. **Cost:** 10 pesos (about 75c U.S.).

**LAKE PÁTZCUARO** is north of town. This is one of Mexico's highest lakes in terms of elevation. Its placid waters are dotted with islands, and a score or more of tiny Tarascan villages ring the shoreline, many accessible only by boat. The distinctive "butterfly" nets that once were the main tool of local fishermen now appear mostly for photographers. The lake still yields the pescado blanco, a small, almost transparent whitefish that is a local favorite.

**MUSEUM OF POPULAR ARTS** (Museo de Artes Populares) is a block s. of the Basilica off Calle Arciga, in the former Colegio de San Nicolás. The exhibits of Michoacán arts and crafts here include white lace rebozos (shawls), hand-painted ceramics and copperware. Behind the museum are the remains of some pre-Columbian stone structures. **Hours:** Tues.-Sun. 9-4:30. **Cost:** 47 pesos (about $3.50 U.S.). **Phone:** (434) 342-1029.

**STIRRUP PEAK** (El Estribo) is about 4 km (2.5 mi.) w. of the main plaza via Calle Ponce de León (beginning at the southwest corner of Plaza Vasco de Quiroga), following signs. Reached by a steep cobblestone road, it overlooks the lake and surrounding villages. The road can be walked or driven; if you choose to hike to the summit, which takes about an hour, it's safer to go on a weekend when there are other people around. 🚻

## PUEBLA, PUEBLA (D-4) pop. 1,539,819

See map page 322.

Puebla (PWEH-blah), capital and commercial center of the state of Puebla, is located in a large valley flanked by four volcanoes: Popocatépetl, Iztaccíhuatl, Malinche and Citlaltépetl (Pico de Orizaba). A product of the Spanish conquest, the city was established in 1531 by colonists to whom Spain had granted land and Indian slaves. Legend maintains that one of these founders, Bishop Julian Garcés, was visited by angels

who showed him where the new settlement was to be located—hence the nickname Puebla de los Angeles, or City of the Angels.

Strategically located along trade routes between the Gulf of Mexico coast and Mexico City, Puebla became a travel stopover between the coast and the interior, and also developed into a major center of the Catholic church; today's city is filled with churches and former convents. By the late 18th century it also was an important producer of pottery and textiles.

History was made at forts Loreto and Guadalupe on May 5, 1862, when about 4,000 poorly armed Mexicans defeated some 6,500 well-trained French troops who invaded the country as part of emperor Napoleon III's attempt to add to his empire. This rare Mexican military victory was greeted with a huge outpouring of national pride, and Gen. Ignacio Zaragoza became a hero, despite the fact that French reinforcements arrived the following year to install Archduke Maximilian as emperor of Mexico while president Benito Juárez's government was still in disarray. The event gave rise to the many Cinco de Mayo celebrations that take place in cities both north and south of the border.

Spain's legacy is still much evident in Puebla. Visually it is represented by the Talavera tiles (azulejos) that adorn buildings both old and new. These colorful hand-painted tiles were introduced from Talavera de la Reina, a town near Toledo. Spanish tilemakers settled in Puebla, which was the first city in Mexico to produce these decorative wares. You'll see Talavera tiles on church domes, fountains, rooftops and on walls in combination with red brick.

The china poblana dress, the national folkloric costume for women, is another poblano icon. It is worn on occasion by little girls as well as older women. Charras (female rodeo riders) and dancers performing the jarabe tapatío (Mexican hat dance) also don the garment.

The traditional ensemble is an ankle-length, sequin-studded red flannel skirt, an embroidered white blouse and a shawl (rebozo) worn around the shoulders and folded across in front. Decorative accents include colorful strands of beads and a red or green head bow. The green, white and red colors replicate the Mexican flag. A monument to La China Poblana, a rather monumental statue standing atop a tiled fountain, is at the northern end of the city at the intersection of Boulevard Héroes del 5 de Mayo and Avenida Defensores de la República.

Puebla also is known for its distinctive cuisine. Mole (mo-LEH), the Náhuatl Indian word for sauce, comes in a variety of guises; many of these complex concoctions were painstakingly developed by Dominican convent nuns. Popular versions are poblano, a blend of chiles and bitter chocolate; pipian, which mixes chiles and pumpkin or squash seeds; and adobo, a pairing of cumin and a variety of regional chiles.

Another signature dish is chiles en nogada, created by the nuns to honor Agustín de Iturbide, emperor of Mexico 1822-23. A large green poblano chile pepper is filled with a mixture of cooked chicken or pork, onions, garlic, raisins and other dried or candied fruit. It is topped with a creamy white sauce made from ground walnuts and sprinkled with parsley and red pomegranate seeds, the colors again recalling the Mexican flag. Restaurant menus normally feature *chiles en nogada* seasonally (July through September).

*Camotes,* confections made of sweet potato paste molded into the shape of a stick and flavored with fruit, are sold by street vendors, along with sweet potatoes, plantains baked in wood-burning stoves and *tacos arabes,* seasoned roast pork rolled into puffy wheat tortillas or pita bread.

The ubiquitous *cemita* is a big bread roll containing meat (usually ham), mild white cheese and avocado and seasoned with chiles or herbs. While these tasty snacks should all be safe to eat, it's best to avoid sno-cones, popsicles and ice cream—even on a hot day—since the water used to make them may not be purified.

Major events include Holy Week, which is observed Palm Sunday to Easter Sunday, and the Puebla State Fair (Feria de Puebla), a monthlong celebration that begins in mid-April and takes place at the fairgrounds within the 5 de Mayo Civic Center complex. The Huey Atlixcóyotl Fiesta is held in late September. This dance and music celebration was once presented as an offering to the god Quetzalcóatl in return for a bountiful harvest season. The festivities take place in the town of Atlixco, southwest of Puebla via Mex. 190-D.

## Practicalities

Hermanos Serdán International Airport is about 22 kilometers (13 miles) west of Puebla via Mex. 190, the Mexico-Puebla Highway (Carretera México-Puebla), at Km marker 91.5 near the town of Huejotzingo. American and United offer nonstop flights from Dallas and Houston, respectively. Low-cost carrier Volaris flies nonstop from Cancún, Monterrey and Tijuana; phone 01 (800) 122-8000 (toll-free long distance within Mexico). Most travelers, however, fly into Mexico City and take a bus to Puebla, which is convenient and easy. *For additional information about airlines see Arriving by Air, page p. 42.*

Puebla-bound buses depart frequently from both the Mexico City airport and the city's eastern bus terminal, Terminal de Autobuses de Pasajeros de Oriente (TAPO). The terminal is near the airport at Calzada Ignacio Zaragoza #200; the closest Metro subway stop is San Lázaro, line 1. The Estrella Roja bus line leaves from the airport and the TAPO terminal. Autobuses de Oriente (ADO) buses also leave for Puebla from the TAPO terminal.

Estrella Roja has its own counter at the airport. The departure time is printed on the ticket; tickets are nonrefundable. The nonstop trip takes a little less than 2 hours; the fare is about $22 (U.S.). Buses arrive at Puebla's main bus station, the Central de Autobuses de Puebla (CAPU), which is located in the northwestern part of the city about 4 kilometers

(2.5 miles) from the *Zócalo.* Estrella Roja buses also stop at the station at Avenida 4 Poniente near Calle 11 Norte (5 blocks west of the *Zócalo*), which is closer to the historic center.

*Taxi Autorizado* kiosks at the CAPU bus terminal sell government-authorized tickets for white-and-yellow taxis. The fare to specific destinations is based on a zone system; maps at the kiosks show the different zones. Pay the kiosk attendant for your ticket and tip the driver (10 percent of the fare is appropriate).

By car from Mexico City, Puebla is about a 3-hour drive via free Mex. 190; the drive time is shortened to about 90 minutes taking toll Mex. 150-D. Mex. 190 is scenic but slow, with more traffic and some bumpy stretches. To access either highway from downtown Mexico City, take the major east-west city thoroughfare Viaducto Miguel Alemán east toward Benito Juárez International Airport, exiting east at the junction with Calzada Ignacio Zaragoza; Zaragoza becomes Mex. 190. Heading east, watch for the signs to access Mex. 150-D.

Most of Puebla's museums and other tourist attractions are within a 4-block walk of the main plaza, or *Zócalo.* For getting around the city public buses are plentiful, and the fare is inexpensive (6 pesos). Exact change is required. Hailing one of the black city cabs that cruise the streets is not recommended. Driving in the historic center also should be avoided, since traffic can be heavy and there are few public parking spaces.

## City Layout

Just as Puebla was long second in importance to Mexico City in New Spain, it is bypassed by many tourists today. There is much to see, however, in this city that was designated a World Heritage Site by UNESCO in 1987. A mix of old and new, Puebla has both imposing glass towers and colonial-era buildings featuring ornamental wrought iron and walls adorned with Talavera tiles.

The Zócalo is a classic Mexican plaza with a bandstand, shoeshine stands and lots of iron benches. It is flanked on three sides by broad stone arches *(portales)* that shelter restaurants, sidewalk cafes and a warren of little shops. Sundays are particularly festive; dressed-up families stroll together after Mass, and in the evening there are sidewalk entertainers and vendors selling balloons and all kinds of snacks.

The surrounding narrow, cobblestone streets form a grid pattern that adheres to the classic blueprint for cities built by the Spanish in Mexico. Although they become poorer and more dilapidated as you head farther away from the city center, the streets in the vicinity of the Zócalo are lined with carefully preserved buildings in a mix of Churrigueresque, baroque and neoclassic architectural styles. Recurring motifs include the liberal use of Talavera tile, ornate white stucco ornamentation known as *alfeñique* (the name comes from a sweet confection made of almond paste) and gray stone carved into all sorts of curlicues, cherubs, gargoyles and other decorative accents.

Noted for its French Renaissance design is City Hall (Palacio Municipal), on the north side of the Zócalo at Portal Hidalgo #14. Intricate stone carvings adorn the exterior of the Theater (Teatro Principal), about 4 blocks northeast of the Zócalo at Avenida 8 Oriente and Calle 6 Norte. Dating from 1760, it is among the oldest theaters in the Americas (although it was rebuilt in the 1930s). The interior can be toured when performances are not taking place; for information check the Puebla State Tourism Office.

A striking contrast is provided by the William O. Jenkins Convention Center (Centro de Convenciones de Puebla), an impressive example of preserving the character of historic buildings—in this case, four ancient textile factories—while grafting on contemporary additions. The complex is worth a visit for its architecture alone. It is located at the eastern end of the historic district along Boulevard Héroes del 5 de Mayo, between avenidas 4 and 10 Oriente and just south of the Church of San Francisco.

The downtown street system is based on numbers rather than names. The northwest corner of the Zócalo is the city center; from this point, the main thoroughfares are north-south Avenida 5 de Mayo/16 de Septiembre and east-west Avenida Palafox y Mendoza/Reforma. East-west streets are even-numbered north of the Zócalo and odd-numbered south of it. Likewise, north-south streets are odd-numbered west of the Zócalo and even-numbered east of it.

Street names also include a direction—north/norte, south/sur, east/oriente or west/poniente—based on the axis of Avenida Reforma and Avenida 5 de Mayo. This makes it a bit easier to find the location of addresses, since the city is essentially divided into four quadrants.

**Puebla State Tourism Office (Secretaría de Turismo):** Avenida 5 Oriente #3, a block south of the Zócalo and across the street from the cathedral. Open Mon.-Sat. 10-7, Sun. 10-1. **Phone:** (222) 246-2044.

**Shopping:** Among the city's long-established Talavera workshops is Uriarte Talavera (Taller de Cerámica Uriarte), 5 blocks west of the Zócalo at Avenida 4 Poniente #911. Factory tours to observe the ceramics being molded, hand painted, fired and cooled are given, and they also will ship your purchases. Tours are offered Monday through Friday afternoons, subject to guide availability; phone (222) 232-1598 to confirm tour schedule.

El Parián Market, 3 blocks east of the Zócalo between calles 6 and 8 Norte, offers typical crafts from this part of Mexico, including Talavera pottery, trees of life and onyx jewelry. The open-air shops are in a pedestrian-only area. Bargaining is expected.

Plazuela de Los Sapos (Plaza of the Toads), bounded by avenidas 3 and 5 Oriente and calles 4 and 8 Sur, is lined with shops offering antique furniture and collectibles as well as new furniture made to look old. The Artists' Neighborhood, in a pedestrian passageway at Avenida 6 Oriente and Calle 6 Norte (behind the Theater), is a concentration of studios where local artists create and sell their work.

**5 DE MAYO CIVIC CENTER** (Centro Cívico 5 de Mayo) is about 15 blks. n.e. of the Zócalo on top of a steep hill (Cerro de Guadalupe). It is best reached by bus. This park, set amid groves of eucalyptus trees, includes several public facilities as well as Forts Loreto and Guadalupe (see separate attraction listing).

Museums include the Regional Museum of Anthropology and History (Museo Regional de Antropología y Historia); the Planetarium (El Planetario); the IMAGINA Interactive Museum (IMAGINA Museo Interactivo); Expo Puebla, an exhibition hall on the Puebla state fairgrounds; and the Relicario Bullring (Plaza de Toros El Relicario). The bubble-domed Reforma Auditorium (Auditorio de la Reforma) seats 2,000.

**Hours:** Museums open Tues.-Sun. 9-1 and 2-6. **Cost:** IMAGINA Interactive Museum 50 pesos (about $3.70 U.S.); 45 pesos (ages 3-12). Regional Museum of Anthropology and History 52 pesos. Planetarium IMAX shows 65 pesos. **Phone:** (222) 213-0289 for IMAGINA museum, or (222) 236-6998 for IMAX show times.

**AFRICAM** is about 16 km (10 mi.) s. of Puebla on the road to Valsequillo, at Km marker 16.5 (follow signs). This ecological park is a bit of Africa on the Mexican high plains, where such animals as lions, tigers, giraffes, buffaloes, deer and peacocks roam freely. Visitors can get out of their cars at certain locations for picture-taking opportunities. The Adventure Zone, a zoo and activities area geared toward kids, features kangaroos, anteaters, meerkats, a bat cave and pony rides. You can also see a live bird show. Buses to Africam depart Tuesday through Sunday from the Zócalo in downtown Puebla.

**Hours:** Daily 10-6. Last admission is at 5. Bird shows daily at 2 and 4. **Cost:** (includes access to Adventure Zone) 232 pesos (about $17 U.S.); 225 pesos (ages 3-11). **Phone:** (222) 281-7000, ext. 272 or 276. GT ⓘ

**AMPARO MUSEUM** is 3 blks. s. of the Zócalo at Calle 2 Sur #708 (at Calle 9 Oriente); street parking in the vicinity is limited. It contains one of the finest collections of pre-Hispanic art in Mexico, as well as pre-Columbian, colonial and modern works. The exhibits are housed in a two-story complex with several outdoor courtyards and fountains.

Two floors are filled with Olmec art, Nayarit clay figurines and other objects, including such whimsical pieces as a figure wearing a long conical hat and another strapped to a bed while a laughing dog peers through the framed headboard. One of the museum's most delightful works is a mural that depicts four angels creating the colonial town of Puebla. Colonial art (arte virreinal) is on the second floor. There also are frequent rotating exhibits. Background information is presented in both Spanish and English.

**Time:** Allow 2 hours minimum. **Hours:** Wed.-Mon. 10-6. **Cost:** 35 pesos (about $2.60 U.S.); 25 pesos (students with ID); free (ages 0-11). Guided tours

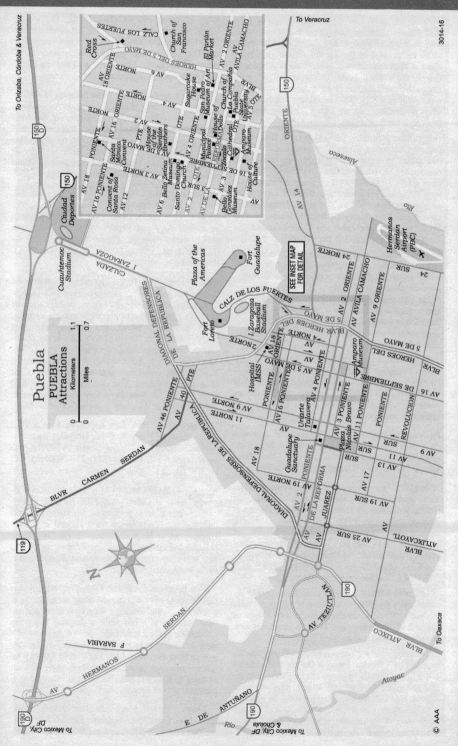

# Puebla
## PUEBLA Attractions

To Orizaba, Córdoba & Veracruz

To Veracruz

3014-16

Cuauhtemoc Stadium

Ciudad Deportes

CALZADA I ZARAGOZA

DIAGONAL DEFENSORES DE LA REPUBLICA

Plaza of the Americas

Fort Guadalupe

CALZ. DE LOS FUERTES

Fort Loreto

I Zaragoza Baseball Stadium

2 NORTE

SEE INSET MAP FOR DETAIL

Hermanos Serdan Airport (PBC)

24 NORTE

24 SUR

ORIENTE

AV 14

AV 9 ORIENTE

AV 2 ORIENTE

AV AVILA CAMACHO

BLVR HEROES DEL S DE MAYO

Hospital IMSS

AV 4 ORIENTE

Amparo Museum

5 DE MAYO

HEROES DEL

BLVR

AV 16

AV 4 PONIENTE

AV 6 PONIENTE

AV 5 DE MAYO

PONIENTE

Uriarte Talavera

AV 3 PONIENTE

Plaza Nicolas Bravo

AV 11 PONIENTE

PONIENTE

REVOLUCION

DE SEPTIEMBRE

AV 40 PONIENTE

AV 46 PONIENTE

AV 9 NORTE

I I NORTE

AV 18

Guadalupe Sanctuary

AV 19 NORTE

AV 2 PONIENTE

AV 25 SUR

SUR

6 AV

AV 11 SUR

AV 13 SUR

AV 17

AV 19 SUR

AV

BLVR CARMEN SERDAN

DE LA REFORMA

JUAREZ

DIAGONAL DEFENSORES DE LA REPUBLICA

BLVR ATLIXCAYOTL

AV TEZIUTLAN

190

To Oaxaca

N

Miles 0  0.7
Kilometers 0  1.1

119

SERDAN

F SARABIA

HERMANOS

AV

190 D

To Mexico City, DF

190

To Mexico City, DF & Cholula

E  DE  ANTUÑANO

Rio

Atoyac

150 D

150

Alseseca

Rio

© AAA

## Inset map detail

CALZ. LOS FUERTES

Red Cross

Church of San Francisco

El Parián Market

AV 2 ORIENTE

AV AVILA CAMACHO

HEROES DELS DE MAYO

AV 8 ORIENTE

AV 6

NORTE

NORTE

AV 16 ORIENTE

AV 4

Sugarcake House

San Pedro Museum of Art

Church of La Compañía

Puebla State University

OTE

AV 4 ORIENTE

AV 2

OTE

House of the Dolls

Cathedral

REFORMA

Amparo Museum

AV 5 OTE

AV 16

PONIENTE

House of the Serdan Brothers

Municipal Palace

Zocalo

OTE

AV 3 NORTE

NORTE

Santa Mónica Convent

Bello Zetina Museum

Santo Domingo Church

AV 6

AV 4 ORIENTE

AV DE LA

SUR

DE SEPTIEMBRE

Bello Gonzalez Museum

House of Culture

AV

AV 18

AV 16 PONIENTE

Convent of Santa Rosa

AV 12

with an English-speaking docent are given for 180 pesos (about $13.35 U.S.) per group (up to 25 people); reservations are required. **Phone:** (222) 229-3850. (H)

**BELLO Y GONZÁLEZ MUSEUM** is a blk. w. of the *Zócalo* at Av. 3 Poniente #302. The museum's collection of art and artifacts was donated to the city by the son of José Luis Bello, a textile magnate and collector. Beautifully hand-carved furniture, glassware, porcelain, gold and silver articles, paintings, ironwork from the 17th to 19th centuries and a large collection of Talavera pottery are all on display, as well as several huge ocean-going travel trunks equipped with hidden locks and latches. **Time:** Allow 1 hour minimum. **Hours:** Tues.-Sun. 10-5. **Cost:** 25 pesos (about $1.85 U.S.). **Phone:** (222) 232-9475. (GT)

**BELLO ZETINA MUSEUM** is at 5 de Mayo #409 next to the Church of Santo Domingo. It displays turn-of-the-20th-century antiques and religious art. **Hours:** Tues.-Sun. 10-3:45. **Cost:** Free. **Phone:** (222) 232-4720.

**CATHEDRAL OF THE IMMACULATE CONCEPTION** (Catedral de la Nuestra Señora de la Inmaculada Concepción) stands on the s. side of the *Zócalo*. The plans for the cathedral, one of the largest in Mexico, were approved in 1562 by Philip II of Spain, but construction was not completed until 1641; it was consecrated in 1649.

The immense building is noted for its elaborately carved facade, great doors, 14 chapels and two bell towers—the tallest in Mexico—that were erected in 1678. Among the extravagantly decorated interior's many highlights are an altar of gray onyx, marble and gold designed in 1799 by Manuel Tolsá, onyx sculptures carved by Tolsá, wood inlay in the choir, lovely tapestries and a collection of rare paintings. The use of cameras and cell phones is prohibited inside the church, and visitors should respect those who are there to worship. **Hours:** Daily 8-12:30 and 4:30-7. **Cost:** Free.

**CHURCH OF LA COMPAÑIA** (Iglesia de la Compañia) is a block e. of the *Zócalo* on Calle 4 Sur. This enormous church, built by Jesuits, features extravagantly detailed exterior stone carvings. Also known as the Church of the Holy Ghost (Templo del Espíritu Santo), it is said to be the final resting place of a local legend, La China Poblana.

Although the story has several interpretations, it is generally agreed that a young girl named Mirrha was born in the early 17th century in India, kidnapped by Portuguese pirates and sold into slavery. She was later adopted by Miguel de Sosa, a well-to-do *poblano* who had her baptized with the name Catarina. Freed to assume a life of piety and religious devotion, Catarina married a Chinese servant named Domingo Suárez—thus earning her nickname—and was revered for her acts of charity, so much so that her characteristic style of dress became universally known as the *china poblana*. **Hours:** Daily 9-7. **Cost:** Free.

**CHURCH OF SAN FRANCISCO** (Templo de San Francisco) is about 6 blks. n.e. of the *Zócalo*, just off Av. 14 Oriente at the corner of Blvd. Héroes del 5 de Mayo. The oldest church in Puebla was founded in 1535; the present edifice was completed in the 18th century. Its imposing north doorway is a good example of the decorative motif known as plateresque. The facade of brick and colorful rectangular tiles is noteworthy.

Off the main altar is a small chapel with a funerary glass box containing the remains of Franciscan friar Sebastián de Aparicio. Before taking his vows, Fray Sebastián was distinguished as one of New Spain's first road builders. He was beatified for his good deeds and purported miracles, and many worshippers come to pay their respects.

**CHURCH OF SANTO DOMINGO** (Iglesia de Santo Domingo) is 3 blks. n. of the *Zócalo* on Av. 5 de Mayo, between avs. 4 Poniente and 6 Poniente. It was completed in the early 17th century and features colorful tile decoration.

Don't miss the spectacularly ornate Chapel of the Rosary (Capilla del Rosario), which has walls and a ceiling completely covered with gold leaf and gilded stucco figures of angels, saints, children and animals. The extravagant altar features a statue of the Virgen del Rosario, crowned and adorned with jewels.

**EX-CONVENT OF SANTA MÓNICA** (Ex-Convento de Santa Mónica) is 9 blks. n. of the *Zócalo* at Av. 18 Poniente #103, just off Av. 5 de Mayo. It was ordered closed when the 1857 Reform Laws abolished monasteries and convents in Mexico; the convent's nuns continued their work in semi-secrecy until 1934.

The museum preserves the dark corridors and austere rooms and includes a collection of religious art; the paintings on velvet by Rafael Morante have retained their brilliant colors after centuries. Guides are available. Entry to the museum is through a house and passageway. **Hours:** Tues.-Sun. 10-5. **Cost:** 39 pesos (about $2.90 U.S.). **Phone:** (222) 232-0178.

**EX-CONVENT OF SANTA ROSA** (Ex-Convento de Santa Rosa) is 7 blks. n.w. of the *Zócalo* at Av. 14 Poniente #305, between calles 3 and 5 Norte. This partially restored convent has a museum (Museo de Arte Popular) with handicraft exhibits and a splendid 18th-century tiled kitchen. According to legend, the traditional chocolate and chile sauce called *mole poblano* was invented here by nuns who wanted to prepare a special dish for the saint's day of their bishop.

A government-sponsored craft shop on the premises sells embroidery, lace and *poblano* craft items. **Hours:** Tues.-Sun. 10-5. **Cost:** 30 pesos (about $2.20 U.S.).

**FORTS LORETO AND GUADALUPE** (Fuertes de Loreto y Guadalupe) are in a park about 2 km (1.2 mi.) n.e. of the city center; take Calle 4 Norte to Blvd. 5 de Mayo, then follow Calzada Zaragoza/Calzada de los Fuertes. The remains of Fort Guadalupe stand on a hill (Cerro de Guadalupe) overlooking the city below; only the walls and cannons remain.

Fort Loreto is about a 20-minute walk downhill. The remodeled fort contains the No Intervention Museum (Museo de la No Intervención), which is dedicated to the Battle of Puebla on May 5, 1862, when a force of 4,000 Mexicans led by General Ignacio Zaragoza defeated an army of 6,500 French troops. The museum houses a collection of oil paintings depicting the battle as well as displays of weapons, uniforms, documents and other items related to this important episode in Mexican history. Museum signage is in Spanish.

Also within the park is a monument to the heroes of the battle. **Time:** Allow 1 hour minimum. **Hours:** Forts open Tues.-Sun. 9-5:30. No Intervention Museum open Tues.-Sun. 10-5. **Cost:** Admission to both forts 47 pesos (about $3.50 U.S.). No Intervention Museum 22 pesos (about $1.65 U.S.). Forts and museum free to all Sun. Taxi fare between the two forts about 25 pesos. The fee to use a video camera is 45 pesos. Cash only.

**GUADALUPE SANCTUARY** (Santuario de Guadalupe) is on Av. Reforma, 6 blks. w. of the *Zócalo*. This is one of the finest examples of the region's traditional architecture.

**HOUSE OF CULTURE** (Casa de la Cultura) is 1 blk. s. of the *Zócalo* at Av. 5 Oriente #5, facing the s. side of the Cathedral. It is housed in the former Archbishop's Palace (Palacio del Obispado), a building in the classic *poblano* style—patterned red brick interspersed with glazed blue-and-white tiles, windows framed in white stucco, and a flat roof embellished with a row of white spikes. It contains a concert and lecture hall as well as the Palafox Library. Free maps of the city can be obtained here. **Hours:** Mon.-Fri. 10-5, Sat.-Sun. 9-6. **Cost:** Free. **Phone:** (222) 246-3186.

**Palafox Library** (Biblioteca Palafoxiana) is on the House of Culture's second floor. Founded in 1646 and believed to be the first public library established in the Americas, it contains some 45,000 books, most of them priceless bound Latin manuscripts. Other valuable tomes include a 1584 atlas printed in Antwerp, Belgium, and a 16th-century Bible in four languages. The library's contents were digitally catalogued in 2010, a process that took 5 years of work and required a team of 30 specialists.

The library is named for Juan de Palafox y Mendoza, a Catholic priest and the bishop of Puebla from 1640 to 1655. The main reason to see it is for the room's ornate beauty. Just 20 feet wide but more than 200 feet long, it's lined with exquisitely carved cedar bookshelves, protected by wire, that rise in three tiers above the worn red-tile floors. At the far end stands a three-story gold altar featuring an oil painting of the Virgin of Trapani.

Photography is not permitted. **Hours:** Tues.-Sun. 10-5. **Cost:** 25 pesos (about $1.85 U.S.).

**NATIONAL MUSEUM OF MEXICAN RAILWAYS** (Museo Nacional de Los Ferrocarriles Mexicanos) is at Calle 11 Norte #1005 (at Av. 10 Poniente), about 6 blks. n.w. of the *Zócalo;* street parking in the vicinity is limited. Housed in a former railway station, the museum's exhibits include repair equipment, a collection of watches from railroad employees, a station diorama, historical photographs and a children's area with costumed characters. The large train yard features several antique and early 20th-century trains, including several that can be walked through.

**Time:** Allow 1 hour minimum. **Hours:** Tues.-Sun. 9-5. Closed Jan. 1 and Christmas. **Cost:** 12 pesos (about 90c U.S.). Cash only.

**REGIONAL MUSEUM OF THE MEXICAN REVOLUTION** (Museo Regional de la Revolución Mexicana) is in the historic center at Av. 6 Oriente #206, between calles 2 and 4 Norte. Also known as the House of the Serdán Brothers, Puebla's most visited museum houses the personal belongings of the Serdán family, who played an important role in launching the revolution against dictator Porfirio Díaz. Don Aquiles Serdán and other patriots were killed in this colonial-style house on Nov. 18, 1910. Visitors can see the living room, kitchen and children's bedroom, the house's dispatch office and a shoe workshop (the family ran a nearby shoe business).

A memorial hall is dedicated to Mexican patriots, and one room features locally crafted, painted ceramic tiles emblazoned with an eagle, the country's national symbol. Other displays include a collection of rifles and cannon balls. A short, well-done video recounts the history of the house. Exhibit information is in Spanish.

Flash photography is not permitted. **Time:** Allow 1 hour, 30 minutes minimum. **Hours:** Tues.-Sun. 10-4:30. Closed Jan. 1 and Christmas. **Cost:** 30 pesos (about $2.20 U.S.); 25 pesos (students with ID). Cash only. **Phone:** (222) 242-1076.

**SAN PEDRO MUSEUM OF ART** (San Pedro Museo de Arte) is 2 blks. n.e. of the *Zócalo* at Calle 4 Norte #203. This museum, housed in the restored Hospital of San Pedro, exhibits paintings, sculpture, ceramics, china and glassware from the Bello Y Gonzalez collection. The second floor displays antique pharmacy jars and other vessels engraved with the names of various plants, herbs and medicines. Rotating temporary exhibitions are devoted to contemporary Mexican artists.

**Time:** Allow 1 hour minimum. **Hours:** Tues.-Sun. 10-5. **Cost:** 30 pesos (about $2.20 U.S.). Separate admission for special exhibits 45 pesos (about $3.35 U.S.). GT

**SUGARCAKE HOUSE** (Casa de Alfeñique) is 3 blks. n.e. of the *Zócalo* at Av. 4 Oriente and Calle 6 Norte. This 17th-century colonial mansion, named for its ornate exterior, was once a residence for visiting dignitaries. Now a museum, it has an archeological and historical collection on the first two floors; the third floor is furnished in period. **Hours:**

Tues.-Sun. 10-5. **Cost:** 25 pesos (about $1.85 U.S.).
**Phone:** (222) 232-0458.

# QUERÉTARO, QUERÉTARO (D-2)
pop. 801,940

Querétaro (keh-REH-tah-roh) lies in a valley at
the base of a hill called the Sangremal. The city was
founded by Otomí Indians long before Europeans
discovered the New World. It was captured by the
Spanish in 1531 and developed as the headquarters
for the Franciscan monks who established missions
throughout Central America, Mexico and California.

Querétaro has played a pivotal role in Mexican
history. The early 19th century saw the city as the
center of rebellion against Spain. Doña Josefa (La
Corregidora) and her husband, the local magistrate,
formed the Society for the Study of Fine Arts to dis-
cuss poetry and politics; two of Mexico's greatest
revolutionary heroes, Father Miguel Hidalgo and
Capt. Ignacio Allende, often attended. In 1810,
when budding plots for national independence were
uncovered, Doña Josefa alerted the principal insurgents of their impending arrest.

The city also was Mexico's capital 37 years later
when U.S. troops took over Mexico City; the Treaty of
Guadalupe-Hidalgo, which ceded California, Arizona
and New Mexico to the United States, was formulated
in 1848 at Querétaro's Academy of Fine Arts. During
the War of Reform (1857-59), President Benito Juárez
made Querétaro his headquarters. Emperor Maximilian's headquarters were here as well; he ended his
3-year reign before a firing squad on the nearby Hill
of the Bells (Cerro de las Campañas), thus ending Europe's dream of controlling Mexico.

Elegant colonial architecture is concentrated in
the historic downtown area, which was designated a
World Heritage Site by UNESCO in 1996. The cobblestone streets are narrow but well maintained,
with pedestrian-only thoroughfares (andadores) linking several plazas.

The central plaza is called Jardín Zenea; north-
south Avenida Corregidora, downtown's main street,
runs along its east side. Band concerts take place at
the plaza on Sunday evenings at 6 p.m. Six blocks
south is the large, tree-shaded Alameda.

Two blocks east of Jardín Zenea is Plaza de Armas (also called Plaza de la Independencia). On the
plaza's west side, at the Portal de Dolores (Avenida
Pasteur #6), is Ecala's House (Casa de Ecala). This
building has what might be the most beautiful 18th-
century baroque facade in the city; note the brick
and stone staircases and the small window with an
elaborate ornamentation of drapes sculpted in stone.
Visitors can walk around the inner courtyard during
normal business hours.

Among other notable downtown buildings is the
Casa de la Marquesa, at Av. Madero #41. In the 18th
century this elegant mansion was the residence of a
wealthy family of royal blood; it now houses a hotel.
The interior courtyard is graced with Moorish-style

arches. Another hotel, the Mesón de Santa Rosa (on
Plaza de Armas at Av. Pasteur #17) has three spectacular courtyards; in the middle one stands an old trough
that once served to water guests' horses.

A block north of the Jardín Zenea at the corner of
avenidas Corregidora and Hidalgo is the Theater of
the Republic (Teatro de la República), built in neoclassic style between 1850 and 1852 and embellished with accents of olive leaves, crowns and
shields. The Mexican Constitution was signed there
in 1917.

A block west of the Jardín Zenea at Avenida Madero and Calle Allende is the Neptune Fountain (Fuente de Neptuno). It was designed by Eduardo Tresguerras, who was responsible for a number of the
city's neoclassic buildings.

Another landmark is the 6-mile-long, 50-foot-high
aqueduct (acueducto), constructed by the Spanish
more than 200 years ago and still supplying the city
with water. Its 74 arches run along the center of
east-west Avenida Zaragoza.

The state of Querétaro is known for its gemstones, especially opals. These should be purchased
only at reputable shops; avoid sidewalk vendors.
Lapidaria de Querétaro, 3 blocks north of Jardín Zenea at the corner of Calle Pasteur and Calle 15 de
Mayo, sells locally mined opals and other semiprecious stones.

The Plaza de Toros Santa María, south of downtown on Avenida Constituyentes, is one of Mexico's
best bullrings, drawing top matadors from Mexico
and Spain. The main season runs from November
through January; phone (442) 216-1617.

**Querétaro State Tourism Office (Secretaría de Tur-
ismo):** Calle Luis Pasteur #4 Norte, just n. of Plaza
de Armas. Open daily 9-8. **Phone:** (442) 238-5067,
or 01 (800) 715-1742 (toll-free long distance within
Mexico).

**CHURCH AND CONVENT OF SANTA CRUZ** (Iglesia y Convento de la Santa Cruz) is several blks. e. of
the historic center at Calle Independencia and Calle
Manuel Acuña. As many as 200 monks once lived in
the mission compound, a well-preserved series of
cloisters and cells complete with an orchard, a kitchen
with a cold storage chamber, several schools and a water reservoir. According to legend, Franciscan missionary Fray Antonio Margil de Jesus buried a wooden
walking stick in the orchard that grew into a tree with
thorns in the shape of a cross.

The monastery also served as self-proclaimed emperor Maximilian's army barracks and, after defeat in
1867, his prison. The ashes of the heroine La Corregidora are encased in a monument behind the church.

**Time:** Allow 1 hour minimum. **Hours:** Church
daily 6 a.m.-9 p.m. Convent Tues.-Sat. 9:30-5:30, Sun.
9-5:30. Short tours in English are given Tues.-Sun.
9-4, subject to guide availability. Closed Catholic holidays. **Cost:** Church free. Convent 10 pesos (about 75c

U.S.). Tipping the tour guide is customary. **Phone:** (442) 212-0235.

**CHURCH OF SAN FRANCISCO** (Iglesia de San Francisco) is opposite Jardín Zenea at the corner of Calle 5 de Mayo and Calle Corregidora. It dates from 1545 and dominates the plaza. The dome's colored tiles were brought from Spain in 1540. The church houses a collection of 17th-, 18th- and 19th-century religious paintings, and a figure of Santiago adorns the doorway. **Hours:** Daily 7:30 a.m.-8 p.m. **Cost:** Free; donations accepted.

**CHURCH OF SANTA CLARA** (Iglesia de Santa Clara) is at the corner of Calle Ignacio Allende and Calle Francisco I. Madero, just w. of the Neptune Fountain. Founded in 1633 and reconstructed during the 18th century by architect Eduardo Tresguerras, Santa Clara had one of Mexico's richest nunneries. It is noted for its ornately carved interior, gilded altarpieces and delicate exterior ironwork. **Hours:** Daily 7:30 a.m.-8 p.m. **Cost:** Free; donations accepted.

**CHURCH OF SANTA ROSA DE VITERBO** (Iglesia de Santa Rosa de Viterbo) is about 4 blks. s.w. of the Jardín Zenea at Av. José María Arteaga and Calle Ezequiel Montes. Oriental influences are visible in this 1752 church's bell tower, fashioned after a pagoda, and in its flying buttresses, flanked by dragon faces. The interior exhibits a profusion of gilt, carved wood with inlaid marble and filigree work. **Hours:** Daily 9-6. **Cost:** Free; donations accepted.

**GOVERNMENT PALACE** (Palacio Gobierno) is at the n. end of Plaza de Armas. Now housing the state of Querétaro offices, it was once the home of Doña Josefa Ortiz, or "La Corregidora" (the mayor's wife), the heroine of the 1810 War of Independence. Under house arrest, she whispered instructions through a keyhole to a messenger to warn insurgents Father Miguel Hidalgo and Capt. Ignacio Allende in the nearby town of Dolores. As a result, Hidalgo immediately issued his famous cry (*grito*) for independence. More than 50 years later, Archduke Maximilian presided over many meetings here. **Hours:** Open during normal business hours.

**HILL OF THE BELLS** (Cerro de las Campañas) is at the western end of downtown via Calle Miguel Hidalgo to Av. Tecnológico, then n. to Av. Justo Sierra. It was the site of Archduke Maximilian's last battle, and it was at this location that he was executed by a firing squad on June 19, 1867.

A monument erected by victorious Mexican rebels in honor of Benito Juárez, who defeated the ill-fated "Emperor of Mexico," is at the top of a hill behind the Capilla de la Piedad. This neoclassic chapel, erected by the Austrian government in 1901, is dedicated to the would-be emperor. Stone markers mark the spots where Maximilian and his two Mexican generals, Miramón and Mejía, were executed.

The city's history is presented in the small Magic of the Past Museum (Museo La Magia del Pasado). The site also features large gardens with manicured trees and shrubs, a small lake, walking trails and playgrounds for kids; it's a pleasant place for an outdoor stroll. The name derives from rocks found in the region that, due to their metallic content, produce a vaguely bell-like sound when struck together.

**Hours:** Park open daily 6-6; museum, chapel and other structures open Tues.-Sun. 10-5. **Cost:** 15 pesos (about $1.10 U.S.); free (ages 0-5).

**MUSEUM OF ART** (Museo de Arte) is at Calle Allende Sur #14. It is housed in a former monastery, the Convent of San Agustín (Convento de San Agustín), an outstanding example of baroque architecture built in 1731 by Mexican architect Ignacio Mariano de las Casas. The building's exterior ornamentation is as impressive as the collection of Mexican colonial and European art inside. **Hours:** Tues.-Sun. 10-6. **Cost:** 30 pesos (about $2.20 U.S.); free to all Tues. **Phone:** (442) 212-2357.

**REGIONAL MUSEUM** (Museo Regional de Querétaro) is on Av. Corregidora next to the Church of San Francisco. Housed in the former monastery, it displays colonial relics; uniforms and weaponry; 17th-, 18th- and 19th-century paintings by Juan Correa, Villalpando, Miguel Cabrera and Luis Rodríguez; and a library of more than 8,000 books, mostly parchment tomes from the 17th and 18th centuries. **Hours:** Tues.-Sun. 9-6. **Cost:** 52 pesos (about $3.85 U.S.).

## REAL DE CATORCE, SAN LUIS POTOSÍ (B-2)

Real de Catorce (ray-ALL day cah-TOR-say) is one of Mexico's most fascinating old mining towns. (The literal translation of the name is "royal of 14," allegedly a reference to the killing of 14 Spanish soldiers by Indian resisters.) Situated in the Sierra de Catorce range at an altitude of 9,000 feet, it has a dry climate, extraordinarily blue skies, peerlessly starry nights and spectacular mountain vistas. The stark countryside—forested to the south, treeless and cacti-strewn to the north—has been featured in several films, including the John Huston classic "The Treasure of the Sierra Madre" and more recently "The Mexican," starring Brad Pitt and Julia Roberts.

Silver was discovered in this region in 1773, and by the late 19th century Real de Catorce had become one of the wealthiest mining towns in the Americas. By the late 19th century it had a population of 15,000, a bullring and shops that sold expensive items imported from Europe.

But although it was rich, the community was isolated. When Mexican dictator Porfirio Díaz journeyed here in 1896 to visit the Santa Ana Mine—the first mine in the country to install water-removing pumps that were powered by electricity—he traveled by train, mule-drawn carriage and finally on horseback in order to reach it. Several years later a tunnel was cut through solid rock to provide access into and out of town.

After an apex of prosperity at the turn of the 20th century, decline set in. The falling price of silver in

1905 initiated an exodus that was exacerbated by the subsequent political and social turmoil of the Mexican Revolution, and the town was all but abandoned. Although Real de Catorce never quite became a ghost town, by 1920 the population had dwindled to a few hundred people eking out a hard-scrabble existence.

While mining never regained its importance (the last process plant shut down in 1990), a slow rebirth had begun in the 1970s as tourists began rediscovering both the glorious mountain scenery and the town's unhurried pace. Entrepreneurs began to move in, renovating crumbling buildings and opening hotels, shops and restaurants. More recently Catorce has seen an influx of artists and filmmakers.

There are a number of ex-haciendas in the surrounding region that date back to the 18th century. Built by the Spanish to supply animals and agricultural products to local mining communities, they passed through various owners after Mexico won its independence and continued to function as ranches until the end of the 19th century. Most of them then gradually fell into disrepair as the *ejido* system of community-owned land was revived in the 1930s by president Lázaro Cárdenas. Today very few of the ex-haciendas have survived intact, with collapsed roofs and weathered walls standing as mute testimony to the past.

This is a place of pilgrimage for Huichol Indians who live in the states of Durango, Jalisco, Nayarit and Zacatecas. They journey to El Quemado, a hilltop that is a revered ceremonial site, and to the surrounding desert scrublands, which make up their spiritual homeland of Wirikuta. The Huichols also come here to participate in religious rituals involving the use of peyote, the common name for a small, spineless species of cactus that grows throughout much of northern Mexico; the buds it produces have a hallucinogenic effect when chewed.

Another important pilgrimage is made by thousands of devout Catholics every year to the Parish of the Immaculate Conception, or parish church, to pay homage to St. Francis of Assisi, the town's patron saint. The church, which dates from 1817, stands in a small plaza between calles Lanzagorta and Constitución; it replaced an older, smaller church building that had a wooden roof. The exterior is neoclassic; inside, frescoes adorn the baptistery and there are several altars. Especially notable is the St. Joseph altar, in the cross vaults under the church dome, which has its original stucco and is decorated with a painting of the Virgin of Guadalupe.

An altar devoted to St. Francis—affectionately known as "Panchito" or "El Charrito"—is in the nave. It features a wood sculpture of the saint, jointed at the arms and legs so that it can be stood on its feet and moved, as well as a painting of Our Lady of Refuge, the patron saint of miners. The image of St. Francis is said to be miraculous, and as a result the church

receives a flow of pilgrims from all over northern Mexico, particularly on Oct. 4, the Day of St. Francis.

Hundreds of *retablos* (small devotional paintings) adorn the walls near the main altar. Created on tinplate by regional artisans, *retablos* can be anything from entreaties by those who are sick to thanks for health, wealth or protection—all expressions of gratitude made to a benefactor saint. They are a distinctly Mexican form of popular art.

Calle Lanzagorta, Catorce's cobblestone main street, is lined with stalls selling religious souvenirs. There are other historic sites as well. Opposite the parish church is the old mint building (Casa de Moneda), where coins were made in 1865 and 1866 before it was shut down by order of Emperor Maximilian. The building has been beautifully restored and now houses the Real de Catorce Cultural Center (Centro Cultural de Real de Catorce), which has rotating temporary art exhibits and a permanent exhibit of machinery from the original mint.

Two blocks west of the mint is Plaza Hidalgo, a pleasant place to relax in the shade of aged trees. There are shops and restaurants on the plaza and along the nearby streets.

At Calle Zaragoza #3 (opposite the northwest corner of the plaza) is Galería Vega M-57, housed in a restored former residence. Real de Catorce is increasingly becoming a magnet for artists, and here you can see contemporary paintings, sculpture, jewelry and silver work by Mexican and foreign artists who live in town. The gallery is open Sat.-Sun. or by appointment; phone (488) 887-5061.

About a block northwest of the plaza via Calle Zaragoza is the Palenque de Gallos, a former cock fighting arena built in the style of a Roman amphitheater; cultural and musical events take place here. A bit farther north on Zaragoza at the edge of town is the bullring, now used for soccer games. Across the street in the cemetery (*panteón*) stands one of the oldest buildings in town, a Franciscan chapel built around 1775. Past the cemetery hikers can follow an old mining road that ends with a view looking out over the high plains that sweep toward the west.

Visitors also can hike into the surrounding countryside. An hour's walk will bring you to the summit of El Quemado; from this hilltop vantage point there are panoramic vistas of the desert below. Another hike can be made to the ruins of the La Concepción Mine, one of many former mines in this region, located high in the hills above the Ogarrio Tunnel. The old mine works, mills and warehouses stand in utter serenity against a backdrop of mountains. **Note:** The terrain is impressively rugged; wear sturdy hiking shoes and a hat and bring water. If you would rather not go it alone, guided horseback, jeep and walking excursions can be arranged.

The largest restaurant in town is Meson de la Abundancia, housed in a handsome 19th-century building on Calle Lanzagorta that was once the Real de Catorce Treasury. The signature dish is *arrachera,* flank steak marinated in a traditional sauce; here the meat is smothered with grilled onions and served with sweet peppers and pico de nopales, a salad of chopped cactus pads, tomatoes, garlic and cilantro.

La Esquina Chata, on Plaza Hidalgo at Calle Lanzagorta #2, is a cafe and bakery that serves breakfast on weekdays and has excellent coffee. Street stalls along Calle Lanzagorta sell tacos, *gorditas*—thick corn tortillas with different fillings—and *chiles rellenos,* roasted green or poblano peppers stuffed with cheese or ground meat, dipped in egg batter and fried.

This is a very low-key place most of the year, with more tourists on weekends than during the week; many shops and restaurants are closed Tuesdays and/or Wednesdays. The Semana Santa and Christmas holidays bring crowds, but the year's biggest event is the Fiesta of San Francisco from late September to mid-October. Thousands of pilgrims, many coming just for a day, descend on Real de Catorce by the busload—and every vehicle must pass through the one-way Ogarrio Tunnel. If you want peace and quiet this is not the time to visit.

## Practicalities

Getting to Real de Catorce is definitely an adventure. The road to town branches off Mex. 57 a little over 3 miles north of Matehuala; watch for the sign that says "Cedral/Real de Catorce." Mostly paved, it runs west about 28 kilometers (17 miles), passing through the rural village of Cedral before reaching a signed junction. At the junction a cobblestone road proceeds south about 24 kilometers (15 miles) to Catorce. **Note:** There are two Pemex stations in Cedral, but no gas stations in Real de Catorce. There are mechanics and tire shops in both towns.

The drive is slow but spectacularly scenic, winding up a mountainside past abandoned buildings before reaching the entrance to the Ogarrio Tunnel. Opened in 1901, the tunnel is just 1.5 miles long but dark, cold and winding. It also is so narrow that vehicles can be accommodated in only one direction at a time. Just inside the tunnel on the right is a tiny chapel, illuminated by an overhead light, that was carved out of solid rock; it honors mine workers and those who lost their lives building the tunnel.

Highway workers at each end direct the flow, and there can be a long wait if traffic is busy. At the other end of the tunnel is a parking area; the fee is $2 (U.S.) for the day and $5 overnight. From the parking area it's a short walk to Calle Lanzagorta, the main street.

If you'd rather have someone else do the driving, buses leave from Matehuala's central bus station (Centro de Autobuses) daily on the hour from 8 a.m. until noon. The last bus departs Catorce for the return to Matehuala at 6 p.m. The station is on Avenida 5 de Mayo, just north of the junction with Mex. 57 and about 2 kilometers (1.2 miles) south of the center of town. The drive takes about 2 hours. One-way fare is 48 pesos.

Passengers switch to a smaller minibus for the trip through the tunnel. Motorists also can park their vehicle outside the tunnel and ride the minibus. The tunnel fee for vehicles is $2 (U.S.); there is no charge for bus passengers. The return trip through the tunnel is free. The minibus can get very crowded on the return trip.

Although tourism is growing, this is still a small town, and there are no banks or currency exchange houses (casas de cambio). Keep pesos on hand if you intend to shop, dine, sightsee or spend the night, since shops, grocery stores, restaurants and hotels don't take credit cards. There is an ATM in the tourist office (Dirección de Turismo), which is located inside the Presidencia Municipal building (across Calle Constitución from the parish church); withdrawal charges can be steep.

For visitors who want more than just a day trip, lodgings range from simple guest houses (casas de huéspedes) to several hotels that occupy restored old buildings. Keep in mind, however, that none of these accommodations have heat, and hot water is limited. The weather can get quite nippy during the winter months, so plan a visit based on your tolerance for cold conditions.

## SAN JUAN DEL RÍO, QUERÉTARO
(D-3) pop. 241,699

San Juan del Río (sahn hwan ·dehl REE-oh), noted for semiprecious stones, woodcarvings, baskets and palm furniture, is located in a prosperous agricultural region that yields corn, dairy products and wine. This picturesque city was once an important stop on the stagecoach route to Mexico City. San Juan del Río features many buildings painted white and enhanced by decorative elements of dark brown carved stone.

Also near San Juan del Río are the Trinidad opal mines. Opals and amethysts are polished in town; gems should be purchased only at established shops.

A short distance northeast of San Juan del Río via Mex. 120 is the resort town of Tequisquiapan (teh-kees-kee-AP-an). This weekend retreat was once popular for its hot-water thermal springs, but competition from local industries for the available water has hurt the spa business. It remains a pretty place to stroll, however, with narrow streets planted with flowering fruit trees and cloaked in brightly colored bougainvillea, and a quaint main plaza surrounded by arcades (portales).

On the plaza's north side is the neoclassic Church of Santa Maria of the Assumption (Templo de Santa María de la Asunción) near the plaza sells rattan furniture and other locally made items.

From Tequisquiapan, continue north on Mex. 120 to Ezequiel Montes; from here, take the paved turnoff west about 10 kilometers (6 miles) to Bernal. Another popular weekend destination, this picturesque little town has craft shops offering wool and cotton clothing. The main attraction, however, is La Peña de Bernal, a huge, pyramid-shaped monolith.

About 38 kilometers (24 miles) north of Tequisquiapan on Mex. 120 is the town of Cadereyta; ask

in town for directions to La Quinta Schmoll, a botanical garden devoted to cacti (more than 4,000 varieties). The garden is open Tues.-Sun. 8-5 and admission is 20 pesos. Phone (441) 276-1071.

This stretch of Mex. 120 through northeastern Querétaro state traverses the Sierra Gorda, part of the eastern Sierra Madre mountain range and a green oasis at the edge of central Mexico's vast semi-desert region. The scenery is impressively rugged; forested peaks rise more than 10,000 feet, while the valleys between them are hot and humid.

Mex. 120 passes through the town of Pinal de Amoles, then makes a series of dramatic ascents and descents to Jalpan. Beginning in the 1750s, Franciscan priest Father Junípero Serra established five missions in this region to evangelize the Chichimeca Indians. These five missions—Jalpan, Concá, Landa, Tancoyol and Tilaco—were designated World Heritage Sites by UNESCO in 2003. Serra went on to found another, more famous chain of missions in Alta (upper) California.

Jalpan's old mission church, the Misión de Jalpan, is beautifully restored. Also in town is the Museum of the Sierra Gorda (Museo de la Sierra Gorda), a former military fort with exhibits offering insight into the region's Indian cultures and Father Serra's evangelical work. It is open Tues.-Sun. 10-6; admission is 10 pesos. Phone (441) 296-0165. **Note:** The museum is undergoing renovations but remains open; hours are erratic and not all exhibits can be seen. Phone ahead for updated information.

## SAN LUIS POTOSÍ, SAN LUIS POTOSÍ
(C-2) pop. 772,604
*See map page 330.*

San Luis Potosí (sahn loo-EES poh-toh-SEE), capital of the state of the same name, was founded in the late 1500s as a mining settlement. The city was the seat of national government under President Benito Juárez in 1863 and again in 1867. The San Luis Plan, drafted by Francisco I. Madero while he was imprisoned in the city by dictator Porfirio Díaz, set the stage for the Revolution of 1910.

Despite a heavy manufacturing presence, today's city is not all soot and smoke. Plaza de Armas, the main square, anchors a well-preserved colonial center. The plaza is flanked by the 18th-century cathedral on the east and the Government Palace (Palacio de Gobierno) on the west.

Two blocks northwest of Plaza de Armas is Founders' Plaza (Plaza de Los Fundadores); 2 blocks east and a block south of Plaza de Armas is Plaza del Carmen. Two blocks west and 2 blocks south of Plaza de Armas is Plaza San Francisco. Each of these plazas is a pleasant spot to observe city life.

The Plaza España bullring is on Avenida Universidad, at the eastern end of downtown near the southeastern corner of Alameda Park. On the north side of this large park is the city's train station,

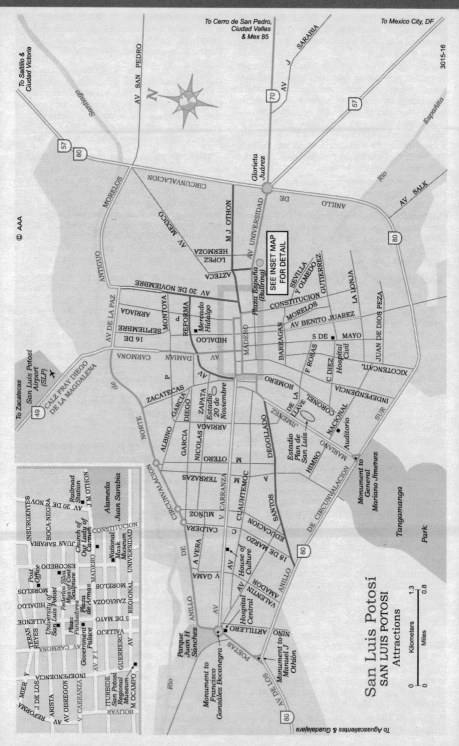

San Luis Potosí
SAN LUIS POTOSI
Attractions

where a series of Fernando Leal frescoes depict the history of transportation in Mexico.

Holy Week (Semana Santa) celebrations are among the city's most traditional as well as most solemn. Various cultural, artistic and gastronomic events lead up to Good Friday, when there is a silent procession through the historic city center. More down to earth is the San Luis Potosí National Fair (Feria Nacional Potosina), normally held the latter half of August, which features bullfights, cockfights, rodeos, carnival rides and agricultural and livestock exhibitions.

San Luis Potosí State Tourism Office (Secretaría de Turismo): in the historic center at Blvd. Manuel José Othón #130, just e. of Plaza de Armas. Open Mon.-Fri. 8-8, Sat. 10-8. Phone: (444) 812-9939.

Shopping: Among the wares on display at the huge Hidalgo Market (Mercado Hidalgo), 4 blocks north of Plaza de Armas, are prized Santa María *rebozos* (shawl-like garments), so gauzy in texture they can be pulled through a woman's wedding ring; pottery; and a candy called *queso de tuna* made from the fruit of the prickly pear cactus. Calle Hidalgo between the market and Plaza de Armas is a pedestrian-only street flanked by numerous shops and stores.

The best place in the city to shop for handicrafts is the government-run FONART store on Plaza San Francisco, which stocks items from all over Mexico. Another good place to browse is La Casa del Artesano, Av. Carranza #540 about 5 blocks west of Plaza de Armas; it sells crafts from the state of San Luis Potosí.

CERRO DE SAN PEDRO is about 8 km (5 mi.) e. out of the city on Av. Universidad (Mex. 70) to a signed turnoff, then 13 km (8 mi.) n., following signs At this partially inhabited ghost town you can see former shops, churches, estates and a hospital. San Pedro was founded in 1583 when several mines in the region began operations. By the late 1940s gold, lead, iron, manganese and mercury deposits had largely been depleted, although local firms continue to extract limited quantities of minerals from the mines. Visitors can enter La Descubridora, the town's first mine. Check with the State Tourism Office or your hotel concierge for information about guided excursions.

CHURCH OF OUR LADY OF EL CARMEN (Iglesia de Nuestra Señora del Carmen) is in the historic center on Plaza del Carmen, a blk. w. of Alameda Park. This ornate church is the city's finest example of Churrigueresque architecture. Its domes are decorated with blue, green, yellow and white tiles. Also note the profusion of carved stone angels, a hallmark of indigenous craftsmanship. The interior contains a carved pulpit, a reredos by Eduardo Tresguerras, paintings by Vallejo and a baroque altar considered one of the most impressive in Mexico.

FEDERICO SILVA MUSEUM OF CONTEMPORARY SCULPTURE (Museo Federico Silva Escultura Contemporánea) is downtown at Av. Alvaro Obregón #80, just n. of Plaza San Juan de Dios (about 3 blks. e. of Plaza de Armas). This is the only museum in Mexico devoted entirely to sculpture, and the first in Latin America to focus on contemporary sculpture. Several large rooms on each of the two floors exhibit oversize metal and plaster sculptures as well as two large mobiles. Time: Allow 1 hour minimum. Hours: Mon. and Wed.-Sat. 10-6, Sun. 10-2. Cost: 30 pesos (about $2.20 U.S.); free to all Sun. Phone: (444) 812-3848.

GOVERNMENT PALACE (Palacio de Gobierno) is just w. of Plaza de Armas. This neoclassic structure dates from 1770. Here Benito Juárez, despite petitions for mercy from wife and children, denied clemency to Archduke Maximilian; the deposed emperor was subsequently executed at Querétaro. A wax tableau and a portrait gallery in the Juárez Room recall the event. Hours: Open to visitors during regular business hours. Cost: Free.

HOUSE OF CULTURE (Casa de la Cultura) is w. of the city center at Av. Carranza #1815. This neoclassic mansion was once the "country house" of wealthy Irish businessman Gerardo Meade Lewis and his Spanish wife Monica Joaquina Sainz-Trapaga. The building, which had former incarnations as a hotel and a school, features beautiful woodwork, ornate doors and window frames and a carved staircase railing.

Both permanent and temporary art exhibits are displayed. There also is a small room containing items related to the city's history. Exhibit information is in Spanish. Time: Allow 1 hour minimum. Hours: Tues.-Sat. 10-5, Sun. 10-2. Cost: 20 pesos (about $1.50 U.S.); 10 pesos (children and senior citizens). Phone: (444) 813-2247.

NATIONAL MASK MUSEUM (Museo Nacional de la Máscara) is in the Zona Centro at Villerías #2, in Plaza Carmen across from the Teatro de la Paz. The museum is housed in an impressively ornate Italianate-style mansion, recently restored, that was built in the 1890s and once belonged to Spanish mining magnate Don Ramon Marti. Permanent exhibits on the first floor include traditional masks representing different historical eras. Many of the masks are placed on fully costumed mannequins to lend a feeling of authenticity.

The restored rooms on the upper level are decorated with period furnishings depicting the wealthy lifestyle enjoyed by the Marti family. Original family heirlooms can be seen in the bedroom, living room, ladies' parlor, men's smoking room, ballroom and chapel. The museum also features temporary exhibits of masks from around the world. Monitors throughout the museum show videos of traditional masked dances in subtitled English, but exhibit background information is in Spanish only.

Time: Allow 1 hour minimum. Hours: Tues.-Fri. 10-6, Sat. 10-5, Sun.-Mon. 10-3. Closed Jan. 1 and Christmas. Cost: 20 pesos (about $1.50 U.S.); 10 pesos (ages 5-12, students and senior citizens). The fee to use a camera is 20 pesos. Free to all Tues. Phone: (444) 812-3025. GT

**SAN POTOSÍ REGIONAL MUSEUM** (Museo Regional Potosino) is at Calle Hermenegildo Galeana #450, a block w. of the Church of San Francisco. Housed in the former Convent of San Francisco, it contains artifacts, historical documents and exhibits relating to the Huastec Indians. The impressively lavish 17th-century Aranzazú Chapel (Capilla de Aranzazú) is in the rear of the building.

The church, remodeled in the 20th century but retaining the original 17th-century sacristy (vestment room) of carved pink stone, is part of the complex as well. **Hours:** Tues.-Sun. 9-5:50. **Cost:** 47 pesos (about $3.50 U.S.). The fee to use a camera is 4 pesos. **Phone:** (444) 812-0358.

## SAN MIGUEL DE ALLENDE, GUANAJUATO (C-2) pop. 160,383

You sense that San Miguel de Allende (pronounced a-YEHN-deh) is special before you even get there. The feeling is reinforced in subtle ways: a family selling snacks along the roadside, a horse and rider clip-clopping contentedly in the distance, brown hills brightened by wildflowers. At this altitude the air has a refreshing coolness, even though the sun is bright. Small clusters of dwellings—tiny cement cubes with tin roofs—and dirt yards exhibit obvious poverty, but somehow seem less grim than the vast shantytowns ringing Mexico City.

Mex. 111, a local two-lane road that branches west off highway Mex. 57-D, is an unlikely gateway to the charm that defines San Miguel. Its outskirts have that everyday scruffiness common to most Mexican towns—dilapidated gas stations mix with newer commercial development in a small-scale version of "suburban sprawl."

But as Mex. 111 twists and turns toward the center of town, things start to change. The street narrows and becomes cobbled. Aged buildings rub shoulders along a sidewalk barely wide enough for one pedestrian, let alone two. Open shop doorways offer quick glimpses of clothing and crafts.

Suddenly you're at a scenic overlook, a pull-off with a small parking area. A few vendors sit beside their wares—piles of woven baskets, perhaps, or neatly arranged rows of painted ceramic figurines. Below a protective wrought-iron fence the town spreads out, filling a bowl-shaped valley. One structure towers above the others: multispired La Parroquía, the parish church (see attraction listing).

San Miguel began as a mission where Indians were evangelized and also taught European weaving and agricultural techniques. As it prospered, the settlement became a local market center for the surrounding haciendas trading in cattle and textiles. Historical significance made its mark as well: Here native son Ignacio Allende, along with Father Miguel Hidalgo y Costilla, a priest from the neighboring town of Dolores Hidalgo, planned the original uprising that led to Mexico's bitter and protracted War of Independence.

In 1926, the Mexican government designated the city a national historic monument, and preservation measures began in earnest. Modern construction was prohibited in the city center; crumbling old buildings were carefully restored. Foreigners began moving in during the 1930s, and today there is an established North American expatriate community of artisans, teachers, writers and part-time residents.

## Practicalities

Del Bajio International Airport is in León, about a 90-minute drive away. American and United offer flights from selected U.S. cities, including Dallas/Fort Worth, Houston and Los Angeles. Polanco Tours, a San Miguel tour company, offers van transportation to and from the airport. One-way fare is about $72 (U.S.) for two passengers, plus $10 for each additional passenger up to six; phone (415) 152-4193. A taxi ride from Querétaro to San Miguel will run about $45. *For additional information about airlines see Arriving by Air, page p. 42.*

"Deluxe" bus service from Mexico City's Terminal Central de Autobuses del Norte is provided daily by ETN; Primera Plus and Pegaso Plus provide first-class service. The trip is nonstop and takes about 3 hours. Second-class service by Flecha Amarilla and Herradura de Plata takes 4 hours and includes a stop in Querétaro and local stops en route. Flecha Amarilla buses also provide frequent service between San Miguel and Guanajuato. The central bus station is on the westward extension of Calle Canal, about 1.5 kilometers (1 mile) west of the center of town. *For additional information about buses see Bus Service, page p. 52.*

Taxis provide flat-rate service between the bus station and downtown, as well as to other locations around the city, for about $3 to $5 (U.S.). There is a *sitio* (cab stand) at the main plaza.

By car, the 180-mile journey from Mexico City takes 3 to 4 hours via Mex. 57-D to the Querétaro toll bypass (watch for the San Miguel exit). The bypass highway crosses Mex. 57-D north of Querétaro and connects with Mex. 111, which proceeds northwest to San Miguel. The trip along two-lane Mex. 111 is slow but scenic, offering views of typical Mexican rural life. From Guanajuato, take Mex. 45 and 45-D south and east toward Celaya, then Mex. 51 north.

**Note:** Street parking is scarce in the congested historic center, and local police do not hesitate to issue violators a ticket. If driving from Mexico City or elsewhere, you may have to park several blocks from the center. If you're staying in town and have a car leave it at your hotel, since almost everything of interest is within walking distance. The altitude may initially tire visitors not used to walking at higher elevations.

Banks along Calle San Francisco exchange currency Mon.-Fri. 9-1:30, but have long lines; the *casas de cambio* (currency exchange houses) located in the vicinity of the main plaza are a quicker alternative.

Internet San Miguel Cyber Café, Calle Mesones #57 (entrance on Calle Reloj), 2 blocks north of the main square, offers full cyber cafe services as well as espresso and cappuccino made from organic Chiapan coffee beans. It's open Mon.-Sat. 9-9, Sun. 10-6.

San Miguel's weather is warm and dry most of the year, but the city rarely experiences the extremes of heat common to much of Mexico. Winter nights can be chilly, and many hotels aren't heated (although some have fireplaces). The rainy season is June through September. In May an extra splash of color is added when the jacaranda trees are covered with purple blooms.

## Exploring Around Town

Some travelers complain that San Miguel's "gentrification," so to speak, has replaced authentic Mexican atmosphere with a touristy vibe—trendy restaurants, pricey boutiques and a lack of local grit. It's true that foreign investors have driven up prices, and the bright orange and red facades add a Disneyesque touch.

But a stroll through the historic center proves that these complaints are primarily quibbles. There is atmosphere to spare, from heavy carved wooden doors to intricate stone carvings adorning the windows of handsome old buildings. Their sheltered inner patios, cool retreats filled with trees, burbling fountains, clipped hedges and flowerpot urns, have a timeless beauty.

You'll see other tourists but also have plenty of opportunities to mingle with locals—perhaps children who shyly ask if you want to buy some gum ("Chicle"?), or an elderly gentleman whiling away the afternoon at El Jardín, the main plaza.

Make the plaza, located between calles San Francisco and Correo, your first stop. Shaded by Indian laurel trees, it's a great place to relax on a wrought-iron bench, listen to the tolling bells of La Parroquía and observe the local scene. Buy a cold drink and plan the day's itinerary. In the evening mariachi bands play, vendors sell carnitas (grilled pork) and churros (doughnut-like fritters), flocks of pigeons flutter and couples stroll. This is the city's heart.

Most attractions are within easy walking distance of the plaza, and the historic center is compact. Wear comfortable shoes; many streets are cobblestoned, and some are steep.

San Miguel's reputation as an arts center was established by the opening of the Allende Institute, southwest of downtown at Calle Ancha de San Antonio #20. One of its American founders, Stirling Dickinson, came to Mexico as a tourist in the 1930s and fell in love with the city. Fountains, arcades and courtyard gardens grace the grounds of the campus, which has extensive classroom space, two art galleries, a theater and a library.

The Bellas Artes Cultural Center (Centro Cultural Bellas Artes), about 2 blocks west of the main plaza at Calle Hernández Macías #75, also is called the Centro Cultural el Nigromante (its official name) and the Centro Cultural Ignacio Ramírez. It is a branch of the well-known National Institute of Fine Arts (Instituto Nacional de Bellas Artes) in Mexico City. The impressive building dates from the mid-18th century and has an immense, tree-shaded courtyard. Several murals are exhibited, including one by David Alfaro Siqueiros. Admission is free.

Helene Kahn Tours conducts English-language walking tours of the city ($20 U.S. per person) as well as guided excursions to out-of-town points of interest, such as the Sanctuary of Atotonilco. Reservations are required; check the website for details.

For information about local happenings, consult the weekly English-language newspaper Atención San Miguel, which is available at the public library (see attraction listing) and the El Colibri bookstore, about 2 blocks east of the main plaza at Calle Sollano #30.

## Shopping

San Miguel is known for regionally produced, high-quality handicrafts. Metalwork—masks, trays, lanterns, picture frames and decorative objects made of tin, copper, brass, bronze and wrought iron—and the work of local silversmiths is particularly worth seeking out. You'll also find pottery, weavings, sculpture, straw items, hand-loomed cambaya cloth (a material frequently used to make skirts), and folk and traditional art. The colonial furniture is some of the finest produced in Mexico.

Most craft and gift shops are open Mon.-Sat. 9-7 and close from 2-4 for the traditional siesta; a few may open briefly on Sunday. Many accept U.S. dollars and/or MasterCard and Visa, and some will pack and ship purchases.

The open-air City Market fills the plaza near the Church of San Felipe Neri, several blocks northeast of the main plaza, and usually spreads onto the surrounding streets. Livestock and fresh produce share space with inexpensive everyday items and souvenirs at the cheaper end of the price scale. The Crafts Market (Mercado de Artesanías) consists of vendor stalls in an alley off Calle Loreto, near the Quinta Loreto Hotel and the City Market.

Pricier boutiques are scattered throughout the historic downtown area. Casa Canal, on Calle Canal, specializes in hand-carved wooden furniture. Casa Maxwell, Calle Canal #14, has an array of Mexican and Latin American folk art. For a large selection of antiques, colonial art and home furnishings, browse through La Antigua Casa Canela, Calle Umaran #20.

Art galleries are concentrated around the main plaza, and exhibit openings are big social events. Two that showcase both regional and national talent are Galería San Miguel, Plaza Principal #14, and Galería Atenea, Calle Jesús #2.

Take a road trip to Galería Atotonilco. From downtown San Miguel, take Calzada de la Aurora (the northward extension of Calle Hidalgo), which becomes Mexico #51 heading to Dolores Hidalgo. Continue north about 8 kilometers (5 miles). At El Cortijo, just past the Escondido Spa, turn left in front of a small stone arch, then left again where the main road veers left. After approximately .65 kilometers (.4 miles), watch for two houses (one yellow and one white) next to each other. Turn right between them and follow the curving driveway to the red gallery building.

Located in a beautiful rural setting on the Río Laja, the gallery carries high-quality handicrafts and antiques from all over Mexico—ceramic jars, vases and platters, colorful baskets, hand-forged ironwork, country-style furniture. Folk art includes whimsical trees of life in different sizes, hand-painted animal wood carvings from Oaxaca, papier-mâché skeletons and *retablos* (small oil paintings of Catholic saints). There's also a nice selection of hand-woven *sarapes* from villages in northern Mexico. The gallery is open by appointment only; phone (415) 185-2225 or (510) 295-4097 (from the United States).

## Dining, Nightlife and Events

Due to San Miguel's expat community there are numerous restaurants offering a wide range of cuisines. They also open and close regularly; check with the State Tourism Office for the current local favorites. The most expensive places are in the upscale hotels, where the dress code may require a sports coat for men. See the Lodgings & Restaurants section for AAA-RATED dining establishments.

You can sip fancy cocktails and dance to DJ-spun hip-hop at the Mint nightclub, located in the same building as the El Petit Four restaurant/bakery (Calle Mesones #99, near the main plaza). Mama Mia's, a bar and restaurant at Calle Umarán #8, has live salsa and jazz bands.

San Miguel celebrates a number of festivals throughout the year. Perhaps the biggest event is the Fiesta of the Archangel San Miguel (Fiesta de San Miguel Arcángel) on Sept. 29, which honors the town's patron saint. The festivities, which extend for several days, take place around the main plaza and along the adjoining streets and include parades, fireworks and regional dance performances.

Holy Week (Semana Santa) celebrations, which begin about 2 weeks before Easter Sunday, include a lavish procession on Good Friday and the burning of Judas effigies on Easter. The traditional and very popular Festival of San Antonio de Padua (Fiesta de San Antonio de Padua) is held on June 13; it features the Los Locos (Crazy Ones) parade, when people dress up in fanciful costumes and masks and parade through the streets to the accompaniment of live music.

The Chamber Music Festival (Festival de Música de Cámara) is held the first 2 weeks of August at the Bellas Artes Cultural Center. The International Festival of Jazz and Blues takes place in mid-November.

San Miguel's traditional *posadas,* with music, canticles and plays dramatizing Mary and Joseph's search for an inn, ring in the holiday season beginning Dec. 16. The State Tourism Office has information about these and other event happenings.

**State Tourism Office:** (Desarrollo Social del Municipio de San Miguel de Allende) is on Calle San Francisco, across from the n. side of El Jardín (the main plaza). Open Mon.-Fri. 8:30-8, Sat. 10-8, Sun. 10-5:30. **Phone:** (415) 152-0900.

**CHURCH OF THE CONCEPTION** (Iglesia de la Concepción) is about 2 blks. w. of the main plaza at calles Canal and Hernández Macías. It was begun in the mid-17th century, although the domed roof—one of the largest in Mexico—was not completed until 1891. While the exterior is worn, inside is a breathtaking *retablo* more than 30 feet tall, decorated with gilded wood and numerous statues. Also notable are the huge oil paintings in both transepts portraying events in the lives of Jesus and Mary. **Time:** Allow 30 minutes minimum. **Hours:** Open daily; Sun. Mass. at 10 a.m. **Cost:** Free; donations accepted. **Phone:** (415) 152-0148.

**CHURCH OF SAN FELIPE NERI** (Oratorio de San Felipe Neri) is at calles Insurgentes and Loreto, 2 blks. n.e. of the main plaza. It was built by San Miguel's Indian population in the early 18th century. The original structure is graced with a lovely facade of pink stone and detailed carvings of saints. The southern exterior, added later, incorporates a baroque style, and the difference is striking. Pass through the low, narrow entrance vestibule to the church's interior, replete with ancient wood benches, rich gold leaf decoration and colorful ceramic statues. The small garden courtyard is a cool and peaceful spot to relax.

**Time:** Allow 1 hour minimum. **Hours:** Daily 8-4 when Mass is not taking place. **Cost:** Free; donations accepted. **Phone:** (415) 152-0521.

**CHURCH OF SAN FRANCISCO** is at the corner of Calle San Francisco and Calle Juárez, 2 blks. from the main plaza. Built in the late 18th century, it is thought to be the work of Eduardo Tresguerras, who contributed to the design of many churches in central Mexico. Construction was financed through donations from wealthy families and the proceeds from bullfights.

The intricate stone carvings gracing the exterior are a fine example of the ornate Churrigueresque style. The high-ceilinged interior contains statues, paintings and more carved stone. The church's shaded outdoor courtyard, complete with stone fountain, is a pleasant spot to rest your feet. **Hours:** Daily 7-2; walk-in visitors are not permitted during services that begin at 7 a.m., 10 and 1. **Cost:** Free; donations accepted.

**HISTORICAL MUSEUM OF SAN MIGUEL DE ALLENDE** (Museo Histórico de San Miguel de Allende) is on Calle Cuna de Allende #1, opposite the s.w. corner of the main plaza; street parking is limited. It was the birthplace of Ignacio Allende, one of the few early leaders of the War of Independence with actual military training. Together, he and Father Miguel Hidalgo organized a ragtag army and plotted strategies for overthrowing Spanish rule.

The two-story building has a central courtyard and exhibits that offer a peek into what life was like in early 19th-century provincial Mexico. A typical kitchen is equipped with a wood-burning stove, fuels and local foodstuffs. Period furniture and artwork in the formal receiving room reflect the opulence enjoyed by the era's privileged citizens. Furnished living areas, a play room and a master bedroom also can be seen. In the courtyard there are small storage granaries, citrus trees and a quiet corner for spiritual contemplation. A mini theater shows a 5-minute film about the history of the house.

**Time:** Allow 1 hour minimum. **Hours:** Tues.-Sun. 9-5. **Cost:** 47 pesos (about $3.50 U.S.); free (ages 0-12). Cash only. **Phone:** (415) 152-2499.

**LA GRUTA HOT SPRINGS** is 10 km (6 mi.) n. of San Miguel on Mex. 51, the road to Dolores Hidalgo, following signs. A hilly green oasis in the midst of a dry, dusty landscape, La Gruta (The Grotto) is one of the most popular of the region's several thermal hot springs.

The 12-acre, tree-shaded site is located just off the highway and has several interconnected pools, each with a lawn and table/chair area. One of the pools is underground, accessed by walking in a dim and narrow tunnel in about 4 feet of water; the tunnel leads to a domed cavern where a jet of warm spring water blasts from a pipe in the wall. The soothing water is non-chlorinated and has no sulfurous odor. Visitors also can indulge in a massage or spa treatment.

Changing rooms, restrooms, lockers and shower facilities are provided. Outdoor wooden stair access is on the rustic side. No outside food or beverages are permitted. **Time:** Allow 2 hours minimum. **Hours:** Daily 7-5. **Cost:** 110 pesos (about $8.15 U.S.). Locker rental fee 50 pesos. Cash only. **Phone:** (415) 185-2162.

**PARISH CHURCH** (La Parroquía) is on Calle Correo, facing the s. side of the main plaza; street parking is limited. Soaring over the plaza, La Parroquía dominates the city. Originally built in the late 17th century in a plain Franciscan style, it was given an imposing facelift 2 centuries later by a local Indian artisan, Zeferino Gutiérrez. With no formal training, he added the present facade of pink-hued sandstone, allegedly using postcard pictures of French Gothic cathedrals as his inspiration.

Inside are murals, vaulted ceilings, side chapels and statues of saints, including St. Michael the Archangel (the church's official name is Parroquía de San Miguel Arcángel). The tomb of Anastasio Bustamante, president of Mexico from 1832-33 and again from 1839-41, is open to the public on Nov. 2. The original bell, cast in 1732, begins ringing early in the morning to summon parishioners. **Time:** Allow 45 minutes minimum. **Hours:** Church open daily 6 a.m.-9 p.m. Sun. Mass held 6 a.m.-1 p.m. and at 6 and 8 p.m. **Cost:** Free; donations accepted. **Phone:** (415) 152-4197.

**PUBLIC LIBRARY** (Biblioteca Pública) is 2 blks. n. of the main plaza at Calle Insurgentes #25. This is the second largest bilingual library in Latin America. Checking the variety of notices posted at the entrance (many in English) is a good way to find out what's going on around town.

A 2-hour house and garden tour of various San Miguel homes departs from the library on Sundays at noon, except on specified Sundays that celebrate Mexican and religious holidays. Tour tickets are available beginning at 11 a.m. Other library-sponsored guided tours visit the former silver mining town of Mineral de Pozos, the nearby communities of Atotonilco, Dolores Hidalgo and Tequisquiapan, and the cities of Guanajuato and Querétaro.

**Hours:** Library open Mon.-Fri. 10-7, Sat. 10-2. Phone ahead to confirm tour schedule. **Cost:** Library free. Tour fee 230 pesos (or $20 U.S.), which benefits programs that help the city's youth. **Phone:** (415) 152-0293.

**SANCTUARY OF ATOTONILCO** (Santuario de Atotonilco) is about 15 km (9 mi.) n. on Mex. 51, then about 3 km (1.9 mi.) s.w. off the highway in the village of Atotonilco. "El Santuario" minibuses make this trip, departing from the bus stop on Calle Puente Umarán (opposite the city market). The church's exterior is plain and worn, but inside is true beauty—walls and arched ceilings covered with writings, poems, paintings and frescoes, most in full color. The Chapel of the Rosario, dedicated to Our Lady of Guadalupe, has an entire wall adorned with gold-framed stations of the cross surrounding a life-size statue of the saint.

Hiring a guide in San Miguel to show you around the church and explain its historical significance makes for a more rewarding experience. **Time:** Allow 30 minutes minimum. **Hours:** Daily 10-6. **Cost:** Free; donations accepted.

**TABOADA SPRINGS** are about 8 km (5 mi.) n. of San Miguel on Mex. 51 (the road to Dolores Hidalgo), then w. following signs to the Hotel Hacienda Taboada. Located on the hotel grounds, these mineral springs feed a thermal spa, which provides a hot soaking and reputed skin benefits. There also are two swimming pools and a large lawn area. Snacks and drinks are available. The buses that go to Atotonilco also stop within walking distance of the spa, but a more convenient means of transportation is to hire a taxi to take you directly to the hotel. **Hours:** Wed.-Mon. 10-6. **Cost:** 300 pesos (about $22 U.S.); 150 pesos (children). **Phone:** (415) 152-9250.

## TEQUILA, JALISCO (C-1) pop. 40,697

This typical Mexican town is about 56 kilometers (35 miles) northwest of Guadalajara, just off Mex. 15. It sits amid extensive plantations devoted to the cultivation of the agave plant, from which the same-named beverage is extracted. Local distilleries (the major one is Sauza) have obtained a patent that prohibits other producers, even those within Mexico, from calling their drink tequila.

Cultivated agave plants resemble a field of spiny blue bayonets. Although the region's indigenous peoples had long drunk the fermented sap, the Spaniards introduced the distilling process. The tough, sword-shaped fronds are stripped from the plant, exposing its "heart," which can weigh more than 100 pounds. The hearts are "cooked" in large copper kettles, and the resulting liquid is transferred to huge tanks. Clear tequila is bottled at once; the golden variety ages in oak casks for up to 7 years.

The Guadalajara Chamber of Commerce organizes a Tequila day trip, the "Tequila Express," in conjunction with Mexican National Railways. The train leaves the Guadalajara rail station, located at Avenida Washington and Calzada Independencia Sur (near Agua Azul Park), Saturdays and Sundays around 10 a.m. en route to the Herradura distillery in the town of Amatitán.

The trip includes mariachi music and tequila tastings on board, a tour of the distillery and a buffet-style lunch. Tickets cost 1,370 pesos (about $101 U.S.); 930 pesos (ages 6-11). They can be purchased at the chamber, Av. Vallarta #4095 (at the corner of Avenida Niño Obrero); phone (33) 3880-9099. Tickets also can be purchased through Ticketmaster in Guadalajara; phone (33) 3818-3800. Reservations should be made at least 10 days in advance.

Tequila lies at the northern base of extinct, 9,797-foot Volcán de Tequila, which has a stopper of hardened lava in its crater. Shards of obsidian, a volcanic glass, are visible in cuts flanking the highway near town. La Toma, a picnic spot with a waterfall and swimming pool, is about 4 kilometers (2.5 miles) northwest of Tequila off Mex. 15. It's in the vicinity of the Santiago River Canyon, a particularly scenic area.

## TLAQUEPAQUE, JALISCO (C-1)
pop. 608,114

Tlaquepaque (tla-keh-PAH-keh), part of the Guadalajara metropolitan area, borders the southeastern side of the city. An important crafts center, it produces the distinctive, hand-painted Tlaquepaque pottery that is prized throughout Mexico. The fragile earthenware is decorated by hand. Many artisans still use the potter's wheel, and visitors can view the work in progress at some pottery shops. Tlaquepaque also is known for blown glass, textiles, jewelry, furniture, copperware and carved wood. The town is a tourist magnet and can get very crowded, but dedicated shoppers won't want to miss out on the huge selection of high-quality handicrafts.

The word "mariachi" seems to have originated in Tlaquepaque. French soldiers garrisoned in the city in the mid-19th century noted that the strolling troubadours performed primarily at weddings, or *mariages*, hence the possible derivation of the term. Mariachi bands perform in the gazebo within Jardín Hidalgo, the main plaza (bounded by the streets Independencia, Guillermo Prieto, Morelos and Francisco I. Madero).

Browsing is easiest along pedestrian-only Calle Independencia. Many of the shops and galleries are housed in refurbished old mansions with thick stone walls and iron gates. Most of the larger shops accept U.S. dollars or payment by credit card, and will arrange to have purchases packed and shipped as well.

Many are closed or open limited hours on Sunday. Under the circular roof of El Parián, a building in the middle of town, are many sidewalk cafes, pleasant spots to relax over a leisurely lunch while the shops close for afternoon *siesta* (usually between 2 and 4).

La Casa Canela, Independencia #258, has showrooms arranged around a lush garden patio. This tasteful shop offers Mexican furniture, papier-mâché artworks and antiques. Tierra Tlaquepaque, Independencia #156, offers wood sculpture, pottery and decorative objects. Sergio Bustamente's fanciful sculptures, known around the world, are featured at the Galería Sergio Bustamente, Calle Independencia #238.

Linea Turquesa (TUR) buses depart regularly for Tlaquepaque and Tonalá (*see separate listing within this region*) from downtown Guadalajara; the trip takes about half an hour. They carry only seated passengers; cheaper city buses carry standing passengers as well and are likely to be crowded. Tell the driver you want to get off at the stop nearest El Parián.

If driving, take Avenida Revolución off Calzada Independencia Sur, heading southeast away from downtown Guadalajara. This road becomes Boulevard Tlaquepaque as it heads into town. At the traffic circle, bear right onto Avenida Niños Héroes, which runs into Calle Independencia after a block.

**Tourist information office:** Calle Guillermo Prieto #80, just n. of the main plaza. Open Mon.-Fri. 9-3, Sat. 9-1. **Phone:** (33) 3635-5756.

**REGIONAL MUSEUM OF CERAMICS** (Museo Regional de la Cerámica) is at Calle Independencia #237, at Calle Alfareros. Housed in an 18th-century building that was formerly a private home, it contains several rooms displaying mostly modern regional pottery pieces as well as some pre-Columbian artifacts. Exhibit information is in Spanish. **Hours:** Tues.-Sun. 11-8. Closed Christmas. **Cost:** Free. **Phone:** (33) 3635-5404.

## TLAXCALA, TLAXCALA (D-4) pop. 89,795

Capital of the same-named state, Tlaxcala (tlas-KAH-lah) is about 75 miles east of Mexico City. This amiable colonial town is off the tourist track, but it's one of Mexico's most picturesque places, and makes for a delightful day trip from Mexico City or Puebla.

Buildings downtown are painted in shades of sepia, deep red and orange. Plaza Constitución, the main square, has neatly trimmed trees, a bandstand and a burbling fountain presented to the city by King Philip III.

On the plaza's north side is the Government Palace (Palacio de Gobierno), with a brick exterior accented by ornately decorated windows and doorways. Inside are extravagantly colorful murals depicting agricultural life and the history of the Tlaxcaltec people, painted in the early 1960s by local artist Desiderio Hernández Xochitiotzin.

Also on the plaza is the baroque Palace of Justice (Palacio de Justicia), with neoclassic touches added

# The Legend of Quetzalcóatl

One of Mexican history's most intriguing mysteries surrounds Quetzalcóatl, a man known for his advocacy of peace and who was believed to have opposed the practice of human sacrifice. Over time, fact and myth have become almost impenetrably tangled, although certain events are reasonably established. The son of Toltec chieftain Mixcóatl, Quetzalcóatl took the full name Ce Acatl Quetzalcóatl (literally, "One Reed Feathered Serpent"). It is believed that he founded the Toltec city of Tollan (Tula); the plumed serpent motif is noticeably evident at this archeological site. A power struggle ensued, and according to legend Quetzalcóatl's rivals conspired to get him drunk and thereby shame him into exile. (A more likely scenario is that the continued invasion of warlike tribes caused a decline in Toltec power.)

The king led his followers, it is said, out of Tula and east toward

the Gulf coast, where he either sailed off, promising to return in a future era, or burned himself alive and was reincarnated as the

© Bartosz Nitkiewicz / Shutterstock.com

morning star. Meanwhile, Quetzalcóatl the myth continued to be invoked, a personage described as light-skinned, blue-eyed and bearded—features different from those of any person the Indians had ever before seen. When Hernando Cortés arrived in the Aztec capital of Tenochtitlan, the emperor Moctezuma believed him to be the returning god—a case of mistaken identity the *conquistador* craftily used to his advantage.

in the 18th century. Inside the Parish Church of St. Joseph (Parroquía de San José), a peach-colored building, is the Chapel of St. Joseph (Capilla de San José), which has an arched ceiling with plaster ornamentation and impressive altarpieces.

Perhaps the finest examples of pre-Columbian artwork in all of Mexico are the mural paintings on view at the ruins of Cacaxtla (ca-CASHT-la). Discovered in 1975, they remain vividly colorful more than a thousand years after their execution. Archeological evidence suggests the city that once stood here reached a peak of development between A.D. 650 and 900, and was abandoned by the beginning of the 11th century.

Cacaxtla's earliest structures were a group of adobe edifices demolished over time and filled in to form a large platform. This process was repeated several times until the foundation reached its present height. Most of the structures seen today are vestiges dating from the latest period of construction. Ceremonial courtyards, tombs and enclosures were repeatedly reconfigured during the site's centuries of occupation.

About 45 kilometers (28 miles) southeast of Tlaxcala is La Malinche National Park. The park's dominant feature is La Malinche, an extinct volcano 14,632 feet high. At the park entrance is Malintzin, a vacation resort run by the Mexican Social Security Institute (IMSS) that offers lodgings, sports facilities and medical services in a wooded setting. Malintzin lies at a 9,840-foot elevation on the northern slopes of the mountain; from a marked exit on Mex. 136 between the towns of Apizaco and Huamantla (the sign reads "Centro Vacacional Malintzi"), a road ascends 14 kilometers (9 miles) to the retreat.

**Tlaxcala State Tourism Office (Secretaría de Turismo):** at the intersection of avenidas Benito Juárez and Lardizábal (behind the Government Palace). The staff speaks English. Open Mon.-Fri. 9-7, Sat.-Sun. 10-6. **Phone:** 01 (800) 509-6557 (toll-free long distance within Mexico).

**CACAXTLA RUINS** are about 17 km (12 mi.) southwest of Tlaxcala. To reach them by car from the center of town, take the road to Nativitas (follow signs) and then watch for the sign about 1.5 km (1 mi.) w. of that town indicating the direction to Cacaxtla and the nearby village of San Miguel del Milagro. The hillside entrance to the site is about a 1-mi. walk from the parking lot. From the Mexico City-Puebla toll road (Mex. 150-D), take the San Martín Texmelucan exit and proceed e. toward Nativitas about 6 km (4 mi.), following signs.

Climb the stairs to reach the Gran Plaza, a broad platform protected by a huge metal roof. In addition to providing rain and sun protection, boardwalks beneath this overhead run right up to the various murals and stone carvings. The largest and most dramatic of the murals is the mythological Mural of the Battle, painted between A.D. 650 and 700. It depicts two groups of warriors—one outfitted in birdlike plumage and feather headdresses, the other cloaked in the skins of

jaguars. The colors—rich blues, reds, yellows and browns—and the depth of detail are startling.

**Note:** The ticket window is about 100 feet inside the ruins complex, which is open per the schedule even if the gate happens to be closed. **Time:** Allow 3 hours minimum. **Hours:** Daily 9-5:30. **Cost:** (includes Xochitécatl site) 62 pesos (about $4.60 U.S.); free (ages 0-12). The fee to use a video camera is 45 pesos. **Phone:** (246) 416-0000. ⏹ ⏹

**Xochitécatl** is about a 2 km (1.2 mi.) walk from Cacaxtla on the other side of a small valley. It was not uncovered until 1994. The large, open-air site consists of three pyramids and the base of a fourth. The Pirámide de la Espiral, named for its circular shape, is thought to have been used for astronomical explorations or built in dedication to Ehecatl, the god of wind. The Pyramid of the Flowers (Pirámide de las Flores), also constructed of rounded stones, has an exceptionally wide base. **Hours:** Daily 9-5:30. **Cost:** included in Cacaxtla Ruins fee.

**EX-CONVENT OF THE ASSUMPTION** (Ex-Convento Francisco de la Asunción) is s.e. of the main plaza and off a smaller plaza, Plaza Xicoténcatl; a cobblestone path leads up a hill to the cathedral. It dates from the early 16th century. The original chapel with its stone baptismal font can be seen. In the Franciscan church are gilded altars, 17th-century religious paintings and an intricately carved and decorated wooden ceiling in *mudéjar* (Moorish) fashion. A lovely open-air chapel features Moorish-style pointed arches. **Hours:** Daily 10-2 and 4-6. **Cost:** Free.

**Tlaxcala Regional Museum** (Museo Regional de Tlaxcala) is in the church's cloister. Exhibits in the whitewashed rooms depict the state's history from prehistoric times to the present. **Hours:** Tues.-Sun. 10-5. **Cost:** 52 pesos (about $3.85 U.S.). **Phone:** (246) 462-0262.

**MUSEUM OF POPULAR ARTS AND TRADITIONS** (Museo de Artes Populares y Tradiciones) is at Blvd. Mariano Sanchez and Calle 1 de Mayo, 3 blks. w. of the main plaza. This small museum exhibits such items as clay water jugs and animal skins. **Hours:** Tues.-Sun. 10-6. **Cost:** 20 pesos (about $1.50 U.S.); 10 pesos (children). **Phone:** (246) 462-2337.

**SANCTUARY OF THE VIRGIN OF OCOTLÁN** (Santuario de la Virgen de Ocotlán) sits atop a high hill about a mile e. of Tlaxcala's town center, in the small hamlet of Ocotlán. It commemorates the supposed appearance of the Virgin of Guadalupe to the Indian Juan Diego Bernardino at this site in 1541. The church is surrounded by a large plaza, with a quiet, shady park across the street. The exterior is quite interesting: an intricately detailed front facade of white stucco, dominated by a large, fluted shell-like design and twin towers made from local cantera stone.

The interior is an explosion of gilded, carved wood ornamentation, with a large altar and several side sconces with life-size statues of saints. The octagonal Dressing Room (Camarín), a chamber where the Virgin's robes were said to be changed, is graced with more carvings of saints and angels. Life's hard realities are underscored by signs on the church's entry door that advertise low-cost services for the poor.

You can hike to the sanctuary from town or take an inexpensive *colectivo* (minivan) designated "Ocotlán"; the driver will stop at the front steps and wait while you visit. **Hours:** Daily 8-6. **Cost:** Donations.

**SANTA ANA CHIAUTEMPAN** is about 3 km (2 mi.) e. of the city center. The village is well known for hand-loomed *sarapes* and beautiful bolts of cloth. Numerous shops sell rugs and *sarapes*. Native craftwork is augmented by the tweeds and woolen bedspreads produced in the Tlaxcala region's modern textile plants.

**TIZATLÁN RUINS** are about 4 km (2.5 mi.) n.e. of town via Mex. 117-D to the Tizatlán turn-off. A wool-weaving settlement established by the Tlaxcaltecs in the mid-14th century, Tizatlán developed into a major trade center. The ruins include a palace built on a small platform and small sanctuaries with murals painted on the altars. These paintings depict wars with the Aztecs, who failed in their attempt to conquer the Tlaxcaltec nation. **Hours:** Tues.-Sun. 10-5. **Cost:** 39 pesos (about $2.90 U.S.).

## TONALÁ, JALISCO (C-1) pop. 478,689

Tonalá (toh-nah-LAH), about 7 kilometers (4 miles) east of Tlaquepaque, was the original site of Guadalajara until 1531, when the Spaniards, repeatedly harassed by hostile Indians, abandoned the area. Many homes in this noted pottery-producing center double as family-run pottery workshops, or *talleres,* and factories here produce many of the wares displayed in Tlaquepaque.

The best days to visit are Thursdays and Sundays, when there is a large open-air *tianguis* (market). Savvy shoppers can obtain excellent buys on glassware, ceramics and papier-mâché crafts, all spread out on the sidewalks in a colorful, enticing hodgepodge.

Tonalá's factories and workshops are concentrated along north-south Avenida de Los Tonaltecas, the main thoroughfare, and in the vicinity of the main plaza, at calles Juárez and Hidalgo. An excellent selection of ceramics can be found at Casa de Artesanos, Av. Tonaltecas Sur #140. The shop/studio of Ken Edwards, Calle Morelos #184, features lovely stoneware items.

Public buses traveling to Tlaquepaque also go to Tonalá. You can take a taxi as well; one-way fare should average about $4 (U.S.) from Tlaquepaque, $7 from Guadalajara. If driving, take the Zapotlanejo Highway (Carretera Zapotlanejo) east out of Tlaquepaque.

**Tourist information office:** downtown at Calle Pedro Moreno #85. Open Mon.-Sat.; phone ahead to confirm hours. **Phone:** (33) 3792-6315.

**NATIONAL MUSEUM OF CERAMICS** (Museo Nacional de la Cerámica) is at Av. Constitución #104, 2 blks. n. of City Hall. Housed in a two-story mansion, it displays a quality collection of pieces from different regions of Mexico dating from pre-Columbian to modern times, as well as displays showing the various methods of creating and firing pottery. Exhibit information is in Spanish. **Hours:** Tues.-Sun. 10-6. Phone ahead to confirm schedule. **Cost:** Free. **Phone:** (33) 3586-6000 Ext. 1412.

## TONANTZINTLA, PUEBLA (D-4)

Tonantzintla (toh-nahn-TSEEN-tlah) *(see Acatepec listing)* is worth a visit just for its amazing church, which dominates the tiny village.

**CHURCH OF SANTA MARÍA TONANTZINTLA** stands on the main plaza. While the yellow and red-tiled exterior looks fairly disciplined, the riotously ornate interior of this 17th-century church is a definitive example of the Churrigueresque architectural style. The walls and dome are completely covered with gilded plaster decorations, painted cherubs and saints garlanded in plumed headdresses. The ornate and colorful motifs include fruits, flowers and birds as well as Christmas themes, and the faces and dress of the human figures are strongly Indian in character.

The name Tonantzintla means "place of our little mother" in the Nahuatl Indian language and is derived from the Aztec goddess Tonantzin. Both this church and the one in neighboring Acatepec are an easy side trip via bus or taxi from Cholula or Puebla. **Note:** Photography is not permitted inside. **Hours:** Daily 10-1 and 3-5. Bus tours depart from Cholula's main plaza approximately every 45 minutes beginning at 10, Tues.-Sun. **Cost:** Church free. Bus tour tickets 95-111 pesos (about $7-$8.20 U.S.).

## TULA, HIDALGO (D-3) pop. 103,919

Tula (TOO-lah), or officially Tula de Allende, was founded by Franciscans in the early 16th century; their fortress-like church, which also dates from that time, still stands. Typical of smaller Mexican towns, it has a non-touristy look and a quiet central plaza bordered with taco stands. Archeologists long believed that the remains of the Toltec capital of Tollan, which means "metropolis" or "large city," were somewhere in this region; however, the exact whereabouts remained a mystery until the Tula ruins were determined to be the site in 1938.

Tula's dominance as a major city in pre-Hispanic Mexico was relatively brief—from about A.D. 950 to 1174, when the Chichimecs, forerunners of the Aztecs, attacked, sacked and burned it. The sculptural figure known as Chac Mool, first found at this site, has become an international artistic symbol of Mesoamerican culture. But the reclining figure—holding a vessel that presumably received still-beating hearts torn from victims' chests during sacrificial ceremonies—underscores the violent nature of Toltec culture.

**TULA RUINS** are about 32 km (20 mi.) off Mex. 57-D (the toll highway to Querétaro) n. through the center of Tula, then 4 km (2.5 mi.) n.w. to the site, following signs. Taxis departing from Tula's main plaza can drop visitors off at the ruins. They constitute what is left of the capital and chief ceremonial center of the Toltecs. The focal point of the ruins is the five-tiered pyramid with a tongue-twisting name, the Temple of Tlahuizcalpantecuitli (Lord of the House of the Morning Star Venus). It dominates the north side of a plaza flanked by colonnaded buildings.

On top of the pyramid stand colossal figures known as the Atlantes (one is a replica). They once supported the roof of a temple that stood atop the pyramid. Each Atlantean is swaddled in a loincloth, its chest protected by stylized butterfly breastplates and its back by shields in the shape of the sun. The figures also sport headgear. This pyramid as well as several others can be climbed, but their steepness makes descending more difficult than ascending.

The museum near the entrance houses professional displays of artifacts found at the site, including huge sandal-clad feet carved from solid rock. Vendors hawking artifact replicas line the path from the museum to the ruins.

The site is not shaded; wear a hat and bring water. **Time:** Allow 1 hour minimum. **Hours:** Tues.-Sun. 9-5. **Cost:** 52 pesos (about $3.85 U.S.). Guided tour fees are negotiable.

## TZINTZUNTZAN, MICHOACÁN (D-2)

**Note:** For current information about safety/security issues in Tzintzuntzan and the state of Michoacán, refer to the U.S. State Department website (travel.state.gov).

Tzintzuntzan (tseen-TSOON-tsahn), a small village on the shore of Lake Pátzcuaro, was once the capital of a powerful Tarascan kingdom. The curious name means "the place of the hummingbirds" in the Tarascan Indian language.

This area is one of the largest sources of inexpensive hand-painted pottery in Mexico. Local artisans decorate their pottery with simple, childlike drawings of swans, fish and native net fishermen. They also weave figurines and table and floor mats out of reeds. Another cottage industry is woodcarving; items range from small wall decorations, dishes and flowerpots to doors, windows and columns.

The restored 16th-century Franciscan Convent of Santa Ana can be visited. The church courtyard is noted for its olive trees, which were planted by Don Vasco de Quiroga despite a Spanish injunction against planting the trees in the New World. Restored *yácatas*, ruins of Tarascan pyramids, are visible from Mex. 120; a paved side road leads to the edge of the site.

Holy Week ceremonies culminate with a series of concerts and performances of classical Spanish plays, staged by residents in the atrium of the Santa Ana Convent. The village's *pastorelas*, medieval dramas based on the Nativity, begin Dec. 16.

During Day of the Dead ceremonies Nov. 1-2, families visit the local cemetery to bring food, drink and other *ofrendas* (offerings) to their deceased relatives.

This ritual, as well as those observed during Holy Week, bring many visitors to towns and villages in the vicinity of Lake Pátzcuaro. Book hotel reservations in nearby Pátzcuaro or Quiroga well in advance.

## URUAPAN, MICHOACÁN (D-2)
pop. 315,350

**Note:** For current information about safety/security issues in Uruapan and the state of Michoacán, refer to the U.S. State Department website (travel.state.gov).

Uruapan (oo-roo-AH-pahn) means "place where the flowers bloom," and the lush vegetation seen throughout the city is a testament to the warm climate (it is nearly 2,000 feet lower in elevation than nearby Pátzcuaro). Orange groves and plantations growing coffee, bananas and especially avocados flourish in the fertile farmland that surrounds the city. Uruapan also is known for hand-painted lacquerware carved from cedar and other native woods.

Uruapan is located in a region that is experiencing ongoing drug cartel violence, and the city has a very visible police and military presence.

**Michoacán State Tourism Office (Delegación de Turismo):** Calle Independencia #18, about 2 blks. northwest of the main plaza. Open Mon.-Sat. 9-2 and 4-7. **Phone:** (452) 524-7199.

**EDUARDO RUIZ PARK** (Parque Eduardo Ruiz) has an entrance at the end of east-west Av. Independencia, about 8 blks. w. of the main plaza. This shady park along the banks of the Río Cupatitzio contains lush subtropical vegetation and fountains with dancing waters propelled by gravity alone; no pumps are used. Numerous footpaths wind along the riverbank.

The river rises at Devil's Knee (Rodilla del Diablo) spring, named—according to legend—for the spot where Lucifer left a kneeling imprint. **Hours:** Daily 8-6. **Cost:** A small entrance fee is charged.

**PARICUTÍN** is n. on Mex. 37 for about 16 km (10 mi.) to the junction with a paved road branching w. 21 km (13 mi.) to the town of Angahuan. Paracutín (pah-ree-koo-TEEN), a now-dormant volcano, sprang from a cornfield in 1943. The blunt-topped cone rises some 1,700 feet above the surrounding valley.

During its brief period of activity, Paricutín destroyed two villages (part of a church protruding from the jumble of boulders is the only remaining evidence of their existence) and forced more than 4,000 people to abandon their homes. The volcanic cone and the weirdly blackened surrounding lava fields can be reached on horseback or by hiking on foot. Guided trips can be arranged in Angahuan, or check with the State Tourism Office in Uruapan.

**REGIONAL MUSEUM OF POPULAR ART** (Museo de Arte Popular) is on Calle Vasco de Quiroga, facing the n. side of the main plaza. It is housed within La Huatapera, a colonnaded building that is a fine example of 16th-century architecture; built under the direction of Spanish bishop Vasco de Quiroga, it was originally a hospital. The museum exhibits artwork by the

Purepecha, Mazahua, Nahua and Otomi Indians—all indigenous peoples of Michoacán—and also has two rooms featuring rotating displays. **Time:** Allow 1 hour minimum. **Hours:** Tues.-Sun. 9:30-1:30 and 3:30-6. Closed Jan. 1, May 1 and Christmas. **Cost:** Free; donations are accepted. **Phone:** (452) 524-3434.

**TZARÁRACUA WATERFALL** (Cascada de Tzarárácua) is just off Mex. 37 about 10 km (6 mi.) s. of town. Here the Río Cupatitzio rushes through a natural stone amphitheater, then drops about 90 feet into a pool within a cool, leafy setting. There is a fairly steep half-mile descent from the parking area down to the falls, but the trail is well marked, and handrails are provided. Buses to Tzarárácua (tsah-RAH-rah-kwah) depart from Uruapan's main plaza on weekends and drop passengers off at the parking lot; a cab ride to the falls is about $5 (U.S.).

## ZACATECAS, ZACATECAS (B-1)
pop. 138,176

**Note:** For current information about safety/security issues in Zacatecas, refer to the U.S. State Department website (travel.state.gov).

Zacatecas (sah-kah-TEH-kahs), capital of the state of the same name, is built in a ravine on the slopes of Cerro de la Bufa, a mountain 8,748 feet high. This centuries-old mining settlement was conquered by the Spaniards in 1548; 40 years later it was bestowed the title of "The Very Noble and Loyal City of Our Lady of the Zacatecas" because of the vast quantities of silver shipped from the region to Spain. Although surrounded by agricultural and cattle-raising lands, Zacatecas continues to be a center for silver mining. The largest mine in the region is 200-year-old El Bote, which is still in operation.

Elaborate old mansions, an aqueduct and stone steps connecting steeply inclined flagstone streets lend Zacatecas a decidedly medieval atmosphere; the historic city center was designated a World Heritage Site by UNESCO in 1993. The beautiful baroque buildings also attest to the great wealth that was generated by the mines.

A wide, divided avenue 5 kilometers (3 miles) long leads east from downtown to the suburb of Guadalupe, the site of an early 18th-century convent. It once served as a base for Franciscan missions established to the north of Mexico in what is now the southwestern United States. The town is noted for its colonial architecture in addition to marquetry (inlaid woodwork) and wool *sarapes* with portraits woven into their designs.

Trancoso, 22 kilometers (14 miles) east of Zacatecas off Mex. 45/49, has one of the most elegant and best preserved old haciendas in Mexico. In Bracho, on the north side of the loop road encircling the city, La Morisma is celebrated the last week in August. During this fiesta, hundreds of local boys and men dressed in Moorish-style costumes act out a battle against a European army for several consecutive days.

**Zacatecas State Tourism Office (Secretaría de Turismo del Estado de Zacatecas):** downtown at Calle Hidalgo #403 (second floor). Open Mon.-Fri. 8-8, Sat.-Sun. 10-6. **Phone:** (492) 922-6751, or 01 (800) 712-4078 (toll-free long distance within Mexico).

**CATHEDRAL** faces the s. side of Plaza de Armas. Begun in 1612 and completed in 1752, it is one of the ultimate expressions of the Mexican baroque style. The extravagant exterior carvings of pink *cantera* sandstone are notable. This is still an active church, and Mass is held daily. **Hours:** Open for services (closes after dark); there is no tour schedule, but visitors can enter the building and quietly look around. **Cost:** Free.

**CERRO DE LA BUFA** (Bufa Hill) overlooks the city from the n.e. Part of the Organos Mountain range, the summit of this rocky outcrop can be reached by taking the Zacatecas Cable Car. At an elevation of 8,770 feet, it offers spectacular panoramic views of the city below and the surrounding mountains. There are also small restaurants and souvenir stands at the summit. You can ride the cable car back down or descend on foot via a series of staircases. Several commemorative equestrian statues stand at the base of the hill.

**Battle of Zacatecas Museum** (Museo Toma de Zacatecas) is next to the chapel. It chronicles the 1914 battle led by Pancho Villa to gain control of the city, one of the decisive conflicts of the Revolution of 1910. Exhibit information is in Spanish. **Hours:** Daily 10-5. **Cost:** 20 pesos (about $1.50 U.S.). **Phone:** (492) 922-8066.

**Patrocinio Chapel** (La Capilla de la Virgen del Patrocinio) is at the summit. Erected in 1728, it is named for the patron saint of miners.

**EL EDÉN MINE** (Mina el Edén) can be reached by car from Mex. 54; when entering the city, follow signs to downtown (Centro), then signs to "Mina el Edén." The mine is just n. on Calle Dovali Jamie from the intersection with Av. Torreón; a nearby landmark is the IMSS Social Security Hospital (Seguro Social Hospital). First operated in the 16th century, El Edén produced great quantities of silver, copper and zinc during its most active period.

A small powered train takes visitors through several of the mine's tunnels before stopping at a small museum with a display of rocks and minerals from around the world. Visitors then proceed on foot while a tour guide provides information about mining processes, the mine's history and the living conditions of the original Indian miners.

Most tours are in Spanish; visitors may want to call ahead to set up a tour with an English-speaking guide. **Time:** Allow 1 hour minimum. **Hours:** Tours daily 10-6 (noon-6 on Jan. 1 and Christmas). **Cost:** 80 pesos (about $5.90 U.S.); 40 pesos (ages 4-11 and 60+). **Phone:** (492) 922-3002.

**FRANCISCO GOITIA MUSEUM** (Museo Francisco Goitia) is s. of the city center at Av. Enrique Estrada #102, across from Enrique Estrada Park. Housed in the former Governor's Mansion, it exhibits works by realist painter and Zacatecas native Goitia (1882-1960) that include a dramatic self-portrait. Sculpture and paintings by other 20th-century Zacatecano artists also are on display. **Hours:** Tues.-Sun. 10-5. **Cost:** 30 pesos (about $2.20 U.S.). **Phone:** (492) 922-0211.

**LA QUEMADA RUINS** are located on a hillside overlooking a valley, about 56 km (35 mi.) s.w. of Zacatecas off Mex. 54. Also known as Chicomostoc Ruins, this archeological site bears traces of narrow streets and the foundations of homes and temples of the Náhuatlac Indians, who settled the valley around 1170. Thought to be destroyed by fire, the city was already a ruin when the Spaniards discovered it in 1535.

Among the remaining structures are a restored pyramid, a palace with 11 standing columns, and the substantial surrounding walls. Since local transportation is unreliable, the ruins are much easier to reach if you have your own vehicle. From the highway it's an uphill, 30-minute walk to the site entrance. Visitors should wear comfortable hiking shoes and bring water. **Hours:** Daily 9-5. **Cost:** 52 pesos (about $3.85 U.S.).

**OUR LADY OF GUADALUPE CONVENT** (Convento de Nuestra Señora de Guadalupe) is about 7 km (4 mi.) s.e. of Zacatecas via Mex. 45/49, in the town of Guadalupe. Local *Ruta* 13 buses depart regularly for Guadalupe from the corner of Calle Salazar and Blvd. López Mateos, near the old bus terminal in downtown Zacatecas.

This enormous convent and baroque church dates from 1707 and once housed Franciscan monks. Rows of corridors lined with paintings and portraits pass cells where the monks spent their time when not ministering to the Indians. Especially noteworthy is the church's Chapel (Capilla de Nápoles), which has a domed roof covered with beautiful gold leaf and a parquet floor elaborately inlaid with zodiac signs and scriptures. It is not always open, so a tip for the guide who grants entrance is appreciated.

**Hours:** Tues.-Sun. 9-6. **Cost:** (includes Museum of Viceregal Art) 52 pesos (about $3.85 U.S.).

**Museum of Viceregal Art** (Museo de Arte Virreinal) is within the convent. It contains paintings of the Virgin of Guadalupe and other works of 18th-century colonial religious art by such artists as Miguel Cabrera, Juan Correa and Cristóbal de Villalpando. Exhibit information is in Spanish. **Hours:** Open same hours as the convent. GT

**PEDRO CORONEL MUSEUM** is on Plaza Santo Domingo, about 2 blks. w. of Plaza de Armas. It houses the outstanding private collection of noted Zacatecan artist and sculptor Pedro Coronel, which includes works by Pablo Picasso, Salvador Dalí, Joan Miró and Marc Chagall.

Other displays include Coronel's tomb and an exhibit of his own sculpture and paintings; pre-Columbian pieces and colonial-era works by Zacatecano artists; Chinese, Indian, Greek and Egyptian art; and a fine collection of Mesoamerican and African masks. **Hours:** Tues.-Sun. 10-5. **Cost:** 30 pesos (about $2.20 U.S.); free (ages 0-9). **Phone:** (492) 922-8021.

**RAFAEL CORONEL MUSEUM** (Museo Rafael Coronel) is n. of the cathedral via Calle Abasolo to Calle San Francisco. It is housed in the 18th-century Convento de San Francisco, abandoned as a convent in 1857. The building's exterior is a mellowed pink, and flowering plants fill the gardens in the interior courtyard.

On display in large, high-ceilinged galleries is an amazing collection of several thousand masks from all over Mexico, donated by Rafael Coronel, younger brother of Pedro. They depict saints as well as grotesque-looking, devilish figures, *conquistadores* and bizarrely imaginative animals. Entirely handmade and decorated with everything from human hair and glitter to steel wool and bones, the masks are a remarkable testament to Mexican artistic ingenuity. There also are impressive dioramas of puppets engaged in such activities as warfare, a bullfight and a wedding, all created by a family of puppet makers from Huamantla, Tlaxcala.

**Hours:** Thurs.-Tues. 10-5. **Cost:** 30 pesos (about $2.20 U.S.). **Phone:** (492) 922-8116. 🍴

**ZACATECAS CABLE CAR** (Teleférico), next to the Hotel Baruk Teleférico y Mina, can be reached from Mex. 45 to Paseo Diaz Ordaz, following signs. Built by Swiss engineers, this cable car system connects the hills Cerro de la Bufa and Cerro Grillo, spanning the northern section of the city. The journey takes 8 minutes, covers a distance of 2,100 feet and overlooks Zacatecas from varying heights. The two enclosed cars hold up to 15 passengers. Parking is available at either end of the run. **Hours:** Cars depart the stations every 15 minutes daily 10-6 (weather permitting). **Cost:** Round-trip fare 100 pesos (about $7.40 U.S.). **Phone:** (492) 922-0745 (for the hotel).

# ZAPOPAN, JALISCO (C-1) pop. 1,243,756

About 7 kilometers (4 miles) northwest of downtown Guadalajara via Avenida Avila Camacho, the sprawling "suburb" of Zapopan (sah-POH-pahn) is the home of the Virgin of Zapopan—often referred to as La Zapopanita ("Little Zapopaner") since her image, made of corn paste, stands a mere 10 inches tall.

Legend alleges that Chimalhuacano Indians, awed by the display of La Zapopanita by a Franciscan friar during the heat of battle against the Spanish, surrendered and were converted to Christianity. In 1734, at the height of an epidemic, she was taken to the towns and villages around Guadalajara. Wherever the virgin appeared, sickness reputedly ceased, and many miracles were subsequently attributed to her.

Each year at dawn on Oct. 12, the statue of the virgin is transported from Guadalajara's cathedral back to her home church, the Basilica of the Virgin of Zapopan. Piety and merrymaking are both in evidence on this occasion. In addition to solemn marchers holding banners, there are marching bands, cowboys on horseback, dancers in native costume and assorted revelers dressed up as if for a giant Halloween party.

Many pilgrims show their devotion by crawling the last kilometer or two on their knees, underscoring the importance of this annual event for the nation's devout Catholics. The homecoming procession from the cathedral to the basilica—a 5-mile route—often involves more than 1 million participants and spectators and is a highlight of Guadalajara's *Fiestas de Octubre* celebration in October.

**BASILICA OF THE VIRGIN OF ZAPOPAN** (Basilica de Nuestra Señora de Zapopan) is at Calle Eva Briseño #152, facing the w. side of Plaza de Las Americas, the main plaza. This massive 17th-century cathedral features an ornate Plateresque exterior and a tiled *mudéjar* dome. In the church courtyard a statue commemorates Pope John Paul II, who gave a mass at the plaza during his 1979 visit. Within the Franciscan monastery adjacent to the basilica is the small Huichol Museum (Museo Huichol); it has displays of beadwork and other handicrafts (all for sale) made by the Huichol Indians of northern Jalisco, Nayarit and Zacatecas.

Buses from downtown Guadalajara go to the basilica; the trip takes about half an hour. **Hours:** Daily 9-8. **Cost:** Free. **Phone:** (33) 3633-6614.

# Southern Mexico

**M**exico's poorest region economically is among its richest in cultural traditions. Many people who live in the states of Oaxaca and Chiapas are descended from the Zapotec, Mixtec and Mayan civilizations that flourished hundreds of years before the Spanish conquest of Mexico. The Maya left behind the ruins of Palenque, Bonampak, Yaxchilan and Tonina, all in Chiapas.

The Zapotecs settled in the Valley of Oaxaca and created the ceremonial center of Monte Albán, which eluded discovery by Spanish *conquistadores.* Much more recently Chiapas, Mexico's southernmost state, made international headlines with the 1994 emergence of the Zapatista National Liberation Army, a guerrilla movement that demanded greater economic opportunities for the region's Indians, or *indígenas.*

Oaxaca is a quintessential Mexican destination; it offers excellent museums, beautiful churches, a vibrant central plaza and Indian markets overflowing with native handicrafts. The distinctive regional cuisine includes everything from subtly spiced *mole* sauces to *panuchos,* fried corn tortillas topped with pork and onions.

Veracruz has the languid ambience of a tropical port (Mexico's oldest and largest) as well as the energy provided by lively music, folk dances and a jolt of *café con leche.* The strong black coffee, laced with hot milk, can be enjoyed at one of the city's many sidewalk cafes. Other Veracruzan specialties are cigars and the *quexquémetl,* a capelike garment decorated with multicolored embroidery.

Little-visited Jalapa is a blend of old and new. Situated on the slopes of Macuiltépetl, a large, tiered hill, the town was a Spanish stronghold and important stagecoach stop between Veracruz and Mexico City. The colonists who followed in the wake of Hernando Cortés almost certainly found the higher altitude and cooler climate a welcome respite from steamy

Veracruz, as well as an environment suitable for the cultivation of coffee and fruit trees.

The picturesque old silver-mining town of Taxco is a popular tourist stop between Mexico City and Acapulco. Sprawled over a rugged hillside in the heart of the Sierra Madre, it hasn't changed that much in outward appearance since the 18th century. The Mexican government prohibits the building of modern structures; older ones—in various stages of preservation—proliferate, along with whitewashed houses, red-tiled roofs and cobblestoned streets.

AAA recommends that travelers consult online U.S. State Department travel advisories when planning traveling abroad. Find this information at http://travel.state.gov/content/passports/english/alertswarnings/mexico-travel-warning.html.

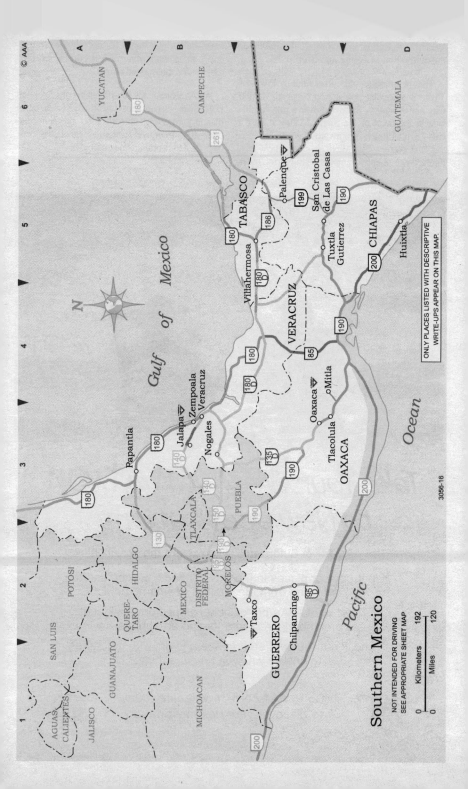

# Southern Mexico

NOT INTENDED FOR DRIVING
SEE APPROPRIATE SHEET MAP

0 Kilometers 192

0 Miles 120

ONLY PLACES LISTED WITH DESCRIPTIVE
WRITE-UPS APPEAR ON THIS MAP.

© AAA

3056-16

# Points of Interest

## CHILPANCINGO, GUERRERO (C-1)
### pop. 241,717

Capital of the state of Guerrero and home to the University of Guerrero, Chilpancingo (cheel-pahn-SEEN-goh) is a bustling college town. It also has historical credentials—the first Congress of Mexico met here in 1813.

Points of interest include the House of the First Revolutionary Congress (Casa del Primer Congreso Revolucionario), La Asunción Church, the city's ancient cemetery and the State Capitol (Palacio de Gobierno), which has some fine murals. The Indian village of Acatlán, 55 kilometers (34 miles) northeast of Chilpancingo via a partially paved road, is noted for hand-loomed and embroidered shawls.

In Chilapa, 54 kilometers (33 miles) east of Chilpancingo, the Day of St. Gertrude on Nov. 16 features whimsically named native dances, including The Seven Vices, The Eight Lunatics, The Old Woman and The Mule. In Chichihualco, 33 kilometers (20 miles) northwest of Chilpancingo, the Fiesta of St. James Sept. 28-29 includes a parade, regional foods and such native dances as Fishermen and Devils.

## JALAPA, VERACRUZ (B-3)

Capital of the state of Veracruz and home to nearly 400,000 people, Jalapa (hah-LAH-pah, but spelled Xalapa in Mexico) doesn't feel like a big city. The natural setting is breathtaking—the black volcanic peaks of the Sierra Madre Oriental rise in the distance, towered over by Pico de Orizaba, Mexico's tallest mountain. Practically every corner offers a vista of the surrounding mountainous terrain.

Jalapa's colonial legacy is evident in the structures flanking older, cobblestone avenues; their red-tiled roofs, wrought-iron balconies, carved wooden doors and window grilles are unmistakably Spanish. Shops and homes are painted in vibrant shades of white, green and deep red. The streets are steep and curving, and also change names and directions frequently; a good city map is an effective navigational aid. Taxis and local buses provide inexpensive transportation to points within the city center.

Begin a morning stroll of downtown Jalapa at the Café la Parroquía, on Calle Zaragoza near the south side of the Government Palace (Palacio de Gobierno). A local gathering place, it has an old-fashioned '50s look and attracts everyone from university professors to families. As in Veracruz, a favorite morning beverage is a *lechero*, a tall glass of strong espresso to which hot milk is added. Tapping your glass with a spoon signals the waiter, who pours the milk from a steaming kettle.

At the corner of calles Enríquez and Revolución, just north of the Government Palace, stands the city's 18th-century Cathedral. The plain white facade is accented by Moorish-style arches and a bell tower clock transported from London. The religious paintings inside are worth a look, as is the sloping floor.

The *chipichipi*, a light but persistent winter rain, and evening mists in summer contribute to Jalapa's reputation as the "flower garden of Mexico." The warmth and moisture create a natural greenhouse effect, and the city is filled with roses, bougainvillea and pine trees. Tree-shaded Juárez Park (Parque Juárez), across Calle Enríquez from the City Hall (Palacio Municipal), is representative of the prevailing lushness. White wrought-iron benches are scattered among pruned hedges and well-tended flower beds at this park, which also is the city's central plaza.

The University of Veracruz gives Jalapa a cultural side. The Agora Arts Center, just off Juárez Park, is a hangout for students and artists and has extensive events listings. The State Theater (Teatro del Estado) on Ignacio de la Llave hosts performances by the ballet and the symphony; phone (228) 817-4177. On Sept. 30, the Day of St. Jerome, the streets are garlanded with flowers and candlelight processions are held.

A few blocks south of Juárez Park on attractively landscaped lakeside grounds is the state-run Casa de Artesanías, where packaged coffee beans and handicrafts by Veracruzan artists are for sale. The indoor market on Calle Altamirano, about 2 blocks north of Juárez Park, is a colorful hodgepodge of assorted trinkets, containers of bubbling *mole* sauces and heaps of dried beans and chiles.

Street vendors frequent Callejón Diamante, a steep little alley off Calle Juan de La Luz Enríquez (a block or so east of Juárez Park). Casual restaurants specialize in regional fare; La Sopa serves a filling *comida corrida* (fixed-price lunch).

Macuiltépetl Park (Parque Macuiltépetl), north of downtown, is an ecological preserve that showcases indigenous flora and fauna. The winding paths offer a bracing climb up one of Jalapa's hillsides, and the views are outstanding.

## Practicalities

The nearest international airport is in Veracruz. From Veracruz, Jalapa is about a 2-hour drive north on Mex. 180 to the town of Cardel, then east on Mex. 140 past numerous coffee plantations.

The central bus station (CAXA) is on Avenida 20 de Noviembre, about a mile east of the downtown area. Here you can make first-class bus connections, arrange for a taxi into town (an otherwise hilly walk) and even grab a bite to eat. It also has a tourist information booth that is open daily. First-class bus service is offered by Autobuses del Oriente (ADO).

# Travel Advisory

It is recommended that travelers check on current conditions in the state of Guerrero (outside the tourist destinations of Acapulco and Ixtapa/Zihuatanejo). The most potentially dangerous areas are the mountainous, remote interior and undeveloped sections of the Pacific coast. Travel is advised only during daylight hours on toll highway Mex. 95D between Mexico City and Acapulco. For additional information, consult the latest Mexico Travel Warning on the U.S. State Department website (travel.state.gov).

**Veracruz State Tourism Office (Subsecretaría de Turismo):** Blvd. Cristóbal Colón #5 in the Torre Animas building, about 3 kilometers (1.9 miles) east of downtown. **Phone:** 01 (800) 712-6666 (toll-free long distance within Mexico).

**GOVERNMENT PALACE** (Palacio de Gobierno) is on the e. side of Plaza Juárez. Ornate fountains face this long, pink, colonial-style building, which serves as the state capitol. Inside are murals by José Chávez Morado, including "Liberation," which depicts humanity's struggle for freedom.

**HACIENDA EL LENCERO** is about 9 km (5.5 mi.) e. of Jalapa off the Xalapa-Veracruz toll road (Mex. 140), then follow signs 1.5 km (1 mi.) to the hacienda. A guided tour of this country estate, a former inn for stagecoaches traveling between Veracruz and Mexico City and later a sugarcane plantation, offers insight into 19th-century hacienda life, a relatively luxurious existence reserved for wealthy plantation owners. The various rooms are furnished with canopied beds, large armoires, hand-carved wood and stone angels, Mexican rugs and ornate light fixtures.

**Time:** Allow 1 hour minimum. **Hours:** Tues.-Sun. 10-5. **Cost:** 35 pesos (about $2.60 U.S.). **Phone:** (228) 820-0270.

**MUSEUM OF ANTHROPOLOGY** (Museo de Antropología de Xalapa) is n.w. of downtown on Av. Xalapa, between avs. Acueducto and 10 de Mayo. It houses a superb collection of artifacts encompassing most of Mexico's gulf coast Indian groups, with an emphasis on the Olmec, Totonac and Huastec cultures. Contrasting vividly with the antiquity of the exhibits is the ultramodern museum building, which incorporates a series of tropically landscaped outdoor patios.

A massive Olmec head is stationed at the museum entrance; several other heads, the largest almost 9 feet tall, are on display in outdoor gardens and indoor galleries. Additional highlights include dramatically lifelike ceramic statues of women wearing belts in the form of writhing serpents; a carved figure in green stone holding an infant with jaguar-like facial features that are characteristically Olmec; and beautifully crafted jade and bone jewelry. The carefully organized displays are augmented by maps that note excavation sites and show where the civilizations flourished.

Information about the exhibits is presented in Spanish only, but headphone audio guides are available in English. **Time:** Allow 2 hours minimum. **Hours:** Tues.-Sun. 9-5. **Cost:** 50 pesos (about $3.70 U.S.); audio guide 20 pesos. An extra fee is charged for the use of a video camera. **Phone:** (228) 815-0920.

## Nearby Destinations

Formal plantings, an arboretum and a palm collection make up Clavijero Botanical Gardens, about 3 kilometers (1.5 miles) south of downtown via the road to Coatepec. En route are views of coffee and banana plantations. Coatepec, a colonial town about

8 kilometers (5 miles) south of Jalapa, is known for the raising of ornamental plants, chiefly orchids. The main plaza is surrounded by small shops selling coffee beans and *heladerías* (ice cream parlors) dishing up exotic flavors.

About 11 kilometers (7 miles) past Coatepec is Xico (HEE-coh), a village where sacks of coffee beans are one of the most common sights. Nearby Texolo Waterfall (Cascada de Texolo) has been put to good scenic use in such films as "Romancing the Stone" and parts of the Harrison Ford espionage adventure "A Clear and Present Danger." The falls cascade into a gorge surrounded by lush greenery. A restaurant is at the site, and pathways allow visitors to observe the falls from different vantage points. Local buses to Coatepec and Xico depart from Jalapa's central bus station.

## MITLA, OAXACA (C-4)

The town of Mitla (MEE-tlah) is about 42 kilometers (26 miles) southeast of Oaxaca and about 1.9 kilometers (3 miles) off Mex. 190. The original city, a religious and ceremonial center, was inhabited by the Zapotecs as early as 800 B.C.; by the 11th or 12th century, the Mixtecs had expelled the Zapotecs from both Mitla and Monte Albán and began to establish their own culture. Mitla prospered up until the time of the Spanish conquest. The name means "place of rest" and refers to the catacombs beneath the Mitla ruins.

Weaving is the principal commercial activity today; woven goods can be purchased almost everywhere. Around Mitla and south along Mex. 190 are outlet stores selling mezcal, a locally produced liquor that packs a wallop. Derived from a variety of the maguey plant, mezcal is a specialty of the state of Oaxaca. The bottle often includes a pickled *gusano* (worm). If imbibed at all, mezcal is best diluted with fruit juice.

**MITLA RUINS** are about 1 km (.6 mi.) n. of the main plaza via Av. Morelos. This site was begun by the Zapotecs but taken over by the Mixtecs, and the architectural style of elaborate cut stonework reflects the latter group. Unlike many Mayan ruins, Mitla was never buried under encroaching jungle, and the structures are well preserved.

Rectangular patios are surrounded by buildings or long, narrow rooms. Underground chambers and cruciform tombs honeycomb the soil beneath these structures. The Hall of Columns, the most important group, is supported by six enormous pillars, each a single stone, and more than 100,000 pieces of cut stones form the intricate mosaic decorating its walls. The most common design is an abstract zigzag pattern. The lack of human, animal and mythological figures sets Mitla apart from other North American archeological sites.

**Note:** Vendors congregate outside the ruins, vociferously hawking fake archeological pieces and a variety of crafts. There also is a craft market near the ruins entrance. Keep in mind, however, that many of the same items can be purchased in town as well, sometimes at lower prices. **Hours:** Daily 8-5. **Cost:** 47 pesos (about $3.50 U.S.). The fee to use a video camera is about $5.

## OAXACA, OAXACA (C-3) pop. 263,357

*See map page 350.*

Oaxaca (wa-HAH-ka), situated in a high valley surrounded by the towering summits of the Sierra Madre del Sur, is one of Mexico's most culturally rewarding destinations. Indian traditions and heritage have remained largely intact in both the state of Oaxaca and in neighboring Chiapas, resulting in a rich and diverse legacy of handicrafts, ethnic celebrations and distinctive cookery. Today descendants of the ancient Zapotec and Mixtec peoples live in numerous rural villages scattered throughout the valley. Regional dialects abound, and for many Oaxaqueños Spanish is a second language.

This strong cultural identity has made Oaxaca one of Mexico's leading art centers. And certainly the city's setting would inspire many an artist. Older buildings are constructed from a volcanic stone that takes on a mellow golden tone in the late afternoon sun. Others are painted bright shades of turquoise and pink. Bougainvillea and roses tumble over walls, scarlet geraniums spill out of huge clay pots, and when the jacaranda trees are in bloom they form masses of purple. Completing this colorful palette is the sky, which is usually an azure blue.

Be sure to sample the local cuisine. Oaxaca is known in particular for *mole*, a sauce that incorporates a number of spices. There are seven varieties, with only *mole negro* employing the chocolate that also turns up in the *mole poblano* sauce of Puebla.

Other Oaxacan specialties include *tamales oaxaqueños*, a mixture of ground corn *(masa)*, shredded chicken and *mole* wrapped in a banana leaf and then steamed; *tlayudas*, crispy, dinner plate-sized corn tortillas topped with a wash of refried beans, meat, lettuce or cabbage, cheese and avocado slices; *picadillo*, spicy shredded pork; *quesillo*, a stringy, mildly flavored white cheese; and corn on the cob basted with lime juice and dusted with chile powder, a favorite street snack. Feeling adventurous? Try *chapulines* (fried grasshoppers) with a squeeze of lime and a dash of chili powder or garlic; they're sold in the food markets and by vendors at Plaza Principal, the city's bustling main square.

## Practicalities

Oaxaca's Xoxocotlán International Airport is about 8 kilometers (5 miles) south of the city off Mex. 175. Transportes Terrestres *colectivo* (shared taxi) and private taxi service between the airport and downtown hotels is easily arranged. Private taxi fare averages 250 pesos (about $18.50 U.S.); *colectivos* are cheaper (about 75 pesos per person). *For additional information about airlines see Arriving by Air, page p. 42.*

United flies nonstop to Oaxaca from Houston. Aeroméxico, phone 01 (800) 021-4000 (toll-free

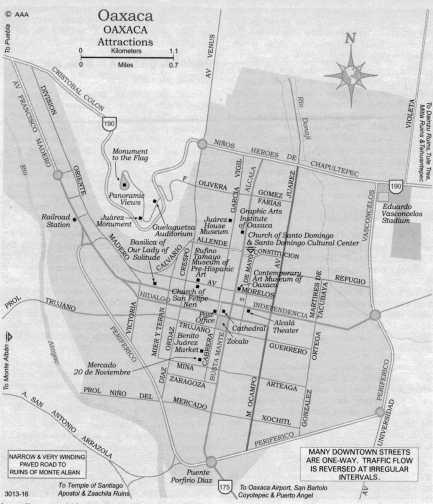

© AAA

# Oaxaca
## OAXACA
### Attractions

Kilometers 0 — 1.1
Miles 0 — 0.7

To Puebla

CRISTOBAL COLON

190

AV FRANCISCO MADERO
DIVISION
ORIENTE
MADERO
CALVARIO
CRESPO
HIDALGO
VICTORIA
MIER Y TERAN
ORDAZ
DIAZ
PERIFERICO
PROL TRUJANO
Atoyac
A. SAN ANTONIO ARRAZOLA

Monument
to the Flag

Panoramic
Views

Juárez
Monument

Railroad
Station

Guelaguetza
Auditorium

Basilica of
Our Lady of
Solitude

AV VENUS

NIÑOS HEROES DE CHAPULTEPEC

AV JUAREZ

Río Donají

Río

190

Eduardo
Vasconcelos
Stadium

VASCONCELOS

VIOLETA

To Danzu Ruins, Tule Tree,
Mitla Ruins & Tehuantepec

F
OLIVERA
GARCIA VIGIL
ALCALA
GOMEZ
FARIAS

Graphic Arts
Institute
of Oaxaca

Juárez
House
Museum

ALLENDE

Rufino
Tamayo
Museum of
Pre-Hispanic
Art

Church of Santo Domingo
& Santo Domingo Cultural Center

CONSTITUCION

Contemporary
Art Museum of
Oaxaca

AV

DE MAYO

MORELOS

MARTIRES DE TACUBAYA

REFUGIO

ORTEGA

Church of
San Felipe
Neri

AV

5

INDEPENDENCIA

Post
Office

TRUJANO

Benito
Juárez
Market

Cathedral

Alcalá
Theater

Zócalo

GUERRERO

BUSTA MANTE

CABRERA

MINA

ZARAGOZA

PROL NIÑO DEL MERCADO

Mercado
20 de Noviembre

M OCAMPO

ARTEAGA

GONZALEZ

XOCHITL

PERIFERICO

UNIVERSIDAD

PERIFERICO

NARROW & VERY WINDING
PAVED ROAD TO
RUINS OF MONTE ALBAN

To Monte Albán

To Temple of Santiago
Apostol & Zaachila Ruins

3013-16

Puente
Porfirio Díaz

175

To Oaxaca Airport, San Bartolo
Coyotepec & Puerto Angel

MANY DOWNTOWN STREETS
ARE ONE-WAY. TRAFFIC FLOW
IS REVERSED AT IRREGULAR
INTERVALS.

long distance within Mexico), offers nonstop connecting flights from Mexico City.

It takes between 5 and 6 hours to drive from downtown Mexico City to Oaxaca via well-signed toll roads Mex. 150-D and Mex. 135-D. After bypassing Puebla and east of the town of Acatzingo, watch for the junction with Mex. 135-D at the town of Cuacnopalan. Mex. 135-D runs south, skirting the cities of Tehuacán and Nochixtlán en route to Oaxaca.

Bus service is available to and from Mexico City, but there are many stops along the 565-kilometer (350-mile) route. "Deluxe" service is provided by UNO and Cristóbal Colón, first-class service by ADO. Oaxaca's first-class bus station is about 1.5 kilometers northeast of downtown at Calzada Niños Héroes de Chapultepec #1036.

Local buses depart from the second-class bus station (about 1 kilometer west of Plaza Principal via Avenida Trujano). They're an economical way to

travel to the archeological ruins and Indian villages, although trips can be excruciatingly slow along the narrow, winding mountain roads. *For additional information about buses see Bus Service, page p. 52.*

Taxis are another way to get around town, and the fare to nearby destinations can be shared among several riders; negotiate the rate before you set out. Fares within the city center average about $4 (U.S.). Taxis line up around Plaza Principal.

Personal safety in Oaxaca means using common sense—precautions such as keeping your car in a lot overnight rather than parking it on the street, storing all valuables out of sight, and staying alert in public places where smooth professional pickpockets operate, like markets and bus stations. Stick to established tourist areas, and avoid driving after dark.

Temperatures are mild to warm throughout the year, averaging in the 70s or 80s during the day and the 50s or 60s at night. May is the hottest month and the height of the dry season; the rainy season is from June through September. At this tropical latitude the sun can be quite strong; take the necessary precautions if you'll be outside all day. Sturdy, comfortable walking shoes also come in handy for exploring the ruins and trekking around the village markets. Avoid wearing skimpy or revealing clothing inside churches.

## Special Events

Oaxaca's festivals draw big crowds, so hotel space should be booked well in advance for the Easter holiday and in July, November and December. The Guelaguetza, meaning "offering," is a centuries-old festival celebrated throughout the state. Community troupes present their regional costumes, dances, songs and music in a specially designed, open-air theater (Auditorio Guelaguetza) built into the side of Cerro del Fortín, the hill in the northern part of the city. To reach the site, take Calzada Madero north to the Mex. 190 junction, then go east on Mex. 190 about 1.6 kilometers (1 mile).

There are numerous Oaxacan folk dance and musical performances, and participating singers, dancers and musicians throw *guelaguetzas* (gifts) to spectators. An evening show presents the legend of Princess Donají, which includes staged re-enactments of battles between Zapotec and Mixtec warriors. Even if you have tickets, arrive early—at least by 8 a.m.—for the best seats. **Note:** Bring water, and wear a hat or appropriate headgear for sun protection.

Performances are given on the two successive Mondays following July 16. (In years when July 18—the anniversary of Benito Juárez's death—falls on a Monday, the dates are July 25 and Aug. 1.) Check in advance with a travel agency, the Oaxaca State Tourism Office or your hotel for the exact dates. Tickets, necessary for the main performances, should be reserved no later than May, preferably through a travel agent; confirm the exact festival dates when you make your reservations.

Holy Week, beginning the Friday before Easter Sunday, brings parades and communion services, and local churches sponsor fairs, concerts and other activities. Oaxaca celebrates the Day of the Dead (Día de Los Muertos) Oct. 31 and Nov. 1 and 2. The markets are ablaze with marigolds and sell all manner of offerings with which to decorate altars built to honor the deceased.

The Fiesta of the Virgen de la Soledad in mid-December is a Christmas season highlight and honors the city's patron saint with processions, fireworks, floats and dances. Dec. 23 brings the Night of the Radishes. For this competition the main plaza is filled with booths displaying radishes carved into all sorts of fanciful shapes. Sweets are served in clay dishes, and after finishing the treat it's customary to fling your dish to the ground so it smashes.

## Shopping

Oaxaca's markets are among Mexico's most fascinating, with head-turning displays of crafts, foodstuffs, household products and curios. If you don't mind the crowds and noise, Saturdays provide the biggest spectacle, drawing Indians who come for miles around to buy and sell. Arrive unburdened so you can maintain your bearings amid the jostling, and be prepared to bargain. A standard opening tactic is offering to pay half the selling price for any item.

Look for leather goods, hand-loomed cottons, jewelry, carved idols and black pottery from the village of San Bartolo Coyotepec. Teotitlán and Ocotlán are weaving and pottery centers, respectively. Carved, brightly painted wooden animals with whimsical or surreal expressions are another specialty. Gold, silver and jade jewelry is often a reproduction of actual pieces found at Monte Albán or designed in a similar style.

The enormous Abastos Market (Mercado de Abastos), southwest of downtown off the Periférico, the loop road that encircles the city, is one of Oaxaca's busiest. It's open daily but is busiest on Saturday, when locals and residents of surrounding villages convene to display their merchandise in a huge warehouse and across blocks of open-air lots and canopied stalls.

This market is packed with such items as shawls, embroidered blouses, leather goods, pottery, woven baskets, rugs, toys, religious ornaments, bird cages, carved and painted wooden animals and woven baskets. The air is filled with the smells of incense, chocolate and tortillas. Abastos also is a produce and livestock market, and there are piles of dried chiles in a rainbow of colors, mounds of garlic bulbs, herbs, unfamiliar vegetables and tropical fruits, along with goats, turkeys and chickens.

Two blocks southwest of Plaza Principal is the older, indoor Benito Juárez Market, again busiest on Saturday. This is primarily a produce market, but you'll also find cheeses, jars filled with *mole* sauces, locally made honey, bags of cacao beans, flowers and household goods. There are numerous food stalls here as well. Use appropriate caution when deciding whether or not to sample snacks; if you can see something being cooked it's usually safe to eat.

Stalls along Calle 20 de Noviembre sell clothing items like coarse-weave woolen sweaters, shawls and capes as well as elaborately embroidered *huipiles* (blouses). In the next block south is the Mercado 20 de Noviembre, where shoppers browse for sandals, straw hats, hammocks, tin ornaments, small pottery jars and animal, bird and angel figurines that hang in strings from the stall awnings. Other merchants specialize in highly polished Oaxacan cutlery—swords, sabers, knives and letter openers.

The Handicrafts Market (Mercado de Artesanías), 4 blocks southwest of Plaza Principal at the corner of calles J.P. García and Zaragoza, offers crafts, pottery and leather goods and also features native textiles. Artisans can be observed as they weave rugs, wall hangings and dresses on simple looms. It's open daily.

If you don't relish the back-and-forth of haggling, focus on the fixed-price stores. The government-run

# Hard Labor in the Cane Fields

Sugar cane, the main source for the raw sugar that is refined to produce the granulated sweetener known the world over, is a member of the grass family. This plant has tall, thick, fibrous stalks that contain a sap rich in sucrose—a sweetening agent for foods and beverages and also a major ingredient in cakes, soft drinks, alcohol, preservatives and many other products.

Sugar cane is grown in many tropical and subtropical parts of the world. Along with olive oil, rice and citrus fruits, it was one of the agricultural products introduced to Mexico by Spanish *conquistadores*. Sugar was a precious commodity during the Spanish colonial era, and sugar haciendas—plantations that were worked by Indian and African slave labor—amassed great wealth for their owners. Sugar cane, which ranks with corn and tomatoes as one of the country's most important cash crops, is grown today in northwestern Mexico with the aid of irrigation, but more commonly in the gulf coast states of Veracruz and Tabasco, where the hot, rainy climate is ideal.

Oaxacan Institute of Artisans (Instituto Oaxaqueño del las Artesanías), Calle García Vigil #809, sells Oaxacan black pottery, rugs and textiles. The store has an English-speaking staff and can ship purchases; phone (951) 514-0861. The Galería Arte de Oaxaca, 3 blocks north and 1 block east of Plaza Principal at Calle Murguía #105, is a gallery featuring the work of noted Oaxacan painters and sculptors.

Between the main plaza and the Church of Santo Domingo Calle M. Alcalá is a pedestrian boulevard lined with high-quality shops. La Mano Mágica, Calle M. Alcalá #203, is a combination art gallery and crafts shop. It's known for finely woven rugs, particularly those by Teotitlán weaver Arnulfo Mendoza, and lovely pieces of regional folk art.

If you'd like to support local artisans, visit MARO (Mujeres Artesanas de las Regiones de Oaxaca), Av. 5 de Mayo #204 between Morelos and Murguía. This cooperative benefiting women in the villages of the Oaxaca Valley offers a variety of handicrafts, including Atzompa and Coyotepec pottery, stamped tinware, leather bags, sandals, belts and toys; phone (951) 516-0670.

Established shops and stores can usually arrange to ship your purchases back home. This is not the case with items purchased at the markets or from village craftspeople, however; always try to obtain a written receipt.

Excursions to area villages can be as rewarding as shopping in the city. The second-class bus station (*see Practicalities*) has bus service to most of the villages; another option is to take an inexpensive taxi from a lot near the Abastos Market. Taxis serve the local population as well and fill up quickly in the morning; a per-person rate is charged. A more convenient way to visit the markets is to hire a private car and driver who will provide transportation and also wait while you shop. Local tour companies offer this service; check with the State Tourism Office for more information.

*Tianguis* (open-air markets) take place on different days. Green-glazed pottery, including bowls from which breasts or lilies whimsically sprout, is the specialty at Atzompa, about 6 kilometers (4 miles) northwest of Oaxaca on Mex. 190. Also look for clay dolls. Market day here is Tuesday. A variety of cheeses and mole sauces can be purchased at the Wednesday market at San Pablo Etla, 14 kilometers (9 miles) northwest on Mex. 190. Thursday's market at Ejutla, 61 kilometers (38 miles) south on Mex. 175, is agriculturally oriented as well.

Zaachila, about 18 kilometers (11 miles) southwest on the road to Cuilapan, also has a Thursday market that does not target tourists but is interesting for its produce and livestock displays and snapshot of Mexican rural life. The raucous Friday market at Ocotlán, about 40 kilometers (25 miles) south on Mex. 175, is perhaps the busiest outside of Oaxaca. *Rebozos* (scarves or shawl-like garments), produce, leather goods, cutlery and whimsical ceramic figurines of women are among the many items for sale.

Other towns are known for a particular craft in which the entire populace seems to be involved. Arrazola, a tiny village southwest of Oaxaca near the ruins of Monte Albán, is noted for carvers who fashion fanciful wooden creatures painted in vivid colors. Second-class buses travel to Arrazola, and local youngsters will take you to the artisans' homes for a small tip.

San Bartolo Coyotepec, about 16 kilometers (10 miles) south of Oaxaca on Mex. 175, is the source of the distinctive black pottery sold in many Oaxaca shops. There are frequent organized bus tours to this village. Items can be purchased at the local factory, in shops around the village plaza or from the potters' homes. Friday is market day.

The village of Guelatao, 63 kilometers (39 miles) north on Mex. 175, has historical significance: It is the birthplace of Mexican president Benito Juárez. Guelatao's monument-studded plaza honors this native son, and lively celebrations are held on his birthday, Mar. 21. The journey to Guelatao offers impressively scenic mountain views at an elevation of around 7,000 feet. To fully enjoy the trip, take a bus; only motorists with nerves of steel should attempt to negotiate the roadway's serpentine bends and potholes.

**Oaxaca State Tourism Office (Secretaría de Desarrollo Turístico):** downtown at Calle Murguía #206 (between Reforma and 5 de Mayo). Open daily 8-8. **Phone:** (951) 516-0123.

**ALCALÁ THEATER** (Teatro Macedonio de Alcalá) is on Av. Independencia at Calle Armienta y Lopez, 2 blks. n.e. of the Zócalo. Built around the turn of the 20th century, the Alcalá reflects the grandiose style public buildings took under the rule of native son and dictator Porfirio Díaz. The interior in particular is impressively opulent. **Hours:** Open only for events; check with the State Tourism Office for schedule information.

**BASILICA OF OUR LADY OF SOLITUDE** (Basilica de la Soledad) is at Av. Independencia #107 (at Av. Galeana), 5 blks. w. of the Zócalo. This massive 17th-century structure, actually a complex of several buildings and a garden, has a richly carved exterior. The basilica is dedicated to the Virgin of Solitude (Virgen de la Soledad). A statue of the Virgin, Oaxaca's patron saint, is displayed above the altar, draped in jewel-encrusted black velvet.

The interior is an extravagant showcase of baroque ornamentation. A museum to the rear of the church displays a replica of the Virgin statue. It also contains glass panels depicting the legend of her arrival in the city and an enormous assemblage of gifts (primarily miniature glass figurines) sent in tribute. Exhibit information is in Spanish. **Hours:** Basilica normally open daily 7-2 and 4-10, museum Mon.-Sat. 10-2 and 4-6; hours may vary. **Cost:** Basilica free; admission to the museum is by donation.

**CATHEDRAL** (Catedral de Oaxaca) faces the n. side of the Zócalo. Begun in 1563, the church was

## Hard Labor in the Cane Fields (continued)

If you're traveling through the fertile farming regions around Veracruz during harvesting season (March and April) you're likely to see—in addition to bananas, cacao trees, and mango and papaya orchards—a waving green sea of sugar cane. Since harvesting cane by machine is difficult, it is still done mainly by hand in centuries-old fashion, which requires a large supply of manual labor.

Generations of *caneros*—essentially serfs toiling the land—have labored in Mexican cane fields. First the fields are burned, which destroys dead leaves and small thorns but leaves the juicy stalks intact. Then the laborers wrap their hands, ankles and feet in layers of old cloth to protect themselves from the bites of poisonous snakes not flushed out during the burning. They wade into 12-foot-tall forests of prickly, razor-sharp cane, cutting it by hand with long machetes in broiling heat and humidity before loading it high onto trucks—all for about $20 (U.S.) per truck.

© satit_srihin / Shutterstock.com

completed about 2 centuries later. Although severely damaged by earthquakes, the rebuilt cathedral, which is constructed of the native greenish stone, still reflects much of its original grandeur. The clock, its works made of wood, was presented by a Spanish king. The facade and central panel above the door are fine examples of baroque craftsmanship. **Time:** Allow 30 minutes minimum. **Hours:** Daily 7 a.m.-9 p.m. Mass is held on a regular schedule. **Cost:** Free.

**CHURCH OF SAN FELIPE NERI** (Iglesia de San Felipe Neri) is on Av. Independencia at Calle Tinoco y Palacios, about 3 blks. n.w. of Plaza Principal. The interior of this 17th-century baroque church features a lavish altar of carved, gilded wood and impressive wall frescoes. **Hours:** Daily 8 a.m.-10 p.m. **Cost:** Free.

**CHURCH OF SANTO DOMINGO** (Templo de Santo Domingo de Guzmán) is 6 blks. n. of the Zócalo at calles Gurrión, Macedonio Alcalá, Berriozábal and Reforma. Founded by the Dominicans in the mid-16th century, it took about a century to complete. Even in a city (and country) of impressive churches, Santo Domingo has a well-deserved reputation as one of the most beautifully ornate. Every square inch of the interior walls and ceilings is covered with extravagant gold leaf, polychrome reliefs and plaster statues. Try to visit in the afternoon, when sunlight pouring through the stained-glass window casts everything in a golden glow.

One particularly noteworthy decoration, on the ceiling under the raised choir loft near the entrance, depicts crowned heads appearing on the branches of the family tree of Santo Domingo de Guzmán, founder of the Dominican order. The adjoining monastery houses the Santo Domingo Cultural Center (see attraction listing). **Time:** Allow 1 hour minimum. **Hours:** Church open to visitors daily 7-1 and 5-8. It is normally closed to walk-in visitors during weddings, which take place regularly. **Cost:** Free. GT

**CONTEMPORARY ART MUSEUM OF OAXACA** (Museo de Arte Contemporáneo de Oaxaca, or MACO) is at Calle M. Alcalá #202, 2 blks. n. of Plaza Principal. It occupies a turn-of-the-18th-century building also known as the House of Cortés (Casa de Cortés), so named for supposedly being a former residence of the conqueror (historians and chronology insist otherwise). Beautifully restored, it features both colonial and contemporary architectural elements. Changing exhibits feature the work of regional as well as international artists. **Hours:** Wed.-Mon. 10:30-8. **Cost:** 20 pesos (about $1.50 U.S.). Cash only. **Phone:** (951) 514-1055.

**DAINZÚ RUINS** are about 24 km (15 mi.) s.e. of Oaxaca on a paved road off Mex. 190, on the way to Mitla; watch for the signed turn-off. Believed to be one of the final evidences of Olmec civilization in the Oaxaca region, their zenith was from around 600 B.C. to A.D. 200, before the better-known Monte Albán. A

pyramidal structure (Edificio A) and a partially restored ball court can be seen, along with artwork portraying ball players and carvings of jaguars, rabbits and dancers. Underground connecting tunnels can be explored, but they are dark, claustrophobic and have steep stairs.

**Time:** Allow 1 hour minimum. **Hours:** Daily 8-5. **Cost:** 39 pesos (about $2.90 U.S.). GT 𝄐

**GRAPHIC ARTS INSTITUTE OF OAXACA** (Instituto de Artes Gráficas de Oaxaca) is at M. Alcalá #507, across from the Church of Santo Domingo. It was created primarily through the efforts of celebrated Oaxacan artist Francisco Toledo. The institute has a collection of more than 5,000 engravings that includes his work, that of fellow Mexicans Rufino Tamayo and José Guadalupe Posada, and international artists. There also is an extensive library of art-related volumes. **Hours:** Daily 9:30-8. **Cost:** Donations. **Phone:** (951) 516-6980.

**JUÁREZ HOUSE MUSEUM** (Museo Casa de Juárez) is about 6 blks. n. of Plaza Principal at Calle Manuel García Vigil #609. This 19th-century colonial home was once owned by Padre Antonio Salanueva. The Salanuevas brought a young Oaxaqueño, Benito Juárez, from the village of Guelatao to live with them; Juárez's resulting education was the springboard for his careers in law and politics. The house is furnished to reflect a typical Oaxacan middle class lifestyle in the 19th century. **Hours:** Tues.-Sun. 10-7. **Cost:** 47 pesos (about $3.50 U.S.). **Phone:** (951) 516-1860.

**MONTE ALBÁN RUINS** are about 10 km (6 mi.) s.w. of Oaxaca; if driving, take Calle Trujano w. out of town across the Río Atoyac; it becomes the narrow, winding road to the ruins. One of Mexico's greatest pre-Columbian sites, Monte Albán presides over the valley of Oaxaca from a mountaintop location. This major religious center was built by the Zapotecs around 600 B.C. atop a summit that was deliberately flattened. At its height around A.D. 300, Monte Albán supported 40,000 inhabitants. The city was taken over in the 10th century by the Mixtecs, who were in turn conquered by the Aztecs, and fell into ruin around the time of the Spanish conquest.

The site's focal point is the Great Plaza, a grassy area about 970 feet long and 650 feet wide, bounded by four large ceremonial platforms. It was leveled by hewing away rock outcroppings. All of the buildings are aligned on a precise north-south axis except for one, an observatory believed to be placed in relation to the stars rather than to compass directions. Many of the structures are roped off.

An I-shaped ball court dominates one corner of the plaza. The Temple of the Dancers (danzantes), on the west side of the plaza, is the oldest building at the site and is named for the elaborate figures carved into its stone slabs. They were first thought to be dancers but may be representations of the diseased or cadavers used for study in a school of medicine.

Some 170 subterranean tombs are scattered throughout the ruins. These contain numerous slab paintings, glyphs, frescoes and stone carvings. Tombs 104 and 105 can be entered by climbing down a ladder, but aren't always open. In 1932, Tomb 7 (near the site entrance) yielded a priceless collection of items, which are on display at the Santo Domingo Cultural Center.

Autobuses Turísticos tour buses depart for Monte Albán several times a day from the Hotel Mesón del Angel, a couple of blocks southwest of Plaza Principal at Calle Mina #518 (at the corner of Calle Mier y Terán). The round-trip fare is about $4 (U.S.). The half-hour ride to the site is very slow but very scenic. There is a museum (with exhibit information in Spanish only), a bookstore and a casual restaurant at the site entrance. Licensed guide service is available for a fee.

**Hours:** Daily 8-5. **Cost:** (includes museum) 64 pesos (about $4.75 U.S.). The fee for using a video camera is about $5. Cash only.

**RUFINO TAMAYO MUSEUM OF PRE-HISPANIC ART** (Museo Rufino Tamayo de Arte Prehispanico) is at Av. José María Morelos #503, 3 blks. n.w. of Plaza Principal. Housed in a restored, 16th-century colonial mansion, it features the private collection of artist Rufino Tamayo, which he donated to his native city. On display are artifacts from Teotihuacán, Nayarit state, and the Olmec, Mayan, Totonac and Aztec civilizations. Figurines, sculptures and other works are handsomely mounted in a series of brightly colored rooms. Exhibit information is in Spanish.

**Hours:** Wed.-Sat. and Mon. 10-2 and 4-7, Sun. 10-3. **Cost:** 40 pesos (about $2.95 U.S.). **Phone:** (951) 516-4750.

**SANTO DOMINGO CULTURAL CENTER** is 5 blks. n. of the Zócalo, next to the Church of Santo Domingo. The building alone makes the center a must-visit—a former Dominican convent that has been beautifully restored to highlight remnants of colonial-era murals and the lovely stonework embellishing arches and stairways. But this also is one of the city's best museums, with exhibits that chart the course of human development in the Valley of Oaxaca.

The showcase display features some 500 pieces of priceless jewelry and art objects—goblets, urns, masks, breastplates—made of gold, turquoise, jade, amber and obsidian that were found in Tomb 7 of the Monte Albán ruins. The museum also contains fascinating, carefully organized collections of regional handicrafts, costumes worn by the different Indian groups within the state, and archeological artifacts. Background information is in Spanish.

The Francisco de Burgoa Library contains more than 30,000 volumes published from the late 15th through the mid-20th centuries. On the grounds (once the site of the convent's orchards) is a garden (Jardín Etnobotánico) with an extensive collection of indigenous plants that have historical and cultural connections to the region. The garden is only accessible as part of a guided tour.

**Time:** Allow 2 hours minimum. **Hours:** Museum Tues.-Sun. 10-6:15. Library reading room Mon.-Fri.

9-3. Botanical garden guided tours in English are given Tues., Thurs. and Sat. at 11 a.m. **Cost:** 64 pesos (about $4.75 U.S.). An audio guide in English can be rented for 60 pesos; inquire at the information desk. Garden guided tour fee 100 pesos (about $7.40 U.S.). **Phone:** (951) 516-2991. GT

**TEMPLE AND EX-CONVENT OF SANTIAGO APOSTOL** is off Calle Vicente Guerrero in the town of Cuilapan, about 16 km (10 mi.) s.w. of Oaxaca via Mex. 131. Better known as Cuilapan de Guerrero, this former Dominican monastery is distinguished by a roofless cloister at the entrance, accentuated by 50-foot-tall columns topped with parapets. The chapel was built in an open-air style to encourage the Indians, who held their religious services outdoors, to attend Mass.

Beyond the cloister is an immense complex of rooms, tunnels and hidden stairways, with enormous portals framed by ornate stonework high atop walls. A museum section displays large, intricately carved stone stela. Next to the monastery are the remnants of a water-driven stone gristmill once used to process wheat. Vicente Guerrero, one of Mexico's first presidents, was executed at this site on Feb. 14, 1831; his remains lie in the base of the Independence Monument in Mexico City.

**Hours:** Daily 10-6. **Cost:** 30 pesos (about $2.20 U.S.). Cash only.

**TULE TREE** (Arbol del Tule) is in the village of Santa María del Tule, about 10 km (6 mi.) s.e. of Oaxaca on Mex. 190. This colossal specimen of a Mexican cypress, or *ahuehuete,* is believed to be at least 2,000 years old. The tree stands in the local churchyard and measures more than 150 feet both in height and around its base. **Hours:** Churchyard open daily 9-5. **Cost:** A small fee is charged to enter the churchyard and see the tree.

**ZAACHILA RUINS** are in Zaachila, about 18 km (11 mi.) s.w. of Oaxaca past the village of Cuilapan; the site, on a hilltop near the church on the main plaza, is marked "Zona Arqueológica." There is limited street parking in the vicinity of the plaza. The name means "place of the Zapoteca kings." A large platform with two sets of stairs descends to the remains of tombs containing ornate carvings, very similar in detail to the zigzag facades that characterize the ruins at Uxmal on the Yucatán Peninsula.

**Time:** Allow 2 hours minimum. **Hours:** Daily 9-6. **Cost:** 39 pesos (about $2.90 U.S.). ⛟

**ZÓCALO** is bordered on the n. by Calle Miguel Hidalgo and on the s. by Calle Valerio Trujano/Vicente Guerrero. Indian laurel trees shade the city's main square, fountains add a soothing burble and a wrought-iron gazebo and bandstand stands at the center. Early evening, when a formal flag-lowering ceremony is performed and people start to gather, is a good time to arrive.

The Zócalo really comes alive at dusk. Street musicians and dancers engage in impromptu performances. Food and handicraft vendors hawk ice cream, roast corn, pineapple chunks, *chorizo* (sausage), musical instruments, balloons, children's toys and tin skeletons dancing on the end of sticks. Band concerts—from brass to marimba to Oaxacan rock—take place regularly.

## PALENQUE, CHIAPAS (C-5) pop. 110,918

The town of Palenque, some 145 kilometers (90 miles) southeast of Villahermosa, has little to offer tourists, although there are hotels and restaurants around its main plaza. It does, however, provide access to the Mayan ruins of Palenque *(see attraction listing),* designated a World Heritage Site by UNESCO in 1987. Occupying the lower foothills of the Sierra Madre in one of Mexico's wettest, most lushly forested regions, Palenque (pah-LEHN-keh) is perhaps the most haunting archeological site in the entire country.

This ancient city most likely began as a farming settlement around 150 B.C. and flourished between A.D. 600 and 800, when it ruled an area covering much of the present-day states of Chiapas and Tabasco. Palenque was abandoned around A.D. 900 for reasons unknown but still debated by historians.

Large-scale excavations in the 1920s under the supervision of Danish explorer Frans Blom *(see San Cristóbal de las Casas)* began clearing away centuries of earth and encroaching jungle. Subsequent excavations have brought to light significant knowledge about Palenque, its inhabitants, its culture and its central role within the Mayan empire.

Travel agencies in Villahermosa, Tuxtla Gutiérrez and San Cristóbal de Las Casas can provide information on reaching Palenque by first-class bus; the trip takes 2 to 3 hours from Villahermosa and about 6 hours from Tuxtla Gutiérrez. Although the ruins can be adequately toured in half a day, staying overnight makes for a less hurried agenda.

From Villahermosa, motorists should take Mex. 186 to Catazajá, then Mex. 199 south to the ruins. Passing through lush countryside, the roadway is generally straight, although slick during the June-through-October rainy season and potholed at any time of year.

Mex. 199 intersects Avenida Juárez about half a mile west of the town's main plaza; the junction is designated by a large statue of a Maya chieftain's head. The road to the ruins branches west off Mex. 199 less than half a mile south of this junction. If you arrive by first-class bus, *colectivo* shuttle buses and taxis run between the center of town and the ruins.

The winter months—November through February—are a better time to visit than in the summer, when it is oppressively hot and humid. Arrive early to avoid both the heat and the crowds, and wear a hat and sunblock for protection from the sun. An all-weather jacket or other rain gear will come in handy at any time. Insect repellent is necessary if you plan on doing any exploring, particularly in the late afternoon.

**Chiapas State Tourism Office (Delegación de Turismo):** on Mex. 199 (Carretera Palenque-Pakal) near the Comfort Inn Palenque. Open Mon.-Sat. 9-9, Sun. 9-1. Information on transportation to the ruins can be obtained here.

**AGUA AZUL WATERFALLS** (Cascadas de Agua Azul) are about 68 km (42 mi.) s. of Palenque via Mex. 199, toward the town of Ocosingo; the entrance is about 4 km (2.5 mi.) w. of the highway via a signed turn-off.

Although not very high, the broad series of cascades plunge dramatically over enormous boulders into clear pools that have a jungle backdrop. Wooden deck platforms provide good views. Swimming is permitted but not recommended; currents can be strong and submerged rocks are hazardous.

Several uphill walkways cover the spread-out grounds, and numerous makeshift huts serve as market stalls and simple eateries. The grounds are also overrun with vendors aggressively hawking their wares. Intentional burning in April and May to clear the jungle can result in a thick haze of smoke. The water also is murky and silt-laden after heavy rains.

The journey to Agua Azul is along a pocked, two-lane blacktop road that winds sinuously through mountainous terrain. Although the views are spectacular, the roadway abuts steep cliffs and there are no shoulders. It also bristles with *topes* (speed bumps). Unless you crave adventure or are very adept at negotiating mountainous terrain, do not attempt the trip in a car.

**Note:** Close to the falls there are locations where local residents not only try and stop traffic to sell beverages, locally grown fruit and other items but may also demand an additional "admission" from unsuspecting tourists. It's safer and easier to visit the falls as part of a guided tour. Travel agencies in Palenque offer day trip packages; inquire along Avenida Juárez near the main plaza. **Hours:** Open daily until dusk. **Cost:** 15 pesos (about $1.10 U.S.) per vehicle. Parking fee 10 pesos. Cash only.

**Misol-Ha** is about 19 km (12 mi.) s. of Palenque off Mex. 199; watch for the signed turn-off. This waterfall is a shorter trip and is equally beautiful; it drops approximately 90 feet into a wide pool. Both Misol-Ha and Agua Azul can be very crowded on weekends and holidays. **Hours:** Open daily. **Cost:** 15 pesos per vehicle.

**PALENQUE RUINS** are about 8 km (5 mi.) s.w. of town via an access road that branches off Mex. 199 a short distance s. of the city cemetery (Panteón Municipal). Despite a remote location, this archeological site is a must-see. The excavated section—small in relation to the city's size during its heyday more than 1,000 years ago—spreads a mile or so from east to west. The ruins here are among the best preserved in Mesoamerica. Stone plaques at each structure offer descriptions in English.

Next to the Temple of the Inscriptions *(see sub-attraction listing)* is Temple XIII, where a tomb was discovered in 1994. Just east of this temple is the Palace, a complex of stepped buildings and four courtyards connected by corridors and an extensive system of underground passageways. The exterior walls are adorned with the beautifully carved, unusually well-preserved panels and stucco reliefs for which Palenque is famous.

Cross the Río Otolum (little more than a stream) to reach the Temple of the Cross, at the southeastern edge of the ruins. It is one of several structures ringing a spacious plaza. Projecting upward from the temple are vertical roof combs, a decorative architectural feature favored by Mayan builders. Inside the building is a small shrine.

Nearby are Temple 14, which contains more stone tablets with carved inscriptions, and the Temple of the Sun, believed to contain the tomb of King Pacal's son, Chan-Bahlum, his successor to the throne. At the site's northern end is the Northern Group of buildings, including a ball court and the Temple of the Count, named for Frederick Waldeck, an early explorer. This structure, the best preserved of the group, is made up of five stepped tiers; its main facade faces east.

Don't miss the museum and visitor center, on the access road about a mile before the ruins entrance. The museum displays reproductions of hieroglyphic panels and artifacts uncovered during the excavations, including the carved tomb of Pacal. Background information is provided in English. Save the museum for the end of your visit, as the air-conditioned interior offers a refreshing respite from the heat.

Most area hotels have in-house tour representatives who can schedule an organized excursion, and there also are several sightseeing tour offices along the main street in the town of Palenque. If you go on your own, official tour guides (identified by their ID badges) can be hired at the ruins entrance; unofficial guides also can be hired for a lower rate. There are numerous vendor stalls at the entrance, and more vendors inside the park selling souvenirs.

**Note:** Visit as early as possible in the morning to beat both the heat and the bus tours. Bring insect repellent, sunscreen, a hat and water (water also is sold outside the ruins). Visitors are permitted to climb most of the structures. **Hours:** Site open daily 8-4. Museum open Tues.-Sun. 8-4. **Cost:** 92 pesos (about $6.80 U.S.; covers separate admissions to the national park and the ruins). The fee to use a video camera is 45 pesos (about $3.65 U.S.). Cash only.

**Temple of the Inscriptions** (Templo de las Inscripciones) is to the right as you enter the site. This 90-foot-tall pyramidal structure is one of Palenque's most impressive. The temple was the final resting place of Pacal, the king who ruled Palenque for almost 70 years beginning at the ripe old age of 12. It is believed to be one of the only temples in Mexico constructed expressly to be a tomb. A steep flight of stone block stairs descends to the royal crypt (closed to visitors). **Note:** Climbing on the pyramid is not permitted.

# PAPANTLA, VERACRUZ (B-3)
pop. 158,599

**Note:** For current information about safety/security issues in the Papantla region, including the El Tajín archeological zone, refer to the U.S. State Department website (travel.state.gov).

Papantla (pah-PAHN-tlah) spreads out over the green foothills of the Sierra Madre Oriental, about 243 kilometers (150 miles) northwest of Veracruz. This was the capital of the Totonac kingdom in the mid-15th century, before it fell to the conquering Aztecs. The vanquished Totonacs extracted a revenge of sorts by aiding Hernando Cortés in defeating the Aztecs. The city remains a center of Totonac culture today, and visitors are likely to see locals wearing native garb: billowing white pants and sailor shirts for men, lacy skirts and embroidered white blouses for women.

This is Mexico's vanilla-producing center, and the distinctively sweet scent frequently hovers in the air. Vanilla bean pods are fashioned into small figures that are sold around town, along with textiles, embroidered clothing and baskets. Souvenir hunters also can try the Hidalgo Market (Mercado Hidalgo), on Avenida 20 de Noviembre just off the northwest corner of the main plaza, for handmade men's and women's clothing.

Papantla is celebrated for its Papantla Flyers (Voladores de Papantla), Totonac Indians who give an exciting rendition of the "Flying Pole" dance. Ropes that have been wound around a 70-foot-tall pole are tied around their waists. Four dancers jump backward off a tiny revolving platform atop the pole, whirling downwards as the ropes unwind. A fifth man, who dances while playing a flute and beating a drum, remains on top of the platform. Each performer revolves around the pole 13 times; the total number of revolutions, 52, equals the number of years in the Aztec religious life cycle.

Before it evolved into a crowd-pleasing spectacle of its own, the dance was part of a pre-Hispanic agricultural ceremony designed to secure the favor of the rain gods and to celebrate the vanilla harvest. The dancers perform up to three times a day during the Festival of Corpus Christi in late May and early June. Papantla's signature annual event, the festival is celebrated with art exhibitions, traditional dances, cockfights and fireworks displays.

Overlooking the city from a hilltop is a giant likeness of a flute-playing *volador,* a monument erected in 1988. There are good views of the surrounding countryside from the base of the statue, which can be reached by walking up Avenida Reforma from the cathedral.

The first-class Autobuses del Oriente (ADO) bus station is at the intersection of avenidas Venustiano Carranza and Benito Juárez, north of Plaza Tellez *(see attraction listing).* From the station there is service to Jalapa and Veracruz.

▼GEM **EL TAJÍN** is about 13 kilometers (8 miles) w. of Papantla via a paved road, following signs. The main reason to come to Papantla is to visit these impressive ruins, which were first discovered in the late 18th century. A major restoration project began in 1992, the same year that El

Tajín (tah-HEEN) was designated a World Heritage Site by UNESCO. Some 40 structures, divided into four sections, have been excavated and restored.

The largest building is the Pyramid of the Niches. Constructed of adobe and stone, its seven terraces are punctuated by 365 deeply recessed niches on all four sides. This pyramid was once painted red, and the niches were black. A smaller pyramid, Building 5, is just to the south.

North of the Pyramid of the Niches in the Tajín Chico section is the Temple of the Columns, which has six richly carved column shafts—three on each side—that once supported a ceiling/roof. Large portions of the roof are scattered below near one of the site's 17 ball courts (six can be visited). The best vantage point of the entire site is from the rear of the Tajín Chico building group.

The museum near the entrance contains display cases of artifacts retrieved from the excavations; information signs are in English and Spanish. Two dioramas depict the site. Also on display are photos of the moon and sun rising over the pyramids.

The Papantla Flyers will perform the well-known flying pole dance just outside the main entrance whenever there are enough tourists—usually tour groups—to form an appreciative audience. A 20-peso donation per person is requested to watch the spectacle, which is not without risk to its daredevil performers; the flyers also will put on a special show for a 400-peso fee.

Stone pathways connect the four sections. Climbing the pyramids is not permitted. Bring a water bottle and wear a hat and sunblock for protection, as the site has little shade. Also pick up a free Spanish-language brochure at the admission desk; it has a good map of the site.

The tourist information office in Papantla can provide information about sightseeing tours to the ruins, although English is not likely to be spoken. Minibuses marked "Chote/Tajín" depart from Avenida 16 de Septiembre at the main plaza (the street running along the uphill side of the cathedral).

From Mexico City, Papantla is a 3- to 4-hour drive via Mex. 130; from Veracruz, Papantla is about 225 kilometers (140 miles) north via Mex. 180. Both highways are safe to drive, although getting to Papantla from Veracruz, visiting the ruins and then returning to Veracruz makes for a very long day. ADO bus service is available from Mexico City and Veracruz to Papantla. Travel (especially by bus) from the state of Tamaulipas, north of Papantla, is not recommended.

**Note:** Expect checkpoint stops (police searching for guns and ammunition) on Mex. 180. This highway also is rough in some places. Avoid driving after dark if possible. **Hours:** Daily 9-5. Tours with a licensed, English-speaking guide are available; guides can be hired at the admission desk. **Cost:** (includes museum) 64 pesos (about $4.75 U.S.); free (ages 0-12). Free to all Sun. The fee to use a video camera is 45 pesos. Guided tour fee 200 pesos for a group of one to eight people; 15 pesos per person for groups of nine or more. Parking is free; give a

tip to the person who watches the cars. Cash only. **Phone:** (784) 842-8354.

**PLAZA TÉLLEZ** is terraced into a hillside in the center of town, between calles Juan Enríquez and José Nuñez. White-tiled and palm-shaded, it has benches inlaid with tile mosaics. On the plaza's south side is the Cathedral of Our Lady of the Assumption (Catedral de Nuestra Señora de la Asunción). Carved into the church's north wall is the Tribute to the Totonac Culture (Homenaje a la Cultura Totonaca), a 165-foot-long stone mural. It depicts Totonac folkloric figures and is dominated by a rendering of the plumed serpent Quetzalcóatl that runs its entire length.

# SAN CRISTÓBAL DE LAS CASAS, CHIAPAS (C-5) pop. 185,917

San Cristóbal (sahn krees-TOH-bahl) de Las Casas is named for Bartolomé de Las Casas, a New World settler and Dominican priest who was appointed bishop of Chiapas in 1545 and became famous for his advocacy on behalf of the indigenous peoples of Mexico and the Caribbean—a position bolstered after he witnessed the atrocities committed by Spanish *conquistadores.* Three years after independence from Spain was won in 1821, San Cristóbal became the Chiapan state capital and remained so until 1892, when the capital was moved to Tuxtla Gutiérrez.

San Cristóbal and Chiapas made international headlines in 1994, Mexico's most politically turbulent year since the 1910 Revolution. Indian guerrillas calling themselves the Zapatista National Liberation Army (in honor of revolutionary leader Emiliano Zapata) occupied San Cristóbal and several other mountain towns, demanding more land and a measure of self-rule for their communities. The rebellion, which left more than 100 dead over 12 days, was a violent reminder that large numbers of poor Indian farmers were not sharing in the country's prosperity.

While social injustices are understandably taken very seriously in Mexico, visitors aren't likely to see evidence of political tension in San Cristóbal outside of the occasional demonstration or graffiti-scrawled wall. Tourism contributes greatly to the local income, and visitors come from around the world; some street vendors sell ski-masked dolls representing Zapatista guerrilla leader Subcomandante Marcos—a popular souvenir—along with the usual trinkets.

The city lies in a highland valley where the surrounding pine and oak forests are sprinkled with orchids and ferns. Here the whitewashed walls and cobblestone streets typical of other Mexican colonial cities have a mystical backdrop of cloud-shrouded mountain peaks. The evening air is redolent with the smoky fragrance of burning *ocote,* a pitch-pine kindling sold in local markets.

Although at a tropical latitude, the altitude, cool weather and frequent fog lend San Cristóbal a decidedly nontropical feeling. And this is where Central America begins, culturally if not politically; the border with Guatemala lies little more than 160 kilometers (100 miles) southeast.

## Practicalities

Getting to remote San Cristóbal takes some planning. The easiest way is to fly into the Tuxtla Gutiérrez or Villahermosa airports. United offers direct service to Villahermosa from Houston. Aeroméxico, phone 01 (800) 021-4000 (toll-free long distance within Mexico), flies to Villahermosa from Mexico City. *For additional information about airlines see Arriving by Air, page p. 42.*

A taxi ride from Tuxtla Gutiérrez to San Cristóbal will cost about $50 (U.S.). The drive from Tuxtla east to San Cristóbal takes about 1.5 hours via Mex. 190. It winds for some 83 kilometers (51 miles) in a series of S-curves around high mountain peaks, frequently above cloud level. The elevation ascends some 5,000 feet between the two cities. The two-lane road passes through beautiful, unspoiled scenery, but slippery pavement during the June-through-October rainy season can make the surface dangerous.

**Note:** If you're unfamiliar with mountain driving, exercise caution. Never drive at a faster speed than conditions warrant, downshift to a lower gear when climbing or going down steep grades, and use particular caution when negotiating curves. Also keep in mind that high elevations often experience changeable weather and can cause headaches or shortness of breath if you're not used to the altitude.

"Deluxe" and first-class bus service to and from Tuxtla Gutiérrez, Palenque, Villahermosa, Oaxaca and Mérida is offered by Autotransportes Cristóbal Colón and ADO. These two lines share a bus terminal at the intersection of Mex. 190 and Avenida Insurgentes, about 9 blocks south of the main plaza. Bus tickets can be purchased at the terminal or at the Ticket Bus agency in downtown San Cristóbal, at Avenida Belisario Domínguez #8 (a block northeast of the main plaza).

Most of San Cristóbal's visitor-related attractions, restaurants and shopping areas are within walking distance of the main plaza. For trips to Indian villages in the vicinity *(see Nearby Destinations)*, passenger vans *(colectivos)* and taxis depart from locations along Mex. 190 in the vicinity of the first-class bus terminal. *Combis* (Volkswagen vans) make regular runs from Mex. 190 (pickup is by the main bus terminal) north to downtown via Avenida Crescencio Rosas. Taxi rides within town average about $3 (U.S.); a knowledge of Spanish will be helpful when determining the exact fare.

Chiapas, Mexico's southernmost state, is largely mountainous and forested, and the stunning natural scenery—from mist-shrouded peaks and cascading waterfalls to steamy jungles inhabited by many kinds of wildlife—makes it a fascinating place to explore. ATC Tours conducts a variety of regional eco-oriented adventures, including bird-watching trips, hikes to observe butterflies and orchids, and hiking and white-water rafting excursions. The San Cristóbal office is at Av. 16 de Septiembre #16 at Calle 5 de Febrero, a block northwest of the main plaza; for information phone (967) 678-2550.

A local tour company that offers city tours is Explorando Chiapas. The guide, Julio Cesar Entzin Mendez, speaks fluent English as well as French and Italian. Sightseeing excursions also can be arranged to the ruins of Palenque, Sumidero Canyon, the Agua Azul and Misol-Ha waterfalls, and the Indian villages of Chamula and Zinacantán. Phone 044 (967) 127-7170 (cellular number); explorandochiapas.com.mx.

## City Layout

Plaza 31 de Marzo, the main plaza, is between avenidas 16 de Septiembre and 20 de Noviembre and calles 5 de Febrero and Guadalupe Victoria. It's a good starting place for exploring downtown. The surrounding colonial-era buildings are stylistically Spanish, although the atmosphere is unmistakably Indian. If you stop here to relax and observe daily life, you'll likely be approached by street vendors (mostly women and children). The scene is especially bustling in the evening, when families congregate and the air is filled with aromas wafting from food carts. Musicians normally play on weekend evenings at the gazebo in the center of the plaza.

On the plaza's north side stands San Cristóbal's 16th-century Cathedral. It was constructed in 1528 and rebuilt in 1693. Some of the exterior carvings of saints are missing their heads. The bright yellow exterior is particularly lovely in the late afternoon sun, and beautifully illuminated at night.

The west side is dominated by the arcaded, yellow-and-white Municipal Palace, distinguished by its numerous arcades. At the plaza's southeast corner is the House of Diego Mazariegos, which dates from the 16th century and now houses a hotel; the building's detailed exterior stonework is an example of the plateresque architectural style.

The narrow streets of the historic center are laid out in an easy-to-navigate grid pattern. As in other Mexican cities, street names change depending on geographical orientation to the main plaza. The principal north-south thoroughfare is called Avenida Insurgentes south of the plaza and General M. Utrilla north of it; Calle Madero, the principal east-west thoroughfare, becomes Diego Mazariegos west of the plaza. Similarly, north-south Avenida 16 de Septiembre changes to Crescencio Rosas south of the plaza; east-west Calle M.A. Flores is named 5 de Febrero west of the plaza.

Opposite the plaza's northwest corner on Avenida 16 de Septiembre is the Museum of Jade (Museo del Jade). Exhibits include jewelry, reproductions of Olmec carvings and a painstaking replica of the sarcophagus lid from the tomb of King Pacal, ruler of Palenque for more than 70 years.

Three blocks south of the plaza, just off Avenida Miguel Hidalgo, is the 1587 Church of El Carmen (Templo del Carmen); a street passes through the middle of its four-story arch. Crowning one of the rolling hills east of the center of town (about 7 blocks east of the plaza via Calle Real de Guadalupe) is the Church of the Virgin of Guadalupe. The view from the top takes in the entire city.

Surrounding the downtown core is a patchwork quilt of neighborhoods *(barrios)* that originally developed around specific trades—carpenters, blacksmiths, candle makers. Today *ladinos*—Mexicans of non-Indian descent—live in these neighborhoods of one-story, pastel-colored stucco houses with red-tiled roofs and wrought-iron window grills.

Mex. 190, the Pan-American Highway, runs through the southern part of town on its way to the Guatemalan border. The official name is Boulevard Juan Sabines, but it's known locally as "El Bulevar."

## Dining, Nightlife and Events

Chiapanecan cuisine incorporates such reliable Mexican standbys as *tamales,* enchiladas and tacos, although they're often enhanced with distinctively flavored herbs and hot sauces. A popular local beverage is *atole,* a lightly sweetened drink made from cornmeal, and vendors outside the cathedral sell corn on the cob and other snacks from their carts. San Cristóbal restaurants also offer numerous vegetarian options.

El Fogón de Jovel, a block west of the main plaza at Av. 16 de Septiembre #11 (at Calle Guadalupe Victoria), has a courtyard and live music, all the better to enjoy such specialties as chicken in *pipián,* a traditional *mole* sauce made from ground pumpkin seeds, chile peppers and other seasonings. Another restaurant close to the main plaza—and a popular local hangout—is Emiliano's Moustache, Calle Crescensio Rosas #7 (at Avenida Mazariegos). The tacos come with various fillings, and tortillas are handmade.

La Paloma is just south of the main plaza at Calle Miguel Hidalgo #3, the pedestrian-only street called the Andador Turístico. This bright, hip little cafe has good Mexican choices like squash flower soup, cactus salad and abalone in chipotle sauce. For something non-Mexican try Restaurant L'Edén, 2 blocks northwest of the main plaza at Calle 5 de Febrero (in the Hotel El Paraíso). The menu features Swiss-inspired dishes, including raclette (melted cheese draped over potatoes) and fondue.

Businesses on Real de Guadalupe cater to tourists, and this also is a convenient place to have breakfast. La Casa del Pan, Real de Guadalupe #55, emphasizes healthy vegetarian dishes made with regionally grown grains and beans. The bread is fresh-baked, and the coffee is a good reason to linger. The shop in the restaurant sells organic coffee beans, raw chocolate and other local products.

Hotel bars and several nightclubs, all in the historic downtown area, offer live music ranging from salsa and jazz to reggae, rock and cover versions of old top 40 hits. The choice is greatest on weekends, but there is something going on almost every night of the week. Musicians play most evenings at El Cocodrilo, in the Hotel Santa Clara (on Avenida Insurgentes across from the south side of the main

plaza). Latino's, a block east of the main plaza at Av. Francisco I. Madero #23, features Latin music.

San Cristóbal's Spring Fair (Feria de la Primavera y de la Paz) takes place the week after Easter. The festivities include parades, bullfights, band concerts, handicraft exhibits, amusement rides and stalls serving an array of regional foods.

The Feast of San Cristóbal, held July 17-25, honors the town's patron saint. Pilgrims carrying torches climb the steep hill to the Church of San Cristóbal *(see attraction listing)* to attend special services. Chiapanecos also celebrate—along with the rest of Mexico—the Days of the Dead Nov. 1 and 2, the Feast Day of the Virgin of Guadalupe Dec. 12 and celebrations of Jesus' birth during the Christmas season.

The Indian village of San Juan Chamula is noted for its religious observances, particularly those celebrated during Holy Week (between Palm Sunday and Easter Sunday). A blend of Christian and pagan rites, the ceremonies take place both inside the village church and on the plaza in front of it. On June 24, a Catholic priest visits the village to baptize newborn children.

Carnaval celebrations, featuring a parade of vivid costumes, are held just before Lent. The rollicking Feast of St. John the Baptist (San Juan Bautista), the patron saint of San Juan Chamula, is observed June 22-25.

**Chiapas State Tourism Office (Secretaría de Turismo):** Av. Miguel Hidalgo #1B, about a block s. of the main plaza. Open Mon.-Sat. 8-8, Sun. 9-2. **Phone:** (967) 678-6570.

Check the bulletin board at the municipal tourist office, in the Municipal Palace building (Ayuntamiento) just off Parque Central near the main plaza, for notices pertaining to cultural events and guided tours, and at each office about arranging excursions to points of interest in and around San Cristóbal. There usually is at least one English-speaking staff member on hand at each office.

**Shopping:** The Municipal Market, 8 blocks north of the main plaza between avenidas General M. Utrilla and Belisario Domínguez, spreads out over blocks and is worth visiting just to observe the colorfully attired merchants and customers. It's open every day but Sunday, when the local village markets take over; Saturday morning is the best time to visit. Produce, flower stands, Chiapan coffee beans and household items dominate the open-air portion; butcher stalls are within the covered section. Be very discreet about taking photographs of vendors or shoppers (or don't take them at all), and watch out for pickpockets.

If you're searching for handicrafts, try the shops along Calle Real de Guadalupe in the blocks just east of the main plaza. The quality is evident in the lovely woolen shawls, *huipiles* (white cotton dresses embroidered with flower and geometric designs), bolts of fabric, leather goods, woven blankets and amber jewelry. Women and children will often approach tourists on the street selling dolls, bracelets and other handmade items.

The government-run House of Crafts (Casa de las Artesanías), 2 blocks south of the main plaza at Calle Niñoes Héroes and Avenida Hidalgo, stocks a representative selection of woolen vests, embroidered blouses and other clothing, amber jewelry, ceramics and textiles. An exhibition room showcases the native dress of villagers in the surrounding Indian communities.

Sna Jolobil, on Calzada Lázaro Cardenas within the Temple and Ex-Convent of Santo Domingo *(see attraction listing)*, is a crafts cooperative run by Tzeltal and Tzotzil Indians, who also handcraft the high-quality merchandise on display. The name means "weaver's house." Another cooperative effort is Taller Leñateros, east of the main plaza at Calle Flavio A. Paniagua #54. In addition to crafts, the workshop—where artisans can be observed on the job—creates ingenious postcards, book binders and writing paper.

La Galeria, Calle Hidalgo #3, spotlights well-known artists and also sells turquoise and silver jewelry. The restaurant above the gallery features live music in the evening.

About 37 kilometers (23 miles) southeast of San Cristóbal via Mex. 190 is the Tzeltal village of Amatenango del Valle, known for its women potters. The pottery is fired by wood rather than in a kiln. You can buy directly from local families, whose wares include simple jugs and pots as well as *animalito* (animal) figures. The women wear *huipiles* embroidered with distinctive red and yellow designs.

**AMBER MUSEUM** (Museo del Ambar) is 3 blks. w. of the main plaza on Av. Diego Mazariegos. Housed in a restored section of the former Ex-Convento de la Merced, this is perhaps the only museum in Mexico devoted to amber, a brownish-yellow, translucent fossil resin that is mined in the nearby Simojovel Valley. On view are sculpted amber pieces carved by local artisans, as well as ancient chunks with fossilized insects inside. Exhibit information is in Spanish and English.

**Hours:** Tues.-Sun. 10-2 and 4-8. **Cost:** 20 pesos (about $1.50 U.S.); 10 pesos (ages 6-10 and 65+). **Phone:** (967) 678-9716.

**CHURCH OF SAN CRISTÓBAL** (Templo de San Cristóbal) is perched atop a hill at the end of Calle Hermanos Domínguez, 4 blks. s. of Plaza 31 de Marzo via Av. Insurgentes. Although you'll have to climb what seems like an endless series of steps up the hill to reach it, the view of the city from the lookout point *(mirador)* at the top is worth it.

The exterior features an eye-catching profusion of intricately detailed stone carvings of saints and biblical figures. The interior is no less ornate, although centuries of soot and smoke from burning incense and candles have left a patina of grime on the many beautiful oil paintings. Vendors congregate outside the church, selling jewelry, crafts, amber, textiles and other items, and if you're practiced at haggling there are good deals to be had. **Note:** This is an active parish church, and walk-in visitors should respect those who are there to worship. **Hours:** Open daily. **Cost:** Free.

**NA-BOLOM MUSEUM** (Casa Na-Bolom) is about 10 blks. n.e. of the main plaza at Av. Vicente Guerrero #33. It celebrates the work of Danish explorer and ethnologist Frans Blom. The colonial-style building, dating from 1891 and now a museum and cultural center, was purchased by Blom in 1950.

Blom conducted extensive research at the Mayan ruins around Palenque and oversaw some of the first excavations at Uxmal, on the Yucatán Peninsula. His wife Gertrude, a journalist and photographer, devoted herself to preserving the rain forest homeland of the reclusive Lacandón Indians. Na-Bolom continues to operate as a private, nonprofit institute dedicated to the preservation of the environment and native cultures.

Guided 90-minute tours of the home take in a collection of pre-Hispanic artifacts put together by Blom; the library, with thousands of volumes about the Maya and Chiapas; a walk through the extensive gardens; and a showing of the film "La Reina de la Selva," about the Lacandón forest and its inhabitants. **Hours:** Museum daily 8-7. Tours in English are offered Tues.-Sun. at 4:30. **Cost:** 40 pesos (about $2.95 U.S.). There is an additional fee of 10 pesos for the tour. Cash only. **Phone:** (967) 678-1418.

**TEMPLE AND EX-CONVENT OF SANTO DOMINGO** is about 5 blks. n. of the main plaza, entered from Av. 20 de Noviembre. Construction of the church was begun in 1547; the extravagantly detailed carvings of saints, angels and decorative accents on its baroque exterior have weathered to a dusty pink. Note the double-headed Hapsburg eagle over the doorway, a symbol of the Spanish monarchy added in the 17th century. The interior features a lavishly ornate pulpit, a gilded altarpiece and gilt-framed *retablos* (religious paintings).

The adjacent convent houses Sna Jolobil, a handicraft showroom selling wool capes, clothing, woven goods and other Indian-made items. **Hours:** Church complex open Tues.-Sun. 10-5. Convent and showroom open Tues.-Sat. 9-2 and 4-6. **Cost:** Convent and showroom 50 pesos (about $3.70 U.S.). Church free.

**Altos Cultural Center** (Centro Cultural de Los Altos) is within the church complex. This museum (the name means "highlands") has displays pertaining to San Cristóbal and Mayan history as well as changing cultural exhibits, with rooms set around a courtyard overlooked by wide balconies. Background information is in Spanish. **Hours:** Tues.-Sun. 9-6. Phone ahead to confirm schedule. **Cost:** 48 pesos (about $3.55 U.S.). **Phone:** (967) 678-1609.

## Nearby Destinations

The ethnic peoples populating the nearby communities north of San Cristóbal are among the most resilient in the country. They have managed to maintain their cultural identity over hundreds of years and also in the face of drastic modernization. Although almost all are members of the Tzeltal, Tzotzil and Chamula tribes, the inhabitants of these mountain villages retain a striking variety of differences in manner of dress, dialect, and religious customs and ceremonies.

Men frequently leave the villages to find work; women tend to the cornfields, take care of the children and run the market stalls. Women are often seen bent under a load of firewood, balanced on their backs with the aid of a strap fitted across the forehead. Among the handicrafts produced by village artisans are wooden musical instruments, leather goods, ceramics, furniture and woven baskets. The best time to visit is during a fiesta or on Sunday morning, when most of the villages have their own market and tourists are most welcomed.

San Juan Chamula, about 10 kilometers (6 miles) northwest of San Cristóbal via a paved road, is the best-known village. Spanish is not spoken, and English is rarely heard. Daily life centers on the town church (Iglesia de San Juan Bautista), where the religious rituals are a fascinating blend of Christian and non-Christian. The church is named for St. John the Baptist, a religious figure who in this region takes precedence over Jesus Christ.

The white stucco structure, which stands next to the main plaza, has a beautifully carved wooden door. Inside the dimness is illuminated by a sea of flickering candles, the tile floor is strewn with pine needles and the smell of incense wafts throughout. There are no pews; people sit on the floor. Statues of saints line the walls, swaddled in layers of brightly colored cloth. While worshipers chant and pray in front of these statues, they figure in church rituals in name only; Catholicism is not observed by the villagers.

You must obtain a 10-peso ticket (about 90c U.S.) to enter the church; tickets are available at the local tourist office on the main plaza. Visitors may stand and observe quietly in the background while prayer or curing rituals are being performed, which often involve rubbing the bodies of the sick with eggs or chicken bones. People also drink from bottles of Coca-Cola—the resultant burping is thought to expel evil spirits from the body—and some imbibe *posh*, a more potent beverage made from fermented sugarcane. Photography is strictly forbidden. Do not wear a hat inside.

Near the church is Ora Ton, a small museum that displays musical instruments and examples of traditional clothing. The ticket allowing admittance to the church includes admission to the museum.

Zinacantán is about 11 kilometers (7 miles) northwest of San Cristóbal; the road to this village forks west off the road to San Juan Chamula and descends into a valley. Zinacantán's side-by-side churches also have floors covered in pine needles, but the rituals here incorporate Catholicism to a greater degree. Photography, both inside and out, is strictly prohibited, and you may be escorted in rather than being allowed to enter on your own. A small fee also is charged.

Unless you feel comfortable assimilating into an unfamiliar culture, a guided trip is the best way to experience a bit of daily life in these villages. Small group tours with an English-speaking guide are offered by the Na-Bolom Museum (see attraction listing). The fee is about $15 (U.S.) per person.

**Note:** A visit to any local village involves sensitivity and respect, as you are an outsider and may well be made to feel like one. Picture taking is forbidden at most events, particularly so inside churches, and residents may not take kindly to being stared at. Photography of any sort is generally objected to, so keep cameras packed. Youthful vendors in San Juan Chamula, many of whom live in desperate poverty, will hawk tourists aggressively.

## TAXCO, GUERRERO (C-2) pop. 104,053

Probably the oldest mining town in North America, Taxco (TAHS-coh) was the Indian village of Tlachco (meaning "place of ball game") when Hernando Cortés' captains discovered rich gold deposits. Initial development began after José de la Borda, a French miner, arrived in 1716 and amassed an immense fortune. Borda's initial impact on the mining industry was carried on by a young American named William Spratling, who came to Taxco in 1929 to write a book. Stranded in Mexico after his publisher went broke, Spratling turned to the silver business. He opened a retail outlet and found apprentices among the local youth, many of whom went on to become proprietors of their own silver shops.

Plaza Borda, Taxco's main square, is typical of those in other old Mexican towns: tree shaded, with benches for relaxation and a bandstand for musical performances. The shops in and around the plaza specialize in silver, and shopping for it is undoubtedly the most popular tourist activity in town. The range of items in Taxco's more than 300 silver shops covers everything from inexpensive trinkets to artistic pieces selling for hundreds of dollars.

The price is usually determined by weight, and many shops sell both retail (menudeo) and wholesale (mayoreo). Always check for the stamp bearing the numerals ".925," which certifies that it is at least 92.5 percent sterling silver, and for the two-letter initials signifying the manufacturer. If you're looking for items at the less expensive end of the scale, try the Silver Market (Mercado de Artesanías Plata), a block or so southeast of Plaza Borda; the stalls here carry a huge selection of rings, chains and other jewelry.

Much pageantry is associated with Holy Week (Semana Santa). On Palm Sunday an image of Christ on a donkey departs the nearby village of Tehuilotepec, east of town, for a processional to Taxco. Candlelit processions by *penitentes* take place nightly, culminating on Holy Thursday, when the Last Supper is staged in front of the Church of Santa Prisca (see attraction listing). The Resurrection re-enactment takes place on Saturday evening, and another processional occurs on Easter Sunday. If you plan on being in town during Holy Week, make hotel reservations in advance.

The weeklong National Silver Fair (Feria Nacional de la Plata), held the last week in November or the

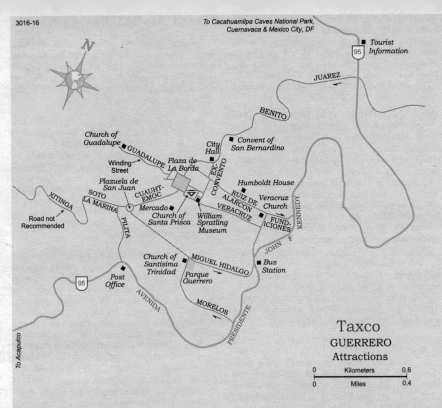

To Cacahuamilpa Caves National Park,
Cuernavaca & Mexico City, DF

■ Tourist
95 Information

JUAREZ

BENITO

Church of
Guadalupe
GUADALUPE
City
Hall
■ Convent of
San Bernardino
Winding
Street
Plaza de
La Borda
Plazuela de
San Juan
CUAUHT-
EMOC
Humboldt House
SOTO
XITINGA
LA MARINA
Mercado ■
RUIZ DE
ALARCON
VERACRUZ
Veracruz
Church
Road not
Recommended
PILITA
Church of
Santa Prisca
William
Spratling
Museum
FUND-
ICIONES
KENNEDY
JOHN F.
Church of
Santísima
Trinidad
MIGUEL HIDALGO
■ Bus
Station
95
Post
Office
Parque
Guerrero
AVENIDA
MORELOS
PRESIDENTE

Taxco
GUERRERO
Attractions

0        Kilometers        0.6
0            Miles          0.4

To Acapulco

© AAA

first week in December, is Mexico's foremost silver-smith competition. Each year judges confer international recognition to artisans whose designs and workmanship are deemed superior.

Another annual event of interest to visitors is Alarcón Days (Jornadas Alarconianas). This cultural and artistic festival offers painting expositions, band serenades in Plaza Borda and musical performances during the last three weekends in May; check with the State Tourism Office for exact dates. Presentations of plays by Juan Ruiz de Alarcón, a Taxco native born of noble Spanish parentage who wrote his works during the same period as Miguel de Cervantes, are given in plazas and city streets.

Steep, narrow roads, infrequent street name designations and many one-way streets make driving in Taxco difficult. Walking is the best way to explore. *Combis* are a convenient and inexpensive means of local transportation; rides in these white Volkswagen minibuses are about 50¢ (U.S.) in town. Taxi fares in town average about $3 to $4; taxis also are available for visiting points of interest in the surrounding area.

A particularly scenic way to appreciate Taxco's mountain setting is by taking a ride on the Monte Gondola, which departs near the entrance to town. The cars hold up to four people, and the views as

they ascend to the Hotel Monte Taxco are spectacular. There are a few shops and a snack bar at the top, and another panoramic vista from the hotel terrace. The cable car operates daily; the last car comes down at 6:50 p.m. A one-way ticket is 45 pesos (about $3.35 U.S.); round trip 65 pesos. The fare for children is 30 pesos one way, 45 pesos round trip. You also can take a taxi back down.

"Tour guides" will eagerly approach visitors around Plaza Borda. Ask to see their credentials, and beware of freelance guides who are not federally licensed or government sponsored. The State Tourism Office can recommend a reliable licensed guide.

**Guerrero State Tourism Office (Secretaría de Fomento Turístico):** Av. J.F. Kennedy #1 (Mex. 95), at the north end of town where the aqueduct arches cross the highway. Open daily 9-8. **Phone:** (762) 622-6616.

**CACAHUAMILPA CAVES NATIONAL PARK** (Parque Nacional Grutas de Cacahuamilpa) is at the intersection of Mex. 166 and Mex. 55, about 32 km (20 mi.) n.e. of Taxco. Spelunkers have burrowed more than 8 miles through the passageways of Grutas de Cacahuamilpa (kah-kah-wah-MEEL-pah) and still haven't reached the end. About half a mile of the vast labyrinth can be viewed from wide, paved pathways.

Huge chambers—100 feet high, 200 feet long and nearly as wide—hold an array of fantastic formations, some of which are enhanced by lighting. Comfortable walking shoes are recommended. Spanish and English-speaking guides lead 90-minute tours of the caverns. Tours depart hourly. **Hours:** Daily 10-5. **Cost:** 75 pesos (about $5.55 U.S.); 65 pesos (ages 6-12); 40 pesos (seniors). **Phone:** (721) 104-0155.

**CHURCH OF SANTA PRISCA** (Iglesia de Santa Prisca) faces the main square. It was funded by José de la Borda in gratitude for his good fortune in mining. Begun in 1751 and completed 7 years later, the church has a beautifully carved facade with twin 130-foot spires flanking a tiled dome. The interior is even more elaborate, a breathtaking profusion of gold-leaf saints and cherubs, 12 highly decorated altars and lovely paintings by Miguel Cabrera, one of Mexico's most celebrated colonial-era artists; Borda spared no expense in making this a beautifully appointed church.

Guides approach visitors outside offering tours. For a few pesos you'll receive some enlightening background information, but determine whether the fee applies to an individual or group tour and make sure the guide speaks understandable English. **Time:** Allow 1 hour minimum. **Hours:** Daily 6:30 a.m.-8 p.m. **Cost:** Free. **Phone:** (762) 622-0184.

**CONVENT OF SAN BERNARDINO** (Ex-Convento de San Bernardino de Siena) is on Plaza del Convento, off Calle Estacadas. It was built by the Franciscan order in 1595 but was destroyed by a fire in 1805; the present neoclassic building dates from 1821. That same year the Plan of Iguala was drafted here by Agustín de Iturbide, a pivotal player in the battle for Mexican independence from Spain. The plan drew the various Mexican social classes into the freedom movement, consolidating previously ineffective efforts. Mexico finally achieved independence several months later.

**HUMBOLDT HOUSE** (Casa Humboldt) is at Calle Juan Ruíz de Alarcón #12. It dates from the 16th century. German naturalist Baron Alexander von Humboldt spent the night in April 1803 while on a scientific journey that included South America and Cuba, hence the name. The restored house, boasting a rich Moorish facade, previously functioned as a convent, a hospital and Taxco's first movie theater. It houses the Museum of Viceregal Art (Museo de Arte Virreinal), which has a small but interesting collection of religious paintings and also hosts special art exhibits.

**Hours:** Tues.-Sun. 10-6. **Cost:** 20 pesos (about $1.50 U.S.). Special exhibits cost extra (about 50 pesos).

**WILLIAM SPRATLING MUSEUM** (Museo Guillermo Spratling) is directly behind the Church of Santa Prisca at Av. Porfirio A. Delgado #1. On display are pre-Columbian art and artifacts, many from Spratling's private collection. **Hours:** Tues.-Sat. 9-5, Sun. 9-3. **Cost:** 39 pesos (about $2.90 U.S.); free to all Sun. **Phone:** (762) 622-1660.

# TLACOLULA, OAXACA (C-3) pop. 19,625

Tlacolula (tlah-coh-LOO-lah), about 38 kilometers (24 miles) east of the city of Oaxaca, dates as far back as 1250. This market center for surrounding Indian communities also is a producer of mezcal, a potent alcoholic beverage distilled from the fermented heart of the maguey plant.

The town is dominated by the imposing Church of the Virgin of the Assumption (Parroquía de la Virgen de la Asunción). The church's adjoining 16th-century, *mudéjar* (Moorish-style) chapel, the Capilla del Señor de Tlacolula, is one of the most beautifully ornate in the state of Oaxaca. Also called the Chapel of Silver, it has an interior bursting with sculptures of angels and saints and gleaming with gold ornamentation. Particularly noteworthy are the angels that flank the main altar, each bearing a silver censer, or incense holder.

Tlacolula's Sunday open-air market *(tianguis)* is notable for its size, authenticity (vendors from the surrounding villages make a day of it, dressing up in colorful regional clothing) and the many intriguing jewels that turn up among the mundane housewares and utilitarian clothing. Market stalls line one side of the arcaded main plaza and wrap around the town church. Tethered goats stand in the churchyard awaiting their fate (most likely ending up barbecued for a family dinner), women carry baskets laden with goods, and food stands offer regional fare like ground *chapulines* (grasshoppers) and hunks of sugar cane. Handicrafts, pottery and leather goods are among the many items for sale.

The plaza and church grounds also are the site of the 5-day Fiesta del Santa Cristo de Tlacolula, which culminates on the second Sunday in October. The festivities include regional dances like the Dance of the Feathers, which incorporates elaborate costumes, and a traditional Mixtec *pelota* (ball game).

**YAGUL RUINS** are about 2.75 km (1.7 mi.) e. of town on Mex. 190 (Km marker 35.5), then 2 km (1.2 mi.) n. of Mex. 190 via a paved road; watch for the signed turn-off. The ruins, which cover the base and side of a large hill, consist of the Triple Tombs (Tumbas Triples), four patios (one a complex of six separate patios), the Room of Consultations and the Palace of Creatures. Dramatic face carvings guard the entrances to the tombs. The ball court here is large and in excellent condition. A marked path leads to the top of the hill; climb it for views that take in the valley and surrounding mountains.

**Time:** Allow 2 hours minimum. **Hours:** Daily 8-5. **Cost:** 47 pesos (about $3.50 U.S.).

# TUXTLA GUTIÉRREZ, CHIAPAS (C-5) pop. 553,374

The discovery of vast oil reserves in Tuxtla Gutiérrez (TOOX-tlah goo-TYEH-rehs) brought an influx of people and wealth to what has become a prosperous commercial hub, which is lower in elevation and therefore steamier than many of the surrounding mountain communities. Tuxtla Gutiérrez also is a distribution point for the region's coffee and tobacco plantations.

Mex. 190 passes through the city; its approach from the west is cluttered with hotels. The hectic downtown area is divided by Avenida Central, the principal thoroughfare, which runs east-west. The main square constitutes two plazas separated by Avenida Central. It is fronted by imposing government buildings, shaded by manicured trees and filled with benches. In the marketplace and in shops near the plaza, such articles as scarves with sewn-on appliques, gold filigree jewelry, boxes of inlaid wood and brightly painted gourds are sold.

At Blvd. Belisario Domínguez #2035 is the government-run Casa de las Artesanías, which has Chiapan handicrafts on display and for sale. First-class bus service is provided by the ADO and OCC bus lines. The first-class bus station is at the corner of Avenida 5 and Blvd. Algarín, next to the Plaza del Sol mall.

Tuxtla is the economic and transportation center of Chiapas, and there is little for tourists to see. But the availability of hotel accommodations make it a good base for travelers touring this part of Mexico. The surrounding countryside is noted for lush scenery, including mountains, canyons, forests and such waterfalls as El Chorreadero.

**Chiapas State Tourism Office (Secretaría de Turismo):** in the western part of the city at Blvd. Dr. Belisario Domínguez #950 in the Plaza de las Instituciones building). **Phone:** (961) 602-5299, or 01 (800) 280-3500 (toll-free long distance within Mexico).

**SUMIDERO CANYON** (Cañon del Sumidero), about 23 km (14 mi.) n. of the city, is reached by a paved mountain road. It features five different lookout points that provide spectacular views of the canyon's sheer walls as they plunge to the Río Grijalva below. Boat tours can be arranged in the town of Chiapa de Corzo, east of Tuxtla Gutiérrez, to observe not only the canyon's gaping cliffs but the river's murky green waters and the surrounding forest's alligators, exotic birds and colorful butterflies.

**ZOOMAT** (Zoológico Miguel Alvarez del Toro) is about 8 km (5 mi.) s.e. of downtown; a taxi ride is about $5 (U.S.). This is one of Mexico's most noteworthy zoos, named in honor of noted Mexican conservationist Miguel Alvarez del Toro. On exhibit is an impressive collection of more than 150 animal species native to Chiapas, including monkeys, tapirs, toucans, anteaters, owls, boa constrictors, iguanas and jaguars. The simulated habitats are so roomy that the animals housed within them appear to be roaming free through the lush vegetation. **Hours:** Tues.-Sun. 8:30-6 (last entry at 4:30). **Cost:** 60 pesos (about $4.45 U.S.); 30 pesos (8:30-10 a.m.). **Phone:** (961) 614-4700.

## VERACRUZ, VERACRUZ (B-3)
### pop. 552,156

Veracruz (veh-rah-CROOS) has traditionally served as a doorway leading to the heart of Mexico

as well as Mexico's gateway to the world. Its long history has been a tumultuous one, inextricably tied to the fortunes and misfortunes of Spain's presence in the New World and the attendant suffering borne out of conquest, war and subjugation. That Veracruz not only survived but blossomed into the festive, culturally vibrant city it is today is no small feat.

In 1518 Spaniard Juan de Grijalva explored the Mexican coastline from the Yucatán Peninsula west to the area around present-day Veracruz. He was followed a year later by Hernando Cortés, a 34-year-old colonist and landowner living in Cuba who set out on an expedition to conquer this uncharted territory, no doubt intrigued by tales of fabulous riches waiting to be plundered. His expedition party—several hundred Spanish soldiers, gunpowder, horses and a contingent of Cuban Indians to bear supplies—landed on the little island of San Juan de Ulúa, in the harbor along which the town was later established.

Cortés founded the first Spanish settlement in Mexico a bit farther up the coast at La Antigua *(see attraction listing)* before marching inland to the Aztec capital of Tenochtitlan and launching the brutal military campaign that resulted in the colonization of the continental Americas. The name he bestowed upon Veracruz—La Villa Rica de la Vera Cruz (Rich Town of the True Cross)—turned out to be prophetic, as the port soon became the main point of departure for Spanish galleons loaded with silver from Mexican mines.

From the beginning Veracruz was bedeviled by pirate raids. Celebrated English privateer John Hawkins met his only defeat here in 1568; attempting to sell slaves in defiance of the Spanish trade monopoly, his powerful fleet was thwarted by a surprise attack. Hawkins' nephew sir Francis Drake was aboard one of two ships that escaped, and he went on to a swashbuckling career raiding Spanish ships. The construction of Fort San Juan de Ulúa *(see attraction listing)* was a response to the constant danger.

The main lure for today's vacationer is the tropical, laid-back setting. Mexicans love Veracruz, but it's unfortunately off the radar of many foreign travelers. The city has both seductive charm and bracing energy. You'll feel it walking along waterfront Paseo de Malecón, where cargo ships, ocean liners and all manner of fishing vessels attest to this seaport's continuing importance.

## City Layout

Central Veracruz is fairly compact and easily negotiated, with streets laid out in a grid pattern. Street names often are posted on the corner buildings at intersections. Since it's hard to get lost, seeing the sights on foot can be a leisurely affair—and you'll want to take it easy from April through October, which is hot and humid. The city also tends to get lots of rain during these months, so an umbrella is a handy item to bring along.

A logical starting point is Plaza de Armas (also called the *Zócalo*). Veracruz's main square is the city's hub and one of the oldest Spanish plazas in

North America. Facing its east side is the 17th-century City Hall (Palacio Municipal). On the south side stands the Cathedral (Catedral de Nuestra Señora de la Asunción), built in 1721, which has a loudly tolling bell tower.

Palm trees and black and white-tiled walkways give the plaza an appropriately tropical look, and the arched arcades, or *portales*, are a distinctive Spanish touch. The arches shelter open-air cafes that are popular places to meet and socialize over coffee in the morning, but it's evenings—after the sun has set and the heat takes a bit of a breather—that the plaza really starts to hum. Vendors hawk their wares and bars offer the regional libation *menjulep*, rum and vermouth mixed with sugar and crushed mint leaf.

The seawall *(malecón)*, a promenade running east from Plaza de Armas, hugs the harbor before turning south to follow the gulf shore. Lined with benches, it offers views of port activity and massive Fort San Juan de Ulúa across the harbor. People fish from concrete breakwater piers, their lines wrapped around small pieces of wood. Intertwined couples, families and sailors on shore leave all stroll along the walkway as vendors hawking *volvones* (puff pastry filled with tuna or chopped beef) exuberantly call out "Guerro!" or "Guerra!" to potential customers.

Facing the harbor at the corner of avenidas Xicotencatl and Aquiles Serdán is the Carranza Lighthouse (Faro Carranza). Mexican president Venustiano Carranza lived in this ornate-looking building during the drafting of the 1917 Mexican constitution; it now contains naval offices.

Elongated Plaza de la República, just north and west of the *malecón*, also faces the harbor. The public buildings along this plaza include the turn-of-the-19th-century Customs House (Aduana Marítima) and the pastel yellow facades of the main post office and the telegraph office.

The Fish Market, on Avenida Landero y Cos just north of Avenida Mariano Arista (2 blocks south of the harbor), is two stories tall and covers an entire block. It displays rows of fresh seafood, live crabs with red claws neatly tied with green seaweed grass and neatly stacked mountains of fish. Food stands offer seafood cocktails *(cócteles)* made with shrimp, oysters or octopus.

Past the *malecón* Boulevard M. Avila Camacho continues on to Playa Villa del Mar, about 4 kilometers (2.5 miles) south of downtown Veracruz. This and the other beaches closest to the city are not the stuff of tourist brochures; the sand is a brownish color and the gulf water is dull green rather than an inviting turquoise. During the week fishermen mend nets or make repairs to their boats. The pace picks up on weekends, with families getting together and vendors selling fresh fish and cold beer against a backdrop of nonstop band music.

## Music, Dance and Cuisine

Artistic expression, most notably in the form of music and dance, is as much a part of the Veracruz character as the balmy breezes blowing off the gulf.

"La Bamba"—popularized by Hispanic pop singer Ritchie Valens in 1959 and remade into an even bigger hit in 1987 by the East Los Angeles band Los Lobos—is actually a Veracruzan folk song. Music also underscores this region's African, Cuban, Spanish and Indian roots.

Plaza de Armas is the site of strolling mariachi players, frequent band concerts and string trios playing guitar, harp and *jarana*, a guitar-shaped, five-stringed instrument. In addition to the ubiquitous mariachis, you're likely to hear the lilting sound of the marimba (a relative of the xylophone), which has wooden keys that the musicians deftly strike with mallets.

The *son jarocho* is quintessentially Veracruzan. Set to a fast, syncopated percussion beat, it features a vigorous strumming of stringed instruments accented by a rhythmically pounded tambourine. The accompanying dance steps are a fandango-derived staccato movement of the heels known as *zapateado*. Son jarocho originated in the 17th and 18th centuries during a time when slaves were imported for plantation agriculture, and many *jarocho* musicians today are of African-Mexican heritage.

The *danzón*, a Cuban import influenced by European ballroom dancing, features gliding movements as partners promenade arm in arm and women wave their fans—maneuvers that don't work up as much of a sweat in this hot and humid city. On Wednesday and Sunday evenings everyone from young children to elderly couples dances the *danzón* at Zamora Park (Parque Zamora), about 7 blocks inland from the waterfront between avenidas Independencia and 5 de Mayo.

The state of Veracruz is known for good coffee, and rival establishments within several blocks of each other are two of the best places to sample the brew. The Gran Café de la Parroquia, on Paseo del Malecón just west of Avenida 16 de Septiembre, is a Veracruz institution. The huge, white-tiled space is especially popular for breakfast, which you should accompany with a *café con leche* served in a tall glass. A concentrated shot of inky black coffee is augmented by hot milk poured by waiters from silver kettles. For a refill, simply clink your spoon against the empty glass.

*Café con leche* also is served at the Gran Café del Portal, on Avenida Independencia across from the southwest corner of Plaza de Armas. Equally cavernous—it covers a city block—the Portal has more meal choices than the Parroquia. For the best atmosphere try to get a table under one of the namesake arches. In the evening it is almost taken over by strolling mariachis and marimba players.

As delectable as the coffee is Veracruzan cuisine, with its emphasis on fresh seafood. *Salsa Veracruzana*—a piquant combination of tomatoes, chiles, onions, garlic, pimentos, capers and green olives sauteed in olive oil—is a perfect accompaniment to fish (or chicken or pasta, for that matter). Broiled red snapper awash in this sauce is *huachinango a la Veracruzana*, which is on almost every restaurant menu in town.

Specialties like *torta de mariscos* (a fluffy omelet) or *filetes relleno* (stuffed fish filets) have rich fillings of oysters, crab and shrimp enlivened with fresh lime juice and herbs. Plantains, sweet potatoes and peanuts (introduced by African slaves) are other essential ingredients in Veracruzan cookery. Peanuts are ground to make sauces for pork or chicken (such as spicy *salsa macha,* which also includes garlic, chiles and olive oil) and even turn up in ice cream. Plantains are fried and served with rice and beans or mashed with garlic and rolled around fillings of cheese or crabmeat.

## Events

Veracruz's party of the year is Carnaval. The celebration rivals New Orleans' Mardi Gras in spectacle and enthusiasm, if not in size. The Veracruz version begins with the "burning of ill humor" and concludes with the funeral of Juan Carnaval. Parades wend their way down waterfront Boulevard Avila Camacho during the 9 days prior to Ash Wednesday, replete with lavishly decorated floats and outrageously attired revelers. Other events, including fireworks, folkloric dance shows and plenty of salsa and other music, take place around Plaza de Armas. Local hotels are booked solid for Carnaval, so if you plan on attending make reservations well in advance.

**Veracruz State Tourism Office:** on the ground floor of City Hall (Palacio Municipal), on the east side of Plaza de Armas. Open Mon.-Sat. 9-8, Sun. 10-6. **Phone:** (229) 934-4208 (English may not be spoken).

**Shopping:** The Hidalgo Market (Mercado Hidalgo) is between avenidas Madero and Hidalgo a block west of Zamora Park (about 7 blocks south of the *Zócalo*). This is one of those Mexican markets that is fascinating to wander through for the sheer variety of wares—everything from live parrots to bushels of produce to animal parts guaranteed to induce squirms.

If you're looking for a trinket to take home, the place to go is Paseo del Malecón; the waterfront boulevard is lined with shops and stalls selling every imaginable type of seashell knickknack, along with embroidered blouses, men's *guayabera* shirts—lightweight, short-sleeved garments worn untucked—coral jewelry, crucifixes and of course, T-shirts. Plaza de las Artesanías, on Paseo del Malecón 2 blocks east of Plaza de Armas, has a mix of souvenirs and high-quality merchandise.

**FORT SAN JUAN DE ULÚA** (Castillo San Juan de Ulúa), in the harbor on Gallega Island, can be reached from coastal hwy. Mex. 180 by taking the Puente Montecitos exit to the port area (Zona Industrial Portuaria); from the city center, take Blvd. Fidel Velazquez to the port area, following signs. This massive fort was built by the Spanish to protect their New World interests. Construction of the thick coral walls began in the 1530s but was not completed until the late 18th century. It later served as a place of incarceration for political prisoners; even Mexican president Benito Juárez was held here.

The floating fortress, declared a historical monument in 1962, is connected to the mainland by a small walking bridge. Visitors can venture into dank prison cells and view guard posts, the remains of cannons and docking areas where gold was stored. Today this ancient rampart is surrounded by huge cargo container ships. A guided tour is recommended, since there is no signage or brochure.

Taxi fare to the fort from the city center is about 70 pesos. Boats depart for the fort from the *malecón,* across from the Hotel Emporio, whenever there are enough passengers; the fee is 35 pesos per person. **Hours:** Tues.-Sun. 9-4:30. One-hour tours with an English-speaking guide are available on request. **Cost:** 52 pesos (about $3.85 U.S.); free (ages 0-12). Free to all Sun. Guided tour fee about 300 pesos. **Phone:** (229) 938-5151.

**LA ANTIGUA** is about 32 km (20 mi.) n. of the city via Mex. 180. This small village, shaded by big trees, was the original site of Veracruz. It contains a ruined 16th-century customs house (Casa de Cortés) as well as the Hermitage (La Ermita del Rosario), reputed to be the oldest church on the American mainland. This is a popular day trip, and there are a couple of small seafood eateries in the vicinity.

**SANTIAGO BULWARK** (Baluarte de Santiago) occupies a city intersection on Calle Canal between avenidas Gomez Farías and 16 de Septiembre (about 5 blks. s. of the harbor and just s. of the *malecón*). Downtown Veracruz has a venerable feel; most of the buildings and churches are more than 150 years old. The city once was surrounded by a defensive wall that incorporated nine fortresses—all protection against pirates—but the only one that remains is the Baluarte de Santiago. It dates from 1635 and stands at what was then the waterfront.

More impressive from the outside than the inside, the stone bulwark is surrounded by cannons. Getting to the main entrance is a challenge; you walk up an almost 45-degree stone incline with no handrail to a small drawbridge that permits access across the "moat" to the entrance door. A museum atop the bulwark contains photos and etchings of old Veracruz and a display of pre-Hispanic gold jewelry discovered by a local fisherman in the 1980s. Be forewarned: the interior is dank and musty.

**Hours:** Tues.-Sun. 9-5. **Cost:** 52 pesos (about $3.85 U.S.).

**TRANVÍAS VERACRUZ** is downtown on Paseo del Malecón, across from the Emporio Veracruz Hotel. Although the narration for this guided tour is in Spanish, it nevertheless offers a good overview of the city. The 45-minute tour route covers 24 historical points of interest, including the Customs House, railroad station, the Teatro de la Reforma and Zamora Park (where an original tour trolley car that was pulled by horses is on display). In between the tour narrative passengers are serenaded by lilting Veracruzan music.

Wear a hat for sun protection; on hot days sitting in the lower level of the double-decker, open-air tour bus will be more comfortable. A red handkerchief identifies Tranvías tour buses. The Tranvías brochure contains a helpful city map. **Hours:** Tours run daily 11-9. Phone ahead to confirm schedule. **Cost:** Tour fee 30 pesos (about $2.20 U.S.). **Phone:** (229) 131-5887 (cellular number).

**VERACRUZ AQUARIUM** (Acuario de Veracruz) is s. of the harbor off Blvd. Manuel A. Camacho (in the Plaza Acuario Mall). This large, well-maintained aquarium is a great family attraction. A variety of marine creatures can be seen in three different habitats: a freshwater gallery, a saltwater gallery and an ocean tank. The freshwater exhibit replicates a tropical jungle, so in addition to tanks of fish there are turtles, crocodiles, boas and toucans. The saltwater tanks feature species from the Gulf of Mexico and the Pacific Ocean, including various colorful tropical fish, lobsters, crabs, rays, shrimp and octopuses.

The ocean tank has sharks, groupers, barracuda, turtles and other species. There also is a section devoted to manatees (the aquarium promotes marine conservation, especially of species indigenous to the Gulf of Mexico). Get an up-close look at sea urchins and crustaceans at an outdoor tide pool, or touch large turtle shells and fossils in the interactive area. The aquarium is connected to a mall that has plenty of restaurants and boutique shops.

**Time:** Allow 1 hour minimum. **Hours:** Daily 9-7 (also 7-7:30 p.m. Fri.-Sun.). **Cost:** 120 pesos (about $9 U.S.); 65 pesos (ages 2-11). **Phone:** (229) 932-7984. GT ⫯

**VERACRUZ NAVAL MUSEUM** (Museo Histórico Naval) is 6 blks. from the waterfront at Calle Mariano Arista #32. It recounts Mexico's naval history from pre-Hispanic times to the present day. The building is remarkable—a two-story structure with a central courtyard and multiple arched entryways, it originally housed the Naval School of Medicine.

Exhibits in some 30 display rooms include Mayan and Aztec-era dugout canoes complete with oars, 19th-century maritime charts, depictions of notable rescue efforts, medical artifacts and a room with hundreds of firearms lining the walls and fashioned into enormous chandeliers. A highlight is the display illustrating the first naval battle that took place in the New World, with large warships built by Hernán Cortes besieged by hundreds of small Aztec vessels. Exhibit information is in Spanish.

**Time:** Allow 1 hour, 30 minutes minimum. **Hours:** Tues.-Sun. 10-5. **Cost:** Free. **Parking:** Free streetside parking is available. ⫯

## Nearby Destinations

The gulf beaches become more attractive the farther out of town you go. About 10 kilometers (6 miles) south of downtown via Boulevard Camacho is Playa Mocambo. Beyond Playa Mocambo, at the mouth of the Río Jamapa, is Boca del Río, a small fishing village known for its open-air seafood restaurants.

If you're looking for quiet beaches, a relaxed pace and a distinct lack of crowds—and you don't mind leaving the city well behind—consider checking out "La Costa Esmeralda" (The Emerald Coast). This 19-kilometer (12-mile) stretch of gulf coast is off Mex. 180 between the towns of Tecolutla and Nautla (about a 2-hour drive north of Veracruz). Much of the coast region is devoted to cattle ranches and farms growing sugar cane and vanilla beans, but along La Costa Esmeralda there are small motels and open-air, thatch-roofed restaurants that serve seafood and shrimp cocktails in tall glasses. Streets wind past colorfully painted bungalows, tropical birds roost in the coconut palms and lounge chairs on grassy lawns look out over the water. Most visitors are content to amble along the brown-sand beaches—and if you avoid the Easter and Christmas holidays you'll probably have them mostly to yourself.

A drive into the surrounding countryside passes large ranches and pastures, tropical fruit orchards and fields of sugar cane. The change in topography can be dramatic—from mangrove swamps and mazes of lagoons and estuaries to lush, mountainous country ideal for growing coffee.

Toll highway Mex. 150-D west from the gulf coast toward Puebla is a spectacularly scenic drive that begins in flat cane fields and ascends through pine forests to elevations as high as 9,000 feet. The route passes snowcapped Pico de Orizaba, at 18,555 feet Mexico's loftiest peak. Highway conditions are excellent, and there are plenty of gas stations. Quaint hamlets as well as larger cities like Córdoba, Fortín de las Flores and Orizaba offer plenty of opportunities for sightseeing, shopping or just taking in the mountain views.

## VILLAHERMOSA, TABASCO (C-4)

Villahermosa (vee-yah-ehr-MOH-sah) was founded in 1519 under the name Santa María de la Victoria. Hernando Cortés established the settlement to commemorate his defeat of an army of Indian warriors who had attacked him during his march toward the Aztec capital of Tenochtitlan. In tribute to their conqueror, the Indians gave Cortés an Indian princess. Baptized Doña Marina, she became Cortés' mistress and trusted translator, an invaluable asset in his conquest of Mexico.

A strategic location on the banks of the navigable Río Grijalva, which flows northward out of rubber, cacao and coffee country, makes the city an important distribution center. The 1970s discovery of some of the world's richest oil fields, as well as the development of extensive hydroelectric projects and successful agricultural programs, energized this hot, humid port. Today Villahermosa is a booming business city and the regional hub for Chiapas, Campeche, Tabasco and eastern Veracruz. It also makes a convenient base from which to explore points of interest in these states.

The city's central downtown area of stores, hotels and restaurants is known as the Zona Luz. It extends from Juárez Park (Parque Juárez) south to Plaza de Armas, the main plaza, and is roughly bounded by

Avenida Zaragoza on the north, Avenida 5 de Mayo on the west, Avenida Allende on the south and waterfront Calle Madrazo (the *malecón*) on the east. Many of the streets are brick-paved pedestrian malls, closed to traffic.

The newer hotel and shopping district, Tabasco 2000, is about 6 kilometers (4 miles) northwest of the Zona Luz; it can be reached via Avenida Ruiz Cortines (Mex. 180), the main east-west thoroughfare. The wealth generated by oil is evident in this complex's contemporary government buildings, upscale hotels and sleek Galerías Tabasco 2000 mall. The Tabasco 2000 area also has the city's nicest accommodations.

First-class bus service to Campeche, Mérida, Mexico City, Palenque, San Cristóbal de Las Casas, Veracruz and other cities is offered by ADO. The ADO bus terminal is at Calle Javier Mina #297 at Calle Lino Merino, about 10 blocks northwest of the Zona Luz and 3 blocks south of Avenida Ruiz Cortines. Taxi fares within the area encompassing the city center north to Avenida Ruiz Cortines average about $2 (U.S.) in shared *colectivo* taxis, about $4 in *especial* taxis. Street signage features arrows indicating the direction of traffic flow, a boon for motorists who must navigate the hectic, congested downtown area.

West of the city are prosperous cacao plantations and the important archeological site of Comalcalco. A driving tour of this region reveals lush countryside that contrasts sharply with Mexico's more common arid expanses. Along Mex. 180 toward Cárdenas are masses of banana plants laden with clusters of fruit, which is sold at roadside stands.

Cárdenas itself is a cacao processing center, and some chocolate plantations and factories offer guided tours (check with travel agencies in Villahermosa). The cacao tree grows everywhere; its large, elliptical pods bear the seeds from which cocoa and chocolate are made. The harvesting season is November through April. Small family-run operations throughout this region grow and process cacao beans that end up as boxes of chocolate. You'll also see mounds of the beans for miles along the highway, drying in the sun.

**Tabasco State Tourism Office (Subsecretaría de Turismo):** Avenida de Los Ríos at the corner of Calle 13 in the Tabasco 2000 complex, past the La Venta Museum and heading west out of downtown. Open Mon.-Fri. 9-3 and 6-8 p.m. **Phone:** 01 (800) 216-0842 (toll-free long distance within Mexico).

**COMALCALCO RUINS** are w. on Mex. 180 to the town of Cárdenas, then n. about 35 km (22 mi.) on Mex. 187 to the town of Comalcalco; the turnoff to the site is about 3 km (2 mi.) farther n., to the right. There are no informational highway signs en route from Villahermosa; watch for signs in Comalcalco that direct visitors to the ruins.

This large site consists of several tall pyramids spread out over grassy meadows and small hills. The structures here were constructed of thin, flat bricks called *tabiques,* covered with a plaster made from ground seashells, rather than the stone used elsewhere

in pre-Hispanic Mexico. Heed the signs warning *No Subir* (Do Not Climb). A small one-room museum contains carved stone figures.

Descendants of the Chontal Maya, who originally inhabited Comalcalco around A.D. 600-900, still live in the area and earn a livelihood as their ancestors did by processing cacao and raising bananas and other fruits. **Note:** This is one of Mexico's hottest regions; visit early in the day and bring a hat or umbrella as a sunscreen. **Hours:** Daily 10-4. **Cost:** 52 pesos (about $3.85 U.S.).

**LA VENTA MUSEUM** (Parque Museo La Venta) is w. of downtown off Av. Ruiz Cortines (Mex. 180), just e. of the Tabasco 2000 complex. This large riverside park has a zoo and is within an archeological zone. A number of large, carved-stone Olmec artifacts discovered in the late 1930s are displayed on trails adjacent to the zoo.

Three colossal stone heads display the wide noses and full, downward-curving lips that are characteristic facial features of Olmec art. Other artifacts include sculptures, stone altars, stela (carved stone tablets) and a tomb. The zoo's jungle-like grounds are inhabited by free-roaming monkeys and deer, birds, crocodiles (confined to a moat) and some caged animals.

Some background information is in English, and English-speaking guides also are available. Visit the park in the morning before it gets too hot. Mosquito repellent is strongly advised. **Time:** Allow 2 hours minimum. **Hours:** Daily 8-5. Last ticket is sold at 4. A sound-and-light show takes place Tues.-Sun. at 7, 8 and 9 p.m.; hours may vary depending on the season. **Cost:** Park admission 40 pesos (about $2.95 U.S.); 10 pesos (ages 6-12). Sound-and-light show 100 pesos (about $7.40 U.S.). Cash only. **Phone:** (993) 314-1652. [¶]

**MUSEUM OF ANTHROPOLOGY** (Museo Regional de Antropología) is s. of downtown at Periférico Carlos Pellicer Camara #511, along the w. bank of the Río Grijalva and adjacent to the Tabasco State Theatre and Cultural College (CICOM). This modern museum exhibits Olmec and Mayan artifacts. The displays are complemented by photographs and maps of the archeological sites from which they were taken. All historical information is in Spanish, and no English-speaking guides are available.

**Time:** Allow 1 hour minimum. **Hours:** Tues.-Sun. 9-4. **Cost:** 20 pesos (about $1.50 U.S.). **Phone:** (993) 312-6344.

# ZEMPOALA, VERACRUZ (B-3)

About 40 kilometers (25 miles) north of Veracruz off Mex. 180, Zempoala (sehm-poh-AH-lah), also known as Cempoala, is the site of remains that once comprised the ceremonial center and fortress of the Totonac Indians. Zempoala was a contemporary of El Tajín (*see Papantla),* although it continued to thrive after El Tajín was abandoned sometime during the 13th century.

It was here that Hernando Cortés gained the first Indian allies in his 1519 campaign to conquer the Aztecs. The *conquistadores* took note of the city because the white stucco buildings, gleaming in the tropical sun, most likely reminded them of silver. He gained the trust of the Totonac chief and his followers, who had been under Aztec rule for the previous 50 years.

**CEMPOALA RUINS** are on the northern edge of town. The site is about a 45-minute drive from Veracruz; watch for the sign indicating the Cempoala turn-off about 7 km (4 mi.) n. of the town of Cardel.

Six major structures remain. The Main Temple (Templo Mayor), constructed of riverbed stones, rises on 13 platforms to about 35 feet and probably resembled similar temples in the Aztec capital of Tenochtitlan. The Temple of the Chimneys (Templo de las Chimeneas) derives its name from a series of semicircular pillars. The Little Faces (Las Caritas), a three-story edifice of boulders and cement, is adorned with niches that once contained small carved faces. At the west end of the site is the Great Pyramid (La Gran Pirámide), which has two staircases that climb to a three-level platform.

First-class buses travel regularly from Veracruz north to Cardel; from Cardel, *colectivos* (minivans) or a taxi can take you to the ruins. **Hours:** Daily 8-5. **Cost:** 47 pesos (about $3.50 U.S.).

# Mexico

# YUCATÁN PENINSULA

AAA recommends that travelers consult online U.S. State Department travel advisories when planning travel abroad. Find this information at http://travel.state.gov/content/passports/english/alertswarnings/mexico-travel-warning.html.

## AKUMAL, QUINTANA ROO—
See The Caribbean Coast p. 392.

## CAMPECHE, CAMPECHE (B-1) pop. 259,005

**HOTEL HACIENDA PUERTA CAMPECHE** (981)816-7508

Historic Vintage Country Inn
$340-$520

THE LUXURY COLLECTION™ **AAA Benefit:**
*Hotels & Resorts* Members save up to 15%, plus Starwood Preferred Guest® benefits!

**Address:** Calle 59 No. 71 92400 **Location:** Between calles 16 and 18; centro of historico city. **Facility:** This hacienda-style lodging is situated behind the fortress walls of the historic part of the city. The unique guest units harken back to a bygone era but with modern comforts and technology. 15 units. 2 stories (no elevator), interior/exterior corridors. **Parking:** street only. **Amenities:** safes. **Dining:** Restaurante La Guardia, see separate listing. **Pool(s):** outdoor. **Activities:** spa. **Guest Services:** valet laundry.

**HOTEL PLAZA CAMPECHE** 981/811-9900
◆◆ **Hotel** $53-$86 **Address:** Calle 10 esq Circuito Baluartes, Centro Historico 24000 **Location:** In Centro Historico. **Facility:** 83 units. 2 stories, interior corridors. **Parking:** no self-parking. **Terms:** cancellation fee imposed. **Amenities:** safes. **Dining:** entertainment. **Pool(s):** outdoor. **Guest Services:** valet laundry.

**HOTEL PLAZA COLONIAL** 981/811-9930
◆◆ **Boutique Hotel** $47-$58 **Address:** Calle 10 No. 15, Centro Historico 24000 **Location:** In Centro Historico. Located in Algunas Fuma Plaza. **Facility:** This charming property has surprisingly elegant touches throughout. Upgrade to a junior suite for optimum comfort. Meets AAA guest room security requirements. 41 units. 4 stories, interior corridors. **Amenities:** safes. **Pool(s):** outdoor. **Guest Services:** valet laundry.

### WHERE TO EAT

**RESTAURANTE LA GUARDIA** 981/816-7508
◆◆◆ International. Fine Dining. $15-$24 **AAA Inspector Notes:** Situated in a UNESCO World Heritage Site and part of a former hacienda, this romantic, fine dining establishment features creative, modern interpretations of Mayan cuisine. **Features:** full bar. **Reservations:** suggested. **Address:** Calle 59 No. 71 **Location:** Between calles 16 and 18; centro of historico city; in Hotel Hacienda Puerta Campeche. **Parking:** valet and street only.

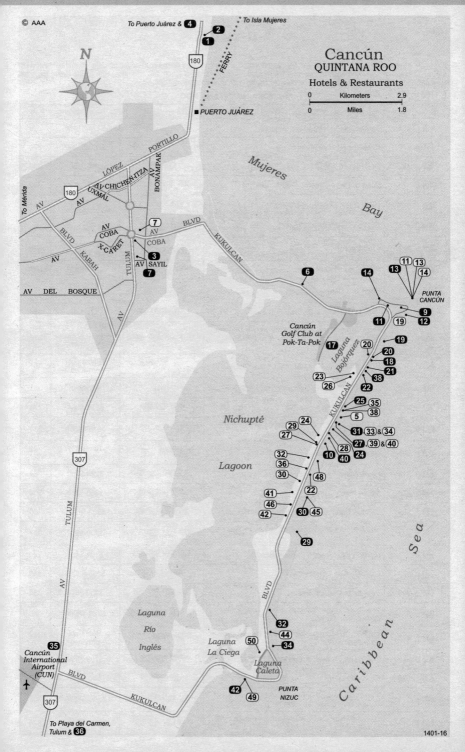

© AAA

To Puerto Juárez & **4**

To Isla Mujeres

**2**

**1**

180

FERRY

■ PUERTO JUÁREZ

PORTILLO

LÓPEZ

AV CHICHEN-ITZA

AV BONAMPAK

180

UXMAL

To Mérida

AV

AV

AV
COBA

X-CARET

BLVD
KABAH

AV

**7**

BLVD
COBA

AV
COBA

AV SAYIL

**3**

**7**

TULUM

AV DEL BOSQUE

AV

# Cancún
## QUINTANA ROO
### Hotels & Restaurants

0  Kilometers  2.9
0  Miles  1.8

*Mujeres*

*Bay*

BLVD

KUKULCAN

**6**

**14**

**11** **13**
**13**

**11** **13**
**14**

PUNTA
CANCÚN

**11**

**9**
**12**

**19**

*Cancún
Golf Club at
Pok-Ta-Pok*

**17**

*Laguna
Bojórquez*

**20**

**19**

**20**

**18**

**21**

**23**

**26**

**38**

**22**

**25** **35**

**5** **38**

KUKULCAN

*Nichupté*

**29** **24**

**27**

**31** **33** & **34**

**27** **39** & **40**

**24**

*Lagoon*

**32**

**36**

**30**

**10**

**28**

**40**

**48**

**41**

**46**

**42**

**22**

**30** **45**

**29**

*Sea*

307

TULUM

AV

*Laguna
Río
Inglés*

*Laguna
La Ciega*

**50**

*Laguna
Caleta*

BLVD

**32**

**44**

**34**

**35**

Cancún
International
Airport
(CUN)

BLVD

KUKULCAN

**42**

**49**

PUNTA
NIZUC

*Caribbean*

307

To Playa del Carmen,
Tulum & **36**

1401-16

# Cancún

This index helps you to "spot" where approved hotels and restaurants are located on the corresponding detailed maps. Hotel daily rate range is for comparison only. Restaurant price range is a combination of lunch and/or dinner. Turn to the listing page for more detailed rate and price information and consult display ads for special promotions.

## CANCÚN, QUINTANA ROO

| Map Page | Hotels | Diamond Rated | Rate Range | Page |
|---|---|---|---|---|
| 1  p. 373 | The Beloved Hotel Playa Mujeres | ◆◆◆◆ | $474-$1450 | 376 |
| 2  p. 373 | Excellence Playa Mujeres | ◆◆◆◆ | $600-$3000 | 376 |
| 3  p. 373 | Oasis Smart | ◆◆ | $87-$150 | 386 |
| 4  p. 373 | Secrets Playa Mujeres Golf & Spa Resort | ◆◆◆◆ | $673-$1480 | 387 |
| 6  p. 373 | Hotel RIU Caribe (See ad p. 380.) | ◆◆◆ | Rates not provided | 381 |
| 7  p. 373 | La Quinta Inn & Suites Cancun | ◆◆◆ | $59-$182 | 384 |
| 9  p. 373 | Aloft Cancun | ◆◆◆ | Rates not provided | 376 |
| 10  p. 373 | Hard Rock Hotel Cancun | ◆◆◆◆ | $617-$896 | 381 |
| 11  p. 373 | Hotel RIU Cancun (See ad p. 380.) | ◆◆◆ | Rates not provided | 381 |
| 12  p. 373 | Krystal Gran Punta Cancun | ◆◆◆ | $125-$280 | 384 |
| 13  p. 373 | Fiesta Americana Grand Coral Beach Cancun Resort & Spa (See ad opposite inside back cover.) | ◆◆◆◆ | $248-$669 | 376 |
| 14  p. 373 | Hotel RIU Palace Las Americas (See ad p. 380.) | ◆◆◆ | Rates not provided | 381 |
| 17  p. 373 | Holiday Inn Express Cancun Zona Hotelera | fyi | $65-$80 | 381 |
| 18  p. 373 | Gran Caribe Real Hotel (See ad on insert, p. 383.) | ◆◆◆ | $288-$564 | 376 |
| 19  p. 373 | Le Blanc Spa Resort (See ad on inside front cover, starting on p. 378.) | ◆◆◆◆◆ | $646-$1350 | 384 |
| 20  p. 373 | Grand Park Royal Cancun Caribe | ◆◆◆ | Rates not provided | 381 |
| 21  p. 373 | Hyatt Zilara Cancun (See ad on insert.) | ◆◆◆◆ | $229-$700 | 384 |
| 22  p. 373 | ME by Melia Cancun | ◆◆◆◆ | $308-$650 | 384 |
| 24  p. 373 | Sandos Cancun Luxury Experience Resort | ◆◆◆◆ | $382-$1031 | 386 |
| 25  p. 373 | The Westin Lagunamar Ocean Resort Villas & Spa Cancun | ◆◆◆◆ | $209-$509 | 387 |
| 27  p. 373 | Marriott CasaMagna Cancun Resort | ◆◆◆◆ | $104-$424 | 384 |
| 29  p. 373 | Omni Cancun Hotel & Villas | ◆◆◆ | $285-$2034 | 386 |
| 30  p. 373 | Paradisus Cancun Resort | ◆◆◆◆ | $350-$870 | 386 |
| 31  p. 373 | The Ritz-Carlton, Cancun (See ad opposite Using Your Guide.) | ◆◆◆◆◆ | $149-$5000 | 386 |
| 32  p. 373 | IBEROSTAR Cancun Golf & Spa Resort (See ad on insert, p. 385.) | ◆◆◆◆ | Rates not provided | 384 |
| 34  p. 373 | The Westin Resort & Spa Cancun | ◆◆◆ | $109-$599 | 387 |
| 35  p. 373 | Courtyard by Marriott Cancun | ◆◆◆ | $80-$148 | 376 |
| 36  p. 373 | Moon Palace Golf & Spa Resort (See ad on inside front cover, starting on p. 378.) | ◆◆◆◆ | $536-$1680 | 386 |
| 38  p. 373 | Beach Palace Cancun (See ad on inside front cover, starting on p. 378.) | ◆◆◆◆ | $436-$716 | 376 |

### CANCÚN, QUINTANA ROO (cont'd)

| Map Page | Hotels (cont'd) | Diamond Rated | Rate Range | Page |
|---|---|---|---|---|
| **40** p. 373 | **Secrets The Vine Cancun** | ◆◆◆◆ | $570-$2200 | 387 |
| **42** p. 373 | NIZUC Resort & Spa | ◆◆◆◆ | $500-$5000 | 386 |

| Map Page | Restaurants | Diamond Rated | Cuisine | Price Range | Page |
|---|---|---|---|---|---|
| **5** p. 373 | Elefanta Indian Cuisine | ◆◆◆ | Indian | $12-$38 | 388 |
| **7** p. 373 | **La Dolce Vita Downtown** | ◆◆◆ | Italian | $15-$30 | 389 |
| **11** p. 373 | **Le Basilic** | ◆◆◆◆◆ | Regional Mediterranean | $33-$78 | 389 |
| **13** p. 373 | Isla Contoy | ◆◆◆ | Regional Caribbean | $18-$43 | 389 |
| **14** p. 373 | **La Joya** | ◆◆◆ | Mexican | $35-$45 | 389 |
| **19** p. 373 | Cambalache | ◆◆◆ | Argentine Steak | $22-$53 | 388 |
| **20** p. 373 | Lorenzillo's | ◆◆◆ | Seafood | $14-$60 | 390 |
| **22** p. 373 | Ruth's Chris Steak House | ◆◆◆ | Steak | $25-$60 | 390 |
| **23** p. 373 | Thai Lounge | ◆◆◆ | Thai | $15-$40 | 390 |
| **24** p. 373 | Limoncello Ristorante | ◆◆◆ | Italian | $15-$40 | 390 |
| **26** p. 373 | La Madonna | ◆◆◆ | Italian | $17-$50 | 389 |
| **27** p. 373 | Hacienda Sisal Mexican Grill | ◆◆◆ | Mexican | $20-$50 | 388 |
| **28** p. 373 | Cenacolo Ristorante Italiano | ◆◆◆ | Italian | $18-$40 | 388 |
| **29** p. 373 | La Destileria | ◆◆◆ | Mexican | $15-$30 | 389 |
| **30** p. 373 | Puerto Madero Steakhouse and Fish Marina | ◆◆◆ | Steak Seafood | $18-$65 | 390 |
| **32** p. 373 | **Harry's Prime Steakhouse & Raw Bar** | ◆◆◆ | International | $20-$50 | 388 |
| **33** p. 373 | **The Club Grill** (See ad opposite Using Your Guide.) | ◆◆◆◆◆ | International | $35-$170 | 388 |
| **34** p. 373 | **Fantino** (See ad opposite Using Your Guide.) | ◆◆◆◆◆ | Mediterranean | $35-$170 | 388 |
| **35** p. 373 | Fred's House Seafood Market and Grill | ◆◆◆ | Seafood | $20-$55 | 388 |
| **36** p. 373 | Crab House Caribe | ◆◆◆ | Mexican Seafood | $15-$43 | 388 |
| **38** p. 373 | **Gustino Italian Grill** | ◆◆◆◆ | Regional Italian | $20-$50 | 388 |
| **39** p. 373 | La Capilla Argentina | ◆◆◆ | Argentine | $10-$60 | 389 |
| **40** p. 373 | Mikado | ◆◆◆ | Asian | $18-$40 | 390 |
| **41** p. 373 | La Habichuela | ◆◆◆ | Mexican | $17-$45 | 389 |
| **42** p. 373 | Captain's Cove Steak & Seafood Grill | ◆◆◆ | Seafood | $20-$40 | 388 |
| **44** p. 373 | Benazuza | ◆◆◆ | International | $75-$75 | 387 |
| **45** p. 373 | **TEMPO Contemporary Cuisine by Martin Berasategui** | ◆◆◆◆ | Regional Spanish | $90-$125 | 390 |
| **46** p. 373 | Cenacolo Mare | ◆◆◆ | Italian Seafood | $15-$40 | 388 |
| **48** p. 373 | Casa Rolandi Gourmet Restaurant & Yacht Club | ◆◆◆ | Italian | $16-$36 | 388 |
| **49** p. 373 | Ramona | ◆◆◆◆ | Northern Mexican | $25-$58 | 390 |
| **50** p. 373 | Navios Mexican Fusion Seafood | ◆◆◆ | Seafood | $12-$40 | 390 |

## CANCÚN, QUINTANA ROO pop. 661,176
- **Restaurants p. 387**
- **Hotels & Restaurants map & index p. 373**

### ALOFT CANCUN
(998)848-9900 **9**

**Hotel**
Rates not provided

**AAA Benefit:** Members save up to 15%, plus Starwood Preferred Guest® benefits!

**Address:** Blvd Kukulcan KM 9, Mz 48 L-8-1 77500 **Location:** 6 mi (10 km) from downtown; centro of Zona Hotelera. **Facility:** Meets AAA guest room security requirements. 177 units. 10 stories, interior corridors. *Bath:* shower only. **Parking:** valet and street only. **Amenities:** safes. **Pool(s):** outdoor. **Activities:** sauna, steamroom, exercise room, massage. **Guest Services:** valet and coin laundry.

### BEACH PALACE CANCUN
(998)891-4110 **38**

**Contemporary Resort Hotel**
$436-$716

**Address:** Blvd Kukulcan KM 11.5 **Location:** Oceanfront. In Zona Hotelera; across from lagoon. **Facility:** This contemporary, all-inclusive resort features spacious guest rooms, a variety of dining options, a luxurious spa and unique rooftop swimming pools. Meets AAA guest room security requirements. 287 units. 14 stories, interior corridors. **Parking:** valet and street only. **Terms:** cancellation fee imposed. **Amenities:** safes. **Dining:** 4 restaurants, entertainment. **Pool(s):** heated outdoor. **Activities:** sauna, hot tub, steamroom, recreation programs, kids club, game room, exercise room, spa. **Guest Services:** valet laundry. *(See ad on inside front cover, starting on p. 378.)*

### THE BELOVED HOTEL PLAYA MUJERES
(998)872-8730 **1**

**Resort Hotel**
$474-$1450

**Address:** Vialidad Paseo Mujeres, Mz 1 Lote 10 SM 3 **Location:** Oceanfront. Bonampak, 4.8 mi (8 km) n, end of the road; beyond Puerto Juárez; in Playa Mujeres Resort and Marina. **Facility:** Contemporary and chic, this resort offers seclusion on a beautiful palm-shaded beach. All of the upscale suites open onto terraces. 109 units, some two bedrooms and efficiencies. 4 stories, exterior corridors. **Parking:** on-site and valet. **Terms:** 4 day cancellation notice. **Amenities:** safes. **Dining:** 4 restaurants, entertainment. **Pool(s):** outdoor, heated outdoor. **Activities:** sauna, hot tub, steamroom, marina, fishing, scuba diving, snorkeling, regulation golf, tennis, recreation programs, kids club, bicycles, playground, game room, trails, exercise room, spa. **Guest Services:** valet laundry.

### COURTYARD BY MARRIOTT CANCUN
(998)287-2200 **35**

**Hotel** $80-$148 **Address:** Blvd Luis Donaldo Colosio KM 12.5 77580 **Location:** 0.5 mi (0.8 km) n of jct Mex 307 and airport exit. **Facility:** 201 units. 4 stories, interior corridors. **Amenities:** safes. **Pool(s):** outdoor. **Activities:** hot tub, exercise room. **Guest Services:** valet and coin laundry, area transportation.

**AAA Benefit:** Members save 5% or more!

### EXCELLENCE PLAYA MUJERES
(998)872-8600 **2**

**Resort Hotel**
$600-$3000

**Address:** Prolongacion Bonampak Lt Terreno **Location:** Oceanfront. 6 mi (10 km) n of downtown; in Playa Mujeres. **Facility:** Located in Cancun's newest resort area, this luxury, all-inclusive resort offers extensive pool areas, multiple upscale restaurants, nightly entertainment and spacious rooms. 450 units, some efficiencies. 1-4 stories, exterior corridors. **Parking:** on-site and valet. **Terms:** age restrictions may apply, 7 day cancellation notice. **Amenities:** safes. **Dining:** 11 restaurants, nightclub, entertainment. **Pool(s):** outdoor, heated outdoor. **Activities:** sauna, hot tub, steamroom, fishing, scuba diving, snorkeling, regulation golf, tennis, recreation programs, bicycles, game room, trails, exercise room, spa. **Guest Services:** valet laundry, area transportation.

### FIESTA AMERICANA GRAND CORAL BEACH CANCUN RESORT & SPA
(998)881-3200 **13**

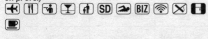

**Resort Hotel**
$248-$669

**Address:** Blvd Kukulcan KM 9.5 Lote 6, Zona Hotelera 77500 **Location:** Oceanfront. Leeward side of Cancun Island. **Facility:** At this impressive resort, the staff caters to your every whim. Features include sophisticated common areas, spacious rooms overlooking the ocean, luxurious spa and expansive beachfront pool areas. Meets AAA guest room security requirements. 602 units. 11 stories, interior corridors. **Parking:** valet only. **Terms:** 5 night minimum stay - seasonal, 7 day cancellation notice. **Amenities:** safes. **Dining:** 4 restaurants, also, Isla Contoy, La Joya, Le Basilic, see separate listings, entertainment. **Pool(s):** outdoor, heated outdoor. **Activities:** sauna, hot tub, steamroom, marina, fishing, scuba diving, snorkeling, recreation programs, kids club, playground, exercise room, spa. **Guest Services:** valet laundry, area transportation. *(See ad opposite inside back cover.)*

### GRAN CARIBE REAL HOTEL
998/881-5500 **18**

**Hotel** $288-$564 **Address:** Blvd Kukulcan KM 11.5, Zona Hotelera **Location:** Oceanfront. Windward side of Cancun Island. **Facility:** 470 units. 2-6 stories, interior/exterior corridors. *Bath:* shower only. **Parking:** on-site and valet. **Terms:** 3 day cancellation notice. **Amenities:** safes. **Dining:** 8 restaurants, entertainment. **Pool(s):** heated outdoor. **Activities:** sauna, hot tub, steamroom, fishing, scuba diving, snorkeling, recreation programs, kids club, bicycles, playground, game room, exercise room, massage. **Guest Services:** valet and coin laundry, rental car service. *(See ad on insert, p. 383.)*

# GRAND VELAS

## Riviera Maya

BEYOND ALL INCLUSIVE, BEYOND ALL COMPARE™

866 868 0992 | velasresorts.com

MERE INCHES
ABOVE SEA LEVEL.
HEAD AND SHOULDERS
ABOVE THE
COMPETITION.

ADULTS ONLY   ALL-INCLUSIVE   1-877-874-0579   LEBLANCSPARESORT.COM

Five Diamond Award

le
blanc
spa resort®

cancun

YOUR KIDS
JUST WON
SHOW
AND TELL

LIVE THE PALACE LIFE

A LIFETIME SUPPLY OF DINNER CONVERSATIONS. INCLUDED.
With five family-friendly resorts in Mexico and Jamaica, the FlowRider®
Double Wave Simulator, Wired Teen Lounge and roughly a million other amazing
amenities, you'll keep enjoying a Palace vacation long after your tan fades.
1.877.874.0579  PalaceResorts.com

PALACE
RESORTS®

AWE-INCLUSIVE™

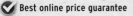

(See map & index p. 373.)

## GRAND PARK ROYAL CANCUN CARIBE

(998)848-7800  **20**

Resort Hotel
Rates not provided

**Address:** Blvd Kukulcan KM 10.5 77500 **Location:** Oceanfront. Windward side of Cancun Island. **Facility:** Rooms at this all-inclusive hotel face the Caribbean; most offer balconies and spectacular views. Poolside and beach-side massages are available. You can dine at multiple themed restaurants. 344 units. 3-7 stories, interior/exterior corridors. **Parking:** on-site and valet. **Terms:** 3 day cancellation notice. **Amenities:** safes. **Dining:** 6 restaurants, entertainment. **Pool(s):** outdoor. **Activities:** sauna, hot tub, steamroom, scuba diving, snorkeling, recreation programs, kids club, playground, exercise room, spa. **Guest Services:** valet laundry, rental car service.

[icons]

## HARD ROCK HOTEL CANCUN

(998)881-3600  **10**

Resort Hotel
$617-$896

**Address:** Blvd Kukulcan KM 14.5 77500 **Location:** Oceanfront. Windward side of Cancun Island. **Facility:** This all-inclusive, rock 'n' roll-themed resort features lagoon- or ocean-view rooms with balconies, and an extensive selection of fun resort activities. The guitar-shaped driveway is a sight to behold. Meets AAA guest room security requirements. 601 units, some two bedrooms. 8-12 stories, interior corridors. **Terms:** 3 day cancellation notice, in season. **Amenities:** safes. *Some:* video games. **Dining:** 5 restaurants, entertainment. **Pool(s):** outdoor, heated outdoor. **Activities:** sauna, hot tub, steamroom, scuba diving, snorkeling, regulation golf, tennis, recreation programs, kids club, game room, exercise room, spa. **Guest Services:** valet laundry.

[icons]

## HOLIDAY INN EXPRESS CANCUN ZONA HOTELERA

(998)883-2200  **17**

[fyi] Hotel  $65-$80 Under major renovation, scheduled to be completed November 2015. **Last Rated:** ▽▽ **Address:** Paseo Pok-Ta-Pok Lote 21 y 22 Zona Hotelera 77500 **Location:** On north side of Cancun Island, off Blvd Kukulcan; 4.2 mi (7 km) from downtown; next to Pok-Ta-Pok Golf Club House. Located in a quiet area. **Facility:** 119 units. 2 stories (no elevator), interior corridors. **Terms:** 3 day cancellation notice-fee imposed. **Pool(s):** outdoor. **Guest Services:** valet laundry.

[icons]

## HOTEL RIU CANCUN

(998)848-7151  **11**

Resort Hotel
Rates not provided

**Address:** Blvd Kukulcan KM 8.5 77500 **Location:** Oceanfront. 6 mi (10 km) from downtown; in Corazon area. **Facility:** The ultra-all-inclusive resort features modern yet elegant lobby areas, well-equipped guest rooms, multiple dining outlets and extensive pool activities. 725 units. 6-15 stories, interior corridors. **Amenities:** safes. **Dining:** 4 restaurants, nightclub, entertainment. **Pool(s):** outdoor. **Activities:** sauna, hot tub, scuba diving, snorkeling, recreation programs, kids club, game room, exercise room, spa. **Guest Services:** valet laundry. *(See ad p. 380.)*

[icons]

## HOTEL RIU CARIBE

(998)848-7850  **6**

Resort Hotel
Rates not provided

**Address:** Blvd Kukulcan KM 5.5, Lote 6-C 77500 **Location:** Oceanfront. 2.6 mi (4.5 km) from downtown; 12.6 mi (21 km) from Cancun International Airport. **Facility:** This all-inclusive resort is centered around a grand strand of beach and boasts an Aztec pyramid-style lobby. The well-equipped guest rooms feature vibrant, contemporary décor. 506 units. 9 stories, interior corridors. **Amenities:** safes. **Dining:** 6 restaurants, entertainment. **Pool(s):** outdoor. **Activities:** hot tub, steamroom, scuba diving, snorkeling, tennis, recreation programs, kids club, playground, game room, exercise room, spa. **Guest Services:** valet laundry, rental car service. *(See ad p. 380.)*

[icons]

## HOTEL RIU PALACE LAS AMERICAS

(998)891-4300  **14**

Resort Hotel
Rates not provided

**Address:** Blvd Kukulcan KM 8.5, Mz 50 77500 **Location:** Oceanfront. Windward side of Cancun Island; in Corazon area. **Facility:** Large guest rooms, ample dining choices and a renowned spa draw visitors to the property from around the world. 372 units. 8 stories, interior corridors. **Amenities:** safes. **Dining:** 6 restaurants, entertainment. **Pool(s):** outdoor, heated outdoor. **Activities:** sauna, hot tub, fishing, scuba diving, snorkeling, recreation programs, playground, exercise room, spa. **Guest Services:** valet laundry. *(See ad p. 380.)*

[icons]

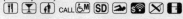

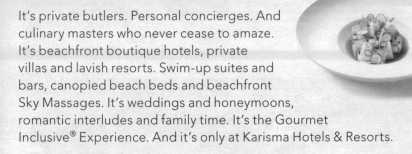

Experience
Gourmet Inclusive.®

It's private butlers. Personal concierges. And culinary masters who never cease to amaze. It's beachfront boutique hotels, private villas and lavish resorts. Swim-up suites and bars, canopied beach beds and beachfront Sky Massages. It's weddings and honeymoons, romantic interludes and family time. It's the Gourmet Inclusive® Experience. And it's only at Karisma Hotels & Resorts.

An experiential, multi-sensory dining adventure at Azul Sensatori Mexico that will challenge any notions of how fine cuisine should look, feel and taste. Behind this pageantry is Chef Jonatán Gómez Luna and his talented culinary team, who've mastered the art and science of cooking to achieve astounding new flavors, textures and shapes.

Riviera Maya, Mexico
Lechiquerestaurant.com

A jewel on a mile long strand of pearl white beach.

El Dorado Royale
a Spa Resort by Karisma

AAA
Four Diamond
Award

A private enclave dedicated to total luxury.

El Dorado
Casitas Royale
by Karisma

AAA
Four Diamond
Award

Beaches. Forests. And one of the largest spas in Riviera Maya.

El Dorado
Seaside Suites
by Karisma

AAA
Four Diamond
Award

A fun, sophisticated and luxurious experience designed to ignite all your senses.

———————————————

AZUL SENSATORI MEXICO
BY KARISMA

Four Diamond Award

---

Barefoot elegance, indigo skies, mouthwatering cuisine and every activity under the Mayan sun.

———————————————

AZUL BEACH
BY KARISMA

Four Diamond Award

---

Mexico's premier all suite, all butler, all gourmet family resort.

———————————————

Generations Riviera Maya
by Karisma

Four Diamond Award

# A FEAST FOR EVERY SENSE.

With inspired cuisine, impeccable service, luxurious accommodations and the prestigious AAA 4 Diamond Award, the Karisma Gourmet Inclusive® Experience is like having all the best things in life handed to you on a silver platter.

Gran Caribe - Cancun

Gran Porto - Playa del Carmen

The Royal Playa del Carmen

## THE BEST HOLIDAYS
## IN THE MOST BEAUTIFUL BEACHES

Get unforgettable moments on a family-friendly
or adults only-romantic in the best All Inclusive of Playa Hotels & Resorts,
on their various destinations; everything with our distinctive:
luxury and exclusivity.

We offer you professional meeting and event planning services
that include a large array of ballrooms and breathtaking
outdoor venues designed for conferences, incentives meetings,
weddings and all special occasions.

### EXCEEDING YOUR EXPECTATIONS

**THE ROYAL**
Playa del Carmen
(Adults Only)

**GRAN CARIBE**
★★★★★
CANCUN

**GRAN PORTO**
★★★★★
PLAYA DEL CARMEN

## USA & CANADA 1-800-760-0944
### www.playaresorts.com

Cancun - Playa del Carmen, Mexico

(See map & index p. 373.)

## HYATT ZILARA CANCUN    (998)881-5600    21

Resort Hotel
$229-$700

**AAA Benefit:** Members save 10%!

**Address:** Blvd Kukulcan KM 11.5, Zona Hotelera 77513 **Location:** Oceanfront. Across from lagoon. **Facility:** Upscale and adult-oriented, this all-inclusive resort offers several dining options, a number of activities and a well-appointed spa. 307 units. 8 stories, interior/exterior corridors. **Parking:** on-site and valet. **Amenities:** safes. **Dining:** 6 restaurants, entertainment. **Pool(s):** heated outdoor. **Activities:** sauna, hot tub, steamroom, fishing, scuba diving, snorkeling, tennis, recreation programs, bicycles, game room, exercise room, spa. **Guest Services:** valet laundry, area transportation. *(See ad on insert.)*

## IBEROSTAR CANCUN GOLF & SPA RESORT
998/881-8000    32

Resort Hotel
Rates not provided

**Address:** Blvd Kukulcan KM 17, Zona Hotelera 77500 **Location:** Oceanfront. Windward side of Cancun Island. **Facility:** A dramatic pyramid structure houses the guest rooms. The property features extensive pool areas and secluded villas situated along a spectacular beach. All rooms have views of the Caribbean. 426 units. 2-9 stories, interior/exterior corridors. **Parking:** on-site and valet. **Amenities:** safes. **Dining:** 6 restaurants, entertainment. **Pool(s):** outdoor, heated outdoor. **Activities:** sauna, hot tub, steamroom, regulation golf, tennis, recreation programs, kids club, game room, exercise room, spa. **Guest Services:** valet laundry. *(See ad on insert, p. 385.)*

## KRYSTAL GRAN PUNTA CANCUN    (998)891-5555    12

Hotel $125-$280 **Address:** Blvd Kukulcan KM 8.5 77500 **Location:** Oceanfront. North end of Zona Hotelera. **Facility:** Meets AAA guest room security requirements. 295 units. 14 stories, interior corridors. **Parking:** on-site and valet. **Terms:** 5 night minimum stay - seasonal, 15 day cancellation notice, in season-fee imposed. **Amenities:** safes. **Dining:** 5 restaurants, entertainment. **Pool(s):** outdoor, heated outdoor. **Activities:** sauna, hot tub, fishing, scuba diving, snorkeling, recreation programs, kids club, exercise room, spa. **Guest Services:** valet laundry.

## LA QUINTA INN & SUITES CANCUN    998/872-9400    7

Hotel $59-$182 **Address:** Ave Tulum SM 4 Mz 14 Lote 2 Entre **Location:** Off Cancun Island; just w of jct Blvd Kukulcan. **Facility:** Meets AAA guest room security requirements. 137 units. 6 stories, interior corridors. **Bath:** shower only. **Amenities:** safes. **Dining:** 2 restaurants. **Pool(s):** outdoor. **Activities:** hot tub, exercise room. **Guest Services:** valet and coin laundry, rental car service, area transportation.

## LE BLANC SPA RESORT    (998)881-4740    19

Contemporary Resort Hotel
$646-$1350

**Address:** Blvd Kukulcan KM 10, Zona Hotelera 77500 **Location:** Oceanfront. Between Plaza Caracol and La Isla Shopping Center; across from Plaza Flamingo, Cancun Island. **Facility:** Modern and comfortable, this beautiful all-inclusive resort caters to the discriminating traveler. Each floor is assigned a butler to ensure the memory of staying here is unforgettable. This is an adult-only property. 260 units. 9 stories, interior corridors. **Parking:** valet only. **Terms:** cancellation fee imposed. **Amenities:** safes. **Dining:** 5 restaurants, entertainment. **Pool(s):** heated outdoor. **Activities:** sauna, hot tub, steamroom, recreation programs, exercise room, spa. **Guest Services:** valet laundry. *(See ad on inside front cover, starting on p. 378.)*

## MARRIOTT CASAMAGNA CANCUN RESORT
(998)881-2000    27

Resort Hotel
$104-$424

**AAA Benefit:** Members save 5% or more!

**Address:** Blvd Kukulcan, Retorno Chac L-41 77500 **Location:** Oceanfront. Blvd Kukulcan KM 16; windward side of Cancun Island. **Facility:** A spacious, luxurious lobby and a large oceanfront pool/activity area complement the stylish rooms at this resort hotel. 450 units. 6 stories, interior corridors. **Terms:** check-in 4 pm. **Amenities:** safes. **Dining:** 3 restaurants, also, La Capilla Argentina, Mikado, see separate listings, entertainment. **Pool(s):** heated outdoor. **Activities:** sauna, hot tub, scuba diving, snorkeling, tennis, recreation programs, kids club, playground, exercise room, spa. **Guest Services:** valet laundry, boarding pass kiosk.

## ME BY MELIA CANCUN    (998)881-2500    22

Contemporary Hotel
$308-$650

**Address:** Blvd Kukulcan KM 12, Zona Hotelera 77500 **Location:** Oceanfront. Blvd Kukulcan KM 12. **Facility:** As the name states, this stylish hotel's focus is on 'me,' the guest, and you'll know that's true the moment you arrive and receive the traditional Mayan salute of arm and hand across the heart. 434 units. 11 stories, interior corridors. **Parking:** on-site and valet. **Amenities:** safes. **Dining:** 5 restaurants, nightclub, entertainment. **Pool(s):** outdoor. **Activities:** sauna, hot tub, steamroom, recreation programs, spa. **Guest Services:** valet laundry.

Families shine brighter at
**IBEROSTAR Hotels & Resorts.**

IBEROSTAR Cancún, water playground

Located on Mexico's most spectacular beaches, IBEROSTAR Hotels & Resorts brings together the best in accommodations, service, recreation and all-inclusive dining. While the children are living it up at the supervised Kids Club, the adults can relax on the beach, in the spa or beside one of the refreshing pools. Book your stay today and look forward to the best of times at Mexico's all-inclusive family destinations.

CANCÚN · RIVIERA MAYA · COZUMEL

AAA Members Save 10%.
To Book Call 888-923-2722.

**IBEROSTAR**
HOTELS & RESORTS

*Enjoy being a star*

(See map & index p. 373.)

## MOON PALACE GOLF & SPA RESORT

(998)881-6000 **36**

**Resort Hotel**
**$536-$1680**

**Address:** Carr Cancun-Chetumal KM 307 77500 **Location:** Oceanfront. Mex 307, 5 mi (8 km) s of Cancun International Airport. **Facility:** This is a very large complex with three sections offering everything from multiple restaurants to all types of water and beach activities. In addition you'll find a luxurious spa and golf course. 2402 units, some kitchens. 3 stories, interior/exterior corridors. **Parking:** on-site and valet. **Terms:** cancellation fee imposed. **Amenities:** safes. **Dining:** 14 restaurants, nightclub, entertainment. **Pool(s):** outdoor, heated outdoor. **Activities:** sauna, hot tub, steamroom, scuba diving, snorkeling, regulation golf, miniature golf, tennis, recreation programs, kids club, bicycles, playground, game room, trails, exercise room, spa. **Guest Services:** valet laundry, area transportation. *(See ad on inside front cover, starting on p. 378.)*

### NIZUC RESORT & SPA

(998)891-5700 **42**

**Resort Hotel $500-$5000 Address:** Blvd Kukulcan KM 21, 260 Lote 1-01 Mz Zona Hotelera 77500 **Location:** Oceanfront. At entrance to Zona Hotelera. **Facility:** This beautiful and expansive resort features rustic and elegant Mayan inspired décor. It not only has a beach with crashing waves but also a nice family beach with limited surf. 274 units, some two bedrooms and efficiencies. 1-6 stories, interior/exterior corridors. **Parking:** valet and street only. **Terms:** 7 night minimum stay - seasonal, 21 day cancellation notice, in season, resort fee. **Amenities:** safes. **Dining:** 5 restaurants, also, Ramona, see separate listing. **Pool(s):** heated outdoor. **Activities:** sauna, hot tub, steamroom, boat dock, snorkeling, tennis, recreation programs, kids club, playground, game room, trails, exercise room, in-room exercise equipment, spa. **Guest Services:** valet laundry, luggage security pick-up, area transportation.

### OASIS SMART

(998)848-8600 **3**

**Hotel $87-$150 Address:** Ave Tulum y Calle Brisa SM 4 CP 77500 **Location:** Off Cancun Island; on Ave Tulum, jct highway to beaches. Located in Old Town Cancun. **Facility:** 119 units. 6 stories, interior corridors. *Bath:* shower only. **Amenities:** safes. **Pool(s):** outdoor. **Activities:** exercise room. **Guest Services:** valet laundry, rental car service.

### OMNI CANCUN HOTEL & VILLAS

(998)881-0600 **29**

**Resort Hotel $285-$2034 Address:** Blvd Kukulcan L-48, M-53 77500 **Location:** Oceanfront. Windward side of Cancun Island. **Facility:** A beachfront location and a range of recreational facilities add appeal to this all-inclusive property, which offers both traditional rooms and full villas. 347 units, some three bedrooms, efficiencies and houses. 3-12 stories, interior corridors. **Parking:** on-site and valet. **Terms:** 3 day cancellation notice, in season. **Amenities:** safes. **Dining:** 6 restaurants, entertainment. **Pool(s):** outdoor. **Activities:** hot tub, steamroom, scuba diving, snorkeling, tennis, recreation programs, kids club, exercise room, spa. **Guest Services:** valet laundry.

## PARADISUS CANCUN RESORT

(998)881-1100 **30**

**Resort Hotel**
**$350-$870**

**Address:** Blvd Kukulcan KM 16.5 77500 **Location:** Oceanfront. Windward side of Cancun Island. **Facility:** One of the largest properties in the Hotel Zone, it offers extensive beach and water activities as well as a spa and several restaurants. For exclusivity, book a room in the hotel's Red Level section. Meets AAA guest room security requirements. 668 units. 6-8 stories, interior corridors. **Parking:** on-site and valet. **Amenities:** safes. **Dining:** 7 restaurants, also, TEMPO Contemporary Cuisine by Martin Berasategui, see separate listing, nightclub, entertainment. **Pool(s):** outdoor, heated outdoor. **Activities:** sauna, hot tub, steamroom, cabanas, fishing, scuba diving, snorkeling, regulation golf, tennis, recreation programs, kids club, playground, game room, exercise room, spa. **Guest Services:** valet laundry.

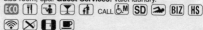

## THE RITZ-CARLTON, CANCUN

(998)881-0808 **31**

**Resort Hotel**
**$149-$5000**

**AAA Benefit:** Unequaled service at special member savings!

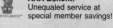

**Address:** Retorno del Rey No. 36, Zona Hotelera 77500 **Location:** Oceanfront. Blvd Kukulcan KM 17.5. **Facility:** Impressive common areas and a refined ambience enhance this hotel's location on a prime section of beach in the middle of the hotel zone. 365 units. 9 stories, interior corridors. **Parking:** valet only. **Terms:** 3 day cancellation notice. **Amenities:** safes. **Dining:** The Club Grill, Fantino, see separate listings, entertainment. **Pool(s):** heated outdoor. **Activities:** sauna, scuba diving, recreation programs, kids club, playground, exercise room, spa. **Guest Services:** valet laundry, area transportation. *(See ad opposite Using Your Guide.)*

## SANDOS CANCUN LUXURY EXPERIENCE RESORT

(998)881-2200 **24**

**Resort Hotel**
**$382-$1031**

**Address:** KM 14 Retorno del Rey 77500 **Location:** Oceanfront. Off Blvd Kukulcan; windward side of Cancun Island. **Facility:** Featuring modern, chic décor, rooms offer striking views of the Caribbean and its occasionally strong and dramatic surf. 214 units. 8 stories, interior corridors. **Parking:** on-site and valet. **Terms:** 3 day cancellation notice-fee imposed. **Amenities:** safes. **Dining:** 4 restaurants, entertainment. **Pool(s):** outdoor, heated outdoor. **Activities:** sauna, hot tub, steamroom, scuba diving, snorkeling, tennis, recreation programs, kids club, playground, exercise room, spa. **Guest Services:** valet laundry.

(See map & index p. 373.)

## SECRETS PLAYA MUJERES GOLF & SPA RESORT
998/283-3600   4

Resort Hotel
$673-$1480

**Address:** Prolongation Bonampak S/N Punta SAM C.P. **Location:** Oceanfront. 6 mi (10 km) n of downtown; in Playa Mujeres. **Facility:** This lovely resort is situated at the remote edge of a nature preserve, providing a sense of peaceful privacy. The calm surf is perfect for swimming, snorkeling, kayaking and sailing. 424 units, some two bedrooms and kitchens. 1-5 stories, exterior corridors. **Parking:** valet only. **Terms:** 4 night minimum stay - seasonal, age restrictions may apply. **Amenities:** safes. **Dining:** 8 restaurants, nightclub, entertainment. **Pool(s):** heated outdoor. **Activities:** sauna, hot tub, steamroom, cabanas, self-propelled boats, scuba diving, snorkeling, regulation golf, tennis, recreation programs, bicycles, game room, trails, exercise room, spa. **Guest Services:** valet laundry, rental car service, area transportation.

## SECRETS THE VINE CANCUN   (998)848-9400   40

Contemporary
Resort Hotel
$570-$2200

**Address:** Retorno del Rey 38, Zona Hotelera 77500 **Location:** Oceanfront. Just e of jct Blvd Kukulcan KM 14.5. **Facility:** This chic, contemporary high-rise is Cancun's newest all-inclusive resort. 'The Vine' takes its name from the property's wine cellar that boasts more than 4,000 bottles and offers daily tastings. 497 units, some two bedrooms. 18 stories, interior corridors. **Parking:** valet only. **Terms:** 4 night minimum stay - seasonal, age restrictions may apply, 3 day cancellation notice. **Amenities:** safes. **Dining:** 7 restaurants, nightclub, entertainment. **Pool(s):** heated outdoor. **Activities:** sauna, hot tub, steamroom, recreation programs, game room, exercise room, spa. **Guest Services:** valet laundry.

## THE WESTIN LAGUNAMAR OCEAN RESORT VILLAS & SPA CANCUN   (998)891-4200   25

Resort
Condominium
$209-$509

**WESTIN** HOTELS & RESORTS **AAA Benefit:** Members save up to 15%, plus Starwood Preferred Guest® benefits!

**Address:** Blvd Kukulcan KM 12.5 Zona Hotelera Lote 18 77500 **Location:** Oceanfront. In Zona Hotelera; across from La Isla Shopping Center. **Facility:** Upscale appointments can be found throughout this oceanfront, vacation ownership property. Spacious rooms and a well-equipped fitness center are other pluses. 592 condominiums. 10 stories, interior corridors. **Parking:** on-site and valet. **Terms:** check-in 4 pm, 3 day cancellation notice-fee imposed. **Amenities:** safes. **Dining:** 4 restaurants. **Pool(s):** heated outdoor. **Activities:** sauna, hot tub, steamroom, miniature golf, tennis, recreation programs, kids club, playground, lawn sports, picnic facilities, exercise room, spa. **Guest Services:** valet and coin laundry.

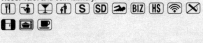

---

Enjoy great member rates and benefits
at AAA/CAA Preferred Hotels

## THE WESTIN RESORT & SPA CANCUN
(998)848-7400   34

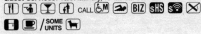

Resort Hotel
$109-$599

**WESTIN** HOTELS & RESORTS **AAA Benefit:** Members save up to 15%, plus Starwood Preferred Guest® benefits!

**Address:** Blvd Kukulcan KM 20 Lote 70 y Zona Hotelera 77500 **Location:** Oceanfront. Windward side of Cancun Island. **Facility:** Designed by a well-known Mexican architect, this attractive property offers upscale amenities and excellent ocean and lagoon beachfront relaxation areas with lounge chairs and attendants. 379 units. 6-7 stories, interior corridors. **Parking:** on-site and valet. **Amenities:** safes. **Dining:** 4 restaurants, entertainment. **Pool(s):** outdoor, heated outdoor. **Activities:** sauna, hot tub, steamroom, tennis, recreation programs, kids club, playground, exercise room, spa. **Guest Services:** valet laundry, rental car service.

## BEACHSCAPE KIN HA VILLAS & SUITES   998/891-5400

fyi Not evaluated. **Address:** Blvd Kukulcan KM 8.5, Zona Hotelera 77500 **Location:** Oceanfront. On north end of beach; just n of Plaza Caracol. Facilities, services, and décor characterize a mid-scale property.

## FIESTA AMERICANA CONDESA CANCUN ALL INCLUSIVE   998/881-4200

fyi Not evaluated; management refused inspection. **Address:** Blvd Kukulcan KM 16.5 **Location:** Oceanfront. Windward side of Cancun Island. Facilities, services, and décor characterize a mid-scale property. Accented by a Mediterranean-style exterior, lush landscaping and refined public areas, this all-inclusive property boasts ocean views from all rooms.

## JW MARRIOTT CANCUN RESORT & SPA   998/848-9600

fyi Not evaluated; management refused inspection. **Address:** Blvd Kukulcan KM 14.5 77500 **Location:** Oceanfront. 2 mi (3.2 km) s of Cancun Convention Center. Facilities, services, and décor characterize an upscale property. Lavish public areas, extensive resort facilities, a world-class spa and excellent service comprise one of Cancun's best-known resorts.

**AAA Benefit:** Members save 5% or more!

## LIVE AQUA CANCUN   998/881-7600

fyi Hotel Did not meet all AAA rating requirements for locking devices in some guest rooms at time of last evaluation on 02/25/2015. **Address:** Blvd Kukulcan KM 12.5, Zona Hotelera 77500 **Location:** Oceanfront. Windward side of Cancun Island. Facilities, services, and décor characterize an upscale property.

## SUN PALACE CANCUN   998/891-4100

fyi Not evaluated. **Address:** Blvd Kukulcan KM 20 77500 **Location:** Oceanfront. Facilities, services, and décor characterize a mid-scale property. *(See ad on inside front cover, starting on p. 378, on inside front cover.)*

## WHERE TO EAT

### BENAZUZA   998/891-5000   44

International. Fine Dining. **AAA Inspector Notes:** Prepare to be wowed by the creations of famed chef Rafael Zafra, whose unique, molecular cuisine is both innovative and delicious. Your experience starts with a cocktail tasting at the bar, then moves into the comfortable dining room to sample the multi-course tasting menu, which features such items as grouper with onion ash, foie gras tacos, and chicken mole with peanuts. **Features:** full bar. **Reservations:** suggested. **Address:** Blvd Kukulcan KM 19.5 77500 **Location:** Blvd Kukulcan KM 19.5; in Oasis Sens Resort. **Parking:** on-site and valet. B D

**(See map & index p. 373.)**

## CAMBALACHE
998/883-0902  19

▼▼▼▼ Argentine Steak. Fine Dining. $22-$53 **AAA Inspector Notes:** For a good steak in a rustic yet elegant atmosphere accented by arched brick ceilings and wine tower walls, head to this spot known for large portions and a wide range of cuts—from New York strip to top sirloin prepared on a either a wood-fired or charcoal grill. Salads and side dishes, such as creamed spinach and loaded baked potatoes, are large enough to share. Service is attentive and professional. It's surprisingly quiet given the location within a shopping mall and next to nightclubs. **Features:** full bar. **Address:** Blvd Kukulcan KM 9 77500 **Location:** Zona Hotelera; in Plaza Forum. **Parking:** on-site and valet. L D LATE CALL M

## CAPTAIN'S COVE STEAK & SEAFOOD GRILL
998/885-0016  42

▼▼▼▼ Seafood. Casual Dining. $20-$40 **AAA Inspector Notes:** In the Zona Hotelera, this restaurant overlooks the lagoon side of the island and affords excellent views of the sunset. A nautical theme sets the atmosphere for seafood prepared with a Mexican flair. Among choices are shrimp scampi, lobster Thermidor, grouper and crab cakes. Good starters include spinach salad with warm bacon dressing or ahi tuna carpaccio. **Features:** full bar, Sunday brunch. **Reservations:** suggested. **Address:** Blvd Kukulcan KM 16.5 77500 **Location:** Opposite Omni Cancun Hotel & Villas. L D

## CASA ROLANDI GOURMET RESTAURANT & YACHT CLUB
998/883-1817  48

▼▼▼ Italian. Fine Dining. $16-$36 **AAA Inspector Notes:** Fresh, well-prepared local seafood and handmade pasta dishes are served by an attentive staff. Creative Italian and Swiss cuisines dominate the menu with an extensive wine list. Beautiful lagoon views make for a memorable dining experience. **Features:** full bar, patio dining. **Reservations:** suggested, for dinner. **Address:** Blvd Kukulcan KM 13.5 77500 **Location:** In Zona Hotelera. **Parking:** valet and street only. L D LATE

## CENACOLO MARE
998/885-2746  46

▼▼▼ Italian Seafood. Fine Dining. $15-$40 **AAA Inspector Notes:** Overlooking the lagoon, this chic new restaurant is a lovely spot to spend a romantic evening. While listening to songs played on a baby grand piano, you'll enjoy homemade pasta, the freshest seafood and excellent wines served by an attentive staff. **Features:** full bar, patio dining. **Reservations:** suggested. **Address:** Blvd Kukulcan KM 14 **Location:** On lagoon side of Zona Hotelera. **Parking:** valet only. L D

## CENACOLO RISTORANTE ITALIANO
998/885-3603  28

▼▼▼ Italian. Fine Dining. $18-$40 **AAA Inspector Notes:** This elegant, contemporary restaurant serves handmade pastas and freshly baked bread. The house specialty is spaghetti with fresh lobster. **Features:** full bar. **Reservations:** suggested. **Address:** Blvd Kukulcan KM 13 77500 **Location:** In Kukulcan Plaza. **Parking:** on-site (fee). L D

## THE CLUB GRILL
998/881-0808  33

◆◆◆◆◆ **AAA Inspector Notes:** The lavish, club-like setting sets the stage for a refined, romantic dining experience. Seafood, steak and game dishes are vividly presented and augmented by local Yucatan and Caribbean flavors. Service is formal and precise. The adjoining lounge is ideal for dancing to live jazz music. **Features:** full bar. **Reservations:** required. Semiformal attire. **Address:** Retorno del Rey No. 36, Zona Hotelera 77500 **Location:** Blvd Kukulcan KM 17.5; in The Ritz-Carlton, Cancun. **Parking:** valet only. *(See ad opposite Using Your Guide.)* D

International Fine Dining
$35-$170

## CRAB HOUSE CARIBE
998/193-0350  36

▼▼▼ Mexican Seafood. Casual Dining. $15-$43 **AAA Inspector Notes:** The fabulous seafood choices featuring crab and lobster are presented tableside for your selection. The menu also offers pastas, steaks and a fun children's menu. The restaurant overlooks the Nichupte Lagoon. **Features:** full bar, patio dining. **Reservations:** suggested. **Address:** Blvd Kukulcan KM 14.7 77500 **Location:** Across from Marriott complex. **Parking:** valet and street only. L D

## ELEFANTA INDIAN CUISINE
998/176-8071  5

▼▼▼ Indian. Casual Dining. $12-$38 **AAA Inspector Notes:** Serving the only authentic Indian food in the Cancun area, this highly decorative restaurant with outdoor palapa seating along the lagoon provides attentive service and a menu that offers tandoori specialties and curry lamb, chicken and shrimp. A nightclub atmosphere prevails after normal restaurant hours. **Features:** full bar. **Reservations:** suggested. **Address:** Blvd Kukulcan KM 12.5 77500 **Location:** In La Isla Shopping Center. **Parking:** on-site (fee). D LATE AC

## FANTINO
998/881-0808  34

◆◆◆◆◆ **AAA Inspector Notes:** The talented chefs have created a specialty menu that features surprising presentations. A chef's tasting menu is offered nightly for those guests that like to sample many courses. The menu is offered paired with or without wines. Refined service and elegant decor are other highlights. **Features:** full bar. **Reservations:** required. Semiformal attire. **Address:** Retorno del Rey No. 36, Zona Hotelera 77500 **Location:** Blvd Kukulcan KM 17.5; in The Ritz-Carlton, Cancun. **Parking:** valet only. *(See ad opposite Using Your Guide.)* D

Mediterranean Fine Dining
$35-$170

## FRED'S HOUSE SEAFOOD MARKET AND GRILL
998/840-6466  35

▼▼▼ Seafood. Fine Dining. $20-$55 **AAA Inspector Notes:** Market fresh seafood is the theme here, where the daily catch of the day is cooked to your liking. As a bonus you'll be treated to an excellent lagoon view and attentive service. **Features:** full bar, patio dining. **Reservations:** suggested. **Address:** Blvd Kukulcan KM 14.5 77500 **Location:** In Zona Hotelera. **Parking:** valet and street only. L D

## GUSTINO ITALIAN GRILL
998/848-9600  38

◆◆◆◆ **AAA Inspector Notes:** Terraced seating provides great views at this classic Italian restaurant, which has a wine cellar and an immense antipasti bar with cured meats, imported cheeses and marinated vegetables. Menu favorites include thick bone-in chops, freshly made ravioli and sweet desserts. **Features:** full bar. **Reservations:** required. **Address:** Blvd Kukulcan KM 14.5 77500 **Location:** 2 mi (3.2 km) s of Cancun Convention Center; in JW Marriott Cancun Resort & Spa. **Parking:** on-site and valet. D CALL M

Regional Italian Fine Dining
$20-$50

## HACIENDA SISAL MEXICAN GRILL
998/848-8220  27

▼▼▼ Mexican. Casual Dining. $20-$50 **AAA Inspector Notes:** Situated in a richly decorated hacienda-style mansion, this restaurant evokes Old Mexico with its soaring ceilings, gilded artwork, courtyards and live mariachi music on most nights at 7 pm. The extensive menu offers standard yet somewhat creative Mexican cuisine, including fajitas, lobster tacos, enchiladas and chile rellenos. The fishbowl margaritas and the guacamole, prepared table side, are outstanding. **Features:** full bar, patio dining, Sunday brunch. **Reservations:** suggested. **Address:** Blvd Kukulcan KM 13.5 77500 **Location:** Between Kukulcan Plaza and The Royal Sands & Spa; on oceanside. **Parking:** on-site and valet. D

## HARRY'S PRIME STEAKHOUSE & RAW BAR
998/840-6550  32

◆◆◆◆ **AAA Inspector Notes:** Elegant surroundings, refined service, live music nightly and a menu boasting top-notch steaks and seafood make this a Cancun must. Though the restaurant specializes in USDA Prime dry-aged beef and chops broiled to perfection, there's also a large assortment of seafood. Good choices include Alaskan king crab, Chilean sea bass, halibut, giant Thai tiger prawns, oysters and lobster from Maine, Australia and the Caribbean. **Features:** full bar. **Reservations:** suggested. **Address:** Blvd Kukulcan KM 14.2, Zona Hotelera 77500 **Location:** Across from The Ritz-Carlton, Cancun; on lagoon side. **Parking:** valet only. L D

International Fine Dining
$20-$50

**(See map & index p. 373.)**

## ISLA CONTOY  998/881-3200  [13]

▼▼▼▼ Regional Caribbean. Casual Dining. $18-$43 **AAA Inspector Notes:** Facing the Caribbean, this indoor/outdoor restaurant features a seafood and pasta market where guests select fresh items to be prepared a la minute. The laid-back atmosphere contrasts well with the elevated cuisine and attentive service. **Features:** full bar. **Address:** Blvd Kukulcan KM 9.5 Lote 6 Zona Hotelera 77500 **Location:** Leeward side of Cancun Island; in Fiesta Americana Grand Coral Beach Cancun Resort & Spa. **Parking:** on-site and valet.

[L] [D] CALL [&M] [K]

## LA CAPILLA ARGENTINA  998/881-2000  [39]

▼▼▼ Argentine. Fine Dining. $10-$60 **AAA Inspector Notes:** Among this comfortable restaurant's décor touches are a Spanish tile floor and Mexican fountain. However, the food is the clear highlight. Servers display fresh cuts of beef and tempting starters, such as gaucho sausage. Expect huge portions of freshly prepared and perfectly spiced cuisine with an Argentine flair. **Features:** full bar. **Reservations:** suggested. **Address:** Blvd Kukulcan, Retorno Chac L-41 77500 **Location:** Blvd Kukulcan KM 16; windward side of Cancun Island; in Marriott CasaMagna Cancun Resort. [B] [D]

## LA DESTILERIA  998/885-1086  [29]

▼▼▼ Mexican. Casual Dining. $15-$30 **AAA Inspector Notes:** Resembling a turn-of-the-20th-century tequila-making ranch, the restaurant is reminiscent of another time. The menu is traditional yet creative with some tableside flambé preparations, such as the delicious beef tenderloin steak with a zesty vodka, Tabasco and Worcestershire sauce. There are more than 100 varieties of tequila on hand to sample or enjoy in a large margarita. The outdoor deck provides a scenic view overlooking the lagoon. Guests are told their satisfaction is guaranteed. **Features:** full bar, patio dining. **Reservations:** suggested. **Address:** Blvd Kukulcan KM 13 77500 **Location:** Blvd Kukulcan; in Zona Hotelera. **Parking:** valet only. [L] [D]

## LA DOLCE VITA DOWNTOWN  998/884-3393  [7]

▼▼▼▼
Italian
Casual Dining
$15-$30

**AAA Inspector Notes:** Between central Cancun and the island proper, this is one of Cancun's earliest Italian restaurants, brought back to life after 30 years. The menu lists an array of options from spinach salad and carpaccio for starters to entrées of osso buco, delicately prepared seafood, risotto, lasagna and ravioli. The garden atmosphere and trained, well-groomed staff enhance the dining experience. **Features:** full bar. **Reservations:** suggested, for dinner. **Address:** Ave Coba 87, SM 3 77500 **Location:** Just w from bridge to Cancun Island. **Parking:** on-site and valet.

[L] [D]

## LA HABICHUELA  998/840-6280  [41]

▼▼▼▼ Mexican. Fine Dining. $17-$45 **AAA Inspector Notes:** Sporting a dramatic Mayan-themed décor and prepares the time-honored family recipes of the Pezzotti family. Favorites include the seafood ceviche, chilled avocado soup and the whole steamed fish served Veracruz style. For dessert, the refined, attentive servers specialize in tableside preparations of crepes flambé as well as strawberry jubilee. **Features:** full bar, patio dining. **Reservations:** suggested. **Address:** Blvd Kukulcan KM 12.6, Zona Hotelera 77500 **Location:** Blvd Kukulcan, lagoon side of Cancun Island; in Zona Hotelera. **Parking:** valet only. [L] [D]

## LA JOYA  998/881-3200  [14]

▼▼▼▼
Mexican
Fine Dining
$35-$45

**AAA Inspector Notes:** Those who dine in the main plaza of this quaint place can discover authentic Mexican cuisine. Distinctive dishes combine national and classic flavors. Entertainment alternates between live mariachis and folklorico music-and-dance shows. **Features:** full bar. **Reservations:** suggested. **Address:** Blvd Kukulcan KM 9.5 Lote 6 Zona Hotelera 77500 **Location:** Leeward side of Cancun Island; in Fiesta Americana Grand Coral Beach Cancun Resort & Spa. **Parking:** valet only. [D]

## LA MADONNA  998/883-4837  [26]

▼▼▼▼ Italian. Fine Dining. $17-$50 **AAA Inspector Notes:** Homemade rich pasta, gourmet pizzas, live lobster and fresh local seafood are just some of the menu highlights. Huge statues the size of three stories, floor-to-ceiling murals including one replica of the Mona Lisa and ornate décor enhance the distinctive European setting. Overlooking activities at the shopping venue, the small patio area on the ground or second level is a nice spot for drinks. **Features:** full bar. **Reservations:** suggested. **Address:** Blvd Kukulcan KM 12.5 77500 **Location:** At La Isla Shopping Center. **Parking:** on-site (fee) and valet. [L] [D] [LATE]

## LE BASILIC  998/881-3200  [11]

▼▼▼▼
Regional
Mediterranean
Fine Dining
$33-$78

**AAA Inspector Notes:** Mediterranean creations feature subtle undertones of French haute cuisine. The elegant dining room, with its pianist and attentive service, encourages romance and celebration. After dinner, diners can step out to the lounge for a nightcap and live nightly entertainment. **Features:** full bar. **Reservations:** suggested. Semiformal attire. **Address:** Blvd Kukulcan KM 9.5 Lote 6 Zona Hotelera 77500 **Location:** Leeward side of Cancun Island; in Fiesta Americana Grand Coral Beach Cancun Resort & Spa. **Parking:** valet only. [D] CALL [&M]

(See map & index p. 373.)

### LIMONCELLO RISTORANTE     998/883-1455   24

▼▼▼ Italian. Casual Dining. $15-$40 **AAA Inspector Notes:** Situated on a picturesque bay, this casual yet refined restaurant offers indoor and outdoor seating. Authentic Italian cuisine is prepared with pasta made on the premises. Menu favorites include the gourmet wood even pizzas, gnocchi, and carpaccio fish and beef. At meal's end, the dessert tray will test even the most dedicated dieter's will power. **Features:** full bar, patio dining. **Reservations:** suggested. **Address:** Blvd Kukulcan KM 10.5 Zona Hotelera 77500 **Location:** Blvd Kukulcan, lagoon side of Cancun Island. **Parking:** valet only.

L   D   🖎

### LORENZILLO'S     998/883-1254   20

▼▼▼ Seafood. Casual Dining. $14-$60 **AAA Inspector Notes:** Named after legendary French pirate Lorenzillo, who came to Mexico in 1683, the long-established restaurant is built over the water on Nichupte Lagoon. The specialty, live lobster, can be selected from the water-filled boat moored in the dining room. Seafood dishes can be cooked in several ways, and six shrimp preparations are offered. Beef and chicken dishes also are available. Tasteful nautical décor and attentive service prevails. **Features:** full bar. **Reservations:** suggested, for dinner. **Address:** Blvd Kukulcan KM 10.5 Zona Hotelera 77500 **Location:** Opposite Grand Caribe Real Cancun. **Parking:** valet only. L   D   LATE

### MIKADO     998/881-2000   40

▼▼▼ Asian. Casual Dining. $18-$40 **AAA Inspector Notes:** Near the entrance of the hotel, the restaurant lets diners choose from both Japanese and Thai selections amid sleek, contemporary Asian décor. Choices include tempura, yellow and green curries, Pad Thai and extensive sushi varieties. **Features:** full bar, patio dining. **Reservations:** suggested. **Address:** Blvd Kukulcan, Retorno Chac L-41 77500 **Location:** Blvd Kukulcan KM 16; windward side of Cancun Island; in Marriott CasaMagna Cancun Resort.

D

### NAVIOS MEXICAN FUSION SEAFOOD     998/885-3848   50

▼▼▼ Seafood. Fine Dining. $12-$40 **AAA Inspector Notes:** Fronting the lagoon at the more remote end of Cancun Island is this popular eatery that's also nice for an intimate meal. Guests can choose to sit inside or dine al fresco on the pier that stretches out over the lagoon. While the kitchen does turn out tasty soups, fresh salads and a few beef and chicken dishes, the menu's primary focus is on seafood, which is served grilled, baked and fried. **Features:** full bar. **Reservations:** suggested. **Address:** Blvd Kukulcan KM 19.5 77500 **Location:** On east end of Cancun Island, lagoon side; across from Sun Palace. L   D

### PUERTO MADERO STEAKHOUSE AND FISH MARINA     998/885-2829   30

▼▼▼ Steak Seafood. Fine Dining. $18-$65 **AAA Inspector Notes:** Overlooking the lagoon, the steak house appeals to well-heeled locals. An extensive wine list complements delicious choices such as ahi tuna, empanadas, Kobe beef and New Zealand lamb. **Features:** full bar, patio dining. **Reservations:** suggested. **Address:** Blvd Kukulcan KM 14 77500 **Location:** In Marina Barracuda. **Parking:** on-site and valet. L   D   LATE   🖎

### RAMONA     998/891-5700   49

▼▼▼ Northern Mexican. Fine Dining. $25-$58 **AAA Inspector Notes:** The elegant dining room and covered patio afford exquisite views of the sea. The attentive staff provides refined, yet personable service. The seasonal menu showcases modern interpretations of traditional cuisine using only the freshest local produce, seafood and spices. A ceviche is a must way to start your meal. **Features:** full bar, patio dining. **Reservations:** suggested. **Address:** Blvd Kukulcan KM 21, 260 Lote 1-01 Mz Zona Hotelera 77500 **Location:** At entrance to Zona Hotelera; in NIZUC Resort & Spa. **Parking:** valet only. D

### RUTH'S CHRIS STEAK HOUSE     998/885-0500   22

▼▼▼ Steak. Fine Dining. $25-$60 **AAA Inspector Notes:** The main fare is steak, which is prepared from several cuts of Prime beef and cooked to perfection, but the menu also lists lamb, chicken and seafood dishes. Guests should come hungry because the side dishes, which are among the a la carte offerings, could make a meal in themselves. **Features:** full bar. **Reservations:** suggested. **Address:** Blvd Kukulcan KM 13.5 **Location:** In Kukulcan Plaza. **Parking:** on-site (fee) and valet. L   D   🖎

### TEMPO CONTEMPORARY CUISINE BY MARTIN BERASATEGUI     998/881-1100   45

▼▼▼ ▼▼▼ Regional Spanish Fine Dining $90-$125 **AAA Inspector Notes:** The dining room's contemporary, minimalist décor is done in shades of white and cream. The eight-course, chef's tasting menu changes regularly. The staff prides itself on professional, attentive service. And of course, the sommelier expertly pairs all courses. **Features:** full bar. **Reservations:** required. **Address:** Blvd Kukulcan KM 16.5 77500 **Location:** Blvd Kukulcan KM 16.5; in Paradisus Cancún Resort. **Parking:** on-site (fee) and valet. D

### THAI LOUNGE     998/176-8070   23

▼▼▼ Thai. Casual Dining. $15-$40 **AAA Inspector Notes:** Dining cabanas and softly-lit palapas spaced for privacy help create a captivating ambience at this restaurant, which has imported Thai chefs and servers to capture a sense of authenticity. Menu highlights include chicken satay, green papaya salad, Pad Thai, and shrimp and chicken curry. The most coveted tables are those situated along the spectacular lagoon front at sunset and should be reserved at least a week ahead of time. **Features:** full bar, patio dining. **Reservations:** suggested. **Address:** Blvd Kukulcan KM 12.5 Zona Hotelera 77500 **Location:** In La Isla Shopping Center; lagoon side of Cancun Island. **Parking:** on-site (fee). D   🔏   🖎

This ends listings for Cancún.

The following page resumes the alphabetical listings of cities in Yucatán Peninsula.

# Destination Caribbean Coast

**T**he Caribbean Coast offers vacationers plenty to do, whether its scuba diving, climbing a pyramid or snorkeling in an underground cenote.

**Y**ou can visit major tourist attractions like the Xcaret and Xel-Ha aquatic parks, or while away an afternoon on little Isla Mujeres, just a short boat ride from Cancún.

© Natchapon L. / Shutterstock.com

© Isabelle Kuehn / Shutter-stock.com

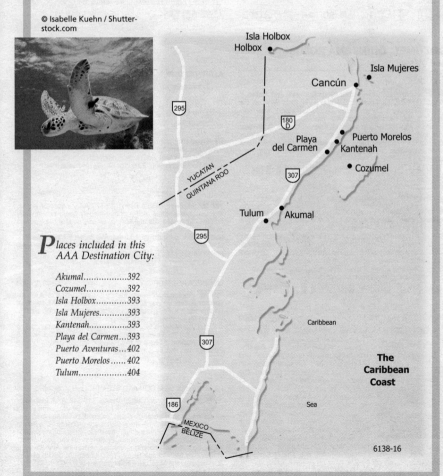

**P**laces included in this AAA Destination City:

The Caribbean Coast

6138-16

# The Caribbean Coast

## AKUMAL, QUINTANA ROO (B-4)

### CATALONIA ROYAL TULUM
984/875-1800

▼▼▼▼
Resort Hotel
$240-$720

**Address:** Carr Cancun-Chetumal KM 264.5 77790 **Location:** Oceanfront. Mex 307 at KM 264.5; on Xpu-Ha Beach. **Facility:** This large all-inclusive adult resort features lavish public areas, modern rooms, excellent service and a wide beach. Guests staying here can choose from standard, deluxe and junior suite rooms. Meets AAA guest room security requirements. 288 units. 3 stories (no elevator), exterior corridors. *Bath:* shower only. **Terms:** 3 night minimum stay - seasonal, age restrictions may apply, 4 day cancellation notice-fee imposed. **Amenities:** safes. **Dining:** 9 restaurants, nightclub, entertainment. **Pool(s):** outdoor. **Activities:** sauna, hot tub, steamroom, motor boats, self-propelled boats, scuba diving, snorkeling, recreation programs, game room, lawn sports, exercise room, spa. **Guest Services:** valet laundry, rental car service.

## COZUMEL, QUINTANA ROO (B-4)
pop. 79,535

### COZUMEL PALACE
(987)872-9430

▼▼▼▼ Hotel. Rates not provided. **Address:** Ave Rafael E Melgar KM 1.5 77600 **Location:** 0.9 mi (1.5 km) sw of ferry pier. **Facility:** 175 units. 5 stories, interior corridors. **Parking:** valet only. **Terms:** 4 day cancellation notice-fee imposed. **Amenities:** safes. **Dining:** 4 restaurants, entertainment. **Pool(s):** outdoor. **Activities:** boat dock, scuba diving, snorkeling, recreation programs, kids club, playground, exercise room, spa. **Guest Services:** valet laundry. *(See ad on inside front cover, starting on p. 378, on inside front cover.)*

### EL CID LA CEIBA BEACH HOTEL
(987)872-0844

▼▼▼ Vacation Rental Condominium. Rates not provided. **Address:** Carr Chankanaab KM 4.5 77600 **Location:** Oceanfront. Adjacent to cruise ship ferry docks. **Facility:** The public areas are open to the sea with snorkeling just a step away. 60 condominiums. 3-12 stories, interior/exterior corridors. **Terms:** 14 day cancellation notice, 3 day off season-fee imposed. **Amenities:** safes. **Dining:** 2 restaurants. **Pool(s):** outdoor. **Activities:** sauna, hot tub, scuba diving, snorkeling, tennis, recreation programs, lawn sports, exercise room, massage. **Guest Services:** valet laundry.

### IBEROSTAR COZUMEL
987/872-9900

▼▼▼▼
Resort Hotel
Rates not provided

**Address:** Carr Costera Sur KM 17.782 77600 **Location:** Oceanfront. At the south end of Carr Costera Sur. **Facility:** This all-inclusive resort at the south end of the island offers a tropical setting with many guest amenities and activities. The guest units are spread out among 48 multi-colored buildings. 306 units, some two bedrooms and efficiencies. 2 stories (no elevator), exterior corridors. *Bath:* shower only. **Amenities:** safes. **Dining:** 4 restaurants, nightclub, entertainment. **Pool(s):** outdoor. **Activities:** hot tub, self-propelled boats, scuba diving, snorkeling, tennis, recreation programs, kids club, playground, lawn sports, exercise room, spa. **Guest Services:** valet laundry, rental car service. *(See ad p. 385.)*

## PRESIDENTE INTERCONTINENTAL COZUMEL RESORT AND SPA
(987)872-9500

▼▼▼▼
Resort Hotel
Rates not provided

**Address:** Carr Chankanaab KM 6.5 77600 **Location:** Oceanfront. 3.9 mi (6.5 km) s of San Miguel on beach road; at La Caleta Yacht Basin. **Facility:** Guests will enjoy the spacious, tropically landscaped grounds with 700 meters of tranquil beach. Rooms feature a private balcony or terrace, most with an ocean view. Snorkeling is steps away. 220 units, some two bedrooms and kitchens. 1-5 stories, interior/exterior corridors. **Parking:** on-site and valet. **Terms:** 5 day cancellation notice, resort fee. **Amenities:** safes. **Dining:** 3 restaurants, also, Alfredo di Roma, see separate listing, entertainment. **Pool(s):** heated outdoor. **Activities:** sauna, hot tub, steamroom, motor boats, self-propelled boats, boat dock, scuba diving, snorkeling, tennis, recreation programs, kids club, playground, game room, lawn sports, exercise room, spa. **Guest Services:** valet laundry, rental car service.

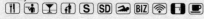

## WHERE TO EAT

### ALFREDO DI ROMA
987/872-9500

◆◆◆
Italian
Fine Dining
$20-$38

**AAA Inspector Notes:** The upscale dining room features floor-to-ceiling plate-glass windows with views of the Caribbean. The signature fettuccine dish is prepared tableside. Occasional live classical guitar music enhances the ambience. **Features:** full bar, patio dining. **Reservations:** required. **Address:** Carr Chankanaab KM 6.5 77600 **Location:** 3.9 mi (6.5 km) s of San Miguel on beach road; at La Caleta Yacht Basin; in Presidente InterContinental Cozumel Resort and Spa. **Parking:** on-site and valet. D

### CARLOS 'N CHARLIE'S
987/869-1647

▼▼ Mexican. Casual Dining. $9-$23 **AAA Inspector Notes:** The Cozumel outpost of this gringo-friendly chain serves tasty burgers, barbecued ribs and shrimp, as well as Mexican favorites such as enchiladas, fajitas and the house specialty, molcajete. **Features:** full bar, patio dining. **Address:** Ave Rafael E Melgar No. 551, LOC BR-2 77600 **Location:** Between Calle 7 and 11 Sur. **Parking:** on-site (fee). L D

### LA CHOZA RESTAURANT
987/872-0958

▼▼ Regional Mexican. Family Dining. $10-$25 **AAA Inspector Notes:** Serving authentic Mexican island dishes, this local favorite offers a fun, casual experience under an open-air palapa. Winning menu choices include fresh ceviche, tasty chile rellenos, fajitas and Veracruz-style fish. Most evenings you'll be entertained by a roving musical trio. **Features:** full bar. **Address:** Ave 10 Sur No. 216 77600 **Location:** 3 blks e of Ave Rafael E Melgar; between Adolfo Rosado Salas and 3rd Sur. **Parking:** street only. B L D AC

### PEPE'S GRILL SEAFOOD AND STEAKHOUSE
987/872-0213

▼▼▼ International. Casual Dining. $15-$42 **AAA Inspector Notes:** *Classic.* An island favorite for nearly 50 years, the eatery specializes in quality steaks, chops, seafood, pasta and more—all with an international twist. Many dishes are prepared table side in a dining room that offers a great view of Cozumel's promenade. A musical trio performs most nights, happy hour. **Reservations:** suggested. **Address:** Ave Rafael E Melgar Esq con Rosado Salas 77600 **Location:** Just s of ferry pier; opposite the Malecon. **Parking:** street only. L D

**SENOR FROG'S**  987/869-1658

▼▼▼ Mexican. Casual Dining. $10-$20 **AAA Inspector Notes:** Part of the chain of Mexican restaurants that also includes Carlos 'n Charlie's, the fun and festive eatery is a great place to eat with the family or rendezvous with friends. The menu is lined with Tex-Mex, American and Mexican favorites, such as chicken wings, quesadillas, fajitas and burritos. After hours, a bar atmosphere prevails. **Features:** full bar, patio dining, happy hour. **Address:** Ave Rafael E Melgar No. 551, LOC AD-1 77600 **Location:** Between Calle 7 and 11 Sur.

L D N

## ISLA HOLBOX, QUINTANA ROO

**AMAITE HOTEL & SPA**  984/875-2217

fyi Not evaluated. **Address:** Ave Benito Juárez Playa S/N **Location:** Oceanfront. Facilities, services, and décor characterize a mid-scale property.

**CASA LAS TORTUGAS PETITE BEACH HOTEL & SPA**
984/875-2129

fyi Not evaluated. **Address:** 20 Oriente Playa Norte **Location:** Oceanfront. Facilities, services, and décor characterize an upscale property.

**CASA SANDRA**  984/875-2171

fyi Not evaluated. **Address:** 40 Oriente Playa Norte **Location:** Oceanfront. On the beach. Facilities, services, and décor characterize a mid-scale property. Here you'll enjoy rustic elegance in paradise.

**HOTEL MAWIMBI**  984/875-2003

fyi Not evaluated. **Address:** 30 Oriente Playa Norte. Facilities, services, and décor characterize a mid-scale property.

### WHERE TO EAT

**BARQUITO BEACH BAR & RESTAURANT**  984/875-2003

▼▼ Mexican. Casual Dining. $10-$40 **AAA Inspector Notes:** On the beach under palms, here's a nice spot to enjoy a laid-back meal of fresh seafood, a frosty margarita or beer, and views of the gulf. **Features:** full bar, patio dining, happy hour. **Reservations:** suggested. **Address:** 30 Oriente Playa Norte **Location:** On the beach; at Hotel Mawimbi. **Parking:** no self-parking.

B L D Ⓚ N

**MANDARINA RESTAURANT BEACH CLUB**  984/875-2129

▼▼▼ International. Casual Dining. $10-$25 **AAA Inspector Notes:** This is the perfect setting for a casual lunch or romantic dinner overlooking the beach and gulf. The creative menu features organic produce and the freshest catch from local fishermen, not to mention excellent baked goods from the in-house bakery. **Features:** full bar, patio dining, happy hour. **Reservations:** suggested. **Address:** 20 Oriente Playa Norte **Location:** On the beach; in Casa Las Tortugas Petite Beach Hotel & Spa. **Parking:** no self-parking.

B L D Ⓚ N

**ROSA MEXICANO**  984/184-1174

▼▼▼ Regional Mexican. Casual Dining. $10-$18 **AAA Inspector Notes:** This small open-air dining room gets crowded quickly with diners enjoying creatively prepared Mexican specialties and fresh-caught local seafood. The friendly staff and unique cocktails make for a lively atmosphere. **Features:** full bar, patio dining. **Reservations:** suggested. **Address:** Tiburon Ballena S/N, Plaza Pueblito 1 **Location:** In Plaza Pueblito, just n of ferry terminal. **Parking:** no self-parking. L D Ⓚ N

## ISLA MUJERES, QUINTANA ROO (A-4)
pop. 16,203

**WORLDMARK ISLA MUJERES**  (998)287-3340

▼▼▼▼ Hotel. Rates not provided. **Address:** Puerto de Abrigo S/N Col. Electricistas 77400 **Location:** Waterfront. Near the airport. **Facility:** 26 units, some efficiencies. 3 stories (no elevator), exterior corridors. **Terms:** check-in 4 pm, 7 day cancellation notice. **Amenities:** safes. **Pool(s):** outdoor. **Activities:** marina, tennis, bicycles, massage. **Guest Services:** valet laundry.

/ SOME UNITS

**HOTEL SECRETO**  998/877-1039

fyi Not evaluated. **Address:** Secc Roca, Lote 11 77400 **Location:** Oceanfront. On north end of island. Facilities, services, and décor characterize a mid-scale property.

**HOTEL VILLA ROLANDI**  998/877-0700

fyi Not evaluated. **Address:** Lotes 15 y 16 Carr Sac-bajo **Location:** Oceanfront. Laguna Mar section of Sac-bajo. Facilities, services, and décor characterize an upscale property.

**ISLA MUJERES PALACE**  998/999-2020

fyi Not evaluated. **Address:** Carr Garrafon Vista Alegre KM 45 77400 **Location:** Oceanfront. 3.6 mi (6 km) s of main ferry terminal; south end of island. Facilities, services, and décor characterize an upscale property. This small couples' resort, located on a white sand beach at the far end of the island, offers a romantic setting for those who want to escape the crowds. *(See ad on inside front cover, starting on p. 378, on inside front cover.)*

### WHERE TO EAT

**PIZZA ROLANDI**  998/877-0429

▼▼▼ Northern Italian. Family Dining. $8-$30 **AAA Inspector Notes:** Focusing on Northern Italian cuisine served in a fun, spirited atmosphere and located within walking distance of the main city pier, the restaurant is a longtime island favorite. **Features:** full bar, patio dining. **Address:** Ave Hidalgo No. 110 **Location:** On Ave Hidalgo walkway, 3 blks e from ferry landing; in Hotel Belmar. **Parking:** no self-parking. L D Ⓚ N

## KANTENAH, QUINTANA ROO

**EL DORADO SEASIDE SUITES BY KARISMA**
984/875-1910

▼▼▼ ▼▼▼
**Resort Hotel**
**$247-$365**

**Address:** KM 95 Carr Cancun-Tulum 77710 **Location:** Oceanfront. In lush Yucatan jungle; between Akumal and Puerto Aventuras; off Mex 307; 20.4 mi (34 km) s of Playa del Carmen. **Facility:** This attractive, adults-only property is located in the jungles not far from famous ruins. Three weekly outdoor events include reggae night, Mexican night and fish market night. Meets AAA guest room security requirements. 380 units. 2-6 stories, exterior corridors. **Parking:** valet only. **Terms:** age restrictions may apply, 3 day cancellation notice-fee imposed. **Amenities:** safes. **Dining:** 8 restaurants, entertainment. **Pool(s):** outdoor. **Activities:** sauna, hot tub, steamroom, self-propelled boats, scuba diving, snorkeling, tennis, recreation programs, bicycles, lawn sports, spa. **Guest Services:** valet laundry. *(See ad on insert, p. 382.)*

ECO ▯ 🛁 Y SD ⌣ 🛗 BIZ 📶 ✕ ▯

## PLAYA DEL CARMEN, QUINTANA ROO
(A-4)
• Restaurants p. 398

**AZUL FIVES BY KARISMA**  (984)877-2750

▼▼▼ ▼▼▼
**Resort Hotel**
**$434-$1070**

**Address:** Fracc El Limonar, Xcalacoco 77710 **Location:** Oceanfront. Fracc Loltun, just n of Playa del Carmen. **Facility:** This large, all-inclusive resort caters to families and offers a variety of room types, including swim-out units. Facilities include multiple pools, a large exercise facility and a gin bar. 480 units, some two bedrooms, three bedrooms and kitchens. 3-4 stories, interior/exterior corridors. **Parking:** valet only. **Terms:** 3 night minimum stay - seasonal and/or weekends, 14 day cancellation notice, 7 day off season-fee imposed. **Amenities:** safes. **Dining:** 11 restaurants, entertainment. **Pool(s):** outdoor, heated outdoor. **Activities:** sauna, hot tub, steamroom, self-propelled boats, scuba diving, snorkeling, tennis, recreation programs, kids club, playground, game room, lawn sports, exercise room, spa. **Guest Services:** valet laundry. *(See ad p. 382.)*

ECO ▯ 🛁 Y 🛗 SD ⌣ BIZ 📶 ✕ ▯

/ SOME UNITS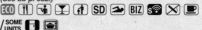

## BANYAN TREE MAYAKOBA                    (984)877-3688

Resort Hotel
$619-$1289

**Address:** Puerto Juárez KM 298 77710 **Location:** Oceanfront. On Mex 307, KM 298 (Carr Federal), 25.8 mi (43 km) s of Cancun. **Facility:** Luxury resort boasts plush guest rooms, private pools, courtyards, and a state-of-the-art spa. Stroll the grounds and enjoy the outstanding landscaping and unique mix of Asian/Mexican architecture. 132 units, some two and three bedrooms. 1-3 stories (no elevator), interior/exterior corridors. **Parking:** valet only. **Terms:** 14 day cancellation notice-fee imposed. **Amenities:** safes. **Dining:** 2 restaurants, also, Saffron, Tamarind, see separate listings, entertainment. **Pool(s):** heated outdoor. **Activities:** sauna, hot tub, steamroom, cabanas, self-propelled boats, snorkeling, regulation golf, tennis, recreation programs, kids club, bicycles, lawn sports, trails, spa. **Guest Services:** valet laundry, luggage security pick-up.

## DESEO HOTEL & LOUNGE                    (984)879-3620

**Boutique Hotel** $135-$145 **Address:** Ave 5A y Calle 12 77710 **Location:** Southwest corner of Calle 12 and Ave 5 walkway. **Facility:** This minimalist-style lodging in the heart of Playa is quiet and sedate during sunlight hours but becomes a local nightspot after dusk. The guest units have a white color palette and unique décor. 15 units. 3 stories (no elevator), interior corridors. **Parking:** on-site (fee). **Terms:** age restrictions may apply, 7 day cancellation notice. **Amenities:** safes. **Pool(s):** outdoor. **Activities:** cabanas. **Guest Services:** valet laundry.

## EL DORADO MAROMA, A BEACHFRONT RESORT BY KARISMA                                    (984)206-3470

**Resort Hotel** $639-$1870 **Address:** Carr Cancun-Tulum KM 55.3 77710 **Location:** Oceanfront. Off Mex 307; in Maroma development. **Facility:** Tranquil and low-key is the atmosphere at this intimate all-inclusive resort. Room types include swim-up units or the original guest rooms in Mi Hotelito. Meets AAA guest room security requirements. 128 units, some kitchens. 2-4 stories, interior/exterior corridors. **Parking:** on-site and valet. **Terms:** age restrictions may apply, 3 day cancellation notice-fee imposed. **Amenities:** safes. **Dining:** 7 restaurants, entertainment. **Pool(s):** outdoor, heated outdoor. **Activities:** sauna, steamroom, self-propelled boats, scuba diving, snorkeling, recreation programs, game room, lawn sports, exercise room, spa. **Guest Services:** valet laundry, rental car service. *(See ad p. 382.)*

## FAIRMONT MAYAKOBA                    (984)206-3000

Resort Hotel
$199-$2200

**Address:** Carr Federal KM 298 77710 **Location:** Oceanfront. On Mex 307, KM 298 (Carr Federal), 25.8 mi (43 km) s of Cancun. **Facility:** Expansive grounds house many pools, gardens and casitas. Some suites have a private infinity plunge pool. Plenty of on-site activities, including a complimentary boat tour through mangrove canals. Meets AAA guest room security requirements. 401 units, some two bedrooms. 1-4 stories, interior/exterior corridors. **Parking:** valet only. **Terms:** 7 day cancellation notice-fee imposed, resort fee. **Amenities:** safes. **Dining:** El Puerto, La Laguna, Las Brisas Restaurant, see separate listings, entertainment. **Pool(s):** outdoor, heated outdoor. **Activities:** sauna, hot tub, steamroom, cabanas, self-propelled boats, snorkeling, regulation golf, tennis, recreation programs, kids club, bicycles, playground, game room, lawn sports, trails, spa. **Guest Services:** valet laundry, rental car service. *(See ad on insert.)*

## FAMILY CONCIERGE AT PARADISUS LA ESMERALDA                                    (984)877-3900

Resort Hotel
Rates not provided

**Address:** AV/Quinta AV Esq 88 **Location:** Oceanfront. 3.1 mi (5 km) s of downtown. **Facility:** Make lasting memories on your next family vacation by staying at this all-inclusive luxury resort with bountiful amenities and personalized service. Some guest units feature private pools. Meets AAA guest room security requirements. 122 units, some two and three bedrooms. 3 stories, interior/exterior corridors. **Parking:** valet only. **Terms:** 3 day cancellation notice-fee imposed. **Amenities:** safes. **Dining:** 12 restaurants, also, Passion by Martin Berasategui, see separate listing, entertainment. **Pool(s):** outdoor, heated outdoor. **Activities:** sauna, hot tub, steamroom, cabanas, motor boats, self-propelled boats, scuba diving, snorkeling, tennis, recreation programs, kids playground, game room, lawn sports, spa. **Guest Services:** valet laundry, boarding pass kiosk, rental car service, luggage security pick-up.

## GRAND HYATT PLAYA DEL CARMEN RESORT   (984)875-1234

**[fyi] Hotel** $155-$750 Too new to rate, opening scheduled for June 2015. **Address:** 1A Ave Esq. Calle 26, Colonia Centro 77710 **Location:** 1A Ave Esq. Calle 26. **Amenities:** 314 units.

**AAA Benefit:**
Members save 10%!

## THE GRAND MAYAN RIVIERA MAYA        (984)206-4000

Resort Hotel
Rates not provided

**Address:** KM 48 Carr Federal Cancun-Playa del Carmen 77710 **Location:** Oceanfront. On Mex 307. **Facility:** This immense property includes multiple theme restaurants including Italian, Asian and Cuban, plus a bar with swinging chairs. In addition, one of only a few permanent Cirque du Soleil venues in the world, offers an amazing live dinner theater show. 750 units, some efficiencies. 3 stories, interior corridors. **Parking:** on-site and valet. **Terms:** check-in 5 pm, 2-7 night minimum stay, 7 day cancellation notice. **Amenities:** safes. **Dining:** 7 restaurants, entertainment. **Pool(s):** outdoor. **Activities:** sauna, hot tub, steamroom, motor boats, self-propelled boats, scuba diving, snorkeling, regulation golf, tennis, recreation programs, kids club, bicycles, playground, game room, lawn sports, exercise room, spa. **Guest Services:** valet and coin laundry, luggage security pick-up, area transportation. *(See ad on insert, p. 467.)*

## GRAND VELAS RIVIERA MAYA            (984)877-4400

Resort Hotel
$610-$1420

**Address:** Carr Cancun-Tulum KM 62 77710 **Location:** Oceanfront. Between Puerto Morelos and Playa del Carmen. **Facility:** Situated on the sugar-white sands of the Riviera Maya, this world class all-inclusive resort offers oversize guest units with exceptional comfort and numerous amenities. 491 units, some two bedrooms. 2-4 stories, interior/exterior corridors. **Parking:** valet only. **Terms:** 7 day cancellation notice, 30 day in season. **Amenities:** safes. **Dining:** 8 restaurants, also, Cocina de Autor, Frida, Piaf, see separate listings, entertainment. **Pool(s):** heated outdoor. **Activities:** sauna, hot tub, steamroom, cabanas, self-propelled boats, scuba diving, snorkeling, recreation programs, kids club, bicycles, playground, game room, lawn sports, spa. **Guest Services:** valet laundry, rental car service, area transportation. *(See ad on insert, p. 377.)*

## GRAN PORTO                    (984)873-4000

**Resort Hotel**
**$174-$892**

**Address:** Ave Constituyentes No. 1 77710 **Location:** Oceanfront. In town; just off Mex 307. **Facility:** A prime beachfront location, a huge pool and an expanded recreational program make this a popular choice. Several room categories are available, including master suites and standard guest units. 287 units. 3 stories, exterior corridors. *Bath:* shower only. **Parking:** on-site and valet. **Terms:** 15 day cancellation notice-fee imposed. **Amenities:** safes. **Dining:** 7 restaurants, entertainment. **Pool(s):** outdoor. **Activities:** sauna, hot tub, steamroom, cabanas, self-propelled boats, scuba diving, snorkeling, tennis, recreation programs, kids club, bicycles, playground, game room, lawn sports, exercise room, spa. **Guest Services:** valet laundry. *(See ad on insert, p. 383.)*

---

## HOLIDAY INN EXPRESS PLAYA DEL CARMEN   (984)206-3434

**Hotel.** Rates not provided. **Address:** Lote 5 y 6 Mz 29 Condominio Playacar 77710 **Location:** Carr Cancun-Tulum, near entrance to Playacar. **Facility:** Meets AAA guest room security requirements. 196 units. 3 stories, interior corridors. *Bath:* shower only. **Amenities:** safes. **Pool(s):** outdoor. **Activities:** exercise room. **Guest Services:** valet laundry.

---

## HOTEL AVENTURA MEXICANA             (984)873-1876

**Boutique Hotel** $114-$280 **Address:** Calle 24 Norte, Mz 55 Lt 10 77710 **Location:** Northeast corner of jct Ave 10 and Calle 24. **Facility:** Attractive garden and pool areas frame this quaint property situated several blocks from the beach. Charming guest units with modest comfort. Beach club privileges. 49 units, some efficiencies. 2-3 stories (no elevator), interior/exterior corridors. *Bath:* shower only. **Parking:** on-site and street. **Terms:** 14 day cancellation notice-fee imposed. **Amenities:** safes. **Pool(s):** outdoor. **Activities:** hot tub, massage.

---

## HOTEL RIU PALACE MEXICO             (984)877-4200

**Resort Hotel**
**Rates not provided**

**Address:** Ave Xaman-Ha, Mz 3 77710 **Location:** E of Mex 307; in Playacar development. **Facility:** The all-inclusive resort offers striking contemporary décor in all areas, modern, well-equipped guest rooms, multiple upscale dining outlets, an excellent beach and pools, plus extensive activities. 434 units. 3 stories (no elevator), interior/exterior corridors. **Amenities:** safes. **Dining:** 6 restaurants, entertainment. **Pool(s):** outdoor. **Activities:** hot tub, steamroom, self-propelled boats, scuba diving, snorkeling, tennis, recreation programs, kids club, playground, game room, lawn sports, exercise room, spa. **Guest Services:** valet laundry. *(See ad p. 380.)*

---

## HOTEL RIU YUCATAN                    (984)877-2050

**Resort Hotel**
**Rates not provided**

**Address:** Ave Xaman-Ha, Mz 3 77710 **Location:** Oceanfront. E of Mex 307; in Playacar development. **Facility:** One of four sister properties located in Playacar, this lodging offers nicely decorated guest units and expansive public areas. There is an array of available activities and an excellent beach. Meets AAA guest room security requirements. 507 units. 3 stories (no elevator), interior/exterior corridors. **Amenities:** safes. **Dining:** 5 restaurants, entertainment. **Pool(s):** outdoor. **Activities:** sauna, hot tub, self-propelled boats, scuba diving, snorkeling, recreation programs, kids club, playground, lawn sports, exercise room, spa. **Guest Services:** valet laundry, rental car service. *(See ad p. 380.)*

---

## IBEROSTAR GRAND PARAISO HOTEL        984/877-2800

**Resort Hotel**
**Rates not provided**

**Address:** Carr Chetumal PTO Juárez KM 309 77710 **Location:** Oceanfront. Hwy Cancun to Playa del Carmen, exit KM 309; in Playa Paraiso. **Facility:** Boasting impressive rooms, the flagship adults-only Iberostar hotel in the Playa Paraiso complex features an ornate Italian theme as well as many all-inclusive amenities and activities. 310 units. 3 stories (no elevator), exterior corridors. **Parking:** valet only. **Terms:** age restrictions may apply. **Amenities:** safes. **Dining:** 6 restaurants, nightclub, entertainment. **Pool(s):** outdoor, heated outdoor. **Activities:** sauna, hot tub, steamroom, motor boats, self-propelled boats, scuba diving, snorkeling, regulation golf, tennis, recreation programs, bicycles, game room, lawn sports, spa. **Guest Services:** valet laundry, boarding pass kiosk, rental car service. *(See ad on insert, p. 385.)*

---

## IBEROSTAR PARAISO BEACH             984/877-2800

**Resort Hotel**
**Rates not provided**

**Address:** Carr Chetumal PTO Juárez KM 309 77710 **Location:** Oceanfront. Hwy Cancun to Playa del Carmen, exit KM 309; in Playa Paraiso. **Facility:** This all-inclusive hotel in the large Iberostar resort complex in Playa Paraiso features Caribbean-influence décor with bright and festive colors. There are plenty of fun activities for the entire family. 424 units. 3 stories (no elevator), exterior corridors. **Amenities:** safes. **Dining:** 7 restaurants, entertainment. **Pool(s):** outdoor. **Activities:** sauna, hot tub, steamroom, motor boats, self-propelled boats, scuba diving, snorkeling, regulation golf, tennis, recreation programs, kids club, bicycles, playground, game room, lawn sports, exercise room, spa. **Guest Services:** valet laundry, rental car service. *(See ad p. 385.)*

### IBEROSTAR PARAISO DEL MAR 984/877-2800

**Resort Hotel**
**Rates not provided**

**Address:** Carr Chetumal PTO Juárez KM 309 77710 **Location:** Oceanfront. Hwy Cancun to Playa del Carmen, exit KM 309; in Playa Paraiso. **Facility:** This all-inclusive hotel in the large Iberostar resort complex in Playa Paraiso features traditional Mexican-Colonial décor and plenty of fun activities for the entire family, including a super-sized pool. 388 units. 3 stories (no elevator), exterior corridors. **Amenities:** safes. **Dining:** 7 restaurants, entertainment. **Pool(s):** outdoor. **Activities:** sauna, hot tub, steamroom, motor boats, self-propelled boats, scuba diving, snorkeling, regulation golf, tennis, recreation programs, kids club, bicycles, playground, game room, lawn sports, exercise room, spa. **Guest Services:** valet laundry, rental car service. *(See ad p. 385.)*

### IBEROSTAR PARAISO LINDO 984/877-2800

**Resort Hotel**
**Rates not provided**

**Address:** Carr Chetumal PTO Juárez KM 309 77710 **Location:** Oceanfront. Hwy Cancun to Playa del Carmen, exit KM 309; in Playa Paraiso. **Facility:** This all-inclusive hotel in Playa Paraiso's large Iberostar resort complex features traditional Mexican décor and plenty of fun activities for the entire family. 448 units. 3 stories (no elevator), exterior corridors. **Amenities:** video games, safes. **Dining:** 6 restaurants, nightclub, entertainment. **Pool(s):** outdoor. **Activities:** sauna, hot tub, steamroom, motor boats, self-propelled boats, scuba diving, snorkeling, regulation golf, tennis, recreation programs, kids club, playground, game room, exercise room, spa. **Guest Services:** valet laundry, rental car service.

### IBEROSTAR PARAISO MAYA 998/877-2800

**Resort Hotel**
**Rates not provided**

**Address:** Carr Chetumal PTO Juárez KM 309 77710 **Location:** Oceanfront. Hwy Cancun to Playa del Carmen, exit KM 309; in Playa Paraiso. **Facility:** This all-inclusive hotel in Playa Paraiso's large Iberostar resort complex features upscale, Mayan-influenced décor and plenty of fun activities for the entire family. 434 units. 3 stories, exterior corridors. **Parking:** on-site and valet. **Amenities:** safes. **Dining:** 5 restaurants, nightclub, entertainment. **Pool(s):** outdoor. **Activities:** sauna, hot tub, steamroom, motor boats, self-propelled boats, scuba diving, snorkeling, regulation golf, tennis, recreation programs, kids club, bicycles, playground, game room, lawn sports, exercise room, spa. **Guest Services:** valet laundry, rental car service. *(See ad on insert, p. 385.)*

### IBEROSTAR QUETZAL 984/877-2000

**Resort Hotel.** Rates not provided. **Address:** Xaman-Ha, Lote Hotelero No 2 77710 **Location:** Oceanfront. In Playacar development. **Facility:** This all-inclusive resort offers many guest amenities and is surrounded by lush foliage that harbors benign wildlife. There's an expansive beach and pool area, plus plenty of theme-dining options. Meets AAA guest room security requirements. 350 units. 3 stories (no elevator), exterior corridors. *Bath:* shower only. **Amenities:** safes. **Dining:** 7 restaurants, nightclub, entertainment. **Pool(s):** outdoor. **Activities:** sauna, hot tub, steamroom, cabanas, motor boats, self-propelled boats, scuba diving, snorkeling, tennis, recreation programs, kids club, bicycles, playground, lawn sports, exercise room, spa. **Guest Services:** valet laundry.

### IBEROSTAR TUCAN 984/877-2000

**Resort Hotel**
**Rates not provided**

**Address:** Ave Xaman-Ha Mz 3 Lote Hotelera 2 Fracc 77710 **Location:** Oceanfront. In Playacar development. **Facility:** This all-inclusive resort offers many guest amenities and is surrounded by lush foliage that harbors benign wildlife. You'll find expansive beach and pool areas, plus plenty of theme-dining options. Meets AAA guest room security requirements. 350 units. 3 stories (no elevator), exterior corridors. *Bath:* shower only. **Amenities:** safes. **Dining:** 7 restaurants, nightclub, entertainment. **Pool(s):** outdoor. **Activities:** sauna, hot tub, steamroom, cabanas, motor boats, self-propelled boats, scuba diving, snorkeling, tennis, recreation programs, kids club, bicycles, playground, lawn sports, exercise room, spa. **Guest Services:** valet laundry. *(See ad p. 385.)*

### MAYAN PALACE RIVIERA MAYA 984/206-4000

**Resort Hotel**
**Rates not provided**

**Address:** KM 48 Carr Federal Cancun-Playa del Carmen 77710 **Location:** Oceanfront. On Mex 307. **Facility:** This large resort complex has several theme restaurant options, including Cuban, Asian and Italian cuisine. Coming to the resort in late 2014 is a permanent Cirque du Soleil dinner theater show. 663 units, some efficiencies. 3 stories, interior corridors. **Parking:** on-site and valet. **Terms:** check-in 5 pm, 2-7 night minimum stay, 7 day cancellation notice. **Amenities:** safes. **Dining:** 8 restaurants, entertainment. **Pool(s):** outdoor. **Activities:** sauna, hot tub, steamroom, self-propelled boats, scuba diving, snorkeling, regulation golf, tennis, recreation programs, kids club, bicycles, playground, game room, lawn sports, exercise room, spa. **Guest Services:** valet and coin laundry, rental car service, area transportation. *(See ad on insert, p. 467.)*

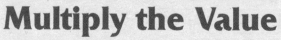

## OCCIDENTAL GRAND XCARET                    (984)871-5400

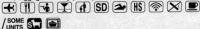 **Resort Hotel.** Rates not provided. **Address:** Carr Chetumal-Puerto Juárez KM 282 77710 **Location:** Oceanfront. Mex 307, KM 282. **Facility:** Adjacent to the world-renowned Xcaret eco-archaeological park, this sprawling all-inclusive resort features river channels, free-form pools, 11 restaurants and a quiet man-made beach with talc-like sand. 750 units. 3 stories, interior/exterior corridors. **Parking:** on-site and valet. **Terms:** 3 night minimum stay - seasonal and/or weekends, 3 day cancellation notice. **Amenities:** safes. **Dining:** 11 restaurants, nightclub, entertainment. **Pool(s):** outdoor. **Activities:** sauna, hot tub, steamroom, cabanas, scuba diving, snorkeling, tennis, recreation programs, kids club, playground, lawn sports, exercise room, spa. **Guest Services:** valet laundry.

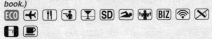

## PARADISUS PLAYA DEL CARMEN LA ESMERALDA
                                                (984)877-3900

**Resort Hotel**
$478-$678

**Address:** Ave Quinta and Calle 12 **Location:** Oceanfront. 3.1 mi (5 km) s of downtown. **Facility:** Bordered by mangroves and an expansive sugar sand beach, this family-friendly all-inclusive resort offers world-class dining, shows and a plethora of activities. Meets AAA guest room security requirements. 370 units. 3 stories, interior/exterior corridors. **Parking:** on-site and valet. **Amenities:** safes. **Dining:** 13 restaurants, nightclub, entertainment. **Pool(s):** outdoor, heated outdoor. **Activities:** sauna, hot tub, steamroom, cabanas, motor boats, self-propelled boats, scuba diving, snorkeling, tennis, recreation programs, kids club, game room, lawn sports, spa. **Guest Services:** valet laundry, rental car service. *(See ad at front of book.)*

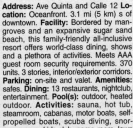

## PARADISUS PLAYA DEL CARMEN LA PERLA
                                                (984)877-3900

**Resort Hotel**
$478-$678

**Address:** Esq 5th Ave and 112 St 77719 **Location:** Oceanfront. 3.1 mi (5 km) s of downtown. **Facility:** Bordered by mangroves and an expansive sugar sand beach, this adults-only all-inclusive resort offers world-class dining, shows and a plethora of activities. Meets AAA guest room security requirements. 272 units. 3 stories, interior/exterior corridors. **Parking:** on-site and valet. **Terms:** age restrictions may apply. **Amenities:** safes. **Dining:** 13 restaurants, also, Passion by Martin Berasategui, see separate listing, nightclub, entertainment. **Pool(s):** outdoor, heated outdoor. **Activities:** sauna, hot tub, steamroom, cabanas, motor boats, self-propelled boats, scuba diving, snorkeling, tennis, recreation programs, playground, game room, lawn sports, spa. **Guest Services:** valet laundry, rental car service, luggage security pick-up. *(See ad at front of book.)*

## RIU PALACE RIVIERA MAYA                    (984)877-2280

**Resort Hotel**
Rates not provided

**Address:** Ave Xaman-Ha, Mz 9 y 10 77710 **Location:** Oceanfront. Off Mex 307, just s of Playa del Carmen; in Playacar development. **Facility:** Marble floors and walls, richly polished wood trim, domed ceilings and chandeliers give this all-inclusive resort's lavish public areas a palatial feel. The pool and beach areas are spectacular. 460 units. 4 stories, interior corridors. **Amenities:** safes. **Dining:** 6 restaurants, entertainment. **Pool(s):** outdoor. **Activities:** sauna, hot tub, self-propelled boats, scuba diving, snorkeling, tennis, recreation programs, kids club, playground, game room, exercise room, spa. **Guest Services:** valet laundry, rental car service. *(See ad p 380.)*

## ROSEWOOD MAYAKOBÁ                          (984)875-8000

**Contemporary Resort Hotel**
$535-$1950

**Address:** Carr Federal KM 298, Solidaridad 77710 **Location:** Oceanfront. On Mex 307, 26.8 mi (43 km) s of Cancún. **Facility:** Built along a network of lagoons and the Caribbean Sea, this resort's suites are strikingly modern in design yet crafted from such indigenous materials as to appear born of the jungle. Meets AAA guest room security requirements. 130 units. 1-2 stories (no elevator), exterior corridors. **Parking:** valet only. **Terms:** 14 day cancellation notice, 90 day in season-fee imposed, resort fee. **Amenities:** safes. **Dining:** 2 restaurants, also, Casa del Lago, see separate listing, entertainment. **Pool(s):** heated outdoor. **Activities:** sauna, hot tub, steamroom, self-propelled boats, scuba diving, snorkeling, regulation golf, tennis, recreation programs, kids club, bicycles, game room, trails, exercise room, spa. **Guest Services:** valet laundry, rental car service, luggage security pick-up, area transportation.

## THE ROYAL PLAYA DEL CARMEN                 (984)877-2900

**Resort Hotel**
Rates not provided

**Address:** Constituyentes No. 2 77710 **Location:** Oceanfront. Downtown; near popular Ave 5 pedestrian area. **Facility:** The all-inclusive, adult-only resort features multiple swimming pools and restaurants as well as an array of activities. All guest units are well appointed with amenities to the hilt. 513 units. 3-4 stories, exterior corridors. **Parking:** on-site and valet. **Terms:** age restrictions may apply, cancellation fee imposed. **Amenities:** safes. **Dining:** 8 restaurants, entertainment. **Pool(s):** heated outdoor. **Activities:** sauna, hot tub, steamroom, motor boats, self-propelled boats, scuba diving, snorkeling, tennis, recreation programs, bicycles, game room, lawn sports, exercise room, spa. **Guest Services:** valet laundry, rental car service, luggage security pick-up. *(See ad on insert, p. 383.)*

## ROYAL SERVICE AT PARADISUS LA PERLA
                                                (984)877-3900

**Resort Hotel**
$478-$678

**Address:** Quinta Avenida Esq 88 **Location:** Oceanfront. 3.1 mi (5 km) s of downtown. **Facility:** This luxuriously appointed property offers guests access to the common areas of three other adjacent hotels. What sets this property apart is the personalized service and extra in-room amenities. Meets AAA guest room security requirements. 122 units. 3 stories, interior/exterior corridors. **Parking:** valet only. **Terms:** age restrictions may apply. **Amenities:** safes. **Dining:** 13 restaurants, nightclub, entertainment. **Pool(s):** outdoor, heated outdoor. **Activities:** sauna, hot tub, steamroom, cabanas, motor boats, self-propelled boats, scuba diving, snorkeling, tennis, recreation programs, game room, lawn sports, spa. **Guest Services:** valet laundry, rental car service, luggage security pick-up.

## SECRETS CAPRI RIVIERA CANCUN   (984)873-4880

**Resort Hotel**
$270-$720

**Address:** Carr Cancun-Chetumal KM 299, Solidaridad 77710 **Location:** Oceanfront. 2 mi (3.2 km) n of Playa del Carmen; just e off Mex 307, follow signs. **Facility:** An all-inclusive resort designed to resemble a Spanish hacienda, it offers upscale public areas, comfortable guest rooms, multiple dining outlets and pool activities in a lagoon-style free-form pool. Meets AAA guest room security requirements. 291 units. 3-5 stories, interior/exterior corridors. **Parking:** on-site and valet. **Terms:** age restrictions may apply. **Amenities:** safes. **Dining:** 6 restaurants, nightclub, entertainment.
**Pool(s):** outdoor, heated outdoor. **Activities:** sauna, hot tub, steamroom, cabanas, motor boats, self-propelled boats, scuba diving, snorkeling, regulation golf, tennis, recreation programs, bicycles, game room, lawn sports, spa. **Guest Services:** valet laundry, rental car service, luggage security pick-up.

## SECRETS MAROMA BEACH RIVIERA CANCUN   (984)877-3600

**Resort Hotel**
$495-$1587

**Address:** Carr Federal 307 Chetumal-Cancun KM 306.5 77710 **Location:** Oceanfront. 10.6 mi (17 km) s of Puerto Morelos; between Puerto Morelos and Playa del Carmen. **Facility:** This oceanfront property caters to upscale travelers with spacious guest units featuring large balconies. Each guest building has its own butler/concierge. 412 units. 3-4 stories, interior/exterior corridors. **Parking:** on-site and valet. **Terms:** 3 day cancellation notice-fee imposed. **Amenities:** safes. **Dining:** 7 restaurants, nightclub, entertainment. **Pool(s):** heated outdoor.
**Activities:** sauna, hot tub, steamroom, self-propelled boats, scuba diving, snorkeling, miniature golf, tennis, recreation programs, bicycles, game room, lawn sports, exercise room, spa. **Guest Services:** valet laundry, rental car service, luggage security pick-up. *(See ad on insert.)*

## VICEROY RIVIERA MAYA   (984)877-3000

**Boutique Hotel**
$605-$2320

**Address:** Ave Fracc 7 Mz 20 Lote 5 y 6 Xcalacoco 77710 **Location:** Oceanfront. Between Playa del Carmen and Puerto Morelos, follow signs; in Princess Hotel complex. **Facility:** Ideal for a romantic getaway, this chic property features individual bungalows scattered about a jungle-like setting. Service is attentive, yet discreet. 41 units. 1 story, exterior corridors. **Parking:** on-site and valet. **Terms:** age restrictions may apply, 14 day cancellation notice-fee imposed. **Amenities:** safes. **Dining:** 2 restaurants. **Pool(s):** heated outdoor. **Activities:** hot tub, steamroom, self-propelled boats, snorkeling, recreation programs, exercise room, spa. **Guest Services:** valet laundry, luggage security pick-up.

## HOTELES CATALONIA RIVERIA MAYA AND YUCATAN BEACH RESORTS AND SPA   984/875-1020

**fyi** Not evaluated. **Address:** Ave Xcacel, Lote 1 **Location:** Oceanfront. In Puerto Aventuras development. Facilities, services, and décor characterize a mid-scale property. Choose the room category to suit your taste at this sprawling resort.

## OCEAN MAYA ROYALE   984/873-4700

**fyi** Not evaluated. **Address:** Carr Federal Chetumal KM 299 77710 **Location:** Oceanfront. Mex 307, KM 299; just n of downtown. Facilities, services, and décor characterize a mid-scale property. All inclusive resort with an array of activities. Guests staying here can choose from six different room categories including junior and honeymoon suites. Balinese beds positioned throughout property.

## PLAYACAR PALACE   984/873-4960

**fyi** Not evaluated. **Address:** Fracc Playacar, Bahiadel Esp Santo 77710 **Location:** Oceanfront. Just n. Facilities, services, and décor characterize an upscale property. All inclusive resort with numerous recreational opportunities and several dining venues. *(See ad on inside front cover, starting on p. 378, on inside front cover.)*

## WHERE TO EAT

### 100% NATURAL   984/873-2242

Natural/Organic Vegetarian. Casual Dining. $8-$20 **AAA Inspector Notes:** Sip on one of the many nutritional beverages made with such ingredients as chaya, spinach, aloe vera and even cactus. The varied menu has a strong vegetarian focus but in addition to the range of salads, soups and ceviches, even one made without fish or seafood, are the Asian-inspired noodle dishes. The knowledgeable staff is well versed in the preparations and the use of ingredients that line the extensive menu. Expect a relaxing ambience. **Features:** beer only, patio dining. **Address:** Ave 5 77710 **Location:** Between 10 Nte bis y 12 Nte bis. **Parking:** no self-parking.

### BIO NATURAL ORGANICS STORE & RESTAURANT   984/267-2208

Natural/Organic Vegetarian. Casual Dining. $7-$14 **AAA Inspector Notes:** This charming little sidewalk eatery offers delightful service in a relaxed environment. Dine here and you will leave feeling healthy because the cuisine centers around organic produce, detox beverages and salads that are sure to wow you. Some menu items have obvious Middle Eastern cuisine influences, such as the falafel and baba ghanoush, but there also is a large selection of quinoa dishes, vegetarian lasagna and a green curry tofu dish. Lunch is served until 5 pm. **Features:** patio dining. **Address:** 126 Calle 26 Nte entre aves 5th y 10th 77710 **Location:** Between aves 5th and 10th; centro. **Parking:** on-site (fee) and street.

### BYBLOS RESTAURANT   984/803-1790

French. Casual Dining. $12-$35 **AAA Inspector Notes:** This very popular and intimate bistro serves an extensive menu of French country cuisine, ranging from the economical daily prix-fixe lunch menu to the more complex à la carte dinner menu featuring foie gras, veal and lamb items in addition to several seafood and vegetarian selections. Service is casual. There's an extensive and well-priced wine list. The property opens at 3 pm, perfect for a late lunch or early dinner. **Features:** full bar, patio dining. **Address:** Calle 14 entre aves 5A y 10A 77710 **Location:** Just off pedestrian area on Calle 14; between aves 5 and 10. **Parking:** street only.

### CANIBAL ROYAL   984/859-1443

Regional Mexican. Casual Dining. $8-$24 **AAA Inspector Notes:** This is a fun, trendy beach club restaurant overlooking the Caribbean. Patrons can stroll in right off the beach for a relaxing bathing suit-and-barefoot meal. There is a minimum per-person charge to obtain a table on the beach. **Features:** full bar, patio dining, happy hour. **Address:** Calle 48 & Mar Caribe 77710 **Location:** On the beach; just n of centro. **Parking:** on-site (fee) and street.

### CARBONCITOS   984/873-1382

Mexican. Casual Dining. $8-$15 **AAA Inspector Notes:** This open-air café, just off the main pedestrian walkway, is a good spot for relaxing and people-watching after shopping. The menu offers a great value for all meals. Cash only. **Features:** full bar, patio dining, happy hour. **Address:** Calle 4 Nte S/N Centro entre 5ta y 10A 77710 **Location:** Between aves 5 and 10; just off pedestrian walkway. **Parking:** no self-parking.

### CASA DEL LAGO   984/875-8000

New Italian. Fine Dining. $19-$46 **AAA Inspector Notes:** The dining room has a chic, multi-level design with a terrace perched over the landscaped grounds and pool. The menu incorporates more than just Italian cuisine and uses many locally sourced products. For lunch there's smoked trout and locally smoked chorizo. Dinner offers such starters as Kobe beef carpaccio and Ensenada clams. The pasta dishes are expertly prepared. Stop by the adjacent lounge before or after dinner as it's an ideal place to enjoy an artisanal tequila or glass of Mexican wine. **Features:** full bar, patio dining. **Reservations:** suggested. **Address:** Carretera Federal KM 298, Solidaridad 77710 **Location:** On Mex 307, 25.8 mi (43 km) s of Cancún; in Rosewood Mayakoba. **Parking:** valet only.

## CASA MEDITERRANEA RISTORANTE ITALIANO
### 984/806-4679

▼▼▼ Italian. Casual Dining. $14-$30 **AAA Inspector Notes:** Tucked into a secret garden, this small intimate open-air restaurant has a loyal following. Featured is fine homemade pasta—including ravioli, bigoli and fettuccine—with a variety of flavorful sauces. Traditional regional entrées, fresh-baked bread and homemade desserts all make for a satisfying and authentic meal. The seasonal open and close dates and hours may vary; call ahead during off season. **Features:** full bar, patio dining. **Address:** 5A Avenida entre calles 6 y 8 77710 **Location:** On Ave 5 pedestrian walkway, between calles 6 and 8; in Marieta Gardens. **Parking:** no self-parking. L D ⊘

## CASA SOFIA
### 984/166-4252

▼▼▼ Italian Pizza. Casual Dining. $6-$12 **AAA Inspector Notes:** Located several blocks from the beach, this restaurant is a big hit with locals and tourists alike. From tossed-in-house pizza to fresh pasta, salads and carpaccio, all dishes are thoughtfully prepared. In a rush? Most items can be prepared to-go, or you can call ahead for pick-up. **Features:** full bar, patio dining. **Address:** Ave Paseo Coba, MZA 3, Fracc Playacar 77710 **Location:** Just w of Coba and 5th aves. **Parking:** street only. L D AC ⊘

## CHEZ CELINE
### 984/803-3480

▼▼ Breads/Pastries Sandwiches. Casual Dining. $8-$10 **AAA Inspector Notes:** This small, authentic French boulangerie and patisserie has a loyal following. Make sure you browse the pastry case to contemplate your after-meal dessert. The open bakery allows you to watch the show. **Features:** beer & wine, patio dining. **Address:** 5ta Ave con Calle 34 77710 **Location:** Jct Calle 34; on pedestrian walkway. **Parking:** no self-parking. B L D ⊘

## COCINA DE AUTOR
### 984/877-4400

▼▼▼▼▼ **AAA Inspector Notes:** Experience the multi-course, inspirational cuisine with a daily changing menu. The artistic presentations and unique, scientific, "molecular" style cuisine creates a very emotional experience. The dapper staff impresses with deft service. **Features:** full bar, patio dining. **Reservations:** required. Semiformal attire. **Address:** Carr Cancun-Tulum KM 62 77710 **Location:** Between Puerto Morelos and Playa del Carmen; in Grand Velas Riviera Maya. **Parking:** valet only. D CALL ⓂM

**Specialty Fine Dining $150**

## CURRY OMM
### 984/873-1516

▼▼ Indian. Casual Dining. $11-$26 **AAA Inspector Notes:** This cozy cafe with distinctive décor inspiration from India is a nice change of pace. The menu offers a bountiful number of curry dishes made with chicken, lamb and vegetables. The dishes are complemented with basmati rice and side dishes of mango chutney. They accept cash only so bring your pesos or dollars. **Features:** full bar, patio dining. **Address:** 10 Ave Sur 77710 **Location:** In Plaza Antigua, just e of entrance to Playacar. **Parking:** on-site (fee). D AC

## DIENTE DE OSO RESTAURANT
### 984/206-1338

▼▼ Burgers. Casual Dining. $11-$19 **AAA Inspector Notes:** If you're craving a burger, here's the place to dine. This is a great spot for people-watching and chatting with the congenial staff while waiting for the burger of your choice to be prepared to your specifications. "Diente de oso" translates into "Tooth of the bear," so most of the burgers are named after bears (think Kodiak and polar). For those on a vegetarian diet there is a quinoa burger. There are various, tempting drink night specials throughout the week. **Features:** full bar, patio dining, happy hour. **Address:** 5th Ave entre calles 30th y 32nd 77710 **Location:** North end of pedestrian walkway between calles 30th and 32nd. **Parking:** no self-parking. B L D AC ⊘ 🐕

## DONA AURELIA
### 984/879-3777

▼▼ Mexican. Casual Dining. $7-$24 **AAA Inspector Notes:** Once you find this restaurant tucked away in a small shopping plaza you will be glad the effort was made. The chef takes great pride in providing a quality experience with authentic Mexican recipes ranging from mole to ceviche. There's also some creativity with a pasta dish à la Mexicana. One popular dish is the tuna prepared with chipotle chile and cilantro. However, the real showstopper is the quail with rose petals prepared in the same style as in the movie "Like Water for Chocolate." **Features:** full bar, happy hour. **Address:** Paseo Xaman Ha Mz 16 Lote 16 77710 **Location:** In Plaza Maya Pakal Playacar. B L D AC ⊘ 🐕

## EL MUELLE CARIBBEAN MARKET
### 984/803-0073

▼▼ Seafood. Casual Dining. $9-$22 **AAA Inspector Notes:** This inviting corner eatery is a great place to savor the freshest seafood around while people-watching from a comfortable vantage point. The Canadian owner/chef really knows his craft after years of honing his skills. The ceviches are outstanding. Highly recommended is the mixed seafood ceviche to satisfy all your seafood cravings. The fish of the day can be prepared fried, grilled or Veracruz-style. For a hearty, savory soup, try the fisherman's seafood soup; it won't disappoint. **Features:** full bar, patio dining. **Address:** 5th Ave esquina Calle 32nd 77710 **Location:** North end of pedestrian walkway; corner of 5th Ave and Calle 32nd. **Parking:** no self-parking. L D AC ⊘

## EL OASIS MARISCOS
### 984/803-2676

▼▼ Mexican Seafood. Casual Dining. $8-$12 **AAA Inspector Notes:** This is the undisputed, go-to place for fresh seafood prepared in a variety of ways using Mexican cuisine techniques and ingredients. Begin with one of the hearty soups or seafood-stuffed empanadas. Entrées range from paella and tender octopus to shrimp prepared six different ways. Fish is served filleted or whole. The decor is whimsical, creating a fun place to linger and relax. Delivery options are available. Open 11 am-7 pm except Friday, Saturday and Sunday when they are open until 8 pm. **Features:** full bar, patio dining. **Address:** 50 Ave Nte, Mz 7, Lote 1 Col. Ejido 77710 **Location:** Between calles 28 Nte and 26 Nte; west side of Carretera 307. L D AC ⊘

## EL OASIS MARISCOS PLAYA
### 984/803-5326

▼▼▼ Mexican Seafood. Casual Dining. $8-$12 **AAA Inspector Notes:** Ideally situated just blocks from the beach, this popular seafood restaurant has a whimsical décor that provides a laid-back ambience ideal for lingering. If you're lucky, you can time your meal outing when the restaurant is stocking their lobster tank with the fresh catch brought in by local fishermen. Over six different types of shrimp dishes are offered as well as seafood tacos and empanadas. The whole fish is sold by the gram and is very tempting. Try the seafood paella for a hearty entrée. **Features:** full bar, patio dining. **Address:** 12 Nte Entre 5th y 10th, Mz 30 77710 **Location:** Center; between 5th and 10th aves. **Parking:** no self-parking. L D AC ⊘

## EL PUERTO
### 984/206-3000

▼▼▼▼ **AAA Inspector Notes:** Overlooking a lagoon and mangroves provides an intimate setting. The chef pushes the boundaries of creativity both in combining specialty ingredients and eye-popping presentations. There is a selection of seafood bar options, including oysters, clams and shrimp. The albacore tuna carpaccio is popular but the steak tartar appetizer has incredible flavor. The entrées include Gulf snook and French-cut veal chop. Some nights local lion fish is an option. Also offered is lifestyle cuisine. **Features:** full bar, patio dining. **Reservations:** required. **Address:** Carr Federal KM 298 77710 **Location:** On Mex 307, KM 298 (Carr Federal), 25.8 mi (43 km) s of Cancun; in Fairmont Mayakoba. **Parking:** valet only. *(See ad on insert.)* D CALL ⓂM

**International Fine Dining $26-$44**

## FRIDA
### 984/877-4400

▼▼▼▼ **AAA Inspector Notes:** Outstanding service, elegant décor and innovative cuisine by Chef Vega create a unique and memorable experience. The gourmet menu provides an excellent opportunity to sample the rich culinary heritage of Mexico. The black bean "cappuccino" is one of the most creative soups you will ever find. To enjoy a multi-course culinary journey be sure to start with an appetizer such as mussels in mole amarillo sauce or the scallops with crispy pork rind. Open days may vary depending on hotel occupancy. **Features:** full bar. **Reservations:** required. Semiformal attire. **Address:** Carr Cancun-Tulum KM 62 77710 **Location:** Between Puerto Morelos and Playa del Carmen; in Grand Velas Riviera Maya. **Parking:** valet only. D

**New Mexican Fine Dining $39-$42**

## FRUTA MADRE
### 984/803-3096

▼▼ Natural/Organic. Casual Dining. $5-$10 **AAA Inspector Notes:** For a healthy change of pace, this colorful café offers a variety of omelettes, creative sandwiches, ravioli dishes and salads featuring organic ingredients. Smoothies and fresh juice combinations are a treat. **Features:** patio dining. **Address:** Ave 10 entre Calle 7, Plaza Paraiso 77710 **Location:** Just n of entrance to Playacar. **Parking:** street only. B L D

### IPANEMA'S BRAZILIAN STEAKHOUSE  984/803-5313
▼▼ ▼▼ Brazilian. Casual Dining. $20-$40 **AAA Inspector Notes:** Diners venturing to this restaurant should come with an appetite as big as Brazil in order to enjoy the bountiful buffet and the more than 20 cuts of meats presented by the roving waiters. Enjoy one of the many fine South American wines with dinner and wear loose fitting clothes so you can eat to your heart's content. The staff is gregarious and engaging. **Features:** full bar. **Address:** Ave 10 Nte esq calle 10 bis 77710 **Location:** On Ave 10, between calles 10 and 12. **Parking:** on-site and street. [L] [D] [LATE]

### KAREN'S SEAFOOD STEAKHOUSE & PIZZA  984/879-4064
▼▼ ▼▼ Mexican. Casual Dining. $10-$30 **AAA Inspector Notes:** A popular place for people-watching, this upbeat spot on the pedestrian walkway has live music daily. The house specialty is shrimp diablo, prepared tableside with flaming flair. **Features:** full bar, patio dining, happy hour. **Address:** Ave 5 77710 **Location:** Between calles 2nd and 4th; on Ave 5 pedestrian walkway. **Parking:** no self-parking. [L] [D] [LATE] [AC]

### LA BARBACOA DE LA PLAYA DEL CARMEN  984/879-4987
▼▼ ▼▼ Mexican. Casual Dining. $6-$15 **AAA Inspector Notes:** Strategically located on an active corner since 1993, the restaurant has a side-street patio. The menu lists popular items, such as fajitas, tacos and quesadillas, as well as a local favorite, tripe soup. The snappy service is comforting in the festive atmosphere. **Features:** full bar, patio dining, happy hour. **Address:** 1 Ave Nte 77710 **Location:** Between Nte 12th and Nte 14th sts. **Parking:** street only.
[B] [L] [D] [24] [AC] [⬧]

### LA CASA DEL AGUA  984/803-0232
▼▼▼ ▼ International. Casual Dining. $14-$48 **AAA Inspector Notes:** This charming restaurant offers rooftop ocean views and a varied menu of European, Mexican and seafood selections. The multi-tiered restaurant features occasional live music, too. A dapper staff is very accommodating and assists guests in navigating the menu, which includes variations of slow-cooked lamb shank, sea bass with romesco sauce, short ribs marinated in dark beer and grouper with a goat cheese sauce. Amazing starters great for sharing include grilled octopus. **Features:** full bar, patio dining. **Reservations:** suggested. **Address:** Ave 5 esq 2 Nte, Col Centro 77710 **Location:** On Ave 5 pedestrian walkway. **Parking:** no self-parking. [L] [D] [AC]

### LA FISHERIA PLAYA  984/147-2543
▼▼▼ ▼ Mexican Seafood. Casual Dining. $17-$21 **AAA Inspector Notes:** After much success in Houston, TX, celebrity chef Aquiles Chavez has recently opened a restaurant in his native country. The décor is bohemian-chic with a tasteful quirkiness. The success of chef Aquiles is no doubt due to his use of the freshest-sourced ingredients combined with his creative twists on classic dishes. The trio of ceviches is a must-try. Also impressive are the whole fried fish, lobster risotto, yellowfin tostadas and the dessert selection. No lunch is served on Monday. **Features:** full bar, patio dining. **Address:** 5th Ave entre de calles 20th y 22nd 77710 **Location:** North end of pedestrian walkway; between calles 20th and 22nd. **Parking:** no self-parking. [D] [AC] [⬧]

### LA LAGUNA  984/206-3000
▼▼▼ ▼ Regional Mexican. Casual Dining. $14-$38 **AAA Inspector Notes:** Dine on the patio overlooking the pool or inside where vaulted wooden ceilings soar above. Foods offered have local flavors, such as prehistoric chicken with chipotle sauce grilled and seasoned as the Mayans did. Prepared using many of the varied chilies found in the countryside, richly flavored sauces enhance your meal. **Features:** full bar, patio dining. **Reservations:** suggested. **Address:** Carr Federal KM 298 77710 **Location:** On Mex 307, KM 298 (Carr Federal), 25.8 mi (43 km) s of Cancun; in Fairmont Mayakoba. **Parking:** valet only. *(See ad on insert.)* [D]

### LA MISSION  984/873-3922
▼▼ ▼▼ Regional Mexican. Casual Dining. $9-$23 **AAA Inspector Notes:** This restaurant has a strong seafood emphasis and is an excellent value. The plentiful multi-course dinner features guacamole, lime chicken soup or dessert in addition to your large flavorful main course. While the eatery does serve lunch, the doors do not open until 2 pm. **Features:** full bar, patio dining. **Address:** 10 Ave Mz 9 entre Ave y 2 Nte 77710 **Location:** Between Calle 2 Nte and Ave Juárez. **Parking:** on-site (fee) and street. [L] [D] [AC]

### LA PARRILLA MEXICAN GRILL  984/873-0687
▼▼ ▼▼ Mexican. Casual Dining. $12-$35 **AAA Inspector Notes:** Plentiful portions of Mexican favorites and a wide variety of grilled meats make this a popular place with travelers and locals alike. The atmosphere is lively, and the second story provides a good spot to watch the action on the busy pedestrian walkway below. **Features:** full bar, patio dining. **Address:** 5A Ave Esq Calle 8 77710 **Location:** On Ave 5 pedestrian walkway at Calle 8. **Parking:** on-site (fee) and street. [L] [D] [LATE] [AC]

### LAS BRISAS RESTAURANT  984/206-3000
▼▼▼ ▼▼▼  **AAA Inspector Notes:** This elegant restaurant features high thatched roof ceilings and an elegant ambience created by glowing candles throughout the dining room. The menu is a fine mix of Latino fusion cuisine with creative and innovative presentation enhancing the dining experience. Starter favorites include Peruvian- and Mexican-style ceviches. Main courses range from Colombian coffee-glazed duck to roasted salmon and pineapple-infused rack of lamb. Opening days may vary depending on hotel occupancy. **Features:** full bar, patio dining. **Reservations:** required. **Address:** Carr Federal KM 298 77710 **Location:** On Mex 307, KM 298 (Carr Federal), 25.8 mi (43 km) s of Cancun; in Fairmont Mayakoba. **Parking:** valet only. *(See ad on insert.)*
Fusion
Fine Dining
$16-$40
[B] [L] [D]

### LAS VENTANAS  984/873-4500
▼▼▼ ▼▼ Fusion. Fine Dining. $125 **AAA Inspector Notes:** A stunningly elegant and chic white dining room awaits your special evening. The waiters are more than just servers, they are dreammakers intent on making your dinner memorable. The multi-course menu changes frequently throughout the year, but the selections are always creative and artistically presented. In order to enjoy the typical five courses, portions are manageable. Entrée favorites include Angus beef, baked sea bass, grilled lamb chops and diver scallops. **Features:** full bar. **Reservations:** required. **Address:** Lote Hotelera No. 6 Fracc Playacar 77710 **Location:** East of MEX 307; in Playacar development; in Occidental Royal Hideaway Resort & Spa. **Parking:** valet only. [D]

### LA VACA GAUCHA  984/803-2084
▼▼ ▼▼ Argentine. Casual Dining. $10-$29 **AAA Inspector Notes:** If you're searching for well-prepared steaks, look no further. Not only is there a huge variety of beef cuts to choose from, the menu is also lined with imported sausage, pastas and gourmet pizzas. If having trouble deciding what cut of beef to order, refer to your place mat's anatomic drawing of a vaca. The service is crisp while a convivial atmosphere prevails. **Features:** full bar, patio dining. **Address:** 5th Ave y Calle 24th 77710 **Location:** North end of pedestrian walkway; corner of 5th Ave and Calle 24th. **Parking:** no self-parking. [L] [D] [AC] [⬧]

### MAIZ DE MAR  984/803-1808
▼▼▼ ▼ New Mexican. Casual Dining. $17-$21 **AAA Inspector Notes:** Another creative concept in dining by famed celebrity chef Enrique Olvera, this place captures the true essence and flavor of Mexican cuisine. The freshest products are sourced locally to create incredible dishes that include a range of ceviches, a lobster burger, and shrimp and pork pozole as well as fish escabeche and an octopus quesadilla. Save room for the floating island dessert made with mango, passion fruit and papaya. It will cap off your delightfully sweet evening. **Features:** full bar, patio dining. **Address:** 5th ave entre de calles 30th y 32nd 77710 **Location:** Between calles 30th and 32nd; in Plaza Cacao. **Parking:** no self-parking. [L] [D] [AC] [⬧]

## MAR DE LAS PAMPAS                     984/803-0765

▼▼▼ Argentine. Casual Dining. $13-$48 **AAA Inspector Notes:** This restaurant on the corner stands out for its obvious romantic ambience set back from the street with attentive service provided by their congenial staff. Make sure to bring a big appetite for the expertly grilled meats with various cuts that will suit most carnivore connoisseurs. If there's no craving for red meat try the grilled tuna, salmon or sea bass. A well rounded wine list is available including many options by the glass. Save room for one of the heavenly inhouse prepared desserts. **Features:** full bar, patio dining. **Address:** 5th Ave y Calle 34 77710 **Location:** Corner of 5th Ave and 34th St; north end of pedestrian walkway. **Parking:** no self-parking.

[B] [L] [D] [AC] [⬟]

## NIKKORI                     984/803-1736

▼▼ Japanese Sushi. Casual Dining. $8-$15 **AAA Inspector Notes:** This Mexican chain of Japanese restaurants is really on a roll, earning a reputation for delicious, well-presented sushi and udon noodle and rice dishes. Sit back with one of the creative beverages as you peruse an encyclopedic menu offering an incredible number of choices. The range of fish includes hamachi, tuna, sea bass and snapper, while seafood choices encompass preparations of shrimp, eel and octopus. **Features:** full bar. **Address:** Ave 10th esquina Calle 32nd 77710 **Location:** Just w of pedestrian walkway; corner of Ave 10th and Calle 32nd. **Parking:** on-site (fee) and street. [L] [D]

## PASSION BY MARTIN BERASATEGUI     984/877-3900

▼▼▼▼ ▼▼▼▼    **AAA Inspector Notes:** Dining here is a
**Fusion**           privileged, unforgettable experience.
**Fine Dining**      From the moment you arrive, you will
**$120**             feel special as the staff guide you
                     through a gastronomic journey. The renowned Chef Berasategui offers here the same exquisitely signature cuisine that made his restaurant in Spain earn so many accolades. The degustation menu features seven-plus courses that will awaken your senses visually, olfactorily and, of course, gustatorily. **Features:** full bar. **Address:** 5A Avenida, Equina Calle 112 **Location:** 3.1 mi (5 km) s of downtown; in Paradisus Playa Del Carmen La Perla. **Parking:** valet only. *(See ad at front of book.)* [D]

## PAVO REAL BY THE SEA               984/135-5559

▼▼▼ Regional Mexican. Casual Dining. $15-$22 **AAA Inspector Notes:** The restaurant's seasonal menu features creative interpretations of regional Mayan cuisine. The freshest of local ingredients result in vibrant flavors. **Features:** full bar, patio dining. **Reservations:** required. **Address:** Carr 307 KM 51 77710 **Location:** Entrance to Maroma. [B] [L] [D]

## PIAF                               984/877-4400

▼▼▼ ▼▼▼    **AAA Inspector Notes:** Luxuriate in the
**French**           romantic setting reminiscent of a 1940's
**Fine Dining**      Parisian cabaret. The French born and
**$27-$39**          trained chef brings his more than two
                     decades of skillful knowledge to create a
                     memorable world class dining experience. From the leek soup with tears of truffles to the sea bass with sea urchin sauce, the outstanding presentations and unique combination of flavors leave an unforgettable impression. The fine cadre of waiters execute service with precision, style and class. **Features:** full bar, patio dining. **Reservations:** required. Semiformal attire. **Address:** Carr Cancun-Tulum KM 62 77710 **Location:** Between Puerto Morelos and Playa del Carmen; in Grand Velas Riviera Maya. **Parking:** valet only. [D] CALL [⬟M]

## THE PUBLIC PLACE                   984/120-3724

▼ International. Casual Dining. $6-$15 **AAA Inspector Notes:** This is a comfy spot to grab a pint and a burger or wings. The rear, uncovered patio is popular on soccer game night with a lot of cheers and booing going on. The menu, at first sight, may seem to have some limitations. But you can expect to enjoy well-prepared, pub-style fare, including fish and chips, Angus beef burgers and bangers with mash. Patrons enjoy the varying beer specials each night. **Features:** full bar, patio dining. **Address:** Ave Aviacion, Plaza Coba 77710 **Location:** Between Paseo Uxmal and 15th Ave Sur. **Parking:** street only. [L] [D] [LATE] [⬟]

## RESTAURANTE NATIVO                  984/147-1753

▼▼ ▼▼ Regional Mexican. Casual Dining. $6-$11 **AAA Inspector Notes:** Situated in two large, thatched-roof palapas, this restaurant specializes in fresh, local cuisine with quite a few vegetarian options. There is an extensive juice menu that includes beet, mango, melon, chaya and papaya. Some of the popular entrées include enchiladas, tacos and various fish preparations. Try the "Nativo," a large platter of tender arrachera steak, cactus, two types of tamales, rice and beans. Locals and tourists alike have been flocking here since 1999. **Features:** full bar, patio dining. **Address:** Ave Benito Juárez S/N, Mz 1 77712 **Location:** Just w of jct of Hwy 307/50 Ave Sur and Ave Benito Juárez; between 55 Ave Nte and 50 Ave Sur.

[B] [L] [D] [LATE] [AC] [⬟]

## RISTORANTE DE BRUNO                 984/873-0553

▼▼ ▼▼ Italian. Casual Dining. $15-$45 **AAA Inspector Notes:** While there may be some mixed reviews and experience with service, the portion size, cost and location of this rustic eatery is undeniably the best for being in the heart of Playa del Carmen. Diners can choose from an array of house-made pasta, pizzas and full-size entrées such as grilled tuna, veal cutlet and swordfish. Often there are times when a minimum per person order is required. There's a good selection of wines by the glass. **Features:** full bar, patio dining. **Reservations:** suggested. **Address:** 5th Ave Nte 77710 **Location:** Between calles 10 y 12. **Parking:** no self-parking. [L] [D] [LATE] [AC]

## ROLANDI'S PIZZERIA PLAYA DEL CARMEN   984/803-4122

▼▼ ▼▼ Italian Pizza. Casual Dining. $12-$29 **AAA Inspector Notes:** This small local chain of pizzerias began with one location in 1979. They quickly became a local favorite and now a tourist sensation. Now offering more than just the 20 different thin crust gourmet pizzas, one with huitlacoche, the current menu features a host of pasta dishes, carpaccio, salads and grilled items. Try the pasta Rolandi a Bolognese-style dish with a touch of habanero, hey you are in Mexico after all! **Features:** full bar. **Address:** Centro Comercial Paseo del Carmen Local 43 77710 **Location:** Centro; south end of commercial pedestrian area. **Parking:** on-site and valet. [L] [D] [LATE]

## SAFFRON                            984/877-3688

▼▼▼▼ Thai. Fine Dining. $18-$30 **AAA Inspector Notes:** This signature restaurant features an open-air atmosphere spread out among three over-the-water decks with views of the mangrove lagoon. This is creative modern Thai cuisine at its best. Guests can enjoy an array of curry dishes and four different types of rice, including jasmine. Start the exploration of the menu with one of the spicy soups or an order of spring rolls. Fish can be ordered steamed or flash fried. Dining here is truly a romantic experience. **Features:** full bar, patio dining. **Reservations:** required. **Address:** Carr Federal Chetumal-Puerto Juárez KM 298 77710 **Location:** On Mex 307, KM 298 (Carr Federal), 25.8 mi (43 km) s of Cancun; in Banyan Tree Mayakoba. **Parking:** valet only. [D] [AC]

## SENOR FROG'S                       984/873-0930

▼▼ ▼▼ Mexican. Casual Dining. $9-$18 **AAA Inspector Notes:** Part of the chain of Mexican restaurants that also includes Carlos 'n Charlie's, the fun and festive eatery is a great place to eat with the family or rendezvous with friends. The menu is lined with Tex-Mex, American and Mexican favorites, such as chicken wings, quesadillas, fajitas and burritos. After hours, a bar atmosphere prevails. **Features:** full bar, patio dining, happy hour. **Address:** Centro Comercial Plaza Marina 77710 **Location:** On the beach. **Parking:** on-site (fee) and street. [L] [D] [LATE] [AC]

## SUR STEAK HOUSE                     984/803-2995

▼▼ ▼▼ Argentine. Casual Dining. $25-$45 **AAA Inspector Notes:** The restaurant specializes in Argentine-style grilled beef, but chicken and fish dishes also appear on the menu. **Features:** full bar, patio dining. **Reservations:** suggested. **Address:** Ave 5 77710 **Location:** On Ave 5 pedestrian walkway, between calles 12 and 14; corner of Ave 5 and Calle Corazon. **Parking:** on-site (fee) and street.

[L] [D] [LATE] [AC] [⬟]

## SUSHICLUB
984/803-2182

▽▽▽ Japanese Sushi. Casual Dining. $7-$17 **AAA Inspector Notes:** This modish corner eatery with chic overtones is just the place to relax in one of their white leather barrel-back chairs to enjoy a mojito or sake while perusing the large menu of sushi options. To whet your appetite, you may want to start with a tempura starter or edamame. The presentations are sure to impress with their eye-popping appeal. **Features:** full bar. **Address:** Ave 10th Mz 61 Lote 7 77710 **Location:** Just w of pedestrian walkway; corner of Ave 10th and Calle 26th. **Parking:** on-site (fee) and street. Ⓑ Ⓛ Ⓓ Ⓛ̲Ⓐ̲Ⓣ̲Ⓔ̲

## SUSHI KEN PLAYA
984/803-5375

▽▽ Japanese Sushi. Casual Dining. $6-$13 **AAA Inspector Notes:** Tucked in a corner, this bright eatery offers an array of Japanese-inspired dishes, including a large sushi menu, teriyaki and udon noodles. There are six different savory soups to choose from as well as five different salads. The tasty gyoza and crunchy vegetable and shrimp tempura are great starters. Special prized sushi rolls on Wednesday and Thursday. **Features:** beer only, patio dining. **Address:** Ave 10 77710 **Location:** Between calles 12 y 14; next to Coco Bongo. **Parking:** on-site and street. Ⓛ Ⓓ

## TAMARIND
984/877-3688

▽▽▽ ▽▽▽
**International Fine Dining**
$22-$105

**AAA Inspector Notes:** This comfortably elegant restaurant prides itself on attentive, personal service. The signature carrot and ginger soup is luscious, but the star of my meal was the deconstructed lemon pie, a unique treat for lovers of lemon desserts. **Features:** full bar. **Reservations:** required. **Address:** Federal Chetumal-Puerto Juárez KM 298 77710 **Location:** On Mex 307, KM 298 (Carr Federal), 25.8 mi (43 km) s of Cancun; in Banyan Tree Mayakoba. **Parking:** valet only. Ⓓ Ⓐ𝒞

## YAXCHE-MAYA CUISINE
984/873-3011

▽▽ Regional Mexican. Casual Dining. $9-$20 **AAA Inspector Notes:** Dine here for a true ancient Mexican experience; both the menu and décor will take you back in time. The stuffed tacos and combo plates are ideal for sharing. Many of the plates take you through a journey of Mayan flavors, and some of the plates are adorned with edible flowers. The exquisitely prepared sauces include a pumpkin seed sauce. **Features:** full bar, patio dining. **Address:** Calle 22 Nte entre aves 5 y 10 77710 **Location:** Just n off Ave 5. **Parking:** on-site (fee). Ⓛ Ⓓ

# PUERTO AVENTURAS, QUINTANA ROO

## BARCELO MAYA PALACE DELUXE
(984)875-1500

▽▽▽ ▽▽▽
**Resort Hotel**
$400-$790

**Address:** Carr Chetumal-Pto. Juárez KM 266.3 Xpu-Ha **Location:** Chetumal Hwy KM 266.6; between Akumal and Puerto Aventuras; 15.6 mi (25 km) s of Playa del Carmen. **Facility:** On the Riviera Maya, this large family resort has plenty of activities to keep all ages busy and happy on vacation. Whether you enjoy shopping, dining or recreation, you will find plenty of options. 756 units. 3 stories, interior/exterior corridors. **Parking:** on-site and valet. **Terms:** 3 day cancellation notice-fee imposed. **Amenities:** safes. **Dining:** 6 restaurants, nightclub, entertainment. **Pool(s):** outdoor.

door. **Activities:** sauna, hot tub, steamroom, self-propelled boats, boat dock, scuba diving, snorkeling, miniature golf, tennis, recreation programs, kids club, playground, game room, lawn sports, exercise room, spa. **Guest Services:** valet laundry, rental car service, luggage security pick-up, area transportation.

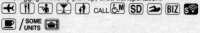

# PUERTO MORELOS, QUINTANA ROO
• Restaurants p. 404

## AZUL BEACH BY KARISMA
(998)872-8080

▽▽▽ ▽▽▽
**Resort Hotel**
$300-$600

**Address:** Carr Federal Cancun, KM 27.5 77580 **Location:** Oceanfront. Bahia Petempich entrance. **Facility:** This resort features upscale appointments throughout and activities for all ages. Of interest is the excellent, well-equipped kids' club. The family suites offer extra child-specific amenities. 148 units. 2-3 stories, exterior corridors. **Parking:** on-site and valet. **Amenities:** safes. **Dining:** 5 restaurants, entertainment. **Pool(s):** outdoor, heated outdoor. **Activities:** sauna, hot tub, steamroom, cabanas, self-propelled boats, snorkeling, recreation programs, kids club, playground, lawn sports, exercise room, spa. **Guest Services:** valet laundry. *(See ad on insert, p. 382.)*

ⒺⒸⓄ ✈ 🍴 🚶 🍸 🏋 Ⓢ̲Ⓓ̲ 🏊 🛝 Ⓑ̲Ⓘ̲Ⓩ̲ 📶 ✖
🖥 💻

## AZUL SENSATORI HOTEL BY KARISMA
(998)872-8450

▽▽▽ ▽▽▽
**Resort Hotel**
$530-$1064

**Address:** Bahia Petempich, KM 27.5 77580 **Location:** Oceanfront. 3.7 mi (6 km) n of Puerto Morelos; 8.7 mi (14 km) s of Cancun International Airport; in Bahia Petempich Complex. **Facility:** An excellent choice for families with young children or teens, this well-appointed resort has a large kids club with its own pool and toys, plus a separate teen lounge, game room and water park. Meets AAA guest room security requirements. 444 units. 4 stories, interior/exterior corridors. **Parking:** on-site and valet. **Terms:** 3 day cancellation notice. **Amenities:** safes. **Dining:** 6 restaurants, also, Le Chique, see separate listing, nightclub, entertainment. **Pool(s):** outdoor, heated outdoor. **Activities:** sauna, hot tub, steamroom, cabanas, self-propelled boats, snorkeling, tennis, recreation programs, kids club, playground, game room, spa. **Guest Services:** valet laundry. *(See ad on insert, p. 382.)*

ⒺⒸⓄ 🍴 🚶 🍸 🏋 Ⓢ̲Ⓓ̲ 🏊 🛝 Ⓑ̲Ⓘ̲Ⓩ̲ 📶 ✖
💻

## DREAMS RIVIERA CANCUN RESORT & SPA
(998)872-9200

▽▽▽ ▽▽▽
**Resort Hotel**
$354-$581

**Address:** Calle 55 SMZ 11 Mz 4 Lote 1-01 77580 **Location:** Oceanfront. 1.5 mi (2.4 km) n of Puerto Morelos. **Facility:** This sprawling all-inclusive resort, reflecting a tropical oasis, offers nine different room categories from which to choose. Many other perks include a world-class spa and gourmet dining. Meets AAA guest room security requirements. 486 units. 5 stories, interior/exterior corridors. **Parking:** valet only. **Terms:** 3 day cancellation notice-fee imposed. **Amenities:** safes. **Dining:** 7 restaurants, nightclub, entertainment. **Pool(s):** outdoor, heated outdoor. **Activities:** sauna, hot tub, steamroom, cabanas, self-propelled boats, scuba diving, snorkeling, recreation programs, kids club, bicycles, playground, game room, lawn sports, exercise room, spa. **Guest Services:** valet laundry, rental car service, luggage security pick-up.

✈ 🍴 🚶 🍸 🏋 CALL Ⓒ̲Ⓜ̲ Ⓢ̲Ⓓ̲ 🏊 📶 ✖
📹 💻 / SOME UNITS 🖥

## EL DORADO CASITAS ROYALE, A SPA RESORT BY KARISMA
(998)872-8030

**Resort Hotel**
$900-$1700

**Address:** Carr Cancun-Tulum KM 45 77710 **Location:** Oceanfront. 5.6 mi (9 km) s of Puerto Morelos. **Facility:** On a 450-acre oceanfront complex, the property offers many room types, including swim-out and plunge pool pool units. Signature gourmet dining adds to the resort's laid-back adult luxury. 205 units. 2 stories (no elevator), exterior corridors. **Parking:** valet only. **Terms:** age restrictions may apply. **Amenities:** safes. **Dining:** 12 restaurants, entertainment. **Pool(s):** outdoor, heated outdoor. **Activities:** sauna, hot tub, steamroom, self-propelled boats, scuba diving, snorkeling, tennis, recreation programs, bicycles, lawn sports, exercise room, spa. **Guest Services:** valet laundry, rental car service, area transportation. *(See ad on insert, p. 382.)*

## EL DORADO ROYALE, A SPA RESORT BY KARISMA
(998)872-8030

**Resort Hotel**
$760-$1400

**Address:** Carr Federal Cancun-Tulum KM 45 77710 **Location:** Oceanfront. 5.6 mi (9 km) s of Puerto Morelos. **Facility:** Stretching over half a mile along the beach, this all-inclusive resort offers spacious rooms, an attentive staff, a wide variety of recreational options and numerous gourmet dining options. 478 units, some two bedrooms and efficiencies. 2-3 stories (no elevator), exterior corridors. **Parking:** on-site and valet. **Terms:** age restrictions may apply. **Amenities:** safes. **Dining:** 11 restaurants, entertainment. **Pool(s):** outdoor, heated outdoor. **Activities:** sauna, hot tub, steamroom, cabanas, self-propelled boats, scuba diving, snorkeling, tennis, recreation programs, bicycles, lawn sports, exercise room, spa. **Guest Services:** valet laundry, rental car service, area transportation. *(See ad on insert, p. 382.)*

## EXCELLENCE RIVIERA CANCUN
998/872-8500

**Contemporary Resort Hotel**
$285-$523

**Address:** KM 328 Carr Cancun-Chetumal 77580 **Location:** Oceanfront. Mex 307, 28 mi (44 km) s of Cancun International Airport; 1.5 mi (2.4 km) n of town. **Facility:** Near the village of Puerto Morelos, this adults-only, all-inclusive resort offers an array of leisure activities. There are six swimming pools and club level accommodations with balcony hot tubs. 440 units. 4 stories, exterior corridors. **Parking:** on-site and valet. **Terms:** 3 night minimum stay, 3 day cancellation notice-fee imposed. **Amenities:** safes. **Dining:** 8 restaurants, nightclub, entertainment. **Pool(s):** outdoor, heated outdoor. **Activities:** sauna, hot tub, steamroom, cabanas, motor boats, self-propelled boats, boat dock, scuba diving, snorkeling, tennis, recreation programs, bicycles, game room, lawn sports, spa. **Guest Services:** valet laundry, boarding pass kiosk, area transportation.

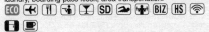

## GENERATIONS RIVIERA MAYA, BY KARISMA
(998)872-8030

**Contemporary Resort Hotel**
$372-$1988

**Address:** Carr Cancun-Tulum KM 45 77710 **Location:** Oceanfront. Cancun-Tulum Hwy; Mex 307 at KM 45. **Facility:** This modern resort concept features 10 different guest room categories that range in size from spacious to over 2,700 square feet. Meets AAA guest room security requirements. 144 units, some two and three bedrooms. 4 stories, interior/exterior corridors. **Parking:** valet only. **Terms:** 3 night minimum stay, cancellation fee imposed. **Amenities:** safes. **Dining:** 5 restaurants, entertainment. **Pool(s):** outdoor, heated outdoor. **Activities:** sauna, hot tub, steamroom, cabanas, self-propelled boats, scuba diving, snorkeling, tennis, recreation programs, kids club, bicycles, lawn sports, exercise room, spa. **Guest Services:** valet laundry, rental car service, area transportation. *(See ad on insert.)*

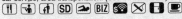

## NOW SAPPHIRE RIVIERA CANCUN
(998)872-8383

**Resort Hotel**
Rates not provided

**Address:** SM 11, Mz 9 77509 **Location:** Oceanfront. Off Mex 307, 1.8 mi (3 km) n, follow signs. **Facility:** This all-inclusive resort's open-air lobby, Mayan theme and beautiful beach/activities area make it a special destination for families. Among dining options you'll find Japanese and French restaurants. 496 units. 3 stories (no elevator), interior/exterior corridors. **Parking:** on-site and valet. **Amenities:** safes. **Dining:** 6 restaurants, nightclub, entertainment. **Pool(s):** outdoor. **Activities:** sauna, hot tub, steamroom, cabanas, self-propelled boats, scuba diving, snorkeling, tennis, recreation programs, kids club, bicycles, playground, game room, lawn sports, exercise room, spa. **Guest Services:** valet laundry, rental car service.

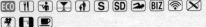

## SECRETS SILVERSANDS RIVIERA CANCUN
(998)193-1800

**Resort Hotel**
$300-$2000

**Address:** Bahia Petempich SM 12, Mz 31 77580 **Location:** Oceanfront. 3.7 mi (6 km) n of Puerto Morelos; 8.7 mi (14 km) s of Cancun International Airport; in Bahia Petempich complex. **Facility:** This luxury all-inclusive, adult only, oceanfront resort offers very spacious suite-style guest units. Gourmet cuisine and live music is a highlight. Enjoy the manager's welcome party on Wednesday. 438 units. 4 stories, interior/exterior corridors. **Parking:** valet only. **Terms:** age restrictions may apply, 14 day cancellation notice, 7 day off season. **Amenities:** safes. **Dining:** 7 restaurants, nightclub, entertainment. **Pool(s):** outdoor, heated outdoor. **Activities:** sauna, hot tub, steamroom, self-propelled boats, scuba diving, snorkeling, tennis, recreation programs, bicycles, game room, exercise room, spa. **Guest Services:** valet laundry, rental car service.

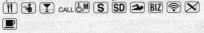

## ZOËTRY PARAISO DE LA BONITA RIVIERA MAYA
(998)872-8300

▽▽▽▽ ▽▽
**Boutique Resort Hotel**
**$508-$2053**

**Address:** Carr Chetumal-Cancun KM 328 77580 **Location:** Oceanfront. Mex 307; Bahia Petempich. **Facility:** The small, secluded resort comprises palatial guest rooms and public areas, a world-class spa and highly personalized service. Meets AAA guest room security requirements. 90 units, some two bedrooms. 2-3 stories (no elevator), exterior corridors. **Parking:** on-site and valet. **Terms:** cancellation fee imposed. **Amenities:** safes. **Dining:** 2 restaurants, also, La Canoa, see separate listing, entertainment. **Pool(s):** heated outdoor. **Activities:** sauna, hot tub, steamroom, cabanas, self-propelled boats, boat dock, scuba diving, snorkeling, tennis, recreation programs, exercise room, spa. **Guest Services:** valet laundry, luggage security pick-up, area transportation. *(See ad on insert.)*

---

**WHERE TO EAT**

### LA CANOA
998/872-8300

▽▽▽▽ ▽▽
**Fusion Fine Dining**
**$30-$45**

**AAA Inspector Notes:** The flavors of North Africa, France and Mexico gracefully collide at this top-notch eatery, making for a dining adventure. Those who are unsure of what to have should ask the chef as he passes the table, and maybe a surprise will be whipped up in your honor. While the menu changes frequently some new items may include foie gras, sea scallops with hazelnut powder, trout with leek sauce and rack of lamb. They are closed on Sunday during the low season. **Features:** full bar, patio dining. **Reservations:** required. Semiformal attire. **Address:** Carr Chetumal-Cancun KM 328 77580 **Location:** Mex 307; Bahia Petempich; in Zoëtry Paraiso de la Bonita Riviera Maya. **Parking:** valet only. *(See ad on insert.)* D

### LE CHIQUE
998/872-8450

▽▽▽▽ ▽▽
**Fusion Fine Dining**
**$150**

**AAA Inspector Notes:** Those fortunate enough to dine here are in store for an unforgettable and emotional experience that will have your senses and imagination soaring. Iron Chef Gomez and his small army of chefs will create magic at your table with more than twenty-five different presentations. Be prepared for a two-hour plus culinary adventure and bring an open mind as well as a good appetite to truly enjoy. This is gourmet fusion cuisine served in refined ambiance with a stupendous waitstaff at its' very best. **Features:** full bar. **Reservations:** required. **Address:** Carr Federal Cancun, KM 27.5 77580 **Location:** 3.7 mi (6 km) n of Puerto Morelos; 8.7 mi (14 km) s of Cancun International Airport; in Bahia Petempich Complex; in Azul Sensatori Hotel by Karisma. **Parking:** valet only. *(See ad on insert.)* D

---

# TULUM, QUINTANA ROO (B-3) pop. 28,263

## DREAMS TULUM RESORT & SPA
984/871-3333

▽▽▽▽ ▽▽
**Resort Hotel**
**$660-$950**

**Address:** Carr Chetumal Puerto Juárez KM 236.7 77780 **Location:** Oceanfront. 3.7 mi (6 km) n of town, off Mex 307. **Facility:** This family friendly, all-inclusive beachfront resort offers plenty of pools, dining choices, beach activities and a nightly Mayan show. 432 units. 2-3 stories, interior/exterior corridors. **Parking:** on-site and valet. **Amenities:** safes. **Dining:** 8 restaurants, nightclub, entertainment. **Pool(s):** heated outdoor. **Activities:** sauna, hot tub, steamroom, self-propelled boats, snorkeling, tennis, recreation programs, kids club, bicycles, playground, game room, lawn sports, spa. **Guest Services:** valet laundry, luggage security pick-up.

---

**WHERE TO EAT**

### CASA JAGUAR
984/155-2328

▽▽▽ Mexican Natural/Organic. Casual Dining. $16-$40 **AAA Inspector Notes:** Dining in the heart of the jungle means that food is prepared without electricity. Walk past your chef at the outdoor brick oven, then into the exotic open-air dining space. Magic fills the air with fresh floral scents everywhere. Eye-popping displays of decorative pottery, hanging lanterns and birdcages create an everlasting impression while a seemingly infinite number of candles light up the night. Specialties include local fish prepared in a banana leaf, ahi tuna tostadas, and fresh ceviche. **Features:** full bar, patio dining. **Address:** Carretera Tulum-Boca Paila, KM 7.5 77780 **Location:** In Zona Hotelera. **Parking:** street only. D

### OSCAR & LALO RESTAURANT, BAR & GRILL
984/115-9965

▽▽▽ Mexican. Casual Dining. $11-$17 **AAA Inspector Notes:** After parking, cross the footbridge and look below to see the myriad of fish. Your jungle garden table, beneath a traditional palapa, is waiting for you just beyond. Each palapa is cooled by tree shade, sporadic breezes and ceiling fans. The cuisine has a strong focus on seafood and all items are made from scratch. Lalo's special is an incredible seafood feast, and the arrachera steak is super tender. Start with the ceviche sampler served in individual shells. **Features:** full bar, patio dining. **Address:** 307 Carretera Federal KM 241 77780 **Location:** 6.8 mi (11 km) n of town. L D

### PIEDRA ESCONDIDA
984/100-1443

▽▽ International. Casual Dining. $8-$20 **AAA Inspector Notes:** This casual gem, on a secluded beach in the center of the hotel zone, features an excellent seafood and pasta menu. **Features:** full bar, patio dining. **Address:** Carr Tulum Ruinas-Boca Paila KM 3.5 77780 **Location:** Beachfront; in Zona Hotelera; in Piedra Escondida Hotel Tulum. B L D

### POSADA MARGHERITA
984/801-8493

▽▽▽ Italian. Casual Dining. $25-$38 **AAA Inspector Notes:** On a beachfront terrace overlooking the Caribbean is this stunning Italian eatery. Enjoy house-baked focaccia, handmade pasta, gourmet pizzas and local fish—all expertly prepared with fresh, organic ingredients. Every inch of the Bohemian-decorated space appears to be highly stylized using indigenous art, potted plants and recycled materials, including old wooden doors and shutters. White-washed wooden tables, and ocean-blue and green vases add to the rustic beach vibe. **Features:** full bar, patio dining. **Address:** Carretera Tulum-Boca Paila KM 4.5 77780 **Location:** Beachfront; in Zona Hotelera. **Parking:** street only. B L D

This ends listings for The Caribbean Coast.

The following resumes the alphabetical listings of cities in Yucatán Peninsula.

## CHICHEN ITZA, YUCATÁN (B-3)

**HOTEL MAYALAND & BUNGALOWS** (985)851-0100
▼▼▼ **Hotel** $114-$714 **Address:** KM 120 Carr Merida-Puerto Juarez 180 97752 **Location:** 6 mi (10 km) s of Cancun-Merida Toll Hwy exit Chichen Itza/Piste. Adjacent to main archaeological area. **Facility:** 92 units. 1-3 stories (no elevator), interior/exterior corridors. **Terms:** 8 day cancellation notice. **Dining:** 2 restaurants, also, Restaurante Mayaland, see separate listing, entertainment. **Pool(s):** outdoor. **Activities:** bicycles, spa. **Guest Services:** valet laundry.

**VILLAS ARQUEOLOGICAS** 985/856-6000
▼▼ **Hotel.** Rates not provided. **Address:** KM 120 Carr Merida-Valladolid **Location:** 6 mi (10 km) s of Cancun-Merida Toll Hwy exit Chichen Itza/Piste. Adjacent to main archaeological area. **Facility:** 43 units. 2 stories (no elevator), exterior corridors. *Bath:* shower only. **Terms:** 3 day cancellation notice, in season. **Amenities:** safes. **Dining:** 2 restaurants. **Pool(s):** outdoor. **Activities:** tennis, game room, massage. **Guest Services:** valet laundry.

**HACIENDA CHICHEN RESORT & YAXKIM SPA** 985/851-0045
[fyi] Not evaluated. **Address:** KM 120 Merida-Puerto Juárez Hwy **Location:** 6 mi (10 km) s of Cancun-Merida Toll Hwy exit Chichen Itza/Piste. Facilities, services, and décor characterize a mid-scale property. Within walking distance of the grand Chichen Itza archaeological zone, this hotel's rooms are spread out among lush jungle gardens. Worth the seclusion.

### WHERE TO EAT

**RESTAURANTE HACIENDA CHICHEN** 985/851-0045
▼▼▼ Regional Mexican. Fine Dining. $11-$35 **AAA Inspector Notes:** In addition to traditional American selections, the menu lists classic Mayan offerings with a modern flair. Seating is offered in the elegant air-conditioned dining room or on the spectacular garden terrace. **Features:** full bar. **Address:** KM 120 Merida-Puerto Juárez Hwy **Location:** 6 mi (10 km) s of Cancun-Merida Toll Hwy exit Chichen Itza/Piste; in Hacienda Chichen Resort & Yaxkim Spa.

**RESTAURANTE MAYALAND** 985/851-0100
▼▼ International. Family Dining. $12-$26 **AAA Inspector Notes:** Located adjacent to the Chichén Itzá ruins, this large restaurant features Mayan dishes such as lime soup and sweet-and-sour pork pibil, as well as empanadas and other specialties. **Features:** full bar. **Reservations:** suggested. **Address:** KM 120 Merida-Puerto Juárez Hwy 97751 **Location:** 6 mi (10 km) s of Cancun-Merida Toll Hwy exit Chichen Itza/Piste; in Hotel Mayaland & Bungalows.

**RESTAURANT LAS MESTIZAS** 985/851-0069
▼▼ Regional Mexican. Casual Dining. $7-$12 **AAA Inspector Notes:** Just a short distance from the world famous Chichen Itza ruins, this spacious restaurant specializes in Yucatecan cuisine. Since 1994, tourists have been coming here to enjoy the well-prepared cuisine using carefully guarded recipes that have been passed down for many generations. Try the panuchos, a crispy tortilla topped with spicy sauce and shredded chicken, as an appetizer. Savory entrées include pavo relleno negro, which is fresh-roasted turkey in a rich, dark sauce made of roasted chiles. **Features:** full bar, patio dining. **Address:** Calle 15 S/N 97751 **Location:** 1 mi (1.5 km) s of Chichen Itza Archeological Zone.

## COZUMEL, QUINTANA ROO—
See The Caribbean Coast p. 392.

## ISLA HOLBOX, QUINTANA ROO—
See The Caribbean Coast p. 393.

## ISLA MUJERES, QUINTANA ROO—
See The Caribbean Coast p. 393.

## IZAMAL, YUCATÁN (B-3) pop. 25,980

**KINICH KAKMO** 988/954-0489
▼▼ Regional Mexican. Casual Dining. $8-$11 **AAA Inspector Notes:** Within walking distance of the pyramid that bears its name, this local favorite is well known for its Yucatecan and Mayan specialties. Attentive servers dressed in traditional attire are knowledgeable about their native cuisine, which includes a variety of chicken and pork entrées as well as a dish featuring venison that's cooked in an underground pit. **Features:** full bar. **Address:** Calle 27 No. 299A **Location:** 1 blk s of Kinich Kakmo Pyramid.

## KANTENAH, QUINTANA ROO—
See The Caribbean Coast p. 393.

## MÉRIDA, YUCATÁN (B-2) pop. 830,732
• Restaurants p. 407

**CASA AZUL HOTEL MONUMENTO HISTORICO** (999)925-5016
▼▼▼▼ Historic Boutique Country Inn $250-$350 **Address:** 347 Calle 60 entre 37 y 35 97000 **Location:** Center; between 35 and 37 sts. **Facility:** This property is an oasis of opulence among the historical streets of Merida. The décor reflects the romance of a bygone era. Elegantly appointed guest units are named after various local barrios. 11 units. 1 story, exterior corridors. **Parking:** valet only. **Terms:** age restrictions may apply, 60 day cancellation notice-fee imposed. **Amenities:** safes. **Pool(s):** outdoor. **Activities:** in-room exercise equipment. **Guest Services:** valet laundry.

**DEL GOBERNADOR HOTEL** (999)930-4141
▼▼ Hotel $60-$84 **Address:** 535 Calle 59 97000 **Location:** 3 blks w of Plaza Grande; jct calles 59 and 66. **Facility:** 86 units. 3 stories (no elevator), exterior corridors. **Pool(s):** outdoor. **Guest Services:** valet laundry.

**FIESTA AMERICANA MERIDA** (999)942-1111
▼▼▼▼ Hotel $145-$285 **Address:** Paseo de Monteo No. 451 97000 **Location:** Paseo de Montejo at Ave Colon; 0.6 mi (1 km) n of main plaza. Located facing historico Paseo de Montejo. **Facility:** You will love the refined atmosphere of the striking atrium lobby and beautiful large pool/terrace with adjacent kids club offered at this elegant, full-service hotel. Meets AAA guest room security requirements. 350 units. 5 stories, interior corridors. *Bath:* shower only. **Parking:** on-site and valet. **Terms:** cancellation fee imposed. **Amenities:** safes. **Dining:** 2 restaurants. **Pool(s):** outdoor. **Activities:** sauna, hot tub, tennis, kids club, exercise room, spa. **Guest Services:** valet laundry.

**FIESTA INN MERIDA** (999)964-3500
▼▼▼ Hotel $83-$185 **Address:** Calle 5B No. 290A x 20A y 60, Col Revolucion 97204 **Location:** Across from convention center. **Facility:** Meets AAA guest room security requirements. 166 units. 10 stories, interior corridors. **Amenities:** safes. **Pool(s):** outdoor. **Activities:** hot tub, exercise room. **Guest Services:** valet laundry.

## HOLIDAY INN EXPRESS MERIDA (999)964-2200

▼▼▼ **Hotel** $65-$105 **Address:** Calle 20A No. 300-A por Calle 5A, Col. Xcumpich 97204 **Location:** Adjacent to convention center. **Facility:** Meets AAA guest room security requirements. 125 units. 7 stories, interior corridors. *Bath:* shower only. **Amenities:** safes. **Pool(s):** outdoor. **Activities:** limited exercise equipment. **Guest Services:** valet laundry, area transportation.

[icons]

## HOLIDAY INN MERIDA (999)942-8800

▼▼▼ **Hotel** $78-$145 **Address:** Ave Colon 498 97000 **Location:** 0.6 mi (1 km) n of Plaza Grande, jct Calle 60 and Ave Colon; just off Paseo de Montejo. **Facility:** 213 units. 5 stories, interior corridors. **Parking:** on-site and valet. **Amenities:** safes. **Dining:** La Veranda, see separate listing, entertainment. **Pool(s):** outdoor. **Activities:** kids club, exercise room. **Guest Services:** valet laundry.

[icons]

## HOTEL CASA DEL BALAM (999)924-8844

▼▼ **Historic Hotel** $100-$180 **Address:** Calle 60 No. 488 97000 **Location:** 2 blks n of Plaza Grande, jct calles 60 and 57. **Facility:** Simple yet distinguished, this is another of Merida's classic colonial-style hotels with an interior courtyard/pool area, traditional Mayan cuisine and a friendly staff. 51 units. 6 stories, exterior corridors. **Amenities:** *Some:* safes. **Pool(s):** outdoor. **Guest Services:** valet laundry.

[icons]

## HOTEL EL CONQUISTADOR (999)940-6400

▼▼▼ **Hotel** $62-$130 **Address:** Paseo de Montejo No. 458 97000 **Location:** Just s of Calle 33. **Facility:** 157 units. 8 stories, interior corridors. **Amenities:** safes. **Pool(s):** outdoor. **Activities:** exercise room. **Guest Services:** valet laundry.

[icons]

## HOTEL PRESIDENTE INTERCONTINENTAL VILLA MERCEDES (999)942-9000

▼▼▼▼ **Historic Boutique Hotel** $110-$185 **Address:** Ave Colon 500 97000 **Location:** 0.6 mi (1 km) n of main plaza; jct Calle 60 and Ave Colon; just off Paseo de Montejo. **Facility:** Treat yourself to this ornate and upscale lodging, at one time a French Embassy. The whimsical, soft-pink exterior, upscale pool courtyard, and refined atmosphere are the highlights here. 127 units. 5 stories, interior corridors. **Parking:** on-site and valet. **Amenities:** safes. **Pool(s):** outdoor. **Activities:** exercise room, massage. **Guest Services:** valet laundry.

[icons]

## HOTEL RESIDENCIAL (999)924-3099

▼▼ **Hotel** $50-$83 **Address:** Calle 59 No. 589 97000 **Location:** 7 blks w of Plaza Grande; jct calles 59 and 76. **Facility:** 66 units. 5 stories, exterior corridors. **Pool(s):** outdoor. **Guest Services:** valet laundry.

[icons]

## HYATT REGENCY MERIDA (999)942-1234

▼▼▼ **Hotel** $85-$190

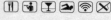

**AAA Benefit:** Members save 10%!

**Address:** Calle 60 No. 344 97000 **Location:** 0.6 mi (1 km) n of main plaza; jct Calle 60 and Ave Colon; just off Paseo de Montejo. **Facility:** 289 units. 17 stories, interior corridors. **Parking:** on-site and valet. **Terms:** 3 day cancellation notice-fee imposed. **Amenities:** safes. **Dining:** Amuza Restaurant, see separate listing. **Pool(s):** outdoor. **Activities:** hot tub, tennis, exercise room. **Guest Services:** valet laundry.

[icons]

## LA HACIENDA XCANATUN CASA DE PIEDRA (999)930-2140

▼▼▼ ▼▼▼ **Historic Country Inn** $260-$310 **Address:** KM 12 Calle 20 S/N, por 19 y 19A **Location:** Just e of Mex 261 at KM 12 Merida-Progreso Hwy, follow signs. Located in Xcanatun hamlet; 0.6 mi (1 km) n of city loop. **Facility:** The beautifully restored former hacienda features Mayan relics, lush gardens and luxurious accommodations in the midst of a quaint hamlet. Visits have been made by Presidents Clinton and Bush. Meets AAA guest room security requirements. 18 units. 1-2 stories (no elevator), exterior corridors. **Terms:** 14 day cancellation notice, in season. **Amenities:** safes. **Pool(s):** outdoor. **Activities:** spa. **Guest Services:** valet laundry.

[icons]

## LA MISION DE FRAY DIEGO (999)924-1111

▼▼ ▼▼ **Country Inn** $162-$237 **Address:** Calle 61 No. 524 97000 **Location:** 2 blks w of Plaza Grande; between calles 64 and 66. **Facility:** 26 units. 1-3 stories (no elevator), exterior corridors. **Parking:** on-site and valet. **Amenities:** safes. **Guest Services:** valet laundry.

[icons]

## ROSAS AND XOCOLATE (999)924-2992

▼▼▼ ▼▼▼ **Boutique Contemporary Hotel** $235-$695 **Address:** Paseo de Montejo 480 y 41 97000 **Location:** Jct Calle 41. **Facility:** Spectacularly contemporary and intimate hotel on the beautiful Paseo de Montejo wows guests with funky amenities including outdoor tubs. Take time to relax by the gorgeous courtyard pool. 17 units. 3 stories (no elevator), exterior corridors. **Parking:** valet and street only. **Amenities:** safes. **Dining:** The Restaurant at Rosas and Xocolate, see separate listing. **Pool(s):** heated outdoor. **Activities:** exercise room, spa. **Guest Services:** valet laundry.

[icons]

Remember, car seats, booster seats and seat belts save lives

## WYNDHAM MERIDA
(999)286-3333

Boutique
Contemporary
Hotel
$72-$115

**Address:** Ave Colon and Calle 6 97000 **Location:** Jct Ave Colon and Calle 6. Located in an upscale area. **Facility:** Opened in 2013, this is a spectacularly contemporary hotel with beautiful marble floors, captivating artwork, a serene pool courtyard area, humongous mattresses and a nine-piece bath amenity package. Meets AAA guest room security requirements. 100 units. 3 stories, exterior corridors. **Amenities:** safes. **Pool(s):** outdoor. **Activities:** hot tub, exercise room. **Guest Services:** valet laundry.

### WHERE TO EAT

## AMUZA RESTAURANT
999/942-1234

Small Plates. Fine Dining. $18-$30 **AAA Inspector Notes:** This chic and contemporary dining room allows guests to watch the chefs in the bustling kitchen as they prepare the food. This is a great place to go with friends and to share dishes. **Features:** full bar. **Reservations:** suggested. **Address:** Calle 60 No. 344 97000 **Location:** 0.6 mi (1 km) n of main plaza; jct Calle 60 and Ave Colon; just off Paseo de Montejo; in Hyatt Regency Merida. **Parking:** on-site and valet.

## HACIENDA TEYA RESTAURANTE
999/988-0800

Regional Mexican. Casual Dining. $10-$22 **AAA Inspector Notes:** *Historic.* This restored henequen hacienda, built in 1683, has rustic furnishings and specializes in Mayan cuisine. The well-prepared entrées include spicy turkey escabeche, crunchy panuchos and cochinita pibil, a slow-roasted pork dish. If you are lucky you may spot one of the several peacocks and deer that roam the grounds. The property is open from 11 am to 6 pm. **Features:** full bar. **Reservations:** suggested. **Address:** KM 12.5 Carr Merida-Cancun 97000 **Location:** 7.8 mi (12.5 km) e of Merida; Merida-Cancun Hwy, just n, follow signs; in Village of Teya.

## LA CHAYA MAYA
999/928-4780

Regional Mexican. Casual Dining. $5-$10 **AAA Inspector Notes:** This small restaurant is popular with locals and tourists. The Mayan medicinal plant Chaya is featured in many of the traditional Yucatan menu items. Portions are large and well-priced. **Features:** beer & wine. **Address:** Calle 62 No. 481 97000 **Location:** Jct calles 62 and 57, 3 blks ne of Plaza Principal; in Centro Historico. **Parking:** on-site (fee).

## LA PIGUA
999/920-3605

Regional Seafood. Casual Dining. $12-$25 **AAA Inspector Notes:** Widely varied fresh seafood is prepared using both classic and innovative approaches. The attentive service staff is knowledgeable. **Features:** full bar. **Reservations:** suggested. **Address:** Calle Cupules No. 505 97000 **Location:** 2 blks w of Fiesta Americana Merida; at Ave Cupules and Calle 35.

## LA VERANDA
999/942-8800

Regional Mexican. Family Dining. $8-$18 **AAA Inspector Notes:** Undecided diners will find a varied choice of Yucatecan dishes and traditional Mexican favorites, which can be chosen from the bountiful breakfast and lunch buffets or ordered a la carte. **Features:** full bar, patio dining. **Address:** Ave Colon 498 97127 **Location:** 0.6 mi (1 km) n of Plaza Grande; jct Calle 60 and Ave Colon, just off Paseo de Montejo; in Holiday Inn Merida. **Parking:** on-site and valet.

## LOS ALMENDROS
999/928-5459

Regional Mexican. Family Dining. $7-$15 **AAA Inspector Notes:** Classic Yucatan cuisine includes pibil-style dishes, fried plantains, pork and chicken marinated in citrus fruits. A favorite choice is a plate of tender, oversized tamales wrapped in banana leaves. Leon beer is popular. **Features:** full bar. **Address:** Calle 50A No. 493 97000 **Location:** 5 blks s of Plaza Grande, jct Calle 57; between calles 57 and 59; adjacent to Museo de Arte Popular de Yucatan and across Parque de la Mejorada.

## OLIVA KITCHEN & BAR
999/923-2248

Italian. Casual Dining. $8-$18 **AAA Inspector Notes:** Be prepared to wait for a table in this teeny dining room, but it's worth it. On the menu you'll find handcrafted pasta, homemade bread and daily specials made with the freshest of ingredients. **Features:** beer & wine. **Address:** Calles 49 y 56, Centro 97000 **Location:** In Centro Historico. **Parking:** no self-parking.

## PANCHO'S RESTAURANT AND PATIO BAR
999/923-0942

Mexican. Casual Dining. $10-$35 **AAA Inspector Notes:** This open-air restaurant, just off the main plaza, offers an excellent selection of regional specialties in a relaxed, lush atmosphere. **Features:** full bar. **Address:** Calle 59 No. 509 97000 **Location:** 1 blk n of main plaza; between aves 60 and 62. **Parking:** no self-parking.

## PORTICO DEL PEREGRINO
999/928-6163

International. Casual Dining. $10-$18 **AAA Inspector Notes:** Situated in a romantic Spanish colonial mansion, this casual restaurant with fine dining undertones is an oasis among the busy streets of Merida. The menu offers a nice blend of Spanish, Mayan and Italian cuisines. Lime soup or ceviche make for excellent starters before moving on to an entree such as red snapper, steak or pork chops. In addition to indoor seating, there are two courtyards for dining al fresco. **Features:** full bar. **Address:** Calle 57 No. 501 por 60 y 62 97000 **Location:** Between calles 60 and 62; downtown Centro Historico. **Parking:** on-site (fee).

## THE RESTAURANT AT ROSAS AND XOCOLATE
999/924-2992

International. Fine Dining. $12-$35 **AAA Inspector Notes:** This trendy, upscale bistro is popular with the lunchtime business crowd and a favorite spot for a dressed-up dinner date. The chef showcases creative interpretations of Yucatecan cuisine on the seasonal menu. **Features:** full bar. **Reservations:** suggested. **Address:** Paseo de Montejo 480 97000 **Location:** Jct Calle 41; in Rosas and Xocolate.

## PLAYA DEL CARMEN, QUINTANA ROO—See The Caribbean Coast p. 393.


## PUERTO AVENTURAS, QUINTANA ROO—See The Caribbean Coast p. 402.


## PUERTO MORELOS, QUINTANA ROO—
See The Caribbean Coast p. 402.


## SANTA ROSA, YUCATÁN

### HACIENDA SANTA ROSA                     999/923-1923

THE LUXURY COLLECTION
*Hotels & Resorts*
Classic Historic Country Inn
$470-$650

**AAA Benefit:** Members save up to 15%, plus Starwood Preferred Guest® benefits!

**Address:** KM 129 Carr Merida Campeche **Location:** Mex 180, 25.2 mi (42 km) w, exit Maxcanu/Halacho, 2.5 mi (4 km) w, 3 mi (5 km) n at fork, then 0.6 mi (1 km) e through village of Santa Rosa de Lima. Located deep in the Yucatan jungle. **Facility:** This beautifully restored, hacienda features upscale accommodations and modern, spacious rooms with antique décor. The unique, signature swimming pool was once a storage tank for the sisal factory. 11 units. 1 story, exterior corridors. **Parking:** valet only. **Amenities:** safes. **Pool(s):** outdoor. **Activities:** bicycles, game room, trails, spa. **Guest Services:** valet laundry.

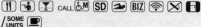


## TEMOZON, YUCATÁN pop. 14,801

### HACIENDA TEMOZON                     999/923-8089

THE LUXURY COLLECTION
*Hotels & Resorts*
Classic Historic Country Inn
$470-$650

**AAA Benefit:** Members save up to 15%, plus Starwood Preferred Guest® benefits!

**Address:** KM 182 Carr Merida-Uxmal 97825 **Location:** Off Mex 261, Merida-Uxmal Hwy, just n at KM 182 (Hacienda Temozon sign), then 5 mi (8 km) n and through the village of Temozon Sur. **Facility:** The beautifully restored ex-hacienda features spacious rooms, lush gardens and luxurious accommodations in the heart of the Yucatan. A massage in the underground cenote is an exotic treat. 28 units. 1 story, exterior corridors. **Parking:** valet only. **Amenities:** safes. **Dining:** Restaurante Hacienda Temozon, see separate listing. **Pool(s):** outdoor. **Activities:** bicycles, game room, spa. **Guest Services:** valet laundry.

### RESTAURANTE HACIENDA TEMOZON          999/923-8089

Regional Mexican. Fine Dining. $10-$30 **AAA Inspector Notes:** This secluded restaurant overlooks the lush gardens of world-famous Hacienda Temozon and serves authentic Yucatecan dishes. Attentive service. **Features:** full bar. **Reservations:** suggested. **Address:** KM 183 Carr Merida-Uxmal 77780 **Location:** Off Mex 261, Merida-Uxmal Hwy, just n at KM 182 (Hacienda Temozon sign), then 5 mi (8 km) n and through the village of Temozon Sur; in Hacienda Temozon.

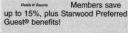


## TIXKOKOB, YUCATÁN pop. 17,176

### HACIENDA SAN JOSE                     999/924-1333

THE LUXURY COLLECTION
*Hotels & Resorts*
Classic Historic Country Inn
$470-$650

**AAA Benefit:** Members save up to 15%, plus Starwood Preferred Guest® benefits!

**Address:** KM 30 Carr Tixkokob-Tekanto 97470 **Location:** 8.7 mi (14 km) s on Carretera to Motul/Cacalchen, just e at KM 30 marker (Hacienda San Jose Cholul sign), 1.2 mi (2 km) on unpaved drive. Located deep in the Yucatan jungle. **Facility:** This beautifully restored hacienda, located in the lush jungle of the Mayan Yucatan, offers modern, spacious rooms with unique, individual décor including jungle showers and outdoor whirlpool bathtubs. 15 units, some cottages. 1 story, exterior corridors. *Bath:* shower only. **Amenities:** safes. **Pool(s):** outdoor. **Activities:** bicycles, trails, spa. **Guest Services:** valet laundry.

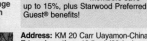


## TULUM, QUINTANA ROO—
See The Caribbean Coast p. 404.


## UAYAMÓN, YUCATÁN

### HACIENDA UAYAMON                     981/813-0530

THE LUXURY COLLECTION
*Hotels & Resorts*
Historic Vintage Country Inn
$540-$730

**AAA Benefit:** Members save up to 15%, plus Starwood Preferred Guest® benefits!

**Address:** KM 20 Carr Uayamon-China-Edzna **Location:** 12.5 mi (20 km) e of Campeche-Merida Hwy 180 exit Edzna-Uayamon, 6.2 mi (10 km) s, then 5 mi (8 km) w, follow signs. **Facility:** In the heart of the Yucatan, this beautifully restored ex-hacienda features lush gardens and luxurious rooms; some units with private outdoor tub. 12 units. 1 story, exterior corridors. **Amenities:** safes. **Dining:** La Casa Principal, see separate listing. **Pool(s):** outdoor. **Activities:** bicycles, spa. **Guest Services:** valet laundry.

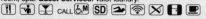

## WHERE TO EAT

### LA CASA PRINCIPAL

981/813-0530

International
Fine Dining
$19-$28

**AAA Inspector Notes:** Situated in the refined setting of the main house, guests can choose to dine on the large veranda or in the well-appointed interior. Knowledgeable servers provide attentive service. Favorite starters are the mixed seafood seviche or the sopa cuatro milpas. Besides a few pasta dishes there is the marinated flank steak stuffed with Dutch cheese or the cobia fish filet steamed in a banana leaf with shrimp, octopus and mussels. The orange blossom crème brûlée is a delightful sweet treat. **Features:** full bar, patio dining. **Reservations:** suggested. **Address:** KM 20 Carr Uayamon-China-Edzna **Location:** 12.5 mi (20 km) e of Campeche-Merida Hwy 180 exit Edzna-Uayamon, 6.2 mi (10 km) s, then 5 mi (8 km) w, follow signs; in Hacienda Uayamon.

B L D 🅧 🔖

### UXMAL, YUCATÁN (B-2)

THE LODGE AT UXMAL

(997)976-2031

♦♦♦ **Boutique Country Inn** $175-$222 **Address:** Mex 261 **Location:** 51.3 mi (85.5 km) s of Merida. Located at main entrance to archaeological zone. **Facility:** Handmade furniture and stained-glass windows reveal a Mayan theme at this property located at the Uxmal ruins. Some units have a traditional thatched ceiling. 40 units. 2 stories (no elevator), exterior corridors. **Terms:** 5 day cancellation notice. **Pool(s):** outdoor. **Activities:** massage. **Guest Services:** valet laundry.

🍴 🛁 🍸 🏊 BIZ 📶 ✕ 🎦 📦 📠

### VALLADOLID, YUCATÁN (B-3) pop. 74,217

EL MESON DEL MARQUES

(985)856-2073

♦♦♦ **Hotel** $68-$204 **Address:** Calle 39 No. 203 Col Centro 97780 **Location:** Between calles 40 and 42, facing the cathedral. **Facility:** Meets AAA guest room security requirements. 82 units. 4 stories (no elevator), exterior corridors. **Terms:** 7 day cancellation notice. **Amenities:** safes. **Pool(s):** outdoor. **Guest Services:** valet laundry.

✈ 🍴 🛁 🍸 SD 🏊 📶 / SOME UNITS 📦 📠

## WHERE TO EAT

RESTAURANTE EL ATRIO DEL MAYAB

985/856-2394

♦♦ Regional Mexican. Casual Dining. $6-$20 **AAA Inspector Notes:** In the heart of downtown, this gourmet restaurant's menu has strong, regional cuisine influences with many Mayan favorites such as poc chuc, cochinita pibil and Valladolid longaniza (a type of sausage). Start your feast off with the cream of chaya soup, a type of spinach. In-house prepared desserts, such as flan, are quite tasty. Enjoy attentive service with the option to sit outside in a garden-inspired atmosphere, or inside the small, air-conditioned dining room. It is open late until 1 am. **Features:** full bar, patio dining. **Address:** 204-A Calle 41 Entre 41 y 40 **Location:** Center. **Parking:** street only. B L D LATE

LA CASONA DE VALLADOLID

985/856-0207

fyi Not evaluated. In the historic downtown area, this place serves typical Yucatecan cuisine in a fine setting. A Mexican folk art shop showcases quality handicrafts from throughout Mexico. **Address:** Calle 41, No. 214 97780 **Location:** Corner of Calle 44.

# *BAJA CALIFORNIA*

AAA recommends that travelers consult online U.S. State Department travel advisories when planning travel abroad. Find this information at http://travel.state.gov/content/passports/english/alertswarnings/mexico-travel-warning.html.

## BUENAVISTA, BAJA CALIFORNIA SUR

**HOTEL BUENA VISTA BEACH RESORT**          624/141-0033

**Resort Hotel.** Rates not provided. **Address:** KM 105 Carr al Sur 23580 **Location:** Oceanfront. On shore of Bahia de Palmas off Mex 1, follow signs. **Facility:** One-story buildings cascade down a hillside to a beach along the Sea of Cortez. The property boasts lush gardens, flowers and fountains. 60 units. 1 story, exterior corridors. *Bath:* shower only. **Terms:** 2-3 night minimum stay - seasonal and/or weekends. **Pool(s):** outdoor. **Activities:** hot tub, boat ramp, fishing, scuba diving, snorkeling, playground, massage. **Guest Services:** valet laundry.

Stay connected with #AAA and #CAA on your favorite social media sites

It's **AMAZING** how much we've **PACKED** into our travel website!

☑ Savings of up to 35% on hotel, air, and car rental

☑ Easy to navigate

☑ Exclusive offers

☑ Support you can trust

You're *good to go* with AAA and CAA.

**Book your vacation at AAA.com/travel or CAA.ca/travel**

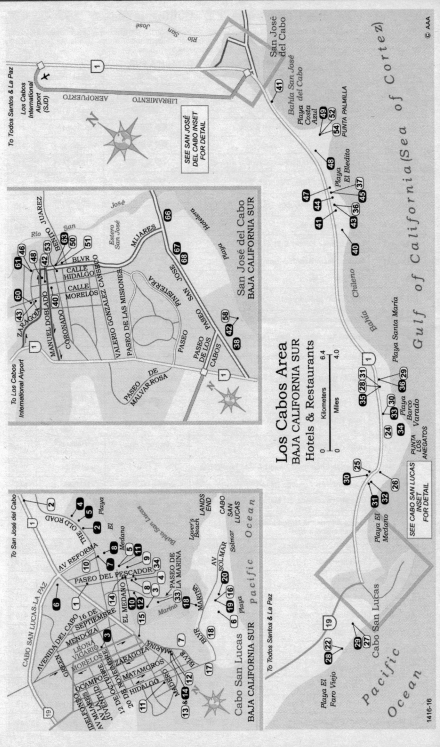

© AAA

Los Cabos Area
BAJA CALIFORNIA SUR
Hotels & Restaurants

Kilometers 6.4
Miles 4.0

1416-16

# Los Cabos Area, Baja California Sur

This index helps you "spot" where approved hotels and restaurants are located on the corresponding detailed maps. Hotel daily rate range is for comparison only. Restaurant price range is a combination of lunch and/or dinner. Turn to the listing page for more detailed rate and price information and consult display ads for special promotions.

## CABO SAN LUCAS, BAJA CALIFORNIA SUR

| Map Page | Hotels | Diamond Rated | Rate Range | Page |
|---|---|---|---|---|
| 2 p. 411 | Villa Del Arco Beach Resort & Grand Spa | ◇◇◇ | $293-$1500 | 417 |
| 3 p. 411 | Hotel Estancia Real Los Cabos | ◇◇ | $67-$104 | 415 |
| 4 p. 411 | Villa del Palmar Beach Resort & Spa | ◇◇◇ | $159-$1400 | 417 |
| 5 p. 411 | Villa La Estancia | ◇◇◇ | $290-$900 | 417 |
| 6 p. 411 | Fairfield Inn by Marriott Los Cabos | ◇◇◇ | $74-$121 | 415 |
| 7 p. 411 | Pueblo Bonito Rose Resort & Spa | ◇◇◇ | Rates not provided | 416 |
| 8 p. 411 | Pueblo Bonito Los Cabos | ◇◇◇ | Rates not provided | 416 |
| 10 p. 411 | ME by Melia Cabo | [fyi] | $225-$1500 | 416 |
| 11 p. 411 | Casa Dorada Resort & Spa Los Cabos | ◇◇◇◇ | $270-$900 | 415 |
| 12 p. 411 | Marina Fiesta Resort & Spa | ◇◇◇ | $150-$774 | 416 |
| 14 p. 411 | Siesta Suites Hotel | ◇◇ | $64-$69 | 417 |
| 18 p. 411 | The Resort at Pedregal | ◇◇◇◇◇ | Rates not provided | 417 |
| 19 p. 411 | Playa Grande Resort & Grand Spa | ◇◇◇◇ | $190-$689 | 416 |
| 20 p. 411 | Solmar All Inclusive Beach Resort | ◇◇ | $198-$488 | 417 |
| 28 p. 411 | Pueblo Bonito Pacifica Resort & Spa | ◇◇◇◇ | Rates not provided | 416 |
| 29 p. 411 | Pueblo Bonito Sunset Beach Resort & Spa | ◇◇◇◇ | Rates not provided | 417 |
| 30 p. 411 | Los Patios Hotel | ◇◇ | Rates not provided | 416 |
| 31 p. 411 | Hotel RIU Palace Cabo San Lucas (See ad p. 380.) | ◇◇◇ | Rates not provided | 415 |
| 32 p. 411 | Hotel RIU Santa Fe (See ad p. 380.) | ◇◇◇ | Rates not provided | 416 |
| 33 p. 411 | Hacienda Encantada Resort & Spa Los Cabos | ◇◇◇ | $198-$424 | 415 |
| 34 p. 411 | Esperanza An Auberge Resort | ◇◇◇◇ | $550-$8500 | 415 |
| 35 p. 411 | Sheraton Hacienda del Mar Golf & Spa Resort Los Cabos | ◇◇◇◇ | $135-$509 | 417 |
| 36 p. 411 | Fiesta Americana Grand Los Cabos All Inclusive Golf & Spa | ◇◇◇◇ | $472-$1800 | 415 |

| Map Page | Restaurants | Diamond Rated | Cuisine | Price Range | Page |
|---|---|---|---|---|---|
| 1 p. 411 | La Golondrina | ◇◇ | Seafood | $16-$60 | 419 |
| 2 p. 411 | La Casona | ◇◇◇ | Continental | $20-$100 | 418 |
| 3 p. 411 | Dos Mares Marina Grill & Bar | ◇◇◇ | Seafood | $10-$25 | 418 |
| 4 p. 411 | Baja Brewing Company | ◇◇ | American | $10-$25 | 418 |
| 5 p. 411 | Bar Esquina | ◇◇◇ | International | $6-$50 | 418 |
| 6 p. 411 | El Farallon | ◇◇◇◇ | Seafood | $30-$100 | 418 |
| 7 p. 411 | Nick-San | ◇◇◇ | Sushi | $15-$60 | 419 |
| 8 p. 411 | Edith's | ◇◇◇ | Seafood | $13-$60 | 418 |
| 9 p. 411 | The Office on the Beach | ◇◇ | Mexican | $10-$54 | 419 |
| 10 p. 411 | Fellini's Ristorante | ◇◇◇ | Italian | $18-$30 | 418 |

| Map Page | Restaurants (cont'd) | Diamond Rated | Cuisine | Price Range | Page |
|---|---|---|---|---|---|
| ⑪ p. 411 | Mi Casa | ◆◆ | Mexican | $15-$30 | 419 |
| ⑫ p. 411 | Pancho's Restaurant & Tequila Bar | ◆◆ | Mexican | $10-$30 | 419 |
| ⑬ p. 411 | Salvatore's | ◆◆ | Italian | $10-$20 | 420 |
| ⑭ p. 411 | Artichoke Heart | ◆◆◆ | International | $19-$50 | 418 |
| ⑮ p. 411 | Ruth's Chris Steak House | ◆◆◆ | Steak | $22-$50 | 419 |
| ⑯ p. 411 | The Brigantine Restaurant | ◆◆◆ | International | $29-$55 | 418 |
| ⑰ p. 411 | Romeo y Julieta Ristorante | ◆◆ | Italian | $10-$25 | 419 |
| ⑱ p. 411 | Puerto San Lucas | ◆◆◆ | International | $12-$45 | 419 |
| ㉒ p. 411 | Restaurante Siempre | ◆◆◆ | Mediterranean | $25-$75 | 419 |
| ㉔ p. 411 | **Cocina del Mar** | ◆◆◆◆ | Mediterranean | $16-$60 | 418 |
| ㉕ p. 411 | Latitude 22+ Roadhouse | ◆◆ | American | $8-$30 | 419 |
| ㉖ p. 411 | Sunset Da Mona Lisa | ◆◆◆ | Mediterranean | $20-$50 | 420 |
| ㉗ p. 411 | **LaFrida Restaurant** | ◆◆◆◆ | Mexican | $25-$144 | 419 |
| ㉘ p. 411 | Pitahayas | ◆◆◆ | Pacific Rim | $30-$50 | 419 |
| ㉙ p. 411 | Rosato | ◆◆◆ | Northern Italian | $22-$72 | 419 |
| ㉚ p. 411 | Los Riscos | ◆◆◆ | Mexican | $15-$40 | 419 |
| ㉛ p. 411 | De Cortez Mezquite Grill and Restaurant | ◆◆◆ | Steak | $30-$50 | 418 |
| ㉝ p. 411 | Hacienda Cocina y Cantina | ◆◆◆ | Regional Mexican | $13-$23 | 418 |
| ㉞ p. 411 | Sharky's Tacos, Beer & Fun | ◆◆ | Regional Mexican | $8-$30 | 420 |

## SAN JOSÉ DEL CABO, BAJA CALIFORNIA SUR

| Map Page | Hotels | Diamond Rated | Rate Range | Page |
|---|---|---|---|---|
| ㊳ p. 411 | **Hyatt Ziva Los Cabos** | ◆◆◆◆ | $163-$700 | 426 |
| ㊵ p. 411 | **Dreams Los Cabos Suites Golf Resort & Spa** | ◆◆◆◆ | Rates not provided | 426 |
| ㊶ p. 411 | Zoëtry Casa del Mar | ◆◆◆◆ | Rates not provided | 427 |
| ㊷ p. 411 | **Cabo Azul Resort** | ◆◆◆◆ | Rates not provided | 425 |
| ㊸ p. 411 | **Las Ventanas al Paraiso, A Rosewood Resort** | ◆◆◆◆◆ | Rates not provided | 426 |
| ㊹ p. 411 | Melia Cabo Real, All Inclusive | ◆◆◆ | Rates not provided | 427 |
| ㊺ p. 411 | **Hilton Los Cabos Beach & Golf Resort** | ◆◆◆◆ | $159-$479 | 426 |
| ㊼ p. 411 | **Marquis Los Cabos All Inclusive Resort & Spa** | ◆◆◆◆ | Rates not provided | 426 |
| ㊽ p. 411 | **The Westin Resort & Spa Los Cabos** | fyi | $219 | 427 |
| ㊾ p. 411 | **One&Only Palmilla** | ◆◆◆◆◆ | Rates not provided | 427 |
| 60 p. 411 | El Encanto Inn Hotel Suites & Spa | ◆◆ | $116-$294 | 426 |
| 61 p. 411 | **Casa Natalia Chic Boutique Hotel** | ◆◆◆ | $165-$475 | 425 |
| 63 p. 411 | Tropicana Inn | ◆◆ | $87-$140 | 427 |
| 66 p. 411 | **Holiday Inn Resort Los Cabos** | ◆◆◆ | Rates not provided | 426 |
| 67 p. 411 | Royal Solaris Los Cabos-All Inclusive Resort & Spa | ◆◆◆ | Rates not provided | 427 |

### SAN JOSÉ DEL CABO, BAJA CALIFORNIA SUR (cont'd)

| Map Page | Hotels (cont'd) | Diamond Rated | Rate Range | Page |
|---|---|---|---|---|
| 68 p. 411 | **Barcelo Grand Faro Los Cabos** | ◈◈◈ | Rates not provided | 425 |

| Map Page | Restaurants | Diamond Rated | Cuisine | Price Range | Page |
|---|---|---|---|---|---|
| 36 p. 411 | **The Restaurant** | ◈◈◈◈ | Regional Mexican | $17-$70 | 428 |
| 37 p. 411 | Restaurant Fenicia | ◈◈◈ | Italian | $20-$45 | 428 |
| 40 p. 411 | Baja Brewing Co | ◈◈ | American | $9-$22 | 427 |
| 41 p. 411 | Restaurante Mama Mia | ◈◈ | Mexican | $12-$35 | 428 |
| 42 p. 411 | La Panga Antigua | ◈◈◈ | Regional Mexican Seafood | $20-$46 | 428 |
| 43 p. 411 | Baan Thai | ◈◈◈ | Asian | $10-$34 | 427 |
| 46 p. 411 | Mi Cocina | ◈◈◈ | International | $15-$45 | 428 |
| 48 p. 411 | Tequila Restaurant | ◈◈◈ | Mediterranean | $15-$50 | 428 |
| 50 p. 411 | Tropicana Bar & Grill | ◈◈ | Seafood | $13-$40 | 428 |
| 51 p. 411 | Don Sanchez Restaurante | ◈◈◈ | Regional Mexican | $14-$27 | 428 |
| 52 p. 411 | Market by Jean-Georges | ◈◈◈◈ | International | $28-$55 | 428 |
| 53 p. 411 | French Riviera Bistro | ◈◈ | French | $7-$20 | 428 |
| 54 p. 411 | Agua | ◈◈◈◈ | Mexican | $18-$49 | 427 |
| 58 p. 411 | **Javier's** | ◈◈◈ | Mexican | $15-$38 | 428 |

# CABO SAN LUCAS, BAJA CALIFORNIA SUR (E-3)

- Restaurants p. 418
- Hotels & Restaurants map & index p. 411

## CASA DORADA RESORT & SPA LOS CABOS

(624)163-5757  **11**

**Address:** Ave El Pescador S/N Col El Medano 23410 **Location:** Oceanfront. 0.7 mi (1.1 km) e of Mex 1 to Paseo del Pescador, just e. **Facility:** Located on popular Medano Beach, this resort offers elegant rooms and fine dining with sweeping views of the famous rock arches. 177 efficiencies, some two and three bedrooms. 7 stories, exterior corridors. **Parking:** valet only. **Terms:** 3 day cancellation notice. **Amenities:** safes. **Dining:** 6 restaurants, entertainment. **Pool(s):** heated outdoor. **Activities:** sauna, hot tub, steamroom, recreation programs, kids club, playground, exercise room, spa. **Guest Services:** valet laundry.

## ESPERANZA AN AUBERGE RESORT

(624)145-6400  **34**

**Address:** Carr Transpeninsular KM 7, Punta Ballena 23410 **Location:** Oceanfront. On Mex 1, 3.6 mi (5.8 km) n of town. **Facility:** This intimate, posh seaside resort features spacious upscale guest rooms with outdoor terraces. A luxurious spa, several pools and dramatic dining enhance the experience. 117 units, some two bedrooms, three bedrooms and kitchens. 3-4 stories, exterior corridors. **Parking:** valet only. **Terms:** 3-7 night minimum stay - seasonal and/or weekends, 30 day cancellation notice. **Amenities:** safes. **Dining:** 3 restaurants, also, Cocina del Mar, see separate listing. **Pool(s):** heated outdoor. **Activities:** hot tub, steamroom, tennis, recreation programs, kids club, bicycles, playground, game room, exercise room, spa. **Guest Services:** valet laundry.

## FAIRFIELD INN BY MARRIOTT LOS CABOS

(624)144-2700  **6**

**Hotel** $74-$121 **Address:** Ave Lazaro Cardenas 2709, Col Medano 23410 **Location:** Mex 1 (Ave Lazaro Cardenas), just sw on Blvd Constituyentes. Next to City Club. **Facility:** Meets AAA guest room security requirements. 128 units. 5 stories, interior corridors. **Amenities:** safes. **Pool(s):** heated outdoor. **Activities:** exercise room. **Guest Services:** valet and coin laundry.

| AAA Benefit: |
|---|
| Members save 5% or more! |

---

## FIESTA AMERICANA GRAND LOS CABOS ALL INCLUSIVE GOLF & SPA

(624)145-6200  **36**

**Address:** Carr Transpeninsular KM 10.3, Lote A-1 23410 **Location:** Oceanfront. On Mex 1, 6 mi (10 km) e of town. Located at Cabo del Sol. **Facility:** On a hillside facing the sea, this luxury resort offers large guest rooms featuring ocean-view balconies and marble baths. 249 units, some two bedrooms. 1-6 stories, exterior corridors. **Parking:** on-site and valet. **Terms:** 3 day cancellation notice-fee imposed. **Amenities:** safes. **Dining:** 7 restaurants, also, Rosato, see separate listing. **Pool(s):** heated outdoor. **Activities:** sauna, hot tub, steamroom, regulation golf, recreation programs, kids club, playground, exercise room, spa. **Guest Services:** valet laundry.

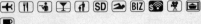

## GRAND SOLMAR LAND'S END RESORT & SPA

(624)144-2500

**fyi** Hotel $614-$8500 Too new to rate, opening scheduled for August 2015. **Address:** Ave Solmar No. 1A 23450 **Location:** Ave Solmar No. 1A. **Amenities:** 244 units. **Terms:** 3 day cancellation notice-fee imposed.

## HACIENDA ENCANTADA RESORT & SPA LOS CABOS

(624)163-5555  **33**

**Address:** Carr Transpeninsular 7.3 KM 23410 **Location:** Oceanfront. On Mex 1, 3.7 mi (6 km) ne of town. **Facility:** This resort's lovely rooms overlook the rocks at the edge of the Sea of Cortez. Elegant furnishings (including poster beds) and attractive artwork evoke Colonial Mexico. 150 units, some efficiencies and kitchens. 4 stories, exterior corridors. **Parking:** valet only. **Terms:** check-in 4 pm, 3-4 night minimum stay - seasonal and/or weekends, 3 day cancellation notice-fee imposed. **Amenities:** safes. **Dining:** 3 restaurants, also, Los Riscos, see separate listing. **Pool(s):** heated outdoor. **Activities:** hot tub, steamroom, recreation programs, playground, exercise room, spa. **Guest Services:** valet and coin laundry, area transportation.

## HOTEL ESTANCIA REAL LOS CABOS

(624)143-7501  **3**

**Hotel** $67-$104 **Address:** Leona Vicario y Revolucion 23410 **Location:** Just n of Lazaro Cardenas. **Facility:** Meets AAA guest room security requirements. 100 units. 3 stories (no elevator), exterior corridors. **Bath:** shower only. **Amenities:** safes. **Pool(s):** Outdoor. **Guest Services:** valet laundry.

## HOTEL RIU PALACE CABO SAN LUCAS

(624)146-7160  **31**

**Address:** Camino Viejo a San Jose 23410 **Location:** Oceanfront. Mex 1, 2.7 mi (4.5 km) e of town via eastbound lateral/access road. **Facility:** A nice all-inclusive choice, the resort has elegant rooms, several restaurants and live entertainment at the pool areas. 642 units. 1-4 stories, exterior corridors. **Terms:** 14 day cancellation notice. **Amenities:** safes. **Dining:** 5 restaurants, nightclub, entertainment. **Pool(s):** heated outdoor. **Activities:** sauna, hot tub, steamroom, tennis, recreation programs, kids club, playground, game room, exercise room, spa. **Guest Services:** valet laundry.

(See ad p. 380.)

(See map & index p. 411.)

## HOTEL RIU SANTA FE
(624)163-6150 **32**

Resort Hotel
Rates not provided

**Address:** Camino Viejo A San Jose Del Cabo 23410 **Location:** Oceanfront. On Mex 1, 2.7 mi (4.5 km) e of town via eastbound access/lateral road. **Facility:** Guest rooms are nicely appointed with marble baths; the expansive public areas offer easy access to Medano Beach. 902 units. 3-4 stories (no elevator), exterior corridors. **Terms:** 14 day cancellation notice. **Amenities:** safes. **Dining:** 5 restaurants, nightclub, entertainment. **Pool(s):** outdoor, heated outdoor. **Activities:** sauna, hot tub, steamroom, tennis, recreation programs, kids club, playground, game room, exercise room, spa. **Guest Services:** valet laundry. *(See ad p. 380.)*

## LOS PATIOS HOTEL
624/145-6070 **30**

**Hotel. Rates not provided. Address:** Carr Transpeninsular KM 4 23450 **Location:** Mex 1, 2.7 mi (4.5 km) e of town via westbound lateral/access road. **Facility:** 76 units. 2 stories (no elevator), exterior corridors. **Bath:** shower only. **Terms:** 2-3 night minimum stay - seasonal and/or weekends. **Amenities:** safes. **Pool(s):** outdoor. **Activities:** hot tub. **Guest Services:** valet laundry.

## MARINA FIESTA RESORT & SPA
(624)145-6020 **12**

Condominium
$150-$774

**Address:** Col La Marina Lote 37 y 38 23410 **Location:** On east side of marina. **Facility:** This pueblo-style complex is located on the marina and features numerous restaurants. Meets AAA guest room security requirements. 155 condominiums. 4-7 stories, exterior corridors. **Parking:** on-site and valet. **Amenities:** safes. **Dining:** 6 restaurants. **Pool(s):** outdoor, heated outdoor. **Activities:** sauna, hot tub, steamroom, recreation programs, playground, exercise room, spa. **Guest Services:** valet laundry, area transportation.

## ME BY MELIA CABO
(624)145-7800 **10**

(fyi)

Boutique Hotel
$225-$1500

Under major renovation, scheduled to be completed December 2015. **Last Rated:** **Address:** Playa El Medano S/N Zona Hotelera 23410 **Location:** Oceanfront. 0.6 mi (1 km) e of Mex 1 via Paseo del Pescador. **Facility:** Catering to a young and trendy adult-oriented crowd, the hotel is located on popular Medano Beach and commands breathtaking views of the famous rocks of Land's End. 151 units. 8 stories, exterior corridors. **Parking:** on-site and valet. **Amenities:** safes. **Dining:** 2 restaurants, nightclub. **Pool(s):** heated outdoor. **Activities:** sauna, hot tub, steamroom, recreation programs, exercise room, spa. **Guest Services:** valet laundry.

## PLAYA GRANDE RESORT & GRAND SPA
(624)145-7575 **19**

Resort Condominium
$190-$689

**Address:** Ave Playa Grande No. 1 23410 **Location:** Oceanfront. 0.9 mi (1.5 km) s of town via Blvd Marina. Located at Land's End. **Facility:** Resembling a colorful seaside village, this expansive resort sits on the sand near the very tip of the Baja Peninsula. 358 condominiums. 4-8 stories, exterior corridors. **Parking:** on-site and valet. **Terms:** check-in 4 pm, 3 day cancellation notice-fee imposed. **Amenities:** safes. **Dining:** 2 restaurants, also, The Brigantine Restaurant, Puerto San Lucas, see separate listings. **Pool(s):** heated outdoor. **Activities:** hot tub, steamroom, miniature golf, tennis, recreation programs, kids club, game room, exercise room, spa. **Guest Services:** valet and coin laundry, area transportation.

## PUEBLO BONITO LOS CABOS
(624)142-9797 **8**

**Resort Condominium. Rates not provided. Address:** Playa El Medano S/N 23410 **Location:** Oceanfront. Mex 1, 0.6 mi (1 km) n of town to Mex 19, 0.5 mi (0.8 km) w to the "Old Road," then just s. **Facility:** Located on popular Medano Beach, the resort boasts expansive grounds. 147 condominiums. 5 stories, exterior corridors. **Parking:** on-site and valet. **Terms:** check-in 4 pm, 14 day cancellation notice-fee imposed. **Amenities:** safes. **Dining:** 2 restaurants. **Pool(s):** heated outdoor. **Activities:** steamroom, recreation programs, exercise room, massage. **Guest Services:** valet laundry.

## PUEBLO BONITO PACIFICA RESORT & SPA
(624)142-9696 **28**

Resort Hotel
Rates not provided

**Address:** Predio Paraiso Escondido S/N 23450 **Location:** Oceanfront. Blvd Marina, 1.1 mi (1.8 km) w via Lazaro Cardenas and Miguel Herrera. **Facility:** Located outside Cabo San Lucas on Sunset Beach, this all-inclusive, adults-only resort boasts elegant guest rooms, spacious baths and upscale bedding. 154 units. 3-5 stories, exterior corridors. **Parking:** on-site and valet. **Terms:** check-in 4 pm, age restrictions may apply, 14 day cancellation notice. **Amenities:** safes. **Dining:** 3 restaurants, also, Restaurante Siempre, see separate listing. **Pool(s):** heated outdoor. **Activities:** sauna, hot tub, steamroom, cabanas, tennis, recreation programs, exercise room, spa. **Guest Services:** valet laundry, area transportation.

## PUEBLO BONITO ROSE RESORT & SPA
(624)142-9898 **7**

Resort Condominium
Rates not provided

**Address:** Playa El Medano S/N 23410 **Location:** Oceanfront. Mex 1, 0.6 mi (1 km) n of town to Mex 19, 0.5 mi (0.8 km) w to the "Old Road," then just s. **Facility:** The elegant lobby and grounds feature classic Italian sculptures, a large reflection pool, a giant free-form pool, koi ponds and tropical birds. Meets AAA guest room security requirements. 260 condominiums. 6 stories, interior corridors. **Parking:** on-site and valet. **Terms:** check-in 4 pm, 14 day cancellation notice-fee imposed. **Amenities:** safes. **Dining:** 3 restaurants, also, Fellini's Ristorante, see separate listing. **Pool(s):** heated outdoor. **Activities:** sauna, hot tub, steamroom, tennis, kids club, exercise room, spa. **Guest Services:** valet laundry.

(See map & index p. 411.)

## PUEBLO BONITO SUNSET BEACH RESORT & SPA
624/142-9999 **29**

WWWWW
**Resort Hotel**
**Rates not provided**

**Address:** Domicilio Conocido S/N 23450 **Location:** Oceanfront. Blvd Marina, 1.1 mi (1.8 km) w via Lazaro Cardenas and Miguel Herrera. **Facility:** The resort's hacienda-style buildings are terraced on the hillside, providing all rooms with a sunset view over the Pacific and a beachside pool. 635 efficiencies, some two and three bedrooms. 2-6 stories, exterior corridors. **Terms:** check-in 4 pm, 14 day cancellation notice. **Amenities:** safes. **Dining:** 8 restaurants, also, LaFrida Restaurant, see separate listing. **Pool(s):** heated outdoor. **Activities:** sauna, hot tub, steamroom, tennis, recreation programs, kids club, exercise room, spa.
**Guest Services:** valet laundry, area transportation.

## THE RESORT AT PEDREGAL
(624)163-4300 **18**

WWWW
**Resort Hotel**
**Rates not provided**

**Address:** Camino del Mar 1 **Location:** Oceanfront. Across from marina, at entrance to Pedregal development. **Facility:** The dramatic entry through a quarter-mile-long mountain tunnel leads guests to this unique and secluded resort. The cliff-side beachfront location provides privacy for a relaxing getaway. Meets AAA guest room security requirements. 96 units, some kitchens and condominiums. 1-4 stories, exterior corridors. **Parking:** valet only. **Terms:** 28 day cancellation notice, 14 day off season. **Amenities:** safes. **Dining:** 2 restaurants, also, El Farallon, see separate listing. **Pool(s):** heated outdoor. **Activities:** sauna, hot tub, steamroom, tennis, recreation programs, kids club, exercise room, spa. **Guest Services:** valet laundry.

## SHERATON HACIENDA DEL MAR GOLF & SPA RESORT LOS CABOS
(624)145-8000 **35**

WWWWW
**Resort Hotel**
**$135-$509**

(S) **Sheraton**
HOTELS & RESORTS

**AAA Benefit:** Members save up to 15%, plus Starwood Preferred Guest® benefits!

**Address:** Corredor Touristico KM 10, Lote D 23410 **Location:** Oceanfront. On Mex 1, 6 mi (10 km) e of town. Located at Cabo del Sol. **Facility:** Situated on the beach, the hotel's tree-shaded mosaic patios offer guests an oasis from the sun and sand; guest rooms are large and comfortable. 270 units, some three bedrooms and kitchens. 2-5 stories, exterior corridors. **Parking:** on-site and valet. **Terms:** 3 day cancellation notice-fee imposed, resort fee. **Amenities:** video games, safes. **Dining:** 3 restaurants, also, De Cortez Mezquite Grill and Restaurant, Pitahayas, see separate listings. **Pool(s):** heated outdoor. **Activities:** sauna, hot tub, steamroom, regulation golf, recreation programs, kids club, playground, game room, exercise room, spa. **Guest Services:** valet laundry, area transportation.

## SIESTA SUITES HOTEL
624/143-2773 **14**

WW **Hotel** $64-$69 **Address:** E Calle Zapata y Guerrero 23400 **Location:** Just n of Blvd Marina; between calles Miguel Hidalgo and Vicente Guerrero; downtown. **Facility:** 19 units, some efficiencies. 4 stories (no elevator), exterior corridors. *Bath:* shower only. **Parking:** on-site and street. **Amenities:** safes. **Dining:** Salvatore's, see separate listing. **Activities:** picnic facilities.

## SOLMAR ALL INCLUSIVE BEACH RESORT
(624)146-7700 **20**

WWW
**Resort Hotel**
**$198-$488**

**Address:** Ave Solmar No. 1 23410 **Location:** Oceanfront. 0.9 mi (1.5 km) s of town via Blvd Marina. Located at Land's End. **Facility:** This beachfront resort features expansive grounds and ample lounging areas; rooms and suites each have a private patio or balcony. 100 efficiencies. 2-5 stories, exterior corridors. **Terms:** check-in 4 pm, 3 day cancellation notice-fee imposed. **Amenities:** safes. **Dining:** 2 restaurants. **Pool(s):** heated outdoor. **Activities:** hot tub, recreation programs, massage. **Guest Services:** valet and coin laundry, area transportation.

## VILLA DEL ARCO BEACH RESORT & GRAND SPA
(624)145-7200 **2**

WWWW **Resort Hotel** $293-$1500 **Address:** KM 0.5 Camino Viejo a San Jose 23410 **Location:** Oceanfront. Mex 1, 0.6 mi (1 km) n of town to Mex 19, 0.5 mi (0.8 km) e to "Old Road," then just n. **Facility:** Guests here can select from fully equipped studios or spacious one-bedroom units with Murphy beds for larger families. The resort features a relaxing tropical pool and a full-service spa. Meets AAA guest room security requirements. 222 condominiums, some two and three bedrooms. 7 stories, exterior corridors. **Parking:** on-site and valet. **Terms:** check-in 4 pm, 3 day cancellation notice. **Amenities:** safes. **Dining:** 4 restaurants. **Pool(s):** heated outdoor. **Activities:** hot tub, snorkeling, tennis, recreation programs, kids club, exercise room, spa. **Guest Services:** valet and coin laundry.

## VILLA DEL PALMAR BEACH RESORT & SPA
(624)145-7000 **4**

WWW **Resort Condominium** $159-$1400 **Address:** KM 0.5 Camino Viejo a San Jose 23450 **Location:** Oceanfront. Mex 1, 0.6 mi (1 km) n of town to Mex 19, 0.6 mi (1 km) e to the "Old Road," then just n. **Facility:** This comfortable resort features spacious, well equipped rooms, a multistory atrium lobby, waterfalls, two tiered pools and a waterslide. Meets AAA guest room security requirements. 465 condominiums. 7-8 stories, interior corridors. **Parking:** on-site and valet. **Terms:** check-in 4 pm, 3 day cancellation notice. **Amenities:** safes. **Dining:** 3 restaurants, entertainment. **Pool(s):** heated outdoor. **Activities:** sauna, hot tub, steamroom, tennis, recreation programs, kids club, exercise room, spa. **Guest Services:** valet and coin laundry.

## VILLA LA ESTANCIA
(624)145-6900 **5**

WWWW **Resort Condominium** $290-$900 **Address:** KM 0.5 Camino Viejo a San Jose 23450 **Location:** Oceanfront. Mex 1, 0.6 mi (1 km) n of town to Mex 19, 0.3 mi (0.5 km) e to the "Old Road," then just n. **Facility:** On Medano Beach, this luxury condominium complex has units with private balconies and views of the ocean and Land's End. Meets AAA guest room security requirements. 70 units, some condominiums. 7 stories, interior/exterior corridors. **Parking:** on-site and valet. **Terms:** check-in 4 pm, 3 day cancellation notice, resort fee. **Dining:** La Casona, see separate listing. **Pool(s):** heated outdoor. **Activities:** sauna, hot tub, steamroom, tennis, kids club, game room, exercise room, spa. **Guest Services:** valet and coin laundry.

(See map & index p. 411.)

## SANDOS FINISTERRA LOS CABOS ALL INCLUSIVE RESORT
624/145-6700

[fyi] Not evaluated. **Address:** Domicilio Conocido 23410 **Location:** Oceanfront. 0.6 mi (1 km) s of town via Blvd Marina. Facilities, services, and décor characterize a mid-scale property. A newly renovated property awaits you.

## TESORO LOS CABOS
624/173-9300

[fyi] Not evaluated. **Address:** Blvd Marina Lote 9 y 10 23410 **Location:** In town; at marina. Facilities, services, and décor characterize a mid-scale property.

## WHERE TO EAT

### ARTICHOKE HEART
624/143-4041  (14)

▼▼▼ International. Fine Dining. $19-$50 **AAA Inspector Notes:** Trendy with contemporary décor, this newer, intimate establishment is sister to Artichoke Heart in Mexico City. Prepared by a talented kitchen and presented by a professional, attentive staff, the seasonal menu focuses on fresh, local and organic ingredients, plus certified Angus beef. House-made pastas with creative sauces and luscious desserts also figure prominently on the menu. **Features:** full bar, patio dining. **Reservations:** suggested. **Address:** Ave Del Pescador No. 4312 23410 **Location:** 0.3 mi (0.5 km) e of Mex 1. **Parking:** valet and street only. (D) (LATE)

### BAJA BREWING COMPANY
624/144-3805  (4)

▼▼ American. Casual Dining. $10-$25 **AAA Inspector Notes:** This brewery's newer location, directly on the marina, features indoor and outdoor seating plus the same changing selection of micro-brewed beers and great pub fare featured at its sister locations at Cabo Villas, and further away in San José del Cabo. **Features:** full bar, patio dining. **Address:** Cabo San Lucas Marina, Puerto Paraiso Mall 23450 **Location:** 0.7 mi (1.1 km) e of Mex 1 to Paseo del Pescador, just w. **Parking:** on-site (fee). (B) (L) (D) (LATE)

### BAR ESQUINA
624/143-1889  (5)

▼▼▼ International. Casual Dining. $6-$50 **AAA Inspector Notes:** This trendy, stylish restaurant features an open demonstration kitchen with seating; there's also a comfortable outdoor dining area. Enjoy creatively prepared seafood specialties with an international flair as well as a variety of wood-fired pizzas. **Features:** full bar, patio dining. **Address:** Ave del Pescador S/N Col El Medano 23410 **Location:** Jct Del Mar de Cortes. **Parking:** on-site and valet. (B) (L) (D) (LATE)

### THE BRIGANTINE RESTAURANT
624/145-7575  (16)

▼▼▼ International. Casual Dining. $29-$55 **AAA Inspector Notes:** Here you'll enjoy a varied menu that includes a mix of casual and upscale international fare. Selections include homemade corn or tortilla soup, spiced pork and beef burgers, ribs, pasta, pizzas, and grilled meat and seafood. As for seating options, you have a choice between the covered open-air terrace and an indoor dining area with bright Mexican decor. **Features:** full bar, patio dining. **Reservations:** suggested. **Address:** Ave Playa Grande No. 1 23410 **Location:** 0.9 mi (1.5 km) s of town via Blvd Marina; in Playa Grande Resort & Grand Spa. (D) (AC)

### COCINA DEL MAR
624/145-6400  (24)

◆◆◆ ▼▼▼ **AAA Inspector Notes:** Al fresco dining underneath the stars and along the dramatic cliffs with waves crashing below and a vast view of the Sea of Cortez is the setting for this unforgettable dining experience. Menus are focused on ingredients that are caught that day from the sea or picked fresh from local organic farms. Guests have a choice of three- or four-course tasting menus that may be paired with wine by the sommelier. On Thursday evening, a short but magical fireworks show is lit off from the beach. **Features:** full bar, patio dining. **Reservations:** suggested. **Address:** Carr Transpeninsular KM 7, Punta Ballena 23410 **Location:** On Mex 1, 3.6 mi (5.8 km) n of town; in Esperanza An Auberge Resort. **Parking:** valet only. (B) (L) (D) (AC)

Mediterranean
Fine Dining
$16-$60

### DE CORTEZ MEZQUITE GRILL AND RESTAURANT
624/145-8000  (31)

▼▼▼ Steak. Fine Dining. $30-$50 **AAA Inspector Notes:** Diners can request a table on the large outdoor terrace overlooking the floodlit beach, or in the elegant semi-open-air dining room with high palapa roofs and upscale Mexican decor. The menu features freshly grilled beef, fish and other seafood, cooked to order. Starters include innovative combinations such as mango-infused lobster bisque with scallop skewers. The outdoor lounge, with its large fire pit, is a nice spot for a before- or after-dinner drink. **Features:** full bar, patio dining. **Reservations:** suggested. **Address:** Corredor Touristico KM 10, Lote D 23410 **Location:** On Mex 1, 6 mi (10 km) e of town; in Sheraton Hacienda del Mar Golf & Spa Resort Los Cabos. **Parking:** on-site and valet. (D)

### DOS MARES MARINA GRILL & BAR
624/143-0582  (3)

▼▼▼ Seafood. Casual Dining. $10-$25 **AAA Inspector Notes:** Don't let the touristy surroundings fool you; this chef-owned gem located on the marina serves some of the best seafood options around. Try the trilogy of ceviche, or the fresh catch of the day, grilled to perfection. Pizzas, pastas and salads are also available. **Features:** full bar, patio dining. **Reservations:** suggested. **Address:** Calle de La Darsena Lote 18 23452 **Location:** On the Marina. **Parking:** street only. (L) (D) (AC)

### EDITH'S
624/143-0801  (8)

▼▼▼ Seafood. Casual Dining. $13-$60 **AAA Inspector Notes:** This popular palapa dining room is a favorite for seafood. Steaks, lamb and chicken are also on the menu. Diners can watch tortillas being made on the mesquite grill. **Features:** full bar. **Reservations:** suggested. **Address:** Camino A Playa El Medano S/N 23410 **Location:** 0.7 mi (1.1 km) s of Mex 1. **Parking:** street only. (D) (AC)

### EL FARALLON
624/163-4300  (6)

▼▼▼ ▼▼▼ Seafood. Fine Dining. $30-$100 **AAA Inspector Notes:** Boasting a dramatic cliffside location, the restaurant treats guests to magnificent views of the mountains and Pacific Ocean. Diners make a selection from the fresh seafood display, and the chef personally cooks it to-order over an open char grill. **Features:** full bar, patio dining. **Reservations:** suggested. **Address:** Calle Camino del Mar No. 1 23455 **Location:** Across from marina, at entrance to Pedregal development; in The Resort at Pedregal. **Parking:** valet only. (D) (AC)

### FELLINI'S RISTORANTE
624/142-9898  (10)

▼▼▼ Italian. Fine Dining. $18-$30 **AAA Inspector Notes:** Terrace dining affords the best view of the bay and famous rocks of Cabo San Lucas. **Features:** full bar, patio dining. **Reservations:** required. **Address:** Playa El Medano S/N 23410 **Location:** Mex 1, 0.6 mi (1 km) n of town to Mex 19, 0.5 mi (0.8 km) w to the "Old Road," then just s; in Pueblo Bonito Rose Resort & Spa. **Parking:** on-site and valet. (D) (LATE)

### HACIENDA COCINA Y CANTINA
624/163-3144  (33)

▼▼▼ Regional Mexican. Casual Dining. $13-$23 **AAA Inspector Notes:** This casual beachfront restaurant overlooks a quiet section of popular Medano beach and the iconic rock formations. Near the marina, it's a great place to watch fishing boats coming and going. **Features:** full bar, patio dining. **Reservations:** suggested. **Address:** Calle Gomez Farias S/N, Colonia El Medano 23410 **Location:** Paseo de La Marina, south gate. (B) (L) (D) (AC)

### LA CASONA
624/145-7000  (2)

▼▼▼ Continental. Fine Dining. $20-$100 **AAA Inspector Notes:** The restaurant's fresh and innovative dishes benefit from expert preparation. The well trained staff is very attentive and helpful with wine pairings. **Features:** full bar, patio dining. **Reservations:** suggested. **Address:** KM 0.5 Camino Viejo a San Jose 23450 **Location:** Mex 1, 0.6 mi (1 km) n of town to Mex 19, 0.3 mi (0.5 km) e to the "Old Road," then just n; in Villa La Estancia. **Parking:** on-site and valet. (B) (D)

---

## Discover a wealth of savings and offers
## on the AAA/CAA travel websites

(See map & index p. 411.)

## LAFRIDA RESTAURANT  624/142-9999 (27)

▽▽▽▽ ▽▽
**Mexican
Fine Dining
$25-$144**

**AAA Inspector Notes:** This elegant restaurant offers you and your better half a romantic setting on its candlelit outdoor terrace, or in the main dining room with its fine Mexican artwork and live pianist. The menu features a nice mix of sophisticated Mexican cuisine. Meals are best finished with after-dinner coffees and liqueurs, some of which are prepared tableside by the highly professional and formal waitstaff. **Features:** full bar, patio dining. **Reservations:** required. **Address:** Predio Paraiso Escondido S/N 23410 **Location:** Blvd Marina, 1.1 mi (1.8 km) w via Lazaro Cardenas and Miguel Herrera; in Pueblo Bonito Sunset Beach Resort & Spa. **Parking:** valet only. D

## LA GOLONDRINA  624/143-0542 (1)

▽▽▽▽ Seafood. Casual Dining. $16-$60 **AAA Inspector Notes:** *Historic.* At a historic trading post, this popular restaurant lets diners relax on the patio under ancient mesquite trees while savoring Mexican-style combination plates of seafood, chicken and beef. **Features:** full bar, patio dining. **Reservations:** suggested. **Address:** Paseo del Pescador S/N 23410 **Location:** Just e of Mex 1; next to City Club. **Parking:** street only. L D ⬧

## LATITUDE 22+ ROADHOUSE  624/143-9282 (25)

▽▽ ▽▽ American. Casual Dining. $8-$30 **AAA Inspector Notes:** The small café and bar boasts great food and attitude. Funky memorabilia is pinned to the walls and ceiling. On the menu are not only great hamburgers and barbecue sandwiches, but also ribs, prime rib, chicken-fried steak and pasta dishes. Ask about the daily local fish specials. Portions are plentiful. Fishermen can bring in their catch for preparation. **Features:** full bar, patio dining. **Address:** KM 4.5 Carr Transpeninsular **Location:** 2.4 mi (4 km) e on Mex 1; next to Costco; behind power plant. B L D 𝕂

## LOS RISCOS  624/163-5555 (30)

▽▽▽▽ Mexican. Fine Dining. $15-$40 **AAA Inspector Notes:** Tables set along cliffs overlooking the Sea of Cortez and Land's End rock formations in the distance is the spectacular setting for this romantic dining experience. Most evenings, strolling musicians, such as a harpist, come by your table to serenade you as you dine. Mesquite-grilled half chicken, rib-eye steak and fresh local fish are prepared with your choice of a side dish. **Features:** full bar, patio dining. **Reservations:** suggested. **Address:** Carr Transpeninsular KM 7.3 23410 **Location:** On Mex 1, 3.7 mi (6 km) ne of town; in Hacienda Encantada Resort & Spa Los Cabos. **Parking:** valet only. D 𝕂

## MI CASA  624/143-1933 (11)

▽▽▽▽ Mexican. Casual Dining. $15-$30 **AAA Inspector Notes:** Strolling musicians liven up this restaurant's enchanting courtyard, which is surrounded by colorful murals. Authentic regional dishes from throughout Mexico include such popular choices as mole poblano fish, roasted pork, filet of beef and grilled chicken. **Features:** full bar, patio dining. **Reservations:** suggested. **Address:** Ave Cabo San Lucas 23410 **Location:** 0.6 mi (1 km) w of Blvd Marina via Lazaro Cardenas; centro. **Parking:** street only. L D

## NICK-SAN  624/143-2491 (7)

▽▽▽▽ Sushi. Casual Dining. $15-$60 **AAA Inspector Notes:** This trendy hot spot serves the freshest fish available. Sit at the sushi bar and watch the chefs expertly prepare sushi rolls, sashimi and chirashi, all presented beautifully. The dining room can get packed during peak times. **Features:** full bar. **Reservations:** suggested. **Address:** Blvd Marina 23450 **Location:** Next to Tesoro Los Cabos Resort. **Parking:** street only. L D

## THE OFFICE ON THE BEACH  624/143-3464 (9)

▽▽ ▽▽ Mexican. Casual Dining. $10-$54 **AAA Inspector Notes:** This is a typical, casual restaurant with tables and chairs on the sand. Stop in for breakfast after a morning walk, or drop by at sunset as shadows fall on El Arco (the arch). Office assistants serve up an assortment of beverages, burgers and enchiladas. Party favors and entertainment enliven theme nights on Monday, Thursday and Sunday. **Features:** full bar, patio dining. **Reservations:** suggested. **Address:** Playa El Medano S/N 23410 **Location:** 0.8 mi (1.2 km) se of Mex 1 via Paseo del Pescador. **Parking:** street only.
B L D 𝕂 ⬧

## PANCHO'S RESTAURANT & TEQUILA BAR  624/143-0973 (12)

▽▽ ▽▽ Mexican. Casual Dining. $10-$30 **AAA Inspector Notes:** Known for its friendly service, this colorful restaurant also boasts the world's largest tequila selection with more than 575 choices. House specialties include tortilla soup, Oaxacan mole and coconut shrimp with mango. **Features:** full bar, patio dining. **Reservations:** suggested. **Address:** Miguel Hidalgo at Calle Zapata 23410 **Location:** In town; just w of Blvd Marina. **Parking:** street only. B L D 𝕂

## PITAHAYAS  624/145-8010 (28)

▽▽▽▽ Pacific Rim. Fine Dining. $30-$50 **AAA Inspector Notes:** Overlooking the beach and the Sea of Cortez, the restaurant lets you relax under the stars while sampling well-presented fresh local seafood and organic vegetables prepared in a variety of styles-- from blackened catch of the day to whole steamed snapper with ying-yang sauce. Also meriting consideration is the "shaked" Angus tenderloin with wasabi mashed potatoes. **Features:** full bar, patio dining. **Reservations:** suggested. **Address:** Corredor Touristico KM 10, Lote D 23410 **Location:** On Mex 1, 6 mi (10 km) e of town; in Sheraton Hacienda del Mar Golf & Spa Resort Los Cabos. **Parking:** on-site and valet. D 𝕂

## PUERTO SAN LUCAS  624/143-0443 (18)

▽▽▽▽ International. Fine Dining. $12-$45 **AAA Inspector Notes:** Perched above the marina, diners will enjoy the view along with well prepared steaks, seafood, pasta and pizzas. The well trained staff graciously assists throughout the dining experience. **Features:** full bar. **Reservations:** suggested. **Address:** Ave Playa Grande 1 23410 **Location:** 0.9 mi (1.5 km) s of town via Blvd Marina; in Playa Grande Resort & Grand Spa. **Parking:** on-site and valet.
L D

## RESTAURANTE SIEMPRE  624/142-9696 (22)

▽▽▽▽ Mediterranean. Fine Dining. $25-$75 **AAA Inspector Notes:** Diners here can select from the beachfront terrace setting or distinct Mexican flavor of the indoor dining area. In the evening, tables are candle lit and the surrounding pool is lit to add to the ambiance. The lunch buffet is extensive. **Features:** full bar, Sunday brunch. **Reservations:** suggested. **Address:** Predio Paraiso Escondido S/N 23450 **Location:** Blvd Marina, 1.1 mi (1.8 km) w via Lazaro Cardenas and Miguel Herrera; in Pueblo Bonito Pacifica Resort & Spa. **Parking:** valet only. B L D

## ROMEO Y JULIETA RISTORANTE  624/143-0225 (17)

▽▽ ▽▽ Italian. Casual Dining. $10-$25 **AAA Inspector Notes:** Pasta, seafood and specialty pizzas are served in this quaint, family-friendly hacienda. **Features:** full bar, patio dining. **Reservations:** suggested. **Address:** Camino del Cerro 23410 **Location:** 0.3 mi (0.5 km) s of town via Blvd Marina; downtown. **Parking:** valet and street only. D

## ROSATO  624/145-6200 (29)

▽▽▽▽ Northern Italian. Fine Dining. $22-$72 **AAA Inspector Notes:** Subdued lighting, candles and soft music set an intimate mood in this sophisticated dining room overlooking the resort and Sea of Cortez. Delicious examples of Northern Italian cooking include a variety of risottos, fresh local seafood and rack of lamb. **Features:** full bar. **Reservations:** suggested. **Address:** Carr Transpeninsular KM 10.3, Lote A-1 23410 **Location:** On Mex 1, 6 mi (10 km) e of town; in Fiesta Americana Grand Los Cabos Golf & Spa Resort. **Parking:** valet and street only. D

## RUTH'S CHRIS STEAK HOUSE  624/144-3232 (15)

▽▽▽▽ Steak. Fine Dining. $22-$50 **AAA Inspector Notes:** The main fare is steak, which is prepared from several cuts of Prime beef and cooked to perfection, but the menu also lists lamb, chicken and seafood dishes. Guests should come hungry because the side dishes, which are among the a la carte offerings, could make a meal in themselves. **Features:** full bar, patio dining. **Reservations:** suggested. **Address:** Lazardo Cardenas esq Cabo Bello S/N Local 41 23450 **Location:** Centro; in Puerto Paraiso Mall. L D LATE

Turn your road trip dreams into reality

with the TripTik® Travel Planner

**(See map & index p. 411.)**

SALVATORE'S　　　　　　　　624/105-1044　(13)

Italian. Casual Dining. $10-$20 **AAA Inspector Notes:** A few blocks from the main strip is this gringo favorite for traditional Italian fare. Large portions of fresh seafood, fish and steak are affordably priced and served in the hotel's moonlit courtyard. Menu highlights include osso buco, lasagna, chicken Parmesan, and steamed Ensanada clams in a garlic and wine sauce. Lending to the tropical atmosphere, tables are set up along a small Mexican-tiled pool among potted palms and hanging star lanterns. Service is quick and friendly. **Features:** full bar, patio dining. **Reservations:** suggested, for dinner. **Address:** E Calle Zapata y Guerrero 23400 **Location:** Just n of Blvd Marina; between calles Miguel Hidalgo and Vicente Guerrero; downtown; in Siesta Suites Hotel. **Parking:** street only.

SHARKY'S TACOS, BEER & FUN　　　　624/143-5513　(34)

Regional Mexican. Casual Dining. $8-$30 **AAA Inspector Notes:** As the name implies, this fun, casual eatery serves a wide variety of local seafood. Fisherman can bring in their own catch and the kitchen will prepare it and provide additional sides. **Features:** full bar, patio dining. **Address:** Paseo del Pescador S/N 23450 **Location:** Just n of Medano Beach. **Parking:** street only.

SUNSET DA MONA LISA　　　　　624/145-8160　(26)

Mediterranean. Fine Dining. $20-$50 **AAA Inspector Notes:** From its cliffside perch, this impressive, open-air, palapa-covered restaurant boasts terrific views of the ocean and Land's End. Guests often arrive early for dinner to sip cocktails and snap photos of the gorgeous sunsets. The kitchen specializes in pasta, seafood and pizza. **Features:** full bar, patio dining. **Reservations:** suggested. **Address:** Carr Transpeninsular KM 6 23410 **Location:** 3.1 mi (5 km) e on Mex 1, 0.6 mi (1 km) s; past Misiones del Cabo. **Parking:** on-site and valet. D

# EL PESCADERO

CERRITOS BEACH CLUB　　　　　624/129-6315

[fyi] Not evaluated. Watch the surfing action from this open-air dining room while you enjoy freshly prepared seafood and local specialties. **Address:** KM 65, Hwy 19 **Location:** At Playa Los Cerritos, just w, follow signs.

# EL ROSARIO, BAJA CALIFORNIA

MAMA ESPINOSA'S　　　　　　616/165-8770

[fyi] Not evaluated. A friendly and reliable respite along the Baja peninsula highway, this historic restaurant serves classic Mexican and seafood specialties. **Address:** KM 55 Carr Transpeninsular **Location:** On Mex 1; town center.

# ENSENADA, BAJA CALIFORNIA (A-1)
pop. 466,814

**BEST WESTERN EL CID**　　　　(646)178-2401

Hotel
Rates not provided

**AAA Benefit:** Save 10% or more every day and earn 10% bonus points!

**Address:** Ave Lopez Mateos No. 993 22800 **Location:** Just w of Ave Blancarte; centro. Located in tourist area. **Facility:** 52 units. 3 stories (no elevator), interior corridors. **Terms:** 3-5 night minimum stay - seasonal and/or weekends, 15 day cancellation notice-fee imposed, resort fee. **Amenities:** Some: safes. **Dining:** El Cid; see separate listing. **Pool(s):** outdoor. **Activities:** hot tub. **Guest Services:** valet laundry.

**CASA DEL SOL HOTEL**　　　　646/178-1570

Motel
Rates not provided

**Address:** Ave Lopez Mateos No. 1001 **Location:** At Ave Blancarte; centro. Located in tourist area. **Facility:** 40 units. 2 stories (no elevator), exterior corridors. *Bath:* shower only. **Dining:** 2 restaurants. **Pool(s):** outdoor. **Activities:** massage.

**CORONA HOTEL & SPA**　　　　646/176-0901

Hotel. Rates not provided. **Address:** Blvd Lazaro Cardenas No. 1442 **Location:** 0.6 mi (1 km) s. **Facility:** 92 units. 4 stories, interior corridors. **Terms:** 3 day cancellation notice. **Amenities:** safes. **Pool(s):** heated outdoor. **Activities:** sauna, hot tub, steamroom, exercise room, spa. **Guest Services:** valet laundry.

**ESTERO BEACH RESORT HOTEL**　　　(646)176-6230

Resort Hotel. Rates not provided. **Address:** PMB 1186, 482 W San Ysidro Blvd 92173 **Location:** Oceanfront. 7 mi (10.5 km) s of town on Mex 1, 1 mi (1.5 km) w on Ave Jose Moreles and Lupita Novelo O. **Facility:** A family-oriented resort on several acres of beachfront grounds. Units are located in several buildings, from modest to upscale. 95 units, some two bedrooms, kitchens and cottages. 2 stories (no elevator), exterior corridors. **Pool(s):** heated outdoor. **Activities:** hot tub, boat ramp, tennis, bicycles, playground, massage. **Guest Services:** coin laundry.

**HACIENDA BAJAMAR**　　　　　(646)155-0151

Resort Hotel. Rates not provided. **Address:** Carr Tijuana-Ensenada KM 77.5 22760 **Location:** On Mex 1-D (toll road) exit Baja Mar; 19.8 mi (33 km) n of town. **Facility:** A golf resort located along a picturesque and peaceful coastline, this Mexican colonial-style hotel surrounds a secluded courtyard. 81 units, some efficiencies. 2 stories (no elevator), interior/exterior corridors. **Terms:** check-in 4 pm, 3 day cancellation notice. **Amenities:** safes. **Pool(s):** heated outdoor. **Activities:** hot tub, regulation golf, miniature golf, tennis, bicycles, playground. **Guest Services:** valet laundry.

**HACIENDA GUADALUPE HOTEL**　　　646/155-2859

Boutique Hotel. Rates not provided. **Address:** KM 81.5 Hwy 3 **Location:** 20 mi (32 km) e of town on Mex 3 (Ruta Del Vino), take 3rd toll road from San Diego. **Facility:** At the rim of the Valley of Guadalupe in the heart of Mexico's wine country, this hotel affords spectacular views from all rooms. 12 units. 2 stories, exterior corridors. *Bath:* shower only. **Terms:** 15 day cancellation notice. **Amenities:** safes. **Pool(s):** heated outdoor. **Activities:** hot tub, massage. **Guest Services:** valet laundry.

**HOTEL CORAL & MARINA**　　　　646/175-0000

Hotel
$97-$116

**Address:** Carr Tijuana-Ensenada No. 3421 **Location:** Waterfront. On Mex 1-D (toll road), 1.8 mi (3 km) n of town at KM 103. **Facility:** 147 units, some two bedrooms, three bedrooms and efficiencies. 6 stories, interior corridors. **Terms:** 5 day cancellation notice-fee imposed. **Amenities:** safes. **Pool(s):** outdoor, heated indoor. **Activities:** sauna, hot tub, steamroom, marina, fishing, tennis, playground, game room, spa. **Guest Services:** valet laundry, area transportation.

## HOTEL CORTEZ       (646)178-2307

Hotel
Rates not provided

▼▼ ▼▼ Hotel. **Address:** Ave Lopez Mateos No. 1089 **Location:** At Ave Castillo; centro. Located in tourist area. **Facility:** 121 units. 2 stories (no elevator), interior/exterior corridors. *Bath:* shower only. **Amenities:** *Some:* safes. **Pool(s):** heated outdoor. **Activities:** limited exercise equipment. **Guest Services:** valet laundry.

🍽️ 🛁 🍷 🏊 📶 / SOME UNITS HS 📞 ☕ 💻

## PUNTA MORRO RESORT       646/178-3507

▼▼ ▼▼ **Hotel. Rates not provided. Address:** KM 106 Carr Tijuana-Ensenada **Location:** Oceanfront. 3.1 mi (5 km) n of town on Mex 1, 0.3 mi (0.5 km) w. **Facility:** 24 units, some two and three bedrooms. 3 stories, exterior corridors. *Bath:* shower only. **Terms:** 7 day cancellation notice. **Amenities:** safes. **Dining:** The Restaurant at Punta Morro, see separate listing. **Pool(s):** heated outdoor. **Activities:** hot tub, massage. **Guest Services:** valet laundry.

🍽️ 🛁 🍷 🏊 BIZ 📶 ✕ 📞 💻 / SOME UNITS AC

## VILLA FONTANA INN       (646)178-3434

Motel
Rates not provided

▼▼ ▼▼ **Address:** Ave Lopez Mateos No. 1050 22800 **Location:** Just w of Ave Blancarte; centro. Located in tourist area. **Facility:** 69 units. 2 stories, exterior corridors. **Pool(s):** outdoor. **Activities:** hot tub. **Guest Services:** valet laundry.

📶 🏊 📶 / SOME UNITS 💻

## ENCUENTRO GUADALUPE ANTIRESORT    646/198-7400

[fyi] Not evaluated. **Address:** Carr Tecate-Ensenada, KM 75 22750 **Location:** Center of town; 50 km ne on Hwy 3. Facilities, services, and décor characterize a mid-scale property.

**WHERE TO EAT**

## BRONCO'S STEAKHOUSE       646/176-4900

▼▼ ▼▼ Mexican Steak. Casual Dining. $8-$26 **AAA Inspector Notes:** This cantina is known for serving great mesquite-grilled steaks, but it's the Saturday and Sunday Mexican breakfast buffets, not to mention the Wednesday lunch spread, that keep locals coming back for more. **Features:** full bar. **Address:** Ave Lopez Mateos No. 1525 **Location:** 0.6 mi (1 km) s of town, cross Ave Guadalupe.

B L D

## EL CID       646/178-1809

▼▼ ▼▼ Mexican. Casual Dining. $8-$28 **AAA Inspector Notes:** A popular spot with both indoor and outdoor seating, you'll find it downtown on the main strip. The menu is loaded with specialties showcasing the diverse flavors of Mexico. Try the combination platter if you can't make up your mind. The delicious flan will do the trick. **Features:** full bar, patio dining. **Address:** Ave Lopez Mateos No. 995-A Zona Centro **Location:** Just w of Ave Blancarte; centro; in BEST WESTERN El Cid. **Parking:** street only.

B L D LATE AC

## EL REY SOL RESTAURANT       646/178-1733

▼▼ ▼▼ ▼ French. Fine Dining. $9-$35 **AAA Inspector Notes:** *Classic.* Family-operated since 1947, this award-winning, formal French restaurant presents a menu that includes highlights such as swordfish with cilantro sauce; fish and shrimp broiled with butter and garlic; and chipotle chicken. The fresh-baked pastries are outstanding. There's also a tea room. **Features:** full bar. **Reservations:** suggested. **Address:** Ave Blancarte No. 130 **Location:** Just n of Ave Lopez Mateos; centro; across from Americas Best Value Inn/Posada El Rey Sol. **Parking:** street only. B L D

## HALIOTIS       646/176-3720

▼▼ ▼▼ Seafood. Casual Dining. $10-$35 **AAA Inspector Notes:** Popular with locals, this family-operated restaurant is just outside the tourist area. Spacious dining rooms are appointed with nautical décor and family pictures. The menu centers on fresh seafood, including the specialty: Pacific abalone grilled in a wine and butter sauce. Other nice choices include scallops in garlic sauce, cheese-stuffed fish, broiled clams and lobster tacos. **Features:** full bar, patio dining. **Address:** Calle Delante 179 **Location:** Mex 1, 0.6 mi (1 km) e; south end of town. L D

## LAS CAZUELAS RESTAURANT       646/176-1044

▼▼ ▼▼ Mexican. Casual Dining. $6-$30 **AAA Inspector Notes:** Fast, friendly service and generous portions of comfort food attract business and family diners all day long to this busy dining room. Breakfast is a special draw. Lobster, abalone, jumbo shrimp stuffed with lobster, chicken adobo, chicken and grilled or baked fish with garlic are a few of the available dishes. **Features:** full bar. **Address:** Ave Sangines No. 6 **Location:** 1.2 mi (2 km) s of town on blvds Lazaro Cardenas and Costero, just e. B L D

## MANZANILLA RESTAURANTE       646/175-7073

▼▼ ▼▼ ▼ Regional Mexican. Fine Dining. $15-$30 **AAA Inspector Notes:** The minimalist décor here is highlighted by pink chandeliers and a vintage bar. Famed chef Benito Molina creates modern Mexican cuisine with a flair. Favorites include the oxtail risotto with wild mushrooms, seared abalone and aged rib-eye steak. **Features:** full bar. **Reservations:** suggested. **Address:** Teniente Azueta 139 22800 **Location:** Centro. **Parking:** street only. L D LATE

## THE RESTAURANT AT PUNTA MORRO       646/178-3507

▼▼ ▼▼ International. Fine Dining. $15-$50 **AAA Inspector Notes:** Set atop a rock overlooking the ocean, this restaurant offers both sunset and city light views. The waves lap beneath the dining room, which features menu selections like calamari steak with "pancake" sauce scented with sage, New Zealand rack of lamb with sangria sauce, prime rib with a biplanes corn basket and chicken breast marinated in balsamic vinegar and virgin olive oil. The lengthy wine list and the flan with Irish cream will complete any meal. **Features:** full bar. **Address:** KM 106 Carr Tijuana-Ensenada **Location:** 3.1 mi (5 km) n of town on Mex 1, 0.3 mi (0.5 km) w; in Punta Morro Resort. B L D

## SANO'S STEAK HOUSE       646/174-4061

▼▼ ▼▼ Steak. Casual Dining. $15-$40 **AAA Inspector Notes:** The restaurant is located in a mission-style building with an open courtyard fronting the lounge. Guests are greeted by personable staff, then escorted to a private booth. The premium steak cuts are aged for at least 21 days, and the menu also boasts a variety of fish, chicken and salmon selections. Fresh herbs, spices and marinated peppers add to the authentic taste. The ambiance, fine service and excellent food make for an enjoyable experience. **Features:** full bar, patio dining. **Reservations:** suggested. **Address:** KM 108 Carr Tijuana-Ensenada **Location:** On Mex 1-D (toll road), 1.8 mi (3 km) n of town at KM 108 Playitas Zona. L D

## LA PAZ, BAJA CALIFORNIA SUR (E-3)

pop. 251,871
• Restaurants p. 422

## ARAIZA PALMIRA       (612)121-6200

▼▼ ▼▼ Hotel $90-$120 **Address:** Blvd Alberto Alvarado Aramburo S/N 23010 **Location:** 1.5 mi (2.5 km) n of town on Carr a Pichilingue. **Facility:** Meets AAA guest room security requirements. 119 units. 3 stories (no elevator), interior corridors. *Bath:* shower only. **Dining:** nightclub. **Pool(s):** outdoor. **Activities:** tennis, picnic facilities. **Guest Services:** complimentary and valet laundry, area transportation.

🍽️ 🏊 BIZ 📶 ✕ 💻 / SOME UNITS 📞

## CLUB EL MORO HOTEL & SUITES       612/122-4084

▼▼ ▼▼ Hotel $85-$171 **Address:** KM 2 Carr a Pichilingue 23010 **Location:** Oceanfront. 1.2 mi (2 km) n of town. **Facility:** 29 units, some two bedrooms and efficiencies. 2 stories (no elevator), exterior corridors. *Bath:* shower only. **Pool(s):** outdoor. **Activities:** hot tub, fishing. **Guest Services:** valet laundry.

🍽️ 🍷 🏊 BIZ 📶 ✕ 🏋️ / SOME UNITS 🍴 📞 📺 💻

**COSTABAJA RESORT & SPA** (612)123-6000

◆◆◆◆ **Contemporary Resort Hotel** $158-$450 **Address:** KM 7.5 Carr a Pichilingue 23010 **Location:** Oceanfront. 4.5 mi (7.5 km) n of town; adjacent to Marina Costa Baja. **Facility:** Located on the bay and marina, this upscale resort features grand public areas and well appointed modern rooms and baths with an open design concept. 115 units. 4 stories, interior/exterior corridors. **Parking:** on-site and valet. **Terms:** 3 day cancellation notice. **Amenities:** safes. **Dining:** 3 restaurants. **Pool(s):** heated outdoor. **Activities:** steamroom, beach access, marina, fishing, scuba diving, snorkeling, regulation golf, tennis, exercise room, spa. **Guest Services:** valet laundry, area transportation.

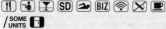

**GRAND PLAZA LA PAZ HOTEL AND SUITES** (612)124-0830

◆◆ **Hotel.** Rates not provided. **Address:** Lote A Marina Nte Fidepaz 23090 **Location:** 3.3 mi (5.5 km) sw on Mex 1 (Abasolo). **Facility:** 54 units, some two and three bedrooms. 2-3 stories (no elevator), exterior corridors. **Amenities:** safes. **Pool(s):** outdoor. **Activities:** sauna, hot tub, exercise room. **Guest Services:** valet laundry.

**HOTEL MARINA SPA & CONVENTION CENTER** 612/121-6254

◇◆◆ **Hotel** $95-$191 **Address:** KM 2.5 Carr a Pichilingue 23010 **Location:** 1.5 mi (2.5 km) n of town. **Facility:** 89 units, some efficiencies. 5 stories, exterior corridors. *Bath:* shower only. **Terms:** 3 day cancellation notice. **Amenities:** *Some:* safes. **Pool(s):** outdoor. **Activities:** hot tub, marina, tennis, spa. **Guest Services:** valet laundry.

**HOTEL MEDITERRANE** 612/125-1195

◆ **Hotel** $67-$102 **Address:** Allende No. 36 23000 **Location:** In town; just e of Paseo Alvaro Obregon. **Facility:** 9 units. 2 stories (no elevator), exterior corridors. *Bath:* shower only. **Parking:** street only. **Terms:** 7 day cancellation notice. **Dining:** Zoe Restaurant, see separate listing. **Guest Services:** valet laundry.

**HOTEL PERLA** 612/122-0777

◆◆ **Hotel** $96 **Address:** Paseo Alvaro Obregon No. 1570 23000 **Location:** On the Malecon; centro. **Facility:** 110 units. 4 stories, interior corridors. *Bath:* shower only. **Parking:** on-site and valet. **Amenities:** safes. **Dining:** Restaurant La Terraza, see separate listing, nightclub. **Pool(s):** outdoor. **Activities:** hot tub, playground. **Guest Services:** valet laundry.

**HOTEL SEVEN CROWN LA PAZ MALECON** 612/128-7788

◆◆ **Hotel** $93-$127 **Address:** Paseo Alvaro Obregon y Lerdo de Tejada 23000 **Location:** On the Malecon; centro. **Facility:** Meets AAA guest room security requirements. 55 units, some efficiencies. 6 stories, interior corridors. *Bath:* shower only. **Parking:** on-site and valet. **Activities:** hot tub. **Guest Services:** valet laundry.

**HYATT PLACE LA PAZ** (612)123-1234

◆◆◆◆ **Hotel** $75-$200

**HYATT PLACE®**
**AAA Benefit:** Members save 10%!

**Address:** Km 7.5 carreterra a pichilingue col. Lomas de Palmira 23010 **Location:** Waterfront. 4.5 mi (7.5 km) n of town; adjacent to Marina Costa Baja. **Facility:** Meets AAA guest room security requirements. 151 units. 5 stories, interior corridors. **Amenities:** safes. **Pool(s):** heated outdoor. **Activities:** exercise room. **Guest Services:** valet laundry, area transportation.

**POSADA DE LAS FLORES LA PAZ** (612)125-5871

◆◆◆◆ **Bed & Breakfast** $150-$250 **Address:** Paseo Alvaro Obregon No. 440 **Location:** Oceanfront. On northern end of town along the Malecon. **Facility:** Offering stunning views of the sunrise and sunset, this antique upscale Mexican hacienda exemplifies authenticity in its furnishings and décor. 8 units. 3 stories (no elevator), exterior corridors. **Parking:** street only. **Terms:** 3 day cancellation notice. **Pool(s):** outdoor. **Guest Services:** valet laundry.

**WHERE TO EAT**

**EL AURA** 612/128-7787

◆◆◆ International. Casual Dining. $10-$30 **AAA Inspector Notes:** The restaurant lays out a breakfast buffet on Sundays. **Features:** full bar, patio dining, Sunday brunch. **Address:** Paseo Alvaro No. 1710 Obregon y Lerdo de Tejeda 23000 **Location:** On the Malecon; centro; in Hotel Seven Crown. **Parking:** street only.
B L D

**LAS TRES VIRGENES** 612/123-2226

◆◆◆ International. Casual Dining. $10-$30 **AAA Inspector Notes:** A casual and elegant outdoor courtyard is the focal point of this local favorite. Entrees are prepared in a wood-fired oven and include such specialties as Porto Nuevo lobster tails, mesquite-grilled filets, and free-range chicken breast. **Features:** full bar, patio dining. **Reservations:** suggested. **Address:** Calle Madero 1130 23000 **Location:** Centro. **Parking:** street only. L D

**LOS MAGUEYES RESTAURANT** 612/128-7846

◆◆ Mexican. Casual Dining. $10-$27 **AAA Inspector Notes:** The restaurant's name means "cactus," and you'll see the real thing growing outside. However, the fresh salsas, crisp salads, tender beef and classic Mexican dishes are anything but prickly. Good choices include the chicken mole and the flank steak grilled with onions. Classic guitar music livens up the atmosphere on weekends. **Features:** full bar. **Address:** Ignacio Allende 512 e/Gmo Prieto y Ramirez 23000 **Location:** Central; jct Allende and Prieto.
B L D

**NIM RESTAURANTE** 612/122-0908

◆◆◆ International. Casual Dining. $15-$25 **AAA Inspector Notes:** Housed in a restored, upscale residence with hand painted tile floors, this chic downtown spot offers an eclectic array of choices like Moroccan lamb tagine with saffron couscous, steamed clams in coconut broth with Serrano chiles, or a savory Vietnamese pho. Check out the on-site wine shop featuring a nice selection of international wines. **Features:** full bar, patio dining. **Reservations:** suggested. **Address:** Revolucion de 1910, esq Hidalgo 23000 **Location:** Centro. **Parking:** street only. L D

**PALERMO'S RISTORANTE** 612/123-1222

◆◆◆ Italian Steak. Fine Dining. $12-$40 **AAA Inspector Notes:** With a prime waterfront location, you can savor the view along with delicious seafood, pasta and steak selections. For something more casual, try one of the gourmet pizzas. Service is refined, without being stuffy. There's live music nightly. **Features:** full bar, patio dining. **Reservations:** suggested. **Address:** Paseo Alvaro Obregon y Hidalgo 23000 **Location:** On the Malecon. **Parking:** street only. L D

**RESTAURANT LA COSTA** 612/122-8808

◆ Seafood. Casual Dining. $10-$35 **AAA Inspector Notes:** This charming restaurant with sandy floors and a palapa roof serves exceptionally fresh seafood dishes. Menu highlights include manta ray or shrimp soup thick with fish and veggies, and Veracruz-style preparations of fish and shellfish. **Features:** full bar, patio dining. **Address:** Navarro y Bahia de La Paz 23060 **Location:** Jct Abasolo, just nw; centro; on the beach. **Parking:** street only. L D

**RESTAURANT LA TERRAZA** 612/122-0777

◆◆ Mexican. Casual Dining. $8-$25 **AAA Inspector Notes:** Popular for its window to the bay and streetside views, the coffee shop-style restaurant offers good food and prompt service. The varied menu lists Mexican favorites, chicken cordon bleu, T-bone steak and filet mignon. **Features:** full bar. **Address:** Paseo Alvaro Obregon No. 1570 23000 **Location:** On the Malecon; centro; in Hotel Perla. **Parking:** street only. B L D

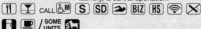

## ZOE RESTAURANT
612/125-1195

▼▼▼ International. Casual Dining. $9-$22 **AAA Inspector Notes:** In front of the hotel, this converted house has black-and-white tile floors, open walls and contemporary décor. Guests can sit in one of several rooms or on the front patio. Made fresh daily on the premises, pasta is used in such preparations as three-cheese ravioli with sage butter. Other favorites include chicken with green curry sauce and fresh salads. **Features:** full bar, patio dining. **Address:** Allende 36 23000 **Location:** In town; just e of Paseo Alvaro Obregon; in Hotel Mediterrane. **Parking:** street only. [D]

# LORETO, BAJA CALIFORNIA SUR (D-3)
### pop. 16,738

## HACIENDA SUITES
613/135-0202

▼▼ Hotel. Rates not provided. **Address:** Salvatierra No. 152 23880 **Location:** 0.6 mi (1 km) e of Mex 1; at town entrance. **Facility:** 42 units. 2 stories (no elevator), exterior corridors. *Bath:* shower only. **Amenities:** safes. **Pool(s):** outdoor. **Guest Services:** valet laundry.

## LA MISION
(613)134-0350

▼▼▼▼ Boutique Hotel. Rates not provided. **Address:** Rosendo Robles S/N Col Centro 23880 **Location:** Waterfront. Mex 1, 1.2 mi (2 km) e on Salvatierra towards Malecon, just n. **Facility:** Overlooking the Malecon and Sea of Cortez, this property was built to emulate the grandeur of classic Mediterranean-style architecture. Guest rooms are spacious and well appointed, each with a terrace. 67 units, some two bedrooms. 4 stories, interior/exterior corridors. **Amenities:** safes. **Dining:** Los Olivos Restaurant, see separate listing. **Pool(s):** outdoor. **Activities:** hot tub, spa. **Guest Services:** valet laundry.

## POSADA DE LAS FLORES LORETO
613/135-1162

▼▼▼ Bed & Breakfast $150-$290 **Address:** Salvatierra esq Madero Col Centro 23880 **Location:** Mex 1, 0.9 mi (1.5 km) e to Calle Independencia, just n to Blvd Benito Juárez, then 0.3 mi (0.5 km) s. **Facility:** Heavy wood furniture and stone floors lend to this hacienda's Old World charm; a glass-bottomed rooftop swimming pool forms the lobby ceiling. 15 units. 3 stories (no elevator), exterior corridors. *Bath:* shower only. **Parking:** street only. **Terms:** 30 day cancellation notice-fee imposed. **Pool(s):** outdoor. **Activities:** spa. **Guest Services:** valet laundry.

## HOTEL VILLA DEL PALMAR AT THE ISLANDS OF LORETO
613/134-1000

[fyi] Not evaluated. **Address:** Carr Transpeninsular KM 84, Ensenada Blanca 23880 **Location:** Oceanfront. Facilities, services, and décor characterize a mid-scale property.

## LORETO BAJA GOLF RESORT & SPA
613/133-0010

[fyi] Not evaluated. **Address:** Blvd Mision de Loreto S/N Fracc Napolo 23880 **Location:** Oceanfront. 4.8 mi (8 km) s on Mex 1, 0.6 mi (1 km) e on Mision San Ignacio, 0.6 mi (1 km) s; in Nopolo. Facilities, services, and décor characterize a mid-scale property. An attractive waterfront property, it's located in an upscale residential area.

### WHERE TO EAT

## 1697 RESTAURANT & PUB
613/135-2538

▼▼ ▼▼ Fusion. Casual Dining. $10-$30 **AAA Inspector Notes:** In an idyllic setting across from the historic town square, the restaurant's chef/owners have concocted a delightful and delicious fusion of Mexican and Italian cuisines. The fresh fish of the day, stuffed with vegetables and bathed in a creamy chipotle sauce is recommended, as are the outstanding wood-fired pizzas. **Features:** full bar, patio dining. **Address:** 14 Calle Davis 23880 **Location:** At town square. **Parking:** street only. [D]

## DOMINGO'S PLACE
613/135-2445

▼▼▼ Steak. Casual Dining. $12-$35 **AAA Inspector Notes:** Rough brick walls, heavy wood doors, and tables with wagon wheel lights contribute to the hacienda-style, ranch atmosphere. The aromas of mesquite-grilled steaks fill the air. Also offered are pork chops, fish and shrimp with garlic butter, tacos, chiles rellenos and hamburgers. **Features:** full bar, patio dining. **Address:** Salvatierra No. 154 23880 **Location:** 0.6 mi (1 km) e of El Nido Mex 1; at town entrance. [L] [D]

## LOS OLIVOS RESTAURANT
613/135-0524

▼▼▼ Mediterranean. Fine Dining. $12-$30 **AAA Inspector Notes:** Diners who opt for the covered terrace seating or a table by the window can watch fishing boats or couples strolling along the malecón. **Features:** full bar, patio dining. **Reservations:** suggested. **Address:** Rosendo Robles S/N Col Centro 23880 **Location:** Mex 1, 1.2 mi (2 km) e on Salvatierra towards Malecon, just n; in La Mision. **Parking:** street only.

[B] [L] [D] CALL [&M]

## MEDITERRANEO
613/135-2577

▼▼ Seafood. Casual Dining. $12-$40 **AAA Inspector Notes:** Diners who choose to sit upstairs on the deck are rewarded with a great view across the malecon. Fresh fish, shellfish and pasta dishes are specialties here. **Features:** full bar, patio dining. **Address:** Malecon Lopez Mateos e Salvatierra e Hidalgo 23880 **Location:** Mex 1, 1.2 mi (2 km) e on Salvatierra towards Malecon, just n. **Parking:** on-site and street. [L] [D]

## MITA GOURMET
613/135-2025

▼▼▼ Regional Mexican. Casual Dining. $10-$25 **AAA Inspector Notes:** In an intimate setting overlooking the historic town square, chef Juan Carlos prepares the fresh fish of the day to guests' specifications. **Features:** full bar, patio dining. **Reservations:** suggested. **Address:** 13 Calle Davis 23880 **Location:** At town square. **Parking:** street only. [L] [D] [⬥]

# LOS BARRILES, BAJA CALIFORNIA SUR

## LOS BARRILES HOTEL
624/141-0024

▼▼ Hotel. Rates not provided. **Address:** 20 de Noviembre 23501 **Location:** 0.6 mi (1 km) e of Mex 1, 0.6 mi (1 km) n. **Facility:** 20 units. 2 stories (no elevator), exterior corridors. *Bath:* shower only. **Pool(s):** outdoor. **Activities:** hot tub.

# MEXICALI, BAJA CALIFORNIA (A-2)
### pop. 936,826
### • Restaurants p. 424

## ARAIZA HOTEL
686/564-1100

▼▼▼ Hotel. $92-$159 **Address:** Blvd Benito Juárez No. 2220 **Location:** From border, 2.6 mi (4.5 km) e on Ave Cristobal Colon, 1.9 mi (3 km) s on Calzada Justo Sierra and Blvd Benito Juárez. **Facility:** 270 units. 3-6 stories, interior corridors. **Terms:** cancellation fee imposed. **Amenities:** safes. **Dining:** Kobu Japanese Cuisine, see separate listing, entertainment. **Pool(s):** outdoor, heated outdoor. **Activities:** hot tub, tennis, game room, exercise room. **Guest Services:** valet and coin laundry.

## CITYEXPRESS HOTELES
(686)564-1650

▼▼▼ Hotel. Rates not provided. **Address:** Blvd Benito Juárez No. 1342 21270 **Location:** From border, 2.6 mi (4.5 km) e on Ave Cristobal Colon, 1.9 mi (3.1 km) s on Calzada Justo Sierra and Blvd Benito Juárez. **Facility:** 117 units. 7 stories, interior corridors. *Bath:* shower only. **Activities:** exercise room. **Guest Services:** valet laundry, area transportation.

## FIESTA INN MEXICALI (686)837-3300

 **Hotel.** Rates not provided. **Address:** Blvd Adolfo Lopez Mateos No. 1029 21000 **Location:** 2.6 mi (4.5 km) s of border, just w. **Facility:** 150 units. 5 stories, interior corridors. **Pool(s):** outdoor. **Activities:** exercise room. **Guest Services:** valet laundry.

## HOTEL CALAFIA MEXICALI 686/568-3311

**Hotel.** Rates not provided. **Address:** Calzada Justo Sierra No. 1495 92231 **Location:** From border, 2.6 mi (4.5 km) s and e on Ave Cristobal Colon, 1.4 mi (2.2 km) s. **Facility:** 172 units. 2-4 stories (no elevator), exterior corridors. **Amenities:** Some: safes. **Pool(s):** outdoor. **Activities:** exercise room. **Guest Services:** valet and coin laundry, area transportation.

## HOTEL COLONIAL (686)556-1312

**Motel.** Rates not provided. **Address:** Blvd Adolfo Lopez Mateos No. 1048 21000 **Location:** 2.6 mi (4.5 km) s of border. **Facility:** 150 units. 2 stories (no elevator), exterior corridors. **Pool(s):** outdoor. **Activities:** limited exercise equipment. **Guest Services:** valet laundry.

## HOTEL LUCERNA (686)564-7000

Hotel
Rates not provided

**Address:** Blvd Benito Juárez No. 2151 21270 **Location:** From border, 2.6 mi (4.5 km) e on Ave Cristobal Colon, 2.3 mi (3.8 km) s on Calzada Justo Sierra and Blvd Benito Juárez. **Facility:** 176 units. 1-6 stories, interior/exterior corridors. **Amenities:** Some: safes. **Dining:** 2 restaurants, also, El Acueducto, Mezzosole Restaurante Italiano, see separate listings. **Pool(s):** outdoor. **Activities:** sauna, exercise room, massage. **Guest Services:** valet laundry, area transportation.

## HOTEL POSADA INN 686/558-6100

**Motel** $56-$65 **Address:** Blvd Lopez Mateos y Torneros No. 939 21000 **Location:** 2.4 mi (4 km) s of border. **Facility:** 49 units. 2 stories (no elevator), exterior corridors. **Amenities:** safes.

## REAL INN MEXICALI (686)557-3600

**Hotel.** Rates not provided. **Address:** Ave de Los Heroes No. 201 21000 **Location:** 2.6 mi (4.5 km) s of border on Blvd Lopez Mateos, just w. **Facility:** 158 units. 8 stories, interior corridors. **Parking:** on-site and valet. **Amenities:** safes. **Dining:** 2 restaurants. **Pool(s):** outdoor. **Activities:** sauna, exercise room. **Guest Services:** valet laundry. Affiliated with Camino Real Hotels.

### WHERE TO EAT

## CASINO DE MEXICALI 686/552-9966

**International. Casual Dining.** $10-$30 **AAA Inspector Notes:** A local favorite for special occasions, the stylish restaurant has a stone entrance, white linen tablecloths, a sprig of greens on each table, designer lighting and an exhibition kitchen. On the menu are prime steaks, chicken parmigiana, fresh fish with herbs, gourmet hamburgers, tacos and burritos. **Features:** full bar. **Address:** Calle L No. 199 **Location:** 2.4 mi (4 km) e of border on Ave Francisco Madero, 0.3 mi (0.5 km) s on Calle K, just e to Calle L. **Parking:** street only. B L D

## EL ACUEDUCTO 686/564-7000

**International. Fine Dining.** $16-$37 **AAA Inspector Notes:** The personable staff goes the extra mile to make sure you have a superior dining experience at this elegant yet casual restaurant. Menu selections range from fresh seafood to savory meats, and it's hard to go wrong with any of the Mexican specialty entrees. **Features:** full bar. **Address:** Blvd Benito Juárez No. 2151 21270 **Location:** From border, 2.6 mi (4.5 km) e on Ave Cristobal Colon, 2.3 mi (3.8 km) s on Calzada Justo Sierra and Blvd Benito Juárez; in Hotel Lucerna. B L D LATE

## EL RINCON DE PANCHITO RESTAURANT 686/567-7718

**Chinese. Casual Dining.** $7-$20 **AAA Inspector Notes:** Accommodating large parties or family celebrations is not a problem at this authentic Cantonese eatery. Specialties include seafood, pork and vegetable entrées. Portions are large enough to share, so come with a hearty appetite. **Features:** full bar. **Address:** Blvd Benito Juárez No. 1900 **Location:** From border, 2.6 mi (4.5 km) e on Ave Cristobal Colon, 1.8 mi (3 km) s on Calzada Justo Sierra and Blvd Benito Juárez. L D LATE

## KOBU JAPANESE CUISINE 686/564-1100

**Asian Fusion. Casual Dining.** $10-$50 **AAA Inspector Notes:** The small dining room is trendy and fun, and serves fresh sushi, sashimi, and specialty rolls, as well as Mexican-inspired items like octopus and chili tostadas, tamarind duck, and a variety of ceviches. **Features:** full bar. **Address:** Blvd Benito Juárez No. 2220 21270 **Location:** From border, 2.6 mi (4.5 km) e on Ave Cristobal Colon, 1.9 mi (3 km) s on Calzada Justo Sierra and Blvd Benito Juárez; in Araiza Hotel. L D

## LOS ARCOS RESTAURANT 686/556-0903

**Mexican Seafood. Casual Dining.** $9-$21 **AAA Inspector Notes:** Festively decorated with fish netting, sculptures and bright colors, the restaurant has lively servers to match. Fresh fish from local waters is the specialty. Open-faced fish tacos with lime are a treat, as is the seafood fiesta for two, which includes a variety of stews of squid and octopus, shredded fish, smoked fish and shrimp, stuffed peppers and perch. Steaks also are available. Top dessert choices are bananas flambe and crepes Suzette. **Features:** full bar. **Address:** Calle Calafia No. 454 **Location:** 2.6 mi (4.5 km) s of border via Blvd Lopez Mateos, just w. L D

## MEZZOSOLE RESTAURANTE ITALIANO 686/564-7000

**Italian. Fine Dining.** $13-$26 **AAA Inspector Notes:** A cool and relaxing atmosphere weaves through the intimate dining room, which has wall and ceiling murals and overlooks the swimming pool. Popular dishes on a menu of pasta, pizza and seafood entrees include seafood linguine, Gorgonzola and beef and chicken prosciutto. **Features:** full bar. **Address:** Blvd Benito Juárez No. 2151 21270 **Location:** From border, 2.6 mi (4.5 km) e on Ave Cristobal Colon, 2.3 mi (3.8 km) s on Calzada Justo Sierra and Blvd Benito Juárez; in Hotel Lucerna. L D LATE

## SAKURA RESTAURANT 686/566-4848

**Japanese. Casual Dining.** $8-$35 **AAA Inspector Notes:** The large complex houses a video bar and karaoke club. Wood paneling, bridges and a rock and water garden with live turtles decorate the dining room. The sushi bar and teppanyaki tables occupy separate areas. Locals frequent the buffet lunch from noon-4 pm daily. **Features:** full bar. **Address:** Blvd Lazaro Cardenas y Calz Fco L Monte **Location:** 2.6 mi (4.5 km) s of border on Blvd Lopez Mateos, just w. L D

# MULEGÉ, BAJA CALIFORNIA SUR (D-3)
pop. 59,114

## LAS CASITAS RESTAURANT 615/153-0019

**Mexican. Casual Dining.** $5-$23 **AAA Inspector Notes:** Popular for breakfast and lunch, the casual patio comes alive Friday night when a mariachi band and folkloric dancers perform during the fiesta buffet. Grilled lobster, fried or ranchero-style garlic chicken, baby back pork ribs and charcoal-broiled fish or shrimp are among the tried-and-true entrees. **Features:** full bar, patio dining. **Address:** Madero No. 50 **Location:** Callejon de Los Estudiantes and Ave Independencia; centro. **Parking:** street only. B L D

## PUNTA CHIVATO, BAJA CALIFORNIA SUR

### POSADA DE LAS FLORES PUNTA CHIVATO
615/155-5600

(fyi) **Not evaluated. Address:** Domicilio Conocido **Location:** Oceanfront. Mex 1 at Palo Verde, 10.2 mi (17 km) e on gravel and dirt road. Facilities, services, and décor characterize a mid-scale property.

## ROSARITO, BAJA CALIFORNIA (A-1)
### pop. 90,668

### ROSARITO BEACH HOTEL & SPA
(619)946-2987

**Resort Hotel**
**$99-$399**

**Address:** Blvd Benito Juárez No. 31 **Location:** On Mex 1-D (toll road) exit south end of town, just prior to toll station, circle right, then just n. **Facility:** In town, this historic resort continues to rebuild to provide modern accommodations. Units are located throughout two-story and high-rise buildings, and range from modest to upscale. 496 units, some two bedrooms, three bedrooms, efficiencies and kitchens. 1-17 stories, interior/exterior corridors. **Parking:** on-site (fee). **Terms:** check-in 4 pm, 2 night minimum stay – seasonal and/or weekends. **Amenities:** Some: safes. **Dining:** Azteca Restaurant, see separate listing. **Pool(s):** outdoor, heated outdoor. **Activities:** sauna, hot tub, steamroom, fishing, tennis, recreation programs, playground, game room, exercise room, spa. **Guest Services:** valet laundry.

**WHERE TO EAT**

### AZTECA RESTAURANT
619/946-2987

**Mexican**
**Casual Dining**
**$5-$33**

**AAA Inspector Notes:** Enjoy a picturesque view from the dining room while sampling Mexican delicacies flavored with fresh herbs. Traditional dishes, prepared to reflect the local culture and ambiance, are enhanced by classic décor and a fireplace. Try the seafood Baja omelet stuffed with shrimp and lobster. Machaca (shredded beef) is always a favorite, and the ceviche (diced fillet of fish marinated in lemon, tomato and chiles) is served with tortillas, which is a meal in itself. **Features:** full bar. **Address:** Blvd Benito Juárez No. 31 **Location:** On Mex 1-D (toll road) exit south end of town, just prior to toll station, circle right, then just n; in Rosarito Beach Hotel & Spa. *Menu on AAA.com* B L D

### EL NIDO STEAKHOUSE
661/612-1430

Steak. Casual Dining. $10-$40 **AAA Inspector Notes:** Rough brick walls, heavy wood posts, an aviary and tables with wagon wheel lights contribute to the eclectic, hacienda-style atmosphere. The aroma of mesquite-grilled steaks fills the air. Also offered are pork chops, fish and shrimp with garlic butter, tacos, chiles rellenos and hamburgers. **Features:** full bar. **Address:** Blvd Benito Juárez 67 **Location:** Centro. **Parking:** on-site and street. L D

### LOS PELICANOS
661/612-1757

Steak. Casual Dining. $7-$30 **AAA Inspector Notes:** Mesquite-broiled steaks and seafood are served in the dining room or on the patio, both of which overlook the ocean. **Features:** full bar, patio dining. **Address:** Calle Ebano 113 **Location:** Just w of Blvd Benito Juárez; on the beach. B L D

## SAN IGNACIO, BAJA CALIFORNIA SUR

### DESERT INN
615/154-0300

(fyi) **Not evaluated. Address:** KM 74 **Location:** 1.6 mi (2.5 km) w of jct Mex 1, towards town plaza. Facilities, services, and décor characterize an economy property.

## SAN JOSÉ DEL CABO, BAJA CALIFORNIA SUR
• Restaurants p. 427
• Hotels & Restaurants map & index p. 411

### BARCELO GRAND FARO LOS CABOS
(624)142-9292  68

**Resort Hotel**
**Rates not provided**

**Address:** Blvd San Jose S/N Secc Hoteles 1 Fonatur 23400 **Location:** Oceanfront. 0.6 mi (1 km) e off Mex 1; in Hotelera Fonatur. **Facility:** Whether for business or families, this all-inclusive resort offers an abundance of activities with numerous restaurants, bars and swimming pools. Meets AAA guest room security requirements. 350 units, some efficiencies. 5 stories, interior corridors. **Amenities:** safes. **Dining:** 5 restaurants, entertainment. **Pool(s):** outdoor, heated outdoor. **Activities:** hot tub, recreation programs, kids club, bicycles, playground, game room, exercise room, spa. **Guest Services:** valet laundry.

### CABO AZUL RESORT
(624)163-5100  42

**Resort Hotel**
**Rates not provided**

**Address:** Paseo Malecon S/N, Lote 11 Fonatur 23400 **Location:** Oceanfront. 1 mi (1.6 km) e of Mex 1. **Facility:** At night, this exotic resort comes to life with its massive flaming torches illuminating the white-washed exterior and jungle-like landscaped paths. 142 kitchen units, some two and three bedrooms. 6 stories, exterior corridors. **Parking:** valet only. **Terms:** check-in 4 pm, 3 day cancellation notice. **Amenities:** safes. **Dining:** 2 restaurants, also, Javier's, see separate listing. **Pool(s):** heated outdoor. **Activities:** sauna, hot tub, steamroom, recreation programs, kids club, playground, exercise room, spa. **Guest Services:** valet and coin laundry.

### CASA NATALIA CHIC BOUTIQUE HOTEL
(624)146-7100  61

**Boutique**
**Contemporary**
**Hotel**
**$165-$475**

**Address:** Blvd Mijares 4-A, Centro 23400 **Location:** Downtown; at town plaza. **Facility:** This is an intimate Mexican-contemporary style inn on palm filled grounds, with waterfalls and fireplaces. Rooms are individually theme-decorated with private terraces, original artwork, and hammocks. Meets AAA guest room security requirements. 19 units. 2-3 stories (no elevator), interior corridors. **Bath:** shower only. **Parking:** street only. **Terms:** age restrictions may apply, 15 day cancellation notice. **Amenities:** safes. **Dining:** Mi Cocina, see separate listing. **Pool(s):** heated outdoor. **Activities:** massage. **Guest Services:** valet laundry, area transportation.

Take your imagination to new destinations with the online AAA/CAA Travel Guides

(See map & index p. 411.)

## DREAMS LOS CABOS SUITES GOLF RESORT & SPA
(624)145-7600  **40**

Resort Hotel
Rates not provided

**Address:** KM 18.5 Carr Transpeninsular 23400 **Location:** Oceanfront. 7.2 mi (12 km) w on Mex 1. Located at Cabo Real. **Facility:** Wide arches open this Spanish hacienda-style resort's airy lobby to a free-form pool, a sandy beach and the sea. 213 units. 4-6 stories, exterior corridors. **Parking:** valet only. **Terms:** 2-7 night minimum stay - seasonal, 15 day cancellation notice, in season-fee imposed. **Amenities:** safes. **Dining:** 5 restaurants, entertainment. **Pool(s):** heated outdoor. **Activities:** sauna, hot tub, steamroom, tennis, recreation programs, kids club, playground, game room, exercise room, spa. **Guest Services:** valet laundry, rental car service.

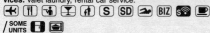

## EL ENCANTO INN HOTEL SUITES & SPA  624/142-0388  **60**

Hotel $116-$294 **Address:** Calle Morelos No. 133 23400 **Location:** Just n of Zaragoza and town square; jct Comonfort. **Facility:** 27 units, some two bedrooms and efficiencies. 2 stories (no elevator), exterior corridors. **Terms:** 2-5 night minimum stay - seasonal and/or weekends, 14 day cancellation notice. **Pool(s):** heated outdoor. **Activities:** sauna, steamroom, spa.

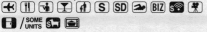

## HILTON LOS CABOS BEACH & GOLF RESORT
(624)145-6500  **45**

Resort Hotel
$159-$479

Hilton
HOTELS & RESORTS

**AAA Benefit:** Members save 5% or more!

**Address:** Carr Transpeninsular KM 19.5 23447 **Location:** Oceanfront. 6.6 mi (11 km) w on Mex 1. Located at Cabo Real. **Facility:** This large resort on a hillside overlooks an infinity swimming pool and the sea and is adjacent to two world-class golf courses. 375 units. 5-6 stories, interior corridors. **Parking:** on-site and valet. **Terms:** 1-7 night minimum stay, cancellation fee imposed. **Amenities:** video games, safes. **Dining:** 4 restaurants, also, Restaurant Fenicia, see separate listing. **Pool(s):** heated outdoor. **Activities:** hot tub, steamroom, regulation golf, tennis, recreation programs, kids club, playground, game room, exercise room, spa. **Guest Services:** valet laundry.

## HOLIDAY INN RESORT LOS CABOS
(624)142-9229  **66**

Resort Hotel
Rates not provided

**Address:** Blvd Mijares S/N, Zona Hotelera 23400 **Location:** Oceanfront. 1.5 mi (2.5 km) e of Mex 1. **Facility:** Next to a fresh-water estuary and natural park, this property accents its scenic setting with pools, organized sports and numerous buffet eateries. 390 units. 3 stories, exterior corridors. **Terms:** 3 night minimum stay - seasonal, 7 day cancellation notice. **Amenities:** *Some:* safes. **Dining:** 5 restaurants, entertainment. **Pool(s):** heated outdoor. **Activities:** tennis, recreation programs, kids club, bicycles, playground, exercise room, massage. **Guest Services:** valet laundry.

## HYATT ZIVA LOS CABOS
624/163-7730  **38**

Resort Hotel
$163-$700

HYATT ZIVA

**AAA Benefit:** Members save 10%!

**Address:** Paseo Malecon S/N Lote-5 **Location:** Oceanfront. 0.4 mi e of Mex 1. **Facility:** This all-inclusive resort sits on a golden sandy beach along the Sea of Cortez. The sprawling property features five free-form swimming pools, including a children's mini water park play area. Meets AAA guest room security requirements. 619 units, some two bedrooms and efficiencies. 7 stories, exterior corridors. **Parking:** on-site and valet. **Amenities:** safes. **Dining:** 7 restaurants, entertainment. **Pool(s):** outdoor, heated outdoor. **Activities:** sauna, hot tub, steamroom, cabanas, tennis, recreation programs, kids club, game room, lawn sports, spa. **Guest Services:** valet laundry, rental car service.

## LAS VENTANAS AL PARAISO, A ROSEWOOD RESORT
(624)144-2800  **43**

Resort Hotel
Rates not provided

**Address:** KM 19.5 Carr Transpeninsular 23400 **Location:** Oceanfront. 6.9 mi (11.5 km) w on Mex 1. Located at Cabo Real. **Facility:** The property's name translates to "window to paradise," a truly applicable name for this beautiful oceanfront resort. The unique, luxurious décor style embraces a native desert ambience. 83 units, some two bedrooms, three bedrooms and kitchens. 2 stories (no elevator), exterior corridors. **Parking:** valet only. **Terms:** 28 day cancellation notice. **Amenities:** safes. **Dining:** 2 restaurants, also, The Restaurant, see separate listing. **Pool(s):** outdoor, heated outdoor. **Activities:** sauna, hot tub, steamroom, cabanas, tennis, exercise room, spa. **Guest Services:** valet laundry, area transportation.

## MARQUIS LOS CABOS ALL INCLUSIVE RESORT & SPA
(624)144-2000  **47**

Contemporary
Resort Hotel
Rates not provided

**Address:** Carr Transpeninsular KM 21.5, Lote 74 23400 **Location:** Oceanfront. 6.6 mi (11 km) w on Mex 1. Located at Cabo Real. **Facility:** This contemporary resort's architectural highlights include an open-air arch and a 36-foot waterfall splashing through the lobby into the pool bar. 235 units. 2-5 stories, interior corridors. **Parking:** valet only. **Terms:** 3-5 night minimum stay - seasonal, 15 day cancellation notice-fee imposed. **Amenities:** safes. **Dining:** 6 restaurants, entertainment. **Pool(s):** heated outdoor. **Activities:** hot tub, steamroom, regulation golf, recreation programs, spa. **Guest Services:** valet laundry, rental car service.

(See map & index p. 411.)

## MELIA CABO REAL, ALL INCLUSIVE    (624)144-2222  44

▽▽▽▽ **Resort Hotel.** Rates not provided. **Address:** KM 19.5 Carr Transpeninsular 23400 **Location:** Oceanfront. 6.6 mi (11 km) w on Mex 1. Located at Cabo Real. **Facility:** Wrapping around palm-shaded grounds and a large free-form pool, these spacious guest rooms have marble floors and light, airy décor. Daily activities include DJ-hosted party events at the pool. 307 units. 1-5 stories, exterior corridors. **Terms:** 2-3 night minimum stay - seasonal and/or weekends, 3 day cancellation notice. **Amenities:** safes. **Dining:** 5 restaurants, entertainment. **Pool(s):** heated outdoor. **Activities:** hot tub, cabanas, tennis, recreation programs, kids club, playground, game room, exercise room, massage. **Guest Services:** valet laundry.

## ONE&ONLY PALMILLA    (624)146-7000  49

▽▽▽▽ ▽▽▽▽
**Resort Hotel**
Rates not provided

**Address:** 7.5 KM Carr Transpeninsular 23400 **Location:** Oceanfront. 2.4 mi (4 km) w on Mex 1. **Facility:** Nine hundred acres of lush, palm-covered grounds surround this long-established Colonial Mexican-style property. Use the world-class spa, get pampered by your butler or stroll the white-sand beach. 173 units, some kitchens and houses. 1-3 stories (no elevator), exterior corridors. **Parking:** valet only. **Terms:** 21 day cancellation notice-fee imposed. **Amenities:** video games, safes. **Dining:** 2 restaurants, also Agua, Market by Jean-Georges, see separate listings. **Pool(s):** heated outdoor. **Activities:** sauna, hot tub, steamroom, regulation golf, tennis, recreation programs, kids club, exercise room, spa. **Guest Services:** valet laundry, area transportation.

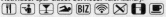

## ROYAL SOLARIS LOS CABOS-ALL INCLUSIVE RESORT & SPA    (624)145-6800  67

▽▽▽▽ **Resort Hotel.** Rates not provided. **Address:** Blvd San Jose, Lote 10 Campo De Golf 23400 **Location:** Oceanfront. 0.4 mi (0.6 km) e. **Facility:** Themed parties are among the many activities organized at this family-friendly resort located on the beach. 390 units. 6 stories, interior corridors. **Bath:** shower only. **Amenities:** safes. **Dining:** 6 restaurants, entertainment. **Pool(s):** heated outdoor. **Activities:** hot tub, scuba diving, tennis, recreation programs, kids club, playground, game room, exercise room, spa. **Guest Services:** valet laundry.

## TROPICANA INN    624/142-1580  63

▽▽▽ **Hotel** $87-$140 **Address:** Blvd Mijares No. 30 23400 **Location:** Centro. **Facility:** 38 units. 2-3 stories (no elevator), exterior corridors. **Terms:** 20 day cancellation notice, in season. **Dining:** Tropicana Bar & Grill, see separate listing. **Pool(s):** heated outdoor. **Activities:** spa. **Guest Services:** valet laundry.

## THE WESTIN RESORT & SPA LOS CABOS    (624)142-9000  48

**fyi**
**Resort Hotel**
$219

**WESTIN** HOTELS & RESORTS
**AAA Benefit:** Members save up to 15%, plus Starwood Preferred Guest® benefits!

Under major renovation, scheduled to be completed September 2015. **Last Rated:** ▽▽▽▽ **Address:** Carr Transpeninsular KM 22.5 23400 **Location:** Oceanfront. 6 mi (10 km) w on Mex 1. **Facility:** Extraordinary architecture creating a window to the sea is the signature of this resort, providing private ocean views from every room. 243 units. 3-9 stories, exterior corridors. **Terms:** closed 12/1-2/29, 3 day cancellation notice-fee imposed, resort fee. **Amenities:** safes. **Dining:** 3 restaurants. **Pool(s):** heated outdoor. **Activities:** sauna, hot tub, steamroom, cabanas, tennis, kids club, exercise room, spa. **Guest Services:** valet laundry.

## ZOËTRY CASA DEL MAR    (624)145-7700  41

▽▽▽▽ ▽▽▽▽ **Resort Hotel.** Rates not provided. **Address:** Carr Transpeninsular KM 19.5 23400 **Location:** Oceanfront. 6.9 mi (11.5 km) w on Mex 1. Located at Cabo Real. **Facility:** With its stone archways, massive wooden doors, courtyard and verdant garden, the resort calls to mind a classic Mexican hacienda. 69 units, some two bedrooms and kitchens. 1-3 stories (no elevator), exterior corridors. **Terms:** 3 night minimum stay - seasonal, 3 day cancellation notice. **Amenities:** safes. **Dining:** 3 restaurants. **Pool(s):** heated outdoor. **Activities:** sauna, hot tub, steamroom, regulation golf, tennis, recreation programs, exercise room, spa. **Guest Services:** valet laundry, area transportation.

## WHERE TO EAT

## AGUA    624/146-7000  54

▽▽▽ ▽▽▽ Mexican. Fine Dining. $18-$49 **AAA Inspector Notes:** Enjoy alfresco dining while perched on a dramatic bluff overlooking the sea. The menu is comprised of Mediterranean fare, which is elegantly presented. The made-from-scratch chicken tortilla soup is a must-try starter topped with diced avocado, tomato and panela cheese. Sautéed Pacific sea bass, homemade fettuccine, and roasted pork chops in a seared foie gras reduction are only a few examples of the excellent fare. **Features:** full bar. **Reservations:** suggested. **Address:** 7.5 KM Carr Transpeninsular 23400 **Location:** 2.4 mi (4 km) w on Mex 1; in One&Only Palmilla. **Parking:** valet only.

## BAAN THAI    624/142-3344  43

▽▽▽ ▽▽▽ Asian. Casual Dining. $10-$34 **AAA Inspector Notes:** Asian teak and bamboo furnishings add to the relaxing ambience of the dining room and patio. Seafood curry, pad thai, lamb shank with herbs, green papaya salad and lettuce-wrapped chicken soon are among the crisply flavored Thai- and Asian-influenced dishes. **Features:** full bar, patio dining. **Address:** Morelos at Alvaro Obregon 24300 **Location:** Just n of Zaragoza and town square. **Parking:** street only.

## BAJA BREWING CO    624/146-9995  40

▽▽▽ American. Casual Dining. $9-$22 **AAA Inspector Notes:** Fans of craft beer will love this small brewery for its variety of specialty brews, best enjoyed around the fire pit on the restaurant's attractive patio. The eclectic, international menu mainly focuses on pub grub, but there's also local seafood, arrachera (flank steak) and pasta, as well as pizzas cooked in a wood-fired oven. The beer-batter bread with tequila butter is a meal in itself. **Features:** full bar, patio dining. **Address:** Morelos S/N No. 1277 E 23400 **Location:** Col Centro, jct Comonfort and Obregon. **Parking:** street only.

(See map & index p. 411.)

**DON SANCHEZ RESTAURANTE**   624/142-2444   51

▼▼▼▼ Regional Mexican. Fine Dining. $14-$27 **AAA Inspector Notes:** In the center of town, this lively yet upscale spot serves delicious, regional Mexican food, including prime steaks from Sonora and the freshest seafood from the Sea of Cortez. In nice weather, the downstairs patio is a lovely spot to enjoy the live music. **Features:** full bar. **Reservations:** suggested. **Address:** Blvd. Antonio Mijares S/N Edificio Eclipse 3 23400 **Location:** Centro. **Parking:** street only.

L   D

**FLORA'S FIELD KITCHEN**   624/355-4564

▼▼▼▼ Natural/Organic. Casual Dining. $15-$38 **AAA Inspector Notes:** Though you have to take a dirt road and drive down a steep hill to get here, you'll be happy you did when you find this hidden gem. Located within the farm where the produce is freshly picked, lies this open-air, tin roof-covered restaurant. You may request to dine at one of the communal tables or privately at one of the garden-style tables. Everything here is organic and made from scratch daily, including the delicious bread that is baked in their wood-fired oven. **Features:** full bar, patio dining, Sunday brunch. **Reservations:** suggested, for dinner. **Address:** Flora Farms, Las Animas Bajas **Location:** 1 mi n of Puerto Los Cabos marina.

B   L   D   AC

**FRENCH RIVIERA BISTRO**   624/142-3350   53

▼▼ French. Casual Dining. $7-$20 **AAA Inspector Notes:** A classically trained master chef, Jacques Chretien treats diners to a wonderful menu of typical French bistro fare and fabulous pastries in this comfortable café. Take a seat in front of the bakery and watch as layers of butter are blended into croissant dough; don't leave the restaurant without at least one. Cassoulet and coq au vin are available to take out in quart size mason jars. **Features:** full bar. **Address:** Plaza Colli Local 10 23400 **Location:** Jct Manuel Doblado and Hidalgo, Colonia Centro. **Parking:** street only.

B   L   D

**JAVIER'S**   624/163-5100   58

▼▼▼▼

Mexican
Fine Dining
$15-$38

**AAA Inspector Notes:** Tiki torches guide the way through the resort's jungle-like landscape to a jaw-dropping grand entrance that's best appreciated at night due to the creative use of fire, water and hanging lanterns. A table near the windows is recommended for stunning views of the beach and distant mountains. Among the tempting menu choices is carne asada made from aged USDA Prime center-cut New York steak with a grilled pasilla chile stuffed with cotija cheese. **Features:** full bar. **Reservations:** suggested. **Address:** Paseo Malecón Lote 11 S/N, Zona Hotelera Fonatur 23400 **Location:** 1 mi (1.6 km) e of Mex 1; in Cabo Azul Resort. **Parking:** valet only.   D   CALL 🅶🅼

**LA PANGA ANTIGUA**   624/142-4041   42

▼▼▼ Regional Mexican Seafood. Fine Dining. $20-$46 **AAA Inspector Notes:** The hacienda setting evokes Old Mexico from a century ago. Star-shaped lights hang from courtyard trees to cast a soft glow over the dining area. Fresh seafood from the Sea of Cortez, as well as steaks are offered. **Features:** full bar, patio dining. **Reservations:** suggested. **Address:** Zaragoza No. 20 23400 **Location:** Just w of Hidalgo; centro. **Parking:** street only.   D

**MARKET BY JEAN-GEORGES**   624/146-7095   52

▼▼▼ ▼▼▼ International. Fine Dining. $28-$55 **AAA Inspector Notes:** This chic restaurant marries innovative cuisine with hip, contemporary decor. Acclaimed chef Jean-Georges Vongerichten has created a menu that allows diners to sample many interesting courses and sides. With starters such as ribbons of tuna, avocado with spicy radish and ginger marinade, or corn ravioli, choices are difficult. Mains include a wide selection of fresh fish and other seafood, grilled beef, lamb or veal, all complemented with distinctive sauces. **Features:** full bar. **Reservations:** suggested. **Address:** 7.5 KM Carr Transpeninsular 23400 **Location:** 2.4 mi (4 km) w on Mex 1; in One&Only Palmilla. **Parking:** valet only.   B   D

**MI COCINA**   624/146-7100   46

▼▼▼ International. Casual Dining. $15-$45 **AAA Inspector Notes:** A casual, yet sophisticated ambience sets the stage for this restaurant's nouvelle Mexican-Euro cuisine. International wines accompany such dishes as grilled shrimp with risotto, pan-seared sea bass on buckwheat soba, grilled lamb with pasta and spinach saffron, and filet mignon on potato leek galette. **Features:** full bar. **Reservations:** suggested. **Address:** Blvd Mijares 4-B, Centro 23400 **Location:** Downtown; at town plaza; in Casa Natalia Chic Boutique Hotel. **Parking:** street only.   L   D   AC

**THE RESTAURANT**   624/144-2800   36

Regional
Mexican
Fine Dining
$17-$70

**AAA Inspector Notes:** Patrons can enjoy elegant dining under the palapa roof or on the open-air patio, which affords views of the sea. In addition, there is a private wine room and beach dining in the sand. Attentive service complements the menu, which lists high-quality dishes prepared with fresh ingredients and a Mexican flair. Steamed parrot fish, roasted cabrilla, Parmesan gnocchi and tender braised short ribs are a few of the items on the ever-changing menu. **Features:** full bar, patio dining. **Reservations:** required. **Address:** KM 19.5 Carr Transpeninsular 23400 **Location:** 6.9 mi (11.5 km) w on Mex 1; in Las Ventanas al Paraiso, A Rosewood Resort. **Parking:** valet only.   B   D   ◩

**RESTAURANTE MAMA MIA**   624/142-3939   41

▼▼ Mexican. Casual Dining. $12-$35 **AAA Inspector Notes:** The menu is split between Mexican and Italian options. You'll find spaghetti bolognese, arrabbiata and brick oven pizzas on the Italian side. Fish tacos, fajitas, chips and salsa populate the Mexican side. The casual, open-air palapa setting overlooks a lovely stretch of sandy beach and affords guests the chance to hear waves crashing while they eat. Reservations are suggested for the very popular theme dinners featuring live entertainment. **Features:** full bar, patio dining. **Address:** Carr Transpeninsular KM 29.5 **Location:** On Mex 1, 1.8 mi (3 km) w of town; in The Coral Baja Resort.   B   L   D

**RESTAURANT FENICIA**   624/145-6500   37

▼▼▼ Italian. Fine Dining. $20-$45 **AAA Inspector Notes:** The pleasant hotel setting overlooks the pool and sea. The Italian menu features a variety of house-made pastas, a selection of mozzarellas and seasonal seafood entrées. **Features:** full bar, patio dining. **Reservations:** suggested. **Address:** Carr Transpeninsular KM 19.5 23447 **Location:** 6.6 mi (11 km) w on Mex 1; in Hilton Los Cabos Beach & Golf Resort. **Parking:** valet only.   D   ◩

**TEQUILA RESTAURANT**   624/142-1155   48

▼▼▼▼ Mediterranean. Fine Dining. $15-$50 **AAA Inspector Notes:** Mexican flavors punctuate the Mediterranean-influenced cuisine on the seasonal menu. Daily, fresh-caught seafood is featured; try the signature dish, tequila shrimp on grilled plantains. The pleasant garden setting occasionally bustles with groups. **Features:** full bar, patio dining. **Address:** Manuel Doblado No. 1011 23400 **Location:** Just w of Blvd Mijares; downtown. **Parking:** street only.   D

**TROPICANA BAR & GRILL**   624/142-2311   50

▼▼ Seafood. Casual Dining. $13-$40 **AAA Inspector Notes:** Fresh seafood and friendly service abound in the large palapa dining room, the comfortable palapa bar and the sidewalk seating area. Specialties are lobster, mahi mahi, ahi tuna and whole red snapper. Breakfasts are popular. **Features:** full bar. **Address:** Blvd Mijares No. 30 23400 **Location:** Centro; in Tropicana Inn. **Parking:** on-site and street.   B   L   D

# TECATE, BAJA CALIFORNIA (A-1)
pop. 101,079

**LA MISION**   665/654-2105

▼▼ Mexican. Casual Dining. $5-$18 **AAA Inspector Notes:** Known for its friendly service and good food, the restaurant serves a variety of sandwiches, soups and salads, as well as seafood, steaks and chicken entrées prepared with a choice of traditional Mexican sauces. **Features:** full bar, Sunday brunch. **Reservations:** required. **Address:** Ave Juárez No. 1110 **Location:** 0.6 mi (1 km) w of town center.   B   L   D

# TIJUANA, BAJA CALIFORNIA (A-1)

pop. 1,559,683
• Restaurants p. 430

## CAMINO REAL TIJUANA    (664)633-4000

▼▼▼ **Hotel.** Rates not provided. **Address:** Paseo de Los Heroes No. 10305, Zona Rio 22320 **Location:** 1.6 mi (2.5 km) se of the border. **Facility:** 263 units. 7 stories, interior corridors. **Parking:** on-site and valet. **Amenities:** safes. **Dining:** 2 restaurants, also, Maria Bonita Cantina, see separate listing. **Activities:** exercise room. **Guest Services:** valet laundry.

## FIESTA INN TIJUANA OTAY AIRPORT    664/979-1900

▼▼▼ **Hotel.** Rates not provided. **Address:** Rampa Aeropuerto No. 16000 **Location:** From Otay Mesa border crossing, 1.8 mi (3 km) s via Carr al Aeropuerto and Calsada Tezhnologico. Located in front of Universidad de Baja California. **Facility:** 142 units. 6 stories, interior corridors. **Pool(s):** outdoor. **Activities:** hot tub, playground, exercise room. **Guest Services:** valet laundry.

## GRAND HOTEL TIJUANA    (664)681-7000

▼▼▼
Hotel
Rates not provided

**Address:** Blvd Agua Caliente No. 4500 **Location:** 1.8 mi (3 km) se of the border via Paseo de Los Heroes, 0.3 mi (0.5 km) s on Ave Rodriguez, just e. Located in a commercial area. **Facility:** 422 units, some two bedrooms. 22 stories, interior corridors. **Parking:** on-site (fee) and valet. **Amenities:** *Some:* safes. **Dining:** 3 restaurants, nightclub. **Pool(s):** heated outdoor. **Activities:** sauna, hot tub, steamroom, tennis, exercise room. **Guest Services:** valet laundry.

## HOLIDAY INN TIJUANA ZONA RIO    (664)636-0000

▼▼▼
Hotel
Rates not provided

**Address:** Paseo de Los Heroes No. 18818, Zona Rio 22320 **Location:** 1.8 mi (3 km) se of the border to Ave Rodriguez, just n to Poniente, 0.3 mi (0.5 km) e. **Facility:** 127 units. 4 stories, interior corridors. *Bath:* shower only. **Pool(s):** outdoor. **Activities:** hot tub, steamroom, exercise room, spa. **Guest Services:** valet laundry.

## HOTEL HACIENDA DEL RIO    664/684-8644

▼▼▼
Hotel
Rates not provided

**Address:** Blvd Rodolfo Sanchez Taboada No. 10606 22320 **Location:** 1.8 mi (3 km) se of the border on Paseo de Los Heroes to Ave Rodriguez, just s, just w. **Facility:** 131 units. 3 stories (no elevator), exterior corridors. **Pool(s):** heated outdoor. **Activities:** exercise room. **Guest Services:** valet laundry, area transportation.

Enjoy great member rates
and benefits at AAA/CAA
Preferred Hotels

## HOTEL LA MESA    664/681-6522

▼▼▼
Motel
Rates not provided

**Address:** Blvd Diaz Gustavo Ordaz No. 12828 22440 **Location:** 1.8 mi (3 km) se of the border on Paseo de Los Heroes, 0.3 mi (0.5 km) s on Ave Rodriguez, 1.6 mi (2.5 km) e on Blvd Agua Caliente. Located in La Mesa area; near casino race course. **Facility:** 139 units. 1-3 stories (no elevator), interior/exterior corridors. **Pool(s):** outdoor. **Activities:** limited exercise equipment. **Guest Services:** valet laundry, area transportation.

## HOTEL LAUSANA OTAY AEROPUERTO    664/973-7600

▼▼▼ **Hotel.** Rates not provided. **Address:** Ave Tijuana 1600; CD Industrial **Location:** From Otay Mesa border crossing, 1.8 mi (3 km) sw via Carr al Aeropuerto and Calle 16. **Facility:** 140 units. 4 stories, interior corridors. **Amenities:** safes. **Pool(s):** heated outdoor. **Activities:** sauna, hot tub, exercise room. **Guest Services:** valet laundry, area transportation.

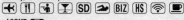

## HOTEL LUCERNA TIJUANA    664/633-3900

▼▼▼
Hotel
Rates not provided

**Address:** Paseo de Los Heroes No. 10902, Zona Rio **Location:** 1.8 mi (3 km) se of the border. **Facility:** 168 units. 2-6 stories, interior/exterior corridors. **Parking:** valet only. **Dining:** 2 restaurants, also, Rivoli Brasserie & Patio, see separate listing. **Pool(s):** outdoor. **Activities:** exercise room. **Guest Services:** valet laundry.

## HOTEL PALACIO AZTECA    (664)681-8100

▼▼ **Hotel** $94-$189 **Address:** Blvd Cuauhtemoc Sur No. 213 Col Davila **Location:** 1.6 mi (2.2 km) s of the border on Paseo de Los Heroes, 0.3 mi (0.5 km) s on Ave Cuauhtemoc (Ave 16 de Septiembre) to Ibarrq, just e, then just n. **Facility:** 201 units. 7 stories, interior corridors. **Parking:** valet only. **Terms:** cancellation fee imposed. **Amenities:** safes. **Pool(s):** outdoor. **Activities:** exercise room. **Guest Services:** valet laundry.

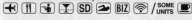

## HOTEL REAL DEL RIO    664/634-3100

▼▼▼ **Hotel.** Rates not provided. **Address:** Jose Ma via Velasco 1409-A, Zona Rio **Location:** 1.6 mi (2.5 km) se of the border on Paseo de Los Heroes to Diego Rivera, just n to Poniente, just e, then just s. **Facility:** 105 units. 5 stories, interior/exterior corridors. *Bath:* shower only. **Amenities:** safes. **Activities:** exercise room. **Guest Services:** valet laundry.

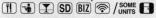

## MARRIOTT TIJUANA    664/622-6600

▼▼▼
Hotel
$103-$169

**AAA Benefit:** Members save 5% or more!

**Address:** Blvd Agua Caliente No. 11553 **Location:** 1.8 mi (3 km) se of the border on Paseo de Los Heroes, 0.3 mi (0.5 km) s on Ave Rodriguez, 0.6 mi (1 km) e. **Facility:** 209 units, some two bedrooms and kitchens. 10 stories, interior corridors. **Parking:** on-site (fee) and valet. **Amenities:** safes. **Pool(s):** heated outdoor. **Activities:** hot tub, exercise room. **Guest Services:** valet laundry.

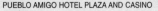

## PUEBLO AMIGO HOTEL PLAZA AND CASINO
664/624-2700

▼▼ **Hotel.** Rates not provided. **Address:** Via Oriente 9211 **Location:** 0.5 mi (0.8 km) se of border, 1st right after border, veer left under bridge to Paseo de Tijuana, just e to Alfonso Reyes, then just s. **Facility:** This property features newly renovated rooms and a lively casino in the atrium lobby. 107 units. 7 stories, interior corridors. **Parking:** on-site and valet. **Amenities:** *Some:* safes. **Activities:** exercise room. **Guest Services:** valet laundry, area transportation.

🅿 ✈ 🍴 🚭 🍸 SD BIZ HS 🛜 / SOME UNITS 📺

## REAL DEL MAR GOLF RESORT AND SPA
664/631-3670

▼▼▼ **Hotel.** Rates not provided. **Address:** KM 19.5 Carr Cuota **Location:** Mex 1-D (toll road) exit Real Del Mar, just e; 11.8 mi (19.5 km) s of the border. **Facility:** 76 efficiencies. 2-3 stories (no elevator), exterior corridors. **Amenities:** *Some:* safes. **Dining:** 2 restaurants. **Pool(s):** heated outdoor. **Activities:** sauna, hot tub, steamroom, regulation golf, tennis, exercise room, spa. **Guest Services:** valet and coin laundry.

🍴 🍸 S SD 🏊 HS 🛜 ✕ 📞 📺
📺 / SOME UNITS 🍳

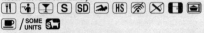

**WHERE TO EAT**

## CASA PLASENCIA
664/686-3604

▼▼▼ **Spanish. Casual Dining. $8-$25 AAA Inspector Notes:** Friendly servers attend to guests in the comfortable dining room. Traditional Spanish recipes are used to prepare numerous tapas and paellas, as well as such dishes as shredded beef with chiles and seasoned chicken breast. **Features:** full bar. **Reservations:** suggested. **Address:** Calle Robirosa No. 250 **Location:** 1.8 mi (3 km) se of border via Paseo de Los Heroes, 0.3 mi (0.5 km) e on Ave Rodriquez to Blvd Agua Caliente, 0.3 mi (0.5 km) e, then just s. **Parking:** on-site and valet. L D

## CHAN'S CUISINE
664/634-2766

▼▼▼ **Szechuan. Casual Dining. $15-$30 AAA Inspector Notes:** The restaurant specializes in tasty platters of Szechuan and Mandarin cuisine. Asian artwork and porcelain vases displayed throughout the restaurant create a Far East ambience. The authentic dishes--ranging from mild to spicy--can be served as combinations dinners or on their own. Chances are excellent you'll be leaving with leftovers in hand. **Features:** full bar. **Address:** Blvd Sanchez Taboada 10880 **Location:** 1.8 mi (3 km) se of border on Paseo de Los Heroes to Ave Rodriguez, just s, then just e. **Parking:** on-site and valet. L D

## CHERIPAN
664/622-9730

▼▼▼ **Argentine. Casual Dining. $10-$25 AAA Inspector Notes:** Located in the "Zona Gastronomica," this highly popular Argentine spot serves up delicious steaks, empanadas, pastas and fresh seafood selections, complemented by an extensive wine and specialty drink list. For something unique, try the tamarind martini. **Features:** full bar. **Reservations:** suggested. **Address:** Calle Escuadron 201-3151 22014 **Location:** 1.8 mi (3 km) se of the border on Paseo de Los Heroes, 0.3 mi (0.5 km) s on Ave Rodriguez, e on Blvd Agua Caliente, then just n. **Parking:** on-site and valet. L D LATE

## EL POTRERO
664/686-3626

▼▼ **Mexican. Casual Dining. $6-$20 AAA Inspector Notes:** Shaped like a large hat, this popular restaurant's walls are covered with cultural artifacts and pictures. Service is thoughtful and casual. Ribeye, New York strip and carne asada are popular steak choices. Chicken can be marinated in polano, conejo or parrilla sauce. Seafood dishes include poached salmon and fish filet in Veracruz sauce. **Features:** full bar. **Address:** Blvd Salinas No. 4700, Col Aviacion **Location:** 1.8 mi (3 km) se of border on Paseo de Los Heroes, 0.3 mi (0.5 km) s on Ave Rodriguez to Blvd Agua Caliente, 0.6 mi (1 km) e, then circle left. B L D LATE

---

## Upgrade to Plus or Premier membership for *more* of the benefits you need most

## EL RODEO
664/686-5640

▼▼ **Steak. Casual Dining. $5-$30 AAA Inspector Notes:** The steak house, which has been serving guests since 1972, specializes in Sonora-style cooking and charcoal-broiled meats. Meals include marinated vegetables, beans, beef broth, a salad and dessert. **Features:** full bar. **Address:** Blvd Salinas No. 1647 22420 **Location:** 1.8 mi (3 km) se of border on Paseo de Los Heroes, 0.3 mi (0.5 km) s on Ave Rodriguez, just e on Ave Gustavo Salinas. L D

## LA ESPADANA
664/634-1488

▼▼ **Mexican. Family Dining. $10-$16 AAA Inspector Notes:** A friendly village feeling envelops the hacienda-style mission building. Popular for families and business companions, the energetic restaurant provides fast service, but there sometimes can be a wait for seating. Among reliable menu offerings are chile rellenos, chicken with mole sauce, pork ribs, grilled beef, enchiladas and fresh pastries. Also popular for breakfast. **Features:** full bar. **Address:** Blvd Sanchez Taboada No. 10813, Zona Rio **Location:** 1.8 mi (3 km) se of border on Paseo de Los Heroes to Ave Rodriguez, just s, just e. B L D LATE

## LOS ARCOS RESTAURANT
664/686-3171

▼▼ **Mexican Seafood. Casual Dining. $10-$25 AAA Inspector Notes:** Festively decorated with fish netting, sculptures and bright colors, the restaurant has lively servers to match. Fresh fish from local waters is the specialty. Open-faced fish tacos with lime are a treat, as is the seafood fiesta for two, which includes stews of squid and octopus, shredded fish, smoked fish and shrimp, stuffed peppers and perch. Steaks also are available. Top dessert choices are bananas flambe and crepes Suzette. **Features:** full bar. **Reservations:** suggested. **Address:** Blvd Salinas No. 1000 **Location:** 1.8 mi (3 km) se of the border on Paseo de Los Heroes, 0.3 mi (0.5 km) s on Ave Rodriguez, just e on Blvd Agua Caliente, then just n on Calle Escuadron. **Parking:** on-site and valet. L D

## MARIA BONITA CANTINA
664/633-4000

▼▼▼ **Mexican. Fine Dining. $11-$25 AAA Inspector Notes:** Select from a variety of traditional Mexican dishes, all tasty, colorful and seasoned with fresh herbs. The botanas, a house specialty, are always an excellent choice. The elegant dining room features a grand piano. **Features:** full bar. **Reservations:** suggested. **Address:** Paseo de Los Heroes No. 10305, Zona Rio **Location:** 1.6 mi (2.5 km) se of the border; in Camino Real Tijuana. L D LATE

## MISION 19
664/634-2493

▼▼▼ **Mexican. Fine Dining. $16-$60 AAA Inspector Notes:** Set in a modern office tower, this sleek space is the perfect setting for contemporary Baja-Mediterranean cuisine. Ingredients are sourced locally, and most are organic. Signature dishes include risotto with huitlacoche and epazote as well as the slow-cooked short ribs with polenta and serrano chiles, topped with a quail egg. The hand-picked wines come from the nearby Guadalupe Valley. **Features:** full bar. **Reservations:** suggested. **Address:** Calle Mision de San Javier 10643, 2nd Floor **Location:** Just s of border; in Zona Rio. **Parking:** on-site and valet. L D 🆇

## RIVOLI BRASSERIE & PATIO
664/633-3900

▼▼▼ **International. Fine Dining. $15-$49 AAA Inspector Notes:** Mural-painted walls decorate the pleasant, peaceful dining room, which has a wall of glass overlooking the courtyard. The well-trained staff serves from a menu offering duck in fig sauce with aromatic lavender, shrimp or lobster with coconut and mango chutney, beef filet Singapore with pureed sweet potato sauce and wasabi. Penne with Gorgonzola, ricotta and mozzarella cheeses and ginger linguine with chicken and shrimp are among the pasta choices. **Features:** full bar, patio dining. **Reservations:** suggested. **Address:** Paseo de Los Heroes No. 10902, Zona Rio **Location:** 1.8 mi (3 km) se of border; in Hotel Lucerna Tijuana. **Parking:** on-site and valet. B L D LATE CALL 📞M

## VILLA SAVERIOS
664/686-6502

▼▼▼ **Mediterranean. Fine Dining. $15-$30 AAA Inspector Notes:** An attractive, modern, Italian-style building houses this large, aroma-filled dining room. Italian and Greek influences are evident in delicious pasta, chicken, beef and seafood dishes. The extensive wine collection surrounds a private dining room in the cellar. **Features:** full bar. **Reservations:** suggested. **Address:** Escuadron No. 201, Rio Zona **Location:** 1.8 mi (3 km) se of the border on Paseo de Los Heroes, 0.3 mi (0.5 km) s on Ave Rodriguez, just e on Blvd Agua Caliente, then just n. **Parking:** on-site and valet. L D

# TODOS SANTOS, BAJA CALIFORNIA SUR

## GUAYCURA BOUTIQUE HOTEL & SPA    (612)175-0800

▼▼▼ **Historic Boutique Hotel** $190-$330 **Address:** Legaspi y Topete S/N, Colonia Centro 23300 **Location:** In Centro Historico. **Facility:** This contemporary gem is hidden in the shell of a renovated historic building that was once the dorm of the local boarding school. Well-appointed rooms feature many upgraded amenities. Meets AAA guest room security requirements. 14 units. 3 stories, interior corridors. **Parking:** street only. **Terms:** closed 9/16-10/16. **Amenities:** safes. **Dining:** Guaycura Restaurant, see separate listing. **Pool(s):** outdoor. **Activities:** hot tub, steamroom, spa. **Guest Services:** valet laundry, area transportation.

## POSADA LA POZA    (612)145-0400

▼▼▼ **Boutique Hotel.** Rates not provided. **Address:** Colonia La Poza 23305 **Location:** Waterfront. Mex 19, 1.2 mi (1.9 km) s via Olachea; south side of town; at La Poza, follow signs. **Facility:** In a secluded location, above a lagoon and palm grove well-suited for bird watching, this beachfront property offers a retreat-like ambience. 8 units. 2 stories, exterior corridors. **Terms:** age restrictions may apply, 30 day cancellation notice. **Amenities:** safes. **Pool(s):** outdoor. **Activities:** sauna, hot tub, beach access, fishing, massage. **Guest Services:** valet laundry.

## TODOS SANTOS INN    (612)145-0040

▼▼▼ **Country Inn** $95-$325 **Address:** Calle Legaspi No. 33 23305 **Location:** Mex 19, just w on Hidalgo, just n; in town. **Facility:** Within the town's historic district, this restored inn has tastefully furnished rooms and tranquil gardens. 8 units. 1 story, exterior corridors. **Parking:** street only. **Terms:** 7 day cancellation notice-fee imposed. **Dining:** La Copa Restaurant & Bar, see separate listing. **Pool(s):** heated outdoor. **Activities:** massage. **Guest Services:** valet laundry.

## HOTEL CALIFORNIA    612/145-0525

**fyi** Not evaluated. **Address:** Benito Juárez S/N Col Centro 23400 **Location:** Centro. Facilities, services, and décor characterize a midscale property.

## RANCHO PESCADERO    612/135-5849

**fyi** Not evaluated. **Address:** Parcela 53, El Pescadero 23005. Facilities, services, and décor characterize an upscale property. Waiting for you is a unique, remote and upscale beachfront inn.

### WHERE TO EAT

## CAFE SANTA FE    612/145-0340

▼▼ Italian. Casual Dining. $15-$40 **AAA Inspector Notes:** Refined Italian dishes are served in an attractively decorated dining room and on the lush, tropical patio. **Features:** full bar, patio dining. **Reservations:** suggested. **Address:** Calle Centenario No. 4 23305 **Location:** Centro. **Parking:** street only.

## CAFFE TODOS SANTOS    612/145-0300

▼▼ Mexican. Casual Dining. $8-$18 **AAA Inspector Notes:** This quiet bakery cafe serves cold sandwiches, hearty soups and organic salads topped with freshly grilled chicken. Guests can take home a loaf of peasant-style bread to enjoy later. **Features:** beer & wine, patio dining. **Address:** No. 33 Centenario 23300 **Location:** Centro. **Parking:** street only.

## GUAYCURA RESTAURANT    612/175-0800

▼▼▼ International. Casual Dining. $12-$40 **AAA Inspector Notes:** Welcome to patio dining at its finest. In a stylish setting you'll enjoy a gourmet experience featuring creatively prepared fresh seafood and local organic produce. **Features:** full bar, patio dining. **Address:** Legaspi y Topete S/N, Colonia Centro 23300 **Location:** In Centro Historico; in Guaycura Boutique Hotel & Spa. **Parking:** street only.

## LA COPA RESTAURANT & BAR    612/145-0020

▼▼ Mexican. Casual Dining. $10-$20 **AAA Inspector Notes:** Located in the heart of the village, this charming spot offers traditional, home-style Mexican cooking. Diners can enjoy their meals in the peaceful courtyard. **Features:** full bar, patio dining. **Address:** Calle Legaspi No. 33 23305 **Location:** Mex 19, just w on Hidalgo, just n; in town; in Todos Santos Inn. **Parking:** on-site and street.

## LA CORONELA    612/145-0525

▼▼ Regional Mexican. Casual Dining. $11-$22 **AAA Inspector Notes:** Located in the famed Hotel California, the restaurant features creative takes on regional Mexican fare, including shrimp-stuffed rellenos, chicken mole, and mesquite-grilled fresh fish. Relax in the bar, or dine on the outdoor garden terrace while soaking up the atmosphere. **Features:** full bar, patio dining. **Address:** Benito Juárez y Marques de Leon 23300 **Location:** Centro; in Hotel California. **Parking:** street only.

## LOS ADOBES DE TODOS SANTOS    612/145-0203

▼▼ Mexican. Casual Dining. $12-$22 **AAA Inspector Notes:** Regional dishes from throughout Mexico have been given a light new touch. Fresh local ingredients enhance such dishes as white fish with cilantro, amaretto and garlic or herbs, chicken mole poblano and pork loin stuffed with mushroom in plum sauce. The kitchen is in a restored historic house, and seating is on the patio. Also on the premises are an internet cafe with coffee and lighter fare, and a wine and tequila bar set in the garden. **Features:** full bar, patio dining. **Address:** Calle Hidalgo between Juárez & Militar 23305 **Location:** Downtown.

## RUMI GARDEN    612/145-1088

▼▼ Asian. Casual Dining. $7-$13 **AAA Inspector Notes:** The restaurant's well-prepared and presented Asian specialties feature fresh seafood and local organic produce. This local favorite gathering spot also hosts great live music. **Features:** full bar. **Address:** 128 Degollado/Pedrajo 23300 **Location:** Hwy 19, at the south entrance to town. **Parking:** on-site and street.

# NORTHWESTERN MEXICO

AAA recommends that travelers consult online U.S. State Department travel
advisories when planning travel abroad. Find this information at
http://travel.state.gov/content/passports/english/alertswarnings/mexico-travel-warning.html.

## ALAMOS, SONORA (C-2) pop. 25,848

### HACIENDA DE LOS SANTOS RESORT & SPA
647/428-0222

Historic Hotel
$155-$950

**Address:** Calle Molina No. 8 **Location:** 2 blks s of main plaza. **Facility:** Built in the late 17th century, this beautifully restored stately hacienda offers manicured gardens and multiple pool areas, along with a theater showing nightly movies; all units have fireplaces. 23 units, some two bedrooms. 1-2 stories (no elevator), exterior corridors. **Parking:** on-site and street. **Terms:** 15 day cancellation notice. **Amenities:** safes. **Dining:** 2 restaurants, also, Hacienda de los Santos Restaurant, see separate listing. **Pool(s):** outdoor, heated outdoor. **Activities:** hot tub, bicycles, exercise room, spa. **Guest Services:** valet laundry.

### HOTEL COLONIAL
647/428-1371

**Historic Country Inn** $128-$366 **Address:** Calle Obregon No. 4 85760 **Location:** 1 blk s of main plaza; centro. **Facility:** This quaint, renovated hacienda, located just off the main plaza, features a spacious courtyard and a rooftop patio with sweeping views. 10 units. 2 stories (no elevator), exterior corridors. *Bath:* shower only. **Parking:** on-site and street. **Terms:** 7 day cancellation notice. **Activities:** picnic facilities. **Guest Services:** valet laundry.

### WHERE TO EAT

### HACIENDA DE LOS SANTOS RESTAURANT
647/428-0222

International. Fine Dining. $8-$38 **AAA Inspector Notes:** Featuring fine dining in an elegant cantina-style dining room or on the spacious patio, this restaurant offers well-prepared Mexican and Continental fare and attentive service. **Features:** full bar, patio dining. **Reservations:** suggested. **Address:** Calle Molina No. 8 **Location:** 2 blks s of main plaza; in Hacienda de los Santos Resort & Spa. **Parking:** on-site and street. [D]

## BAHIA KINO, SONORA

### JORGE'S RESTAURANT
662/242-0049

Seafood. Casual Dining. $5-$23 **AAA Inspector Notes:** The restaurant serves fresh seafood, as well as beef and chicken, with a nice view of the beach and sea, especially from the available outside seating; lobster is available in season. **Features:** full bar, patio dining. **Address:** Mar de Cortez y Alicantes **Location:** 4.8 mi (8 km) nw on beach highway; just w of Kino Bay RV Park. [B] [L] [D]

## CASAS GRANDES, CHIHUAHUA
pop. 10,587

### LAS GUACAMAYAS BED AND BREAKFAST
636/692-4144

[fyi] Not evaluated. **Address:** Ave 20 de Noviembre y Zona Arqueologica No. 1101 **Location:** Ave Allende, southwest main plaza; just nw of Paquime Ruins. Facilities, services, and décor characterize an economy property.

## CEROCAHUI, CHIHUAHUA

### HOTEL MISION DE CEROCAHUI
635/456-5294

**Hotel.** Rates not provided. **Address:** Bahuichivo Station **Location:** 10.8 mi (18 km) from Bahuichivo Station. Located in a remote area; accessible only by train. **Facility:** 41 units. 1 story, exterior corridors. *Bath:* shower only. **Terms:** 20 day cancellation notice. **Pool(s):** outdoor. **Activities:** game room. **Guest Services:** area transportation.

### MARGARITAS CEROCAHUI WILDERNESS LODGE
635/456-0245

[fyi] Not evaluated. **Address:** Bahuichivo Station **Location:** 13.2 mi (22 km) from Bahuichivo Station; 4.9 mi (8 km) from Cerocahui center. Facilities, services, and décor characterize an economy property.

## CHIHUAHUA, CHIHUAHUA (C-3)
pop. 819,543, elev. 4,690'

### BEST WESTERN HOTEL MIRADOR
614/432-2200

[fyi] Not evaluated. **Address:** Ave Universidad 1309 31240 **Location:** On Mex 45; 6 blks s of Pancho Villa Monument. Facilities, services, and décor characterize a mid-scale property.

**AAA Benefit:**
Save 10% or more every day and earn 10% bonus points!

### CASA GRANDE HOTELES BUSINESS PLUS
614/439-4444

[fyi] Not evaluated. **Address:** Ave Tecnologico 4702 **Location:** 4.2 mi (7 km) n on Mex 45. Facilities, services, and décor characterize a mid-scale property.

### FIESTA INN
614/429-0100

[fyi] Not evaluated. **Address:** 2801 Blvd Ortiz Mena 31250 **Location:** 1.2 mi (2 km) at Minnesota St. Facilities, services, and décor characterize a mid-scale property.

### HOLIDAY INN EXPRESS
614/442-2200

[fyi] Not evaluated. **Address:** Ave Cristobal Colon 11390 **Location:** 4.8 mi (8 km) n on Mex 45. Facilities, services, and décor characterize a mid-scale property.

### HOLIDAY INN HOTEL & SUITES CHIHUAHUA
614/439-0000

[fyi] Not evaluated. **Address:** Escudero 702 31240 **Location:** On Mex 45; 6 blks s of Pancho Villa Monument. Facilities, services, and décor characterize a mid-scale property.

### HOTEL HAMPTON INN CHIHUAHUA
614/439-8000

[fyi] Not evaluated. **Address:** Periferico de La Juventud No. 6100 **Location:** Jct Mex 16 to Ave Cuauhtemoc. Facilities, services, and décor characterize a mid-scale property.

**AAA Benefit:**
Members save up to 10%!

### HOTEL SICOMORO
614/214-2500

[fyi] Not evaluated. **Address:** Blvd Ortiz Mena 411 31230 **Location:** 2 mi (3.2 km) nw on Ave Universidad to VW dealer, just sw on Americas to Pemex Station, 1 mi (1.6 km) s. Facilities, services, and décor characterize a mid-scale property.

### THE HOTEL SOBERANO CHIHUAHUA
614/429-2929

[fyi] Not evaluated. **Address:** Barranca del Cobre No. 3211 31125 **Location:** 4.8 mi (8 km) nw on Cuauhtemoc Bypass. Facilities, services, and décor characterize a mid-scale property.

MICROTEL INN & SUITES BY WYNDHAM CHIHUAHUA
614/432-2525

**fyi** Not evaluated. **Address:** Periferico de La Juventud, No. 3304 31250 **Location:** Jct Polytecnico. Facilities, services, and décor characterize an economy property.

POSADA TIERRA BLANCA
614/415-0000

**fyi** Not evaluated. **Address:** Niños Heroes No. 102 31000 **Location:** Just n of Plaza de Armas. Facilities, services, and décor characterize an economy property.

QUALITY INN SAN FRANCISCO CHIHUAHUA
614/439-9000

**fyi** Not evaluated. **Address:** Calle Victoria 409 **Location:** Just off main plaza; centro of downtown. Facilities, services, and décor characterize a mid-scale property.

## WHERE TO EAT

EL RETABLO
614/415-5545

**fyi** Not evaluated. Mingle with the locals who frequent this comfortable, cozy spot at lunchtime for traditional northern Mexican cuisine along the lines of green chile salsa with a real kick to it, and slow-cooked pork that melts in your mouth. Locally made tiles and handsome wood tables and chairs crafted by local artisans enhance the décor. **Address:** Blvd Ortiz Mena 1810 **Location:** 2 mi (3.2 km) nw.

GARUFA RESTAURANTE ARGENTINO
614/430-0417

**fyi** Not evaluated. You'll enjoy the excellent quality, well-prepared beef at this eating establishment serving Argentinian-style food. **Address:** Periferico de La Juventud No. 3108 **Location:** Jct Mex 16 to Ave Cuauhtemoc.

LOS CANDILES
614/429-2929

**fyi** Not evaluated. This elegant, fine dining restaurant is appointed in upscale décor and affords commanding city views. Highlights of the eclectic menu include beef, seafood and fowl prepared in a blend of international and Mexican styles. **Address:** Barranca del Cobre No. 3211 **Location:** 4.8 mi (8 km) nw on Cuauhtemoc Bypass; in The Hotel Soberano Chihuahua.

RESTAURANT DEL HOTEL SICOMORO
614/413-5445

**fyi** Not evaluated. Service is swift, competent and friendly at this lively restaurant, where the menu features a good mix of tasty Continental and Mexican food. **Address:** Blvd Ortiz Mena 411 **Location:** 2 mi (3.2 km) nw on Ave Universidad to VW dealer, just sw On Americas to Pemex Station, 1 mi (1.6 km) s; in Hotel Sicomoro.

RESTAURANTE BAR LA CALESA
614/416-0222

**fyi** Not evaluated. Uniformed staff circulate through the semi-formal dining room, which is appointed with crisp linens. On the menu is a fine selection of steaks made from quality beef (including a truly impressive New York-cut steak), Mexican food and delectable desserts. Red chile salsa is both piquant and tasty. **Address:** Ave Juárez 3300 Col Centro **Location:** 1.1 mi (1.8 km) e on Mex 45.

RESTAURANTE DEGA
614/439-9000

**fyi** Not evaluated. Inside a popular downtown hotel, the dining room is usually busy with local businesspeople and hotel guests. Near the cathedral and central plaza area, this restaurant is convenient to shopping and sightseeing. The menu keeps both locals and tourists happy with a good mix of Continental cuisine and Mexican dishes. **Address:** Calle Victoria 409 **Location:** Just off main plaza; centro of downtown; in Quality Inn San Francisco Chihuahua.

## CIUDAD JUÁREZ, CHIHUAHUA
pop. 1,332,131, elev. 5,000'

BEST WESTERN PLUS PLAZA JUAREZ
656/613-1310

**fyi** Not evaluated. **Address:** Avenida Lincoln No. 722, Zona Pronaf 32315 **Location:** 2.1 mi (3.5 km) s of Bridge of the Americas. Facilities, services, and décor characterize a mid-scale property.

**AAA Benefit:**
Save 10% or more every day and earn 10% bonus points!

HAMPTON INN-CIUDAD JUAREZ
656/227-1717

**fyi** Not evaluated. **Address:** Blvd Tomas Fernandez No. 7770 **Location:** Jct Tomas Fernandez and Vicente Guerrero, just e. Facilities, services, and décor characterize a mid-scale property.

**AAA Benefit:**
Members save up to 10%!

HOLIDAY INN EXPRESS
656/629-6000

**fyi** Not evaluated. **Address:** 3745 Paseo Triunfo de La Republica **Location:** 2.4 mi (4 km) e on Chihuahua Hwy (Mex 45). Facilities, services, and décor characterize a mid-scale property.

HOTEL CASA GRANDE
656/629-4000

**fyi** Not evaluated. **Address:** Ave Tecnologico 3620 **Location:** 6.2 mi (10 km) e on Chihuahua Hwy (Mex 45). Facilities, services, and décor characterize a mid-scale property.

HOTEL KRYSTAL
656/629-0994

**fyi** Not evaluated. **Address:** Ave Tecnologico 3750 **Location:** 6 mi (10 km) e on Chihuahua Hwy (Mex 45). Facilities, services, and décor characterize a mid-scale property.

HOTEL LUCERNA
656/629-9900

**fyi** Not evaluated. **Address:** Paseo Triunfo de La Republica 3976 **Location:** 2.3 mi (3.9 km) e on Chihuahua Hwy (Mex 45). Facilities, services, and décor characterize a mid-scale property.

SHANGRI-LA RESTAURANT
656/613-0033

**fyi** Not evaluated. This is a popular dining spot for tourists, local business people and El Paso, Texas residents who live just across the border. Skilled staff prepare and serve authentic Chinese dishes in a semiformal setting. **Address:** Ave de Las Americas 133 **Location:** 2.7 mi (4.5 km) sw of Bridge of the Americas.

## CREEL, CHIHUAHUA (C-3) elev. 7,650'

BEST WESTERN THE LODGE AT CREEL HOTEL & SPA
(635)456-0071

**WWW WW** Hotel $62 **Address:** Ave Lopez Mateos No. 61 Creel (Copper Canyon) 33200 **Location:** Centro. **Facility:** 37 units. 1-2 stories (no elevator), interior/exterior corridors. **Terms:** 2 night minimum stay - seasonal and/or weekends, cancellation fee imposed. **Dining:** Sierra Madre Restaurant, see separate listing. **Activities:** sauna, hot tub, bicycles, playground, exercise room, massage. **Guest Services:** valet laundry, area transportation.

**AAA Benefit:**
Save 10% or more every day and earn 10% bonus points!

VILLA MEXICANA CREEL MOUNTAIN LODGE   (635)456-0666

**WWW** Vacation Rental Cabin. Rates not provided. **Address:** Calle Lopez Mateos S/N **Location:** 0.6 mi (1 km) se. Adjacent to RV park. **Facility:** Rustic log cabins with heaters; each with picnic table and charcoal grill. 31 cabins. 1 story, exterior corridors. **Terms:** 3 day cancellation notice. **Activities:** playground, game room. **Guest Services:** coin laundry, area transportation.

MARGARITA'S PLAZA MEXICANA
635/456-0108

**fyi** Not evaluated. **Address:** Elefido Batista S/N **Location:** Southwest main plaza; centro. Facilities, services, and décor characterize an economy property.

SIERRA MADRE RESTAURANT
635/456-0071

**WWW WW** Mexican. Casual Dining. $12-$14 **AAA Inspector Notes:** Tasty food, such as roasted pork served with grilled apples, is served in a lodge-style atmosphere that includes a fireplace. **Features:** full bar, patio dining. **Address:** Calle Lopez Mateos 61 **Location:** Centro; in BEST WESTERN The Lodge At Creel Hotel & Spa.

## CULIACAN, SINALOA pop. 858,638

**FIESTA INN**                667/759-5900

[fyi] Not evaluated. **Address:** Blvd Jose Diego No. 1676 Pte **Location:** 1.2 mi (2 km) n of Centro Historico; in Plaza Forum Center Mall. Facilities, services, and décor characterize a mid-scale property.

**HOTEL EXECUTIVO**                667/713-9300

[fyi] Not evaluated. **Address:** Blvd Fco Madero & Ave Obregon **Location:** Just n of jct Blvd Francisco I Madero and Ave Alvaro Obregon; centro. Facilities, services, and décor characterize a mid-scale property.

**HOTEL SAN LUIS LINDA VISTA**                667/759-2000

[fyi] Not evaluated. **Address:** Rio Sinaloa No. 1 **Location:** 1.1 mi (1.8 km) s on Ave Alvaro Obregon. Facilities, services, and décor characterize a mid-scale property.

**RAMADA HOLA CULIACAN**                667/716-5850

[fyi] Not evaluated. **Address:** Ave Juan Carrasco, 606 N Cross Rosa **Location:** Jct aves Juan Carrasco and Rosales. Facilities, services, and décor characterize a mid-scale property.

## DELICIAS, CHIHUAHUA pop. 137,935

**HOTEL CASA GRANDE**                639/474-0404

[fyi] Not evaluated. **Address:** Ave 6 Oriente 601 **Location:** 6 blks e of centro; just w of Mex 45. Facilities, services, and décor characterize an economy property.

**WHERE TO EAT**

**LOS NOGALES RESTAURANTE**                639/474-0404

[fyi] Not evaluated. Featured are well-prepared Mexican specialties, as well as a good selection of meat, poultry and seafood dishes. The well-appointed dining room is in the covered atrium of the hotel. **Address:** Ave 6 Oriente 601 **Location:** 6 blks e of centro; just w of Mex 45; in Hotel Casa Grande.

## DIVISADERO, CHIHUAHUA

**HOTEL DIVISADERO BARRANCAS**                614/415-1199

 Hotel. Rates not provided. **Address:** Divisadero Station **Location:** Near Divisadero Train Station **Location:** 52 units. 2 stories (no elevator), interior/exterior corridors. *Bath:* shower only. **Terms:** 3 day cancellation notice.

## EL FUERTE, SINALOA pop. 97,536

**HOTEL EL FUERTE**                (698)893-0226

 **Historic Country Inn.** Rates not provided. **Address:** Montesclaros No. 37 **Location:** Just w of the Old Fort. **Facility:** You'll feel as if you've just stepped back in time while staying at this historic hacienda, located just a block away from the Old Fort. 44 units. 2 stories (no elevator), exterior corridors. *Bath:* shower only. **Guest Services:** valet laundry.

**HOTEL POSADA DEL HIDALGO**                698/893-1194

 **Historic Hotel.** Rates not provided. **Address:** Hidalgo 101 **Location:** Mex 15, just s of KM 55, 33 mi (55 km) e on rural paved road; just ne of main plaza. **Facility:** Portions of this historic building were constructed in 1890. Attractive gardens surround the guest rooms. 69 units. 2 stories (no elevator), exterior corridors. *Bath:* shower only. **Pool(s):** outdoor. **Activities:** hot tub, massage.

**WHERE TO EAT**

**RESTAURANT EL MESON DEL GENERAL**                698/893-0260

 Regional Mexican. Casual Dining. $8-$16 **AAA Inspector Notes:** Just a block off the main plaza, this restaurant serves generous portions of regional favorites. **Features:** full bar, patio dining. **Address:** B Juárez 202 **Location:** Just s; in main plaza. [L] [D]

## GOMEZ PALACIO, DURANGO pop. 327,985

**BEST WESTERN POSADA DEL RIO**                871/714-3399

[fyi] Not evaluated. **Address:** Ave Francisco I Madero 144 Sur **Location:** 2.4 mi (4 km) s on Mex 49 (which becomes Fco Madero) to Ave Juárez; downtown. Facilities, services, and décor characterize a mid-scale property.

> **AAA Benefit:**
> Save 10% or more every day and earn 10% bonus points!

**WHERE TO EAT**

**EL PARADOR**                871/714-3399

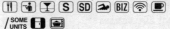 Continental. Casual Dining. $8-$17 **AAA Inspector Notes:** Well-prepared tender meat, savory poultry and fresh seafood specialties are at the heart of a menu that also includes hearty soup, well-stacked sandwiches and spicy Mexican specialties. **Features:** full bar, Sunday brunch. **Address:** Ave Francisco I Madero 144 Sur **Location:** 2.4 mi (4 km) s on Mex 49 (which becomes Fco Madero) to Ave Juárez; downtown; in BEST WESTERN Posada del Rio.

[B] [L] [D]

## GUAMUCHIL, SINALOA

**HOTEL YORK**                673/732-5611

[fyi] Not evaluated. **Address:** Carr Internacional KM 1528 **Location:** 0.9 mi (1.5 km) n. Facilities, services, and décor characterize an economy property.

## HERMOSILLO, SONORA (B-2) pop. 784,342

**FIESTA INN HERMOSILLO**                (662)289-2200

 Hotel $80-$120 **Address:** Blvd Eusebio Kino 375 **Location:** 2.7 mi (4.5 km) n on Mex 15. **Facility:** 155 units. 5 stories. interior corridors. **Pool(s):** heated indoor. **Activities:** exercise room. **Guest Services:** valet laundry.

🍽 🍸 [S] [SD] 🏊 [BIZ] 📶 💻 / SOME UNITS 📶 📺

**HAMPTON INN BY HILTON HERMOSILLO**                (662)313-9000

 Hotel $69-$129 **Address:** 172 Paseo Rio Sonora 83270 **Location:** Jct Mex 15, just e. Across from Galerias Mall. **Facility:** 151 units. 8 stories, interior corridors. *Bath:* shower only. **Terms:** 1-7 night minimum stay, cancellation fee imposed. **Amenities:** safes. **Pool(s):** heated outdoor. **Activities:** exercise room. **Guest Services:** valet and coin laundry, rental car service, area transportation.

> **AAA Benefit:**
> Members save up to 10%!

✈ 🍽 🍸 🏊 [BIZ] [HS] 📶 ✕ 📶 💻

**HOLIDAY INN HERMOSILLO**                662/289-1700

 Hotel $70-$110 **Address:** Blvd Eusebio Kino y Ramon Corral **Location:** 2.3 mi (3.8 km) ne on Mex 15. **Facility:** Meets AAA guest room security requirements. 133 units. 3 stories, interior/exterior corridors. **Amenities:** safes. **Pool(s):** outdoor. **Activities:** exercise room. **Guest Services:** complimentary and valet laundry.

🍽 🍸 [SD] 🏊 [BIZ] 📶 ✕ 💻 / SOME UNITS [HS] 📶

**HOTEL ARAIZA HERMOSILLO**                662/109-1700

 Hotel $116-$155 **Address:** Blvd Eusebio Kino 353 **Location:** 2.4 mi (4 km) ne on Mex 15. Located in a commercial area. **Facility:** 159 units. 4 stories, interior/exterior corridors. **Pool(s):** outdoor. **Activities:** exercise room. **Guest Services:** valet and coin laundry.

🍽 🍸 [SD] 🏊 [BIZ] 📶 💻 / SOME UNITS 📶 📺

**HOTEL FIESTA AMERICANA HERMOSILLO**      (662)259-6000

▼▼▼ **Hotel** $90-$150 **Address:** Blvd Eusebio Kino 369 **Location:** 2.7 mi (4.5 km) n on Mex 15; in Zona Hotelera. **Facility:** 221 units. 9 stories, interior corridors. **Amenities:** safes. **Dining:** 2 restaurants, also, El Rincon, see separate listing, entertainment. **Pool(s):** outdoor. **Activities:** tennis, exercise room. **Guest Services:** valet laundry.

**WHERE TO EAT**

**EL RINCON**                           662/259-6000

▼▼▼ Mexican Steak. Fine Dining. $16-$30 **AAA Inspector Notes:** Those who visit this high-end dining room will enjoy an extensive selection of prime Sonoran steaks cooked to order over a wood fire, as well as other regional favorites like traditional cheese soup and flank steak tacos. **Features:** full bar. **Address:** Blvd Eusebio Kino 369 **Location:** 2.7 mi (4.5 km) n on Mex 15; in Hotel Fiesta Americana Hermosillo. ⌊L⌋ ⌊D⌋ ⌊LATE⌋

**RESTAURANT PALOMINOS**               662/212-2700

▼▼▼ Steak. Casual Dining. $10-$40 **AAA Inspector Notes:** Outstanding Sonoran steak is the hallmark of this popular establishment. In addition, such regional favorites as queso fundido and fresh seafood from the nearby Sea of Cortez are offered. **Features:** full bar. **Address:** 72 Galeana 83270 **Location:** Jct Paseo Rio Sonora; in front of the Government Center. **Parking:** on-site and street.

⌊L⌋ ⌊D⌋ ⌊LATE⌋

**SONORA STEAK**                       662/210-0313

▼▼▼ Steak. Casual Dining. $11-$25 **AAA Inspector Notes:** Steaks, cut from premium local beef and weighed tableside, are charcoal grilled to 'al carbon' perfection at this restaurant. The house specialty rib-eye is particularly flavorful, and makes for a grand meal when accompanied by one of the tasty, decoratively prepared salads. **Features:** full bar, patio dining. **Address:** Blvd Eusebio Kino 914 **Location:** On Mex 15; in Zona Hotelera. ⌊L⌋ ⌊D⌋ ⌊LATE⌋

# JUAN MATA ORTIZ, CHIHUAHUA
pop. 2,000

**ADOBE INN**                          636/661-7135

⌊fyi⌋ Not evaluated. **Address:** Calle del Parque No. 4000 **Location:** 0.5 mi (0.8 km) nw of railroad crossing. Facilities, services, and décor characterize an economy property.

# LOS MOCHIS, SINALOA

**HOTEL SANTA ANITA**                  668/816-7046

⌊fyi⌋ Not evaluated. **Address:** Ave Gabriel Leyva y Hidalgo **Location:** Downtown. Facilities, services, and décor characterize a mid-scale property.

**PLAZA INN HOTEL & CONVENTION CENTER**    668/816-0800

⌊fyi⌋ Not evaluated. **Address:** Aves Gabriel Leyva y L Cardenas S/N **Location:** 0.3 mi (0.5 km) e. Facilities, services, and décor characterize a mid-scale property.

**WHERE TO EAT**

**OWEN'S RESTAURANT & STEAKS**         668/816-0938

▼▼ Steak. Casual Dining. $7-$17 **AAA Inspector Notes:** Although this place is decorated much like an American coffee shop, the service and cuisine it offers are more refined. In addition to a fine breakfast selection, food choices include a wide variety of steaks. At dinner, service is semi-formal. Well upholstered booths, comfortable chairs and a roomy dining room are the features of this comfortable, popular eatery. **Features:** full bar. **Reservations:** suggested. **Address:** Aves Gabriel Leyva y L Cardenas S/N **Location:** 0.3 mi (0.5 km) e; in Plaza Inn Hotel & Convention Center.

⌊B⌋ ⌊L⌋ ⌊D⌋ ⌊LATE⌋

**RESTAURANTE SANTA ANITA**            668/818-7046

▼▼▼ International. Casual Dining. $9-$22 **AAA Inspector Notes:** Mexican charm prevails at this hotel restaurant. The food represents a good selection of international cuisine, including some pleasing Mexican items. **Features:** full bar. **Address:** Ave Gabriel Leyva y Hidalgo **Location:** Downtown; in Hotel Santa Anita.

⌊B⌋ ⌊L⌋ ⌊D⌋

# NAVOJOA, SONORA pop. 157,729

**BEST WESTERN HOTEL DEL RIO**          642/425-5300

▼▼▼ **Hotel.** Rates not provided. **Address:** Pesqueira Norte S/N **Location:** On Mex 15; at south end of bridge over Rio Mayo. **Facility:** 65 units, some two bedrooms. 2 stories (no elevator), exterior corridors. **Bath:** shower only. **Terms:** resort fee. **Pool(s):** outdoor. **Activities:** picnic facilities. **Guest Services:** valet laundry.

**AAA Benefit:**
Save 10% or more every day and earn 10% bonus points!

**HOTEL EL MAYO**                       (642)422-6828

▼▼ **Hotel** $42-$80 **Address:** Otero y Jimenez **Location:** Just s of jct Mex 15 and Son 13 to Otero y Jimenez, just e. **Facility:** 48 units, some efficiencies. 2 stories (no elevator), exterior corridors. **Terms:** 7 day cancellation notice. **Pool(s):** outdoor. **Activities:** hot tub, bicycles, picnic facilities, limited exercise equipment. **Guest Services:** valet laundry.

**WHERE TO EAT**

**TIP'S RESTAURANTE**                   642/422-9028

▼ Mexican. Casual Dining. $6-$18 **AAA Inspector Notes:** Although it resembles an American coffee shop, the restaurant offers mostly Mexican cuisine. Patrons will find all the traditional dishes, such as enchiladas, tacos and burritos. Try the carne adobada plate: it's exceptional. **Features:** beer & wine. **Address:** Pesquiera y J O de Dominguez **Location:** On Mex 15 through town; 2 blks s of Alamos turn off; centro. ⌊B⌋ ⌊L⌋ ⌊D⌋

## NOGALES, SONORA pop. 220,292, elev. 3,674'

**LA ROCA**        520/313-6313

▼▼▼ Mexican. Casual Dining. $10-$25 **AAA Inspector Notes:** Just a short stroll from the international border crossing, this long-standing favorite features delicious regional Mexican cuisine served by an attentive, refined waitstaff. Enjoy live music in the evenings while sipping on one of their famous fresh-made margaritas. Don't miss the assortment of upscale shops on the lower level. **Features:** full bar. **Address:** Calle Elias 91 84010 **Location:** Centro; just s of the pedestrian crossing. **Parking:** on-site and street. [L] [D]

## PALOMAS, CHIHUAHUA

**THE PINK STORE**        656/666-0106

▼▼ Mexican. Casual Dining. $6-$18 **AAA Inspector Notes:** This large and lively restaurant is a favorite across-the-border stop. Patrons can sip a frosty margarita and shop in the attached curio shop while waiting for a table. The extensive menu lists hearty portions of flavorful Mexican favorites, such as tacos and enchiladas. **Features:** full bar, patio dining. **Address:** Ave 5 de Mayo 113 **Location:** I-10 exit 82A, just s of border crossing on Mex 24 (Ave 5 de Mayo). [B] [L] [D]

## POSADA BARRANCA, CHIHUAHUA

**HOTEL POSADA BARRANCA MIRADOR**        635/578-3020

▼▼ Hotel. Rates not provided. **Address:** Estacion Posada Barranca **Location:** Just s of Posada Barranca Train Station. **Facility:** 65 units. 3 stories (no elevator), exterior corridors. *Bath:* shower only. **Terms:** 3 day cancellation notice. **Activities:** game room. **Guest Services:** area transportation.

**RANCHO POSADA BARRANCA**        668/818-7046

▼ Hotel. Rates not provided. **Address:** Estacion Posada Barranca **Location:** Just n of Posada Barranca Train Station. **Facility:** 23 units. 2 stories, exterior corridors. *Bath:* shower only. **Terms:** 5 day cancellation notice-fee imposed. **Guest Services:** area transportation. [BIZ] 📡 ✖ 📺 📺 🏊

## PUERTO PEÑASCO, SONORA (B-1) pop. 57,342

**BELLA SIRENA**        638/382-8021

▼▼▼ Condominium $113-$351 **Address:** Blvd Paseo de Las Dunas KM 3.7 83550 **Location:** Oceanfront. Jct Blvd SG Brown and Cholla Bay Rd, 2.7 mi (4 km) w, follow signs. Located on Sandy Beach. **Facility:** This gated beachfront property features luxurious accommodations, all with water views, and lovely grounds with multiple pool areas. 35 condominiums. 8-12 stories, exterior corridors. **Terms:** check-in 4 pm, 10 day cancellation notice-fee imposed. **Amenities:** *Some:* safes. **Pool(s):** outdoor, heated outdoor. **Activities:** hot tub, tennis, picnic facilities. **Guest Services:** complimentary laundry.

🍴 🍸 SD 🏊 📡 ✖ 🛏 📦 📺

**CASA BLANCA GOLF VILLAS**        638/382-8021

▼▼▼ **Resort Condominium** $109-$189 **Address:** Blvd Paseo de Las Dunas, KM 3.5 83550 **Location:** Oceanfront. Jct Blvd SG Brown and Cholla Bay Rd, 2.7 mi (4 km) w, follow signs. Located on Sandy Beach. **Facility:** This newer property, with some buildings still under construction, features luxury condos with views of the Sea of Cortez and an 18-hole professional putting course. 11 condominiums. 3-7 stories, exterior corridors. **Terms:** off-site registration, check-in 4 pm, 10 day cancellation notice-fee imposed. **Pool(s):** outdoor. **Activities:** picnic facilities. **Guest Services:** complimentary laundry.

🍴 SD 🏊 📡 ✖ 🛏 📦 📺

**HOTEL PENASCO DEL SOL**        (638)383-0300

▼▼▼
Hotel
$84-$230

**Address:** Paseo Las Glorias No. 1 83550 **Location:** Oceanfront. Centro; at west end of 13th St. **Facility:** 208 units, some three bedrooms. 5 stories, exterior corridors. **Terms:** check-in 4 pm. **Amenities:** safes. **Dining:** Miguel's, see separate listing. **Pool(s):** heated outdoor. **Activities:** hot tub. **Guest Services:** valet laundry.

🍴 🛏 🍸 SD 🏊 BIZ 📡
✖ 📺 /SOME UNITS 🏊 🛏 📦

**HOTEL PLAYA BONITA**        (638)383-2586

▼▼ ▼▼
Hotel
$65-$185

**Address:** Paseo Balboa No. 100 **Location:** Oceanfront. Centro; east end of Sandy Beach. Located on Playa Bonita. **Facility:** 124 units, some two bedrooms and efficiencies. 4 stories, interior corridors. **Terms:** 8 day cancellation notice. **Pool(s):** outdoor. **Activities:** hot tub, picnic facilities, spa.

🍴 🍸 🏊 BIZ HS 📡 ✖
/SOME UNITS 🛏 📦 📺

**LAS PALOMAS BEACH & GOLF RESORT**        (638)108-1000

▼▼▼ ▼▼▼
Resort
Condominium
$124-$350

**Address:** Blvd Costero No. 150, Col Sandy Beach 83550 **Location:** Oceanfront. Jct Blvd SG Brown, 1.2 mi (2 km) w on Cholla Blvd, 0.6 mi (1 km) s. Located on Sandy Beach. **Facility:** Fronting a beautiful Sea of Cortez beach, this property's luxurious condos feature upscale furnishings and appointments. 350 condominiums. 11-15 stories, exterior corridors. **Terms:** check-in 4 pm, 10 day cancellation notice-fee imposed. **Dining:** 2 restaurants, also, Citron Fine Cuisine, see separate listing. **Pool(s):** outdoor, heated outdoor. **Activities:** hot tub, regulation golf, recreation programs, playground, picnic facilities, exercise room, massage. **Guest Services:** complimentary laundry.

🍴 🍸 SD 🏊 📡 ✖ 🛏 📦 📺 /SOME UNITS HS

## MAYAN PALACE PUERTO PENASCO    638/383-0400

**Resort Hotel**
**$225-$305**

**Address:** KM 24 Carr Puerto Penasco Caborca 83550 **Location:** Oceanfront. Jct Sonora Hwy 8, 14.4 mi (24 km) e, 3.4 mi (5.7 km). **Facility:** In addition to well-appointed rooms and striking public areas, this luxury resort boasts a fine beach and an 18-hole golf course. 263 units, some efficiencies. 3-8 stories, interior corridors. **Parking:** on-site and valet. **Terms:** check-in 5 pm, 2-7 night minimum stay, 7 day cancellation notice. **Amenities:** safes. **Dining:** 3 restaurants, also, Bakal, see separate listing. **Pool(s):** outdoor, heated indoor. **Activities:** sauna, steamroom, fishing, scuba diving, snorkeling, regulation golf, tennis, recreation programs in season, game room, exercise room, spa. **Guest Services:** valet and coin laundry. *(See ad on insert, p. 467.)*

### PRINCESA DE PENASCO    638/382-8020

**Condominium** $101-$215 **Address:** Blvd Costero KM 3.7 S/N, Camino de La Cholla 83550 **Location:** Jct blvds Benito Juárez and SG Brown, 3.7 mi (5.9 km) w on Blvd SG Brown through roundabout at Pemex via Cholla Bay Rd, just sw. **Facility:** One of the first condo developments on Sandy Beach, this property has spacious units, attractive furnishings and some master baths with beachfront windows. 105 condominiums. 6 stories, exterior corridors. **Terms:** check-in 4 pm, cancellation fee imposed. **Pool(s):** outdoor, heated outdoor. **Activities:** hot tub, picnic facilities, exercise room. **Guest Services:** complimentary laundry.

### SONORAN SEA RESORT    (638)382-8253

**Resort Condominium** $125-$315 **Address:** Camino de la Cholla KM 3.7 S/N 83550 **Location:** Oceanfront. Jct Blvd SG Brown and Cholla Bay Rd, 2.2 mi (3.7 km) w, follow signs. Located on Sandy Beach. **Facility:** Set on a great stretch of beach, this luxury vacation property offers a wide range of recreational activities. Each guest unit sports a unique décor. 115 condominiums. 10 stories, exterior corridors. **Terms:** check-in 4 pm, 10 day cancellation notice-fee imposed. **Pool(s):** outdoor, heated outdoor. **Activities:** hot tub, tennis, playground, picnic facilities, exercise room. **Guest Services:** complimentary laundry.

### SONORAN SKY RESORT    (638)108-2100

**Condominium** $208-$518 **Address:** Camino Costero No. 600 Col Ferr Playa 83550 **Location:** Oceanfront. Jct Blvd SG Brown, 1.2 mi (2 km) w on Cholla Bay Rd, 0.8 mi (1.1 km) s through roundabout, then just sw. Located on Sandy Beach. **Facility:** This high-rise facility offers upscale, attractive rooms with a large patio or balcony overlooking the negative-edge pool and beach. Enjoy happy hour daily at the only beach bar along Sandy Beach. 40 condominiums. 15 stories, exterior corridors. **Terms:** check-in 4 pm, 10 day cancellation notice-fee imposed. **Pool(s):** outdoor, heated outdoor. **Activities:** hot tub, playground, picnic facilities, exercise room. **Guest Services:** complimentary laundry.

### SONORAN SPA RESORT    (638)382-8060

**Condominium** $105-$275 **Address:** Camino de La Cholla KM 3.7 S/N **Location:** Oceanfront. Jct Blvd SG Brown and Cholla Bay Rd, 2.2 mi (3.7 km) w, follow signs. Located on Sandy Beach. **Facility:** A sister property of the adjacent Sonoran Sea Resort, the well-appointed, beachside condominiums offer ample amenities including pools and a gym. 120 condominiums. 8 stories, interior corridors. **Terms:** check-in 4 pm, 10 day cancellation notice-fee imposed. **Dining:** Sonoran Grill Restaurant & Bar, see separate listing. **Pool(s):** outdoor, heated outdoor. **Activities:** hot tub, tennis, picnic facilities, exercise room, spa. **Guest Services:** complimentary laundry.

### SONORAN SUN RESORT    638/383-0200

**Condominium** $124-$624 **Address:** Camino de La Cholla KM 3.7 S/N 83550 **Location:** Oceanfront. Jct Blvd SG Brown and Cholla Bay Rd, 2.7 mi (4 km) w, follow signs. Located on Sandy Beach. **Facility:** The resort has well decorated units, all with an attractive marble bath and an ocean-view patio or balcony. 115 condominiums. 10 stories, exterior corridors. **Terms:** check-in 4 pm, 10 day cancellation notice-fee imposed. **Amenities:** *Some:* safes. **Pool(s):** outdoor, heated outdoor. **Activities:** hot tub, tennis, picnic facilities, exercise room, spa. **Guest Services:** complimentary laundry.

### THE RESORTS AT MIRAMAR    638/388-6642

**fyi** Not evaluated. **Address:** KM 24 Carr Puerto Penasco Caborca 83550 **Location:** Oceanfront. Jct Sonora Hwy 8, 14.4 mi (24 km) e, 3.4 mi (5.7 km) s. Facilities, services, and décor characterize a mid-scale property.

## WHERE TO EAT

### AL CAPONE'S PIZZA & BEER    638/388-6737

Italian. Casual Dining. $5-$15 **AAA Inspector Notes:** Here's a fun, festive spot serving delicious pizza, pasta, salads and wings, as well as fresh seafood specials that change seasonally. Locals and visitors alike mingle in the bar area watching sports on big-screen TVs or enjoying live music. **Features:** full bar, patio dining, happy hour. **Address:** Calle Sinaloa y Quintana Roo 83550 **Location:** Jct Juárez Blvd, 0.5 mi (0.8 km) e on Fremont Blvd, just s. **Parking:** on-site and street. L D LATE

### BAKAL    638/383-0400

Continental. Casual Dining. $10-$29 **AAA Inspector Notes:** This plantation-style restaurant features themed buffet nights as well as delicious a la carte items. The wonderful Sunday brunch is not to be missed. **Features:** full bar, Sunday brunch, happy hour. **Reservations:** suggested. **Address:** KM 24 Carrera Penasco-Caborca 83550 **Location:** Jct Sonora Hwy 8, 14.4 mi (24 km) e, 3.4 mi (5.7 km); in Mayan Palace Puerto Penasco. **Parking:** on-site and valet. B D CALL 🄼

### CASA DEL CAPITAN    638/383-5698

Seafood. Casual Dining. $9-$18 **AAA Inspector Notes:** Fresh, local seafood prepared Mexican-style is the specialty of the house at this hilltop restaurant overlooking the harbor. Needless to say, the bay and ocean views are marvelous. **Features:** full bar, patio dining. **Address:** Lote 1 y 2 Fracc del Cerro 83550 **Location:** Centro; on hill above Old Port; next to lighthouse. L D

### CITRON FINE CUISINE    638/108-1000

**Continental**
**Casual Dining**
**$12-$30**

**AAA Inspector Notes:** An impressive lounge with fieldstone walls and high ceilings makes for a fine first impression. Attentive servers will assist throughout the meal, serving classic Mexican, Italian and American favorites. **Features:** full bar, patio dining, Sunday brunch. **Reservations:** suggested. **Address:** Blvd Costero No. 150, Col Sandy Beach 83550 **Location:** Jct Blvd SG Brown, 1.2 mi (2 km) w on Cholla Blvd, 0.6 mi (1 km) s; in Las Palomas Beach & Golf Resort. B D CALL 🄼

### DON JULIO BAR & GRILL    638/388-0056

Regional Steak. Casual Dining. $10-$19 **AAA Inspector Notes:** Delicious Sonoran-style steaks, seafood and Mexican favorites line the menu at this festive restaurant, which also offers a daily breakfast buffet. The attentive waitstaff helps with ordering, while mariachi players stroll through the attractive dining room. **Features:** full bar. **Address:** Blvd Fremont y Ave Sinaloa 83550 **Location:** Centro; across from Plaza Fremont. B L D

### THE HUT BAR & GRILL    638/382-8648

American. Casual Dining. $7-$14 **AAA Inspector Notes:** Refreshing ocean breezes blow through this palapa-roofed beach restaurant, which resembles a tiki hut. Sipping a frozen margarita at the bar is nice way to start. Moving on to the menu, items such as hearty burgers and fried shrimp baskets appeal to diners of all ages. Those in search of entertainment will enjoy the live music offered Thursday, Friday and Saturday nights. **Features:** full bar, patio dining. **Address:** Camino de La Cholla KM 3.7 S/N 83550 **Location:** Jct Blvd SG Brown and Cholla Bay Rd, 2.2 mi (3.7 km) w, just sw; in front of Sonoran Sea Resort. L D

**THE LIGHTHOUSE RESTAURANT BAR**    638/383-2389

International. Casual Dining. $11-$18 **AAA Inspector Notes:** Patrons can dine by rock 'n' roll or jazz music at the lively eatery and lounge, which overlooks the town and the harbor. Local seafood and beef are prepared in a variety of international styles. Lunch is served on the weekends. **Features:** full bar, patio dining, happy hour. **Address:** Fracc del Cerro Lotes 2 y 2Bis **Location:** Centro; on top of hill at Old Port. D

**MARE BLU RISTORANTE**    638/383-0656

Italian. Casual Dining. $12-$20 **AAA Inspector Notes:** Directly on the oceanfront in Sandy Beach, the restaurant has huge windows that offer stunning views of the Sea of Cortez. Creative presentations enhance classic Italian and Continental menu choices such as seafood cioppino, homemade stuffed ravioli and velvety tiramisu. **Features:** full bar, patio dining. **Address:** Camino de La Cholla KM 3.7 83550 **Location:** Jct Mex 8 and La Cholla Rd, 2.3 mi (3.7 km) w, 0.6 mi (1 km) s at sign; adjacent to Reef RV Park. D

**MAX'S CAFE**    638/383-1011

American. Casual Dining. $5-$14 **AAA Inspector Notes:** A pleasant, casual atmosphere prevails at this café, which serves a great breakfast burrito and offers a fine selection of coffee drinks. At lunch there's a nice line-up of sandwiches, as well as a daily soup special. Free Wi-Fi is another plus. **Features:** full bar, patio dining. **Address:** Calle Trece No. 15 83550 **Location:** Centro; across from Hotel Penasco del Sol. B L D

**MIGUEL'S**    638/383-0300

International. Casual Dining. $8-$18 **AAA Inspector Notes:** Overlooking the pool area, the restaurant lays out a sumptuous breakfast buffet and also serves hearty lunches and dinners with fine wines. The chef creates plates that look as wonderful as they taste. Local and American dishes, including shrimp enchiladas and margarita pizza, share space on the menu. **Features:** full bar. **Address:** Paseo Las Glorias No. 1 83550 **Location:** Centro; at west end of 13th St; in Hotel Penasco del Sol. B L D CALL M

**SONORAN GRILL RESTAURANT & BAR**    638/382-8089

International. Casual Dining. $7-$14 **AAA Inspector Notes:** Owned by expatriate Americans, this casual eatery features a wide variety of Mexican and American favorites. Lunch is served on weekends. **Features:** full bar, patio dining. **Address:** Camino de La Cholla KM 3.7 S/N **Location:** Jct Blvd SG Brown and Cholla Bay Rd, 2.2 mi (3.7 km) w, follow signs; in Sonoran Spa Resort. D

## SAN CARLOS, SONORA

**MARINATERRA HOTEL AND SPA**    (520)303-7515

Hotel $100-$215 **Address:** Calle Gabriel Estrada S/N 85506 **Location:** Waterfront. 7 mi (11.5 km) w on San Carlos turn-off. **Facility:** 112 units. 7 stories, interior/exterior corridors. **Amenities:** safes. **Pool(s):** outdoor. **Activities:** hot tub, marina, fishing, scuba diving, snorkeling, playground, exercise room, spa. **Guest Services:** valet laundry.

**SAN CARLOS PLAZA HOTEL, RESORT & CONVENTION CENTER**    622/225-3000

fyi Not evaluated. **Address:** Paseo Mar Bermejo Nte No. 4 85506 **Location:** 11 mi (18.5 km) w on San Carlos turn-off. Facilities, services, and décor characterize a mid-scale property.

## WHERE TO EAT

**BLACKIE'S RESTAURANT & BAR**    622/226-1525

International. Casual Dining. $10-$28 **AAA Inspector Notes:** Just the place for a fun evening; dine on sumptuous local seafood, chicken, or fine beef cuts, or try some of the international flavors on the menu. You'll also find a good selection of cocktails, wine and beer to liven up your meal. **Features:** full bar. **Address:** Blvd M F Beltrones KM 10.3 S/N **Location:** 6.4 mi (10.7 km) nw on Mex 15, 6.2 mi (10.3 km) w on San Carlos turn-off. L D

**CHARLY'S ROCK**    622/226-0888

Regional Seafood. Casual Dining. $5-$24 **AAA Inspector Notes:** This quaint, thatched-roof establishment provides a spectacular view of the sea. Enjoy grilled lobster (in season), seafood salads, soups and fresh fish prepared several ways. **Features:** full bar. **Address:** Blvd M F Beltrones KM 9 **Location:** 6.4 mi (10.7 km) nw on Mex 15, 5.6 mi (9.3 km) w on San Carlos turn-off. L D

# NORTHEASTERN MEXICO

**AAA recommends that travelers consult online U.S. State Department travel advisories when planning travel abroad. Find this information at http://travel.state.gov/content/passports/english/alertswarnings/mexico-travel-warning.html.**

## CIUDAD VICTORIA, TAMAULIPAS

HAMPTON INN BY HILTON        834/153-7070

(fyi) Not evaluated. **Address:** Blvd Tamaulipas 2539 **Location:** On Mex 85 (Blvd Tamaulipas), just s of Mex 101. Facilities, services, and décor characterize a mid-scale property.

**AAA Benefit:** Members save up to 10%!

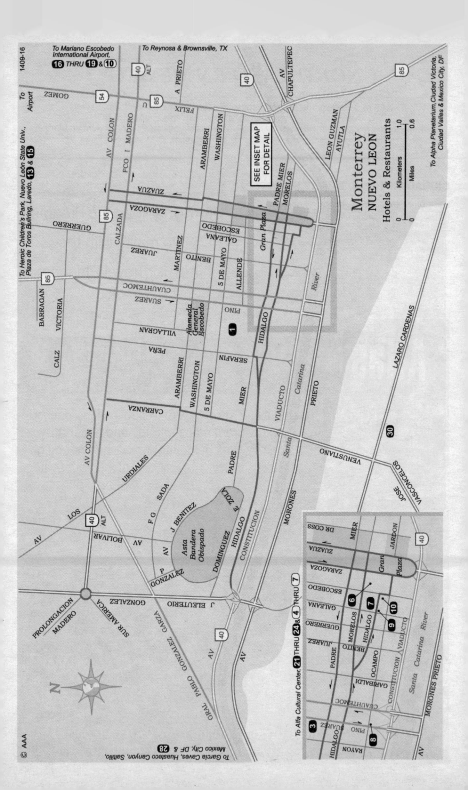

Monterrey
NUEVO LEON
Hotels & Restaurants

Kilometers
0        0.6        1.0
Miles

# ✈ Airport Hotels

| Map Page | GENERAL MARIANO ESCOBEDO INTERNATIONAL AIRPORT | Diamond Rated | Rate Range | Page |
|---|---|---|---|---|
| **17** p. 440 | Courtyard by Marriott Monterrey Airport, 0.9 mi (1.5 km) n of main terminal entrance | ◆◆◆ | $74-$121 | 442 |
| **19** p. 440 | Fairfield Inn by Marriott Monterrey Airport, 0.9 mi (1.5 km) n of main terminal entrance | ◆◆ | $48-$79 | 442 |
| **18** p. 440 | Hampton Inn by Hilton Monterrey Aeropuerto, 0.9 mi (1.5 km) n of main terminal entrance | ◆◆◆ | Rates not provided | 442 |
| **16** p. 440 | One Monterrey Aeropuerto, 0.9 mi (1.5 km) n of main terminal entrance | ◆ | Rates not provided | 443 |

# Monterrey

This index helps you "spot" where approved hotels and restaurants are located on the corresponding detailed maps. Hotel daily rate range is for comparison only. Restaurant price range is a combination of lunch and/or dinner. Turn to the listing page for more detailed rate and price information and consult display ads for special promotions.

## MONTERREY, NUEVO LEÓN

| Map Page | Hotels | Diamond Rated | Rate Range | Page |
|---|---|---|---|---|
| **1** p. 440 | Hampton Inn Monterrey Galerias Obispado | ◆◆◆ | $105-$120 | 442 |
| **3** p. 440 | **Safi Royal Luxury Towers** | ◆◆◆ | $110-$210 | 443 |
| **6** p. 440 | Hotel Macroplaza Monterrey | ◆◆ | $70-$125 | 442 |
| **7** p. 440 | Fiesta Americana Centro Monterrey | ◆◆◆ | $100-$230 | 442 |
| **8** p. 440 | Fiesta Inn Centro | ◆◆ | $90-$135 | 442 |
| **9** p. 440 | **Sheraton Ambassador Monterrey Hotel** | [fyi] | $160-$250 | 443 |
| **10** p. 440 | Gran Hotel Ancira | ◆◆◆ | $90-$175 | 442 |
| **13** p. 440 | BEST WESTERN Royal Courts | ◆◆ | Rates not provided | 442 |
| **15** p. 440 | Wyndham Garden Monterrey Norte | ◆◆ | $85 | 443 |
| **16** p. 440 | One Monterrey Aeropuerto | ◆ | Rates not provided | 443 |
| **17** p. 440 | Courtyard by Marriott Monterrey Airport | ◆◆◆ | $74-$121 | 442 |
| **18** p. 440 | Hampton Inn by Hilton Monterrey Aeropuerto | ◆◆◆ | Rates not provided | 442 |
| **19** p. 440 | Fairfield Inn by Marriott Monterrey Airport | ◆◆ | $48-$79 | 442 |
| **21** p. 440 | Holiday Inn Express Galerias-San Jeronimo | ◆◆◆ | $100-$180 | 442 |
| **22** p. 440 | **Hotel Quinta Real Monterrey** | ◆◆◆◆ | $185-$310 | 443 |
| **23** p. 440 | Presidente InterContinental Monterrey | ◆◆◆ | $145-$275 | 443 |
| **24** p. 440 | Hotel Camino Real Monterrey | ◆◆◆◆ | $145-$285 | 442 |
| **28** p. 440 | Hilton Garden Inn Monterrey | ◆◆◆ | $75-$130 | 442 |
| **30** p. 440 | **Safi Royal Luxury Valle** | ◆◆◆◆ | $185-$260 | 443 |

| Map Page | Restaurants | Diamond Rated | Cuisine | Price Range | Page |
|---|---|---|---|---|---|
| **4** p. 440 | Bice Ristorante | ◆◆◆ | Italian | $10-$13 | 444 |
| **5** p. 440 | Restaurante Safi | ◆◆◆ | Mexican | $8-$20 | 444 |
| **6** p. 440 | Kyo Grill | ◆◆◆ | Japanese | $20-$58 | 444 |
| **7** p. 440 | Wall St. Steakhouse | ◆◆◆ | Steak | $15-$45 | 444 |
| **10** p. 440 | El Papalote Aeropuerto | ◆◆ | Mexican | $12-$28 | 444 |

# MONTERREY, NUEVO LEÓN (C-2)

pop. 1,135,550
- Restaurants p. 444
- Hotels & Restaurants map & index p. 440

## BEST WESTERN ROYAL COURTS
81/8305-1900  **13**

**Hotel.** Rates not provided. **Address:** Ave Universidad No. 314 **Location:** On Mex 85, 5.1 mi (8.5 km) s of toll road to Nuevo Laredo; on northern city outskirts. Located in a busy commercial area. **Facility:** 82 units. 2-3 stories (no elevator), exterior corridors. **Bath:** shower only. **Terms:** 30 day cancellation notice-fee imposed, resort fee. **Amenities:** Some: safes. **Pool(s):** outdoor. **Guest Services:** valet laundry, area transportation.

**AAA Benefit:**
Save 10% or more every day and earn 10% bonus points!

## COURTYARD BY MARRIOTT MONTERREY AIRPORT
(81)8196-7900  **17**

**Hotel** $74-$121 **Address:** Carr Miguel Alemán KM 23.7 **Location:** At entrance to General Mariano Escobedo International Airport. **Facility:** 205 units. 5 stories, interior corridors. **Amenities:** Some: safes. **Pool(s):** outdoor. **Activities:** exercise room. **Guest Services:** valet and coin laundry, area transportation.

**AAA Benefit:**
Members save 5% or more!

## FAIRFIELD INN BY MARRIOTT MONTERREY AIRPORT
(81)8196-8900  **19**

**Hotel** $48-$79 **Address:** Ave Rogelio Gonzalez Caballero No. 150 66600 **Location:** On Carr Miguel Alemán; at entrance to General Mariano Escobedo International Airport. **Facility:** 206 units. 3 stories, interior corridors. **Pool(s):** outdoor. **Activities:** exercise room. **Guest Services:** valet laundry, area transportation.

**AAA Benefit:**
Members save 5% or more!

## FIESTA AMERICANA CENTRO MONTERREY
81/8319-0900  **7**

**Hotel** $100-$230 **Address:** Corregidora No. 519 Zona Rosa **Location:** In downtown historico Zona Rosa. **Facility:** Meets AAA guest room security requirements. 207 units. 13 stories, interior corridors. **Parking:** on-site and valet. **Amenities:** Some: safes. **Pool(s):** heated indoor. **Activities:** sauna, exercise room. **Guest Services:** valet laundry.

## FIESTA INN CENTRO
81/8150-2200  **8**

**Hotel** $90-$135 **Address:** Ave Pino Suarez No. 1001, Col Centro **Location:** Jct aves Pino Suarez and Ocampo. **Facility:** Meets AAA guest room security requirements. 231 units. 13 stories, interior corridors. **Pool(s):** indoor. **Activities:** exercise room. **Guest Services:** valet laundry.

## GRAN HOTEL ANCIRA
(81)8150-7000  **10**

**Historic Hotel** $90-$175 **Address:** Ocampo, No. 443 Ote **Location:** Southwest corner of Plaza Hidalgo; entrance only by one-way eastbound Ave Hidalgo. Located in the historico main plaza. **Facility:** This neoclassic landmark in the center of the historical district boasts a grand marbled lobby combined with contemporary amenities and service. Meets AAA guest room security requirements. 244 units. 5 stories, interior corridors. **Parking:** on-site and valet. **Amenities:** video games, safes. **Pool(s):** outdoor. **Activities:** sauna, hot tub, exercise room. **Guest Services:** valet laundry.

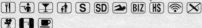

## HAMPTON INN BY HILTON MONTERREY AEROPUERTO
81/8196-8500  **18**

**Hotel.** Rates not provided. **Address:** Carr Miguel Alemán KM 23.7 **Location:** At entrance to General Mariano Escobedo International Airport. **Facility:** 181 units. 5 stories, interior corridors. **Terms:** 1-7 night minimum stay, cancellation fee imposed. **Pool(s):** outdoor. **Activities:** exercise room. **Guest Services:** valet and coin laundry, area transportation.

**AAA Benefit:**
Members save up to 10%!

## HAMPTON INN MONTERREY GALERIAS OBISPADO
81/8625-2450  **1**

**Hotel** $105-$120 **Address:** Ave Gonzalitos 415 S **Location:** Across from Galerias Mall. Located in modern Galerias District. **Facility:** Meets AAA guest room security requirements. 223 units. 7 stories, interior corridors. **Terms:** 1-7 night minimum stay, cancellation fee imposed. **Dining:** 2 restaurants. **Pool(s):** outdoor. **Activities:** exercise room. **Guest Services:** valet laundry, area transportation.

**AAA Benefit:**
Members save up to 10%!

## HILTON GARDEN INN MONTERREY
(81)8122-8000  **28**

**Hotel** $75-$130 **Address:** Blvd Antonio L Rodriguez No. 1880 64650 **Location:** On Hwy Monterrey-Saltillo, along Ave Constituyentes at Torres Morada and suspension bridge (Tirantes). **Facility:** 150 units. 5 stories, interior corridors. **Terms:** 1-7 night minimum stay, cancellation fee imposed. **Amenities:** safes. **Pool(s):** heated indoor. **Activities:** exercise room. **Guest Services:** valet laundry, area transportation.

**AAA Benefit:**
Members save up to 10%!

## HOLIDAY INN EXPRESS GALERIAS-SAN JERONIMO
(81)8389-6000  **21**

**Hotel** $100-$180 **Address:** 1082 Ave San Jeronimo **Location:** Just w of Galerias Mall. **Facility:** Meets AAA guest room security requirements. 170 units. 5 stories, interior corridors. **Parking:** on-site and valet. **Amenities:** safes. **Pool(s):** outdoor. **Activities:** exercise room. **Guest Services:** valet and coin laundry.

## HOTEL CAMINO REAL MONTERREY
(81)8133-5400  **24**

**Contemporary Hotel** $145-$285 **Address:** Ave Diego Rivera No. 2492 **Location:** Between Lazaro Cardedes and Ave Batallon de San Patricio. Located in main financial district. **Facility:** This place is full of wows with guest rooms that are large and feature eight-foot-long marble desks and ultra contemporary bathrooms with red floor-to-ceiling sliding glass doors. Meets AAA guest room security requirements. 254 units. 17 stories, interior corridors. **Parking:** on-site and valet. **Amenities:** safes. **Dining:** 2 restaurants, also, Bice Ristorante, Kyo Grill, see separate listings. **Pool(s):** heated outdoor. **Activities:** hot tub, exercise room, spa. **Guest Services:** valet laundry.

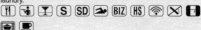

## HOTEL MACROPLAZA MONTERREY
81/8380-6000  **6**

**Hotel** $70-$125 **Address:** Morelos 574 Ote **Location:** In front of Plaza Zaragoza; in downtown Centro Historico. Located in a busy commercial area. **Facility:** Meets AAA guest room security requirements. 203 units. 9 stories, interior corridors. **Amenities:** safes. **Dining:** entertainment. **Pool(s):** heated indoor. **Activities:** sauna, hot tub, steamroom, exercise room. **Guest Services:** valet and coin laundry.

**(See map & index p. 440.)**

## HOTEL QUINTA REAL MONTERREY

(81)8368-1000 **22**

**Hotel**
**$185-$310**

**Address:** Diego Rivera No. 500 **Location:** Across from Plaza Fiesta San Agustin. Located in an upscale financial district. **Facility:** Bedazzling colonial architecture and upscale décor enhance the property, which features a rotunda registration area, life-size artwork and palatial furnishings. Meets AAA guest room security requirements. 165 units. 5 stories, interior corridors. **Parking:** on-site (fee) and street. **Amenities:** safes. **Pool(s):** heated indoor. **Activities:** hot tub, exercise room, massage. **Guest Services:** valet laundry. Affiliated with Preferred Hotels & Resorts.

## ONE MONTERREY AEROPUERTO

(81)1156-9950 **16**

**Hotel.** Rates not provided. **Address:** Blvd Aeropuerto Lotes 12 **Location:** Across from General Mariano Escobedo International Airport. **Facility:** 126 units. 7 stories, interior corridors. *Bath:* shower only. **Guest Services:** coin laundry.

## PRESIDENTE INTERCONTINENTAL MONTERREY

(81)8368-6000 **23**

**Hotel** $145-$275 **Address:** Ave Vasconcelos 300 Oriente 66260 **Location:** In upscale Valle financial district. **Facility:** This traditional, business-class hotel has expansive public areas, striking marble floors, tastefully decorated guest rooms and an outdoor lawn area that's family friendly on Saturday and Sunday. Meets AAA guest room security requirements. 305 units, some kitchens. 10 stories, interior corridors. **Parking:** on-site (fee) and valet. **Amenities:** safes. **Dining:** 2 restaurants, also, Wall St. Steakhouse, see separate listing. **Pool(s):** heated indoor. **Activities:** sauna, hot tub, steamroom, tennis, spa. **Guest Services:** valet laundry.

## SAFI ROYAL LUXURY TOWERS

81/8399-7000 **3**

**Hotel**
**$110-$210**

**Address:** Ave Pino Suarez 444 Sur **Location:** From Monterrey-Nuevo Laredo toll road, s on Ave Universidad to Ave Pino Suarez, then s to northern edge of downtown. Adjacent to Alameda Park. **Facility:** Meets AAA guest room security requirements. 244 units. 3-7 stories, interior/exterior corridors. **Amenities:** safes. **Pool(s):** heated outdoor. **Activities:** hot tub, exercise room. **Guest Services:** valet laundry.

**Dream. Plan. Go.**
*TripTik® Travel Planner*

AAA.com/ttp

## SAFI ROYAL LUXURY VALLE

(81)8100-7000 **30**

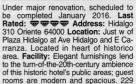

**Hotel**
**$185-$260**

**Address:** Diego Rivera 555 Valle Ote 66269 **Location:** In Valle financial district. **Facility:** Prepare yourself for a refined European ambience, which permeates this hotel located in the upscale Valle financial district. You'll revel in the spacious rooms with upscale furniture. 220 units. 14 stories, interior corridors. **Parking:** on-site and valet. **Terms:** 3 day cancellation notice-fee imposed, resort fee. **Amenities:** safes. **Dining:** Restaurante Safi, see separate listing. **Pool(s):** heated outdoor. **Activities:** hot tub, exercise room. **Guest Services:** valet laundry.

## SHERATON AMBASSADOR MONTERREY HOTEL

(81)8380-7000 **9**

**fyi**
**Historic Hotel**
**$160-$250**

**AAA Benefit:** Members save up to 15%, plus Starwood Preferred Guest® benefits!

Under major renovation, scheduled to be completed January 2016. **Last Rated:** **Address:** Hidalgo 310 Oriente 64000 **Location:** Just w of Plaza Hidalgo at Ave Hidalgo and E Carranza. Located in heart of historico area. **Facility:** Elegant furnishings lend to the turn-of-the-20th-century ambience of this historic hotel's public areas; guest rooms are modern and spacious. 229 units. 11 stories, interior corridors. **Parking:** valet only. **Amenities:** safes. **Dining:** entertainment. **Pool(s):** outdoor. **Activities:** hot tub, tennis, massage. **Guest Services:** valet laundry.

## WYNDHAM GARDEN MONTERREY NORTE

81/8305-2400 **15**

**Hotel** $85 **Address:** Ave Universidad 501 Nte **Location:** 4.8 mi (8 km) s of Mex 85 and Monterrey-Nuevo Laredo (toll road); 1 mi (1.7 km) n of Universidad de Nuevo Leon. **Facility:** Meets AAA guest room security requirements. 235 units. 6 stories, interior corridors. **Pool(s):** outdoor. **Activities:** exercise room. **Guest Services:** valet laundry.

## CROWNE PLAZA MONTERREY

81/8319-6000

**fyi** Not evaluated. **Address:** Ave Constitution Ote 300 **Location:** Just w of Plaza Hidalgo. Facilities, services, and décor characterize a mid-scale property.

## HOLIDAY INN EXPRESS AEROPUERTO

81/8288-1200

**fyi** Not evaluated. **Address:** Blvd Aeropuerto No. 400 66600 **Location:** At entrance to General Mariano Escobedo International Airport. Facilities, services, and décor characterize a mid-scale property.

## HOLIDAY INN MONTERREY CENTRO

81/8228-6000

**fyi** Not evaluated. **Address:** Padre Mier 194 Pte **Location:** 0.4 mi (0.7 km) w of Grand Plaza; jct Padre Mier and Ave Garibaldi. Facilities, services, and décor characterize a mid-scale property.

## HOLIDAY INN MONTERREY VALLE

81/8133-0808

**fyi** Not evaluated. **Address:** Ave Lazaro Cardenas No. 2305 66260 **Location:** In upscale Valle District. Facilities, services, and décor characterize a mid-scale property.

(See map & index p. 440.)

**WHERE TO EAT**

**BICE RISTORANTE**  81/8133-5400  ④

▼▼▼▼ Italian. Fine Dining. $10-$13 **AAA Inspector Notes:** The sleek, modern Italian décor features a floor-to-ceiling wine rack that requires a ladder. The attentive, friendly staffers serve intriguing signature dishes such as aromatic mushroom risotto, rich lasagna and a lively frutti di mare capellini. **Features:** wine only. **Reservations:** suggested. **Address:** Ave Diego Rivera No. 2492 66269 **Location:** Between Lazaro Cardedes and Ave Batallon de San Patricio; in Hotel Camino Real Monterrey. **Parking:** valet and street only.

⒝ ⒧ ⒟ (LATE)

**EL PAPALOTE AEROPUERTO**  81/8145-0055  ⑩

▼▼▼ Mexican. Casual Dining. $12-$28 **AAA Inspector Notes:** This eatery caters to airport-area businesses with variety of tender Mexican beef, grilled poultry and fresh seafood combos. Guests are greeted with chips and three types of salsa. For dessert, try the chilled flan. It's cool, refreshing and satisfying. **Features:** patio dining, happy hour. **Address:** Blvd Aeropuerto No. 400 66600 **Location:** At entrance to General Mariano Escobedo International Airport.

⒧ ⒟

**KYO GRILL**  81/8133-5426  ⑥

▼▼▼▼ Japanese. Fine Dining. $20-$58 **AAA Inspector Notes:** Leave one world behind by crossing the bridge over the gurgling stream and enter a spectacular temple with a 20-foot stone Buddha, decorative accents that dazzle the mind and a fusion of Asian and Mexican. The jicama-wrapped crab and avocado is worth a try. **Features:** full bar. **Reservations:** suggested. **Address:** Ave Diego Rivera No. 2492 **Location:** Between Lazaro Cardedes and Ave Batallon de San Patricio; in Hotel Camino Real Monterrey. **Parking:** on-site and valet. ⒟ CALL Ⓛ Ⓜ

**LOS ARCOS RESTAURANT**  81/8347-2301

▼▼ Mexican Seafood. Casual Dining. $10-$25 **AAA Inspector Notes:** A well-known local favorite that is casual and friendly. Try the light and refreshing Mexican-style shrimp cocktail with pico de gallo and avocado or the hot steamy shrimp ball soup. **Features:** full bar. **Address:** Ave Ignacio Morones Prieta No. 2414 64710 **Location:** In financial district. ⒧ ⒟ ⊠

**RESTAURANTE SAFI**  81/8100-7000  ⑤

▼▼▼ Mexican. Casual Dining. $8-$20 **AAA Inspector Notes:** This popular full-service restaurant features a la carte menu as well as a massive 100-item buffet for breakfast, lunch and dinner with seafood, Mexican, Italian and American selections. All breads and pastries are homemade. **Features:** full bar. **Address:** Ave Diego Rivera No. 555 Valle Ote 66269 **Location:** In financial district; in Safi Royal Luxury Valle. **Parking:** on-site and valet. ⒝ ⒧ ⒟

**SIRLOIN STOCKADE**

▼▼ Steak. Quick Serve. $9-$11 **AAA Inspector Notes:** The steakhouse lines up buffet items, including pizza, tacos, soups, salads and desserts, providing both excellent variety and a good value. Rotating theme nights allow for the sampling of sushi, barbecue and seafood. The buffet may also serve to complement a quality steak. **Bar:** beer & wine. ⒧ ⒟ ⊠

*For additional information, visit AAA.com*
**LOCATIONS:**
**Address:** Ave Alfonso Reyes 110 Nte, Col Anahuac **Location:** Just n of Ciudad Universitaria; next to HEB Shopping Complex. **Phone:** 81/8352-9902

**Address:** Ave Lazaro Cardenas Pte 2510 **Location:** On Ave Lazaro Cardenas at Diego Rivera. **Phone:** 81/8625-7325

**Address:** Ave Eugenio Garza Sada No. 3750 **Location:** Just off Malaga St; in Mas Palomas District. **Phone:** 81/8103-0521

**Address:** Ave Insurgentes No. 2500 **Location:** In Galerias District. **Phone:** 81/8333-1032

**Address:** Carr Miguel Aleman No. 5391 67129 **Location:** In Plaza Sirloin Lindavista; in Colonia Riveras de la Purisima. **Phone:** 81/8394-5428

**WALL ST. STEAKHOUSE**  81/8368-6000  ⑦

▼▼▼ Steak. Fine Dining. $15-$45 **AAA Inspector Notes:** This city landmark is known for its American-sized cuts of juicy, sizzling steaks. An elegant dining room, polished staff and wide-ranging wine list add up to an exceptional experience. The spinach salad, with fried Brie and raspberry vinaigrette, wakes up your taste buds for the coming attractions. **Features:** full bar. **Reservations:** suggested. **Address:** Ave Vasconcelos 300 Ote 66260 **Location:** In financial district; in Presidente InterContinental Monterrey. **Parking:** on-site (fee) and valet. ⒧ ⒟

## SALTILLO, COAHUILA (C-2) pop. 725,123, elev. 5,245'

**AMERICAN HOTEL EXPRESS**  844/438-8800

(fyi) Not evaluated. **Address:** Carr Saltillo-Monterrey No. 9000 **Location:** 10.8 mi (18 km) on Saltillo to Monterrey Hwy (libre). Facilities, services, and décor characterize a mid-scale property.

**CAMINO REAL SALTILLO**  844/438-0000

(fyi) Not evaluated. **Address:** Blvd Los Fundadores No. 2000 Col Los Cerritos **Location:** 3.6 mi (6 km) se on Mex 57 from Mex 40; on eastern city outskirts. Facilities, services, and décor characterize an upscale property.

**DOUBLETREE SUITES BY HILTON HOTEL SALTILLO**  844/438-7000

(fyi) Not evaluated. **Address:** Blvd Venustiano Carranza 8800 **Location:** 10.8 mi (18 km) n on Saltillo to Monterrey Hwy (libre). Facilities, services, and décor characterize a mid-scale property.

**AAA Benefit:**
Members save 5% or more!

**HAMPTON INN BY HILTON ZONA AEROPUERTO**  844/450-4500

(fyi) Not evaluated. **Address:** 6580 Carr Saltillo-Monterrey **Location:** 11.4 mi (19 km) n on Saltillo to Monterrey Hwy (libre). Facilities, services, and décor characterize a mid-scale property.

**AAA Benefit:**
Members save up to 10%!

**QUALITY INN & SUITES SALTILLO EUROTEL**  844/438-8888

(fyi) Not evaluated. **Address:** Blvd V Carranza No. 4100 **Location:** 0.6 mi (1 km) s from Glorieta; at N Ortiz G and Blvd V Carranza. Facilities, services, and décor characterize an economy property.

**WHERE TO EAT**

**RESTAURANT LA CANASTA**  844/415-8050

▼▼▼ Regional Mexican. Casual Dining. $7-$28 **AAA Inspector Notes:** Fireplaces lend to the restaurant's elegant, yet informal, country-style décor. You'll find ample parking behind this place, which is north of downtown. Among examples of popular regional Mexican dishes is the house specialty: mole poblano. This eatery is popular for both leisure dining and power lunches. Service is friendly and efficient. **Features:** full bar, Sunday brunch. **Reservations:** suggested. **Address:** Blvd V Carranza 2485 25280 **Location:** 0.8 mi (1.3 km) from Glorieta; at N Ortiz G and Blvd V Carranza. **Parking:** on-site and valet. ⒧ ⒟ (LATE) ⊠

## SAN NICOLAS DE LOS GARZA, NUEVO LEON pop. 443,273

### FIESTA INN MONTERREY LA FE-AIRPORT          81/8319-7500

**fyl** Not evaluated. **Address:** Ave Miguel Alemán No. 105 Col La Fe **Location:** At entrance to airport. Facilities, services, and décor characterize a mid-scale property.

## TORREON, COAHUILA pop. 639,629

### BEST WESTERN HOTEL POSADA DEL RIO EXPRESS
871/750-7500

**fyl** Not evaluated. **Address:** Blvd Independencia No. 3837 27018 **Location:** On Mex 40; near Industrial City turn off. Facilities, services, and décor characterize a mid-scale property.

**AAA Benefit:** Save 10% or more every day and earn 10% bonus points!

### CROWNE PLAZA TORREON          871/729-9600

**fyl** Not evaluated. **Address:** Blvd Torreon Matamoros No. 4050 **Location:** Off Diagonal Reforma; centro. Facilities, services, and décor characterize a mid-scale property.

### FIESTA INN TORREON GALERIAS          871/749-3300

**fyl** Not evaluated. **Address:** Periferico Raul Lopez Sanchez No. 6000 **Location:** On Mex 40; in Galerias Shopping Center. Facilities, services, and décor characterize a mid-scale property.

### HAMPTON INN TORREON AEROPUERTO GALERIAS
871/705-1550

**fyl** Not evaluated. **Address:** Periferico Raul Lopez Sanchez 10995 **Location:** Just nw of jct Carr Santa Fe. Facilities, services, and décor characterize a mid-scale property.

**AAA Benefit:** Members save up to 10%!

### HOLIDAY INN EXPRESS TORREON          871/729-6000

**fyl** Not evaluated; located in remote area. **Address:** Blvd Independencia 1133 Ote **Location:** Just ne on Mex 30. Facilities, services, and décor characterize a mid-scale property.

### HOTEL MISION TORREON          871/729-4300

**fyl** Not evaluated. **Address:** Paseo de La Rosita 910 27250 **Location:** Jct Paseo de La Rosita and Diagonal de Los Fuentes, just w. Facilities, services, and décor characterize a mid-scale property.

### MARRIOTT TORREON          871/895-0000

**fyl** Not evaluated. **Address:** Blvd Independencia 100 Pte **Location:** 1.2 mi (2 km) ne on Mex 30. Facilities, services, and décor characterize an upscale property.

**AAA Benefit:** Members save 5% or more!

### WHERE TO EAT

#### MARTIN'S RESTAURANT          871/729-6440

◈◈ Mexican. Casual Dining. $8-$30 **AAA Inspector Notes:** Locally popular, this coffee shop-style restaurant serves a good selection of reasonably priced American sandwiches, burgers, steaks, soups and Mexican food. Don't miss the luscious desserts. **Features:** full bar. **Address:** Blvd Independencia 1133 Ote **Location:** Just ne on Mex 30; in Holiday Inn Express Torreon.
B  L  D  LATE

#### SIRLOIN STOCKADE          871/718-4884

◈◈ Steak. Quick Serve. $9-$11 **AAA Inspector Notes:** The steakhouse lines up buffet items, including pizza, tacos, soups, salads and desserts, providing both excellent variety and a good value. Rotating theme nights allow for the sampling of sushi, barbecue and seafood. The buffet may also serve to complement a quality steak. **Features:** full bar. **Address:** Blvd Independencia 2270 **Location:** On eastbound access road of Mex 40-D (toll road).
L  D  ⬲

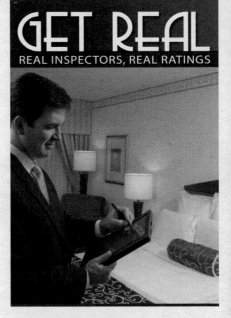

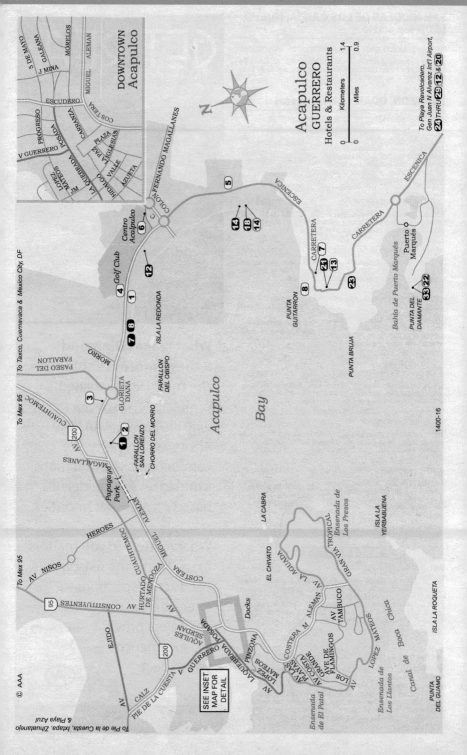

DOWNTOWN ACAPULCO

Acapulco GUERRERO
Hotels & Restaurants

Acapulco Bay

# THE PACIFIC COAST

**AAA recommends that travelers consult online U.S. State Department travel advisories when planning travel abroad. Find this information at http://travel.state.gov/content/passports/english/alertswarnings/mexico-travel-warning.html.**

## Acapulco

This index helps you "spot" where approved hotels and restaurants are located on the corresponding detailed maps. Hotel daily rate range is for comparison only. Restaurant price range is a combination of lunch and/or dinner. Turn to the listing page for more detailed rate and price information and consult display ads for special promotions.

### ACAPULCO, GUERRERO

| Map Page | Hotels | Diamond Rated | Rate Range | Page |
|---|---|---|---|---|
| **1** p. 446 | Hotel Emporio Acapulco | ▼▼▼ | $75-$130 | 449 |
| **7** p. 446 | Fiesta Americana Villas Acapulco | ▼▼▼ | $277-$526 | 448 |
| **8** p. 446 | Holiday Inn Resort Acapulco | ▼▼▼ | $91-$356 | 448 |
| **12** p. 446 | Hotel Elcano | ▼▼ | $98-$270 | 449 |
| **14** p. 446 | Casa Inn Acapulco, Mexico | ▼▼ | $100-$158 | 448 |
| **18** p. 446 | **Grand Hotel Acapulco & Convention Center** | ▼▼▼ | $85-$190 | 448 |
| **21** p. 446 | **Hotel Las Brisas Acapulco** | ▼▼▼▼ | $260-$900 | 449 |
| **23** p. 446 | Camino Real Acapulco Diamante | ▼▼▼ | $345-$739 | 448 |
| **24** p. 446 | The Fairmont Acapulco Princess | ▼▼▼ | $143-$1248 | 448 |
| **25** p. 446 | The Fairmont Pierre Marques | ▼▼▼ | $132-$615 | 448 |
| **26** p. 446 | Holiday Inn Acapulco La Isla | ▼▼▼ | $107-$209 | 448 |
| **27** p. 446 | **Mayan Palace Regency Golf** *(See ad on insert, p. 467.)* | ▼▼▼ | $255-$305 | 449 |
| **29** p. 446 | **The Grand Mayan Acapulco** *(See ad on insert.)* | ▼▼▼▼ | $331-$397 | 448 |
| **33** p. 446 | **Banyan Tree Cabo Marques** | ▼▼▼▼▼ | $285-$1535 | 448 |

| Map Page | Restaurants | Diamond Rated | Cuisine | Price Range | Page |
|---|---|---|---|---|---|
| ① p. 446 | La Mansion | ▼▼ | Steak | $30-$50 | 450 |
| ② p. 446 | Sunset | ▼▼ | International Fusion | $10-$15 | 450 |
| ③ p. 446 | Fisher's Acapulco | ▼▼ | Seafood | $10-$28 | 449 |
| ④ p. 446 | Hard Rock Cafe | ▼▼ | American | $10-$24 [SAVE] | 449 |
| ⑤ p. 446 | Suntory Acapulco | ▼▼▼ | Japanese | $16-$45 | 450 |
| ⑥ p. 446 | Su Casa | ▼▼ | Continental | $14-$32 | 450 |
| ⑦ p. 446 | Tony's Asian Bistro | ▼▼ | Asian Fusion | $18-$40 | 450 |
| ⑧ p. 446 | Kookaburra | ▼▼▼ | Seafood | $18-$35 | 449 |
| ⑫ p. 446 | **Tabachin ChopHouse** | ▼▼▼▼ | Steak | $40-$60 | 450 |
| ⑬ p. 446 | **Bellavista** | ▼▼▼▼ | International | $23-$55 | 449 |
| ⑭ p. 446 | El Pescador | ▼▼ | International | $14-$30 | 449 |
| ⑳ p. 446 | **Saffron** | ▼▼▼ | Thai | $30-$55 | 450 |
| ㉒ p. 446 | La Nao | ▼▼▼ | International | $30-$50 | 450 |

## ACAPULCO, GUERRERO   pop. 789,971
• Hotels & Restaurants map & index p. 446

### BANYAN TREE CABO MARQUES    (744)434-0100  **33**

Contemporary Hotel
$285-$1535

**Address:** Blvd Cabo Marques, Lote 1 39907 **Location:** Oceanfront. 1.5 mi (2.2 km) off Mex 200 (Airport Hwy); in Punta Diamante. **Facility:** Luxurious and spacious public areas showcase breathtaking views at this remote location with unique architecture that provides ultimate privacy. Meets AAA guest room security requirements. 45 units. 1 story, exterior corridors. **Terms:** 3 night minimum stay - seasonal and/or weekends, 3 day cancellation notice. **Amenities:** safes. **Dining:** 2 restaurants, also, La Nao, Saffron, see separate listings. **Pool(s):** outdoor. **Activities:** recreation programs, exercise room, spa. **Guest Services:** valet laundry, area transportation.

### CAMINO REAL ACAPULCO DIAMANTE    (744)435-1010  **23**

Hotel $345-$739 **Address:** Carr Escenica KM 14, Baj Catita S/N Fracc Pichilinque **Location:** Oceanfront. 8.1 mi (13 km) se on Mex 200 (Airport Hwy); overlooking Bahia de Puerto Marques. Located in a secluded residential area. **Facility:** Meets AAA guest room security requirements. 157 units. 5-9 stories, interior corridors. **Parking:** on-site (fee) and valet. **Terms:** 2-5 night minimum stay - seasonal, resort fee. **Amenities:** safes. **Dining:** 3 restaurants. **Pool(s):** outdoor. **Activities:** sauna, steamroom, snorkeling, recreation programs in season, kids club, exercise room, spa. **Guest Services:** valet laundry.

### CASA INN ACAPULCO, MEXICO    744/435-2000  **14**

Hotel $100-$158 **Address:** Ave Costera Miguel Aleman No. 2310 **Location:** 5 mi (8 km) e; across from Walmart and casino. Located in a busy commercial area. **Facility:** 328 units, some efficiencies. 16 stories, interior corridors. **Bath:** shower only. **Parking:** on-site (fee). **Pool(s):** outdoor. **Activities:** playground, exercise room. **Guest Services:** valet and coin laundry.

### THE FAIRMONT ACAPULCO PRINCESS    (744)469-1000  **24**

Resort Hotel $143-$1248 **Address:** Costera de Las Palmas S/N Col. Granjas del Marquez 39890 **Location:** Oceanfront. 12.1 mi (19.3 km) se, off Mex 200 (Airport Hwy). Located in a quiet area. **Facility:** An enormous hotel with beautiful and sprawling tropical grounds, this property is away from the hustle and bustle of downtown. Some guest rooms have ocean views. 1011 units, some two bedrooms and efficiencies. 10-14 stories, interior corridors. **Parking:** on-site (fee) and valet. **Amenities:** safes. **Dining:** 6 restaurants, entertainment. **Pool(s):** outdoor. **Activities:** sauna, hot tub, steamroom, regulation golf, tennis, recreation programs, kids club, playground, exercise room, spa. **Guest Services:** valet laundry.

### THE FAIRMONT PIERRE MARQUES    (744)435-2600  **25**

Classic Resort Hotel $132-$615 **Address:** Playa Revolcadero S/N Col. Granjas del Marquez **Location:** Oceanfront. 10.9 mi (17.5 km) se, off Mex 200 (Airport Hwy). Located in a quiet beachside setting. **Facility:** Acapulco's iconic hotel is situated on 50 private acres. The original portion of the hotel was once part of the 95-room home of famous industrialist John Paul Getty. 229 units. 1-5 stories, exterior corridors. **Parking:** on-site and valet. **Amenities:** safes. **Dining:** 3 restaurants, also, Tabachin ChopHouse, see separate listing. **Pool(s):** outdoor. **Activities:** regulation golf, tennis, recreation programs in season, kids club, playground, exercise room. **Guest Services:** valet laundry, area transportation.

### FIESTA AMERICANA VILLAS ACAPULCO    (744)435-1600  **7**

Vacation Rental Condominium $277-$526 **Address:** Ave Costera Miguel Aleman 97 39690 **Location:** Oceanfront. 3.3 mi (5.3 km) e. Located in busy commercial area. **Facility:** Attractive and bustling public areas. The large terrace pool area overlooks Acapulco Bay. 324 condominiums. 19 stories, interior corridors. **Parking:** valet only. **Terms:** 3 day cancellation notice. **Amenities:** safes. **Dining:** 3 restaurants. **Pool(s):** outdoor. **Activities:** steamroom, recreation programs, kids club, playground, spa. **Guest Services:** complimentary and valet laundry.

### GRAND HOTEL ACAPULCO & CONVENTION CENTER
(744)469-1234  **18**

Hotel
$85-$190

**Address:** Ave Costera Miguel Aleman No. 1 39869 **Location:** Oceanfront. 5 mi (8 km) e. Located on the bay next to Icacos Navy Base. **Facility:** 573 units. 23 stories, interior corridors. **Parking:** on-site (fee) and valet. **Terms:** 3 night minimum stay - seasonal, 3 day cancellation notice, in season-fee imposed. **Amenities:** Some: safes. **Dining:** 3 restaurants, also, El Pescador, see separate listing. **Pool(s):** outdoor. **Activities:** sauna, steamroom, recreation programs in summer, exercise room, spa. **Guest Services:** valet laundry, area transportation.

### THE GRAND MAYAN ACAPULCO    744/469-6000  **29**

Resort Hotel
$331-$397

**Address:** Ave Costera de Las Palmas No. 1121 39900 **Location:** Oceanfront. 13.8 mi (22 km) se, off Mex 200 (Airport Hwy). **Facility:** On expansive grounds, this luxurious, family-friendly property features lakes, a lazy river and a huge reflecting pool at the entry. Meets AAA guest room security requirements. 352 units, some two bedrooms and efficiencies. 10 stories, interior corridors. **Parking:** on-site (fee) and valet. **Terms:** check-in 5 pm, 2-7 night minimum stay, 7 day cancellation notice-fee imposed. **Amenities:** safes. **Dining:** 5 restaurants, entertainment. **Pool(s):** outdoor. **Activities:** sauna, hot tub, steamroom, regulation golf, tennis, recreation programs, kids club, playground, game room, exercise room, spa. **Guest Services:** valet and coin laundry, area transportation. *(See ad on insert.)*

### HOLIDAY INN ACAPULCO LA ISLA    (744)435-6500  **26**

Hotel $107-$209 **Address:** Blvd de Las Naciones No. 2000, Col La Zanja 39906 **Location:** Just n of La Isla Shopping Village. **Facility:** Meets AAA guest room security requirements. 101 units. 6 stories, interior corridors. **Terms:** 3 night minimum stay - seasonal, 3 day cancellation notice. **Amenities:** safes. **Pool(s):** outdoor. **Activities:** exercise room. **Guest Services:** coin laundry.

### HOLIDAY INN RESORT ACAPULCO    (744)435-0500  **8**

Hotel $91-$356 **Address:** Ave Costera Miguel Aleman No. 2311 39900 **Location:** Oceanfront. 3.4 mi (5.4 km) e. Located on the bay in a heavy-commercial area. **Facility:** 220 units. 15 stories, interior corridors. **Bath:** shower only. **Parking:** valet only. **Terms:** 2-3 night minimum stay - seasonal. **Amenities:** safes. **Pool(s):** outdoor. **Activities:** recreation programs, kids club, limited exercise equipment. **Guest Services:** valet laundry.

(See map & index p. 446.)

HOTEL ELCANO                                    (744)435-1500  **12**

WWW **Hotel** $98-$270 **Address:** Ave Costera Miguel Alemán 75 39690 **Location:** Oceanfront. 3.8 mi (6 km) e. Located on the bay in a busy commercial area. **Facility:** 180 units. 10 stories, interior corridors. **Parking:** on-site and valet. **Amenities:** safes. **Pool(s):** outdoor. **Activities:** recreation programs in summer, exercise room, massage. **Guest Services:** valet laundry.

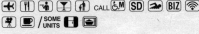

HOTEL EMPORIO ACAPULCO                    (744)469-0505  **1**

WWW **Contemporary Resort Hotel** $75-$130 **Address:** Ave Costera Miguel Alemán No. 121 39670 **Location:** Oceanfront. 2.6 mi (4.5 km) w; near Glorieta de La Diana traffic circle. Located on the bay in a busy commercial area. **Facility:** A good value, this beachfront hotel has lush, tropical gardens. Guest rooms are in two modern towers, and all units feature a balcony with a sea view. Meets AAA guest room security requirements. 422 units. 14 stories, exterior corridors. **Parking:** on-site (fee) and valet. **Amenities:** safes. **Dining:** 2 restaurants, also, Sunset, see separate listing. **Pool(s):** outdoor. **Activities:** sauna, hot tub, steamroom, recreation programs, kids club, playground, exercise room, spa. **Guest Services:** valet laundry.

HOTEL LAS BRISAS ACAPULCO        (744)469-6900  **21**

WWWW
**Retro Resort Hotel**
$260-$900

**Address:** Carr Escenica No. 5255 39867 **Location:** 7.1 mi (11.3 km) se on Mex 200 (Airport Hwy). Located in residential area. **Facility:** The hotel's picturesque, hillside location offers spectacular ocean, city and bay views. Duplex cottages feature either a private or semi-private swimming pool. Meets AAA guest room security requirements. 251 units. 1 story, exterior corridors. **Terms:** 3 night minimum stay - seasonal, 15 day cancellation notice, in season-fee imposed. **Amenities:** safes. **Dining:** 2 restaurants, also, Bellavista, see separate listing. **Pool(s):** outdoor.

**Activities:** sauna, steamroom, scuba diving, snorkeling, tennis, recreation programs, kids club, exercise room, spa. **Guest Services:** valet laundry, area transportation.

MAYAN PALACE REGENCY GOLF     744/469-6000  **27**

WWW
**Resort Hotel**
$255-$305

**Address:** Ave Costera de Las Palmas No. 1121 39900 **Location:** 13.8 mi (22 km) se, off Mex 200 (Airport Hwy); in Punta Diamante resort area. Located in a quiet setting. **Facility:** The property features lush gardens, unique Aztec-style construction in the lobby and an expansive pool area with a water park. All guest rooms have a balcony. 190 units, some efficiencies. 3 stories, interior corridors. **Parking:** on-site and valet. **Terms:** check-in 5 pm, 2-7 night minimum stay, 7 day cancellation notice-fee imposed. **Amenities:** safes. **Dining:** entertainment. **Pool(s):** outdoor.

**Activities:** regulation golf, recreation programs, kids club, playground, exercise room. **Guest Services:** valet and coin laundry, area transportation. *(See ad on insert, p. 467.)*

Pick up colorful, top-quality
travel guides and atlases
at AAA/CAA offices

HOTEL CROWNE PLAZA ACAPULCO             744/440-5555

[fyi] Not evaluated; management refused inspection. **Address:** Ave Costera Miguel Alemán 1803 39670 **Location:** Oceanfront. 2.8 mi (4.5 km) w. Facilities, services, and décor characterize a mid-scale property.

ONE ACAPULCO COSTERA                          744/435-0470

[fyi] Not evaluated. **Address:** Ave Costera Miguel Alemán No.16 39850 **Location:** 5 mi (8 km) e. Facilities, services, and décor characterize an economy property.

PARK ROYAL ACAPULCO                             744/440-6565

[fyi] Not evaluated. **Address:** Costera Guitarron 110 Fracc Playa Guitarron 39867 **Location:** Oceanfront. 5.9 mi (9.5 km) se off Carr Escenica, follow signs. Facilities, services, and décor characterize a mid-scale property.

QUINTA REAL ACAPULCO                             744/469-1500

[fyi] **Hotel** Did not meet all AAA rating requirements for locking devices in some guest rooms at time of last evaluation on 03/05/2014. **Address:** Paseo de La Quinta No. 6 Fracc Real Diamante 39907 **Location:** Oceanfront. 1.3 mi (2 km) off Mex 200 (Airport Hwy); in Punta Diamante. Facilities, services, and décor characterize a mid-scale property.

## WHERE TO EAT

BELLAVISTA                                    744/469-6900  **13**

WWWW
**International
Fine Dining**
$23-$55

**AAA Inspector Notes:** The restaurant serves creative cuisine in an elegant atmosphere. You'll enjoy dining outside, where every table has a spectacular view of Acapulco Bay. The menu consists of lobster, shrimp, duck, beef, chicken and pasta dishes. **Features:** full bar, patio dining. **Reservations:** required. **Address:** Carr Escenica No. 5255 39867 **Location:** 7.1 mi (11.3 km) se on Mex 200 (Airport Hwy); in Hotel Las Brisas Acapulco. **Parking:** on-site and valet.

EL PESCADOR                                   744/469-1234  **14**

WW International. Casual Dining. $14-$30 **AAA Inspector Notes:** This casual, open-air beachfront restaurant offers great views of Acapulco Bay from most of the tables. The menu features a good mix of international fare, including grilled fish, seafood, meats and pasta. You'll also find lighter options such as burgers, pizza and entrée salads. **Features:** full bar. **Reservations:** suggested. **Address:** Ave Costera Miguel Alemán No. 1 39869 **Location:** 5 mi (8 km) e; in Grand Hotel Acapulco & Convention Center.

FISHER'S ACAPULCO                             744/484-9148  **3**

WW Seafood. Casual Dining. $10-$28 **AAA Inspector Notes:** This bustling restaurant features an extensive variety of fresh seafood prepared in regional styles. Try the crab tostadas, seafood pasta or oysters on the half shell. **Features:** full bar. **Address:** Ave Costera Miguel Alemán No. 1926 **Location:** In Galeria Diana. **Parking:** valet only.

HARD ROCK CAFE                                744/484-0047  **4**

WW American. Casual Dining. $10-$24 **AAA Inspector Notes:** Rock 'n' roll memorabilia decorates the walls of the popular theme restaurant. Live music on the weekends contributes to the bustling atmosphere. On the menu is a wide variety of American cuisine—from burgers and sandwiches to seafood, steaks and pasta. **Features:** full bar. **Address:** Ave Costera Miguel Alemán No. 37 Fracc Costa Azul 39850 **Location:** 4 mi (6.4 km) e of downtown. **Parking:** valet and street only.

KOOKABURRA                                    744/446-6020  **8**

WWW Seafood. Fine Dining. $18-$35 **AAA Inspector Notes:** Named after the unusual bird that inhabits Mexico, Kookaburra presents creative preparations of seafood such as shrimp, crab, lobster, octopus and local marlin, many tinged with citrus flavorings. Desserts are fun and tempting. **Features:** full bar. **Reservations:** suggested. **Address:** La Isla Shopping Village, Local 10 y 11 39670 **Location:** In La Isla Shopping Village, Acapulco Diamante. **Parking:** on-site (fee) and valet.

(See map & index p. 446.)

LA MANSION                          744/481-0796  ①

▼▼ ▼▼ Steak. Casual Dining. $30-$50 AAA Inspector Notes: Prime beef cuts are the star attraction at this popular chain restaurant with a comfortable ambiance. Those who'd rather have traditional Mexican food will find suitable choices on the extensive menu. Steaks are served on heavy wooden plates with handles with some selections prepared table side. Features: full bar. Reservations: suggested. Address: Ave Costera Miguel Alemán 81-26 39670 Location: 3.8 mi (6 km) e. Parking: valet only. L D ◣

LA NAO                               744/434-0100  ㉒

▼▼▼▼ International. Casual Dining. $30-$50 AAA Inspector Notes: From the extensive breakfast buffet to the à la carte dinner menu, this elegant restaurant's creative interpretations of Mexican cuisine have an Asian flair. Enjoy patio dining with an expansive view of the open Pacific. Features: full bar, patio dining, Sunday brunch. Address: Blvd Cabo Marques, Lote 1 39907 Location: 1.5 mi (2.2 km) off Mex 200 (Airport Hwy); in Punta Diamante; in Banyan Tree Cabo Marques. Parking: valet only. B L D

SAFFRON                             744/434-0100  ⑳

▼▼▼▼ ▼▼▼▼
Thai
Fine Dining
$30-$55

AAA Inspector Notes: Here's a fine choice if you crave exquisite Thai cuisine served in a romantic atmosphere, complete with Pacific waves crashing on the rocks below. Features: full bar. Reservations: suggested. Address: Blvd Cabo Marques, Lote 1 39907 Location: 1.5 mi (2.2 km) off Mex 200 (Airport Hwy); in Punta Diamante; in Banyan Tree Cabo Marques. Parking: valet only.
D ◣

SU CASA                             744/484-4350  ⑥

▼▼ ▼▼ Continental. Casual Dining. $14-$32 AAA Inspector Notes: Perched on a mountainside, this intimate restaurant offers fabulous views of Acapulco Bay. The dining area is on a large open-air terrace with archways that are lined with twinkling lights and flower baskets. The ambience is romantic and the food is well-prepared. While Su Casa offers a wide variety of Continental cuisine, the adjoining dining room and sister restaurant, La Margarita, offers more traditional Mexican food. Features: full bar. Reservations: suggested, in season. Address: Anahuac No. 110, Lomas de Costa Azul Location: Jct Ave Costera Miguel Alemán and Calle Cristobal Colon, 0.6 mi (1 km) nw. Parking: no self-parking. D Ⓐ ◣

SUNSET                              744/469-0505  ②

▼▼ ▼▼ International Fusion. Casual Dining. $10-$15 AAA Inspector Notes: This open-air restaurant overlooks the pool and beachfront and has a tropical feel. The menu features a variety of fresh seafood and shellfish prepared in typical regional style, yet with a creative flair. Be sure to request a table on the second-floor terrace to enjoy the view. Features: full bar, patio dining. Reservations: suggested. Address: Ave Costera Miguel Alemán No. 121 39670 Location: 2.6 mi (4.5 km) w; near Glorieta de La Diana traffic circle; in Hotel Emporio Acapulco. Parking: on-site (fee) and valet.
L D Ⓐ ◣

SUNTORY ACAPULCO                    744/484-8088  ⑤

▼▼ ▼▼ Japanese. Casual Dining. $16-$45 AAA Inspector Notes: Entrée selections are prepared before your eyes, teppanyaki style (on a flat-surface plate grill), and feature combinations of fresh seafood, poultry and beef. Sushi rolls and sashimi are offered as well. Dining room windows overlook the tropical garden with teppanyaki tables also available on the terrace. Features: full bar. Reservations: suggested. Address: Ave Costera Miguel Alemán No. 36 39850 Location: 4.7 mi (7.5 km) e. Parking: valet only.
L D LATE ◣

TABACHIN CHOPHOUSE                  744/435-2600  ⑫

▼▼▼▼ ▼▼▼▼
Steak
Fine Dining
$40-$60

AAA Inspector Notes: Steaks and seafood are served in stylish, refined surroundings by extremely attentive and congenial servers. An extensive, well-thought-out wine list adds to the experience. Features: full bar. Reservations: suggested. Address: Costera de Las Palmas S/N 39890 Location: 10.9 mi (17.5 km) se, off Mex 200 (Airport Hwy); in The Fairmont Pierre Marques. Parking: on-site and valet. D ◣

TONY'S ASIAN BISTRO                 744/446-5492  ⑦

▼▼▼▼ Asian Fusion. Fine Dining. $18-$40 AAA Inspector Notes: Reservations are a must for this intimate dining room overlooking Acapulco Bay. Creative French-Asian cuisine is expertly prepared by Chef Nguyen and presented by his attentive staff. Features: full bar. Reservations: required. Address: Escenica Las Brisas S/N, Guitarron Location: In Palladium Discoteque. Parking: valet only. D

This ends listings for Acapulco.
The following resumes the alphabetical listings of cities in The Pacific Coast.

Take Your
*Imagination*
to New Destinations

**Use AAA Travel Guides online to explore the possibilities.**

❯ Tour popular places in the U.S., Canada, Mexico and the Caribbean from the comfort of your home.

❯ Read what AAA's professional inspectors say about area hotels, restaurants and attractions.

❯ Check out the best stuff to see and do, with itineraries to ensure you won't miss a thing.

**Go to AAA.com/travelguide today to discover your next destination.**

# BAHÍAS DE HUATULCO, OAXACA (D-5)

## BEST WESTERN POSADA CHAHUE (958)587-0945

**Hotel** $78-$147 **Address:** Mixie y Mixteco, Bahia de Chahue 70989 **Location:** 4.9 mi (8 km) from centro. **Facility:** 30 units. 3 stories (no elevator), exterior corridors. **Terms:** 3 day cancellation notice-fee imposed. **Amenities:** safes. **Dining:** 2 restaurants. **Pool(s):** outdoor. **Activities:** exercise room. **Guest Services:** valet laundry, area transportation.

**AAA Benefit:** Save 10% or more every day and earn 10% bonus points!

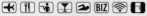
/ SOME UNITS

## CAMINO REAL ZAASHILA (958)583-0300

**Resort Hotel** $115-$401 **Address:** Blvd Benito Juárez 5 70989 **Location:** Oceanfront. In Tangolunda Zona Hotelera. **Facility:** Set on a peaceful bay in the heart of Huatulco, this resort features a unique architectural design with its white-washed walls and stunning tropical pool. 151 units, some two bedrooms and efficiencies. 2-3 stories (no elevator), exterior corridors. **Parking:** valet only. **Terms:** 4 night minimum stay - seasonal and/or weekends, 4 day cancellation notice-fee imposed. **Amenities:** safes. **Dining:** 3 restaurants. **Pool(s):** outdoor. **Activities:** hot tub, tennis, limited exercise equipment, spa. **Guest Services:** valet laundry.

/ SOME UNITS

## DREAMS HUATULCO RESORT AND SPA (958)583-0400

**Resort Hotel** $212-$474

**Address:** Blvd Benito Juárez No. 4 70989 **Location:** Oceanfront. At Bahia de Tangolunda. **Facility:** In a beautiful private cove with a powder-sand beach and incredible views, this well-appointed all-inclusive resort offers plenty of activities for all members of the family. 421 units. 6 stories, interior corridors. *Bath:* shower only. **Terms:** 7 night minimum stay - seasonal and/or weekends, 21 day cancellation notice. **Amenities:** safes. **Dining:** 6 restaurants, entertainment. **Pool(s):** outdoor. **Activities:** sauna, hot tub, steamroom, cabanas, recreation programs, kids club, bicycles, playground, game room, exercise room, spa. **Guest Services:** valet laundry, area transportation.

## LAS BRISAS HUATULCO (958)583-0200

**Resort Hotel** $210-$320

**Address:** Bahia de Tangolunda Lote 1 70989 **Location:** Oceanfront. In Tangolunda Zona Hotelera. **Facility:** This 55-acre resort complex has a series of buildings set on a cliff overlooking a peaceful bay with spectacular views from its guest rooms. Both all-inclusive and European plans are offered. 484 units. 3 stories (no elevator), exterior corridors. *Bath:* shower only. **Amenities:** safes. **Dining:** 5 restaurants, entertainment. **Pool(s):** outdoor. **Activities:** snorkeling, tennis, recreation programs, kids club, playground, game room, exercise room, massage. **Guest Services:** valet laundry.

## QUINTA REAL HUATULCO (958)581-0428

**Boutique Hotel** $175-$289 **Address:** Blvd Benito Juárez Lote 2 70989 **Location:** Oceanfront. In Tangolunda Zona Hotelera. **Facility:** A stunning cliffside setting provides outstanding views of the bay. The property descends to the beach, where you'll find a lovely tropical pool. 28 units. 2-3 stories (no elevator), exterior corridors. **Parking:** on-site and valet. **Terms:** 3 night minimum stay - seasonal and/or weekends, 7 day cancellation notice. **Amenities:** safes. **Dining:** 2 restaurants. **Pool(s):** outdoor. **Activities:** snorkeling, tennis, massage. **Guest Services:** valet laundry, area transportation. Affiliated with Preferred Hotels & Resorts.

## SECRETS HUATULCO RESORT & SPA (958)583-0500

**Resort Hotel** $266-$564

**Address:** Blvd Benito Juarez Seccion Hotelera Lote 8, Bahia de Conejos **Location:** Oceanfront. Jct Mex 200, 1.2 mi (2 km) s; in Bahia de Conejos. **Facility:** This new resort has a large, secluded beach with palapas and water activities, plus oversize swimming pools with beverage service. 399 units. 3 stories, interior/exterior corridors. **Parking:** on-site and valet. **Terms:** 7 night minimum stay - seasonal and/or weekends, age restrictions may apply, 21 day cancellation notice. **Amenities:** safes. **Dining:** 8 restaurants, nightclub, entertainment. **Pool(s):** outdoor. **Activities:** sauna, hot tub, steamroom, snorkeling, tennis, recreation programs, game room, exercise room, spa. **Guest Services:** valet laundry, area transportation.

## HOTEL VILLABLANCA 958/587-0606

**[fyi] Hotel** Did not meet all AAA rating requirements for locking devices in some guest rooms at time of last evaluation on 10/16/2014. **Address:** Blvd Benito Juárez S/N 70989 **Location:** In Bahia Chahue; corner of Zapoteco and Blvd Benito Juárez. Facilities, services, and décor characterize an economy property.

---

## WHERE TO EAT

## ALEBRIJES RESTAURANT BAR 958/581-0504

**International. Casual Dining. $8-$22 AAA Inspector Notes:** Located on hotel row, this combination restaurant/bar specializes in tasty Mexican fare and snappy yet personable service. Good appetizer choices include chunky guacamole, fried calamari or one of the many soups. Charcoal-grilled meats are the house specialty. **Features:** full bar. **Address:** Blvd Benito Juárez 22 70989 **Location:** Centro of Tangolunda Zona Hotelera; in Hotel Plaza Tangolunda. **Parking:** on-site and street. **B** **L** **D**

## DON PORFIRIO LOBSTER & STEAK HOUSE 958/581-0001

**International. Casual Dining. $10-$25 AAA Inspector Notes:** Smack dab in the middle of hotel row is this al fresco eatery that's known for firing up the grill streetside. The menu focuses on steaks, including rib-eye, porterhouse and churrasco, but also lists Mexican specialties such as fajitas and a variety of ceviches. For seafood lovers there is a seafood fountain for two. Several menu items are prepared tableside. **Features:** full bar. **Address:** Tangolunda Zona Hotelera 70989 **Location:** Centro of Tangolunda Zona Hotelera; across from Dreams Huatulco Resort and Spa and Crown Pacific Huatulco. **Parking:** street only. **L** **D**

## GIORDANA'S DELIZIE ITALIANE 958/583-4324

**Italian. Casual Dining. $7-$15 AAA Inspector Notes:** Utilizing fresh local ingredients, the menu features handmade pasta and pizza along with seafood. The dining area is mostly open air. **Features:** beer & wine, patio dining. **Address:** Gardenia esq. Palma Real, La Crucesita Centro 70989 **Location:** Jct Gardenia and Palma Real, just n of La Crucesita Plaza. **Parking:** street only. **L** **D** CALL

## OCEAN BAR AND GRILL 713/874-2203

**Seafood. Casual Dining. $8-$18 AAA Inspector Notes:** This chic open air palapa not only has a fantastic view but is steps away from Playa Arrocito. A wonderful place to enjoy a perfect margarita and expertly prepared seafood using the freshest ingredients. From the ceviche to shrimp alajillo, any meal in this setting is a treat for the senses. **Features:** full bar, patio dining. **Address:** Lote 2 Mza 4, Residencial El Arr 70989 **Location:** Located in Cosmos Residences on Playa Arrocito. **L** **D** **LATE**

## TERRA COTTA 958/587-1903

**Mexican Seafood. Casual Dining. $8-$18 AAA Inspector Notes:** The freshest of local seafood is featured here and prepared using regional recipes. Starting with the green apple salad to the dorado with mango salsa a light and refreshing lunch will give you room to sample the luscious house flan. The downtown location is convenient for strolling the many downtown shops. **Features:** full bar. **Address:** Gardenia No. 902 70989 **Location:** Just n of La Crucesita Plaza. **Parking:** street only. **B** **L** **D**

# BUCERIAS, NAYARIT

## ROYAL DECAMERON COMPLEX
329/298-1135

Resort Hotel $156-$282 **Address:** Lazaro Cardenas No. 150 63732 **Location:** On Mex 200 exit n through Decameron gates; centro. **Facility:** The all-inclusive resort features comfortable rooms with a bright Mexican decor, a good choice of dining options and various entertainment programs. 620 units. 4-5 stories, exterior corridors. **Amenities:** safes. **Dining:** 7 restaurants, entertainment. **Pool(s):** outdoor. **Activities:** scuba diving, snorkeling, tennis, recreation programs, bicycles, playground, game room, exercise room, spa. **Guest Services:** valet laundry.

## SUITES COSTA DORADA
329/298-0046

Hotel $90-$291 **Address:** Lazaro Cardenas No. 156 Sur 63732 **Location:** Oceanfront. Centro. **Facility:** 27 units, some two bedrooms, three bedrooms, efficiencies and kitchens. 6 stories, interior corridors. **Parking:** street only. **Amenities:** safes. **Dining:** Karen's Place Beachfront Restaurant, see separate listing. **Pool(s):** outdoor.

## WHERE TO EAT

## ADAUTO'S ON THE BEACH
329/298-2790

Seafood. Casual Dining. $13-$36 **AAA Inspector Notes:** Diners can sit right on the beach with their toes touching the sand or in the indoor dining room, which has a high palapa roof. Seafood is a specialty on a menu of local and regional fare. Highlights include shrimp fajitas, fresh local lobster, combination platters and homemade Mexican dishes. **Features:** full bar, patio dining. **Address:** Ave del Pacifico No. 11A 63732 **Location:** Centro. **Parking:** street only.

## ADRIANO'S
329/298-0088

Mexican. Casual Dining. $8-$22 **AAA Inspector Notes:** This colorful restaurant serves fresh, made-to-order tacos, nachos, fish, seafood and more. Tables are available directly on the beach or in the covered open-air dining area decorated with bright Mexican art. On weekends it has a beach club feel with a blend of happy locals and tourists hanging out for some fun in the sun. **Features:** full bar, patio dining. **Address:** Ave del Pacifico, No. 2 63732 **Location:** Directly on the beach; centro. **Parking:** street only.

## ADRIATICO
329/298-6038

Italian. Fine Dining. $16-$32 **AAA Inspector Notes:** Lush tropical plants and tranquil water fountains surround the open-air dining area, which sits under a high palapa roof. Freshly prepared Italian dishes include innovative pasta, meat, lamb and fish and other seafood selections. Live music is featured Tuesday through Saturday. **Features:** full bar, patio dining. **Reservations:** suggested. **Address:** Lazaro Cardenas S/N 63732 **Location:** Centro. **Parking:** street only.

## ARMI GRANO'S ENCORE RESTAURANT JAZZ LOUNGE
329/298-0140

International. Casual Dining. $8-$30 **AAA Inspector Notes:** Breakfast and lunch attract locals with hearty portions at very reasonable prices. Dinner draws crowds for the professional jazz entertainment and a fine, mixed menu. Highlights include fresh local fish and seafood, some Asian and Mexican specialties as well as a good pasta selection. All are welcome and many folks stop by for a late-night dessert and coffee, or perhaps a cocktail. The open-air setting is comfortable with lots of tropical plants tempting you to linger longer. **Features:** full bar, patio dining. **Address:** 51 Lazaro Cardenas 63732 **Location:** Centro; 3 blks n of Royal Decameron Hotel. **Parking:** street only.

## EL CHIVERO
329/298-0612

Seafood. Casual Dining. $8-$22 **AAA Inspector Notes:** This laid-back beach eatery is the perfect spot for fresh local fish and seafood, tasty shrimp or light Mexican fare. Hamburger hounds are in for a treat as this place serves them up hot and sizzling. A two-for-one cocktail special is offered for most of the day. **Features:** full bar, patio dining. **Address:** Ave Pacifico No. 9 63732 **Location:** Directly on the beach; centro. **Parking:** street only.

## IXTA RESTAURANT BAR
329/298-3486

Mexican. Casual Dining. $8-$22 **AAA Inspector Notes:** Check out this popular local hangout for well-prepared, regional Mexican fare. All the food is made-to-order, so your meal may take a while to arrive. But we think you'll agree it's well worth the wait. Phone ahead for the current schedule of evening entertainment, which on select nights amps up the festive atmosphere. **Features:** full bar, happy hour. **Reservations:** suggested. **Address:** Lazaro Cardenas No. 500 63732 **Location:** Between Javier Mlna and Agustin Melgar; centro. **Parking:** street only.

## KAREN'S PLACE BEACHFRONT RESTAURANT
329/298-3176

International. Casual Dining. $12-$25 **AAA Inspector Notes:** In the evening, candlelit tables lend to the romantic ambience at this relaxed open-air restaurant, where diners enjoy beach views as they feast on fresh pasta, seafood or fine steak. No credit cards are taken at lunch. **Features:** full bar, patio dining, Sunday brunch. **Reservations:** suggested, for dinner. **Address:** Lazaro Cardenas No. 156 Sur 63732 **Location:** Centro; in Suites Costa Dorada. **Parking:** street only.

## MARK'S BAR & GRILL
329/298-0303

International. Fine Dining. $15-$31 **AAA Inspector Notes:** Reservations are highly recommended for this popular establishment, which presents an innovative menu in an upscale yet comfortable setting. Offerings include hot and cold appetizers, including fresh flat-bread selections, and fire-baked pizzas as well as fresh pasta dishes, seafood and grilled meats. Stuffed whole baby chicken is a popular choice. Homemade desserts provide a decadent indulgence. Patrons can sit indoor or on the patio. **Features:** full bar, patio dining. **Reservations:** suggested. **Address:** Lazaro Cardenas No. 56 63732 **Location:** Centro. **Parking:** street only.

## MAR Y SOL - THE LOBSTER HOUSE
329/296-1914

Seafood. Casual Dining. $8-$22 **AAA Inspector Notes:** Enjoy the sound of crashing ocean waves as you dine directly on the beach with your toes in the sand. This is the perfect setting to enjoy freshly prepared local fish and seafood with a Mexican flair. It is fun to test your bargaining skills with the local vendors, who will bring their crafts right to your table. **Features:** full bar, patio dining. **Address:** Ave Pacifico No. 4 63732 **Location:** On the beach; town center. **Parking:** street only.

## MESON BAY RESTAURANT
329/298-1634

Seafood. Casual Dining. $8-$23 **AAA Inspector Notes:** At the beachside eatery, patrons can watch the breakers while dining on fresh seafood. Shrimp, lobster and fresh red snapper are perfectly baked. There's a bar here, too, with giant margaritas that demand quick attention. **Features:** full bar, patio dining. **Address:** Calle Lazaro Cardenas No. 17 63732 **Location:** Centro. **Parking:** street only.

## MEZZOGIORNO RISTORANTE ITALIANO
329/298-0350

Italian. Fine Dining. $9-$28 **AAA Inspector Notes:** This popular eatery attracts both loyal locals and the tourist market. Several tables in the stunning setting directly overlook the beach. Ocean breezes blow through the open-air dining room, which has a thatched palapa roof. The menu focuses on fresh, homemade pasta dishes filled with the likes of seafood and chicken, and flavored with rich sauces. **Features:** full bar, patio dining. **Reservations:** required, dinner. **Address:** Ave del Pacifico No. 33 63732 **Location:** Centro. **Parking:** street only.

## ROSA MEXICANA
329/298-0063

Mexican. Casual Dining. $12-$22 **AAA Inspector Notes:** A delightful, open-air tropical garden setting is the perfect backdrop for an evening indulging in freshly prepared home-style Mexican cuisine. A highlight is the fresh salsa prepared table side. Some nights, live music sets a romantic mood. Twice per week, mariachi musicians fosters a festive atmosphere. Phone ahead for the schedule to select the entertainment suited to your mood. **Features:** full bar, patio dining. **Address:** Ave Lazaro Cardenas No. 90B 63732 **Location:** Centro. **Parking:** street only.

## SANDRINA'S RESTAURANT AND BOUTIQUE 329/298-0273

▼▼▼ Mediterranean. Casual Dining. $12-$23 **AAA Inspector Notes:** Here you'll find a lovely back patio setting with a garden of tropical plants. The menu features some interesting options with lots of Greek and local influences. What makes it fun is that all the plates and glasses are handmade Mexican pottery and glass done in vibrant colors; you'll be tempted to shop in the upscale boutique after your meal. Open at 3 pm for late lunch; a light menu is offered. Heavier dinner entrées are served after 6 pm. Save room for dessert. **Features:** full bar, patio dining. **Reservations:** suggested. **Address:** Lazaro Cardenas 33 63732 **Location:** At J. Morelos; centro. **Parking:** street only.  L  D  🍷

## COLIMA, COLIMA (C-2) pop. 146,904

### BEST WESTERN HOTEL CEBALLOS (312)316-0100

▼▼ **Hotel** $76-$86 **Address:** Portal Medellin No. 12 28000 **Location:** Centro. 5 stories. 2 stories, interior corridors. *Bath:* shower only. **Terms:** 2 night minimum stay - seasonal and/or weekends, cancellation fee imposed. **Amenities:** *Some:* safes. **Dining:** 2 restaurants. **Pool(s):** outdoor. **Activities:** limited exercise equipment. **Guest Services:** valet laundry.

**AAA Benefit:**
Save 10% or more every day and earn 10% bonus points!

🍽 🍷 BIZ 📶 ✕ / SOME UNITS 🛏 💻

### FIESTA INN COLIMA (312)316-4444

▼▼▼ **Hotel** $100-$130 **Address:** Prolongacion Blvd Camino Real No. 101 Col. El Diezmo 28010 **Location:** Next to University of Colima. Across from convention center. **Facility:** 104 units. 3 stories, interior corridors. *Bath:* shower only. **Pool(s):** heated outdoor. **Activities:** playground, exercise room. **Guest Services:** valet and coin laundry. 🍽 🚶 🍷 🏊 BIZ 📶 💻

### HOTEL LOS CANDILES SA 312/312-3212

▼▼ **Hotel** $60-$120 **Address:** Blvd Camino Real No. 399 28010 **Location:** 0.9 mi (1.5 km) ne on Mex 54. **Facility:** 75 units. 3 stories (no elevator), interior/exterior corridors. **Amenities:** safes. **Pool(s):** outdoor. **Guest Services:** valet laundry.
🍽 🍷 🏊 BIZ 📶 ✕ / SOME UNITS 🐾

## IXTAPA, GUERRERO (C-3)

• **Restaurants p. 454**

### BARCELO IXTAPA BEACH 755/555-2000

▼▼▼ **Resort Hotel** $294-$737

**Address:** Blvd Ixtapa S/N 40884 **Location:** Oceanfront. South end of Zona Hotelera. **Facility:** The hotel has an atrium lobby with panoramic elevators. Attractive guest rooms feature modern décor and newly renovated bathrooms. Many units with a balcony and ocean view. 398 units. 4-12 stories, interior corridors. **Parking:** on-site and valet. **Amenities:** safes. **Dining:** 6 restaurants, entertainment. **Pool(s):** outdoor. **Activities:** sauna, hot tub, steamroom, scuba diving, tennis, recreation programs, kids club, bicycles, playground, game room, exercise room, spa. **Guest Services:** valet laundry.

ECO ✈ 🍽 🚶 🍷 🏋 S SD 🏊 BIZ 📶 🛏 💻

### CAPELLA IXTAPA RESORT AND SPA (755)555-1100

▼▼▼ ▼▼▼ **Boutique Resort Hotel** $200-$950 **Address:** Blvd Paseo Playa Linda, Zona Hotelera II 40880 **Location:** Waterfront. At Playa Linda. **Facility:** Set against a hillside, this intimate resort features incredible views from all areas, including the two infinity pools and several restaurants. 59 units. 7 stories, exterior corridors. *Bath:* shower only. **Parking:** valet only. **Terms:** 5 night minimum stay - seasonal, age restrictions may apply, 60 day cancellation notice, in-season resort fee imposed. **Amenities:** safes. **Dining:** 3 restaurants. **Pool(s):** outdoor. **Activities:** sauna, hot tub, steamroom, limited beach access, recreation programs, bicycles, exercise room, spa. **Guest Services:** valet laundry, boarding pass kiosk.

✈ 🍽 🚶 🍷 🏋 SD 🏊 BIZ 📶 ✕ 🛏 💻
/ SOME UNITS 🅂🛏

### EMPORIO IXTAPA (755)555-0800

▼▼▼ **Hotel** $84-$209 **Address:** Blvd Ixtapa S/N 40880 **Location:** Oceanfront. In centro of Zona Hotelera. **Facility:** Meets AAA guest room security requirements. 219 units, some two bedrooms. 11 stories, interior corridors. *Bath:* shower only. **Terms:** check-in 4 pm, 2 night minimum stay - seasonal, 7 day cancellation notice, in season. **Amenities:** safes. **Dining:** 2 restaurants. **Pool(s):** outdoor. **Activities:** hot tub, tennis, recreation programs in season, exercise room, spa. **Guest Services:** valet laundry.

🍽 🚶 🍷 🏋 CALL 🅲🅼 SD 🏊 📶 ✕ 🛏 💻

### HOTEL FONTAN IXTAPA BEACH RESORT (755)553-1666

▼▼▼ **Hotel** $156-$242 **Address:** Blvd Ixtapa S/N 40880 **Location:** Oceanfront. In centro of Zona Hotelera. **Facility:** 472 units. 8 stories, interior corridors. *Bath:* shower only. **Terms:** 7 day cancellation notice, in season-fee imposed. **Dining:** 4 restaurants. **Pool(s):** outdoor. **Activities:** recreation programs, kids club, bicycles, playground, limited exercise equipment. **Guest Services:** valet laundry.

🍽 🚶 🍷 🏋 📶 / SOME UNITS 🛏 💻

### LAS BRISAS IXTAPA (755)553-2121

▼▼▼▼ ▼▼▼▼ **Resort Hotel** $98-$915

**Address:** Playa Vista Hermosa S/N 40880 **Location:** Oceanfront. At Playa Vista Hermosa. **Facility:** All rooms at this architecturally rich property feature ocean views and private balconies with hammocks; some units with private pools. 416 units, some two bedrooms. 12 stories, interior corridors. *Bath:* shower only. **Parking:** on-site and valet. **Terms:** check-in 4 pm, 4 night minimum stay - seasonal, 3 day cancellation notice, in season. **Amenities:** safes. **Dining:** 3 restaurants, also, La Brisa II, Portofino Ristorante, Restaurant El Mexicano, see separate listings. **Pool(s):** outdoor. **Activities:** tennis, recreation programs, kids club, playground, exercise room, massage. **Guest Services:** valet laundry.

🍽 🚶 🍷 🏋 CALL 🅲🅼 S SD 🏊 BIZ 🅂🅷🅂
🆂 📶 🛏 💻

### POSADA REAL IXTAPA (755)553-1745

▼▼ **Hotel** $149-$302 **Address:** Blvd Ixtapa S/N 40884 **Location:** Oceanfront. North end of Zona Hotelera. **Facility:** 110 units. 4 stories, interior corridors. *Bath:* shower only. **Amenities:** safes. **Pool(s):** outdoor. **Activities:** miniature golf, kids club. **Guest Services:** valet laundry.

🍽 🚶 🍷 🏊 📶 ✕ 💻

### PRESIDENTE INTERCONTINENTAL IXTAPA AN ALL INCLUSIVE RESORT (755)553-0018

▼▼ ▼▼ **Resort Hotel** $291-$489

**Address:** Blvd Ixtapa S/N 40880 **Location:** Oceanfront. In centro of Zona Hotelera. **Facility:** A few rooms have a hammock on the balcony facing the bay with a private palapa area; many units afford ocean views. 420 units. 3-11 stories, interior corridors. **Parking:** on-site and valet. **Terms:** 3 night minimum stay - seasonal, 7 day cancellation notice, in season-fee imposed. **Amenities:** *Some:* safes. **Dining:** 6 restaurants, entertainment. **Pool(s):** outdoor. **Activities:** sauna, tennis, recreation programs, kids club, bicycles, playground, exercise room, massage. **Guest Services:** valet laundry.

🍽 🚶 🍷 🏋 SD 🏊 BIZ 📶 / SOME UNITS 🛏 💻

## SUNSCAPE DORADO PACIFICO BEACH RESORT
(755)553-2025

**Hotel**
**$169-$500**

**Address:** Paseo de Ixtapa S/N Lote 3-A 40880 **Location:** Oceanfront. North end of Zona Hotelera. **Facility:** 285 units. 13 stories, interior corridors. *Bath:* shower only. **Terms:** 3 day cancellation notice. **Amenities:** safes. **Dining:** 6 restaurants, entertainment. **Pool(s):** outdoor. **Activities:** sauna, hot tub, steamroom, tennis, recreation programs, kids club, playground, game room, exercise room, spa. **Guest Services:** valet laundry.

### AZUL IXTAPA ALL INCLUSIVE BEACH RESORT AND CONVENTION CENTER
755/555-0000

[fyi] **Hotel** Did not meet all AAA rating requirements for locking devices in some guest rooms at time of last evaluation on 03/10/2014. **Address:** Paseo Punta Ixtapa Lote 2 40880 **Location:** Oceanfront. Facilities, services, and décor characterize a mid-scale property. This activity-oriented, all-inclusive resort is at Playa Linda, across from Ixtapa Island. Here you'll find huge swimming pools, a swim-up bar and many dining choices.

### GRAND AZUL IXTAPA
755/555-0000

[fyi] **Hotel** Did not meet all AAA rating requirements for locking devices in some guest rooms at time of last evaluation on 03/10/2014. **Address:** Blvd Punta Ixtapa Lote 2, Zona Hotelera II 40880 **Location:** Oceanfront. At Playa Linda; across from Ixtapa Island. Facilities, services, and décor characterize an upscale property.

### HOLIDAY INN
755/555-0500

[fyi] **Not evaluated. Address:** Ave Paseo de Las Palmas 40880 **Location:** North end of Zona Hotelera; jct Paseo Agua de Correa. Facilities, services, and décor characterize a mid-scale property.

### PACIFICA RESORT IXTAPA
755/555-2500

[fyi] **Hotel** Did not meet all AAA rating requirements for locking devices in some guest rooms at time of last evaluation on 03/14/2014. **Address:** Paseo de La Colina, Col Vista Hermosa **Location:** Oceanfront. Follow signs to Vista Hermosa. Facilities, services, and décor characterize a mid-scale property.

### PACIFICA SPA
755/555-0460

[fyi] **Hotel** Did not meet all AAA rating requirements for locking devices in some guest rooms at time of last evaluation on 03/14/2014. **Address:** Calle Fragatas Lote F17 Secc Hotelera II 40884 **Location:** Follow signs to Playa Vista Hermosa. Facilities, services, and décor characterize an upscale property. This small boutique-style hotel is located on a hillside and features contemporary décor as well as a thalasso (seawater) pool for spa treatments.

### WHERE TO EAT

### BECCOFINO RESTAURANT AND BAR
755/553-1770

Northern Italian. Casual Dining. $16-$40 **AAA Inspector Notes:** A Mediterranean atmosphere pervades the seaside dining room and the beautiful teak wood deck, which is perched right on the water. Plentiful seafood is nicely prepared in Italian-style dishes. Main dishes also include preparations of chicken and beef. Formally set tables and waterside views of the marina set the ambiance at this attractive dining spot. **Features:** full bar. **Reservations:** suggested. **Address:** Veleros No. 6 Local 3, Marina Plaza 40880 **Location:** 0.9 mi (1.5 km) n of Zona Hotelera to Blvd Ixtapa; at Plaza Marina Ixtapa.

### CASA MORELOS
755/553-0578

Mexican. Casual Dining. $7-$25 **AAA Inspector Notes:** Authentic Mexican fare served in an open-air, cantina-like setting keeps tourists and locals coming back for more. In the shopping area and restaurant row of the hotel zone, this popular eatery attracts diners with a menu that mixes the flavors of Mexico with some favorites from back home. Choices range from hot-and-spicy fajitas to enchiladas to simply broiled steak or seafood. **Features:** full bar, patio dining. **Address:** Zona Commercial, La Puerta Local 9/10/18 40884 **Location:** In centro of Zona Hotelera.

### DEBORAHS CHILI BEANS
755/553-3313

Regional Mexican. Casual Dining. $5-$22 **AAA Inspector Notes:** Bright Mexican appointments decorate the casual eatery's bi-level open-air dining room. Chile peppers pop up in interesting photographs and pictures showing the different degrees of peppers and their degree of heat. The menu lists a wide range of casual Mexican and American fare, not to mention well-priced breakfasts. **Features:** full bar, patio dining. **Address:** Blvd Ixtapa S/N 40880 **Location:** Across from Emporio Ixtapa. **Parking:** street only.

### EL FARO RESTAURANTE
755/555-2500

International. Fine Dining. $18-$32 **AAA Inspector Notes:** Diners are treated to an outstanding view of Ixtapa from this prime hilltop location. The open-air dining room provides a truly romantic setting complete with live entertainment. On the menu you'll find a fine mix of global fare, including fresh seafood, pasta, meat and poultry dishes. **Features:** full bar, patio dining. **Reservations:** suggested. **Address:** Paseo de Las Colina, Col. Vista Hermosa 40880 **Location:** Follow signs to Vista Hermosa; in Pacifica Resort Ixtapa.

### EL GALEON RESTAURANT-BAR
755/553-2150

Seafood. Casual Dining. $15-$40 **AAA Inspector Notes:** The distinctive, open-air restaurant resembles a Spanish galleon, parked pierside with seating on its upper decks, and affords a good view of the many yachts and boats housed at the marina. The menu includes pasta, seafood, chicken and beef selections, prepared in the Continental style. The service is attentive and courteous, and the servers are knowledgeable. **Features:** full bar. **Reservations:** suggested. **Address:** Veleros No. 6 Local 3, Marina Plaza 40880 **Location:** 1 mi (1.5 km) n of Zona Hotelera to via Blvd Ixtapa; at marina.

### EL TIBURON DE LA COSTA
755/553-0074

Seafood. Casual Dining. $8-$18 **AAA Inspector Notes:** A favorite of locals, this is the sister restaurant of the same name in San Jose Ixtapa, where many would take the 20-minute drive to enjoy excellent, fresh-caught fish and shellfish. Traditional preparations include ceviche, cocktails, aguachiles, grilled fish and shrimp with a variety of flavorful sauces. Shrimp al ajillo is served whole with the shell and head on, which makes for messy but fun eating. **Features:** full bar. **Address:** Paseo de Las Garzas S/N. **Location:** Jct Paseo del Rincon; in Ixtapa Palace.

### EMILIO'S PIZZERIA
755/553-1583

Pizza. Casual Dining. $13-$25 **AAA Inspector Notes:** This casual, two-level eatery serves a variety of small and large thin crust pizzas, including some unique topping combinations, baked in a wood-fired brick oven. You'll also find salads and a few pasta entrées. **Features:** full bar. **Address:** Paseo de Las Garzas 2 y 2A 40880 **Location:** North end of Zona Hotelera, just ne. **Parking:** on-site and street.

### LA BRISA II
755/553-2121

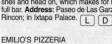

**Mediterranean**
**Fine Dining**
**$29-$41**

**AAA Inspector Notes:** The romantic terraces overlook the sea below. On the menu are delicious fresh seafood, steaks and pasta entrées. A few menu items are flambéed tableside. **Features:** full bar. **Reservations:** required. **Address:** Playa Vista Hermosa S/N 40880 **Location:** At Playa Vista Hermosa; in Las Brisas Ixtapa. **Parking:** on-site and valet.

### LA FUSION RESTAURANT-BAR
755/553-0225

Mexican. Casual Dining. $8-$17 **AAA Inspector Notes:** This casual upstairs restaurant overlooks the main boulevard. The chef's specialty, shrimp al ajillo, is well prepared and definitely a must try. Also featured are fresh fish and shrimp served with a variety of healthy sauces. Live music is featured many nights during the week. **Features:** full bar. **Address:** Blvd Ixtapa S/N **Location:** In Zona Hotelera, across from Emporio Hotel. **Parking:** street only.

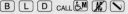

**Remember, car seats, booster seats and seat belts save lives**

## MAMMA NORMA AND DEBORAH
755/553-0274

▼▼ American. Family Dining. $7-$23 AAA Inspector Notes: Set back in a small shopping center, a casual covered patio and a menu featuring wholesome, home-cooked cuisine make this a favorite with locals and tourists alike. Menu highlights include homemade soups, salads and sandwiches, as well as some Mexican specialties and grilled items such as chicken, steak and seafood. If deep-sea fishermen bring in their own fresh catch, the restaurant is happy to cook it for them. Features: full bar. Address: Ixtapa Plaza Local 5 40884 Location: Centro of Zona Hotelera; across from Presidente InterContinental Ixtapa, An All Inclusive Resort. Parking: on-site and street. B L D 🅰️ ⊠

## PORTOFINO RISTORANTE
755/553-2121

▼▼▼

Italian
Fine Dining
$21-$43

AAA Inspector Notes: The formal, intimate, fine dining restaurant is characterized by an elegant dining room, tuxedoed maitre d' and imaginatively prepared Italian cuisine. The well-trained, formally attired staff delivers smooth, practiced service. Features: full bar. Reservations: required. Address: Playa Vista Hermosa S/N 40880 Location: At Playa Vista Hermosa; in Las Brisas Ixtapa. Parking: on-site and valet. D CALL 🅰️M 🅰️

## RESTAURANT EL MEXICANO
755/553-2121

▼▼▼

Mexican
Fine Dining
$14-$38

AAA Inspector Notes: This moderately upscale spot prepares steaks, chicken and seafood in a traditional Mexican style. The atmosphere is reflective of a 16th-century colonial hacienda. Features: full bar. Reservations: required. Address: Playa Vista Hermosa S/N 40880 Location: At Playa Vista Hermosa; in Las Brisas Ixtapa. Parking: on-site and valet. D

## RUBEN'S HAMBURGERS
755/553-0027

▼ Burgers. Quick Serve. $5-$10 AAA Inspector Notes: Many folks notice the lack of fast food restaurants in this area of Mexico and crave a good old fashioned burger. That's why this popular open-air eatery has been around for years serving up hearty homemade hamburgers, chicken burgers, tasty fries and a variety of sides. They also have a take-out counter. Features: beer only, patio dining. Address: Andador Punta San Esteban S/N 40880 Location: In Zona Hotelera; Centro Comercial Flamboyant. Parking: street only.

L D 🅰️ ⊠

# LA CRUZ DE HUANACAXTLE

## MATLALI HOTEL
322/115-7700

▼▼▼ ▼▼

Boutique Hotel
$220-$625

Address: Carr La Cruz Punta de Mita KM 0.2 Location: In Puerto Bahia complex. Facility: Clusters of spacious suites and multi-bedroom villas have been created in a lush, tropical setting. Here you'll find a perfect balance and harmony of nature with a lagoon pool and hiking trail. Meets AAA guest room security requirements. 40 units, some two bedrooms, three bedrooms, kitchens and condominiums. 4 stories, interior/exterior corridors. Bath: shower only. Parking: valet only. Terms: resort fee. Amenities: safes. Pool(s): outdoor, heated outdoor. Activities: steamroom, exercise room, spa. Guest Services: complimentary and valet laundry, area transportation.

🍴 🧖 🍸 CALL 🅰️M SD 🏊 BIZ HS 🛜 ✕ 🚪 🖥 / SOME UNITS 🅂HS 📷

## MANZANILLO, COLIMA (C-1) pop. 161,420
• Restaurants p. 456

## BARCELO KARMINA PALACE DELUXE
314/331-1300

▼▼▼ ▼▼

Resort Hotel
$240-$450

Address: Ave Vista Hermosa No. 13 28867 Location: Oceanfront. Mex 200, Peninsula de Santiago. Facility: The resort has seven connected pools that eventually lead down to a private sheltered lagoon and lots of ocean activities. 324 units. 7 stories, interior corridors. Amenities: safes. Dining: 4 restaurants, nightclub, entertainment. Pool(s): outdoor. Activities: steamroom, self-propelled boats, scuba diving, snorkeling, tennis, recreation programs, kids club, game room, exercise room, spa. Guest Services: valet laundry.

ECO 🍴 🧖 🍸 🏋️ SD 🏊

BIZ 🛜 🅿️ 🖥

## BEST WESTERN LUNA DEL MAR
314/331-0220

▼▼ Hotel. Rates not provided. Address: Ave Lazaro Cardenas 1301-A 28210 Location: Oceanfront. 1.9 mi (3 km) off Mex 200; in Las Brisas; on Playa Azul. Facility: Meets AAA guest room security requirements. 68 units, some two bedrooms and efficiencies. 4-5 stories (no elevator), interior/exterior corridors. Terms: 3-5 night minimum stay - seasonal and/or weekends, 10 day cancellation notice-fee imposed, resort fee. Pool(s): outdoor. Activities: hot tub, spa. Guest Services: valet laundry.

**AAA Benefit:**
Save 10% or more every day and earn 10% bonus points!

🍴 🧖 🍸 🏊 BIZ HS 🛜 / SOME UNITS 🅿️

## CAMINO REAL MANZANILLO
(314)331-1740

▼▼▼ Boutique Hotel. Rates not provided. Address: Paraiso No. 11 Col Residencial Salagua 28869 Location: Oceanfront. 0.9 mi (1.5 km) off Mex 200, follow signs. Facility: The oceanfront hotel, with a large pool and intimate spa, features standard business class rooms, spacious suites and bi-level units, each with a contemporary Mexican flair. 63 units, some two and three bedrooms. 4 stories, exterior corridors. Parking: on-site and valet. Amenities: safes. Dining: 2 restaurants, also, Restaurante La Huerta Cafe, see separate listing. Pool(s): outdoor. Activities: sauna, hot tub, exercise room, spa. Guest Services: valet laundry.

🍴 🧖 SD 🏊 🅂HS 🛜 🅿️ 🖥

## CITYEXPRESS MANZANILLO
(314)331-3030

▼▼▼ ▼▼

Hotel
$71-$79

Address: Blvd Miguel de La Madrid Hurtado No. 1845 28218 Location: 1.9 mi (3 km) off Mex 200; on Playa Azul. Facility: 116 units. 7 stories, interior corridors. Bath: shower only. Pool(s): outdoor. Activities: exercise room. Guest Services: valet laundry.

🍴➕ S SD 🏊 BIZ HS 🛜

✕ / SOME UNITS 🅿️ 🖥 🖥

## DOLPHIN COVE INN
(314)334-1515

▼▼▼ Hotel $110-$250 Address: Ave Vista Hermosa S/N 28860 Location: Oceanfront. 7.2 mi (11.5 km) nw on Mex 200, 1.5 mi (2.5 km) s on Peninsula Santiago. Facility: 50 units, some two bedrooms, efficiencies and kitchens. 4 stories (no elevator), exterior corridors. Bath: shower only. Amenities: Some: safes. Dining: Paradise Restaurant, see separate listing. Pool(s): outdoor. Guest Services: coin laundry.

🍴 🧖 🍸 SD 🏊 🛜 🅿️ 🖥 🖥

## GRAND ISLA NAVIDAD RESORT    (314)331-0500

▽▽▽▽ ▽▽▽▽
**Resort Hotel**
$229-$425

**Address:** Circuito de Los Marinos S/N 28838 **Location:** Oceanfront. Mex 200, 3.8 mi (6 km) n of Cihuatlan, 11.3 mi (18 km) w. **Facility:** An impressive complex, this luxurious resort hotel features golf, beach and spa facilities. The refined service is excellent. 199 units, some two and three bedrooms. 10 stories, exterior corridors. **Parking:** valet only. **Terms:** resort fee. **Amenities:** safes. **Dining:** 4 restaurants, also, Antonio's, La Plazuela, La Terraza, see separate listings, entertainment. **Pool(s):** outdoor, heated outdoor. **Activities:** hot tub, marina, fishing, scuba diving, snorkeling, regulation golf, tennis, recreation programs, bicycles, exercise room, spa. **Guest Services:** valet laundry.

[icons]

## HOLIDAY INN EXPRESS MANZANILLO    314/331-2330
▽▽▽▽ **Hotel** $90-$125 **Address:** Blvd Miguel de La Madrid 424 **Location:** Zona Industrial Tapeixtles. **Facility:** 112 units. 6 stories, interior corridors. *Bath:* shower only. **Amenities:** safes. **Pool(s):** outdoor. **Activities:** exercise room. **Guest Services:** valet laundry, area transportation.

[icons] / SOME UNITS

## HOTEL EJECUTIVO    314/333-2265
▽▽▽▽ **Hotel** $86-$113 **Address:** Blvd Costera Miguel de La Madrid KM 11.5 **Location:** Off Mex 200, 1.9 mi (3 km); on Playa Azul. **Facility:** 24 units. 3 stories (no elevator), interior/exterior corridors. **Parking:** street only. **Amenities:** safes. **Dining:** La Pergola, see separate listing. **Pool(s):** outdoor. **Activities:** exercise room, massage. [icons] / SOME UNITS

## HOTEL LA POSADA    314/333-1899
▽▽ **Motel** $58-$78 **Address:** Lazaro Cardenas No. 201 28210 **Location:** 1.9 mi (3 km) off Mex 200; in Las Brisas; on Playa Azul. **Facility:** Meets AAA guest room security requirements. 24 units, some efficiencies. 1-2 stories (no elevator), exterior corridors. *Bath:* shower only. **Pool(s):** outdoor. **Guest Services:** coin laundry.

[icons] / SOME UNITS

## HOTEL PEZ VELA    314/334-2616
▽▽ **Hotel** $68-$86 **Address:** Central S/N Col. Salagua Ave 28869 **Location:** 0.9 mi (1.5 km) off Mex 200; next to Walmart. **Facility:** 21 units. 2 stories (no elevator), interior corridors. *Bath:* shower only. **Amenities:** safes. **Dining:** La Cabana del Mono, see separate listing. **Pool(s):** outdoor. [icons]

## LAS ALAMANDAS    (322)285-5500

▽▽▽▽
**Hotel**
$371-$2399

**Address:** KM 85 Carr Barra de Navidad 48850 **Location:** Oceanfront. Mex 200, KM 85, follow signs. **Facility:** Set on 1,500 acres of a private reserve, this exclusive resort features a private airstrip and three beaches. 16 units, some two bedrooms. 1-2 stories (no elevator), exterior corridors. **Amenities:** safes. **Pool(s):** outdoor. **Activities:** tennis, bicycles, playground, exercise room, massage. **Guest Services:** coin laundry.

[icons] CALL / SOME UNITS

Keep your focus safely
on the road when driving

## LAS HADAS GOLF RESORT & MARINA    (314)331-0101

▽▽▽▽ ▽▽▽▽
**Resort Hotel**
$284-$520

**Address:** Ave Vista Hermosa S/N 28867 **Location:** 7.2 mi (11.5 km) nw on Mex 200, 1.5 mi (2.5 km) s on Peninsula Santiago. **Facility:** Arabesque buildings set in a private cove at the base of rugged hills form a striking sight at this property complete with beach and marina. 232 units, some two bedrooms. 1-5 stories, interior/exterior corridors. **Parking:** valet only. **Amenities:** safes. **Dining:** 5 restaurants, also, Los Delfines, Restaurant Legazpi, see separate listings, entertainment. **Pool(s):** outdoor. **Activities:** marina, fishing, scuba diving, snorkeling, regulation golf, tennis, recreation programs, kids club, exercise room, spa. **Guest Services:** valet laundry, area transportation.

[icons]

## LOS ANGELES LOCOS    315/351-5020
▽▽ **Resort Hotel** $190-$240 **Address:** Carr Federal No. 200 KM 20 28830 **Location:** Mex 200, KM 20, 1.9 mi (3 km), follow signs. **Facility:** This family resort is very activity-oriented and appeals to all age groups. It is located in a remote area, about 45 minutes from the Manzanillo airport, on a lovely stretch of beach. 204 units. 4 stories (no elevator), exterior corridors. **Amenities:** safes. **Dining:** 4 restaurants, entertainment. **Pool(s):** heated outdoor. **Activities:** steamroom, scuba diving, snorkeling, tennis, recreation programs, playground, exercise room, massage. **Guest Services:** valet laundry. [icons] CALL

## PUNTA SERENA VILLAS AND SPA    315/351-5427
▽▽▽ **Hotel** $250-$300 **Address:** Carr Federal No. 200, KM 20 48850 **Location:** Oceanfront. Mex 200 at KM 20, follow signs 1.9 mi (3 km). **Facility:** 24 units. 2 stories (no elevator), exterior corridors. **Terms:** age restrictions may apply. **Amenities:** safes. **Pool(s):** heated outdoor. **Activities:** sauna, hot tub, steamroom, exercise room, spa. **Guest Services:** valet laundry.

[icons]

## TESORO MANZANILLO    (314)331-2200

▽▽▽
**Resort Hotel**
$154-$215

**Address:** Ave de La Audencia L-1 28867 **Location:** 7.2 mi (11.5 km) nw on Mex 200, 1.6 mi (2.5 km) s on Peninsula Santiago. **Facility:** Frequented by tourists from the United States and Canada, this resort has lively entertainment as well as fine beaches. 331 units. 19 stories, interior corridors. **Terms:** off-site registration. **Amenities:** safes. **Dining:** 4 restaurants, entertainment. **Pool(s):** outdoor. **Activities:** hot tub, steamroom, fishing, scuba diving, snorkeling, tennis, recreation programs, kids club, playground, game room, exercise room, spa. **Guest Services:** valet laundry.

[icons] / SOME UNITS

## WHERE TO EAT

### ANTONIO'S    314/331-0500

▽▽▽▽ ▽▽▽▽
**International Fine Dining**
$25-$39

**AAA Inspector Notes:** Guests enjoy the luxurious ambiance of the dining room, where tables are set with fresh red roses and elegant candles. The traditional menu also features some fresh local and regional options with a Mexican flair. The chef enjoys teasing the palate with changing complements such as flaky vegetable rolls, melon sorbet and house-made chocolates throughout the course of the meal. It's appropriate that in this hacienda-style setting, the bar would feature more than 200 tequilas. **Features:** full bar. **Reservations:** required. **Address:** Circuito de Los Marinos S/N 28830 **Location:** Mex 200, 3.8 mi (6 km) n of Cihuatlan, 11.3 mi (18 km) w; in Grand Isla Navidad Resort. **Parking:** valet only. [D]

## BISTRO MARINA
314/335-0900

▼▼▼▼ International. Fine Dining. $15-$30 **AAA Inspector Notes:** An innovative menu and al fresco dining at candlelit patio tables are what's in store for those who choose this peaceful, Marina Las Hadas bistro. The servers excel at tableside preparations, including tempting dishes such as pasta prepared in a giant bowl made of cheese. Bacon-wrapped shrimp is another excellent choice. Flambé coffee is a house specialty, and makes for the perfect finish to an evening here. **Features:** full bar, patio dining. **Address:** Marina Las Hadas S/N 28867 **Location:** At Marina Las Hadas.

## EL TABLAO BY MARINA LAS HADAS
314/109-8202

▼▼ International. Casual Dining. $14-$22 **AAA Inspector Notes:** You'll dine under the stars at this popular spot overlooking the boats at the marina. Feast on local shrimp and grilled fish, or sink your teeth into tangy barbecue ribs. The ambience is bright and inviting, and will make you want to linger. **Features:** full bar, patio dining. **Address:** Marina Las Hadas S/N **Location:** At Marina Las Hadas. **Parking:** street only.

## LA CABANA DEL MONO
314/334-2616

▼▼ Seafood. Casual Dining. $8-$18 **AAA Inspector Notes:** This comfortable spot is popular with locals for its tropical atmosphere. You'll also get a kick out of watching the restaurant's caged monkeys swing to live musical entertainment. The menu is loaded with fresh, local seafood, as well as some excellent grilled items. Among the must-trys: ceviche, seafood cocktail and the homemade soups. **Features:** full bar, patio dining. **Address:** Central S/N Col. Salagua Ave 28869 **Location:** 0.9 mi (1.5 km) off Mex 200; next to Walmart; in Hotel Pez Vela. **Parking:** street only.

## LA HUERTA
314/333-2079

▼▼ Seafood Steak. Casual Dining. $8-$28 **AAA Inspector Notes:** This large, open-air dining room is a great place to sample fresh local fish and seafood, prepared to order in hearty portions. Overlooking the beach, it's a nice spot to listen to the crashing waves as you feast on the bounty of the sea. **Features:** full bar, patio dining. **Address:** Blvd Costero Miguel de La Madrid No. 873 28869 **Location:** On Playa Azul.

## LA PERGOLA
314/333-2265

▼▼▼▼ International. Casual Dining. $14-$30 **AAA Inspector Notes:** This casual eatery gives you a choice of sitting indoors or on the outdoor terrace. The varied menu includes wood-fire-baked pizzas, fresh pastas and grilled seafood. You'll see plenty of locals gathered at the comfortable bar, soaking up the laid-back atmosphere. **Features:** full bar, patio dining. **Reservations:** suggested. **Address:** Blvd Costera Miguel de La Madrid KM 11.5 28869 **Location:** Off Mex 200, 1.9 mi (3 km); on Playa Azul; in Hotel Ejecutivo. **Parking:** street only.

## LA PLAZUELA
314/331-0500

▼▼ International. Casual Dining. $8-$30 **AAA Inspector Notes:** This casual restaurant features a light menu of varied International and Mexican fare in a relaxed setting overlooking the pool. A small indoor dining area also is available for rainy days. In season they offer a fresh fish market concept for diner, where meals are weighed in to be priced and cooked to order in any style desired. **Features:** full bar, patio dining. **Address:** Circuito de Los Marinos S/N 28830 **Location:** Mex 200, 3.8 mi (6 km) n of Cihuatlan, 11.3 mi (18 km) w; in Grand Isla Navidad Resort.

## LA TERRAZA
314/331-0500

▼▼▼ International. Casual Dining. $19-$38 **AAA Inspector Notes:** Candlelit tables and live guitar entertainment enhance the romantic atmosphere at the open-air restaurant. You'll enjoy stunning views of the bay as you explore the chef's seasonally changing menu of innovative fare. **Features:** full bar, patio dining. **Reservations:** required. **Address:** Circuito de Los Marinos S/N 28830 **Location:** Mex 200, 3.8 mi (6 km) n of Cihuatlan, 11.3 mi (18 km) w; in Grand Isla Navidad Resort. **Parking:** valet only.

## LA TOSCANA
314/333-2515

▼▼ International. Casual Dining. $9-$20 **AAA Inspector Notes:** Diners can spy the culinary action in the restaurant's open, outdoor kitchen while heading for their table, where they're presented with a dry-erase menu board listing the evening's Mexican and seafood choices. Most seating is on the outdoor patio, where the sounds of live music and crashing waves fill the air. **Features:** full bar. **Reservations:** suggested. **Address:** Blvd Miguel de La Madrid KM 7 28869 **Location:** 1.9 mi (3 km) off Mex 200; on Playa Azul.

## LOS DELFINES
314/331-0101

▼▼▼ Seafood. Fine Dining. $12-$35 **AAA Inspector Notes:** A stunning oceanfront setting perfectly complements the fine menu of freshly prepared seafood. The covered, open-air dining room features a cool ocean breeze and a relaxed, romantic ambience. **Features:** full bar, patio dining. **Reservations:** suggested. **Address:** Ave Vista Hermosa S/N 28867 **Location:** 7.2 mi (11.5 km) nw on Mex 200, 1.5 mi (2.5 km) s on Peninsula Santiago; in Las Hadas Golf Resort & Marina. **Parking:** on-site (fee).

## MARINA GRILL
314/336-5006

▼▼▼ Steak. Casual Dining. $15-$29 **AAA Inspector Notes:** A delightful setting overlooking the marina and candlelit tables make this a great choice for a romantic dining experience. The specialty here is grilled meats, and they are fabulous. To start the meal, the staff will prepare fresh salsa tableside to your own spice comfort level while you decide which cut of meat you prefer. Then sit back, relax and enjoy the ambiance and glittering lights of Manzanillo in the distance. **Features:** full bar, patio dining. **Reservations:** required. **Address:** Marina Puerto Las Hadas S/N 28867 **Location:** At Marina Puerto Las Hadas. **Parking:** street only.

## PARADISE RESTAURANT
314/334-1515

▼▼ International. Casual Dining. $7-$20 **AAA Inspector Notes:** Stunning views and huge portions of well-prepared casual fare are in store for you at this hillside restaurant. The hand-coated coconut shrimp is fabulous. The salads are fresh and creatively prepared. Another solid choice is one of the hearty pasta dishes. In the mood for a good old burger and fries? They're on the menu as well. Be aware that the hillside location means it's a steep walk from the lobby. Phone ahead if you're interested in the very popular Italian or lobster theme nights. **Features:** full bar, patio dining. **Address:** Ave Vista Hermosa S/N 28860 **Location:** 7.2 mi (11.5 km) nw on Mex 200, 1.5 mi (2.5 km) s on Peninsula Santiago; in Dolphin Cove Inn.

## RESTAURANTE LA HUERTA CAFE
314/331-1740

▼▼▼ International. Casual Dining. $7-$29 **AAA Inspector Notes:** Diners enjoy stunning views of the ocean and mountains from the covered open terrace. The menu offers a good mix of international and Mexican fare. At night, romantic candlelit tables complement the lights of the skyline. **Features:** full bar, patio dining. **Reservations:** suggested. **Address:** Paraiso No. 11 Col Residencial Salagua 28869 **Location:** 0.9 mi (1.5 km) off Mex 200, follow signs; in Camino Real Manzanillo.

## RESTAURANT EL VAQUERO
314/333-8005

▼▼ Steak. Casual Dining. $9-$28 **AAA Inspector Notes:** Sometimes you just crave a grilled steak, and that's what you're going to get at this local hot spot. Cowboy, rib, T-bone or even a freshly grilled giant burger are what draw crowds to this popular hangout. The dining room features bright Mexican décor, and the choice of sitting in a covered, open-air setting, or an enclosed air-conditioned section. Live music adds to the nightly fun. **Features:** full bar. **Address:** Crucero Las Brisas No. 19 Col Del Pacifico 28869 **Location:** 1.9 mi (3 km) w off Mex 200; on Playa Azul.

## RESTAURANT LEGAZPI
314/331-0101

▼▼▼▼ ▼▼

Continental Fine Dining $20-$35

**AAA Inspector Notes:** This upscale restaurant features a fine menu and staff skilled in tableside preparation. Live piano entertainment enhances the ambience. **Features:** full bar. **Reservations:** required. **Address:** Ave Vista Hermosa S/N 28867 **Location:** 7.2 mi (11.5 km) nw on Mex 200, 1.5 mi (2.5 km) s on Peninsula Santiago; in Las Hadas Golf Resort & Marina.

## RISTORANTE POCCO PAZZO
314/336-8533

▼▼ Italian. Casual Dining. $9-$16 **AAA Inspector Notes:** In the mood for well-prepared, home-style Italian fare loaded with rich tomato sauces, gobs of melted cheese and plenty of garlic? It's tough to beat this restaurant's gourmet pizzas, outstanding baked lasagna, delicious pasta dishes, grilled meats and seafood selections. Your meal is best enjoyed on the peaceful patio overlooking the marina. **Features:** full bar. **Address:** Local 18 y 19 Comercial Marina Las Hadas 28867 **Location:** At Marina Manzanillo. **Parking:** street only.

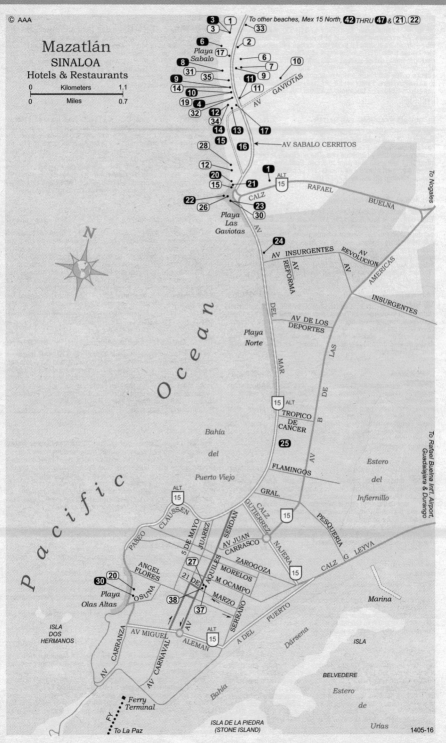

© AAA

# Mazatlán
## SINALOA
### Hotels & Restaurants

Kilometers  0 — 1.1
Miles  0 — 0.7

To other beaches, Mex 15 North, 42 THRU 47 & 21 22

Playa Sabalo

AV GAVIOTAS

AV SABALO CERRITOS

Playa Las Gaviotas

CALZ

RAFAEL    BUELNA

To Nogales

AV INSURGENTES

AV REFORMA

AV REVOLUCION

AV AMERICAS

INSURGENTES

AV DE LOS DEPORTES

DEL    MAR

DE    LAS

Playa Norte

Pacific Ocean

Bahía

del

Puerto Viejo

TROPICO DE CANCER

FLAMINGOS

AV

Estero del Infiernillo

PESQUERIA

To Rafael Buelna Int'l Airport, Guadalajara & Durango

CLAUSSEN

PASEO

5 DE MAYO

JUAREZ

AV JUAN CARRASCO

SERDAN

CALZ GUTIERREZ

ZAROGOZA

NAJERA

CALZ G LEYVA

GRAL.

ANGEL FLORES

21 DE

AQUILES

MORELOS

M OCAMPO

MARZO

SERRANO

A DEL    PUERTO

Marina

OSUNA

Playa Olas Altas

AV CARRANZA

AV MIGUEL    ALEMAN

AV    CARNAVAL

Dársena

ISLA BELVEDERE

Estero de

Urías

ISLA DOS HERMANOS

FY

Ferry Terminal

To La Paz

ISLA DE LA PIEDRA (STONE ISLAND)

Bahía

1405-16

# Mazatlán

This index helps you "spot" where approved hotels and restaurants are located on the corresponding detailed maps. Hotel daily rate range is for comparison only. Restaurant price range is a combination of lunch and/or dinner. Turn to the listing page for more detailed rate and price information and consult display ads for special promotions.

## MAZATLÁN, SINALOA

| Map Page | Hotels | Diamond Rated | Rate Range | Page |
|---|---|---|---|---|
| **1** p. 458 | Cityexpress Mazatlan | ◆◆ | $70-$95 | 461 |
| **3** p. 458 | **Hotel Pueblo Bonito Mazatlan** | ◆◆◆ | $165-$280 | 462 |
| **4** p. 458 | The Inn at Mazatlan | ◆◆◆ | $110-$280 | 462 |
| **6** p. 458 | Oceano Palace Beach Hotel | ◆◆ | $115-$130 | 462 |
| **8** p. 458 | The Palms Resort of Mazatlan | ◆◆◆ | $130-$165 | 462 |
| **9** p. 458 | El Cid El Moro Beach Hotel | ◆◆ | $120-$240 | 461 |
| **10** p. 458 | Royal Villas Resort | ◆◆◆ | $160-$370 | 463 |
| **11** p. 458 | El Cid Granada Country Club | ◆◆ | $80-$160 | 461 |
| **12** p. 458 | Hotel Costa de Oro | ◆◆ | $100-$170 | 462 |
| **13** p. 458 | El Cid Castilla Beach Hotel | ◆◆◆ | $105-$210 | 461 |
| **14** p. 458 | Motel Marley | ◆◆ | $85-$100 | 462 |
| **15** p. 458 | Suites Lindamar | ◆◆ | $65-$95 | 463 |
| **16** p. 458 | Azteca Inn | ◆◆ | $55-$85 | 461 |
| **17** p. 458 | BEST WESTERN Hotel Posada Freeman Zona Dorada | ◆◆ | Rates not provided | 461 |
| **20** p. 458 | Hotel Playa Mazatlan | ◆◆◆ | $115-$180 | 462 |
| **21** p. 458 | Quality Inn Mazatlan | ◆◆◆ | $64-$92 | 462 |
| **22** p. 458 | Ramada Resort & Spa Mazatlan | ◆◆ | $114-$320 | 462 |
| **23** p. 458 | Emporio Mazatlan | ◆◆◆ | $110-$250 | 461 |
| **24** p. 458 | Don Pelayo Pacific Beach | ◆◆ | $64-$140 | 461 |
| **25** p. 458 | Hotel Aguamarina-Mazatlan | ◆◆ | $65-$160 | 461 |
| **30** p. 458 | BEST WESTERN Posada Freeman | ◆◆◆ | Rates not provided | 461 |
| **42** p. 458 | **Pueblo Bonito Emerald Bay Resort & Spa** | ◆◆◆◆ | $245-$360 | 462 |
| **45** p. 458 | Mayan Sea Garden/Mayan Palace Mazatlan *(See ad on insert, p. 467.)* | ◆◆◆ | $529-$634 | 462 |
| **46** p. 458 | **Crowne Plaza Resort Mazatlan** | ◆◆◆◆ | $100-$180 | 461 |
| **47** p. 458 | **RIU Emerald Bay Hotel** *(See ad p. 380.)* | ◆◆◆ | Rates not provided | 463 |
| Map Page | Restaurants | Diamond Rated | Cuisine | Price Range | Page |
| **1** p. 458 | Cilantro's | ◆◆ | International | $8-$25 | 463 |
| **2** p. 458 | Los Zapares | ◆◆ | Mexican | $8-$15 | 464 |
| **3** p. 458 | Angelo's Restaurant | ◆◆◆ | Italian | $20-$35 | 463 |
| **6** p. 458 | Villa Italia | ◆◆ | Italian | $11-$18 | 465 |
| **7** p. 458 | La Casa Country Restaurant | ◆◆ | Steak | $10-$30 | 464 |
| **9** p. 458 | Carlos & Lucia's Restaurant Bar & Grill | ◆◆ | Cuban | $7-$17 | 463 |
| **10** p. 458 | Restaurant Casa Loma | ◆◆ | International Seafood | $15-$22 | 464 |
| **11** p. 458 | El Patio | ◆◆ | Argentine | $6-$25 | 463 |
| **12** p. 458 | Terraza Playa | ◆◆ | International | $8-$20 | 465 |
| **14** p. 458 | La Concha | ◆◆ | Steak | $8-$25 | 464 |

| Map Page | Restaurants (cont'd) | Diamond Rated | Cuisine | Price Range | Page |
|---|---|---|---|---|---|
| ⑮ p. 458 | Vittore | ◆◆◆ | Italian | $10-$20 | 465 |
| ⑰ p. 458 | Chili's Pepper | ◆◆ | Mexican | $7-$16 | 463 |
| ⑲ p. 458 | La Hacienda de la Flor | ◆◆◆ | Mexican | $9-$28 | 464 |
| ⑳ p. 458 | El Shrimp Bucket | ◆◆ | Seafood | $7-$20 | 463 |
| ㉑ p. 458 | Restaurante La Marina | ◆◆◆ | International | $7-$24 | 465 |
| ㉒ p. 458 | Los Candiles Restaurante | ◆◆◆ | International | $13-$22 | 464 |
| ㉖ p. 458 | Panchos Restaurant | ◆◆ | International | $7-$16 | 464 |
| ㉗ p. 458 | Pedro & Lola | ◆◆◆ | Mexican | $8-$18 | 464 |
| ㉘ p. 458 | Las Rejas Restaurante | ◆◆ | International | $8-$19 | 464 |
| ㉚ p. 458 | Condimento | ◆◆◆ | International | $7-$20 | 463 |
| ㉛ p. 458 | Oasis Restaurant | ◆◆ | International | $8-$18 | 464 |
| ㉜ p. 458 | Papagayo | ◆◆◆ | International | $10-$22 | 464 |
| ㉝ p. 458 | Panchos | ◆◆ | Mexican | $7-$18 | 464 |
| ㉞ p. 458 | Adobes Restaurant and Bar | ◆◆ | International | $10-$21 | 463 |
| ㉟ p. 458 | Munchkins Restaurant and Sports Bar | ◆ | American | $6-$15 | 464 |
| ㊲ p. 458 | Il Mosto | ◆◆◆ | Mediterranean | $10-$20 | 463 |
| ㊳ p. 458 | Casa Canobbio | ◆◆ | Italian | $8-$18 | 463 |

## MAZATLÁN, SINALOA (A-1) pop. 438,434

- Restaurants p. 463
- Hotels & Restaurants map & index p. 458

### AZTECA INN
669/913-4477 **16**

🚤🚤 **Motel** $55-$85 **Address:** Ave Playa Gaviotas No. 307 82110 **Location:** 4.6 mi (7.3 km) nw. **Facility:** 74 units. 3 stories (no elevator), exterior corridors. *Bath:* shower only. **Pool(s):** outdoor. **Guest Services:** valet laundry.

### BEST WESTERN HOTEL POSADA FREEMAN ZONA DORADA
(669)989-4400 **17**

🚤🚤 **Hotel.** Rates not provided. **Address:** Ave Camaron Sabalo 777 82110 **Location:** Oceanfront. 5.3 mi (8.5 km) nw; in Zona Dorado. **Facility:** Meets AAA guest room security requirements. 50 units. 5 stories, interior corridors. *Bath:* shower only. **Terms:** 3-5 night minimum stay - seasonal and/or weekends, 30 day cancellation notice-fee imposed, resort fee. **Amenities:** safes. **Pool(s):** outdoor. **Guest Services:** valet laundry.

**AAA Benefit:**
Save 10% or more every day and earn 10% bonus points!

### BEST WESTERN POSADA FREEMAN
(669)985-6060 **30**

🚤🚤🚤 **Hotel.** Rates not provided. **Address:** Ave Olas Atlas No. 79 82000 **Location:** In Centro Historico. **Facility:** 71 units. 12 stories, interior corridors. *Bath:* shower only. **Terms:** 3-5 night minimum stay - seasonal and/or weekends, 30 day cancellation notice-fee imposed, resort fee. **Amenities:** safes. **Pool(s):** outdoor. **Guest Services:** valet laundry.

**AAA Benefit:**
Save 10% or more every day and earn 10% bonus points!

### CITYEXPRESS MAZATLAN
(669)989-6000 **1**

🚤🚤 **Hotel** $70-$95 **Address:** Ave del Toreo No. 91 82120 **Location:** Jct Ave Rafael Buelna. **Facility:** Meets AAA guest room security requirements. 110 units. 5 stories, interior corridors. *Bath:* shower only. **Pool(s):** outdoor. **Activities:** limited exercise equipment. **Guest Services:** valet laundry.

### CROWNE PLAZA RESORT MAZATLAN
(669)988-0324 **46**

**Hotel**
**$100-$180**

**Address:** Blvd Sabalo Cerritos No. 3110, Marina Mazatlan 82100 **Location:** Oceanfront. In Marina Mazatlan District. **Facility:** The resort's stunning beachfront location and bright, contemporary décor attract beach lovers in droves. Refined accommodations and fine dining round out an upscale experience. Meets AAA guest room security requirements. 90 units, some two bedrooms and efficiencies. 18 stories, exterior corridors. **Amenities:** safes. **Dining:** Los Candiles Restaurante, see separate listing. **Pool(s):** heated outdoor. **Activities:** exercise room, spa. **Guest Services:** valet laundry.

### DON PELAYO PACIFIC BEACH
669/983-1888 **24**

🚤🚤 🚤🚤 **Hotel** $64-$140 **Address:** Ave del Mar No. 1111, Col Flamingos **Location:** 2.5 mi (4 km) nw. **Facility:** 162 units, some efficiencies. 5-10 stories, interior/exterior corridors. *Bath:* shower only. **Pool(s):** outdoor. **Activities:** hot tub, game room, exercise room. **Guest Services:** valet laundry.

### EL CID CASTILLA BEACH HOTEL
(669)989-6969 **13**

🚤🚤🚤 **Resort Hotel** $105-$210 **Address:** Ave Camaron Sabalo S/N 82110 **Location:** Oceanfront. 5.4 mi (8.7 km) nw; in Camaron Sabalo Zona Hotelera. **Facility:** Part of the massive El Cid Resort Complex, this mid-level high-rise property offers a huge lobby, ample public areas, beautiful ocean views and two pools and four restaurants. 500 units. 4-15 stories, interior corridors. **Parking:** valet only. **Amenities:** safes. **Dining:** 4 restaurants. **Pool(s):** heated outdoor. **Activities:** sauna, hot tub, regulation golf, tennis, recreation programs, exercise room, spa. **Guest Services:** valet laundry.

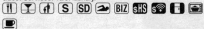

### EL CID EL MORO BEACH HOTEL
(669)989-6969 **9**

🚤🚤🚤 **Resort Hotel** $120-$240 **Address:** Ave Camaron Sabalo S/N 82110 **Location:** Oceanfront. 5.4 mi (8.7 km) nw; in Camaron Sabalo Zona Hotelera. **Facility:** Within the El Cid complex of 3 adjacent hotels, this impressive tower property has a mall with fine shops, as well as a beach, swimming pools and restaurants. It features 3 pools and 2 restaurants. Meets AAA guest room security requirements. 314 units, some efficiencies. 28 stories, interior corridors. **Parking:** on-site and valet. **Amenities:** safes. **Dining:** La Concha, see separate listing. **Pool(s):** heated outdoor. **Activities:** hot tub, regulation golf, tennis, recreation programs, exercise room, spa. **Guest Services:** valet laundry.

### EL CID GRANADA COUNTRY CLUB
(669)989-6969 **11**

🚤🚤 **Hotel** $80-$160 **Address:** Ave Camaron Sabalo S/N 82110 **Location:** Oceanfront. 5.4 mi (6.5 km) nw; in Camaron Sabalo Zona Hotelera; across from El Cid Castilla Beach Hotel. **Facility:** 120 units, some efficiencies. 3 stories, interior corridors. **Parking:** valet only. **Amenities:** safes. **Dining:** El Patio, see separate listing. **Pool(s):** heated outdoor. **Activities:** sauna, hot tub, regulation golf, tennis, recreation programs, exercise room, spa. **Guest Services:** valet laundry.

### EMPORIO MAZATLAN
(669)983-4611 **23**

🚤🚤🚤 **Hotel** $110-$250 **Address:** Ave Camaron Sabalo 51 82110 **Location:** Oceanfront. 4.1 mi (6.5 km) nw. **Facility:** Meets AAA guest room security requirements. 133 units. 4 stories, exterior corridors. *Bath:* shower only. **Parking:** on-site and valet. **Amenities:** safes. **Dining:** Condimento, see separate listing. **Pool(s):** heated outdoor. **Activities:** hot tub, exercise room. **Guest Services:** valet laundry.

### HOTEL AGUAMARINA-MAZATLAN
669/981-7080 **25**

🚤🚤 **Hotel** $65-$160 **Address:** Ave del Mar 110 82000 **Location:** 2.1 mi (3.3 km) nw. **Facility:** 111 units, some efficiencies. 3 stories (no elevator), interior/exterior corridors. *Bath:* shower only. **Pool(s):** heated outdoor. **Guest Services:** valet laundry.

---

**(See map & index p. 458.)**

### HOTEL COSTA DE ORO                          (669)913-5344  **12**

 **Resort Hotel** $100-$170 **Address:** Ave Camaron Sabalo No. 710 82110 **Location:** Oceanfront. 5.5 mi (8.8 km) nw. **Facility:** This is a perfect lodging for all as some rooms have simple, rustic décor and furnishings, while the suites with kitchenettes are far more modern and spacious. 230 units, some efficiencies. 3-10 stories, exterior corridors. *Bath:* shower only. **Dining:** Adobes Restaurant and Bar, see separate listing. **Pool(s):** heated outdoor. **Activities:** hot tub, scuba diving, snorkeling, tennis, exercise room. **Guest Services:** valet laundry.

### HOTEL PLAYA MAZATLAN                        (669)989-0555  **20**

 **Hotel** $115-$180 **Address:** Ave Playa Gaviotas No. 202 82110 **Location:** Oceanfront. 4.6 mi (7.3 km) nw; on Las Gaviotas Beach. **Facility:** 408 units. 3-5 stories, interior/exterior corridors. *Bath:* shower only. **Amenities:** safes. **Dining:** 2 restaurants, also, Terraza Playa, see separate listing, entertainment. **Pool(s):** heated outdoor. **Activities:** hot tub, exercise room, spa. **Guest Services:** valet laundry.

### HOTEL PUEBLO BONITO MAZATLAN

(669)989-8900  **3**

Hotel
$165-$280

**Address:** Ave Camaron Sabalo 2121 82110 **Location:** Oceanfront. 7.8 mi (12.5 km) nw. **Facility:** 247 efficiencies, some two bedrooms. 4-5 stories, exterior corridors. **Parking:** valet only. **Terms:** check-in 4 pm. **Amenities:** safes. **Dining:** 3 restaurants, also, Angelo's Restaurant, Cilantro's, see separate listings. **Pool(s):** heated outdoor. **Activities:** hot tub, recreation programs, exercise room, massage. **Guest Services:** valet laundry.

### THE INN AT MAZATLAN                         (669)913-5500  **4**

 **Resort Hotel** $110-$280 **Address:** 6291 Ave Camaron Sabalo 82110 **Location:** Oceanfront. Just n of Ave Castro. In heart of Zona Dorada section. **Facility:** Comprising three towers, the fabulous public areas, pools and spacious condo units are upscale, while standard rooms are less so, yet all have striking ocean views. The restaurant is a city landmark. 215 units, some two bedrooms, efficiencies and kitchens. 4-10 stories, interior corridors. **Parking:** valet and valet only. **Amenities:** safes. **Dining:** 2 restaurants, also, Papagayo, see separate listing, entertainment. **Pool(s):** outdoor, heated outdoor. **Activities:** exercise room. **Guest Services:** valet laundry, rental car service.

### MAYAN SEA GARDEN/MAYAN PALACE MAZATLAN

(669)989-4000  **45**

 **Hotel** $529-$634 **Address:** Calz Sabalo-Cerritos S/N 82100 **Location:** Oceanfront. 0.6 mi (1 km) n of marina. **Facility:** 268 units, some efficiencies and kitchens. 4-12 stories, exterior corridors. *Bath:* shower only. **Terms:** check-in 5 pm, 2-7 night minimum stay, 7 day cancellation notice. **Amenities:** safes. **Dining:** 2 restaurants. **Pool(s):** outdoor, heated outdoor. **Activities:** game room, exercise room, spa. **Guest Services:** valet and coin laundry. **(See ad on insert, p. 467.)**

### MOTEL MARLEY                                 669/913-5533  **14**

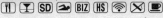 **Extended Stay Motel** $85-$100 **Address:** Ave Playa Gaviotas No. 226 82110 **Location:** Oceanfront. 4.7 mi (7.5 km) nw; on Las Gaviotas Beach. **Facility:** 16 efficiencies, some two bedrooms. 2 stories (no elevator), exterior corridors. *Bath:* shower only. **Pool(s):** outdoor. **Guest Services:** valet laundry.

### OCEANO PALACE BEACH HOTEL                    (669)913-0666  **6**

**Hotel** $115-$130 **Address:** Ave Camaron Sabalo S/N 82110 **Location:** Oceanfront. 7.5 mi (12 km) nw. **Facility:** 256 units, some efficiencies. 6 stories, interior corridors. **Amenities:** safes. **Dining:** 2 restaurants. **Pool(s):** heated outdoor. **Activities:** hot tub, exercise room. **Guest Services:** valet laundry.

### THE PALMS RESORT OF MAZATLAN                 (669)913-2222  **8**

**Hotel** $130-$165 **Address:** Ave Camaron Sabalo 696 82110 **Location:** Oceanfront. 5.8 mi (9.2 km) nw. **Facility:** Meets AAA guest room security requirements. 190 units, some efficiencies. 6 stories, interior corridors. *Bath:* shower only. **Parking:** on-site and valet. **Amenities:** safes. **Dining:** 3 restaurants, also, Oasis Restaurant, see separate listing. **Pool(s):** heated outdoor. **Activities:** tennis, exercise room. **Guest Services:** valet and coin laundry.

### PUEBLO BONITO EMERALD BAY RESORT & SPA

(669)989-0525  **42**

Resort Hotel
$245-$360

**Address:** Ave Ernesto Coppel Campana S/N 82110 **Location:** Oceanfront. Just past Marina Mazatlan on Emerald Bay. **Facility:** This luxurious beach resort has sumptuous public areas, refined guest rooms, an enormous three-tiered pool area and the finest spa I've seen anywhere. It's truly a dream. Meets AAA guest room security requirements. 378 units, some two bedrooms, efficiencies and kitchens. 2-4 stories, interior corridors. **Parking:** on-site and valet. **Terms:** check-in 4 pm. **Amenities:** safes. **Dining:** 5 restaurants. **Pool(s):** heated outdoor. **Activities:** sauna, hot tub, steamroom, fishing, snorkeling, tennis, recreation programs, spa. **Guest Services:** valet laundry.

### QUALITY INN MAZATLAN                          (669)989-2323  **21**

**Hotel** $64-$92 **Address:** Bugambilias 100 82110 **Location:** In heart of Golden Zone. **Facility:** 89 units. 3 stories, interior corridors. *Bath:* shower only. **Amenities:** safes. **Pool(s):** outdoor. **Activities:** hot tub, exercise room. **Guest Services:** valet laundry.

### RAMADA RESORT & SPA MAZATLAN                  (669)983-5333  **22**

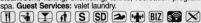 **Resort Hotel** $114-$320 **Address:** Ave Playa Gaviotas No. 100 82110 **Location:** Oceanfront. 4.4 mi (7 km) nw; on Las Gaviotas Beach. **Facility:** This basic hotel features well-tended grounds, a large swimming pool, comfortable guest rooms and suites. You can enjoy beach views from their restaurant. 200 units, some two bedrooms and efficiencies. 8 stories, exterior corridors. **Amenities:** safes. **Dining:** 2 restaurants. **Pool(s):** outdoor. **Activities:** sauna, hot tub, scuba diving, snorkeling, exercise room. **Guest Services:** valet laundry.

---

## Ask your AAA/CAA club about travel money and other financial services for travelers

**(See map & index p. 458.)**

## RIU EMERALD BAY HOTEL    669/989-7900   47

▼▼▼▼
**Resort Hotel**
Rates not provided

**Address:** Ave Sabalo-Cerritos No. 3404 82112 **Location:** Oceanfront. Just past Marina Mazatlan on Emerald Bay. **Facility:** This elegant all-inclusive resort fronts a fine stretch of beach and offers entertainment and activities programs, a refined lobby and pool areas. Honeymoon and hot tub suites are available. Meets AAA guest room security requirements. 716 units. 22 stories, interior corridors. **Parking:** on-site and valet. **Terms:** check-in 4 pm. **Amenities:** safes. **Dining:** 4 restaurants, entertainment. **Pool(s):** outdoor. **Activities:** recreation programs, playground, game room, exercise room, spa. **Guest Services:** valet laundry, rental car service. *(See ad p. 380.)*

🍴 🍸 SD ⛵ BIZ SHS 📶 ✕ 🔒

## ROYAL VILLAS RESORT    (669)916-6161   10

▼▼▼▼ Hotel $160-$370 **Address:** Ave Camaron Sabalo No. 500 82110 **Location:** Oceanfront. 5.3 mi (8.5 km) nw; in Zona Dorada. **Facility:** 111 units, some two bedrooms, three bedrooms, efficiencies and kitchens. 12 stories, interior corridors. **Parking:** valet only. **Amenities:** *Some:* safes. **Dining:** 2 restaurants, also, La Hacienda de la Flor, see separate listing, entertainment. **Pool(s):** heated outdoor. **Activities:** hot tub, recreation programs, exercise room, spa. **Guest Services:** valet and coin laundry.

🍴 🍸 🛋 ⛵ BIZ HS 📶 🔒 🖥 ☕

## SUITES LINDAMAR    669/913-5533   15

▼▼▼ Hotel $65-$95 **Address:** Ave Playa Gaviotas No. 222 82110 **Location:** Oceanfront. 4.7 mi (7.5 km) nw; on Las Gaviotas Beach. **Facility:** 12 kitchen units. 3 stories (no elevator), exterior corridors. **Bath:** shower only. **Pool(s):** outdoor.

🍴+ ⛵ HS 📶 ☷ 🔒 🖥 /SOME UNITS ☕

## ADOBES RESTAURANT AND BAR    669/913-5344   34

▼▼▼ International. Casual Dining. $10-$21 **AAA Inspector Notes:** Whether it's the extensive breakfast buffet, a light bite at lunch or a full surf-and-turf meal, the views and the casual ambience are sure to please. Diners can select from hot starters such as cream of corn or traditional tortilla soup, then move on to mains such as fajitas, pasta dishes, or grilled steak and seafood. Both inside and outdoor terrace dining are available. **Features:** full bar, patio dining. **Reservations:** suggested. **Address:** Ave Camaron Sabalo No. 710 82110 **Location:** 5.5 mi (8.8 km) nw; in Hotel Costa de Oro.

B L D ⋯

## ANGELO'S RESTAURANT    669/989-8900   3

▼▼▼▼ Italian. Casual Dining. $20-$35 **AAA Inspector Notes:** Here you'll devour roasted red peppers, cured meats and marinated vegetables as a prelude to great pasta dishes. This place also is famous for perfectly cooked-to-order steaks. The setting is casual yet refined. **Features:** full bar. **Reservations:** required. **Address:** Ave Camaron Sabalo 2121 82110 **Location:** 7.8 mi (12.5 km) nw; in Hotel Pueblo Bonito Mazatlan. **Parking:** valet only. D

## CARLOS & LUCIA'S RESTAURANT BAR & GRILL    669/913-5677   9

▼▼▼ Cuban. Casual Dining. $7-$17 **AAA Inspector Notes:** Cuban cuisine is served in a relaxed, pleasant atmosphere. Guests can sit on the patio or in the indoor dining room. The Cuban sandwich is a must-try, and the imperial shrimp is fit for a king or queen. **Features:** full bar, patio dining. **Reservations:** suggested. **Address:** Ave Camaron Sabalo S/N 82110 **Location:** Across from The Palms Resort. **Parking:** street only. B L D ⋯

## CASA CANOBBIO    669/910-1417   38

▼▼▼ Italian. Casual Dining. $8-$18 **AAA Inspector Notes:** Here you'll find a great spot to take in the sights and sounds of the popular Plaza Machado while dining on fresh, home-style Italian fare. Made-to-order pizzas, tasty pastas and a few daily fish and meat specials can be paired with a nice glass of wine. The large, outdoor patio is the perfect place to sit and listen to the buzz of the Historic Center and do some people-watching. The staff doesn't mind if you choose to linger longer and soak up the ambiance. **Features:** full bar, patio dining. **Address:** Heriberto frias y Constitucion 82000 **Location:** In Centro Historico at Plaza Machado. **Parking:** street only.

L D ⋯ ⋯

## CHILI'S PEPPER    669/913-0069   17

▼▼ Mexican. Casual Dining. $7-$16 **AAA Inspector Notes:** This casual beachfront eatery is the perfect spot to relax and unwind with a jumbo margarita and some tasty Mexican fare. The open-air dining room offers fabulous ocean views, and the staff provides warm and friendly service. In addition to Mexican specialties, the menu lists grilled meats and fresh seafood, including shrimp, as well as some casual American fare. **Features:** full bar, patio dining. **Reservations:** suggested. **Address:** Ave Camaron Sabalo 82110 **Location:** 6.3 mi (10 km) nw; directly overlooking the beach. **Parking:** street only.

B L D ⋯ ⋯

## CILANTRO'S    669/989-8900   1

▼▼▼ International. Casual Dining. $8-$25 **AAA Inspector Notes:** A great spot for a casual meal, the open-air restaurant's spectacular oceanfront setting lends to its popularity with tourists and locals alike. Because reservations are not accepted, diners should be prepared to wait, but heading to the bar for a decadent cocktail and complimentary chips and salsa helps bide the time. The menu lists a good variety of freshly grilled items, including lobster, beef and seafood. **Features:** full bar, patio dining. **Address:** Ave Camaron Sabalo 2121 82110 **Location:** 7.8 mi (12.5 km) nw; in Hotel Pueblo Bonito Mazatlan. **Parking:** valet only.

B L D ⋯

## CONDIMENTO    669/983-4822   30

▼▼▼ International. Casual Dining. $7-$20 **AAA Inspector Notes:** Diners here enjoy the wonderful setting overlooking the beach and ocean from the outdoor terrace as well as the brightly decorated indoor dining area. The menu features a fine selection of regional Mexican and international fare from the a la carte menu as well as extensive buffet options in high season. **Features:** full bar, patio dining. **Reservations:** suggested. **Address:** Ave Camaron Sabalo 51 82110 **Location:** 4.1 mi (6.5 km) nw; in Emporio Mazatlan.

B L D ⋯ ⋯

## EL PATIO    669/913-3333   11

▼▼▼ Argentine. Casual Dining. $6-$25 **AAA Inspector Notes:** A casual poolside eatery by day, this place transforms into an intimate Argentinean grill house in the evening. Guests dine under the stars on the open-air patio and enjoy fine cuts of meat, fish and seafood, grilled to order. This is a busy place, so dinner reservations are a must. **Features:** full bar, patio dining. **Reservations:** required, for dinner. **Address:** Ave Camaron Sabalo S/N 82110 **Location:** 5.4 mi (8.7 km) nw; in Camaron Sabalo Zona Hotelera; across from El Cid Castilla Beach Hotel; in El Cid Granada Country Club.

B L D ⋯ ⋯

## EL SHRIMP BUCKET    669/981-6350   20

▼▼ Seafood. Casual Dining. $7-$20 **AAA Inspector Notes:** Shrimp served in a clay bucket with fries is the signature dish at the popular cafe, which features an outdoor sidewalk section that affords fine views of the malecon and ocean. Sunsets here are a treat. **Features:** full bar, patio dining. **Address:** Olas Atlas No. 11 82110 **Location:** 5 blks sw of Plaza de La Republica. **Parking:** street only.

L D ⋯

## IL MOSTO    669/985-4366   37

▼▼▼ Mediterranean. Casual Dining. $10-$20 **AAA Inspector Notes:** This prime people-watching spot has an outdoor patio facing historic Plaza Machado. The menu features a delicious mix of Mediterranean favorites, including pasta dishes, fresh fish, shrimp and other seafood. **Features:** full bar, patio dining. **Reservations:** suggested. **Address:** Plazuela Machado 82000 **Location:** In Centro Historico. **Parking:** no self-parking.

L D ⋯

(See map & index p. 458.)

**LA CASA COUNTRY RESTAURANT**     669/916-5300   7
♦♦ ♦♦ Steak. Casual Dining. $10-$30 **AAA Inspector Notes:** A great place for a hearty steak dinner and a side of wild Western atmosphere, this restaurant is a favorite with locals and tourists alike, as evidenced by the usual wait for seating. However, you won't mind when the wait is rewarded with heaping portions of fine steaks, corn on the cob and a steaming baked potato. In season, festive cowboy entertainment adds to the fun. **Features:** full bar. **Reservations:** suggested. **Address:** Ave Camaron Sabalo S/N 82100 **Location:** 5.9 mi (9.5 km) nw. L D

**LA CONCHA**     669/913-3333   14
♦♦ ♦♦ Steak. Casual Dining. $8-$25 **AAA Inspector Notes:** Diners can choose from the oceanfront open-air patio section or one of two levels of interior dining room extending down to the beach from the lobby level. The menu has a fun mix of grilled fare with an 'Aussie' flavor. Among options are grilled steaks from the 'Barbie' with corn on the cob or fresh local fish and seafood. **Features:** full bar, patio dining. **Reservations:** suggested. **Address:** Ave Camaron Sabalo S/N 82110 **Location:** 5.4 mi (8.7 km) nw; in Camaron Sabalo Zona Hotelera; in El Cid El Moro Beach Hotel. **Parking:** valet only. B L D

**LA HACIENDA DE LA FLOR**     669/916-6161   19
♦♦ ♦♦ ♦♦ Mexican. Casual Dining. $9-$28 **AAA Inspector Notes:** Lending to the cozy restaurant's festive feel are distinctive Mexican décor and live music each evening. Staff members are skilled at tableside and flambe presentations. The menu incorporates a good mix of Mexican and international fare. **Features:** full bar. **Reservations:** suggested. **Address:** Ave Camaron Sabalo No. 500 82110 **Location:** 5.3 mi (8.5 km) nw; in Zona Dorada; in Royal Villas Resort. **Parking:** valet only. L D

**LAS REJAS RESTAURANTE**     669/913-5100   28
♦♦ ♦♦ International. Casual Dining. $8-$19 **AAA Inspector Notes:** Dine on the patio listening to the crashing waves, or inside the bright, modern dining room. The menu offers a choice of light snacktype fare, which is great for a relaxing day on the beach. You'll also find more substantial dinners, including rack of ribs, grilled steaks or fresh local seafood. The nightly entertainment in the adjacent lounge livens up the ambiance. **Features:** full bar, patio dining. **Address:** Ave Playa Gaviotas 212 82110 **Location:** 4.6 mi (7.3 km) nw; on Las Gaviotas Beach; in Las Flores Beach Resort. B L D

**LOS ARCOS RESTAURANT**     669/913-9577
♦♦ ♦♦ Mexican Seafood. Casual Dining. $6-$20 **AAA Inspector Notes:** A shrimp lover's paradise, this popular restaurant delights locals and tourists alike with its fine selection of fresh local shrimps and seafood, cooked in every way imaginable. From fresh tasty starters such as a traditional chilled shrimp cocktail to coconut, garlic, Mexican spiced or Hawaiian pineapple jumbo shrimps, you're sure to be satisfied. The dining room is brightly decorated with a distinct Mexican theme and features pleasant evening entertainment. **Features:** full bar. **Reservations:** suggested. **Address:** Ave Camaron Sabalo No. 1019 82110 **Location:** 5.4 mi (8.7 km) nw; in Camaron Sabalo Zona Hotelera. L D

**LOS CANDILES RESTAURANTE**     669/988-0324   22
♦♦ ♦♦ ♦♦ International. Fine Dining. $13-$22 **AAA Inspector Notes:** The staff will pamper you in this refined facility, which boasts beautiful ocean views. Here you'll enjoy a wide variety of flavorful seafood, pasta and Mexican dishes. The organic salad with honeyyogurt dressing is healthy and satisfying as is the grilled fish served over steamed vegetables. This is an excellent spot, whether you crave a simple sandwich or a multi-course feast. **Features:** full bar, patio dining. **Address:** Blvd Sabalo Cerritos No. 3110, Marina Mazatlan 82100 **Location:** In Marina Mazatlan District; in Crowne Plaza Resort Mazatlan. B L D LATE CALL M

**LOS ZAPARES**     669/913-1400   2
♦♦ ♦♦ Mexican. Casual Dining. $8-$15 **AAA Inspector Notes:** This festive restaurant serves a wide range of freshly prepared Mexican fare from different regions of the country. Before your meal, you'll enjoy watching salsa being prepared tableside to your preferred level of spiciness. On some evenings, live musical entertainment features Mexican or Country Western singers. The bright décor is marked by colorful wall murals and paintings. **Features:** full bar. **Address:** Ave Camaron Sabalo No. 2601 82100 **Location:** 7.5 mi (12 km) nw. **Parking:** street only. L D

**MUNCHKINS RESTAURANT AND SPORTS BAR**     669/916-6180   35
♦♦ American. Casual Dining. $6-$15 **AAA Inspector Notes:** A popular local hangout, this casual eatery is known for its juicy burgers, tender steaks, spicy chicken wings and all-you-can-eat meaty barbecue ribs. **Features:** full bar. **Address:** Ave Camaron Sabalo 550 82100 **Location:** In Golden Zone. **Parking:** street only. L D

**OASIS RESTAURANT**     669/913-2222   31
♦♦ ♦♦ International. Casual Dining. $8-$18 **AAA Inspector Notes:** Dine in the sea breeze, overlooking the ocean and under the stars. This casual open-air restaurant features a stunning location perfect for listening to the crashing waves and eating your favorite Mexican or international fare. The menu ranges from hearty burgers and pastas, to sizzling fajitas and any-way-you-like-them shrimp. It's also a great place to grab a cocktail and watch the sunset. **Address:** Ave Camaron Sabalo No. 696 82100 **Location:** 5.8 mi (9.2 km) nw; in The Palms Resort of Mazatlan. L D M

**PANCHOS**     669/913-3040   33
♦♦ ♦♦ Mexican. Casual Dining. $7-$18 **AAA Inspector Notes:** Even if you opt to dine on the casual outdoor patio, take time to admire the amazing Mexican artwork and décor accents inside this comfortable restaurant, as it really adds to the enjoyment of a meal here. The menu is rich in local and regional Mexican specialties, with a strong emphasis on fish, seafood, and naturally, fresh shrimp (a Mazatlan specialty) prepared any way you'd like. As a thank you, after your meal the waiter will usually set you up with a complimentary shot of tequila. Cheers! **Features:** full bar. **Address:** Ave Camaron Sabalo No. 1614 L-B 82110 **Location:** 7.8 mi (12.5 km) nw. **Parking:** no self-parking. B L D

**PANCHOS RESTAURANT**     669/914-0911   26
♦♦ ♦♦ International. Casual Dining. $7-$16 **AAA Inspector Notes:** You'll likely have to wait for a table at always-hopping Panchos, but you'll be treated to outstanding views and great food once you're seated. From the second-floor dining area, large panoramic windows and bright, festive decor enhance the setting, while the main, lower-level area offers covered patio seating. The nice selection of casual fare includes Mexican, seafood and American specialties. **Features:** full bar. **Address:** Ave Playa Gaviotas No. 408 82110 **Location:** 4.4 mi (7 km) nw; on Las Gaviotas Beach. **Parking:** no self-parking. B L D M

**PAPAGAYO**     669/913-4151   32
♦♦ ♦♦ ♦♦ International. Casual Dining. $10-$22 **AAA Inspector Notes:** Serving a luscious mix of traditional international fare, plus plenty of local seafood, the restaurant offers seating in its upscale dining room or on a lovely outdoor terrace cooled by the ocean breeze. **Features:** full bar, patio dining. **Reservations:** suggested. **Address:** Ave Camaron Sabalo S/N 82110 **Location:** Just n of Ave Castro; in The Inn at Mazatlan. B L D

**PEDRO & LOLA**     669/982 2589   27
♦♦ ♦♦ ♦♦ Mexican. Casual Dining. $8-$18 **AAA Inspector Notes:** Besides having a great menu selection of Mexican and international fare, this restaurant is simply a fun place to dine. Across from the bustling Plaza Machado in the heart of the historic center, this place gives you plenty to watch while dining. It is wise to phone ahead to try to reserve an outside table in the center of the action. The restaurant often features live entertainment. **Features:** full bar. **Reservations:** suggested. **Address:** Ave Constitucion esq con Carnaval 82000 **Location:** In Centro Historico; at Plaza Machado. **Parking:** street only. L D M

**RESTAURANT CASA LOMA**     669/913-5398   10
♦♦ ♦♦ International Seafood. Casual Dining. $15-$22 **AAA Inspector Notes:** You'll be wowed by this popular restaurant that blends well-prepared Italian cuisine and some Mexican dishes on its diverse menu. Don't overlook the outstanding wine list. Enjoy your meal on the romantic garden terrace, or more formal interior dining room. **Features:** full bar. **Reservations:** suggested. **Address:** Ave Playa Gaviotas, No. 104 Fracc Gaviotas 82110 **Location:** 4.9 mi (7.8 km) nw. **Parking:** on-site and street. L D

(See map & index p. 458.)

**RESTAURANTE LA MARINA** 669/913-3333 (21)

▼▼▼▼ International. Casual Dining. $7-$24 **AAA Inspector Notes:** A stylish dining experience awaits. From the open patio, patrons are treated to a marvelous view of white yachts in the marina. Seafood, as well as fowl and meats, is skillfully prepared and attractively presented. **Features:** full bar. **Address:** Ave Camaron Sabalo S/N 82110 **Location:** 8.4 mi (13.5 km) nw; north end of Zona Hotelera; in El Cid Marina Beach Hotel. **Parking:** on-site and valet.

(B) (L) (D) (✎)

**TERRAZA PLAYA** 669/989-0555 (12)

▼▼▼ International. Casual Dining. $8-$20 **AAA Inspector Notes:** This open-air restaurant offers excellent views of the ocean and a refreshing sea breeze. The casual menu features a good selection of Mexican and North American fare. You can walk up directly from the beach or through the lobby of the hotel. A great spot to watch the sunset while dining or enjoying a cocktail. **Features:** full bar, patio dining. **Address:** Ave Playa Gaviotas No. 202 82110 **Location:** 4.6 mi (7.3 km) nw; on Las Gaviotas Beach; in Hotel Playa Mazatlan.

(B) (L) (D) (AC)

**VILLA ITALIA** 669/913-0311 (6)

▼▼ Italian. Casual Dining. $11-$18 **AAA Inspector Notes:** Thick lasagna, rich frutti di mare, and saucy Alfredo Italian specialties are served indoors and on the casual patio. The outdoor brick oven wafts a wonderful aroma baking pizzas and specialty breads. **Features:** full bar. **Reservations:** suggested. **Address:** Ave Camaron Sabalo S/N **Location:** 5 mi (8 km) nw; in front of Hotel El Cid.

(L) (D) (✎)

**VITTORE** 669/986-2424 (15)

▼▼▼ Italian. Fine Dining. $10-$20 **AAA Inspector Notes:** A wood-burning pizza oven, trattoria ambience, open air dining room and pleasant patio all add up to a memorable Italian dining experience. **Features:** full bar. **Reservations:** suggested. **Address:** Ave Playa Gaviotas No. 100 82110 **Location:** 4.4 mi (7 km) nw; on Las Gaviotas Beach; across from Ramada Resort & Spa Mazatlan.

(L) (D) (✎)

## NUEVO VALLARTA, NAYARIT
• **Restaurants p. 469**

**BEL AIR COLLECTION RESORT AND SPA VALLARTA**
(322)226-1050

▼▼▼▼ Hotel $120-$210 **Address:** Blvd Costero No. 800 Sur 63732 **Location:** Oceanfront. Mex 200 exit Nuevo Vallarta, 1.3 mi (2 km) n. **Facility:** 215 units, some efficiencies. 7 stories, exterior corridors. **Amenities:** safes. **Dining:** 4 restaurants, also, Palm Terrace, see separate listing. **Pool(s):** heated outdoor. **Activities:** recreation programs, kids club, exercise room, spa. **Guest Services:** valet laundry.

(🍴) (🛎) (👤) (🏊) (BIZ) (📶) (✕) (🔌) (💻)
/ SOME UNITS (HS) (🧳)

**CLUB HOTEL RIU JALISCO** (322)226-6600

▼▼▼▼
Resort Hotel
Rates not provided

**Address:** Ave de Los Cocoteros Riviera Nayarit 63732 **Location:** Oceanfront. Mex 200 exit Nuevo Vallarta, 1.3 mi (2 km) n. **Facility:** This huge all-inclusive resort features a prime beachfront location and a variety of dining options. In addition to ever-changing entertainment programs, you'll find an abundance of activities. 700 units. 6 stories, exterior corridors. **Amenities:** safes. **Dining:** 5 restaurants, nightclub, entertainment. **Pool(s):** outdoor. **Activities:** sauna, hot tub, scuba diving, snorkeling, recreation programs, kids club, game room, exercise room, spa. **Guest Services:** valet laundry. (See ad p. 380.)

(🍴) (🍷) (👤) (🏊) (BIZ) (📶) (✕) (🔌)

## DREAMS VILLAMAGNA NUEVO VALLARTA
(322)226-8700

Resort Hotel
$451-$629

**Address:** Paseo de Los Cocoteros, Lotes 32 y 33 63732 **Location:** Oceanfront. Mex 200 exit Nuevo Vallarta, 1.3 mi (2 km) n. **Facility:** This deluxe all-inclusive resort features spacious suites with an upscale contemporary design, all with private hot tubs on the balconies. Guests can select either ocean or tropical view. 229 units. 8-9 stories, exterior corridors. **Parking:** valet only. **Amenities:** safes. **Dining:** 5 restaurants, entertainment. **Pool(s):** outdoor, heated outdoor. **Activities:** sauna, hot tub, scuba diving, snorkeling, tennis, recreation programs, kids club, bicycles, spa. **Guest Services:** valet laundry.

## THE GRAND BLISS
322/226-4000

Boutique Contemporary Hotel
$396-$473

**Address:** Ave Paseo de Las Moras S/N Fracc 63735 **Location:** Mex 200 exit Nuevo Vallarta, 1.3 mi (2 km) n. **Facility:** Thanks to colorful artwork and hip, contemporary décor, the hotel lobby is a stunner. Rooms are spacious and include a balcony. 168 units, some two bedrooms. 9 stories, interior corridors. **Parking:** on-site (fee) and valet. **Terms:** check-in 5 pm, 2-7 night minimum stay, 7 day cancellation notice-fee imposed. **Amenities:** safes. **Pool(s):** heated outdoor. **Activities:** recreation programs. **Guest Services:** valet laundry, area transportation. Affiliated with Mayan Resorts. (See ad on insert, p. 467.)

## GRAND LUXXE
322/226-4000

Contemporary Resort Hotel
$671-$804

**Address:** Ave Paseo de Las Moras S/N Fracc Nautico Turistico 63735 **Location:** Mex 200 exit Nuevo Vallarta, 1.3 mi (2 km) n. **Facility:** Contemporary design marks the resort's spacious units. Guests enjoy personal attention from their private floor concierge, who will also provide butler services. 789 units, some two bedrooms, three bedrooms, efficiencies and kitchens. 9 stories, interior corridors. **Parking:** on-site (fee) and valet. **Terms:** 2-7 night minimum stay, 7 day cancellation notice-fee imposed. **Amenities:** safes. **Dining:** 6 restaurants, also, The Burger Custom Made, Epazote, Punta Arena, see separate listings, entertainment. **Pool(s):** outdoor, heated outdoor. **Activities:** hot tub, regulation golf, recreation programs, spa. **Guest Services:** valet and coin laundry, luggage security pick-up. Affiliated with Mayan Resorts. (See ad on insert, p. 467.)

Visit AAA.com/searchfordiscounts

to save on travel, shopping,

dining and attractions

## THE GRAND MAYAN NUEVO VALLARTA
322/226-4000

Resort Hotel
$344-$412

**Address:** Paseo de Las Moras S/N 63735 **Location:** Mex 200 exit Nuevo Vallarta, 1.3 mi (2 km) n. **Facility:** This huge resort complex features outstanding public facilities. Guests enjoy trolley transportation throughout the property grounds. 792 units, some efficiencies. 9 stories, interior corridors. **Parking:** on-site (fee) and valet. **Terms:** check-in 5 pm, 2-7 night minimum stay, 7 day cancellation notice-fee imposed. **Amenities:** safes. **Dining:** 5 restaurants, also, Gong, Samba Restaurant, Tramonto, see separate listings. **Pool(s):** heated outdoor. **Activities:** hot tub, scuba diving, snorkeling, regulation golf, recreation programs, spa. **Guest Services:** valet and coin laundry, area transportation. (See ad on insert, p. 467.)

## GRAND VELAS RIVIERA NAYARIT
(322)226-8000

Resort Hotel
$900-$1300

**Address:** Ave Cocoteros Sur No. 98 63735 **Location:** Oceanfront. Mex 200 exit Nuevo Vallarta, 1.3 mi (2 km) n. **Facility:** This all-inclusive, luxurious spa retreat offers outstanding facilities and a prime beachfront setting. The dining options are decadent leaving guests feeling full and pampered. 267 units, some two bedrooms. 9 stories, interior corridors. **Parking:** valet only. **Amenities:** safes. **Dining:** 5 restaurants, also, Frida, Lucca, Piaf, see separate listings, entertainment. **Pool(s):** outdoor, heated outdoor. **Activities:** sauna, hot tub, steamroom, scuba diving, snorkeling, tennis, recreation programs, kids club, bicycles, spa. **Guest Services:** valet laundry. (See ad opposite title page, on insert.)

## HARD ROCK HOTEL VALLARTA
(322)226-8470

Resort Hotel
$380-$700

**Address:** Paseo de Los Cocoteros 19 Villa 8 Naut Turist 63735 **Location:** Oceanfront. Mex 200 exit Nuevo Vallarta, 1.3 mi (2 km) n. **Facility:** The all-inclusive beachfront resort features many dining options, a huge tropical pool and nightly entertainment. Rooms are spacious and hip. 348 units. 6-8 stories, interior corridors. **Amenities:** Some: video games. **Dining:** 6 restaurants, entertainment. **Pool(s):** heated outdoor. **Activities:** hot tub, scuba diving, kids club, spa. **Guest Services:** valet laundry.

## HOTEL RIU VALLARTA
322/226-7250

Resort Hotel
Rates not provided

**Address:** Ave de Los Cocoteros S/N Lote K 63732 **Location:** Oceanfront. Mex 200 exit Nuevo Vallarta, 1.3 mi (2 km) n. **Facility:** In addition to a variety of dining options, guests at this all-inclusive resort can partake in well-planned activities (held day and night) that cater to all age groups. 550 units. 9 stories, interior corridors. **Amenities:** safes. **Dining:** 4 restaurants, entertainment. **Pool(s):** outdoor. **Activities:** scuba diving, snorkeling, recreation programs, kids club, exercise room, spa. **Guest Services:** valet laundry. (See ad p. 380.)

A theatrical & culinary experience like no other

# JOYÀ

## BY CIRQUE DU SOLEIL®

Only at Vidanta Riviera Maya

## MARIVAL RESIDENCES & WORLD SPA    (322)226-9740

Resort Hotel
$472-$708

**Address:** Ave Paseo de Los Cocoteros Lote 53 Villa 8 11 63732 **Location:** Oceanfront. Mex 200 exit Nuevo Vallarta, 1.3 mi (2 km) n. **Facility:** Guests enjoy full hotel services when staying in the property's luxurious, fully equipped residences. The all-inclusive plan includes access to a private beach club. 169 kitchen units, some two and three bedrooms. 2-6 stories, exterior corridors. **Parking:** valet only. **Amenities:** safes. **Dining:** 4 restaurants. **Pool(s):** heated outdoor. **Activities:** tennis, recreation programs, kids club, playground, spa. **Guest Services:** valet and coin laundry, area transportation.

## MARIVAL RESORT AND SUITES    (322)226-8200

Resort Hotel
$261-$509

**Address:** Blvd Paseo Cocoteros S/N 63732 **Location:** Oceanfront. Mex 200 exit Nuevo Vallarta, 1.2 mi (2 km) n. **Facility:** A primo beachfront location, excellent dining options and spacious accommodations all add up to top-rate, family-oriented all-inclusive resort. 497 units, some two and three bedrooms. 3-6 stories, interior corridors. **Amenities:** safes. **Dining:** 6 restaurants, entertainment. **Pool(s):** heated outdoor. **Activities:** scuba diving, snorkeling, tennis, recreation programs, kids club, exercise room, spa. **Guest Services:** valet and coin laundry.

## MAYAN PALACE NUEVO VALLARTA    322/226-4000

Resort Hotel
$265-$317

**Address:** Paseo de Las Moras S/N 63732 **Location:** Mex 200 exit Nuevo Vallarta, 1.3 mi (2 km) n. **Facility:** Guests enjoy comfortable rooms with a distinct Mexican décor. The impressive resort's huge pool overlooks the ocean. 100 units, some efficiencies. 7 stories, interior corridors. **Parking:** valet only. **Terms:** check-in 5 pm, 2-7 night minimum stay, 7 day cancellation notice-fee imposed, resort fee. **Amenities:** safes. **Dining:** 3 restaurants, also, Havana Moon, see separate listing, entertainment. **Pool(s):** heated outdoor. **Activities:** regulation golf, recreation programs, game room. **Guest Services:** valet and coin laundry. *(See ad on insert, p. 467.)*

## MAYAN SEA GARDEN NUEVO VALLARTA    322/226-4000

Hotel
$159-$218

**Address:** Paseo de Las Moras S/N 63735 **Location:** Mex 200 exit Nuevo Vallarta, 1.3 mi (2 km) n. **Facility:** 182 units, some efficiencies. 7 stories, exterior corridors. **Parking:** on-site (fee) and valet. **Terms:** check-in 5 pm, 2-7 night minimum stay, 7 day cancellation notice-fee imposed. **Amenities:** safes. **Pool(s):** heated outdoor. **Activities:** recreation programs. **Guest Services:** valet and coin laundry.

## OCCIDENTAL GRAND NUEVO VALLARTA ALL INCLUSIVE
(322)226-9800

**Contemporary Resort Hotel** $284-$335 **Address:** Paseo de Los Cocoteros No. 18 63732 **Location:** Oceanfront. Mex 200 exit Nuevo Vallarta, 1.3 mi (2 km) n. **Facility:** Guests are greeted by bright, contemporary décor and stunning ocean views from the lobby lounge. You'll also enjoy the large tropical pool and the extensive, well-landscaped grounds. 274 units, some two bedrooms, efficiencies and kitchens. 5 stories, interior corridors. **Parking:** on-site and valet. **Amenities:** safes. **Dining:** 4 restaurants, entertainment. **Pool(s):** heated outdoor. **Activities:** tennis, recreation programs, kids club, bicycles, playground, exercise room, massage. **Guest Services:** valet laundry.

## PARADISE VILLAGE BEACH RESORT & SPA    (322)226-6770

**Resort Hotel** $160-$198 **Address:** Paseo de Los Cocoteros No. 1 63732 **Location:** Oceanfront. Mex 200 exit Nuevo Vallarta, 1.3 mi (2 km) n. **Facility:** Even a zoo is featured at this large-scale resort with such amenities as three pools, a fine beach, several restaurants and many shops. 698 units, some two bedrooms, three bedrooms. 8 stories, interior corridors. **Amenities:** safes. **Dining:** 5 restaurants, also, El Faro de Tulum, Il Pescatore Ristorante, Kaybal Terrace, Mayapan, see separate listings, entertainment. **Pool(s):** heated outdoor. **Activities:** fishing, scuba diving, snorkeling, regulation golf, tennis, recreation programs, bicycles, playground, exercise room, spa. **Guest Services:** valet and coin laundry.

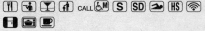

## RIU PALACE PACIFICO    (322)176-0090

Resort Hotel
Rates not provided

**Address:** Ave de Los Cocoteros Lote G 63735 **Location:** Oceanfront. Mex 200 exit Nuevo Vallarta, 1.5 mi (2.4 km) n. **Facility:** This beachfront all-inclusive resort features an elegant lobby with a European ambiance, a great selection of dining options and nightly entertainment. Guest rooms are spacious and well equipped. 450 units. 8 stories, interior corridors. **Amenities:** safes. **Dining:** 5 restaurants, entertainment. **Pool(s):** heated outdoor. **Activities:** sauna, hot tub, recreation programs, spa. **Guest Services:** valet laundry. *(See ad p. 380.)*

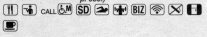

## SAMBA VALLARTA    (322)226-8250

**Hotel** $230-$280 **Address:** Ave Costera y La Playa S/N 63732 **Location:** Oceanfront. Mex 200 exit Nuevo Vallarta, 1.3 mi (2 km) n. **Facility:** 183 units. 4 stories, interior corridors. **Amenities:** safes. **Dining:** 4 restaurants, entertainment. **Pool(s):** heated outdoor. **Activities:** hot tub, steamroom, fishing, scuba diving, tennis, recreation programs, kids club, playground, game room, exercise room, massage. **Guest Services:** valet laundry.

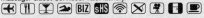

## VILLA DEL PALMAR FLAMINGOS BEACH RESORT AND SPA    (322)226-8100

Resort Hotel
$296-$579

**Address:** Paseo de Los Cocoteros No. 750 Sur 63732 **Location:** Oceanfront. Mex 200 exit Nuevo Vallarta, 1.3 mi (2 km) n. **Facility:** In a prime oceanfront setting, this family-oriented resort features a tropical pool and beach, fully-equipped studios and suites with large balconies and full kitchens. 277 units, some two bedrooms, three bedrooms, efficiencies and kitchens. 8 stories, exterior corridors. **Parking:** on-site and valet. **Amenities:** safes. **Dining:** 2 restaurants, also, El Patron, see separate listing. **Pool(s):** heated outdoor. **Activities:** sauna, hot tub, steamroom, spa. **Guest Services:** valet laundry.

## VILLA LA ESTANCIA
(322)226-9700

Hotel
$278-$618

**Address:** Paseo de Los Cocoteros No. 750 Sur 63732 **Location:** Oceanfront. Mex 200 exit Nuevo Vallarta, 1.3 mi (2 km) n. **Facility:** Located beachfront, the hotel offers spacious, luxury studio units and one-bedroom suites, each fully equipped for upscale leisure. 245 units, some two bedrooms, three bedrooms, efficiencies and kitchens. 8-10 stories, exterior corridors. **Parking:** valet only. **Amenities:** video games, safes. **Dining:** 2 restaurants, also, La Casona, see separate listing. **Pool(s):** heated outdoor. **Activities:** hot tub, recreation programs, spa. **Guest Services:** valet laundry.

### WHERE TO EAT

THE BURGER CUSTOM MADE
322/226-4000
Burgers. Casual Dining. $14-$26 **AAA Inspector Notes:** Not your typical burger restaurant, this place serves exotic specialty burgers made with fine Angus beef, complimented by a fun assortment of condiments and sides. A lineup of other grilled specialties rounds out the menu. Enjoy the ocean breeze on the outdoor patio, or feast in the chic, interior dining area. **Features:** full bar, patio dining. **Address:** Ave Paseo de Las Moras S/N Fracc Nautico Turistico 63735 **Location:** Mex 200 exit Nuevo Vallarta, 1.3 mi (2 km) n; in Grand Luxxe. **Parking:** on-site (fee) and valet.

CIAO!
322/152-6594
Pizza Steak. Casual Dining. $12-$30 **AAA Inspector Notes:** Surrounded by lush tropical greenery, you'll dine under the stars at this cute, patio-style eatery. They specialize in fresh gourmet pizzas but also cook up some hearty steaks and starters. Live entertainment adds to the ambiance and makes you want to linger longer. **Features:** full bar, patio dining. **Address:** Paseo de Los Cocoteros No. 35 63732 **Location:** Mex 200 exit Nuevo Vallarta, 1.3 mi (2 km) n. **Parking:** on-site and street.

EL FARO DE TULUM
322/226-6770
International. Casual Dining. $10-$25 **AAA Inspector Notes:** Open-air dining and an oceanfront setting attract diners to the lovely restaurant, but tasty and creative dishes keep them coming back. The menu blends contemporary Mexican cuisine and seafood specialties. Service is warm and personable, and the setting is comfortable. **Features:** full bar, patio dining. **Address:** Paseo de Los Cocoteros No. 1 63732 **Location:** Mex 200 exit Nuevo Vallarta, 1.3 mi (2 km) n; in Paradise Village Beach Resort & Spa.

EL PATRON
322/226-8100
Mexican. Casual Dining. $10-$45 **AAA Inspector Notes:** Diners can sit indoors or on the terrace, where ocean breezes can be enjoyed. The menu lists a nice mix of local and regional fare. **Features:** full bar, patio dining. **Reservations:** suggested. **Address:** Paseo de Los Cocoteros No. 750 Sur 63732 **Location:** Mex 200 exit Nuevo Vallarta, 1.3 mi (2 km) n; in Villa Del Palmar Flamingos Beach Resort and Spa. **Parking:** valet only.

EL TIGRE CLUB HOUSE RESTAURANT
322/226-6770
International. Casual Dining. $8-$17 **AAA Inspector Notes:** Offering light fare in a casual setting, this pleasant restaurant overlooks the Paradise Village golf course. During the week, the menu features hearty breakfast and light lunches of salads, sandwiches, pastas and burgers. Live entertainment adds spice to the Sunday brunch, where guests can enjoy all-you-can-drink champagne. **Features:** full bar, patio dining, Sunday brunch. **Reservations:** suggested. **Address:** Paseo de Los Cocoteros No. 1 63732 **Location:** Mex 200 exit Nuevo Vallarta, 1.3 mi (2 km) n; at El Tigre Golf Clubhouse.

## EPAZOTE
322/226-2400

Mexican
Fine Dining
$17-$27

**AAA Inspector Notes:** Dining here you'll enjoy unique Mexican cuisine while gazing at some striking, contemporary art in the lobby of the Grand Luxxe. If you prefer the tropical feel, there's also an elegant outdoor patio. The chef has crafted an interesting menu that celebrates regional Mexican fare, providing a chance to experience different cooking styles. Don't be alarmed when you're served 'rat tails'; they're just one of the many types of hot chile peppers offered. **Features:** full bar. **Reservations:** suggested. **Address:** Ave Paseo de Las Moras S/N Fracc Nautico Turistico 63735 **Location:** Mex 200 exit Nuevo Vallarta, 1.3 mi (2 km) n; in Grand Luxxe. **Parking:** on-site (fee) and valet.

ESTUDIO CAFE
322/297-0820
Mexican. Casual Dining. $8-$18 **AAA Inspector Notes:** You'll find this down-to-earth cafe packed on Saturday and Sunday mornings for the very popular breakfast and waterside art show. You may have to wait for a table, but this spot by the marina is a relaxing place to hang out. The menu features freshly prepared home-style fare with a Mexican touch, and always has changing daily specials. **Features:** full bar, patio dining. **Address:** Paseo de La Marina No. 31 63735 **Location:** At Marina Nuevo.

ETC. BEACH CLUB BAR & RESTAURANT
322/297-0174
International. Casual Dining. $8-$15 **AAA Inspector Notes:** Here you'll find a great place to hang out and kick-back for the afternoon while munching on fresh, locally made fare. You're encouraged to stay as long as you want, play at the beach and relax at the club. Lunch begins at 11 am and lasts until 7 pm, so you can even catch an early dinner or a glass of wine before the sun sets. **Features:** full bar, patio dining. **Address:** Paseo de Los Cocoteros No. 36 63735 **Location:** Directly on the beach; in Zona Hotelera.

FAJITA REPUBLIC TROPICAL GRILL
322/297-2277
American. Casual Dining. $9-$27 **AAA Inspector Notes:** As the name implies, fajitas are a must-order at this open-air restaurant, a fun spot to kick back with a cold cerveza or margarita. In addition to the usual fajita suspects (beef, chicken, shrimp), you'll find exotic choices such as lobster tail. For a taste of home, try the fall-off-the-bone barbecued ribs special. At night, drop-down bamboo lights lend to the tropical ambiance. Strolling musicians provide the soundtrack. And if you sit on the balcony, you may even meet the resident raccoon. **Features:** full bar, patio dining. **Reservations:** suggested. **Address:** Paseo de Los Cocoteros Lote 8, Villa 8 63732 **Location:** Mex 200 exit Nuevo Vallarta, 1.3 mi (2 km) n.

## FRIDA
322/226-8000

Mexican
Fine Dining
$20-$40

**AAA Inspector Notes:** From the thoughtful menu planning to the bright and colorful décor, it's the attention to detail that makes this a truly memorable fine dining experience. The chef uses timeless recipes to create an extensive menu featuring freshly prepared Mexican fare from various regions of the country. The wine list offers a nice variety of Mexican wines. Servers specialize in tableside preparations; don't miss the made-to-order guacamole. **Features:** full bar. **Reservations:** required. Semiformal attire. **Address:** Ave Cocoteros Sur No. 98 63735 **Location:** Mex 200 exit Nuevo Vallarta, 1.3 mi (2 km) n; in Grand Velas Riviera Nayarit. **Parking:** valet only.

GONG
322/226-4000
Asian. Casual Dining. $15-$28 **AAA Inspector Notes:** For those who love a variety in cooking, this is a winning choice. Patrons choose from freshly prepared sushi and a variety of specialty fried rice dishes, or they can opt to go for the gusto with the Peking duck specialty. The milieu is delightful. A lovely fountain and huge Asian statue serve as backdrop for the open-air patio tables. Inside, you'll dine in a dramatic setting, complete with soaring ceilings and plush, red velvet drapes. **Features:** full bar, patio dining. **Reservations:** required. **Address:** Paseo de Las Moras S/N 63735 **Location:** Mex 200 exit Nuevo Vallarta, 1.3 mi (2 km) n; in The Grand Mayan Nuevo Vallarta. **Parking:** valet only.

**GUIDO NAPOLI ITALIAN RESTAURANT**    322/297-1061

▼▼▼ Italian. Casual Dining. $8-$18 **AAA Inspector Notes:** Casual, home-style Italian fare is what makes this place special and keeps the locals coming back for more. Expect to find made-to-order pizzas and fresh, well-prepared pasta dishes in hearty portions. Both indoor and outdoor patio dining is available. The friendly staff is great, making it a fun place to eat. **Features:** full bar, patio dining. **Address:** Blvd Nayarit Villa 5 Local 2 63732 **Location:** Mex 200 exit Nuevo Vallarta, 1.3 mi (2 km) n. **Parking:** street only. [D] [AC] [⬡]

**HAVANA MOON**    322/226-4000

▼▼▼ International. Casual Dining. $12-$25 **AAA Inspector Notes:** This casual restaurant features an upbeat, contemporary decor on the inside and a romantic open-air dining terrace overlooking the ocean. The menu features a good mix of international fare and caters well to families. As the name suggests, guests can gaze up at the moon and stars on clear nights. **Features:** full bar, patio dining. **Reservations:** suggested. **Address:** Paseo de Las Moras S/N 63732 **Location:** Mex 200 exit Nuevo Vallarta, 1.3 mi (2 km) n; in Mayan Palace Nuevo Vallarta. **Parking:** valet only. [D] [AC]

**IL PESCATORE RISTORANTE**    322/226-6670

▼▼▼ Italian. Fine Dining. $11-$32 **AAA Inspector Notes:** Set on the peaceful side of the marina, the open-air restaurant boasts a romantic setting and a fine menu of freshly prepared Italian cuisine. The chef features fresh local seafood, including a particularly popular grilled lobster entrée served with a side of tasty pasta. The eatery proves to be a wonderful spot to linger over a glass of wine and a fine meal. **Reservations:** suggested. **Address:** Paseo de Los Cocoteros No. 1 63732 **Location:** Mex 200 exit Nuevo Vallarta, 1.3 mi (2 km) n; in Paradise Village Beach Resort & Spa. [D]

**KAYBAL TERRACE**    322/226-6770

▼▼▼ Seafood. Casual Dining. $20-$35 **AAA Inspector Notes:** A snack bar by day, this space transforms by night into a romantic beachfront restaurant where fine fresh local and regional seafood is served on a terrace under the twinkling stars. Some nights feature special theme menus and live entertainment. **Features:** full bar, patio dining. **Reservations:** suggested. **Address:** Paseo de Los Cocoteros No. 1 63732 **Location:** Mex 200 exit Nuevo Vallarta, 1.3 mi (2 km) n; in Paradise Village Beach Resort & Spa. [D] [AC]

**LA CASONA**    322/226-9700

▼▼▼ Steak. Fine Dining. $32-$45 **AAA Inspector Notes:** Live music boosts the atmosphere on the open-air terrace and in the semi-enclosed dining room. Tropical night breezes cool diners as they savor succulent steaks and fine international fare. **Features:** full bar, patio dining. **Reservations:** suggested. **Address:** Paseo de Los Cocoteros No. 750 Sur 63732 **Location:** Mex 200 exit Nuevo Vallarta, 1.3 mi (2 km) n; in Villa La Estancia. **Parking:** valet only. [B]

**LA DOLCE VITA**    322/297-0403

▼▼▼ Italian. Casual Dining. $10-$22 **AAA Inspector Notes:** A bustling atmosphere, friendly servers and a great selection of cooked-to-order pizzas, pasta and grilled items make this a very popular spot. Reservations aren't taken, but the wait for a table passes quickly at the bar, a nice spot for a pre-meal drink. The dining room is air conditioned, but on pleasant days the cozy outdoor patio is the place to be. **Features:** full bar, patio dining. **Address:** Ave Paseo de Las Palmas No. 2 63732 **Location:** Mex 200, 2nd entrance to Nuevo Vallarta; at La Plaza 3.14. **Parking:** street only. [L] [D]

**LA LAGUNA TINO'S**    329/297-0221

▼▼▼ Seafood. Casual Dining. $10-$22 **AAA Inspector Notes:** The delightful open-air eatery fronts a lagoon filled with sea turtles. Iguana sightings are also a good bet in this natural setting. The menu features both local and regional Mexican fare with an emphasis on fresh fish and seafood. Cooked-to-order shrimp is one of the house specialties. **Features:** full bar, patio dining. **Address:** La Jarretaderas S/N 63735 **Location:** At 2nd entrance to Nuevo Vallarta. [L] [D] [AC]

**LE COIN DES AMIS**    322/297-7457

▼▼▼ French. Casual Dining. $12-$23 **AAA Inspector Notes:** These guys are now well established and a favorite with many locals. Offering a great variety of fine cuisine, an ever-changing blackboard menu reflects the freshest ingredients of the season. The chef prepares a good assortment of sauces in the traditional French fashion. I enjoyed the rich cordon bleu with a creamy mushroom sauce--a rare find in the area. The covered outdoor patio area is relaxing, and a small indoor area also is available. **Features:** full bar, patio dining. **Address:** Blvd Nayarit No. 400 Local 3 63732 **Location:** Mex 200 exit Nuevo Vallarta, 1.3 mi (2 km) n. **Parking:** street only. [B] [L] [D] [AC]

**LUCCA**    322/226-8000

Italian Fine Dining $20-$38

**AAA Inspector Notes:** A pianist entertains guests who sit down in the elegant dining room to a fine meal of classic Italian cuisine. **Features:** full bar. **Reservations:** required. **Address:** Ave Cocoteros Sur No. 98 63735 **Location:** Mex 200 exit Nuevo Vallarta, 1.3 mi (2 km) n; in Grand Velas Riviera Nayarit. **Parking:** valet only. [D]

**MAYAPAN**    322/226-6770

▼▼ International. Casual Dining. $12-$32 **AAA Inspector Notes:** Sea breezes wash over the large open-air terrace, where patrons sit down to international dishes prepared with Mexican touches. Live entertainment enhances the atmosphere most evenings. It's a good idea to phone ahead for information about theme nights, which may include barbecue or Western nights. **Features:** full bar, patio dining. **Reservations:** suggested. **Address:** Paseo de Los Cocoteros No. 1 **Location:** Mex 200 exit Nuevo Vallarta, 1.3 mi (2 km) n; in Paradise Village Beach Resort & Spa. [D] [AC]

**NICKSAN**    322/297-2464

▼▼▼ Japanese Sushi. Casual Dining. $12-$28 **AAA Inspector Notes:** The blending of Japanese cuisine with traditional Mexican fare is the chef's innovative specialty. For example, take the raw tuna with mango and chile. It's a simple combination, yet surprisingly the interplay of flavors is intriguing and exotic. Obviously, fresh fish and seafood play key roles on the menu. But there also are traditional tempura and teriyaki dishes for the less adventurous. Befitting the cuisine, both the dining room and outdoor patio offer peaceful settings. **Features:** full bar, patio dining. **Address:** Paseo Cocoteros No. 53 63732 **Location:** Mex 200 exit Nuevo Vallarta, 1.3 mi (2 km) n. **Parking:** street only. [L] [D]

**PALM TERRACE**    322/226-1050

▼▼ International. Casual Dining. $7-$20 **AAA Inspector Notes:** This restaurant's outdoor patio boasts a wonderful oceanfront setting. The menu is casual and varied. Some evenings, the patio transforms into a grill, where fine cuts of beef, chicken and seafood are cooked to order. On cooler evenings, you may want to opt for the elegant, indoor dining area. **Features:** full bar, patio dining. **Address:** Blvd Costero No. 800 Sur 63732 **Location:** Mex 200 exit Nuevo Vallarta, 1.3 mi (2 km) n; in Bel Air Collection Resort and Spa Vallarta. [B] [D]

**PIAF**    322/226-8000

▼▼▼▼ French Fine Dining $22-$44

**AAA Inspector Notes:** Classic French cuisine is presented in a serene room with sunset views over the ocean. The attentive staff will see to your every need, offering dishes such as foie gras terrine, escargot, and veal kidneys with Dijon mustard sauce. You may choose to end your meal with the peach melba, which is a cool delight, or the enticing saffron crème brûlée. **Features:** full bar. **Reservations:** required, for non-hotel guests. **Address:** Ave Cocoteros Sur No. 98 63735 **Location:** Mex 200 exit Nuevo Vallarta, 1.3 mi (2 km) n; in Grand Velas Riviera Nayarit. **Parking:** valet only. [D]

**PORTO BELLO BISTRO AND LOUNGE**    322/297-6719

▼▼▼ Italian. Casual Dining. $15-$30 **AAA Inspector Notes:** For good Italian fare, both traditional and innovative, it's tough to beat this restaurant offering indoor and outdoor terrace dining. Very popular with locals and visitors alike, it's a wise move to phone ahead for reservations. **Features:** full bar, patio dining. **Reservations:** suggested. **Address:** Ave Nayarit Lote 22 Villa 5 63732 **Location:** At Centro Comercial Nuevo Vallarta Plaza and Business Center Local 4. **Parking:** street only. [L] [D]

## PRIME 159
322/297-6442

⬥⬥⬥ Steak. Casual Dining. $12-$35 **AAA Inspector Notes:** The restaurant's upbeat, contemporary dining room offers a fine spot to feast on well-portioned, grilled-to-order steaks, chops and seafood. If the weather's nice, an outdoor table with a view of the boats is a nice option. For those who want to catch the big game on TV, there's also seating in the sports bar. **Features:** full bar, patio dining. **Reservations:** suggested. **Address:** Nuevo Vallarta Plaza & Business Center Local 13 63732 **Location:** In Centro Comercial Nuevo Vallarta Plaza and Business Center. **Parking:** valet only.

L  D

## PUNTA ARENA
322/226-4000

⬥⬥⬥ Seafood. Casual Dining. $18-$48 **AAA Inspector Notes:** Palms sway in the sea breeze. At night, the tables in the open-air dining room are candlelit, setting a romantic mood. The service is warm and personable, and the waiters go out of their way to provide a wonderful dining experience. Menu highlights include tasty soups, a variety of hot and cold appetizers, pastas and a selection of fresh seafood and grilled meats. **Features:** full bar, patio dining. **Reservations:** suggested. **Address:** Ave Paseo de Las Moras S/N Nautico Turistico 63735 **Location:** Mex 200 exit Nuevo Vallarta, 1.3 mi (2 km) n; in Grand Luxxe. D

## RESTAURANT RIVIERA GRILL
322/297-6545

⬥⬥⬥ International. Casual Dining. $16-$28 **AAA Inspector Notes:** At this hidden treasure, set off the main tourist road in Nuevo Vallarta, the owners have created a tranquil garden patio setting, full of tropical plants and trees. The candlelit tables and live entertainment set the tone for a relaxing and memorable dining experience. The varied menu always features fresh fish and seafood, as well as a variety of typical Mexican dishes. We also enjoy the homemade pastas. Many items are sized for sharing. Save room for the exotic desserts. **Features:** full bar, patio dining. **Address:** Paseo de Los Cocoteros No. 33 63732 **Location:** Mex 200 exit Nuevo Vallarta, 1.3 mi (2 km) n. D

## RINCON DE BUENOS AIRES
322/297-4950

⬥⬥ Steak. Casual Dining. $12-$28 **AAA Inspector Notes:** This is a great spot to indulge in a fine grilled steak and good old-fashioned baked potato. The chefs broil your meal over a wood fire, creating an amazing flavor. With a fun children's play area in the restaurant's garden, this is a perfect place for family dining. **Features:** full bar, patio dining. **Address:** Blvd Nayarit No. 250 63735 **Location:** Off Mex 200, 2nd entrance to Nuevo Vallarta.

L  D

## SAMBA RESTAURANT
322/226-4000

⬥⬥⬥ International. Casual Dining. $12-$30 **AAA Inspector Notes:** This open-air restaurant overlooks the huge Grand Mayan Resort's pool and fountain. The menu features a nice mix of International fare; grilled meats and seafood are the specialties. **Features:** full bar, patio dining. **Reservations:** suggested. **Address:** Paseo de Las Moras S/N 63735 **Location:** Mex 200 exit Nuevo Vallarta, 1.3 mi (2 km) n; in The Grand Mayan Nuevo Vallarta. **Parking:** on-site and valet. B  L  D

## TRAMONTO
322/226-4000

⬥⬥⬥ International. Fine Dining. $15-$45 **AAA Inspector Notes:** Chic contemporary design characterizes the main dining room, while a breezier feel prevails on several covered patio areas. The innovative menu features fine Italian and international fare. **Features:** full bar, patio dining. **Reservations:** suggested, for non-hotel guests. **Address:** Paseo de Las Moras S/N 63735 **Location:** Mex 200 exit Nuevo Vallarta, 1.3 mi (2 km) n; in The Grand Mayan Nuevo Vallarta. **Parking:** on-site (fee). D

## PUERTO ESCONDIDO, OAXACA

## HOTEL SANTA FE
(954)582-0170

⬥⬥ **Hotel.** Rates not provided. **Address:** Calle del Morro S/N 71980 **Location:** 0.5 mi (0.8 km) s of town off Mex 200, just w to Playa Zicatela. **Facility:** 60 units. 3 stories (no elevator), exterior corridors. *Bath:* shower only. **Terms:** 30 day cancellation notice, 7 day off season. **Amenities:** safes. **Dining:** restaurant, see separate listing. **Pool(s):** outdoor. **Activities:** beach access. **Guest Services:** valet laundry.

## POSADA REAL PUERTO ESCONDIDO
954/582-0133

**fyi** Not evaluated. **Address:** Blvd Benito Juárez S/N 71980 **Location:** 1.4 mi (2.2 km) n of jct Mex 200 and 131, 0.6 mi (1 km) s of airport, 0.3 mi (0.5 km) w; in Zona Hotelera. Facilities, services, and décor characterize an economy property.

### WHERE TO EAT

## HOTEL SANTA FE RESTAURANT
954/582-0170

⬥⬥ International. Casual Dining. $12-$27 **AAA Inspector Notes:** This open-air restaurant features a thatched roof, leather tables and chairs and an outstanding view of the ocean from its raised balcony. The menu has a strong focus on vegetarian fare but also lists pasta dishes, Mexican specialties and made-to-order shrimp, fish and other seafood. **Features:** full bar, patio dining. **Address:** Calle del Morro S/N 71980 **Location:** 0.5 mi (0.8 km) s of town off Mex 200, just w to Playa Zicatela; in Hotel Santa Fe. **Parking:** street only. B  L  D

## COCO'S
954/582-0133

**fyi** Not evaluated. Lush tropical gardens surround this beachfront eatery's lovely setting, which overlooks the pool and ocean. The menu features a mix of light and international fare, including burgers, sandwiches and nachos, as well as grilled fish, seafood and chicken. A children's menu is also offered. **Address:** Blvd Benito Juárez S/N 71980 **Location:** 1.4 mi (2.2 km) n of jct Mex 200 and 131, 0.6 mi (1 km) s of airport, 0.3 mi (0.5 km) w; in Posada Real Puerto Escondido.

## HACIENDA RESTAURANT
954/582-0133

**fyi** Not evaluated. A peaceful feel marks the covered open-air dining room, which overlooks a tropical pool and gardens. The menu focuses on simple fare, including Mexican and international specialties such as shrimp cocktail filled with fresh shrimp and chopped avocado, tortilla soup and preparations of pasta, grilled chicken and seafood. **Address:** Blvd Benito Juárez S/N 71980 **Location:** 1.4 mi (2.2 km) n of jct Mex 200 and 131, 0.6 mi (1 km) s of airport, 0.3 mi (0.5 km) w; in Zona Hotelera; in Posada Real Puerto Escondido.

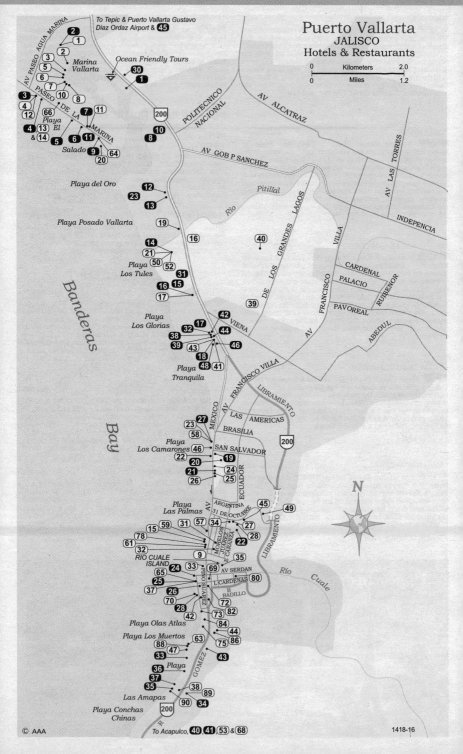

# Puerto Vallarta
## JALISCO
### Hotels & Restaurants

Kilometers 0 — 2.0
Miles 0 — 1.2

To Tepic & Puerto Vallarta Gustavo
Diaz Ordaz Airport & 45

Ocean Friendly Tours

Marina
Vallarta

AV PASEO AGUA MARINA

PASEO DE LA MARINA

Playa El Salado

Playa del Oro

Playa Posado Vallarta

Playa Los Tules

Playa Los Glorias

Playa Tranquila

Playa Los Camarones

Playa Las Palmas

RÍO CUALE ISLAND

Playa Olas Atlas

Playa Los Muertos

Playa

Las Amapas

Playa Conchas Chinas

Banderas Bay

POLITECNICO NACIONAL

AV ALCATRAZ

AV GOB P SANCHEZ

Río Pitillal

AV LAS TORRES

INDEPENCIA

DE LOS GRANDES LAGOS

AV FRANCISCO VILLA

CARDENAL

PALACIO

PAVOREAL

RUISEÑOR

ABEDUL

AV FRANCISCO VILLA

LIBRAMIENTO

AV LAS AMERICAS

BRASILIA

SAN SALVADOR

ECUADOR

ARGENTINA

31 DE OCTUBRE

AV MEXICO

MORELOS

JUAREZ

I DE CARANZA

PINO SUAREZ

GOMEZ

AV SERDAN

L. CARDENAS

B BADILLO

Río Cuale

N

To Acapulco, 40 41 53 & 68

© AAA

1418-16

# Puerto Vallarta

This index helps you "spot" where approved hotels and restaurants are located on the corresponding detailed maps. Hotel daily rate range is for comparison only. Restaurant price range is a combination of lunch and/or dinner. Turn to the listing page for more detailed rate and price information and consult display ads for special promotions.

## PUERTO VALLARTA, JALISCO

| Map Page | Hotels | Diamond Rated | Rate Range | Page |
|---|---|---|---|---|
| **1** p. 472 | Comfort Inn | ▼▼ | $60-$125 | 478 |
| **2** p. 472 | **Casa Velas Hotel Boutique** *(See ad on insert.)* | ▼▼▼▼ | $500-$800 | 478 |
| **3** p. 472 | Velas Vallarta Suite Resort & Convention Center *(See ad on insert.)* | ▼▼▼ | $440-$720 | 482 |
| **4** p. 472 | **CasaMagna Marriott Puerto Vallarta Resort & Spa** *(See ad on p. 479.)* | ▼▼▼ | $80-$378 | 478 |
| **5** p. 472 | Melia Vacation Club Puerto Vallarta | ▼▼▼ | $440 | 481 |
| **6** p. 472 | **Mayan Palace Puerto Vallarta** *(See ad on insert, p. 467.)* | ▼▼▼ | $265-$317 | 481 |
| **7** p. 472 | Vamar Vallarta All Inclusive Marina & Beach Resort | ▼▼ | $146-$250 | 482 |
| **8** p. 472 | Crown Paradise Club | ▼▼▼ | $187-$281 | 478 |
| **9** p. 472 | **The Westin Resort and Spa Puerto Vallarta** | ▼▼▼▼ | $85-$450 | 483 |
| **10** p. 472 | Crown Paradise Golden-Adults All Inclusive | ▼▼▼ | $303-$454 | 478 |
| **11** p. 472 | Villa Vera Puerto Vallarta | ▼▼ | $93-$123 | 482 |
| **12** p. 472 | Hacienda Buenaventura Hotel Spa & Beach Club | ▼▼ | $140-$200 | 478 |
| **13** p. 472 | **Krystal Puerto Vallarta** | ▼▼▼ | $100-$200 | 481 |
| **14** p. 472 | Holiday Inn Resort Puerto Vallarta | ▼▼ | $109-$139 | 480 |
| **15** p. 472 | Friendly Vallarta | ▼▼▼ | $194-$300 | 478 |
| **16** p. 472 | **Fiesta Americana Puerto Vallarta All Inclusive & Spa** | ▼▼▼ | $245-$480 | 478 |
| **17** p. 472 | Las Palmas by the Sea | ▼▼ | $144-$290 | 481 |
| **18** p. 472 | **Sheraton Buganvilias Resort & Convention Center** | ▼▼▼ | Rates not provided | 482 |
| **19** p. 472 | **Buenaventura Grand Hotel & Spa Puerto Vallarta** | ▼▼▼ | $176-$400 | 477 |
| **20** p. 472 | Hotel El Pescador | ▼▼ | $88-$190 | 480 |
| **21** p. 472 | Hotel Rosita | ▼▼ | $88-$190 | 480 |
| **22** p. 472 | Hacienda San Angel | ▼▼▼▼ | $435-$750 | 480 |
| **23** p. 472 | **Hilton Puerto Vallarta Resort** | ▼▼▼▼ | $249-$569 | 480 |
| **24** p. 472 | Casa Dona Susana | ▼▼ | $78-$102 | 477 |
| **25** p. 472 | **Playa Los Arcos Beach Resort & Spa** | ▼▼ | $88-$145 | 481 |
| **26** p. 472 | Los Arcos Suites | ▼▼ | $89-$110 | 481 |
| **27** p. 472 | **Villa Premiere Hotel & Spa** | ▼▼▼▼ | $157-$341 | 482 |
| **28** p. 472 | Hotel San Marino | ▼▼ | $120-$220 | 480 |
| **30** p. 472 | Holiday Inn Express Puerto Vallarta | ▼▼▼ | $90-$140 | 480 |
| **31** p. 472 | Villa del Palmar | ▼▼ | $141-$387 | 482 |
| **32** p. 472 | Plaza Pelicanos Grand Beach Resort | ▼▼▼ | $290 | 481 |
| **33** p. 472 | **Hyatt Ziva Puerto Vallarta** | ▼▼▼▼ | $163-$720 | 481 |
| **34** p. 472 | **Hotel Mousai** *(See ad on insert.)* | ▼▼▼▼▼ | $500-$750 | 480 |

## PUERTO VALLARTA, JALISCO (cont'd)

| Map Page | Hotels (cont'd) | Diamond Rated | Rate Range | Page |
|---|---|---|---|---|
| 35 p. 472 | BEST WESTERN PLUS Suites Puerto Vallarta | ◇◇◇ | Rates not provided | 477 |
| 36 p. 472 | Costa Sur Resort & Spa | ◇◇ | $100-$200 | 478 |
| 37 p. 472 | Garza Blanca Preserve, Resort & Spa *(See ad on insert.)* | ◇◇◇◇ | $320-$420 | 478 |
| 38 p. 472 | Sunset Plaza Beach Resort & Spa | ◇◇◇◇ | $329-$411 | 482 |
| 39 p. 472 | Plaza Pelicanos Club Beach Resort | ◇◇ | $211 | 481 |
| 40 p. 472 | Barcelo Puerto Vallarta | ◇◇◇ | $286-$372 | 477 |
| 41 p. 472 | Casa Iguana Hotel de Mismaloya | ◇◇ | $105-$133 | 477 |
| 42 p. 472 | Canto Del Sol Plaza Vallarta | ◇◇ | $193-$209 | 477 |
| 43 p. 472 | Hotel Grand Miramar Puerto Vallarta | ◇◇◇ | $251-$552 | 480 |
| 44 p. 472 | Villas Vallarta by Canto del Sol | ◇◇ | $75-$85 | 482 |
| 45 p. 472 | Hotel One Puerto Vallarta Aeropuerto | ◇◇ | $60-$120 | 480 |
| 46 p. 472 | Now Amber | ◇◇◇◇ | $454-$1210 | 481 |
| 48 p. 472 | Secrets Vallarta Bay | ◇◇◇◇ | $500-$1390 | 482 |

| Map Page | Restaurants | Diamond Rated | Cuisine | Price Range | Page |
|---|---|---|---|---|---|
| 1 p. 472 | Emiliano | ◇◇◇◇ | International | $12-$35 | 484 |
| 2 p. 472 | Victor's Place Cafe Tacuba Restaurant | ◇◇ | Mexican | $8-$17 | 487 |
| 3 p. 472 | Rincon de Buenos Aires | ◇◇ | Argentine Steak | $10-$30 | 487 |
| 4 p. 472 | La Ribera Restaurant | ◇◇ | Steak | $12-$24 | 485 |
| 5 p. 472 | Terrazza di Roma Ristorante Italiano | ◇◇◇ | Italian | $8-$26 | 487 |
| 6 p. 472 | Fajita Banana Tropical Grill & Bar | ◇◇ | American | $9-$17 | 484 |
| 7 p. 472 | Las Palomas Doradas | ◇◇ | International | $8-$20 | 486 |
| 8 p. 472 | Porto Bello Ristorante Italiano | ◇◇◇ | Italian | $14-$40 | 487 |
| 9 p. 472 | Vitea Oceanfront Bistro | ◇◇◇ | International | $8-$25 | 488 |
| 10 p. 472 | D'z Route 66 Rock N Roll Diner | ◇◇ | American | $6-$18 | 484 |
| 11 p. 472 | Las Casitas | ◇◇◇ | International | $15-$28 | 486 |
| 12 p. 472 | Andrea Gourmet | ◇◇◇ | International | $10-$35 | 483 |
| 13 p. 472 | Mikado | ◇◇◇ | Japanese | $20-$35 | 486 |
| 14 p. 472 | La Estancia | ◇◇◇ | Mexican | $16-$24 | 485 |
| 15 p. 472 | Viejo Vallarta | ◇◇ | Mexican | $10-$22 | 487 |
| 16 p. 472 | Pizzeria La Dolce | ◇◇ | Italian Pizza | $8-$16 | 487 |
| 17 p. 472 | La Leche | ◇◇◇ | International | $17-$28 | 485 |
| 19 p. 472 | De Santos | ◇◇◇ | International | $12-$25 | 484 |
| 20 p. 472 | Arrecifes Seafood and Steakhouse | ◇◇◇ | Seafood Steak | $18-$30 | 483 |
| 21 p. 472 | Restaurante Mariaches | ◇◇ | Mexican | $14-$20 | 487 |
| 22 p. 472 | Mariscos Tino's | ◇◇ | Seafood | $15-$25 | 486 |
| 23 p. 472 | Murales | ◇◇◇ | Mexican | $11-$23 | 486 |
| 24 p. 472 | La Dolce Vita Ristorante Bar | ◇◇ | Italian | $12-$29 | 485 |
| 25 p. 472 | Paradise Burger | ◇◇ | American | $8-$18 | 486 |

| Map Page | Restaurants (cont'd) | Diamond Rated | Cuisine | Price Range | Page |
|---|---|---|---|---|---|
| 26 p. 472 | La Chata de Guadalajara | ♦♦ | Mexican | $8-$22 | 485 |
| 27 p. 472 | Cafe des Artistes | ♦♦♦ | French | $20-$28 | 483 |
| 28 p. 472 | Hacienda San Angel Gourmet | ♦♦♦ | International | $21-$47 | 484 |
| 31 p. 472 | Trio Restaurant | ♦♦♦ | Mediterranean | $18-$29 | 487 |
| 32 p. 472 | The Blue Shrimp Restaurant | ♦♦♦ | Seafood | $16-$40 | 483 |
| 33 p. 472 | Oscar's Fine Cuisine | ♦♦♦ | International | $9-$30 | 486 |
| 34 p. 472 | **El Arrayan** | ♦♦♦ | Mexican | $16-$24 | 484 |
| 35 p. 472 | The River Cafe | ♦♦♦ | International | $12-$30 | 487 |
| 37 p. 472 | Kaiser Maximilian | ♦♦♦ | Austrian | $15-$27 | 484 |
| 38 p. 472 | Blanca Blue | ♦♦♦ | International | $12-$30 | 483 |
| 39 p. 472 | Las Adelitas | ♦♦ | Mexican | $9-$22 | 485 |
| 40 p. 472 | Las Carmelitas | ♦♦ | Mexican | $18-$28 | 485 |
| 41 p. 472 | **La Villita** | ♦♦ | International | $10-$25 | 486 |
| 42 p. 472 | Daiquiri Dick's | ♦♦♦ | International | $16-$29 | 484 |
| 43 p. 472 | Gaviotas | ♦♦♦ | International | $15-$29 | 484 |
| 44 p. 472 | **Vista Grill** | ♦♦♦♦ | International | $20-$32 | 488 |
| 45 p. 472 | Si Senor | ♦♦♦ | Mexican | $15-$35 | 487 |
| 46 p. 472 | El Andariego Restaurante and Bar | ♦♦ | Mexican | $8-$30 | 484 |
| 47 p. 472 | **La Palapa Restaurante and Bar** | ♦♦♦ | International | $16-$50 | 485 |
| 49 p. 472 | Barcelona Tapas | ♦♦♦ | Spanish | $9-$24 | 483 |
| 50 p. 472 | La Guacamaya Restaurant | ♦♦ | International | $10-$22 | 485 |
| 52 p. 472 | Piaceres Restaurant | ♦♦♦ | International | $14-$25 | 487 |
| 53 p. 472 | Le Kliff Restaurante and Bar | ♦♦♦ | Seafood | $16-$45 | 486 |
| 57 p. 472 | La Bodeguita Del Medio | ♦♦ | Cuban | $8-$18 | 485 |
| 58 p. 472 | La Corona | ♦♦♦ | International | $16-$29 | 485 |
| 59 p. 472 | Cheeky Monkey | ♦♦ | American | $8-$18 | 483 |
| 61 p. 472 | Mi Querencia | ♦♦ | Mexican | $8-$20 | 486 |
| 63 p. 472 | Si Senor Mexican Restaurant and Beach Club | ♦♦♦ | Mexican | $10-$28 | 487 |
| 64 p. 472 | El Palmar | ♦♦♦ | International | $12-$30 | 484 |
| 65 p. 472 | Mi Pueblito Restaurant | ♦♦ | International | $8-$25 | 486 |
| 66 p. 472 | Sonora Grill Prime | ♦♦♦ | Steak | $16-$40 | 487 |
| 68 p. 472 | Chico's Paradise | ♦♦ | Mexican | $10-$24 | 483 |
| 69 p. 472 | Margarita Grill | ♦♦ | Mexican | $9-$24 | 486 |
| 70 p. 472 | Archie's Wok | ♦♦♦ | Asian | $10-$25 | 483 |
| 72 p. 472 | Fajita Republic | ♦♦ | Mexican | $10-$22 | 484 |
| 73 p. 472 | Coco Tropical | ♦♦♦ | International | $10-$29 | 483 |
| 75 p. 472 | La Piazzetta Ristorante Olas Altas | ♦♦ | Italian | $9-$20 | 485 |
| 78 p. 472 | La Posta | ♦♦ | Italian | $9-$22 | 485 |

| Map Page | Restaurants (cont'd) | Diamond Rated | Cuisine | Price Range | Page |
|---|---|---|---|---|---|
| ⑧⓪ p. 472 | La Vaca Argentina | ▼▼▼ | Steak | $18-$43 | 486 |
| ⑧② p. 472 | No Way José! | ▼▼▼ | Mexican | $15-$22 | 486 |
| ⑧④ p. 472 | The Sea Monkey Restaurant & Bar on the Beach | ▼▼ | American | $8-$18 | 487 |
| ⑧⑥ p. 472 | El Palomar de los Gonzalez | ▼▼▼ | International | $18-$38 | 484 |
| ⑧⑧ p. 472 | Langostino's Bar & Restaurant | ▼▼ | Seafood | $9-$25 | 485 |
| ⑧⑨ p. 472 | Hiroshi | ▼▼▼ | Japanese | $18-$82 | 484 |
| ⑨⓪ p. 472 | Bocados Bites & Meats | ▼▼▼ | Steak | $18-$30 | 483 |

# PUERTO VALLARTA, JALISCO
pop. 255,681
- **Restaurants p. 483**
- **Hotels & Restaurants map & index p. 472**

## BARCELO PUERTO VALLARTA
(322)226-0660 **40**

**Resort Hotel**
**$286-$372**

**Address:** Zona Hotelera Sur KM 11.5 No. 4900 48390 **Location:** Oceanfront. 7.2 mi (11.5 km) s of town center. **Facility:** This all-inclusive resort is loaded with recreational activities and guest room amenities. You'll also find a great view of Los Arcos, and live shows each evening. 316 units, some two bedrooms. 9 stories, exterior corridors. **Amenities:** safes. **Dining:** 4 restaurants, entertainment. **Pool(s):** heated outdoor. **Activities:** hot tub, steamroom, fishing, scuba diving, snorkeling, tennis, recreation programs, kids club, playground, game room, spa. **Guest Services:** valet laundry.

ECO ⓘ ✏ ⓨ ⓕ CALL 🔲 Ⓢ SD ➹ 👷
BIZ $HS 📶 🗗 🖵

## BEST WESTERN PLUS SUITES PUERTO VALLARTA
(322)226-0191 **35**

**Hotel.** Rates not provided.
**Address:** Carr a Barra de Navidad KM 8.5, Zona Hotelera Sur 48390 **Location:** Oceanfront. On Airport Hwy (Mex 200), 5.3 mi (8.5 km) s. **Facility:** 120 units, some two bedrooms. 10 stories, exterior corridors. **Terms:** 3-6 night minimum stay - seasonal and/or weekends, 30 day cancellation notice-fee imposed, resort fee. **Amenities:** *Some:* safes. **Dining:** 2 restaurants. **Pool(s):** heated outdoor. **Activities:** limited beach access, tennis, exercise room, spa. **Guest Services:** valet laundry.

ⓘ ✏ ⓨ ➹ BIZ 📶 ✕ 🗗 🖵

> **AAA Benefit:**
> Save 10% or more every day and earn 10% bonus points!

## BUENAVENTURA GRAND HOTEL & SPA PUERTO VALLARTA
(322)226-7000 **19**

**Resort Hotel**
**$176-$400**

**Address:** Ave Mexico 1301, Col 5 de Diciembre 48350 **Location:** Oceanfront. 0.6 mi (1 km) n on Airport Hwy (Mex 200). **Facility:** This busy all-inclusive hotel is close to the bustle of the town, yet on the outskirts. Rooms have comfortable décor and modern amenities. 232 units. 5 stories, interior corridors. **Amenities:** safes. **Dining:** 3 restaurants, entertainment. **Pool(s):** heated outdoor. **Activities:** hot tub, recreation programs, kids club, exercise room, spa. **Guest Services:** valet laundry.

ⓘ ✏ ⓨ SD ➹ BIZ HS
📶 ✕ 🗗 🖵

## CANTO DEL SOL PLAZA VALLARTA
(322)226-0123 **42**

**Hotel**
**$193-$209**

**Address:** Jose Clemente Orozco No. 125 48333 **Location:** Oceanfront. 1.6 mi (2.5 km) n off Airport Hwy (Mex 200); in Zona Hotelera Norte. **Facility:** 265 units, some efficiencies. 4 stories, interior corridors. *Bath:* shower only. **Parking:** on-site (fee). **Amenities:** safes. **Dining:** 4 restaurants, entertainment. **Pool(s):** heated outdoor. **Activities:** tennis, recreation programs, kids club, exercise room, massage. **Guest Services:** valet laundry.

ⓘ ⓨ ⓕ ➹ BIZ HS 📶
✕ / SOME UNITS 🗗 🖵

## CASA DONA SUSANA
322/226-7100 **24**

**Hotel $78-$102 Address:** Manuel M Dieguez No. 171 48380 **Location:** Centro; in Zona Romantica. **Facility:** 42 units, some efficiencies. 4 stories, interior corridors. *Bath:* shower only. **Terms:** age restrictions may apply. **Amenities:** safes. **Pool(s):** heated outdoor. **Activities:** beach access. **Guest Services:** valet laundry.

ⓘ+ ➹ HS 📶 🗗 / SOME UNITS 🖵

## CASA IGUANA HOTEL DE MISMALOYA
322/228-1162 **41**

**Hotel $105-$133 Address:** Ave 5 de Mayo No. 455 **Location:** 7.2 mi (11.5 km) s of town center. **Facility:** 50 efficiencies, some two and three bedrooms. 4 stories (no elevator), exterior corridors. *Bath:* shower only. **Pool(s):** heated outdoor. **Activities:** hot tub, exercise room.

ⓘ ⓨ ➹ BIZ HS 📶 🗗 / SOME UNITS 🖵

(See map & index p. 472.)

## CASAMAGNA MARRIOTT PUERTO VALLARTA RESORT & SPA
(322)226-0000 **4**

Resort Hotel
$80-$378

**MARRIOTT**

**AAA Benefit:** Members save 5% or more!

**Address:** Paseo La Marina Norte 435 48354 **Location:** 3.1 mi (5 km) n on Airport Hwy (Mex 200); in Marina Vallarta. **Facility:** Here you'll enjoy a prime location and extensive tropical landscaping both inside and out. The modern, well-appointed rooms feature balconies. 433 units. 5-9 stories, interior corridors. **Terms:** check-in 4 pm, 3 day cancellation notice. **Amenities:** safes. **Dining:** 4 restaurants, also, La Estancia, Las Casitas, Mikado, see separate listings. **Pool(s):** heated outdoor, heated indoor. **Activities:** sauna, hot tub, steamroom, tennis, recreation programs, kids club, spa. **Guest Services:** valet laundry. (See ad p. 479.)

## CASA VELAS HOTEL BOUTIQUE
322/226-8060 **2**

Boutique Resort Hotel
$500-$800

**Address:** 311 Pelicanos Marina Vallarta 48354 **Location:** At Marina Vallarta Golf Course. **Facility:** This gated resort features private villas or spacious guestrooms, many with private dip pool and views of the adjoining golf course. 80 units. 4 stories, interior/exterior corridors. **Parking:** valet only. **Terms:** age restrictions may apply. **Amenities:** safes. **Dining:** Emiliano, see separate listing. **Pool(s):** heated outdoor. **Activities:** sauna, hot tub, steamroom, recreation programs, exercise room, spa. **Guest Services:** valet laundry, area transportation. (See ad on insert.)

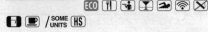

## COMFORT INN
(322)226-7979 **1**

Hotel $60-$125 **Address:** Blvd Francisco Medina Ascencio No. 3965 48335 **Location:** Just off Airport Hwy (Mex 200); adjacent to Marina Vallarta. **Facility:** 121 units, some two bedrooms. 5 stories, interior corridors. **Bath:** shower only. **Amenities:** safes. **Pool(s):** outdoor. **Guest Services:** valet laundry.

## COSTA SUR RESORT & SPA
322/226-8050 **36**

Hotel $100-$200 **Address:** Carr Barra de Navidad KM 4.5 48390 **Location:** Oceanfront. KM 4.5 Carr Puerto Vallarta a Barra de Navidad. **Facility:** 205 units, some two bedrooms, efficiencies and kitchens. 9-14 stories, interior/exterior corridors. **Bath:** shower only. **Amenities:** safes. **Pool(s):** outdoor, heated outdoor. **Activities:** kids club, exercise room, spa. **Guest Services:** valet laundry.

## CROWN PARADISE CLUB
(322)226-6868 **8**

Resort Hotel $187-$281 **Address:** Ave Las Garzas No. 1 48333 **Location:** 3 mi (4.8 km) n off Airport Hwy (Mex 200). **Facility:** This family-oriented property offers an outstanding program for children with an extensive kids club, special menus in the restaurants and an active pool area. Some rooms have bunk beds. 253 units. 4 stories, exterior corridors. **Amenities:** safes. **Dining:** 4 restaurants, nightclub, entertainment. **Pool(s):** heated outdoor. **Activities:** hot tub, scuba diving, snorkeling, tennis, recreation programs, kids club, playground, game room, exercise room, spa. **Guest Services:** valet laundry.

## CROWN PARADISE GOLDEN-ADULTS ALL INCLUSIVE
(322)226-6800 **10**

Resort Hotel $303-$454 **Address:** Paseo de las Garzas No. 3 48333 **Location:** 3 mi (4.8 km) n off Airport Hwy (Mex 200). **Facility:** This all-inclusive, adults-only resort on a lovely stretch of beach welcomes guests who are 18 and over; rooms are spacious and well appointed. 214 units, some efficiencies. 7-8 stories, exterior corridors. **Terms:** age restrictions may apply. **Amenities:** safes. **Dining:** 4 restaurants, nightclub, entertainment. **Pool(s):** heated outdoor. **Activities:** hot tub, scuba diving, snorkeling, tennis, recreation programs, exercise room, spa. **Guest Services:** valet laundry.

## FIESTA AMERICANA PUERTO VALLARTA ALL INCLUSIVE & SPA
(322)226-2100 **16**

Hotel
$245-$480

**Address:** Blvd Fco Medina Ascencio KM 2.5 48333 **Location:** Oceanfront. 2.5 mi (4 km) n on Paseo de Las Palmas, off Airport Hwy (Mex 200). **Facility:** Here you will find a truly upscale and distinctly Mexican design throughout the public areas and guest rooms. A tropical pool and a great beachfront location complete the package. 291 units. 9 stories, interior corridors. **Parking:** on-site (fee) and valet. **Amenities:** safes. **Dining:** 8 restaurants, entertainment. **Pool(s):** heated outdoor. **Activities:** recreation programs, spa. **Guest Services:** valet laundry.

## FRIENDLY VALLARTA
(322)226-4600 **15**

Resort Hotel $194-$300 **Address:** KM 2.5 Blvd Fco Medina Ascencio 2199 48333 **Location:** Oceanfront. 2.5 mi (4 km) n on Ave de Las Palmas, off Airport Hwy (Mex 200). **Facility:** This all-inclusive resort offers spacious rooms with distinct Mexican décor. All units have either a balcony or patio, and many boast an ocean view. Guests will enjoy the nightly entertainment. 300 units. 5-14 stories, interior corridors. **Amenities:** safes. **Dining:** 4 restaurants, entertainment. **Pool(s):** heated outdoor. **Activities:** sauna, hot tub, steamroom, scuba diving, tennis, recreation programs, kids club, spa. **Guest Services:** valet laundry.

## GARZA BLANCA PRESERVE, RESORT & SPA
322/176-0700 **37**

Resort Hotel
$320-$420

**Address:** KM 7.5 Carr a Barra de Navidad **Location:** Oceanfront. KM 7.5 Carr a Barra de Navidad. **Facility:** The most difficult decision is whether to book an oceanfront room, or a clifftop unit with sweeping views from up high. The tropical grounds are outstanding. 168 units, some two bedrooms, three bedrooms, efficiencies and kitchens. 8-12 stories, interior/exterior corridors. **Parking:** valet only. **Terms:** check-in 4 pm. **Amenities:** safes. **Dining:** 3 restaurants, entertainment. **Pool(s):** heated outdoor. **Activities:** sauna, hot tub, steamroom, self-propelled boats, fishing, scuba diving, snorkeling, tennis, recreation programs, spa. **Guest Services:** valet and coin laundry. (See ad on insert.)

## HACIENDA BUENAVENTURA HOTEL SPA & BEACH CLUB
322/226-6667 **12**

Hotel $140-$200 **Address:** Blvd Fco Medina Ascencio 2699 48300 **Location:** 3 mi (4.8 km) n; just off Airport Hwy (Mex 200). **Facility:** 155 units. 2-4 stories (no elevator), interior corridors. **Parking:** on-site and street. **Amenities:** Some: safes. **Dining:** 3 restaurants. **Pool(s):** heated outdoor. **Activities:** hot tub, beach access, recreation programs, spa. **Guest Services:** valet laundry.

# YOUR GATEWAY
## TO RELAXATION

**EXLUSIVE DEALS
FOR AAA MEMBERS**

**MARRIOTT** RESORT
CASAMAGNA
PUERTO VALLARTA

**RESERVE**
**1 888 236 2427**

**PUERTOVALLARTAMARRIOTT.COM**

(See map & index p. 472.)

**HACIENDA SAN ANGEL**      (322)222-2692   **22**

▽▽▽ ▽▽▽ **Hotel** $435-$750 **Address:** Miramar 336 Col Centro 48300 **Location:** Centro; 3 blks e of town square. **Facility:** Set high on a hill, this charming hidden treasure in the heart of Puerto Vallarta has luxurious rooms spread throughout a series of connected villas. 20 units. 2-3 stories (no elevator), interior/exterior corridors. **Parking:** street only. **Terms:** age restrictions may apply. **Amenities:** safes. **Dining:** Hacienda San Angel Gourmet, see separate listing. **Pool(s):** heated outdoor. **Guest Services:** valet laundry.

🍽 🛎 🍸 🏊 🛜 ✕ 📱 /SOME UNITS 🐾

**HILTON PUERTO VALLARTA RESORT**
     (322)176-1176   **23**

▽▽▽ ▽▽▽
**Resort Hotel**
**$249-$569**

Ⓗ **Hilton** HOTELS & RESORTS    **AAA Benefit:** Members save 5% or more!

**Address:** Ave de Las Garzas 136-1 48333 **Location:** Oceanfront. 3 mi (4.8 km) n off Airport Hwy (Mex 200). **Facility:** Bright, vibrant décor sets the tone for this luxurious, all-inclusive resort set on a wide stretch of beach. The views are fabulous, and some rooms feature private plunge pools. 259 units. 4-8 stories, interior corridors. **Parking:** valet only. **Terms:** off-site registration, 1-7 night minimum stay, cancellation fee imposed. **Amenities:** safes. **Dining:** 4 restaurants, entertainment. **Pool(s):** heated outdoor. **Activities:** sauna, hot tub, steamroom, scuba diving, snorkeling, recreation programs, kids club, spa. **Guest Services:** valet laundry.

🍽 🛎 🍸 🏋 SD 🏊 🛁 BIZ SHS 📶 ✕
📱 💻

**HOLIDAY INN EXPRESS PUERTO VALLARTA**
     (322)226-7760   **30**

▽▽▽ **Hotel** $90-$140 **Address:** Blvd. Francisco Medina Ascencio 3974 **Location:** Directly across from Plaza Marina. **Facility:** 115 units. 7 stories, interior corridors. *Bath:* shower only. **Amenities:** safes. **Pool(s):** outdoor. **Activities:** hot tub, exercise room. **Guest Services:** valet laundry.

🍽➕ SD 🏊 BIZ HS 📶 ✕ 💻
/SOME UNITS 📱 💻

**HOLIDAY INN RESORT PUERTO VALLARTA**
     (322)226-1700   **14**

▽▽▽ **Hotel** $109-$139 **Address:** Blvd Fco Medina Ascencio S/N KM 3.5 48300 **Location:** Oceanfront. 2.5 mi (4 km) n on Airport Hwy (Mex 200). **Facility:** 307 units. 9-18 stories, interior corridors. **Amenities:** safes. **Dining:** 3 restaurants, also, La Guacamaya Restaurant, Piaceres Restaurant, Restaurante Mariaches, see separate listings, entertainment. **Pool(s):** heated outdoor. **Activities:** hot tub, fishing, scuba diving, tennis, recreation programs, kids club, game room, exercise room, massage. **Guest Services:** valet laundry.

🍽 🛎 SD 🏊 BIZ 📶 ✕ 💻
/SOME UNITS 🐾 HS

**HOTEL EL PESCADOR**      (322)176-1100   **20**

▽▽ **Hotel** $88-$190 **Address:** Paraguay No. 1117 Col S de Diciembre 48350 **Location:** Oceanfront. 2 blks n of the Malecon. **Facility:** 103 units. 3 stories, exterior corridors. *Bath:* shower only. **Parking:** on-site and street. **Pool(s):** outdoor.

🍽 🛎 🍸 🏊 BIZ HS 📶 ✕

**HOTEL GRAND MIRAMAR PUERTO VALLARTA**
     (322)221-5120   **43**

▽▽▽ ▽▽▽
**Hotel**
**$251-$552**

**Address:** Paseo de Los Corales 139 48390 **Location:** 1.2 mi (2 km) on Carra Barra de Navidad, 0.6 mi (1 km), follow signs. **Facility:** Sweeping views greet guests at this amazing clifftop location. A series of pools, a rooftop lounge and a jungle setting complete the package. Rooms are oversized with a distinct Mexican design. 112 units, some two bedrooms, three bedrooms, efficiencies and kitchens. 6 stories, interior corridors. **Parking:** valet only. **Amenities:** safes. **Dining:** 3 restaurants. **Pool(s):** outdoor, heated outdoor. **Activities:** sauna, hot tub, steamroom, exercise room, spa. **Guest Services:** valet laundry, area transportation.

🍽 🛎 🍸 🏋 🏊 BIZ 📶 ✕ 📱 📷 💻

**HOTEL MOUSAI**      322/176-0710   **34**

▽▽▽ ▽▽▽
**Boutique**
**Contemporary**
**Hotel**
**$500-$750**

**Address:** KM 7.5 Carretera a Barra de Navidad **Location:** Oceanfront. KM 7.5 Carretera a Barra de Navidad. **Facility:** This chic hotel offers the ultimate in contemporary design in its rooms and public areas. Highly personalized service complete with a mid-day "siesta" hammock service sets this apart from the rest. Meets AAA guest room security requirements. 73 units. 17 stories, interior corridors. *Bath:* shower only. **Parking:** valet only. **Terms:** age restrictions may apply. **Amenities:** safes. **Dining:** Hiroshi, see separate listing. **Pool(s):** heated outdoor. **Activities:** sauna, steamroom, scuba diving, snorkeling, recreation programs, trails, spa. **Guest Services:** valet laundry. *(See ad on insert.)*

🍽 🛎 🍸 SD 🏊 🛁 BIZ SHS 📶 ✕ 📱 💻

**HOTEL ONE PUERTO VALLARTA AEROPUERTO**
     322/176-1040   **45**

▽▽ **Hotel** $60-$120 **Address:** 3987 Blvd Francisco Medina Ascencio **Location:** Directly n of airport on Airport Hwy (Mex 200). **Facility:** 126 units. 5 stories, interior corridors. *Bath:* shower only. **Pool(s):** outdoor. **Guest Services:** valet and coin laundry.

🍽➕ CALL 🦻M 🏊 BIZ 📶 ✕

**HOTEL ROSITA**      322/176-1111   **21**

▽▽ **Hotel** $88-$190 **Address:** Paseo Diaz Ordaz No. 901 48300 **Location:** Oceanfront. Downtown; at beginning of the Malecon. **Facility:** 114 units. 4 stories, exterior corridors. *Bath:* shower only. **Parking:** street only. **Pool(s):** outdoor.

🍽 🛎 🍸 🏊 BIZ HS 📶 ✕ /SOME UNITS 📱

**HOTEL SAN MARINO**      322/222-3050   **28**

▽▽ **Hotel** $120-$220 **Address:** Rodolfo Gomez No. 111 Col E Zapata 48380 **Location:** Oceanfront. Centro; in Zona Romantica. **Facility:** 163 units. 5-8 stories, exterior corridors. *Bath:* shower only. **Parking:** street only. **Amenities:** safes. **Dining:** 2 restaurants. **Pool(s):** outdoor. **Activities:** recreation programs, spa.

🍽 🍸 🏊 📶 ✕

---

# Stay connected with #AAA and #CAA

# on your favorite social media sites

(See map & index p. 472.)

## HYATT ZIVA PUERTO VALLARTA

322/226-5000 **33**

**Resort Hotel**
$163-$720

**AAA Benefit:** Members save 10%!

**Address:** KM 3.5 Carr a Barra de Navidad **Location:** Oceanfront. KM 3.5 Carr a Barra de Navidad. **Facility:** This luxurious all-inclusive resort boasts an excellent beachfront location with stunning views. Rooms are decorated in a chic Mexican style; some units have balcony hot tubs. 335 units. 12 stories, interior corridors. **Parking:** on-site and valet. **Amenities:** safes. **Dining:** 4 restaurants, entertainment. **Pool(s):** heated outdoor. **Activities:** sauna, hot tub, steamroom, self-propelled boats, scuba diving, snorkeling, recreation programs, kids club, playground. **Guest Services:** valet laundry, rental car service.

## KRYSTAL PUERTO VALLARTA

322/226-0700 **13**

**Resort Hotel**
$100-$200

**Address:** Ave de Las Garzas S/N Zona Hotelera Norte 48300 **Location:** Oceanfront. 2.8 mi (4.5 km) n off Airport Hwy (Mex 200). **Facility:** A huge, beachfront resort on acres of tropical landscaping offers standard hotel rooms, beachfront units or ground-level villas with private pools. 260 units. 3-4 stories, interior/exterior corridors. **Parking:** on-site (fee). **Amenities:** safes. **Dining:** 4 restaurants, entertainment. **Pool(s):** outdoor. **Activities:** hot tub, scuba diving, snorkeling, tennis, recreation programs, kids club, playground, exercise room, spa. **Guest Services:** valet laundry.

## LAS PALMAS BY THE SEA

(322)226-1220 **17**

**Resort Hotel** $144-$290 **Address:** Blvd Francisco Medina Ascencio KM 2.5 48333 **Location:** Oceanfront. 1.6 mi (2.5 km) n off Airport Hwy (Mex 200). **Facility:** This popular, always-bustling property offers all-inclusive packages. The beachfront location and casual ambiance make for a perfect laid-back vacation. 225 units. 5 stories, interior/exterior corridors. **Bath:** shower only. **Parking:** street only. **Amenities:** safes. **Dining:** 2 restaurants, entertainment. **Pool(s):** outdoor. **Activities:** hot tub, scuba diving, snorkeling, recreation programs, kids club, playground, massage. **Guest Services:** valet laundry.

## LOS ARCOS SUITES

322/226-7100 **26**

**Hotel** $89-$110 **Address:** Manuel M Dieguez No. 164 48380 **Location:** Centro; in Zona Romantica. **Facility:** 44 efficiencies. 4 stories, exterior corridors. **Bath:** shower only. **Amenities:** safes. **Pool(s):** heated outdoor. **Activities:** beach access. **Guest Services:** valet laundry.

## MAYAN PALACE PUERTO VALLARTA

322/226-6000 **6**

**Resort Hotel**
$265-$317

**Address:** Paseo de La Marina Sur No. 220 48354 **Location:** Oceanfront. 3.1 mi (5 km) off Mex 200; in Marina District. **Facility:** Authentic Mexican décor is found throughout this resort, which features a peaceful lagoon in addition to a huge pool, all in an oceanfront setting. 213 units, some efficiencies. 5-7 stories, interior corridors. **Parking:** valet only. **Terms:** check-in 5 pm, 2-7 night minimum stay, 7 day cancellation notice-fee imposed. **Amenities:** safes. **Dining:** 2 restaurants. **Pool(s):** heated outdoor. **Activities:** recreation programs, exercise room, massage. **Guest Services:** valet laundry.

*(See ad on insert, p. 467.)*

## MELIA VACATION CLUB PUERTO VALLARTA

(322)226-3002 **5**

**Resort Hotel** $440 **Address:** Paseo de La Marina Sur Lote No. 7 48354 **Location:** Oceanfront. 3.1 mi (5 km) n off Airport Hwy (Mex 200); in Marina District. **Facility:** This large resort caters to families. Features include on-site babysitting, a kids club for 5-11 year olds and activities for teens. Ask for bunk bed rooms with child-friendly amenities. 318 units. 4-9 stories, interior corridors. **Amenities:** safes. **Dining:** 5 restaurants, entertainment. **Pool(s):** heated outdoor. **Activities:** scuba diving, snorkeling, tennis, recreation programs, kids club, playground, game room, exercise room, spa. **Guest Services:** valet laundry.

## NOW AMBER

(322)226-2840 **46**

**Resort Hotel**
$454-$1210

**Address:** David Alfaro Siqueiros No. 164 48333 **Location:** Oceanfront. Just n of town center; in Zona Hotelera Las Glorias. **Facility:** This luxurious, family-oriented resort has an extensive kids club, a teen club and a professional entertainment team. A wide selection of dining options suits all tastes. 327 units. 8-15 stories, interior corridors. **Parking:** valet only. **Amenities:** safes. **Dining:** 5 restaurants, nightclub, entertainment. **Pool(s):** outdoor, heated outdoor. **Activities:** sauna, hot tub, steamroom, scuba diving, snorkeling, tennis, recreation programs, kids club, game room, spa. **Guest Services:** valet laundry, rental car service.

## PLAYA LOS ARCOS BEACH RESORT & SPA

(322)226-7100 **25**

**Hotel**
$88-$145

**Address:** Olas Altas 380 48380 **Location:** Oceanfront. Centro; in Zona Romantica. **Facility:** 169 units, some efficiencies and kitchens. 4 stories, interior/exterior corridors. **Bath:** shower only. **Amenities:** safes. **Dining:** Mi Pueblito Restaurant, see separate listing, entertainment. **Pool(s):** heated outdoor. **Activities:** hot tub, recreation programs, spa. **Guest Services:** valet laundry.

## PLAZA PELICANOS CLUB BEACH RESORT

322/226-2700 **39**

**Hotel** $211 **Address:** Diego Rivera No. 120 Zona Hotelera Las Glorias 48330 **Location:** In Zona Hotelera Las Glorias. **Facility:** 200 units. 3 stories (no elevator), interior corridors. **Amenities:** safes. **Dining:** 3 restaurants. **Pool(s):** outdoor, heated outdoor. **Activities:** beach access, tennis, recreation programs, kids club, exercise room, massage. **Guest Services:** valet laundry.

## PLAZA PELICANOS GRAND BEACH RESORT

(322)226-2700 **32**

**Hotel** $290 **Address:** Jose Clemente Orozco 131 48330 **Location:** Oceanfront. 1.6 mi (2.5 km) n off Airport Hwy (Mex 200). **Facility:** 100 units. 3 stories, interior/exterior corridors. **Amenities:** safes. **Dining:** 5 restaurants, entertainment. **Pool(s):** heated outdoor. **Activities:** scuba diving, snorkeling, recreation programs, kids club, game room, exercise room, massage. **Guest Services:** valet laundry.

Remember, car seats, booster seats
and seat belts save lives

(See map & index p. 472.)

### SECRETS VALLARTA BAY    (322)226-2900  48

Contemporary
Resort Hotel
$500-$1390

**Address:** David Alfaro Siqueiros No. 164 48333 **Location:** Oceanfront. Just n of town center; in Zona Hotelera Las Glorias. **Facility:** Guests at this contemporary, adult-oriented, all-inclusive resort will enjoy the luxurious amenities. In addition, you'll have full access to facilities at the adjoining Now Amber property. 271 units. 8-15 stories, interior corridors. **Parking:** valet only. **Terms:** age restrictions may apply. **Amenities:** safes. **Dining:** 10 restaurants, nightclub, entertainment. **Pool(s):** outdoor, heated outdoor. **Activities:** sauna, hot tub, steamroom, scuba diving, snorkeling, tennis, recreation programs, spa. **Guest Services:** valet laundry, rental car service.

### SHERATON BUGANVILIAS RESORT & CONVENTION CENTER    (322)226-0404  18

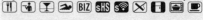

Resort Hotel
Rates not provided

**AAA Benefit:** Members save up to 15%, plus Starwood Preferred Guest® benefits!

**Address:** Blvd Francisco Medina Ascencio 999 48333 **Location:** Oceanfront. Just n of town center. **Facility:** This large complex features two large pools with swim-up bars and a fine oceanfront location; it is walking distance from the popular downtown area. 473 units. 13 stories, interior corridors. **Amenities:** safes. **Dining:** 4 restaurants, also, Gaviotas, La Villita, see separate listings. **Pool(s):** heated outdoor. **Activities:** tennis, recreation programs, kids club, spa. **Guest Services:** valet laundry.

### SUNSET PLAZA BEACH RESORT & SPA    (322)226-2757  38

Boutique Resort
Hotel
$329-$411

**Address:** Diego Rivera No. 121, Zona Hotelera Las Glorias 48330 **Location:** Oceanfront. 1.6 mi (2.5 km) n off Airport Hwy (Mex 200); in Zona Hotelera Las Glorias. **Facility:** Simultaneously chic and family-friendly, this beachfront property has a relaxing adults' pool, a family pool, a vibrant kids club and a raised sun deck with three outdoor hot tubs. 100 units, some kitchens. 15 stories, interior corridors. **Parking:** valet only. **Amenities:** safes. **Dining:** 3 restaurants. **Pool(s):** heated outdoor. **Activities:** hot tub, tennis, recreation programs, kids club, playground, exercise room, spa. **Guest Services:** valet laundry.

### VAMAR VALLARTA ALL INCLUSIVE MARINA & BEACH RESORT    322/221-1177  7

 Hotel $146-$250 **Address:** Ave Paseo de La Marina Sur S/N Marina 48354 **Location:** 3.1 mi (5 km) on of Airport Hwy (Mex 200); in Marina District. **Facility:** 253 units, some two bedrooms, three bedrooms and efficiencies. 3-9 stories, exterior corridors. **Dining:** 3 restaurants, entertainment. **Pool(s):** outdoor. **Activities:** sauna, steamroom, scuba diving, snorkeling, recreation programs, bicycles, playground, spa. **Guest Services:** valet laundry.

### VELAS VALLARTA SUITE RESORT & CONVENTION CENTER    (322)226-9500  3

 Resort Hotel $440-$720 **Address:** Ave Costera S/N LH-2 Marina Vallarta 48354 **Location:** Oceanfront. 3.1 mi (5 km) n on Airport Hwy (Mex 200); in Marina District. **Facility:** Interlocking pools are set around lush tropical gardens at this all-inclusive resort on a lovely stretch of beach; choose a suite or studio unit. 344 efficiencies, some two and three bedrooms. 8-9 stories, exterior corridors. **Parking:** valet only. **Terms:** check-in 4 pm. **Amenities:** safes. **Dining:** 3 restaurants, also, Andrea Gourmet, La Ribera Restaurant, see separate listings. **Pool(s):** heated outdoor. **Activities:** tennis, recreation programs, kids club, exercise room, spa. **Guest Services:** valet laundry. *(See ad on insert.)*

### VILLA DEL PALMAR    (322)226-1400  31

 Hotel $141-$387 **Address:** Blvd Fco Medina Ascencio KM 2.5 48300 **Location:** Oceanfront. 2.5 mi (4 km) n on Airport Hwy (Mex 200). **Facility:** 517 efficiencies, some two bedrooms. 4-8 stories, interior/exterior corridors. **Amenities:** safes. **Dining:** 3 restaurants. **Pool(s):** outdoor, heated outdoor. **Activities:** tennis, recreation programs, exercise room, spa. **Guest Services:** coin laundry.

### VILLA PREMIERE HOTEL & SPA    (322)226-7040  27

Hotel
$157-$341

**Address:** San Salvador 117, Col 5 Diciembre 48350 **Location:** Oceanfront. 0.6 mi (1 km) n on Airport Hwy (Mex 200). **Facility:** This luxurious hotel offers highly personalized service and is adult oriented. Upon arrival, guests are welcomed with a complimentary beverage and an instantly relaxing neck massage. 83 units. 7 stories, interior corridors. **Parking:** valet and street only. **Terms:** age restrictions may apply. **Amenities:** safes. **Dining:** La Corona, Murales, see separate listings. **Pool(s):** heated outdoor. **Activities:** sauna, steamroom, spa. **Guest Services:** valet laundry.

### VILLAS VALLARTA BY CANTO DEL SOL    (322)226-0123  44

 Hotel $75-$85 **Address:** Pablo Picasso S/N 48333 **Location:** 1.6 mi (2.5 km) n off Airport Hwy (Mex 200); in Zona Hotelera Norte. **Facility:** 152 units, some two bedrooms, efficiencies and kitchens. 3 stories, exterior corridors. *Bath:* shower only. **Parking:** on-site (fee). **Amenities:** safes. **Pool(s):** outdoor. **Guest Services:** valet laundry.

### VILLA VERA PUERTO VALLARTA    (322)221-1015  11

 Hotel $93-$123 **Address:** Paseo de La Marina Sur No. 210 48354 **Location:** Waterfront. In Marina District. **Facility:** 65 units, some efficiencies. 3 stories (no elevator), exterior corridors. **Terms:** check-in 4 pm. **Amenities:** safes. **Pool(s):** outdoor. **Guest Services:** valet laundry.

(See map & index p. 472.)

## THE WESTIN RESORT AND SPA PUERTO VALLARTA
(322)226-1100  **9**

▼▼▼ ▼▼▼
**Resort Hotel**
**$85-$450**

**WESTIN**
HOTELS & RESORTS

**AAA Benefit:** Members save up to 15%, plus Starwood Preferred Guest® benefits!

**Address:** Paseo de La Marina Sur No. 205 Marina Vallarta 48354 **Location:** Oceanfront. 3.1 mi (5 km) n on Airport Hwy (Mex 200); in Marina Vallarta. **Facility:** This handsome beachfront hotel has excellent facilities and attractive rooms. Guests enjoy the lobby's contemporary Mexican décor, accented with local art pieces, as well as the huge tropical pools. 280 units. 14 stories, interior corridors. **Terms:** 7 day cancellation notice-fee imposed, resort fee. **Amenities:** safes. **Dining:** 3 restaurants, also, Arrecifes Seafood and Steakhouse, El Palmar, see separate listings. **Pool(s):** heated outdoor. **Activities:** sauna, hot tub, steamroom, tennis, recreation programs, playground, spa. **Guest Services:** valet laundry.

[icons]

## ANDREA GOURMET
322/221-0091  **12**

▼▼▼ International. Casual Dining. $10-$35 **AAA Inspector Notes:** The elegant dining room features candlelit tables and both indoor and outdoor terrace seating. Mexico-influenced contemporary décor complements a fine menu of Continental and Italian cuisine. **Features:** full bar. **Reservations:** suggested. **Address:** Ave Costera 585 S/N LH-2 Marina Vallarta 48354 **Location:** 3.1 mi (5 km) n on Airport Hwy (Mex 200); in Marina District; in Velas Vallarta Suite Resort & Convention Center. **Parking:** valet only.

[B] [L] [D]

## ARCHIE'S WOK
322/222-0411  **70**

▼▼▼ Asian. Casual Dining. $10-$25 **AAA Inspector Notes:** Dishing up excellent, freshly prepared Pan Asian fare, this restaurant is sure to please those craving coconut ginger soup, cashew chicken or perhaps barbecued pork ribs. Fresh herbs and spices complement the tasty fare. And although reservations aren't taken, guests don't mind the wait when it's rewarded with food as good as this. **Features:** full bar. **Address:** Francisca Rodriguez 130, El Centro 48380 **Location:** In Zona Romantica. **Parking:** no self-parking.

[L] [D]

## ARRECIFES SEAFOOD AND STEAKHOUSE
322/226-1100  **20**

▼▼▼ Seafood Steak. Fine Dining. $18-$30 **AAA Inspector Notes:** With a relaxing sea breeze blowing, dine under the stars on the large open-air terrace. The chef offers a tempting menu of fine, fresh local and regional fish and seafood as well as grilled-to-order steaks. Choose from a wide range of side dishes, which are sized for sharing. **Features:** full bar, patio dining. **Reservations:** required. **Address:** Paseo de La Marina Sur No. 205 48354 **Location:** 3.1 mi (5 km) n on Airport Hwy (Mex 200); in Marina District; in The Westin Resort and Spa Puerto Vallarta. [D] CALL [icons]

## BARCELONA TAPAS
322/222-0510  **49**

▼▼▼ Spanish. Casual Dining. $9-$24 **AAA Inspector Notes:** Set high on a hill, the restaurant offers stunning views of town from its open-air terrace. A wide range of tapas, as well as large orders of paella, are perfect for group dining. **Features:** full bar, patio dining. **Address:** Matamoros y 31 de Octubre S/N 48310 **Location:** Old Town Center. **Parking:** street only. [L] [D] [icon]

---

## BLANCA BLUE
322/176-0700  **38**

▼▼▼▼ International. Fine Dining. $12-$30 **AAA Inspector Notes:** Your first decision is whether to dine on the large open-air terrace next to the glowing fire pit, or in the seductive formal dining room with candlelit tables. Once that choice has been made you have the decision of which one of the chef's creations you're in the mood for. Most diners like to start with one of the specialty margaritas from the extensive in-house tequila selection. The international cuisine is fresh and innovative, and prepared with a Mexican flair. **Features:** full bar, patio dining. **Reservations:** suggested. **Address:** Carr a Barra de Navidad KM 7.5 48390 **Location:** 4.5 mi (7.5 km) s of town. **Parking:** valet only. [B] [L] [D]

## THE BLUE SHRIMP RESTAURANT
322/223-1840  **32**

▼▼▼ Seafood. Casual Dining. $16-$40 **AAA Inspector Notes:** This is the spot for shrimp lovers. As the name suggests, the popular restaurant specializes in fresh shrimp in everything from tangy cocktails to pay-the-pound options. The chef cooks them in a variety of ways, including tequila, freshly breaded coconut and the frequently ordered garlic-seasoned. Also available are huge local lobsters, some meat options and a tasty salad bar. Great beachfront location. **Features:** full bar, patio dining. **Reservations:** suggested. **Address:** Olas Altas No. 336 48380 **Location:** In Zona Romantica; south side; overlooking beach. **Parking:** street only.

[B] [L] [D] [icon]

## BOCADOS BITES & MEATS
322/176-0700  **90**

▼▼▼ Steak. Casual Dining. $18-$30 **AAA Inspector Notes:** Set high on a hill, this spot offers striking views from its open-air patio and is a favorite place to watch the sunset. On the menu of contemporary cuisine you'll find fine cuts of steak and a variety of side dishes perfect for sharing. The chic lounge and indoor dining area also are popular. **Features:** full bar, patio dining. **Reservations:** suggested. **Address:** Carr a Barra de Navidad KM 7.5 48390 **Location:** In Zona Hotelera Sur. [D] [icon]

## CAFE DES ARTISTES
322/222-3228  **27**

▼▼▼ French. Fine Dining. $20-$28 **AAA Inspector Notes:** Guests can select from dining in the air-conditioned elegant dining room or the open-air upper-level garden patio to enjoy the night breeze. Fine live music filters through to both areas as well as the upscale lounge. The menu features a fine mix of local and regional specialties and is ever changing to reflect the best of the season. **Features:** full bar, patio dining. **Reservations:** required. **Address:** Guadalupe Sanchez 740 48351 **Location:** Centro. [D] [icon]

## CHEEKY MONKEY
322/222-8938  **59**

▼▼ American. Casual Dining. $8-$18 **AAA Inspector Notes:** Using beer and margarita specials as bait, this bi-level restaurant on the Malecon lures in tourists who quickly discover the fun atmosphere, friendly service and good food make it worth sticking around. The menu lists plenty of munchies, such as nachos and wings, as well as tasty pizzas, burgers, sandwiches and pastas. Offering great bang-for-the-buck and excellent ocean views, it's no surprise this place is always busy. **Features:** full bar, patio dining. **Address:** Corono No. 3 Altos 48300 **Location:** On the Malecon. **Parking:** street only. [L] [D] [icon] [icon]

## CHICO'S PARADISE
322/223-6005  **68**

▼▼ Mexican. Casual Dining. $10-$24 **AAA Inspector Notes:** This is a must when visiting Vallarta, mostly for its unique riverside atmosphere. You'll dine on one of several open-air terraces overlooking a small tropical waterfall. The canopy adventures operate from here, so there's always lots of action to watch while you eat. The menu lists fresh, home-style Mexican fare, plus barbecue ribs and meat, grilled fish and other seafood items. The homemade guacamole is worth the visit alone. Don't forget to bring a bathing suit for a pre- or post-meal swim. **Features:** full bar, patio dining. **Address:** KM 20 Carr A Colima 48294 **Location:** On KM 20 Carr A Colima. **Parking:** street only. [B] [L] [icon]

## COCO TROPICAL
322/222-5485  **73**

▼▼▼ International. Casual Dining. $10-$29 **AAA Inspector Notes:** Nightly live entertainment and a great location overlooking the ocean draw plenty of locals to this place. You'll find them hanging out in the bar, as well as participating in some of the restaurant's special theme nights. A tropical feel prevails on the open-air terrace, where you'll want to linger after enjoying well-prepared Mexican and international fare. **Features:** full bar, patio dining. **Reservations:** suggested. **Address:** Rincon Madreperla No. 105-2 48399 **Location:** Directly overlooking the beach; in Zona Romantica. **Parking:** no self-parking. [L] [D] [icon]

(See map & index p. 472.)

### DAIQUIRI DICK'S
322/222-0566  (42)

▼▼▼ International. Casual Dining. $16-$29 **AAA Inspector Notes:** Diners appreciate not only the prime beachfront location but also the contemporary design of the trendy dining room. Such innovative dishes as grilled asparagus, pork chops with espresso sauce and lobster tacos complement the décor. Key lime pie finishes a meal with style. **Features:** full bar, patio dining. **Reservations:** suggested. **Address:** Olas Atlas 314 48380 **Location:** In Zona Romantica. **Parking:** street only. B L D 🅰️

### DE SANTOS
322/221-3090  (19)

▼▼▼ International. Casual Dining. $12-$25 **AAA Inspector Notes:** A very cool place with unique décor, it has rustic wood floors and tabletops, a long bar, and in the rear, a fully open concept kitchen complete with a wood-fired pizza oven. A small outdoor patio area is another seating option. The menu is a mix of Italian fare, grilled meats, pastas and Mexican specialties. It has become a local favorite for family gatherings. Friday and Saturday nights the tone changes with live bands; it is wise to call ahead and check the schedule. **Features:** full bar, patio dining. **Address:** Blvd Francisco Medina Ascencio No. 2485 48300 **Location:** At Peninsula Plaza. D

### D'Z ROUTE 66 ROCK N ROLL DINER
322/209-0760  (10)

▼▼ American. Casual Dining. $6-$18 **AAA Inspector Notes:** The D'z guys have done a great job creating a fabulous old-style diner in a covered, outdoor patio setting. As for the décor, think checkered-tile floors, hot rod cars and photos of old movie stars and entertainers. The menu, made to look like a record album cover, features all the diner classics: juicy burgers, homemade fries and ice cream floats. The marina location makes it a nice spot for people-watching. Oldies music adds to the fun. **Features:** patio dining. **Address:** Paseo de La Marina 3 Local No. 6 48335 **Location:** At Marina Vallarta. **Parking:** street only. B L D 🅰️

### EL ANDARIEGO RESTAURANTE AND BAR
322/223-2100  (46)

◆◆ Mexican. Casual Dining. $8-$30 **AAA Inspector Notes:** Boasting an excellent reputation, this well-established eatery has been serving homemade Mexican fare for more than 25 years. Several tasting platters and hearty entrée portions ensure you don't leave hungry. The ambiance is relaxed and the simple dining room features a fine wall mural of Old Town Puerto Vallarta. A two-for-one margarita special is offered daily from noon to 5 pm. **Features:** full bar. **Address:** Col. 5 de Diciembre 48310 **Location:** 0.6 mi (1 km) n on Airport Hwy (Mex 200). **Parking:** no self-parking. B L D

### EL ARRAYAN
322/222-7195  (34)

◆◆◆
**Mexican**
**Casual Dining**
**$16-$24**

**AAA Inspector Notes:** This bright, festive restaurant features an authentic Mexican feel both in decor and menu choices. All courses are made to order, and great care has been taken to offer a wide array of flavors and spice levels. **Features:** full bar. **Reservations:** suggested. **Address:** Allende No. 344 El Centro 48351 **Location:** Just e of Matamoros; centro. **Parking:** street only. D

### EL PALMAR
322/226-1100  (64)

▼▼▼ International. Casual Dining. $12-$30 **AAA Inspector Notes:** Here you will find a varied international menu with some fresh local and regional specials. The peaceful setting overlooks the tropical pool area. It is a great place to relax and have nice quiet meal. **Features:** full bar, patio dining. **Address:** Paseo de La Marina Sur No. 205 Marina Vallarta 48354 **Location:** 3.1 mi (5 km) n on Airport Hwy (Mex 200); in Marina Vallarta; in The Westin Resort and Spa Puerto Vallarta. B L D 🅰️

### EL PALOMAR DE LOS GONZALEZ
322/222-0795  (86)

▼▼▼ International. Fine Dining. $18-$38 **AAA Inspector Notes:** At this restaurant, set high on a hill, you'll enjoy a stunning view of Puerto Vallarta's sparkling lights while dining on either the open-air or covered terrace. Candlelit tables add to the romantic ambiance. The menu lists an abundance of fresh local fish and seafood as well as a wide mix of international fare. For a special treat, try one of the flaming coffees, which the staff will skillfully prepare table side. Although they take credit cards tips are accepted in cash only. **Features:** full bar, patio dining. **Reservations:** suggested. **Address:** Aguacate No. 425 Col. Alta Vista 48380 **Location:** Just s of town, follow signs from Airport Hwy (Mex 200). **Parking:** street only. D 🅰️

### EMILIANO
322/226-6688  (1)

◆◆◆ ◆◆◆
**International**
**Fine Dining**
**$12-$35**

**AAA Inspector Notes:** Guests enter through secured gates and graceful lobby of the hotel before being awed by cascading waters leading to a midnight blue pool, which will be the backdrop for an enjoyable meal. Menu options might include sweet plantain and black bean turnover in a sweet cream sauce, a salad of tender lobster and sliced pineapple in a citric vinaigrette or maybe beef medallions in a blue agave sauce with cracked black pepper. **Features:** full bar, patio dining. **Reservations:** required, for non-hotel guests. **Address:** 311 Pelicanos Marina Vallarta 48354 **Location:** At Marina Vallarta Golf Course; in Casa Velas Hotel Boutique. **Parking:** valet only. B L D

### FAJITA BANANA TROPICAL GRILL & BAR
322/221-3154  (6)

▼▼ American. Casual Dining. $9-$17 **AAA Inspector Notes:** US-style ribs, burgers and, of course, fajitas, are served at the eatery, which lets guests sit in an open-air setting and view the boats in the marina. There is also a bar and lounge. Patrons might overindulge on the all-you-can-eat ribs. **Features:** full bar, patio dining. **Address:** Puesta del Sol Loc 17 Marina Vallarta 48354 **Location:** In Marina Vallarta. **Parking:** street only. L D 🅰️

### FAJITA REPUBLIC
322/222-3131  (72)

▼▼ Mexican. Casual Dining. $10-$22 **AAA Inspector Notes:** Sizzling fajitas flamed with tequila are a specialty at this casual eatery, a fun spot to kick back with a cool drink and feast on some well-prepared Mexican fare. **Features:** full bar, patio dining. **Address:** Basilio Badillo 188 48380 **Location:** At Olas Altas and Pino Suarez; in Old Town. **Parking:** street only. L D 🅰️

### GAVIOTAS
322/226-0404  (43)

▼▼▼ International. Fine Dining. $15-$29 **AAA Inspector Notes:** Contemporary. Sophisticated. This relaxed spot often has live entertainment and offers indoor or outdoor patio dining. The menu lists a nice variety of well-prepared international dishes, but the highlights are Mexican specialties such as cactus salad, tortilla soup and steak and seafood items. The skillfully prepared desserts are wonderful. **Features:** full bar, patio dining. **Reservations:** required. **Address:** Blvd Francisco Medina Ascencio 999 48333 **Location:** Just n of town center; in Sheraton Buganvilias Resort & Convention Center. D

### HACIENDA SAN ANGEL GOURMET
322/222-2692  (28)

▼▼▼ International. Fine Dining. $21-$47 **AAA Inspector Notes:** High on a hill overlooking the town below, the restaurant boasts wonderful panoramic views from its covered, open-air terrace. At sunset, it's wise to phone ahead and request one of the highly coveted tables with a view. The menu features a fine mix of international fare with a Mexican flair. In addition to classic meat, seafood and pasta dishes, there are good traditional Mexican choices such as black bean soup, chile poblano and chicken mole. Live entertainment spices up the ambiance. **Features:** full bar, patio dining. **Reservations:** required. Semiformal attire. **Address:** Miramar 336 Col Centro 48300 **Location:** Centro; 3 blks e of town square; in Hacienda San Angel. **Parking:** street only. D 🅰️

### HIROSHI
322/176-0710  (89)

▼▼▼ Japanese. Casual Dining. $18-$82 **AAA Inspector Notes:** Greeting you upon arrival are chic, contemporary décor and sweeping views from the hilltop location. The menu is great for exploring exotic Asian fare with a twist. Portions are sized for sampling and a chef's à la minute menu is also offered. Fresh fish and seafood are always incorporated into the menu, which also includes sashimi, hand rolls, tofu and Kobe steak options. **Features:** full bar, patio dining. **Reservations:** required. **Address:** KM 7.5 Carr a Barra de Navidad **Location:** KM 7.5 Carretera a Barra de Navidad; in Hotel Mousai. **Parking:** valet only. D CALL 🅶

### KAISER MAXIMILIAN
322/223-0760  (37)

▼▼▼ Austrian. Fine Dining. $15-$27 **AAA Inspector Notes:** European décor and ambience punctuate the indoor dining room and the sidewalk area. A few Austrian specialties stand out on the menu. Coffee and pastries are served at a separate coffee bar. **Features:** full bar, patio dining. **Reservations:** suggested. **Address:** Olas Altas No. 38B 48380 **Location:** In Zona Romantica. **Parking:** street only. D

(See map & index p. 472.)

### LA BODEGUITA DEL MEDIO   322/223-1585   57

▼▼▼▼ Cuban. Casual Dining. $8-$18 **AAA Inspector Notes:** A taste of Cuba on the Mexican Riviera, this casual eatery offers a nice variety of tapas and shareable starters, as well as hearty entrées. Tasty Cuban specialties such as slow-cooked pork, rice and peas, and plantains are ever-popular. The bi-level restaurant, located in the heart of the Malecón, boasts lovely ocean views from its upper level. **Features:** full bar. **Address:** Paseo Diaz Ordaz 858 48300 **Location:** On the Malecón. **Parking:** street only.  L  D  🅰🅲  🗕

### LA CHATA DE GUADALAJARA   322/222-5529   26

▼▼ Mexican. Casual Dining. $8-$22 **AAA Inspector Notes:** In a great location overlooking the Malecon, this well-established restaurant presents a menu of home-style Mexican cuisine for breakfast, lunch and dinner. The excellent cuisine is freshly prepared and served in hearty portions. Strolling mariachis often play here, making for a festive atmosphere. **Features:** full bar, patio dining. **Address:** Paseo Diaz Ordaz No. 708 48300 **Location:** On the Malecon. **Parking:** no self-parking.  B  L  D  🅰🅲

### LA CORONA   322/226-7040   58

▼▼▼▼ International. Fine Dining. $16-$29 **AAA Inspector Notes:** This casual restaurant features a mixed menu of international fare with a Mexican flair. Dining on the peaceful terrace makes this a nice spot to escape the hustle and bustle of the downtown area. Menu highlights include fine fish, seafood and top-quality meats. Well-prepared desserts put a sweet, finishing touch on a relaxing meal. **Features:** patio dining. **Reservations:** required, for non-hotel guests. **Address:** San Salvador 117, Col 5 Diciembre 48350 **Location:** 0.6 mi (1 km) n on Airport Hwy (Mex 200); in Villa Premiere Hotel & Spa. **Parking:** street only.  D

### LA DOLCE VITA RISTORANTE BAR   322/222-3852   24

▼▼▼ Italian. Casual Dining. $12-$29 **AAA Inspector Notes:** Reservations aren't taken at this popular, bi-level Italian restaurant, where long waits for a table are the norm. Most folks pass the time in the bar, having a drink and enjoying the view of the Malecón. Once seated (many tables have excellent ocean views), the kitchen does not disappoint. The pizzas, cooked in a wood-burning oven, are outstanding. The seafood is fresh. And the homemade pasta dishes are flavored with wonderfully rich sauces. **Features:** full bar. **Address:** Ave P Diaz Ordaz No. 674 48300 **Location:** On the Malecón, along beachfront road; centro. **Parking:** street only.  L  D

### LA ESTANCIA   322/226-0000   14

▼▼▼ Mexican. Casual Dining. $16-$24 **AAA Inspector Notes:** High ceilings, marble floors and lots of tropical plants help create the perfect setting for an enjoyable meal. Service is friendly and personable. The menu features a good selection of well-prepared Mexican fare (the tortilla soup and shrimp fajitas are standouts). Those in search of a tranquil spot to dine should request a table on the small outdoor patio. **Features:** full bar. **Reservations:** suggested. **Address:** Paseo La Marina Norte 435 48354 **Location:** 3.1 mi (5 km) n on Airport Hwy (Mex 200); in Marina Vallarta; in CasaMagna Marriott Puerto Vallarta Resort & Spa.  B  D

### LA GUACAMAYA RESTAURANT   322/226-1700   50

▼▼▼ International. Casual Dining. $10-$22 **AAA Inspector Notes:** Diners can select from a daily international hot and cold buffet or a varied a la carte menu that includes grilled meats, fish and seafood, as well as burgers, sandwiches and pastas. Many tables in the peaceful, covered open-air setting overlook the beach. **Features:** full bar. **Address:** Blvd Fco Medina Ascencio S/N KM 3.5 48300 **Location:** 2.5 mi (4 km) n on Airport Hwy (Mex 200); in Holiday Inn Resort Puerto Vallarta.  B  L  D  🅰🅲

### LA LECHE   322/293-0900   17

▼▼▼▼ International. Fine Dining. $17-$28 **AAA Inspector Notes:** This delightful restaurant features a striking contemporary décor of bright white. The ever-changing menu is listed on a blackboard to reflect the freshest use of local and seasonal ingredients. An outdoor patio also is available. **Features:** full bar, patio dining. **Reservations:** suggested. **Address:** Blvd Francisco Medina Ascencio KM 2.5 48333 **Location:** 2.5 mi (4 km) n on Paseo de Las Palmas, off Airport Hwy (Mex 200).  D

### LANGOSTINO'S BAR & RESTAURANT   322/222-0894   88

▼▼ Seafood. Casual Dining. $9-$25 **AAA Inspector Notes:** This is a great place to kick back, relax and enjoy home-style prepared fresh fish, seafood and Mexican fare. Locals enjoy the daily happy hour as a start to their evening. The place has a beach club ambiance by day. At night, go the romantic route with candlelit beach dining. Don't be afraid to get your feet wet as the tides often crash up to the tables. **Features:** full bar, patio dining, happy hour. **Address:** Manual M. Dieguez 109 48380 **Location:** Directly on the beach; at New Town Pier. **Parking:** street only.  B  L  D  🅰🅲  🗕  🐾

### LA PALAPA RESTAURANTE AND BAR   322/222-5225   47

▼▼▼▼ **AAA Inspector Notes:** Casual elegance and a prime beachfront setting are the main attractions. During the day, diners can take a break from the sun and have a wonderful light or full entree lunch on the sand or in the main dining room. At night, the setting is romantic as diners hear the roar of the waves. Live entertainment is featured in the lounge day and night. The menu features a range of local and International fare including fresh seafood, fajitas and beef selections. **Features:** full bar, patio dining. **Reservations:** suggested, for dinner. **Address:** Pulpito No. 105-3 Col. Emiliano Zapata 48380 **Location:** On Playa de Los Muertos. **Parking:** street only.  B  L  D  🅰🅲

International Casual Dining $16-$50

### LA PIAZZETTA RISTORANTE OLAS ALTAS   322/222-7911   75

▼▼ Italian. Casual Dining. $9-$20 **AAA Inspector Notes:** Always buzzing with happy diners, this Italian eatery in the Romantic Zone dishes up tasty, home-style pasta dishes and pizzas. Throw in a friendly staff and great value, and it's no wonder this place has been a local favorite for years. **Features:** patio dining. **Address:** Olas Altas & Rodolfo Gomez 48380 **Location:** In Zona Romantica. **Parking:** street only.  D  🅰🅲

### LA POSTA   322/222 0941   78

▼▼ Italian. Casual Dining. $9-$22 **AAA Inspector Notes:** Located in the old post office building, this space has been transformed into a wonderful eatery serving up well-prepared Italian and local fare. The bi-level dining room features a small courtyard patio as well as views of the Malecón and ocean. **Features:** full bar, patio dining. **Address:** Morelas No. 444 48380 **Location:** On the Malecón. **Parking:** no self-parking.  L  D  🅰🅲

### LA RIBERA RESTAURANT   322/221-0091   4

▼▼ Steak. Casual Dining. $12-$24 **AAA Inspector Notes:** Reservations are not taken at this casual open-air restaurant, which overlooks the ocean. Diners who don't opt for the daily buffet can order such a la carte dishes as the tasty specialty grilled steaks. **Features:** full bar, patio dining. **Address:** Ave Costera S/N LH-2 Marina Vallarta 48354 **Location:** 3.1 mi (5 km) n on Airport Hwy (Mex 200); in Marina District; in Velas Vallarta Suite Resort & Convention Center. **Parking:** valet only.  B  L  D  🅰🅲

### LAS ADELITAS   322/293-7778   39

▼▼ Mexican. Casual Dining. $9-$22 **AAA Inspector Notes:** Here you'll find hearty portions of tasty Mexican fare and a festive atmosphere. Large wall murals featuring cowboys and mariachi players add to the ambiance, as do the bright costumes worn by the servers. The restaurant is known for its large, meaty ribs, but also serves great, home-style, local specialties as well as the popular jumbo margaritas. **Features:** full bar. **Address:** Ave Fluvial Vallarta No. 234 48300 **Location:** Airport Hwy (Mex 200), just e.  B  L  D  🅰🅲

### LAS CARMELITAS   322/293-3112   40

▼▼ Mexican. Casual Dining. $18-$28 **AAA Inspector Notes:** This restaurant beckons you to come as its lights twinkle high on the mountain each night. You will not be disappointed when you make the journey as you'll find a comfortable open-air terrace offering spectacular views and a menu of fresh, home-style Mexican fare. It is cash only, and a minimum charge of 100 pesos per person is collected at the lower level entrance on arrival; the amount is later deducted from your dinner bill. This is a must-do when visiting the area. **Features:** full bar, patio dining. **Address:** Camino a la Aguacatera KM 1.2 48380 **Location:** Just past the tunnel grande, just up the mountain.  D  🅰🅲

(See map & index p. 472.)

**LAS CASITAS**  322/226-0000  **11**

▼▼▼ International. Casual Dining. $15-$28 AAA Inspector **Notes:** This oceanfront open-air dining room provides a perfect setting for a casual and romantic dining experience. The chef showcases innovation in preparations and presentations of starters and grilled-to-order meats and seafood. **Features:** full bar, patio dining. **Reservations:** suggested. **Address:** Paseo La Marina Norte 435 48354 **Location:** 3.1 mi (5 km) n on Airport Hwy (Mex 200); in Marina Vallarta; in CasaMagna Marriott Puerto Vallarta Resort & Spa. **B L D**

**LAS PALOMAS DORADAS**  322/221-0470  **7**

▼▼ International. Casual Dining. $8-$20 AAA Inspector **Notes:** Near the sailboats and yachts in the marina, the boardwalk cafe serves fresh fish, American-style steaks and Mexican cuisine. Margaritas are enormous, and the food is freshly prepared. **Features:** full bar, patio dining. **Address:** Club de Tenis, Puesta Local Marina Vallarta 48335 **Location:** In Marina Vallarta. **Parking:** street only. **B L D**

**LA VACA ARGENTINA**  322/224-0908  **80**

▼▼▼ Steak. Casual Dining. $18-$43 AAA Inspector Notes: Known for its huge cuts of grilled meats, this chic restaurant is a steak lover's paradise. The chef will take the time to grill your selection perfectly to order. All meals include all-you-can-eat fresh salad, plus there's an abundance of tasty side dishes to compliment your meal. Not in the mood for beef? Fresh fish, seafood and pasta dishes also are offered. **Features:** full bar, patio dining. **Reservations:** suggested. **Address:** Francisco Medina Ascencio Blvd 48333 **Location:** 2.5 mi(4 km) n of Airport Hwy (Mex 200). **Parking:** valet and street only. **L D**

**LA VILLITA**  322/226-0404  **41**

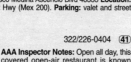

International
Casual Dining
$10-$25

**AAA Inspector Notes:** Open all day, this covered open-air restaurant is known throughout the area for its wonderful Sunday brunch buffet, complete with mariachi players. The rest of the week, this place remains equally enjoyable but quieter. Buffet breakfasts are followed by varied a la carte lunch and dinner menus. Guests can go lighter with burgers, sandwiches and entrée salads or more substantial with fine fresh seafood or grilled meats. Nice sea breezes cool this close-to-the-ocean retreat. **Features:** patio dining, Sunday brunch. **Address:** Blvd Francisco Medina Ascencio 999 48333 **Location:** Just n of town center; in Sheraton Buganvilias Resort & Convention Center. **B L D**

**LE KLIFF RESTAURANTE AND BAR**  322/228-0666  **53**

▼▼▼ Seafood. Fine Dining. $16-$45 AAA Inspector Notes: On a cliff overlooking the ocean, the restaurant is known for its spectacular views. Many patrons reserve a table so they can dine while watching the sunset. Marriage proposals are common in this romantic setting. The menu lists a wonderful selection of fine Continental cuisine, with fresh local seafood a specialty. **Features:** full bar, patio dining. **Reservations:** suggested. **Address:** Carr a Barra de Navidad KM 17.5 S/N 48294 **Location:** On Carr a Barra de Navidad KM 17.5. **L D**

**MARGARITA GRILL**  322/222-9755  **69**

▼▼ Mexican. Casual Dining. $9-$24 AAA Inspector Notes: Always bustling, this casual hot spot provides diners with well-prepared, home-style Mexican fare and a lively atmosphere. Local musicians create a lovely ambiance. Menu highlights include made-at-the-table guacamole, sizzling fajitas, and fresh corn and flour tortillas. **Features:** full bar, patio dining. **Address:** Pino Suarez No. 321 Col. Emiliano Zapata 48380 **Location:** Jct Basilio Badillo; centro; in Zona Romantica. **Parking:** no self-parking. **L D**

**MARISCOS TINO'S**  322/223-2803  **22**

▼▼ Seafood. Casual Dining. $15-$25 AAA Inspector Notes: This popular, centrally located eatery offers a wide selection of fish and seafood, freshly prepared in both Mexican and American styles. In addition to casual indoor dining, there are also outside tables on the second floor's wraparound balcony, which overlooks the city streets and the Malecon. **Features:** full bar, patio dining. **Address:** Paseo Diaz Ordaz 920 Local 31 48300 **Location:** At the Malecon; at Plaza Small Vallarta. **L D**

**MIKADO**  322/221-0004  **13**

▼▼▼ Japanese. Casual Dining. $20-$35 AAA Inspector **Notes:** The restaurant incorporates a Japanese sushi bar and teppanyaki tableside cooking done by entertaining chefs. The setting is tranquil with an indoor garden and an authentic feel of Asia created by wood walkways leading to the main entrance. **Features:** full bar. **Reservations:** suggested. **Address:** Paseo La Marina Norte 435 48354 **Location:** 3.1 mi (5 km) n on Airport Hwy (Mex 200); in Marina Vallarta; in CasaMagna Marriott Puerto Vallarta Resort & Spa. **D**

**MI PUEBLITO RESTAURANT**  322/226-7100  **65**

▼▼ International. Casual Dining. $8-$25 AAA Inspector **Notes:** In the heart of the Romantic Zone, this bustling beachfront restaurant serves good grilled steaks, seafood and international fare. It is wise to phone ahead and reserve a table for special theme nights featuring a buffet and Mexican folkloric show. **Features:** full bar, patio dining. **Address:** Olas Atlas 380 48380 **Location:** Centro; in Zona Romantica; in Playa Los Arcos Beach Resort & Spa. **Parking:** street only. **B L D** **AC**

**MI QUERENCIA**  322/222-7701  **61**

▼▼ Mexican. Casual Dining. $8-$20 AAA Inspector Notes: Massive margaritas and flaming fajitas are the specialties of the house at this restaurant located at the far end of the Malecon. Bright Mexican décor, friendly service and a varied menu of local and international fare make this a nice choice. **Features:** full bar. **Address:** Morelos 426 48310 **Location:** On the Malecon. **Parking:** no self-parking. **B L D** **AC**

**MURALES**  322/226-7040  **23**

▼▼▼ Mexican. Casual Dining. $11-$23 AAA Inspector **Notes:** Overlooking the pool, the fine Mexican restaurant gives patrons the choice of indoor or terrace seating, the latter of which overlooks the pool. The menu blends innovative Mexican and regional dishes, with a focus on fresh fish and other seafood. Fine Mexican artwork enhances the appeal of the dining room. **Features:** full bar, patio dining. **Reservations:** required, for non-hotel guests. **Address:** San Salvador 117 Col 5 de Diciembre 48350 **Location:** 0.6 mi (1 km) n on Airport Hwy (Mex 200); in Villa Premiere Hotel & Spa. **D**

**NO WAY JOSÉ!**  322/223-2853  **82**

▼▼ Mexican. Casual Dining. $15-$22 AAA Inspector **Notes:** This bright, festive spot is a local favorite for freshly prepared Mexican fare, so it's best to phone ahead and reserve if you want to dine at a specific time. Otherwise, grab one of the sidewalk lounge tables and enjoy a pre-dinner cocktail. Be sure to bring a hearty appetite as the menu is so tempting you may want to overindulge and try the flambé bananas for dessert. **Features:** full bar, patio dining. **Reservations:** suggested. **Address:** 5 de Febrero No. 260, Col. Emiliano Zapata 48380 **Location:** Jct Ignacio L. Vallarta; in Zona Romantica. **Parking:** street only. **D** **AC**

**OSCAR'S FINE CUISINE**  322/223-0789  **33**

▼▼▼ International. Casual Dining. $9-$30 AAA Inspector **Notes:** On Isla Rio Cuale and overlooking the ocean, this covered open-air restaurant serves as a great setting for a romantic meal. Freshly grilled steaks, fish and other seafood share menu space with several pasta selections. Live entertainment often enhances the atmosphere at night. After dinner, patrons can stroll on the nearby pier. **Features:** full bar, patio dining. **Address:** Isla Rio Cuale Local 1 48380 **Location:** At Isla Rio Cuale. **Parking:** street only. **B L D** **AC**

**PARADISE BURGER**  322/223-2328  **25**

▼▼ American. Casual Dining. $8-$18 AAA Inspector Notes: In the mood for a juicy burger or some tasty onion rings? This should fit the bill. Also on the menu are wings, fish and chips, hearty sandwiches, salads and ribs. The prime oceanfront location has some balcony seating offering a great view. **Features:** full bar, patio dining. **Address:** Paseo Diaz Ordaz No. 740 48300 **Location:** On the Malecon; facing ocean. **Parking:** street only. **L D** **AC**

(See map & index p. 472.)

**PIACERES RESTAURANT**   322/226-1700   52

▼▼▼ International. Casual Dining. $14-$25 **AAA Inspector Notes:** The chef's attention to detail helps make a meal at this elegant restaurant a memorable one. Formal service sets the stage for a fine mix of Italian fare, which includes fresh pasta dishes and grilled meats and seafood. **Features:** full bar. **Reservations:** suggested. **Address:** Blvd Fco Medina Ascencio S/N KM 3.5 48300 **Location:** 2.5 mi (4 km) n on Airport Hwy (Mex 200); in Holiday Inn Resort Puerto Vallarta. D

**PIZZERIA LA DOLCE**   322/224-0455   16

▼▼ Italian Pizza. Cafeteria. $8-$16 **AAA Inspector Notes:** This pizzeria offers a choice of indoor seating or covered patio dining in a new zone of town that's always bustling with activity. The pizzas are amazing and made right before your eyes in the wood-fired pizza oven. The result is a thin-crust, gourmet-style pie oozing with flavor. If you're in the mood for pasta, you'll find plenty of dishes to choose from. **Features:** full bar, patio dining. **Address:** S/N Francisco Medina Ascencio Blvd 48333 **Location:** 2.5 mi(4 km) n on Airport Hwy (Mex 200). **Parking:** on-site and valet. L D

**PORTO BELLO RISTORANTE ITALIANO**   322/221-0003   8

▼▼▼ Italian. Casual Dining. $14-$40 **AAA Inspector Notes:** This elegant restaurant offers diners a choice of indoor or outdoor patio in the relaxed, yet sophisticated style that is so common in the area. The menu features a wide variety of fine Italian cuisine with antipasto platters for sharing, fresh homemade pastas, veal and seafood offerings. Although portions are hearty, try to save room for the fabulous selection of homemade desserts, the ultimate in decadence. **Features:** full bar, patio dining. **Reservations:** suggested, for dinner. **Address:** Marina del Sol Local 7 Marina Vallarta 48335 **Location:** In Marina Vallarta. **Parking:** street only. L D

**RESTAURANTE MARIACHES**   322/226-1700   21

▼▼ Mexican. Casual Dining. $14-$20 **AAA Inspector Notes:** Bright Mexican décor and servers dressed in traditional mariachi costumes enhance the festive feel at this casual restaurant. Examples of traditional favorites include fajitas with corn tortillas and grilled seafood with rich sauces. Meals come with fresh salsa and tortilla chips. Servers have a selection of mariachi hats that diners can don for a souvenir snapshot. **Features:** full bar. **Reservations:** suggested. **Address:** Blvd Fco Medina Ascencio S/N KM 3.5 48300 **Location:** 2.5 mi (4 km) n on Airport Hwy (Mex 200); in Holiday Inn Resort Puerto Vallarta. D

**RINCON DE BUENOS AIRES**   322/221-2260   3

▼▼ Argentine Steak. Casual Dining. $10-$30 **AAA Inspector Notes:** This casual eatery features hearty portions of prime beef. Servers will display the huge cuts of meat tableside to help diners make their selection. Kebobs, seafood, and poultry are also featured. The chefs grill all meals to order over a wood fire, making the flavor sensational. **Features:** full bar. **Reservations:** suggested. **Address:** Malecon de La Marina Royal Pacific Local 126-127 48335 **Location:** In Marina Vallarta. **Parking:** street only. D AC

**THE RIVER CAFE**   322/223-0788   35

▼▼▼▼ International. Casual Dining. $12-$30 **AAA Inspector Notes:** A tranquil setting awaits diners who wish to escape from the bustling city streets to a peaceful oasis overlooking the river. Lucky diners may spot some large iguanas sunning themselves in the heat of the day. At night, a romantic atmosphere is created with candlelit tables and pleasant background music. The menu offers light and full lunch entrees and a sophisticated dinner menu featuring fine Continental cuisine. **Features:** full bar, patio dining. **Reservations:** suggested, for dinner. **Address:** Isla Rio Cuale Local 4 48380 **Location:** Centro; at Isla Rio Cuale. **Parking:** no self-parking. B L D AC

**THE SEA MONKEY RESTAURANT & BAR ON THE BEACH**   322/222-2174   84

▼▼ American. Casual Dining. $8-$18 **AAA Inspector Notes:** Here you can choose to eat directly on the beach under a sun umbrella, or on the covered open-air terrace. The atmosphere is fun and laid-back, which is what life is supposed to be like on the beach. The menu features plenty of casual fare, including home-style Mexican and American favorites such as burgers and wings. This place is well known for its value-priced buckets of beer and jumbo margaritas. **Features:** full bar, patio dining, happy hour. **Address:** 174 Aquiles Serdan 48380 **Location:** In Zona Romantica. B L D AC 🖫 🍴

**SI SENOR**   322/113-0064   45

▼▼▼ Mexican. Casual Dining. $15-$35 **AAA Inspector Notes:** This cantina serves freshly prepared Mexican fare in a bright, festive atmosphere. Diners start off their meals with fresh tortillas and spicy salsa, compliments of the house, and then proceed to the main course of flaming fajitas, tasty tacos or grilled meats or seafood. Fresh tortillas are always available. **Features:** full bar, patio dining. **Reservations:** suggested. **Address:** Josefa Ortiz de Dominguez No. 274 48351 **Location:** Jct Calle Guadalupe Sanchez; centro. **Parking:** no self-parking. L D AC

**SI SENOR MEXICAN RESTAURANT AND BEACH CLUB**   322/222-0577   63

▼▼▼ Mexican. Casual Dining. $10-$28 **AAA Inspector Notes:** A great location directly on the beach, a relaxed ambiance and fresh, well-prepared Mexican fare make this a hit with locals and tourists alike. At night, dining on the beach offers a romantic feel; during the day it also serves as a beach club. The chef features fine cuisine from various regions of the country, as well as Tex-Mex selections. There's always a showcase of fresh shrimp, which can be cooked any way you like. **Features:** full bar, patio dining. **Address:** Playa-Amapas No. 114 48380 **Location:** In Zona Romantica. **Parking:** street only. B L D AC

**SONORA GRILL PRIME**   322/221-3124   66

▼▼▼ Steak. Casual Dining. $16-$40 **AAA Inspector Notes:** Passing by this chic, typically packed dining room, it's hard not to stop and take a look. This covered, open-air steakhouse fosters a club-like feel, complete with a glass-walled kitchen so you can watch the chefs sizzle your meal selection. Fine cuts of beef, including Sterling Silver and USDA Prime, are the house specialty. **Features:** full bar. **Reservations:** suggested. **Address:** Paseo de La Marina 121 Fracc 48335 **Location:** At Marina Vallarta. **Parking:** street only. L D

**TERRAZZA DI ROMA RISTORANTE ITALIANO**   322/221-0871   5

▼▼▼ Italian. Fine Dining. $8-$26 **AAA Inspector Notes:** A charming, awning-covered pier at the water's edge is part of the setting at this restaurant. The menu lists pizza and a full range of Italian pasta and meat dishes, as well as both American and Mexican breakfast selections. **Features:** full bar, patio dining. **Address:** Condominio Puesta del Sol Local 2 48354 **Location:** In Marina Vallarta. **Parking:** street only. B L D

**TRIO RESTAURANT**   322/222-2196   31

▼▼▼ Mediterranean. Fine Dining. $18-$29 **AAA Inspector Notes:** Fine European cuisine is what you'll find at this very popular dining spot located in the central part of the city. It also features a pleasant mix of local and bistro decor, live music and generous drinks. It is popular with the American and European expatriate communities. **Features:** full bar. **Reservations:** suggested. **Address:** Guerrero No. 264 48310 **Location:** 3 blks n of the Malecon; centro. **Parking:** street only. D

**VICTOR'S PLACE CAFE TACUBA RESTAURANT**   322/221-2808   2

▼▼ Mexican. Casual Dining. $8-$17 **AAA Inspector Notes:** Always packed, this place draws you in to see what all the hype is about. What you'll find are exceedingly nice people and good home-style Mexican food. There's American fare as well, including breakfast served all day at excellent prices. To top it off, the outdoor patio offers relaxing views of the marina. Inside, diners enjoy a festive Mexican ambience. **Features:** full bar, patio dining. **Address:** Condominio Las Palmas Local 9 Fracc. Marina Vallarta 48354 **Location:** At Marina Vallarta. **Parking:** street only.

 B L D AC ⬚

**VIEJO VALLARTA**   322/222-8558   15

▼▼ Mexican. Casual Dining. $10-$22 **AAA Inspector Notes:** After climbing up to the building's third floor, you'll be delighted to find a bright, festive restaurant offering stunning views of the ocean and Vallarta's famed Malecon (seaside promenade). The menu features a good mix of home-style Mexican fare, including tasty shrimp cocktails, spicy tortilla soup, sizzling fajitas and fresh fish. The hot, homemade tortillas are outstanding. **Features:** full bar. **Address:** Morelos 484 Altos 48300 **Location:** Centro; directly overlooking the Malecon. **Parking:** street only. L D AC

(See map & index p. 472.)

## VISTA GRILL
322/222-3570 ④④

▽▽▽▽ ▽▽▽▽
International
Fine Dining
$20-$32

**AAA Inspector Notes:** In addition to the tantalizing menu, diners here enjoy an outstanding view of Vallarta from the restaurant's prime hilltop location. The contemporary décor and live entertainment in the open-air lounge complement the chef's innovative menu. Highlights include fresh seafood, slow-roasted pork and freshly grilled meats with exotic sauces. This is a great spot to watch the sunset. **Features:** patio dining. **Reservations:** suggested. Semiformal attire. **Address:** Pulpito No. 377 Col. Emiliano Zapata 48380 **Location:** Just s of town, follow signs from Airport Hwy (Mex 200). **Parking:** street only. Ⓓ

## VITEA OCEANFRONT BISTRO
322/222-8703 ⑨

▽▽▽ International. Casual Dining. $8–$25 **AAA Inspector Notes:** Overlooking the New Malecon area of town, the bustling oceanfront eatery sports a bright and airy decor. A European Riviera theme weaves through the innovative menu, which incorporates grilled items, seafood, meats and poultry. The excellent desserts merit at least a few bites. **Features:** full bar, patio dining. **Reservations:** suggested. **Address:** Libertad 2 y Malecon Centro 48380 **Location:** At the Malecon Centro; oceanfront. **Parking:** street only.

Ⓑ Ⓛ Ⓓ ⒦

This ends listings for Puerto Vallarta. The following resumes the alphabetical listings of cities in The Pacific Coast.

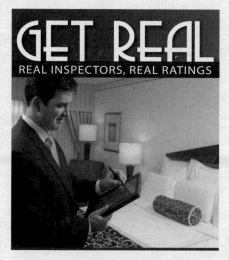

## PUNTA MITA, NAYARIT

## CASA DE MITA
329/298-4114

▽▽▽▽ ▽▽▽▽
Bed & Breakfast
$675-$835

**Address:** Calle Playa Caneyeras S/N **Location:** Oceanfront. Mex 200, 11.3 mi (18 km) on Punta Mita Rd, Higuera Blanco turn off, 1.1 mi (1.8 km) w to bridge Puente Cauyeros, then 0.7 mi (1.1 km) on beach access road. **Facility:** This property is an exclusive, luxury, seaside B&B where the included meals emphasize fine dining. 8 units. 3 stories (no elevator), exterior corridors. **Bath:** shower only. **Terms:** age restrictions may apply. **Amenities:** safes. **Pool(s):** heated outdoor. **Activities:** snorkeling, limited exercise equipment. **Guest Services:** valet laundry.

## FOUR SEASONS RESORT PUNTA MITA, MEXICO
(329)291-6000

▽▽▽▽ ▽▽▽▽
Resort Hotel
$750-$2000

**Address:** Punta Mita Bahia de Banderas 63734 **Location:** Oceanfront. Puerto Vallarta Airport, 29.2 mi (46.7 km) n. **Facility:** This exclusive resort overlooks the ocean and a beach. It caters to couples and families who enjoy outdoor activities rather than nightlife. The tropical grounds and landscaping are outstanding. 173 units. 1-3 stories (no elevator), exterior corridors. **Parking:** valet only. **Terms:** cancellation fee imposed, resort fee. **Amenities:** safes. Some: video games. **Dining:** 4 restaurants, also, Aramara, Bahia Ocean Grill and Bar, see separate listings, entertainment. **Pool(s):** heated outdoor. **Activities:** hot tub, steamroom, fishing, scuba diving, snorkeling, regulation golf, tennis, recreation programs, kids club, playground, game room, spa. **Guest Services:** valet and coin laundry, boarding pass kiosk.

## GRAND PALLADIUM VALLARTA RESORT AND SPA
329/226-9900

▽▽▽ **Resort Hotel** $384 **Address:** Costa Banderas KM 11.5 **Location:** Oceanfront. Mex 200 exit Punta Mita Rd, 6.9 mi (11 km) s to entrance. **Facility:** This all-inclusive resort offers a relaxing, fun atmosphere and a stunning oceanfront location; activities are available for all ages. 419 units. 3 stories (no elevator), exterior corridors. **Amenities:** safes. **Dining:** 6 restaurants, entertainment. **Pool(s):** outdoor. **Activities:** sauna, hot tub, scuba diving, snorkeling, tennis, recreation programs, kids club, game room, spa.

## HOTEL CINCO
(329)291-5005

▽▽▽ ▽▽▽
Condominium
$320-$760

**Address:** Ave El Anclote No. 5 63734 **Location:** Oceanfront. In town center. **Facility:** At this upscale beachfront property, guests enjoy spacious condostyle units with contemporary décor. A beach-level pool caters to families; the rooftop pool and lounge is for adults only. 9 condominiums. 4 stories, interior corridors. **Bath:** shower only. **Parking:** on-site and street. **Amenities:** safes. **Dining:** Tuna Blanca by cafe des artistes, see separate listing. **Pool(s):** heated outdoor. **Activities:** sauna, hot tub, steamroom, exercise room, spa. **Guest Services:** complimentary and valet laundry.

## IBEROSTAR PLAYA MITA
329/298-4280

**Resort Hotel**
**Rates not provided**

**Address:** Camino Ingreso a Litibu, Lote 2 63734 **Location:** Oceanfront. Mex 200, 11.3 mi (18 km) on Punta Mita Rd, follow signs; in Litibu complex. **Facility:** Located on an outstanding stretch of beach, the property offers many relaxing options. Sit by the ocean, lounge by the huge tropical pool or wander the extensive grounds. 452 units. 4 stories, exterior corridors. **Parking:** valet only. **Amenities:** safes. **Dining:** 7 restaurants, entertainment. **Pool(s):** heated outdoor. **Activities:** sauna, hot tub, steamroom, scuba diving, snorkeling, tennis, recreation programs, kids club, playground, game room, spa. **Guest Services:** valet laundry. *(See ad on insert.)*

[icons] CALL 🛒 S SD 🏊 BIZ 🛜 ✕ 🛗 💻 / SOME UNITS

## RANCHOS BANDERAS ALL SUITE RESORT BY MARIVAL GROUP
329/291-7000

**Condominium** $170-$585 **Address:** Carr a Punta de Mita KM 8.3 **Location:** Oceanfront. Carr a Punta de Mita KM 8.3. **Facility:** At this hidden gem you'll find the perfect spot for a quiet retreat. Highlights include lush tropical grounds, a bi-level pool with a waterfall, and a pristine beach area. 49 condominiums. 4 stories, exterior corridors. **Bath:** shower only. **Amenities:** safes. **Pool(s):** outdoor, heated outdoor. **Activities:** recreation programs, limited exercise equipment, spa. **Guest Services:** coin laundry.

[icons]

## THE ROYAL SUITES PUNTA DE MITA BY PALLADIUM
329/226-9900

**Hotel** $457 **Address:** Costa Banderas KM 11.5 **Location:** Oceanfront. Mex 200 exit Punta Mita Rd, 6.9 mi (11 km) s to entrance. **Facility:** 100 units. 3 stories (no elevator), interior/exterior corridors. **Terms:** age restrictions may apply. **Amenities:** safes. **Pool(s):** heated outdoor. **Activities:** recreation programs, spa.

[icons]

## THE ST. REGIS PUNTA MITA RESORT
(329)291-5800

**Resort Hotel**
$350-$1200

**ST REGIS**

**AAA Benefit:** Members save up to 15%, plus Starwood Preferred Guest® benefits!

**Address:** Lote H-4 Cond Maestro Ramal Carr Federal 200 KM 19.5 63734 **Location:** Oceanfront. Puerto Vallarta Airport, 29.2 mi (46.7 km) n; Mex 200, 11.3 mi (18 km) on Punta Mita Rd. **Facility:** This stunning oceanfront resort features clusters of luxurious guest units set on more than 22 acres of beautifully landscaped tropical grounds. 120 units, some two and three bedrooms. 2 stories (no elevator), exterior corridors. **Parking:** valet only. **Terms:** cancellation fee imposed, resort fee. **Dining:** 3 restaurants, also, Carolina at The St. Regis Punta Mita Resort, see separate listing. **Pool(s):** heated outdoor. **Activities:** hot tub, scuba diving, snorkeling, recreation programs, kids club, spa. **Guest Services:** valet laundry.

[icons]

## WHERE TO EAT

## ARAMARA
329/291-6000

**Asian Fine Dining**
$21-$35

**AAA Inspector Notes:** This elegant dining room offers both indoor and outdoor terrace dining. The chef has created an innovative menu of contemporary Asian cuisine, which includes popular choices such as thinly-sliced steak cooked on a hot stone. Another menu highlight is the spiny lobster risotto with a soy sauce glaze. Specialty dessert souffles end any meal on a sweet note. **Features:** full bar, patio dining. **Reservations:** suggested. **Address:** Punta Mita de Banderas 63734 **Location:** Puerto Vallarta Airport, 29.2 mi (46.7 km) n; in Four Seasons Resort Punta Mita, Mexico. **Parking:** valet only. D

## BAHIA OCEAN GRILL AND BAR
329/291-6000

Steak. Casual Dining. $21-$45 **AAA Inspector Notes:** This open-air restaurant's beachfront location affords great views of the ocean. Patrons combine simple grilled foods with exotic and creative dipping sauces in self-made creations. The chef encourages guests to be adventuresome. **Features:** full bar, patio dining. **Reservations:** suggested. **Address:** Punta Mita Bahia de Banderas 63734 **Location:** Puerto Vallarta Airport, 29.2 mi (46.7 km) n; in Four Seasons Resort Punta Mita, Mexico. **Parking:** valet only. D 🅰

## THE BLUE SHRIMP RESTAURANT
329/2915212

Seafood. Casual Dining. $12-$32 **AAA Inspector Notes:** Here you'll find a relaxed yet sophisticated setting with stunning views of the ocean. The covered, open-air dining room is the perfect spot to enjoy freshly prepared fish and seafood. The house specialty is shrimp, made any way you like. Don't miss the restaurant's fresh, hot tortillas. After the kitchen closes at 11 pm, the restaurant becomes a chic lounge. **Features:** full bar, patio dining. **Address:** Ave El Anclote No. 10 63734 **Location:** Beachfront; in town center. **Parking:** street only. L D 🅰

## CAROLINA AT THE ST. REGIS PUNTA MITA RESORT
329/291-5800

**International Fine Dining**
$35-$52

**AAA Inspector Notes:** This elegant dining room features a unique contemporary design with a choice of both indoor and outdoor patio dining. Guests may enjoy a pre- or post-dinner cocktail in the unique lounge. The chef offers an innovative menu that changes often to reflect fresh seasonal ingredients. A tableside flambé coffee is the perfect finale. **Features:** full bar, patio dining. **Reservations:** required. **Address:** Lote H-4 Cond Maestro Ramal Carr Federal 200 KM 19.5 63734 **Location:** Puerto Vallarta Airport, 29.2 mi (46.7 km) n; Mex 200, 11.3 mi (18 km) on Punta Mita Rd; in The St. Regis Punta Mita Resort. **Parking:** valet only. D

## EL DORADO
329/291-6296

International. Casual Dining. $10-$22 **AAA Inspector Notes:** Perfect for those who want to hang out on the beach all day, this casual eatery has umbrella-shaded tables, as well as a bi-level covered patio. From tasty shrimp cocktails and seafood platters to burgers and Mexican fare, the menu aims to please all palates. **Features:** full bar, patio dining. **Address:** Playa El Anclote S/N 63734 **Location:** Directly on the beach; in town center. **Parking:** street only. B L D 🅰 🗲

## MARGARITAS RESTAURANT
329/291-5107

Mexican. Casual Dining. $10-$20 **AAA Inspector Notes:** This laid-back beachfront restaurant enjoys good word-of-mouth for its humongous margaritas and generous portions of cooked-to-order Mexican food; shrimp is the house specialty. Sheltered by palapa umbrellas, the dining tables are set directly on the beach. **Features:** full bar, patio dining. **Address:** Ave El Anclote No. 14 63734 **Location:** In town center. **Parking:** street only. L D 🅰

## MARISCOS TINO'S
329/291-6473

Seafood. Casual Dining. $10-$21 **AAA Inspector Notes:** Located on the beach and set under a large palapa roof, this casual open-air joint is perfect for a laid-back lunch or dinner. The menu lists a nice mix of fresh fish and seafood as well as Mexican favorites and some lighter fare. **Features:** full bar, patio dining. **Address:** Ave El Anclote No. 64 Nvo Cora **Location:** Directly on the beach; in town center. **Parking:** on-site and street. L D 🅰 🗲

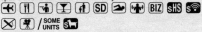

Trust the recommendations
of AAA/CAA travel experts
to make a good trip great

**ORIGINAL ANCLOTE RESTAURANT - BAR**  329/291-6361

▼▼▼ Seafood. Casual Dining. $8-$22 **AAA Inspector Notes:** Here's a great spot to watch the surfers, sink your feet into the sand and enjoy an abundance of fresh local fish and seafood. You'll find a laid-back beach club ambiance with some tables located on the beach, while others are shaded under a large palapa roof. **Features:** full bar, patio dining. **Address:** Ave El Anclote S/N 63734 **Location:** Beachfront; in town center. **Parking:** street only. ⬜L ⬜D ⬜AC

**SI SENOR**  329/291-6652

▼▼▼ Mexican. Casual Dining. $12-$28 **AAA Inspector Notes:** Offering a delightful setting both day and night, this outstanding beachfront restaurant has a tunnel of palm trees, creating shade and a tropical ambience. The menu features fresh fish and seafood prepared with a Mexican flair. Servers take pride in bringing the catch of the day selections to the table and describing preparation options. Before leaving, take time to appreciate the restaurant's innovative display of Mexican pottery. **Features:** full bar, patio dining. **Reservations:** suggested, for dinner. **Address:** El Anclote S/N 63734 **Location:** Centro. **Parking:** street only. ⬜L ⬜D

**TUNA BLANCA BY CAFE DES ARTISTES**  329/291-5414

▼▼▼ International. Casual Dining. $8-$45 **AAA Inspector Notes:** Sophisticated yet relaxed, this trendy spot is very popular with locals who appreciate innovative cuisine. A cool sea breeze blows through the open-air beachfront dining area, where entertainment comes courtesy of a live pianist and the sizzling culinary action in the exhibition kitchen. In addition to a prix fixe menu, diners will also find nice a la carte selections. At lunch, expect a more casual beach club feel and a simpler menu with lots of fresh fish, ceviche and sandwiches. **Features:** full bar, patio dining. **Reservations:** suggested. **Address:** Ave El Anclote No. 7 63734 **Location:** In town center; in Hotel Cinco. **Parking:** street only. ⬜L ⬜D ⬜AC

## RINCON DE GUAYABITOS, NAYARIT

**DECAMERON LOS COCOS**  327/274-0191

▼ Resort Hotel $142-$210 **Address:** Retorno Las Palmas 63727 **Location:** Centro. **Facility:** A complete village on its own, this beachfront resort consists of a series of buildings and pools spread out over a large area. It is less than a block from the beach. 240 units. 2-4 stories, exterior corridors. **Amenities:** safes. **Dining:** 4 restaurants, entertainment. **Pool(s):** outdoor. **Activities:** tennis, recreation programs, bicycles, playground, game room, massage.

⬜ ⬜ ⬜ ⬜

**VILLA CORONA DEL MAR BED AND BREAKFAST**  327/274-0912

▼▼▼ Bed & Breakfast $120-$250 **Address:** 15 Retorno Gaviotas 63726 **Location:** Mex 200 exit Rincon de Guayabitos westbound, 0.6 mi (1 km) n. **Facility:** Beautifully converted into a B&B, this villa boasts wonderful grounds and a center courtyard with a spacious tropical pool area. 9 units, some two bedrooms and cottages. 1-3 stories (no elevator), interior/exterior corridors. **Bath:** shower only. **Parking:** street only. **Pool(s):** outdoor. **Activities:** beach access, tennis, massage.

⬜ ⬜ ⬜ ⬜ ⬜ / SOME UNITS ⬜ ⬜ ⬜

**WHERE TO EAT**

**BESO DEL SOL STEAKHOUSE**  327/274-0659

▼▼ Steak. Casual Dining. $10-$18 **AAA Inspector Notes:** Here's a nice spot to enjoy a hearty, grilled steak or some tangy barbecued ribs in a comfortable setting with Spanish décor. Look out for the daily specials, which include your first beer or glass of wine. This place is a definite hit with locals and visiting 'snowbirds.' Cash only. **Features:** full bar. **Address:** Ave Sol Nuevo No. 103 63726 **Location:** Centro. **Parking:** no self-parking. ⬜B ⬜L ⬜D ⬜AC

**RESTAURANT VILLANUEVA**  327/274-0391

▼▼ International. Casual Dining. $8-$15 **AAA Inspector Notes:** Seasonal local residents (or 'snowbirds') from 'el norte' flock to this open-air restaurant for tasty food, good music and the casual 'dinner party with friends' atmosphere. The varied menu features regional Mexican and international fare. **Features:** full bar, patio dining. **Address:** Retorno Ceibas No. 3 63726 **Location:** North end of beach. **Parking:** street only. ⬜B ⬜L ⬜D ⬜AC

**SALVADOR'S RESTAURANT**  322/151-7702

▼▼▼ Seafood. Casual Dining. $8-$16 **AAA Inspector Notes:** A friendly place to kick back and feast on fresh seafood, this family-owned-and-operated eatery has been packing in regulars and newcomers alike since 1980. Weekday specials include all-you-can-eat shrimp on Tuesdays and Fridays, and on Thursdays there's a seafood dinner platter that will feed up to five people. The good food and fabulous beachfront location mean nights can get very busy; it is wise to phone ahead for reservations or make them in person during the day. **Features:** full bar, patio dining. **Address:** Returno Las Palmas S/N 63726 **Location:** Directly on the beach, north side of town. **Parking:** no self-parking. ⬜B ⬜L ⬜D ⬜AC ⬜

**VISTA GUAYABITOS**  327/274-2589

◆ International. Casual Dining. $10-$28 **AAA Inspector Notes:** Looking up high in the sky, you'll be drawn to this delightful, covered, open-air terrace-style restaurant overlooking the beach. Both day and night, diners are enticed by the hilltop location. At lunch you'll find a mix of casual favorites such as burgers and soups as well as a full range of well-prepared Mexican and international specialties. At night, a romantic ambiance prevails with candlelit tables overlooking the sparkling lights of the town below. **Features:** full bar, patio dining. **Address:** Carr a Los Ayala KM 1.5 63726 **Location:** Directly up the hill from the beach. ⬜L ⬜D ⬜AC

## ZIHUATANEJO, GUERRERO

See also Ixtapa, Guerrero p. 453

**LA CASA QUE CANTA**  (755)555-7030

▼▼▼ ▼▼▼
**Boutique Hotel**
$295-$885

**Address:** Camino Escenico S/N Playa La Ropa 40880 **Location:** Playa Ropa, 5.6 mi (9 km) n of airport; Mirador, follow signs to Playa La Ropa sector. **Facility:** On a cliff with bay views, this elegant property is decorated with fine Mexican folk art and offers a real romantic getaway. Stair climbing is required to reach most areas of hotel. 27 units, some houses. 3-6 stories, exterior corridors. **Bath:** shower only. **Terms:** 7 night minimum stay - seasonal, age restrictions may apply, 28 day cancellation notice, in season-fee imposed. **Amenities:** safes. **Dining:** 2 restaurants. **Pool(s):** outdoor. **Activities:** limited beach access, recreation programs, exercise room, spa. **Guest Services:** valet laundry.

⬜ ⬜ ⬜ ⬜ ⬜ ⬜ HS ⬜ ⬜ ⬜ ⬜

**VICEROY ZIHUATANEJO**  (755)555-5500

▼▼▼ ▼▼▼
**Boutique Hotel**
$176-$1450

**Address:** Playa La Ropa S/N 40895 **Location:** Oceanfront. 6.3 mi (10 km) n of airport, follow signs. **Facility:** Palms, lagoons and tropical gardens surround this service-oriented hotel, which features a fine restaurant. Some guest rooms have private plunge pools. 46 units, some two bedrooms. 1-3 stories (no elevator), exterior corridors. **Bath:** shower only. **Parking:** on-site and valet. **Terms:** 7 night minimum stay - seasonal, 14 day cancellation notice, in season, resort fee. **Amenities:** safes. **Dining:** 2 restaurants. **Pool(s):** outdoor. **Activities:** tennis, recreation programs in season, exercise room, spa. **Guest Services:** valet laundry.

⬜ ⬜ ⬜ ⬜ ⬜ ⬜ BIZ HS ⬜ ⬜ / SOME UNITS ⬜ ⬜ ⬜

**HOTEL LAS PALMAS**  755/557-0634

fyi Not evaluated. **Address:** Lot 5, Playa Blanca 40880 **Location:** On Playa Blanca, s of airport. Facilities, services, and décor characterize a mid-scale property. Guest rooms at this boutique hotel feature private terraces, hammocks and wonderful ocean views. Some units feature private plunge pools.

**TENTACIONES HOTEL & RESTAURANTS**        755/544-8383

[fyi] Not evaluated. **Address:** Camino Escenico a Playa Ropa, Lote 97-C 40880 **Location:** On La Ropa Beach Rd; above Playa Madera. Facilities, services, and décor characterize an upscale property.

## WHERE TO EAT

**COCONUTS**        755/554-2518

International. Fine Dining. $16-$27 **AAA Inspector Notes:** *Historic.* This restaurant, located in a pedestrian-only alleyway, occupies the delightful open courtyard of a historic building. The patio is filled with lush trees and fairy lights that set a romantic tone. The chef's international menu features fine cuts of meat, fresh fish and other seafood, house-made pasta and some Mexican fare. **Features:** full bar. **Reservations:** suggested. **Address:** Pasaje Agustin Ramirez l 40880 **Location:** Centro; entrance from Calle Juan N. Alvarez or Calle Vincente Guerrero. **Parking:** street only.

**KAU-KAN RESTAURANT**        755/554-8446

Seafood. Casual Dining. $16-$30 **AAA Inspector Notes:** Sunsets are lovely from this restaurant's rooftop patio, which offers a romantic view of the bay. A fine selection of wine and spirits complements an array of delicious seafood offerings, including red snapper, stingray and octopus. Nightly specials available. **Features:** full bar. **Reservations:** suggested. **Address:** Carr Escenica Lote No. 7 Cd La Madera S/N 40880 **Location:** On La Ropa Beach Rd; above Playa Madera. **Parking:** valet only.

**LA CASA VIEJA**        755/554-9770

Regional Mexican. Casual Dining. $8-$18 **AAA Inspector Notes:** This local favorite has a rustic, charming vibe. Authentic, regional menu items are served by friendly, efficient waiters. Offered on Thursdays is a traditional lunch of pozole with either chicken, pork or seafood. Live music makes for a fun atmosphere. **Features:** full bar, Sunday brunch. **Address:** Josefa Ortiz de Dominguez 7 La Madera **Location:** Centro. **Parking:** street only.

**LA PERLA**        755/554-2700

Seafood. Casual Dining. $9-$35 **AAA Inspector Notes:** Right on the beach, you can dine under the palapas with tables in the sand at this eatery that serves fresh, simply prepared seafood, including red snapper, lobster, octopus and clams. Jumbo shrimp is plentiful, and patrons can order it cooked the way they like it. **Features:** full bar. **Address:** Playa La Ropa S/N 40880 **Location:** Playa La Ropa. *(See ad at front of book.)*

**MAR Y CIELO**        755/555-7000

Seafood. Fine Dining. $10-$20 **AAA Inspector Notes:** A spectacular setting and attentive service create a truly romantic dining experience. The talented chef uses only the freshest of local seafood and other seasonal ingredients to create a unique, ever-changing menu. **Features:** full bar, patio dining. **Reservations:** suggested. **Address:** Camino Escenico S/N **Location:** Playa Ropa, 5.6 mi (9 km) n of airport; Mirador, follow signs to Playa La Ropa sector; in La Casa Que Canta. **Parking:** valet only.

**RISTORANTE IL MARE**        755/554-9067

Italian. Casual Dining. $12-$35 **AAA Inspector Notes:** Set on a cliff at La Madera Beach, this casual dining spot boasts wonderful views and serves modern Italian and Greek cuisine, including a variety of pastas. **Features:** full bar, patio dining. **Reservations:** suggested. **Address:** Carretera Escenica a La Ropa Beach S/N 40880 **Location:** Follow signs to Playa La Ropa sector.

**TENTACIONES**        755/544-8383

[fyi] Not evaluated. Seafood and international fusion cuisine is offered along with spectacular views. A surprise, five-course meal is served and reservations are required. **Address:** Camino Escenico a Playa La Ropa, Lote 97-C, Col. La Madera 40880 **Location:** On La Ropa Beach Rd; in Tentaciones Hotel & Restaurants.

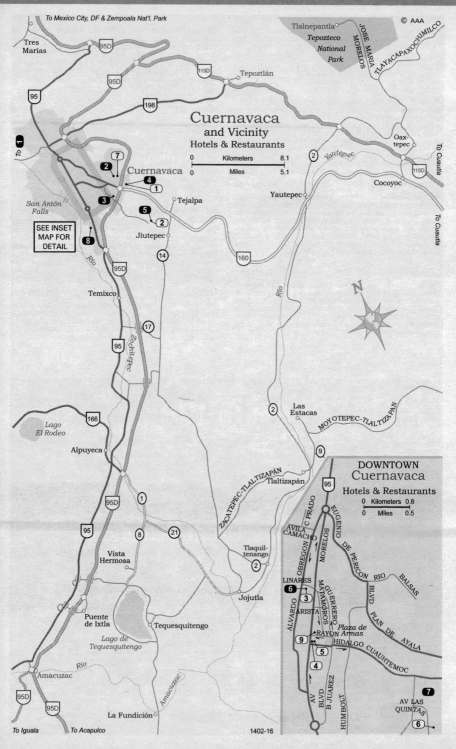

To Mexico City, DF & Zempoala Nat'l. Park

© AAA

Tres Marías

Tlalnepantla

Tepozteco National Park

Tepoztlán

95D

115D

95D

198

95

Cuernavaca
and Vicinity
Hotels & Restaurants

Oax-tepec

To Cuautla

7

Cuernavaca

2

Yautepec

Cocoyoc

115D

0    Kilometers    8.1
0    Miles    5.1

4

1

Tejalpa

Yautepec

San Antón Falls

3

5

2

160

Rio

SEE INSET MAP FOR DETAIL

8

Jiutepec

14

Rio

N

Río

95D

Temixco

17

Zochitepec

95

Las Estacas

2

MOYOTEPEC-TLALTIZAPAN

166

Lago El Rodeo

9

DOWNTOWN
Cuernavaca
Hotels & Restaurants

Alpuyeca

ZACATEPEC-TLALTIZAPÁN

Tlaltizapán

95

0    Kilometers    0.8
0    Miles    0.5

95D

1

8

21

2

Tlaquil-tenango

C PRADO

ÁVILA CAMACHO

EUGENIO DE PERICON

RIO

BALSAS

OBREGON

SOTERO

Vista Hermosa

LINARES

6

3

GUERRERO

MATAMOROS

BLVD PLAN DE AYALA

Jojutla

ALVARADO

ARISTA

Plaza de Armas

Puente de Ixtla

Tequesquitengo

9

RAYON

HIDALGO

CUAUHTEMOC

5

Lago de Tequesquitengo

4

Río

Amacuzac

AV BLVD B JUAREZ

HUMBOLT

AV LAS QUINTAS

7

95D

Amacuzac

6

95D

La Fundición

To Iguala    To Acapulco

1402-16

# MEXICO CITY AND VICINITY

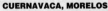

**AAA recommends that travelers consult online U.S. State Department travel advisories when planning travel abroad. Find this information at http://travel.state.gov/content/passports/english/alertswarnings/mexico-travel-warning.html.**

## Cuernavaca and Vicinity

This index helps you "spot" where approved hotels and restaurants are located on the corresponding detailed maps. Hotel daily rate range is for comparison only. Restaurant price range is a combination of lunch and/or dinner. Turn to the listing page for more detailed rate and price information and consult display ads for special promotions.

### CUERNAVACA, MORELOS

| Map Page | Hotels | Diamond Rated | Rate Range | Page |
|---|---|---|---|---|
| **1** p. 492 | Hotel Racquet | ▽▽▽ | $121-$287 | 494 |
| **2** p. 492 | Hotel Argento | ▽▽▽ | $128-$153 | 494 |
| **3** p. 492 | Hotel Vista Hermosa | ▽▽▽ | $92-$160 | 494 |
| **4** p. 492 | **Hotel & Spa Hacienda de Cortes** | ▽▽▽▽ | $182-$464 | 494 |
| **5** p. 492 | Camino Real Sumiya, Cuernavaca | ▽▽▽ | $233-$389 | 494 |
| **6** p. 492 | **Las Mañanitas Hotel Garden Restaurant & Spa** | ▽▽▽▽ | $280-$580 | 494 |
| **7** p. 492 | **Hosterias Las Quintas** | ▽▽▽ | $110-$250 | 494 |
| **8** p. 492 | Holiday Inn Express & Suites Cuernavaca | ▽▽▽ | $73-$244 | 494 |

| Map Page | Restaurants | Diamond Rated | Cuisine | Price Range | Page |
|---|---|---|---|---|---|
| ① p. 492 | La Casona Restaurant | ▽▽▽ | Regional Mexican | $10-$28 | 495 |
| ② p. 492 | Restaurant Sumiya | ▽▽▽ | Asian | $18-$24 | 495 |
| ③ p. 492 | **Las Mañanitas Restaurant** | ▽▽▽ | Mexican | $16-$45 | 495 |
| ④ p. 492 | Casa Hidalgo | ▽▽▽ | International | $8-$22 | 495 |
| ⑤ p. 492 | 1521 El Paraiso | ▽▽ | Mexican | $7-$22 | 494 |
| ⑥ p. 492 | Las Quintas | ▽▽ | Regional Steak | $9-$25 | 495 |
| ⑦ p. 492 | El Madrigal Restaurant Bar | ▽▽▽ | Mexican Specialty | $10-$35 | 495 |
| ⑨ p. 492 | La India Bonita Restaurante & Bar | ▽▽ | Mexican | $6-$25 | 495 |

# CUERNAVACA, MORELOS (C-2)

pop. 365,168, elev. 5,058'
• Hotels & Restaurants map & index p. 492

## CAMINO REAL SUMIYA, CUERNAVACA          777/329-9888  **5**

WWW Resort Hotel $233-$389 **Address:** Interior de Fracc Sumiya S/N, Col Jose Parres **Location:** 1.8 mi (3 km) se of Mex 95-D (toll road) exit Mex 160 (Cuernavaca-Cuautla Rd), follow signs. **Facility:** Authentic Japanese architecture, gardens and artwork are featured on the expansive grounds of this property located in a private, residential area. Meets AAA guest room security requirements. 163 units. 4 stories, exterior corridors. **Parking:** on-site and valet. **Terms:** 3 day cancellation notice. **Amenities:** safes. **Dining:** 2 restaurants, also, Restaurant Sumiya, see separate listing. **Pool(s):** outdoor, heated outdoor. **Activities:** sauna, steamroom, tennis, recreation programs in season, playground, exercise room, massage. **Guest Services:** valet laundry.

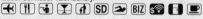

## HOLIDAY INN EXPRESS & SUITES CUERNAVACA
(777)310-5333  **8**

WWW Hotel $73-$244 **Address:** 133 Avenida Morelos Sur **Location:** In Las Palmas area. **Facility:** Meets AAA guest room security requirements. 124 units. 7 stories, interior corridors. **Amenities:** safes. **Pool(s):** heated outdoor. **Activities:** exercise room. **Guest Services:** valet and coin laundry.

## HOSTERIAS LAS QUINTAS          777/362-3949  **7**

WWWW
Country Inn
$110-$250

**Address:** Blvd Diaz Ordaz No. 9, Col Cantarranas **Location:** 1.8 mi (3 km) e of Cortes Palace, off Ave Cuauhtemoc at Ave Las Quintas 107. Located in a quiet residential area. **Facility:** Spacious, tropical grounds. Colonial-style inn. Some rooms with fireplace. All rooms with ceiling fans. Variety of suites and junior suites available. Meets AAA guest room security requirements. 121 units. 2 stories (no elevator), interior/exterior corridors. **Parking:** on-site and valet. **Terms:** 3 day cancellation notice. **Amenities:** safes. **Dining:** Las Quintas, see separate listing. **Pool(s):** outdoor, heated outdoor. **Activities:** sauna, hot tub, steamroom, recreation programs, kids club, exercise room, spa. **Guest Services:** valet laundry.

## HOTEL & SPA HACIENDA DE CORTES
777/315-8844  **4**

WWWW
Classic Historic
Country Inn
$182-$464

**Address:** Plaza Kennedy No. 90, Col Atlacomulco Jiutepec 62560 **Location:** Mex 95-D (toll road) exit Jojutla, just e to 1st traffic light, then 1.3 mi (2 km) s to Jiutepec, follow signs; in Atlacomulco Colonia of Jiutepec. **Facility:** Founded in the mid-1500's and once a retreat for the aristocrats of New Spain, this former hacienda comprises beautiful gardens, unique guest rooms with buildings and some furnishings from the period. 54 units. 1-4 stories, exterior corridors. **Parking:** on-site and valet. **Terms:** 3 day cancellation notice. **Amenities:** safes. **Dining:** La Casona Restaurant, see separate listing. **Pool(s):** heated outdoor. **Activities:** sauna, hot tub, playground, exercise room, spa. **Guest Services:** valet laundry.

## HOTEL ARGENTO          (777)316-3282  **2**

WWW Hotel $128-$153 **Address:** Ave Rio Mayo 1001 62290 **Location:** Mex 95-D (toll road) exit Ave Rio Mayo, 0.8 mi (1.3 km) w. **Facility:** Meets AAA guest room security requirements. 63 units. 2 stories (no elevator), interior/exterior corridors. *Bath:* shower only. **Parking:** on-site and valet. **Amenities:** safes. **Pool(s):** heated outdoor. **Activities:** recreation programs in season, playground, exercise room. **Guest Services:** valet laundry.

## HOTEL RACQUET          (777)101-0350  **1**

WWW Hotel $121-$287 **Address:** Ave Francisco Villa 100, Fracc Rancho Cortes 62120 **Location:** 0.5 mi (0.8 km) n of Zapata's monument, follow signs. **Facility:** 52 units. 4 stories (no elevator), interior/exterior corridors. **Parking:** on-site and valet. **Amenities:** safes. **Pool(s):** heated outdoor. **Activities:** miniature golf, tennis, playground, game room, exercise room, spa. **Guest Services:** valet laundry.

## HOTEL VISTA HERMOSA          777/315-2374  **3**

WWW Country Inn $92-$160 **Address:** Rio Panuco No. 600 62290 **Location:** Mex 95-D (toll road) exit Ave Rio Mayo, 0.6 mi (1 km) sw on Calle Diana, sw on Ave Rio Mayo, then 0.7 mi (1.2 km) s; corner of Rio Papaloapan. Located in a quiet residential area. **Facility:** Colonial in style, this inn has a large, tranquil courtyard garden. Some guest rooms feature a private garden terrace. Street-side rooms have double-paned windows. 40 units, some two bedrooms. 2 stories (no elevator), interior/exterior corridors. **Parking:** valet only. **Amenities:** safes. **Pool(s):** heated outdoor. **Activities:** playground. **Guest Services:** valet laundry.

## LAS MAÑANITAS HOTEL GARDEN RESTAURANT & SPA          (777)362-0000  **6**

WWWW
Classic
Country Inn
$280-$580

**Address:** Ricardo Linares 107 Col Centro 62000 **Location:** Just e of Mex 95. **Facility:** Tropical gardens surround the colonial-style inn. A few rooms feature fireplaces; some units with private patio and fountain. There's a large meeting facility adjacent to the inn. 27 units, some two bedrooms. 2 stories (no elevator), interior/exterior corridors. **Parking:** valet only. **Terms:** 7 day cancellation notice. **Amenities:** safes. **Dining:** Las Mañanitas Restaurant, see separate listing. **Pool(s):** heated outdoor. **Activities:** sauna, hot tub, steamroom, spa. **Guest Services:** valet laundry.

## BARCELO CUERNAVACA EJECTIVO          777/322-3924

[fyi] Not evaluated. **Address:** Coronel Ahumanda 203, Col. Lomas del Mirador 62450 **Location:** Mex 95-D (toll road) exit Plan de Ayala St. Facilities, services, and décor characterize an economy property.

## WHERE TO EAT

## 1521 EL PARAISO          777/312-4499  **5**

WW Mexican. Casual Dining: $7-$22 **AAA Inspector Notes:** The centrally located restaurant is a perfect spot for a respite from sightseeing. Ample sidewalk seating and a menu of classic, reasonably priced Mexican dishes, including parrilladas and molcajetes, are offered. **Features:** full bar. **Address:** Hidalgo No. 1, Col Centro 62000 **Location:** Downtown; near Cortes Palace. **Parking:** street only. [B] [L] [D] [K] [N]

Visit the AAA/CAA senior driver sites
for resources to help you drive safely longer

(See map & index p. 492.)

**CASA HIDALGO**                                   777/312-2749  (4)

▼▼▼▼ International. Casual Dining. $8-$22 **AAA Inspector Notes:** Take the elevator up and dine on the balcony or attractive terrace overlooking the Cortes Palace and the zócalo, or relax in the third-floor bar. The central location makes this place a nice stop if you're in the downtown area. Live music on weekends. **Features:** full bar. **Reservations:** suggested. **Address:** Jardin de Los Heroes No. 6/Hidalgo No. 6, Col Centro 62000 **Location:** Downtown; facing Cortes Palace. **Parking:** valet only.  L  D  🛇

**EL MADRIGAL RESTAURANT BAR**                     777/100-7700  (7)

▼▼▼▼ Mexican Specialty. Fine Dining. $10-$35 **AAA Inspector Notes:** Dine on the covered terrace at this spacious, beautifully designed Mexican colonial-style restaurant with wonderful works of art adorning the walls and tranquil views of the gardens and waterfall. Contemporary Mexican and international cuisine is prepared. Ask about the Sunday specials. Patio heaters warm the space in cooler weather. **Features:** full bar, patio dining. **Reservations:** suggested. **Address:** Sonora No. 115, Col. Vista Hermosa 62290 **Location:** Mex 95-D (toll road) exit Ave Rio Mayo, just nw to Ave San Diego, then just w; jct Ave San Diego, just n. **Parking:** valet only.

B  L  D  🄰🄲  🛇

**LA CASONA RESTAURANT**                           777/315-8844  (1)

▼▼▼ Regional Mexican. Casual Dining. $10-$28 **AAA Inspector Notes:** Established in the 1500s, the famous hacienda offers a quiet dining respite in its cool garden courtyard patio or inside the historic restaurant, once a former sugar mill and now where patrons dine beneath an amazing canopy of trees. Brunch is offered on Saturday and Sunday. **Features:** full bar, patio dining, Sunday brunch. **Reservations:** suggested. **Address:** Plaza Kennedy No. 10, Col Atlacomulco Jiutepec 62560 **Location:** Mex 95-D (toll road) exit Jojutla, just e to 1st traffic light, then 1.3 mi (2 km) s to Jiutepec, follow signs; in Atlacomulco Colonia of Jiutepec; in Hotel & Spa Hacienda de Cortes. **Parking:** on-site and valet.

B  L  D  🄰🄲  🛇

**LA INDIA BONITA RESTAURANTE & BAR**   777/312-5021  (9)

▼▼ Mexican. Casual Dining. $6-$25 **AAA Inspector Notes:** Classic. Since 1933, Cuernavaca's oldest restaurant has been serving traditional Mexican cuisine in a Spanish colonial home that was the former residence of U.S. Ambassador Dwight W. Morrow. Patio dining is available in the garden area. Live music is featured in the evenings and ballet folklorico on most Saturdays at 8 pm. **Features:** full bar, Sunday brunch. **Address:** Morrow 15-B, Col. Centro 62000 **Location:** Between aves Morelos and Matamoros; centro. **Parking:** street only.  B  L  D  🄰🄲  🛇

**LAS MAÑANITAS RESTAURANT**                       777/362-0019  (3)

▼▼▼▼
Mexican
Fine Dining
$16-$45

**AAA Inspector Notes:** The restaurant in a colonial country inn offers dining on the terrace amid meticulously manicured lawns and gardens with strolling peacocks and flamingos. **Features:** full bar, patio dining. **Reservations:** suggested. **Address:** Ricardo Linares 107 Col Centro 62000 **Location:** Just e of Mex 95; in Las Mañanitas Hotel Garden Restaurant & Spa. **Parking:** valet only.

B  L  D  🄰🄲  🛇

**LAS QUINTAS**                                    777/362-3949  (6)

▼▼ Regional Steak. Casual Dining. $9-$25 **AAA Inspector Notes:** Dine surrounded by the delightful gardens and a koi pond. The menu features steaks, seafood and Mexican cuisine. **Features:** full bar, patio dining, Sunday brunch. **Address:** Blvd Diaz Ordaz No. 9, Col Cantarranas **Location:** 1.8 mi (3 km) e of Cortez Palace, off Ave Cuauhtemoc at Ave Las Quintas 107; in Hosterias Las Quintas. **Parking:** on-site and valet.  B  L  D  🄰🄲  🛇

**RESTAURANT SUMIYA**                              777/329-9888  (2)

▼▼▼▼ Asian. Casual Dining. $18-$24 **AAA Inspector Notes:** In a tranquil setting overlooking the lush Japanese gardens, this restaurant offers varied Asian-style preparations and a large Sunday buffet. **Features:** full bar, patio dining, Sunday brunch. **Reservations:** suggested. **Address:** Interior de Fracc Sumiya S/N, Col Jose Parres **Location:** 1.8 mi (3 km) se of Mex 95-D (toll road) exit Mex 160 (Cuernavaca-Cuautla Rd), follow signs; in Camino Real Sumiya, Cuernavaca. **Parking:** on-site and valet.  L  D  🛇

**DAICHI TEPPAN & STEAKHOUSE**                     777/322-0348

**[fyi]** Not evaluated. Dine at the teppanyaki tables in an inviting ambiance. Sushi also is served. **Address:** Ave San Diego No. 304, Col. Vista Hermosa **Location:** Mex 95-D (toll road) exit Ave Rio Mayo, just nw to Ave San Diego, then just w.

**LOS COLORINES**                                  777/311-7301

**[fyi]** Not evaluated. Traditional and some local Mexican dishes are served in a casual, colorful atmosphere. **Address:** Ave Emiliano Zapata 598 62170 **Location:** Centro.

**OCEAN DRIVE RESTAURANT**                         777/228-0106

**[fyi]** Not evaluated. A variety of seafood appetizers, ceviche and entrées are served at this casual restaurant. **Address:** Ave San Diego No. 20, Col. Vista Hermosa 62290 **Location:** Mex 95-D (toll road) exit Ave Rio Mayo, just nw to Ave San Diego, then just w.

**RINCON DEL BIFE RESTAURANTE-BAR**                777/315-4794

**[fyi]** Not evaluated. Beef and seafood are the primary focus at this restaurant that is open for breakfast, lunch and dinner. **Address:** San Diego No. 1001, Col. Vista Hermosa 62290 **Location:** Mex 95-D (toll road) exit Ave Rio Mayo, just nw to Ave San Diego, then just w; just e from jct Sonora.

## IXTAPAN DE LA SAL, MÉXICO (C-2)
pop. 33,541, elev. 6,311'

**HOTEL BUNGALOWS LOLITA**                         721/143-0016

**[fyi]** Not evaluated. **Address:** Blvd Arturo San Roman 33 **Location:** 0.9 mi (1.5 km) n on Mex 55. Facilities, services, and décor characterize a mid-scale property.

**IXTAPAN DE LA SAL MARRIOTT HOTEL & SPA**  721/143-2010

**[fyi]** Not evaluated. **Address:** Jose Ma Morelos S/N Fracc Bugambilias **Location:** Just w of Mex 55. Facilities, services, and décor characterize a mid-scale property.

**AAA Benefit:**
Members save 5% or more!

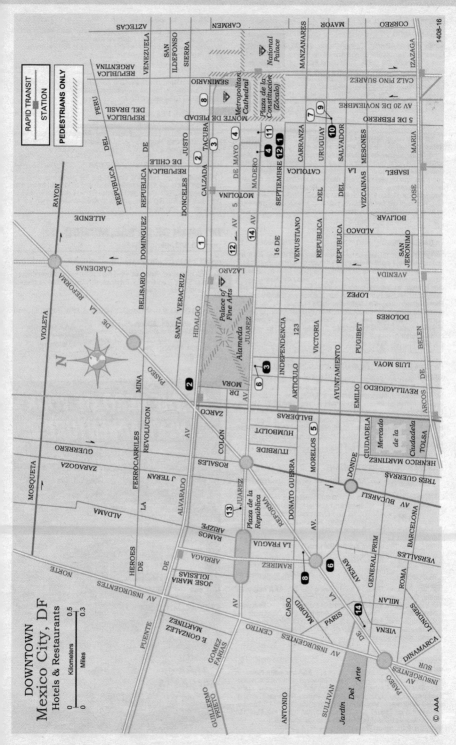

DOWNTOWN
Mexico City, DF
Hotels & Restaurants

RAPID TRANSIT
STATION
PEDESTRIANS ONLY

© AAA

1408-16

# Mexico City

## Downtown Mexico City

This index helps you "spot" where approved hotels and restaurants are located on the corresponding detailed maps. Hotel daily rate range is for comparison only. Restaurant price range is a combination of lunch and/or dinner. Turn to the listing page for more detailed rate and price information and consult display ads for special promotions.

### MEXICO CITY, DISTRITO FEDERAL

| Map Page | Hotels | Diamond Rated | Rate Range | Page |
|---|---|---|---|---|
| **1** p. 496 | Gran Hotel Ciudad de Mexico | ▽▽▽ | $130-$245 | 506 |
| **2** p. 496 | Hotel De Cortes | fyi | Rates not provided | 507 |
| **3** p. 496 | **Hilton Mexico City Reforma** | ▽▽▽▽ | $129-$239 | 506 |
| **4** p. 496 | Zocalo Central | ▽▽▽ | $129-$200 | 509 |
| **6** p. 496 | Fiesta Americana Reforma | ▽▽▽ | Rates not provided | 505 |
| **8** p. 496 | **Le Meridien Mexico City** | ▽▽▽▽ | $285-$410 | 508 |
| **10** p. 496 | Hampton Inn & Suites Mexico City-Centro Historico | ▽▽▽ | $95-$125 | 506 |
| **12** p. 496 | NH Centro Historico | ▽▽▽ | $1349-$1805 | 508 |
| **14** p. 496 | Emporio Reforma | ▽▽▽ | Rates not provided | 505 |

| Map Page | Restaurants | Diamond Rated | Cuisine | Price Range | Page |
|---|---|---|---|---|---|
| 1 p. 496 | Los Girasoles | ▽▽▽ | Regional Mexican | $8-$22 | 511 |
| 2 p. 496 | Hosteria de Santo Domingo | ▽▽ | Regional Mexican | $10-$22 | 511 |
| 3 p. 496 | Cafe de Tacuba | ▽▽ | Regional Mexican | $6-$20 | 510 |
| 4 p. 496 | Restaurante Mercaderes Cafe | ▽▽▽ | International | $10-$32 | 512 |
| 5 p. 496 | Meson del Cid | ▽▽ | Spanish | $10-$45 | 511 |
| 6 p. 496 | El Cardenal | ▽▽▽ | Mexican | $20-$65 | 510 |
| 7 p. 496 | Garabatos | ▽▽ | Mexican Breads/ Pastries | $10-$22 | 511 |
| 8 p. 496 | La Casa de la Sirenas | ▽▽ | Mexican | $13-$38 | 511 |
| 9 p. 496 | Fisher's Centro | ▽▽ | Mexican Seafood | $10-$28 | 511 |
| 11 p. 496 | MUMEDI Cafe | ▽▽ | International | $7-$15 | 511 |
| 12 p. 496 | La Opera Restaurant Bar | ▽▽▽ | Regional Mexican | $12-$25 | 511 |
| 13 p. 496 | Gotan Restaurante Argentino | ▽▽ | Steak | $8-$18 | 511 |
| 14 p. 496 | El Cardenal | ▽▽▽ | Mexican | $10-$30 | 510 |

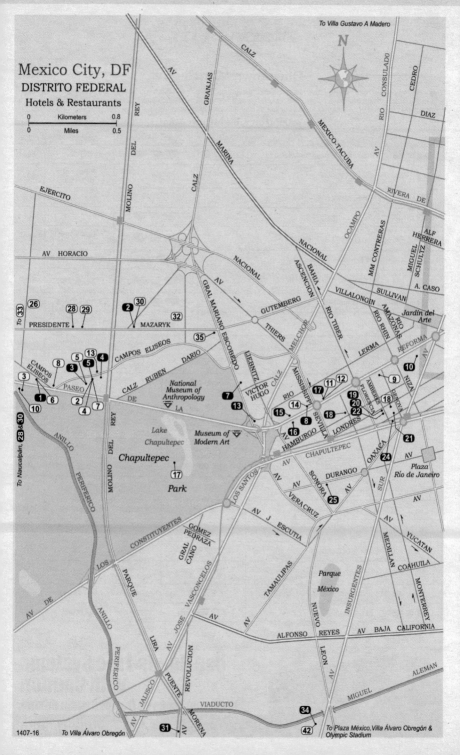

Mexico City, DF
DISTRITO FEDERAL
Hotels & Restaurants

Kilometers  0.8
Miles  0.5

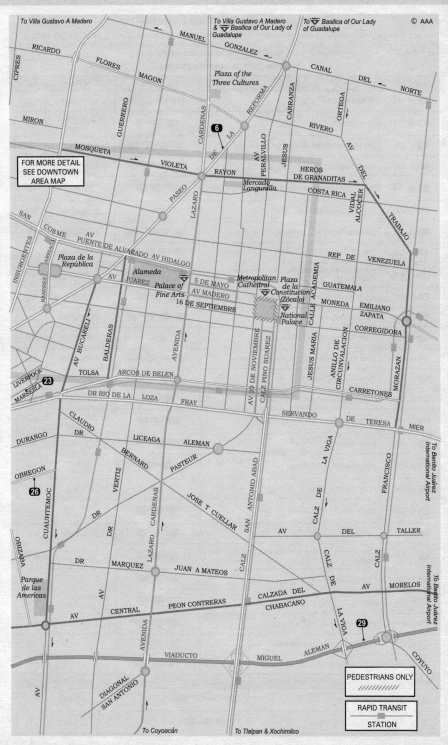

© AAA

To Villa Gustavo A Madero

To Villa Gustavo A Madero & Basilica of Our Lady of Guadalupe

To Basilica of Our Lady of Guadalupe

RICARDO
CIPRES
FLORES
MAGON
MANUEL
GONZALEZ
CANAL
DEL
NORTE
MIRON
GUERRERO
CARRANZA
RIVERO
ORTEGA
MOSQUETA
Plaza of the Three Cultures
6
LA
REFORMA
DE
AV PERALVILLO
JESUS
AV DEL
TRABAJO

FOR MORE DETAIL SEE DOWNTOWN AREA MAP

VIOLETA
RAYON
Mercado Lagunilla
HEROS DE GRANADITAS
COSTA RICA
VIDAL ALCOCER

SAN
COSME
ARRIAGA
INSURGENTES
AV PUENTE DE ALVARADO   AV HIDALGO
Plaza de la República
REP DE VENEZUELA

RAMIREZ
AV JUAREZ
Alameda
Palace of Fine Arts
5 DE MAYO
AV MADERO
16 DE SEPTIEMBRE
Metropolitan Cathedral
Plaza de la Constitución (Zócalo)
National Palace
CALLE ACADEMIA
GUATEMALA
MONEDA
EMILIANO ZAPATA
CORREGIDORA

LIVERPOOL
MARSELLA
23
AV BUCARELI
BALDERAS
TOLSA
ARCOS DE BELEN
AVENIDA
AV 20 DE NOVIEMBRE
CALZ PINO SUAREZ
JESUS MARIA
ANILLO DE CIRCUNVALACION
MORAZAN
CARRETONES

DR RIO DE LA   LOZA
FRAY
SERVANDO
DE   TERESA
MIER

CLAUDIO
DR
LICEAGA
ALEMAN
LA VIGA
FRANCISCO

To Benito Juárez International Airport

DURANGO
BERNARD
VERTIZ
PASTEUR
SAN ANTONIO ABAD
OBREGON
26
CUAUHTEMOC
DR
LAZARO   CARDENAS
JOSE T CUELLAR
AV
CALZ DE
DEL
TALLER
OBIZABA
DR
MARQUEZ
JUAN A MATEOS
CALZ
CALZ DE
CALZ

Parque de las Americas
AV
CENTRAL
PEON CONTRERAS
CALZADA DEL
CHABACANO
LA VIGA
AV   MORELOS

To Benito Juárez International Airport

AV
AVENIDA
DIAGONAL SAN ANTONIO
VIADUCTO
MIGUEL
ALEMAN
29
COYUYO

To Coyoacán

To Tlalpan & Xochimilco

PEDESTRIANS ONLY

RAPID TRANSIT
STATION

# Mexico City, Distrito Federal

This index helps you "spot" where approved hotels and restaurants are located on the corresponding detailed maps. Hotel daily rate range is for comparison only. Restaurant price range is a combination of lunch and/or dinner. Turn to the listing page for more detailed rate and price information and consult display ads for special promotions.

## MEXICO CITY, DISTRITO FEDERAL

| Map Page | Hotels | Diamond Rated | Rate Range | Page |
|---|---|---|---|---|
| **1** p. 498 | **W Mexico City** | ◆◆◆◆ | $239-$569 | 509 |
| **2** p. 498 | Hotel Habita | ◆◆◆ | Rates not provided | 507 |
| **3** p. 498 | **JW Marriott Hotel Mexico City** | ◆◆◆◆ | $159-$470 | 507 |
| **4** p. 498 | **Hyatt Regency Mexico City** | ◆◆◆◆ | $160-$500 | 507 |
| **5** p. 498 | **Hotel Presidente InterContinental Mexico City** | ◆◆◆ | Rates not provided | 507 |
| **6** p. 498 | **Krystal Grand Reforma Uno** | [fyi] | $128-$221 | 508 |
| **7** p. 498 | **Camino Real Polanco Mexico City** | ◆◆◆◆ | $130-$585 | 505 |
| **8** p. 498 | **The St. Regis Mexico City** | ◆◆◆◆ | $350-$605 | 509 |
| **10** p. 498 | **Marriott Reforma Mexico City** *(See ad on back cover.)* | ◆◆◆◆ | $159-$309 | 508 |
| **13** p. 498 | Fiesta Americana Grand Chapultepec | ◆◆◆ | $132-$410 | 505 |
| **15** p. 498 | Marquis Reforma Hotel & Spa | ◆◆◆◆ | $192-$714 | 508 |
| **16** p. 498 | **Four Seasons Hotel Mexico D.F.** | [fyi] | $290-$4565 | 506 |
| **17** p. 498 | **Sheraton Mexico City Maria Isabel Hotel** | ◆◆◆◆ | $300-$600 | 509 |
| **18** p. 498 | **Galeria Plaza Reforma** | ◆◆◆ | $143-$228 | 506 |
| **19** p. 498 | Hotel Plaza Florencia | ◆◆ | $88-$143 | 507 |
| **20** p. 498 | NH Mexico City *(See ad on insert.)* | ◆◆◆ | Rates not provided | 508 |
| **21** p. 498 | **Hotel Geneve** | ◆◆◆ | $104-$540 | 507 |
| **22** p. 498 | Hotel Century Zona Rosa | ◆◆ | Rates not provided | 507 |
| **23** p. 498 | Hotel Posada Viena | ◆ | $73-$84 | 507 |
| **24** p. 498 | BEST WESTERN Royal Zona Rosa | ◆◆◆ | Rates not provided | 505 |
| **25** p. 498 | La Casona | ◆◆◆ | $110-$165 | 508 |
| **26** p. 498 | **Four Points by Sheraton Mexico City, Colonia Roma** | ◆◆◆ | Rates not provided | 505 |
| **28** p. 498 | Sheraton Santa Fe | ◆◆◆ | $150-$350 | 509 |
| **29** p. 498 | Holiday Inn Dali Aeropuerto | ◆◆◆ | Rates not provided | 506 |
| **30** p. 498 | Fiesta Americana Santa Fe | ◆◆◆ | $199-$461 | 505 |
| **31** p. 498 | **Radisson Flamingos Mexico City** | ◆◆◆ | $104-$200 | 508 |
| **34** p. 498 | Crowne Plaza Hotel de Mexico | ◆◆◆ | $175-$255 | 505 |

| Map Page | Restaurants | Diamond Rated | Cuisine | Price Range | Page |
|---|---|---|---|---|---|
| 2 p. 498 | **Au Pied de Cochon** | ◆◆◆◆ | Regional French Seafood | $30-$85 | 510 |
| 3 p. 498 | El Lago Chapultepec | ◆◆◆ | Regional New World | $15-$75 | 510 |

| Map Page | Restaurants (cont'd) | Diamond Rated | Cuisine | Price Range | Page |
|---|---|---|---|---|---|
| ④ p. 498 | **Alfredo Di Roma** | ▽▽▽ | Italian | $18-$40 | 510 |
| ⑤ p. 498 | **Brasserie Lipp** | ▽▽▽ | Regional French | $32-$64 | 510 |
| ⑥ p. 498 | Solea Restaurant | ▽▽▽ | Regional Mexican | $10-$38 | 512 |
| ⑦ p. 498 | The Palm Restaurant | ▽▽▽ | American | $15-$55 | 512 |
| ⑧ p. 498 | Los Almendros | ▽▽▽ | Regional Mexican | $15-$30 | 511 |
| ⑨ p. 498 | Cafeteria Los Naranjos | ▽▽ | Mexican | $8-$22 | 510 |
| ⑩ p. 498 | Meridiem Restaurante | ▽▽▽ | International | $11-$25 | 511 |
| ⑪ p. 498 | Manhattan Deli | ▽▽ | Deli | $12-$35 | 511 |
| ⑫ p. 498 | Cocina Amici | ▽▽▽ | Italian | $14-$32 | 510 |
| ⑬ p. 498 | Agua y Sal Cebicheria | ▽▽▽ | Seafood | $16-$25 | 509 |
| ⑭ p. 498 | Restaurant Diana | ▽▽▽▽ | Regional Mexican | $15-$45 | 512 |
| ⑰ p. 498 | Del Bosque Restaurante | ▽▽▽ | Continental | $12-$33 | 510 |
| ⑱ p. 498 | Restaurante Fonda El Refugio | ▽▽▽ | Regional Mexican | $13-$25 | 512 |
| ㉖ p. 498 | Torre d Castilla | ▽▽▽ | Spanish | $10-$70 | 512 |
| ㉘ p. 498 | Rincon Argentino Restaurante | ▽▽▽ | Argentine | $25-$56 | 512 |
| ㉙ p. 498 | Dulce Patria en las Alcobas | ▽▽▽▽ | Regional Mexican | $20-$40 | 510 |
| ㉚ p. 498 | Aqua Restaurante | ▽▽ | Regional Mexican | $9-$28 | 510 |
| ㉜ p. 498 | Pujol Restaurante | ▽▽▽▽ | New Mexican | $90 | 512 |
| ㉝ p. 498 | **La Hacienda de los Morales** | ▽▽▽ | Regional Mexican | $18-$40 | 511 |
| ㉟ p. 498 | Morimoto Mexico City | ▽▽▽ | Japanese | $20-$88 | 511 |
| ㊷ p. 498 | Dolce Mexico | ▽▽ | New Mexican | $10-$22 | 510 |

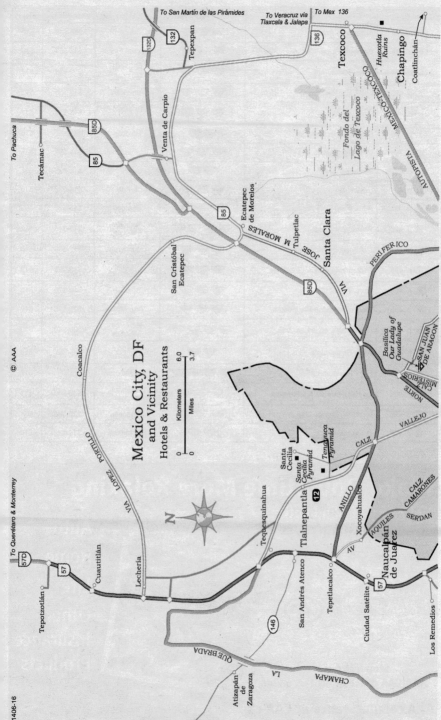

© AAA

## Mexico City, DF
### and Vicinity
#### Hotels & Restaurants

Kilometers
0        6.0

Miles
0        3.7

To San Martín de las Pirámides

To Veracruz via Tlaxcala & Jalapa

To Mex 136

132
132D
Tepexpan

136
Texcoco

Huexotla Ruins

Chapingo
Coatinchán

MÉXICO-TEXCOCO

AUTOPISTA

Venta de Carpio

Fondo del Lago de Texcoco

To Pachuca

85D

85

Tecámac

Ecatepec de Morelos

85

San Cristóbal Ecatepec

JOSÉ M MORALES

Tulpetlac

Santa Clara

85D

VIA

PERIFÉRICO

Coacalco

Basílica Our Lady of Guadalupe

SAN JUAN DE ARAGÓN

CALZ MISTERIOS

NORTE

VIA LÓPEZ PORTILLO

VALLEJO

CALZ.

Tenayuca Pyramid

Santa Cecilia

Santa Cecilia Pyramid

12

Tequesquinahua

Tlalnepantla

ANILLO

Xocoyahualco

CALZ CAMARONES

SERDAN

To Querétaro & Monterrey

57D

57

Tepotzotlán

Cuautitlán

Lechería

San Andrés Atenco

Tepetlacalco

AV

AQUILES

Naucalpán de Juárez

57

Ciudad Satélite

Los Remedios

146

QUEBRADA

LA CHAMAPA

Atizapán de Zaragoza

N

1406-16

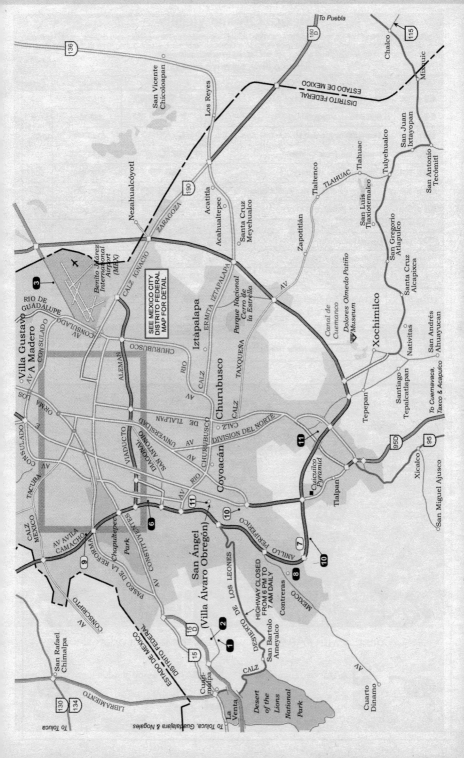

To Puebla

150 D

115

Chalco

Mixquic

San Vicente
Chicoloapan

Los Reyes

ESTADO DE MEXICO

DISTRITO FEDERAL

San Juan
Ixtayopan

San Antonio
Tecómitl

136

190

Nezahualcóyotl

ZARAGOZA

Acatitla

Acahualtepec

Santa Cruz
Meyehualco

Tlaltenco

Zapotitlán

TLAHUAC

Tlahuac

San Luis
Tlaxiotemalco

Tulyehualco

San Gregorio
Atlapulco

Santa Cruz
Alcapixca

Benito Juárez
International
Airport (MEX)

CALZ IGNACIO

3

RIO DE
GUADALUPE

SEE MEXICO CITY
DISTRITO FEDERAL
MAP FOR DETAIL

ERMITA IZTAPALAPA

Parque Nacional
Cerro de
la Estrella

Canal de
Cuemanco

AV

Dolores Olmedo Patiño
Museum

Xochimilco

Nativitas

San Andrés
Ahuayucan

Iztapalapa

AV CONSULADO

Villa Gustavo
A A Madero

CONSULADO

CHURUBUSCO

CALZ

RIO

TAXQUEÑA

Churubusco

AV

Santiago
Tepalcatlalpan

Tepepan

95D

95

Xicalco

San Miguel Ajusco

ALEMAN

AV DE LOS

NORMA

AV

UNIVERSIDAD

RIO CHURUBUSCO

DE TLALPAN

DIVISION DEL NORTE

Coyoacán

To Cuernavaca,
Taxco & Acapulco

11

Cuicuilco
Pyramid

Tlalpan

AV CONSULADO

TACUBA

VIADUCTO

DIAGONAL

SAN ANTONIO

AV

AV

11

10

ANILLO PERIFERICO

7

10

CALZ
MEXICO

AV AVILA
CAMACHO

Chapultepec
Park

PASEO DE LA REFORMA

AV CONSTITUCION

6

AV

San Ángel
(Villa Álvaro Obregón)

DE LOS LEONES

8

MEXICO

Contreras

9

AV CONSCRIPTO

ESTADO DE MEXICO
DISTRITO FEDERAL

15
D

15

2

1

DESIERTO

HIGHWAY CLOSED
FROM 6 PM TO
7 AM DAILY

San Bartolo
Ameyalco

AV

San Rafael
Chimalpa

130

134

LIBRAMIENTO

Cuaji
malpa

La
Venta

CALZ

Desert
of the
Lions
National
Park

AV

Cuarto
Dinamo

To Toluca

To Toluca, Guadalajara & Nogales

## Mexico City and Vicinity

This index helps you "spot" where approved hotels and restaurants are located on the corresponding detailed maps. Hotel daily rate range is for comparison only. Restaurant price range is a combination of lunch and/or dinner. Turn to the listing page for more detailed rate and price information and consult display ads for special promotions.

### MEXICO CITY, DISTRITO FEDERAL

| Map Page | Hotels | Diamond Rated | Rate Range | Page |
|---|---|---|---|---|
| **1** p. 502 | The Westin Santa Fe Mexico City | ◈◈◈ | $165-$365 | 509 |
| **2** p. 502 | **Hilton Mexico City Santa Fe** | ◈◈◈◈ | $89-$359 | 506 |
| **3** p. 502 | **Courtyard by Marriott Mexico City Airport** | ◈◈◈ | $139-$229 | 505 |
| **6** p. 502 | **Holiday Inn Trade Center** | ◈◈◈ | $110-$350 | 506 |
| **8** p. 502 | Pedregal Palace Hotel | ◈◈ | $109-$132 | 508 |
| **10** p. 502 | Radisson Paraiso Perisur Hotel Mexico City | ◈◈◈ | $130-$450 | 508 |
| **11** p. 502 | Fiesta Inn Periferico Sur | ◈◈◈ | $99-$225 | 505 |

| Map Page | Restaurants | Diamond Rated | Cuisine | Price Range | Page |
|---|---|---|---|---|---|
| **7** p. 502 | Rosato Ristorante | ◈◈◈ | Italian | $9-$25 | 512 |
| **9** p. 502 | Sir Winston Churchill's | ◈◈◈ | British | $22-$68 | 512 |
| **10** p. 502 | Saks San Angel | ◈◈◈ | Regional Mexican | $12-$28 | 512 |
| **11** p. 502 | Restaurante San Angel Inn | ◈◈◈◈ | Traditional Continental | $25-$60 | 512 |

### TLALNEPANTLA, MÉXICO

| Map Page | Hotel | Diamond Rated | Rate Range | Page |
|---|---|---|---|---|
| **12** p. 502 | Crowne Plaza Mexico Norte Tlalnepantla | ◈◈◈ | Rates not provided | 514 |

LET'S GET SOCIAL

Connect with #AAA and #CAA for the latest updates.

AAA.com/Facebook
AAA.com/Googleplus
AAA.com/Twitter
YouTube.com/AAA

CAA Social Media: CAA.ca/social

# MEXICO CITY, DISTRITO FEDERAL
pop. 8,851,080
- **Restaurants p. 509**
- **Hotels & Restaurants map & index p. 496**

## BEST WESTERN ROYAL ZONA ROSA    (55)9149-3000  24

▼▼▼▼ **Hotel.** Rates not provided. **Address:** Amberes No. 78 06600 **Location:** In Zona Rosa; jct Ave Chapultepec and Liverpool St. **Facility:** Meets AAA guest room security requirements. 162 units. 20 stories, interior corridors. **Parking:** valet only. **Terms:** 5 day cancellation notice-fee imposed, resort fee. **Amenities:** safes. **Pool(s):** heated outdoor. **Activities:** steamroom, exercise room, massage. **Guest Services:** valet laundry.

**AAA Benefit:**
Save 10% or more every day and earn 10% bonus points!

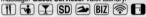

## CAMINO REAL POLANCO MEXICO CITY
(55)5263-8888  7

**Classic Historic Hotel**
**$130-$585**

**Address:** Mariano Escobedo No. 700 Col. Nueva Anzures 11590 **Location:** Between Victor Hugo and Kent, just n of Diana Cir; Periferico exit Ave Presidente Masaryk, then w. **Facility:** The flagship property of the upscale Mexican chain, this large, distinguished hotel was designed by architect Ricardo Legorreta to resemble an Aztec pyramid. 712 units, some two bedrooms and kitchens. 5 stories, interior corridors. **Parking:** on-site (fee) and valet. **Amenities:** safes. **Dining:** 7 restaurants, also, Morimoto Mexico City, see separate listing, entertainment. **Pool(s):** heated outdoor. **Activities:** massage. **Guest Services:** valet laundry.

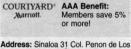

## COURTYARD BY MARRIOTT MEXICO CITY AIRPORT
(55)4631-4000  3

**COURTYARD Marriott**
**Hotel**
**$139-$229**

**AAA Benefit:** Members save 5% or more!

**Address:** Sinaloa 31 Col. Penon de Los Banos 15520 **Location:** In Terminal 1. **Facility:** Meets AAA guest room security requirements. 288 units. 4 stories, interior corridors. **Parking:** on-site (fee). **Amenities:** safes. **Activities:** exercise room. **Guest Services:** valet laundry.

## CROWNE PLAZA HOTEL DE MEXICO    (55)1164-1164  34

▼▼▼▼ **Hotel** $175-$255 **Address:** Calle Dakota No. 95, Col Naples **Location:** Just n of Ave Insurgentes; adjacent to Mexico City World Trade Center. **Facility:** Meets AAA guest room security requirements. 310 units. 11 stories, interior corridors. **Parking:** on-site (fee) and valet. **Amenities:** safes. **Dining:** 3 restaurants, also, Dolce Mexico, see separate listing. **Activities:** sauna, hot tub, steamroom, exercise room, spa. **Guest Services:** valet laundry.

Visit AAA.com/searchfordiscounts

to save on travel, shopping,

dining and attractions

## EMPORIO REFORMA    (55)5566-7766  14

▼▼▼▼ **Boutique Hotel.** Rates not provided. **Address:** Paseo de La Reforma 124 Col. Juárez 06600 **Location:** On Paseo de La Reforma, just ne of Ave Insurgentes. **Facility:** In a prime location, this European-style hotel offers cozy, well-appointed guest units with many amenities. Meets AAA guest room security requirements. 145 units. 5-11 stories, interior corridors. **Parking:** on-site (fee) and valet. **Amenities:** safes. **Dining:** 2 restaurants. **Activities:** exercise room. **Guest Services:** valet laundry, area transportation.

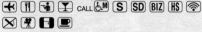

## FIESTA AMERICANA GRAND CHAPULTEPEC
(55)2581-1500  13

▼▼▼▼ **Hotel** $132-$410 **Address:** Mariano Escobedo 756 Col Anzures 11590 **Location:** On Mariano Escobedo, jct Paseo de La Reforma. **Facility:** 203 units, some efficiencies. 20 stories, interior corridors. **Parking:** on-site (fee) and valet. **Amenities:** safes. **Activities:** sauna, hot tub, steamroom, exercise room, spa. **Guest Services:** valet laundry.

## FIESTA AMERICANA REFORMA    (55)5140-4100  6

▼▼▼▼ **Hotel.** Rates not provided. **Address:** Paseo de La Reforma 80 06600 **Location:** Southwest quarter of Glorieta Cristobal Colon. **Facility:** 616 units. 25 stories, interior corridors. **Parking:** on-site (fee) and valet. **Amenities:** safes. **Dining:** 2 restaurants, entertainment. **Activities:** sauna, steamroom, exercise room, massage. **Guest Services:** valet laundry.

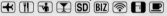

## FIESTA AMERICANA SANTA FE    (55)1105-5000  30

▼▼▼▼ **Hotel** $199-$461 **Address:** Calle 3 No. 55, Col Lomas de Santa Fe **Location:** 7.2 mi (12 km) w on Paseo de La Reforma (which becomes Prolongacion Reforma) exit Joaquin Gallo, just s on Vasco de Quiroga, then just s on Santa Fe; in Santa Fe District. **Facility:** 172 units, some kitchens. 10 stories, interior corridors. **Parking:** on-site (fee) and valet. **Terms:** cancellation fee imposed. **Amenities:** safes. **Dining:** Rosato Ristorante, see separate listing. **Pool(s):** heated indoor. **Activities:** exercise room. **Guest Services:** valet laundry.

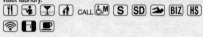

## FIESTA INN PERIFERICO SUR    (55)5096-9300  11

▼▼▼▼ **Hotel** $99-$225 **Address:** Periferico Sur 5530 Col Pedregal de Carrasco **Location:** Just s of Tlalpan Ave. **Facility:** 212 units. 12 stories, interior corridors. **Parking:** on-site (fee) and valet. **Amenities:** safes. **Pool(s):** heated indoor. **Activities:** hot tub, exercise room. **Guest Services:** valet laundry, area transportation.

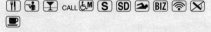

## FOUR POINTS BY SHERATON MEXICO CITY, COLONIA ROMA
(55)1085-9500  26

**FOUR POINTS BY SHERATON**
**Hotel**
**Rates not provided**

**AAA Benefit:** Members save up to 15%, plus Starwood Preferred Guest® benefits!

**Address:** Alvaro Obregon 38 06700 **Location:** Jct Ave de Los Insurgentes, 0.5 mi (0.8 km) e. **Facility:** 90 units. 8 stories, interior corridors. *Bath:* shower only. **Parking:** valet only. **Terms:** 3 day cancellation notice. **Amenities:** safes. **Activities:** exercise room, massage. **Guest Services:** valet laundry.

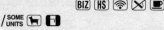

(See map & index p. 496.)

## FOUR SEASONS HOTEL MEXICO D.F.
(55)5230-1818 **16**

**[fyi]**
**Hotel**
**$290-$4565**

Under major renovation, scheduled to be completed February 2016. **Last Rated:** ▼▼▼▼▼ **Address:** Paseo de La Reforma 500 Col Juárez 06600 **Location:** On Paseo de La Reforma. Adjacent to Chapultepec Park. **Facility:** 240 units. 8 stories, interior corridors. **Parking:** on-site (fee) and valet. **Amenities:** safes, hot tub, interior corridors. **Dining:** 3 restaurants, also, Reforma 500, see separate listing, entertainment. **Pool(s):** heated outdoor. **Activities:** sauna, hot tub, exercise room, massage. **Guest Services:** valet laundry, area transportation.

[icons] ✈ 🛏 🚶 ⅄ ♿ CALL &M
S SD 🏊 BIZ $HS 📶 ✕ 🎬 🗄
/ SOME UNITS 🛏🐾 📠 🖥


## GALERIA PLAZA REFORMA
(55)5230-1717 **18**

▼▼▼▼▼
**Hotel**
**$143-$228**

**Address:** Hamburgo No. 195 Col Juárez 06600 **Location:** In Zona Rosa; between Valsovia and Lancaster. **Facility:** Dominating the city's famed Zona Rosa galleries, restaurants and boutiques, this recently renovated full-service hotel offers guests fine dining, a complete business center and a tour agency. Meets AAA guest room security requirements. 433 units. 11 stories, interior corridors. **Parking:** on-site (fee) and valet. **Amenities:** safes. **Dining:** 2 restaurants. **Pool(s):** heated outdoor. **Activities:** exercise room. **Guest Services:** valet laundry.

🍴 🚶 ⅄ CALL &M S SD 🏊 BIZ 📶 ✕
🎬 🗄 🖥


## GRAN HOTEL CIUDAD DE MEXICO
(55)1083-7700 **1**

▼▼▼ Classic Historic Hotel $130-$245 **Address:** 16 de Septiembre No. 82 06000 **Location:** Just w of the Zócalo; in Centro Historico. **Facility:** Recently renovated, this historic landmark features an Art Nouveau atrium lobby with a spectacular 1908 Tiffany stained-glass ceiling and an ornate wrought iron elevator that evokes the era. 60 units. 4 stories, interior corridors. **Parking:** on-site (fee) and valet. **Amenities:** safes. **Dining:** 2 restaurants. **Activities:** exercise room. **Guest Services:** valet laundry.

🍴 🚶 ⅄ SD BIZ HS 📶 ✕ 🖥


## HAMPTON INN & SUITES MEXICO CITY-CENTRO HISTORICO
(55)8000-5000 **10**

▼▼▼▼ Historic Hotel $95-$125
**Address:** Calle 5 de Febrero No. 24 Centro Historico 06060 **Location:** In heart of Centro Historico; 2 blks s of Zocalo Mayor. **Facility:** Magnificently restored to its 1800 opulence, highlights include walls covered in hand-painted ceramic tiles, wrought iron railings and long large windows. Meets AAA guest room security requirements. 108 units. 6 stories, interior corridors. **Parking:** valet only. **Terms:** 1-7 night minimum stay, cancellation fee imposed. **Amenities:** safes. **Dining:** Fisher's Centro, Garabatos, see separate listings. **Activities:** exercise room. **Guest Services:** valet and coin laundry.

**AAA Benefit:** Members save up to 10%!

🍴 🚶 📶 S SD BIZ HS 📶 🖥
/ SOME UNITS 🗄 📠


## HILTON MEXICO CITY REFORMA
(55)5130-5300 **3**

▼▼▼ ▼▼▼
**Contemporary Hotel**
**$129-$239**

(Ⓗ) **Hilton** HOTELS & RESORTS
**AAA Benefit:** Members save 5% or more!

**Address:** Ave Juárez No. 70, Col. Centro 06010 **Location:** Facing Alameda Park; in Centro Historico. **Facility:** The downtown high-rise features upscale, contemporary décor; the upper rooms offer a spectacular view of the city. 456 units. 27 stories, interior corridors. **Parking:** on-site (fee) and valet. **Terms:** 1-7 night minimum stay, cancellation fee imposed. **Amenities:** safes. **Dining:** 3 restaurants, also, El Cardenal, see separate listing. **Pool(s):** heated outdoor, heated indoor. **Activities:** hot tub, steamroom, tennis, exercise room, spa. **Guest Services:** valet laundry.

✈ 🍴 🚶 ⅄ CALL &M S SD 🏊 BIZ $HS
📶 ✕ 🎬 🗄 🖥 / SOME UNITS 📠


## HILTON MEXICO CITY SANTA FE
555/985-9000 **2**

▼▼▼ ▼▼▼
**Hotel**
**$89-$359**

(Ⓗ) **Hilton** HOTELS & RESORTS
**AAA Benefit:** Members save 5% or more!

**Address:** Antonio Dovali Jaime 70 **Location:** 7.2 mi (12 km) w on Paseo de La Reforma (which becomes Prolongacion Reforma) exit Joaquin Gallo, just s on Vasco de Quiroga, then just s on Santa Fe; in Santa Fe District. **Facility:** This beautifully sleek hotel has many unique features, including a Barbie-themed guest room that will delight any young girl. The property also offers direct access to a large, upscale shopping mall. 260 units. 13-16 stories, interior corridors. **Bath:** shower only. **Parking:** on-site (fee) and valet. **Terms:** 1-7 night minimum stay, cancellation fee imposed. **Amenities:** safes. **Dining:** 2 restaurants. **Pool(s):** heated outdoor. **Activities:** exercise room. **Guest Services:** valet laundry, boarding pass kiosk, rental car service, luggage security pick-up.

✈ 🍴 🚶 ⅄ CALL &M 🏊 BIZ $HS 📶 ✕
🗄 🖥 / SOME UNITS 🛒 📠


## HOLIDAY INN DALI AEROPUERTO
(55)5036-0990 **29**

▼▼▼ Hotel. Rates not provided. **Address:** Viaducto Rio de La Piedad, Col Magdalena Mix **Location:** 0.4 mi (0.6 km) n of Congreso de La Union Ave. **Facility:** Meets AAA guest room security requirements. 150 units. 6 stories, interior corridors. **Bath:** shower only. **Amenities:** safes. **Activities:** sauna, hot tub, exercise room. **Guest Services:** valet laundry.

✈ 🍴 🚶 ⅄ SD BIZ HS 📶 ✕ 🖥
/ SOME UNITS 🗄


## HOLIDAY INN TRADE CENTER
(55)5278-9950 **6**

▼▼▼
**Hotel**
**$110-$350**

**Address:** Ave Revolucion 583 **Location:** Colonia San Pedro de Los Pinos; Ave Revolucion S at Calle 23. **Facility:** 188 units. 7 stories, interior corridors. **Amenities:** safes. **Activities:** sauna, steamroom, game room, exercise room, massage. **Guest Services:** valet and coin laundry, area transportation.

✈ 🍴 🚶 ⅄ CALL &M SD
BIZ HS 📶 ✕ 🎬 🖥
/ SOME UNITS 🗄

(See map & index p. 496.)

### HOTEL CENTURY ZONA ROSA          (55)5726-9911  **22**

◆◆◆ **Hotel.** Rates not provided. **Address:** Liverpool St 152 06600 **Location:** In Zona Rosa. **Facility:** 141 units. 21 stories, interior corridors. **Parking:** on-site (fee) and valet. **Amenities:** safes. **Pool(s):** heated outdoor. **Activities:** exercise room. **Guest Services:** valet laundry.

[icons]

### HOTEL DE CORTES          (55)5518-2181  **2**

**[fyi] Historic Boutique Hotel.** Rates not provided. Under major renovation, scheduled to be completed May 2016. **Last Rated:** ◆◆◆ **Address:** Ave Hidalgo 85, Col Centro **Location:** Across from Alameda Park; in Centro Historico. **Facility:** Built in 1610 as a lodging, this is the first hostel of the New World. Guest rooms and bathrooms are ultra modern and feature sleek, upscale yet minimalist themes. 26 units, some two bedrooms. 3 stories (no elevator), exterior corridors. **Parking:** valet only. **Amenities:** safes. **Guest Services:** valet laundry.

[icons]

### HOTEL GENEVE          (55)5080-0800  **21**

◆◆◆
Historic Hotel
$104-$540

**Address:** Londres 130 06600 **Location:** In Zona Rosa; 0.3 mi (0.5 km) s of Paseo de La Reforma. **Facility:** This 100+year-old property in the heart of the Zona Rosa offers a refined, Old World atmosphere that features hand-carved antique furnishings and original artwork. All rooms offer modern conveniences. 222 units. 4-5 stories, interior corridors. **Parking:** valet only. **Amenities:** safes. **Dining:** 2 restaurants, entertainment. **Activities:** sauna, steamroom, exercise room, massage. **Guest Services:** valet laundry, area transportation.

[icons]

### HOTEL HABITA          55/5282-3100  **2**

◆◆◆ **Hotel.** Rates not provided. **Address:** Ave Presidente Masaryk No. 201 **Location:** In Polanco Zone; jct La Martine. **Facility:** 36 units. 6 stories, interior corridors. **Parking:** valet only. **Amenities:** safes. **Dining:** Aqua Restaurante, see separate listing. **Pool(s):** heated outdoor. **Activities:** sauna, hot tub, exercise room, massage. **Guest Services:** valet laundry, area transportation.

[icons]

### HOTEL PLAZA FLORENCIA          (55)5242-4700  **19**

◆◆ **Hotel** $88-$143 **Address:** Florencia 61 06600 **Location:** In Zona Rosa; just s of Paseo de La Reforma. **Facility:** 142 units. 12 stories, interior corridors. **Parking:** valet only. **Amenities:** safes. **Dining:** 2 restaurants. **Activities:** exercise room. **Guest Services:** valet laundry.

[icons]

### HOTEL POSADA VIENA          (55)5566-0700  **23**

◆ **Hotel** $73-$84 **Address:** Marsella No. 28 06600 **Location:** Just off Dinamarca. **Facility:** 88 units, some two bedrooms. 4-5 stories, interior corridors. **Bath:** shower only. **Guest Services:** valet laundry.

[icons]

### HOTEL PRESIDENTE INTERCONTINENTAL MEXICO CITY          (55)5327-7700  **5**

◆◆◆◆
Hotel
Rates not provided

**Address:** Campo Eliseos 218 Col. Polanco 11560 **Location:** In Polanco Zone; on Paseo de La Reforma, 0.8 mi (1.3 km) w of Periferico; opposite Chapultepec Park and National Auditorium. **Facility:** 661 units, some two bedrooms and efficiencies. 42 stories, interior corridors. **Parking:** on-site (fee) and valet. **Amenities:** video games, safes. **Dining:** 4 restaurants, also, Alfredo Di Roma, Au Pied de Cochon, The Palm Restaurant, see separate listings. **Activities:** spa. **Guest Services:** valet laundry, area transportation.

[icons]

### HYATT REGENCY MEXICO CITY          (55)5083-1234  **4**

◆◆◆◆
Hotel
$160-$500

HYATT REGENCY
**AAA Benefit:** Members save 10%!

**Address:** Campos Eliseos 204 Col Polanco Chapultepec 11560 **Location:** In Polanco Zone; jct Campos Eliseos and Andres Bello St; 1 blk from National Museum of Anthropology. **Facility:** Multiple art exhibits decorate the lobby of this high-rise, which provides a full array of business and leisure facilities. 755 units. 38 stories, interior corridors. **Parking:** on-site and valet. **Terms:** cancellation fee imposed. **Amenities:** safes. **Dining:** 3 restaurants. **Pool(s):** heated indoor. **Activities:** sauna, steamroom, tennis, recreation programs, massage. **Guest Services:** valet laundry.

[icons]

### JW MARRIOTT HOTEL MEXICO CITY          (55)5999-0000  **3**

◆◆◆◆
Hotel
$159-$470

JW MARRIOTT
**AAA Benefit:** Members save 5% or more!

**Address:** Andres Bello No. 29 11560 **Location:** On Paseo de La Reforma; opposite Chapultepec Park and National Auditorium. **Facility:** This luxurious hotel is designed to meet the needs of both the business traveler and tourist alike. Some rooms boast outstanding views of the city from many angles. Meets AAA guest room security requirements. 312 units, some two bedrooms. 26 stories, interior corridors. **Parking:** on-site (fee) and valet. **Amenities:** safes. **Dining:** Brasserie Lipp, see separate listing. **Pool(s):** heated outdoor. **Activities:** sauna, hot tub, steamroom, exercise room, massage. **Guest Services:** valet laundry, area transportation.

[icons]

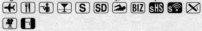

(See map & index p. 496.)

## KRYSTAL GRAND REFORMA UNO    55/5063-1000  [6]

[fyi]
Hotel
$128-$221

Under major renovation, scheduled to be completed October 2015. **Last Rated:** ▽▽▽▽ **Address:** Paseo de La Reforma No. 1 **Location:** Jct Ave de La Republica. **Facility:** 500 units. 20 stories, interior corridors. **Parking:** on-site (fee) and valet. **Amenities:** safes. **Dining:** 3 restaurants. **Pool(s):** heated indoor. **Activities:** sauna, hot tub, steamroom, exercise room, spa. **Guest Services:** valet laundry.

## LA CASONA    55/5286-3001  [25]

▽▽▽▽ **Country Inn** $110-$165 **Address:** Durango 280 Colonia Roma **Location:** Corner of Durango and Cozumel. **Facility:** Located in a quiet residential area and reminiscent of a mansion, this older hotel has large rooms, period furnishings and plenty of artwork. Meets AAA guest room security requirements. 29 units. 2 stories (no elevator), interior corridors. **Parking:** on-site (fee). **Amenities:** safes. **Activities:** steamroom, exercise room. **Guest Services:** valet laundry.

## LE MERIDIEN MEXICO CITY    (55)5061-3000  [8]

▽▽▽▽ ▽▽▽▽
Hotel
$285-$410

*Le* MERIDIEN  **AAA Benefit:** Members save up to 15%, plus Starwood Preferred Guest® benefits!

**Address:** Paseo de La Reforma No. 69, Col Tabacalera 06030 **Location:** On Paseo de La Reforma at Monumento Colon. **Facility:** On a bustling, attractive boulevard, this architecturally dramatic hotel offers contemporary rooms with spacious seating areas. 160 units. 19 stories, interior corridors. **Parking:** on-site (fee) and valet. **Amenities:** safes. **Pool(s):** heated indoor. **Activities:** hot tub, exercise room. **Guest Services:** valet and coin laundry.

## MARQUIS REFORMA HOTEL & SPA    (55)5229-1200  [15]

▽▽▽▽ ▽▽▽▽ **Hotel** $192-$714 **Address:** Paseo de La Reforma 465 06500 **Location:** 0.5 mi (0.8 km) sw of jct Insurgentes; opposite Chapultepec Park. **Facility:** Located near famed Chapultepec Park, the dramatic exterior of pink granite and blue glass gives way to a plush, expensively furnished lobby and well-appointed guest rooms. Meets AAA guest room security requirements. 209 units. 11 stories, interior corridors. **Parking:** valet only. **Amenities:** safes. **Dining:** 3 restaurants, entertainment. **Pool(s):** heated indoor. **Activities:** sauna, hot tub, steamroom, exercise room, spa. **Guest Services:** valet laundry.

## MARRIOTT REFORMA MEXICO CITY    (55)1102-7030  [10]

▽▽▽▽ ▽▽▽▽
Hotel
$159-$309

MARRIOTT

**AAA Benefit:** Members save 5% or more!

**Address:** Paseo de La Reforma 276 Col Juárez 06600 **Location:** Just w of Ave Insurgentes. **Facility:** For business and leisure travelers alike, this upscale hotel offers refined public areas and modern guest rooms with comfortable baths. Meets AAA guest room security requirements. 322 units. 16 stories, interior corridors. **Parking:** on-site (fee) and valet. **Amenities:** safes. **Dining:** 2 restaurants, entertainment. **Pool(s):** heated outdoor, heated indoor. **Activities:** sauna, hot tub, steamroom, exercise room, spa. **Guest Services:** valet laundry. *(See ad on back cover.)*

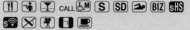

## NH CENTRO HISTORICO    (55)5130-1850  [12]

▽▽▽▽ **Hotel** $1349-$1805 **Address:** Palma 42 Centro 06010 **Location:** 3 blks sw of the Zocalo, just s of 16 de Septiembre; downtown Centro Historico. **Facility:** Meets AAA guest room security requirements. 105 units. 6 stories, interior corridors. **Parking:** on-site (fee) and valet. **Amenities:** safes. **Activities:** exercise room. **Guest Services:** valet laundry.

## NH MEXICO CITY    (55)5228-9928  [20]

▽▽▽▽ **Hotel.** Rates not provided. **Address:** Liverpool 155, Zona Rosa **Location:** In Zona Rosa; between Amberes and Florencia. **Facility:** 302 units. 17 stories, interior corridors. **Parking:** valet only. **Amenities:** safes. **Pool(s):** heated outdoor. **Activities:** exercise room. **Guest Services:** valet laundry. *(See ad on insert.)*

## PEDREGAL PALACE HOTEL    (55)5681-6855  [8]

▽▽▽▽ **Hotel** $109-$132 **Address:** 3487 Periferico Sur **Location:** Just off Periferico Sur exit Luis Cabrera. **Facility:** 64 units. 7 stories, interior corridors. **Bath:** shower only. **Parking:** valet only. **Amenities:** safes. **Activities:** hot tub, steamroom, exercise room. **Guest Services:** valet laundry.

## RADISSON FLAMINGOS MEXICO CITY    (55)5627-0220  [31]

▽▽▽▽
Hotel
$104-$200

**Address:** Ave Revolucion No. 333, Col Tacubaya 11870 **Location:** Jct Viaducto Presidente Miguel Alemán, just s; in Colonia Tacubaya. **Facility:** Meets AAA guest room security requirements. 252 units. 15 stories, interior corridors. **Parking:** valet only. **Amenities:** video games, safes. **Activities:** sauna, steamroom, game room, exercise room, massage. **Guest Services:** valet laundry.

## RADISSON PARAISO PERISUR HOTEL MEXICO CITY    (55)5927-5959  [10]

▽▽▽▽ **Hotel** $130-$450 **Address:** Cuspide 53, Col Parques del Pedregal **Location:** Adjacent to main Periferico; in southern part of city. Across from Perisur Mall. **Facility:** 237 units. 10 stories, interior corridors. **Parking:** on-site (fee) and valet. **Amenities:** safes. **Dining:** 2 restaurants. **Activities:** sauna, exercise room, massage. **Guest Services:** valet laundry, area transportation.

(See map & index p. 496.)

## THE ST. REGIS MEXICO CITY    (55)5228-1818  [8]

**Contemporary Hotel** $350-$605 **Address:** Paseo de La Reforma 439, Col. Cuauhtemoc 06500 **Location:** Paseo de La Reforma at Rio Mississippi St; opposite Glorieta La Diana. **Facility:** This gleaming hotel tower offers spacious, upscale units complete with high-tech conveniences and a butler assigned to each room. Meets AAA guest room security requirements. 189 units. 16 stories, interior corridors. **Parking:** on-site (fee) and valet. **Terms:** cancellation fee imposed. **Amenities:** safes. **Dining:** Restaurant Diana, see separate listing, entertainment. **Pool(s):** heated indoor. **Activities:** sauna, hot tub, steamroom, kids club, exercise room, spa. **Guest Services:** valet laundry, area transportation.

**AAA Benefit:** Members save up to 15%, plus Starwood Preferred Guest® benefits!

## SHERATON MEXICO CITY MARIA ISABEL HOTEL    (55)5242-5555  [17]

**Hotel** $300-$600

**AAA Benefit:** Members save up to 15%, plus Starwood Preferred Guest® benefits!

**Address:** Paseo de La Reforma No. 325, Col Cuauhtemoc 06500 **Location:** Next to US Embassy, opposite Angel de La Independencia Monument. **Facility:** This long-standing upscale property is on the famed Paseo de La Reforma. Executive rooms feature comfortable, over-stuffed chairs with ottomans. 755 units, some two bedrooms. 19-22 stories, interior corridors. **Parking:** on-site (fee) and valet. **Terms:** cancellation fee imposed. **Amenities:** safes. **Dining:** 2 restaurants, also, Cocina Amici, Manhattan Deli, see separate listings, entertainment. **Pool(s):** heated outdoor. **Activities:** sauna, steamroom, tennis, exercise room, massage. **Guest Services:** valet laundry.

## SHERATON SANTA FE    (55)5258-8500  [28]

**Hotel** $150-$350 **Address:** Guillermo Gonzalez Camarena 200 01210 **Location:** 7.2 mi (12 km) w on Paseo de La Reforma (which becomes Prolongacion Reforma) exit Joaquin Gallo, just s on Santa Fe; in Santa Fe District. **Facility:** Meets AAA guest room security requirements. 190 units. 10 stories, interior corridors. **Parking:** on-site (fee) and valet. **Terms:** closed 10/27-10/31, cancellation fee imposed. **Amenities:** safes. **Dining:** 3 restaurants. **Activities:** sauna, exercise room, massage. **Guest Services:** valet laundry.

**AAA Benefit:** Members save up to 15%, plus Starwood Preferred Guest® benefits!

---

Discover a wealth of savings

and offers on the AAA/CAA

travel websites

---

## THE WESTIN SANTA FE MEXICO CITY    (55)5089-8000  [1]

**Hotel** $165-$365 **Address:** Javier Barros Sierra 540 Lomas Santa Fe **Location:** 7.2 mi (12 km) w on Paseo de La Reforma (which becomes Prolongacion Reforma) exit Joaquin Gallo, just s on Vasco de Quiroga, then just s on Santa Fe; in Santa Fe District. **Facility:** This dramatic glass high-rise features ultra-modern public areas and large, nicely decorated guest rooms. From the rooftop pool/spa you'll enjoy great views of surrounding Santa Fe. Meets AAA guest room security requirements. 259 units. 11 stories, interior corridors. **Parking:** on-site (fee) and valet. **Terms:** cancellation fee imposed. **Amenities:** safes. **Dining:** 2 restaurants. **Pool(s):** heated outdoor. **Activities:** sauna, hot tub, exercise room, spa. **Guest Services:** valet laundry, area transportation.

**AAA Benefit:** Members save up to 15%, plus Starwood Preferred Guest® benefits!

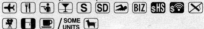

## W MEXICO CITY    (55)9138-1800  [1]

**Contemporary Hotel** $239-$569

**AAA Benefit:** Members save up to 15%, plus Starwood Preferred Guest® benefits!

**Address:** Campos Eliseos 252 Col Polanco 11560 **Location:** Just off Ave Paseo de La Reforma; in Polanco District. **Facility:** One of the newest hotels in this tony neighborhood, the property offers spacious high-tech guest rooms featuring hip, urban decor. 237 units. 25 stories, interior corridors. **Parking:** on-site (fee) and valet. **Amenities:** safes. **Dining:** Solea Restaurant, see separate listing. **Activities:** sauna, hot tub, steamroom, exercise room, spa. **Guest Services:** valet laundry, area transportation.

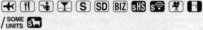

## ZOCALO CENTRAL    (55)5130-5130  [4]

**Hotel** $129-$200 **Address:** Cinco de Mayo y Zocalo Centro Historico 06000 **Location:** Just w of Zocalo. **Facility:** Meets AAA guest room security requirements. 105 units. 7 stories, interior corridors. **Parking:** valet only. **Amenities:** safes. **Dining:** 2 restaurants. **Activities:** sauna, steamroom, exercise room. **Guest Services:** valet laundry.

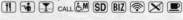

## HOLIDAY INN EXPRESS & SUITES AT WTC    55/1164-1160

[fyi] Not evaluated. **Address:** Dakota No. 95 Col Napoles 03810 **Location:** Just n of Ave Insurgentes. Facilities, services, and décor characterize a mid-scale property.

## HOLIDAY INN EXPRESS REFORMA    55/9150-5900

[fyi] Not evaluated. **Address:** Paseo de La Reforma No. 208 Col Juarez 06600 **Location:** Just w of jct Ave Insurgentes. Facilities, services, and décor characterize a mid-scale property.

## HOTEL ROYAL PEDREGAL    55/5449-4000

[fyi] Not evaluated. **Address:** Periferico Sur 4363 **Location:** Adjacent to main Periferico; in southern part of city; 0.3 mi (0.5 km) n from Perisur Mall. Facilities, services, and décor characterize a mid-scale property.

## WHERE TO EAT

## AGUA Y SAL CEBICHERIA    55/5282-2746  [13]

**Seafood. Casual Dining.** $16-$25 **AAA Inspector Notes:** This is a seafood lover's paradise in a colorful, casual and lively atmosphere. Sit at the open demonstration kitchen and watch the chefs create your ceviche and seafood cocktail from the extensive list while enjoying a plate of shrimp al ajillo tacos or sharing a plancha de frutas de mar with your dinner date. **Features:** full bar, patio dining. **Reservations:** required. **Address:** Campos Eliseos 199-A, Col Polanco **Location:** Just off Ave Paseo de La Reforma; in Polanco District. **Parking:** on-site (fee) and valet. [L] [D] [LATE]

(See map & index p. 496.)

## ALFREDO DI ROMA
55/5327-7700 ④

▼▼▼
**Italian**
**Fine Dining**
**$18–$40**

**AAA Inspector Notes:** This elegant restaurant uses a deli-style case to show off its cheeses, hard salami, imported prosciutto and fresh pasta. House specialties include a buttery fettuccine Alfredo prepared tableside. The wine list is extensively hedonistic. **Features:** full bar. **Reservations:** suggested. **Address:** Campos Eliseos 218 Col. Polanco 11560 **Location:** In Polanco Zone; on Paseo de La Reforma, 0.8 mi (1.3 km) w of Periferico; opposite Chapultepec Park and National Auditorium; in Hotel Presidente InterContinental Mexico City. **Parking:** on-site and valet. Ⓛ Ⓓ

## AQUA RESTAURANTE
55/5282-3100 ㉚

▼▼ Regional Mexican. Casual Dining. $9–$28 **AAA Inspector Notes:** If the mood strikes for casual yet intriguing dining, this is a nice choice. At breakfast you'll find an extensive buffet. Before or after dinner, enjoy a cocktail in the rooftop bar. **Features:** full bar, patio dining. **Address:** Ave Presidente Masaryk No. 201 **Location:** In Polanco Zone; jct La Martine; in Hotel Habita. **Parking:** valet only.

Ⓛ Ⓓ ⓛⒶⓉⒺ ◣

## AU PIED DE COCHON
55/5327-7700 ②

▼▼▼▼▼
**Regional**
**French**
**Seafood**
**Fine Dining**
**$30–$85**

**AAA Inspector Notes:** This elegant French restaurant specializes in seafood like its namesake in France. On the menu you'll find pate, French onion soup, a wide variety of fresh oysters and live lobsters in classic preparations. Add a renowned wine cellar and impeccable service, and you've got an unforgettable experience. **Features:** full bar, Sunday brunch. **Reservations:** suggested. **Address:** Campos Eliseos 218 Col. Polanco 11560 **Location:** In Polanco Zone; on Paseo de La Reforma, 0.8 mi (1.3 km) w of Periferico; opposite Chapultepec Park and National Auditorium; in Hotel Presidente InterContinental Mexico City. **Parking:** on-site (fee) and valet.

Ⓑ Ⓛ ㉔ ◣

## BRASSERIE LIPP
55/5281-3434 ⑤

▼▼▼▼
**Regional**
**French**
**Fine Dining**
**$32–$64**

**AAA Inspector Notes:** All the way from the Left Bank of Paris, Chef Jacques-Olivier Borja brings his legendary restaurant (established in 1880) to the swanky Polanco district. Specialty dishes include various shellfish, imported Kobe or Black Angus beef, and several flambé desserts, including a Baked Alaska with fresh, charred meringue. **Features:** full bar. **Reservations:** suggested. **Address:** Andres Bello No. 29 11560 **Location:** On Paseo de La Reforma; opposite Chapultepec Park and National Auditorium; in JW Marriott Hotel Mexico City. **Parking:** valet only.

Ⓑ Ⓛ Ⓓ ⓛⒶⓉⒺ ◣

## CAFE DE TACUBA
55/5518-4950 ③

▼▼ Regional Mexican. Casual Dining. $6–$20 **AAA Inspector Notes:** *Historic.* Originally the palace of royalty, the cafe features hand-carved stone columns, hand-painted tiles and frescoes, making this place tremendously popular with tourists. The menu offers a variety of traditional Mexican dishes; the Oaxacan tamale is a treat. **Features:** full bar. **Address:** Tacuba No. 28 06010 **Location:** Downtown; near Zocalo; in historico area. **Parking:** valet only.

Ⓑ Ⓛ Ⓓ ⒶⒸ

## CAFETERIA LOS NARANJOS
55/5705-2800 ⑨

▼▼ Mexican. Casual Dining. $8–$22 **AAA Inspector Notes:** Excellent variety of Mexican and American dishes for budget-minded travelers visiting Paseo de La Reforma. **Features:** full bar. **Address:** Paseo de La Reforma 105 06030 **Location:** Southwest quarter of Glorieta Cristobal Colon; centro; in Hotel Sevilla Palace. **Parking:** on-site (fee) and valet. Ⓑ Ⓛ Ⓓ

## COCINA AMICI
55/5242-5555 ⑫

▼▼▼ Italian. Casual Dining. $14–$32 **AAA Inspector Notes:** A contemporary look throughout the dining room complements the innovative menu at this popular spot, which specializes in fine Italian cuisine. Menu highlights include fresh tomato and mozzarella cheese salads, Caesar salads or homemade soups, followed by an extensive array of rich pastas, veal, poultry or fish selections. The desserts are a menu highlight worth saving room for. **Features:** full bar, Sunday brunch. **Reservations:** suggested. **Address:** Paseo de la Reforma No. 325, Col Cuauhtemoc **Location:** Next to US Embassy, opposite Angel de La Independencia Monument; in Sheraton Maria Isabel Hotel & Towers. **Parking:** on-site (fee) and valet.

Ⓛ Ⓓ ⓛⒶⓉⒺ ◣

## DEL BOSQUE RESTAURANTE
55/5263-6906 ⑰

▼▼▼ Continental. Fine Dining. $12–$33 **AAA Inspector Notes:** Floor-to-ceiling glass panel walls overlook one of Chapultepec's lakes. Pleasing all palates are unique dishes such as duck breast, sea bass and ravioli. **Address:** Margen Oriente del Lago Menor 11839 **Location:** In Chapultepec Park, 2nd section. **Parking:** valet only.

Ⓑ Ⓛ Ⓓ

## DOLCE MEXICO
55/1164-1164 ㊷

▼▼ New Mexican. Casual Dining. $10–$22 **AAA Inspector Notes:** Unique combination of Mexican and Italian cuisine. Custom pizzas bake in the brick oven while you place chicharrónes, pasilla chile and fried tortilla strips into your caldo tlalpeno. **Features:** full bar. **Address:** Calle Dakota No. 95, Col Napoles **Location:** Just n of Ave Insurgentes; adjacent to Mexico City World Trade Center; in Crowne Plaza Hotel de Mexico. **Parking:** on-site (fee) and valet.

Ⓛ Ⓓ ⓛⒶⓉⒺ

## DULCE PATRIA EN LAS ALCOBAS
55/3300-3999 ㉙

▼▼▼ ▼▼▼ Regional Mexican. Fine Dining. $20–$40 **AAA Inspector Notes:** Renowned chef Martha Ortiz delights patrons in this stylish monument to innovative, modern Mexican cuisine. Dishes such as the divine squash blossom soup dressed with flowers, and the pork in mole amarillo are presented with a dramatic, whimsical flair. The accomplished waitstaff recommends unique cocktails and will help guide through the extensive wine list featuring Mexican selections. **Features:** full bar. **Reservations:** suggested. **Address:** Anatole France 100, Col. Polanco 11560 **Location:** At Presidente Masaryk. **Parking:** street only. Ⓛ Ⓓ ⓛⒶⓉⒺ ◣

## EL CARDENAL
55/5130-5300 ⑥

▼▼▼ Mexican. Fine Dining. $20–$65 **AAA Inspector Notes:** Folks line up early to dine at this establishment, which serves national Mexican cuisine cooked with the freshest of ingredients. As one would expect, service is attentive and swift. **Features:** full bar. **Reservations:** suggested. **Address:** Ave Juárez No. 70, Col. Centro 06010 **Location:** Facing Alameda Park; in Centro Historico; in Hilton Mexico City Reforma. **Parking:** on-site (fee) and valet.

Ⓑ Ⓛ Ⓓ ◣

## EL CARDENAL
55/5521-3080 ⑭

▼▼▼ Mexican. Casual Dining. $10–$30 **AAA Inspector Notes:** *Historic.* In the heart of the historical zone, this converted home is world-renowned for classic Mexican dishes like escamoles (fried ant eggs) and a variety of moles. The place is usually bustling with both locals and visitors alike. **Features:** full bar. **Reservations:** suggested. **Address:** Palma 23 Centro Historico 06000 **Location:** Between Ave Cinco de Mayo and Francisco I Madero. **Parking:** no self-parking. Ⓑ Ⓛ Ⓓ ⒶⒸ

## EL LAGO CHAPULTEPEC
55/5515-9586 ③

▼▼▼▼ Regional New World. Fine Dining. $15–$75 **AAA Inspector Notes:** The restaurant offers truly fine dining as captains take orders and relay to service attendants. Offerings include many tableside preparations and house specialties. Dramatic tiered seating in the elegant dining spot afford views over the beautiful lake. **Features:** full bar, patio dining, Sunday brunch. **Reservations:** suggested. Semiformal attire. **Address:** Lago Mayor 2 da, Chapultepec Park **Location:** In new section of Chapultepec Park; near National Museum of Natural History. **Parking:** on-site (fee) and valet.

Ⓑ Ⓛ Ⓓ

**(See map & index p. 496.)**

## FISHER'S CENTRO — 55/5521-8867 (9)

▼▼ ▼▼ Mexican Seafood. Casual Dining. $10-$28 **AAA Inspector Notes:** This bustling restaurant serves an extensive variety of fresh seafood. Try the crab tostadas, seafood pasta or oysters. **Features:** full bar. **Address:** Calle 5 de Febrero No. 24, Centro Historico 06060 **Location:** In heart of Centro Historico; 2 blks s of Zocalo Mayor; in Hampton Inn & Suites Mexico City-Centro Historico. **Parking:** no self-parking. [L] [D] [◣]

## GARABATOS — 55/5518-4551 (7)

▼▼ ▼▼ Mexican Breads/Pastries. Casual Dining. $10-$22 **AAA Inspector Notes:** This popular Mexican diner features a bakery with hard-to-resist pastries. **Features:** full bar. **Address:** Calle 5 de Febrero No. 24 Centro Historico 06060 **Location:** In heart of Centro Historico; 2 blks s of Zocalo Mayor; in Hampton Inn & Suites Mexico City-Centro Historico. **Parking:** valet only. [B] [L] [D]

## GOTAN RESTAURANTE ARGENTINO — 55/5535-2136 (13)

▼▼ ▼▼ Steak. Casual Dining. $8-$18 **AAA Inspector Notes:** This locally popular restaurant is very small with a warm and inviting atmosphere. Excellent imported beef from Uruguay is expertly grilled. For non-meat eaters there's homemade pasta, lovingly prepared using Viviana's grandmother's recipes. Save room for dessert as a variety of family favorite treats are on the menu. **Features:** beer & wine. **Address:** Pedro Baranda 17, Col. Tabacalera **Location:** Just n of jct Ave de La Republica and Paseo de La Reforma. **Parking:** street only. [L] [D] [AC]

## HOSTERIA DE SANTO DOMINGO — 55/5510-1434 (2)

▼▼ ▼▼ Regional Mexican. Family Dining. $10-$22 **AAA Inspector Notes:** *Classic Historic.* Serving complex yet authentic Mexican dishes since 1840, this city landmark's walls are covered with photos of celebrity guests. Chiles en nogada is served daily. Another good menu choice is the 'Wild Chicken,' a breast marinated in red adobado sauce, grilled and served with roasted nopal (prickly pear). **Features:** full bar. **Address:** Belisario Domingues 70, Centro Historico 06010 **Location:** 2 blks n of National Cathedral and Zocalo. **Parking:** on-site (fee). [B] [L] [D] [AC]

## LA CASA DE LA SIRENAS — 55/5704-3545 (8)

▼▼ ▼▼ Mexican. Casual Dining. $13-$38 **AAA Inspector Notes:** Located along a walkway behind the main cathedral, this restaurant is housed in a building that dates to the 1700s. The entrance is adorned with carved stone mermaids, hence the "Sirenas" name. Authentic Mexican dishes are best enjoyed on the third-floor terrace, which overlooks the back of the cathedral. **Features:** full bar. **Address:** Republica de Guatemala No. 32 06000 **Location:** In Centro Historico. **Parking:** no self-parking. [L] [D] [AC] [◣]

## LA HACIENDA DE LOS MORALES — 55/5283-3054 (33)

▼▼▼▼▼

Regional Mexican Fine Dining $18-$40

**AAA Inspector Notes:** Surrounded by beautiful gardens with fountains, the restored hacienda boasts large courtyards and dining rooms suited to relaxing, refined dining. Excellent quality ingredients go into dishes that are served in ample portions. **Features:** full bar, patio dining. **Reservations:** suggested. **Address:** Vazquez de Mella 525 11510 **Location:** Just s of Ejercito Nacional; in Polanco District. **Parking:** valet only. [L] [D] [LATE] [AC] [◣]

## LA OPERA RESTAURANT BAR — 55/5512-8959 (12)

▼▼▼▼▼ Regional Mexican. Casual Dining. $12-$25 **AAA Inspector Notes:** *Historic.* This historic restaurant, which once catered to affluent opera goers, offers an Old World ambience not to be missed. A visit here is not complete without looking up at the ceiling to spot the bullet hole left by the legendary Pancho Villa. **Features:** full bar. **Address:** 10 Cinco de Mayo, Centro Historico **Location:** Downtown. **Parking:** no self-parking. [L] [D] [LATE]

## LOS ALMENDROS — 55/5531-7307 (8)

▼▼▼▼▼ Regional Mexican. Casual Dining. $15-$30 **AAA Inspector Notes:** Known for Mayan-influenced cuisine, the restaurant transports diners to the Yucatan. A must on any tourist's itinerary, this spot offers an unforgettable experience. A well-rounded meal might start with savory, but not spicy, panuchos de cochinita pibil; center on arroz con pollo with platanos fritos; and end with cerveza Leon. **Features:** full bar. **Reservations:** suggested. **Address:** Campos Eliseos No. 164 **Location:** In Polanco Zone; corner of Campos Eliseos and Arquimedes, just e. **Parking:** valet and street only. [B] [L] [D] [◣]

## LOS GIRASOLES — 55/5510-0630 (1)

▼▼▼▼▼ Regional Mexican. Casual Dining. $8-$22 **AAA Inspector Notes:** Created as a place to serve pre-Columbian recipes that have been handed down for generations, the restaurant is conveniently located near museums and the Zocalo. Menu items range from traditional tortilla soup and duckling in blackberry sauce to such adventurous choices as fried worms, ant eggs and grasshoppers. I highly recommend the cilantro soup, as well as the turkey with tamarind mole sauce. Third-floor seating offers views of historic buildings, and outside dining also is available. **Features:** full bar, patio dining. **Address:** Calle de Tacuba **Location:** Between calles 8 and 10; in historico downtown district; in front of Plaza Manuel Tolsa. **Parking:** valet and street only. [L] [D]

## MANHATTAN DELI — 55/5242-5555 (11)

▼▼ ▼▼ Deli. Casual Dining. $12-$35 **AAA Inspector Notes:** Finding a New York-style deli in the heart of Mexico City is quite a surprise, but this one is located directly beside the U.S. Embassy, so it fits right in. In addition to classic deli fare, you can feast on tacos, quesadillas and more Mexican favorites. An extensive salad bar also is offered, along with soup, entrée and dessert bars. You'll find a variety of bagel and croissant sandwiches on the à la carte menu. **Features:** full bar. **Address:** Paseo de La Reforma No. 325, Col Cuauhtemoc 06500 **Location:** Next to US Embassy, opposite Angel de La Independencia Monument; in Sheraton Maria Isabel Hotel & Towers. **Parking:** on-site (fee) and valet. [B] [L] [D] [LATE]

## MERIDIEM RESTAURANTE — 55/5273-3599 (10)

▼▼▼▼▼ International. Casual Dining. $11-$25 **AAA Inspector Notes:** Large windows overlook a lake and fountain at this spot that also has an attractive patio. Guests can order a la carte or try the buffet. **Features:** full bar, patio dining, Sunday brunch. **Reservations:** suggested. **Address:** Margen Poniente Lago Mayor, 2 da **Location:** In second section of Chapultepec Park; near National Museum of History. **Parking:** valet only. [B] [L] [D]

## MESON DEL CID — 55/5512-7629 (5)

▼▼ ▼▼ Spanish. Casual Dining. $10-$45 **AAA Inspector Notes:** Since 1972, this establishment has been preparing classic and contemporary Spanish cuisine, including daily specials. A unique, medieval prix fixe dinner and show is offered Saturdays at 8:30 pm. **Features:** full bar. **Reservations:** suggested. **Address:** Humbolt No. 61, Col Centro 06000 **Location:** Between Articulo 123 and Morelos; in downtown Centro Historico. **Parking:** valet only. [L] [D] [LATE]

## MORIMOTO MEXICO CITY — 55/5262-6264 (35)

▼▼▼▼▼ Japanese. Casual Dining. $20-$88 **AAA Inspector Notes:** Chef Morimoto brings his innovative and highly acclaimed Japanese cuisine to Mexico City. The modern décor is almost as impressive as the creative and artful food presentations. The toro tartare is an outstanding choice, along with the braised black cod in a ginger-soy reduction. **Features:** full bar. **Reservations:** suggested. **Address:** Mariano Escobedo No. 700 Col. Nueva Anzures 11590 **Location:** Between Victor Hugo and Kent, just n of Diana Cir; Periferico exit Ave Presidente Masaryk, then w; in Camino Real Polanco Mexico City. **Parking:** on-site (fee) and valet. [L] [D]

## MUMEDI CAFE — 55/5510-8609 (11)

▼▼ ▼▼ International. Casual Dining. $7-$15 **AAA Inspector Notes:** Unique is what to expect at this bustling café. Not only is the menu creative, using local ingredients in unexpected forms, but also the architecture and art lend a stylish, contemporary feel. Worth a stroll is the attached gallery and shop, featuring many Mexican modern artists. **Address:** Francisco I Madero No. 74 **Location:** Col Centro, on pedestrian walkway just n of Zócalo. [B] [L] [D] [LATE] [AC]

(See map & index p. 496.)

THE PALM RESTAURANT     55/5327-7700   (7)

▼▼▼▼ American. Fine Dining. $15-$55 **AAA Inspector Notes:** This bustling restaurant is noted for Prime, dry-aged steaks and Nova Scotia lobsters. The huge portions are delivered by an attentive staff in an atmosphere that is fun and lively. At the end of the meal, servers present tempting pastries tableside. Caricature-lined walls lend to the feeling that patrons are dining in an art gallery. Even if you bring a good appetite you still may leave with a doggy bag. **Features:** full bar. **Reservations:** suggested. **Address:** Campo Eliseos 218 Col. Polanco 11560 **Location:** In Polanco Zone; on Paseo de La Reforma, 0.8 mi (1.3 km) w of Periferico; opposite Chapultepec Park and National Auditorium; in Hotel Presidente InterContinental Mexico City. **Parking:** on-site (fee) and valet. L D LATE N

PUJOL RESTAURANTE     55/5545-4111   (32)

▼▼▼ ▼▼▼ New Mexican. Fine Dining. $90 **AAA Inspector Notes:** The restaurant features an upscale dining room, an interesting, contemporary Mexican menu and an extensive wine list. You may want to bring a Spanish dictionary to translate the creative menu choices, which include fabulous seafood and duck dishes. Wine flights are available for the connoisseur. **Features:** full bar. **Reservations:** required. Semiformal attire. **Address:** F Petrarca 254 Polanco 11570 **Location:** Between Horacio and Homero; in Polanco District. **Parking:** on-site (fee) and valet. L D LATE

**REFORMA 500**     55/5230-1818

▼▼▼ ▼▼▼

Mediterranean
Fine Dining
$15-$45

**AAA Inspector Notes:** The kitchen's Mediterranean concepts employ premium local ingredients. Preparations are complex and presentations distinctive. You can dine in the elegant dining room or on the outdoor terrace overlooking the refined courtyard. **Features:** full bar, patio dining, Sunday brunch. **Reservations:** suggested. **Address:** Paseo de La Reforma 500 Col Juárez 06600 **Location:** On Paseo de La Reforma; in Four Seasons Hotel Mexico D.F. **Parking:** valet only. B L D N

RESTAURANT DIANA     55/5228-1818   (14)

▼▼▼ ▼▼▼ Regional Mexican. Fine Dining. $15-$45 **AAA Inspector Notes:** Modern Mexican cuisine is served in a refined dining room overlooking the famed Diana fountain at one of the city's major intersections. Undecided about which glass of wine to enjoy with your meal? The professional waiter will roll the wine cart to your table and pour a tasting to help make up your mind. **Features:** full bar, patio dining. **Reservations:** suggested. **Address:** Paseo de La Reforma 439, Col. Cuauhtemoc 06500 **Location:** Paseo de La Reforma at Rio Mississippi St; opposite Glorieta La Diana; in The St. Regis Mexico City. **Parking:** valet only. B L D LATE N

RESTAURANTE FONDA EL REFUGIO     55/5525-8128   (18)

▼▼▼ Regional Mexican. Casual Dining. $13-$25 **AAA Inspector Notes:** Quaint countryside décor lends to the informal atmosphere at this longtime, local favorite restaurant. Excellent preparation marks dishes that journey through the culinary regions of Mexico. Don't pass up the margarita—one of the city's best. **Features:** full bar. **Address:** Liverpool 166 **Location:** In Zona Rosa. L D LATE

RESTAURANTE MERCADERES CAFE     55/5510-2213   (4)

▼▼▼ International. Casual Dining. $10-$32 **AAA Inspector Notes:** A great location in the city's historical center, across from the cathedral and a few blocks from the Palace of Fine Arts, makes this the perfect spot to break or end your sightseeing day. Although the menu is in Spanish only, the waiters will display the various cuts of steaks that are the featured specialty. They are grilled to order and arrive in hearty portions. Also offered are seafood, pasta and Mexican selections. **Features:** full bar. **Address:** Ave Cinco de Mayo No. 57 Centro Historico **Location:** In Centro Historico. **Parking:** valet only. B L D

---

RESTAURANTE SAN ANGEL INN     55/5616-2222   (11)

▼▼▼ ▼▼▼ Traditional Continental. Fine Dining. $25-$60 **AAA Inspector Notes:** Historic. In a renovated 18th-century hacienda, the renowned dining room is surrounded by gardens and patios. Have a drink and unwind in any of the courtyard gardens or elegant rooms, then settle in at your table in the ornate main dining room and appreciate the excellent service. The menu focuses on haute Mexican cuisine. But your gaze may be drawn elsewhere, as this is a place you'll likely see Mexico City's glitterati. **Features:** full bar, Sunday brunch. **Reservations:** required. **Address:** Diego Rivera No. 50 esq Altavista **Location:** 7 blks w of Insurgentes Sur; 5 blks e of Anillo Periferico; in San Angel Inn. **Parking:** valet only. L D LATE N

RINCON ARGENTINO RESTAURANTE     55/5254-8775   (28)

▼▼▼ ▼▼▼ Argentine. Casual Dining. $25-$56 **AAA Inspector Notes:** The name translates to "corner of Argentina," which is manifested in a bohemian atmosphere, tender cuts of grilled beef and attentive, personalized service. **Features:** full bar. **Reservations:** suggested. **Address:** Ave Presidente Masaryk No. 177 11570 **Location:** In Polanco Zone. **Parking:** on-site (fee) and valet. L D LATE N

ROSATO RISTORANTE     55/1105-5000   (7)

▼▼▼ Italian. Casual Dining. $9-$25 **AAA Inspector Notes:** This eatery's classic Italian selections are prepared with fresh and imported ingredients. The crab-stuffed ravioli topped with a rich pomodoro sauce is best accompanied by a glass of crisp Chianti. **Features:** full bar. **Reservations:** suggested. **Address:** Calle 3 No. 55, Col Lomas de Santa Fe **Location:** 7.2 mi (12 km) w on Paseo de La Reforma (which becomes Prolongacion Reforma) exit Joaquin Gallo, just s on Vasco de Quiroga, then just s on Santa Fe; in Santa Fe District; in Fiesta Americana Santa Fe. **Parking:** on-site and valet. B L D N

SAKS SAN ANGEL     55/5616-1601   (10)

▼▼▼ Regional Mexican. Casual Dining. $12-$28 **AAA Inspector Notes:** This place gets very busy during the Saturday artisan market. The patio is a good spot to people-watch with a glass of wine from the extensive list. In addition to well-prepared appetizers and entrées you'll find house-baked bread and pastries. **Features:** full bar, patio dining. **Reservations:** suggested. **Address:** Plaza San Jacinto 6, Col San Angel **Location:** On Plaza San Jacinto. **Parking:** no self-parking. B L D CALL &M

SIR WINSTON CHURCHILL'S     55/5280-6070   (9)

▼▼▼ British. Fine Dining. $22-$68 **AAA Inspector Notes:** The menu features fine English and international cuisine, including Churchill's favorite, roast prime rib of beef served with Yorkshire pudding and fresh horseradish. Graced with lovely gardens, the atmosphere is elegant and refined. There's live piano music daily from 1 to 5 pm. **Features:** full bar, patio dining. **Reservations:** suggested. **Address:** Blvd M Avila Camacho 67 11560 **Location:** Jct Volcan; enter Paseo and Palmas; in Polanco District. **Parking:** valet only. L D LATE

SOLEA RESTAURANT     55/9138-1800   (6)

▼▼▼ Regional Mexican. Casual Dining. $10-$38 **AAA Inspector Notes:** Steak and seafood dishes are prepared with fresh ingredients and a Mexican twist at this hip, contemporary restaurant. Among the seating options are a private dining room and a communal table. **Features:** full bar. **Reservations:** suggested. **Address:** Campos Eliseos 252 Col Polanco 11560 **Location:** Just off Ave Paseo de La Reforma; in Polanco District; in W Mexico City. **Parking:** valet only. B L D

TORRE D CASTILLA     55/5281-0906   (26)

▼▼▼ Spanish. Fine Dining. $10-$70 **AAA Inspector Notes:** Set in a castle, this restaurant gives you a true sense of medieval Europe with its distressed wood floors, wall murals and stone walls. The menu features a wonderful mixture of fine Spanish cuisine, complete with a broad selection of hot and cold appetizers, or tapas, and a good selection of meat, poultry and seafood. Jumbo shrimp in garlic sauce is a popular dish. The menu is in Spanish, so it's a good idea to bring a language book and a sense of adventure. The patio is inviting. **Features:** full bar. **Reservations:** suggested. **Address:** Esopo 31 Polanco 11530 **Location:** Jct Ave Presidente Masaryk; near Cuban Embassy; follow FFCC and Horacio. **Parking:** valet only. L D LATE

(See map & index p. 496.)

EL BAJIO                                      55/5234-3763

[fyi] Not evaluated. The popular chain's original location serves authentic country-style Mexican food. Must-order items include mole de olla (beef soup), marinated shredded pork panuchos, Mexican rice with plantains and fish a la Veracruzana with capers, olives, tomatoes and bell pepper. **Address:** Ave Cuitlahuac No. 2709 **Location:** Just e of Ave Tlahuac; in Colonia Iztapalapa.

EL BAJIO REFORMA 222                          55/5511-9117

[fyi] Not evaluated. This is one of the newer locations of a popular Mexican chain serving authentic country-style Mexican food, including mole de olla beef soup, marinated shredded pork panuchos, Mexican rice with plantains and fish a la Veracruzana with capers, olives, tomatoes and bell pepper. Service is quick. **Address:** Ave Paseo de La Reforma 222, Col. Juárez 06500 **Location:** Just w of Ave Insurgentes; in Reforma 222 shopping mall.

## This ends listings for Mexico City.
## The following resumes the alphabetical listings of cities in Mexico City and Vicinity.

# TEOTIHUACÁN, MÉXICO pop. 53,010

QUINTO SOL HOTEL                              594/956-1881

♥♥ **Hotel.** Rates not provided. **Address:** Ave Hidalgo No. 26, Barrio Purificacion **Location:** On road leading to pyramids. **Facility:** 38 units. 2 stories (no elevator), interior corridors. *Bath:* shower only. **Amenities:** safes. **Pool(s):** outdoor. **Guest Services:** valet laundry.

[icons] / SOME UNITS [icons]

VILLAS ARQUEOLOGICAS TEOTIHUACAN              594/956-0909

♥♥ **Hotel.** Rates not provided. **Address:** Periferico Sur S/N **Location:** Adjacent to main archeological zone, off Mex 132. **Facility:** 43 units. 2 stories (no elevator), exterior corridors. **Amenities:** safes. **Dining:** 2 restaurants. **Pool(s):** outdoor. **Activities:** hot tub, playground, massage. **Guest Services:** valet laundry.

[icons] / SOME UNITS [icons]

### WHERE TO EAT

RESTAURANT LA GRUTA                           594/956-0104

♥♥ Regional Mexican. Family Dining. $12-$25 **AAA Inspector Notes:** At the entrance to the pyramids, the restaurant occupies an immense cave at the foot of the mountain. Live shows are presented on Saturday at 3:30 pm, and Sunday at 3:30 and 5:30 pm. **Features:** full bar, patio dining. **Address:** Zona Arqueologica Teotihuacan S/N 55800 **Location:** Adjacent to main archeological zone.

[L] [D] [AC]

# TEPOZTLÁN, MORELOS (C-3) pop. 41,629, elev. 5,579'

POSADA DEL TEPOZTECO                          (739)395-0010

♥♥♥ **Historic Country Inn.** Rates not provided. **Address:** Paraiso No. 3, Barrio de San Miguel 62520 **Location:** Just w of main plaza. **Facility:** Overlooking the mountains in a village that dates back to pre-conquest Mexico, this heritage house offers clay tile floors, arched entries and hand-painted accents evoking traditional Mexico. 21 units. 2 stories (no elevator), exterior corridors. **Terms:** 4 day cancellation notice. **Amenities:** safes. **Pool(s):** heated outdoor. **Activities:** tennis, playground, massage. **Guest Services:** valet laundry.

[icons]

XACALLAN HOTEL PUEBLO MAGICO                  739/395-4999

[fyi] Not evaluated. **Address:** Calle de Olvido No. 9 62520 **Location:** Corner of Condessa Barrio de San Miguel. Facilities, services, and décor characterize an economy property.

### WHERE TO EAT

LOS COLORINES                                 739/395-0198

♥♥ Regional Mexican. Casual Dining. $4-$9 **AAA Inspector Notes:** On the town's main street, this casual Mexican restaurant has colorful, festive decor with multicolored flags hanging from the ceiling. The menu includes some classic Mexican dishes as well some unique local dishes not found elsewhere. **Features:** full bar, patio dining. **Address:** Ave del Tepozteco No.13 Barrio la Santisima 62520 **Location:** Centro. **Parking:** street only. [B] [L] [D] [AC]

RESTAURANT AXITLA                             739/395-0519

♥♥ Regional Mexican. Family Dining. $8-$15 **AAA Inspector Notes:** Hidden in the steep hills of this ancient Aztec town, the restaurant's lush gardens provide a relaxed dining retreat. Patrons enjoy beautiful views as they savor authentic Mexican dishes such as mole, chicken enchiladas or even the classic trout amandine. Refreshing aguas frescas, such as agua de Jamaica or tamarindo, are made from exotic fruit and flowers. **Features:** full bar, patio dining. **Address:** Ave del Tepozteco S/N **Location:** At far north end of Ave del Tepozteco; near the start of trail to pyramid. **Parking:** street only.

[L] [D] [AC] [icon]

## TEQUESQUITENGO, MORELOS
elev. 3,083'

HOTEL HACIENDA VISTA HERMOSA      734/345-5361

**fyi** Not evaluated. **Address:** KM 7 Carr Alpuyeca **Location:** 5.1 mi (8.5 km) se of Alpuyeca interchange off Mex 95 and 95-D (toll road); 0.9 mi (1.5 km) n of Lake Tequesquitengo. Facilities, services, and décor characterize a mid-scale property.

## TLALNEPANTLA, MÉXICO pop. 664,225
• Hotels & Restaurants map & index p. 502

CROWNE PLAZA MEXICO NORTE TLALNEPANTLA    (55)5228-9500   **12**

 **Hotel.** Rates not provided. **Address:** Ave Roberto Fulton 2-A 54000 **Location:** 0.5 mi (0.8 km) e of jct Mex 57 at Tlalnepantla de Baz; north of Mexico City limits. **Facility:** 126 units, some two bedrooms. 9 stories, interior corridors. **Amenities:** safes. **Activities:** sauna, steamroom, tennis, exercise room. **Guest Services:** valet laundry.

## TOLUCA, MÉXICO (B-2) pop. 819,561, elev. 8,790'

DEL REY INN HOTEL      (722)277-1010

Hotel
Rates not provided

**Address:** Carr Mex Toluca KM 63.5 50160 **Location:** 2.4 mi (4 km) e on Mex 15. **Facility:** 250 units. 2-5 stories, interior corridors. **Amenities:** safes. **Pool(s):** heated indoor. **Activities:** hot tub, game room, exercise room. **Guest Services:** valet laundry.

/ SOME UNITS

QUINTA DEL REY      (722)275-8000

Hotel
Rates not provided

**Address:** Paseo Tollocan Ote No. 500 52170 **Location:** 5.7 mi (9.5 km) e on Mex 15. **Facility:** 66 units, some two bedrooms. 3 stories, interior corridors. **Amenities:** safes. **Pool(s):** heated indoor. **Activities:** sauna, hot tub, steamroom, playground, game room, exercise room, spa. **Guest Services:** valet laundry, area transportation.

QUINTA DEL REY EXPRESS      (722)235-8888

 **Hotel.** Rates not provided. **Address:** San Antonio 102 50200 **Location:** Blvd Aeropuerto Miguel Alemán Valez, off southbound lane departing from airport grounds. Located near Toluca International airport. **Facility:** Meets AAA guest room security requirements. 122 units. 3 stories, interior corridors. **Bath:** shower only. **Amenities:** safes. **Pool(s):** heated indoor. **Activities:** exercise room. **Guest Services:** valet laundry, area transportation.

CROWNE PLAZA HOTEL TOLUCA      722/477-1000

**fyi** Not evaluated. **Address:** Paseo del Tollocan 750 Ote **Location:** Mex 15 (Toluca-Mexico City) Paseo Tollocan exit Ave Albert Einstein. Facilities, services, and décor characterize a mid-scale property.

# CENTRAL MEXICO

AAA recommends that travelers consult online U.S. State Department travel advisories when planning travel abroad. Find this information at http://travel.state.gov/content/passports/english/alertswarnings/mexico-travel-warning.html.

## ABASOLO, GUANAJUATO pop. 84,332

HOTEL BALNEARIO SPA LA CALDERA                429/693-0020

[fyi] Not evaluated; located in remote area. **Address:** Libramiento Carr KM 29 36970 **Location:** Mex 45 (Mexico/Guadalajara Frwy) to Mex 90 (Guadalajara), south of Irapuato. Facilities, services, and décor characterize an economy property. A fun family-oriented full service resort built around a natural hot spring, the hotel offers a retreat-like ambiance.

## AGUASCALIENTES, AGUASCALIENTES
(C-1) pop. 797,010, elev. 6,193'

### HOTEL MARRIOTT AGUASCALIENTES        449/139-4060

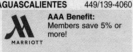

Contemporary Hotel
$105-$391

**AAA Benefit:** Members save 5% or more!

**Address:** Blvd Zacatecas Norte S/N Col Trojes de Alonso **Location:** In northern part of city, just n of city loop Aguascalientes Norte. Adjacent to Altaria Shopping Complex. **Facility:** This refined, contemporary high-rise hotel has elegant public spaces, including an outdoor sitting area with stone fire pits. The large, comfortable guest rooms feature upgraded bedding. 287 units. 15 stories, interior corridors. **Parking:** on-site (fee) and valet. **Amenities:** safes. **Dining:** Condimento, see separate listing. **Pool(s):** heated outdoor. **Activities:** hot tub, exercise room, massage. **Guest Services:** valet laundry.

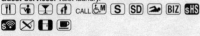

FIESTA INN AGUASCALIENTES                     449/149-0200

[fyi] Not evaluated. **Address:** Mahatma Gandhi 302 Sur **Location:** 0.6 mi (1 km) s on Leon Hwy (Mex 45). Facilities, services, and décor characterize a mid-scale property.

GRAN HOTEL ALAMEDA                            449/970-3800

[fyi] Not evaluated. **Address:** Alameda 821 **Location:** On east side, 3 blks e of Ave de La Convencion. Facilities, services, and décor characterize a mid-scale property.

HOTEL FIESTA AMERICANA AGUASCALIENTES
                                              449/910-0500

[fyi] Not evaluated. **Address:** Calle Los Laureles No. 401 **Location:** Just w of Ave Americas; near Plaza de Toros. Facilities, services, and décor characterize an upscale property.

HOTEL FRANCIA AGUASCALIENTES                  449/918-7300

[fyi] Not evaluated. **Address:** Ave Fco I Madero No. 113-A **Location:** Just e of Plaza Principal; in Centro Historico. Facilities, services, and décor characterize a mid-scale property.

HOTEL ONE AGUASCALIENTES SAN MARCOS    449/994-6660

[fyi] Not evaluated. **Address:** Laureles 404 Col. Las Flores **Location:** Just w of Ave Americas; near Expo Plaza. Facilities, services, and décor characterize an economy property.

QUINTA REAL AGUASCALIENTES                    449/978-5818

[fyi] Not evaluated. **Address:** Ave Aguascalientes Sur 601 20270 **Location:** On south side, just e of jct Blvd Jose Chavez and Ave Aguascalientes. Facilities, services, and décor characterize an upscale property.

CONDIMENTO                                    449/139-4060

Mexican. Casual Dining. $12-$35 **AAA Inspector Notes:** This restaurant offers delicious dishes served with a Mexican flair. Specialties include a variety of fresh-made pastas with your choice of flavorful sauces. The juicy Mexican-style skirt steak is tender and enhanced with traditional corn with aromatic poblano peppers. The décor is bright, festive and elegant. **Features:** full bar, Sunday brunch. **Address:** Blvd Zacatecas Norte S/N Col Trojes de Alonso **Location:** In northern part of city, just n of city loop Aguascalientes Norte; in Hotel Marriott Aguascalientes. **Parking:** on-site (fee) and valet. [B] [L] [D]

## AJIJIC, JALISCO

AJIJIC PLAZA SUITES                           376/766-0383

Motel $45-$65 **Address:** Calle Colon No. 33 45920 **Location:** Centro. Across from main plaza. **Facility:** 10 units. 1 story, exterior corridors. Bath: shower only. **Parking:** street only. **Pool(s):** outdoor.

HOTEL REAL DE CHAPALA                         376/766-0014

Hotel $110-$130 **Address:** Paseo del Prado No. 20 45920 **Location:** Between Blvd Ajijic and Chapala; in La Floresta area. **Facility:** 85 units. 2 stories (no elevator), interior/exterior corridors. **Amenities:** safes. **Pool(s):** outdoor, heated outdoor. **Activities:** hot tub, tennis. **Guest Services:** valet laundry.

LA NUEVA POSADA                               376/766-1344

Country Inn $95-$115 **Address:** Donato Guerra No. 9 45920 **Location:** Just se of main plaza. **Facility:** The inn overlooks Lake Chapala. Some rooms have balconies; all feature Mexican-Colonial décor, colorful artwork, and comfortable furnishings. 19 units, some two bedrooms. 3 stories (no elevator), interior corridors. Bath: shower only. **Dining:** La Taberna, see separate listing. **Pool(s):** outdoor.

LOS ARTISTAS BED & BREAKFAST                  376/766-1027

Bed & Breakfast $78-$98 **Address:** Constitucion No. 105 45920 **Location:** Centro. **Facility:** The eclectically decorated guest lounge is graced with the owner's art collection; a manicured garden offers outdoor interest. Spacious rooms sport distinct Mexican décor and tile floors. 6 units. 1 story, interior/exterior corridors. Bath: shower only. **Pool(s):** outdoor.

LA TABERNA                                    376/766-1344

International. Casual Dining. $10-$19 **AAA Inspector Notes:** Popular with the town's American residents, the restaurant serves Continental, American and Mexican cuisine. Some tables in the elegantly furnished dining room offer views of the garden and patio. Located near the shore of Lake Chapala, a good lake-viewing room, and a spacious, shaded patio, give you two choices of setting. Attentive, semiformal service by a well-trained, uniformed staff accompanies the fine food. **Features:** full bar, patio dining. **Reservations:** suggested. **Address:** Donato Guerra No. 9 45920 **Location:** Just se of main plaza; in La Nueva Posada. [B] [L] [D]

## CELAYA, GUANAJUATO pop. 468,469

### CASA INN CELAYA                    461/598-6700

[fyi] Not evaluated; located in remote area. **Address:** Ave Torres Landa No. 202 **Location:** Carr Panamericana exit Libramiento Nor-Poniente southbound, just s to Ave Torres Landa; Carr Mexico Japon exit Ave Tecnologico northbound, just w; jct Calle Francisco Juárez; adjacent to Plaza Galerias Tecnologico. Facilities, services, and décor characterize a mid-scale property.

### HOTEL FIESTA INN CELAYA            461/618-8600

[fyi] Not evaluated; located in remote area. **Address:** Carr Panamericana KM 5 S/N 38060 **Location:** Just w of Villagran-Celaya Hwy. Facilities, services, and décor characterize a mid-scale property.

## CIUDAD VALLES, SAN LUIS POTOSÍ
pop. 167,713

### SIERRA HUASTECA INN                481/382-8300

[fyi] Not evaluated. **Address:** Blvd Don Antonio 151 79090 **Location:** On Mex 85, just s; jct Mex 70. Facilities, services, and décor characterize a mid-scale property.

## DOLORES HIDALGO, GUANAJUATO
(C-2) pop. 148,173, elev. 6,517'

### HOTEL HIDALGO                      418/182-2683

◆ **Hotel.** Rates not provided. **Address:** Hidalgo No. 15 Centro **Location:** 2 blks e of main plaza. Across from hospital and half a block from bus terminal. **Facility:** 30 units. 3 stories (no elevator), interior corridors. **Amenities:** safes. **Activities:** exercise room. **Guest Services:** coin laundry. [🍴] [SD] [HS] [🛜] [✕] [AC]

### HOTEL EL RELICARIO                 418/120-0712

[fyi] **Hotel** Did not meet all AAA rating requirements for viewports/peepholes in some guest rooms at time of last evaluation on 05/20/2015. **Address:** 12 Calzada de Los Heroes 37800 **Location:** Just n of Monumento de Los Heroes. Facilities, services, and décor characterize an economy property.

### PARADOR DON JOSE                   418/185-9008

◆◆ Regional Mexican. Family Dining. $4-$12 **AAA Inspector Notes:** You'll find this place just outside of town on the highway to San Luis de La Paz. A casual family restaurant, it offers buffet and a la carte dining in a casual friendly atmosphere. I love the large portions and just made gorditas and fideo. **Features:** beer & wine. **Address:** Carr a San Luis de La Paz KM 6 37800 **Location:** On highway to San Luis de La Paz, 0.4 mi (0.6 km) from town. [B] [L] [D] [◣]

### RESTAURANTE PLAZA                  418/182-0259

◆◆ Regional Mexican. Casual Dining. $8-$18 **AAA Inspector Notes:** *Classic.* Facing the city plaza, this 60-year-old restaurant is a local favorite and offers a wide variety of Mexican dishes. Fresh-ground coffee is a house specialty. Daily specials include a three-course dinner for less than $8. Try the enchiladas Potosinas for a unique twist on a centuries old dish. **Features:** full bar, Sunday brunch. **Address:** Plaza Principal No. 17B 37800 **Location:** Opposite south side of main plaza. **Parking:** street only. [B] [L] [D] [AC]

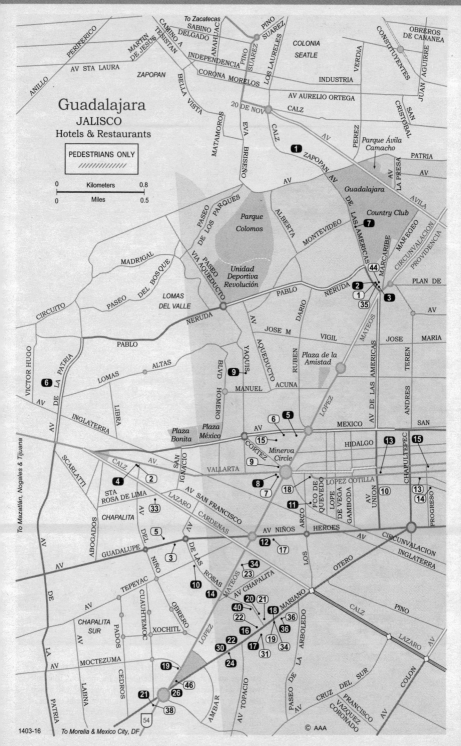

# Guadalajara
## JALISCO
### Hotels & Restaurants

PEDESTRIANS ONLY
/////////////

Kilometers
0 ——— 0.8
0 ——— 0.5
Miles

To Morelia & Mexico City, DF

© AAA

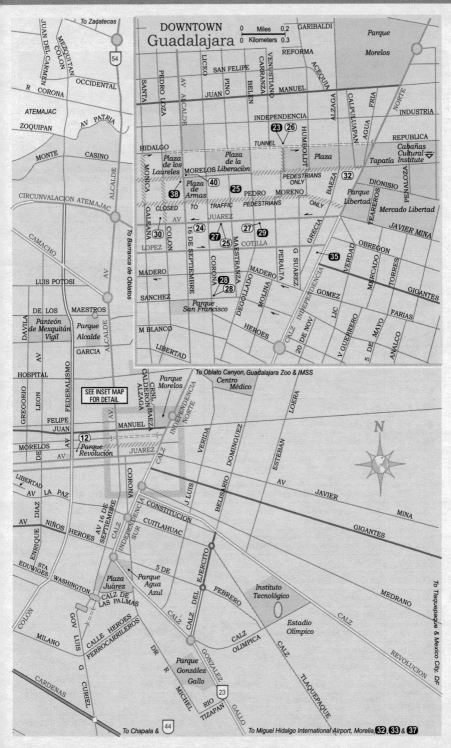

# Guadalajara

| ✈ Airport Hotels | | | | |
|---|---|---|---|---|
| Map Page | **DON MIGUEL HIDALGO Y COSTILLA INTERNATIONAL AIRPORT** | Diamond Rated | Rate Range | Page |
| **37** p. 518 | Holiday Inn Express Guadalajara Aeropuerto, 3.7 mi (6 km) | ▼▼▼ | $80-$175 | 524 |

## Guadalajara

This index helps you "spot" where approved hotels and restaurants are located on the corresponding detailed maps. Hotel daily rate range is for comparison only. Restaurant price range is a combination of lunch and/or dinner. Turn to the listing page for more detailed rate and price information and consult display ads for special promotions.

### GUADALAJARA, JALISCO

| Map Page | Hotels | Diamond Rated | Rate Range | Page |
|---|---|---|---|---|
| **1** p. 518 | Hotel Country Plaza | ▼▼▼ | $90-$110 | 524 |
| **2** p. 518 | **Grand Fiesta Americana Guadalajara Country Club** | ▼▼▼▼ | $150-$190 | 523 |
| **3** p. 518 | **NH Collection Guadalajara** | ▼▼▼▼ | $130-$220 | 525 |
| **4** p. 518 | Camino Real Guadalajara | ▼▼▼ | $240-$272 | 523 |
| **5** p. 518 | **Quinta Real Guadalajara** | ▼▼▼▼ | $350-$388 | 525 |
| **6** p. 518 | Holiday Inn Express Guadalajara UAG | ▼▼▼ | $95-$128 | 524 |
| **7** p. 518 | Aloft Guadalajara | ▼▼▼ | $200 | 523 |
| **8** p. 518 | Hotel Fiesta Americana Guadalajara | ▼▼▼ | $118-$343 | 524 |
| **9** p. 518 | Quinta Ganz | ▼▼ | $150 | 525 |
| **10** p. 518 | Clarum 101 | ▼▼▼▼ | $80-$120 | 523 |
| **11** p. 518 | Hotel Plaza Diana | ▼▼▼ | $79-$99 | 524 |
| **12** p. 518 | Holiday Inn Select | ▼▼▼ | $95-$117 | 524 |
| **13** p. 518 | **Villa Ganz Boutique Hotel** | ▼▼▼ | $180-$250 | 526 |
| **14** p. 518 | Guadalajara Plaza Ejecutivo Lopez Mateos | ▼▼▼ | $66-$104 | 523 |
| **15** p. 518 | Trocadero Suites | ▼▼ | $70-$100 | 525 |
| **16** p. 518 | **Fiesta Inn Guadalajara Expo** | ▼▼▼ | $105-$226 | 523 |
| **17** p. 518 | Hotel Guadalajara Plaza Expo Business Class | ▼▼▼ | $80-$100 | 524 |
| **18** p. 518 | **Hilton Guadalajara** | ▼▼▼▼ | $89-$259 | 524 |
| **19** p. 518 | **Hotel Presidente InterContinental Guadalajara** | ▼▼▼▼ | $147-$171 | 525 |
| **20** p. 518 | Real Inn | ▼▼▼ | $80-$155 | 525 |
| **21** p. 518 | Crowne Plaza Guadalajara | ▼▼▼ | $84-$119 | 523 |
| **22** p. 518 | Cityexpress Expo Guadalajara | ▼▼ | $85-$100 | 523 |
| **23** p. 518 | Hotel de Mendoza | ▼▼ | $120-$135 | 524 |
| **24** p. 518 | Holiday Inn Express Guadalajara Expo | ▼▼▼ | $90-$120 | 524 |
| **25** p. 518 | Hotel Frances | ▼▼ | $54-$97 | 524 |
| **26** p. 518 | **Staybridge Suites** | ▼▼▼ | $90-$100 | 525 |
| **27** p. 518 | Holiday Inn & Suites Guadalajara-Centro Historico | ▼▼▼ | $95-$115 | 524 |
| **28** p. 518 | **Hotel Morales Historical & Colonial Downtown Core** | ▼▼▼ | $85-$100 | 524 |
| **29** p. 518 | Hotel Real Inn Guadalajara Centro | ▼▼▼ | $50-$100 | 525 |

## GUADALAJARA, JALISCO (cont'd)

| Map Page | Hotels (cont'd) | Diamond Rated | Rate Range | Page |
|---|---|---|---|---|
| 30 p. 518 | Ibis Hotel | ◆◆ | $53-$83 | 525 |
| 32 p. 518 | Hampton Inn by Hilton Guadalajara Aeropuerto | ◆◆◆ | $92-$144 | 523 |
| 33 p. 518 | **Holiday Inn Express Guadalajara Iteso** | ◆◆◆ | $86-$125 | 524 |
| 34 p. 518 | **Hotel RIU Plaza Guadalajara** *(See ad p. 380.)* | ◆◆◆◆ | Rates not provided | 525 |
| 35 p. 518 | BEST WESTERN Gran Hotel Centro Historico | ◆◆ | Rates not provided | 523 |
| 36 p. 518 | **The Westin Guadalajara** | ◆◆◆◆ | $99-$299 | 526 |
| 37 p. 518 | Holiday Inn Express Guadalajara Aeropuerto | ◆◆◆ | $80-$175 | 524 |
| 38 p. 518 | One Hoteles | ◆◆ | $60-$100 | 525 |
| 40 p. 518 | **Hampton Inn by Hilton Guadalajara Expo** | ◆◆◆ | $69-$132 | 523 |

| Map Page | Restaurants | Diamond Rated | Cuisine | Price Range | Page |
|---|---|---|---|---|---|
| 1 p. 518 | Cuatro Estaciones | ◆◆◆ | International | $13-$30 | 526 |
| 2 p. 518 | Maria Bonita | ◆◆◆ | Regional Mexican | $13-$24 | 528 |
| 3 p. 518 | El Tango | ◆◆◆ | Argentine Steak | $12-$22 | 526 |
| 5 p. 518 | La Pasta | ◆◆◆ | Italian | $9-$20 | 527 |
| 6 p. 518 | La Matera | ◆◆ | Argentine Steak | $9-$21 | 527 |
| 7 p. 518 | La Franda | ◆◆◆ | International | $8-$25 | 527 |
| 9 p. 518 | Pomodoro | ◆◆ | Italian | $7-$16 | 528 |
| 10 p. 518 | Santo Coyote | ◆◆◆ | Mexican | $15-$28 | 528 |
| 12 p. 518 | El Sacromonte | ◆◆◆ | Regional Mexican | $11-$22 | 526 |
| 13 p. 518 | Recco Restaurant | ◆◆ | Italian | $9-$25 | 528 |
| 14 p. 518 | Suehiro | ◆◆◆ | Japanese | $15-$24 | 528 |
| 15 p. 518 | La Tequila | ◆◆ | Regional Mexican | $10-$18 | 527 |
| 17 p. 518 | La Trattoria de Guadalajara | ◆◆ | Italian | $8-$20 | 527 |
| 18 p. 518 | La Dolce Vita | ◆◆ | Italian | $8-$18 | 527 |
| 19 p. 518 | Angus Butcher House Restaurant and Bar | ◆◆ | Steak | $13-$30 | 526 |
| 21 p. 518 | Stock Cafe | ◆◆ | International | $8-$22 | 528 |
| 22 p. 518 | Manolo Campestre | ◆◆ | Mexican | $9-$20 | 528 |
| 23 p. 518 | Chardonnay | ◆◆◆◆ | International | $15-$30 | 526 |
| 24 p. 518 | La Chata de Guadalajara | ◆◆ | Mexican | $8-$15 | 527 |
| 25 p. 518 | Dolce Mexico | ◆◆ | International | $7-$16 | 526 |
| 26 p. 518 | La Forja | ◆◆◆ | International | $8-$20 | 527 |
| 27 p. 518 | Stock Cafe | ◆◆ | International | $8-$22 | 528 |
| 28 p. 518 | El Ruedo | ◆◆ | International | $8-$15 | 526 |
| 30 p. 518 | La Fonda de San Miguel Arcangel | ◆◆ | Mexican | $12-$23 | 527 |
| 31 p. 518 | La Flor de Calabaza | ◆◆ | International | $10-$18 | 527 |
| 32 p. 518 | El Mexicana Restaurant Turistico | ◆◆ | Mexican | $8-$16 | 526 |
| 33 p. 518 | Los Arcos | ◆◆ | Seafood | $10-$22 | 527 |

| Map Page | Restaurants (cont'd) | Diamond Rated | Cuisine | Price Range | Page |
|----------|---------------------|---------------|---------|-------------|------|
| ㉞ p. 518 | **Los Vitrales** | ◈◈ | International | $10-$18 | 528 |
| ㉟ p. 518 | Olio Bistro | ◈◈◈ | Mediterranean | $10-$22 | 528 |
| ㊱ p. 518 | Grill and Vine | ◈◈◈ | International | $10-$22 | 526 |
| ㊳ p. 518 | La Fuente | ◈◈ | International | $10-$18 | 527 |
| ㊵ p. 518 | La Antigua Restaurant Bar | ◈◈ | Mexican | $8-$18 | 527 |
| ㊸ p. 518 | La Estancia Gaucha | ◈◈◈ | Steak | $15-$28 | 527 |
| ㊻ p. 518 | Frutas Y Flores | ◈◈ | International | $12-$35 | 526 |

## GUADALAJARA, JALISCO pop. 1,495,189

- Restaurants p. 526
- Hotels & Restaurants map & index p. 518

### ALOFT GUADALAJARA
(33)1598-8800  **7**

WWWW Hotel $200 **Address:** Ave de Las Americas 1528 44630 **Location:** At Colonia Country Club. **Facility:** 142 units. 24 stories, interior corridors. *Bath:* shower only. **Terms:** cancellation fee imposed. **Amenities:** safes. **Pool(s):** heated outdoor. **Activities:** exercise room. **Guest Services:** valet and coin laundry.

**AAA Benefit:** Members save up to 15%, plus Starwood Preferred Guest® benefits!

### BEST WESTERN GRAN HOTEL CENTRO HISTORICO
(333)613-9781  **35**

WW Hotel. Rates not provided. **Address:** 168 S Calzada independencia 44100 **Location:** Jct Lopez Cotilla; in Centro Historico. **Facility:** Meets AAA guest room security requirements. 176 units. 10 stories, interior corridors. *Bath:* shower only. **Pool(s):** outdoor. **Guest Services:** valet laundry.

**AAA Benefit:** Save 10% or more every day and earn 10% bonus points!

### CAMINO REAL GUADALAJARA
(33)3134-2424  **4**

WWWW Hotel $240-$272 **Address:** Ave Vallarta No. 5005 45040 **Location:** 3.8 mi (6 km) nw on Mex 15. **Facility:** 205 units. 2 stories (no elevator), exterior corridors. **Parking:** on-site and valet. **Amenities:** safes. **Dining:** 2 restaurants, also, Maria Bonita, see separate listing. **Pool(s):** outdoor, heated outdoor. **Activities:** playground, exercise room, massage. **Guest Services:** valet laundry.

### CITYEXPRESS EXPO GUADALAJARA
(33)3880-3700  **22**

WWWW Hotel $85-$100 **Address:** Ave Mariano Otero No. 1390 Frac. Rinconada del Sol 45055 **Location:** 2.1 mi (3.5 km) w; near Expo Convention Center. **Facility:** 145 units. 8 stories, interior corridors. *Bath:* shower only. **Activities:** exercise room. **Guest Services:** valet laundry, area transportation.

### CLARUM 101
33/1201-7507  **10**

WWWW WWW Boutique Hotel $80-$120 **Address:** Parque Juán Diego No. 101 45050 **Location:** At Col. Chapalita. **Facility:** Located in an upscale residential neighborhood, this small boutique hotel has a unique, contemporary design. The owners have created a chic ambiance throughout the property. 9 units. 3 stories (no elevator), interior corridors. *Bath:* shower only. **Parking:** on-site and street. **Amenities:** safes. **Guest Services:** valet laundry.

### CROWNE PLAZA GUADALAJARA
(33)3634-1034  **21**

WWWW Hotel $84-$119 **Address:** Ave Lopez Mateos Sur No. 2500 45050 **Location:** 4.5 mi (7.2 km) s on Mex 15 and 80; off Glorieta Mariana Otero. **Facility:** 202 units. 2-9 stories, interior/exterior corridors. **Parking:** on-site (fee) and valet. **Amenities:** safes. **Dining:** La Fuente, see separate listing. **Pool(s):** heated outdoor. **Activities:** sauna, playground, exercise room, massage. **Guest Services:** valet laundry.

### FIESTA INN GUADALAJARA EXPO
(33)3669-3200  **16**

WWWW Hotel $105-$226 **Address:** Ave Mariano Otero 1550 45055 **Location:** 2.1 mi (3.5 km) w; near Expo Convention Center. **Facility:** 158 units. 8 stories, interior corridors. **Amenities:** safes. **Pool(s):** heated outdoor. **Activities:** exercise room. **Guest Services:** valet laundry.

### GRAND FIESTA AMERICANA GUADALAJARA COUNTRY CLUB
(33)3648-3500  **2**

WWWW WWWW Hotel $150-$190 **Address:** Ave Americas No. 1551 44630 **Location:** Directly across from the Country Club at Ave Lopez Mateos. **Facility:** This chic hotel features upscale Mexican décor in both its public areas and guest rooms. Take time to view the fine art pieces throughout, which are enhanced by exotic floral arrangements. 207 units. 19 stories, interior corridors. *Bath:* shower only. **Parking:** valet only. **Amenities:** safes. **Dining:** Cuatro Estaciones, see separate listing. **Activities:** exercise room, spa. **Guest Services:** valet laundry.

### GUADALAJARA PLAZA EJECUTIVO LOPEZ MATEOS
(33)3208-4400  **14**

WWWW Hotel $66-$104 **Address:** Ave Lopez Mateos 2128 44150 **Location:** 4.2 mi (7 km) s on Mex 15 and 80. **Facility:** 142 units. 2-7 stories, interior/exterior corridors. **Parking:** valet only. **Pool(s):** heated outdoor. **Activities:** exercise room. **Guest Services:** valet laundry.

### HAMPTON INN BY HILTON GUADALAJARA AEROPUERTO
(33)3164-1800  **32**

WWWW Hotel $92-$144 **Address:** 7012 Solidaridad Ave 45690 **Location:** 3.7 mi (6 km) s of Don Miguel Y. Hidalgo International Airport. **Facility:** 156 units. 7 stories, interior corridors. **Terms:** 1-7 night minimum stay, cancellation fee imposed. **Pool(s):** outdoor. **Activities:** exercise room. **Guest Services:** valet laundry.

**AAA Benefit:** Members save up to 10%!

### HAMPTON INN BY HILTON GUADALAJARA EXPO
(33)1598-9000  **40**

WWWW Hotel $69-$132

**AAA Benefit:** Members save up to 10%!

*Hampton* by HILTON

**Address:** Ave de Las Rosas 3030 44500 **Location:** Jct Ave Lope. **Facility:** 143 units. 6 stories, interior corridors. *Bath:* shower only. **Terms:** 1-7 night minimum stay, cancellation fee imposed. **Amenities:** safes. **Activities:** exercise room. **Guest Services:** valet laundry, area transportation.

(See map & index p. 518.)

## HILTON GUADALAJARA
(33)3678-0505 **18**

Hotel
$89-$259

**AAA Benefit:** Members save 5% or more!

Hilton
HOTELS & RESORTS

**Address:** Ave de Las Rosas No. 2933 44540 **Location:** At Expo Convention Center and World Trade Center. **Facility:** A spacious lobby, meeting and dining facilities, plus a shopping area and smooth, polished service contribute to the upscale ambiance of this big-city hotel. 450 units. 20 stories, interior corridors. **Parking:** on-site (fee) and valet. **Terms:** 1-7 night minimum stay, cancellation fee imposed. **Amenities:** safes. **Dining:** Angus Butcher House Restaurant and Bar, Los Vitrales, see separate listings. **Pool(s):** heated outdoor. **Activities:** steamroom, exercise room, spa. **Guest Services:** valet laundry.

## HOLIDAY INN & SUITES GUADALAJARA-CENTRO HISTORICO
(33)3560-1200 **27**

Hotel $95-$115 **Address:** Ave Juárez 211-103 44100 **Location:** Centro. **Facility:** 90 units, some efficiencies. 5 stories, interior corridors. **Bath:** shower only. **Amenities:** safes. **Dining:** Dolce Mexico, see separate listing. **Activities:** limited exercise equipment. **Guest Services:** valet and coin laundry.

## HOLIDAY INN EXPRESS GUADALAJARA AEROPUERTO
(33)3001-5900 **37**

Hotel $80-$175 **Address:** 7012 Carr Chapala 45690 **Location:** 3.7 mi (6 km) s of Don Miguel Y Hidalgo International Airport. **Facility:** Meets AAA guest room security requirements. 108 units. 7 stories, interior corridors. **Pool(s):** outdoor. **Activities:** exercise room. **Guest Services:** valet laundry, area transportation.

## HOLIDAY INN EXPRESS GUADALAJARA EXPO
(33)5000-8080 **24**

Hotel $90-$120 **Address:** Ave Mariano Otero No. 2397 **Location:** Just w of Expo Convention Center and World Trade Center. **Facility:** 152 units. 4 stories, interior corridors. **Bath:** shower only. **Amenities:** safes. **Pool(s):** heated outdoor. **Activities:** exercise room. **Guest Services:** valet laundry.

## HOLIDAY INN EXPRESS GUADALAJARA ITESO
33/3884-1234 **33**

Hotel
$86-$125

**Address:** Ave Camino Al Iteso No. 8650 A-10 45601 **Location:** Jct Periferico. **Facility:** 95 units. 4 stories, interior corridors. **Bath:** shower only. **Amenities:** safes. **Activities:** exercise room. **Guest Services:** valet laundry, area transportation.

## HOLIDAY INN EXPRESS GUADALAJARA UAG
(33)3648-0060 **6**

Hotel $95-$128 **Address:** Ave Patria No. 999 45110 **Location:** At University of Guadalajara Campus UAG. **Facility:** 200 units. 4 stories, interior corridors. **Bath:** shower only. **Amenities:** safes. **Pool(s):** heated outdoor. **Activities:** hot tub, exercise room. **Guest Services:** valet laundry.

## HOLIDAY INN SELECT
(33)3122-2020 **12**

Hotel $95-$117 **Address:** Ave Niños Heroes No. 3089 44500 **Location:** 0.3 mi (0.5 km) s of Minerva Fountain. **Facility:** 220 units. 14 stories, interior corridors. **Parking:** on-site (fee). **Amenities:** safes. **Pool(s):** heated outdoor. **Activities:** steamroom, exercise room. **Guest Services:** valet laundry.

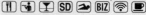

## HOTEL COUNTRY PLAZA
(33)3208-4633 **1**

Hotel $90-$110 **Address:** Prolonguacion Ave Americas 1170 45160 **Location:** 5 mi (8 km) w. **Facility:** 119 units. 4 stories, interior corridors. **Amenities:** Some: safes. **Pool(s):** heated outdoor, heated indoor. **Activities:** hot tub, exercise room. **Guest Services:** valet laundry.

## HOTEL DE MENDOZA
(33)3942-5151 **23**

Hotel $120-$135 **Address:** Venustiano Carranza 16 44100 **Location:** In historico district; opposite Degollado Theatre. **Facility:** 104 units. 6 stories, interior corridors. **Parking:** on-site (fee) and valet. **Amenities:** safes. **Dining:** La Forja, see separate listing. **Pool(s):** outdoor. **Activities:** hot tub, exercise room. **Guest Services:** valet laundry.

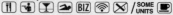

## HOTEL FIESTA AMERICANA GUADALAJARA
(33)3818-1400 **8**

Hotel $118-$343 **Address:** Aurelio Aceves No. 225 44110 **Location:** On Minerva Cir; jct aves Vallarta and Lopez Mateos. Located in a busy commercial area. **Facility:** 391 units. 22 stories, interior corridors. **Parking:** on-site (fee) and valet. **Amenities:** safes. **Dining:** La Franda, see separate listing. **Activities:** exercise room. **Guest Services:** valet laundry.

## HOTEL FRANCES
33/3613-1190 **25**

Historic Hotel $54-$97 **Address:** Maestranza No. 35 44100 **Location:** In historico district; centro. **Facility:** This charming hotel has tremendous character with its wood floors and high chandeliers in the lobby. 65 units, some two bedrooms. 4 stories, interior corridors. **Parking:** valet only.

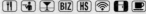

## HOTEL GUADALAJARA PLAZA EXPO BUSINESS CLASS
(33)3669-0215 **17**

Hotel $80-$100 **Address:** Mariano Otero No. 3261 44550 **Location:** At Expo Convention Center and World Trade Center. **Facility:** 204 units. 4 stories, interior corridors. **Amenities:** Some: safes. **Dining:** La Flor de Calabaza, see separate listing. **Pool(s):** outdoor. **Activities:** exercise room. **Guest Services:** valet laundry.

## HOTEL MORALES HISTORICAL & COLONIAL DOWNTOWN CORE
(33)3658-5232 **28**

Boutique Hotel
$85-$100

**Address:** Ave Ramon Corona No. 243 44100 **Location:** Jct Priscilano Sanchez; in Centro Historico. **Facility:** A truly authentic Mexican hotel located in the heart of the historic district, this is a very special place to stay. In days gone by, this site was frequented by bullfighters. 98 units. 4 stories, interior corridors. **Parking:** valet only. **Amenities:** safes. **Dining:** El Ruedo, see separate listing. **Pool(s):** heated outdoor. **Activities:** exercise room. **Guest Services:** valet laundry.

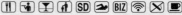

## HOTEL PLAZA DIANA
(33)3540-9700 **11**

Hotel $79-$99 **Address:** Ave Agustin Yanez No. 2760 44500 **Location:** 3 mi (5 km) n. **Facility:** 151 units. 5 stories, interior corridors. **Parking:** valet only. **Amenities:** safes. **Pool(s):** heated indoor. **Activities:** exercise room. **Guest Services:** valet laundry, area transportation.

(See map & index p. 518.)

## HOTEL PRESIDENTE INTERCONTINENTAL GUADALAJARA (33)3678-1234 **19**

Hotel
$147-$171

**Address:** Ave Lopez Mateos Sur y Moctezuma 45050 **Location:** 4.2 mi (7 km) s on Mex 15 and 80; across from Plaza del Sol. **Facility:** This large, upscale, city hotel features impressive marble-trimmed public areas, secured parking and proximity to a high-end shopping mall. 423 units. 13 stories, interior corridors. **Parking:** on-site (fee) and valet. **Amenities:** safes. **Dining:** Frutas Y Flores, see separate listing, entertainment. **Pool(s):** heated outdoor. **Activities:** sauna, hot tub, steamroom, exercise room. **Guest Services:** valet laundry.

## HOTEL REAL INN GUADALAJARA CENTRO (33)3613-7500 **29**

Hotel $50-$100 **Address:** Ave Juárez 123 44100 **Location:** In Centro Historico. **Facility:** 197 units. 7 stories, interior corridors. **Parking:** on-site (fee). **Amenities:** safes. **Dining:** Stock Cafe, see separate listing. **Activities:** steamroom, exercise room. **Guest Services:** valet laundry. Affiliated with Camino Real Hotels.

## HOTEL RIU PLAZA GUADALAJARA (33)3880-7500 **34**

Hotel
Rates not provided

**Address:** Ave Lopez Mateos No. 830 44500 **Location:** At Col. Chapalita. **Facility:** Seen for miles around, this contemporary high-rise offers a chic design throughout. Guests enjoy the vibrant colors and mood lighting in the lounge, hallways and spacious guest rooms. 558 units. 42 stories, interior corridors. **Parking:** on-site (fee) and valet. **Amenities:** safes. **Dining:** 2 restaurants, also, Chardonnay, see separate listing. **Pool(s):** heated outdoor. **Activities:** spa. **Guest Services:** valet laundry. (See ad p. 380.)

## IBIS HOTEL (33)3880-9600 **30**

Hotel $53-$83 **Address:** Ave Mariano Otero 1400 44520 **Location:** 2.1 mi (3.5 km) w; near Expo Convention Center. **Facility:** 159 units. 4 stories, interior corridors. *Bath:* shower only.

## NH COLLECTION GUADALAJARA (33)3648-9500 **3**

Contemporary
Hotel
$130-$220

**Address:** Calle Sao Paulo No. 2334, Col. Providencia 44630 **Location:** Jct Ave Americas. **Facility:** In a commercial/residential area, this upscale hotel features unique, contemporary décor. Rooms have floor-to-ceiling mirrors and huge bathrooms with "rain" showers. 137 units. 14 stories, interior corridors. **Parking:** valet only. **Amenities:** safes. **Activities:** exercise room. **Guest Services:** valet laundry.

## ONE HOTELES (33)3942-4350 **38**

Hotel $60-$100 **Address:** Ave 16 de Septiembre No. 16 44100 **Location:** In Centro Historico; directly across from the cathedral. **Facility:** 146 units. 8 stories, interior corridors. *Bath:* shower only. **Parking:** no self-parking. **Guest Services:** complimentary and valet laundry.

## QUINTA GANZ 33/3120-1416 **9**

Vacation Rental Condominium $150 **Address:** 3048 Ave Garibaldi 44680 **Location:** Between Juán Palomar y Arias and Beethoven. **Facility:** In a residential neighborhood, these spacious, bi-level vacation rentals are fully loaded. There's a tranquil garden courtyard/pool area as well. 10 condominiums. 2 stories (no elevator), exterior corridors. *Bath:* shower only. **Terms:** off-site registration, age restrictions may apply. **Pool(s):** outdoor.

## QUINTA REAL GUADALAJARA 33/3669-0600 **5**

Hotel
$350-$388

**Address:** Ave Mexico No. 2727, Col Vallarta Norte 44680 **Location:** 2 blks n of Minerva Fountain; near Ave Lopez Mateos. **Facility:** Fine art, well-appointed rooms and manicured grounds add an elegant sophistication to this property. 76 units, some three bedrooms. 3-5 stories, interior corridors. **Parking:** valet only. **Amenities:** safes. **Pool(s):** outdoor. **Activities:** hot tub, exercise room, massage. **Guest Services:** valet laundry. Affiliated with Preferred Hotels & Resorts.

## REAL INN (33)3880-7700 **20**

Hotel $80-$155 **Address:** Ave Mariano Otero 1326 44510 **Location:** Opposite Expo Convention Center and World Trade Center. **Facility:** 163 units. 9 stories, interior corridors. **Parking:** on-site (fee) and valet. **Amenities:** safes. **Dining:** Stock Cafe, see separate listing. **Activities:** exercise room, massage. **Guest Services:** valet laundry. Affiliated with Camino Real Hotels.

/ SOME UNITS

## STAYBRIDGE SUITES (33)3880-3610 **26**

Extended Stay
Hotel
$90-$100

**Address:** Ave Mariano Otero 2682 45050 **Location:** Jct Ave Lopez Mateos. **Facility:** 117 units, some two bedrooms and efficiencies. 10 stories, interior corridors. **Parking:** valet only. **Amenities:** safes. **Pool(s):** heated outdoor. **Activities:** exercise room. **Guest Services:** valet and coin laundry.

/ SOME UNITS

## TROCADERO SUITES 33/3120-1416 **15**

Extended Stay Hotel $70-$100 **Address:** Lopez Cotilla No. 1188, Col Americana 44160 **Location:** Between Atenas and Robles Gil. **Facility:** 6 efficiencies. 1 story, exterior corridors. *Bath:* shower only. **Amenities:** safes. **Guest Services:** valet laundry.

/ SOME UNITS

---

# AAA Vacations® packages ...
## exciting itineraries and exclusive values

(See map & index p. 518.)

## VILLA GANZ BOUTIQUE HOTEL  (33)3120-1416   13

Boutique Hotel
$180-$250

**Address:** Lopez Cotilla No. 1739, Col Americana 44160 **Location:** Between Union and Chapultepec. **Facility:** A beautifully restored home which offers guests a chance to stay in an authentic Mexican hacienda in a central location. 10 units. 2 stories (no elevator), interior corridors. **Terms:** age restrictions may apply. **Amenities:** safes. **Guest Services:** valet laundry.

[icons]

## THE WESTIN GUADALAJARA  (33)3880-2700  36

Boutique
Contemporary
Hotel
$99-$299

**WESTIN** HOTELS & RESORTS **AAA Benefit:** Members save up to 15%, plus Starwood Preferred Guest® benefits!

**Address:** Ave de Las Rosas No. 2911 44530 **Location:** Adjacent to Expo Convention Center and World Trade Center. **Facility:** This shimmering glass high-rise hotel features a contemporary look throughout with fine modern art and a wonderful lobby level lounge with a small garden patio. Rooms are spacious and chic. 221 units. 27 stories, interior corridors. **Parking:** valet only. **Amenities:** safes. **Dining:** Grill and Vine, see separate listing. **Activities:** massage. **Guest Services:** valet laundry.

[icons]

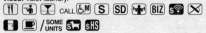

## WHERE TO EAT

### ANGUS BUTCHER HOUSE RESTAURANT AND BAR
33/3671-4627  19

Steak. Casual Dining. $13-$30 **AAA Inspector Notes:** A true Western atmosphere with a Mexican flair sets the tone at this popular steakhouse. Although beef is the main draw, the menu also lists some Mexican dishes and a good selection of hot and cold appetizers. The staff attire lends to a Vegas nightclub feel, which is an interesting mix of themes. **Features:** full bar. **Reservations:** suggested. **Address:** Ave de Las Rosas No. 2933 **Location:** At Expo Convention Center and World Trade Center; in Hilton Guadalajara. **Parking:** on-site (fee). [L] [D]

### CHARDONNAY
33/3880-7500  23

International. Fine Dining. $15-$30 **AAA Inspector Notes:** A contemporary design and cozy intimate setting are the perfect backdrop for the fine menu selection you will find here. The chef entices diners with complimentary starters, fresh breads and a wide selection of fresh local, regional and International fare. An excellent wine list completes the experience. Many like to enjoy a pre- or post-meal beverage in the adjacent lobby lounge that features a chic upbeat ambiance. **Features:** full bar. **Reservations:** suggested. **Address:** Ave Lopez Mateos No. 830 44500 **Location:** At Col. Chapalita; in Hotel RIU Plaza Guadalajara. **Parking:** on-site (fee) and valet. [D] CALL [GM]

### CUATRO ESTACIONES
33/3648-3500  1

International. Casual Dining. $13-$30 **AAA Inspector Notes:** Upbeat contemporary dining marks the large dining room, where patrons peruse a fine international menu. Locals frequent the featured buffet breakfast, which winds up around noon, but also take advantage of the varied a la carte options at lunch and dinner. **Features:** full bar. **Reservations:** suggested. **Address:** Ave Americas No. 1551 44630 **Location:** Directly across from the Country Club at Ave Lopez Mateos; in Fiesta Americana Grand Guadalajara Country Club. **Parking:** on-site (fee). [B] [L] [D]

### DOLCE MEXICO
33/3560-1200  25

International. Casual Dining. $7-$16 **AAA Inspector Notes:** On the second floor of the Holiday Inn and Suites in the city's historic zone, the dining room is a popular choice for its hearty buffet breakfast and à la carte lunch and dinner selections. The terrace overlooks the elegant hotel lobby and bustling city streets. Light, casual fare along the lines of burgers, sandwiches and salads is a solid bet, as are spicy Mexican dishes and grilled meats and seafood. **Features:** full bar, patio dining. **Address:** Ave Juárez 211-103 44100 **Location:** Centro; in Holiday Inn & Suites Guadalajara-Centro Historico. [B] [L] [D] [icon]

### EL MEXICANA RESTAURANT TURISTICO  33/3658-0345  32

Mexican. Casual Dining. $8-$16 **AAA Inspector Notes:** Live folkloric entertainment throughout the day means this restaurant feels like a full-time Mexican fiesta. Local and regional home-style Mexican fare is served in a large dining room featuring floor-to-ceiling wall murals. On Saturdays and Sundays, the restaurant presents full folkloric ballet shows. **Features:** full bar. **Address:** Morelos No. 79 Plaza Tapatia 44100 **Location:** In Centro Historico. **Parking:** street only. [L] [D]

### EL RUEDO
33/3658-5232  28

International. Casual Dining. $8-$15 **AAA Inspector Notes:** Just off the lobby of the Hotel Morales, the delightful dining room has fine stone archways and a Mexican water fountain. Grilled meats and chicken share menu space with lighter fare, including burgers and sandwiches, and some tasty Mexican selections. **Features:** full bar. **Address:** Ave Ramon Corona No. 243 44100 **Location:** Jct Prisciliano Sanchez; in Centro Historico; in Hotel Morales Historical & Colonial Downtown Core. **Parking:** valet only. [B] [L] [D]

### EL SACROMONTE
33/3825-5447  12

Regional Mexican. Casual Dining. $11-$22 **AAA Inspector Notes:** Billowy fabric drapes the ceiling, while the soft glow of candlelight emanating from punctured-tin light fixtures reflects off small mirrors along yellow and ochre stucco courtyard walls. Locals and a few knowledgeable international visitors love both the casual ambience and the honest native cuisine in this neighborhood restaurant. **Features:** full bar. **Reservations:** suggested. **Address:** Pedro Moreno No. 1398 Col Americana 44140 **Location:** Just e of Ave Chapultepec. **Parking:** valet only. [L] [D] [icon] [icon]

### EL TANGO
33/3647-9981  3

Argentine Steak. Casual Dining. $12-$22 **AAA Inspector Notes:** This bustling eatery serves huge portions of freshly grilled meats. Tableside, the servers present a platter of beef cuts and helps diners make their selection. Each meal comes with a green salad, fresh vegetables, potatoes and pasta. A pianist tickles the ivories, spicing up the ambience in the lively, Argentina-themed dining area. **Features:** full bar. **Reservations:** suggested. **Address:** Ave Guadalupe, No. 1004 45050 **Location:** Across from Glorieta Chapalita. **Parking:** no self-parking. [B] [L] [D]

### FRUTAS Y FLORES
33/3678-1234  46

International. Casual Dining. $12-$35 **AAA Inspector Notes:** Here you'll enjoy a fine selection of varied fare in a refined, relaxing atmosphere. On the menu, which aims to please all palates, you'll find light sandwiches and entrée salads as well as grilled meats, fish and seafood. Sauces utilize local and regional herbs and spices. The extensive breakfast buffet is a local favorite, and is a great way to start a leisurely day. **Features:** full bar. **Address:** Ave Moctezuma 3515 45050 **Location:** 4.2 mi (7 km) s on Mex 15 and 80; across from Plaza del Sol; in Hotel Presidente InterContinental Guadalajara. **Parking:** on-site (fee). [B] [L] [D]

### GRILL AND VINE
33/3880-2700  36

International. Casual Dining. $10-$22 **AAA Inspector Notes:** A chic, contemporary dining room and a varied menu to suit all taste buds await diners here. The convenient location directly across from the Expo Convention Center makes it a good choice for the business traveler. **Features:** full bar, patio dining. **Address:** Ave de Las Rosas No. 2911 44530 **Location:** Adjacent to Expo Convention Center and World Trade Center; in The Westin Guadalajara. **Parking:** on-site (fee) and valet. [B] [L] [D]

**(See map & index p. 518.)**

### LA ANTIGUA RESTAURANT BAR          33/3563-6570  (40)

▼▼ Mexican. Casual Dining. $8-$18 **AAA Inspector Notes:** This is a delightful find that you may miss if you don't look up to the second level of this old building in the center of the historic district, directly in front of the cathedral. From the large, colorful upper-level dining room, the open windows offer excellent views of all the activity below. Breakfast features a very popular buffet, as do some luncheons. The à la carte menu lists traditional Mexican dishes. There's live mariachi entertainment most days. **Features:** full bar. **Address:** Morelos 371 44100 **Location:** In Centro Historico; directly across from cathedral. **Parking:** no self-parking.

[B] [L] [D]

### LA CHATA DE GUADALAJARA          33/3613-0588  (24)

▼▼ Mexican. Casual Dining. $8-$15 **AAA Inspector Notes:** While it may be difficult to find bilingual staff members, the menu of traditional favorites--from fresh guacamole and zesty chiles rellenos to spicy meat dishes--enables guests and servers alike to speak a common language. Hand-painted tile accents decorate the cheerful, bright yellow dining room, a block from Place d'Arms and a nice respite from the crowds in the historic town center. **Features:** full bar. **Address:** Ave Ramon Corona No. 126 44100 **Location:** Jct aves Juárez and Ramon Corona; centro. **Parking:** street only.

[B] [L] [D] CALL Ⓛ [M]

### LA DOLCE VITA          33/3615-3424  (18)

▼▼ Italian. Casual Dining. $8-$18 **AAA Inspector Notes:** This bustling, locally popular eatery dishes up well-prepared Italian fare, ranging from fresh pastas and gourmet pizzas to grilled meat, chicken and seafood dishes. The casual dining room features bright décor, flat-screen TVs and soccer memorabilia, while the large street front patio allows patrons to dine al fresco. **Features:** full bar, patio dining. **Address:** Ave Lopez Cotilla No. 1976 44130 **Location:** At Col. Arcos Vallarta. **Parking:** street only. [L] [D] [◥]

### LA ESTANCIA GAUCHA          33/3817-1808  (44)

▼▼▼ Steak. Casual Dining. $15-$28 **AAA Inspector Notes:** Quite simply, here you'll sink your teeth into perfectly grilled fine cuts of meat in huge portions. The food is fresh and simple. Locals love this place, so phone ahead to make a reservation, especially if you prefer outdoor patio dining. **Features:** full bar, patio dining. **Address:** Ave Americas No. 1545 44630 **Location:** Jct Calle Soa Paulo. **Parking:** on-site (fee). [L] [D]

### LA FLOR DE CALABAZA          33/3669-0215  (31)

▼▼ International. Casual Dining. $10-$18 **AAA Inspector Notes:** Lingering over breakfast with good friends is a tradition in the heart of Mexico, and the huge morning buffet spread at this restaurant is a real treat. Live piano music and big boisterous dining groups make for a bustling atmosphere early in the day. Later, the ambience takes a quieter, more relaxed turn featuring a business luncheon buffet as well as an a la carte menu. **Features:** full bar. **Address:** Mariano Otero No. 3261 44550 **Location:** At Expo Convention Center and World Trade Center; in Hotel Guadalajara Plaza Expo Business Class. [B] [L] [D]

### LA FONDA DE SAN MIGUEL ARCANGEL   33/3613- 0809  (30)

▼▼ Mexican. Casual Dining. $12-$23 **AAA Inspector Notes:** In a converted convent in the heart of the historic district, the courtyard-like setting features high ceilings and star-shaped hanging lanterns. Lending to the Mexican atmosphere are colorful tables and hand-carved chairs graced with designs of tropical birds. Live birds in cages surround the restaurant. Pleasant evening entertainment comes courtesy of a live pianist. The menu offers a good mix of home-style Mexican fare. **Features:** full bar. **Reservations:** suggested. **Address:** Donato Guerra No. 25 44100 **Location:** Centro; in historico district. **Parking:** street only. [B] [L] [D]

### LA FORJA          33/3942-5151  (26)

▼▼ International. Casual Dining. $8-$20 **AAA Inspector Notes:** Guests enjoy the Old World atmosphere of the elegant restaurant, which is just off the lobby of the Hotel De Mendoza. The menu is a good mix of Continental fare, including preparations of beef, seafood and spicy Mexican dishes. **Features:** full bar. **Reservations:** suggested. **Address:** Venustiano Carranza 16 44100 **Location:** In historico district; opposite Degollado Theatre; in Hotel de Mendoza. **Parking:** on-site (fee). [L] [D] [◥]

### LA FRANDA          33/3818-1400  (7)

▼▼▼ International. Casual Dining. $8-$25 **AAA Inspector Notes:** This casual restaurant is well known for its extensive daily breakfast buffet, which rivals an upscale brunch. At lunch and dinner, the a la carte menu boasts excellent steaks and other grilled items. The décor is simple and comfortable. **Features:** full bar. **Address:** Aurelio Aceves No. 225 44110 **Location:** On Minerva Cir; jct aves Vallarta and Lopez Mateos; in Hotel Fiesta Americana Guadalajara. **Parking:** on-site (fee). [B] [L] [D]

### LA FUENTE          33/3634-1034  (38)

▼▼▼ International. Casual Dining. $10-$18 **AAA Inspector Notes:** If you want to experience a real Guadalajara tradition, this is the place. Locals flock here for the popular breakfast buffet that extends until noon daily. It is a great place for lingering over the morning with good food and lots of coffee. The rest of the day features a mixed à la carte menu with some Mexican specialties. A lovely patio area faces the tropical courtyard. **Features:** full bar, Sunday brunch. **Address:** Ave Lopez Mateos Sur No. 45050 **Location:** 4.5 mi (7.2 km) s on Mex 15 and 80; off Glorieta Mariana Otero; in Crowne Plaza Guadalajara. [B] [L] [D] CALL Ⓛ [M]

### LA MATERA          33/3616-1626  (6)

▼▼▼ Argentine Steak. Casual Dining. $9-$21 **AAA Inspector Notes:** A fun and bustling atmosphere and a diverse menu make this a place where locals love to dine. In addition to a good mix of wood-fire-baked pizzas and tasty pasta dishes, patrons can order meats and seafood cooked over an open grill. Hearty portions leave diners stuffed and satisfied. **Features:** full bar, patio dining. **Reservations:** suggested. **Address:** Ave Mexico No. 2891 44140 **Location:** Just n of Mineva Fountain, near Ave Lopez Mateos. **Parking:** street only.

[L] [D] [✗] [◥]

### LA PASTA          33/3121-1374  (5)

▼▼▼ Italian. Casual Dining. $9-$20 **AAA Inspector Notes:** Although spacious, this contemporary restaurant's dining room has a patio-like feel, complete with tropical trees and plants. A tasty selection from the antipasto salad bar is nice starter. Moving on to the main menu, diners will find a fine selection of classic Italian fare as well as grilled meats, chicken and seafood. Complementing the cuisine is a strong wine list. **Features:** full bar. **Reservations:** suggested. **Address:** Ave Guadalupe No. 1357 45040 **Location:** Close to Glorieta Chapalita. **Parking:** valet only. [L] [D] [◥]

### LA TEQUILA          33/3640-3440  (15)

▼▼ Regional Mexican. Casual Dining. $10-$18 **AAA Inspector Notes:** Lending to the relaxed atmosphere and interesting décor are large murals of Mexican villages and huge photographs of the Mexican countryside. To start, fresh salsa is prepared tableside to the diner's preferred spice level. Up next is a tasty Mexican bean salad. The menu lists a wide range of local and regional Mexican fare; all meals come with fresh, hot tortillas. Those with a fondness for spirits should not pass up a frozen margarita or a shot of one of the many featured tequilas. **Features:** full bar. **Reservations:** suggested. **Address:** Ave Mexico 2830 44140 **Location:** Just n of Minerva Fountain. **Parking:** street only. [L] [D]

### LA TRATTORIA DE GUADALAJARA          33/3122-1817  (17)

▼▼ Italian. Casual Dining. $8-$20 **AAA Inspector Notes:** Located on busy Avenida de Los Niños Héroes, and popular with locals and tourists alike, this bright, comfortable restaurant offers authentic Italian entrées and an accomplished selection of appetizers and wines. A salad bar is included with most menu items and there is always an anti pasta bar. **Features:** full bar. **Reservations:** suggested. **Address:** Ave de Los Niños Heroes 3051 44500 **Location:** Just e of jct Ave Lopez Mateos. **Parking:** valet only. [L] [D]

### LOS ARCOS          33/3122-3719  (33)

▼▼ Seafood. Casual Dining. $10-$22 **AAA Inspector Notes:** From the moment you arrive you're transported from the bustling city to a bright, seaside atmosphere complete with seashells, tropical colors and even a palapa umbrella. The focus here is shrimp of all sizes and preparation styles. Shrimp cocktails, soups, grilled shrimp, coconut shrimp, garlic shrimp--whatever you crave, they can prepare. The servings are huge, but you will want to keep on eating as they do a great job with their specialty. **Features:** full bar. **Address:** Calz. Lazaro Caradenas 3359 45040 **Location:** At Fracc Jardines de San Ignacio. [L] [D] CALL Ⓛ [M]

(See map & index p. 518.)

## LOS VITRALES
33/3678-0505  (34)

International
Casual Dining
$10-$18

**AAA Inspector Notes:** This spot is very popular for the extensive buffet breakfast that goes until noon and tempts diners to linger over the morning. Lunch and dinner feature a mixed menu of casual International fare, including some American favorites such as burgers and steaks as well as home-style Mexican fare, pastas and home-made soup. The contemporary décor is bright and inviting. **Features:** full bar. **Address:** Ave de Las Rosas No. 2933 44540 **Location:** At Expo Convention Center and World Trade Center; in Hilton Guadalajara. **Parking:** on-site (fee) and valet.

(B) (L) (D)

## MANOLO CAMPESTRE
33/3122-2244  (22)

Mexican. Casual Dining. $9-$20 **AAA Inspector Notes:** This roomy, bustling restaurant is a winning choice for tasty Mexican fare. The traditional Mexican décor features leather chairs as well as plenty of plants and greenery. The varied menu lists everything from tortilla soup to fine cuts of fresh, local beef. Special platters are offered on weekends. **Features:** full bar. **Address:** Ave Mariano Otero 1510 45055 **Location:** Near Expo Convention Center. **Parking:** on-site (fee). (L) (D)

## MARIA BONITA
33/3134-2434  (2)

Regional Mexican. Casual Dining. $13-$24 **AAA Inspector Notes:** This bustling, upscale restaurant dishes up hearty portions of tasty, regional Mexican cuisine. The contemporary décor features a huge mosaic tile wall adorned with pictures of the famous Maria Bonita. Sports junkies can catch the big game on large flat-screen TVs. **Features:** full bar. **Reservations:** suggested. **Address:** Ave Vallarta No. 5005 45040 **Location:** 3.8 mi (6 km) nw on Mex 15; in Camino Real Guadalajara. **Parking:** on-site (fee).

(B) (L) (D)

## OLIO BISTRO
33/3817-1180  (35)

Mediterranean. Casual Dining. $10-$22 **AAA Inspector Notes:** Here you will find an excellent wine list to complement the innovative menu of tapas, pastas and fine meats. The open-air concept allows you to enjoy a garden-like atmosphere in the middle of the busy commercial area. Before ordering their main course, the locals seem to enjoy sharing a mixture of appetizers as they sip fine wine and tequila. I enjoyed the vibrant atmosphere. **Features:** full bar. **Reservations:** suggested. **Address:** Ave Americas 1501 44630 **Location:** Jct Calle Soa Paulo. **Parking:** on-site (fee).

(L) (D) (M) (N)

## POMODORO
33/3793-1111  (9)

Italian. Casual Dining. $7-$16 **AAA Inspector Notes:** The bustling eatery serves good home-style Italian fare, in hearty portions and flavored with rich sauces. Diners can mix-n-match pastas and sauces to suit their mood. This place is very popular and reservations are advised. **Features:** full bar. **Address:** Lopez Mateos Nte. 145 44110 **Location:** Jct Ave Vallarta. **Parking:** on-site (fee). (L) (D)

## RECCO RESTAURANT
33/3825-0724  (13)

Italian. Casual Dining. $9-$25 **AAA Inspector Notes:** Hearty servings of lasagna and tasty osso buco make this centrally-located Italian restaurant a nice change of pace. The Caesar salad is 'magnifico,' as are the desserts. The shady outdoor patio provides a good lunch spot, as well as a pleasant setting for an evening meal. **Features:** full bar, patio dining. **Reservations:** suggested. **Address:** Libertad 1981 44100 **Location:** Just e of Ave Chapultepec. **Parking:** on-site and street. (L) (D) (N)

## SANTO COYOTE
33/3616-6978  (10)

Mexican. Casual Dining. $15-$28 **AAA Inspector Notes:** In the former U.S. Consul General's residence, the Nuevo Mexican eatery features several open-air rooms with hand-painted murals, romantic pixie and candle lighting and views of a courtyard garden. Cabrito (goat) and excellent baby back ribs, topped with tamarind and pepper sauce, are roasted over a wood fire in the open kitchen and grill. **Features:** full bar, patio dining. **Reservations:** suggested. **Address:** Lerdo de Tejada No. 2379 44150 **Location:** Just e of Ave Chapultepec. **Parking:** valet only.

(B) (L) (D) CALL (M) (N)

## STOCK CAFE
33/3880-7705  (21)

International. Casual Dining. $8-$22 **AAA Inspector Notes:** Bright, contemporary décor and a casual, varied menu offer guests a chance to relax after a hard day's work. Sink your teeth into hearty, homemade burgers or tasty pasta dishes. Or wine and dine with a cut of fine steak. The made-to-order, fire-oven pizzas are a popular item and the chef will split the ingredients on one order if requested. **Features:** full bar. **Address:** Ave Mariano Otero 1326 **Location:** Opposite Expo Convention Center and World Trade Center; in Real Inn. **Parking:** on-site (fee). (B) (L) (D)

## STOCK CAFE
33/3613-7500  (27)

International. Casual Dining. $8-$22 **AAA Inspector Notes:** Bright, contemporary style and a mixed menu of casual fare make this a popular choice for those exploring the historic center. The extensive buffet breakfast is a popular option. The menu features hearty pastas, burgers and sandwiches. **Features:** full bar. **Address:** Ave Juárez 123 44100 **Location:** In Centro Historico; in Hotel Real Inn Guadalajara Centro. **Parking:** on-site (fee). (B) (L) (D)

## SUEHIRO
33/3826-0094  (14)

Japanese. Casual Dining. $15-$24 **AAA Inspector Notes:** Specializing in Japanese-style tableside preparation, the restaurant features table grills, which are used to cook wonderfully flavorful beef, shrimp and chicken dishes. You'll also find a full sushi, teriyaki and tempura menu. A tranquil Japanese garden can be viewed through the large windows and enhances the overall dining experience. **Features:** full bar. **Reservations:** suggested. **Address:** Ave La Paz 1701 44100 **Location:** 4 blks e of Ave Chapultepec. **Parking:** valet only. (L) (D)

This ends listings for Guadalajara.

The following resumes the alphabetical listings of cities in Central Mexico.

## Take Your Imagination to New Destinations

### Use AAA Travel Guides online to explore the possibilities.

❯ Tour popular places in the U.S., Canada, Mexico and the Caribbean from the comfort of your home.

❯ Read what AAA's professional inspectors say about area hotels, restaurants and attractions.

❯ Check out the best stuff to see and do, with itineraries to ensure you won't miss a thing.

### Go to AAA.com/travelguide today to discover your next destination.

© AAA

Avenida Subterránea Miguel Hidalgo is for inbound traffic only with street level exits just beyond the Hidalgo Market, at Plazuela de los Ángeles, at Jardín Unión and terminus at Plaza de Allende. It is 3 km. long.

To México City, DF or León & Pípila Statue

To ⛪ Church of La Valenciana / Cubilete Mountain, 🔟 🔢 & ①

Cantador Park

C PARDO

AV SUBTERRANEA MIGUEL HIDALGO

JUAREZ 5 DEMAYO

ESCALERA SALGADO

MENDIZABAL

State Historical Museum (Alhóndiga de Granaditas)

JUAN VALLE

POCITOS

Plazuela de los Ángeles

ALONZO

Diego Rivera Museum

3

Plaza de la Paz

4    3

TENAZA

Jardín Unión  9

EL SOL

8    5    12

MANUEL DOBLADO

Don Quixote Iconographic Museum

HIDALGO

Plaza de Allende

CALLE SANGRE DE CRISTO

CALLE BELAUNZARAN

Las Embajadoras Park

C SEBASTIAN

San Jerónimo Park

N

CALLE

PASEO DE LA PRESA

CALLE PASTITA

Antillón Park

8

CONDE DE VALENCIANA

MARQUES DE RAYAS

13 & 14

To Presa de la Olla

Las Acacias Park

## Guanajuato
### GUANAJUATO
### Hotels & Restaurants

| 0 | Kilometers | 0.3 |
|---|---|---|
| 0 | Miles | 0.2 |

1404-16

## Guanajuato

This index helps you "spot" where approved hotels and restaurants are located on the corresponding detailed maps. Hotel daily rate range is for comparison only. Restaurant price range is a combination of lunch and/or dinner. Turn to the listing page for more detailed rate and price information and consult display ads for special promotions.

### GUANAJUATO, GUANAJUATO

| Map Page | Hotels | Diamond Rated | Rate Range | Page |
|---|---|---|---|---|
| 3 p. 529 | Hotel San Diego | ▽▽ | $65-$110 | 531 |
| 4 p. 529 | El Meson de los Poetas | ▽▽ | $80-$145 | 531 |
| 8 p. 529 | **Quinta Las Acacias** | ▽▽▽▽ | $235-$450 | 531 |
| 9 p. 529 | **1850 Hotel Boutique** | ▽▽▽▽ | $250-$450 | 531 |
| 10 p. 529 | Casa Estrella de la Valenciana | ▽▽▽ | $180-$255 | 531 |
| 11 p. 529 | Camino Real Guanajuato | ▽▽▽ | $155-$340 | 531 |
| 12 p. 529 | Edelmira Boutique Hotel | ▽▽▽ | $145-$230 | 531 |
| 13 p. 529 | Hotel Hacienda Mision Guanajuato | ▽▽ | $120-$265 | 531 |
| 14 p. 529 | Holiday Inn Express Guanajuato | ▽▽ | $80-$145 | 531 |

| Map Page | Restaurants | Diamond Rated | Cuisine | Price Range | Page |
|---|---|---|---|---|---|
| 1 p. 529 | Restaurant Real de la Esperanza | ▽▽▽ | Continental | $7-$14 | 531 |
| 3 p. 529 | La Tasca de la Paz Restaurant Bar | ▽▽ | International | $5-$12 | 531 |
| 5 p. 529 | Casa Valadez | ▽▽▽ | International | $12-$28 | 531 |
| 8 p. 529 | La Capellina | ▽▽▽ | International | $9-$18 | 531 |

## GUANAJUATO, GUANAJUATO (C-2)
pop. 171,709, elev. 6,649'
• Hotels & Restaurants map & index p. 529

### 1850 HOTEL BOUTIQUE (473)732-2795 [9]

▼▼▼▼ ▼▼▼▼
**Historic Boutique Hotel**
$250-$450

**Address:** Jardin de La Union No. 7, Col Centro 36250 **Location:** In Centro Historico. **Facility:** Most would be surprised to learn this stylish, contemporary inn was once a historic palace. The upscale décor and attentive service will make you feel like a royal guest. 20 units. 4 stories, interior corridors. *Bath:* shower only. **Parking:** no self-parking. **Amenities:** safes. **Activities:** exercise room, spa. **Guest Services:** valet laundry, boarding pass kiosk, area transportation.

### CAMINO REAL GUANAJUATO (473)102-1500 [11]

▼▼▼ **Historic Hotel** $155-$340 **Address:** Alhondiga No. 100 36020 **Location:** 1.2 mi (2 km) ne on Mex 110 (Dolores Hidalgo Hwy). **Facility:** Among the city's finest hotels. Distinct architecture, dramatic views and a central location are highlights of this hotel. Meets AAA guest room security requirements. 105 units. 6 stories, interior/exterior corridors. *Bath:* shower only. **Parking:** on-site (fee) and valet. **Amenities:** safes. **Pool(s):** heated outdoor. **Activities:** exercise room. **Guest Services:** valet laundry.

### CASA ESTRELLA DE LA VALENCIANA (473)732-1784 [10]

▼▼▼ **Bed & Breakfast** $180-$255 **Address:** Callejon Jalisco No. 10 **Location:** 2.1 mi (3.5 km) nw on Mex 110 (Dolores Hidalgo Hwy), just w, follow signs. **Facility:** Tucked atop a hill across from the noted Valenciana church, this spectacular property overlooks a valley and offers elegant accommodations. 8 units. 2 stories (no elevator), interior/exterior corridors. **Terms:** check-in 4 pm. **Amenities:** safes. **Pool(s):** outdoor. **Activities:** hot tub, tennis, massage. **Guest Services:** valet laundry.

### EDELMIRA BOUTIQUE HOTEL 473/732-3743 [12]

▼▼▼ **Historic Boutique Country Inn** $145-$230 **Address:** Allende No. 7, Col Centro 36250 **Location:** Jct Allende and Jardin de La Union. **Facility:** Fall in love with this unique, contemporary small lodging in the heart of the city at the edge of Jardin de La Union. This property provides an excellent base for easily exploring the city on foot. Meets AAA guest room security requirements. 27 units. 5 stories, interior corridors. *Bath:* shower only. **Parking:** on-site and valet. **Amenities:** safes. **Pool(s):** heated indoor. **Activities:** hot tub, limited exercise equipment, massage. **Guest Services:** valet laundry.

### EL MESON DE LOS POETAS (473)732-0705 [4]

▼▼ **Hotel** $80-$145 **Address:** Positos No. 35 Esq con Juan Valle 36000 **Location:** Just w of Jardin de La Union; centro. **Facility:** 34 units, some two bedrooms, efficiencies and kitchens. 9 stories (no elevator), some safes. **Parking:** on-site (fee). **Terms:** 7 day cancellation notice, in season. **Amenities:** *Some:* safes. **Guest Services:** valet laundry.

### HOLIDAY INN EXPRESS GUANAJUATO (473)735-2000 [14]

▼▼▼ **Hotel** $80-$145 **Address:** Euquerio Guerrero No. 120 **Location:** On Mex 110 (toll road); at entrance to town; sw on Mex 110 (non-toll), 0.6 mi (1 km) w. **Facility:** Meets AAA guest room security requirements. 165 units. 5 stories, interior corridors. **Terms:** cancellation fee imposed. **Amenities:** safes. **Pool(s):** heated indoor. **Activities:** exercise room. **Guest Services:** valet and coin laundry, area transportation.

### HOTEL HACIENDA MISION GUANAJUATO (473)732-3980 [13]

▼▼▼ **Historic Hotel** $120-$265 **Address:** Camino Antiguo a Marfil KM 2.5 36050 **Location:** 1.6 mi (2.5 km) w; at entrance to town on Mex 110 (Dolores Hidalgo Hwy). **Facility:** On the 'libramiento' city bypass is where you'll find this charming, historic lodging. Once a hacienda, it has thick stone walls, clay tile floors, period furnishings and austere, older rooms. 138 units, some two bedrooms. 2-3 stories (no elevator), interior corridors. *Bath:* shower only. **Pool(s):** outdoor. **Guest Services:** valet laundry.

### HOTEL SAN DIEGO 473/732-1300 [3]

▼▼▼ **Hotel** $65-$110 **Address:** Jardin de La Union No. 1 36000 **Location:** Centro. Located in a historico commercial district. **Facility:** 43 units, some two bedrooms. 5 stories, interior corridors. *Bath:* shower only. **Parking:** no self-parking. **Guest Services:** valet laundry.

### QUINTA LAS ACACIAS (473)731-1517 [8]

▼▼▼ ▼▼▼
**Classic Country Inn**
$235-$450

**Address:** Paseo de La Presa No. 168 36000 **Location:** Centro; across from Acacia Park. **Facility:** This spectacular, historic, renovated home with many contemporary rooms is nestled in the hills in a lovely setting next to La Presa and Parque Las Acacias. Some suites include blissful steam baths. 16 units. 2-5 stories (no elevator), interior/exterior corridors. **Terms:** age restrictions may apply. **Amenities:** safes. **Activities:** hot tub, massage. **Guest Services:** valet laundry, area transportation.

## WHERE TO EAT

### CASA VALADEZ 473/732-0311 [5]

▼▼▼ International. Fine Dining. $12-$28 **AAA Inspector Notes:** Ask for an outdoor table to really feel the vibes of this famous colonial city. An attentive staff welcomes guests with the classic warmth of Mexico. There's nothing like their refreshing homemade watermelon juice to enhance crowd-pleasers like coconut shrimp, Mexican specialties, pastas, steaks and spectacular salads. **Features:** full bar, patio dining. **Reservations:** suggested. **Address:** Jardin de La Union No. 3 36000 **Location:** In Centro Historico; corner of Jardin de La Union, across from Teatro Juárez. **Parking:** no self-parking.

### LA CAPELLINA 473/732-7224 [8]

▼▼▼ International. Casual Dining. $9-$18 **AAA Inspector Notes:** Attentive service and live music in the evenings make this a perfect choice for surprisingly good international fare served in an upscale, yet casual setting. Specialties include pasta, seafood and a superb wine list. **Features:** full bar. **Address:** Sopena No. 3 36000 **Location:** In Centro Historico, just e of Teatro Juárez. **Parking:** no self-parking.

### LA TASCA DE LA PAZ RESTAURANT BAR 473/734-2225 [3]

▼▼▼ International. Casual Dining. $5-$12 **AAA Inspector Notes:** In a historic building, this lovely little café offers a variety of international selections. Sidewalk seating is fun for people watching and friendly, attentive servers make this a peaceful spot for chilling out. Sopa Azteca and the large ensalada Griega are house specialties. **Features:** full bar. **Address:** Plaza de La Paz No. 28 Zona Centro 36000 **Location:** Centro; in Plaza de La Paz; across from Basilica. **Parking:** no self-parking.

### RESTAURANT REAL DE LA ESPERANZA 473/732-1041 [1]

▼▼▼ Continental. Casual Dining. $7-$14 **AAA Inspector Notes:** On the outskirts of the city, this eatery is well worth the short drive. Built on the ruins of a 16th-century chapel, the restaurant preserves its roots with a church facade and cobblestone steps. The interior is done in soft, muted colors and decorated with some nice consignment art. On the menu you'll see traditional Mexican fare such as milanesa (breaded steak), arrachera (marinated skirt steak) and fideo (Mexican pasta soup). Save room for one of the delicious dessert crepes. **Features:** full bar. **Address:** Carr A Dolores Hidalgo KM 5 36000 **Location:** 3.3 mi (5.5 km) on Mex 110 (Dolores Hidalgo Hwy), just ne of Valencia.

# LEON, GUANAJUATO pop. 1,436,480

## COURTYARD BY MARRIOTT AT THE POLIFORUM
(477)295-9400

Hotel
$87-$143

**COURTYARD Marriott. AAA Benefit:** Members save 5% or more!

**Address:** Blvd Francisco Villa **Location:** Jct Blvd Adolfo Lopez Mateos; at Poliforum complex. **Facility:** Meets AAA guest room security requirements. 140 units, some kitchens. 14 stories, interior corridors. **Parking:** on-site (fee) and valet. **Amenities:** safes. **Pool(s):** heated outdoor. **Activities:** exercise room. **Guest Services:** valet and coin laundry, boarding pass kiosk.

## FIESTA INN LEON
(477)710-0500

Hotel $85-$145 **Address:** Blvd Adolfo Lopez Mateos 2702 Ote 37530 **Location:** On Mex 45; jct Blvd M Escobedo. **Facility:** Meets AAA guest room security requirements. 160 units. 3 stories, interior corridors. **Amenities:** safes. **Pool(s):** outdoor. **Activities:** playground, exercise room. **Guest Services:** valet laundry.

## HOLIDAY INN CENTRO DE CONVENCIONES
(477)710-0040

Hotel $100-$155 **Address:** Blvd Adolfo Lopez Mateos No. 1501 37270 **Location:** On Mex 45, jct Blvd Chichimecas. **Facility:** 177 units. 5 stories, interior corridors. **Amenities:** safes. **Pool(s):** heated indoor. **Activities:** exercise room. **Guest Services:** valet laundry.

## HOLIDAY INN LEON MEXICO
(477)710-0003

Hotel $90-$110 **Address:** Ave Adolfo Lopez Mateos No. 1308 **Location:** 2.2 mi (3.5 km) se on Mex 45. **Facility:** 175 units. 5 stories, interior corridors. **Amenities:** safes. **Pool(s):** heated indoor. **Activities:** exercise room. **Guest Services:** valet laundry, rental car service.

## HOTEL HOTSSON LEON
(477)719-8000

Hotel
$165-$210

**Address:** Blvd Adolfo Lopez Mateos No. 1102 37270 **Location:** On Mex 45; between Merida and Pampas sts. Across from Centro Estrella. **Facility:** Very cool and beautiful hotel features dramatic public areas, upscale guest rooms, a contemporary pool area and expansive grounds including a 1700s chapel. Meets AAA guest room security requirements. 211 units, some two bedrooms. 8 stories, interior corridors. **Parking:** on-site and valet. **Amenities:** safes. **Dining:** 2 restaurants. **Pool(s):** heated outdoor. **Activities:** tennis, exercise room, spa. **Guest Services:** valet laundry, rental car service.

## RADISSON POLIFORUM PLAZA HOTEL LEON
(477)710-0022

Hotel $95-$160 **Address:** Blvd Adolfo Lopez Mateos 2611 Ote **Location:** Across street from Poliforum complex. **Facility:** Meets AAA guest room security requirements. 160 units. 4 stories, interior corridors. **Parking:** on-site and valet. **Amenities:** safes. **Dining:** entertainment. **Pool(s):** heated outdoor. **Activities:** exercise room. **Guest Services:** valet laundry.

## ARGENTILIA RESTAURANT
477/718-3394

Argentine Steak. Casual Dining. $7-$23 **AAA Inspector Notes:** In a restored historic hacienda, this steakhouse caters to meat lovers with cuts of beef prepared Argentine-style and grilled over mesquite wood. **Features:** full bar. **Reservations:** suggested. **Address:** Ave Cerro Gordo No. 12 **Location:** 1.2 mi (1.9 km) w on Ave Lopez Mateos to Ave Campestre, 1.3 mi (2 km) s to dead end. **Parking:** on-site (fee) and valet.

## FRASCATI RISTORANTE-PIZZERIA
477/773-7154

Italian. Casual Dining. $8-$24 **AAA Inspector Notes:** Pasta, pizza, marinated veggies and other Italian staples are dished up in a casually upscale atmosphere. This local favorite features modern design with hardwood floors, a brick boveda ceiling, limestone walls and a hip bar area. **Features:** full bar. **Reservations:** suggested. **Address:** Ave Cerro Gordo 201A **Location:** At Plaza Mayor Mall. **Parking:** valet and street only.

## LA ESTANCIA ARGENTINA RESTAURANTE
477/763-3070

Argentine Steak. Casual Dining. $8-$24 **AAA Inspector Notes:** This popular eatery with a trendy, contemporary atmosphere is a favorite of local business people. Quality cuts of meat are presented for selection then grilled on an open parilla. Fresh fish and savory pasta dishes are also on the menu. The dessert cart carries a tempting assortment of freshly baked pastries, pies and cakes. A separate indoor playground is a treat for families. **Features:** full bar. **Reservations:** suggested. **Address:** Blvd Adolfo Lopez Mateos S/N 37270 **Location:** 2.2 mi (3.5 km) se on Mex 45; across from Plaza del Zapato. **Parking:** valet and street only.

## SIRLOIN STOCKADE
477/718-4689

Steak. Quick Serve. $9-$11 **AAA Inspector Notes:** The steakhouse lines up buffet items, including pizza, tacos, soups, salads and desserts, providing both excellent variety and a good value. Rotating theme nights allow for the sampling of sushi, barbecue and seafood. The buffet may also serve to complement a quality steak. **Features:** beer & wine. **Address:** Blvd Maria Clutier No. 2002 **Location:** Jct Blvd Manuel J Clouthier; in Plaza Mayor Shopping Complex.

# MATEHUALA, SAN LUIS POTOSÍ
pop. 91,522

## LAS PALMAS MIDWAY INN
488/882-0002

**fyi** Not evaluated; located in remote area. **Address:** Hwy 57 (KM 617) **Location:** On Mex 57, by north jct entrance road to town. Facilities, services, and décor characterize a mid-scale property.

## LAS PALMAS RESTAURANT
488/882-0002

**fyi** Not evaluated. Diners take to the relaxing atmosphere to unwind and replenish, with the help of the well-trained staff. The menu centers on Continental fare. **Address:** Hwy 57 (KM 617) **Location:** On Mex 57, by north junction entrance road to town; in Las Palmas Midway Inn.

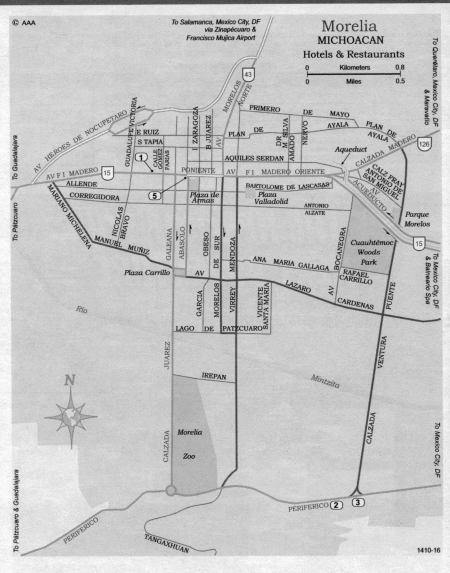

© AAA

To Salamanca, Mexico City, DF
via Zinapécuaro &
Francisco Mujica Airport

## Morelia
### MICHOACAN
**Hotels & Restaurants**

| 0 | Kilometers | 0.8 |
| 0 | Miles | 0.5 |

To Querétaro, Mexico City, DF & Maravatío

43

MORELOS NORTE

PRIMERO   DE   MAYO

GUADALUPE VICTORIA

E RUIZ

S TAPIA

PLAN   DE

NERVO

AYALA

PLAN DE AYALA

AV HEROES DE NOCUPETARO

I ZARAGOZA

B JUAREZ

AV

DR M SILVA

AMADO

Aqueduct

CALZADA MADERO

126

CALZ FRAY ANTONIO DE SAN MIGUEL

To Guadalajara

AV F I MADERO

15

CALLE GOMEZ FARIAS

1

AQUILES SERDAN

PONIENTE   AV   F I MADERO ORIENTE

AV ACUEDUCTO

ALLENDE

CORREGIDORA

5

Plaza de Armas

BARTOLOME DE LASCASAS
Plaza Valladolid

ANTONIO ALZATE

Parque Morelos

To Pátzcuaro

MARIANO MICHELENA

NICOLAS BRAVO

MANUEL MUÑIZ

GALEANA

ABASOLO

OBESO

DE SUR

MENDOZA

ANA   MARIA   GALLAGA

BOCANEGRA

Cuauhtémoc Woods Park

RAFAEL CARRILLO

15

To Mexico City, DF & Balneario Spa

Plaza Carrillo

AV

Río

GARCIA

MORELOS

VIRREY

VICENTE SANTA MARIA

LAZARO

AV

CARDENAS

PUENTE

LAGO   DE   PATZCUARO

JUAREZ

IREPAN

Mintzita

VENTURA

N

Morelia Zoo

CALZADA

To Mexico City, DF

To Pátzcuaro & Guadalajara

PERIFERICO

PERIFERICO   2   3

PERIFERICO

TANGAXHUAN

1410-16

## Morelia

This index helps you "spot" where approved hotels and restaurants are located on the corresponding detailed maps. Hotel daily rate range is for comparison only. Restaurant price range is a combination of lunch and/or dinner. Turn to the listing page for more detailed rate and price information and consult display ads for special promotions.

### MORELIA, MICHOACÁN

| Map Page | Restaurants | Diamond Rated | Cuisine | Price Range | Page |
|----------|-------------|---------------|---------|-------------|------|
| ① p. 533 | Fonda Las Mercedes | ▽▽▽ | Mexican | $15-$20 | 535 |
| ② p. 533 | Las Trojes Restaurant-Bar | ▽▽▽ | Mexican | $13-$22 | 535 |
| ③ p. 533 | San Miguelito Restaurante | ▽▽▽ | Regional Mexican | $23-$30 | 535 |
| ⑤ p. 533 | Restaurante Hotel Virrey de Mendoza | ▽▽▽ | Regional Mexican | $12-$18 | 535 |

## MORELIA, MICHOACÁN (D-2) pop. 729,279, elev. 6,399'
• Hotels & Restaurants map & index p. 533

### BEST WESTERN PLUS GRAN HOTEL MORELIA
443/322-8000

**fyi** Not evaluated. **Address:** Aves Camelinas & Ventura Puente 58070 **Location:** On Periferico, just w of jct Calzada Ventura; at Convention Center. Facilities, services, and décor characterize a mid-scale property.

**AAA Benefit:** Save 10% or more every day and earn 10% bonus points!

### CANTERA DIEZ HOTEL BOUTIQUE
443/312-5419

**fyi** Not evaluated. **Address:** Blvd Benito Juárez No. 63, Centro Historico 58000 **Location:** Centro; across from the cathedral. Facilities, services, and décor characterize an upscale property. The guest rooms surround the courtyard in this restored, 300-year-old colonial building, which offers contemporary amenities in an upscale style.

### HOLIDAY INN EXPRESS MORELIA
443/315-7100

**fyi** Not evaluated. **Address:** Paseo de La Republica 5000 58270 **Location:** 4 mi (6.7 km) se on Periferico. Facilities, services, and décor characterize a mid-scale property.

### HOLIDAY INN-MORELIA
443/314-3111

**fyi** Not evaluated. **Address:** Ave Camelinas No. 3466 58279 **Location:** 3.8 mi (6.3 km) se on Periferico. Facilities, services, and décor characterize a mid-scale property.

### HOTEL DE LA SOLEDAD
443/312-1888

**fyi** Not evaluated; located in remote area. **Address:** Ignacio Zaragoza 90, Centro Historico 58000 **Location:** Just n of the cathedral. Facilities, services, and décor characterize a mid-scale property.

### HOTEL VIRREY DE MENDOZA
443/312-0633

**fyi** Not evaluated. **Address:** Ave Madero Poniente 310, Col Centro 58000 **Location:** Centro; just w of the cathedral. Facilities, services, and décor characterize an upscale property. From a stained-glass ceiling to original art, Old World elegance imbues this hotel built in the 17th century; some units furnished in superb antiques.

### TUROTEL
443/333-1300

**fyi** Not evaluated. **Address:** Ave Aqueducto No. 3805, Col. Fray Antonio de Lisboa 58254 **Location:** Jct aves Aqueducto and Camelinas (Periferico). Facilities, services, and décor characterize a mid-scale property.

### VILLA MONTANA HOTEL & SPA
443/314-0231

**fyi** Not evaluated. **Address:** Patzimba No. 201, Vista Bella 58090 **Location:** 2 mi (3.3 km) s off Mex 15 via Periferico (Ave Camelinas), s on Tangaxhuan. Facilities, services, and décor characterize an upscale property.

### VILLA SAN JOSE HOTEL & SUITES
443/324-4545

**fyi** Not evaluated. **Address:** 77 Patzimba No. 77, Col Vista Bella 58090 **Location:** 1.9 mi (3.3 km) s off Mex 15 via Periferico, s on Tangaxhuan. Facilities, services, and décor characterize a mid-scale property.

### WHERE TO EAT

### FONDA LAS MERCEDES
443/312-6113  ①

▼▼▼ Mexican. Casual Dining. $15-$20 **AAA Inspector Notes:** A great starting or ending point for exploring the beautiful historic center of town, the downtown restaurant serves local specialties and some Continental dishes. The menu includes oysters, salmon, chicken, pasta, beef and Mexican specialties. Distinctively decorated dining rooms mix colonial and contemporary styles; the courtyard patio is another seating option. The professional, uniformed waitstaff provides semiformal service. **Features:** full bar, patio dining. **Reservations:** suggested. **Address:** Leon Guzman No. 47 **Location:** Just w of the cathedral; near jct Ave Madero Pte; in historico district. **Parking:** street only. ⓛ ⓓ 🅐🅒

### LAS TROJES RESTAURANT-BAR
443/324-3283  ②

▼▼▼ Mexican. Casual Dining. $13-$22 **AAA Inspector Notes:** Named after the traditional housing of the indigenous people of Morelia, this rustic yet sophisticated restaurant welcomes families to dine on steak, soups and salads prepared Mexican style. Complimentary starters might include tangy cucumber or nopales salad, or homemade salsa. Service is attentive and somewhat formal. **Features:** full bar. **Reservations:** suggested. **Address:** Juan Sebastian Bach No. 51 **Location:** 1.9 mi (3.3 km) s off Mex 15 via Periferico, just s on Mozart, just e. **Parking:** valet only. ⓛ ⓓ 🅐🅒 ◼

### RESTAURANTE HOTEL VIRREY DE MENDOZA
443/312-0633  ⑤

▼▼▼ Regional Mexican. Fine Dining. $12-$18 **AAA Inspector Notes:** Classic. This elegant dining room makes for a memorable experience. Here you'll enjoy well-prepared, regional Michoacan favorites. Charalitos fresh from Lake Patzcuaro are a crunchy treat, and the Sopa Tarasca is a house specialty. **Features:** full bar, patio dining. **Reservations:** suggested. **Address:** Ave Madero Poniente 310, Col Centro 58000 **Location:** Centro; just w of the cathedral; in Hotel Virrey de Mendoza. **Parking:** on-site (fee) and valet. ⓑ ⓛ ⓓ 🅐🅒

### SAN MIGUELITO RESTAURANTE
443/324-4411  ③

▼▼▼ Regional Mexican. Fine Dining. $23-$30 **AAA Inspector Notes:** In the afternoon, a lively crowd gathers for lunch at this Colonial-style restaurant with unique décor. On the menu is a good selection of tender steaks, tasty chicken dishes and fresh salads, reinforced by tasty margaritas. It's a fun place. **Features:** full bar. **Reservations:** suggested. **Address:** Ave Camelinas S/N, Fracc La Loma 58290 **Location:** 2.1 mi (3.5 km) off Mex 15 via Periferico; across from convention center. **Parking:** valet only. ⓛ ⓓ 🅐🅒

## PÁTZCUARO, MICHOACÁN (D-2)
pop. 87,794, elev. 7,131'

### BEST WESTERN POSADA DE DON VASCO
434/342-0227

**fyi** Not evaluated. **Address:** Ave de Lazaro Cardenas No. 450 61600 **Location:** 1.5 mi (2.5 km) n on Calz de Las Americas. Facilities, services, and décor characterize a mid-scale property.

**AAA Benefit:** Save 10% or more every day and earn 10% bonus points!

### LA MANSION DE LOS SUEÑOS
434/342-5708

**fyi** Not evaluated. **Address:** Ibarra No. 15, Centro 61600 **Location:** Centro. Facilities, services, and décor characterize an upscale property.

### WHERE TO EAT

### PRISCILLAS
434/342-5708

▼▼▼ Regional International. Fine Dining. $12-$25 **AAA Inspector Notes:** Menu offerings are presented in an elegant, refined dining room, or in the more casual setting of a courtyard under the stars. Juicy beef tenderloin served with scalloped potatoes is a house specialty. Finish your meal with a selection from the fresh pastry-loaded dessert cart. **Features:** full bar. **Reservations:** suggested. **Address:** Ibarra No. 15, Centro 61600 **Location:** Centro; in La Mansion de los Sueños. **Parking:** street only. ⓑ ⓛ ⓓ 🅐🅒

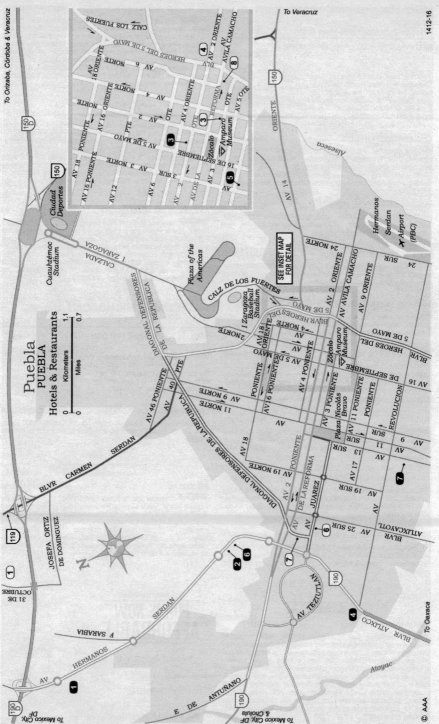

Puebla
PUEBLA
Hotels & Restaurants

© AAA

1412-16

## Puebla

This index helps you "spot" where approved hotels and restaurants are located on the corresponding detailed maps. Hotel daily rate range is for comparison only. Restaurant price range is a combination of lunch and/or dinner. Turn to the listing page for more detailed rate and price information and consult display ads for special promotions.

### PUEBLA, PUEBLA

| Map Page | Hotels | Diamond Rated | Rate Range | Page |
|---|---|---|---|---|
| **1** p. 536 | Marriott Real Puebla | ▽▽▽ | $104-$171 | 538 |
| **2** p. 536 | **Presidente InterContinental Puebla** | ▽▽▽▽ | $109-$220 | 538 |
| **3** p. 536 | Gilfer Hotel | ▽▽ | $49-$68 | 538 |
| **4** p. 536 | Courtyard by Marriott Puebla Las Animas | ▽▽▽ | $70-$115 | 538 |
| **5** p. 536 | Quinta Real Puebla | ▽▽▽▽ | $103-$345 | 538 |
| **6** p. 536 | Holiday Inn Express Puebla | ▽▽▽ | $65-$95 | 538 |
| **7** p. 536 | **Holiday Inn Puebla La Noria** | ▽▽▽ | $75-$120 | 538 |

| Map Page | Restaurants | Diamond Rated | Cuisine | Price Range | Page |
|---|---|---|---|---|---|
| 1 p. 536 | El Mural de los Poblanos Restaurant Tradicional | ▽▽▽ | Regional Mexican | $8-$32 | 539 |
| 3 p. 536 | Vittorio's Cafe - Pizzeria | ▽▽ | Italian Pizza | $8-$25 | 539 |
| 4 p. 536 | Casareyna Restaurante | ▽▽▽ | Regional Mexican | $8-$25 | 538 |
| 6 p. 536 | Chimichurri | ▽▽▽ | Argentine Steak | $15-$30 | 538 |
| 7 p. 536 | Pizzeria Napoli | ▽▽ | Pizza | $7-$15 | 539 |
| 8 p. 536 | Cinco Cocina Urbana | ▽▽▽ | Regional Mexican Small Plates | $8-$18 | 539 |

# PUEBLA, PUEBLA (D-4) pop. 1,539,819, elev. 7,091'
• Hotels & Restaurants map & index p. 536

## COURTYARD BY MARRIOTT PUEBLA LAS ANIMAS
(222)477-2100  **4**

▽▽▽ **Hotel** $70-$115 **Address:** Ave 31 Poniente No. 3333 **Location:** Jct Blvd Atlixco; in Las Animas district. **Facility:** Meets AAA guest room security requirements. 154 units. 7 stories, interior corridors. **Parking:** on-site (fee) and valet. **Amenities:** safes. **Pool(s):** heated outdoor. **Activities:** playground, exercise room. **Guest Services:** valet laundry, area transportation.

**AAA Benefit:**
Members save 5% or more!

## GILFER HOTEL
222/309-9800  **3**

▽▽ **Hotel** $49-$68 **Address:** Calle 2 Oriente No. 11, Centro Historico 72000 **Location:** 2 blks e of Zócalo. **Facility:** Meets AAA guest room security requirements. 92 units. 8 stories, interior corridors. **Parking:** on-site and valet. **Terms:** age restrictions may apply. **Amenities:** Some: safes. **Guest Services:** valet laundry.

## HOLIDAY INN EXPRESS PUEBLA
(222)303-0303  **6**

▽▽▽ **Hotel** $65-$95 **Address:** Ave Hermanos Serdan No. 45, Col. Amor 72140 **Location:** S of Mex 190-D (toll road). **Facility:** Meets AAA guest room security requirements. 189 units. 7 stories, interior corridors. **Bath:** shower only. **Amenities:** safes. **Pool(s):** heated indoor. **Activities:** exercise room. **Guest Services:** valet and coin laundry, area transportation.

## HOLIDAY INN PUEBLA LA NORIA
(222)211-9000  **7**

▽▽▽ **Hotel** $75-$120

**Address:** Circ. Juan Pablo II No. 1936, Col Ex Hacienda la Noria 72140 **Location:** Federal Rd Mexico-Puebla S to Cir Juan Pablo II. **Facility:** Meets AAA guest room security requirements. 150 units. 15-25 stories, interior corridors. **Parking:** on-site and valet. **Amenities:** safes. **Pool(s):** outdoor. **Activities:** exercise room. **Guest Services:** valet laundry.

## MARRIOTT REAL PUEBLA
(222)141-2000  **1**

▽▽▽ **Hotel** $104-$171 **Address:** Ave Hermanos Serdan 807, Col. San Rafael Poniente 72000 **Location:** Mex 190-D (toll road) exit Centro Puebla, just s. **Facility:** Meets AAA guest room security requirements. 296 units. 2-3 stories, interior/exterior corridors. **Amenities:** safes. **Dining:** 2 restaurants. **Pool(s):** heated outdoor. **Activities:** tennis, playground, exercise room. **Guest Services:** valet laundry.

**AAA Benefit:**
Members save 5% or more!

## PRESIDENTE INTERCONTINENTAL PUEBLA
(222)213-7070  **2**

▽▽ ▽▽ **Hotel** $109-$220

**Address:** Ave Hermanos Serdan 141, Col Amor 72140 **Location:** S of Mex 190-D (toll road). **Facility:** The hotel boasts dramatically ornate public areas, an attractive central pool courtyard and contemporary, well-equipped guest rooms. Meets AAA guest room security requirements. 200 units. 5 stories, interior/exterior corridors. **Parking:** on-site and valet. **Amenities:** safes. **Dining:** 2 restaurants. **Pool(s):** heated outdoor. **Activities:** sauna, exercise room, spa. **Guest Services:** valet laundry, area transportation.

## QUINTA REAL PUEBLA
(222)229-0909  **5**

▽▽ ▽▽ **Classic Historic Hotel** $103-$345 **Address:** 7 Poniente No. 105, Centro Historico 72000 **Location:** Just sw of plaza. **Facility:** A central courtyard accents this 16th-century convent, now a hotel. A variety of recently renovated rooms feature high ceilings and tasteful, modern décor. Meets AAA guest room security requirements. 84 units. 4 stories, interior/exterior corridors. **Bath:** shower only. **Amenities:** safes. **Activities:** exercise room, massage. **Guest Services:** valet laundry. Affiliated with Preferred Hotels & Resorts.

## BEST WESTERN REAL DE PUEBLA
222/230-0122

**fyi** Not evaluated. **Address:** 5 Calle 5 Poniente No. 2522, Col La Paz 72160 **Location:** Between aves Reforma and Juárez. Facilities, services, and décor characterize an economy property.

**AAA Benefit:**
Save 10% or more every day and earn 10% bonus points!

## MESONES SACRISTIA HOTEL
222/232-4513

**fyi** Not evaluated. **Address:** 6 Sur 304 Callejon de Los Sapos, Centro Historico 72000 **Location:** On Callejon de Los Sapos (Alley of the Toads); centro. Facilities, services, and décor characterize a mid-scale property.

## WHERE TO EAT

## CASAREYNA RESTAURANTE
222/232-0032  **4**

▽▽▽ Regional Mexican. Fine Dining. $8-$25 **AAA Inspector Notes:** A visit to Puebla wouldn't be complete without sampling traditional mole poblano. Casareyna provides a comfortable and modern ambiance to enjoy award winning moles along with a variety of Mexican wines. Take time to visit the Talavera workshop that features many unique designer ceramics. **Features:** full bar, patio dining. **Reservations:** suggested. **Address:** Privada 2 Oriente 1007, Col. Centro, Paseo de San Francisco 72000 **Location:** Just e of Blvd Heroes del 5 de Mayo; adjacent to Gardens of San Francisco. **Parking:** on-site (fee) and valet.

## CHIMICHURRI
222/249-1534  **6**

▽▽▽ Argentine Steak. Casual Dining. $15-$30 **AAA Inspector Notes:** This Argentinian restaurant offers a good variety of nicely prepared steaks and seafood. Be sure to request the non-smoking section if that is what you desire. Dining on the terrace also is an option. **Features:** full bar, patio dining. **Reservations:** suggested. **Address:** 27 Sur No. 701 72160 **Location:** Jct Ave Juárez. **Parking:** valet only.

(See map & index p. 536.)

**CINCO COCINA URBANA**   222/246-0001   8

▼▼▼ Regional Mexican Small Plates. Casual Dining. $8-$18 **AAA Inspector Notes:** This kitchen's young chef showcases a unique menu featuring creative interpretations of local street food using traditional recipes and cooking techniques. The dining room is small and chic, making for a fun atmosphere. **Features:** full bar. **Reservations:** suggested. **Address:** Calle 3 Oriente 627, Centro Historico **Location:** Jct Blvd Heroes del 5 de Mayo. **Parking:** valet only. B L D

**EL MURAL DE LOS POBLANOS RESTAURANT TRADICIONAL**   222/242-6696   1

▼▼▼ Regional Mexican. Casual Dining. $8-$32 **AAA Inspector Notes:** Located in the historical center, this jewel of a restaurant offers guests cordial attentive service and classic creations from Puebla. A variety of moles and traditional selections are prepared with fresh ingredients. A good selection of mezcals. The large mural on the wall depicts the famous people who contributed to the enhancement of Puebla. If you have time, schedule a mole cooking class with the talented young chef. It will be well worth it! **Features:** full bar. **Reservations:** suggested. **Address:** 16 de Septiembre no. 506 Centro Historico **Location:** 1 blk e of main Cathedral plaza; jct 7 Oriente. B L D

**PIZZERIA NAPOLI**   222/621-9650   7

▼▼ Pizza. Casual Dining. $7-$15 **AAA Inspector Notes:** This popular neighborhood pizzeria has welcoming and friendly service. The pizza oven is in the dining room so you can watch your pie or calzone being baked before your eyes. Portions are easily shareable, but never share your salami! **Features:** beer & wine. **Address:** 29 Sur No. 129 **Location:** Just n of Ave Juárez. **Parking:** street only. L D 🍺 🚫

**VITTORIO'S CAFE - PIZZERIA**   222/232-7900   3

▼▼ Italian Pizza. Casual Dining. $8-$25 **AAA Inspector Notes:** The restaurant has been dishing up tasty brick-oven pizzas for more than 30 years. Try one of the unique pizza toppings, such as mole poblano or huitlacoche. Not craving pizza? The menu also lists some pasta dishes and a few local specialties. Dine inside, or if you're in the mood for people-watching, ask for a sidewalk table. There is live music Friday and Saturday nights. **Features:** full bar. **Address:** Portal Morelos 2 Sur No. 106, Centro Historico 72000 **Location:** Under one of the portals in front of the Zocalo. **Parking:** street only. B L D LATE 🍺 🚫

# QUERÉTARO, QUERÉTARO (D-2)

pop. 801,940, elev. 6,078'
• Restaurants p. 540

**CASA INN QUERETARO MEXICO**   (442)101-4100

▼▼▼ Hotel $140-$295 **Address:** Paseo de Monte Mirande Oeste No. 2 **Location:** Mex 57, 0.5 mi (0.8 km) s of central bus terminal. **Facility:** Meets AAA guest room security requirements. 195 units. 11 stories, interior corridors. **Amenities:** safes. **Pool(s):** outdoor. **Activities:** sauna, hot tub, steamroom, exercise room. **Guest Services:** valet laundry, area transportation.

♿ 🍽 🛎 🍸 SD 🏊 BIZ HS 🛜 ✕ 🖥 📶

**FIESTA INN QUERETARO**   442/196-0000

▼▼▼
Hotel
$95-$155

**Address:** Ave 5 de Febrero, No. 108 **Location:** On Mex 57, 0.6 mi (1 km) n of jct Mex 45 and 45-D (toll road) exit Ave 5 de Febrero. **Facility:** Meets AAA guest room security requirements. 225 units, some efficiencies. 3 stories, interior corridors. **Terms:** 2 night minimum stay - weekends, 3 day cancellation notice-fee imposed. **Amenities:** safes. **Pool(s):** heated outdoor. **Activities:** playground, exercise room. **Guest Services:** valet laundry.

🍽 🛎 🍸 S SD 🏊 BIZ
🛜 ✕ 📶 / SOME UNITS 🖥 📶

**HAMPTON INN BY HILTON QUERETARO TECNOLOGICO**   (422)153-2800

▼▼▼ Hotel $79-$86 **Address:** Blvd Bernardo Quintana 4100-1 76100 **Location:** 1 mi (1.6 km) nw of Calzada de Los Arcos. **Facility:** Meets AAA guest room security requirements. 178 units. 8

| AAA Benefit: |
| Members save up to 10%! |

stories, interior corridors. **Terms:** 1-7 night minimum stay, cancellation fee imposed. **Pool(s):** outdoor. **Activities:** exercise room. **Guest Services:** valet and coin laundry, area transportation.

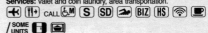

**HILTON GARDEN INN QUERETARO**   (442)256-3636

▼▼▼ Hotel $85-$128 **Address:** Prol. Ignacio Zaragoza 99 76180 **Location:** Just w of Queretaro-Mexico City Hwy. **Facility:** Meets AAA guest room security requirements. 102 units. 7 sto-

| AAA Benefit: |
| Members save up to 10%! |

ries, interior corridors. *Bath:* shower only. **Terms:** 1-7 night minimum stay, cancellation fee imposed. **Amenities:** safes. **Pool(s):** heated outdoor. **Activities:** exercise room. **Guest Services:** valet and coin laundry, area transportation.

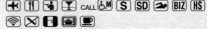

**HOLIDAY INN EXPRESS QUERETARO**   (442)215-0020

▼▼▼ Hotel. Rates not provided. **Address:** Ave 5 de Febrero No. 110-Bis 76010 **Location:** On Mex 57, 0.6 mi (1 km) n of jct Mex 45 and 45-D (toll road) exit Ave 5 de Febrero. **Facility:** Meets AAA guest room security requirements. 101 units. 8 stories, interior corridors. *Bath:* shower only. **Amenities:** safes. **Activities:** hot tub, exercise room. **Guest Services:** valet laundry.

🍽 CALL 🛎M S SD BIZ HS 🛜 ✕ 📶
/ SOME UNITS 🖥 📶

**HOLIDAY INN QUERETARO CENTRO HISTORICO**   (442)192-0202

▼▼▼ Hotel $155-$260 **Address:** Ave 5 de Febrero No. 110, Niños Heroes 76010 **Location:** On Mex 57, 0.6 mi (1 km) n of jct Mex 45 and 45-D (toll road) exit Ave 5 de Febrero. **Facility:** Meets AAA guest room security requirements. 234 units. 3 stories, interior corridors. **Amenities:** safes. **Dining:** 2 restaurants, also, Los Arcos Restaurant, see separate listing, entertainment. **Pool(s):** heated outdoor. **Activities:** hot tub, playground, game room, exercise room. **Guest Services:** valet and coin laundry.

♿ 🍽 🛎 SD 🏊 BIZ 🛜 ✕ 🖥 📶
/ SOME UNITS HS

**HOME2 SUITES BY HILTON**   (442)368-3030

▼▼▼ Extended Stay Hotel $76-$89 **Address:** Gasa de Incorporacion a Carretera Queretaro 76100 **Location:** Mex 57 exit Juriquilla, just sw.

| AAA Benefit: |
| Members save up to 10%! |

**Facility:** Meets AAA guest room security requirements. 97 units, some efficiencies and kitchens. 4 stories, interior corridors. **Terms:** 1-7 night minimum stay, cancellation fee imposed. **Amenities:** safes. **Pool(s):** heated outdoor. **Activities:** hot tub, exercise room. **Guest Services:** valet and coin laundry.

🍽 🛎 🍸 CALL 🛎M S SD 🏊 BIZ HS 🛜
✕ 🖥 📶 📶

**HOTEL DONA URRACA**   (442)238-5400

▼▼▼▼ Boutique Hotel $214-$292 **Address:** Ave 5 de Mayo No. 117 **Location:** In historico downtown; just e of Plaza de Armas. **Facility:** Located within a few blocks of Queretaro's loveliest plazas, this hotel features spacious rooms with Mexican modern décor, luxurious amenities and each unit's comfortable seating area is a bonus. Meets AAA guest room security requirements. 24 units. 2 stories, interior corridors. **Parking:** on-site and valet. **Amenities:** safes. **Pool(s):** heated outdoor. **Activities:** hot tub, steamroom, bicycles, spa. **Guest Services:** valet laundry.

🍽 🛎 🍸 CALL 🛎M SD 🛜 ✕ 🖥 📶
/ SOME UNITS HS

## HOTEL FIESTA AMERICANA QUERETARO

(442)192-9999

Hotel
$132-$320

**Address:** Blvd Bernardo Quintana No. 4050 Col. Alamos **Location:** Just nw of Calzada de Los Arcos. Located in modern-commercial complex. **Facility:** This colonial-style hotel's public areas please the eye with arched ceilings and back-lit marble walls. Guest rooms are spacious and recently renovated with Mexican modern furnishings and décor. Meets AAA guest room security requirements. 173 units, some efficiencies. 5 stories, interior corridors. **Parking:** valet and street only. **Terms:** age restrictions may apply. **Amenities:** safes. **Pool(s):** heated outdoor. **Activities:** hot tub, exercise room, massage. **Guest Services:** valet laundry, area transportation.

## HOTEL HACIENDA JURICA QUERETARO

(442)218-0022

**Historic Hotel** $156-$325 **Address:** Paseo Jurica Esquina Paseo del Meson S/N 76100 **Location:** Mex 57 exit Jurica, 2.5 mi (4 km) w; end of Jurica development. **Facility:** The large, spread-out, converted 17th-century hacienda boasts period structures and furnishings as well as attractive landscaping and artistic cobblestone walkways. Meets AAA guest room security requirements. 182 units. 2 stories (no elevator), interior corridors. **Parking:** on-site and valet. **Amenities:** safes. **Dining:** Los Hules, see separate listing. **Pool(s):** heated outdoor. **Activities:** miniature golf, tennis, playground, exercise room, spa. **Guest Services:** valet laundry.

## HOTEL REAL DE MINAS TRADICIONAL

442/216-0444

**Hotel** $58-$89 **Address:** Ave Constituyentes 124 Pte **Location:** On Mex 45 (Celaya Libre), just w of jct Mex 57. Next to the bull ring. **Facility:** Meets AAA guest room security requirements. 200 units, some two and three bedrooms. 2 stories (no elevator), interior corridors. *Bath:* shower only. **Amenities:** safes. **Pool(s):** heated outdoor. **Activities:** miniature golf, tennis, exercise room. **Guest Services:** valet laundry.

## LA CASA DE LA MARQUESA

442/212-0092

**Classic Historic Country Inn** $220-$380 **Address:** Madero No. 41 Esq Allende 76000 **Location:** Downtown; in historico district. **Facility:** Beautiful courtyards and luxurious rooms characterize this stunning 1700s country inn, formerly home to emperors and presidents. 13 units. 3 stories (no elevator), interior/exterior corridors. **Parking:** valet only. **Terms:** age restrictions may apply. **Dining:** El Comedor de la Marquesa, see separate listing. **Activities:** massage. **Guest Services:** valet laundry, area transportation.

## ONE QUERETARO PLAZA GALERIAS

(442)101-8800

**Hotel** $85-$145 **Address:** Ave 5 de Febrero No. 108-A, Col Niños Heroes 76010 **Location:** On Mex 57, 0.6 mi (1 km) n of jct Mex 45 and 45-D (toll road) exit Ave 5 de Febrero. **Facility:** Meets AAA guest room security requirements. 126 units. 7 stories, interior corridors. *Bath:* shower only. **Guest Services:** valet and coin laundry.

## PLAZA CAMELINAS

(442)192-3900

**Hotel** $68-$378 **Address:** Ave 5 de Febrero No. 28 **Location:** Between aves Zaragoza and Constituyentes. **Facility:** 168 units. 3 stories, interior corridors. *Bath:* shower only. **Parking:** on-site and valet. **Amenities:** safes. **Pool(s):** heated outdoor. **Activities:** recreation programs, playground, game room, exercise room. **Guest Services:** valet laundry.

## STAYBRIDGE SUITES QUERETARO

(442)103-2900

**Extended Stay Hotel** $110-$220 **Address:** Carr San Luis - Que No. 10685 76127 **Location:** On Mex 57 southbound exit Jurica, just s. **Facility:** Meets AAA guest room security requirements. 135 units, some two bedrooms, efficiencies and kitchens. 4 stories, interior corridors. *Bath:* shower only. **Amenities:** safes. **Pool(s):** heated outdoor. **Activities:** hot tub, exercise room. **Guest Services:** complimentary and valet laundry, area transportation.

## TUROTEL QUERETARO

442/251-8100

**Hotel** $85-$140 **Address:** No. 2107 Col Ampl Cimatario **Location:** On Mex 57, 0.6 mi (1 km) n of jct Mex 45 and 45-D (toll road) exit Ave Cimatario. **Facility:** Meets AAA guest room security requirements. 36 units. 4 stories, interior corridors. *Bath:* shower only. **Amenities:** safes. **Pool(s):** outdoor. **Activities:** exercise room. **Guest Services:** complimentary laundry.

## DOUBLETREE BY HILTON HOTEL QUERETARO

442/368-3000

[fyi] Not evaluated. **Address:** Luis M Vega y Monroy 410, Col Cimatario 76030 **Location:** Just e of Ave Louis Pasteur. Facilities, services, and décor characterize a mid-scale property.

**AAA Benefit:**
Members save 5% or more!

## GRAN HOTEL QUERETARO

442/251-8050

[fyi] **Hotel Address:** Juárez Sur No. 5 Centro Historico 76000 **Location:** In Centro Historico. Facilities, services, and décor characterize a mid-scale property.

## QUINTA ZOE

442/365-7818

[fyi] Not evaluated. **Address:** Vergara Sur 22, Col Centro **Location:** Centro; just sw of Plaza de Armas. Facilities, services, and décor characterize an economy property. A quaint, unique and American owned B&B in a central location.

**WHERE TO EAT**

## CHUCHO EL ROTO

442/212-4295

**Mexican. Casual Dining.** $8-$26 **AAA Inspector Notes:** Named after Mexico's Robin Hood, this colonial-style spot facing the famed Plaza de Armas offers uniquely regional dishes like tlayudas--a piece of meat hidden in a pyramid-shaped tamale bathed in classic ranchero red sauce. At night, live music pumps up the energy level. **Features:** full bar, patio dining, happy hour. **Reservations:** suggested. **Address:** Luis Pasteur 16 76000 **Location:** Plaza de Armas; in Centro Historico. **Parking:** no self-parking.

B  L  D  CALL

## COCONO GUSTO MEXICANO

442/223-2022

**Mexican. Fine Dining.** $12-$40 **AAA Inspector Notes:** Steps from the historic aqueduct arches, the food is exotically Mexican with classic ceviche, a variety of moles and six salsas, including Mayan xnipec. The manager details the seasonally changing daily specials and fresh seafood selections. **Features:** full bar. **Reservations:** suggested. **Address:** Blvd Bernardo Quintana No.18, Col La Calesa 76020 **Location:** Just n of aqueduct arches. **Parking:** valet only.

L  D

## EL COMEDOR DE LA MARQUESA

442/212-0092

**Regional International. Fine Dining.** $15-$45 **AAA Inspector Notes:** *Historic.* Although the menu is Mexican, it exhibits notable European influences in such dishes such as lamb chops with mint sauce and fusilli Alfredo. **Features:** full bar. **Reservations:** suggested. **Address:** Madero No. 41 Esq Allende 76000 **Location:** Downtown; in historico district; in La Casa de la Marquesa. **Parking:** valet and street only.

B  L  D

---

Ask your AAA/CAA club about travel money
and other financial services for travelers

## EMILIA

442/218-8455

▼▼▼ Regional Italian. Fine Dining. $12-$35 **AAA Inspector Notes:** Located at the entrance to the upscale Jurica development, this casually upscale restaurant focuses on Italian fare, including pizza cooked in a wood-burning oven, pasta and chicken dishes and steak. Mexican specialties round out the menu. The interior, with its high ceilings and brick arches, is reminiscent of an old hacienda. Outside you'll find a beautiful garden patio. This place has become a very popular spot in the upscale Jurica area. **Features:** full bar, patio dining. **Reservations:** suggested. **Address:** Priv de Los Industriales No. 105 76100 **Location:** Just off Mex 57, s on frontage road, at entrance to Jurica zona. L D

## JOSECHO

442/216-0201

▼▼▼ Regional International. Fine Dining. $15-$29 **AAA Inspector Notes:** The restaurant, popular among the business class, features Continental and Mexican dishes served by a well-trained staff in a contemporary, stylish dining room. Menu highlights include New Zealand lamb chops, Kobe beef, Dover sole and medallions of beef with huitlacoche topping. You'll find a variety of nicely complementing vintages on the impressive wine list. **Features:** full bar. **Reservations:** suggested. **Address:** Dalia No. 1, Fracc Orquideas 76000 **Location:** On Mex 45 (Celaya Libre), just w of jct Mex 57. **Parking:** valet only. L D

## LOS ARCOS RESTAURANT

442/192-0202

▼▼ Mexican. Casual Dining. $11-$25 **AAA Inspector Notes:** This colonial-style restaurant offers both a buffet and a la carte service. On the menu you'll find a wide, flavorful array of classic Mexican soups, salads and entrées, including chicken enchiladas, fried tacos, steaks and seafood dishes. Don't miss the house-made desserts. **Features:** full bar, Sunday brunch. **Address:** Ave 5 de Febrero No. 110, Niños Heroes 76010 **Location:** On Mex 57, 0.6 mi (1 km) n of jct Mex 45 and 45-D (toll road) exit Ave 5 de Febrero; in Holiday Inn Queretaro Centro Historico. **Parking:** on-site (fee) and valet.

B L D

## LOS HULES

442/218-0022

▼▼ Regional Mexican. Fine Dining. $6-$18 **AAA Inspector Notes:** Overlooking the majestic grounds of a 1600s former hacienda, the restaurant lets guests savor Mexican cuisine indoors or on a garden terrace. There's a breakfast buffet for those that are very hungry or in a hurry as well as a la carte selection for lingering over your meal. **Features:** full bar, patio dining, Sunday brunch. **Address:** Paseo Jurica Esquina Paseo del Meson S/N **Location:** Mex 57 exit Jurica, 2.5 mi (4 km) w; end of Jurica development; in Hotel Hacienda Jurica Queretaro. **Parking:** on-site and valet.

B L D

## MARISCOS SINALOA

442/217-1374

▼▼ Seafood. Casual Dining. $12-$28 **AAA Inspector Notes:** Sporting simple décor and offering fast-paced service, this inland restaurant serves Sinaloan-style seafood that is very fresh. This is a great place to linger with a savory seafood cocktail, or a whole grilled redfish accompanied by fresh-made tortillas and salsas. **Features:** full bar, patio dining. **Address:** Prol. Tecnologico No. 1002 76100 **Location:** Just s of Ave Bernardo Quintana. L D

## RESTAURANTE BAR 1810

442/161-0192

◆◆ International. Casual Dining. $10-$19 **AAA Inspector Notes:** International and Mexican specialties are served in a lively atmosphere. On the varied menu are pasta dishes, glazed duck, steaks, fish and shrimp. Chile en nogada--poblano peppers stuffed with sweetly seasoned ground beef and topped with walnut sauce and pomegranate seeds--serves as a good introduction to regional cuisine. The outdoor patio is on the Plaza de Armas and offers prime opportunities for interesting people-watching. **Features:** full bar, patio dining, Sunday brunch. **Reservations:** suggested. **Address:** Andador La Libertad No. 62 **Location:** Plaza de Armas; in Centro Historico. **Parking:** street only.

B L D

## SUSHI ITTO

442/215-6048

◆◆ Sushi. Casual Dining. $9-$18 **AAA Inspector Notes:** Featuring Japanese food served fast in a casual setting, the restaurant boasts an extensive menu, a full bar and both indoor and outdoor seating. My favorites include the California roll and chicken teriyaki. **Features:** full bar, patio dining. **Address:** Ave Constituyentes Poniente No. 180 **Location:** On Mex 45 (Celaya Libre), just w of jct Mex 57. **Parking:** on-site and street.

L D

# REAL DE CATORCE, SAN LUIS POTOSÍ

## HOTEL RUINAS DEL REAL

488/887-5066

fyi Not evaluated. **Address:** Libertad S/N **Location:** Jct Lerdo de Tejada. Facilities, services, and décor characterize a mid-scale property.

# SAN JUAN DEL RÍO, QUERÉTARO (D-3)

### pop. 241,699, elev. 6,498'

## FIESTA AMERICANA HACIENDA GALINDO

(427)271-8200

▼▼▼ Classic Historic Hotel $135-$290 **Address:** Carr a Amealco KM 5 76800 **Location:** On Mex 57, 23 mi (37 km) e, exit KM 172, 3.8 mi (6 km) s on Mex 120 toward Galindo, exit Amealco Galindo. Located in the country. **Facility:** Spectacular 16th-century hacienda has been converted and is extensively decorated with period art; beautiful grounds, pools, stables and a chapel. Meets AAA guest room security requirements. 168 units. 3 stories (no elevator), interior corridors. **Parking:** on-site and valet. **Amenities:** safes. **Pool(s):** heated outdoor. **Activities:** miniature golf, tennis, bicycles, playground, game room, exercise room. **Guest Services:** valet laundry.

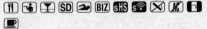

## HOLIDAY INN EXPRESS

427/101-9200

fyi Not evaluated. **Address:** Ave Paseo Central No. 23, Fracc Industrial Valle de Oro 76803 **Location:** On Paseo Central, just n of Camino A Santa Cruz. Facilities, services, and décor characterize a mid-scale property.

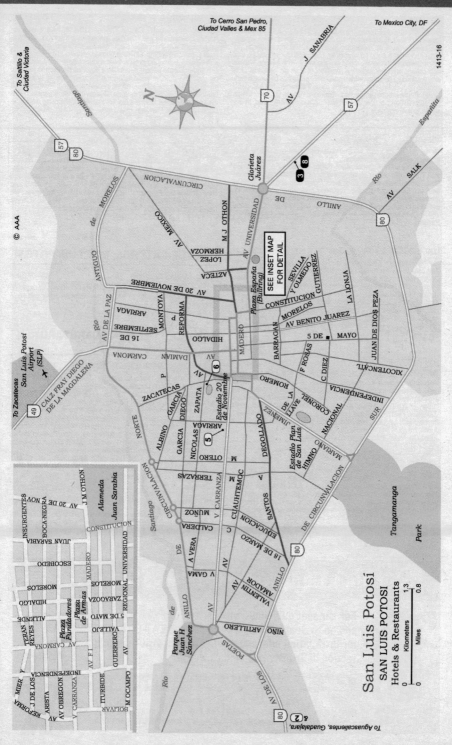

San Luis Potosí
SAN LUIS POTOSI
Hotels & Restaurants

To Cerro San Pedro,
Ciudad Valles & Mex 85

To Mexico City, DF

To Saltillo &
Ciudad Victoria

To Zacatecas

San Luis Potosi
Airport (SLP)

To Aguascalientes, Guadalajara

© AAA

1413-16

Glorieta
Juárez

J SANABRIA

AV

Española

Río

AV SALK

ANILLO DE

CIRCUNVALACION

de MORELOS

ANTIGUO

AV MEXICO

M J OTHON

AV UNIVERSIDAD

HERMOZA

LOPEZ

AZTECA

Plaza España
(Bullring)

SEE INSET MAP
FOR DETAIL

SEVILLA
Y OLMEDO

GUTIERREZ

CONSTITUCION

LA LONJA

AV 20 DE NOVIEMBRE

REFORMA

HIDALGO

MADERO

MORELOS

AV BENITO JUAREZ

JUAN DE DIOS PEZA

BARRAGAN

5 DE MAYO

XICOTENCATL

AV DE LA PAZ

ARRIAGA

16 DE SEPTIEMBRE

MONTOYA

CARMONA

DAMIAN

AV

F ROSAS

C DIEZ

INDEPENDENCIA

CORONEL

NACIONAL

SUR

P

DIEGO

GARCIA

ZACATECAS

ZAPATA

Estadio 20
de Noviembre

ROMERO

DE LA
LLAVE

JIMENEZ

Estadio Plan
de San Luis

MARIANO

ALBINO

GARCIA

NICOLAS

ARRIAGA

DEGOLLADO

HIMNO

OTERO

M

NORTE

TERRAZAS

CUAUHTEMOC

V

SANTOS

A

DE CIRCUNVALACION

Tangamanga
Park

CIRCUNVALACION

Santiago

MUÑOZ

CALDERA

C

EDUCACION

80

DE

A VERA

AV

V GAMA

AV

18 DE MARZO

ANILLO

VALENTIN AMADOR

Parque
Juan H
Sánchez

de

ANILLO

AV

NIÑO ARTILLERO

Río

AV DE LOS POETAS

80

4 2

INSET MAP:

J M OTHON

INSURGENTES

BOCA NEGRA

AV 20 DE NOV

Alameda

Juan Sarabia

JUAN SARABIA

CONSTITUCION

MADERO

REGIONAL UNIVERSIDAD

ESCOBEDO

MORELOS

ZARAGOZA

5 DE MAYO

HIDALGO

ALLENDE

TERAN

REFORMA

REYES

Plaza
Fundadores

Plaza
de Armas

GUERRERO

VALLEJO

AV

AV CARMONA

MIER Y

J DE LOS

ARISTA

V OBREGON

V CARRANZA

BOLIVAR

INDEPENDENCIA

ITURBIDE

M OCAMPO

80

57

70

57

80

49

N

3 8

6

5

Kilometers   1,3
Miles         0,8

0
0

## San Luis Potosi

This index helps you "spot" where approved hotels and restaurants are located on the corresponding detailed maps. Hotel daily rate range is for comparison only. Restaurant price range is a combination of lunch and/or dinner. Turn to the listing page for more detailed rate and price information and consult display ads for special promotions.

### SAN LUIS POTOSÍ, SAN LUIS POTOSÍ

| Map Page | Hotels | Diamond Rated | Rate Range | Page |
|---|---|---|---|---|
| **3** p. 542 | Holiday Inn Express San Luis Potosi | ▼▼▼ | Rates not provided | 544 |
| **8** p. 542 | Courtyard by Marriott | ▼▼▼ | $73-$120 | 544 |

| Map Page | Restaurants | Diamond Rated | Cuisine | Price Range | Page |
|---|---|---|---|---|---|
| ② p. 542 | La Boveda | ▼▼▼ | International | $12-$30 | 544 |
| ⑤ p. 542 | La Oruga y La Cebada | ▼▼ | Mexican | $7-$15 | 544 |
| ⑥ p. 542 | Restaurante La Gran Via | ▼▼▼ | International | $8-$22 | 544 |

## SAN LUIS POTOSÍ, SAN LUIS POTOSÍ

(C-2) pop. 772,604, elev. 6,157'
• Hotels & Restaurants map & index p. 542

### COURTYARD BY MARRIOTT                    (444)834-5700  [8]

▼▼▼ Hotel $73-$120 **Address:** Ave Benito Juárez No. 1220 78399 **Location:** 1.8 mi (3 km) s on Mex 57. **Facility:** 155 units. 6 stories, interior corridors. **Amenities:** *Some:* safes. **Pool(s):** heated indoor. **Activities:** hot tub, exercise room. **Guest Services:** valet and coin laundry, area transportation.

**AAA Benefit:** Members save 5% or more!

### HOLIDAY INN EXPRESS SAN LUIS POTOSI          (444)499-9000  [3]

▼▼▼ Hotel. Rates not provided. **Address:** Ave Benito Juárez No. 1270 78399 **Location:** 1.8 mi (3 km) s on Mex 57. **Facility:** 124 units. 7 stories, interior corridors. *Bath:* shower only. **Pool(s):** heated outdoor. **Activities:** hot tub, exercise room. **Guest Services:** valet laundry, area transportation.

### CITY SUITES                               444/826-9900

[fyi] Not evaluated. **Address:** Carr 57 No. 1530, Zona Industrial **Location:** On Mex 57, 0.6 mi (1 km) se. Facilities, services, and décor characterize a mid-scale property.

### HILTON SAN LUIS POTOSI                    444/825-0125

[fyi] Not evaluated. **Address:** Avenida Real de Lomas 1000 78210 **Location:** 2.1 mi (3.5 km) sw on Carr SLP-Guadalajara. Facilities, services, and décor characterize an upscale property.

**AAA Benefit:** Members save 5% or more!

### HOLIDAY INN QUIJOTE                       444/834-4100

[fyi] Not evaluated. **Address:** Carr Central S/N Zona Industrial 78090 **Location:** 3 mi (5 km) se on Mex 57. Facilities, services, and décor characterize a mid-scale property.

### HOTEL REAL DE MINAS                       444/499-8400

[fyi] Not evaluated. **Address:** Carr 57 Central KM 426.6 **Location:** On Mex 57; 0.6 mi (1 km) se of Glorieta Juárez; 0.3 mi (0.5 km) s of Distribuidora Juárez. Facilities, services, and décor characterize an economy property.

### HOTEL REAL PLAZA                          444/814-6055

[fyi] Not evaluated. **Address:** Ave Venustiano Carranza 890 **Location:** In heart of downtown. Facilities, services, and décor characterize an economy property.

### WHERE TO EAT

### LA BOVEDA                                 444/825-0125  [2]

▼▼▼ International. Fine Dining. $12-$30 **AAA Inspector Notes:** Beef and seafood figure prominently in the Mexican specialties served in this elegant dining room, which is located inside an upscale hotel. A buffet is offered at lunch. **Features:** full bar, Sunday brunch. **Reservations:** suggested. **Address:** Avenida Real de Lomas 1000 78210 **Location:** 2.1 mi (3.5 km) sw on Carr SLP-Guadalajara; in Hilton San Luis Potosi. **Parking:** on-site and valet.

[B] [L] [D]

### LA ORUGA Y LA CEBADA                      444/812-4508  [5]

▼▼ Mexican. Casual Dining. $7-$15 **AAA Inspector Notes:** Tucked away on a tight side street, this small, local favorite is worth seeking out. The menu includes classic regional dishes such as spicy enchiladas Potosinas and tender arrechera steak. **Features:** full bar. **Address:** Callejon de Lozada No. 1 **Location:** Centro. **Parking:** street only. [B] [L] [D]

### RESTAURANTE LA GRAN VIA                   444/812-2899  [6]

▼▼▼ International. Fine Dining. $8-$22 **AAA Inspector Notes:** Translated to read the great street, this well known local favorite delights diners with a delicious variety of classic Mexican dishes in an informal and relaxed setting. **Features:** full bar. **Address:** Ave Venustiano Carranza No. 560 78000 **Location:** Colonia Centro, nw of jct aves Venustiano Carranza and de Reforma. **Parking:** valet and street only. [L] [D]

## SAN MIGUEL DE ALLENDE, GUANAJUATO (C-2) pop. 160,383, elev. 6,134'

### ANTIGUA VILLA SANTA MONICA                415/152-0427

▼▼▼ Historic Country Inn $221-$336 **Address:** Fray Jose Guadalupe Mojica No. 22 **Location:** Facing Benito Juárez Park. **Facility:** This very attractive, intimate inn sits on well-landscaped grounds, in a building over 230 years old. The unique rooms all face an interior courtyard. 12 units. 1 story, exterior corridors. **Amenities:** safes. **Pool(s):** outdoor. **Guest Services:** valet laundry.

### ATOTONILCO EL VIEJO RANCHO HOTEL          415/185-2131

▼▼ Hotel $132-$195 **Address:** Carr Santuario Atotonilco S/N **Location:** 0.6 mi (1 km) w off Dolores Hidalgo Hwy to Atotonilco. **Facility:** 32 units. 2 stories (no elevator), exterior corridors. **Amenities:** safes. **Pool(s):** heated outdoor, heated indoor. **Activities:** hot tub, tennis, recreation programs in season, playground, game room, exercise room, spa. **Guest Services:** valet laundry.

### BELMOND CASA DE SIERRA NEVADA   (415)152-7040

▼▼▼▼ Historic Country Inn $350-$550

**Address:** Hospicio No. 35 37700 **Location:** Just se of main plaza; 1/2 blk off Recreo. **Facility:** Various buildings on elegant grounds with beautiful gardens, period antiques and exceptional service make this hotel a wonderful and memorable experience. Some suites have a small private pool. Meets AAA guest room security requirements. 37 units. 2 stories (no elevator), exterior corridors. **Parking:** on-site (fee) and valet. **Terms:** 7 day cancellation notice-fee imposed. **Amenities:** safes. **Dining:** Andanza at Casa de Sierra Nevada, see separate listing. **Pool(s):** heated outdoor. **Activities:** spa. **Guest Services:** valet laundry, area transportation.

### CASA DE LOS OLIVOS HOTEL                  415/154-9874

▼▼▼ Bed & Breakfast $215-$300 **Address:** Correo 30, Centro 37700 **Location:** East of Jardin; in Centro Historico. **Facility:** Sophisticated and intimate, this comfy hotel in the heart of town offers tastefully decorated rooms, a pleasant rooftop terrace. Meets AAA guest room security requirements. 5 units. 1 story, exterior corridors. **Parking:** valet and street only. **Terms:** age restrictions may apply. **Amenities:** safes. **Activities:** massage. **Guest Services:** valet laundry.

### CASA LIZA                                 (415)152-0352

▼▼▼ Bed & Breakfast $180-$240 **Address:** Bajada del Chorro No. 7 Centro 37700 **Location:** 3 blks se of main plaza; between Recreo and Calle de Chorro. Located at the edge of the historico district. **Facility:** Lush gardens invite outdoor lounging at this B&B notable for its guest room décor. The property sits in a quiet neighborhood only a city park only steps away. Many units with fireplace. 9 units, some kitchens and cottages. 2 stories (no elevator), exterior corridors. **Activities:** hot tub. **Guest Services:** valet laundry.

## CASA PUESTA DEL SOL
415/152-0220

▼▼▼ **Bed & Breakfast** $120-$190 **Address:** Fuentes No. 12 **Location:** Jct Pedro Vargas (Queretaro Hwy), just e on Santo Domingo, just ne. **Facility:** High in the residential area above the village and tucked into a tiered garden, you'll find a waterfall with fountains to cool the day at this inn. 7 units, some two bedrooms and kitchens. 2 stories (no elevator), interior/exterior corridors. **Parking:** street only. **Activities:** massage. **Guest Services:** valet laundry.

🚪 🍽️ BIZ 🛜 ✕ AC /SOME UNITS 🐾 🛗 🖨️

## CASA SCHUCK BOUTIQUE B&B
(415)152-0657

▼▼▼ **Bed & Breakfast** $246-$351 **Address:** Bajada de La Garita No. 3 37700 **Location:** 4 blks e of main plaza. **Facility:** A lovely fountained courtyard and a rooftop patio with a view to the Parroquia provide guests a tranquil environment and scenic surroundings. 10 units. 2 stories (no elevator), exterior corridors. **Parking:** no self-parking. **Terms:** age restrictions may apply. **Amenities:** safes. **Pool(s):** outdoor. **Activities:** massage. **Guest Services:** valet laundry.

🚪 🍽️ 🏊 BIZ 🛜 ✕ AC 🛎️

## HOTEL COQUETE
415/152-2289

▼ **Hotel** $161-$275 **Address:** Cuadrante No. 3 37700 **Location:** 1 blk e of main plaza; centro. **Facility:** Meets AAA guest room security requirements. 14 units. 3 stories (no elevator), interior corridors. **Parking:** valet only. **Terms:** 5 day cancellation notice. **Pool(s):** outdoor. **Guest Services:** valet laundry.

🏊 🛜 /SOME UNITS HS AC 🖨️

## HOTEL HACIENDA TABOADA
415/152-9250

▼▼ **Hotel** $152-$248 **Address:** KM 8 Carr a Dolores Hidalgo Hwy **Location:** 4.8 mi (8 km) on San Miguel de Allende Dolores Hidalgo Hwy (Mex 51), 1.8 mi (3 km) w, follow signs. Located in a quiet area. **Facility:** 70 units. 3 stories (no elevator), exterior corridors. **Terms:** cancellation fee imposed. **Pool(s):** heated outdoor. **Activities:** hot tub, tennis, recreation programs in season, playground, exercise room, spa. **Guest Services:** valet laundry.

🍽️ 🏊 🛗 🛜 ✕

## HOTEL MATILDA
(415)152-1015

▼▼▼ **Boutique Contemporary Hotel** $524-$1322 **Address:** Aldama No. 53, Col Centro 37700 **Location:** 3 blks s of Plaza Principal. **Facility:** A surprising treat, this contemporary property is hidden behind a colonial-style courtyard wall. A luxurious full-service spa with custom apothecary services is on the premises. Meets AAA guest room security requirements. 32 units. 3 stories, interior corridors. **Parking:** valet only. **Amenities:** safes. **Dining:** Moxi, see separate listing. **Pool(s):** heated outdoor. **Activities:** exercise room, spa. **Guest Services:** valet laundry, boarding pass kiosk, area transportation.

🚪 🍽️ 🛗 🛎️ SD 🏊 HS 🛜 ✕ 🐾 🖨️ /SOME UNITS 🍽️ 🖨️

## HOTEL MONTEVERDE BEST INNS
415/152-1814

**fyi** **Hotel.** Rates not provided. Under major renovation, scheduled to be completed December 2015. **Last Rated:** ▼▼ **Address:** Volantores No. 2, Col Centro **Location:** 0.5 mi (0.8 km) nw of central plaza, jct Calzada de La Luz and Mex 57. **Facility:** 40 units. 2 stories (no elevator), exterior corridors. **Bath:** shower only. **Terms:** 2-5 night minimum stay - seasonal and/or weekends, 30 day cancellation notice-fee imposed, resort fee. **Guest Services:** valet laundry.

🍽️ 🛗 🛎️ SD 🛜 AC

## HOTEL POSADA DE LA ALDEA
415/152-1022

▼ **Historic Hotel** $117-$170 **Address:** Calle Ancha de San Antonio No. 15 37700 **Location:** 0.6 mi (1 km) s on Mex 49 (Celaya Hwy). **Facility:** Within walking distance of the plaza, this hotel on the southwest end of town offers wireless Internet in all rooms and ample parking. This is one of the town's few hotels with air conditioning. Meets AAA guest room security requirements. 65 units. 3 stories, interior corridors. **Bath:** shower only. **Terms:** 5 day cancellation notice. **Pool(s):** heated outdoor. **Activities:** tennis, exercise room. **Guest Services:** valet laundry.

🍽️ 🛗 🛎️ CALL 🈁M 🏊 BIZ 🛜 ✕

## LA PUERTECITA BOUTIQUE HOTEL
(415)152-5011

▼▼▼ **Country Inn** $238-$322

**Address:** Santo Domingo No. 75 37740 **Location:** Jct Pedro Vargas (Queretaro Hwy), 0.4 mi (0.6 km) e. Located in affluent Atascadero neighborhood. **Facility:** On a hilltop overlooking the city, the inn's picturesque gardens and waterfalls create a retreat-like ambiance. Many rooms feature fireplaces. 24 units. 3 stories (no elevator), interior/exterior corridors. **Parking:** on-site and valet. **Amenities:** safes. **Dining:** La Puertecita Restaurante, see separate listing. **Pool(s):** outdoor, heated outdoor. **Activities:** hot tub, exercise room, massage. **Guest Services:** valet laundry, area transportation.

🚪 🍽️ 🛗 🛎️ 🏊 🛜 AC

## ROSEWOOD SAN MIGUEL DE ALLENDE
(415)152-9700

▼▼▼ ▼▼▼ **Hotel** $290-$2580 **Address:** Nemesio Diez 11, Colonia Centro 37700 **Location:** Just e of jct San Antonio; 5 blks se of main plaza. Located in a quiet residential area. **Facility:** These luxurious, hacienda-style accommodations feature large, dramatic guest rooms, balconies and landscaped areas. The property's circular design makes the refined, central courtyard a focal point. 67 units. 4 stories, interior corridors. **Parking:** valet only. **Amenities:** safes. **Dining:** 1826 Restaurant, Luna, see separate listings. **Pool(s):** heated outdoor. **Activities:** sauna, hot tub, steamroom, recreation programs, kids club, exercise room, spa. **Guest Services:** valet laundry, area transportation.

🚪 🍽️ 🛗 🛎️ 🏋️ CALL 🈁M S SD 🏊 BIZ HS 🛜 ✕ 🐾 🖨️ /SOME UNITS 🍽️ 🖨️ 🖨️

## VILLA MIRASOL HOTEL
(415)152-6685

▼▼ **Bed & Breakfast** $115-$180 **Address:** Pila Seca No. 35 **Location:** Just 4 blks sw of main plaza. **Facility:** A quiet location lends a relaxing ambiance to this lodging, which combines style with comfort and convenience. 12 units, some efficiencies. 3 stories (no elevator), exterior corridors. **Parking:** street only. **Terms:** 15 day cancellation notice-fee imposed. **Guest Services:** valet laundry.

🍽️ BIZ 🛜 ✕ /SOME UNITS AC 🖨️ 🖨️ 🖨️

## DOS CASAS LUXURY BED & BREAKFAST
415/154-4073

**fyi** Not evaluated. **Address:** Quebrada 101 37700 **Location:** 4 blks e of main plaza. Facilities, services, and décor characterize an upscale property. Upscale décor and furnishings await.

## HACIENDA DE GUADALUPE HOTEL BOUTIQUE
415/121-0700

**fyi** Not evaluated. **Address:** Hidalgo No. 4, Col Centro 37700 **Location:** Just n of Plaza Principal. Facilities, services, and décor characterize an upscale property. In a great location, the property boasts beautiful, newly restored architecture.

## HOTEL CASA ROSADA
415/154-5410

**fyi** Not evaluated. **Address:** Cuna de Allende 12; Colonia Centro 37700. Facilities, services, and décor characterize a mid-scale property.

---

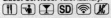
**WHERE TO EAT**

## 1826 RESTAURANT
415/152-9701

▼▼ ▼▼▼ Regional Mexican. Fine Dining. $12-$35 **AAA Inspector Notes:** The talented chef presents a unique and creative interpretation of regional cuisine. Attentive, personalized service and upscale décor add to an excellent dining experience. The chef's own specialties, such as dual-colored gazpacho, are not to be missed. **Features:** full bar, patio dining, Sunday brunch. **Reservations:** suggested. **Address:** Nemesio Diez 11, Col Centro 37700 **Location:** Just e of jct San Antonio; 5 blks se of main plaza; in Rosewood San Miguel de Allende. **Parking:** valet and street only. B L D CALL 🈁M

## ANDANZA AT CASA DE SIERRA NEVADA
415/152-7040

▼▼▼ Traditional Continental. Fine Dining. $8-$27 **AAA Inspector Notes:** *Historic.* Most would never guess this eatery sits just southeast of the bustling main plaza; its lovely garden courtyard provides upscale tranquility...perfect for special occasions. For a more formal outing, request the dining room. The Continental menu is diverse in its offerings. **Features:** full bar, patio dining. **Reservations:** suggested. **Address:** Hospicio 42 37700 **Location:** Just se of main plaza; 1/2 blk off Recreo; in Belmond Casa de Sierra Nevada. **Parking:** valet and street only. B L D AC

## ANTIGUA TRATTORIA ROMANA
415/152-3790

▼▼▼ ◆ Italian. Casual Dining. $9-$25 **AAA Inspector Notes:** Popular with locals and near the Instituto Allende, this hide-away prepares a modest selection of rich pasta entrées in a friendly, laid-back, village-style atmosphere. **Features:** full bar. **Address:** Codo No. 9 **Location:** 3 blks s of main plaza. **Parking:** street only.

 L D AC

## APERI
415/152-0941

▼▼▼▼ ◆ New International. Fine Dining. $22-$30 **AAA Inspector Notes:** Within this historic building is a surprisingly chic and stylish dining room where chef Matteo Salas brings inspired creativity to a constantly changing seasonal menu with bold, complex flavors and unique presentations. The chef's table—featuring a specially created menu and "ringside" seats in the kitchen—is the city's hottest ticket. **Features:** full bar, patio dining. **Reservations:** required. **Address:** 101 Quebrada **Location:** Jct Umaran, just w of Jardin. **Parking:** valet only. L D ✎

## EL PEGASO
415/152-1351

▼▼▼ ◆ International. Casual Dining. $8-$20 **AAA Inspector Notes:** Few of the city's many restaurants offer the charming service for which this place is known—friendly and laid-back but with an eye and instinct for anticipating a diner's every need. The international menu offers something for everyone, including chicken enchiladas, a tasty Reuben sandwich and sushi. Among the varied desserts are cakes, flan and pies. Local artists' creations, some quite humorous, line the walls. **Features:** full bar. **Address:** Corregidora No. 6 **Location:** 1 blk w of main plaza; centro. **Parking:** street only.

B L D AC

## EL TEN TEN PIE RESTAURANTE
415/152-7189

▼▼▼ ◆ Mexican. Casual Dining. $8-$14 **AAA Inspector Notes:** You'll find this subdued sidewalk café just behinds the famed Parroquia cathedral. The name means quick little snacks, such as huevos rancheros, enchiladas, breaded steak and chicken sandwiches. Thursday through Saturday evenings you'll hear really cool yet spicy live jazz and Latin music. **Features:** beer & wine, patio dining. **Address:** Cuna de Allende 19 37700 **Location:** Jct Calle Cauadrante, 1 blk s of main plaza. **Parking:** no self-parking.

B L D AC ✎

## EL TOMATO, COCINA ARGENTINA
415/154-6390

▼▼▼ ◆ Argentine. Casual Dining. $6-$10 **AAA Inspector Notes:** This diminutive, friendly eatery features Argentinian fusion fare and is famous for its juicy steaks and flaky empanadas. The staff makes you feel at home while the décor provides a warm, home like ambience. **Features:** beer & wine. **Address:** Mesones No. 62 A & B, Centro **Location:** Just n of main plaza. **Parking:** street only.

L D AC

## HANK'S NEW ORLEANS CAFE
415/152-2645

▼▼▼ ◆ Cajun. Casual Dining. $15-$23 **AAA Inspector Notes:** Fresh shrimp cocktail, spicy jambalaya, and blacken seafare served in stylish, contemporary surroundings offering a definite American experience. **Features:** full bar, Sunday brunch. **Reservations:** suggested. **Address:** Hidalgo No. 12 37700 **Location:** Just n of main plaza; centro. **Parking:** street only. L D LATE AC

## HECHO EN MEXICO
415/154-6383

▼▼▼ ◆ International. Casual Dining. $8-$22 **AAA Inspector Notes:** The bilingual staff greets guests with friendly smiles. Southern touches enhance dishes such as sweet potato casserole, while others, such as cactus salad, center on Mexican elements. Dessert portions are big enough to share. Simple décor characterizes the inviting enclosed courtyard at this spot next to Instituto Allende. **Features:** full bar, patio dining. **Address:** Calle Ancha de San Antonio 8 37700 **Location:** 1 blk w from Pila Seca and Zacateros. **Parking:** street only. L D AC

## LA CASA DEL DIEZMO
415/154-4034

▼▼▼ ◆ Regional Mexican. Casual Dining. $9-$18 **AAA Inspector Notes:** The owners recently moved to central Mexico from Merida and opened this stylish Yucatecan restaurant. Discover all the classics like lime soup, cochinita pibil and tikin xic-style fish in this beautiful colonial setting while being attended to by the gracious owners. **Features:** full bar, patio dining. **Reservations:** suggested. **Address:** De Jesus 36, Col Centro 37700 **Location:** 3 blks s of main plaza, between calles Cuadrante and Terraplen. **Parking:** street only.

 L D AC

## LA MEZCALERIA
415/121-5354

▼▼ ◆ International Small Plates. Casual Dining. $8-$18 **AAA Inspector Notes:** This cozy restaurant features a seasonal menu of creative tapas based on the cuisine of Oaxaca. On the menu you'll find perfectly cooked, whole-grilled octopus, as well as huitlacoche-stuffed mushrooms. Make a point of trying a flight from the extensive list of mescal, to sip straight-up or in a creative cocktail. **Features:** patio dining. **Reservations:** suggested. **Address:** 47 Correo **Location:** Just e of Jardin. **Parking:** no self-parking.

L D AC

## LA PARADA
415/152-0473

▼▼▼ ◆ Peruvian Small Plates. Casual Dining. $8-$18 **AAA Inspector Notes:** Looking for something a bit different? This cozy dining room serves up both authentic Peruvian food and distinctive charm. **Features:** full bar, patio dining. **Reservations:** suggested. **Address:** 94 Recreo **Location:** South of Jardin.

L D AC

## LA PUERTECITA RESTAURANTE
415/152-5011

▼▼▼ ◆ Regional International. Casual Dining. $11-$26 **AAA Inspector Notes:** Creative dishes in this hideaway location utilize seasonal, local ingredients. The huitlacoche crepes are a savory treat. Servings are plentiful, and service is friendly. **Features:** full bar. **Reservations:** suggested. **Address:** Santo Domingo No. 75 37740 **Location:** Jct Pedro Vargas (Queretaro Hwy), 0.4 mi (0.6 km) e; in La Puertecita Boutique Hotel. B L D AC

## LUNA
415/152-9700

▼▼▼ ◆ Mexican Small Plates. Casual Dining. $10-$20 **AAA Inspector Notes:** Enjoy breathtaking, 360-degree views of the city and a beautiful sunset while sampling an upscale, international tapas menu and sipping excellent margaritas or other creative cocktails. **Features:** full bar. **Reservations:** required. **Address:** 11 Nemesio Diaz **Location:** Just e of jct San Antonio; 5 blks se of main plaza; in Rosewood San Miguel de Allende. **Parking:** on-site (fee) and valet.

L D CALL  AC ✎

## MAMA MIA RESTAURANTE
415/152-2063

▼▼ ◆ Italian. Casual Dining. $10-$35 **AAA Inspector Notes:** Bohemian intimacy in a fun patio setting makes for a great place to enjoy fresh-made Italian specialties. The menu features crepes filled with zucchini flowers and corn mushrooms, seafood soup and enchiladas. At night, soft jazz and Latin music fills the air. **Features:** full bar, patio dining. **Reservations:** suggested. **Address:** De Jesus 8 37700 **Location:** 2 blks w of main plaza. **Parking:** street only.

L D LATE AC ✎

## MOXI
415/152-1015

▼▼▼ ◆ Regional New World. Fine Dining. $18-$35 **AAA Inspector Notes:** Enrique Olvera, of Mexico City's famed Pujol restaurant, has now opened Moxi (Otomi for 'craving') for an ultra-contemporary and exciting experience. I loved the lump crabmeat encased in paper thin wafers of potato. The wheat risotto with spinach, mini potatoes and a delicately poached egg is what dreams are made of. Mine anyway. **Features:** full bar, patio dining. **Reservations:** suggested. **Address:** Aldama No. 53, Col Centro 37700 **Location:** 3 blks s of Plaza Principal; in Hotel Matilda. **Parking:** valet only. L D CALL

## THE RESTAUARANT
415/154-7877

▼▼▼ ◆ New World. Casual Dining. $10-$28 **AAA Inspector Notes:** This place serves haute, exciting cuisine on a small side street near the Zocalo. Enjoy duck, crab cakes and exotic burgers artistically presented by a very knowledgeable staff. **Features:** full bar, patio dining, Sunday brunch. **Reservations:** suggested. **Address:** Soliano 16, Col Centro 37700 **Location:** 3 blks se from main plaza. **Parking:** street only. L D AC

## TIO LUCAS
415/152-4996

▼▼▼ ◆ Regional Steak. Casual Dining. $10-$25 **AAA Inspector Notes:** Specializing in American cuts, the restaurant offers thick steaks, juicy and full of flavor. However, it's the staff that truly makes the difference at this small and inviting spot. Personalized attention makes meals memorable in the lovely enclosed courtyard, which has a fountain, greenery and tin-star lanterns. Entertainers perform regularly. Delicious crepes prepared tableside are a fitting dessert choice. **Features:** full bar, patio dining. **Reservations:** suggested. **Address:** 103 Mesones Centro 37700 **Location:** 2 blks w of main plaza. **Parking:** valet and street only. L D AC

## XIPAL
415/154-5410

▼▼▼ Mexican. Fine Dining. $8-$20 AAA Inspector Notes: This colonial 1726 structure was formerly part of cathedral La Parroquia. On the refined, rooftop terrace you'll dine on fresh-made dishes made with locally sourced ingredients. The highly personalized service made me feel like I owned the place. Features: full bar, patio dining. Reservations: suggested. Address: Cuna de Allende 12, Colonia Centro 37700 Location: Jct Calle Cuadrante; in Hotel Casa Rosada. Parking: valet only.

## SILAO, GUANAJUATO pop. 173,024

### HAMPTON INN BY HILTON SILAO AEROPUERTO
(472)135-1000

▼▼▼ Hotel $68-$152 Address: Carr 45 Silao-Leon KM 152 y 550 Location: 4 mi (6.4 km) n of Mex 110 toll road to Guanajuato. Located in a quiet area, just n of city limits. Facility: Meets AAA guest room security requirements. 110 units. 6 stories, interior corridors. Terms: 1-7 night minimum stay, cancellation fee imposed. Amenities: safes. Pool(s): heated outdoor. Activities: exercise room. Guest Services: valet laundry, area transportation.

**AAA Benefit:** Members save up to 10%!

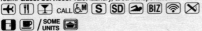

### HOLIDAY INN EXPRESS SILAO-AEROPUERTO BAJIO
(472)722-8000

▼▼▼ Hotel $80-$155 Address: Libramiento Nte No. 3360 36169 Location: On Mex 45 exit Silao. Facility: Meets AAA guest room security requirements. 165 units. 5 stories, interior corridors. Amenities: safes. Pool(s): heated indoor. Activities: exercise room. Guest Services: valet and coin laundry.

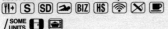

## TLAQUEPAQUE, JALISCO (C-1)
pop. 608,114

### CASA DE LAS FLORES
33/3659-3186

▼▼▼ Bed & Breakfast $100-$110 Address: Santos Degollado No. 175 45500 Location: Centro; 4 blks s of Plaza Hidalgo. Facility: Near the center of town, in a restored historic home, this B&B features colorful décor and artwork. A well-tended garden makes for a nice spot to relax. 7 units. 2 stories (no elevator), exterior corridors. Bath: shower only. Parking: on-site and street. Terms: age restrictions may apply. Guest Services: coin laundry.

### LA VILLA DEL ENSUENO
(33)3635-8792

▼▼▼ Boutique Hotel $120-$156 Address: Florida 305 45500 Location: 0.6 mi (1 km) w of El Parian. Facility: Although a wall makes the exterior of this property seem nondescript, the interior features fine examples of uniquely Mexican décor. The large rooms are colorfully decorated in the local style. 20 units, some efficiencies. 2 stories (no elevator), interior corridors. Pool(s): outdoor. Activities: hot tub. Guest Services: valet laundry.

### QUINTA DON JOSE BOUTIQUE HOTEL
33/3635-7522

▼▼▼ Boutique Hotel $80-$175 Address: Reforma No. 139 Centro 45500 Location: Centro. Facility: In the heart of town, this property has a variety of rooms, from singles to family units. All rooms feature classic Mexican décor, including colorful tiles, furniture and artwork. 19 units, some two bedrooms and kitchens. 2 stories (no elevator), interior/exterior corridors. Dining: TlaquePasta, see separate listing. Pool(s): outdoor. Guest Services: valet laundry.

## WHERE TO EAT

### ADOBE RESTAURANTE & BAR
33/3657-2792

▼▼▼ Mexican. Casual Dining. $12-$22 AAA Inspector Notes: Combined with a pottery and crafts shop, this colorful, lively restaurant and cantina serves large portions of well-prepared beef and chicken as well as a good selection of spirits. Homemade tortillas are always available. Festive, live entertainment adds to the ambiance. Features: full bar, patio dining. Address: Francisco de Miranda No. 27 45500 Location: Centro. Parking: street only.

### CASA FUERTE RESTAURANTE
33/3639-6481

▼▼▼ Mexican. Casual Dining. $12-$22 AAA Inspector Notes: This lively restaurant presents a fine menu of freshly prepared Mexican fare. Diners can request seating on the street-front patio, in the lovely open-air center courtyard or in the more sophisticated interior dining room. Live music adds to the ambiance. Menu highlights include stuffed peppers, sizzling fajitas and freshly grilled fish and other seafood. The tortillas here are always fresh. Features: full bar, patio dining. Reservations: suggested. Address: Independencia No. 224 45500 Location: Centro. Parking: street only.

### CASA LUNA
331/591-4735

▼▼▼ Mexican. Fine Dining. $12-$22 AAA Inspector Notes: Here in the heart of town you'll find truly authentic Mexican food and décor. Meals can be taken on the bustling sidewalk patio, in the courtyard patio where live music livens the setting, or inside surrounded by bright art. The chef has created a menu that blends both traditional and contemporary Mexican dishes in a creative and tempting way. The highly trained staff go out of their way to ensure you have an enjoyable, memorable dining experience. Features: full bar, patio dining. Address: Independencia No. 211 45500 Location: Centro. Parking: street only.

### EL ABAJENO TLAQUEPAQUE CAMPESTRE
333/635-9015

▼▼ Mexican. Casual Dining. $8-$16 AAA Inspector Notes: Very popular, the restaurant's large garden courtyard is a nice spot to enjoy local and regional Mexican eats. Also big here: barbecued steaks, chicken and ribs. On Saturdays and Sundays, diners should arrive early for the folkloric show at 4:30 pm. Features: full bar, patio dining. Reservations: suggested. Address: Ave Juárez 231 45500 Location: Jct Francisco Miranda.

### EL PATIO
33/3635-1108

▼▼▼ Mexican. Casual Dining. $9-$20 AAA Inspector Notes: Reservations are highly recommended at this bustling, authentic Mexican restaurant. Plants and flowers surround the wonderful patio courtyard, which has a festive feel thanks to live entertainment. Fresh tortillas, which factor into many of the home-style Mexican dishes, are prepared before your eyes. Groups should order a few of the featured platters. A large glass case near the entrance displays hard-to-resist desserts. Features: full bar, patio dining. Reservations: suggested. Address: Calle Peatonal Independencia No. 186 45500 Location: Centro. Parking: no self-parking.

### REAL SAN PEDRO
33/3659-3631

▼▼▼ Regional Mexican. Casual Dining. $12-$40 AAA Inspector Notes: Trendy, yet still able to maintain an old-fashioned Mexican art village feel, this lovely restaurant is set in a shaded courtyard complete with bubbling fountains. The sound of live music fills the air. Fine Mexican fare and exotic game fill the menu. Features: full bar. Address: Independencia No. 163 45500 Location: Centro. Parking: street only.

### TLAQUEPASTA
33/3635-7522

▼▼ International. Casual Dining. $9-$20 AAA Inspector Notes: This is a wonderful place to have a comfortable meal in a real Mexican village. The huge bright Mexican paintings on the adobe walls set the tone on arrival and from then on a pleasant staff and live music complete the package. The menu changes daily and is offered on a large white board reflecting the freshest of local and regional ingredients. Pasta and Mexican fare are equally represented. They open for lunch Friday, Saturday and Sunday at 2 pm. Features: full bar, patio dining. Address: Reforma No. 139 Centro 45500 Location: Centro; in Quinta Don Jose Boutique Hotel.

## URUAPAN, MICHOACÁN (D-2) pop. 315,350, elev. 5,491'

**HOLIDAY INN URUAPAN**     452/503-3700

[fyi] Not evaluated. **Address:** Blvd Industrial No. 1705, Col Villa Uruapan **Location:** Hwy Mexico-Morelea-Uruapan to Blvd Industrial. Facilities, services, and décor characterize a mid-scale property.

**HOTEL MANSION DEL CUPATITZIO**     452/523-2100

[fyi] Not evaluated. **Address:** Calz de La Rodilla del Diablo No. 20 **Location:** 0.3 mi (0.5 km) se of Mex 37 on Calz Fray Juan de San Miguel. Facilities, services, and décor characterize a mid-scale property.

### WHERE TO EAT

**RESTAURANTE MANSION DEL CUPATITZIO**     452/523-2100

▼▼▼▼ Mexican. Casual Dining. $7-$20 **AAA Inspector Notes:** Situated in a colonial-era mansion, this restaurant features a striking dining room as well as a beautiful patio set among lush gardens. The excellent appetizer sampler consists of quesadillas, crispy mini-tacos, grilled fajitas and enchiladas adorned with julienned onions and chiles. If you'd like to try a classic Mexican dish, we recommend the milanesa (breaded chicken or steak) with boiled chayote. **Features:** full bar, patio dining. **Address:** Calz de La Rodilla del Diablo No. 20 **Location:** 0.3 mi (0.5 km) se of Mex 37 on Calz Fray Juan de San Miguel; in Hotel Mansion del Cupatitzio. [B] [L] [D] [🍷] [🚭]

## ZACATECAS, ZACATECAS (B-1) pop. 138,176, elev. 8,115'

**HOTEL BARUK-TELEFERICO**     (492)922-0745

▼▼▼▼ Hotel. Rates not provided. **Address:** Paseo Diaz Ordaz No. 602, Col Centro **Location:** Adjacent to tramway station. On hilltop overlooking Zacatecas. **Facility:** 73 units, some two bedrooms, three bedrooms and kitchens. 1 story, interior corridors. **Amenities:** safes. **Activities:** exercise room. **Guest Services:** valet laundry.

[🍴] [🛎️] [🍸] [SD] [BIZ] [HS] [📶] [▭]
/ SOME UNITS [🍴] [🛗]

**HOTEL EMPORIO ZACATECAS**     (492)925-6500

▼▼▼▼
Historic Hotel
Rates not provided

**Address:** Ave Hidalgo No. 703 **Location:** On Plaza de Armas; centro. Located in historical district; opposite cathedral. **Facility:** Many of the property's rooms overlook a courtyard with a fountain, while some have patios. 113 units. 6 stories, interior corridors. **Parking:** on-site (fee) and valet. **Amenities:** safes. **Activities:** sauna, exercise room. **Guest Services:** valet laundry.

[🍴] [🛎️] [🍸] [SD] [BIZ] [HS] [📶]
[🚭] [🛗] [▭]

**SANTA RITA HOTEL**     (492)925-1194

▼▼▼▼ Boutique Hotel. Rates not provided. **Address:** Ave Hidalgo No. 507 98000 **Location:** Centro Historico. **Facility:** The colonial exterior belies the contemporary guest rooms featuring laminate flooring, luxurious bedding and modern light fixtures. 41 units. 7 stories, interior corridors. **Parking:** valet only. **Amenities:** safes. **Activities:** exercise room, spa. **Guest Services:** valet laundry.

[🍴] [🛎️] [🍸] [SD] [BIZ] [📶] [🛗]

**FIESTA INN ZACATECAS**     492/491-4930

[fyi] Not evaluated. **Address:** Calzada Heroes de Chapultepec KM 13 **Location:** On Carr Zacatecas-Morelos, just n of University de Durango. Facilities, services, and décor characterize a mid-scale property.

**HOTEL HACIENDA BARUK**     492/924-6666

[fyi] Not evaluated. **Address:** Heroes de Chapultepec 801 98054 **Location:** 2.4 mi (4 km) ne of centro on Guadalajara Rd; jct Mex 54. Facilities, services, and décor characterize a mid-scale property.

**MISION ARGENTO INN**     492/925-1718

[fyi] Not evaluated. **Address:** Ave Hidalgo No. 407 Centro **Location:** In Centro Historico. Facilities, services, and décor characterize a mid-scale property.

**QUINTA REAL ZACATECAS**     492/922-9104

[fyi] Not evaluated. **Address:** Ave Ignacio Rayon No. 434, Col Centro 98000 **Location:** 5 blks w of cathedral; beside Elcubo Aqueduct on Ave Gonzalez Ortega. Facilities, services, and décor characterize an upscale property.

### WHERE TO EAT

**LA PLAZA RESTAURANT**     492/922-9104

▼▼▼▼ Continental. Fine Dining. $12-$30 **AAA Inspector Notes:** This famous, elegant dining room overlooks the picturesque ruins of a historic bullring. Fresh seafood and savory cuisine from all sections of Mexico are complemented by an extraordinary wine list. The classic, formal service includes waiters wearing white gloves. **Features:** full bar. **Reservations:** suggested. **Address:** Ave Ignacio Rayon No. 434, Col Centro **Location:** 5 blks w of cathedral; beside Elcubo Aqueduct on Ave Gonzalez Ortega; in Quinta Real Zacatecas. **Parking:** valet only. [B] [L] [D] [LATE]

**LOS DORADOS DE VILLA**     492/922-5722

▼▼ Mexican. Casual Dining. $8-$17 **AAA Inspector Notes:** For traditional Northern Mexican cuisine, there aren't many better places than this tiny restaurant, which is appointed in folkloric decor. For a true taste of regional cuisine--and as they say, 'When in Rome ...'--enchiladas Zacatecanas stands out. The staff takes great pride in making menu items a la minute so guests can sit back, relax and rest assured it will be worth the wait. Reservations are highly recommended; those who don't make one risk being disappointed. **Features:** beer only. **Reservations:** suggested. **Address:** Plazuela de Garcia No. 1314 **Location:** Centro; north of cathedral; next to Museo Rafael Coronel. **Parking:** street only. [L] [D] [LATE] [🚭]

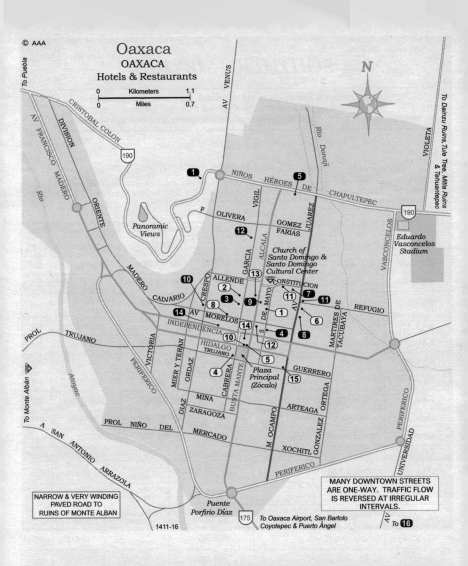

© AAA

# Oaxaca
## OAXACA
### Hotels & Restaurants

Kilometers  0 — 1.1
Miles  0 — 0.7

To Puebla

AV FRANCISCO MADERO

CRISTOBAL COLON

DIVISION

190

ORIENTE

Río Atoyac

MADERO

CALVARIO

PROL TRUJANO

PERIFERICO

VICTORIA

MIER Y TERAN

ORDAZ

DIAZ

PROL NIÑO DEL

A SAN ANTONIO ARRAZOLA

To Monte Albán

**NARROW & VERY WINDING PAVED ROAD TO RUINS OF MONTE ALBAN**

Panoramic Views

F

OLIVERA

CRESPO

GARCIA

ALLENDE

MORELOS

INDEPENDENCIA

HIDALGO

TRUJANO

CABRERA

BUSTAMANTE

MINA

ZARAGOZA

MERCADO

Puente Porfirio Díaz

1411-16

175

To Oaxaca Airport, San Bartolo Coyotepec & Puerto Ángel

AV VENUS

NIÑOS HÉROES DE CHAPULTEPEC

VIGIL

ALCALA

GOMEZ FARIAS

JUAREZ

**Church of Santo Domingo & Santo Domingo Cultural Center**

CONSTITUCION

DE MAYO

5

AV

MARTIRES DE TACUBAYA

REFUGIO

GUERRERO

ORTEGA

GONZALEZ

ARTEAGA

XOCHITL

M OCAMPO

PERIFERICO

Río Donají

190

VASCONCELOS

Eduardo Vasconcelos Stadium

N

To Dainzu Ruins, Tule Tree, Mitla Ruins & Tehuantepec

VIGUERA

PERIFERICO

UNIVERSIDAD

AV To ⑯

1 5

10 12 13 14 8 3 2 9 11 7 11 6 1 4 8 14 10 12 5 4 15

**MANY DOWNTOWN STREETS ARE ONE-WAY. TRAFFIC FLOW IS REVERSED AT IRREGULAR INTERVALS.**

# SOUTHERN MEXICO

AAA recommends that travelers consult online U.S. State Department travel advisories when planning travel abroad. Find this information at http://travel.state.gov/content/passports/english/alertswarnings/mexico-travel-warning.html.

## Oaxaca

This index helps you "spot" where approved hotels and restaurants are located on the corresponding detailed maps. Hotel daily rate range is for comparison only. Restaurant price range is a combination of lunch and/or dinner. Turn to the listing page for more detailed rate and price information and consult display ads for special promotions.

### OAXACA, OAXACA

| Map Page | Hotels | Diamond Rated | Rate Range | Page |
|---|---|---|---|---|
| ❶ p. 549 | Hotel Fortin Plaza | ♦♦ | $96-$225 | 551 |
| ❸ p. 549 | Casa Oaxaca | ♦♦♦ | $180-$330 | 551 |
| ❹ p. 549 | Casa Antigua | ♦♦♦ | $96-$133 | 551 |
| ❺ p. 549 | Holiday Inn Express Oaxaca Centro Historico | ♦♦♦ | Rates not provided | 551 |
| ❼ p. 549 | Parador Del Dominico | ♦♦ | $63-$126 | 551 |
| ❽ p. 549 | Casa de las Bugambilias B&B | ♦♦♦ | $90-$145 | 551 |
| ❾ p. 549 | ABU Hotel | ♦♦ | $74-$119 | 551 |
| ❿ p. 549 | La Casa de los Milagros | ♦♦♦ | $92-$130 | 551 |
| ⓫ p. 549 | AZUL de Oaxaca Hotel & Galeria | ♦♦♦ | $130-$540 | 551 |
| ⓬ p. 549 | Hotel La Casona de Tita | ♦♦♦ | $210-$277 | 551 |
| ⓮ p. 549 | Parador San Miguel Oaxaca | ♦♦♦ | $97-$230 | 551 |

| Map Page | Restaurants | Diamond Rated | Cuisine | Price Range | Page |
|---|---|---|---|---|---|
| ① p. 549 | Carbon de Palo | ♦♦♦ | Northern Mexican | $7-$22 | 551 |
| ② p. 549 | Zicanda | ♦♦♦ | Northern Mexican | $12-$18 | 552 |
| ④ p. 549 | El Asador Vasco | ♦♦♦ | Regional Mexican | $10-$27 | 552 |
| ⑤ p. 549 | La Casa de la Abuela | ♦♦ | Regional Mexican | $8-$15 | 552 |
| ⑥ p. 549 | La Olla Restaurante Galeria | ♦♦ | Regional Mexican | $8-$18 | 552 |
| ⑧ p. 549 | Catedral Restaurante and Bar | ♦♦♦ | Regional Mexican | $12-$28 | 552 |
| ⑩ p. 549 | La Primavera | ♦♦ | Regional Mexican | $6-$15 | 552 |
| ⑪ p. 549 | Casa Oaxaca, El Restaurante | ♦♦♦ | Regional Mexican | $14-$35 | 552 |
| ⑫ p. 549 | La Catrina de Alcala | ♦♦♦ | Regional Mexican | $12-$22 | 552 |
| ⑬ p. 549 | Los Danzantes | ♦♦♦ | Northern Mexican | $12-$30 | 552 |
| ⑭ p. 549 | El Portal del Marques Restaurante | ♦♦ | International | $8-$20 | 552 |
| ⑮ p. 549 | Cafe Bistrot Epicurio | ♦♦♦ | Italian | $10-$18 | 551 |
| ⑯ p. 549 | Casa Mayordomo | ♦♦ | Regional Mexican | $10-$25 | 552 |

## OAXACA, OAXACA (C-3) pop. 263,357, elev. 5,084'
• Hotels & Restaurants map & index p. 549

### ABU HOTEL (951)516-4900 **9**
Hotel $74-$119 **Address:** Murguia 104, Centro Historico 68000 **Location:** Just north of Zocalo; between Macedonio Alcala and 5 de Mayo. **Facility:** 53 units. 3 stories, interior corridors. *Bath:* shower only. **Parking:** on-site (fee) and valet. **Amenities:** safes. **Guest Services:** valet laundry.

### AZUL DE OAXACA HOTEL & GALERIA (951)501-0016 **11**
Historic Boutique Country Inn $130-$540 **Address:** Abasolo 313, Centro 68000 **Location:** Just north of Zocalo; between Avenida Juárez and Pino Suárez. **Facility:** This unique, contemporary small inn was designed and decorated by four well-known Mexican artists: Francisco Toledo, Rubén Leyva, José Villalobos and Luis Zárate. A gallery also showcases their artwork. 21 units. 2 stories (no elevator), interior corridors. **Parking:** street only. **Amenities:** safes. **Activities:** bicycles, massage. **Guest Services:** valet laundry.

### CASA ANTIGUA (951)501-1240 **4**
Country Inn $96-$133 **Address:** 5 de Mayo 206 68000 **Location:** Between Matamoros and Morelos; in Centro Historico. **Facility:** This quaint and charming property is in the heart of the Colonial center. 15 units. 3 stories (no elevator), exterior corridors. **Parking:** on-site (fee). **Terms:** 3-7 night minimum stay - seasonal and/or weekends. **Amenities:** safes. **Guest Services:** valet laundry.

### CASA DE LAS BUGAMBILIAS B&B (951)516-1165 **8**
Bed & Breakfast $90-$145 **Address:** Reforma No. 402 Col Centro 68000 **Location:** Between Constitucion and Abasolo; in historico downtown. **Facility:** This inn features a delightful Mexican décor throughout its public areas and guest rooms. The owners have taken great care to make all rooms unique by incorporating fine local art pieces. 9 units, some two bedrooms. 2 stories (no elevator), interior corridors. **Parking:** on-site (fee). **Terms:** 3-5 night minimum stay - seasonal and/or weekends, 30 day cancellation notice-fee imposed. **Amenities:** safes. **Guest Services:** valet laundry.

### CASA OAXACA (951)514-4173 **3**
Country Inn $180-$330 **Address:** Garcia Vigil 407 68000 **Location:** 4 blks n of Zocalo; between M. Bravo and Ignacio Allende; in historico downtown. **Facility:** Peaceful and serene, the inn features rooms surrounding a lovely courtyard where local artists' work is displayed. 7 units. 3 stories, interior corridors. **Terms:** 3-7 night minimum stay - seasonal and/or weekends, 15 day cancellation notice-fee imposed. **Amenities:** safes. **Pool(s):** outdoor. **Activities:** sauna, massage. **Guest Services:** valet laundry.

### HOLIDAY INN EXPRESS OAXACA CENTRO HISTORICO (951)512-9200 **5**
Hotel. Rates not provided. **Address:** Diaz Quintas No. 115 68040 **Location:** Corner of Diaz Quintas and Jacabo DaleVuelta; just n of Centro Historico. **Facility:** 100 units. 3 stories, interior corridors. *Bath:* shower only. **Amenities:** safes. **Pool(s):** outdoor. **Activities:** hot tub, exercise room. **Guest Services:** valet laundry.

### HOTEL FORTIN PLAZA (951)515-7777 **1**
Hotel $96-$225 **Address:** Ave Venus 118, Col Estrella 68040 **Location:** On north side; in Colonia Estrella on Mex 190. **Facility:** 108 units. 7 stories, interior corridors. **Amenities:** safes. **Pool(s):** heated outdoor. **Activities:** exercise room. **Guest Services:** valet laundry, area transportation.

### HOTEL LA CASONA DE TITA (951)516-1400 **12**
Historic Bed & Breakfast $210-$277 **Address:** Garcia Vigil 805, Centro 68000 **Location:** Jct Cosijopi. **Facility:** This small and intimate property is walking distance of the historic district but far enough away to enjoy a peaceful stay. 6 units. 1 story, interior/exterior corridors. **Parking:** street only. **Terms:** age restrictions may apply, 15 day cancellation notice. **Amenities:** safes. **Guest Services:** valet laundry.

### LA CASA DE LOS MILAGROS (951)501-2262 **10**
Bed & Breakfast $92-$130 **Address:** Matamoros No. 500-C 68000 **Location:** Jct Crespo; between M. Bravo and Morelos; in historico downtown. **Facility:** This small B&B offers very spacious and well-appointed public areas, including a large living room and attractive courtyard area. 3 units. 2 stories (no elevator), interior corridors. *Bath:* shower only. **Parking:** on-site (fee). **Terms:** 3-7 night minimum stay - seasonal and/or weekends, 30 day cancellation notice. **Amenities:** safes. **Activities:** massage. **Guest Services:** valet laundry.

### PARADOR DEL DOMINICO (951)513-1812 **7**
Hotel $63-$126 **Address:** Pino Suárez Col. Centro No. 410 68000 **Location:** Between Constitucion and Abasolo; in Centro Historico. **Facility:** 32 units. 3 stories (no elevator), interior corridors. *Bath:* shower only. **Terms:** 3 night minimum stay - seasonal and/or weekends, 3 day cancellation notice. **Amenities:** safes. **Guest Services:** valet laundry.

### PARADOR SAN MIGUEL OAXACA (951)514-9331 **14**
Historic Country Inn $97-$230 **Address:** Ave Independencia No. 503 68000 **Location:** Between Tinoco y Palacios and Porfirio Diaz; in historico downtown. **Facility:** This lovely inn has an attractive center courtyard as well as an upper-level deck for your enjoyment. Tastefully decorated rooms feature a fine Mexican theme and modern amenities. 23 units. 3 stories (no elevator), interior corridors. **Parking:** on-site (fee). **Amenities:** safes. **Activities:** massage. **Guest Services:** valet laundry.

### LA CATRINA DE ALCALA HOTEL 951/514-5705
Not evaluated. **Address:** Macedonio Alcala No. 102 68000 **Location:** Between Morelos and Independencia aves. Facilities, services, and décor characterize a mid-scale property. Just off the pedestrian walk near the Zócalo, this new, small inn features a unique, contemporary style.

### QUINTA REAL OAXACA 951/501-6100
Not evaluated; management refused inspection. **Address:** 5 de Mayo 300 68000 **Location:** 4 blks n of Zocalo; between Murguia and Abasolo sts; centro. Facilities, services, and décor characterize a mid-scale property. This picturesque 16th-century convent has arched cloisters and a fountain in the courtyard. Rooms have high ceilings, colorful décor and modern amenities.

**WHERE TO EAT**

### CAFE BISTROT EPICURIO 951/514-9750 **15**
Italian. Casual Dining. $10-$18 **AAA Inspector Notes:** If you're looking for a change of cuisine, this downtown restaurant is worth the stroll away from the main plaza. Wood fired pizzas, perfectly prepared pastas and Italian entrées plus an attentive staff make for a memorable meal. **Features:** full bar. **Address:** Vincente Guerrero No. 319 Col Centro 68000 **Location:** Just e of Zocolo. **Parking:** no self-parking.

### CARBON DE PALO 951/516-8116 **1**
Northern Mexican. Fine Dining. $7-$22 **AAA Inspector Notes:** Small and cozy, this modern dining room with attentive service features a well executed and creative menu showcasing local ingredients. From the Organic Carbon de Palo salad to the deconstructed osso buco ravioli and ending with a luscious fried squash cheese cake with guayaba salsa your taste buds will be handsomely rewarded. **Features:** full bar. **Address:** 5 de Mayo No. 311 Col Centro 68000 **Location:** Just se of Santo Domingo. **Parking:** no self-parking.

**CASA MAYORDOMO**　951/516-6113　[16]

▼▼ Regional Mexican. Casual Dining. $10-$25 **AAA Inspector Notes:** Within walking distance of El Zocalo, this restaurant is sure to please everyone with a wide assortment of mole, and chiles stuffed with diced chicken, tomatoes, almonds, raisins and more. **Features:** full bar. **Address:** Calle Alcala No. 302 68000 **Location:** At Calle Mariano Matamoros. **Parking:** no self-parking.

[B] [L] [D] [◣]

**CASA OAXACA, EL RESTAURANTE**　951/516-8531　[11]

▼▼▼ Regional Mexican. Fine Dining. $14-$35 **AAA Inspector Notes:** A nice example of Oaxaca's slow-food movement, this restaurant offers a creative menu featuring local, fresh and organic ingredients in unique preparations. Salsa is prepared tableside and adjusted for your palate. The grilled, whole baby octopus with huitlacoche is quite the sight and sublime in flavor. **Features:** full bar, patio dining. **Reservations:** suggested. **Address:** Constitucion 104-A, Col Centro 68000 **Location:** Between 5 de Mayo and Reforma, just s of Santo Domingo. **Parking:** no self-parking.　[L] [D] [K]

**CATEDRAL RESTAURANTE AND BAR**　951/516-3285　[8]

▼▼ Regional Mexican. Fine Dining. $12-$28 **AAA Inspector Notes:** This centrally located restaurant presents a fine menu of local and regional Mexican fare, including moles, spicy sauces, grilled meats, poultry, seafood and, of course, freshly prepared tortillas. The lovely and sophisticated setting includes candlelit tables and a Mexican-style fountain in the courtyard area. **Features:** full bar, Sunday brunch. **Reservations:** suggested. **Address:** Garcia Vigil No. 105 68000 **Location:** In Centro Historico. **Parking:** no self-parking.　[B] [L] [D] [◣]

**EL ASADOR VASCO**　951/514-4755　[4]

▼▼ Regional Mexican. Casual Dining. $10-$27 **AAA Inspector Notes:** *Historic.* The restaurant allows you to dine amid the entertaining surroundings of the Zócalo. On the second floor of a historic building facing the main square, terrace seating is highly sought after on any given night. The menu's international influences include local Oaxacan cuisine as well as some Basque specialties. If you seek a more casual experience, opt for The Tavern dining area. **Features:** full bar, patio dining. **Address:** Portal de Flores No. 10A 68000 **Location:** On west side of Zocalo. **Parking:** no self-parking.

[L] [D] [K] [◣]

**EL PORTAL DEL MARQUES RESTAURANTE**
951/514-4118　[14]

▼▼ International. Casual Dining. $8-$20 **AAA Inspector Notes:** *Historic.* With more than 60 years of experience, this restaurant prides itself in serving the best in regional, national and international dishes. A cadre of servers attired in traditional Mexican dress serve well-prepared soups, salads and Mexican-influenced entrées, such as chicken mole and tamales. A local favorite is the chapulines, tasty fried grasshoppers. **Features:** full bar, patio dining. **Address:** Portal de Claveria S/N 68000 **Location:** Corner of Portal de Mercedes and Portal de Claveria; facing Zocalo. **Parking:** no self-parking.　[B] [L] [D] [K] [◣]

**LA CASA DE LA ABUELA**　951/516-3544　[5]

▼▼ Regional Mexican. Family Dining. $8-$15 **AAA Inspector Notes:** The professional waitstaff serves freshly prepared and tasty meals in a great location. The well-seasoned mixed grill which includes pork chops, ribs, chicken breast and Mexican sausage is a hearty favorite. The simply decorated dining room's second-level seating provides an optimal vantage point for viewing the lively ambience of the plaza. **Features:** full bar, patio dining. **Reservations:** suggested. **Address:** Ave Hidalgo 616 Altos 68000 **Location:** Overlooking Zocalo. **Parking:** no self-parking.

[L] [D] [K] [◣]

**LA CATRINA DE ALCALA**　951/514-5704　[12]

▼▼▼ Regional Mexican. Casual Dining. $12-$22 **AAA Inspector Notes:** Situated in a decorative atrium, this gourmet Mexican restaurant offers fine cuisine with regional influences from the Isthmus of Tehuantepec. The talented chef utilizes fresh local products, so the menu changes based on seasonality and availability of ingredients. House specialties include duck al higo, pork adobo, chapulines (grasshoppers) and a variety of moles. The professional waitstaff, attired in traditional dress, aims to please. **Features:** full bar. **Address:** Macedonio Alcala No. 102 68000 **Location:** Between aves Morelos and Independencia; in Centro Historico district. **Parking:** no self-parking.　[B] [L] [D] [K]

**LA OLLA RESTAURANTE GALERIA**　951/516-6668　[6]

▼▼ Regional Mexican. Casual Dining. $8-$18 **AAA Inspector Notes:** This cozy café is popular for the fresh, local and organic products used in the creative menu. The flor de calabaza soup is luscious with a striking, artistic presentation using fresh squash flowers. The house-made flan is a special meal-ending treat. **Features:** full bar. **Address:** Reforma No. 402, Centro Historico 68000 **Location:** Between Constitucion and Abasolo; adjacent to Casa de las Bugambilias B&B. **Parking:** street only.　[B] [L] [D] [K]

**LA PRIMAVERA**　951/516-2595　[10]

▼▼ Regional Mexican. Casual Dining. $6-$15 **AAA Inspector Notes:** On the Zocalo, in the center of action, this authentic Oaxacan restaurant serves various moles, stuffed peppers and typical dishes of the area. **Features:** full bar. **Address:** Ave Hidalgo con Portal de Flos 68000 **Location:** In historico downtown area. **Parking:** no self-parking.　[B] [L] [D] [LATE] [K] [◣]

**LOS DANZANTES**　951/501-1184　[13]

▼▼▼ Northern Mexican. Fine Dining. $12-$30 **AAA Inspector Notes:** Enjoy regional cuisine with a creative, modern flair while dining amongst unique architecture. The poblano chile relleno with huitlacoche, goat cheese and chapulines is an excellent introduction to these local favorites. Luscious desserts with an after-dinner mescal make for a fine finish. **Features:** full bar. **Reservations:** suggested. **Address:** Macedonio Alcala 403-4, Col Centro 68000 **Location:** On pedestrian walkway, between M Bravo and Ignacio Allende; just s of Santo Domingo Convent. **Parking:** no self-parking.

[L] [D] [K]

**ZICANDA**　951/501-0715　[2]

▼▼▼ Northern Mexican. Casual Dining. $12-$18 **AAA Inspector Notes:** Creatively prepared and presented contemporary Oaxacan cuisine is featured in this colorful and lively restaurant. From the flavorful chileatole soup to the rich complex sauces of cured pork belly with mole rojo and octopus Veracruzano, your palate will not be disappointed. **Features:** full bar. **Address:** Garcia Vigil No. 409-A Col Centro 68000 **Location:** Just n of Zocalo. **Parking:** no self-parking.

[L] [D] [LATE] [K]

**EL REFECTORIO**　951/501-6100

[fyi] Not evaluated. Diners enjoy live Mexican music and a varied menu of regional Mexican and international fare at this stunning setting in the middle of a converted historic convent. A choice of terrace or indoor seating is offered. **Address:** 5 de Mayo 300 68000 **Location:** 4 blks n of Zocalo; between calles Murguia and Abasolo; centro; in Quinta Real Oaxaca.

# PALENQUE, CHIAPAS (C-5) pop. 110,918

**BEST WESTERN MAYA PALENQUE**　916/345-0780

[fyi] Not evaluated. **Address:** Merle Green y Ave Juárez S/N **Location:** At Glorieta La Cabeza Maya. Facilities, services, and décor characterize a mid-scale property.

> **AAA Benefit:**
> Save 10% or more every day and earn 10% bonus points!

**CHAN-KAH RESORT VILLAGE**　916/345-1100

[fyi] Not evaluated. **Address:** KM 3 Carr a Las Ruinas **Location:** 1.1 mi (1.8 km) n of main entrance to Palenque ruins. Facilities, services, and décor characterize a mid-scale property.

**HOTEL MISION PALENQUE PARK PLAZA**　916/345-0241

[fyi] Not evaluated. **Address:** Rancho San Martin de Porres 29960 **Location:** 4 blks e of centro, follow signs. Facilities, services, and décor characterize a mid-scale property.

**HOTEL NUTUTUN PALENQUE**　916/345-0100

[fyi] Not evaluated. **Address:** KM 3.5 Carr Palenque-Ocosingo 29960 **Location:** 3 mi (5 km) s on Mex 199 to Agua Azul. Facilities, services, and décor characterize an economy property.

**HOTEL PLAZA PALENQUE**　916/345-0555

[fyi] Not evaluated. **Address:** KM 27 Carr Caletaja-Palenque **Location:** 0.6 mi (1 km) n on Mex 199. Facilities, services, and décor characterize a mid-scale property.

**EL HUACHINANGO FELIZ**      916/345-4642

▼▼ Seafood. Casual Dining. $8-$18 **AAA Inspector Notes:** The establishment's name translates to 'The Happy Snapper.' A popular open-air restaurant, it features fresh seafood prepared in a variety of styles; all portions are generous and sharable. The shrimp al ajillo is especially flavorful. **Features:** full bar. **Address:** Ave Hidalgo S/N, Col La Canada 29960 **Location:** In La Canada. **Parking:** street only. [L] [D] [K] [N]

**RESTAURANTE MAYA CANADA**      916/345-0216

▼▼ Regional Mexican. Casual Dining. $5-$18 **AAA Inspector Notes:** This open-air restaurant serves local Mayan specialties. Prices are economical with the daily prix fixe menu, a great value featuring three courses and a drink. Free Wi-Fi. **Features:** full bar. **Address:** Ave Hidalgo S/N, Col La Canada 22960 **Location:** In La Canada. **Parking:** street only. [B] [L] [D] [K] [N]

## PLAYA DE CHACHALACAS

**HOTEL PUNTA REAL RESORT AND SPA**      296/962-6035

[fyi] **Hotel** Did not meet all AAA rating requirements for sprinklers/smoke detectors in some guest rooms at time of last evaluation on 04/09/2014. **Address:** Carlos Saenz De La Pena S/N **Location:** Oceanfront. 21 mi (35 km) on Mex 180 (Veracruz/Xalapa Hwy) to Playa de Chachalacas, 9.3 mi (15 km) passing through village of Ursulo Galvan, ne at Tres Caminos, follow signs. Facilities, services, and décor characterize a mid-scale property.

## SAN CRISTÓBAL DE LAS CASAS, CHIAPAS (C-5) pop. 185,917, elev. 6,888'

**HOLIDAY INN SAN CRISTOBAL ESPANOL**      (967)678-0045

▼▼▼ Hotel $93-$128 **Address:** Ave 1st de Marzo No. 15 29200 **Location:** Corner of aves 1st de Marzo and Crescencio Rosas; in Centro Historico district. **Facility:** 79 units. 3 stories (no elevator), interior/exterior corridors. **Amenities:** safes. **Activities:** exercise room. **Guest Services:** valet laundry.

[] [] [Y] [SD] [BIZ] [] [X] []

**MANSION DE LOS ANGELES**      967/678-1173

▼▼ **Historic Country Inn** $60-$90 **Address:** Calle Francisco I. Madero No. 17 29200 **Location:** Between aves Insurgentes and Benito Juárez, just e of central plaza; in Centro Historico district. **Facility:** In an ideal location, this 17th century former mansion features a Mexican motif and angel theme throughout the property. 20 units. 3 stories (no elevator), interior corridors. *Bath:* shower only. **Parking:** on-site and valet. **Guest Services:** valet laundry.

[] [SD] [] [K]

**HOTEL MANSION DEL VALLE**      987/678-2582

[fyi] **Hotel** Did not meet all AAA rating requirements for locking devices in some guest rooms at time of last evaluation on 10/14/2013. **Address:** Calle Diego de Mazariegos No. 39, Barrio de La Merced 29240 **Location:** In Centro Historico; just w of jct Cinco de Mayo; adjacent to Museo Culturas Populares. Facilities, services, and décor characterize an economy property.

**HOTEL MISION GRAND SAN CRISTOBAL DE LAS CASAS**      967/678-0928

[fyi] Not evaluated. **Address:** Francisco I. Madero No. 19 29200 **Location:** Jct Blvd Benito Juárez; in Centro Historico. Facilities, services, and décor characterize an economy property. This well-maintained boutique hotel offers many guest amenities and is conveniently located.

**TIERRA Y CIELO HOTEL**      967/678-1053

[fyi] Not evaluated. **Address:** Ave Benito Juárez No. 1 29200. Facilities, services, and décor characterize a mid-scale property. Well-maintained boutique hotel with many guest amenities. Convenient location in the historic center.

**COCINA EL AGRENTINO PARRILLA**      967/631-7150

▼▼ Argentine Steak. Casual Dining. $8-$22 **AAA Inspector Notes:** This bustling Argentine grill serves large portions of aged beef, chicken and seafood plus side dishes. There is particularly efficient service. **Features:** full bar. **Address:** Real de Guadalupe No. 13-D 29200 **Location:** Just e of Zocalo. **Parking:** no self-parking. [L] [D] [K]

**RESTAURANTE PLAZA REAL**      967/678-0992

▼▼ International. Casual Dining. $15-$30 **AAA Inspector Notes:** *Historic.* Located in a historic 19th century building, this restaurant serves well-prepared Mexican and international dishes. Tortilla soup and cactus salad are favorite starters. Fajitas are a good dinner choice, and great for sharing. The menu also lists a nice line-up of pasta dishes and pizzas. Must-try desserts include creme brulee and apple strudel. **Features:** full bar, Sunday brunch. **Address:** Calle Real de Guadeloupe No. 5 29200 **Location:** In Centro Historico; on Real de Guadeloupe pedestrian walkway; just e of Ave General Utrilla; in House of Congress Building. **Parking:** no self-parking.

[B] [L] [D] [K] [N]

**TIERRA Y CIELO RESTAURANTE**      967/678-1053

▼▼▼ Northern Mexican. Fine Dining. $12-$22 **AAA Inspector Notes:** This trendy restaurant's outstanding chef showcases creative variations of local cuisine using fresh seasonal ingredients. The chia seed-crusted salmon with mango was seared to perfection, and the meal-ending pear torte had just the right amount of spicy chocolate flavor. **Features:** full bar. **Address:** Ave Benito Juárez No. 1 29200 **Location:** Just e of Zocalo; between Madero and Guadalupe; in Centro Historico; in Tierra Y Cielo Hotel. **Parking:** valet only.

[B] [L] [D]

## TAXCO, GUERRERO (C-2) pop. 104,053, elev. 5,897'

**HOTEL MONTE TAXCO**      762/622-1300

[fyi] Not evaluated. **Address:** Fracc Lomas de Taxco S/N 40200 **Location:** On steep mountain, just n of Mex 95; at entrance of city. Facilities, services, and décor characterize an economy property.

**POSADA DE LA MISION**      762/622-0063

[fyi] Not evaluated. **Address:** Cerro de La Mision 32 40230 **Location:** On Mex 95; opposite Pemex station. Facilities, services, and décor characterize an economy property.

**PUEBLO LINDO**      762/622-3481

[fyi] Not evaluated. **Address:** Miguel Hidalgo No. 30, Colonia Centro 40200 **Location:** Centro. Facilities, services, and décor characterize a mid-scale property. This newer boutique hotel offers a wonderful view of the town and is convenient to the main plaza (Plaza Borda) and historic sites. Pool on-site, too.

**HOTEL MONTE TAXCO RESTAURANTE**      762/622-1300

[fyi] Not evaluated. Take the teleferico up and reserve the terrace to ensure the best view of Taxco below. Mostly Mexican favorites are offered. **Address:** Fracc Lomas de Taxco S/N 40200 **Location:** On steep mountain, just n of Mex 95; at entrance of city; in Hotel Monte Taxco.

**LOS VIKINGOS RESTAURANTE**      762/622-3481

[fyi] Not evaluated. The spectacular view from the terrace makes dining here a pleasure anytime, but especially at breakfast or at sunset. **Address:** Miguel Hidalgo No. 30 40200 **Location:** Centro; in Pueblo Lindo.

## TUXTLA GUTIÉRREZ, CHIAPAS (C-5)
### pop. 553,374

**CROWNE PLAZA TUXTLA GUTIERREZ** (961)617-2200

▼▼▼ Hotel. Rates not provided. Address: Blvd Belisario Dominguez KM 1081B Location: 3 mi (4.5 km) w on Mex 190; adjacent to Holiday Inn Tuxtla Gutierrez. Facility: 112 units, some efficiencies. 6 stories, interior corridors. Amenities: safes. Dining: 2 restaurants. Pool(s): outdoor. Activities: exercise room. Guest Services: valet laundry.

[icons]

**FIESTA INN TUXTLA GUTIERREZ** (961)617-1300

▼▼▼ Hotel. $160-$210 Address: Prolongacion del anillo de Circunvalacion S/N 29060 Location: Just e of Galerias Blvd Shopping Center. Facility: 120 units. 9 stories, interior corridors. Bath: shower only. Amenities: safes. Pool(s): outdoor. Activities: exercise room. Guest Services: valet laundry, area transportation.

[icons]

**HILTON GARDEN INN TUXTLA GUTIERREZ** 961/617-1800

▼▼▼ Hotel. $67-$83 Address: Blvd Belisario Dominguez No. 1641 29000 Location: Jct Blvd Castillos. Facility: 167 units. 6 stories, interior corridors. Terms: 1-7 night minimum stay, cancellation fee imposed. Amenities: safes. Pool(s): heated outdoor. Activities: hot tub, exercise room. Guest Services: valet laundry.

**AAA Benefit:**
Members save up to 10%!

[icons]

**HOLIDAY INN TUXTLA GUTIERREZ** (961)617-1000

▼▼▼ Hotel. Rates not provided. Address: Blvd Belisario Dominguez KM 1081 Location: 3 mi (4.5 km) w on Mex 190; adjacent to Crowne Plaza Tuxtla Gutierrez. Facility: 108 units. 2 stories, interior corridors. Bath: shower only. Parking: valet and street only. Amenities: safes. Dining: Restaurant di Piu, see separate listing, entertainment. Pool(s): outdoor. Activities: exercise room. Guest Services: valet laundry, area transportation.

[icons]

**CAMINO REAL TUXTLA GUTIERREZ** 961/617-7777

[fyi] Not evaluated. Address: Blvd Belisario Dominguez No. 1195 29000 Location: Jct Ave Central and Blvd Belisario Dominguez. Facilities, services, and décor characterize an upscale property.

**HOLIDAY INN EXPRESS TUXTLA GUTIERREZ LA MARIMBA**
961/618-9500

[fyi] Not evaluated. Address: Ave Central No. 1254 Col Central 29000 Location: Jct 22th Poniente. Facilities, services, and décor characterize a mid-scale property.

### WHERE TO EAT

**ASADOR CASTELLANO** 961/602-9000

▼▼▼ Steak Seafood. Fine Dining. $20-$60 AAA Inspector Notes: Offering refined service in an upscale setting, this restaurant is popular with the local and visiting business set. Enjoy a variety of aged cuts of beef and expertly prepared regional seafood along with a nice bottle of red wine from the extensive list. Features: full bar. Reservations: suggested. Address: Blvd Belisario Dominguez No. 2320-A, Col Las Granjas 29000 Location: Just e of Galerias Blvd Shopping Center. [L] [D]

**LA MANSION** 961/617-7733

▼▼▼ Steak. Fine Dining. $15-$45 AAA Inspector Notes: The restaurant offers a refined dining experience, complete with a dapper, attentive waitstaff. On the menu you'll find a fine selection of Angus beef, chicken and a few fish dishes. Very tempting are the delicious selections from the dessert trolley. Features: full bar. Reservations: suggested. Address: Blvd Belisario Dominguez No. 1195 29060 Location: Jct Ave Central and Blvd Belisario Dominguez; in Camino Real Tuxtla Gutierrez. Parking: valet only. [L] [D] [LATE]

**RESTAURANT DI PIU** 961/617-1000

▼▼▼ International. Fine Dining. $12-$25 AAA Inspector Notes: Located across from a large shopping mall, this restaurant offers shoppers and businessmen a selection of well-prepared fresh seafood, aged steaks and traditional pasta dishes. Live music is featured on weekends, making for a lively night spot. Features: full bar, patio dining. Reservations: suggested. Address: Blvd Belisario Dominguez KM 1081 29000 Location: 3 mi (4.5 km) w on Mex 190; adjacent to Crowne Plaza Tuxtla Gutierrez; in Holiday Inn Tuxtla Gutierrez. [L] [D]

## VERACRUZ, VERACRUZ (B-3) pop. 552,156

**CAMINO REAL VERACRUZ** (229)923-5500

▼▼▼ Hotel. $204-$445 Address: Blvd Manuel Avila Camacho No. 3650, Fracc Costa de Oro 94299 Location: Oceanfront. 3.8 mi (6 km) sw from Plaza de Armas; in Costa de Oro area of Boca del Rio. Facility: Meets AAA guest room security requirements. 156 units. 12 stories, interior corridors. Parking: on-site and valet. Amenities: safes. Dining: 2 restaurants. Pool(s): heated outdoor. Activities: fishing, playground, exercise room. Guest Services: valet laundry.

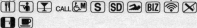

**EMPORIO VERACRUZ** (229)989-3300

▼▼▼ Hotel $76-$318

Address: Paseo del Malecon 244 91700 Location: Waterfront. On the Malecon; jct Xicotencalt. Facility: Meets AAA guest room security requirements. 223 units. 9 stories, interior corridors. Parking: on-site and valet. Amenities: safes. Dining: 2 restaurants, also, Los Canarios Restaurante Bar Cafe, see separate listing. Pool(s): outdoor, heated indoor. Activities: sauna, hot tub, recreation programs, kids club, exercise room, spa. Guest Services: valet laundry, area transportation.

[icons]

**GALERIA PLAZA VERACRUZ** (229)989-0505

▼▼▼ Hotel. Rates not provided. Address: Blvd Adolfo Ruiz Cortines No. 3495 94294 Location: In Boca del Rio area. Adjacent to Plaza Las Americas. Facility: 258 units. 6 stories, interior/exterior corridors. Parking: on-site and valet. Amenities: safes. Dining: 2 restaurants. Pool(s): heated indoor. Activities: hot tub, steamroom, kids club, exercise room, massage. Guest Services: valet laundry, area transportation.

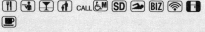

**HILTON GARDEN INN** (229)923-0201

▼▼▼ Hotel. $100-$120 Address: Manuel Avila Camacho S/N, Boca del Rio Location: Oceanfront. 3 mi (4.8 km) sw from Plaza de Armas. Facility: Meets AAA guest room security requirements. 108 units. 5 stories, interior corridors. Terms: 1-7 night minimum stay, cancellation fee imposed. Amenities: safes. Pool(s): heated outdoor. Activities: exercise room. Guest Services: valet laundry.

**AAA Benefit:**
Members save up to 10%!

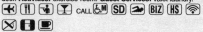

**HOTEL VERACRUZ CENTRO HISTORICO** (229)989-3800

▼▼ Hotel. $67-$200 Address: Ave Independencia S/N, Esq. Miguel Lerdo 91700 Location: Jct M Lerdo St; near Zocalo. Located in historico area of downtown. Facility: 116 units. 6 stories, interior corridors. Bath: shower only. Parking: on-site and valet. Amenities: safes. Dining: 2 restaurants. Pool(s): heated outdoor. Guest Services: valet laundry.

**COMFORT INN VERACRUZ**     229/923-1206

[fyi] Not evaluated. **Address:** Blvd Manuel Avila Camacho S/N 91910 **Location:** Jct Bartolome de Las Casas. Facilities, services, and décor characterize an economy property.

**FIESTA AMERICANA VERACRUZ**     229/989-8989

[fyi] **Hotel** Did not meet all AAA rating requirements for locking devices in some guest rooms at time of last evaluation on 04/22/2015. **Address:** Prol Blvd Manuel Avila Camacho S/N, Fracc Costa de Oro 94299 **Location:** Oceanfront. 3.8 mi (6 km) sw from Plaza de Armas in Boca del Rio area. Facilities, services, and décor characterize an upscale property.

**HOLIDAY INN VERACRUZ BOCA DEL RIO**     229/923-2050

[fyi] Not evaluated. **Address:** Blvd Adolfo Ruiz Cortines N 4298, Fracc. Costa de Oro 94299 **Location:** 5 mi (8 km) sw from Plaza de Armas on Blvd Veracuz Mocambo. Facilities, services, and décor characterize a mid-scale property.

**HOLIDAY INN VERACRUZ CENTRO HISTORICO**
    229/932-4052

[fyi] Not evaluated. **Address:** Ave Morelos No. 225 Col. Centro 91700 **Location:** Centro. Facilities, services, and décor characterize a mid-scale property.

**WHERE TO EAT**

**CASA USCANGA**     297/973-7115

Regional Seafood. Family Dining. $7-$15 **AAA Inspector Notes:** Great for families on a budget, this quaint restaurant is located on a lagoon in the small town of Mandinga about 20 minutes from the Boca del Rio area, and offers a variety of fresh seafood. Strolling musicians play the typical music of Veracruz, local traditional dancers perform and 45 minute boat tours of the lagoon are offered for a fee. A children's play area is available. The restaurant closes around 6 pm daily due to the mosquitoes. **Address:** Calle Principal S/N 95250 **Location:** From Boca del Rio (centro), follow Mex 145 (Anton Lizardo), 5 mi (8 km), exit Mandinga, then 1 mi (1.6 km) s.

L   K  

**GRAN CAFE DE LA PARROQUIA**     229/932-1855

Regional Coffee/Tea Seafood. Family Dining. $8-$25 **AAA Inspector Notes:** *Historic.* In existence for more than 200 years, the well-known cafe and full-service restaurant is adjacent to the main waterfront walkway, el malecon, which always teems with locals. Servers make a big show of preparing the popular cafe con leche. You are brought a cup of triple espresso coffee, which you clink with a spoon when you're ready for the scalding milk. A roaming server comes by and raises the large metal teapot way up, and brings it back down as they pour the milk into your cup. **Features:** full bar, patio dining. **Address:** Insurgentes Veracruzanos, Paseo del Malecon No. 340 91700 **Location:** On the Malecon waterfront walkway; between aves Gomez and 16 de Septiembre. **Parking:** street only.

B   L   D   LATE   CALL M

**GRAN CAFE DE LA PARROQUIA**     229/130-0200

Regional Mexican. Casual Dining. $6-$15 **AAA Inspector Notes:** This 'new' sister restaurant (the original has been in existence for more than 200 years and is located in downtown Veracruz) offers the same menu of simply prepared fish, beef, sandwiches and delicious coffee. Clink your glass with your spoon when you want the roaming server to add hot, scalding milk to your cup of triple espresso. **Features:** patio dining. **Address:** Blvd Adolfo Ruiz Cortines 1815 94294 **Location:** Jct Jardines de Virginia; in Boca del Rio area.

B   L   D   CALL M

**GRAN CAFE DEL PORTAL**     229/931-2759

Regional Mexican. Family Dining. $6-$14 **AAA Inspector Notes:** Open from 7 am to midnight, this cafe is housed in a building dating from 1824 and offers a varied menu with simply prepared food, including Mexican appetizers, seafood (be sure to ask what is recommended), sandwiches and steaks. Sidewalk seating and live marimba music nightly. A few famous people have dined here, including Benito Juarez and Harry S. Truman. **Features:** patio dining. **Address:** Ave Independencia No. 1187 91700 **Location:** Jct Zamora; across from the cathedral. **Parking:** street only.

B   L   D   LATE   CALL M

**LOS CANARIOS RESTAURANTE BAR CAFE**     229/989-3300

Regional Mexican. Casual Dining. $6-$25 **AAA Inspector Notes:** Views of the harbor and well-prepared fresh fish and beef are served, sometimes with a Spanish flair. Recommended is the ceviche. A nice selection of wines is available. Smoking is permitted in a separate, enclosed room. On weekends, try the seafood brunch. **Features:** full bar, Sunday brunch. **Address:** Paseo del Malecon 244 91700 **Location:** On the Malecon; jct Xicotencalt; in Emporio Veracruz. **Parking:** valet and street only.

L   D   CALL M

**MARISCOS VILLA RICA RESTAURANTE**     229/922-3743

Regional Seafood. Casual Dining. $11-$40 **AAA Inspector Notes:** Among Mexico's best-known seafood restaurants, here you can dine under the large palapa with its open windows, which offer beautiful views of the gulf, sandy beaches and large, frond-laden palms. On the extensive menu you'll find snails, octopus, crunchy seafood tostadas, refreshing ceviche, clams, aros de calamar (squid cooked in their own ink) and all types of fish caught that morning. Whole sea bass is scored across its thick side for effect. **Features:** full bar. **Address:** Calzada Mocambo No. 527 Col Boca del Rio 94294 **Location:** In Mocambo neighborhood; in Boca del Rio area.

L   D   K  

**ROSATO RESTAURANTE**     229/989-8989

[fyi] Not evaluated. This charming restaurant features Italian cuisine and is open for late night dining. **Address:** Prol Blvd Manuel Avila Camacho S/N, Fracc Costa de Oro 94299 **Location:** 3.8 mi (6 km) sw from Plaza de Armas; in Boca del Rio area; in Fiesta Americana Veracruz.

# VILLAHERMOSA, TABASCO (C-4)

• Restaurants p. 556

**HOLIDAY INN EXPRESS VILLAHERMOSA TABASCO 2000**     (993)310-4650

Hotel
Rates not provided

**Address:** Periferico Carlos Pellicer Camara No. 4000 86037 **Location:** In tourist and commercial area known as La Choca. **Facility:** 88 units. 4 stories, interior corridors. *Bath:* shower only. **Amenities:** safes. **Pool(s):** heated outdoor. **Activities:** exercise room, massage. **Guest Services:** valet laundry, area transportation.

**HOTEL MAYA TABASCO**     (993)358-1111

Hotel $86 **Address:** Ave Adolfo Ruiz Cortinez No. 907 86000 **Location:** Just w of Ave Francisco Mina. **Facility:** 151 units. 6 stories, interior corridors. *Bath:* shower only. **Amenities:** safes. **Pool(s):** outdoor. **Guest Services:** valet laundry, area transportation.

**HYATT REGENCY VILLAHERMOSA**     (993)310-1234

Hotel
$95-$215

HYATT REGENCY®

**AAA Benefit:** Members save 10%!

**Address:** Ave Juárez No. 106, Col Lindavista 86050 **Location:** 0.8 mi (1.5 km) n on Mex 180; near Tabasco 2000 Commercial Complex. **Facility:** 207 units. 9 stories, interior corridors. **Parking:** on-site and valet. **Terms:** cancellation fee imposed. **Amenities:** safes. **Pool(s):** outdoor. **Activities:** exercise room, massage. **Guest Services:** valet laundry, area transportation.

Remember, car seats, booster seats and seat belts save lives

## VILLAHERMOSA MARRIOTT HOTEL

(993)310-0201

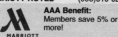

Contemporary Hotel

$110-$154

**AAA Benefit:** Members save 5% or more!

**Address:** Prolongacion Paseo Tabasco 1407/Tabasco 2000 86030 **Location:** Just off Paseo Tabasco, 4 blks nw of jct Ave Adolfo Ruiz Cortinez. **Facility:** 267 units, some two bedrooms. 11 stories, interior corridors. **Parking:** on-site (fee) and valet. **Amenities:** safes. **Dining:** entertainment. **Pool(s):** outdoor. **Activities:** playground, exercise room, spa. **Guest Services:** valet laundry, area transportation.

## HILTON VILLAHERMOSA & CONFERENCE CENTER

993/313-6800

**fyi** Not evaluated. **Address:** Ave Adolfo Ruiz Cortinez Ote KM 12.8 86280 **Location:** Just s of entrance to Villahermosa Airport. Facilities, services, and décor characterize a mid-scale property.

**AAA Benefit:** Members save 5% or more!

## REAL INN

993/310-1600

**fyi** Not evaluated. **Address:** Paseo de La Choca No. 107 86035 **Location:** Periferico Carlos Pellicer, jct Paseo Tabasco. Facilities, services, and décor characterize a mid-scale property.

## ASADOR CASTELLANO

993/316-9909

Steak Seafood. Fine Dining. $20-$60 **AAA Inspector Notes:** Offering refined service in an upscale setting, this restaurant is popular with the local and visiting business set. Enjoy a variety of aged cuts of beef and expertly prepared regional seafood along with a nice bottle of red wine from the extensive list. **Features:** full bar, patio dining, happy hour. **Reservations:** suggested. **Address:** Paseo La Choca No. 120, Tabasco 2000 86035 **Location:** Col. Tabasco 2000; in La Choca business zone.

## GOURMET MX

993/316-3939

International. Casual Dining. $9-$37 **AAA Inspector Notes:** The young and dynamic chef of this trendy new restaurant features a regularly changing menu using many local and regional items. The smoked cheese from Tenosique with honey to the Robalo with jicama fettuccine with momo pesto are just a sample of the many unique creations to be shared with your dining companions. **Features:** full bar, patio dining. **Address:** Calle Cardenas Local 450 Col Atasta 86030

## JANGADA RESTAURANTE

993/316-2895

Seafood. Casual Dining. $10-$25 **AAA Inspector Notes:** This popular seafood restaurant features an extensive buffet plus tableside offerings, including soups, sushi and desserts. The à la carte menu also showcases regional seafood specialties, such as banana leaf-wrapped fish with achiote sauce. **Features:** full bar. **Address:** Paseo La Choca 126-A 86035 **Location:** Col. Tabasco 2000; in La Choca business zone.

# Club Contacts in Mexico

The Mexican Automobile Association (Asociación Mexicana Automovilística, or AMA) has branch offices in Mexico that may be able to help visiting AAA/CAA members or provide roadside assistance in the event of a vehicle breakdown. Members also are eligible for discounted repair fees. For information phone 01 (800) 911-0262 (toll-free long distance within Mexico). AMA headquarters is located in Mexico City at Av. Orizaba #7 at Avenida Chapultepec (behind the Metro Insurgentes station), just outside the Zona Rosa in the Roma neighborhood (M: Insurgentes, line 1).

As part of the "AAA Discounts & Rewards" program and an alliance between AAA/CAA and AMA, U.S. and Canadian members can enjoy savings with program partners. For information about "Ahorra con AMA" partners, go to the AAA Discounts & Rewards section of www.AAA.com on your club's website. Member admission discounts at the Xcaret, Xplor and Xel-Ha theme parks also are given for phone purchases; for information phone (888) 885-5187 (toll-free from the United States).

# Speaking of Spanish

ON THE FOLLOWING PAGES are listed some of the Spanish phrases and sentences that are most useful to an English-speaking visitor in Mexico. Although not essential, a basic knowledge of the language will be helpful. Most Mexicans who deal with tourists speak at least some English, and those who don't will be only too glad to help you along with your attempts at Spanish. Fortunately, the language is not that difficult to speak. A little study of the following rules of pronunciation will be sufficient to make yourself understood.

Even if your knowledge of Spanish is rudimentary, using such everyday expressions as por favor (please), gracias (thank you), buenos días (good morning), buenas tardes (good afternoon) and buenas noches (good evening) shows respect. Mexicans are very polite and use these terms all the time; you should also. Good manners mean more than being able to speak the language fluently.

## Pronunciation

The pronunciation of the Spanish language presents very few difficulties. The spelling is almost phonetic; nearly every letter has one sound that it retains at all times.

**Vowels**
A—pronounced as "a" in father.
E—pronounced as "e" in them.
I—pronounced as "e" in me.
O—pronounced as "o" in hold.
U—pronounced as "oo" in food.

**Consonants**
Consonants do not differ materially from those in English. The few differences are as follows:
b and v—in Mexico are pronounced as in "boy."
c—is pronounced with an "s" sound before e and i. Otherwise it has a "k" sound. Ex. cinco—seen-koh.
g—is soft, like a strong English "h," when it precedes e and i. Ex. gente—hente. In all other cases, it is a hard "g" as in go. Ex. gato—gahtoh. If gu precedes an e or i, the "g" has a hard sound and the "u" is not pronounced. Ex. guerra—geh-rah, guiso—geeh-so. If the "u" has an umlaut it is pronounced güera—gweh-rah, güiro—gwee-roh.

h—always silent, except after c, which makes a "ch" sound as in English.
j—pronounced like the English "h."
ll—pronounced like the English "y." Ex. caballo—kah-BAH-yo.
ñ—combination of "n" and "y," like cognac. Ex. niño—neenyoh.
qu—pronounced like "k." Ex. que—keh.
r—in Mexico the "r" is trilled; the "r" at the beginning of a word and the double "rr" are trilled quite strongly.
x—pronounced as in English, and also pronounced like the English "s" as in Xochimilco (soh-chih-MEEL-coh), and the English "h," as in México (ME-hee-coh). In Mexico "x" also is used to represent the "sh" sound in native languages, as in Xel-Ha (Shehl-HAH).
z—in Mexico is always pronounced like the English "s."

ch, ll, ñ—these are all letters in the Spanish alphabet and are found after the single letter: "ch" after "c," "ll" after "l," "ñ" after "n."

**Diphthongs**

Spanish diphthongs are pronounced as very swift omissions of the component vowels.

Ex. "ue" as in weh—fuente.

Ex. "au" as in English ouch—gaucho.

**Accent or Stress**

1. The stress falls on the next to the last syllable when a word ends in a vowel, "n" or "s."

Ex. hombre—OHM-breh.

Ex. hablan—AH-blahn.

Ex. estos—EHS-tos.

2. The stress falls on the last syllable when the word ends in a consonant other than "n" or "s."

Ex. hablar—ah-BLAR.

3. In some cases an accent mark will be found over a vowel. This does not change the pronunciation of that vowel but indicates that the stress falls on that syllable.

Ex. gramática—grah-MAH-teeh-cah.

# Words and Phrases

Note: All nouns in Spanish are either masculine or feminine, and there are two words meaning "the": el is used before masculine nouns, la before feminine nouns. Masculine words end with an o, feminine words end with an a (although there are a few exceptions). An adjective agrees in gender with the noun it modifies. The plural of el is los, of la is las. After words given on these pages the gender is indicated by (m.) for masculine, (f.) for feminine. For instance, say el hotel and los hoteles; la posada and las posadas. The word "usted," meaning "you," is abbreviated Ud.

## Language

| | |
|---|---|
| Do you understand English? | ¿Entiende Ud. el inglés? |
| I do not speak Spanish | No hablo español. |
| Yes, sir; no, madam | Si, señor; no, señora. |
| Very little | Muy poco. |
| I do not understand | No entiendo. |
| Do you understand me? | ¿Me entiende Ud.? |
| Please speak slowly | Por favor hable despacio. |
| I wish to speak with an interpreter | Quisiera hablar con un intérprete. |
| What did you say? | ¿Cómo dice? |

## Polite Phrases

| | |
|---|---|
| Good morning | Buenos días. |
| Good afternoon | Buenas tardes. |
| Good night | Buenas noches. |
| Goodbye; see you later | Adios; hasta la vista. |
| Thank you | Gracias. |
| Yes; very good | Sí; muy bien. |
| Please | Por favor. |
| Excuse me | Perdóneme. |
| I am very sorry | Lo siento mucho. |

## To Explain Your Needs

| | |
|---|---|
| I need; we need | Necesito; necesitamos. |
| I would like to telephone | Quisiera telefonear. |
| I am hungry; we are hungry | Tengo hambre; tenemos hambre. |
| I am thirsty; we are thirsty | Tengo sed; tenemos sed. |
| I am cold; we are cold | Tengo frío; tenemos frío. |
| I am warm; we are warm | Tengo calor; tenemos calor. |
| I am tired; we are tired | Estoy cansado; estamos cansados. |
| I am sick; we are sick | Estoy enfermo; estamos enfermos. |
| The child is sick; tired | El niño (la niña) está enfermo (a); cansado (a). |
| Men's room, ladies' room | El baño de hombres, de damas. |
| Fire | Fuego (m.). |
| Help | Auxilio; socorro (m.). |

## Time

| | |
|---|---|
| today | hoy |
| the morning | a mañana |
| tomorrow | mañana |
| noon | el mediodía |
| yesterday | ayer |
| the afternoon | la tarde |

| | |
|---|---|
| tonight | esta noche |
| night | la noche |
| last night | anoche |
| midnight | la media noche |
| What time is it? | ¿Qué hora es? |
| It is one o'clock | Es la una. |
| It is ten minutes past two | Son las dos y diez. |
| It is quarter past three | Son las tres y cuarto. |
| It is a quarter of five | Es un cuarto para las cinco. |
| It is 25 minutes of six | Son veinticinco para las seis. |
| It is half past four | Son las cuatro y media. |

## Days of the Week

| | |
|---|---|
| Sunday | domingo (m.) |
| Monday | lunes (m.) |
| Tuesday | martes (m.) |
| Wednesday | miércoles (m.) |
| Thursday | jueves (m.) |
| Friday | viernes (m.) |
| Saturday | sábado (m.) |

## Months of the Year

| | |
|---|---|
| January | enero (m.) |
| February | febrero (m.) |
| March | marzo (m.) |
| April | abril (m.) |
| May | mayo (m.) |
| June | junio (m.) |
| July | julio (m.) |
| August | agosto (m.) |
| September | septiembre (m.) |
| October | octubre (m.) |
| November | noviembre (m.) |
| December | diciembre (m.) |

## Colors

| | |
|---|---|
| white | blanco |
| black | negro |
| gray | gris |
| brown | café |
| red | rojo |
| pink | rosa |
| blue; dark blue | azul; azul oscuro |
| green; light green | verde; verde claro |
| purple | morado |
| yellow | amarillo |

## Useful Adjectives

**Note: These adjectives are in their masculine forms. End them with an "a" if you want the feminine form (except for grande, tarde and fácil, which are used for both genders).**

| | |
|---|---|
| bad | malo |
| high | alto |
| beautiful | bello |
| kind | bondadoso |
| cheap | barato |
| large | grande |
| clean | limpio |
| late | tarde |
| difficult | difícil |
| low | bajo |
| dirty | sucio |
| polite | cortés |
| early | temprano |
| sharp | agudo |
| easy | fácil |
| slow | lento |
| expensive | caro |

| | |
|---|---|
| small | pequeño |
| fast | rápido |
| ugly | feo |
| good | bueno |
| unkind | despiadado, duro |
| long | largo |
| short | corto |
| narrow | angosto |
| dangerous | peligroso |

## Numerals

| | | | | |
|---|---|---|---|---|
| 1. uno | 8. ocho | 15. quince | 30. treinta | 90. noventa |
| 2. dos | 9. nueve | 16. diez y seis | 31. treinta y uno | 100. cien |
| 3. tres | 10. diez | 17. diez y siete | 40. cuarenta | 200. doscientos |
| 4. cuatro | 11. once | 18. diez y ocho | 50. cincuenta | 500. quinientos |
| 5. cinco | 12. doce | 19. diez y nueve | 60. sesenta | 1,000. mil |
| 6. seis | 13. trece | 20. veinte | 70. setenta | 1,000,000. un |
| 7. siete | 14. catorce | 21. veintiuno | 80. ochenta | millón |

## Points of the Compass

north..........norte (m.)     south..........sur (m.)     east...........este (m.)     west...........oeste (m.)

Note: In addresses, east is oriente, abbreviated Ote.; west is poniente, abbreviated Pte.

## At the Border

| | |
|---|---|
| passport | pasaporte |
| tourist card | tarjeta de turista |
| age | edad |
| marital status | estado civil |
| single | soltero |
| married | casado |
| widowed | viudo |
| divorced | divorciado |
| profession or occupation | profesión; ocupación |
| vaccination card | certificado de vacuna |
| car owner's title (registration) | título de propiedad (registro) |
| driver's license | licencia de manejar |
| year of car | modelo (o año) |
| make (Ford, Plymouth, etc.) | marca |
| license plate number and state | número y estado de placa |
| chassis and motor number | número de chasis y motor |
| number of doors | número de puertas |
| number of cylinders | número de cilindros |
| number of passengers | número de pasajeros |

## On the Road

| | |
|---|---|
| highway | carretera (f.) |
| road | camino (m.) |
| street | calle (f.) |
| avenue | avenida (f.) |
| boulevard | bulevar (m.) |
| corner | esquina (f.) |
| kilometer | kilómetro (m.) |
| block | cuadra (f.) |
| left side | lado izquierdo (m.) |
| right side | lado derecho (m.) |
| Please show me the road to | Enséñeme el camino a. . . . |
| How far is? | ¿Qué tan lejos está. . . ? |
| Can we get to. . . before dark? | ¿Podemos llegar a. . . antes del anochecer? |
| Is this road dangerous? | ¿Es peligroso este camino? |
| Is that road in good condition? | ¿Está en buen estado ese camino? |
| Is it paved or is it a dirt road? | ¿Está pavimentado o es de tierra? |
| Go straight ahead. | Siga adelante. |
| Turn to the right; left. | Vuelta a la derecha; izquierda. |
| What city, town, is this? | ¿Qué ciudad, pueblo, es éste? |
| Where does this road lead? | ¿A dónde va este camino? |

## In Case of Car Trouble

| | |
|---|---|
| I want to ask you a favor. | Quiero pedirle un favor. |
| My car broke down. | Se me descompuso el carro. |
| I need a tow truck. | Necesito una grúa. |
| My lights don't work. | Mis faros no funcionan. |
| My engine's overheating. | Mi motor se está sobrecalentando. |
| I have run out of gasoline. | Se me acabó la gasolina. |
| Is there a gasoline station near here? | ¿Hay alguna gasolinería cerca de aquí? |
| Is there a garage near here? | ¿Hay algún taller cerca? |
| Please send a mechanic. | Por favor mándeme un mecánico. |
| May I go with you to get a mechanic? | ¿Puedo ir con usted a conseguir un mecánico? |
| Do you have a rope to tow my car? | ¿Tiene un cable para remolcar mi carro? |
| The starter does not work. | El arranque no funciona. |
| Can you help me push the car to one side of the road? | ¿Puede ayudarme a empujar el coche a un lado del camino? |
| Do you want to be my witness? | ¿Quiere ser mi testigo? |
| Do you want to help me change a tire? | ¿Quiere ayudarme a cambiar una llanta? |

## Arriving in Town

| | |
|---|---|
| Is English spoken here? | ¿Se habla inglés aquí? |
| Where is the center of town? | ¿Dónde está el centro de la ciudad? |
| May I park here? | ¿Puedo estacionarme aquí? |
| Could you recommend a good restaurant; a good small hotel; a first class hotel? | ¿Puede Ud. recomendar un buen restaurante; unbuen hotel pequeño; un hotel de primera clase? |
| Please direct me to the nearest post office | Por favor diríjame a la oficina de correos mas cercana. |
| I wish to telephone, to telegraph, to cable | Quiero telefonear, telegrafiar, cablegrafiar. |
| Please direct me to the railroad station, the bus station | Por favor diríjame a la estación del ferrocarril, a la estación del autobús. |
| Where is X Street, X Square, the X Hotel? | ¿Dónde está la Calle X, la Plaza X, el Hotel X? |
| How often does the bus go by? | ¿Que tan seguido pasa el autobús? |
| Does the streetcar stop here? | ¿Para aquí el tranvía? |
| I wish to change some money. | Quiero cambiar dinero. |
| What is the rate of exchange? | ¿Cuál es el tipo de cambio? |
| I want to cash a check. | Quiero cambiar un cheque. |
| I have lost my traveler's checks. | He perdido mis cheques de viajero. |
| Where can I find a policeman, a hairdresser, a doctor, a drug store? | ¿Dónde puedo hallar un policía, un peinador, un médico, una farmacia? |
| Where is the police station; the chamber of commerce; the automobile club? | ¿Dónde está la comisaría, la cámara de comerciola asociación automovilística? |
| Where can I find guidebooks, road maps, postcards, American newspapers? | ¿Dónde se pueden hallar guías turísticas, mapas de carreteras, tarjetas postales, periódicos norteamericanos? |

## At the Hotel

| | |
|---|---|
| hotel | hotel (m.) |
| inn | posada (f.) |
| guesthouse | casa de huéspedes (f.) |
| apartment house | apartamentos (m.) |
| furnished room | cuarto amueblado (m.) |
| stairway | escalera (f.) |
| bedroom | recámara (f.) |
| bathroom | cuarto de baño (m.) |
| kitchen | cocina (f.) |
| towel | toalla (f.) |
| washcloth | toallita facial (f.) |
| soap | jabón (m.) |
| air conditioning | aire acondicionado |
| room | cuarto (m.) |
| hot water | agua caliente |
| office | oficina (f.) |
| elevator | elevador (m.) |

| | |
|---|---|
| dining room | comedor (m.) |
| guest | huésped (m.) |
| manager | gerente |
| office employee | empleado de oficina |
| maid | camarera (f.) |
| key | llave (f.) |
| porter | mozo (m.) de servicios |
| bellboy | botones (m.) |
| ice water | agua con hielo |

| | |
|---|---|
| I want a single room, with bath | Deseo un cuarto para una persona, con baño. |
| I want a room for two, with twin beds | Deseo un cuarto para dos, con camas gemelas. |
| I want two connecting rooms | Deseo dos cuartos comunicados. |
| On the lower floor; upper floor | En el piso bajo; piso alto. |
| A front room; a back room | Un cuarto al frente; al fondo. |
| Do you have hot running water? | ¿Hay agua corriente y caliente? |
| What is the price? | ¿Cuál es el precio? |
| What is the minimum rate? | ¿Cuál es el precio mínimo? |
| Do you accept checks in payment? | ¿Acepta Ud. cheques en pago? |
| Is there a garage? | ¿Hay garage? |
| Please call me at six o'clock | Hágame el favor de llamarme a las seis. |
| Where is the ladies' room, men's room? | ¿Dónde está el lavabo de señoras, de señores? |
| Will you have the baggage brought up? down? | ¿Quiere Ud. hacer subir. . . .bajar el equipaje? |
| We are leaving tomorrow | Partimos mañana. |
| We are staying several days. . . Just tonight. | Nos quedaremos aquí unos pocos días. . . .solamente esta noche. |
| Please send these clothes to the laundry | Hágame el favor de mandar esta ropa a la lavandería. |
| Please clean and press this suit | Hágame el favor de limpiar y planchar este traje. |
| I want it today; tomorrow. | Lo quiero hoy; mañana. |
| Where is a barber shop? | ¿Dónde hay una peluquería? |
| I wish my bill, please. | Quiero mi cuenta, por favor. |
| Please forward my correspondence to this address. | Por favor reexpida mi correspondencia a esta dirección. |
| Do you want to prepare a lunch for us to carry with us? | ¿Quiere Ud. prepararnos un almuerzo para llevárnoslo? |

## At the Garage

| | |
|---|---|
| Fill up the gasoline tank; the radiator | Llene el tanque de gasolina; el radiador. |
| Give me five, ten, fifteen, twenty liters | Deme cinco, diez, quince, veinte litros. |
| Do you have unleaded gasoline? | ¿Tiene gasolina sin plomo? |
| How much is gasoline per liter? | ¿Cuánto vale el litro de gasolina? |
| Check the oil; change the oil, antifreeze | Vea el aceite; cambie el aceite, anticongelante. |
| Please lubricate the car; wash the car | Favor de lubricar el automóvil; lavar el automóvil. |
| Please tighten the brakes; adjust the brakes | Favor de apretar los frenos; ajustar los frenos. |
| Please tune the engine; change the spark plugs | Favor de afinarme el motor; cambiar las bujías. |
| My tire has a puncture. Can you repair it? | Mi llanta está picada. ¿Puede repararla? |
| The tire is flat. | La llanta está desinflada. |
| Put water in the battery. | Por favor, ponga agua en la batería. |
| The horn is not working. | La bocina no funciona. |
| The battery needs charging | La batería necesita carga. |
| Please replace this headlamp | Por favor, cámbieme este farol. |
| the fan belt | la banda del ventilador. |
| the radiator hose | la manguera del radiador. |
| The gas line is clogged | La tubería de gasolina está tapada. |
| My engine's overheating | Mi motor se está sobrecalentando. |
| The exhaust is choked | Está obstruido el tubo de escape. |
| The steering gear is out of order | La dirección está descompuesta. |
| The radiator leaks | El radiador gotea. |
| The clutch slips | El clutch se derrapa. |
| The gasoline tank is leaking | El tanque de gasolina está goteando. |
| There is a short circuit | Hay un cortocircuito. |
| The windshield wiper does not work | El limpiavidrios del parabrisa no funciona. |
| The taillight does not work | La calavera no funciona. |
| The water pump does not work | La bomba de agua no funciona. |
| Please clean the windshield | Favor de limpiar el parabrisa. |
| When will the repairs be finished? | ¿Cuándo terminará la reparación? |

How much do I owe you? ........................................ ¿Cuánto le debo?

## In Restaurants

| | |
|---|---|
| breakfast | desayuno (m). |
| lunch | almuerzo (m.) |
| midday meal | comida (f.) |
| dinner; supper | cena (f.); merienda (f.) |
| spoon | cuchara (f.) |
| cup | taza (f.) |
| glass | vaso (m.) |
| napkin | servilleta (f.) |
| bill | cuenta (f.) |
| tip | propina (f.) |
| knife | cuchillo (m.) |
| fork | tenedor (m.) |

### Meat, Eggs, Fish

| | |
|---|---|
| bacon | tocino (m.) |
| beef | carne (f.) de res (m.) |
| beefsteak | bistec (m.) |
| chicken | pollo (m.) |
| duck | pato (m.) |
| egg | huevo (m.) |
| fried | frito |
| soft-boiled | tibio |
| hard-boiled | duro |
| fish | pescado (m.) |
| ham | jamón (m.) |
| lamb | carne (f.) de carnero (m.) |
| lamb chops | chuletas (f.) de carnero (m.) |
| meat | carne (f.) |
| omelet | omelete de huevo (m.) |
| pork | carne (f.) de puerco (m.) |
| roast | asado (m.) |
| sausage | salchicha (f.) |
| turkey | guajolote (m.); pavo (m.) |
| veal | ternera (f.) |

### Vegetables

| | |
|---|---|
| salad | ensalada (f.) |
| beans | frijoles (m.) |
| beets | betabeles (f.) |
| cabbage | repollo (m.); col (f.) |
| corn; young corn | maiz (m.); elote (m.) |
| lettuce | lechuga (f.) |
| onion | cebolla (f.) |
| peas | chícharos (m.) |
| potatoes | papas (f.) |
| rice | arroz (m.) |
| string beans | ejotes (m.) |
| sweet potatoes | camotes (m.) |
| tomatoes | jitomates (m.) |
| vegetables | legumbres (f.); verduras (f.) |

### Bread

| | |
|---|---|
| bread | pan (m.) |
| crackers | galletas (f.) |
| toast | pan tostado (m.) |

### Beverages, Liquors

| | |
|---|---|
| beer | cerveza (f.) |
| brandy | brandy (m.) |
| coffee | café (m.) |
| with cream | con crema (f.) |
| without cream | sin crema |
| gin | ginebra (f.) |
| juice | jugo (m.) |

milk ........................................................................leche (f.)
rum ........................................................................ron (m.)
tea..........................................................................té (m.)
whiskey ..................................................................whisky (m.)
table wine...............................................................vino de mesa (m.)

### Sweets
dessert....................................................................postre (m.)
sweet rolls..............................................................pan dulce (m.)
cake .......................................................................pastel (m.)
candies ..................................................................dulces (m.)
cookies...................................................................galletas (f.)
custard ...................................................................flan (m.)
ice cream ...............................................................helado (m.)
sherbets .................................................................nieves (f.)
pastries ..................................................................pasteles (m.)
pie...........................................................................pastel (m.)

### Fruits, Nuts
apple.......................................................................manzana (f.)
avocado ..................................................................aguacate (m.)
banana....................................................................plátano (m.)
cantaloupe ..............................................................melón (m.)
figs ..........................................................................higos (m.)
fruit..........................................................................fruta (f.)
grapes.....................................................................uvas (f.)
guava.......................................................................guayaba (f.)
grapefruit.................................................................toronja (f.)
lemon.......................................................................limón amarillo (m.)
lime (sweet) ............................................................limón (m.)
nuts..........................................................................nueces (f.)
olives.......................................................................aceitunas (f.)
orange......................................................................naranja (f.)
peach.......................................................................durazno (m.)
peanuts...................................................................cacahuates (m.)
pecans.....................................................................nueces (f.)
pineapple ................................................................piña (f.)
strawberries ...........................................................fresas (f.)
walnut .....................................................................nuez (f.) de castilla
watermelon .............................................................sandía (f.)

### Miscellaneous
sugar.......................................................................azúcar (m.)
salt ..........................................................................sal (f.)
pepper.....................................................................pimienta (f.)
butter.......................................................................mantequilla (f.)
soup; broth..............................................................sopa (f.); caldo (m.)
cheese ....................................................................queso (m.)
honey.......................................................................miel de abejas (f.)
cigarette; cigar .......................................................cigarrillo (m.); puro (m.)
Please bring me the menu........................................Por favor tráigame el menú.
I like my meat rare, medium, well done .....................Quiero la carne roja, término medio, bien cocida

# Fiestas and Holidays

NOTE: The dates listed here for local celebrations are often variable and may be moved forward or back when the fiesta must be celebrated on a specific day of the week or time of the month or year. Confirm dates in advance with your hotel, at a local tourist information office or at city hall.

## National Holidays

All banks and most businesses close on these days.

| | |
|---|---|
| Jan. 1 | New Year's Day (Año Nuevo) |
| Feb. 5 | Constitution Day (Día de la Constitución) commemorates the Constitutions of 1857 and 1917. |
| Mar. 21 | Birthday of Benito Juárez, Mexican president and national hero. |
| May 1 | Labor Day (Primero de Mayo), with workers' parades throughout the country. |
| May 5 | Battle of Puebla (Batalla de Puebla), commonly known as Cinco de Mayo, commemorates the Mexican victory over the French at Puebla in 1862. |
| June 1 | Navy Day |
| Sept. 1 | The president of Mexico delivers the annual State of the Union Address (Informe Presidencial). |
| Sept. 16 | Mexican Independence Day (Día de la Independencia). The president presides at the ceremony of the *Grito de Dolores* in Mexico City's *Zócalo*, or sometimes at the parish church in Dolores Hidalgo, Gto., where Father Miguel Hidalgo y Costilla issued the *Grito* in 1810. Special celebrations take place in each state capital and start the night of Sept. 15. |
| Oct. 12 | Discovery of the New World by Christopher Columbus, known as Día de la Raza (Day of the Race). |
| Dec. 25 | Christmas Day (Navidad). Plays, religious ceremonies. |

## Fiestas and Fairs in Mexico

The following fiestas and holiday periods are celebrated in many parts of the country.

| | |
|---|---|
| Jan. 6 | Day of the Three Kings (Día de los Santos Reyes) features an exchange of gifts in accordance with the three gift-bearing wise men and is the culmination of Christmas festivities. This also is the day when *Rosca de Los Reyes* (King's Loaf) is served. The round, doughnut-like cake has a plastic doll inside; if you are served the slice containing the doll, tradition says you must host a party on Candlemas Day. |
| Feb. (varies) | Carnaval is a 5-day celebration beginning the weekend before Lent and exuberantly celebrated with parades, floats and dancing in the streets. Especially festive in port cities like Ensenada, B.C.; La Paz, B.C.S.; Mazatlán, Sin.; and Veracruz, Ver. |
| Feb. 2 | Candlemas (Día de la Candelaria) is celebrated with processions, dancing, music and food to observe the passing of winter. |
| Mar. 19 | St. Joseph's Day (Día de San José). Especially colorful in Tamuín, S.L.P. |
| Palm Sunday to Easter Sunday | Holy Week (Semana Santa). Particularly impressive are the candlelight processions in Taxco, the Passion Play in Iztapalapa (Mexico City), and the Processions of Silence in San Luis Potosí, S.L.P. and San Miguel de Allende, Gto. Other notable observances occur in Pátzcuaro, Mich.; Querétaro, Qro.; Tzintzuntzan, Mich.; and Zinacantán, Chis. |
| Holy Saturday | Judas Day. Grotesque papier-mâché figures representing Judas are burned the day before Easter Sunday. Especially dramatic in Mexico City and vicinity. |
| May 3 | Holy Cross Day (Día de la Santa Cruz). Construction workers decorate and mount crosses on buildings at construction sites, followed by picnics and fireworks. |
| June 24 | Saint John the Baptist Day (Día de San Juan Bautista) is celebrated with fairs, religious festivities and crowd-pleasing spectacles associated with water dunking. |
| Aug. 15-16 and 20-22 | Celebration for the Day of the Virgin of Charity and Assumption Day (Día de la Asunción). Flowers and sawdust adorn the streets for processions and special masses. Especially significant in Huamantla, Pue. Fair, Indian dances, *tianguis*. |
| Oct. 4 | St. Francis' Day. Especially interesting in Real de Catorce, S.L.P., and San Francisquito, Son. |
| Nov. 1-2 | Day of the Dead (Día de Los Muertos). A 2-day religious festival celebrated throughout Mexico and marked by visits to cemeteries, flower and culinary offerings, candlelight vigils, elaborately decorated home altars and general merrymaking. It is especially impressive on Isla Janitzio, Mich. Other noteworthy observances take place in Tzintzuntzan, Mich.; Oaxaca, Oax.; and Chiapa de Corzo, Chis. |

| | | |
|---|---|---|
| **Nov. 20** | | Revolution Day (Día de la Revolución). Not a national holiday, but a day marking the anniversary of the Mexican Revolution of 1910 with speeches and official ceremonies. |
| **Dec. 8** | | Immaculate Conception. San Juan de los Lagos, Jal., and Pátzcuaro, Mich. are among the many towns with noteworthy celebrations. |
| **Dec. 12** | | Feast Day of the Virgin of Guadalupe. Religious festival that pays tribute to the Guadalupe Virgin. This is Mexico's largest religious pilgrimage. Especially dramatic in Mexico City and Monterrey, N.L., but celebrations take place throughout the country. |
| **Dec. 16-Jan. 6** | | Las Posadas. A candlelit procession ending at a nativity scene is part of the re-enactment of Mary and Joseph's search for shelter in Bethlehem. The entire country celebrates, and some of the programs are quite impressive. |
| **Dec. 31** | | New Year's Eve and Thanksgiving (Fin de Año y Día de Gracias). Especially vibrant in Mexico City, where empty eggshells filled with confetti and food coloring are tossed into the air. |

# Other Selected Local Festivals and Events

| | | |
|---|---|---|
| **Jan. 17** | Taxco, Gro. | St. Anthony's Day. Blessing of pets and other animals in the parish church. |
| **Jan. 18** | Taxco, Gro. | Day of Santa Prisca, town patroness, begins with parishioners singing early morning wake-up songs (mañanitas) to the Virgin. Celebration and dancing last all day. |
| **Feb. 1-3** | San Blas, Nay. | Blessing of the Sea. Dancing and horse races. |
| **Mar. 6** | Taxco, Gro. | Day of Our Lord of Xalpa. Indian dances include Los Tlacololeros, Santiagos, Diablos and Pescadores. |
| **Mar. 18-Apr. 4** | Tonalá, Jal. | Ceramics Fair. Handicraft exhibits and sales. |
| **Mar. or Apr.** | Uruapan, Mich. | Palm Sunday celebration with a huge, weeklong ceramics contest and exhibition, handicraft sales. |
| **Apr. 1-7** | Cuernavaca, Mor. | Flower Fair. Exhibits and competitions in floriculture and gardening. Sound-and-light show; popular entertainers. |
| **Apr. 16-May 6** | Aguascalientes, Ags. | San Marcos Fair. A major commercial, industrial and agricultural exposition. Handicrafts, local food and beverages, bullfights, exhibits. |
| **Apr. 20-26** | Tuxtla Gutiérrez, Chis. | Fiesta of St. Mark the Evangelist. A regional commercial and crafts fair, with charreadas, theatrical presentations, marimba contests and sports events. |
| **Apr. (last week)** | Villahermosa, Tab. | Tabasco State Fair. People from throughout the state present their music, dances and traditions. Folkloric ballet. |
| **May (last 3 weekends)** | Taxco, Gro. | Alarcón Days. Cultural and artistic festival with band serenades, musical performances and presentations of plays by Taxco-born playwright Juan Ruiz de Alarcón. |
| **May (3 weeks)** | Morelia, Mich. | Michoacán State Fair (Feria de Morelia). Handicrafts, livestock and agricultural exhibitions, regional dances, bullfights. Fireworks on May 18 mark the anniversary of the city's founding in 1541. |
| **May 3-15** | Tepic, Nay. | Fiesta of St. Isador the Farmer. A commercial and cultural fair that includes the blessing of seeds, animals and water. |
| **May 17-June 3** | Chihuahua, Chih. | Fiesta of Santa Rita. A major fair with commercial exhibits, cultural events, food and Indian dances. |
| **May 20-June 10** | Monterrey, N.L. | Commercial and agricultural fair. |
| **May 20-30** | Tequisquiapan, Qro. | National Wine and Cheese Fair. Tastings and sales, tianguis, cultural events. |
| **June (1st Thurs.)** | Temascalcingo, Mex. | Corpus Christi Thursday. Blessing of farm animals and equipment; children in Indian costumes. |
| **June 15-July 2** | Tlaquepaque, Jal. | National Ceramics Fair and June Fiestas. Craft competitions, exhibits and demonstrations; cultural events. |
| **June 29** | Zaachila, Oax. | Fiesta of St. Peter and St. Paul. |
| **June 18** | Papantla, Ver. | Corpus Christi Day and Vanilla Festival. The famous Flying Pole dancers perform in their place of origin. Regional food and beverages, booths with vanilla products. |
| **July 25** | Santiago Tuxtla, Ver. | Day of St. James the Apostle. Líseres (in which participants wear jaguar costumes), Negritos and other local Indian dances. |
| **Mid- to late July (two successive Mondays)** | Oaxaca, Oax. | Guelaguetza (Festival of Cooperation). Elaborate, dynamic folkloric festival with dances, regional costumes, music and food. |
| **July 20-Aug. 5** | Santa Ana Chiautempan, Tlax. | National Sarape Fair (Feria Nacional del Sarape). This fair takes place simultaneously with the celebration of the town's patron saint on July 26. |
| **Aug. (variable)** | Santa Clara del Cobre, Mich. | Copper Fair. Copper handicrafts. Indian dancers, floats. |

# Highway Signs

Stop

No Passing

Horizontal Clearance

Maximum Weight (Metric Tons)

No Pedestrians

Parking Limit

One-Hour Parking

No Left Turn

No U Turn

No Parking

Keep to the Right

Inspection

No Trucks

Pedestrians Keep Left

Speed Limit (In K.P.H.)

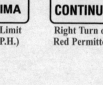
Right Turn on Red Permitted

No Bicycles

Keep Right

Do Not Enter

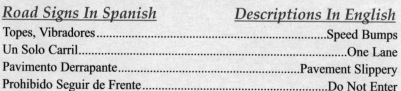

## Road Signs In Spanish

## Descriptions In English

Topes, Vibradores..........................................Speed Bumps
Un Solo Carril..............................................One Lane
Pavimento Derrapante..................................Pavement Slippery
Prohibido Seguir de Frente...........................Do Not Enter
Vado...........................................................Dip

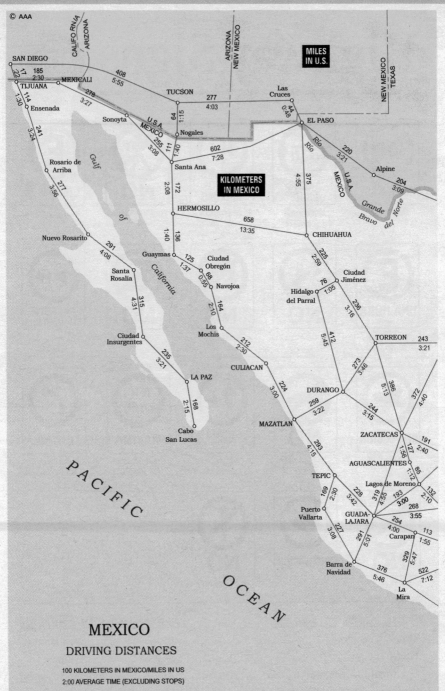

© AAA

CALIFORNIA / ARIZONA

ARIZONA / NEW MEXICO

NEW MEXICO / TEXAS

**MILES IN U.S.**

SAN DIEGO

185
2:30

1 / :22

114
1:30

TIJUANA

MEXICALI

408
5:55

278
3:27

241
3:24

Ensenada

Sonoyta

U.S.A.
MEXICO

TUCSON

277
4:03

64
1:15

Las
Cruces

44
0:48

EL PASO

Rio

220
3:21

Alpine

204
3:09

Rosario de
Arriba

277
3:59

265
3:08

111
1:41

Nogales

602
7:28

375
4:55

U.S.A.
MEXICO

Grande

Bravo   del

del   Norte

Gulf

Santa Ana

172
2:08

**KILOMETERS
IN MEXICO**

Nuevo Rosarito

291
4:08

HERMOSILLO

136
1:40

658
13:35

CHIHUAHUA

225
2:59

of

Guaymas

125
1:37

Ciudad
Obregón

68
0:55

Ciudad
Jiménez

Santa
Rosalia

315
4:31

California

Navojoa

Hidalgo
del Parral

76
1:05

238
3:16

Ciudad
Insurgentes

235
3:21

164

2:10

Los
Mochis

212
2:30

412
5:45

TORREON

243
3:21

LA PAZ

168
2:15

CULIACAN

224
3:00

273
3:46

386
5:13

372
4:40

Cabo
San Lucas

DURANGO

259
3:22

244
3:15

ZACATECAS

191
1:56

127
2:40

MAZATLAN

293
4:15

AGUASCALIENTES

85
1:12

132
2:10

TEPIC

169
2:00

228
3:42

Lagos de Moreno

319
4:55

193
3:00

268
3:55

Puerto
Vallarta

227
3:08

GUADA-
LAJARA

291
5:01

254
4:00

Carapan

113
1:55

Barra de
Navidad

376
5:46

329
5:47

522
7:12

La
Mira

*PACIFIC*

*OCEAN*

# MEXICO

## DRIVING DISTANCES

100 KILOMETERS IN MEXICO/MILES IN US

2:00 AVERAGE TIME (EXCLUDING STOPS)

3632-16

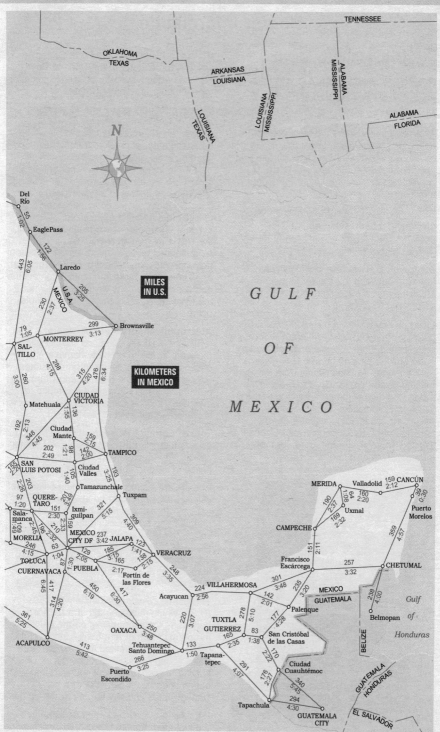

# Border Information

## Traveling to Mexico

### FOR U.S. AND CANADIAN RESIDENTS TRAVELING TO MEXICO

AAA recommends that travelers consult online U.S. State Department travel advisories when planning travel abroad. Find this information at http://travel.state.gov/content/passports/english/alertswarnings/mexico-travel-warning.html.

**Border crossing requirements:** Travelers are required to present proper travel documents for travel to Mexico and to return to the United States.

**Air travel:** U.S. and Canadian citizens traveling between the United States and Mexico by air are required to show a valid passport.

**Land or sea travel:** A passport or passport card, or other U.S. official ID (not including a state-issued driver's license), is required to enter Mexico by land or sea. U.S. citizens returning to the United States from Mexico by land or sea are required to present proper travel documents according to the Western Hemisphere Travel Initiative. Approved documents include a passport or passport card, Enhanced Driver's License or Trusted Traveler program card; for more information refer to the U.S. Department of

State's website travel.state.gov. Canadian citizens should refer to the Canada Border Services Agency website cbsa-asfc.gc.ca for requirements to re-enter Canada.

**Children:** Minors under age 18 traveling alone or with someone other than a parent or legal guardian are required to present a notarized letter of consent from at least one absent parent giving permission to travel only if the minor is departing (not entering) Mexico, is traveling by air or sea or is using Mexican documents to travel. However, because airline or Mexican immigration officials may request a notarized letter of consent under other circumstances as well, the U.S. Embassy in Mexico City recommends that any minor traveling without both parents carry a notarized consent letter at all times. For more information contact the embassy, the nearest Mexican consulate or the Mexican National Immigration Institute (INM).

**Automobile insurance:** Full coverage from a reliable Mexican insurance company is required, including property damage and public liability. AAA offices in border states (along with offices in Nevada and Utah) can provide Mexican automobile insurance to members. U.S. or Canadian automobile insurance is not valid in Mexico.

**Tourist permits:** When traveling to Mexico as a tourist you must obtain an FMM tourist permit. You must show a valid passport or passport card to obtain a permit.

Permits are issued at immigration offices at official points of entry and at some Mexican tourism offices. You must have a valid tourist permit if you remain within the border zone—the area within 20 to 30 kilometers (12 to 19 miles) of the U.S. border, depending on the Mexican state—for more than 72 hours, or if you travel beyond the border zone.

The permit costs approximately $24.50 (U.S.), which must be paid at a Mexican bank (see the list of banks on the back of the permit form) or at a bank window at the border. You are required to show the "Fee Paid" stamp on your tourist permit when leaving Mexico. It is recommended that you obtain your tourist permit before leaving the United States and pay the fee at the border.

If traveling by air, the permit is distributed on the flight and the fee is included in the airline

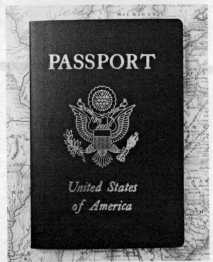

ticket price. If arriving by cruise ship, the fee is collected when disembarking or is included in the cruise fare if the stay is longer than 72 hours.

## Exemptions:

- Visitors traveling by sea, staying less than 72 hours and remaining in the seaport.
- Visitors traveling by land to destinations within the border zone and staying less than 72 hours.
- Visitors traveling by land beyond the border zone, staying less than 72 hours and limiting their visit to the following destinations/tourist corridors: Tijuana to Ensenada, Baja California; Sonoyta to Puerto Peñasco, Sonora; Ciudad Juárez to Paquime, Chihuahua; Piedras Negras to Santa Rosa, Coahuila; and Reynosa to Presa Cuchillo, Nuevo León.
- Business travelers with a business visa; students (as defined by Mexican immigration laws) with a student visa (contact a Mexican consulate for business/student visa information).

## Permit validity:

- The permit is valid for up to 180 days.
- A multiple-entry permit allows unlimited visits into and out of Mexico within the 180-day period.
- In Baja California a tourist permit is good for a maximum of 180 days per year and 30 days per visit.
- A tourist permit not used within 90 days of issue becomes void.
- Visitors should carry their tourist permit with them at all times while in Mexico.
- If a permit is lost, obtain a duplicate from local immigration officials (write down the tourist permit number and keep it separate from the permit to expedite this process).
- Permits are required to be turned in to Mexican immigration officials at the border when you depart the country.
- If you choose to remain in Mexico beyond the permit validity period an extension must be requested from immigration authorities prior to the expiration date.
- Violation of the laws governing tourist permits may result in subsequently being refused entry into Mexico and/or incurring a substantial fine.

Vehicle travel beyond the border zone requires a government-issued temporary vehicle importation permit and a promise to return vehicle form. These two documents are not required in Baja California unless the vehicle is put on a ferry bound for the mainland. They also are not required for travel to the following destinations in the state of Sonora: Rocky Point (Puerto Peñasco), Guaymas, San Carlos, Bahía Kino and other locations west of Mex. 15, as well as cities along Mex. 15 (Magdalena, Santa Ana, Hermosillo).

An Only Sonora permit is acceptable if driving is confined within the state east of Mex. 15 as well as south of Empalme (about 350 miles south of the U.S. border). The permit can be obtained at Banjercito offices in Agua Prieta (opposite Douglas, Ariz.), Cananea (on Mex. 2 southwest of Agua Prieta) and Empalme (on Mex. 15 at Km marker 98, just south of the Guaymas bypass).

To obtain the temporary vehicle importation permit and promise to return vehicle form at an official point of entry (immigration checkpoint), the vehicle owner must have a valid (unexpired) tourist permit, a valid international major credit card and a current vehicle license/registration receipt (the original and two copies). Information on the application for temporary vehicle importation and on the promise to return form must match; the same requirements apply to both.

An administration fee plus tax must be paid with a major international credit card (American Express, Mastercard or Visa) at the official point of entry (mainland border crossing or ferry crossing from Baja California to the mainland) in order to receive a temporary importation permit windshield sticker. The credit card must be in the vehicle owner's name and issued by a U.S. or Canadian bank or lending institution. Vehicle owners who don't have a major credit card must post a bond ($200 to $400 based on vehicle value) with a Mexican bonding firm (Afianzadora) at the point of entry. Cash, checks, money orders or credit cards issued by a Mexican bank are not accepted.

## More about temporary importation permits:

- Generally issued for 180 days, the same length as the tourist permit.
- Only one permit will be issued per person, for one motorized vehicle at a time.
- Carry the permit with you; do not leave it in the vehicle.
- Return permit, promise to return vehicle form and windshield sticker to Mexican customs officials at the Banjercito office

at the border before or on the expiration date shown on the form, or be subject to a fine.
- If the permit or form is lost or stolen, Mexican customs offices can issue replacement documentation provided you obtain a certified document attesting to the loss from your homeland (U.S. or Canada) embassy or consulate.
- If you remain in Mexico beyond the authorized time period and without the proper documentation, your car will be immediately confiscated.

**Pets:** U.S. visitors may bring a dog, cat or bird into Mexico with government approval. A pet health certificate signed not more than 15 days before the animal enters Mexico and a pet vaccination certificate showing proof of treatment for rabies, hepatitis and leptospirosis are required at the border for each animal. A pet permit fee is charged at the time of entry.

# Leaving Mexico

## FOR U.S. AND CANADIAN RESIDENTS LEAVING MEXICO

**When leaving the country:**
- FMM tourist permits, temporary vehicle importation permits, promise to return vehicle forms and windshield stickers must be returned to Mexican immigration and customs officials at the departure or border checkpoint (or at an interior inspection point).

© Barry Singleton / Shutterstock.com

- Those entering Mexico with a motor vehicle must leave the country with the vehicle.
- At highway stations near the U.S. border, Mexican agricultural officials will inspect vehicles traveling north that are carrying any fruits, vegetables, houseplants and other plant matter.
- You must have an export certificate to take official cultural artifacts (excluding handicrafts) out of the country.
- Religious or archeological artifacts may not be taken out of the country.

**Returning to the United States or Canada:**

U.S. citizens returning from Mexico by land or sea are required to present proper travel documents; refer to the U.S. Department of State website for the most current information. Canadian citizens entering the United States are subject to the rules governing entry to the U.S. by foreign nationals; refer to the Canadian Border Services Agency website for requirements to re-enter Canada.

**U.S. exemptions:**
- You may bring back duty-free articles not exceeding $800 in retail value from a stay abroad of at least 48 hours.
- The exemption is allowed once every 30 days.
- A family (related persons living in the same household) may combine exemptions; i.e., a family of six would be entitled to $1,600 worth of goods duty-free on one declaration, even if the articles claimed by one member exceed that individual's $800 amount.
- Duty must be paid on all items in excess of the exemption amount.
- Payment of duty is required upon arrival.
- Gifts taken across the U.S./Mexico border are considered to be for personal use and are included in the $800 exemption.
- Articles purchased and left behind for alterations or other reasons do not qualify for the $800 exemption when shipped at a later date.
- The $800 exemption may include no more than 1 liter of alcoholic beverages and no more than 200 cigarettes and 100 cigars.

**Restricted or prohibited articles:** An agricultural quarantine bans the importation of certain fruits, vegetables, plants, livestock, poultry and meats. All food products brought into the United States must be declared. The U.S. Department of Agriculture also prohibits bringing back any type of pet. Visit the Animal and Plant Health Inspection Service (APHIS) website or U.S. Customs at cbp.gov for more information.

One foreign-made article carrying a protected U.S. trademark (i.e., camera, binoculars, musical instrument, jewelry or watch) may normally be brought into the United States under your personal exemption, provided it is for your private use and not sold within 1 year of importation.

The following are prohibited: narcotics and dangerous drugs, drug paraphernalia, obscene articles and publications, seditious or treasonable matter, lottery tickets, hazardous items (fireworks, dangerous toys, toxic or poisonous substances) and switchblade knives. Goods originating in the following embargoed countries are prohibited: Western Balkans, Burma, Ivory Coast, Cuba, Democratic Republic of Congo, Iran, Iraq, Liberia, Sierra Leone, Sudan, Syria and Zimbabwe.

If you plan to bring back items made of fur or whalebone, any animal skin other than cowhide leather, or any product manufactured wholly or in part from any type of wildlife, contact the U.S. Fish and Wildlife Service's Office of Law Enforcement, 4401 N. Fairfax Dr., MS-LE-3000, Arlington, VA 22203. Phone (703) 358-1949 for regulations; fws.gov/le.

**Alcoholic beverages:** Both federal and state laws apply. If regulations conflict, state laws regarding import limits supersede.

U.S. residents 21 years of age or older may bring into the United States 1 liter of alcohol duty-free once every 30 days. However, if you arrive in a state that permits a lesser amount than what you have legally brought into the United States, state law prevails.

**Gifts:** Gifts in packages with a total retail value not exceeding $100 may be sent to friends or relatives in the United States free of U.S. customs duty or tax, provided no recipient receives more than one gift shipment per day. Gifts may be sent to more than one person in the same package if they are individually wrapped and labeled with each recipient's name. Perfumes valued at more than $5 retail, tobacco products or alcoholic beverages may not be included in gift packages, which should be clearly marked with the designation "Unsolicited Gift," the gift giver's name and the retail value of the contents.

**Duties:** A flat rate duty of 3 percent is applied to the first $1,000 (fair retail value) worth of merchandise in excess of the $800 customs exemption. A sales receipt constitutes proof of value. Family members residing in one household and traveling together may group articles for application of the flat-duty rate, which may be taken once every 30 days. Articles must accompany you to the U.S. border.

**Canadian exemptions:** Citizens who have been outside Canada at least 48 hours may bring back duty- and tax-free goods not exceeding $400 (CAN) in retail value. The exemption can be claimed any number of times a year. Citizens who have been outside Canada 7 days or more may bring back duty- and tax-free goods not exceeding $750 (CAN) in retail value. The $750 exemption can be claimed regardless of any $400 exemption taken on a previous trip and requires a written declaration. The two exemptions may not be combined.

Citizens may claim duty- and tax-free entry for articles (excluding tobacco products or alcoholic beverages) not exceeding $50 (CAN) in retail value when returning from a trip abroad of at least 24 hours. Items brought into Canada under a personal exemption must be for personal or household use, souvenirs or gifts.

**Canadian limitations (on either the $400 or $750 exemption):** 50 cigars, 200 cigarettes, 200 tobacco sticks, 200 grams (6.4 ounces) of tobacco, 40 ounces (1.1 liters) of liquor, 53 imperial ounces of wine and 300 ounces (8.5 liters) of beer or ale (equivalent to 24 12-ounce bottles/cans). All exemptions are individual and may not be combined with that of another person to cover an article valued at more than the maximum exemption. You may be asked to prove the length of your visit outside Canada. Dated sales receipts for goods or services constitute valid proof.

All declared goods associated with the $400 personal exemption must accompany the purchaser to the Canadian border. Declared goods associated with the $750 personal exemption may follow the purchaser by mail.

While AAA makes every effort to provide accurate and complete information, AAA makes no warranty, express or implied, and assumes no legal liability or responsibility for the accuracy or completeness of any information contained herein.

# Points of Interest Index

## Index Legend

## BRIDGES

## BUILDINGS, OFFICE

## BUILDINGS, PUBLIC; CAPITOL; CITY HALL

**SIGHTSEEING TOURS**

# Bed & Breakfast Hotels Index

Some bed and breakfasts listed below might have historical significance.
Those properties are also referenced in the Historical index.

# Country Inns Index

Some of the following country inns can also be considered as bed-and-breakfast operations.

# Historical Hotels & Restaurants Index

Some of the following historical lodgings can also be considered as bed-and-breakfast operations.

# Resorts Index

Many establishments are located in resort areas; however, the following
places have extensive on-premises recreational facilities:

## Resorts (cont'd)

## YUCATÁN PENINSULA
### ACCOMMODATIONS

## Resorts (cont'd)

# Comprehensive City Index

Here is an alphabetical list of all cities and places appearing in this Travel Guide. Each city includes the state in which it is located. Page numbers under the POI column indicate where points of interest text begins. Page numbers under the H&R column indicate where lodging and restaurant listings begin.

## Comprehensive City Index (cont'd)

## Comprehensive City Index (cont'd)

# Get Involved and Keep Teens Safe

Exploring the countryside or visiting nearby cities can be perfect opportunities to teach your teens good habits and rules of the road—before and after they learn to drive.

**Get resources from AAA/CAA:**

- Tools to improve driving skills
- Information about driver's licensing
- Tips to avoid distracted driving
- Advice for keeping insurance costs down
- A model parent-teen driving agreement

Visit TeenDriving.AAA.com or DriveRight.CAA.ca

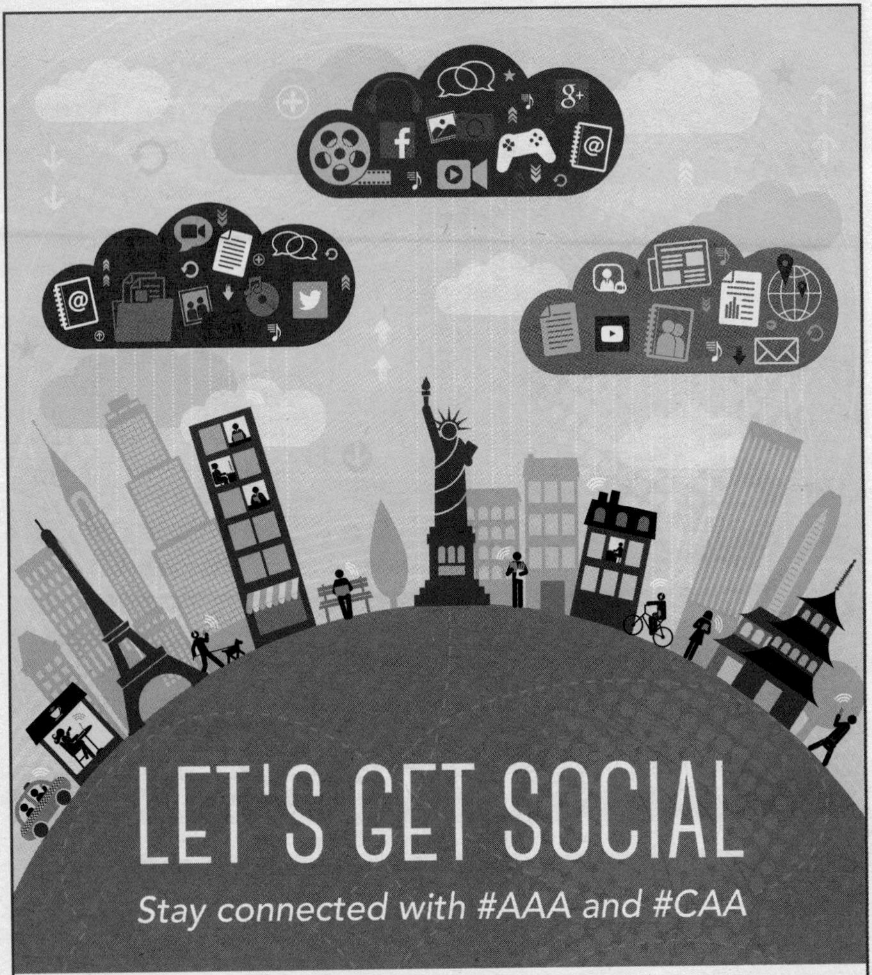
LET'S GET SOCIAL
Stay connected with #AAA and #CAA

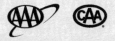

# THE FREEDOM TO GET
## where you want to go

Take advantage of valuable resources from the leading authority on senior driver safety and mobility:

- Assess your driving fitness
- Maintain your driving skills to drive safely longer
- Get expert advice

Before you hit the open road, make the AAA or CAA senior driving site the first stop on your journey.

604

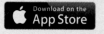

**Grand
Fiesta Americana**
CORAL BEACH CANCÚN

THE *Grand*
CLUB

For the discerning traveler searching a personalized high-quality service that frames a well-deserved vacation.
VIP status at the adults only Grand Club Lounge, outstanding panoramic views of the Caribbean, private concierge and butler brings the true meaning of Mexican hospitality. But if it's sun you are searching for, the family friendly Grand Beach Club & Sundeck will turn into your own oasis.

**Stay for 5 or more nights and get $1,000 resort credit to enjoy in different experiences at the resort (\*)**

Toll free: 1 888 830 9008
coralbeachcancunresort.com  🅕 🅣 📷 / GrandCoralBeach

Sabre: FH24223 | Amadeus: FHCUN700 | Worldspan: FHCUN50 | Apollo: FH19076

(\*) Promotion subject to availability. Prior reservation is needed.

LVX
*Preferred*
HOTELS & RESORTS